NATURAL RESOURCES LAW

PRIVATE RIGHTS AND THE PUBLIC INTEREST

■ ■ ■

by

Eric T. Freyfogle
Swanlund Chair and Professor of Law
University of Illinois

Michael C. Blumm
Jeffrey Bain Faculty Scholar & Professor of Law
Lewis and Clark Law School

Blake Hudson
Burlington Resources Professor in Environmental Law
Edward J. Womac, Jr. Professor in Energy Law
Joint Appointment
LSU Law Center
LSU School of the Coast and Environment

AMERICAN CASEBOOK SERIES®

© 2015 LEG, Inc. d/b/a West Academic
    444 Cedar Street, Suite 700
    St. Paul, MN 55101
    1-877-888-1330

Printed in the United States of America

ISBN: 978-0-314-28912-4

To the memory of our great teacher,
mentor, and friend, Joseph P. Sax

~ ETF, MCB, BH ~

For Jane

~ ETF ~

For Kathleen, for everything

~ MCB ~

For Eliza, Campbell, and Ridley

~ BH ~

PREFACE

For many decades, natural resources law has been a mainstay of the law school curriculum, with good reason. The physical things of daily life begin as elements of the natural world. Our food, heat, shelter, clothing, cars, computers—all start as natural resources, which someone, somewhere, has severed from the natural fabric and reshaped for human use. Nature's elements provide recreational opportunities and pleasing surroundings. They sustain the ecological processes upon which all life depends.

This text provides an overview of natural resources law in the United States. It is meant chiefly for use in an introductory course, one that covers the subject as a whole and supplies a foundation for advanced courses on water, federal lands, oil and gas, mining, renewable energy, and similar topics.

We view this book as a selective, yet rich overview of natural resources law, not an encyclopedic attempt to cover a subject that is multi-faceted and yet overlapping. We attempt in this text to provide students with a glimpse of the abundant historical context of natural resources law, yet expose them to complexities of managing natural resources in the 21st century.

In an effort to provide a manageable teaching vehicle for professors and an accessible text for students, we've pared the material to 900 pages. We view this size as ideal for a one-semester, two- or three-credit course. The material can be covered in its entirety in the latter, and in the former, there is considerable room for professors to select material to emphasize natural resources of particular interest.

The book differs from other natural resources casebooks in two fundamental ways.

First, it pays full attention to natural resources on private lands and avoids undue emphasis on federal lands. Over 60 percent of the United States is privately owned, and most natural resource production takes place there. Private lands are particularly important in states east of the 100th meridian—that is, east of the Rocky Mountains—because the vast bulk of federally owned lands are west of there. We do not shortchange resources on federal lands; they appear in many chapters, and two chapters are devoted entirely to them. But our coverage is meant to survey the field broadly without overlapping too much with a specialized federal-lands course.

The second difference has to do with the ways we tie together the various bodies of natural resources law. Our overall arrangement is conventional: we address particular resources separately, after introductory material that considers the topic broadly. But within these chapters we draw comparisons among the various bodies of natural resources law to invite students to consider how the law addresses common issues in varied ways. A bit more needs to be said about this.

As the first chapter explains, natural resources law coordinates uses of nature by people. It does so by dividing nature into pieces, or use-rights, and then making these pieces or rights available to potential users. The law does this functional work—dividing nature, specifying the terms of rights, and making them available—in every resource setting, whether it is water, oil and gas, timber, grazing, recreation, geothermal energy, and so on. As the text proceeds, we identify these functions of natural resources law and take note of the different ways that the law performs them in different resources settings. By doing so, we are able to spot common issues and compare answers.

To take one example, natural resources law in various settings has made resources available to potential users (that is, it has allocated resources) on a first-in-time basis. It does so, for instance, in the case of wild animals, water flows (in prior appropriation jurisdictions), and mining rights on federal lands. When we draw lines between these bodies of law, what we see are that first-in-time allocation systems pretty much always pose three issues or challenges that lawmakers need to resolve as they craft their first-in-time rules. They must: (i) explain clearly *what action* is needed to be taken first; (ii) provide some level of *protection against interference* for those who are undertaking to perform the required action; and (iii) provide rules that allow for the *precise dating* of an action, to determine who has been first, when the required action takes a period of time to perform. By comparing the laws on wild animals, water diversion, and mineral prospecting, we can see how these three functions have been performed in each body of law and draw lessons accordingly.

One reason why we take time to draw these comparisons, and talk directly about the recurring functions of natural resources law, is that we believe it helps students prepare for law practice. Sometimes the elements of resource-use rights are prescribed directly by law. Those who acquire the resource rights are governed and constrained by these binding legal terms. To illustrate: when a wild animal lawfully taken into captivity escapes and returns to something like its natural habitat, the hunter's rights come to an end; the governing law, that is, sets a durational limit on private rights in the wild animal.

In many settings, however, the natural resources law operates quite differently. It merely provides terms for resource use-rights that apply only when and if the people involved in creating the right do not displace them with differing terms of their own choosing. Here we might consider the case of a landowner who sells her subsurface mineral rights to another person. What rights does the buyer have to use the land surface to extract the underlying minerals? Natural resources law, as we will see, provides an answer; it specifies the surface-use rights of mineral-rights owners. But the law's provisions in this setting serve only as back-up (default) rules. They apply only when the landowner and mineral-rights buyer do not, in their agreement, come up with a different arrangement. The private actors can override the law's provisions by writing their own rules.

When practicing natural resources law, lawyers are often called upon to draft agreements or deeds that, in effect, create particular natural resource use-rights and define their elements. For instance, a lawyer representing a fee simple landowner might draft an agreement creating rights to hunt on the land, or to remove timber or graze livestock, or to exploit particular minerals. A well-drafted agreement ought to provide all of the material terms of the use-right being created (for instance, what resource-activity the rights holder can undertake, where, and for how long; what protections the rights holder enjoys while acting; whether the rights are transferable or divisible, and so on). A lawyer can draft a sound, complete agreement if she begins with a clear sense of the key elements of use-rights generally; if she is aware of the key terms that need to be prescribed to set forth a use-right fully. It helps also to have awareness of the many ways that a key term might be drafted or expressed, drawing upon the relevant rules in various bodies of natural resources law. To return to the example of durational limits on use rights: what are the many ways that resources law has prescribed them (they are ubiquitous)? A good lawyer will, of course, know the back-up answers that the law provides to fill a gap in an incomplete agreement. But she will know also ways to alter a back-up answer and perhaps make it more appropriate for a particular situation or client. A lawyer who drafts a resource-use agreement, starting with a blank page, needs to know more than simply the elements of the applicable body of natural resources law.

Our principal focus on private lands allows us to raise fundamental issues concerning the nature of land and usufructuary ownership that students first encountered in their Property classes. The text also emphasizes state regulation, a subject too often overlooked in natural resources law classes, although we also explore federal regulation under statutes like the Clean Water Act, the Endangered Species Act, and the Migratory Bird Treaty Act, since they too play a prominent role in natural resources law on private lands.

Although our debts are many, we wish to express our thanks particularly to the late Joe Sax, who was a guiding light to us throughout our careers and to whom we dedicate this book. His loss is an enormous one to the legal academy and the next generation of our students. We hope this endeavor helps to fill that void.

ERIC T. FREYFOGLE
MICHAEL C. BLUMM
BLAKE HUDSON

December 2014

ACKNOWLEDGMENTS

We could not have produced this book without the indefatigable editorial assistance of Professor Blumm's crackerjack research assistant, Angela Ostrowski '15, and we're grateful for her heroic efforts. No less indispensable was Lisa Frenz, stellar word processor at Lewis and Clark Law School, who formatted the book and managed to mold innumerable drafts into a manageable whole.

Professor Blumm also is grateful for the research efforts of Andrea Lang '15, Kara Tebeau '15, and Kevin Fisher '15. Professor Hudson would like to thank his research assistant, Gavin Dunn '15. We're confident that all will soon make their marks on natural resources law.

Editors' Note

We've eliminated most footnotes; those that remain are numbered consecutively within each chapter; we did not retain their original footnote numbers. We also eliminated as unnecessary most parallel case citations, generally retaining only cites to West reporters, except where unavailable or where reference to a state reporter was necessary to indicate a cite to a particular page. We indicate deletions of a sentence or two with ellipses; we indicate deletions of larger blocks of material with asterisks. Generally, we omit concurring or dissenting opinions without notation.

SUMMARY OF CONTENTS

TABLE OF CONTENTS

TABLE OF CASES

The principal cases are in bold type.

NATURAL RESOURCES LAW

PRIVATE RIGHTS AND THE PUBLIC INTEREST

CHAPTER 1

AN OVERVIEW

▪ ▪ ▪

This initial chapter introduces natural resources law by briefly surveying the field to gain a sense of its recurring issues and themes before turning, in later chapters, to explore the laws dealing with particular resources. We can begin this survey, getting a sense of why the field exists and what it does, by imagining a group of settlers who arrive in a new landscape and who have full liberty to decide for themselves how they will use it. We can populate our imagined scene with fictional settlers who stand high on a mountainside and gaze over a vast open landscape, unoccupied by any people and ungoverned by any laws. How might they settle this new land? In what ways might they use it? Who would do the using and who will make the decisions about use? The group could simply let individuals wander off, one by one, and use the land however they might prefer. But this approach could succeed over time only if their numbers remain small and only if individuals refrain from stealing or invading one another's privacy. Even if the people are unusually well behaved, resource uses by one person will inevitably conflict with the activities of someone else. What happens when two people want to use the same part of nature at the same time? What happens when one proposed land or resource use conflicts with another one? And what about land uses (for instance, large-scale irrigation) that are possible only if people work together?

What is likely to happen is that our fictional settlers will come up with formal or informal laws that govern uses of their landscape. In some manner, they will allocate to individuals and to small groups rights to use nature in particular ways and in specific places. The options they have in doing this are nearly infinite, in terms of the precise ways they might define these use rights and then make them available for acquisition. The people could retain some use rights for the shared enjoyment of each person individually. They could reserve other use rights for collective exercise, to provide particular services or benefits for the people as a whole. No doubt many use rights will go to individuals, families, and small groups; rights to build homes, for instance, to plant crops, and to operate stores. As for allocation methods, the assembled people could give these use rights away, sell them, offer them to the first taker, or employ a variety of public-interest considerations. Like the use rights themselves, methods for allocating resources (one of the law's key functions) come in a wide variety of shapes and sizes.

The ways these people go about their resource-allocation work will depend to some degree upon the land itself, in terms of its natural features. Methods that make sense in one landscape may make little sense elsewhere. Even more, the methods they choose will depend upon the people themselves, their numbers, their values, and their hopes. As these policy determinants change over time, change will also come in the ways people use nature and in how they resolve their inevitable resource use squabbles. Changed conditions and changed values are likely to stimulate changes in the rules governing land and resource uses.

And thus we have our topic: *Natural resources law* is the expansive body of rules and processes governing the ways people interact with nature. At its core are rules that define and protect specific rights to make use of nature. Many use rights will be held by individuals, what we would call *private* property. Other use rights will be held for communal use or to provide shared services, what we call *public* property. But we shall need to employ this private-public distinction with some care. Public and private interests—or, as we might term them, shared and individual interests—are present pretty much everywhere in natural resources law. Use rights cannot be squeezed into two distinct categories. Both public and private rights are given shape by law; both of them have to do with using nature, and both are aimed at fostering the good of the social whole. Public property is often used by private actors who hold rather secure rights to do so. On the other side, the public has legitimate (albeit contested) interests in the way most private property is used. Public and private interests in natural resources are thus complexly mixed.

Another categorization that we need to employ carefully is the familiar line between owning *land* and owning some discrete *component of nature*; owning, for instance, a mineral deposit, a grazing right, or a stand of trees. As commonly understood, natural resources law deals with the latter; property law covers the former. But "land" as a legal concept is usefully understood as a bundle of rights to use the elements of nature that exist in a defined place. It is a compilation of resource use rights, packaged together and then allocated and traded as a unit. As for what use rights such a bundle might include—what resources come with land when you buy it—lawmakers must decide for themselves. There is no Platonic ideal for "land" that lawmakers can turn to for guidance. Over time and among cultures, the rights of land ownership have varied widely in time and place. To say that a person owns land really tells us almost nothing unless we know something about the surrounding culture and applicable legal regime. When we conceive of land ownership this way— as a package of use rights rather than as a monolithic entity—we are more apt to be attentive to its many details and to spot the ways it changes over time. Making matters more complex is the fact that landowners routinely fragment their bundle of rights, selling off one or more resource use rights while retaining others. (Although as we will see, the law does not always allow this fragmentation; some resource use rights are attached to land and cannot be severed.) Thus, a landowner's bundle often changes shape due to voluntary actions.

Beyond these points, we have the complexity that arises in natural resources law because one person's activities can readily affect what other people do. Here we confront countless questions about how the rights of one person should fit together with the use rights of someone else. Sometimes the conflict is between two people who are adjacent landowners (as when landowner A's mining operation pollutes neighbor B's groundwater). Instead, one might be a landowner and the other the holder of a right to use a natural resource (for instance, an oil and gas lease) located in the same place. Or they might both possess narrowly tailored rights to use different resources on the same land parcel (for instance, a right to graze livestock and a right to hunt). Whatever the situation, conflict can and will arise. One of the prime tasks or functions of natural resources law is to define resource use rights so as to anticipate these conflicts, avoiding them whenever possible and resolving them later when avoidance is not possible. We shall see how the law does this in various settings. In doing so, we will also compile a list of pretty much all of the ways that the law might do this, so we can compare the legal approaches.

Like all law, natural resources law is dynamic. Its evolution over time will also be part of our story. Nature's parts can gain or lose ecological or economic value due to scarcity, to rising human populations, to new technology, and to shifts in ethics and aesthetics. (As for losing value, nineteenth-century Americans often saw far more economic value in seaweed and the ice on lake surfaces than we do today.) Advances in ecological knowledge also play a prominent role, as we heighten our awareness of the ecological ripple effects that given resource uses can stimulate. Over the past century, there have been increasing calls for more integrated resource management and at larger spatial scales, at the level of the watershed, the ecosystem, or the fishery. Moreover, we now perceive, more clearly than in the past, considerable costs in allowing individuals to use their separate parts of nature however they see fit. Indeed, according to many observers, important land-use goals can be achieved only when decisions are made or coordinated at relatively large spatial scales.

Landscape-scale resource management can succeed fully only if it remains attentive to the inevitable fluctuations in nature itself. How many cattle can a pasture hold, for instance? How many lobsters can be harvested from a fishery, when, and of what size? The answers vary, from place to place and from time to time, often due to forces that people only dimly understand. Individual users, of course, can and should make many of these decisions; we have good reasons to propose, as an overall policy ideal, that individual users ought to possess as much independent authority over their resources as they can safely exercise. But individual management has its limits, even among individuals who are well-meaning, far-sighted community members. Many land-use goals are attainable only by coordinated action at a scale well above the individual-parcel level. As economists have long pointed out, the good discipline of the market is not strong enough to keep the land healthy for future generations.

In addition to these important points, we need to keep in mind that private property has some morally problematic sides to it. Private property depends for its existence upon the willingness of people collectively to protect and enforce private rights. Private property cannot exist in the absence of communal governance, nor without police and courts available to protect it. Take away public protection in the form of law and government and we end up with the free-for-all of the unregulated commons—the nightmare of all resource use arrangements. Private ownership is actually messier, more complicated, and a more fascinating institution than we might suppose.

Natural resources law is as venerable a field as any part of Anglo-American legal culture. From its first beginnings, the law has been called upon to resolve disputes over nature. Ever since, natural resources law has been on the move, along with society itself. Hardly any era, though, has seen as much change as the past half-century.

Today, pressures are strong to create new types of resource use rights, in parts of nature once deemed valueless in order to extend the reach of private property. At the same time, the inherited concept of land as an expansive bundle of use rights is under stress. Bundles are being fragmented, so that more resource use rights are separately held, often in collective or communal hands (for instance, ranch lands subject to conservation easements that prohibit development). Important questions are being raised about the presumed ability of resource-owners to degrade or destroy what they own. Should the ownership of farmland, for instance, include the power to erode its soils or to emit non-point source water pollution unchecked? All the while, new forms of resource governance are bubbling up, albeit with resistance and a good deal of intellectual confusion. Beneath it all are the undercurrents that animate modern society generally—the endless tensions between freedom versus control; the individual versus the collective; the present versus the future; and humankind versus the larger organic whole.

A. WHAT COMES WITH LAND?

Nearly every legal system over time has allowed individuals and groups to take control of particular portions of the land's surface, with varying rights to keep outsiders from using the land without their permission. But landownership can take many forms, so a recurring issue—an inescapable one for lawmakers—is to decide the components of nature that are part of the bundle of rights that a landowner acquires. Which resource use rights should be placed into the bundle called land, and which use rights should either be made available as discrete assets under separate resource-allocation schemes and/or be kept in common ownership? To illustrate: should one who acquires land obtain, as part of the package, rights to the minerals beneath the surface, to the water in an adjacent lake, to the wildlife that scampers across fields, or (to look ahead to chapter 3, p. 128) to the seaweed deposited on the foreshore? The case below addressed that question in the context of nineteenth century mining camp law, a fertile source of early American natural resources law.

HICKS V. BELL

Supreme Court of California
3 Cal. 219 (1853)

[Hicks claimed ownership of a mining claim along 200 yards of the bed of the Yuba River under local mining camp rules. He alleged that Bell had unlawfully trespassed by mining on about 90 feet of Hicks' prior claim while Hicks was working the upper part of the claim, and Bell knew of its existence. Bell defended on the basis that Hicks lacked actual possession of the lower 90 feet, but the trial court concluded that Hicks had constructive possession of the whole 200 yards. The California Supreme Court affirmed in the opinion below. In reaching its decision, the Supreme Court considered the English common law rule of mineral ownership, which reserved ownership of gold and silver in the Crown, not the landowner, and whether that rule was appropriate for federal lands in California.]

HEYDENFELDT, J.

The objection that the record discloses that there was no actual possession, is not good, because it appears there was actual possession of a portion adjacent to the premises in dispute, and, as I understand it, constructive possession of the latter was claimed by the rules and customs of miners on that part of the river. . . .

* * *

The main reliance in this case of the appellants is, that the land in question is the public land of the United States, and therefore the statutes of this State, which recognize the possessions of miners, which provide for their protection, and require mining claims to be decided according to the rules and regulations of bodies of miners, at each particular mining locality, are mere police regulations, and are invalid to confer any right, such as that of possession, or to enable the recovery thereof.

This position involves the decision of the question, to whom do the mines of gold and silver belong? To arrive at a satisfactory solution, it is only necessary to examine a few of the leading authorities.

According to the common law of England, mines of silver and gold are termed royal mines, and are the exclusive property of the Crown. Blackstone says, vol. 1, p. 294: "A twelfth branch of the royal revenue, the right to mines, has its original from the king's prerogative of coinage, in order to supply him with materials, and therefore those mines which are properly royal, and to which the king is entitled, when found, are only those of silver and gold. By the old common law, if gold or silver be found in mines of base metal, according to the opinion of some, the whole was a royal mine, and belonged to the king." And he cites 2 Just. 577.

* * *

Blackstone, it will be seen, attributes the origin of the law to the right of coinage. Plowden says, that the reason is because gold and silver are most excellent things, and the law has appointed them to the person who is most excellent, and that was the king. It is, however, immaterial as to the reason for its origin; the law has been settled beyond question, as it is declared by the earliest and most distinguished judges, and to this time has never been disputed. See Bainbridge on the Law of Mines and Minerals, where the authorities are collected.

This doctrine of the law has been acted upon in some, and probably in many, of the States in the Union. In Pennsylvania, it was the subject of legislation as early as 1787. In that year, by an act establishing a land office, she reserves for the use of the Commonwealth, one-fifth of all gold and silver ore. See Dunlap's Laws of Pennsylvania.

In New York, as early as 1789, an act of the legislature was passed, exempting the discoverers of gold and silver mines from paying to the people of the State as sovereign thereof, any portion or dividend of the yield, for the space of 21 years from the time of giving notice of the discovery; and forbidding the working of the same after the expiration of that term. See 1 Laws of New York, 124.

Again, in 1827, another act was passed, which declares that all mines of gold and silver discovered, or hereafter to be discovered, within this State, shall be the property of the people of this State, in their right of sovereignty. See 1 Revised Statutes, 281.

This was in effect but a re-enactment of the common law, which vested the right in the State government as the successor of the king.

It is hardly necessary at this period of our history, to make an argument to prove that the several States of the Union, in virtue of their respective sovereignties, are entitled to the *jura regalia* [rights which belong to the King—Eds.] which pertained to the king at common law.

* * *

In reference to the ownership of the public lands, the United States only occupied the position of any private proprietor, with the exception of an express exemption from State taxation. The mines of gold and silver on the public lands are as much the property of this State, by virtue of her sovereignty, as are similar mines in the lands of private citizens. She has, therefore, solely the right to authorize them to be worked; to pass laws for their regulation; to license miners; and to affix such terms and conditions as she may deem proper, to the freedom of their use. In her legislation upon this subject, she has established the policy of permitting all who desire it, to work her mines of gold and silver, with or without conditions; and she has wisely provided that their conflicting claims shall be adjudicated by the rules and customs which may be established by bodies of them working in the same vicinity.

According to this enactment, the case under consideration has been tried and decided, and for aught that is disclosed by the record, the decision is consonant with right and justice. Judgment is affirmed.

NOTES

1. *Prospectors and constructive possession.* **Hicks v. Bell**, decided not long after California joined the Union, offers a glimpse into life during the gold rush. Miners were piling on top of one another to control the best mining spots—initially in river beds and later, as these were panned out, in ore formations away from the water. Note that the argument here dealt with a single mining claim, staked out on a first-in-time basis in accordance with local custom. The claim extended 200 yards along the Yuba River, a dimension no doubt mandated by local custom. The second-in-time miner encroached upon 90 feet of this claim. This 90-foot section was the entire subject matter of the lawsuit (and loaded with more than fool's gold, one hopes).

Justice Heydenfeldt's decision established an important rule that applied in mining territory: a prospector who properly stakes out a claim has the exclusive right to work it. So long as the miner is using part of the claim, he has "constructive possession" of the whole of the claim. If another miner shows up and begins working the same claim, he has wrongfully disrupted the possession of the first miner, even though there is no actual physical interference with what the first miner is doing. The idea of constructive possession is, of course, difficult to apply in practice unless defined precisely by local custom or agreement.

2. *The twelfth branch of royal revenue, and what comes with land?* Gold and silver mines in England were claimed by the English Crown. They were owned by the King (or Queen), not in a *proprietary* capacity (as the King would own a farm or castle), but in a *sovereign* capacity—the same capacity as the King owned land beneath navigable waterways and wild game. These rights passed to the states once Independence was declared or, later, as each state entered the Union. But what was a state to do with its mineral rights, and how did this state ownership relate to land ownership? To the modern reader *Hicks* reaches an unexpected outcome. The common (and accurate) understanding today is that landowners in the United States own all the minerals beneath the surface, gold and silver included. What accounts for the ruling?

Hicks is a surprising case and by no means expresses contemporary law (under which minerals belong to the surface owner, whether public or private). The ruling is nonetheless useful because it gives us good background on the ownership of mines at common law, and because it highlights a fundamental policy question that each jurisdiction needs to answer. Which minerals (and other resources) go with the land surface, and which do not? The question could receive widely varied answers. Governments around the world have come up with a variety of them. (As you might guess from the extreme wealth of various state-run oil companies around the globe, landowners do better in the United States than elsewhere.) The law governing gold and silver is also useful because it illustrates one of the many ways that the United States tailored the inherited common law to suit the circumstances and cultural values of America. Particularly when it came to property, lawmakers paid attention to what England's courts had said but felt free to make even major legal changes to the common law system.

3. *The law of the mining camp.* In *Hicks* the court decided that certain minerals belonged to the state and were available for separate acquisition. As for how a person could gain ownership of this state-controlled resource, the court was willing to defer to the de facto code that arose in the mining camps (largely borrowed from mining regions in Europe): mines go to the first person to discover a valuable deposit and to stake out (or "locate") the claim in accordance with local mining customs. Note that two steps were involved in the court's legal reasoning, and the court could have taken the first step and not the second. The court could have announced that the minerals belonged to the state (step one), but then announced that the first-in-time system was of no legal effect (step two).

The ruling in *Hicks* no doubt made sense to Californians during the gold rush era. The case dealt with land owned by the distant federal government. Fueled by an anti-federal bias, Californians were apparently happy to carve up and carry away minerals on federal lands. The problem that quickly arose concerned the application of *Hicks* to private land. Private owners were not so happy to have outsiders enter their lands, discover gold, and then claim a right to mine it.

As it turned out, the rule announced in *Hicks v. Bell* did not survive the decade as a principle of state property law. The California court reversed itself in *Moore v. Smaw*, 17 Cal. 199, 218 (1861), shifting to the majority American rule that all solid subsurface minerals belong to the owner of the land surface. (An intriguing, half-way step toward reversing *Hicks* was made by the court in 1859 in *Boggs v. Merced Mining Co.*, 14 Cal. 279. The court decided that, while the state owned the minerals underneath private land, it had not granted to the public a general license to enter private lands to engage in mining. In so ruling, the court reaffirmed the public's ownership, but then withheld from the public the necessary right of access.)

As for mining law on federal lands today, it bears many similarities to the system described in *Hicks*. We take it up in later, in chapter 8 (pp. 690–731). We will also look at the more important and vastly different law of mining that applies on all other lands in chapter 5 (pp. 363–425). Finally, we will have occasion to return to the distinction between sovereign and proprietary powers once held by the King, and see other natural resources that the King owned in a sovereign sense (e.g., wildlife, p. 247).

4. *The progeny of* Hicks. Although the precise holding in *Hicks* would prove short-lived, the ruling played a key role in stimulating two legal developments of immense importance in shaping resource use in the American West. First, the idea emerged that the customary law of the mining camp, with its first-in-time allocation system, applied on federally owned land, and that this law would be viewed chiefly as a component of *state* rather than *federal* law. Mining law was thus subject to variation among the states, even when mining took place on federal land. Congress soon gave its approval to this legal arrangement in statutes enacted over the ensuing decade and a half. That lawmaking work culminated in the Mining Law of 1872, which still provides the framework for mining today. *Hicks*, in sum, survived in part as the law governing public lands, as we shall see in chapter 8 (pp. 690–708).

The second post-*Hicks* development had to do with a resource that miners soon found essential for their new, hydraulic mining methods: water. If first-in-time made sense among competing miners on federal lands, neither of whom owned the land surface, then it seemed to make equally good sense to allocate water the same way. In the case of water, though, the common law was much clearer. Under it, rights to divert and consume water belonged to riparian landowners alone. There was no other way to gain a right to use surface water. But with the landowning federal government thousands of miles away and apparently disinterested, the California Supreme Court was left to decide itself between two trespassers on the federal lands. As between trespasser A and trespasser B—neither a riparian landowner—which one should get the water? The only rule that made any sense—the rule used, for instance, in finding law to resolve a dispute between two finders—was the rule that the first water user got to keep the water until the riparian landowner showed up to claim it. Thus was born the prior appropriation system of water allocation (which we consider in detail in chapter 6 at pp. 460–535), and the key precedent relied upon was *Hicks v. Bell*. See Eric T. Freyfogle, Lux v. Haggin *and the Common Law Burdens of Modern Water Law*, 57 U. Colo. L. Rev. 485 (1986).

5.   *Ancillary right: minerals, and what else?* Note one problem that quickly arises when we allow one person to acquire rights to minerals underneath land owned by someone else. The miner needs to gain access to the minerals, and often needs to alter the land surface significantly in order to extract the minerals. The California court was well aware of this issue. It made specific mention of the fact that, in England, the King's ownership rights in gold and silver were accompanied by "full liberty to dig, and carry away the ores, and with all such incidents thereto as are necessary to be used for getting them." Plainly, this formulation of the King's rights made mining the paramount use of the land surface. The King apparently could disrupt and displace whatever the surface owner was doing, without need to compromise or make reasonable accommodation (what else would we expect, when the King made the laws?)

Perhaps the California court viewed this arrangement as sensible in California mountains owned by the federal government; after all, what other value did this rocky land have? But the story was quite otherwise in lands that did clearly have other uses. On such lands, it was not so obvious that a mining-first policy was socially wise. A policy that favored miners discouraged surface owners from investing in other surface-use activities. This conflict over surface uses could be avoided by shifting to the legal approach in which surface and minerals were combined in a single owner. When the subsurface minerals all were owned by the surface owner, the surface owner could decide which resource use would take priority. When a surface owner severed the mineral rights and conveyed them to someone else, the parties to the transaction could negotiate as to the surface-use rights that the mineral buyer received.

We turn more directly to the issue of ancillary rights—a key topic in natural resources law—later in this chapter. It returns repeatedly in later chapters.

6.   *The federal government as proprietor.* A final note on the legal status of federal lands: The court's ruling was made easier because of the then-prevailing assumption among courts that the federal government as landowner "only occupied the position of any private proprietor, with the exception of an express exemption from State taxation." Today the legal understanding is vastly different. Congress holds nearly unlimited lawmaking powers for federal lands under the Property Clause of the Constitution (Art. IV, § 3, cl.2). Any laws it enacts preempt state law on federally owned lands (and even reach some activities on private lands). *Kleppe v. New Mexico*, 426 U.S. 529 (1976). State mining law applies on federal lands only because and so long as Congress tolerates it, although a

shift in that longstanding policy would plainly need to consider existing property rights. Much natural resources law today has to do with the resources on federally owned lands, how they are managed, and the types of use rights that private citizens can gain in them. Chapters 8 and 9 focus on these federal lands, including federal mining rights, but federal land law arises in various other chapters as well, particularly concerning wetland regulation in chapter 3 (pp. 217–245).

B. USE RIGHTS, COMMON POOLS, AND GOVERNANCE REGIMES

Many natural resource use rights are attached to land in the legal sense; that is, the person who owns the land either owns the resource in place or has exclusive rights to exploit the resource. (We shall explore that distinction soon.) Other use rights, however, are owned separately as discrete assets. These use rights are particularly frequent in settings involving what are termed common-pool resources—parts of nature that are not feasibly divided in any spatial sense and that are best used as a single resource by one or multiple users. Many common-pool settings involve parts of nature that do not stay in place or that are subject to considerable fluctuation in their physical existence (for instance, fish that swim great distances, and fish populations that fluctuate over time). Further, many particular common pools are valuable not for just a single resource but because they contain different types of resources, with discrete use rights that are defined differently for the different resources. These features of common-pool settings further complicate the work of defining use rights, accommodating conflicts among the users, and taking into account nature's dynamism. As we shall see, natural resources law for obvious reasons pays close attention to nature and its dynamism—and to the particular ways that people might exploit or otherwise use particular natural resources.

Use rights are central to natural resources law in much the same way that the abstract tract of land—Greenacre or Blackacre—has long been central to land law. In the case of use rights, there really is no abstract model that provides the benchmark for describing and comparing particular legal variants. Use rights do have common features to them— for instance, they describe what resource can be used, where, in what ways, and for how long—but their elements are so varied that it is not really possible to identify or construct any overall paradigm use right. Perhaps the key points to emphasize are that nature itself plays a central role in defining the rights and so does the technology that people use to take advantage of it.

Particularly in common-pool settings, but in others as well, use rights are embedded into governance regimes of one sort or another. That is, the terms of use rights are often subject to legal modification over time through governance systems in which they are embedded. These governance systems—in which the users might well play a considerable role—may also be used to resolve the inevitable conflicts among users. Some resource-related activities are mild enough that individual owners can act in near isolation from other users. But many resource activities require oversight or communal input of some sort, whether to enhance the resource's overall productivity (for instance a lobster fishery off the Maine coast or a producing oil and gas field) or to protect the land's lasting health and beauty. Often, governance regimes are erected in nested, hierarchical form, from the local level to ever broader spatial scales. When multiple levels exist, rules are then needed to specify the proper governance roles at each level.

Just as resource use rights do not fit neatly into categories of public and private, so too governance regimes come in diverse shapes and sizes. Best known are the law-making engines of constituted civil governments, whether federal, state, or local. But natural resources lawyers have always had an element of imagination that other lawyers have lacked(!). Governance regimes can take many other forms, blending private and public. Resource users in particular settings could create their own governance regimes without consulting outsiders (and have done so, many times). The resulting institutions could look like a typical homeowners' association in a residential subdivision, like a drainage district set up by landowners in a farm landscape, or—to anticipate the next case—like the communal management regime set up by gillnet fishermen in the Columbia River.

MARINCOVICH V. TARABOCHIA

Supreme Court of Washington
787 P.2d 562 (1990)

[The plaintiffs, commercial gillnet fishermen on the lower Columbia River and members of the Altoona Snag Union, sought to enjoin other commercial gillnetters on the lower Columbia River from fishing in the territory they claimed because the defendants lacked "drift rights"— exclusive rights to fish in a particular area—issued by the Union.]

DOLLIVER, J.

Plaintiffs are members of the Altoona Snag Union, Inc., which pools together funds collected from its members in order to coordinate the yearly removal of snags and debris from areas of the river where gillnet fishing would otherwise be impossible.

Snags are most commonly cleared from drifts, which are expanses of water over which gillnet fishermen set their nets. Certain drifts on the lower Columbia River have long been recognized and maintained according to local custom and usage. The State of Washington

Department of Fisheries issues snagging permits to individual fishermen for the purpose of authorizing snag removal.

Membership in the Altoona Snag Union is evidenced by ownership of a "drift right", by which the union gives an exclusive right to fish a particular drift where snags have been removed. Drift rights have traditionally been treated as valuable personal property and have been passed to family members through probate and divorce proceedings. It is undisputed fishermen have paid valuable consideration for their drift rights.

Membership in the union is exclusive. Agreement to help pay for snag clearing does not make one a member; instead, a person interested in joining must locate an already existing right and purchase it with the union's approval. Enforcement of drift rights occurs in a variety of ways, all of which include some degree of intimidation and, in some cases, threats to life and property. The most common form of enforcement is "corking". This entails placing one's fishing net so close to that of the offending fisherman that the offender is forced to remove his net from the water to avoid ripping or tearing.

In October 1985, plaintiffs filed a complaint for damages and injunctive relief against defendants arising from a dispute over an area of the river not clearly controlled under the drift right system. The trial court imposed a permanent injunction against the defendants and ordered them to stop interfering with plaintiffs' fishing operations. Defendants filed a counterclaim challenging the legality of plaintiffs' drift rights. In February 1987, defendants filed a motion for summary judgment on this issue. The trial court concluded that before a material issue of fact can arise, plaintiffs must possess a basic legal right to exclude others from fishing the cleared drifts. Finding no such right existed, the trial court granted defendants' summary judgment motion. The court granted a stay of judgment pending the outcome of plaintiffs' appeal.

The Court of Appeals affirmed the trial court's ruling. *Marincovich v. Tarabochia*, 769 P.2d 866 (Wash. App. 1989). We also affirm.

* * *

Plaintiffs argue local custom and usage constitute a sufficient legal basis for recognizing they have a proprietary interest in drift rights; as such, they assert the trial court erred by granting summary judgment in favor of defendants on this issue. Plaintiffs base their position on essentially three separate arguments: analogy to trade use and custom as applied in contract law; reliance on customary water appropriation principles as a means to perfecting a legal right; and the notion that because the Department of Fisheries issues snagging permits, these permits impliedly give the holders the exclusive right to fish the areas they have cleared.

We reject plaintiffs' analogy to contract law under the facts of this case. As the Court of Appeals succinctly stated, the cases plaintiffs cite in support of their argument have to do with applying custom and trade use to interpret contracts or otherwise to flesh out rights already recognized by law. *Marincovich,* 769 P.2d at 867. In this case, neither contracts nor rights previously given legal recognition are at issue. For this reason, the Court of Appeals properly rejected plaintiffs' argument.

Nor do we accept plaintiffs' argument that under customary water appropriation principles, their drift rights should be legally recognized. Article 21, section 1, of the Washington Constitution provides that the use of the waters in this state for irrigation, mining, and manufacturing purposes shall be deemed a public use. In addition, 43 U.S.C. § 661 also recognizes rights to the use of water for mining and other such purposes when the same have been recognized by local custom, laws, and the decisions of courts. Neither of these provisions, nor the case law cited by plaintiffs in support of their argument, convince us this case should be analyzed under this theory. See *Isaacs v. Barber,* 38 P. 871 (Wash. 1894); *Tenem Ditch Co. v. Thorpe,* 20 P. 588 (Wash. 1889); *Hunter v. United States,* 388 F.2d 148 (9th Cir.1967); *Department of Parks v. Department of Water Admin.,* 530 P.2d 924 (Idaho 1974). See also Frank Trelease, *Coordination of Riparian and Appropriative Rights to the Use of Water*, 33 Tex.L.Rev. 26 (1954). The appropriated use of water is not analogous to the recognition of drift rights for fishing.

We also reject plaintiffs' argument that the Department of Fisheries, by issuing snag removal permits, has impliedly given permit holders the exclusive right to fish the areas they clear. The Department of Fisheries has been given the duty to promote orderly fisheries and to enhance and improve commercial fishing within the state. RCW 75.08.012. It does this in part by issuing snagging permits since the permits enable it to discern between those persons who are legally clearing snags and those who may be fishing illegally. Nothing in the record or the case law supports plaintiffs' argument that this somehow carries with it the exclusive right to fish the areas covered by the individual permits.

It has long been established in Washington and Oregon that citizens enjoy equal access to the navigable waters of their respective states. *Morris v. Graham*, 47 P. 752 (Wash. 1897); *Radich v. Fredrickson,* 10 P.2d 352 (Or. 1932); *Driscoll v. Berg,* 293 P. 586 (Or. 1930); *Johnson v. Jeldness,* 167 P. 798 (Or. 1917); *Hume v. Rogue River Packing Co.,* 92 P. 1065 (Or. 1907). In addition, this court has previously held the State, in its sovereign capacity, owns the fish in its waters. *Washington Kelpers Ass'n v. State,* 502 P.2d 1170 (Wash. 1972), *cert. denied,* 411 U.S. 982

(1973). As such, individual fishermen cannot assert a property right over the fish until they are caught. *Washington Kelpers Ass'n,* 502 P.2d at 1173 (quoting *Vail v. Seaborg,* 207 P. 15, 17 (Wash. 1922)). These cases establish the fact plaintiffs do not enjoy a legal right to portions of public waters to the exclusion of other citizens of this state.

In its memorandum opinion, the trial court found *Radich v. Fredrickson,* 10 P.2d 352 (Or. 1932) to be analogous to the present case. In *Radich,* gillnet fishermen sued to enjoin other fishermen from erecting a fish trap which would have severely interfered with their ability to fish the river. *Radich,* 10 P.2d at 353. The court held defendants did not have a right to set up fish traps since to do so would interfere with the right to fish the public waters of the state, a right shared equally by all citizens. *Radich,* 10 P.2d at 355.

It is interesting to note the plaintiffs in *Radich* had established an operation similar to the one established by plaintiffs in this case. The fishermen would clear snags from the river and take turns fishing the drifts to the exclusion of fishermen who did not participate in the clearing efforts. *Radich,* 10 P.2d at 355. However, *Radich* is distinguishable from the present case in one important aspect; namely, under the system enjoyed in that case, any fisherman who wanted to help clear snags was invited to fish. *Radich,* 10 P.2d at 355. In the present case, however, the same interest in helping to clear snags is not enough to gain access to the drifts. Instead, the inquiring individual must locate and purchase, with the union's approval, an already existing drift right before he will be allowed to fish the drifts.

The cases cited and discussed above establish that local custom and usage do not support legal recognition of plaintiffs' drift rights. This is true even though drift rights have existed in Oregon and Washington for many years. As the Court of Appeals stated, plaintiffs claim would arrogate to them rights owned in common by all of the people of the state. *Marincovich,* 69 P.2d at 867. We affirm the Court of Appeals.

A final comment: Although not necessary to the disposition of this case, we recognize the trial court's reluctance in ruling against plaintiffs in this case. In the words of the trial court:

> [T]here is no dispute as to the allegation that the denial of the rights asserted by plaintiff would result in, (1) chaos in the use of the drifts; (2) economic detriment to those holders of the drift rights; (3) to avoid overcrowding, no additional fishermen should be used on those drifts.

Clerk's Papers, at 174–75. We also are sympathetic to these concerns. However, under RCW 75.08, regulation of the particular issues raised in this case is vested within the Department of Fisheries. That Department, by allowing plaintiffs to carry out snag clearing for many years, may have allowed plaintiffs to operate under the impression their drift rights were legally enforceable. By this opinion that impression comes to an end. The problems presented in this case must be resolved by departmental rules and regulations, not by the self help of the Altoona Snag Union. Only the Department is in a position to establish the orderly promotion of gillnet fishing on the Columbia River.

NOTES

1. *The origin of property?* *Marincovich* gives us a useful glimpse into the way property rights emerge. An assertion commonly encountered in basic property law courses is that private property arises when an individual takes physical possession of an unowned thing; first occupancy, it is said, is the origin of property. This can be apt from an individual's perspective, but it is true only if (i) a governance regime already exists that recognizes private property rights, and (ii) the governance regime allows people to gain ownership by taking possession in this way. Unless these conditions are met, we have merely the king-of-the-hill world of might makes right. Property rights actually come second; a governance regime of some sort, formal or informal, must come first. But how does such a regime of property rights itself first come into existence? The basic answer is simple: somehow, a group of people need to come together and make rules governing uses of nature—much like our fictional settlers arriving in a new land.

Once a people do create some sort of property-rights regime, what options do they have in terms of making property rights available to individuals? First occupancy is one possibility, but as we shall see, it is only one of many resource-allocation methods. At common law, its role in allocating property was in fact quite modest compared with other allocation methods. It had little or no role in allocating land, for instance, or in allocating the many forms of intangible property rights that were so important before the modern age. Rarely, in fact, did private ownership begin with first possession rather than by way of grant from above or other collective action.

As best we can tell, how did the informal (but apparently well-enforced) system of property rights in *Marincovich* come into existence? Many current holders of drift rights apparently acquired their rights by purchase. But how did the first holders gain their rights? Can we imagine the true origin of individual property rights in this fishery?

2. *Managing the common pool.* The fishery discussed in *Marincovich* provides a classic example of a common-pool resource that can remain productive over the long-term only if the uses of it are controlled carefully. But how can control take place, when gillnet fishing is done by individuals and small groups competing with one another? What must the local fishermen do (and thus wield the power to do) to keep their fishery intact and prevent over-harvesting? They obviously must be able to exclude outsiders, or else their internal harvest limits will go for naught. But what else is

necessary? More generally, what does it take for a group of individuals acting together to manage a commons successfully over the long-run?

In the end, the main weakness of the Snag Union's system was that the members collectively lacked the legitimate power to protect their fishery against invasion by outsiders. On this issue, their story offers a classic illustration of how property rights—whether individual or group—exist only to the extent recognized and protected by law. Union members settled rights among themselves, but their rights were not binding on outsiders who rejected their system and were not bound by law to respect it. As for other challenges that confronted the Snag Union's governance system, we hear little about them. No doubt questions and conflicts arose among Union members as to their relative rights—who was authorized to catch, where, how much, and when? These were questions that the internal governance system had to resolve, with answers that very likely shifted over time with changes in fishing populations, fishing methods, and other factors.

3. *Restrictions on sale, and who decides?* One of the key issues of a resource use right is the power (if any) of the owner to transfer the right to someone else. In the case of the Snag Union, the court mentioned that individual owners of drift rights could sell them only "with the union's approval." Does this sound like an undue restriction on individual rights, or is such a restraint on alienation perhaps a necessary fixture of an effective resource-management regime? Does the Union perhaps have a legitimate need to screen potential purchasers and to prohibit sales to people who they sense will not adequately abide by their rules?

One way to understand *Marincovich* is as a dispute, not chiefly about private use rights, but about the identity of the governing body. Would the legitimate governing body be the Snag Union and its leaders, or would it instead be the state? The Snag Union's governance arose by private action, without any sanction by the state. Apparently, it was efficient, effective, and low cost. The effect of the court's ruling was to undercut the effectiveness of that private governance, thereby replacing private governance with public governance. Was the shift a wise one in policy terms? We can answer the question, of course, only be undertaking a comparative study of the relative merits and demerits of the two governance regimes and the possibilities of blending them. Public lawmakers could choose to vest governance powers in the Snag Union, subject perhaps to various limits that in effect turned the Union into a quasi-public body. The Union, that is, could operate as a management intermediary between the state and the individual fishers.

4. *Gaining rights by prescription.* Although the Snag Union presented three legal arguments to the court, only one had much merit: the Union's claim that it ought to control the fishing territory because it was first in time to take possession, and because it had used the fishery productively for years. Implicit here was the claim that Union fishermen had mixed their labor with the fishery, adding value to it by removing snags. The addition of this value gave rise to a moral claim to the fishery under the labor theory of property.

More explicit was the fishermen's claim that their long-continued use of the fishery was tantamount to the acquisition of an easement by prescription. Why did the court reject the plaintiffs' first-in-time/prescription argument? As a policy matter, should it have done so?

At the beginning of the nineteenth century, fishermen often took exclusive control of fisheries in navigable waters by reliance upon the law of prescription. E.g., *Carson v. Blazer*, 2 Binn. 475 (Pa. 1810); *Pitkin v. Olmstead*, 1 Root 217 (Conn. 1790); *Freary v. Cooke*, 14 Mass. 488 (1779). See *Acquisition of Title by Prescription*, 19 Am. Jurist 96 (1838). The practice was apparently widespread and tolerated, but it did not fit easily into the law, and courts from an early point expressed uncertainty about it. As the century progressed, courts turned against the idea, embracing the line of reasoning used in *Marincovich*: navigable waters are open to public fishing, and no person can claim exclusive rights in them, no matter how long the use. See e.g., *Shrunk v. Schuylkill Navigation Co.*, 14 Serg. & Rawle 71 (Pa. 1826). This new, anti-monopoly reasoning aligned with the economic liberalism that dominated society in the decades before the Civil War. We shall take a close look at public rights in waterways in Chapter 3, including the public trust doctrine (pp. 178–217).

5. *The power of government to alienate public rights.* Note the appellate court's favorable quotation (from the trial court record) on how a refusal to recognize the plaintiffs' rights in the fishery would bring "chaos in the use of the drifts." Why would this be so? Are other outcomes also possible—such as an end to snag removal and an end to net fishing at the mouth of the river? And could there be environmental benefits to this outcome? This last question would be difficult to answer without knowing the ensuing ecological effects. We would also need to know the overall effects, if any, on total fish harvests, since an end to fishing in the river's mouth could well produce larger harvests elsewhere. Snag removal might increase predation of young fish by eliminating places for them to hide, thereby reducing overall fish harvests. Beyond that, could it be more efficient to refrain from harvesting the fish at the river's mouth and instead wait until the migrating fish get nearer to their natal streams, where they are easier to catch?

The resolution of this predictable chaos on the fishing grounds, the court makes clear, was a matter for administrative rather than judicial action. Only the Department of Fisheries (or the state legislature presumably) had the power "to establish the orderly promotion of gillnet fishing on the Columbia River." But if it is legitimate for a state agency to allow private parties to take over a public fishery, why would it be illegitimate for a court to do so? After all, the public would suffer in the same way if denied access to a valuable fishery by a state agency instead of the Snag Union. If exclusive private rights in fact conflict unduly with the public's rights to fish, how then could an agency fairly create exclusive fishing territories? In terms of its legal jurisdiction (which the court did not explore), the state Department of Fisheries may or may not possess the legal power to close the fishery to public fishing, and doing so may or may not be consistent with public rights guaranteed by the federal navigation servitude (see chapter 3, pp. 243–244).

6. *The coercive side of private rights.* Before leaving *Marincovich* we might pause to consider the plight of fishermen outside the Snag Union, those who wanted to fish in the area but were excluded from doing so by the Snag Union. Wasn't the Snag Union's assertion of control unfair to them, perhaps a restriction of their liberty? The obvious answer: indeed, it was unfair and an interference with individual liberty, and necessarily so. But that is the way private property in nature always works!

One person or a group can gain rights over a part of nature only at the expense of other people. To allow A to take over a piece of land (or a fishery), giving her the power to exclude outsiders, is necessarily to deprive all other people of their liberties to enter and use what A now owns. Here, the effect of the Snag Union system was to attempt to gain for Union members a limited private property right in their territory. Note, however, that this was not likely an exclusive property right, in terms of *all* uses of the waters. The public presumably remained free to use the same waters for other purposes. What the fishermen collectively asserted was merely an exclusive right to harvest the fish in their self-defined territory.

7. *The homesteading comparison.* As the American West was settled, eager homesteaders often moved onto federal lands that were not yet surveyed and open to settlement. Squatting did not give the first arrivals an automatic preference, but squatters frequently found ways to gain ownership of their lands once the government did put the lands up for sale. From time to time, Congress would validate squatting retroactively by means of "preemption" statutes, while claiming to discourage it prospectively. (The General Preemption Act of 1841 did authorize prospective preemption under certain, much-abused circumstances.)

Another method used by initial first settlers to protect their unauthorized claims was to form "claims associations," in which members agreed to respect one another's squatting claims by not bidding for occupied land and by warding off outside bidders. See George Cameron Coggins, Charles F. Wilkinson & John D. Leshy, *Federal Public Land and Resources Law* 75–76 (5th ed. 2002). The practice held true in the frontier Midwest early in the nineteenth century:

> Not only did settlers mutually acknowledge the rights of squatters to their improvements [on land that they had settled], but they acted together to defend these customary rights against legal encroachments. According to Pascal P. Enos, registrar at the Springfield office in the 1820s, there were no instances "of any person bid[d]ing more than the Govt. prices, or any persons bid[d]ing against a person that held by possession." Speculators were probably intimidated in Springfield, as they were elsewhere, by associations of squatters showing up en masse to protect their claims. In Wisconsin in 1835, according to one contemporary report,

"if a speculator should bid on a settler's farm, he was knocked down and dragged out of the land office, and if the striker was prosecuted and fined, the settlers paid the expense by common consent among themselves." "A kind of common-law was established by common consent and common necessity," John Reynolds wrote, "that the improvements on congress land shall not be purchased by any person except he who made the improvement."

James Mack Faragher, *Sugar Creek: Life on the Illinois Prairie* 55 (1986).

Preemption was conceptually distinct from homesteading, which involved more than just taking possession of land. (It differed also, of course, in being an *ex post* validation of seizing land, rather than an *ex ante* authorization.) Homesteaders typically had to cultivate, irrigate, build upon, or otherwise improve a portion of their homestead before gaining secure title. As an allocation system, therefore, homesteading was not merely a rule of first occupancy. In practice, homestead laws were "liberally applied in favor of the entryman," which brought the system closer to allocation by first possession. *Stewart v. Penny*, 238 F.Supp. 821 (D. Nev. 1965) (concluding that homesteader had satisfied the 20-acre cultivation requirement on arid land, even though crops had entirely failed due to "freezing, depredations by mice, rabbits, and other rodents, and invasions of ranging livestock").

C. CONFLICTS AMONG USERS AND THE LEGAL METHODS OF ADDRESSING THEM

In many natural settings, a particular resource can be used by different users at the same time, perhaps in different ways but perhaps in the same way. When this happens, their resource use activities can easily conflict, just as activities by neighboring landowners can conflict. One of the law's main tasks is to provide rules to resolve such clashes. It can attempt to forestall disputes by providing clear guidance to resource users in advance, so that they know what they can do and what they must avoid. If such *ex ante* measures do not succeed, the law needs to provide for resolving conflicts *ex post*. The following case, also involving gillnet fishing on the Columbia River, illustrates the problem and one legal method of dealing with it.

COLUMBIA RIVER FISHERMEN'S PROTECTIVE UNION v. CITY OF ST. HELENS

Supreme Court of Oregon
87 P.2d 195 (1939)

[Commercial gillnetters fishing for salmon in the Columbia River claimed that municipal and industrial water polluters—from the city and from pulp and paper mills—were damaging their livelihoods due to their pollution. They charged the dischargers with maintaining a public nuisance.]

BEAN, J.

* * *

Plaintiffs, as gill net fishermen, have a special interest, distinct from the public in fishing their drift which will be protected in a court of equity against destruction by acts of the defendants, which destroy their nets and interfere with their fishing. . . .

It is stated in the plaintiffs' brief that the lower court sustained the demurrer on the grounds that the complaint shows these plaintiffs have suffered no special and peculiar injury differing in kind from that suffered by the public, and therefore they cannot maintain this suit. The defendants rely largely upon this rule, and cite as authority for sustaining their position the decision in the case of *Kuehn v. Milwaukee*, 53 N.W. 912 (Wis. 1892). Suffice it to say that this rule has not been followed in the state of Oregon, but a different rule has been adopted in numerous cases.

To delete the fish from the Columbia and Willamette rivers is to prevent the plaintiffs from pursuing their vocations and earning their livelihood fishing with gill nets in the portions of the rivers where they have been accustomed to fish.

* * *

There is a vital distinction between the rights of plaintiffs, who are accustomed to fishing in the river and have a license so to do, and the rights of other citizens of the state, who never fish in the river and do not intend to and are interested only in a general way in the benefit the state receives by the prosecution of a valuable industry, so that surely the plaintiffs have a special interest differing widely from the interest of the public in fishing in the portions of the river mentioned.

* * *

Numerous suits have been maintained in the courts of this state to prevent interference with the right of fishing. The difference between this case and the several others cited above is in degree. There is a greater degree of interference in the present case than in the cases heretofore prosecuted.

Enormous quantities of salmon are found in the Columbia and Willamette rivers and are of extensive commercial value. The salmon industry has grown to great proportions and has been one of the principal industries of the state of Oregon for many years. Thousands of citizens of Oregon earn their livelihood by catching salmon, and the business aggregates hundreds of thousands of dollars annually. All the citizens of Oregon have a common right to fish in the waters mentioned in the complaint, and to deprive any one citizen of that right is to violate the state constitution. On its admission to the Union, Oregon was vested with the title to the land under navigable waters within the state, subject to the public right of navigation and to the common right of the citizens of the state to fish. *Monroe v. Withycombe*, 165 P. 227 (Or. 1917). In the latter case, where the opinion was written by Mr. Justice Harris, plaintiffs brought suit to enjoin the interference of fishing rights in the Columbia River. The case, in principle, is like the one at bar.

Fish are classified as *ferae naturae*. While the ownership of the fish in question, before they are taken, is in the state of Oregon, as far as ownership can be established, this suit is not brought for the purpose of obtaining the salmon but to protect the right of fishermen to pursue their vocation of fishing. *Monroe v. Withycombe*, 165 P. 227.

* * *

Strandholm v. Barbey, 26 P.2d 46 (Or. 1933), was a case brought to protect the fishing rights of plaintiff in the Columbia [R]iver, which had been interfered with by the construction of a wharf and three fish traps by defendant. At . . . page 52 of 26 P.2d we find the language of Mr. Justice Rossman: "We are therefore satisfied that, since the wharf interferes with long-established fishing rights possessed by the plaintiff, he is entitled to a decree enjoining the maintenance of the wharf beyond the line just mentioned."

* * *

Radich v. Fredrickson, 10 P.2d 352 (Or. 1932), is a case where thirty-three gill net fishermen, as plaintiffs, brought a suit to protect their rights and to restrain the construction of a fish trap and interfering with the rights of plaintiffs to fish. The syllabus reads: "Maintenance of fish traps should be enjoined where it prevented fishing with gill nets in adjacent navigable waters." [10 P.2d at 353.]

Section 39–603, Oregon Code Supplement 1935, prohibits the pollution of streams and public waters of the state by depositing any deleterious substance or any substances which do or may render the waters of a stream, or any other body of water, destructive of fish life.

Section 40–213, Oregon Code 1930, prohibits depositing deleterious substances, explosives or poisons, or using the same in the waters of the state.

The regulatory power of a state extends not only to the taking of its fish, but also over the waters inhabited by the fish. Its care of the fish would be of no avail if it had no power to protect the waters from pollution. 11 R.C.L. 1047, § 35. See *Eagle Cliff Fishing Co. v. McGowan*, 137 P. 766 (Or. 1914). We read in 11 R.C.L. 1039, § 26, as follows: "But, on the other hand, a member of the public who is specially injured by the maintenance of a nuisance, may abate it or maintain an equitable action for relief therefrom. Thus, if one exercising his right to take fish from a common fishery is obstructed by a nuisance, he may abate the obstruction."

* * *

The jurisdiction of equity courts to grant relief by injunction in a proper case against a nuisance, either public or private, is undoubted and well-settled, and wherever the circumstances of the case are such that adequate redress cannot be obtained elsewhere, equity will afford relief. 14 Enc. of Pl. & Pr. 1118; 1 Am. & Eng. Enc. of Law, 2d Ed. 64. . . .

* * *

The provision for a statutory penalty for polluting a stream is not a bar to prosecuting a suit to prevent the same. 26 C.J. 619, § 36.

NOTES

1. *What is the legal right?* Is *Fishermen's Protective Union* consistent with *Marincovich*? If gillnet fishermen have no property rights in their fishing territories, what then is the special legal interest they possess that allows them to sue for interferences with their fishing operations? If not a property right in the resource, what is it? Are there legal protections that resource-harvesters enjoy that do not amount to property rights?

The legal rule embraced by the court is widely accepted. Fishers in navigable waterways, open to public use, typically can recover for lost profits under a nuisance-like standard when they can show substantial harm unreasonably imposed. See e.g., *Union Oil Co. v. Oppen*, 501 F.2d 558 (9th Cir. 1974). The fact that they engage in fishing and suffer reduced fish catches is sufficient to satisfy the "special injury" standing requirement that applies in public nuisance actions.

2. *Protection in the rush to capture.* As *Marincovich* and *Fishermen's Protective Union* explain, fish and other wildlife are owned by the state in a special sovereign, trust-like capacity for the benefit of the people collectively. Subject to the substantial limits imposed by state fish and game laws, wild animals are typically available for capture by licensed takers on a first-in-time basis.

Is it useful to think of *Fishermen's Protective Union* as a case dealing not with property rights, but with the protection a person enjoys while engaged in the process of resource acquisition? When resources are made available to the first taker, the rush to capture can lead to wild, dangerous behavior as each person tries to be first. To keep the whole process fair and safe, rules of conduct can be necessary. We will return to the issue of first-in-time resource allocation in later chapters, where we will see decisions that involve this exact policy issue.

3.   *Nature and multiple use.* Another way to consider this decision is to focus on the plaintiff fishermen together with the polluters. The polluters are also using the river, and their use of it (to carry off pollution) is not per se illegitimate. Thus, we have a conflict between two users of a single natural resource. Which use will take priority? As we resolve this paradigmatic resource use conflict, should the law aim to produce one winner and one loser, or should it strive instead to find ways that allow both users of the river to co-exist? These questions permeate natural resources law in every resource setting. When drafting resource use agreements, private lawyers also need to grapple with this issue as they go about defining how the recipient of a use right can and cannot make use of the resource.

Consider the major ways that this conflict, and countless ones like it, might be resolved.

a.   We could use *nature as the baseline,* prescribing as the guiding rule that anyone can use a resource so long as its natural conditions remain fundamentally unchanged. The idea here is that, when all resource uses are mild and leave nature mostly unaltered, few conflicts will arise among competing users. We shall see this idea at work in, for instance, various forms of water law and drainage law. The obvious downside to this approach, recognized at the dawn of the industrial revolution if not before, was that it did not permit users to exploit a resource intensively and largely banned activities that were distinctly polluting and noisy. To critics this approach seemed to inhibit economic development unduly.

b.   Another possibility is to look to *priority in time.* Whichever user is first gets to keep using the resource without interference by those who show up later. This idea makes many appearances in natural resources law, and we shall dwell on the issues that commonly arise and require resolution when the method is used. One difficulty with this approach is that it can encourage waste. Another is that it can favor resource uses that are less socially and economically desirable than those that have come later. First does not always mean best.

c.   A third possibility is to assess the competing uses in terms of their *reasonableness,* or how much they promote the common good. The term "reasonable" is notoriously vague, so we would have to explain what it means. Does it refer just to the type of resource use? To its efficiency? To its suitability for the location where it is conducted? To its value in relation to competing uses of the same resource? This approach, of course, is the one incorporated into nuisance law, both public (as in *Fishermen's Protective Union*) and private. The underlying idea is that unreasonable activities can be halted in favor of those that are reasonable. One limitation of this dispute-resolution method is that it fails to provide clear guidance when conflict occurs between or among resource uses that are all reasonable. Then, some other dispute-resolution principle needs to be brought in, such as priority in time.

d.   Yet another possibility is to carve up the resource and then allocate fair shares of it to each interested user, employing a *correlative rights* approach. This approach, as we shall see, is widely used in oil and gas fields to reduce conflicts caused by a strict rule of capture. It is a workable approach when a resource can be quantified in advance and divided into shares and when exploitation of a share by one person does not interfere with the actions of other users. When these facts are not present, it may be infeasible to use this approach.

e.   A fifth possibility is to focus on the ability of the competing users to make alterations in their practices so as to diminish the conflict. That is, we could seek out possibilities for *accommodation,* then press for change by the party that can more easily diminish the conflict by altering her resource use practices. We shall see that this idea has crept into mining law and makes an appearance in some definitions of "reasonable use" employed in water law, perhaps even in implementation of the public trust doctrine.

f.   Of course, the law could do nothing, and leave the parties to resolve things as they see fit. But note that this approach is by no means a neutral, hands-off approach by government. When the law allows parties to act as they see fit, it has essentially chosen to *favor the party whose resource use is more intensive.* In the case of Columbia River fishing, to allow the parties to act as they like is in effect to favor the polluters over the fishermen (given that the fishing does not disrupt the polluters). If we decide to let the market rule—leaving the parties to negotiate an agreement privately—we have chosen this sixth option, deliberately favoring the intensive resource user.

g.   Lastly, we could choose a process-oriented solution. Instead of dictating a particular resolution of the dispute, the law could create (or stimulate) a *private governance body of resource users,* which possesses the power to decide which resource uses will take place and on what terms. The Altoona Snag Union illustrated this approach.

Keep these options in mind for continued reflection, for they will reappear regularly. Indeed, much of what follows in this book elaborates upon these seven conflict-resolution options, illustrating how they appear in various corners of resources law and how lawmakers over time have chosen (and re-chosen) among them and, quite often, combined them. A central theme of what follows has to do with the rise of option c, reasonable use, which has largely displaced options a and b (although option a has enjoyed a modest resurgence in the context of resources set aside for wildlife and recreation). We shall also see a growing role for the accommodation idea of option e. As for the final option, it has made only cameo appearances to date. Its heyday likely has not yet come.

4.   *Accommodation I: a seventeenth-century example.* One way to allow multiple people to use the same land or waterway at the same time, for

different and possibly conflicting purposes, is to define use rights in the resource carefully so that the uses conflict as little as possible. The difficulties of performing this task vary greatly, as one would expect, depending upon the nature of the various resource uses and the degree of conflict that can arise among them. On this issue, consider the following summary of a resource use arrangement quite different from our own. This approach, too, centered around private property rights, but it defined and allocated the rights in ways suited to a much different economy and culture.

This summary considers the land-use patterns and arrangements employed by the seventeenth-century Algonquians, who inhabited much of New England and bordering Canada at the time the first English-speaking settlers arrived. As you read the excerpt take note, not just of the ways use rights were defined and allocated, but of how the use rights were apparently made more productive through tribal land-management efforts:

> The countryside of early New England was divided among numerous Indian villages, each generally inhabited by a couple hundred residents. The leader or sachem of each village held sovereign title as village representative to all of the village lands. Boundaries among villages, although subject to occasional change, were relatively clear and respected. In many instances, sachems owed homage to higher or stronger sachems of the same tribe, and some villages at times had easement-like rights to use or to cross lands held by other villages. But generally, the village was the basic unit of sovereign land ownership with tribal land co-ownership rare or unknown.

> The average Indian group that comprised a single village migrated seasonally on the lands it owned. Village groups in northern areas with climates hostile to agriculture were pure hunter-gatherer societies. Villages in areas where agriculture was possible typically lived on their agricultural lands in the warm months; like their northern compatriots, they migrated farther inland during colder months and dispersed themselves for hunting. A village group usually changed its camp locations only after a number of years, when agricultural fertility had declined, firewood had become scarce, or a site had otherwise become undesirable. Such seasonal migrations were possible because the Indians were content with insubstantial, portable dwellings and possessed few personal belongings. Southern tribes set aside village lands for hunting, burning the land regularly to aid travel and to remove low-level shrubs that hindered the hunter's sighting of animals. . . .

> Individual Indian families generally possessed and tilled their own agricultural lands. Such lands were privately owned and used until soil fertility declined or the village changed its camp location, at which point the lands were abandoned without afterthought. Indians commonly mixed several crops—corn, beans and squash, for

example—in a single field, a technique that produced fields that seemed messy and overgrown in comparison to the clean, single-crop English fields but that yielded substantial benefits by reducing weeds, preserving soil moisture, and increasing crop yields. . . .

The Indian land tenure system's incorporation of diverse forms of individual and group ownership is particularly worthy of scrutiny. In their use of property, the Indians clearly embraced a system of private ownership, although they carved up property rights much differently than the colonists did and retained more property rights for communal use. Indian families owned exclusively the land on which their wigwams or other dwellings stood. This exclusive right of use continued until the family abandoned the land. Village agricultural lands were divided up and owned by individual families, with each family's ownership rights in the farm lands continuing only so long as the family made actual use of the lands. The family's rights did not include many of the privileges Europeans commonly associated with ownership: a user could not (and saw no need to) prevent other village members from trespassing or gathering nonagricultural food on such lands, and had no conception of deriving rent from them. Planting fields were 'possessed' by an Indian family only to the extent that it would return to them the following year. In this, they were not radically different in kind from other village lands. . . .

In short, an Indian who "owned" agricultural lands simply had a usufruct right—an exclusive right for the period of ownership to use the land for agricultural purposes. Ownership interests in all other Indian lands—the "clam banks, fishing ponds, berry-picking areas, hunting lands, the great bulk of a village's territory"—were even more clearly limited to usufruct rights and even more distinctly fragmented. Rights to collect edible wild plants and birchbark for canoes, to catch fish and shellfish, to hunt populous roaming animals such as deer and turkeys, and to set snares and traps for less numerous or more sedentary creatures were all viewed as separate land use rights and all subject to different use allocation schemes.

Thus, an Indian who "owned" land possessed only one or more rights to use the land for a particular purpose. Some uses, such as use of a wigwam site, were exclusive uses, while others, such as the right to take migratory birds from the land, were retained in common by the village and not allocated to individuals. Significantly, some rights that are currently associated with land ownership, such as the right to amass and hold land that is in excess of personal needs and the right to transfer for value unneeded land to another person, were alien to Indian land tenure practices and cultures (until introduced by the colonists) and were not rights that belonged to anyone, individually or communally. . . .

Eric T. Freyfogle, *Book Review, Land Use and the Study of Early American History*, 94 Yale L. J. 717, 720–23 (1985) (citations omitted).

D. ANCILLARY RIGHTS AND TAILORING LAW TO NATURE

As already noted, natural resources law over the generations has paid considerable attention to the natural features of lands and resources. It has defined rights in ways that take them into account, while attending also to the ways people have exploited resources and the problems they face doing so. Rights are not defined abstractly; they are highly contextual.

The next opinion is our first look at an important body of resources law, the prior appropriation method of allocating rights to use surface waters. As we shall see later, most states treat the right to use surface water as one of the resource-rights that are part of land that a person acquires when gaining land; it comes with the land when she buys it. In many of the more arid states of the American West, the decision was made to sever water from land and make it available as a discrete resource use right. As the name of the doctrine suggests, the right to use surface water was mostly allocated on a first-in-time basis and disputes among water users were resolved on the same basis.

The decision to treat water as a distinct resource created new problems even as it helped avoid problems associated with the English common law rule of riparian rights. One motivation for rejecting riparian rights was to allow use of surface water far from the water source, sometimes miles away. The idea made sense at the time given the prevailing desire simply to promote economic activities and resource exploitations. But how was the owner of the water right to get the water to the place of use when other people (often the federal government) owned the land in between, and what if the transport effort required the installation of ditches or pipelines and pumps? Without effective ways to gain rights to transport the water, the new water-law system could be frustrated.

The following opinion is complex and will require careful reading. In the end, the legal issue at stake was a simple one: was injecting groundwater into an aquifer for storage a trespass that overlying surface owners could maintain? The court gave a direct, simple answer: no. In the course of reaching that answer (and getting to the legal question), the opinion offers a first-rate survey of relevant Colorado law (dealing, as we shall see, with property rights in land as well as water). In doing so, it introduces several key issues that regularly arise in natural resources law. It is worth careful study even though, on many points, Colorado law is somewhat atypical.

PARK COUNTY BOARD OF COMMISSIONERS V. PARK COUNTY SPORTSMEN'S RANCH, LLP

Supreme Court of Colorado
45 P.3d 693 (2002)

[The Park County Board of County Commissioners, James B. Gardner, and Amanda Woodbury (landowners) and Park County Sportsmen's Ranch, LLP (PCSR) own property in South Park, Colorado. PCSR filed an application with the water court for permission (a conditional water rights decree) to use subsurface geological formations as part of a complex plan to exploit its groundwater rights more efficiently. The landowners objected to PCSR's application to the water court. They agreed that PCSR as holder of groundwater rights had the legal power, without their permission, to *move* water under their lands (that is, injecting the water in one place and removing it in another), but it had no right simply to *store* the water beneath their lands. Storing water without their consent was a subsurface trespass. The water court ruled that PCSR as holder of a water right had the legal power to store the water beneath the ground as well as use the subsurface for water movement. PCSR's project therefore did not require either the landowners' consent or condemnation and payment to them of just compensation for subsurface storage rights. The landowners appealed.]

HOBBS, J.

* * *

The Water Court determined that: (1) artificial recharge activities involving the movement of underground water into, from, or through aquifers underlying surface lands of the Landowners would not constitute a trespass; and (2) PCSR's proposed project would not require the Landowners' consent or condemnation and the payment of just compensation under the provisions of Article XVI, sections 14 and 15, section 37–87–101(1), or the other statutes the Landowners invoke, because the project did not involve the construction of any facilities on or in the Landowners' properties. We agree with the Water Court and uphold its judgment.

* * *

B. *Landowners' Trespass Claim*

* * *

On appeal, the Landowners take no exception to the passage of augmentation water through the aquifers underlying their lands. They also concede that PCSR's proposed project does not involve the construction of any facilities on or within their properties. However, they contend that use of the aquifers for "storage" of PCSR's artificially recharged water within their properties would constitute a trespass. This novel proposition has attracted several amicus briefs arguing that artificial recharge, augmentation, and storage of water in aquifers are authorized by Colorado law and do not require the consent of overlying landowners, unless the project facilities are located on or within the overlying landowners' properties.

To support their theory, the Landowners invoke our decisions in *Walpole v. State Board of Land Commissioners,* 163 P. 848 (Colo. 1917) and *Wolfley v. Lebanon Mining Co.,* 4 Colo. 112 (1878). The Landowners invoke *Walpole* and *Wolfley* for the assertion that their "fee ownership includes the space underneath the land" and therefore they have a right to withhold consent and require compensation for PCSR's project. In *Walpole,* . . . we said:

> Land has an indefinite extent upward and downward from the surface of earth, and therefore includes whatever may be erected upon it, and whatever may lie in a direct line between the surface and the center of the earth.

Walpole, 163 P. at 849–50. In *Wolfley,* we said: "At common law a grant of land carries with it all that lies beneath the surface down to the center of the earth." *Wolfley,* 4 Colo. at 114.

The Water Court found that "Plaintiffs have not alleged that their use, benefit and enjoyment of the estate will be invaded or compromised in any way." The Landowners simply assert that common-law principles entitle them to control the storage space in aquifers underneath the surface of their lands and grant them a remedy in trespass against migration of PCSR's water laterally into their property. The Ohio Supreme Court has rejected a very similar contention in *Chance v. BP Chemicals, Inc.,* 670 N.E.2d 985 (Ohio 1996). In that case, a property owner claimed that the migration of injected liquid into portions of a very deep aquifer underlying its property constituted a trespass. Determining that the injectate mixed with "waters of the state" in the aquifer, the Ohio Supreme Court rejected the property owner's claim of ownership and trespass based on the *cujus* doctrine. It stated:

> Our analysis above concerning the native brine illustrates that appellants do not enjoy absolute ownership of waters of the state below their properties, and therefore underscores that their subsurface ownership rights are limited. As the discussion in *Willoughby Hills*[1] makes evident, ownership rights in today's world are not so clear-cut as they were before the advent of airplanes and injection wells.

---

[1] See *Willoughby Hills v. Corrigan,* 278 N.E.2d 658, 664 (Ohio 1972) (stating that "the doctrine of the common law, that the ownership of land extends to the periphery of the universe, has no place in the modern world") (citing *United States v. Causby,* 328 U.S. 256 (1946)).

Consequently, we do not accept appellants' assertion of absolute ownership of everything below the surface of their properties. Just as a property owner must accept some limitations on the ownership rights extending above the surface of the property, we find that there are also limitations on property owners' subsurface rights. We therefore extend the reasoning of *Willoughby Hills,* that absolute ownership of air rights is a doctrine which "has no place in the modern world," to apply as well to ownership of subsurface rights.

Chance, 670 N.E.2d at 992.

We find the Ohio Supreme Court's discussion of state waters and limitations upon absolute subsurface ownership rights to be of particular significance to the case before us, in light of Colorado's strong constitutional, statutory, and case law holding all water in Colorado to be a public resource and allowing holders of water rights decrees the right of passage for their appropriated water through and within the natural surface and subsurface water-bearing formations. The Arizona Court of Appeals has rejected a claim of property ownership rights very similar to the Landowners' claim in this case. See *W. Maricopa Combine, Inc. v. Ariz. Dep't of Water Resources,* 26 P.3d 1171, 1176 (Ariz. Ct. App.2001); see also *Los Angeles v. San Fernando,* 537 P.2d 1250, 1297 (Cal. 1975) (recognizing ground water storage by artificial recharge and stating that the "fact that spread water is commingled with other ground water is no obstacle to the right to recapture the amount by which the available conglomerated ground supply has been augmented by the spreading.")

* * *

C.   *Tributary Aquifer Hydrology*

Legislators, administrators, and judges generally have a better understanding of surface water systems than ground water systems. See Robert Jerome Glennon & Thomas Maddock, *The Concept of Capture: The Hydrology and Law of Stream/Aquifer Interactions,* Forty-Third Annual Rocky Mountain Mineral Law Institute § 22.02, at 22–7 (1997). Some states that allocate their surface water by the principles of prior appropriation nevertheless allocate ground water by a rule of capture that permits overlying landowners to possess the ground water appearing under their land without regard to the effect of its extraction upon other ground water and surface water users. However, such a rule of capture defies hydrologic reality and impairs the security and reliability of senior water use rights that depend on an interconnected ground and surface water system. Colorado law contains a presumption that all ground water is tributary to the surface stream unless proved or provided by statute otherwise. *Safranek v. Town of Limon,* 228 P.2d 975, 977 (Colo. 1951).

An aquifer is a subsurface water bearing formation. Hydrologic continuity exists if there is a hydrologic connection between a surface stream and the water table of an aquifer. Glennon & Maddock, *supra,* at 22–7 to 22–8. The water moves through a shared, permeable layer. Ground water, in an interconnected hydrologic system, provides a base flow for surface streams through the saturated layer of the water bearing formation. Water added to a ground water system can increase the flow of the surface stream; conversely, well pumping that results in lowering the water table can deplete the surface stream.

Aquifers consist of unsaturated and saturated zones. The unsaturated zone contains both air and water in the spaces between the grains of sand, gravel, silt, clay, and cracks within the rock. See *Ground Water and Surface Water, A Single Resource,* U.S. Geological Survey Circular 1139, at 6 (1999) [hereinafter *USGS*]. The movement of water in the unsaturated zone above the water table is controlled by gravity and capillary forces. Georg Matthess, *The Properties of Groundwater* 173 (1982). In the saturated zone, these voids are completely filled with water. *USGS* at 6. The upper surface of the saturated zone is the water table. *Id.* Water that infiltrates the land surface moves vertically downward through unsaturated areas to the water table to become ground water. Once the water has infiltrated the soil, its passage downward to join the ground water depends on the geologic structures and rock composition. See Elizabeth M. Shaw, *Hydrology in Practice* 124 (2d ed. 1989). Storativity can be calculated for confined and unconfined aquifers. *Id.* at 128. The ground water typically moves laterally within the ground water system. *USGS* at 7. Well pumping creates a cone of depression, with the point of the inverted cone occurring at the bottom of the well pipe. This causes surrounding water in the aquifer to flow into the cone from all sides. See *Fellhauer v. People,* 447 P.2d 986, 992 (Colo. 1968).

The interaction between streams and tributary aquifers occurs in three basic ways: streams gain water from inflow of ground water into the surface stream, streams lose water to the aquifer from outflow from the stream, or do both by gaining water from aquifers in some reaches and losing it to aquifers in other reaches. *USGS* at 9. Without human intervention, the surface/ground water interconnected system "exists in a state of approximate equilibrium" which implies "a long-term balance between natural recharge and discharge processes in a groundwater basin." Glennon & Maddock, cited above, at 22–10.

"Recharge," whether natural or artificial, is "the accretion of water to the upper surface of the saturated zone." *USGS* at 6. "Discharge" is the contribution of aquifer water that migrates to the surface. *Id.* "Storage" is the retention of ground water in the aquifer for a temporal period. The length of the retention time depends upon the specific characteristics of the aquifer:

> Aquifers have two main functions in the underground phase of the water cycle. They store water for varying periods in the underground reservoir, and they act as pathways or conduits to pass water along through the reservoir. Although some are more efficient as pipelines (e.g., cavernous limestones) and some are more effective as storage reservoirs (e.g., sandstones), most aquifers perform both functions continuously.

John C. Manning, *Applied Principles of Hydrology* 156 (1987). . . .

* * *

Under the Landowners' property ownership theory, each landowner would have a cause of action against PCSR or any other person attempting to pursue a conditional water rights application for storage of water in the aquifer. However, we determine that the General Assembly, in authorizing the use of aquifers for storage of artificially recharged waters pursuant to decreed conjunctive use projects, has further supplanted the Landowners' common-law property ownership theory.

Conjunctive use projects are water projects that employ the natural water bearing formations—on the land's surface and in the aquifers—in the exercise of decreed water use rights according to their priority vis-à-vis all other decreed water rights. We now discuss the General Assembly's authorization for such projects.

D. *Statutory Authorization for Conjunctive Use Projects*

When parties have use rights to water they have captured, possessed, and controlled, they may place that water into an aquifer by artificial recharge and enjoy the benefit of that water as part of their decreed water use rights, if the aquifer can accommodate the recharged water without injury to decreed senior water rights.

This authority resides in a number of statutory sections that implement the "Colorado Doctrine," which is that all water in the state is a public resource dedicated to the beneficial use of public and private agencies, as prescribed by law. See *Chatfield E. Well Co. v. Chatfield E. Prop. Owners Ass'n,* 956 P.2d 1260, 1268 (Colo. 1998).

Sections 37–92–305(9)(b) and (c) provide that the Water Court may issue a conditional decree for storage of water in underground aquifers if the applicant can and will lawfully capture, possess, and control water for beneficial use which it then artificially recharges into the aquifer. Section 37–87–101(1) provides that the right to store water of a natural stream is a right of appropriation in order of priority, and section 37–87–101(2) provides that underground aquifers can be used for storage of water that the applicant artificially recharges into the aquifer pursuant to a decreed right.

The storage definition of section 37–92–103(10.5), 10 C.R.S. (2001), contains a two-part definition. The statute provides:

> "Storage" or "store" means the impoundment, possession, and control of water by means of a dam. Waters in underground aquifers are not in storage or stored *except to the extent waters in such aquifers are placed there by other than natural means with water to which the person placing such water in the underground aquifer has a conditional or decreed right.*

Id. (emphasis added). The first part defines "storage" as the impoundment, possession, and control of water by means of a dam and describes the typical reservoir, which is a constructed impoundment. The second definition contemplates the artificial recharge of water into the aquifer for "storage" and describes the circumstances under which a decree may be issued for aquifer storage. Thus, the legislature contemplated a two-step process: that a person will capture, possess, and control water and then artificially recharge it into the aquifer for storage and subsequent use, pursuant to a decreed water right.

* * *

Construing the General Assembly's wording and intent and effectuating evident legislative purposes, we determine that the General Assembly has authorized the issuance of decrees for artificial recharge and storage of water in an aquifer when the decree holder lawfully captures, possesses, and controls water and then places it into the aquifer for subsequent beneficial use. . . .

We now turn to water use rights and property ownership rights under Colorado law.

E.   *Water Use Rights and Land Ownership Rights Under Colorado Law*

[The court began its discussion of state law by surveying the history of water law, beginning in the early English cases and continuing through the first rulings by Colorado courts.]

When first announcing the Colorado Doctrine, we said that "rules respecting the tenure of private property must yield to the physical laws of nature, whenever such laws exert a controlling influence." *Yunker v. Nichols,* 1 Colo. 551, 553 (1872) (Hallett, C.J.).

> When the lands of this territory were derived from the general government, they were subject to the law of nature, which holds them barren until awakened to fertility by nourishing streams of water, and the purchasers could have no benefit from the grant

without the right to irrigate them. It may be said, that all lands are held in subordination to the dominant right of others, who must necessarily pass over them to obtain a supply of water to irrigate their own lands, and this servitude arises, not by grant, but by operation of law.

Yunker, 1 Colo. at 555. Commenting on the 1861 Territorial Act, Justice Wells, in *Yunker,* confirmed this principle:

> I conceive that, with us, the right of every proprietor to have a way over the lands intervening between his possessions and the neighboring stream for the passage of water for the irrigation of so much of his land as may be actually cultivated, is well sustained by force of the necessity arising from local peculiarities of climate. . . . But it appears to me that this right must rest altogether upon the necessity rather than upon the grant which the statute assumes to make. . . .

> It seems to me, therefore, that the right springs out of the necessity, and existed before the statute was enacted, and would still survive though the statute were repealed.

Id. at 570 (Wells, J., concurring).

We followed *Yunker's* lead with *Coffin v. Left Hand Ditch Co.,* 6 Colo. 443 (1882), holding that an appropriator could capture water from a stream and transport it to another watershed, using streams in both watersheds to convey the appropriated water to its place of beneficial use. . . .

Accordingly, by reason of Colorado's constitution, statutes, and case precedent, neither surface water, nor ground water, nor the use rights thereto, nor the water-bearing capacity of natural formations belong to a landowner as a stick in the property rights bundle. Section 37–87–103, 10 C.R.S. (2001), for example, codifies this longstanding aspect of the Colorado Doctrine. It provides that water appropriated by means of a reservoir impoundment and then released for travel to its place of beneficial use shall enjoy the right of passage through the natural formation in the administration of water use rights.

* * *

F.   *Accommodation of Water Use*
Rights and Land Ownership Rights

Upon adoption of Colorado's constitution, the state struck an accommodation between two kinds of property interests—water use rights and land rights—by requiring the owners of water use rights to obtain the consent of, or pay just compensation to, owners of land in, upon, or across which the water right holders constructed dams, reservoirs, ditches, canals, flumes, or other manmade facilities for the diversion, conveyance, or storage of water. See Colo. Const. art. XVI, § 7; Colo. Const. art. II, §§ 14 & 15; § 37–86–102, 10 C.R.S. (2001).

But, this requirement does not extend to vesting in landowners the right to prevent access to the water source or require compensation for the water use right holder's employment of the natural water bearing surface and subsurface formations on or within the landowners' properties for the movement of its appropriated water. Our decision in *Southwestern,* reaffirming the Colorado Doctrine, is adverse to the Landowners' property right and just compensation claims in this regard.

* * *

In deference to the laws of nature, which we held to be foundational in *Yunker v. Nichols,* Colorado law does not recognize a land ownership right by which the Landowners can claim control of the aquifers as part of their bundle of sticks. To the contrary, "[a]s knowledge of the science of hydrology advanced, it became clear that natural streams are surface manifestations of extensive tributary systems, including underground water in stream basins," *Three Bells Ranch Assocs. v. Cache La Poudre Water Users Ass'n,* 758 P.2d 164, 170 (Colo. 1988), and passage of appropriated water through the natural streams is part of the Colorado law of water use rights.

However, Article XVI, section 7 does subject the construction of artificial water facilities on another's land to the payment of just compensation and grants a right of private condemnation for the construction of such waterworks:

> All persons and corporations shall have the right of way across public, private and corporate lands for the construction of ditches, canals and flumes for the purpose of conveying water for domestic purposes, for the irrigation of agricultural lands, and for mining and manufacturing purposes, and for drainage, upon payment of just compensation.

Colo. Const. art. XVI, § 7. . . .

In sum, the holders of water use rights may employ underground as well as surface water bearing formations in the state for the placement of water into, occupation of water in, conveyance of water through, and withdrawal of water from the natural water bearing formations in the exercise of water use rights. See *Coffin,* 6 Colo. at 449; *Larimer County Reservoir Co. v. Luther,* 9 P. 794, 795–96 (Colo. 1885) (holding that an appropriator can use the natural non-navigable stream for water storage); *People v. Emmert,* 597 P.2d 1025, 1028 (Colo. 1979) (stating that section 5 of Article XVI of the Colorado Constitution "was primarily intended to preserve the historical appropriation system of water rights upon which the irrigation economy in Colorado was founded"); *Danielson v. Vickroy,* 627 P.2d 752, 756 (Colo. 1981) (stating that the purpose of the Ground Water Management Act was to permit the full economic development of designated ground water resources); *Bayou Land Co. v. Talley,* 924 P.2d 136, 146 (Colo. 1996) (holding that Congress did not grant ownership of water along with land grants and the General Assembly's statutory provisions control); *Chatfield E. Well Co. v. Chatfield E. Prop. Owners Ass'n,* 956 P.2d 1260, 1268 (Colo. 1998) (stating that water is a public resource and the "right to use nontributary ground water outside of a designated basin is purely a function of statute and landowners do not have an absolute right to ownership of water underneath their land"); *Park County Sportsmen's Ranch v. Bargas,* 986 P.2d 262, 275 (Colo. 1999) (holding that ground water beneath lands in South Park is tributary and is subject to the doctrine of prior appropriation).

We reject the Landowners' claim that the *cujus* doctrine provides them with a property right to require consent for artificial recharge and storage of water in aquifers that extend through their land. Water is not a mineral. See *Andrus v. Charlestone Stone Prods.,* 436 U.S. 604, 615 (1978). The law of minerals and property ownership we relied on in *Walpole* and *Wolfley* is inapplicable to water and water use rights.[2]

G. *Condemnation for Constructed Waterworks*

We now address the Landowners' contention that certain statutory provisions, in combination with Article II, sections 14 and 15 of the Colorado Constitution, evidence legislative intent to require consent or the payment of just compensation for the right of storage occupancy in aquifers extending through the Landowners' properties.

* * *

The Colorado Constitution prohibits the taking of private property for public or private use without the property owner's consent, but provides five exceptions to this prohibition, four of which pertain to constructed water facilities. Article XVI, section 7:(1) provides for access to the water source across the lands of others, embodying the common-law right-of-way rule for artificial water structures we first articulated in *Yunker v. Nichols;* and (2) requires compensation for the construction of water project features on the land of those who do not consent. Article II,

---

[2] We decline to extend principles of mineral law to water law in Colorado for additional reasons. Ownership of oil and gas is a private right closely tied to property ownership; it logically follows that the right to ownership, extraction, and storage of mineral resources would remain sticks in the property owner's bundle of sticks. Water is a public resource, and any rights to it are usufructuary. Mineral law is a special body of law derived from special circumstances. See *Chance v. BP Chems., Inc.,* 77 Ohio St.3d 17, 670 N.E.2d 985, 991 (1996) ("We find the situation before us is not analogous to those present in oil and gas cases, around which a special body of law has arisen based on special circumstances not present here.").

section 14 further recognizes and addresses the private right of condemnation for the construction of waterworks:

> Private property shall not be taken for private use unless by consent of the owner, except for private ways of necessity, and except for reservoirs, drains, flumes, or ditches on or across the lands of others for agricultural, mining, milling, domestic or sanitary purposes.

Colo. Const. art. II, § 14.[3] Article II, section 15 establishes a compensation requirement for such takings:

> Private property shall not be taken or damaged, for public or private use, without just compensation. Such compensation shall be ascertained by a board of commissioners, of not less than three freeholders, or by a jury. . . .

Colo. Const. art II, § 15.

[The court next considered several state statutes, concluding that they did not alter this constitutional rule governing compensation.]

Article XVI, section 7, Article II, sections 14 and 15, and section 37–87–101(1) establish a private right of condemnation of private property through eminent domain for "those interests in real property reasonably necessary for the construction, maintenance, or operation of any water storage projects." Section 37–87–101(1) provides in full:

> The right to store water of a natural stream for later application to beneficial use is recognized as a right of appropriation in order of priority under the Colorado constitution. No water storage facility may be operated in such a manner as to cause material injury to the senior appropriative rights of others. Acquisition of those interests in real property reasonably necessary for the construction, maintenance, or operation of any water storage reservoir, together with inlet, outlet, or spillway structures or other facilities necessary to make such reservoir effective to accomplish the beneficial use or uses of water stored or to be stored therein, may be secured under the laws of eminent domain.

§ 37–87–101(1), 10 C.R.S. (2001).

The first two sentences of this subsection clearly provide that storage for subsequent use of natural stream waters is a constitutionally protected appropriative right, the exercise of which must not cause

---

[3] We conclude that this provision's reference to condemnation for "reservoirs" on or across the lands of others refers to artificial structures constructed on or in land to hold water in storage, as each of the remaining terms in the provision is an artificial structure and reservoirs are generally understood to be flat water impoundments constructed for the purpose of damming water. . . .

material injury to decreed senior appropriative rights. The third sentence plainly pertains to facilities that the holder of a water use right constructs to divert, store, or convey water in the exercise of decreed rights. See *Roaring Fork*, 36 P.3d at 1232.

In the case before us, the proposed project facilities include constructed wells, dams, recharge reservoirs, and other water works, but the project does not include the location of any artificial features on or in the Landowners' properties. Thus, PCSR would not need the consent of the Landowners or an easement, nor would it have to pay just compensation to them, and no trespass occurs simply as the result of water moving into an aquifer and being contained or migrating in the course of the aquifer's functioning underneath the lands of another.

* * *

We agree with the Water Court's holding that artificially recharging an aquifer "is analogous to the use of an unconfined aquifer or natural stream for transport." This comports with longstanding principles of Colorado water law that have allowed passage of the appropriator's water across the lands of another. . . .

* * *

The Water Court did not err in concluding that PCSR's recharge, augmentation, and storage activities in aquifers pursuant to a decreed water use right would not constitute a trespass or require condemnation and the payment of just compensation, unless project features are constructed on or in the Landowners' properties. Accordingly, we affirm the Water Court's judgment.

NOTES

1. *Ancillary rights and the efficient use of resources.* In its effort to promote the full use of water, Colorado lawmakers made significant changes to the common law, not just of water rights but of landed property rights. It is useful to identify exactly what they did and why to each of these bodies of law.

On the water side, those who gain rights to use water under the prior appropriation system have certain rights to use land in order to exploit their water fully, chiefly rights to transport the water to the place where it will be used. According to the court, they can cross private land to get to the water, and they can convey the water to their place of use employing natural channels and subsurface formations on land belonging to other people, without seeking permission. In a sense, these land-use rights are ancillary and attached to the primary water rights. The law, in other words, bundles legal entitlements together to promote more efficient use: a person who acquires water gets certain land-use rights along with the water. The practice is in fact widespread in natural resources law; those who gain rights in a specific resource need access to it, and quite often need to make incidental uses of neighboring land to enjoy a resource fully. A familiar example: public boaters on navigable rivers can make incidental uses of adjacent private lands to portage around obstacles in the river.

This specific dispute, of course, has to do with the subsurface-use rights of water-rights holders. All parties to the litigation agreed that a water right carried with it the power to *transport* the water through naturally existing subsurface cavities. What they disagreed about was whether the owner of a water right could *store* the water underground. The court says the water owner can do so. What reasoning does it employ in getting to that result? Does the reasoning seem to be motivated mostly by the state's longstanding desire to promote the full use of water, even when that means curtailing the property rights of landowners? Or does the reasoning instead have more to do with recognition that courts might have trouble distinguishing between the use of the subsurface for water transport (often very slow transport) and the use of the subsurface for storage?

On the side of landed property rights, Colorado has changed the law of trespass in material ways, denying owners the right to halt certain invasions of their lands. As early Colorado lawmakers saw things, water was the scarce commodity, and it was more important that water be used efficiently than it was that landowners have a full right to exclude. The outcome of this policy was a new understanding of landownership that takes into account a land parcel's physical features. Land that is crossed by a physical feature (a gully, for instance) capable of conveying water on or below the surface does not carry the same rights to exclude as do other types of land. Differences like this in landowner rights arise regularly in natural resources law (for instance, state game laws may allow hunting on certain lands and not others; zoning ordinances may similarly prohibit mining in some places and not others).

We should note also that the court's opinion is permeated by a sense that owners of land and valuable resources need to take into account the respective needs of one another. Note the title that the court gives to part II.F. of its opinion: "Accommodation of Water Use Rights and Land Ownership Rights." This obligation to accommodate recurs regularly in natural resources law, and with increasing frequency. Indeed, it is an idea that might well have a considerable future, as courts identify new ways in which accommodation can increase resource use efficiency and decrease ecological degradation.

2. *The complexities of modern water law. Park County* is a challenging decision to read because it presumes a rather advanced knowledge of water law. Three basic points will help: a *conditional water rights* decree in Colorado is a judicial declaration that a water user is undertaking the steps necessary to gain an appropriative water right; once all the steps are taken (basically, physically diverting the water and applying it to a beneficial use),

the new water right will ripen and, in terms of temporal priority, will date back in time to the date of the conditional water rights decree. The decree is conditional on completion of all the steps; if the steps are not completed in a timely manner, the right ends.

A *plan of augmentation and exchange* involves a situation in which a party that wants to use water from one source (typically where water is fully appropriated) can gain the right to do so by replacing the water it is removing with water from elsewhere. The idea may seem strange but in many physical settings makes good sense in terms of reducing the costs of transporting and storing water. As for *conjunctive use*, it is a broad term that covers various arrangements by which surface water is used in conjunction with groundwater.

3. *Law versus nature.* Whenever nature is divided into discrete natural resources, problems arise in defining where one resource ends and the next begins. Water law is no exception. In nature, surface and groundwater are often closely connected hydrologically. A well drilled next to a river can easily draw water out of the river. Disputes are inevitable when surface water is allocated in one way and groundwater in another. Even when both forms of water are allocated based on priority in time, we can easily have a holder of a relatively recent groundwater right taking water indirectly from the holder of a much older surface water right—and legally so, if the temporal priority schemes for the two types of water are entirely separate. Note how Colorado has attempted to address the problem: its law "contains a presumption that all ground water is tributary to the surface stream unless proved or provided by statute otherwise."

4. *Private condemnation: passageways for water flows.* It is a surprise to many students of the law (new and old alike) to learn that many states have statutes that expressly authorize takings of private property for private use, as Colorado does in the context of water. As best we can tell from this opinion, when can a Colorado water user condemn a right to use private land upon payment of just compensation? As for the constitutionality of such takings, it may be useful to back up and think first about the property rights that landowners have. If a state from the beginning has reserved the right to reclaim land to devote to particular types of private uses, is the exercise of that reserved right a taking of private property? Could we view it instead as merely taking advantage of a pre-existing limit on the rights that the landowner has always possessed?

Condemnation is one of the legal mechanisms that facilitate resource reallocation over time. In many settings, market mechanisms for reallocation do not work well. This is particularly true when a particular proposed activity requires the use of a specific piece of land or resource. If the owner of that land or resource has the power to refuse use, the activity may not take place. In negotiations related to the use of that land or resource, there is only one potential seller. The situation creates a natural monopoly, which displaces market forces. In their efforts to promote the full use of natural resources, legislators have long authorized condemnation as a way to overcome this type of market failure. The guiding idea has been that the full use of natural resources serves the public good. Property law should not empower particular individuals to frustrate that public good, even while it insists on compensation when landowners and resource-owners are deprived of private rights.

E. USING NATURE, AND THE SHIFTING CONCEPT OF HARM

We end this overview of natural resources law by turning to the issue of ecological degradation, and how it has played out in the field. Many resource use activities, of course, are directly governed by environmental laws and, in the case of resources on public lands, by environmentally-aimed public laws that govern such resources. But the influence of environmental considerations is much broader, as we shall see. Step by step, particular parts of nature have come to seem more valuable to lawmakers and worth protecting. In the case of privately-owned resources, this has often meant limitations on how owners can use what they own, both landowners and owners of discrete resources. The following opinion is illustrative. The case concerns a natural resource that has, over the centuries and millennia, often been abused by peoples to their long-term detriment. Indeed, abuse of this resource has often contributed to the downfall of entire civilizations. The opinion also brings into our survey issues regarding state regulatory power and the constitutional provisions that protect private property owners from unfair legal changes.

WOODBURY COUNTY SOIL CONSERVATION DISTRICT V. ORTNER

Supreme Court of Iowa
279 N.W.2d 276 (1979)

[An adjacent landowner, Matt, filed a complaint with the county soil conservation district, alleging that his land was being damaged by water and soil erosion from the neighboring farms owned by Ortner and Schrank. The district determined that the Ortner and Schrank farms were exceeding the statutory erosion limits, and consequently issued an administrative order requiring compliance with applicable standards by either seeding the land for pasture or for hay or terracing it. The latter would cost the Ortners some $12,000 and the Schranks around $1,500 and perhaps make some land untillable. State funding was available to defray part of these costs. The Ortners and Schranks challenged the statute as unconstitutional, and a trial court agreed, declaring that the statute placed an unreasonable burden on landowners. This appeal followed.]

LeGrand, J.

* * *

The two specific issues raised on this appeal are: Did the trial court err in holding § 467A.44 unconstitutional and did the trial court err in finding that the acceptable soil loss limit on the property is ten tons per acre per year? The second of these may be disregarded because the parties admit there is no support in the record for the trial court's finding that the acceptable soil loss is ten tons per acre per year. Actually the testimony shows without dispute that the acceptable loss limit is five tons per acre per year. The Ortners and Schranks concede as much and we give this no further consideration. The only question before us, therefore, is the constitutional one involving both federal and state constitutional provisions.

In considering the constitutionality of legislative enactments, we accord them every presumption of validity and find them unconstitutional only upon a showing that they clearly infringe on constitutional rights and only if every reasonable basis for support is negated. *Bryan v. City of Des Moines*, 261 N.W.2d 685, 687–88 (Iowa 1978); *Chicago Title Insurance Co. v. Huff*, 256 N.W.2d 17, 25 (Iowa 1977); *John R. Grubb, Inc. v. Iowa Housing Finance*, 255 N.W.2d 89, 92–93 (Iowa 1977).

Important to our decision here is a determination as to whether the restrictions and conditions imposed by ch. 467A, The Code, amount to a taking of property under eminent domain or simply a regulation under the police power of the state. The latter entitles the property owner to no compensation; the former requires that he be paid for the appropriation of his property for public use.

We recognized this distinction in *Hinrichs v. Iowa State Highway Commission*, 152 N.W.2d 248, 255 (Iowa 1967) as follows:

> "Eminent domain" is the taking of private property for a public use for which compensation must be given. On the other hand "Police Power" controls and regulates the use of property for the public good for which no compensation need be made.

Even the exercise of police power, however, may amount to a taking if it deprives a property owner of the substantial use and enjoyment of his property. See *Phelps v. Board of Supervisors*, 211 N.W.2d 274, 276 (Iowa 1973). The point at which police power regulation becomes so oppressive that it results in a taking is impossible of general definition and must be determined on the circumstances of each case. *Penn Central Transportation Co. v. City of New York*, 438 U.S. 104, 124 (1978); *Iowa Natural Resources Council v. Van Zee*, 158 N.W.2d 111, 116 (Iowa 1968); *Benschoter v. Hakes*, 8 N.W.2d 481, 485–86 (Iowa 1943). See also 16 Am.Jur.2d, *Constitutional Law* § 290 (1964).

In *Van Zee* and *Hakes* we stated that the test is whether the "collective benefits [to the public] outweigh the specific restraints imposed [on the individual]." Factors of particular importance include the "economic impact of the regulation on the claimant and, particularly, the extent to which the regulation has interfered with distinct investment backed expectations." To be considered also is the "character of the governmental action." See *Penn Central*, 437 U.S. at 124. It is important therefore to consider the nature of the public interest involved and the impact of the restrictions placed on defendants' use of their land by ch. 467A, The Code.

It should take no extended discussion to demonstrate that agriculture is important to the welfare and prosperity of this state. It has been judicially recognized as our leading industry. See *Benschoter v. Hakes*, 8 N.W.2d at 486.

The state has a vital interest in protecting its soil as the greatest of its natural resources, and it has a right to do so. *Iowa Natural Resources Council v. Van Zee*, 158 N.W.2d at 118. This is the purpose of ch. 467A as is apparent from this declaration of purpose contained in § 467A.2:

> It is hereby declared to be the policy of the legislature to provide for the restoration and conservation of the soil and soil resources of this state and for the control and prevention of soil erosion and for the prevention of erosion, floodwater, and sediment damages, and thereby to preserve natural resources, control floods, prevent impairment of dams and reservoirs, assist and maintain the navigability of rivers and harbors, preserve wild life, protect the tax base, protect public lands and promote the health, safety and public welfare of the people of this state.

This same subject receives further legislative treatment in § 467A.43 as follows:

> To conserve the fertility, general usefulness, and value of the soil and soil resources of this state, and to prevent the injurious effects of soil erosion, it is hereby made the duty of the owners of real property in this state to establish and maintain soil and water conservation practices or erosion control practices, as required by the regulations of the commissioners of the respective soil conservation districts.

Defendants' argument is two-fold. They assert first that the statute amounts to a taking of private property without just compensation. Next, they say the statute is an unreasonable and illegal exercise of the state's police power.

We hold defendants have failed to establish § 467A.44 is unconstitutional. Its provisions are reasonably related to carrying out the announced legislative purpose of soil control, admittedly a proper exercise of police power.

While this imposes an extra financial burden on defendants, it is one the state has a right to exact. The importance of soil conservation is best illustrated by the state's willingness to pay three-fourths of the cost. In Ortner's case, the state's share is $36,760.50 and in Schrank's it is $4,413.00. The remainder to be paid by defendants ($12,253.50 by Ortner and $1,471.00 by Schrank) is still substantial, but not unreasonably so. A law does not become unconstitutional because it works a hardship. *Chicago Title Insurance Co.*, 256 N.W.2d at 25; *Diamond Auto Sales, Inc. v. Erbe*, 105 N.W.2d 650, 652 (Iowa 1960). The argument that one must make substantial expenditures to comply with regulatory statutes does not raise constitutional barriers. See *Northwestern Laundry v. City of Des Moines*, 239 U.S. 486, 491–92 (1916).

There is conflicting testimony concerning the effect which either proposal—permanent seeding or terracing—will have on future farming operations, the necessity for additional equipment, the possibility of other alternatives, diminution in farm income, and decrease in value of the land. This is not the kind of clear and compelling evidence necessary as a premise for holding a statute unconstitutional.

What we have already said is relevant, too, on defendants' claim the regulations established by the soil conservation district amount to a taking of their property without compensation in violation of the federal and state constitutions.

As we have already pointed out, an exercise of police power may be so sweeping in its scope and so all inclusive in its operation that it becomes a taking rather than a regulation. However, this did not happen here. Defendants still have the use and enjoyment of their property, limited only by the necessity to prevent soil erosion beyond allowable standards.

Each case must be determined on its own facts. Our conclusion on the facts here is that the record does not support the trial court's finding of unconstitutionality. We have reviewed the authorities relied on by defendants and have given particular attention to *Penn Central Transportation Co. v. City of New York*, 437 U.S. at 124, where the factors important to deciding if there has been a taking without compensation are discussed. We are unable to agree they help defendants' position.

Defendants raise one other objection. They say the statute is invalid because it is designed "solely as a means of furthering the purely private property interests of a very limited class of landowners" rather than for the benefit of the public generally. This is based on § 467A.47 which, they allege, provides for action by the soil conservation district upon the complaint of one damaged by erosion, rather than upon the initiative of the district itself. We believe this argument ignores other sections of the act under which the soil conservation district is authorized to act. See § 467A.44(3), under which the commissioners may require owners to act, and § 467A.52, under which, in limited circumstances, they may take independent action. See also *Miller v. Schoene*, 276 U.S. 272, 281 (1928), where a similar provision was held unobjectionable. We find no merit to this complaint.

The judgment of the trial court is reversed and the case is remanded for such other proceedings as may be appropriate.

NOTES

1. *The basic limits on using nature.* A central principle in all of property law, applicable to natural resources and to land, is that owners should use what they own so as to cause no harm. Over the past century, that principle has often been transformed by courts and legislatures into a requirement that land and resource uses not be unreasonable. But what types of activities and effects qualify as harm, and how do we determine whether a particular land or resource use is unreasonable? And who should get to decide? Many times, legislatures and regulatory bodies get involved in the work of giving specific meaning to these general limits on ownership, as the Iowa legislature did with the farmlands at issue in this dispute. Such rules, whether common law, statutory or regulatory, set forth one of the key elements of a resource use right: how the owner can use it. In many settings, the limits are designed to reduce conflicts that arise among resource owners. In other settings the rules aim to halt wasteful or degrading practices that frustrate public policies favoring the wise use of resources. As we study particular bodies of law, we will call attention to this critical issue: How can the owner of a resource use it, and how are private rights tailored to reduce or forestall actions that seem harmful or in other ways contrary to sound public policy?

As we shall see, the "do-no-harm" limit—and related requirements that resource uses be reasonable—have long been linked to normative standards that evolve over time as society itself evolves. The concept of "harm" has shifted meaning from generation to generation and, along with it, the limits on how owners can use their resources. The history of nuisance law, for instance, features many illustrations of land uses that once were harmful and later deemed benign, or that were benign and later deemed harmful. Similar change has taken place in the idea of reasonable use as it applies in water law, drainage law, and elsewhere. Indeed, if we were to look for a background principle of property law, it might well be the constancy of gradual change.

2. *Assessing the effects of regulation: where to start?* In *Woodbury County*, the landowners contended that the regulatory limits protecting soil interfered with their property rights to such an extent that they deserved compensation under the just compensation clause. The regulations, they said, went too far; they were not reasonable limits that restrained activities that were now legitimately viewed as harmful. In various forms, this question

often arises persistently in natural resources law. To resolve it in a given setting, the first step is to determine how the regulations under challenge affect the private property rights involved. Have the regulations altered landowner rights and, if so, how grave has the change been? The inclination of many people is to begin with the assumption that landowners can rather freely do whatever they please unless they are causing obvious, grave harm. When a statute or regulation comes along to ban a land-use activity, its effect is thus to take away from the landowner the legal right to engage in that activity. This could well be true, but is it necessarily always true? What baseline of property rights should we use when judging the effects of some new law on them? And how do we decide whether a new law is simply a normal updating of ownership norms, the type of legal change that lawmakers (courts mostly) have undertaken for generations, or whether instead it actually takes away property? To make a before-and-after comparison of the regulation, we need to know the "before" part.

To explore this issue, it is useful to imagine how this soil-erosion dispute might be interpreted if the case had involved an action in private or public nuisance, and a court had decided that the soil erosion qualified as a nuisance. If that happened, it would likely seem that the soil-protection ruling was simply an implementation of a pre-existing limitation on landowner rights, and therefore did not deprive the owner of any pre-existing property rights. But if a court in private litigation could decide that a resource use activity involved an improper nuisance, should legislators and regulatory agencies be able to make the same determination, perhaps after studying an issue in more detail and with greater expertise than a court can bring to bear? We can phrase the issue more broadly: When it comes to specifying the elements of owning nature, whether land or some particular resource, what component(s) of government should do the lawmaking?

Like all other bodies of law, property law can get out of date and need amendment. In many states, courts have stepped aside and decided that only the legislature or an administrative agency ought to perform this important work. But is this wise? Are there settings where courts ought to continue the lawmaking function that their judicial predecessors performed for centuries? And if, in fact, legislatures are better able to keep the law up to date, is there a reason why statutory change would be viewed with greater suspicion than common law change?

3. *The expansive police power.* In any event, as this discusssion illustrates, courts for many decades have been highly deferential to legislatures and administrative bodies when called upon to assess the constitutionality of new laws governing land and resource uses. A new law is likely to run afoul of the constitutional ban on the taking of private property without just compensation only if it (i) deprives a landowner of all economic use of the property or (ii) permits a "permanent physical occupation" of private land by someone else. See Michael C. Blumm & Lucus Ritchie, Lucas's *Unlikely Legacy: The Rise of Background Principles as Categorical Takings Defenses*, 29 Harv. Envtl. L. Rev. 321 (2005) (concluding that

background principles of state property and nuisance law frequently lead to judicial rejection of landowner compensation claims). Thus, for instance, a statute that prohibits mining in a region is unlikely to run afoul of constitutional limits unless the land has literally no value for any other purpose. What happens, though, when mining rights to the land have been severed and sold, and then a new law bans all mining? The effect of such a law then is to deprive the mining rights of all value (at least if the market views the law as an enduring, unchangeable limit). Is a ban on mining *illegitimate* as applied to a person who only holds mining rights because it deprives the property right of all economic value while at the same time *legitimate* for a neighboring landowner who holds both surface and subsurface rights? The issue to date has no clear answer.

4. *A right to degrade?* In the past, the do-no-harm rule has largely applied to harms that cross boundary lines—harms that a landowner imposes on neighbors or on the public at large. *Woodbury County* is evidence that the idea of harm can include (and in various settings does include) harm that an owner imposes on his own land or specific resources. In the view of many, such degradation is harmful to the community as such and/or to future generations. These rules raise a critical question: should private owners of nature possess the right to degrade what they own in ecological terms (admitting, of course, the difficulty of deciding what is and is not degradation)? Presumably, an owner of nonrenewable resources must have a right to consume them (otherwise, of what value are they?). But what about renewable resources that, if well-tended, could last essentially forever in human timeframes? Could an owner's property rights in such resources include merely the right to use the resources, not the right to overuse or degrade them? With some frequency, the law now says yes.

5. *A wildlife law comparison.* One setting in which the law expresses a dislike of waste, even by an owner, arises under state laws regulating hunting. Many state game laws include provisions that prohibit hunters from "wasting" the meat of game animals. Even though they own the meat lawfully, they cannot simply leave it to rot. Such a statute was applied in *State v. Huebner*, 827 P.2d 1260 (Mont. 1992), to a hunter who shot a mountain goat and took only the head, horns, and cape of the animal. The court upheld the hunter's criminal conviction against a claim that the definition of waste was unconstitutionally vague. It also ruled that the statute required no showing of intent but rather imposed absolute liability. The effect of such statutes is to tailor the property rights that hunters gain in big game animals so as to incorporate considerations of public policy. We shall see more limits on property rights in wild animals—alive or dead—in chapter 4.

6. *A lighter note: "resources" as moral agents.* The materials in this chapter have all dealt with disputes among people with respect to parts of nature. But the law has not always had this sharp focus. Consider the ancient common law principle of *deodand*, under which property rights in an object were forfeited to the state if the object was implicated in a human

death—for instance, a stack of logs or a horse involved in a fatal accident. J.H. Baker, *An Introduction to English Legal History* 322 (2d ed. 1979). More alien to modern sensibilities was the practice centuries ago of holding animals morally responsible for harms caused to people and their property.

THE HISTORICAL AND CONTEMPORARY PROSECUTION AND PUNISHMENT OF ANIMALS

Jen Girgen
9 Animal Law 97, 98–99 (2003)

"Once upon a time,"—and we might well begin in that manner because the story is as fantastic as a fairy tale—animals were held to be as liable as men for their criminal acts and torts.

In 1386, in Falaise (France), an alleged female killer mangled the face and arms of a child, thereby causing the child's death. The defendant was brought before the local tribunal, and after a formal trial she was declared guilty of the crime. True to *lextalionis*, or "eye-for-an-eye" justice, the court sentenced the infanticidal malefactor first to be maimed in her head and upper limbs and then to be hanged. A professional hangman carried out the punishment in the public square near the city hall. The executioner, officially decreed to be a "master of high works," was issued a new pair of gloves for the occasion "in order that he might come from the discharge of his duty, metaphorically at least, with clean hands, thus indicating that, as a minister of justice, he incurred no guilt in shedding blood."

This particular trial and execution is interesting both because of the retaliatory nature of the punishment and the fact that the village commemorated the execution with a fresco painted on a wall in the south transept of the local Church of the Holy Trinity. However, the case is especially significant because of the fact that the defendant was a pig.

Today, it would seem peculiar for a community to prosecute and punish an animal for a criminal or other offense. We would like to believe that our present-day criminal justice system is too sophisticated to resort to holding animals accountable for the harms they sometimes cause. Not so long ago, however, animal trials and executions, such as that of the Falaise sow, were a regular part of our Western jurisprudential history.

A. *The Two Kinds of Trials*

Medieval animal trials are most appropriately thought of as two distinct proceedings, depending upon the transgressing animal's offense and species. If the animal caused a public nuisance (typically involving the destruction of crops intended for human consumption), the transgression was addressed by church officials in an ecclesiastical court. Alternatively, when an animal caused physical injury or death to a human being, the animal was tried and punished by a judge in a secular court. . . .

In spite of their nontraditional defendants, both the ecclesiastical and secular courts took these proceedings very seriously and strictly adhered to the legal customs and formal procedural rules that had been established for human criminal defendants. The community, at its own expense, provided the accused animals with defense counsel, and these lawyers raised complex legal arguments on behalf of the animal defendants. In criminal trials, animal defendants were sometimes detained in jail alongside human prisoners. Evidence was weighed and judgment decreed as though the defendant were human. Finally, in the secular court, when the time came to carry out the punishment (usually lethal), the court procured the services of a professional hangman, who was paid in a like manner as for the other, more traditional, executions he performed.

CHAPTER 2

CONTROLLING AND USING NATURE: THE BASICS

■ ■ ■

Natural resources law builds upon the basic law of property, particularly in the case of those resources that are owned or controlled by landowners. As the first case in the chapter illustrates, property law also helps define the elements of particular discrete resource use rights. In this chapter we review quickly the laws of trespass and private nuisance, before moving on to consider in more depth the elements of easement law. Many resource use rights take the form of easements, or similar arrangements. It is essential for lawyers in the field to know easement law quite thoroughly.

A. TRESPASS AND PRIVATE NUISANCE

STATE V. CORBIN
Minnesota Court of Appeal
343 N.W.2d 874 (1984)

LANSING, J.

This is a case of first impression, construing the 1979 amendment to Minn.Stat. § 100.273, subd. 7 (1982) allowing a hunter to trespass on unposted agricultural land to retrieve a wounded animal without permission of the landowner. The State brought this appeal, pursuant to Rule 28.04, subd. 1, Minn.R.Crim.P., following a pretrial order by the trial court that it would instruct the jury that Minn.Stat. § 100.273, subd. 7, provided a defense in a misdemeanor trespass complaint. We affirm.

The facts, as stipulated, are as follows. On November 6, 1982, Jay Corbin, Ronald Niebuhr and other members of their hunting party requested permission to hunt at the Soost farms. Wayne and Ed Soost told the hunters they could hunt in the woods but could not go "through the standing corn." The next day, the hunters returned and asked if they could get a wounded deer out of the corn field. Ed Soost refused to allow the retrieval of the deer until he got his corn picked. Later, Soost became suspicious and went to his corn field "to see what the Sam Hill was down on the other end of the field." Soost learned that Corbin and Niebuhr had entered the corn field to retrieve the wounded deer. The corn field was part of the Soost property that was not posted with "no trespassing" signs. The Faribault County Sheriff's Office was contacted and Corbin and Niebuhr were charged with trespassing. . . .

The sole issue on appeal is whether a hunter commits a trespass prohibited under Minn.Stat. § 100.273, subd. 3, by retrieving a wounded deer from unposted agricultural land after being told not to do so by the landowner.

Minn.Stat. § 100.273, subd. 3, provides:

> No person shall enter upon any land not his own regardless if it is agricultural land with intent to take any wild animals after being notified not to do so, either orally by the owner, occupant or lessee, or by signs erected pursuant to subdivision 6

This section, which applies both to agricultural and nonagricultural land, became effective in 1978. *See* Laws of Minnesota 1978, Chapter 794, Section 2. In 1979, the legislature made a number of changes to Minn.Stat. § 100.273. One of these changes, incorporated in subdivision 2, requires affirmative permission to hunt on agricultural land. This subdivision reads, in part:

> No person shall enter upon the agricultural lands of another with the intent of hunting big or small game * * * unless and until the permission of the owner, occupant, or lessee is obtained.

See Laws of Minnesota 1979, Chapter 291, Section 4.

As part of the same legislative act, subdivision 7 was amended to create a limited exception for entry without permission to retrieve a wounded animal from agricultural lands that are not posted:

> During the season for taking big or small game, a hunter may on foot retrieve a wounded big or small game animal from agricultural land of another which is not posted pursuant to subdivision 6, without permission of the landowner, and shall then leave as soon as possible.

See Laws of Minnesota 1979, Chapter 291, Section 4.

Corbin and Niebuhr obtained the initial permission necessary to enter upon Soost's land to hunt deer. Whether their subsequent entry into the cornfield to retrieve the wounded deer constituted a trespass depends upon the interpretation of subdivision 7. This subdivision allows hunters to trespass in certain instances to retrieve a wounded animal *without permission* of the landowner. The State would interpret "without permission" to mean "without having received a refusal." The defendants, on the other hand, maintain that "without permission" allows entry even after a refusal has been received.

In construing the statute, we are aided by several principles. First, penal statutes must be construed strictly; any reasonable doubt must be interpreted in favor of the defendant. *State v. Olson,* 325 N.W.2d 13, 19 (Minn.1982); *State v. Haas,* 159 N.W.2d 118, 121 (Minn. 1968). Second, specific provisions of an act prevail over prior, general provisions. Minn.Stat. § 645.26, subd. 1 (1982); *Fink v. Cold Spring Granite Co.,* 115 N.W.2d 22, 26 (Minn. 1962). Finally, we "cannot supply that which the legislature purposely omits or inadvertently overlooks." *Northland Country Club v. Commissioner of Taxation,* 241 N.W.2d 806, 809 (Minn. 1976), quoting *Wallace v. Commissioner of Taxation,* 184 N.W.2d 588 (Minn. 1971).

In light of the misdemeanor penalty for violating subdivision 3, this statute is penal in nature. Second, subdivision 7 was enacted after subdivision 3 and is the more specific subdivision because it regulates a narrower range of activity. Finally, a plain reading of the entire statute suggests a purposeful omission of the construction urged by the State. The parallel subdivisions create gradations of protection and categories of notice, including written permission, oral permission, oral notice, and notice by posting signs. *See* Minn.Stat. § 100.273, subds. 2, 3, 5, 6. Subdivision 3 specifically provides two methods for a property owner to warn a hunter about trespassing-signs and oral notice. Subdivision 7, which is the subdivision at issue, includes only one method of notice: posting. Therefore, the inference exists that the legislature purposely omitted an oral notice provision in subdivision 7.

We note that this interpretation allows limited entry on unposted *agricultural* land to retrieve a wounded animal after an oral notice not to do so, but would prohibit a similar entry on unposted *nonagricultural* land. Because the statute generally defines a more protected status for agricultural lands, an anomaly is created.

The legislature may desire to address this by (a) requiring affirmative permission to enter agricultural land regardless of the presence of a wounded animal, or (b) placing greater weight on the refusal of permission to enter agricultural land, or (c) providing an additional limited exception for hunters to enter nonagricultural land to retrieve wounded animals. Until it does so, we believe that statutory construction requires the interpretation given by the trial court. If a landowner wishes to avoid this temporary intrusion on agricultural land, the owner should post the land, pursuant to Minn.Stat. § 100.273, subd. 6.

Affirmed.

NOTES

1. *Procedure and the elements of trespass.* This case, plainly, is a criminal prosecution brought by a state, not a civil action brought by a

landowner. Private parties seeking to enforce their rights generally must do so themselves; they cannot expect government officials to step in and help them. Certain interferences with property rights, however, are crimes as well as civil wrongs, trespass to land among them. Criminal actions are harder to prove because the burden of proof is higher, and crimes often require showings of specific knowledge or intent on behalf of the alleged trespasser, matters that need not be proven in a civil case. Further, prosecutors must be convinced to bring a criminal suit, and many will not do so unless a trespasser enters land after being expressly told to stay away, a requirement often not needed to bring a civil case. Nonetheless, the two bodies of law largely overlap. Criminal trespass builds on and helps protect the property rights of landowners as specified by property law. (Given the discretion of overburdened prosecutors, commonly posted warnings that "trespassers will be prosecuted" need to be understood as an expression of a landowner's hopes; prosecutors make their own decisions.)

As *Corbin* implies, a landowner can bring a trespass action by showing a direct, physical invasion of private land that the owner has not authorized, expressly or implicitly. Trespass is an intentional tort, but intention in this instance simply means the trespasser intended to do what she did. Mistake of boundary lines is not typically an excuse. The invasion, though, does have to be direct and visible, a requirement that causes problems in the case of small particles, chemicals, odors, and the like. In the case of indirect, invisible or slow-developing interferences, the proper remedy is an action in private nuisance. As the following case explains, courts and practicing lawyers sometimes have difficulty drawing (or finding) the line between trespass and nuisance. As we will also see, a plaintiff in private nuisance must show substantial and unreasonable harm in order to obtain relief. No such requirements exist in the case of trespass.

2.   *The shifting law of trespass. Corbin* provides a good opportunity not just to see the law of trespass in action but to get a glimpse of some of the changes legislatures have made to it in their ongoing efforts at law reform. In what ways did the Minnesota legislature change the state law of trespass with each of its statutory enactments? Why might some of its statutes have applied only to agricultural lands (keeping in mind that, in many states, the vast bulk of all lands are agricultural)? Are agricultural lands more (or less) worthy of protection? More (or less) prone to trespass? And what weight in their deliberations should lawmakers give to the desires of hunters (often rural landowners themselves, of course)?

3.   *Hunting as a resource use right.* The statutes at issue in *Corbin* do more than just specify the powers of landowners to exclude. They have the effect also of prescribing the legal rights of hunters to enter private land without permission. By doing so, they help specify the contours of this resource use right, a right open to anyone who complies with state licensing requirements and game laws. As it tinkered with trespass law, the state legislature sought to accommodate these sometimes conflicting resource-related rights. Landowners typically like to be left alone, but lawmakers

sometimes curtail their rights to exclude when, by doing so, they can promote the more full use of the state's resources.

4. *Hunting in early America; or, we become like our parents.* Read carefully, *Corbin* contains a slight hint of the old law of hunting that prevailed in colonial America and well into the nineteenth century. We can get a direct look at it by considering a hunting case from the early nineteenth century with facts not dissimilar to *Corbin*. In *M'Conico v. Singleton*, 2 MillConst. 244, 9 S.C.L. 244 (S.C.Const.App.1818)—"an action of trespass, *quare clausum fregit*" [literally, "wherefore he broke the close"—Eds.]—a rural landowner "warned and ordered the defendant not to hunt on his lands." Despite the warning the hunter-defendant "rode over, and hunted deer on his unenclosed and unimproved lands." The trial court rejected the claim of trespass, as did the appellate court:

> Until the bringing of this action, the right to hunt on unenclosed and uncultivated lands has never been disputed, and it is well known that it has been universally exercised from the first settlement of the country up to the present time; and the time has been, when, in all probability, obedient as our ancestors were to the laws of the country, a civil war would have been the consequence of an attempt, even by the legislature, to enforce a restraint on this privilege. It was the source from whence a great portion of them derived their food and raiment, and was, to the devoted huntsman, (disreputable as the life now is,) a source of considerable profit. The forest was regarded as a common, in which they entered at pleasure, and exercised the privilege; and it will not be denied that animals, *ferae naturae*, are common property, and belong to the first taker. If, therefore, usage can make law, none was ever better established. . . .

> Having come to the conclusion, that it is the right of the inhabitants to hunt on unenclosed lands, I need not attempt to prove that the dissent or disapprobation of the owner cannot deprive him of it; for I am sure it never yet entered the mind of any man, that a right which the law gives, can be defeated at the mere will and caprice of an individual.

M'Concico reflects an earlier era of American history, a time when the law showed its revolutionary heritage and its disdain for English laws and practices that, a few generations earlier, had seemed oppressive to ordinary citizens. One of the great complaints of colonists against mother England had to do with the barbarous hunting rules that applied there. Back in England, they complained, a person had to own land to hunt. Not so in the free country of America, where people could roam the countryside at will, regardless of land boundaries. So valued was this hunting right in Vermont that it was (and still is) expressly incorporated into the state constitution as a right of citizens to hunt on all unenclosed rural land, regardless of land ownership. At the Pennsylvania convention ratifying the federal constitution, delegates proposed that the federal Bill of Rights include a provision guaranteeing a common right to hunt on all unenclosed land. See Jeffrey Omar Usman, *The Game Is Afoot: Constitutionalizing the Right to Hunt and Fish in the Tennessee Constitution*, 77 Tenn. L. Rev. 57 (2009). These Revolutionary-era constitutional provisions should not be confused with recently adopted ones protecting hunting, which do not open private lands to hunting and largely solidify the legal status quo. On the recent amendments see, in addition to the just-cited article, see Stephen P. Halbrook, *The Constitutional Right to Hunt: New Recognition of an Old Liberty in Virginia*, 19 Wm. & Mary Bill Rts. J. 197 (2010). We shall see these again in chapter 4 (pp. 259–260 (hunter harassment statutes), 300–302 (clash over hunting and animal cruelty statutes)).

Many states today allow rural landowners to exclude public hunters but require them often to post conspicuous no-hunting signs and sometimes to take other steps. A few states in effect penalize landowners who do close their lands to public hunting by denying them certain benefits (e.g., the ability to get compensated for livestock killed by wild animals). A survey of current law is offered in Mark R. Sigmon, *Note, Hunting and Posting on Private Land in America*, 54 Duke L. J. 549 (2004).

5.   *Grazing livestock, then and now.* The right to hunt on unenclosed land was less important economically to early Americans than the similar rights to graze livestock, gather firewood, and otherwise forage. In much of the country until the Civil War (and even later in places) landowners had no right to exclude wandering livestock from lands that they had not lawfully enclosed with sturdy fences. As the Supreme Court of Alabama generalized in an 1854 ruling, all unenclosed lands of the state by law were "a common pasture for the cattle and stock of every citizen." *Nashville & Chattanooga Railroad Co. v. Peacock*, 25 Ala. 229 (1854). The high court of Georgia expressed the same legal rule in a case brought by a railroad hoping to avoid liability for killing livestock that had wandered onto its tracks. In rejecting the idea that the livestock was trespassing, the court noted the vast change in landed property rights that the railroad's theory would entail:

> Such Law as this [labeling the horse a trespasser] would require a revolution in our people's habits of thoughts and action. A man could not walk across his neighbor's unenclosed land, nor allow his horse, or his hog, or his cow, to range in the woods nor to graze on the old fields, or the "wire grass," without subjecting himself to damages for a trespass. Our whole people, with their present habits, would be converted into a set of trespassers. We do not think that such is the Law.

Macon & Western Railroad Co. v. Lester, 30 Ga. 911 (1860). In a 1880 ruling, the Nebraska Supreme Court declined an opportunity to revise the law of trespass to halt public uses of unenclosed land. "If the time has arrived for such change," it asserted, "the legislature, and not the court, is the place where it should be inaugurated." *Delaney v. Errickson*, 6 N.W. 600, 601 (Neb. 1880).

Vestiges of this former attitude toward livestock grazing remain, particularly in parts of the United States that are designated by statute, regulation, or local custom as "open" grazing areas—meaning that landowners who want to keep livestock off their lands must take the initiative to fence them out. A glimpse at this system and at the legal issues related to it is offered in *Maguire v. Yanke*, 590 P.2d 85 (Idaho 1978).

6.   *A right to roam?* While the United States in recent decades has leaned increasingly in the direction of landowners and their rights to keep outsiders away, Great Britain has moved in a much different direction. It has opened many types of uncultivated rural lands to public recreational use, recognizing and expanding a public "right to roam." The trend is considered sympathetically by Kevin Gray, Dean of Trinity College, Cambridge, in *Pedestrian Democracy and the Geography of Hope*, 1 J. Human Rights & Envt. 45 (2010) (promoting a "human right to engage more closely with the natural world and to enjoy access to the regenerative benefits afforded by wild and open spaces"), and in Jerry L. Anderson, *Britain's Right to Roam: Redefining the Landowner's Bundle of Sticks*, 19 Geo. Int. Envtl. L. Rev. 375 (2007); John A. Lovett, *Progressive Property in Action: The Land Reform (Scotland) Act 2003*, 89 Neb. L. Rev. 739 (2011). In Britain and many other countries, the law protects the ability of landowners to halt interferences with what they do; it gives lesser power to halt harmless entries onto their lands. Assessments looking beyond Britain are offered in Heidi Gorowitz Robertson, *Rationale for Limiting the Right to Exclude*, 23 Geo. Int. Envtl. L. Rev. 211 (2011); Jerry L. Anderson, *Comparative Perspectives on Property Rights: The Right to Exclude*, 56 J. Legal Educ. 539 (2006). From a natural resources law perspective, these statutes expand the powers of the public to enjoy nature through recreation, one of today's most valuable resource use rights in economic terms.

––––––––––

The fundamental law that protects a landowner in her use and enjoyment of land—as opposed to protection against physical invasion (trespass)—is the law of private nuisance. It is an all-purpose remedy that an owner can bring to obtain either damages for an interference with a land use or an injunction halting the interference. The word nuisance is simply a French term meaning harm and, on its own, tells us little. The idea it expresses is that a landowner who has been harmed can go to court and get relief. The term also expresses the idea that one who owns land cannot use it in a way that causes harm to someone else. Nuisance law is thus a *source* and *protection* of property rights as well as a *limit* on how an owner can use what she owns.

The following case introduces nuisance law and contrasts it with trespass law. It also shows again (as in *Corbin*) how resource-related uses can clash and how legislatures can step in to prescribe rules to resolve the clashes, sometimes distinctly favoring one use over another. They often do so (as in *Corbin* and the following case) by revising the elements of the remedies that protect the resource users. By altering the remedies, they indirectly change the rights that people enjoy.

MOON V. NORTH IDAHO FARMERS ASSOCIATION
Idaho Supreme Court
96 P.3d 637 (2004)

BURDICK, J.

The defendant-seed growers are appealing the district court's decision holding the amendments to I.C. § 22–4801 et seq., which were passed by the 2003 Legislature, unconstitutional. This Court granted a permissive appeal of this interlocutory order. For the reasons outlined below, we hold the recently enacted amendments to be in conformity with the Idaho and United States Constitutions.

Factual and Procedural Background

The plaintiffs are individuals claiming sensitivity to grass smoke, who filed an action against various seed growers in north Idaho who traditionally burn the post-harvest straw and stubble in their fields as part of their farming activities. The plaintiffs' complaint, filed in June of 2002, asserted among others, claims of nuisance and trespass. The plaintiffs filed for a preliminary injunction in July of 2002, seeking to enjoin the defendant-seed growers from burning their Kentucky bluegrass fields. The district court, in August 2002 took testimony from the plaintiffs' medical experts, State officials from Washington and Idaho, class members and grass farmers. The district court issued findings of fact and conclusions of law and ultimately granted the preliminary injunction to abate the injury caused by the field burning of the grass farmers and required the posting of a bond.

In September of 2002, however, the Idaho Supreme Court granted the defendant-seed growers' request for a writ of prohibition, after concluding that the injunction exceeded in some respects the district court's jurisdiction. The Court enjoined the district court from enforcing the terms of the preliminary injunction against the grass burners.

The plaintiffs sought and were granted certification as a class and were granted leave to amend their complaint to assert a punitive damage claim. Thereafter, in the early spring of 2003, several bills related to field burning were under consideration by the Idaho legislature. The district court held a hearing on April 11, 2003, where the impact of the various bills was discussed with respect to the plaintiffs' property and their statutory rights to abate the nuisance and/or enjoin the trespass caused by the grass burners' smoke.

In April 2003, after Governor Kempthorne signed House Bill 391 into law, the plaintiffs filed a motion to the district court to declare the law unconstitutional as applied to the facts of this case. HB 391, which was passed as an emergency measure, amended the Smoke Management and Crop Residue Disposal Act of 1999, I.C. § 22–4801 et seq., and effectively extinguished liability for all North Idaho grass farmers that burn in compliance with its provisions. Of particular significance, HB 391 amended portions of I.C. § 22–4803 and added a new statute, I.C. § 22–4803A.

The district court heard the motion of the plaintiffs, arguing the unconstitutionality of I.C. § 22–4803A(6), which reads as follows:

> (6) Crop residue burning conducted in accordance with section 22–4803 Idaho Code, shall not constitute a private or public nuisance or constitute trespass. Nothing in this chapter shall be construed to create a private cause of action against any person who engages in or allows crop residue burning of a field or fields required to be registered pursuant to section 22–4803(3) Idaho Code, provided such activities are conducted in accordance with chapter 49, title 22, Idaho Code, and rules promulgated thereunder.

On June 4, 2003, the district court issued an order holding HB 391 unconstitutional. The district court held: (1) that HB 391 effects an unconstitutional taking of property without prior compensation or due process; (2) that HB 391 imposes a limitation that is not in the interests of the common welfare and thus violative of Article I, § 1 of the Idaho Constitution; and (3) that HB 391 is a "local or special law" in violation of Article III, § 19 of the Idaho Constitution. The district court concluded that for two months of the year, August and September, "the burning invades and destroys two of the three fundamental aspects of the plaintiffs' property rights . . . possession and use." The district court also ruled that by affirmatively granting the grass burners the right to maintain the nuisance on the plaintiffs' property, the State imposed an easement on the plaintiffs' land. . . .

Issues on Appeal

1.   Did the district court err in finding HB 391 is an unconstitutional "taking" of private property under both the Idaho and United States Constitutions?

2.   Did the district court err in finding that HB 391 is a violation of Article I, § 1 of the Idaho Constitution, because the "limitation" imposed

by the amendments were not in the "interests of the common welfare"?
. . .

Discussion

HB 391 affected amendments to portions of I.C. §§ 22–4801, –4803 and –4804 and added an entirely new section, I.C. § 22–4803A. The plaintiffs' motion dated April 30, 2003, challenged the constitutionality of HB 391 in several respects.

In asserting their challenge to the statute, the plaintiffs contended that the immunity conferred by I.C. § 22–4803A(6) to the grass farmers who burn their fields results in a taking of private property without the payment of compensation in violation of federal and state constitutional provisions. The statute at issue provides in relevant part: "Crop residue burning conducted in accordance with section 22–4803, Idaho Code, shall not constitute a private or public nuisance or constitute a trespass." The district court determined that I.C. § 22–4803A(6) is unconstitutional because it takes property without prior compensation in violation of the Fifth Amendment to the federal Constitution.

The just compensation clause of the Fifth Amendment of the United States Constitution provides that no person shall "be deprived of life, liberty, or property, without due process of law, nor shall private property be taken for public use, without just compensation." The Idaho Constitution also guarantees its citizens the right of due process if private property is taken for a public use, pursuant to Article I, § 13, and provides for just compensation for such a taking, pursuant to Article I, § 14. The question this Court must answer, then, is whether the grant of immunity to the grass farmers can be deemed a "taking" from the plaintiffs. In other words, have the plaintiffs been deprived, by the statute, of their common law right to bring a nuisance action and/or a trespass action, without remuneration.

Idaho case law has defined "trespass" to apply to the wrongful interference with the right of exclusive possession of real property, while the tort of private "nuisance" applies to the wrongful interference with the use and enjoyment of real property. *Mock v. Potlatch Corp.*, 786 F.Supp. 1545 (D. Idaho 1992). *See also Carpenter v. Double R Cattle Co., Inc.*, 669 P.2d 643 (Idaho 1983) ("But where an invasion of property is merely incidental to the use of adjoining property, and does not physically interfere with possession of the property invaded, it generally has been classified as a nuisance rather than a trespass."); I.C. § 52–101 (defining nuisance as "anything which is injurious to health [. . .] or an obstruction to the free use of property, so as to interfere with the comfortable enjoyment of life or property."). A useful differentiation between trespass and nuisance is found in a case that the district court found to be squarely on point, in which the Iowa Supreme Court noted: "Trespass comprehends an actual physical invasion by tangible matter. An invasion which constitutes a nuisance is usually by intangible substances, such as noises or odors." *Bormann v. Board of Supervisors,* 584 N.W.2d 309 (Iowa 1998), *cert. den. sub nom, Girres v. Bormann,* 525 U.S. 1172 (1999), *citing Ryan v. City of Emmetsburg,* 4 N.W.2d 435, 439 (Iowa 1942). Thus, in the plaintiffs' situation, an action could be said to lie in nuisance and in trespass, respectively, given the invasion of the thick, oppressive smoke generated by the farmers' burning and the particulates emitted from the smoke onto the plaintiffs' land.

In *Covington v. Jefferson County,* 53 P.3d 828 (Idaho 2002), the increased noises, offensive odors, dust, flies, and litter caused by the operation of the landfill near the Covingtons' property formed the basis of their claim of inverse condemnation. In their amended complaint, they alleged that their property was impaired by the operation of the landfill by an amount in excess of 25% of the property's total value, which they claimed amounted to a taking for which they were entitled to compensation. The Court analyzed the elements of the claim, including whether the Covingtons' property was invaded or appropriated to the extent of a taking, and determined as a matter of law that the Covingtons had failed to allege a taking under either the state or the federal constitution. *Id.* at 831.

According to the *Covington* court, before an owner is entitled to compensation for a violation of Article I, § 14 of the Idaho Constitution, his property must be "taken" and not merely "damaged." *Id.*at 832, *citing Powell v. McKelvey,* 53 P.2d 626, 632–33 (Idaho 1935). This conclusion was based on the language of the constitutional provision that contains only the word "taken" and which has not authorized the collection of damages where there is no actual physical taking of the property. *Id.* at 780, 53 P.3d at 831, *citing Idaho-Western Ry. Co. v. Columbia Conference of Evangelical Lutheran Augustana Synod,* 119 P. 60, 65 (Idaho 1911). The Court also held that under the United States Constitution, a physical invasion or a regulatory taking, which permanently deprives the owner of "all economically beneficial uses" of his land, requires compensation. *Id., citing Lucas v. South Carolina Coastal Council,* 505 U.S. 1003 (1992).

The case presently before the Court is not an inverse condemnation case but as in *Covington,* deals with a regulatory taking. *Covington,* 53 P.3d at 832. Although a footnote in *Covington* indicates that "[t]his activity may constitute a nuisance claim which is not before this court," the opinion does not address whether the elimination of such a nuisance claim by act of the legislature could or could not be deemed a taking. The determination of whether or not there was a taking is a matter of law to be resolved by the trial court. *Rueth v. State,* 596 P.2d 75 (Idaho 1979). The trial court should also determine the nature of the property interest so taken. *Tibbs v. City of Sandpoint,* 603 P.2d 1001, 1004 (Idaho 1979).

The taking asserted by the plaintiffs is not a physical taking because the plaintiffs' land is not appropriated and because the smoke complained of does not result in a loss of access or of any complete use of the property. *See Hughes v. State of Idaho,* 328 P.2d 397 (Idaho 1958) (impairment of a right of access constituted a 'taking of property'). *See also Covington,* cited above (where there has been no loss of access to or denial of any use of the Covingtons' property). The taking asserted then, is in the nature of a regulatory taking, but the plaintiffs have not claimed a permanent deprivation of all economically beneficial uses of their land. As such, under the Idaho Constitution, which does not allow less than a total deprivation of use or denial of access, and under *Lucas,* 505 U.S. 1003, there is no taking in violation of the state or the federal constitution. *See also Tahoe-Sierra Preservation Council, Inc. v. Tahoe Regional Planning Agency, et al.,* 535 U.S. 302 (2002) (holding no categorical taking had occurred because the regulations had only a temporary impact on the petitioners' fee interest in the properties); *cf. Renninger v. State, et al.,* 213 P.2d 911 (Idaho 1950) (a taking requiring just compensation occurs when the state inflicts permanent and irreparable injury on land).

The district court, in analyzing the extent of the taking, concluded that "[a]ny destruction, interruption, or deprivation by the common, usual and ordinary use of property is by the weight of authority a taking of one's property in violation of the constitutional guaranty." *Knowles v. New Sweden Irr. Dist.,* 101 P. 81, 86 (Idaho 1908), *as cited in Hughes v. State,* 328 P.2d 397, 401 (Idaho 1958). As noted above, the destruction of access and deprivation of the use of property may be compensable, but the mere interruption of the use of one's property, as it is less than a permanent (complete) deprivation, does not mandate compensation. This Idaho authority relied upon by the district court has since been overruled by the Supreme Court's interpretation of the scope of a taking. *Covington,* cited above.

The district court also relied on *Renninger v. State,* 213 P.2d 911 (Idaho 1950), for the proposition that just compensation is warranted even when the taking is intermittent. This proposition is derived from cases cited in *Renninger* holding that where a *structure* causes 'permanent liability to *intermittent* but inevitably recurring overflows' it is taking. *Id., citing Sanguinetti v. United States,* 264 U.S. 146 (1924). The physical structure in *Sanguinetti* was a dam, and the servitude created by reason of the intermittent overflow was held to be a partial taking. *See id.* In *Renninger,* the structure that led to injury to the land was a bridge—distinguishing it from the smoke created by the field burning in the case at hand.

Another proposition cited by the district court, which is not the holding of *Renninger,* is a quote from *Pumpelly v. Green Bay & Mississippi Canal Co.,* 80 U.S. 166 (1871):

where real estate is actually invaded by superinduced additions of water, earth, sand or other material . . . so as to effectually destroy or impair its usefulness, it is a taking, within the meaning of the Constitution, and that this proposition is not in conflict with the weight of judicial authority in this country, and certainly not with sound principle.

Id. at 181. Rather, in *Renninger,* where the plaintiff sought to recover damages in inverse condemnation for the injury caused by the bridge built by the State, the Court held that when the state inflicts permanent and irreparable injury on the land without making any compensation, there is a violation of Article I, § 14 of the Idaho Constitution. The district court's reading of *Renninger* is inaccurate.

Next, the district court concluded that the right to maintain a nuisance is an easement, citing the Restatement of Property § 451, at 2912 (1944), which provides: "An affirmative easement entitles the owner thereof to use the land subject to the easement by doing acts which, were it not for the easement, he would not be privileged to do." As explained by the comments to § 451:

> In many cases, the use an owner of an affirmative easement is entitled to make enables him to intrude upon the land subject to the easement in ways which, were it not for the easement, would make him a trespasser upon the land. On the other hand, it may entitle him to do acts on his own land which, were it not for the easement, would constitute a nuisance."

Id. cmt. (1944). Idaho, however, has not adopted the Restatement; moreover, in the case before the Court, the smoke created by the burning of the fields is the "nuisance or trespass" immunized by the statute, I.C. § 22–4803A(6). This immunity thus entitles the grass farmers to invade the property of the plaintiffs' with the smoke from their burning fields, while preventing the plaintiff landowners from full possession, use, and quiet enjoyment of their land and denying them a remedy from the invasion from the farmers' smoke.

The district court followed the reasoning of the court in *Bormann v. Board of Supervisors.* In *Bormann,* the Iowa Supreme Court recalled long-standing law that the right to maintain a nuisance is an easement, 584 N.W.2d at 315–16, *citing Churchill v. Burlington Water Co.,* 62 N.W. 646, 647 (Iowa 1895), which holding is consistent with the *Restatement of Property* § 451. The court characterized the nuisance immunity provision in section 352.11(1)(a) of the Iowa Code as creating an easement in the property affected by the nuisance (the servient tenement) in favor of the applicants' land (the dominant tenement). *Id.* at 316. Concluding that easements are property interests subject to the just compensation requirements of the Iowa and the Federal Constitutions, the court ruled that the approval of the application for an agricultural area pursuant to 352.11(1)(a) conferred immunity, which resulted in the Board's taking of easements in the neighbors' properties for the benefit of the applicants. *Id.* at 321. The court concluded that the legislature had exceeded its authority by authorizing the use of property in such a way as to infringe on the rights of others by allowing the creation of a nuisance without the payment of compensation, compelling the court to hold "that portion of Iowa Code section 352.11(1)(a) that provides for immunity against nuisances unconstitutional and without any force and effect." *Id.* at 321–322.

There is no direct authority in Idaho holding that the right to maintain a nuisance is an easement. . . .

The challenge in *Bormann* was one of inverse condemnation by the landowners when the Board of Supervisors failed to seek condemnation in court. 584 N.W.2d at 311–12. The landowners claimed an invasion of their property by the Board's approval of an application for an agricultural area designation, the effect of which was an immediate interference with the plaintiffs' enjoyment and use of their land and a corresponding, measurable loss of the property's value. The *Bormann* court found historical support for allowing compensation for interferences short of a physical taking or touching of the land in *Pennsylvania Coal Co. v. Mahon,* 260 U.S. 393 (1922) (statute that was an attempt to condemn property and deny the owner coal company the occupancy and right to mine his property viewed as a taking of an interest without any physical intrusion) and *Richards v. Washington Terminal Co.,* 233 U.S. 546, 34 S.Ct. 654 (1914) (recognizing the taking of a property interest or right to be free from 'special and peculiar' governmental interference with enjoyment and eliminating the requirement of a physical taking or touching). The *Bormann* court looked to more recent United States Supreme Court cases drawing a distinction between *per se* takings as outlined in *Lucas v. South Carolina Coastal Council,* 505 U.S. 1003 (1992), and all other cases involving regulatory takings, which are to be examined on a case-by-case basis, calling for a balancing test that is one of reasonableness, to determine at which point the exercise of police power becomes a taking. *Bormann,* 584 N.W.2d at 316–17, *citing Penn Cent. Transp. Co. v. New York City,* 438 U.S. 104, 124 (1978).

The district court in deciding whether the farmers' grass burning effected a taking also relied on *Richards v. Washington Terminal Co.,* 233 U.S. 546 (1914), as cited in *Bormann,* 584 N.W.2d at 319, which awarded compensation for the gases and smoke emitted from engines in the tunnel, which constituted "special and peculiar" damage resulting in diminution of the value of the plaintiff's property. *Richards,* 233 U.S. at 557. The grass farmers correctly argue here, that the plaintiffs have not alleged any "special and peculiar" damage so as to bring themselves within the scope of a private nuisance as contemplated by *Richards,* but only such damages as naturally and unavoidably result from the field burning and are shared generally by property owners whose lands lie within the range of the inconveniences necessarily incident to proximity to the fields being burned. . . .

The grass farmers argue that the plaintiffs have failed to identify Idaho authority for the proposition that the Legislature is foreclosed from abolishing nuisance or trespass causes of action that have not yet accrued. Article XXI, § 2 of the Idaho Constitution provides that the legislature has the power to modify or repeal common law causes of action. It is well established that "it is the province of the Legislature, and not the court, to modify the rules of the common law." *Moon v. Bullock,* 151 P.2d 765, 771 (Idaho 1944). The Court has held that the Legislature can abolish common law causes of action entirely or impose statutes of limitation without violating Article I, § 18. *Hawley v. Green,* 117 Idaho 498, 788 P.2d 1321 (1990). More recently, the Court determined that no one has a vested right to a particular common law or necessarily, to a statutory cause of action. *Osmunson v. State,* 17 P.3d 236, 239 (Idaho 2000). . . .

Accordingly, we hold that that the provision of Idaho Code § 22–3806A(6) granting immunity to the grass farmers does not represent an unconstitutional taking under either the state or federal constitution.

II.

The district court ruled that HB 391 violates Article I, § 1 of the Idaho Constitution. The district court applied the test of *Newland v. Child,* 254 P.2d 1066, 1069 (Idaho 1953) to analyze whether I.C. § 22–4803A(6) promoted the common welfare and placed a reasonable limitation on the plaintiffs' inalienable right "to possess and protect property" conferred by Article I, § 1. Disagreeing with the Legislature's findings and making an independent finding that Kentucky bluegrass can be grown without burning, as is done in Oregon and Washington, the district court determined that the limitation imposed by the statute was not "in the interests of the common welfare."

The plaintiffs' challenge to the statute is a facial challenge, invoking a standard requiring the challenger to establish that no set of circumstances exist under which the Act would be valid. *United States v. Salerno,* 481 U.S. 739, 745 (1987); *see also Village of Hoffman Estates v. Flipside, Hoffman Estates, Inc.,* 455 U.S. 489, 498 (1982); *State v. Newman,* 696 P.2d 856, 863 (Idaho 1985), *citing Steffel v. Thompson,* 415 U.S. 452 (1974). Because there clearly are some interests of the common welfare being protected by the Legislature's action in allowing field burning, we cannot say that the plaintiffs have met their burden to show no conceivable constitutional application for this legislation. There were no facts presented at this stage of the case, and accordingly, an "as applied" challenge is not available to the plaintiffs. . . .

The district court erred in holding I.C. § 22–4803A(6) unconstitutional because it violated Article I, § 1 of the Idaho Constitution.

NOTES

1.   *Trespass, nuisance, and the resolution of resource use conflicts.* *Moon* involves a typical clash between neighboring landowners, one involved in a relative intensive use, one involved in a more sensitive activity. Individually, the activities are sensible enough. It is the combination, the proximity of one to the other, which gives rise to the conflict. Which one will the law favor, directly or indirectly? Because property rights reside on both sides, there is no "pro-property" stance that one could take. To favor one side—arguably expanding the rights of that owner—is to disfavor the other, arguably diminishing the rights on that side.

To bring an action in private nuisance a landowner (or tenant) needs to show that she has been significantly harmed in her actual use and enjoyment of land under circumstances in which the imposition of the harm seems unreasonable. The wrongful act must be either intentional or negligent. Whether harm is substantial is an issue of fact for the fact-finder to resolve. Plainly, there is no easy way to distinguish substantial harms from those that are insufficiently substantial. Typically, the plaintiff must show a decrease in her ability to use the land; it is not enough to claim simply annoyance with neighbors or aesthetic harm. A decline in land value is also usually not adequate as evidence of substantial harm, although it is relevant.

How did the Idaho legislature go about resolving disputes involving grass burning? As you answer this question, pay attention to the regulatory system that was put in place and the role of regulatory agency. The court's ruling also gives us another look at the law of regulatory takings, which imposes a limit on precisely this kind of legal change that curtails private property rights (even as it, in different ways, also expands private rights).

2.   *The link between rights and remedies.* *Moon* presents an especially clear explanation of the links between private property *rights* and the *remedies* that the law provides to protect them. Practically speaking, property rights exist only to the extent of the legal remedies that exist to vindicate them. Alter the remedies, and the property rights themselves necessarily change. As the old legal adage puts it (with some overstatement), there is no right without a remedy.

To see this reality is to understand why, for centuries, students of the common law centered their studies around the various legal remedies, not on bodies of substantive law as students do today. Even at the end of the nineteenth century, legal study centered on what we would call *causes of action*—what were then called *forms of action*, and what earlier lawyers talked about as *writs*. A study of property law would thus center around the study of trespass, nuisance, and other less familiar remedies for invasions of private rights. As for the remedies themselves, the court in *Moon* is particularly clear in upholding the power of state lawmakers to alter them: "[N]o one has a vested right to a particular common law or necessarily, to a statutory cause of action." To change remedies is to change the underlying rights, however. Thus, *Moon* effectively recognizes the broad powers of lawmakers to redefine what private property means, in terms of the rights and responsibilities of property owners. The two main pillars of land ownership are trespass and nuisance. To revise these remedies, as the Idaho legislature did, is to alter land ownership at its core.

3.   *The element of intent.* Nearly all nuisances involve ongoing conduct; it is rare for a nuisance suit to relate to a one-time event, although such cases do arise. In the instance of ongoing activities, the defendant clearly intends to continue the current activity, even though it is causing harm. This mental state is adequate to satisfy the intent requirement of nuisance. It is not necessary to show that the defendant intended to cause harm, or even knew that harm would take place before beginning. Courts typically require a showing of negligence only when harm is caused by a one-time event, typically accidents, such as overturned trucks or railroad cars that emit gases. Even then, if harm arises because of a dangerous condition maintained by the defendant, a court may determine that the harm was intentional in the sense of clearly foreseeable. See, e.g., *Wendinger v. Forst Farms, Inc.*, 662 N.W.2d 546 (Minn. App. 2003) ("a defendant intentionally causes nuisance harm when he maintains the condition causing the harm after having been apprised of its effect upon the plaintiff's use and enjoyment of land," citing Dan B. Dobbs, *The Law of Torts* (2000)).

4.   *The causation conundrum.* The *sic utere tuo* principle announces boldly that landowners should use what they own so as to cause no harm. Harm is a key question, and so is the issue of causation. It seems axiomatic that the party causing the harm should be the one to stop. This insight, though, is often hard to apply because conflicts among land uses (as in *Moon*) require two parties before they arise. So who causes the harm?

One tempting answer is to say that the harm is caused by the land use that began later in time. It was the second land use that created the problem, and the first should thus be protected. The problem with this approach is that it, in effect, gives the first landowner the power to curtail what neighboring landowners can do. Is this fair, particularly to neighboring owners who might have owned adjacent lands for many years? Also, when the law routinely favors the first land use in an area, it can end up protecting land uses that are less socially valuable or economically productive than later land uses. On this point, consider note 6, below.

Yet another tempting answer to "who caused the harm" is to point the finger at the land use that is more intensive—the one that is noisy, that produces light, odors or vibrations or that is unsightly or anxiety-producing.

This approach would protect the more sensitive of two land uses while curtailing the more intensive one. Thus, a factory might be deemed a nuisance if a residence is constructed next door. Here again, though, the law might end up favoring a land use that is, all things considered, less socially valuable or economically productive. And it can seem unfair for the law to decide suddenly that a land use that has been perfectly fine for years is a nuisance because of something a neighboring landowner has recently done.

Inevitably, lawmakers and legal scholars have been prone to want to shift to a legal standard that takes all relevant facts into account and that seeks to promote justice in light of them. This approach has the virtue of being flexible and attentive to peculiar circumstances. The downside of it is that such an approach is inherently vague and unpredictable. It is the epitome of the *ex post* approach to dispute resolution, the approach that vests broad discretion in the court called upon to resolve the dispute. Until the court hands down a ruling, landowners do not know what protections they enjoy and what land-use limits they face, making it is hard to plan and hard to know when one has the right to complain.

5.   *The Restatement of Torts.* A number of courts, struggling to bring clarity to the law of nuisance, have looked for guidance to the *Restatement of Torts (Second)* and cited or even expressly adopted language taken from several of its provision. On the issue of intent, the Restatement sets forth the prevailing view: a landowner acts with intent not just when he "acts for the purpose of causing" the interference, but when he "knows that it is resulting or is substantially certain to result from his conduct." (§ 825). Thus, in the typical case of an ongoing alleged nuisance, intent is clearly present.

It is on the issue of unreasonableness that the Restatement has proved most useful, even though its language is vague. Most courts, in their tests for nuisance, require a showing of substantial harm and an element of unreasonableness. The Restatement blends the two requirements together under the question of reasonableness. On that issue the Restatement includes several key elements (italics added):

a.   Action is unreasonable "if the harm resulting from the invasion is *severe* and greater than the other should be required to bear without compensation." § 829A.

b.   Action is unreasonable if the harm is *significant* and the actor's conduct is "contrary to common standards of decency." § 829.

c.   Action is unreasonable "if the harm is *significant* and it would be practicable for the actor to avoid the harm in whole or in part without undue hardship." § 830.

d.   Action is unreasonable if the harm is *significant* and "the particular use or enjoyment interfered with is well suited to the character of the locality" *and* "the actor's conduct is unsuited to the character of the locality." § 831.

e.   Action is unreasonable if "the harm caused by the conduct is *serious* and the financial burden of compensating for this and similar harm to others would not make the continuation of the conduct not feasible." § 826.

f.   Finally, an action is unreasonable if the "the gravity of the harm outweighs the utility of the actor's conduct." § 826. For this purpose, the utility of the actor's conduct is determined by looking at "the social value that the law attaches to the primary purpose of the conduct," "the suitability of the conduct to the character of the locality," and "the impracticability of preventing or avoiding the invasion."

Note that the Resetatement calls for an overt balancing of harm and utility only under item f., above, not in the case of items a. through e. Also significant is the drafter's use of varied terms to describe the severity of the harm that must be shown. The key words are in italics, and have, of course, slightly different meanings. On that point, it is important also that the balancing test in f. does not require a separate showing that the harm be significant. These provisions, like all statutory provisions, must be read with great care!

In assessing the significance (or severity or seriousness) of the harm, the Restatement draws attention to "the extent of the harm involved," "the character of the harm involved," "the social value that the law attaches to the type of use or enjoyment invaded," "the suitability of the particular use or enjoyment invaded to the character of the locality," and "the burden on the person harmed of avoiding the harm." § 827.

6.   *Industrialism and the decline of first in time.* As best we can tell (given the scanty historical record), the *sic utere tuo*, do-no-harm common law rule in the pre-industrial era typically operated to favor the land use that was earlier in time. The *sic utere tuo* rule was set forth rather strictly, and in its original form did not require an injured landowner to show that the harm was substantial or that the imposition of the harm under the circumstances was unreasonable. (The law, though, did not apparently bother with modest harms.) The requirements of significant harm and unreasonableness crept in during the shift to industrialism and helped make it possible by allowing railroads, factories, and other businesses to engage in more intensive land uses, even though they caused harm.

It has largely been forgotten (except by historians) that the reasonableness of a land use first appeared in the law as a *defense* raised by a landowner who was accused of violating the do-no-harm rule. See Jeremiah Smith, *Reasonable Use of One's Own Property as a Justification for Damage to a Neighbor*, 17 Colum. L. Rev. 383 (1917). Under *sic utere tuo* a landowner who imposed harm on a neighbor was supposed to be responsible for it. Causation seemed to be determined chiefly by looking to which landowner was present first. In urban and industrial settings, landowners accused of causing harm began defending themselves in nuisance actions by, in effect, admitting that they had caused harm but claiming that they had the right to impose the harm. They had the right to do so when they were using their lands for ordinary or customary purposes; or, to use language that soon emerged, so long as they were using their land reasonably. The idea that landowners could use their lands reasonably, even if it harmed others, largely gained judicial approval. And in time, reasonableness shifted from being a defense to becoming a required element of the plaintiff's nuisance action. Under this new approach, it was up to the plaintiff to show that the imposition of the harm under the circumstances was unreasonable.

This evolution in the law has been commented on by various historians. One of them, Morton Horwitz, points to a key ruling from New York (about the time of *Pierson v. Post*), the case of *Palmer v. Mulligan*, 3 Cai. R. 307, 1 Am. Dec. 270 (N.Y. Sup. 1805), as a sign of the changing legal times. While New York was still a colony Palmer constructed a sawmill on a river, with an associated dam that partially blocked the river. The dam raised a head of water to supply power for the sawmill and also helped to collect and store logs being floated to the mill. Later, an upstream landowner constructed essentially an identical dam and mill. The effect was to interfere with Palmer's use of his property. Under the existing law, Palmer deserved to win his case because the new user was causing him harm.

The conservative judges on the bench, including James Kent, voted to uphold that law and the system of private rights based on it. Palmer was wronged and deserved relief, they stated. But the majority, led by Brockholst Livingston, decided to deviate from the old way of determining harm. The old way essentially gave Palmer a monopoly on using the river and thus stifled competition, Livingston explained. To favor Palmer was to undercut the ability of the upstream landowner to do what Palmer had done, when the upstream owner held identical property rights. *See* Morton J. Horwitz, *The Transformation of American Law, 1780–1860*, at 31–42 (1977). Trends in nuisance and property law are also considered in J. Willard Hurst, *Law and the Conditions of Freedom in the Nineteenth-Century United States* (1956); William W. Fisher III, *The Law of the Land: An Intellectual History of American Property Doctrine, 1776–1880* (Ph.D. diss., Harvard U, 1991); Louise A. Halper, *Nuisance, Courts and Markets in the New York Court of Appeals, 1850–1915*, 54 Albany L. Rev. 301 (1990); Paul M. Kurtz, *Nineteenth Century Anti-Entrepreneurial Nuisance Injunctions: Avoiding the Chancellor*, 17 Wm. & Mary L. Rev. 621 (1976); Harry Scheiber, *Instrumentalism and Property Rights: A Reconsideration of American 'Styles of Judicial Reasoning' in the 19th Century*, 1975 Wisc. L. Rev. 1; and Kenneth J. Vandevelde, *The New Property in the Nineteenth Century: The Development of the Modern Conception of Property*, 29 Buff. L. Rev. 325 (1980).

7.   *Ecological degradation as a nuisance.* Among the types of activities that are today viewed as potentially harmful—even though not viewed that way generations ago—are landowner activities that disrupt basic natural processes and ecological functions. Could private nuisance law play a role in combating ecological degradation, particularly when landowners significantly

alter ecologically sensitive lands with spillover effects on surrounding landowners? Litigation so far has been slight, but the possibility has drawn considerable interest. See, e.g., J.B. Ruhl, *Making Nuisance Ecological*, 58 Case West. Res. L. Rev. 753 (2008); Christine A. Klein, *The New Nuisance: An Antidote to Wetland Loss, Sprawl, and Global Warming*, 48 B.C. L. Rev. 1155 (2007). A much-discussed ecological nuisance case is *Cook v. Sullivan*, 829 A.2d 1059 (N.H. 2003) (building home in wetland is a private nuisance due to spillover effects). More litigation has sought to challenge pesticide-use practices as nuisances, particularly when they interfere with nearby organic farming. See, *e.g.*, Alexandra B. Klass, *Bees, Trees, Preemption, and Nuisance: A New Path to Resolving Pesticide Land Use Disputes*, 32 Ecol. L. Q. 763 (2005). The *Woodbury County* ruling in chapter 1 (p. 42), relating to a state soil-protection law, might be viewed as a legislative illustration of ecological nuisance.

8.   *Nuisance* per se *and compliance with zoning and other regulations.* Many courts in their nuisance rulings refer to a longstanding distinction between land uses that are nuisances "per se" and those that are nuisances "in fact" (or, in older terms, "per accidens"). The former are land uses that are nuisances in all locations regardless of circumstances, the latter land uses that are nuisances by reason of the ways they are operated or their locations and surroundings. The distinction has largely been discarded as unhelpful in resolving common law cases, but the terms are still put to use and many ordinances do in effect label particular land uses as nuisances per se. Of greater influence today is whether a land use challenged as a nuisance is subject to zoning or other regulation and, if so, whether it is in compliance. Land uses that comply with regulatory schemes, particularly detailed ones, are more likely for that reason to avoid nuisance liability, although regulatory compliance does not guarantee immunity from damages. By the same token, a violation of zoning or regulatory standards can be used to help establish the unreasonableness of a land use. Many environmental statutes, federal and state, expressly provide that they do not displace common law remedies.

9.   *Coming to the nuisance and right-to-farm laws.* In note 6, above, we comment on the declining influence of first-in-time as a way of resolving land-use disputes in the early and mid-nineteenth century, particularly in settings in which protection for the first user would halt an economically productive land use. First-in-time, though, hardly disappeared as an important factor when assessing the reasonableness of a land use, particularly when a plaintiff complained of a land use in existence when the plaintiff arrived on the scene. Courts that denied relief to such plaintiffs sometimes reasoned that the plaintiffs deserved no relief because they "came to the nuisance." The "coming to the nuisance" doctrine as a strict rule is accepted nowhere. The near-universal view is that expressed in Section 840D of the Restatement (Second) of Torts, entitled "Coming to the Nuisance": "The fact that the plaintiff has acquired or improved his land after a nuisance interfering with it has come into existence is not in itself sufficient to bar his action, but it is a

factor to be considered in determining whether the nuisance is actionable." Common *b* to the Section gives the rationale:

> The rule generally accepted by the courts is that in itself and without other factors, the "coming to the nuisance" will not bar the plaintiff's recovery. Otherwise the defendant by setting up an activity or a condition that results in the nuisance could condemn all the land in his vicinity to a servitude without paying any compensation, and so could arrogate to himself a good deal of the value of the adjoining land. The defendant is required to contemplate and expect the possibility that the adjoining land may be settled, sold or otherwise transferred and that a condition originally harmless may result in an actionable nuisance when there is later development

Various legislative enactments, however, have embraced coming to the nuisance as a way of protecting particular favored industries that run of risk of being challenged as nuisances. Most popular have been "right to farm" laws, which insulate certain agricultural activities from nuisance liability so long as they operate in accordance with applicable regulations (typically written, critics contend, by pro-agricultural agencies). An overview is offered in Rusty Rumley, *A Comparison of the General Provisions Found in Right-to-Farm Statutes*, 12 Vt. J. Envtl. L. 327 (2011).

B. EASEMENTS AND LICENSES

Many natural resource use rights take the form of easements, licenses or similar arrangements in which the holder has a right to enter land owned by someone else to engage in a particular resource-related activities. When easements and licenses arise through private action, which is the useful way of creation, the parties to the transaction can tailor rights as they see fit, given the resource user more or fewer powers. Often, though, agreements are incomplete, and courts are left to fill-in the gaps that they parties have left.

GOSS V. C.A.N. WILDLIFE TRUST, INC.
Maryland Court of Appeals
852 A.2d 996 (2004)

KRAUSER, J.

We are asked to decide whether the right to hunt and fish on an adjoining property owner's land, when that right has been acquired by deed, is a "license" or a "profit a prendre." In this instance, we conclude it is a profit a prendre. . . .

Approximately thirty years ago, Charles F. Deffinbaugh sold two of his 380 acres of land to Charles R. Goss and Geraldine E. Goss as tenants by the entireties for the sum of $10.00. In the deed transferring the property, Deffinbaugh "grant[ed] to the [Gosses] . . . and to those invited guests at their camp all hunting and fishing rights and the use of the creek waters on the whole tract of land" that he owned. The Gosses then erected a hunting camp on the two acres so that Mr. Goss, an avid hunter, could hunt on Deffinbaugh's land.

In the years that followed that transaction, Deffinbaugh conveyed several other small portions of his property; seven of those conveyances included a grant of the right to hunt and fish on his land. On February 11, 1977, Deffinbaugh sold the rest of his property, which then consisted of 323 acres, to Carl C. Benson and Charlotte A. Benson. [The property was then acquired by C.A.N. Wildlife Trust, Inc., a closely held family corporation formed by Donald H. Nixon and his two sons largely for the purpose of acquiring title to the Deffinbaugh property. When Mr. Goss died, his widow transferred the 2 acres with hunting rights to herself and her daughter, Christine Franklin. In 2001, Goss and Franklin, who were not interested in hunting, purported to assign the hunting rights to the Cooks, who used the rights and gave permission to a friend, Jacob Kasecamp, to hunt as well. Although not relevant to the dispute, the Cooks were in the process of purchasing the two acres from Goss and Franklin. The Trust then filed to suit, contending that the hunting rights were no longer valid. According to the court, the single issue in the case was this: "Did the deed granting hunting and fishing rights on an adjoining property to Charles and Geraldine Goss create a profit a prendre or a license, and, if it created a profit a prendre, does the profit a prendre run with the land?"]

Discussion

Appellants claim that the Goss deed created, not a license, but a profit a prendre to hunt and fish on the Deffinbaugh property, which is now owned by the Trust. That profit, appellant maintains, was assignable to others, such as the Cooks. The circuit court disagreed. Observing that the language of the deed conferring hunting and fishing rights on the Gosses "did not use terms such as heirs or assigns that would suggest an intention to make [those rights] assignable" in the granting clause, the court found that Goss and her invited guests "were given the personal privilege to hunt or fish on the [Trust's] adjoining acreage" and nothing more. The Goss deed, it declared, "created a license, not an easement or profit a prendre" and the "purported assignment of July 18, 2001," to the Cooks was accordingly a "nullity."

To understand how the circuit court reached that conclusion, we must first define the terms central to its analysis: "license," "easement," and "profit a prendre." To define the first two terms, we need look no further than Maryland caselaw, but to define the third term—profit a prendre—we must look further afield and delve into the caselaw of other jurisdictions and the works of respected authorities.

The difference between a "license," on the one hand, and an easement (and, by implication, a profit a prendre), on the other, is that "a license is merely a personal privilege to do some particular act or series of acts on [another's] land without possessing any estate or interest therein," while an easement is "an interest in land" that grants the right to use that land for a specific purpose. *Griffith v. Montgomery County,* 57 Md.App. 472, 485, 470 A.2d 840 (1984); see *Black's Law Dictionary* 527 (7th ed.1999). Moreover, a license, as a "mere personal privilege," ceases upon the death of the grantor or grantee, while an easement, as an interest in land, may be both transferable and inheritable. *Griffith,* 57 Md.App. at 485, 470 A.2d 840.

A profit a prendre ("profit"), like an easement, is an incorporeal interest in land. But, while an easement confers a right to use another's land for a specific limited purpose, a profit a prendre confers the right to enter upon another's land and remove something of value from the soil or the products of the soil, see *Chester Emery Co. v. Lucas,* 112 Mass. 424 (1873); *Hanson v. Fergus Falls Nat'l Bank,* 65 N.W.2d 857 (Minn. 1954); *Anderson v. Gipson,* 144 S.W.2d 948 (Tex.Civ.App., 1940); *see also* 25 *Am.Jur.2d Easements & Licenses* § 4, at 573–74 (1996), something which an easement impliedly forbids. *See Anderson,* 144 S.W.2d at 950 ("[A]n easement implies that the owner thereof shall take no profit from the soil. . . ."). Moreover, unlike an easement, "it is within the statute of frauds and requires a writing for its creation." *Id.; see also Hanson,* 65 N.W.2d at 861.

Since "the right of hunting on premises is an incorporeal right growing out of the soil," *Hanson,* 65 N.W.2d at 863, that right, when conveyed by a deed, constitutes a profit a prendre. *See Fairbrother v. Adams,* 378 A.2d 102, 104 (Vt. 1977); *see also Hanson,* 65 N.W.2d at 860; *Anderson,* 144 S.W.2d at 950. The Gosses, having received from Deffinbaugh by deed two acres of land and "all hunting and fishing rights" on Deffinbaugh's adjoining property, obtained a "profit a prendre" to hunt and fish upon Deffinbaugh's property. *See Fairbrother,* 378 A.2d at 104; *see also* Hanson, 65 N.W.2d at 860; *Anderson,* 144 S.W.2d at 950. But that does not end our inquiry. The next question is what type of profit a prendre did the Gosses receive from Deffinbaugh.

Like an easement, a profit can be either appurtenant to land or in gross. *See Hanson,* 65 N.W.2d at 860–61. Once we have determined which of these two types of profits the Gosses received from Deffinbaugh, we shall know whether they could have transferred the profit to the Cooks without also transferring their land. If the profit exists to serve a dominant estate, the profit is appurtenant to that estate and can only be transferred or alienated along with the dominant estate. *See* 25 *Am.Jur.2d*, cited above, at 574; *see also Hanson,* 65 N.W.2d at 861; *Hopper v. Herring,* 67 A. 714, 715–16 (N.J. 1907). Conversely, if the profit does not exist to serve a dominant estate, it is a profit in gross, and may be transferred or alienated separate and apart from the dominant estate. *See* 28A *C.J.S. Easements* § 9, at 179–80; *see also Hanson,* 65 N.W.2d at 861, 863; *Beckwith v. Rossi,* 175 A.2d 732 (Me. 1961).

That feature—the transferability of a profit a prendre in gross—distinguishes it from an easement in gross. In short, an easement in gross cannot be transferred while a profit in gross can. *See* 28A C.J.S., *supra,* at 180, 184; *see also Hanson,* 65 N.W.2d at 861. That is because a profit in gross "has the character of an estate in the land" itself that exists independent of ownership of land. *Hanson,* 65 N.W.2d at 863; *see* 28A *C.J.S.,* cited above at 180; *see also Hanson,* 65 N.W.2d at 861. In sum, a profit a prendre is closely related to an easement, but, unlike an easement, it affords the grantee an opportunity to share in the products or profits of the grantor's land and a profit in gross can be transferred apart from the dominant estate. *See* 28A *C.J.S.,* cited above, at 171–85; *see also Hanson,* 65 N.W.2d at 861–62; *Anderson,* 144 S.W.2d at 950.

To determine what type of profit the Gosses received, we look to the deed which granted the profit. *See Hanson,* 65 N.W.2d at 861–62. As we do, we note that the "cardinal rule in the construction of deeds" is that the intention of the parties governs the transaction. *Calvert Joint Venture #140 v. Snider,* 816 A.2d 854 (Md. 2003). To determine that intent, we must consider the language of the deed in light of the facts and circumstances surrounding the transaction. *See id.* The "true test" of what was meant by the language of the deed is "what a reasonable person in the position of the parties would have thought it meant." *Chesapeake Isle, Inc. v. Rolling Hills Dev. Co.,* 237 A.2d 1 (1968); *see also James v. Goldberg,* 256 Md. 520, 527, 261 A.2d 753 (1970).

Where the grant or reservation is for an exclusive right to the products of the soil, such as minerals or game, the grant reflects a general intent of the parties to sever the estate in the products of the land from the surface estate, allowing the severed estate to be freely transferred or assigned. *See Calvert Joint Venture,* 373 Md. at 50, 816 A.2d 854; *see also Chester Emery Co.,* 112 Mass. at 435 (holding that the grant of "all the iron ore, metals, and minerals in and upon the tract" was a "grant of an estate in the mines and minerals"). But, where the grant is nonexclusive, it reflects an intent to create an incorporeal hereditament that cannot be severed from or further transferred without the dominant estate. *See Johnstown Iron Co. v. Cambria Iron Co.,* 32 Pa. 241, 246 (1858) (finding that a grant of a privilege to mine on the grantor's lands in common with him was an incorporeal hereditament to mine); *Gloninger v. Franklin Coal Co.,* 55 Pa. 9, 16 (1867) (noting that where the grantor reserves a right to mine along with the grantee, the grantee receives an incorporeal hereditament to mine).

When the profit is created in conjunction with the transfer of a particular parcel of land for its benefit, the profit is appurtenant to that parcel. *See Council v. Sanderlin,* 111 S.E. 365, 368 (N.C. 1922) (holding that where the grantee received a tract of land and a profit to hunt, the profit could only be transferred along with ownership of the premises conveyed); *see also Hopper,* 67 A. at 716 (holding that where the grantee received a sawmill and the right to take gravel from the grantor's property to maintain the mill's dam, the profit to remove gravel was appurtenant to the sawmill); *Grubb v. Grubb,* 74 Pa. 25, 33–34 (1873) (holding that the right to take coal from one tract of land to benefit another tract was appurtenant to the second tract because the right added value to that land). *See generally Clayton v. Jensen,* 240 Md. 337, 346, 214 A.2d 154 (1965) (stating that an easement established for benefit of a particular tract of land is an "appurtenant right" that passes with ownership of the benefited tract). And, the profit may not be transferred without also conveying the land to which it is appurtenant. *See id.; see also Grubb,* 74 Pa. at 33–34.

The Gosses' profit was appurtenant to the two acres they received from Deffinbaugh. Because the profit was granted in the same deed that transferred the two acres of land, the profit to hunt and fish on Deffinbaugh property was part and parcel of that transaction and inseparable from it. *See Sanderlin,* 111 S.E. at 368; *see also Grubb,* 74 Pa. at 33–34. Indeed, the two acre tract was purchased by the Gosses for a hunting camp. It was of little or no value to them without the attendant right to hunt and fish on Deffinbaugh's property. Moreover, the deed did not convey to them an exclusive right to hunt and fish on that property. As noted, Deffinbaugh conveyed that same right to the purchasers of seven other pieces of his land. Thus, the Gosses' profit a prendre was appurtenant to the land they purchased from Deffinbaugh.

And, like all profits appurtenant, the Gosses' hunting and fishing rights could not be transferred without conveying the land to which they are appurtenant. *See Sanderlin,* 111 S.E. at 368; *see also Hanson,* 65 N.W.2d at 861; *Grubb,* 74 Pa. at 33–34. Thus, the 1997 transfer of those rights from Goss to herself and Franklin was valid because the rights were in fact conveyed with the title to the two acres of land. On the other hand, the 2001 purported assignment of the hunting and fishing rights to the Cooks was not valid because Goss and Franklin did not also convey, with that assignment, ownership of the two acres. Accordingly, we shall affirm the judgment of the circuit court, but not without noting that, in doing so, we do not address the import or impact of the December 2001 lease agreement.

NOTES

1. *Reading the case.* This dispute raised two basic questions: did the hunting right given to the Gosses in the early 1970s still exist and, if so, who owned it? To answer those questions, the court had to raise and answer another one: what type of interest in land did the Gosses receive? In the court's view, once it determined the type of interest that was created it could put the hunting right in a legal box and would then know its legal attributes. The court would know how long the property right lasted and whether it could be conveyed, with or without the land.

How did the court go about assigning a legal category to the legal interest that the Gosses received? The first step was to decide whether it was a *license* or, instead, a *profit* (a special type of easement that allows its holder to take something of value off the land of another). As the court noted, a hunting right can take the form of a profit. It can also, however, take the form of a license, and quite often does. Why did the court conclude that this right is a profit rather than a license? It puts emphasis on the fact that the hunting right was created and conveyed at the time that the two-acre tract of land was conveyed and for use in connection with that tract. This suggests, the court said, that the interest was a profit. Its reasoning here was sound, but the court might have elaborated a bit more.

The whole point for the Gosses in buying the land was to hunt on the much larger land tract next to it. They likely would not have wanted the two acres without the attached hunting right. This suggests that they sought, and obtained, a hunting right that was of similar duration to the land (that is, perpetual), a right that the owner of the larger tract could not terminate at will. Overall, whether the parties created a license or an easement is simply a matter of intent. On the facts, the court concluded that the parties intended a hunting right best categorized as a profit. Might the outcome have been different if the hunting right had been agreed to later, after the two acres were sold? If it took place later, might the court also pay attention to whether it was purchased or given for free? (Yes to both questions; a right given for free is likely a license.) Yet another key point: a profit is an interest in land that is properly conveyed by a written deed, as it was here. In contrast, a license can be created orally or by a writing that does not include words of conveyance. The fact that the interest here was conveyed in a deed is yet another important fact that the court implicitly weighs.

With this first step taken, how did the court take the next one: deciding whether the profit attaches to the two acres of land or whether instead it is held personally by the Gosses? The court's role, it stated, was to study the deed and figure out the parties' intentions. Intentions are revealed, not just in the deed language, but by surrounding facts and circumstances. Again, what facts seemed relevant in determining that the benefit of this profit was meant to attach to the land and to be used only in conjunction with the land? On this point, the court observed that the profit was nonexclusive. Can you surmise why the profit's nonexclusive nature might make it more likely that the parties intended a profit that was appurtenant to the two-acre tract?

2.   *The types of interests. Goss* provides a good introduction to the types of privately created use rights in land (non-possessory interests) that parties can create by agreement. Before listing and surveying them, it is worth keeping in mind that a given transaction could be interpreted as conveying a *possessory* interest in the land rather than a *nonpossessory* interest. A conveyance could transfer the land itself (a *fee interest*), and many disputes center on whether a fee was intended rather than an easement. Also, a conveyance could transfer a *leasehold* interest. A lease gives exclusive possession of some part of real estate to a lessee for a particular period of time. (The term lease is regularly misused, and courts often interpret "lease" documents as creating licenses or easements instead; see note 6, below)

A *license* is, in essence, mere permission by a landowner for someone else to enter the land and do something on it. It is not an interest in property. If the license is created as part of a bilateral binding contract, then the benefit of the license can be a contractual right. Licenses are exceedingly common in everyday life. Movie theater tickets are licenses. Invitations to enter a store or someone's home create licenses. No writing or special language is needed to create a license. Indeed, a license can arise implicitly whenever a landowner seems to consent to allowing people to enter her private land.

An *easement* is something much more substantial and durable. An easement is a type of interest in land. As the court here noted, it is termed an *incorporeal* interest meaning that it has no physical body; it does not give the holder an exclusive right to possess any part of the land. Instead, an easement is a use right, although possibly quite valuable all the same. As an interest in real property, it must comply with the Statute of Frauds and can be created and transferred only by a document that satisfies the Statute, subject to some narrow exceptions which we will discuss below. In addition, it is a property interest that can and usually should be recorded in the county recorder's office. A document transferring a property interest can be recorded only if it satisfies various formalities in terms of form and acknowledgment. As *Goss* noted, an interest in land that is transferred using such a document, particularly a document that employs formal words of conveyance, is more likely viewed as an easement.

At one time a *profit* (or *profit a prendre*) was viewed as a distinct type of property interest. Today it is often viewed as a particular type of easement— an easement that allows the holder to enter someone's land and remove something, typically some part of nature (trees, grass, minerals, water). Courts are more likely to view a profit as transferable (see below), but that legal conclusion is based mostly on the presumed intentions of the parties. By tradition, a right to hunt is termed a profit, although one might quibble with the application. Wildlife on private land is not owned by the landowner; it is owned by the state, and state permission is needed to kill or capture it. All the landowner conveys is the right to come on the land and engage in an activity like hunting.

Important in *Goss* was whether the profit was attached to the two-acre tract—that is, whether it was *appurtenant* to it—or whether it was an interest in property held simply by the Gosses as individuals; that is, held *in gross*. This distinction significantly affects transferability. Courts entertain a preference to interpret an easement as appurtenant when in doubt. Other relevant factors in drawing the distinction are mentioned in *Goss* and in the first note. To those we can add a further, useful question: is the easement one that could be enjoyed by someone who does not own the putative dominant estate, and if so how fully? Note that an easement can be appurtenant even if the dominant estate is not adjacent to the servient estate. Thus, for instance, a right-of-way to reach a beach from a public road in a residential development can be appurtenant to all lots in the development, even those that are distant from the access path.

A final bit of terminology: the rights of the holder of an easement to use a tract of land take precedence over the activities of the owner of that tract. The owner of the land cannot interfere unreasonably (or perhaps at all) with the exercise of the easement. The easement is thus the dominant property interest, and the rights of the land owner are subordinate. A land parcel with an appurtenant easement is termed the *dominant estate*; the land that is subject to an easement is the *servient estate*.

3. *Duration and termination.* How long an interest lasts, and when and how it can be terminated, are matters for the parties to decide. Courts look to the parties' intentions to resolve such questions. That said, though, courts (as in *Goss*) are strongly inclined to categorize interests, and then to determine their duration and other attributes based on the category. Private intent and legal categories are thus intertwined.

Licenses are presumed to be personal to the recipient and cannot be transferred. (If a license is an enforceable contract right, it is possible to assign the right under contract law.) Licenses presumably end upon the death of the holder. They also presumably end upon the death of the person granting the license, on the theory that they are nothing more than permission by the landowner to enter the land, a permission that terminates with the person's death. A defining feature of licenses is that they can always be terminated at any time by the person granting them unless they have ripened into an easement or termination would be inequitable. Termination of a license might violate a contractual agreement between the parties and, if it does, contract damages might be owed. But the license termination is still valid. Licenses last only so long as the grantor wants them to last.

Easements cannot be terminated by the grantor unless the grantor has expressly reserved the right to do so. As for their duration generally, it is more variable. They can be perpetual, and are presumed to be unless the parties otherwise agree. The parties can define their duration, though, as they see fit (*e.g.*, a specific number of years or until some event occurs), so party intentions are important. Courts sometimes conclude that an easement given for a particular purpose comes to an end when that purpose can no longer be served. (Thus, a profit to remove minerals would likely end when all the minerals are removed.) In addition, as we will see (pp. 92–100), easements can be abandoned by the holder, in which case they simply come to an end. (Abandonment does not mean that the easement is transferred back to the servient estate owner; the easement is extinguished and the servient estate is thus no longer encumbered by it.)

Another method of termination arises from the rule that a person cannot create or hold on easement on his own land. If the owner of the servient estate somehow acquires the easement on his land, the easement automatically ends by operation of the doctrine of *merger*. Merger most often happens when the dominant and servient estate come into single ownership. Finally, an easement can be lost through significant misuse that overburdens the servient estate or by means of adverse use that amounts to prescription. We will return to the issue of easement duration later in this chapter (pp. 89–101); one of the key functions of natural resources law is to specify how long a given right lasts.

4. *Transferability. Goss* gives a good primer also on the rules of transfer—another key element in any resource use right. As noted, licenses are not transferable unless the parties otherwise agree (although contract rights can be assigned). Appurtenant easements can be and are transferred along with the dominant estate. They transfer even if not mentioned in the deed conveying the land, and even if the land purchasers are unaware of them. Appurtenant easements cannot be severed and sold separately; indeed, older precedent suggests that an attempt to do so can terminate the easement. The difficult transfer questions have to do with easements in gross (whether or not they qualify as profits). The court in this case repeats a long-held view that profits can be transferred, while other easements in gross cannot be. This distinction, indeed, was the reason for drawing the line among these types of easements.

Most courts today look to the intentions of the parties on the issue of transferability, and to allow parties to resolve this issue as they see fit. They do not simply ask whether an easement is or is not a profit. A common presumption today is that any easement of commercial value is likely transferable, while easements that are more personal in nature are not. The fact that an easement is exclusive is more likely to make it transferable, as is the fact that the recipient paid money for it. On this point, various facts and circumstances are relevant. A common question that courts ask is whether the identity of the easement-holder is relevant to the owner of the servient estate. Landowners are often willing to grant an easement to a friend or family member but not to a stranger; when the personal connection seems important, a court will be prone to view the easement as non-transferable.

Related to the issue of transfer is whether an easement can be divided and used by multiple parties. We will take that issue up below (pp. 87–88), when considering exclusive versus nonexclusive easements and the often rocky relationships between the easement holder and the servient estate owner.

5. *A personal right to hunt.* Rights to hunt are increasingly common in rural America as less and less land is open to free public use. In many parts of the country (and elsewhere in the world), hunting and fishing are the most valued land uses. Rights to hunt can and do take various legal forms. In one dispute, for instance, a deed transferred a right of way to a duck hunting club. In it, the grantor reserved the right for each of her four named sons to hunt on the club's grounds. Each son had the right to designate one of his own sons to exercise the rights instead. The court ruled thatthese hunting rights were "noncommercial easements in gross" and were limited by their terms to the exact people named. As "a mere personal interest in the property," the rights were not assignable or inheritable. Therefore, when one of the original four sons died, the right of that son ended and could not be exercised by his sons. *Maw v. Weber Basin Water Conservancy District*, 436 P.2d 230 (Utah 1968).

6. *Interpreting confused language.* As courts go about interpreting deeds, they often discount the technical legal terms used by the parties. They reason that nonlawyers commonly misuse legal words, and that their job as courts is to implement the parties' intentions. For instance, in *Seven Lakes Development Co. v. Maxson*, 144 P.3d 1239 (Wyo. 2006), a deed transferring land contained the following language "Hunting and fishing privileges are extended to all lands now owned by grantor, or hereafter acquired by grantor in said Sections 22 and 27, but said privileges must not be commercialized by grantees herein;" and "These covenants are to run with the land and shall be binding on grantors and grantees and all persons claiming under them." The court held that, despite the parties' use of the terms "privileges" and "covenants," the transaction transferred to the grantees profits a prendre that were appurtenant to their lands. The transaction did not create, as grantor's successor in interest argued, a revocable, nontransferable license that was personal to the original grantor and grantees.

Perhaps even more stark, as a ruling ignoring language, is *Boyce v. Cassese*, 941 So.2d 932 (Ala. 2006). A multi-page formal agreement between the parties purported to convey a license, and the agreement used the term license consistently throughout, but the court nevertheless held that the agreement created an easement.

HUNKER V. WHITACRE-GREER FIREPROOFING COMPANY

Ohio Court of Appeals
801 N.E.2d 469 (2003)

DONOFRIO, J.

[John Whitacre in 1995 granted a non-exclusive easement on 2,000 acres to a hunting club, Gully Ridge Hounds, of which he was a member, allowing the club to engage in "horseback riding, fox hunting with horses and hounds, and hill topping with horses and horse-drawn vehicles and four-wheel vehicles (or motor vehicles)." For various reasons the club broke up. A new club of the same name was formed and retained the easement. Whitacre and others formed a second club, which also engaged in fox hunting on the land based on Whitacre's rights as landowner. Gully Ridge Hounds sought and obtained from the trial court an injunction prohibiting Whitacre as servient estate owner from also hunting fox on the land. On appeal, Whitacre raised two issues. The first was whether the original easement was ambiguous when it provided that Gully Ridge Hounds obtained the "non-exclusive right" to engage in the listed activities.]

Appellants [Whitacre and his business, which co-owned the land] assert that the question before this court is: What is the ordinary and commonly understood meaning of the agreement language providing "the non-exclusive right . . . to use . . . property . . . for . . . fox hunting." Appellants argue that a non-exclusive right is commonly understood to mean a right that does not exclude others from the same right. Accordingly, appellants continue, the commonly understood meaning of the words granting a non-exclusive right to fox hunt would mean that such right does not exclude appellants or others from fox hunting.

Appellants note that at trial appellees argued that the phrase "non-exclusive right to fox hunt" was merely a recognition of the fact that previous easements had been granted that encumbered the premises, such as oil and gas leases, and that the defendants contemplated that they might grant future easements to generate an economic benefit to them. Appellants, however, contend that because the phrase "non-exclusive" adverbially modifies only "the right to fox hunt," the phrase is not reasonably susceptible of appellees' interpretation that it somehow relates only to present or future oil, gas, or other easements.

For these reasons, appellants conclude that the language regarding the non-exclusive right to fox hunt was not reasonably susceptible of two different meanings, particularly the meaning offered by appellees, and that the trial court therefore erred in permitting parol evidence for the purpose of construing that phrase.

The construction of written contracts and conveyances is a matter of law. *Alexander v. Buckeye Pipe Line Co.* (1978), 53 Ohio St.2d 241, 7 O.O.3d 403, 374 N.E.2d 146, paragraph one of the syllabus. We review questions of law *de novo. Nationwide Mut. Fire Ins. Co. v. Guman Bros. Farm*, 73 Ohio St.3d 107, 108, 652 N.E.2d 684 (1995).

Where terms in an existing contract are clear and unambiguous, a court cannot create a new contract by finding an intent not expressed in the clear language employed by the parties. *Long Beach Assn., Inc. v.*

Jones (1998), 82 Ohio St.3d 574, 577, 697 N.E.2d 208, citing *Alexander,* 53 Ohio St.2d at 246, 374 N.E.2d 146: " 'Common words appearing in a written instrument will be given their ordinary meaning unless manifest absurdity results, or unless some other meaning is clearly evidenced from the face or overall contents of the instrument.' " . . .

In the present case, the trial court took careful effort to analyze the extrinsic evidence the parties presented to conclude that appellees held an exclusive right to fox hunt. But we need not reach this analysis because the conveyance language is not ambiguous. Extrinsic evidence is admissible to ascertain the intent of the parties only when a contract is unclear or ambiguous, or when circumstances surrounding an agreement give the plain language special meaning. *Graham v. Drydock Coal Co.,* 76 Ohio St.3d 311, 314, 667 N.E.2d 949 (1996).

The phrase, "non-exclusive right, privilege, and permission . . . , to enter upon and use the real property of Grantors, . . . for the sole purpose of horseback riding, fox hunting with horses and hounds, and hill topping with horses and horse-drawn vehicles and four-wheel vehicles" is not ambiguous. In this phrase, the words "non-exclusive right" to fox hunt are clear. We must look at these words using their ordinary, everyday meaning. . . . [T]he common meaning of "non-exclusive" right to fox hunt is that other people can fox hunt because the holder of the non-exclusive right does not have the power to exclude others from fox hunting.

Appellees argue that the "non-exclusive" language is reasonably susceptible of two constructions: the first, as espoused by appellants, and the second being simply a recognition that other easements were already in place as encumbrances on the property or that others were contemplated by appellants in the future. However, the easement language, without any extrinsic evidence does not lead to this conclusion. It is only upon the examination of extrinsic evidence that one might reasonably conclude that the language is susceptible of two or more interpretations. Within the agreement itself there is no mention of other easements, such as oil or gas leases, as appellees suggest. And since we are not to consider extrinsic evidence unless the language in the conveyance is reasonably susceptible of two or more meanings, we cannot conclude that the "non-exclusive right . . . for . . . fox hunting" is ambiguous. Accordingly, appellants' first assignment of error has merit.

Appellants' second assignment of error states: "The trial court erred by interpreting a non-exclusive easement to use property for fox hunting, to exclude the owner and his assigns from using the same property for fox hunting."

In its judgment entry, the trial court stated:

Whether two hunt clubs can schedule joint "use" of the 2,000 acres is not relevant. The recreational easement agreement at issue, as construed, precludes joint use and joint scheduling. It is a moot point. However, the weight of the trial testimony supports a finding that two clubs cannot physically "hunt" the 2,000 acres together on any regular basis as such overuse of such a limited area would diminish, or totally eliminate, the quarry being hunted. Any "second hunt" would amount to "unreasonable" interference with plaintiffs' rights.

Assuming that the right transferred to appellees in the agreement was a non-exclusive right to fox hunt, appellants argue that the trial court erred in determining that any fox hunting by appellant was unreasonable *per se* under Section 8 of the agreement, which provides:

> (8) Grantors and their successors and assigns shall have the full right and privilege to use the Premises, *provided that Grantors shall not unreasonably interfere with the rights granted to Grantee hereunder.*" (Emphasis added.)

Appellants contend that this section was clearly intended to demonstrate that they retained the full right to use their own property while not unreasonably interfering with the rights granted to appellees. If the right to fox hunt is non-exclusive, appellants continue, it cannot be unreasonable to allow two competing groups to fox hunt, because a non-exclusive right to fox hunt clearly contemplates that the owner also has the right to fox hunt. Appellants concede that there is some "gray area" as to how much they can fox hunt before they unreasonably interfere with appellees' right to fox hunt. However, appellants urge that the language defining the easement clearly contemplates that it is not exclusive, and that both they and appellees have the right to fox hunt. Accordingly, appellants conclude, the issue cannot be resolved by simply saying, as the trial court did, that too much fox hunting would eliminate the quarry being hunted, and that therefore appellants may not engage in fox hunting.

As stated above, the trial court concluded that the easement was exclusive. Thus, appellants could not fox hunt on the property. This should have ended the trial court's decision. Instead, the court went on to issue an advisory opinion regarding what the evidence demonstrated *if* it had found that the easement was non-exclusive. The court should not have reached this issue. The question of whether appellants have unreasonably interfered with appellees' easement has not yet arisen. Appellants have not, to this date, unreasonably interfered with appellees' non-exclusive right to fox hunt. Because appellees possess a non-exclusive right to fox hunt, all hunting by appellants cannot be said to be an unreasonable interference. Accordingly, appellants' second assignment of error has merit.

For the reasons stated above, the trial court's decision is hereby reversed, and the permanent injunction is lifted.

WAITE, J., concurring.

Although I agree with most of the reasoning used in the majority opinion, I believe that we must also resolve whether there has been an unreasonable interference with appellees' nonexclusive right to hunt on appellants' property. In so doing, it is important to review the differences between an exclusive and nonexclusive easement.

The right to hunt or fish on property owned by another is given through a type of easement known as a profit à prendre. 1 *Restatement of the Law 3d, Property* (2000) 12, Section 1.2. "A profit à prendre is an easement that confers the right to enter and remove [such things as] timber, minerals, oil, gas, game, or other substances from land in the possession of another." *Id.*

A profit à prendre, as well as most other types of easements, may be exclusive or nonexclusive. These are legal terms of art encompassing (1) the persons who may be excluded and (2) the uses or area from which those persons may be excluded. *Id.* at 14, Section 1.2.:

> At one extreme, the holder of the easement or profit has no right to exclude anyone from making any use that does not unreasonably interfere with the uses authorized by the servitude. For example[,] the holder of a private roadway easement in a public road has no right to exclude anyone from using the road. . . . At the other extreme, the holder of the easement or profit has the right to exclude everyone, including the servient owner, from making any use of the land within the easement boundaries. In between are easements where the servitude holder can exclude anyone except the servient owner and others authorized by the servient owner (usually called 'nonexclusive easement')

Unless the easement agreement states otherwise, the servient owner may make any use of the property that does not unreasonably interfere with the enjoyment of the servitude. 1 *Restatement of the Law 3d, Property* (2000) 581, Section 4.9. "All residual rights remain in the possessory estate-the servient estate." *Id.* at 582; *see also* 1 *Thompson on Real Property* (1980) 472, Section 135:

> In the absence of detailed arrangements between them, it is assumed that the owner of the servitude and the holder of the servient estate are intended to exercise their respective rights and privileges in a spirit of mutual accommodation.

The terms of the fox hunting easement in the instant case must be interpreted with an understanding of the aforementioned commonly accepted legal principles. Based on these principles, there is no ambiguity in the language of the easement agreement. Appellants granted a nonexclusive easement for the purpose of fox hunting (among other things), and there were no restrictions placed on appellants' residual rights except for the promise not to "unreasonably interfere with the rights granted to" appellees. This latter provision is already implied in the very grant of the easement in the first place, and does not materially change the nature of the easement. Seeing that the easement agreement does not place any other restrictions on appellants' use of their property, the law presumes that appellants, as the grantors of the easement, have reserved the right to fox hunt on their property or to issue other nonexclusive easements for fox hunting, within reasonable limits. . . .

Once we have determined that the agreement does not contain an exclusive easement, our review is not ended, because there remains an open question as to whether appellants have unreasonably interfered with appellees' right to fox hunt. . . .

The majority opinion affirmatively declares that "[a]ppellants have not, to this date, unreasonably interfered with appellees' nonexclusive right to fox hunt." It appears from this statement that the majority has implicitly concluded that appellants' actions were reasonable. While I agree with the majority's conclusion, I find it necessary to explain this decision.

The trial court found that it was physically impossible for two groups to regularly fox hunt on appellants' property because it would "diminish, or totally eliminate, the quarry being hunted." On this basis, the trial court held that it would be unreasonable for anyone other than appellees to fox hunt on appellants' property. The trial court has fundamentally misunderstood what the parties actually agreed in their easement. Appellants did not agree to supply live foxes or well-rested foxes or, for that matter, any foxes at all. The easement agreement merely allows appellees the right to hunt for any foxes that happen to be on appellants' property.

The holder of a servient estate generally has no duty to the beneficiary of an easement or profit to maintain the condition of the servient estate. 1 *Restatement of the Law 3d, Property* (2000) 631, Section 4.13. There is nothing in the easement language that created a duty for appellants to maintain foxes on their property, or to keep the foxes in prime condition for the enjoyment of the hunters. There is nothing in the easement language guaranteeing that appellees would find any foxes on the property. Appellees' attempt to imply such duties and terms adds new elements to the easement to which the parties did not agree.

Appellees allegation that appellants unreasonably interfered with their right to hunt presumes that some right was actually curtailed by appellants. Appellees must prove at trial that appellants prevented them from hunting on their property. There is nothing in the record indicating that appellants prevented appellees from entering the property at any time for the purpose of fox hunting. . . .

NOTES

1.   *What did the parties decide?* According to the court, this dispute was resolved simply by referring to the language of the easement agreement. As it interpreted the agreement, the court was unwilling to consider extrinsic evidence because it believed the language was clear. If the court had considered extrinsic evidence, what facts might it have weighed? Is it likely that Whitacre, who helped set up and run the fox-hunting club, contemplated the possibility of granting fox-hunting rights to someone else? Further, recall the willingness of courts, noted above, to ignore language used in easements and instead to seek to implement the intentions of the parties. If a court, as in *Boyce v. Cassese*, cited in note 6, page 81, can conclude that a "license agreement" is in fact an easement agreement, why not entertain the possibility that a nonexclusive easement was meant to be exclusive? (Other courts might well have considered external evidence.) Perhaps the governing rule is this: courts follow clear language unless they think the parties did not mean what they said.

2.   *Exclusive or not?* Easements by their nature are typically nonexclusive, and courts interpret them that way unless the evidence suggests a contrary intent. It is often difficult to determine whether an easement was or was not meant to be exclusive. One factor is whether more than one actor could engage in the activity authorized by the easement. The price paid is also relevant, particularly in the case of a profit. If the price reflects the full value of a resource on the servient estate (for instance, the value of all standing timber), a court is likely to say that an easement to cut timber is exclusive. Similarly, an easement to graze livestock, if tailored to take full advantage of available forage, is likely to be deemed exclusive. Exclusive means both that the servient owner cannot grant a similar easement to someone else, and that the servient owner cannot engage in the authorized activity herself. Still, the starting assumption is that an easement is nonexclusive.

3.   *Dividing or sharing an easement.* Closely related to the issues of easement transfer and exclusivity is the question whether an easement holder can divide the easement in some way among multiple users or otherwise share its use. Generally, a *nonexclusive* easement cannot be divided. It would make little sense for the holder of a nonexclusive easement to divide the easement and purport to sell rights to multiple purchasers, perhaps in direct competition with owner of the servient estate. On the other hand, an *exclusive* easement typically can be divided and otherwise shared so long as the overall use stays within the scope of the easement and does not overburden the servient estate. The need to respect the overall easement

scope and avoid overburdening the estate are the guiding principles. They set the limits, for instance, as to how many friends or family members can be invited to enjoy a recreational easement that is not transferable or divisible.

A special case is presented when land with an appurtenant easement is divided. Typically, each part of the dominant estate continues to enjoy the appurtenant easement, again subject to the rule that overall use must remain within the original easement scope and not overburden the servient estate.

4. *Using and changing the servient estate.* The owner of a servient estate retains the right to use it fully so long as there is no interference with easement use by the easement holder. Further, there is no obligation to keep the servient estate in a condition that benefits the easement holder. In *Hunker*, the landowner, as the concurrence put it, "did not agree to supply live foxes or well-rested foxes or, for that matter, any foxes at all." What happens, though, when changes in the servient estate essentially destroy the value of an easement? The issue comes up regularly in hunting-related cases given that the value of land for hunting depends on its value as wildlife habitat. A few courts have limited what servient estate owners can do to the land, but most leave the servient owner unconstrained absent an express restriction.

In *Deer Field Hunting Club, Inc. v. Swayze Plantation*, 998 S.2d 1235 (La. App. 2008), the court ruled that significant timber harvesting on the 640-acre servient estate did not interfere with hunting rights. In *Mikesh v. Peters*, 284 N.W.2d 215 (Iowa 1979), the court allowed the servient owner to clear the land completely, drain a pond, and plant the entire tract in corn; the servient owner, the court stated, could make free use of the property "absent an express covenant to the contrary or malicious bad faith destruction of the clearly designated object (i.e., game or its habitat) of the right." 284 N.W.2d at 219. On the other hand, the court in *Deer Slayers, Inc. v. Louisiana Motel and Investment Corp.*, 434 So.2d 1183 (La. App. 1983), concluded that a servient-estate owner acted wrongfully by converting 800 to 900 acres of a wooded 1,800-acre tract to soybean production and removing all merchantable timber from the remaining acres. In *Figliuzzi v. Caracjou Shooting Club*, 516 N.W.2d 410 (Wis. 1994), the court decided that a servient owner wrongly interfered with an 1896 grant of hunting rights by constructing a 26-unit condominium on the 42-acre tract.

5. *Maintaining the easement.* Easement agreements sometimes do (and certainly should) cover the issue of maintaining the easement—who can or must do it, and in what way. In the absence of agreement, courts rely on long-established rules. The servient estate owner has no maintenance or repair obligation. The easement holder has the *right* to engage in reasonable repairs and, indeed, to make improvements as needed (for instance, paving a right of way), so long as the improvements do not overburden the servient estate. On the other hand, the easement holder has no *duty* to the servient owner to keep the easement well-maintained. Maintenance and repairs are

sufficient so long as the easement's condition does not disrupt use of the servient estate or create dangers that could lead to liability for the servient owner. A further wrinkle: when multiple people can use an easement (typically, a right-of-way), they are each obligated under the equitable doctrine of contribution to share maintenance expenses fairly, whether or not they have agreed to do so.

6. *Relocating the easement.* Quite often the owner of a servient estate that is crossed by a right-of-way would like to relocate the route of the right-of-way to allow for different use of the servient estate. Can it be done without the permission of the easement holder? The longstanding rule was that location changes were impermissible without the easement owner's consent. Over time, courts have pressed parties to easements to accommodate one another whenever reasonably possible (further evidence of the rising influence of accommodation as a dispute-resolution principle). In many recent instances, courts on the facts have concluded that easement owners have consented or acquiesced in changes in easement location, or are estopped from challenging the changes, if they have remained silent while the change was made at substantial expense to the servient estate owner. In *Sweezy v. Neel*, 904 A.2d 1050 (Vt. 2006), the court allowed a servient estate owner to bend a right-of-way several meters around a new home addition. The court, however, refused to change the general common law rule requiring consent. It declined in particular to embrace the recommendation of the Restatement (Third) of Property: Servitudes (2000) that servient owners possess the right to make unilateral changes so long as changes (i) do not significantly lessen the utility of the easement, (ii) do not increase the burdens on the owner of the easement in its use and enjoyment, and (iii) do not otherwise frustrate the purpose for which the easement was created. Massachusetts is among the states that has embraced the new Restatement approach. For an application in a contentious dispute on Martha's Vineyard involving a beach-access route—featuring an 8-day trial focused on relocation—see *Carlin v. Cohen*, 895 N.E.2d 793 (Mass. App. 2008). Flexibility and fairness can come at a cost!

As noted several times, one of the fundamental terms of any resource use right is the time period that it lasts—its duration. A fee simple absolute in land is permanent, unless the duration is shortened by private agreement or the land is taken by government through eminent domain or for nonpayment of taxes. Virtually all other rights to use nature are limited in duration, by design or in practice. Sometimes the limit is express and intended. Sometimes it is implicit or comes about because of something the resource owner did or failed to do.

Because many resource use rights are created through the agreement of private parties, they can include a wide variety of terms relating to duration, including provisions that authorize renewals or that allow resource use rights to continue for more extended periods if particular actions are taken. As one would expect, many appellate decisions dealing with duration center on the interpretation of ambiguous provisions in private agreements. Other decisions look to the circumstances surrounding a transaction and attempt to discern the parties' intent from external evidence. Ultimately, though, courts find it necessary to provide back-up rules of law that specify the duration of resource use rights when the parties have failed to do so, including (as we shall see later) rules dealing with abandonment. Legislatures have also gotten into the act, often enacting statutes that promote the policy of ensuring that natural resources are put to good use. Duration issues thus present the same tensions that we have seen elsewhere in natural resources law, between the *private intent* of the parties and *public policy*.

TATUM V. GREEN

Alabama Supreme Court
535 So.2d 87 (1988)

ALMON, J.

The appellants, Luther T. Tatum and his wife Shelba Tatum and Don Swain and his wife Ray Deena Swain, brought a declaratory judgment action against Margaret Green, seeking to have the trial court declare that Green had no easement across their property . . .

In December 1963, Green's father purchased from the U.S. Government a parcel of property situated in St. Clair County. As part of the transaction, Mr. Green also purchased a "perpetual road right-of-way easement" over the adjoining land. In 1967 and 1968 a portion of Mr. Green's property was flooded by the creation of Neeley Lake. Part of the property that was flooded was that portion of Mr. Green's land to which the easement connected. This portion of the land is still covered with water and the easement no longer touches the property above the water line.

On May 1, 1981, the appellants purchased the property over which the easement purchased by Mr. Green runs. On November 11, 1981, Margaret Green became the owner of her father's property by inheritance.

The appellants brought this action for declaratory judgment to have the right-of-way extinguished and to receive monetary damages from Green for trespass and nuisance. The trial court entered judgment in favor of Green; appellants contend that the trial court erred in finding that Green has a right-of-way over their property.

The general rule is that an easement given for a specific purpose terminates as soon as the purpose ceases to exist, is abandoned, or is rendered impossible of accomplishment. *Sasser v. Spartan Food Systems, Inc.,* 452 So.2d 475 (Ala.1984). Thus, if the easement was granted to

Green's father solely for the purpose of access by land to his property, the easement would be extinguished, since the easement no longer reaches the property. *Id.*

The Court must look to the written instrument to determine the scope of the grant. *City of Montgomery v. Maull,* 344 So.2d 492 (Ala.1977).

The deed from the U.S. Government to Green's father did not specify the purpose for which the easement was given but simply granted "a perpetual road right-of-way easement."

If the language is ambiguous or uncertain in any respect, the surrounding circumstances, including the construction placed on the language by the parties, are taken into consideration so as to carry out the intention of the parties. *Id.* Furthermore, if subject to interpretation, the extent of the easement depends on the intention of the parties as gathered from the terms of the deed and the situation of the land. *Cobb v. Allen,* 460 So.2d 1261 (Ala.1984).

Evidence presented at trial shows that at the time of the grant of the easement engineers from Alabama Power Company had already conducted surveys to determine which lands would be flooded by the construction of Neeley Lake. This evidence tends to show that the parties to the deed were aware of the fact that the easement would cease to be connected to Mr. Green's property due to the construction of the lake. The trial court could have reasonably determined under these circumstances that the easement was also granted to provide Mr. Green access to the lake after its construction. Since access to the lake is a purpose that is still in existence, the easement is also still in existence.

The judgment of the trial court is affirmed.

NOTES

1.   *Intent vs. public policy. Tatum* provides a quick introduction to some of the basic rules governing the duration of resource use rights. The opinion is brief, but there is much to learn from it. As you consider the case, keep in mind the tension between two approaches that the court could take on this issue: implementing the intent of the parties, and pursuing a public interest goal or goals that could override what the parties intended. Discerning private intent is often a difficult job, particular where, as here, the original parties to the written document are no longer around and cannot testify as to their designs. Here, the deed governing the easement specifically stated that the easement would be perpetual. Why did this express statement not resolve the dispute immediately? Given this language, why did the court proceed to probe the likely intentions of the parties as to how the easement would be used?

2.   *The life cycle of resource use rights.* The court tells us that an easement "given for a specific purpose" can come to an end in several ways—

by abandonment (that is, the owner intentionally gives it up), when the purpose can no longer be fulfilled (impossibility), and when the purpose ceases to exist. Note that the second and third of these causes of termination are related. In the case of each rationale we need to know the chief purpose of the easement. How did the court in *Tatum* figure out the purpose of the easement? What facts did it view as relevant?

Pause for a moment to think about the rules of law that the court discussed. Land ownership is a perpetual property right (unless expressly limited) and cannot be abandoned. Given this rule, why might the law allow for abandonment of a resource use easement? Keep in mind that a landowner who buys a fee simple absolute for a specific purpose does not lose her rights simply because her initial intended purpose has come to an end or cannot be fulfilled. A fee simple absolute is perpetual, and the owner can use the land for any lawful purpose. Why then do courts treat easements differently? Put otherwise, why do we not we simply look at *what* the purchaser bought (here, a "perpetual" easement) instead of wondering *why* the purchaser bought what she did? The answer, clearly, has something to do with public policies. But in what way?

Tatum did not give clear answers to these questions, but we can likely make good guesses. Lawmakers (courts included) have long favored the full use of land and resources as a matter of public policy. If the owner of this easement can no longer use it, why not let someone else take it over? Perhaps the more pertinent consideration relates to the owner of the servient estate. The easement restricts what that landowner can do on his land. If the easement remains alive and unused, the owner of the servient estate is restricted unnecessarily, and the public loses whatever indirect benefits might come from a full use of the servient estate. This reality could motivate courts to bring resource use rights to an end when they are no longer being used. Yet, even if we agree with this reasoning, why not let the parties work things out for themselves? If the easement is largely worthless to its owner, why not let the landowner come forward and offer to buy the easement back, thereby (as a matter of property law) automatically extinguishing it?

MOODY V. ALLEGHENY VALLEY LAND TRUST

Pennsylvania Supreme Court
976 A.2d 484 (2009)

GREENSPAN, J.

In this appeal, we hold that as long as the requirements of Section 1247(d) of the National Trails System Act are met, a railroad right-of-way is "railbanked" regardless of whether the rail operator agrees to resuscitate service. Accordingly, we affirm the Superior Court's decision below.

Railbanking is the preservation of an easement that was previously used as a rail thoroughfare by allowing interim trail use on the right-of-way, subject to revitalization of rail service at a later date, consistent with the requirements of Section 1247(d) of the National Trails System Act, 16 U.S.C. §§ 1241–1251 ("National Act").

The right-of-way, or easement, at issue here is a section of former railroad track in Armstrong County, Pennsylvania. Appellants are landowners of the servient estates. Conrail, the former holder of the contested right-of-way, obtained permission from the Interstate Commerce Commission (ICC) (now the Surface Transportation Board (STB)) to abandon rail service on the right-of-way. After receiving permission to abandon service, Conrail entered into an agreement with Appellee Armstrong County Conservancy (the Conservancy) to convey the right-of-way to an organization nominated by the Conservancy. The Conservancy nominated a rails-to-trails organization, the Allegheny Valley Land Trust (the AVLT), to receive the right-of-way. In early 1992, Conrail conveyed the right-of-way to the AVLT by quitclaim deed; the AVLT appended a Declaration of Railbanking to the quitclaim deed upon recording it. Conrail turned over responsibility for maintenance of road crossings and bridges on the right-of-way to the AVLT, the Conservancy, and Armstrong County.

In 1995, Appellants filed a complaint against Conrail and Appellees the AVLT, the Conservancy, Armstrong Rails to Trails Association, and the officers of these organizations. Appellants sought to enjoin alleged trespasses and to obtain a declaratory judgment that Conrail had abandoned the right-of-way and therefore their property was no longer subject to an easement. The Armstrong County Court of Common Pleas found that the right-of-way had been abandoned and that the servient estates were therefore no longer subject to an easement. On appeal, the Superior Court reversed, holding that evidence of cessation of rail service coinciding with transfer of the right-of-way to a "rails-to-trails" organization cannot support a determination that the property was abandoned to Appellants under state law. *Moody v. Allegheny Valley Land Trust*, 930 A.2d 505, 507 (Pa.Super.2007). . . .

In this case, the parties agree on all material facts, but characterize the legal import of those facts very differently. The essence of the dispute is whether an effort to railbank a railroad right-of-way via the private railbanking process can be effective if the railroad does not agree to be bound to resuscitate service if directed to do so at a later date. We hold that the manner of railbanking at issue here was effective and a railbanking did result. Accordingly, Appellants' claim that the right-of-way was abandoned, and the easement over their land extinguished, is without merit and we therefore affirm the Superior Court. . . .

With regard to abandonment of such easements, this Court has stated:

In evaluating whether the user abandoned the property, the court must consider whether there was an intention to abandon the property interest, together with external acts by which such intention is carried into effect. *Lawson v. Simonsen,* 490 Pa. 509, 417 A.2d 155, 160 (1980); *see also Burnier v. Dep't of Envtl. Resources,* 148 Pa.Cmwlth. 530, 611 A.2d 1366, 1368 (Pa.Cmwlth.1992). In order to establish the abandonment of a right-of-way, the evidence must show that the easement holder intended to give up its right to use the easement permanently. *Thompson v. R.R. Preservation Society,* 612 A.2d 450, 453 (Pa. Super. 1992). "Such conduct must consist of some *affirmative act* on his part which renders use of the easement impossible, or of some *physical obstruction* of it by him in a manner that is inconsistent with its further enjoyment." *Id.* (emphasis in original); *see also Piper v. Mowris,* 351 A.2d 635, 640 (Pa.1976). Mere nonuse by the railroad does not amount to abandonment. *Lawson,* 417 A.2d at 160; *see also Burnier,* cited above.

Buffalo Township v. Jones, 813 A.2d 659, 664–65 (Pa. 2002).

Appellants argue that Conrail's application for and receipt of permission to abandon the rail lines it had maintained on the right-of-way in question, combined with what they characterize as Conrail's "refusal to railbank," satisfy the test for abandonment of an easement as laid out in *Buffalo Township.* There, however, this Court held that a railbanking effort substantially similar to the one at issue here was effective. The only legally significant difference between this case and *Buffalo Township* is that in this case, the railroad holding the right-of-way did not *explicitly* agree to resuscitate rail service on the right-of-way in the future if directed to do so. Apparently, Appellants see Conrail's failure to agree to be *bound* to resuscitate service as constituting a "refusal to railbank," despite the fact that Conrail sold the right-of-way to the AVLT, a qualified railbanking organization. Moreover, that organization did, in fact, convert the right-of-way to trail use while maintaining its viability as a rail thoroughfare, in every way consistent with the goals and procedures of private railbanking.

The agreement between Conrail and the AVLT provides that Conrail can provide rail service in the future. In addition, the AVLT appended a Declaration of Railbanking to the deed. With this Declaration the AVLT confirmed that it would preserve the right-of-way for future rail use while allowing interim trail use, consistent with Section 1247(d) of the National Act, which provides:

in the case of interim use of any established railroad rights-of-way pursuant to donation, transfer, lease, sale, or otherwise in a manner consistent with [the National Act], if such interim use is subject to restoration or reconstruction for railroad purposes, such interim use shall not be treated, for purposes of any law or rule of law, as an abandonment of the use of such rights-of-way for railroad purposes.

16 U.S.C. § 1247.

Viewing the transactions in the instant case in their entirety, we hold that Conrail's sale of the right-of-way to a qualified railbanking organization like AVLT, that filed a Declaration of Railbanking at the time the deed was recorded, did not result in abandonment of the right-of-way. Conrail owned a right-of-way; it sold that right of way to an organization that a) planned to use it as a right-of-way and b) planned to hold it subject to revitalization of rail lines in accordance with the requirements of Section 1247(d) of the National Act and consistent with the railbanking requirements established in *Buffalo Township*, 813 A.2d at 670. . . .

Amici Pennsylvania Department of Conservation and Natural Resources, Pennsylvania Department of Transportation, and Rails-to-Trails Conservancy each emphasize the strong policy reasons supporting recognition and enforcement of railbanking. They point to the legislative concerns underlying both the National Act and the Pennsylvania's Rails to Trails Act, 32 P.S. §§ 5611–5622 (the State Act), which authorizes Pennsylvania's Department of Environmental Resources to develop rail-trails, and also authorizes counties and municipalities to accept title to railroad rights-of-way by quitclaim or warranty deed. Both the National and State Acts "display a strong legislative policy encouraging the preservation of railroad rights-of-way by using existing rights-of-way for interim recreational trail use." *Buffalo Township*, 813 A.2d at 667. *Amici* point out that rail transport is extremely efficient and is currently undergoing its largest development boom in more than a century. Revitalization of rail lines may well be essential to revitalizing the nation's economy in the coming years. The legislative intent of the National and State Acts expresses an interest in preserving railroad easements even where rail service is no longer active, and Section 1247(d) of the National Act places appropriate conditions on when preservation of such easements can be effective.

In *Buffalo Township,* this Court pointed to the rail operator's continuing obligation by agreement to restore rail service as a factor leading to the conclusion that a railbanking had occurred. 813 A.2d at 670. However, such continuing obligation is not the only requirement we must consider in evaluating the instant situation. Given the strong public policy interests that support promotion of railbanking, and this Court's holding in *Buffalo Township* that compliance with Section 1247(d) is the essential test, our decision that no abandonment occurred here follows the letter and spirit of *Buffalo Township*. A contrary holding would undermine *Buffalo Township* and the National and State Acts that informed it. . . .

Appellants nonetheless argue that, by recognizing a railbanked right-of-way here, the Superior Court effected a taking of their property for which they are owed just compensation in accordance with the Takings Clause of the Fifth Amendment to the United States Constitution, and the Eminent Domain Clause of the Pennsylvania Constitution. While the United States Supreme Court has determined that it is possible for a railbanking to result in a taking, *see Preseault v. ICC,* 494 U.S. 1, 8 (1990), the Court nonetheless upheld the National Act and stated that when determining the breadth of an easement, courts should look to state law, as "[s]tate law generally governs the disposition of reversionary interests." *Id.* In determining whether a railbanking had effected a taking in light of the United States Supreme Court's earlier decision, the Federal Circuit looked first to whether the rail operator's interest was fee simple or an easement; second, to whether the easements' terms were "limited to use for railroad purposes, or did they include future use as public recreational trails;" and third, to whether the easements had been extinguished by abandonment. *Preseault v. United States,* 100 F.3d 1525, 1533 (Fed.Cir.1996) (applying Vermont state law to hold that a particular railroad easement was not broad enough to allow subsequent trail use).

Although Appellants argue that the Federal Circuit's *Preseault* opinion directs that the railbanking in the instant case effected a taking of their land, we do not agree. The language of that opinion implies that an easement's terms can either limit the easement to railroad purposes, or explicitly include future use as public recreational trails, but we note these two alternatives are not exclusive. *Id.* (stating that one determinative issue is whether "the terms of the easements [were] limited to use for railroad purposes, *or* . . . include[d] future use as public recreational trails") (emphasis added). Of course, in its reasoning, the Federal Circuit relied on governing state law to determine the scope of the easement in question. *See* 100 F.3d at 1541 (looking to Vermont law to determine the scope of the easement)

Indeed, both *Preseault* cases look to state law to determine the scope of the easement in question, a crucial determination in evaluating a takings claim under these circumstances. Therefore we must look at the instant easement itself to establish its extent under Pennsylvania law. "[I]n construing a deed . . . it is not what the parties may have intended by the language used but what is the meaning of the words" that determines what interest is conveyed therein. *Teacher v. Kijurina,* 76 A.2d 197, 200 (Pa. 1950). The deed that created the easement at issue here referred to it as a "right of way," and contained the following *habendum* clause: "To have and to hold the said rights and privileges to the use of [Conrail], so long as the same shall be required for the use and purposes of said Road, in as full, perfect and ample a manner as may be necessarily required for the purposes hereby intended." R.R. 76a.[1]

The plain language of the deed's *habendum* clause refers to the right-of-way over Appellants' land as a "Road." It is this property interest in the "Road" that Conrail conveyed to the AVLT. A road is "[a]n open, generally public way for the passage of vehicles, people, and animals," "[t]he surface of a road; a roadbed," "[a] course or path," or "a railroad." By the plain language of the deed's *habendum* clause, there is no reason to confine our understanding of the easement grant as allowing rail service, but not preservation for future rail service. Fundamentally, the deed and its *habendum* clause create an easement to allow travel through the servient estates. Subsequent holders of the easement may not transgress its boundaries, but they do not transgress the use for which it was granted when they use it for hiking and biking. Interim trail use is consistent with the terms of the easement grant. . . .

Importantly, Conrail's intent to abandon rail service on the right-of-way must not be confused with Conrail's alleged intent to abandon the right-of-way itself, an intent that is incompatible with the actions Conrail took in selling the right-of-way. It is beyond dispute that Conrail intended to abandon its rail service on the right-of-way, and took steps to effectuate that by, among other things, selling the right-of-way to AVLT. However, as the Superior Court wisely observed, the evidence presented cannot support both the conclusion that Conrail meant to extinguish the right-of-way via abandonment and that it meant to sell the right-of-way to a qualified railbanking organization such as AVLT. 930 A.2d at 507. . . .

Railbanking, properly conceived, is a method of rail maintenance and preservation rather than a departure from the intentions and purposes of the easement at the time it was granted. The deed's *habendum* clause grants the easement for "so long as the same shall be required for the use and purposes of said Road, in as full, perfect and ample a manner as may be necessarily required for the purposes hereby intended." R.R. 76a. Railbanking provides conservation of this right-of-way in a rail-ready state during a period when rail service is not feasible, and this is not a departure from the intended "use and purposes" of the easement. On the contrary, consistent with the terms of the easement and the policies behind the National Act, railbanking preserves rail networks for the purposes of rail service in the future. Preservation of a resource for the purposes of using that resource as it was used initially is not a departure from the broadly-stated terms of the easement. . . .

---

[1] The easement at issue in the *Preseault* cases did not involve comparable *habendum* clause language.

NOTES

1. *Reading the case. Moody* revisits the issue of easement scope, giving insights to the culturally hot-button context of rails-to-trails conversions. It also introduces issues of easement termination, particularly by abandonment.

Here, the conveyance at issue stated that the grantor was transferring a "right of way" to the Railroad. It referred to the right-of-way as a "Road" and provided that the grantee could enjoy the corridor "in as full, perfect and ample a manner as may be necessarily required for the purposes hereby intended." An initial question (logically, not in terms of the court's reasoning) had to do with the scope of this easement. In what ways did it allow the grantees to use the right-of-way? The language itself was not expressly limited. Would it be appropriate for a court to take note of the context and construe the grant as conveying only a right of way for railroad purposes? Alternatively, was the language sufficiently unambiguous that the court, like the court in the fox-hunting case of *Hunker* (p. 81), might properly refuse to consider extrinsic evidence?

As for abandonment, the court recited the long-established rule that abandonment requires proof that an easement holder intended to relinquish the easement. Mere nonuse, courts have said endlessly, does not establish an intent to abandon. Here, the railroad immediately moved to shift its easement to a new use when it ceased using it for railroad purposes. It viewed the easement as valuable, and took clear steps to retain it. On these facts, why was abandonment even a serious claim? What evidence was there that the railroad intended to give up this valuable property right as opposed to ending its current pattern of easement use? The facts as presented by the court suggest that the easement here was merely being transferred from one owner to another and from one permitted use to another—clear evidence that no abandonment had taken place. If so, why did the court spend time talking about the railbanking program?

2. *Railroad corridors.* Precedents such as *Moody*, without regard for how they come out, inevitably have limited value. The outcome of litigation turns on the language of railroad grants and variations in language have been vast. Some railroad grants are interpreted to transfer fee simple interests in land, so the land can be used for any purpose. Occasionally, courts have interpreted language limiting use to rail purposes as a fee simple determinable or fee simple on a condition subsequent. See, e.g., *Swaby v. Northern Hills Regional Railroad Authority*, 769 N.W.2d 798 (S.D. 2009). Most are interpreted as easements, but the scope of the easement can vary greatly. (In some states, all railroad rights acquired by condemnation are interpreted as easements.)

A critical issue in rails-to-trails projects is whether the corridor can be used for hiking, biking, and other recreational purposes. Sometimes the answer is yes, other times no, depending on the easement's express language. A related issue, almost always missed, is whether, in the case of an easement that can be used for recreation, the scope of the easement includes the right to maintain vegetation along the corridor free of interference by servient estate owners. Rail corridors typically average 80 to 100 feet in width, far more than is needed for hiking and biking. Can servient farmland owners plant corn up to the edge of the hiking and biking trail or is prairie preservation or reforestation along the corridor an ancillary, protected easement use? A rail-corridor easement is a type of resource use right, and like all rights the scope of the easement—exactly how it can be used—is a vital element of the easement yet often not set forth with adequate clarity.

3. *Railroad abandonment, economics, and the cultural context.* For reasons worth pondering, rails-to-trails conversions have been highly contentious, particularly among libertarian and "property rights" organizations. Conversions to trails, according to studies, add value to surrounding lands; they are economic improvements upon railroads. Moreover, when rail corridors were set up many decades ago, servient owners typically received full value for the land taken; purchasers since then have often paid nothing for the land burdened by the rights of way and are not taxed on it. Economics aside, though, strident claims are made that conversions are unfair to servient landowners. This cultural component seems to be at work in various judicial rulings and legislative chambers as well. Application of the longstanding law of abandonment would almost never lead to a conclusion that a rail-line has been abandoned. Why would a railroad abandon an easement rather than simply retain it for possible future use? Nonetheless, courts have occasionally found abandonment despite strenuous efforts by railroads to make clear their actual intent to retain them. This durational limit—the right lasts only until abandoned—can thus be an imprecise one when courts are inclined to favor easement termination.

A partial explanation for the cultural and legal clashes over railroad easement might lie in a failure to keep distinct the two issues of easement scope and abandonment. A rails-to-trails conversion is not possible if trail use is outside the easement scope, without regard to abandonment. If trail use is permitted, a shift to trail use should provide conclusive evidence that no abandonment has taken place. Moreover, if trail use (or other use) is permitted, then ending rail service and removing tracks should provide no more than modest, circumstantial evidence of an intent to abandon the easement (as opposed to abandoning rail service). To observers not sensitive to these legal issues, a conversion from rails to trails can seem to deprive servient owners of their land and to take from them, without compensation, a new easement. In any event, it is easy for citizens generally, regardless of policy slant, to fail to see that judicial precedents are highly dependent on the exact language of deeds.

4. *Railroad grants and the Supreme Court.* In *Marvin M. Brandt Revocable Trust v. United States*, 134 S.Ct. 1257 (2014), the U.S. Supreme Court waded uneasily into the world of federally granted railroad rights-of-way, producing an 8–1 decision by Chief Justice Roberts that reflected a confused view of the action required for abandonment of an easement—which, as just noted, requires both intent and non-use, not merely the latter,

which the majority opinion seemed to assume. The case concerned an 1875 land grant, in which the 10th Circuit—a court with considerable experience interpreting railroad grants—ruled the federal government retained a reversionary interest after the railroad stopped railroad use, regardless of whether the grant was judicially construed as a fee or an easement. Therefore, the government had the authority, under the "railbanking" provision of the National Trails System Act, 16 U.S.C. s. 1247(d), to change the purpose of the retained lands from railroad use to public hiking use. The Supreme Court reversed.

According to a leading commentator, "the [*Brandt*] decision did not rely on the law, the history, or the policy of preserving public lands; it relied instead on the supposed audacity of the government to change its mind." Danya C. Wright, *A New Era of Lavish Land Grants: Taking Public Property for Private Use and* Brandt Revocable Trust v. United States, 28 Probate and Property no. 5 (forthcoming 2014) (concluding that adjacent landowners, through 5th Amendment compensation, obtained a windfall from the federal treasury, "with an added bonus to their lawyers," that "they never bought, expected, or received a deed for").

5.   *Railroads and utilities.* Easement-scope issues often arise in the context of utility lines, particularly with the advent of cables that carry internet communications, television signals, and other data streams. Does an easement given to a utility for "telephone lines," for instance, include the right to hang, on the telephone poles, lines for cable television or internet service? Cases again turn on the exact language of easements. See e.g., *Grady v. Narragansett Electric Co.*, 962 A.2d 34 (R.I. 2009) (easement for poles and wires interpreted broadly). Some courts construe them narrowly. See e.g., *Marcus Cable Associates v. Krohn*, 90 S.W.3d 697 (Tex. 2002) (easement for electric transmission does not authorize installation of cable television lines). Others, though, acknowledge that the public interest is served by expanded communications, and that even narrowly tailored utility easements should be construed to allow new data lines, at least when (as usual) the addition of new lines does not noticeably increase the burden on servient estate owners. See e.g., *C/R TV, Inc. v. Shannondale*, 27 F.3d 104 (4th Cir. 1994).

6.   *Conservation easements and their duration.* Many states have enacted statutes authorizing a new form of easement (a negative rather than affirmative easement) that allows the easement-holder to restrict use of a servient estate to promote conservation aims. Such an easement is itself a valuable natural resource right, even if not literally a use right. Easements created under these statutes differ widely in their terms. Some allow continuation of particular land uses, such as farming or grazing. Others restrict almost all intensive human land uses. Easements can last for particular time periods (and often do, when purchased by government entities), but they can also, like all other easements, be perpetual in duration. Many easements are donated to conservation groups by servient estate owners. A difficult issue in some settings is figuring out who can enforce an easement. One of the few rulings is *Tennessee Environmental Council v.*

Bright Par 3 Associates, L.P., 2004 WL 419720 (Tenn. App. 2004) (allowing private citizen enforcement of a conservation easement when the easement holder, the City of Chattanooga, refused to do so).

Conservation easements have sometimes encountered cultural resistance not unlike that encountered by rails-to-trails conversions. Perpetual property rights are the norm, and no one complains when property is given, for instance, to the Roman Catholic church for perpetual church use. The idea of devoting lands permanently to conservation, however, troubles some. One claim is that conservation easements over time can stand in the way of development useful to a community. A related claim is that conservation easements can lose their conservation value over time due to shifts in surrounding uses and fluctuating wildlife populations. If conservation easements stand in the way of desired growth, or if they no longer achieve the original conservation goals, should they be terminated? The issue is considered in Nancy C. McLaughlin, *Rethinking the Perpetual Nature of Conservation Easements*, 29 Harv. Envtl. L. Rev. 421 (2005); Barton H. Thompson, Jr., *The Trouble With Time: Influencing the Conservation Choices of Future Generations*, 44 Nat. Res. J. 601 (2004).

One response to this concern has been to argue that easements can be released through private negotiations and agreement: private transactions can accommodate needs to shift to new land uses in this context as well as any other. Transaction costs are by no means high; indeed, disputes often involve a single party on each side. It might be, of course, that a conservation group does not want to sell its property rights, but that problem is common to a system of private property law generally. If the public interest is strong enough, condemnation could be used to acquire the interest involuntarily. A more particular problem arises when an easement is donated to a conservation group under terms by which the easement cannot be released by its holder, at least without court approval under the law of trusts. This problem, again, is not limited to conservation settings—churches might also be unable to sell land. But to some observers it seems more troubling in the land-conservation context. A legal solution to it would seem to be a statute authorizing conservation groups to relinquish conservation easements, despite strings attached by donors, if the money is entirely used to conserve similar land nearby.

7. *Easement termination through misuse.* The materials so far have noted various ways that easements can come to an end—by voluntary action, because of built-in duration limits, through abandonment, by merger, and by prescription. Yet another method, more rare, is that an easement can be lost through significant misuse that overburdens the servient estate. A recent case considering (and rejecting) a claim to terminate an easement for overuse is *Steed v. Solso*, 246 P.3d 697 (Mont. 2010).

DRAYTON V. CITY OF LINCOLN CITY
Oregon Court of Appeals
260 P.3d 642 (2011)

BREWER, C.J.

Plaintiff brought several claims against defendants Scott and Andrea Torrance and the City of Lincoln City arising from a longstanding dispute among the parties about aspects of the operation of plaintiff's landscaping business that resulted in the deposit of windblown dust and dirt onto adjoining property owned by the Torrances. Among other claims, plaintiff sought a prescriptive easement to shield his activities. As pertinent here, the Torrance defendants counterclaimed for public and private nuisance and for trespass, seeking damages and an injunction. The trial court entered a judgment in favor of plaintiff on the prescriptive easement claim and on defendants' counterclaims. Defendant Scott Torrance appeals, and we affirm.

Defendant raises six assignments of error on appeal . . . [W]e review the trial court's legal conclusions for legal error and are bound by the court's findings on the parties' equitable claims and defenses, unless there is no evidence to support them; we presume that disputed facts in the record were decided consistently with the court's ultimate conclusion. *State v. D.R.*, 239 Or.App. 576, 579, 244 P.3d 916 (2010).

Viewed under that standard, and without unnecessary detail, we recite the pertinent evidence in accordance with the trial court's findings. Plaintiff and the Torrance defendants own adjoining parcels of property in Lincoln City. Plaintiff's predecessor in interest started a landscaping business in 1984, supplying gravel, rocks, bark dust, compost, topsoil, and sand to customers. Plaintiff bought the property and landscaping business in 1991. Since 1984, the same products have been stored, moved, and sold on plaintiff's property. Small particulates of landscaping material, primarily consisting of bark dust, have regularly blown onto the Torrances' adjoining property since plaintiff's predecessor started the business in 1984. The frequency and degree of the intrusion have varied over time, depending on variables such as wind, weather, and the volume of business inventories. Over time, improvements were removed from the Torrances' property. Before and after the removal of those improvements, all the Torrance property was regularly invaded by the materials, "both by what you could see in the residue on the ground and in the buildings and on the buildings[.]"

The Torrances purchased their property in 2002, and they opened a nursery business on that property in 2004. In 2006, the Torrances complained to a Lincoln City code enforcement officer about the material blowing from plaintiff's property onto their property. As a result of an ensuing investigation, the city cited plaintiff for violating Lincoln City

Municipal Code section 12.08.050(b) by committing "land disturbing activity causing erosion or deposits of material on the property of another." The municipal court eventually found plaintiff guilty of violating the ordinance, which constituted an infraction. In 2006, plaintiff brought this action against defendants, seeking, in addition to his claims against the Torrances, to enjoin the city from enforcing the ordinance against plaintiff. As discussed, the Torrances filed counterclaims, and the equitable claims, defenses, and counterclaims were tried to the court, while the counterclaim for damages was presented to a jury. The court found that plaintiff had established a prescriptive easement, and it dismissed the counterclaims. Defendant appeals from the ensuing judgment.

Three of defendant's assignments of error challenge the trial court's failure to admit into evidence and, indeed, give conclusive effect to, with respect to the public nuisance counterclaim, the Lincoln City Municipal Court judgment that convicted plaintiff of the violation of the ordinance. The trial court declined to admit that judgment on the ground that, under OEC 403, any relevance that it might have to the public nuisance counterclaim was substantially outweighed by its unfairly prejudicial effect. The court dismissed that counterclaim on the ground that the Torrances had adduced no other evidence to show that plaintiff had committed a public nuisance. As discussed below, those rulings were not error.

This case involves the doctrines of public nuisance and private nuisance. As we have explained

> The doctrines of public nuisance and private nuisance have different origins and protect different interests. However, many of the governing rules are the same. A public nuisance is an unreasonable interference with a right that is common to all members of the public. Because the primary responsibility for preventing public nuisances is with the public authorities, a private action to enforce that right requires proof that the plaintiff suffered an injury distinct from the injury that the public as a whole suffered. A private nuisance is an unreasonable non-trespassory interference with another's private use and enjoyment of land. The right to recover is in the person whose land is harmed. *See Smejkal v. Empire Lite-Rock, Inc.,* 274 Or. 571, 574, 547 P.2d 1363 (1976); *Raymond v. Southern Pacific Co.,* 259 Or. 629, 634, 488 P.2d 460 (1971); *Restatement (Second) of Torts* (1979) §§ 821A, 821B, 821D; introductory note (1979)."

Mark v. Dept. of Fish and Wildlife, 158 Or.App. 355, 359–60, 974 P.2d 716 (1999).

For purposes of this case, one of the important differences between the two doctrines is that, although a person can obtain a prescriptive right to maintain a private nuisance, the same cannot be said for public nuisances. *Foster Auto Parts, Inc. v. City of Portland,* 171 Or.App. 278, 282, 15 P.3d 573 (2000). The basis for the difference is that the statute of limitations and, hence, the prescriptive period to acquire an interest in land does not run for a public nuisance, and the private landowner whose land would be affected by the easement can oppose the use as a public nuisance even though the landowner has allowed the use to continue over the prescriptive period. *See, e.g., Smejkal,* 274 Or. at 574–77, 547 P.2d 1363.

With those principles in mind, we turn to defendant's arguments that the trial court erred in excluding from evidence and not giving preclusive effect to the municipal court judgment. The central problem with defendant's argument regarding the admissibility and evidentiary effect of that judgment is that, contrary to his assertion, it would not have established that plaintiff's activities constituted a public nuisance. As noted, a judgment that plaintiff had violated the ordinance did not depend on the fact that he had done anything with respect to public property; rather, it was based on a determination that plaintiff had conducted land-disturbing activities that had either caused erosion or deposits of material on the property "of another." Consistently with the nature of defendant's complaint to the city's code enforcement officer, the primary focus of the municipal court's memorandum opinion was on the effect of plaintiff's activities on defendants' "adjacent property." In one passage of its memorandum opinion, the court stated that the city had presented evidence that "wind and rain caused earth and sand to be blown from [plaintiff's] property and deposited upon public property (the public street) and private property." However, that recital was not necessary to establish that plaintiff had violated the ordinance. *See Nelson v. Emerald People's Utility District,* 318 Or. 99, 104, 862 P.2d 1293 (1993) (in order to be preclusive, issue decided in earlier case must have been "actually litigated and essential to a final decision on the merits in the prior proceeding").

More importantly, although the recital and the judgment itself might have been minimally relevant as foundational evidence toward establishing that plaintiff had committed a public nuisance, that evidence did not demonstrate that plaintiff had unreasonably interfered with a right common to the public. Neither the judgment nor any recital contained therein established any fact apart from what plaintiff had readily acknowledged, namely, that he and his predecessor had engaged in activities that caused deposits of material on the property of another. . . . Because there was no evidence that plaintiff's activities had unreasonably interfered with a public right, the trial court did not err in dismissing defendants' counterclaim for public nuisance.

We turn, then, to defendant's contentions that the trial court erred (1) in concluding that plaintiff had proved his prescriptive easement claim and (2) in dismissing the remaining counterclaims for private nuisance and trespass. Unlike a claim for public nuisance, claims for private nuisance and trespass can be overcome by clear and convincing proof of a supervening prescriptive right. *Arrien v. Levanger,* 263 Or. 363, 372, 502 P.2d 573 (1972); *Restatement (Second) of Torts* § 821C comment e (1965). Thus, if there was clear and convincing evidence to support the trial court's conclusion that plaintiff had established a prescriptive easement over the Torrances' property, the court properly dismissed the remaining counterclaims.

To establish a prescriptive easement, plaintiff had to prove open, notorious use of the land, adverse to the rights of defendants and their predecessors, for a continuous and uninterrupted period of 10 years. *Thompson v. Scott,* 270 Or. 542, 546, 528 P.2d 509 (1974). To satisfy the open and notorious requirement, the use of the easement must have been such that defendants and their predecessors had a reasonable opportunity to learn of its existence and nature. *Baylink v. Rees,* 159 Or.App. 310, 317, 977 P.2d 1180 (1999). Open use for a period of 10 years creates a presumption that the use is adverse to the owner's rights. *Feldman v. Knapp,* 196 Or. 453, 470–72, 250 P.2d 92 (1952). Finally, to show continuous and uninterrupted use for more than 10 years, plaintiff had to prove that he or his predecessor used the property in a normal manner throughout such a period, irrespective of characteristic ebbs and flows. *Frady v. Portland General Elec. Co.,* 55 Or.App. 344, 637 P.2d 1345 (1981) (holding that, in order to establish a prescriptive easement, the plaintiff did not have to show that its use of the land was exclusive or constant, only that it was consistent with the character of the claimed easement).

The evidence recited above was sufficient to establish, clearly and convincingly, that plaintiff and his predecessor had satisfied each of the requirements to establish a prescriptive easement over the Torrances' property for purposes of engaging in the challenged activities. It follows that the trial court did not err in entering a judgment in favor of plaintiff on that claim and in dismissing the counterclaims for private nuisance and trespass.

Affirmed.

NOTES

1.   *Gaining resource rights by prescription.* As *Drayton* shows, it is possible to gain by prescription the right to engage in a *private* nuisance,

such as a polluting activity, by complying with the elements of prescription. The court noted (as others have done) that it is not possible to gain the right to engage in a *public* nuisance. Why might that be the case? On the facts here, why did the court rather quickly reject the claim that Drayton was engaged in a public nuisance? Note that the law of prescription puts Drayton in a rather awkward position. To press a claim of easement by prescription Drayton needs to assert that he is engaged in a private nuisance. If he loses this claim, however, he has in effect conceded liability for private nuisance.

2.   *Negative easements, and a pro-development slant.* Drayton in effect gained the right to continue an intensive resource use, despite harm caused to the neighbor, by being first in time to engage in the land use (1984 versus 2004). The law thus operates to reconcile disputes based on first in time, at least when the first land use begins early enough to satisfy the statute of limitations. It is worth noting, though, that courts do not similarly favor the first-in-time user when the first use is a sensitive one. A sensitive user sometimes claims to have acquired a right to a negative easement by prescription, limiting a neighbor's ability to interfere with the sensitive use. But courts uniformly deny that negative easements can be acquired by prescription. See *e.g., Hefazi v. Stiglitz*, 862 A.2d 901 (D.C. App. 2004) (refusing to recognize a claimed easement to light reaching a window on property boundary, thus allowing neighbor to build a wall that completely covered the window). Several states even ban such prescriptive rights by statute. See James W. Ely, Jr. & Jon W. Bruce, *The Law of Easements and Licenses in Land* § 5:30 (Supp. 2011). This legal approach, plainly, favors intensive activities at the expense of more sensitive ones, reflecting the pro-development policies embraced in the nineteenth century.

It is worth noting that American law started in a different place, allowing landowners under the doctrine of *ancient lights* to acquire rights to prohibit neighbors from blocking light and air when they had relied on the light or air for 20 years or more. See, e.g., *Robeson v. Pittenger*, 2 N.J. Eq. 57 (1838) ("as a general rule, in a case of ancient lights, where they have existed for upwards of twenty years undisturbed, the owner of the adjoining lot has no right to obstruct those lights"). This common law rule was one of many that changed in the nineteenth century to facilitate more intensive development, particularly in urban areas.

Recognition of a negative easement is sometimes rejected on the ground that it limits development of neighboring land, which is true. But recognition of a prescriptive right to engage in a private nuisance similarly interferes with neighboring land uses, perhaps as much or more. A more commonly offered reason for the distinction is that, in the case of a negative easement, the neighbor has no ability to file suit against the adverse claimant to halt the adverse use (or put otherwise, that the activity by the claimant is not really adverse). A sensitive land use is not a private nuisance that can be halted, nor is it a trespass. As for this rationale and the purported distinction, however, we might return to the facts in *Drayton*. The Torrances were timely in complaining about the interference with their landscaping business once they started it in 2004. At that point in time, Drayton's activity was a private nuisance, just as he asserted. But was it a private nuisance for the entire period of the statute of limitations? We do not really know, but it might not have been. Recall that, to bring an action in private nuisance, a landowner must show substantial harm that has been unreasonably imposed. If the Torrances land was, in fact, not being used until 2004, then its owner (the Torrances and their predecessor) had no ability to bring a private nuisance action. Drayton's activity then was not adverse to them; it did not become adverse, in the sense of constituting a nuisance, until the Torrances began their activity. Should the period of prescription, then, have started only from that date? This outcome is usefully compared with the case of the claimed negative easement. In that setting, too, the conflict arises only when both lands are being used in ways that create a conflict.

A more refined way to justify the law's current shape is to say that a purchaser of land might well have no notice that a neighbor is claiming a negative easement. (Perhaps true in some cases, although not true in others—such as *Hefazi*, cited above, where the window was right on the property line.) But if notice is the issue, could we allow negative easements to arise by prescription subject to a requirement that the claimant give notice to the neighboring landowner?

At the base of this issue, as we've seen before, is a fundamental question on how we reconcile conflicting land uses. Should we favor the use first in time? The use that is more intensive? Uses that are consistent with natural conditions? (On this, you might re-read note 3 after the *Columbia River Fishermen's* case on page 20.)

C. EMINENT DOMAIN

A central legal feature of all private property rights in nature is the power retained by government to acquire any property from a private owner upon payment of just compensation when the property is publicly needed. This power—of eminent domain, as it is often termed in the United States, or of expropriation, the term used elsewhere—has long been an important feature of natural resources law and remains central to the study of natural resources law.

Useful background on this governmental power is offered in Susan Reynolds, *Before Eminent Domain: Toward a History of Expropriation of Land for the Common Good* (2010). A British historian, mostly of the medieval period, Reynolds has examined expropriation in various countries up to 1800, including Britain and the United States. (Her title, *Before Eminent Domain*, highlights that the term eminent domain gained usage only after 1800, and chiefly in the United States.) According to Reynolds, "the principle that land might be taken from individuals when the community needed it has been so generally accepted that it did not need to be stated or argued until quite recent times." (p. 11) Lawmaking communities, that is, did not vest in landowners, as part of their ownership rights, the power to resist the community's call to relinquish land when needed for a public purpose. What was debated and, over time, insisted upon, was that government compensate landowners when taking their lands for public purposes. Reynolds concluded that, in early Norman England, only the church and nobles received compensation. But the idea of compensation for all landowners entered the law in the high middle ages, even if the duty to pay was not always fulfilled (pp. 31–35).

By the eighteenth century, the British Parliament insisted that expropriations take place only when authorized by statute, a move that was part of a larger effort to centralize governmental control and curtail the independent powers of local governments and nobles. In colonial British North America, governments often paid compensation for land taken. Still, as Reynolds reports, "unoccupied or unenclosed land, for instance, could in some areas and at some times be taken without compensation, though not necessarily without argument." (pp. 78–79) In sum, Reynolds relates, the power of government to acquire land for the public interest was not seriously questioned and, by the year 1800, was widely (although not universally) understood that landowners should receive compensation. What was often debated, apparently at all times, was whether a particular expropriation did or did not serve the common good.

The limitation in the Constitution on eminent domain is contained in the Fifth Amendment, which states: "nor shall private property be taken for public use, without just compensation." As written, the limitation (like all provisions of the Bill of Rights) restricted only actions by the federal government. Not until a century later was it applied to the states by way of the Fourteenth Amendment. Meanwhile, however, nearly all states in the nineteenth century added similar provisions to their state constitutions, although in some instances only after continuing for decades to take certain types of land (e.g., land for new roads through rural areas) without paying. (The stories of the various states are complex and often peculiar; Pennsylvania, for instance, long followed the practice in state land grants of giving grantees an extra 6 percent so that the state might later fairly return and reclaim some of it for roads.)

The inclusion of the federal provision for compensation in the Fifth Amendment was due, it seems, to the personal initiative of James Madison, the chief drafter of the Bill of Rights. The provision was not among those requested by the various states which insisted on a Bill of Rights as a condition for ratifying the Constitution. The result is a lack of good evidence as to Madison's intent. According to Susan Reynolds, there is no evidence that the term "public use" was meant to be more restrictive than "public purpose" or "common good." (p. 107).

Madison was clearly supportive of a right to property, but to him, as to many others of his day and later (particularly Thomas Jefferson), the "right" was to *acquire* property on easy terms; that is, a right to resist land monopolies by the wealthy and to gain land for subsistence living (or better) on easy terms. See William B. Scott, *In Pursuit of Happiness: American Conceptions of Property form the Seventeenth to the Twentieth Century* 36–70 (1977). (Madison agreed that property was based on positive law, not on natural law. William M. Treanor, *Note, The Origins and Original Significance of the Just Compensation Clause of the Fifth Amendment*, 94 Yale L. J. 694, 710 (1985).) Madison seemed in favor of laws authorizing forfeiture without compensation of land that an owner failed to cultivate or drain, and he introduced a bill in Virginia expressly confirming the rights of the public to hunt on unenclosed land. John F. Hart, *Land Use Law in the Early Republic and the Original Meaning of the Takings Clause*, 94 Nw. U. L. Rev. 1099, 1129, 1137–39 (2000).

From earliest days, American colonies (and later the states) wanted their natural resources put to good use. They did not care to see private owners leave valuable resources unused when other citizens were ready and willing to use them. They particularly disliked having rare resources—for instance, prime spots to build water-powered mills—left unused given that their exploitation enhanced the local economy. (An especially vivid illustration was a 1777 Virginia statute that authorized a person, accompanied by a justice of the peace, to enter and prospect for minerals on any unenclosed land; a prospector who found valuable minerals could extract them without the landowner's permission, while paying damages to the landowner. See Hart, cited above, at 1121.

States also wanted landowners to have road access to their lands. They wanted canals and then rail and telegraph lines to cross the countryside, without being halted by uncooperative private landowners. They did not like mining sites to go unused because miners could not get needed water to their sites. Sometimes governments got involved in this condemnation work. In many settings, however, legislatures gave specific, narrow condemnation authority to private actors when their actions would promote the public good. This trend began with statutes that authorized owners of mill dams to flood neighboring property, paying for the harm but without requiring the neighbor's consent. Similar statutes authorized private businesses to condemn good mill sites. Such authorizations were widely upheld when mills were used to provide public services such as grinding grain for farmers. Many states—though not all—also upheld their validity when water power was used simply for private manufacturing. The guiding thought, in states where such actions were allowed, was that expropriation was for a public use when it brought about the prosperity of the larger community.

The story of expropriation to promote resource use and economic development is told by historian Harry N. Scheiber in various writings, including *Property Law, Expropriation, and Resource Allocation by Government, 1789–1910*, 33 J. of Econ. Hist. 232 (1973), *reprinted in* Lawrence Friedman & Harry Scheiber, eds, *American Law and the Constitutional Order* (1978). In this study Scheiber continues the story into the late nineteenth century:

> The heyday of expropriation as an instrument of public policy designed to subsidize private enterprise can probably be dated as beginning in the 1870s and lasting until about 1910. During that era of alleged laissez faire (which in fact was a period of broad-ranging public subsidies for business), all the constitutional stops were pulled out.

> No longer did judges or framers of state constitutions rely so much upon sophistries about "public use." Instead, they now merely paused to assert prescriptively that one private interest or another—mining, irrigation, lumbering, or manufacturing—was so vitally necessary to the commonweal as to be a public use by inference. In some of the western states, they went beyond that; without verbal evasion, they simply declared certain types of private enterprises to be "public" in their constitutions. All this was done, moreover, despite the availability of the Fourteenth Amendment—an instrument which the courts readily used when they decided to invalidate state laws to regulate private enterprise. . . .

> Colorado blazed the path of eminent-domain law for the West. That state's constitutional convention of 1875–76 adopted a provision that private property might be taken for private use "for private ways of necessity, . . . reservoirs, drains, flumes, or ditches on or across the lands of others, for mining, milling, domestic, or sanitary purposes." Other Rocky Mountain states followed this model closely. In the Idaho constitutional convention of 1889, the debate over expropriation produced a sharp clash of farming interests against miners. Neither interest group stood for an abstraction that can be termed "vested rights"; rather, each wanted the upper hand in the rivalry to exploit common resources. The bitter debate over what one delegate termed "a doctrine that is anti-republican in every respect, . . . contrary to the right to hold property . . . or to pursue happiness" ended in a compromise. Idaho's constitution thus declared as a public use all uses of land for irrigation and drainage purposes, for the draining and working of mines including "the working thereof, by means of roads, railroad, tramways, cuts, tunnels, shafts, hoisting works, dumps or other

necessary means to their complete development, or any other use necessary to the complete development of the material resources of the state." For these purposes might private property be expropriated upon payment of compensation.

Takings for resource development and economic prosperity were not without their critics, and various states along the way did strike down statutes as violations of the public use requirement. As Scheiber reported, however, the United States Supreme Court largely took a hands-off attitude, deferring to local judgments and leaving it to political processes to strike a reasonable balance.

Eminent domain controversies today pose two central legal issues arising from the language of the just compensation clause: when is expropriation done for a "public use," and what is "just compensation." The just-compensation issue raises issues that apply broadly to all types of property; there is little that is different in the natural resources area. It is on the first issue, of public use, where natural resources law has had its own peculiar features (as the Scheiber article displayed).

On its face, the term "public use" suggests that land may be taken only if it will be used by the public in some way, perhaps literally open to the public (as a park), perhaps also if used by a government entity (as a military base). The Supreme Court, however, has interpreted the term more broadly, in line, it seems, with the historical record developed by Reynolds and others. The Court handed down a leading, unanimous ruling on public use in 1984, *Hawaii Housing Authority v. Midkiff*, 467 U.S. 229 (1984), which defined public use sufficiently loosely that any purpose for which government could regulate under the police power was adequate to satisfy the public use requirement. "The 'public use' requirement," the Court announced, "is thus coterminous with the scope of a sovereign's police powers." 467 U.S. at 240. "To be sure, the Court's cases have repeatedly stated that 'one person's property may not be taken for the benefit of another private person without a justifying public purpose, even though compensation be paid.' [citations omitted] . . . But where the exercise of the eminent domain power is rationally related to a conceivable public purpose, the Court has never held a compensated taking to be proscribed by the Public Use Clause." *Id.* at 240–41.

By the time the public use requirement returned to the Supreme Court two decades later, American culture had shifted and distrust of government was on the rise. *Kelo v. City of New London*, 545 U.S. 469 (2005), involved a dispute over a plan by the City of New London to acquire land along its waterfront to promote community revitalization. Some of the land taken would be made available for use by private businesses not open to the public. The issue as distilled was whether a government could exercise eminent domain to promote economic development. In its 5–4 ruling, the majority largely put that issue aside. It ruled instead that the key issue, in deciding whether the public use limit was satisfied, was whether a condemnation action aimed to provide a private benefit rather than to serve a public purpose. Dissenting justices sought to interpret the provision to ban condemnation that promoted economic development, even when public leaders strongly desired it; they were inclined to limit the broad language of *Midkiff* based on the peculiar facts of that case. The majority reasoned as follows:

> [T]he City would no doubt be forbidden from taking petitioners' land for the purpose of conferring a private benefit on a particular private party. See *Midkiff,* 467 U.S. at 245 ("A purely private taking could not withstand the scrutiny of the public use requirement; it would serve no legitimate purpose of government and would thus be void"); *Missouri Pacific R. Co. v. Nebraska,* 164 U.S. 403 (1896). Nor would the City be allowed to take property under the mere pretext of a public purpose, when its actual purpose was to bestow a private benefit. The takings before us, however, would be executed pursuant to a "carefully considered" development plan. 843 A.2d at 536 (Conn. 2004). The trial judge and all the members of the Supreme Court of Connecticut agreed that there was no evidence of an illegitimate purpose in this case. Therefore, as was true of the statute challenged in *Midkiff,* 467 U.S. at 245, the City's development plan was not adopted "to benefit a particular class of identifiable individuals." . . .

> The disposition of this case therefore turns on the question whether the City's development plan serves a "public purpose." Without exception, our cases have defined that concept broadly, reflecting our longstanding policy of deference to legislative judgments in this field. . . .

> Viewed as a whole, our jurisprudence has recognized that the needs of society have varied between different parts of the Nation, just as they have evolved over time in response to changed circumstances. Our earliest cases in particular embodied a strong theme of federalism, emphasizing the "great respect" that we owe to state legislatures and state courts in discerning local public needs. See *Hairston v. Danville & Western R. Co.,* 208 U.S. 598, 606–607 (1908) (noting that these needs were likely to vary depending on a State's "resources, the capacity of the soil, the relative importance of industries to the general public welfare, and the long-established methods and habits of the people"). For more than a century, our public use jurisprudence has wisely eschewed rigid formulas and intrusive scrutiny in favor of affording legislatures broad latitude in

determining what public needs justify the use of the takings power. . . .

Petitioners contend that using eminent domain for economic development impermissibly blurs the boundary between public and private takings. Again, our cases foreclose this objection. Quite simply, the government's pursuit of a public purpose will often benefit individual private parties. For example, in *Midkiff,* the forced transfer of property conferred a direct and significant benefit on those lessees who were previously unable to purchase their homes. . . . The owner of the department store in *Berman* objected to "taking from one businessman for the benefit of another businessman," 348 U.S. at 33, referring to the fact that under the redevelopment plan land would be leased or sold to private developers for redevelopment. Our rejection of that contention has particular relevance to the instant case: "The public end may be as well or better served through an agency of private enterprise than through a department of government—or so the Congress might conclude. We cannot say that public ownership is the sole method of promoting the public purposes of community redevelopment projects." *Id.,* at 34. . . .

Kelo, 545 U.S. 477, 482–83.

BRIDLE BIT RANCH COMPANY V. BASIN ELECTRIC POWER COOPERATIVE

Supreme Court of Wyoming
118 P.3d 996 (2005)

HILL, C.J.

Employing its powers of eminent domain, the Respondent, Basin Electric Power Cooperative (Basin), sought to condemn a right-of-way through a portion of Campbell County in order to build a 230-kilovolt (kV) power transmission line. Basin asserted that the transmission line was necessary so as to provide additional electrical power to areas of Campbell County where coal bed methane (CBM) is being developed and to otherwise enhance the availability and reliability of electrical service to that area. Basin is a regional wholesale electric generation and transmission cooperative that supplies wholesale electricity to its distribution cooperatives. Powder River Energy Corporation (PRECorp) is a Wyoming non-profit corporation and is one of Basin's distribution cooperative members. PRECorp provides electricity at retail to its customers in Northeastern Wyoming, including Campbell County.

Basin was able to reach settlements with approximately 82% of the private landowners affected by the transmission line, as well as with the United States Forest Service. At the time of the hearing on this stage of the condemnation action (the "taking"), Basin had not yet reached agreements with two groups of landowners, nor with The State of Wyoming, Office of State Land and Investments (State Lands), or the Bureau of Land Management (BLM). Case No. 04–134 is a challenge to the district court's order granting Basin immediate possession of the lands owned by a group of landowners to whom we will refer collectively as "the Bridle Bit Group." Case No. 04–136 is a similar challenge to that same order by another group of landowners to whom we will refer as "the Roush Group." . . .

Issues

The Bridle Bit Group raises these issues:

A. Did the district court commit clear error in finding Basin located the transmission line in the manner most compatible with greatest public good and least private injury?

B. Did the district court err in finding that a perpetual easement for transmission lines is permitted under Wyoming law? . . .

Facts and Proceedings

During the winter of 2000, Basin began looking at selecting a route for an additional power transmission line in Campbell County. By letter dated December 21, 2000, Basin submitted the following inquiry to PSC:

Basin Electric Power Cooperative (Basin Electric) is currently reviewing its resources for supplying wholesale power to its member Powder River Energy Corporation (PRECORP). PRECORP has experienced a sudden and rather substantial increase in its membership load because of the development of coal bed methane in the Powder River Basin.

While Basin Electric is considering several options for power supply, the first phase of an overall program needs to move forward expeditiously so that Basin Electric can meet its power supply obligations. Our studies show that Basin Electric needs approximately 40–50 MW [megawatt] of capacity in place in the PRECORP service territory on or before May of 2002. . . .

[To supply this power to its various members, Basin needed to construct further transmission lines, which would cross both private and federal land.] . . .

[Basin applied to the state for a certificate of public convenience and necessity to support its proposed project, which was necessary if it was a public utility. The applicable state commission decided, however, that Basin was not a public utility because it did not serve the public directly.]

During 2001, Basin began the process of obtaining easements from landowners and public entities. As a part of this process, Basin had a consultant prepare an environmental assessment as required by the U.S. Forest Service and a 25-year, renewable easement was obtained from that federal agency in 2003. The record is unclear as to what, if any, compensation was paid for that easement, although it appears that the only cost associated with that easement is an application fee. The easement may be renewed. Basin was able to obtain easements from about 82% of the affected landowners, but had not as yet obtained firm commitments for easements from State Lands or the BLM. With respect to State Lands, an application for an easement had been submitted, but such an easement is not acted upon until the applicant for the easement has obtained access from all necessary private landowners. When such easements are approved by State Lands, they are generally for a period of 35 years, but may be for longer periods of time, including perpetuity. With respect to the BLM, Basin had been offered a 30-year easement that could be renewed and that easement could be for as long as 50 years. The BLM does not require the payment of compensation for the easement, nor is there a fee for the renewal process.

On January 30, 2004, Basin filed a complaint for condemnation seeking to take the lands of those private landowners who had not yet settled with Basin. . . .

Discussion

[The court first agreed with the state commission that Basin was not a public utility because it did not serve the public directly. In the course of that discussion it included comments about the power of eminent domain in the state.]

With respect to condemnation of private land, the Wyoming Constitution provides, at art. 1, § 32:

> § 32.   Eminent domain. Private property shall not be taken for private use unless by consent of the owner, except for private ways of necessity, and for reservoirs, drains, flumes or ditches on or across the lands of others for agricultural, mining, milling, domestic or sanitary purposes, nor in any case without due compensation.

. . . .

Wyo. Stat. Ann. § 1–26–815 (LexisNexis 2005) provides:

§ 1–26–815. Right of eminent domain granted; ways of necessity for authorized businesses; purposes; extent.

(a) *Any person, association, company or corporation authorized to do business in this state may appropriate by condemnation a way of necessity over, across or on so much of the lands or real property of others as necessary for the location, construction, maintenance and use of* reservoirs, drains, flumes, ditches including return flow and wastewater ditches, underground water pipelines, pumping stations and other necessary appurtenances, canals, *electric power transmission lines and distribution systems,* railroad trackage, sidings, spur tracks, tramways, roads or mine truck haul roads required in the course of their business for agricultural, mining, exploration drilling and production of oil and gas, milling, electric power transmission and distribution, domestic, municipal or sanitary purposes, or for the transportation of coal from any coal mine or railroad line or for the transportation of oil and gas from any well.

(b) The right of condemnation may be exercised for the purpose of:

(i) Acquiring, enlarging or relocating ways of necessity; and

(ii) Acquiring easements or rights-of-way over adjacent lands sufficient to enable the owner of the way of necessity to construct, repair, maintain and use the structures, roads or facilities for which the way of necessity is acquired.

(c) A way of necessity acquired hereunder shall not exceed one hundred (100) feet in width on each side of the outer sides or marginal lines of the reservoir, drain, ditch, underground water pipeline, canal, flume, power transmission line or distribution system, railroad trackage, siding or tramway unless a greater width is necessary for excavation, embankment or deposit of waste from excavation. In no case may the area appropriated exceed that actually necessary for the purpose of use for which a way of necessity is authorized.

* * *

As a private corporation, Basin may condemn private property to obtain a right-of-way (way of necessity) across the lands of other private persons and entities. Wyo. Stat. Ann. § 1–26–815. The landowners argue here that Basin cannot be pursuing a private interest and, at the same time, argue that its business is vested with a public interest. However, the statute does not appear to preclude such a circumstance. The Wyoming Constitution does not prohibit such a "taking," and the landowners involved in this litigation do not make such an argument. . . .

Did Basin Comply With Condemnation Statutes

The condemnation process is governed by statute. . . . Wyo. Stat. Ann. § 1–26–504 (LexisNexis 2005) provides:

§ 1–26–504. Requirements to exercise eminent domain.

(a) Except as otherwise provided by law, the power of eminent domain may be exercised to acquire property for a proposed use only if all of the following are established:

> (i) The public interest and necessity require the project or the use of eminent domain is authorized by the Wyoming Constitution;

> (ii) The project is planned or located in the manner that will be most compatible with the greatest public good and the least private injury; and

> (iii) The property sought to be acquired is necessary for the project.

(b) Findings of the public service commission, the interstate commerce commission and other federal and state agencies with appropriate jurisdiction are prima facie valid relative to determinations under subsection (a) of this section if the findings were made in accordance with law with notice to condemnees who are parties to the condemnation action and are final with no appeals from the determinations pending.

Wyo. Stat. Ann § 1–26–509 (LexisNexis 2005) provides:

§ 1–26–509. Negotiations; scope of efforts to purchase.

(a) A condemnor shall make reasonable and diligent efforts to acquire property by good faith negotiation. . . .

The Bridle Bit Group contends that Basin did not locate the transmission line in a manner most compatible with the greatest public good and the least private injury. Wyo. Stat Ann. § 1–26–504(a)(ii) This is based on Basin's admitted decision to avoid public lands in favor of private lands as one factor used in selecting the route ultimately chosen. Other routes were available to Basin that used somewhat more public land, but Basin chose a route that included only a small amount of public land. The Bridle Bit Group asserts that this decision by Basin was arbitrary and capricious, as well as an act made in bad faith and constituted an abuse of its discretion with respect to the location of the transmission line.

The Roush Group contends that Basin failed to demonstrate that public interest and necessity require the project at issue and that Basin's proposed route does not comply with the requirement that the project be located so as to do the greatest public good and the least private harm. Wyo. Stat. Ann. § 1–26–504(a)(i) and (ii). Those landowners contend that the project is designed solely for the benefit of PRECorp so that it can provide electricity for CBM development, but that there is no evidence that the public interest and necessity require the project. . . . Further, the Roush Group asserts that Basin failed to negotiate in good faith as required by Wyo. Stat. Ann. § 1–26–509. . . .

Basin contends that the route was chosen after considerable thought and study, and that it listened to the concerns of landowners. Basin considered the following factors in selecting the route now at issue: (a) Tie-in or connections to the existing electrical system infrastructure; (b) physical limitations, such as topography, railroad crossings, existing improvements, and dry lakebeds; (c) landowner concerns; (d) costs of construction; (e) reliability and safety matters (e.g., avoiding paralleling existing high power transmission lines); (f) minimizing the number of landowners being crossed; (g) minimizing impact to government property; (h) minimization of visual impact; (i) environmental concerns; (j) avoidance of archeological sites; and (k) avoidance of cultivated property. Basin ascertained that, given that the transmission line was necessary, the proposed route (and the bottom line is that it had to pick a route) was the most compatible with the greatest public good and the least private injury. . . .

. . . . Before filing an eminent domain complaint, a condemnor must make reasonable, diligent, and good faith efforts to negotiate with the condemnee. Wyo. Stat. Ann. § 1–26–509 (LexisNexis 2001). Efforts made in compliance with the statutes constitute prima facie evidence of the condemnor's good faith. Wyo. Stat. Ann. § 1–26–510 (LexisNexis 2001).

54 P.3d at 1282–83.

In *Wyoming Resources Corporation v. T-Chair Land Company,* 2002 WY 104, ¶¶ 13–14, 49 P.3d 999, 1003–04 (Wyo.2002) we held:

> The taking of private property for a private way of necessity is recognized as valid in Wyoming because "[t]here is a public interest in giving access by individuals to the road and highway network of the state as a part and an extension thereof for economic reasons and the development of land as a resource for the common good, whether residential or otherwise." *Hulse v. First American Title Co. of Crook County,* 2001 WY 95, ¶ 30, 33 P.3d 122, ¶ 30 (Wyo.2001). "[T]he right to condemn a way of necessity under constitutional and statutory provisions is an expression of public policy against landlocking property and rendering it useless." Id.; see Coronado Oil Co., 603 P.2d at 410.

The legislature has enacted the eminent domain and private road establishment acts so that access will be available to permit mineral estate owners to realize the full benefit of their property ownership and landlocked property will not be rendered useless.

Did Basin Demonstrate Public Interest and Necessity

It is evident from the above-described standard of review that this Court has ascribed a broad meaning to the phrase "public interest and necessity," and that is consistent with the overall tenor of Wyoming's eminent domain statutes. *See* 2A *Nichols on Eminent Domain,* § 7.02[3] at 7–29—7–35 (3rd ed.2004); and 29A C.J.S. *Eminent Domain* § 29 (1992). *Nichols* identifies three core criteria for this analysis: "(1) That the taking affect a community as distinguished from a single individual; (2) That the use to which the taken property is applied is authorized by law; (3) That the title taken not be invested in a person or corporation as private property to be used and controlled as private property unless the public receives some public benefit as a result of the private possession." 2A *Nichols,* § 7.02[3] at 7–35.

The evidence presented by Basin plainly demonstrated the need for additional electric power to PRECorp's service territory and that additional power would inure to the benefit of the public in that locality, both in terms of the additional power itself and the reliability of service in the area. The landowners presented no evidence to contradict Basin's comprehensive studies that established the ever-increasing demand for more electric power. The district court's findings that Basin demonstrated that the project was necessary and in the public interest is unassailable and we affirm it here.

Did Basin Demonstrate That the Project Was Most Compatible With the Greatest Public Good and Least Private Harm

The landowners' argument in this regard focuses almost entirely on Basin's decision to avoid public lands. However, the record is replete with evidence that Basin considered many alternative routes and finally settled on the one at issue here for a variety reasons, one of which was the avoidance of public lands. . . .

Again, the record amply demonstrates that Basin did examine several alternate routes, but ultimately had to make a decision as to which one best fulfilled all of the various criteria that went into making a decision to move forward with the project and begin the process of acquiring the necessary rights-of-way and access easements. Several years have been devoted to that effort. . . .

We conclude that the district court's determination that the transmission line was located in such a manner so as to be the most compatible with the greatest public good and the least private harm is correct.

Did Basin Negotiate in Good Faith

The landowners contend that Basin did not negotiate in good faith as required by the statute. There is little, if any, dispute that Basin negotiated in good faith with respect to the amount of money to be paid for the easements and accesses. . . . [The court also concluded that Basin negotiated in good faith over the location of the transmission line. It set aside for separate consideration the duration of the easements that Basin sought.]

Should the Easements Be Perpetual

We embark on this discussion with a reference to Wyo. Stat. Ann. § 1–26–515, which provides for the termination of condemned easements, such as those at issue here, because of nonuse, upon certain transfers or attempted transfers of the easement by the condemnor, and where a new use is not identical to the original use. The landowners contend that since the Forest Service will give only a 25-year easement, the State a 35-year easement, and the BLM a 30-year easement, their property should not be saddled with perpetual easements. Although the circumstances with the State are somewhat different, with both the Forest Service and the BLM renewal of the easement is a matter of formality and does not require the payment of additional compensation. It is the goal of the landowners (who apparently might settle for a 50-year term) to require that compensation be renegotiated after, e.g., 50 years, so that future generations will derive benefit from the land as well.

The district court did not characterize the easements as perpetual. Rather it found that the easements would be required for "an unlimited length of time." Evidence adduced at trial showed that existing electrical transmission infrastructure had been in place for over 50 years and would continue to be needed for the indefinite future. As a general rule, easements may be perpetual, or for an indefinite duration, or for so long as they are needed for their intended purpose or so long as the necessity continues. 4 *Powell on Real Property* § 34.19, at 34–179—34–184 (2001); 25 Am.Jur.2d *Easements and Licenses* § 94 (2004).

The landowners have not cited pertinent authority that convinces us that the district court erred in determining that the easements were for an indefinite period of time, although they are, of course, limited by a use consistent with Wyo. Stat. Ann. § 1–26–515.

[The court affirmed the trial court in all respects, upholding the private condemnation.]

NOTES

1. *Consistent with* Kelo? Although handed down several months after the Supreme Court's ruling in *Kelo*, *Bridle Bit Ranch* makes no reference to the ruling and does not raise expressly the public use limit on condemnations. (Many other rulings from western states have been similarly confident that their state statutes satisfied *Kelo* and have not addressed the public use issue; see, e.g., *In re Tonko*, 154 P.3d 397 (Colo. 2007).) Had the

issue been raised more expressly would the condemnation have been allowed? Are the "public interest" and "greatest public good" determinations under state law essentially the same as the "public purpose" test that *Kelo* uses to interpret the public use requirement? Note the court's various references to the public interest in promoting full access to private land. The public has an interest, the court contended, in the "the development of land as a resource for the common good, whether residential or otherwise."

Pipeline cases continue to stimulate arguments about whether condemnation by a private company in a given setting is adequately connected to the public interest to meet constitutional muster. A common conclusion is that the pipeline needs to be open to use by an entity other than the one constructing it; the pipeline owner must be, that is, in at least a limited sense a common carrier. See, e.g., *Texas Rice Land Partners, Ltd. v. Denbury Green Pipeline-Texas, LLC,* 363 S.W.3d 192 (Tex. 2012) (requiring a reasonable probability that a pipeline will carry gas owned by someone in addition to the pipeline owner); *Smith v. Arkansas Midstream Gas Services Corp.,* 377 S.W.3d 199 (Ark. 2010) (pipeline can be common carrier if use by even a small number of others can be fairly anticipated in the future). We will return to this issue in the context of rights to use the subsurface in *Anderson v. Beech Aircraft Corp.,* 699 P.2d 1023 (Kan. 1985), in chapter 5 (p. 353), in which the state authorized condemnation of subsurface storage rights by a natural gas public utility but not by other gas owners seeking places to store their gas.

2.   *The special language in* Kelo. Natural resources law professionals welcomed recognition by the majority in *Kelo* of the variations in natural settings of the states and the consequent varied needs of states to craft property rules to promote good resource use. "Viewed as a whole," the Court stated, "our jurisprudence has recognized that the needs of society have varied between different parts of the Nation," and it reflected the propriety of deferring to states "in discerning local public needs. See *Hairston v. Danville & Western R. Co.,* 208 U.S. 598, 606–607 (1908) (noting that these needs were likely to vary depending on a State's 'resources, the capacity of the soil, the relative importance of industries to the general public welfare, and the long-established methods and habits of the people')." *Kelo,* 545 U.S. at 482–83. On this point, we might recall the language used by the Colorado Supreme Court in the *Park County* ruling in chapter 1 (p. 29); the power of private condemnation to acquire rights to build water diversion structures was, in the arid lands of Colorado, in the public interest, even when the structure had only one private user.

3.   *The carefully crafted state statute.* The facts of *Bridle Bit* illustrate with some vividness the challenges companies face attempting to construct long-distance lines through lands with multiple owners, public and private. (We will see another illustration of this in chapter 4, p. 314) with a 678-mile pipeline crossing private and federal lands, in *Center for Biological Diversity v. U.S. Bureau of Land Management,* 698 F.3d 1101 (9th Cir. 2012). Quite often the exploitation of a particular natural resource can take place only

when such lines are successfully sited—lines that get water, power or other needed materials to the site and lines that carry away the resource. States could construct these lines themselves, at public expense, raising no public-use issues. But states save tax money by leaving it to private parties to do so.

The Wyoming statute discussed in the *Bridle Bit* opinion is worth careful study, for it reflects a fine-tuned accommodation of public and private interests. A private party can exercise eminent domain only under the precise circumstances authorized by the legislature and only by following the process set forth. In Wyoming, the power can be exercised not just when it promotes the public interest but when it also satisfies a necessity test. Even then the project must be planned to promote the greatest public good with the least private injury (a test that is, logically, not possible to satisfy in the technical sense (elaborated by mathematicians) because one cannot maximize two variables at once). Note also the process requirements for reasonable, diligent, and good faith negotiations with landowners to acquire rights privately.

The concluding language of this opinion is worth remembering as a general statement concerning the duration of easements: "As a general rule, easements may be perpetual, or for an indefinite duration, or for so long as they are needed for their intended purpose or so long as the necessity continues." At some point, the court implied, these easements will come to an end, and the servient lands will no longer be burdened by them.

4. *Public and state reaction to* Kelo. The majority opinion in *Kelo* flowed rather easily from the reasoning of the Court's ruling in *Midkiff*, although the facts of *Midkiff were unusual*. The *Kelo* decision came across in public media, however, as an apparent change in the law. Indeed, a widely embraced assumption was that the idea of using eminent domain to promote economic development, shifting property from one private owner to another, was something new. Public outcry was considerable, leading many state legislatures to enact statutes of one form or another to reduce the ability of governments in their states (though not the federal government, which would be immune from such laws) to exercise eminent domain to promote private economic development. Some provisions narrowly protect the primary residences of landowners. Others limit condemnations in the name of economic development when property is shifting to private hands. Variant state statutes protect all forms of property from condemnations that involve transferring land from one private owner to another, whether or not expressly motivated by development aims. The various state provisions are sympathetically reviewed and evaluated in Ilya Somin, *The Limits of Backlash: Assessing the Political Response to* Kelo, 93 Minn. L. Rev. 2100 (2009). As a result of these state statutes, the more significant public use limit on condemnations by states and local governments is, in most states, imposed by state law, not by the federal constitution.

Even before the *Kelo* ruling, various state courts—many of which had long been less willing to interpret public use broadly—were expressing reservations about condemnations that involved shifting property from one owner to another. See., e.g., *Southwestern Illinois Development Authority v. National City Environmental, LLC*, 768 N.E.2d 1 (Ill. 2002) (disallowing condemnation of parking lot for private racetrack); *County of Wayne v. Hathcock*, 684 N.W.2d 765 (Mich. 2004) (disallowing a condemnation for private business and technology park); *Manufactured Housing Communities of Washington v. Washington*, 13 P.3d 183 (Wash. 2000) (disallowing a state law allowing tenants of mobile home lots rights of first refusal to purchase lots if landowner decided to sell).

D. REEXAMINING THE OWNERSHIP PARADIGM

RIGHTS OF OWNERSHIP OR RIGHTS OF USE?—THE NEED FOR A NEW CONCEPTUAL BASIS FOR LAND USE POLICY

Lynton K. Caldwell
15 Wm. & Mary L. Rev. 759 (1974)

We conclude this survey of the basics of property law as they affect natural resources by considering a provocative essay by a leading political scientist who played a key role in drafting the National Environmental Policy Act of 1969. In it, he questioned whether we should move even further than we have away from the idea that a landowner should control nearly all of the natural resources within the owner's bounded space, instead treating more parts of nature as distinct use rights. In the essay, the author criticizes the conventional concept of land ownership as "detrimental to rational land use, obstructive to the development of related environmental policies, and deceptive to those innocent individuals who would trust it for protection." He called for "a new conceptual basis for land use" in order "to reconcile the legitimate rights of the users of land with the interest of society in maintaining a high quality environment." His proposed new conceptual basis centered on the following elements, which draw upon largely forgotten writings by leading land economists and land planners from the 1920s and 1930s.

First, rights of ownership should be redefined to apply not to land itself but to specific rights to occupy or use particular parcels of land, or both, in accordance with publicly established criteria. Rights to use might be bought and sold, and could confer possession, but the land itself would cease to be the representative symbol of these rights. The ultimate repository for such rights would be in society, and their administration, while through government, could involve extensive citizen participation.

Second, rights of occupancy would be defined by law, with land classified according to its economic and ecological capabilities, and would be regulated by provisions specifying the obligations of occupancy and governing the acquisition of additional rights. The term "rights" would encompass those activities in relation to the land in which the occupant or user might freely engage, as well as those aspects of privacy and of security from external damage or annoyance which society through government would undertake to defend and protect. Obligations concomitant to custody of land would include, in addition to traditional restriction against public nuisance, measures designed to protect air and water quality, the integrity of ecosystems, and the character of the landscape, whether manmade or natural. The classification system, allocating specific rights to particular areas or parcels of land, would be the product of public planning. For any given piece of land, only those rights allocated to it could be exercised, although not all available right would have to be exercised. Furthermore, a purchaser might buy some but not all of the rights pertaining to a parcel of land; he could, for example, purchase the right to farm without also obtaining the rights to mine or to develop the land. The combination of rights and obligations thus defined could apply to communities and public authorities, as well as individuals and corporation. Such application would be especially important with respect to land used for public works, such as power plants, energy transmission lines, airports, highways, military installations, scientific research, recreation, historic preservation, and natural resources development.

Finally, taxation would apply to the economic value of the rights actually possessed and exercised, not to the land itself or in anticipation of rights that *might* be obtained for the particular piece of land. The tax rate could be adjusted to compensate the public for any burden, such as air pollution, that a particular land use might place upon a community. This system would put an end to the practice of assessing land at its presumed market value regardless of its use. The owner of the right to farm a tract of land, for example, could be taxed only in relation to that right, even though the farm was surrounded by land for which highly taxed development rights had been granted. In addition, since capital gains in land per se would not be obtainable, the owner of the right to farm a piece of land could not follow the present practice of holding land off the market in anticipation of an increase in its value. He could not develop the land or sell development rights to others unless he possessed such rights, and any changes in the use of land not included among the rights already possessed by the user would require purchase of additional rights from the appropriate public authority. . . .

A major objective of these changes in land law would be to assure that publicly created values in land would accrue to the public. Thus, increases in the value of land at newly constructed interchanges on interstate highways would afford no opportunity for profit to the existing land users. Whether development rights or franchises would be granted would depend upon considerations of areal physical planning and public necessity and convenience. . . .

A secondary purpose of the proposed changes would be prevention of socially and ecologically harmful speculation in development. Although a grant of development rights would confer limited authority to change the uses of land in certain ways, major environmental changes, such as development of a shopping center involving public services and transportation, would require an additional franchise. . . .

A virtue of the foregoing approach to land use policy is that decisions affecting the public would in effect become public decisions, a circumstance that occurs imperfectly, if at all, under the laws currently prevailing in most states. The decisional process could be made more open and explicit than generally is the case under the system of private land ownership. The "rights to use" approach would direct public action away from litigation and toward planning and administration. . . .

The principal effect of the foregoing propositions would be to take from private persons, individual or corporate, the power to effect significant alterations in the environment without public consent. It does not follow, however, that the power of environmental planning and management would be transferred to public bureaucracy. Use of citizen boards of review and open planning sessions, as well as provision for input from science and the design arts, could result in more socially and ecologically responsible land use decisions than might be expected under the existing technicalities of land use law.

The objectives of these propositions are, in a very fundamental sense, conservative. They are intended to preserve and to conserve, to encourage and to enforce responsibility toward society and posterity, and to reduce the likelihood of rash and destructive uses of land and resources. . . .

CHAPTER 3

WATERWAYS, ADJACENT LANDS, AND THE PUBLIC TRUST

■ ■ ■

In this chapter we begin our look at particular natural resources. We start with waterways and lands adjacent or connected to them, including wetlands and beaches. The land-water boundary region has long been a central focus of natural resources law, and for reasons that are easily grasped. The land-water line is imprecise and often highly variable in natural terms. The presence of water gives rise to apparent and often immediate ecological interconnections among competing land and water uses. And waterways and nearby lands are vital to a wide range of public activities and have been publicly used as long as humans have lived near water. It is in this natural setting, perhaps above all, in which abstract notions of property rights collide with the realities of dynamic nature. Not surprisingly, a high percentage of regulatory takings cases that reach the United States Supreme Court have dealt with the land-water edge.

We begin by looking at beaches, once of great importance for a variety of economic activities, now largely thought about in terms of recreation opportunities. From there we turn to the law governing property lines that are bounded by shifting waterways and then to public rights to use waterways as such, including incidental use rights in adjacent private lands. Following that we take up use rights in non-navigable waters when the underlying land is privately owned. Among the most contentious issues having to do with lands and water are those that consider the ability of landowners either to drain their lands or to keep water from encroaching on their lands. Our coverage of this topic begins with common law principles before turning, late in the chapter, to the various statutes and regulations designed to protect hydrologic systems from undue disruption. Along the way we look at the public trust doctrine, a body of law that arose out of the land-water boundary and that protects public interests in it. The doctrine has been extended in some jurisdictions beyond these lands and waters; those extended applications are also taken up here. We conclude the chapter with a look at the chief federal regulatory program affecting the land-water edge: the permit program authorized by section 404 of the Clean Water Act.

A. BEACHES AND THE FORESHORE

MATHER V. CHAPMAN

Supreme Court of Errors of Connecticut
40 Conn. 382 (1873)

SEYMOUR, C.J.

The first count of the plaintiffs' declaration is in trespass for the taking and converting to his own use by the defendant of large quantities of sea-weed alleged to be the proper goods and estate of the plaintiffs. This sea-weed was cast upon the shore adjoining the defendant's land,[1] and was there, below high-water mark, taken by the defendant and converted to his own use. The Court of Common Pleas, against the request of the plaintiffs, instructed the jury, in substance, that sea-weed cast and left upon the shore (that is, between ordinary high and low-water mark) *prima facie* belongs to the public and may lawfully be appropriated by the first occupant.

To this charge the plaintiffs object, and the principal question in the case arises upon this objection.

A different question arises under the second count, which will be considered in its proper place.

It is conceded that by the settled law of Connecticut the title of a riparian proprietor terminates at ordinary high-water mark. It is also conceded that though his title in fee thus terminates, yet he has certain privileges in the adjoining waters.

Among the most important of these privileges are—(1.) That of access to the deep sea. (2.) The right to extend his lands into the water by means of wharves, subject to the qualification that he thereby does no injury to the free navigation of the water by the public. (3.) The right by accretion to whatever lands by natural or artificial means are reclaimed from the sea, subject however to certain qualifications not necessary here to be mentioned.

The plaintiffs claim that among the privileges of the riparian proprietor is also that of the exclusive right to the sea-weed which is cast upon the shore and left there by the receding tide.

In respect to the weed cast by extraordinary floods upon the land of the proprietor and there left above ordinary high-water mark, the law of this state is settled, in conformity with what we understand to be the

---

[1] [Ed.: It is possible that the court meant the plaintiff's land, since the plaintiff's argument was that the defendant took the seaweed from the foreshore that existing between the plaintiff's land and the water. Apparently, though, the defendant did own nearby land, and in fact the roles of the parties are largely reversed on the second issue in this case: it is the plaintiff, also a seaweed harvester, who seeks to make use of the defendant's land.]

common law of England. The owner of the soil has it *ratione soli*. No other person can then take it without a trespass upon the owner's land, and as owner of the land he is deemed to be constructively the first occupant.

But below high-water mark the soil does not belong to the owner of the upland. The sea-weed in dispute was not taken from the plaintiffs' land, and their title, if they have a title, is not *ratione soli*. No trespass on the plaintiffs' land was committed by the defendant in taking the weed, for the taking of which recovery is sought in this count.

Upon what ground then can the plaintiffs sustain the title which they claim to the weed? While it was floating on the tide it was *publici juris*. Why, when it is left on the shore by the receding tide, should it become their property?

In Massachusetts and Maine, by virtue of the Colonial Ordinance of 1641, the individual title of proprietors adjoining navigable water extends to low-water mark. Sea-weed left by the receding tides being then on private property, the owner of the soil has title *ratione soli*, not only to sea-weed but to other articles cast upon and left on the shore. Thus in *Barker v. Bates*, 13 Pick., 255, a stick of timber was thrown up and had lodged on the shore within the old colony of Plymouth. The question is largely discussed by Shaw, Ch. J., whether the ordinance of 1641 extends to the colony of Plymouth. That being settled, the learned judge proceeds to say: "Considering it as thus established that the place upon which this timber was thrown and had lodged was the soil and freehold of the plaintiff, the defendants cannot justify their entry for the purpose of taking away or marking the timber. We are of opinion that such entry was a trespass, and that, as between the plaintiff and defendant, the plaintiff had in virtue of his title to the soil the preferable right of possession, and that the plaintiff has a right to recover the agreed value of the timber."

The cases therefore in Massachusetts and Maine which decide that sea-weed left on the shore belongs to the riparian proprietor have no application here. In New Hampshire the Massachusetts ordinance is adopted as law. . . .

In the case we are called on to decide the sea-weed could not be regarded as a marine increase of the plaintiffs' land, for it had not reached their land and was not attached to it nor connected with it. To be a marine increase it must form part and parcel of the land itself. Being between high and low-water mark, at each returning tide it would be afloat, and even in Massachusetts sea-weed when afloat is *publici juris*, although floating over soil which is private property.

The sea-weed in this suit is not treated as part of the real estate which by small and imperceptible degrees had become part of the plaintiffs' land. It is treated as personal property, and the defendant is sued for taking it as such and converting it to his own use. In the case of *Emans v. Turnbull* the plaintiff's title was held good upon a liberal construction of the *jus alluvionis*, which implies that the weed had then become part and parcel of the plaintiff's land and must therefore have been above or upon ordinary high-water mark. Title to personal property *jure alluvionis* would be a novelty in the law. 2 Black. Com., 262. Title by accretion is substantially the same as by alluvion. Both are modes of acquiring title to real property.

Title however to personal property may be acquired by what in law is called accession, but to acquire title by accession the accessory thing must be united to the principal, so as to constitute part and parcel of it. "Accessio" is defined by Bouvier as "a manner of acquiring the property in a thing which becomes *united* with that which a person already possesses." The plaintiffs therefore seem to us to have no title by alluvion, or by accretion, or by accession, certainly none *ratione soli*, and they cannot be regarded as first occupants by construction merely because of the *propinquity* of their land to the property in dispute. . . .

[T]he right of taking sea-weed would seem to stand on the same ground as the right of taking fish. We see no reason for making a distinction between the vegetable and animal products of the ocean. Neither in the state of nature is the property of any one; the title to both depends upon the first occupancy. It is agreed that while afloat both are alike common; why, when the tide recedes and leaves shellfish and sea-weed on the shore, should the sea-weed belong to the riparian proprietor when confessedly the shell-fish remains common property?

We think the charge of the judge in regard to the first count was correct. In respect to the second count a different question arises.

The plaintiffs under that count claimed to recover for the throwing off from the defendant's upland upon the shore a small heap of sea-weed which had been gathered by the plaintiffs and laid there. The plaintiffs claimed the right to pile it on the upland where it was piled, and the defendant denied the right and justified the removal of the heap as a nuisance. The conveyances upon which this question depends are as follows.

Prior to January 7th, 1847, John J. Avery was the owner of a large tract of land in the town of Groton lying contiguous to the waters of Fishers' Island Sound, divided into two farms, and bounding southerly for some distance on "salt water." On that day he conveyed to his son, Albert L. Avery, the south part of the farm, reserving "all the sea-manure privilege of the shore east of the mow lots north of Pine Island, & c., with the privilege of piling up said sea-manure on the shore, and then re-carting to the north farm; for the use of his son Erastus Avery, or whosoever should improve his said north farm." The plaintiffs claimed title under the foregoing deed to Erastus Avery. . . .

The court charged the jury that, as the plaintiffs are limited by their deeds to piling sea-weed *"on the shore,"* they had no right by virtue of their deeds and reservations therein to pile it upon the *upland.* The defendant's argument is that the word "shore" has a definite and inflexible meaning in law, denoting the space between ordinary high and low-water mark. It is true that the word is now generally used in treatises on navigable waters in that sense, but Lord Hale says there be three kinds of shore. (Hale *de Jure Maris*, chap. 6.) One of these three kinds is the space between high and low-water mark. Both the other kinds embrace portions of the land above ordinary high-water mark.

Webster, in his Dictionary, defines shore thus:—"The coast or land adjacent to the ocean, sea or a large lake or river." He says we use the word to express the land near the border of the sea or of a great lake to an indefinite extent, as when we say "a town stands on the shore." Bouvier defines shore as "land on the side of the sea or a lake or river." He gives to the compound word "sea-shore" the more limited meaning of land between high and low-water mark.

The privilege of piling the manure above high-water mark, on the margin of the land granted, is a valuable privilege and a proper subject of reservation, for it reserves a right in the thing granted, but the land below ordinary high-water mark not belonging to the grantor, the reservation of a right to pile sea-weed there would be the reservation of a right not in nor upon the land granted, but wholly outside of it. The reservation ought to be construed as reserving something which but for the reservation would have passed by the deed; but the right to pile sea-weed between high and low-water mark is a right which, as we have already seen, does not pertain to the riparian proprietor. Besides, such a right would be of small value, if indeed of any value, for each returning tide would probably scatter the pile.

In regard to this count, we think the construction given to the reservation was wrong, and therefore advise a new trial. In this opinion the other judges concurred.

NOTES

1. *Transient property rights.* Given the court's conclusion in *Mather,* what is the legal status of seaweed that is floating at high tide above the foreshore (the area of beach between high and low tide)? If the ebbing tide leaves the seaweed on the foreshore, who then owns it? If the next tide picks it up again, who owns? And if that tide pushes it slightly above the high-tide line and deposits it again, what is its legal status? Should the answers to any

of these questions depend upon whether the private land is posted against trespassers?

As for giving the seaweed to the landowner when it is deposited *above* the usual high-tide line, what did the landowner do to deserve it? If the seaweed grew in public waters and was public property while growing, why should the landowner now get to claim it, simply because ocean waves deposited it on her land? Could we decide instead that it remains public property wherever it is deposited, subject to the rule that a person harvesting it cannot be a trespasser? In a later chapter, we will see that wild animals that enter private land remain publicly owned, at least as long as they remain alive. Anyone with lawful access to the land can capture them, assuming compliance with hunting regulations. Like wild animals, most seaweed varieties are not affixed to the soil.

2.   *Digging for worms:* In *People v. Brennan*, a nonresident of Queens County, New York, was arrested for digging sand worms between high- and low-water marks on the shores of Little Neck Bay. The village that included the beach required *non*residents to obtain licenses to take "fish bait from shores within or bounding upon the village." In the course of sustaining the Depression-Era conviction, despite its overt discrimination against nonresidents, the court commented on the law of the foreshore in New York:

> The right of the public to use the foreshore for passing, repassing, fishing, bathing and purposes of navigation is open to no manner of doubt. . . .

> The rights of the public in the foreshore are of a restricted nature and include only passing, fishing, bathing, hunting and navigation. In none of these activities is there any disturbance of the soil. Sand worms, however, can be obtained only by digging—oftentimes to a considerable depth. In the case at bar it is claimed that such digging on the shores of Little Neck bay has undermined the sea walls, although there is nothing in this record to substantiate the contention. Does the right of the public go the distance of permitting an actual disturbance of the soil? In Johnson v. May (189 App. Div. 196, a decision by the Second Department) it was held that a bather could not lawfully drive four stakes in the ground for the purpose of erecting a temporary sun shelter. In the strong dissenting opinion of Mr. Justice Davis in *Stewart v. Turney* (203 App. Div. 486) the right of a hunter to erect a temporary blind between high and low-water marks was denied. . . .

> It has long been settled law that the public cannot gather seaweed from the foreshore. (*Parsons v. Miller*, 15 Wend. 561; *Nolan v. Rockaway Park Imp. Co.*, 76 Hun, 458; Emans v. Turnbull, 2 Johns. 313; 45 C. J. 507.) These cases sustain the view that the public right in the foreshore is both qualified and narrowly restricted. . . .

Principles governing the rights of the public in the land between high and low-water marks have their roots in ancient times and primitive conditions. With the improvement of the gasoline engine and the consequent increase of traffic by land and sea, the owner of water front property is now subject to constant attack from both front and rear. To minimize this the Legislature has appropriated vast sums to provide shore front playgrounds which are freely placed at the disposal of all the people. A very substantial part of this burden of expense has fallen upon the inhabitants of Nassau county. Conceivably the Legislature had these conditions in mind in delegating some measure of authority in such matters to the trustees of incorporated villages. As was said by the Court of Appeals in *Klein v. Maravelas* (219 N. Y. 383): 'The needs of successive generations may make restrictions imperative to-day which were vain and capricious to the vision of times past.'

People v. Brennan, 255 N.Y.S. 331 (Nassau County, 1931).

3. *Law of the foreshore.* An indication of the former importance of this body of law can be gained simply by looking at the bulk of what was (and still is, though little used) the leading Anglo-American legal treatise on the subject, Stuart A. Moore, *A History of the Foreshore and the Law Relating Thereto* (3d ed. 1888). As the court in *Mather* noted, different legal rules about foreshore ownership are followed in Massachusetts and Maine based on colonial charters. In these states, landowners own to the low-tide mark, not the high-tide mark. A few other Atlantic coast states also follow this rule. In these states, however, landowner rights in the foreshore are subject to various public uses of it. In Massachusetts, for instance, the public has rights to use this land for fishing, fowling, and navigation. *Pazolt v. Director of Division of Marine Fisheries,* 631 N.E.2d 547 (Mass. 1994). Contemporary treatises on property law typically shortchange foreshore issues. Two useful introductions, reflecting differing policy slants, are offered in Comment, 31 Mich. L. Rev. 1134 (1933), and Winthrop Taylor, *The Seashore and the People*, 10 Cornell L. Q. 303 (1925). This once-important, experience-filled body of law has largely disappeared from legal study and is fading from legal memory.

Members of the public can use the foreshore only if they can get to it without trespassing on private land, and access routes sometimes are widely separated. Towns that have highly desirable beaches sometimes restrict public access by controlling parking in lots and along streets near access points, allowing parking only by town residents with appropriate stickers for their vehicles. A related strategy is to leave access points unmarked and poorly maintained so that nonresidents have trouble finding them. Owners of large sections of beaches sometimes also attempt to curtail public use by making access to the beach more difficult—and, at times, erecting fences that unlawfully block public access. *See* Jane Costello, *Beach Access: Where Do You Draw the Line in the Sand?*, N.Y. Times, Jan. 21, 2005.

4. *Ancillary rights: temporary storage.* The second issue in *Mather* seemingly has to do with a rather ordinary issue of deed interpretation, but it is connected to a natural-resources issue of considerable significance. Imagine a person trying to harvest seaweed to use as fertilizer on farm fields. The harvester needs to gather a large quantity of seaweed, far more than he could possibly carry. What is he to do? One possibility is to put the gathered seaweed in piles, then come back later and load the piles onto a wagon. But note the danger here. If the pile is left on the foreshore, the seaweed could wash away or be considered unowned.

Practically speaking, if a seaweed harvester cannot safely leave the seaweed piled on the foreshore, where is he to put it? Is it reasonable to say that he can place the pile on private land, adjacent to the foreshore, as an adjunct or ancillary right to his right to use the foreshore—something akin to the canoeist who is allowed to step onto private land to portage around a river rapids? Hasn't the *Mather* court unwittingly diminished the value of the public's harvesting right on the foreshore by failing to think about the practical elements of its exercise? Issues such as this arise repeatedly in natural resource law: what ancillary rights do resource owners require so as to make reasonable use of their resources?

CITY OF DAYTONA BEACH V. TONA-RAMA, INC.

Supreme Court of Florida
294 So.2d 73 (1974)

ADKINS, C.J.

Defendant [McMillan and Wright, Inc.] has owned water front property in Daytona Beach, Florida, for more than 65 years and operated on the property an ocean pier extending 1,050 feet over the Atlantic Ocean as a recreation center and tourist attraction. Defendant provided such attractions as fishing space, helicopter flights, dances and skylift.

The tract of land upon which the pier begins extends 102 feet north and south along the ocean front and approximately 1,050 feet landward of the mean high water mark. This area of approximately 15,300 square feet is an area of dry sand and is covered by water only on rare occasions during extremely high tide and during hurricanes. Defendant secured a permit for and constructed the observation tower which precipitated this litigation. The circular foundation of the tower is 17 feet in diameter and the diameter of the tower is four feet. It occupies an area of approximately 225–230 square feet of the 15,300 square feet of land to which defendant holds record title. The observation tower is an integral part of the pier and can only be entered from the pier.

Oceanward and easterly of the dry sand area is the foreshore, that is, the area between the high and low water marks and is designated herein as the hard or wet sand area.

Building permit was issued by the City for construction of the tower after public hearings. After the permit was issued, the tower was constructed at a cost of over $125,000.

Plaintiff [Tona-Rama, Inc.] operated an observation tower near the site of the pier of defendant and protested the issuance of the permit. When work in connection with the erection of the tower had progressed to completion of test borings and other arrangements, plaintiff commenced this action against defendant for a declaratory judgment and injunctive relief to prevent the erection of defendant's public observation tower. Among other contentions, plaintiff alleged that by continuous use of the property for more than 20 years, the public had acquired an exclusive prescriptive right to the use of the land of defendant. . . .

The land in question is a parcel of white, powdery sand running between the hard-packed driving surface of Daytona Beach and the existing seawalls. By stipulation of the parties, the land is above the normal high water mark and would be subject to being covered by the waters of the Atlantic Ocean only during hurricanes or extremely high tides.

We recognize the propriety of protecting the public interest in, and right to utilization of, the beaches and oceans of the State of Florida. No part of Florida is more exclusively hers, nor more properly utilized by her people than her beaches. And the right of the public of access to, and enjoyment of, Florida's oceans and beaches has long been recognized by this Court.

White v. Hughes, 139 Fla. 54, 190 So. 446 (1939), was a suit brought to recover damages from injuries received by plaintiff White when struck by an automobile driven by defendant on the beach of the Atlantic Ocean between high and low water marks, the hard or wet sand area. The Florida Statute had declared the hard sand area to be a public highway. The trial court instructed the jury that the public in using the beach for the purpose of bathing and recreation had "rights at least equal" to the rights of motorists on that part of the beach. This instruction was held to be error, the Court saying:

> There is probably no custom more universal, more natural or more ancient, on the sea-coasts, not only of the United States, but of the world, than that of bathing in the salt waters of the ocean and the enjoyment of the wholesome recreation incident thereto. The lure of the ocean is universal; to battle with its refreshing breakers a delight. Many are they who have felt the lifegiving touch of its healing waters and its clear dust-free air. Appearing constantly to change, it remains ever essentially the same.

The Sovereign state may in the interest of the general welfare authorize the beach or shore to be appropriately used as a public highway. And most of our Florida beaches, when the tide is out, afford marvelously perfect highways, which are obliterated and re-built twice each day by the unseen hand of the Almighty. However, we are of the opinion that such an authorization for highway uses must be subject to reasonable use of the beach or shore for its primary and long established public purposes, for which the State holds it in trust, and subject to lawful governmental regulations.

For the above reasons we hold that the right of the public to use the beach for bathing and recreational purposes is superior to that of the motorists driving automobiles thereon.' 190 So. 446, pp. 448–450.

It is possible for the public to acquire an easement in the beaches of the State by the finding of a prescriptive right to the beach land. *City of Miami Beach v. Undercliff Realty & Investment Co.*, 21 So.2d 783 (Fla. 1945), and *City of Miami Beach v. Miami Beach Improvement Co.*, 14 So.2d 172 (Fla. 1943). However, in both of the cases cited above and relied upon by the District Court of Appeal, First District, in the case *sub judice*, this Court declined to find such prescriptive right in the public because of the absence of an adverse nature in the public's use of private beach land.

This Court in City of Miami Beach v. Undercliff Realty & Investment Co., said:

It is true that in the earlier days preceding the remarkable development of Miami Beach, when it had a small population, many persons used the beach for bathing, sunning and other recreational purposes. The fact that the upland owners did not prevent or object to such use is not sufficient to show that the use was adverse or under a claim of right. It has not been shown that there has been an open, notorious, continuous and uninterrupted use of the beach by the public, in derogation of the upland proprietors' rights, for a period of twenty years, or for any period.' 21 So.2d 783, p. 786.

This Court in *Downing v. Bird*, 100 So.2d 57 (Fla.1958), set forth the test for right of access by prescription:

In either prescription or adverse possession, the right is acquired only by actual, continuous, uninterrupted use by the claimant of the lands of another, for a prescribed period. In addition The use must be adverse under claim of right and must either be with the knowledge of the owner or so open, notorious, and visible that knowledge of the use by and adverse claim of the claimant is imputed to the owner. In both rights the use or possession must be inconsistent with the owner's use and enjoyment of his lands and must not be a permissive use, for the use must be such that the owner has a right to a legal action to stop it, such as an action for trespass or ejectment.

If the use of an alleged easement is not exclusive and not inconsistent with the rights of the owner of the land to its use and enjoyment, it would be presumed that such use is permissive rather than adverse. Hence, such use will never ripen into easement. . . .

In the case *sub judice*, the land in issue is occupied in part by the Main Street pier, a landmark of the Daytona Beach oceanfront for many years, and the land and pier are owned by the defendant. The pier is used as a recreation center and tourist attraction. It is utilized for fishing and dances, and offers a skylift and helicopter flights by the present owner.

That portion of the land owned by defendant which is not occupied by the pier has been left free of obstruction and has been utilized by sunbathing tourists for untold decades. These visitors to Daytona Beach, including those who have relaxed on the white sands of the subject lands, are the lifeblood of the pier. As such, they have not been opposed, but have been welcomed to utilize the otherwise unused sands of petitioner's oceanfront parcel of land.

The sky tower, which was substantially completed when the trial judge's order halted it, consists of a metal tower rising 176 feet above the ocean and a 25-passenger, air-conditioned gondola which was to be boarded from the pier to rise, rotating slowly, to the top of the tower, remain rotating at the top for a few minutes, and then descend. The tower utilizes a circle of sand only 17 feet in diameter. A building permit was issued in October, 1969, and the project was completed, representing an investment of over $125,000, by the time the hearings were held.

[Both the trial court and the appellate court decided that the public had acquired a beach-use easement by prescription, and ordered the tower removed. The Supreme disagreed.]. . . . The public has continuously, and over a period of several decades, made uninterrupted use of the lands in issue. However, neither the trial court, nor the District Court, reached the other requirement for prescription to be properly effective—adverse possession inconsistent with the owner's use and enjoyment of the land.

The use of the property by the public was not against, but was in furtherance of, the interest of the defendant owner. Such use was not injurious to the owner and there was no invasion of the owner's right to the property. Unless the owner loses something, the public could obtain no easement by prescription. *J. C. Vereen & Sons v. Houser,* cited above.

Even if it should be found that such an easement had been acquired by prescription, the defendant-owner could make any use of the land consistent with, or not calculated to interfere with, the exercise of the easement by the public. See Tiffany Real Property, (Third Edition), Vol. 3, Section 811. The erection of the sky tower was consistent with the recreational use of the land by the public and could not interfere with the exercise of any easement the public may have acquired by prescription, if such were the case.

The beaches of Florida are of such a character as to use and potential development as to require separate consideration from other lands with respect to the elements and consequences of title. The sandy portion of the beaches are of no use for farming, grazing, timber production, or residency-the traditional uses of land-but has served as a thoroughfare and haven for fishermen and bathers, as well as a place of recreation for the public. The interest and rights of the public to the full use of the beaches should be protected. Two states, Oregon and Hawaii, have used the 'customary rights doctrine' to afford the rights in beach property. *State ex rel. Thornton v. Hay,* 462 P.2d 671 (Or. 1969); *In re: Ashford,* 440 P.2d 76 (Haw. 1968). See also W. Roderick Bowdoin, *Easements: Judicial and Legislative Protection of the Public's Rights in Florida's Beaches,* 25 Fla. L. Rev. 586 (1973).

As stated in *Tiffany Real Property*, (Third Edition), Vol. 3, § 935:

In England, persons of a certain locality or of a certain class may have, by immemorial custom, a right to make use of land belonging to an individual. Thus, there may be a custom for the inhabitants of a certain town to dance or play games on a particular piece of land belonging to an individual, or to go thereon in order to get water. So there may be a custom for fishermen to dry nets on certain land, or for persons in a certain trade (victualers) to erect booths upon certain private land during a fair. The custom, to be valid, "must have continued from time immemorial, without interruption, and as of right; it must be certain as to the place, and as to the persons; and it must be certain and reasonable as to the subject matter or rights created. . . .

If the recreational use of the sandy area adjacent to mean high tide has been ancient, reasonable, without interruption and free from dispute, such use, as a matter of custom, should not be interfered with by the owner. However, the owner may make any use of his property which is consistent with such public use and not calculated to interfere with the exercise of the right of the public to enjoy the dry sand area as a recreational adjunct of the wet sand or foreshore area.

This right of customary use of the dry sand area of the beaches by the public does not create any interest in the land itself. Although this right of use cannot be revoked by the land owner, it is subject to appropriate governmental regulation and may be abandoned by the public. The rights of the owner of the dry sand area may be compared to rights of a part-owner of a land-locked nonnavigable lake, as described in *Duval v. Thomas*, 114 So.2d 791 (Fla.1959).

Testimony was presented that the public's presence on the land and its use of the land was not adverse to the interest of defendant, but rather that the defendant's Main Street pier relied on the presence of such seekers of the sea for its business. Thus, the issue of adversity was clearly raised and the evidence failed to show any adverse use by the public. In fact, the construction of the sea tower was consistent with the general recreational use by the public. The general public may continue to use the dry sand area for their usual recreational activities, not because the public has any interest in the land itself, but because of a right gained through custom to use this particular area of the beach as they have without dispute and without interruption for many years.

NOTES

1. *Customary rights in beaches.* This litigation as a legal matter had to do with public rights in beaches, but it was brought, you will note, not by a public-interest group seeking to protect public rights but by a competing private landowner with a competing waterfront tower. Presumably, the competing tower-owner also had, on its side, various public users of the beach who were willing to assert their beach-access rights, and thus allow the court to consider the interests of the public.

The court said little about what it termed the hard or wet sand beach—below the high-tide line. It said little because this property is owned by the state and subject to the public trust doctrine protecting public use-rights (considered later in this chapter, pp. 178–217). The public plainly had rights to use this portion of the beach. The litigation focused instead on possible public rights to use the dry beach above that. Why did the court reject the contention that the public had acquired an easement by prescription? As for the claim of customary use rights, what did members of the public need to show in order to gain recognition of such rights?

The court concluded that the public did have customary rights to use the dry beach. It also said, however, that customary use "does not create any interest in the land itself" even though "this right of use cannot be revoked by the land owner." If the customary right is not an interest in the land, what is it? As best we can tell (making some guesses), how does a customary right to use the beach differ from an easement to use the beach?

2. *Prescriptive rights.* Only a few states recognize the legal rule that the public can gain rights to dry beaches based on customary use. In other

states, public rights typically take the form of easements, obtained either through prescription or by transfer from landowners. New Jersey has recognized extensive public use rights by drawing upon the public trust doctrine. See, *e.g., Raleigh Ave. Beach Assn. v. Atlantis Beach Club, Inc.*, 879 A.2d 112 (N.J. 2005) (discussing ability of private owner of dry sand beach to impose reasonable charges for services rendered to public users of the beach). One of the editors claims that the Oregon customary rights beach doctrine is actually part of the public trust doctrine. See Michael C. Blumm & Erika Doot, *Oregon's Public Trust Doctrine: Public Rights in Waters, Wildlife, and Beaches,* 42 Envtl. L. 375, 407-11 (2012) (discussing *Thorton v. Hay*, 462 P.2d 671 (Or. 1969); and *Stevens v. City of Cannon Beach*, 854 P.2d 449 (O. 1993), cert. denied 510 U.S. 1207, 1211–12 (1994) (Scalia, dissenting)). More on the public trust doctrine and its application to beaches appears below.

B. WATERWAYS AS BOUNDARIES

BABEL V. SCHMIDT

Court of Appeals of Nebraska
17 Neb. App. 400, 765 N.W.2d 227 (2009)

SIEVERS, J.

This appeal involves conflicting claims of ownership to riparian land in the form of islands located between the banks of the Platte River in Merrick County, Nebraska. In a sentence, the resolution of the dispute depends upon whether the legally effective boundary is the present "thread of the stream" or whether there was an avulsive event proved, which, while changing the location of the thread of the stream, would not change the legal boundary between the owners from what it was at the time of the avulsive event. . . .

Babel and the Schmidts own property on the south bank and the north bank, respectively, of the Platte River near Chapman in Merrick County, and as a result, they own the riparian lands consisting of islands between their respective banks of the Platte River. Who owns what island land is the crux of the lawsuit.

So that our factual recitation is more understandable, we begin by defining the legal concept of the "thread of the stream." In *Monument Farms, Inc. v. Daggett,* 520 N.W.2d 556, 562 (Neb. 1994), we said:

> The thread or center of a channel, as the term is employed, must be the line which would give the owners on either side access to the water, whatever its stage might be, and particularly at its lowest flow. *State v. Ecklund,* 147 Neb. 508, 23 N.W.2d 782 (1946). In other words, the thread of the stream is the deepest groove or trench in the bed of a river channel, the last part of the bed to run dry. . . .

[At the time of the litigation the thread of the Platte River ran between Islands No. 5 and No. 3. Island No. 3 had always been on the Schmidts' side of the river. The Schmidts claimed that the river formerly ran so that most of Island No. 5 was also on their side of the river. Due to a sudden event, according to the Schmidts, the thread of the river jumped northward so that Island No. 5 was no longer within their property boundaries. Because the river shifted due to avulsion (a sudden shift) rather than accretion and reliction (gradual processes, described below), property boundaries should have stayed where they were and not moved along with the thread of the river. The dispute thus dealt with the ownership of Island No. 5.]

The core question before us in this appeal, remembering that our review is *de novo* on the record, is whether there was sufficient evidence adduced by the Schmidts to show that avulsion occurred that altered the course of the river from the channel south of Island No. 5 to the current thread of the stream located between Island No. 3 and Island No. 5 sometime between the 1858 GLO survey and the 1921 survey of Island No. 3, the timeframe asserted during oral argument—although we note that the Schmidts' answers to interrogatories in evidence would extend the time period to 1938. However, in the final analysis, whether the end of the timeframe is 1921 or 1938 is of no consequence. . . .

The law of avulsion and accretion is well settled in Nebraska. Avulsion is a sudden and perceptible loss of or addition to land by the action of water, or a sudden change in the bed or course of a stream. *Monument Farms, Inc. v. Daggett,* 520 N.W.2d 556 (Neb. 1994). Avulsion is a change in a stream that is violent and visible and arises from a known cause, such as a freshet or a cut through which a new channel has formed. *See Conkey v. Knudsen,* 4 N.W.2d 290 (Neb. 1942), *vacated on other grounds* 143 Neb. 5, 8 N.W.2d 538 (1943). On the other hand, accretion is the process of gradual and imperceptible addition of solid material, called alluvion, thus extending the shoreline out by deposits made by contiguous water; reliction is the gradual withdrawal of the water from the land by the lowering of its surface level from any cause. *Monument Farms, Inc. v. Daggett,* cited above. In summary, the changes wrought by accretion versus avulsion involve processes that are markedly different, and each process has a different consequence for the boundary between the land-owners on opposite banks of the river.

Where the thread of the main channel of a river is the boundary line between two estates and it changes by the slow and natural processes of accretion and reliction, the boundary follows the channel. *Ziemba v. Zeller,* 86 N.W.2d 190 (Neb. 1957). Accretion, regardless of which bank to which it adds ground, leaves the boundary still at the center of the channel. *See Anderson v. Cumpston,* 606 N.W.2d 817 (Neb. 2000); *Lienemann v. County of Sarpy,* 16 N.W.2d 725 (Neb. 1944); *Conkey v.*

Knudsen, cited above; *Monument Farms, Inc. v. Daggett,* cited above. On the other hand, avulsion has no effect on boundary, but leaves it in the center of the old channel. *See Lienemann v. County of Sarpy,* cited above. *See also O'Connor v. Petty,* 146 N.W. 947 (Neb. 1914) (holding that change by avulsion in main channel of Missouri River does not change boundary between states of Iowa and Nebraska). The applicability of the law of avulsion is not dependent upon the navigability of the waterway. *Anderson v. Cumpston,* cited above.

A party who seeks to have title in real estate quieted in him on the ground that it is accretion to land to which he has title has the burden of proving the accretion by a preponderance of the evidence. *State v. Matzen,* 250 N.W.2d 232 (Neb. 1977). The burden to show that the channel of the river changed by avulsion obviously would be the same. . . .

Past cases have illustrated the sorts of events that constitute avulsion. *See Anderson v. Cumpston,* cited above (party admitted that change in thread of Platte River was brought about suddenly by artificial structures and diversion, thus doctrine of avulsion applied and boundary remained in center of old channel); *Ziemba v. Zeller,* cited above (based on photographs and eyewitness reports, construction of diversion dam and riprapped dike some 700 to 800 feet long, which shut off main channel, constituted avulsion); *Ingraham v. Hunt,* 68 N.W.2d 344 (Neb. 1955) (flash floods that suddenly, violently, and visibly moved channel of river far toward north of original channel can be considered avulsion); *Conkey v. Knudsen,* cited above (evidence was sufficient to show ice gorge created by spring floods in 1910 altered course of Missouri River and constituted avulsion, not accretion). It is noteworthy that no such similar events as described in the foregoing cases are identified in the evidence as the avulsive event allegedly at work in the present case. . . .

The only evidence as to whether an avulsive act altered the course of the river came from Graves and Joeckel. Graves was asked if he had an opinion, based on his training as a surveyor, as to why there would be a channel currently across Island No. 3 that is not indicated in the GLO survey of 1858. In response, Graves said:

> [T]here must have been a smaller—a small stream that went through there and something has, erosion or whatever, caused through the time since it was surveyed until—even from the time they originally surveyed until 1921, it actually had—must have grown quite a bit. . . . And there's something—probably was a small island, small channel through there and something made it grow to be a larger one, got more water at that point than it had or stopped going in different directions. Some reason that all of a sudden it became a lot because if it was that big, it should have showed up on the GLO.

Graves also testified that in his personal opinion, not as a surveyor, but, rather, as a person familiar with the river, he did not know exactly what caused the river to change course but suspected a flood or ice jam. . . .

Graves' unchallenged testimony shows that the location of the thread of the stream has changed, making Babel's Island No. 5 bigger and the Schmidts' Island No. 3 smaller. However, in order for the Schmidts to prevail on their counterclaims—meaning that the boundary is not the thread of the stream—the Schmidts' burden, under the legal principles we have outlined above, is to prove that the change occurred by avulsion. Graves' testimony simply does not prove avulsion, although it does show a change in the course of the river, but at an unknown point in time. . . .

We turn next to the Schmidts' claim that the testimony of Joeckel, an associate professor of soil science and geology at the University of Nebraska-Lincoln, establishes that the change in the course of the river is due to avulsion. Joeckel testified about two soil samples that he took from Island No. 5 by digging holes with a spade and one sample taken from Island No. 3 in the same fashion. The samples were taken from the center of the northeastern portion of Island No. 3 (labeled "A" on the map in exhibit 46), from the northern edge of Island No. 5 near the thread of the stream (labeled "B" on the map in exhibit 46), and from the center of the northeastern part of Island No. 5 (labeled "C" on the map in exhibit 46). Joeckel testified that the soil profile of site A was broadly similar to site B and that both sites had thick "A and C horizons" and relatively no "B horizon." A soil horizon, according to Joeckel's testimony, is a layer within a soil sample that exists because of differences in chemical, physical, and biological processes at different depths below the land surface of the soil, measured from the surface of the land downward. In reference to the soil sample from site B, Joeckel testified:

> These soils are all developed in river sediment. So we kept digging, basically, as deep as we could go by hand with the spade, down to 85 centimeters. So no evidence for there being more than one unit of sediment being deposited on that site, hence, came to the conclusion that the soil was developed in a single episode, single length of time after deposition had ceased at the site.

As to the soil sample from site C, Joeckel stated that it was obviously a different profile from either site A or B. Joeckel testified that site C had much more geomorphic activity and episodes of sedimentation and soil development. He stated that site C had been subject to more regular flooding and sedimentation events than either site A or B, which had been subject to fewer, if any, severe floods. Joeckel did not opine that any particular soil samples resulted from accretion or avulsion. When asked whether the soil profile at site C was consistent with accretion land, Joeckel limited his testimony to discussion of the thickness of the soil horizons at each site and his conclusions that site C had more episodes of sedimentation and soil development than either site A or B.

The Schmidts argue Joeckel's testimony about the three soil samples shows that site C was formed by accretion and that an avulsive event occurred at some point to separate site A from site B, because the two sites are now located on different islands, whereas, according to the Schmidts' argument, they were once part of the same island. The Schmidts further argue that Joeckel's testimony about the soil samples shows the thread of the stream changed in a dramatic fashion so as to have bisected the original island and that as such, they have shown an avulsive event that requires the property boundary to be located along the original thread of the stream. Consequently, according to the Schmidts' argument, the original boundary of Island No. 3 and its southern meanders, which corresponds with the channel south of Island No. 5 as alleged by the Schmidts, is the effective boundary between the lands of Babel and the Schmidts, rather than the current thread of the stream.

The problem is that Joeckel did not testify to the conclusions that the Schmidts argue. While Joeckel did testify to finding differences in the soil at sites A and B when compared to site C, he did not offer an opinion as to when the soil patterns he found at the three sites were formed— particularly in relation to the surveys in evidence that go back as far as 1858. Joeckel did testify that the soil pattern he observed at sites A and B were likely created in "a single episode, single length of time after deposition had ceased at the site." Whether the land in question was identifiable as having remained intact through the substantial change in the river has been seen as relevant to avulsion. *See United States v. Wilson,* 433 F.Supp. 57 (N.D. Iowa 1977); *Jeffrey v. Grosvenor,* 157 N.W.2d 114 (Iowa 1968). While we see the evidence regarding the soils at sites A and B as supporting the avulsion theory to a degree, it does not carry the Schmidts' burden of proof by itself. We so conclude because there is no evidence as to when such "single episode" occurred, what caused it, or whether a "single episode" in the language of soil science, the basis upon which Joeckel testified, has the same hallmarks as the legal concept of avulsion, which requires a sudden and violent change in the course of the river. . . . No evidence was offered which would enable a fact finder to say what the avulsion event was, how and why it occurred, and when it occurred—no particular day, month, year, or even decade being identifiable from the evidence. And, of course, it follows from the foregoing that no one testified to witnessing the event, nor was any historical record proffered—evidence that would clearly help satisfy the "perceptible" requirement for an avulsive event. . . .

These various elements that constitute the hallmarks of an avulsive event simply are absent from the evidentiary record.... This sparse evidence—that, at best, merely suggests the possibility of avulsion, but of an unknown nature, from an unknown cause, and occurring at an unknown time between 1858 and either 1921 or 1938—is simply insufficient to carry the Schmidts' burden of proving that the change in the river's course occurred from avulsion.

NOTES

1. *Meandering rivers as boundaries.* This opinion aptly summarized a rule of property law of considerable importance to countless landowners with rivers as property boundaries. Rivers meander over time, sometimes quite considerably, particularly broad, shallow rivers in flat terrain. Landowners can easily gain and lose many acres over a period of years due to gradual accretion and reliction. The rule considered in *Babel* distinguishes between gradual shifts and more sudden ones. Predictably, such a line is hard to draw at times: How sudden and rapid must a change be to qualify as avulsion rather than accretion and reliction? Moreover, it can be challenging, when avulsion takes place, to delineate precisely the pre-avulsion boundary line. Adding complexity to this important body of law are changes made to waterways in whole or in part not by nature but by people, changes that ought to be excluded from this rule. As we'll see below, many Western states define property boundaries based on the high (or mean-high) water lines in a river, not based on the thread of the river. The state then retains ownership of the land underneath the water. This different approach to property boundaries does not do away with the law of accretion and avulsion; it still determines whether a boundary shifts along with a shifting river (the shifting border is then at the mean high-water line, not at the river's thread).

The same issue arises when a waterway forms the boundary of a state or other political jurisdiction. In the case of state boundaries, the starting point of legal inquiry is with the federal statutes that admitted the competing states into the union. Enabling Acts specify the boundaries of a new state. Congress has sometimes defined state boundaries based on the location of a river at the time the state gained admission to the Union, with the boundary remaining fixed despite shifts in the river. In a few settings, a state boundary has been set, not at the thread of the river, but on one of the banks. Thus, along the Ohio River between Illinois and Kentucky, the border is on the Illinois bank of the river. Private property boundaries are largely defined by state property law and are thus affected by the locations of state boundaries; states cannot define a property boundary so that it includes land in another state.

2. *Avulsion along ocean fronts.* As we have seen, the boundaries of private land that fronts on an ocean or arm of an ocean usually extend to the mean high-tide mark. Like river-front boundaries, these boundaries can and do change as a result of physical forces. Such shifts usually take the form of

accretion and reliction. What happens, though, when an avulsive event, such as a hurricane, takes place? Would property boundaries remain as they were before the avulsive event if the effect was to deprive the public of its longstanding rights in the foreshore?

A rare dispute confronting the issue led to the ruling in *Severance v. Patterson*, 345 S.W.3d 18 (Tex. 2010), which arose out of the coastline shift caused by Hurricane Rita in 2005. Texas follows the common rule that the rights of landowners extend to the mean high-tide line. Under Texas law, the high-tide line remains the property boundary, both when the line moves through accretion and reliction and when it moves through avulsion. The state of Texas also holds various public-access easements to use dry sand beaches above the high-tide line. In *Severance* the court held that, when these public easements in the foreshore shifted landward and seaward as the high-tide line moved by accretion and reliction, the dry-sand easements did not move when the high-tide line shifted suddenly by avulsion. In that event, the state had to reestablish new public easements. On the broader issue, see Donna R. Christie, *Of Beaches, Boundaries, and SOBs*, 25 J. Land Use & Envtl. L. 19 (2009).

C. RIGHTS IN NAVIGABLE AND NON-NAVIGABLE WATERS

STATE V. MCILROY

Supreme Court of Arkansas
268 Ark. 227, 595 S.W.2d 659 (1980)

HICKMAN, J.

W. L. McIlroy and his late brother's estate, owners of 230 acres in Franklin County, sought a chancery court declaration that their rights as riparian landowners on the Mulberry River were, because the stream was not a navigable river, superior to the rights of the public.

McIlroy joined as defendants the Ozark Society, a conservationist group, and two companies that rent canoes for use on the Mulberry and other Ozark Mountain streams. The State of Arkansas, intervening, claimed the Mulberry was a navigable stream and the stream bed the property of the state, not the McIlroys.

The Ozark Society and the other defendants generally claimed that the Mulberry was a navigable stream but that even if the court found otherwise, a public easement in the Mulberry should be recognized. The defendants also argued that the public had acquired a prescriptive easement in the river and that the act admitting Arkansas into the Union placed the Mulberry in the public domain . . . . .

As we define the term "navigable" we find the Mulberry River, as it passes through McIlroy's property, to be navigable. Consequently, we reverse the chancellor's decree in that regard. Our decision precludes the necessity to discuss any of the other issues raised on appeal.

The Mulberry River, located in northwest Arkansas, heads up in the Ozark Mountains and flows in a westerly direction for about 70 miles until it joins the Arkansas River. It could best be described as an intermediate stream, smaller than the Arkansas River, the lower White and Little Red Rivers and other deep, wide rivers that have been used commercially since their discovery. But neither is it like the many small creeks and branches in Arkansas that cannot be regularly floated with canoes or flatbottomed boats for any substantial period of time during the year. The Mulberry is somewhere in between. It is a stream that for about 50 or 55 miles of its length can be floated by canoe or flatbottomed boat for at least six months of the year. Parts of it are floatable for longer periods of time. The Mulberry is a typical rock-bottomed Ozark Mountain stream, flowing with relatively clear water and populated by a variety of fish. Smallmouth bass favor such a stream and populate the Mulberry.

For most of its distance it is a series of long flat holes of water interrupted by narrower shoals. These shoals attract the canoeists. McIlroy describes the stream as following a tortuous course; canoeists find it an exciting stream testing the skill of an experienced canoeist. Watergaps, affairs of wire or boards erected across the stream to hold cattle, have at times been erected but, according to W. L. McIlroy, they go down with the first rise of water. It is not a stream easily possessed. In recent years, the Mulberry has claimed the lives of several canoeists.

Annually, since 1967, the Ozark Society has sponsored for its members one or more float trips on the Mulberry River. These trips take them through McIlroy's property, which is located about 23 miles up the river from where the Mulberry enters the Arkansas. McIlroy said he had a confrontation with Ozark Society members in 1975 when about 600 people put in at a low water bridge on his property. The bridge, near Cass, serves a county road, and is undisputably a public bridge. Canoeists and fishermen have regularly used it as an access place to the river. . . .

This is essentially a lawsuit about the river as it passes through McIlroy's property. W. L. McIlroy testified that just below the bridge is a long hole of water, perhaps the longest on that stretch of the river, which is about 100 feet wide; it narrows to a shoal. He said a man could wade the water almost any time of the year. He claimed the river could sometimes not be canoed for an entire year. He said dry spots usually existed for six to eight months of the year. He denied seeing a canoe before 1974. However, from 1947 to 1971, McIlroy was in California. During that time he would spend only a week or so a year in Arkansas.

The great preponderance of the evidence conflicts with McIlroy's estimate of the river. It is floatable for at least six months of the year.

According to a pamphlet, "The Float Streams of Arkansas," published by an Arkansas state agency, the floating season is October through June. This is for a course from a point considerably upstream from McIlroy's property to the river's mouth, a distance of about 50 miles. Numerous canoeists testified they had floated the Mulberry through the Cass area, mostly in the spring of the year. It was not disputed, however, that at times, usually in the summer months, the Mulberry could not be floated.

The evidence by testimony and exhibits demonstrates conclusively that the Mulberry had been used by the public for recreational purposes for many years. It has long been used for fishing and swimming and is today also popular among canoeists.

[The court's summary of the testimony of many canoeists who used the river is omitted.]

Besides McIlroy's testimony, several other local landowners testified or their stipulated testimony was presented. Woody Woolsey, who had lived most of his life next to the river, said he considered the stream private. He said he first saw a canoe in 1974. George Freeman, living nearby for 50 years, said he expected people to get permission to use the stream. He considered the stream private property.

Al Wiederkehr bought land on the Mulberry in 1966 and agreed he thought the Mulberry private property. He said his land was posted. The former sheriff of Franklin County, W. D. Gober, who built a cabin on the McIlroy property, said he first saw canoes in 1974. The testimony of five others was offered to the effect that the Mulberry was private property or used only with permission.

The original government plat made of this area in 1838 was introduced and shows the "Mulberry Creek" was "meandered" by the surveyors. Meander lines are those representing the border line of a stream and such lines are considered prima facie evidence of navigability. *Lutesville Sand & Gravel Co. v. McLaughlin*, 26 S.W.2d 892 (Ark. 1930).

The facts presented prove that the Mulberry River at the point in question is capable of recreational use and has been used extensively for recreational purposes. We must now decide whether such a stream is navigable.

Determining the navigability of a stream is essentially a matter of deciding if it is public or private property. *See State v. Korrer*, 148 N.W. 617 (Minn.), *supp. op.* 148 N.W. 1095 (Minn. 1914). Navigation in fact is the standard modern test of navigability, and, as embroidered by the federal courts, controls when navigation must be defined for federal purposes maritime jurisdiction, regulation under the Commerce Clause, and title disputes between the state and federal governments. *See Hitchings v. Del Rio Woods Recreation & Park District*, 127 Cal.Rptr. 830

(1976); *Day v. Armstrong,* 362 P.2d 137 (Wyo.1961). Otherwise, the states may adopt their own definitions of navigability. *Donnelly v. United States,* 228 U.S. 243 (1913).

While navigation in fact is widely regarded as the proper test of navigability, *St. Louis, Iron Mountain & Southern Railroad Co. v. Ramsey,* 13 S.W. 931 (Ark. 1890), it is a test which should not be applied too literally. For example, it has been said a stream need not be navigable at all its points or for the entire year to be navigable. *Economy Light & Power Co. v. United States,* 256 U.S. 113 (1921). The real issue in these cases is the definition of navigation in fact.

Arkansas has adopted the standard definition of navigability. *Lutesville Sand & Gravel Co. v. McLaughlin,* cited above. That test, which was similar to the general test used by the federal courts, defines navigability in terms of a river's potential for commercial usefulness; that is, whether the water could be used to remove the products of the surrounding land to another place. That definition reads:

> . . . Nor is it necessary that the stream should be capable of floating boats or rafts the whole, or even the greater part of the year. Upon the other hand, it is not sufficient to impress navigable character that there may be extraordinary times of transient freshets, when boats might be floated out. For, if this were so, almost all insignificant streams would be navigable. The true criterion is the dictate of sound business common sense, and depends on the usefulness of the stream to the population of its banks, as a means of carrying off the products of their fields and forests, or bringing to them articles of merchandise. If, in its natural state, without artificial improvements, it may be prudently relied upon and used for that purpose at some seasons of the year, recurring with tolerable regularity, then in the American sense, it is navigable, although the annual time may not be very long. Products may be ready and boats prepared, and it may thus become a very great convenience and materially promote the comfort and advance the prosperity of the community. But it is evident that sudden freshets at uncertain times cannot be made available for such purposes. No prudent man could afford the expense of preparation for such events, or could trust to such uncertainty in getting to market. The result of the authorities is this, that usefulness for purposes of transportation, for rafts, boats or barges, gives navigable character, reference being had to its natural state, rather than to its average depth the year round. (citing authorities). *Id.,* 26 S.W.2d at 893.

Therefore, a river is legally navigable if actually navigable and actually navigable if commercially valuable.

However, in the case of *Barboro v. Boyle*, 178 S.W. 378 (Ark. 1915), this Court foresaw, no doubt, that things would change in the future and that recreation would become an important interest of the people of Arkansas. The language in the *Barboro* case is almost prophetic. While adhering to the standard definition of navigability, with its dependence upon a commercial criterion, the Court went on to say:

> It is the policy of this state to encourage the use of its water courses for any useful or beneficial purpose. There may be other public uses than the carrying on of commerce of pecuniary value. The culture of rice is being developed in this state and the waters of the lake could be used for the purpose of flooding the rice fields and for other agricultural purposes. As the population of the state increases, the banks of the lake may become more thickly populated, and the water could be used for domestic purposes. Pleasure resorts might even be built upon the banks of the lake and the water might be needed for municipal purposes. Moreover, the waters of the lake might be used to a much greater extent for boating, for pleasure, for bathing, fishing and hunting than they are now used. (Emphasis added.) *Id.*, 178 S.W. at 380.

Since that time no case presented to us has involved the public's right to use a stream which has a recreational value, but lacks commercial adaptability in the traditional sense. Our definition of navigability is, therefore, a remnant of the steamboat era.

However, many other states have been presented with this same problem. Back in 1870, the Massachusetts Supreme Court found a stream navigable that could only be used for pleasure. The stream was about two feet deep at low water. The court stated:

> If water is navigable for pleasure boating, it must be regarded as navigable water though no craft has ever been upon it for the purpose of trade or agriculture. *Attorney General v. Woods,* 108 Mass. 436, 440 (1870).

In Ohio, the court recently was faced with this problem and decided to change its definition of navigation. The Ohio court said:

> We hold that the modern utilization of our water by our citizens requires that our courts, in their judicial interpretation of the navigability of such waters, consider their recreational use as well as the more traditional criteria of commercial use. *State ex*

rel. v. Newport Concrete Co., 336 N.E.2d 453, 457 (Ohio App. 1975).

Applying a "public trust" to the Little Miami River, the Ohio court found that the State of Ohio ". . . holds these waters in trust for those Ohioans who wish to use the stream for all legitimate uses, be they commercial, transportational, or recreational." *State ex rel. v. Newport Concrete Co.*, cited above.

Michigan reached a similar conclusion in 1974. Navigability in Michigan was significantly affected by whether logs had been, or could be, floated down a stream. That "floatable test" had been used by the Michigan court until it was confronted with the same problem that we have. Michigan readily admitted that its definition needed to be changed:

We therefore hold that members of the public have the right to navigate and to exercise the incidents of navigation in a lawful manner at any point below high water mark on waters of this state which are capable of being navigated by oar or motor propelled small craft. *Kelley, ex. rel. MacMullan v. Hallden*, 214 N.W.2d 856, 864 (Mich. 1974).

For examples of other states that have adopted similar definitions of navigation, see: *People v. Mack*, 97 Cal.Rptr. 448 (1971); *Lamprey v. State*, 53 N.W. 1139 (Minn. 1893); *Luscher v. Reynolds,* 56 P.2d 1158 (Or. 1936).

Arkansas, as most states in their infancy, was mostly concerned with river traffic by steamboats or barges when cases like *Lutesville, supra,* were decided. We have had no case regarding recreational use of waters such as the Mulberry. It may be that our decisions did or did not anticipate such use of streams which are suitable, as the Mulberry is, for recreational use. Such use would include flat bottomed boats for fishing and canoes for floating or both. There is no doubt that the segment of the Mulberry River that is involved in this lawsuit can be used for a substantial portion of the year for recreational purposes. Consequently, we hold that it is navigable at that place with all the incidental rights of that determination.

McIlroy and others testified that the reason they brought the lawsuit was because their privacy was being interrupted by the people who trespassed on their property, littered the stream and generally destroyed their property. We are equally disturbed with that small percentage of the public that abuses public privileges and has no respect for the property of others. Their conduct is a shame on us all. It is not disputed that riparian landowners on a navigable stream have a right to prohibit the public from crossing their property to reach such a stream. The McIlroys' rights in this regard are not affected by our decision. While there are laws prohibiting such misconduct, every branch of Arkansas' government should be more aware of its duty to keep Arkansas, which is a beautiful state, a good place to live. No doubt the state cannot alone solve such a problem, it requires some individual effort of the people. Nonetheless, we can no more close a public waterway because some of those who use it annoy nearby property owners, than we could close a public highway for similar reasons.

In any event, the state sought a decision that would protect its right to this stream. With that right, which we now recognize, goes a responsibility to keep it as God made it.

NOTES

1. *Waterways open under state law. McIlroy* is a state-law decision setting forth a legal conclusion based on Arkansas property law. As the court explains, its ruling has to do with the scope of both public rights in waterways and the private rights of adjacent riparian landowners. In Arkansas (and most states in the East), landowners own the soil beneath waterways; various states in the West, in contrast, retain ownership of lands submerged beneath traditionally navigable waters. Thus, in Arkansas and elsewhere, the public owns and has extensive rights in the water that flows across and alongside the private land but not in the streambed. The juxtaposition of public and private rights inevitably raises boundary issues, as *McIlroy* illustrates.

McIlroy expresses the near unanimous view that waterways are open to public travel, including recreation, when they are navigable. Many states express this rule either by statute or by constitutional provision. *E.g.*, S. C. Const. Art. XIV § 4: "All navigable waters shall forever remain public highways free to the citizens of the State and the United States. . . ." (under which, according to state courts, commercial use is not required; pleasure traffic is also protected, *Brownlee v. S.C. Dept. of Health and Envtl. Control*, 676 S.E.2d 116, 121 (S.C. 2009)). The legal test for navigability looks simply to whether a waterbody can in fact be used for travel. It is a factual test that considers the size and regularity of a water flow and whether people can actually navigate on it. Beyond this generalization, states seem to deviate. What types of boats or other objects (*e.g.*, floating logs) must a waterway be able to sustain to qualify as navigable? How much of the year must it be usable? All states agree that natural obstacles do not undercut navigability if it is possible to get around them. Also, human-made obstacles, including dams, typically do not affect navigability. But even with agreement on these points, conflicts are common, in part because no verbal test for navigability can be so clear that people of differing temperaments will apply it with the same results. Among the points of disagreement is the scope of public rights in backwaters when water levels are high.

McIlroy expressly embraces a recreational-use definition of navigability for purposes of recreational travel. The court suggested that this is an expansion of public rights, although actually this was by no means clear on the facts; the waterway at issue in the dispute might well have been navigable under any standard. As for a commercial-use test, it is worth recognizing that the main commercial use of the vast majority of waterways today is renting boats and guide services for recreation. These would seem to be a commercial activity, akin to the commerce created by the paying customers of a hotel or restaurant.

A few states in the past decade or two, encouraged by "property rights" groups, have sought to curtail public property rights in waterways, and with occasional success. *See, e.g., Givens v. Ichauway, Inc.,* 493 S.E.2d 148 (Ga. 1997) (suggesting a river must be capable of floating a barge that is 245 feet long, 35 feet wide, with a 7 foot 6 inch draft). On the other side, a number of states extend public use rights to waterways that have not been considered navigable or whose status is unclear. The court in *Alaska Public Easement Defense Fund v. Andrus,* 435 F.Supp. 664 (D. Alaska 1977), interpreted the Alaska constitution, with its reservation of all waters in the state "for common use," as extending public rights to non-navigable waterways. A prominent ruling is *Day v. Armstrong,* 362 P.2d 137 (Wyo. 1961), recognizing public rights to engage in recreational uses of non-navigable waters. A ruling largely following *Day* was *Conatser v. Johnson,* 194 P.3d 897 (Utah 2008). In these latter two jurisdictions, public rights in non-navigable waters are more limited than in navigable ones (see notes after the next case, p. 158).

2. *Waterways open under federal law.* Public rights in waterways are quite legally complex, largely because various federal laws play key roles that are poorly understood, if they are known about at all. Indeed, a common, erroneous assumption is that waterway access is simply a matter of state law.

Notice that in *McIlroy* one of the canoeists' arguments was that the river at issue was open to the public as a matter of federal statutory law: the statute admitting Arkansas into the Union. The court had no need to reach that federal issue because it concluded that the river was open under state law. Presumably, the court would have addressed the federal issue had state law not kept the river open. In fact, lawyers could have reached more widely into various sources of federal law to protect public rights in the waterway. They could have cited 33 U.S.C. § 10, providing that all navigable rivers in the region covered by the Louisiana Purchase "shall be and forever remain public highways." They could have cited 33 U.S.C. § 403, banning all obstructions of navigable waters except those permitted by federal law. Further, they could have cited the federal navigation servitude, a "dominant servitude" on all submerged lands subject to it, *United States v. Rands,* 389 U.S. 121, 122–23 (1967); a "permanent easement that [is] a preexisting limitation" upon the title of all such submerged lands, including lands held by private owners. *Lucas v. South Carolina Coastal Council,* 505 U.S. 1003, 1028 (1992). "When a navigational servitude exists, it gives rise to the right of the public to use those waterways" to which it applies. *Dardar v. Lafourche Realty Co.,* 985 F.2d 824, 832 (5th Cir. 1993). We return to the navigation servitude at the end of this chapter.

The possible clash between state and federal law, and the primacy of federal law when it protects a wider range of public rights, can be seen by comparing two contemporaneous rulings from Georgia. Under state law, only the largest waterways, capable of floating large commercial barges, are apparently open. *Givens v. Ichauway*, 493 S.E.2d 148 (Ga. 1997). According to a federal court, a whitewater river in Georgia with rapids, rocks, and shifting currents, usable by kayaks after rains, was open as a matter of federal law under the navigation servitude. *Atlanta School of Kayaking, Inc. v. Douglasville-Douglas-County Water and Sewer Authority*, 981 F.Supp. 1469 (N.D. Ga. 1997).

In states other than Arkansas, other federal laws may apply to protect public rights, including state enabling acts. Thus, states formed out of the former Northwest Territory apparently remain subject to the Northwest Ordinance of 1787, which provided that navigable waterways flowing into either the Mississippi or St. Lawrence Rivers, together with portage routes between such rivers, "shall be common highways, and forever free." 1 Stat. 51, 52 note (1789), re-enacted at 1 Stat. 51 (1789). According to the chief interpretive decision, *Economy Light & Power Co. v. United States*, 256 U.S. 113, 122 (1921), the Ordinance remains valid and in effect to the extent that "it established public rights of highway in navigable waters"; on that point (but perhaps only on that point), the Ordinance was "no more capable of repeal by one of the states than any other regulation of interstate commerce enacted by the Congress." (Various Supreme Court rulings from the 1880s and early 1890s did curtail the Ordinance to the extent needed for states to authorize bridges and waterway improvements.) The Wisconsin Supreme Court relied in part on the Northwest Ordinance in upholding public rights in *Diana Shooting Club v. Husting*, 145 N.W. 816 (Wisc.1914).

This story of federal waterway rights continues after the next case, which looks at the scope of public rights (fishing, hunting, trapping, bathing). Later we will consider the important role of the public trust doctrine in defining and protecting public rights (pp. 178–217).

3. *Navigable waters and human alterations.* One of many questions that arise about public rights has to do with public rights in waterways created or expanded by human effort. A leading ruling is *Vaughn v. Vermillion Corp.*, 444 U.S. 206 (1979), which concluded that human-made canals are not covered by the navigation servitude but that such a canal is covered, and thus open to public use, if was created "in part by means of diversion or destruction of a preexisting natural navigable waterway." Most states seem to conclude that a human-made water body does not become navigable simply because it is connected to a navigable waterway. And in *Kaiser Aetna v. United States*, 444 U.S. 164 (1979), a companion to *Vaughn*, the Supreme Court ruled that a government agency could not open a private waterbody to public access without paying just compensation. *Kaiser Aetna* implicitly assumed that, under applicable state law, the property owner had the right to exclude the public under the facts, and that the particular landowner involved was being singled out for special, ill treatment. Various

states, on the hand, take the view that a landowner who voluntarily connects a private lake to a navigable waterway thereby loses the right to exclude the public under state property law. *State v. Head,* 498 S.E.2d 389 (S.C. App. 1997); *Mentor Harbor Yachting Club v. Mentor Lagoons, Inc.,* 163 N.E.2d 373 (Ohio 1959). A later ruling from Arkansas, citing *McIlroy,* concluded as a matter of state property law that water on private land became open to public use due to an Army Corps of Engineers project on nearby land. *Arkansas River Rights Committee v. Echubby Lake Hunting Club,* 126 S.W.3d 738 (Ark. 2003).

MUNNINGHOFF V. WISCONSIN CONSERVATION COMMISSION
Supreme Court of Wisconsin
38 N.W.2d 712 (1949)

[Munninghoff sought a muskrat farm license from the state for lands owned and leased by him in Oneida County that were submerged by the Wisconsin River. The state conservation commission refused to issue the license on the ground that relevant state statute did not authorize the granting of a trapping license in navigable waters. The right to trap muskrats in navigable waters, the commission said, was a public right, which meant that the state could not authorize exclusive rights to raise and trap muskrats in it. Continuing to believe that the state could and should authorize his trapping (thereby recognizing that the public had no trapping rights), Munninghoff appealed.]

MARTIN, J.

* * *

It is admitted that the lands upon which Munninghoff desires to operate a muskrat farm are his own lands, and are located under the navigable waters of the Wisconsin river. These waters became navigable by the erection by the Rhinelander Paper Company of a dam in the year 1906, which dam flooded the land in question and it has been flooded since that time.

The issues in this case are whether the conservation commission, pursuant to sec. 29.575, Stats., can license privately owned lands lying under navigable waters, and whether such muskrat farming is an incident to navigation.

The muskrat farm law was originally passed in 1919. [As amended, § 29.575(1) provides:] "The owner or lessee of any lands within the state of Wisconsin suitable for the breeding and propagating of muskrats . . . shall have the right upon complying with the provisions of this section to establish, operate and maintain on such lands a muskrat . . . farm, for the purpose of breeding, propagating, trapping and dealing in muskrats." . . .

[Under Wisconsin law, it] is not essential to the public easement that the capacity for navigation be continuous throughout the year to make it navigable or public. It is sufficient that a stream has periods of navigable capacity ordinarily recurrent from year to year and continuing long enough to make the stream usable as a highway. *Willow River Club v. Wade*, 76 N.W. 273 (Wisc. 1898). The capacity for floating logs to market during the spring freshets which normally lasts six weeks was held to make a stream navigable. *Falls Mfg. Co. v. Oconto River Imp. Co.* et al., 58 N.W. 257 (Wisc. 1894). . . .

[T]he meaning of [§ 29.575(1) was] construed in *Krenz v. Nichols*, 222 N.W. 300, 303 (Wisc. 1928), wherein it was stated:

> The state, under its police power, and to carry out its trust, passed the statute in question. So far as it affects the public, the statute is reasonable, and is not contrary to any provision of the federal or state Constitution. Nor do we think it is contrary to the decision of this court in *Diana Shooting Club v. Husting,* 156 Wis. 261, 145 N.W. 816, Ann.Cas.1915C, 1148. In that case the court upheld the right of a citizen of the state to hunt from a boat in the navigable inland streams of the state, notwithstanding that the boat should be on the waters over the lands of a private owner. The court there said that was a right incident to the right of navigation, and that the right of navigation was free to all the citizens of the state upon such waters, by virtue of the Ordinance of 1787, the Enabling Act of the state Constitution, and the constitutional provision thereto. . . .

In Wisconsin the owner of the banks of the stream is the owner of the bed, regardless of whether the stream is navigable or non-navigable. The owner of the submerged soil of a running stream does not own the running water, but he does have certain exclusive rights to make a reasonable use of the water as is passes over or along his land. For instance, he may erect a pier for navigation; he may pump part of the water out of the stream to irrigate his crops; his cattle may be permitted to drink of it; and his muskrats may use it to gather vegetation for the construction of muskrat houses or for food.

It is not within the power of the state to deprive the owner of submerged land of the right to make use of the water which passes over his land, or to grant the use of it to a non-riparian. The riparian's exclusive right to use the water arises directly from the fact that non-riparians have no access to the stream without trespass upon riparian lands.

In the present case the respondent would make use of the water flowing over or past his land in permitting the muskrats to swim in the water, gather feed found in the water or in the bed of the river, build muskrat houses on the bed where the water is shallow, and dig runways in the banks from underneath the surface of the water to their burrows in the banks above the water line.

In general, the rights of the public to the incidents of navigation are boating, bathing, fishing, hunting, and recreation. See *Doemel v. Jantz,* 193 N.W. 393 (Wisc. 1923). Trapping is not included for it is an incident of land use. See *Johnson v. Burghorn,* 179 N.W. 225, 228 (Mich. 1920). Appellant asserts that float trapping does not require the use of the bottom. However, floats for float trapping are always anchored to the bottom and any method of anchoring or securing a float would, of necessity, require the use of the land or the bottom. The right to use the running water of the bed for float trapping is not included in the easement of navigation. To float trap in navigable water constitutes a trespass upon the submerged land for which the trespasser may be prosecuted by the owner of the soil and enjoined from using the public water for that purpose.

The muskrats on a muskrat farm have been bought and paid for by the licensee. They are his personal property whether they are swimming in the waters above his lands or running along on the dry land within the limits of his licensed premises. The presence of the muskrats in a navigable stream covering privately owned lands does not entitle a trespasser to take them any more than a trespasser would be entitled to seize domestic ducks in the same stream. But if a muskrat should leave a licensed area, he becomes *ferae naturae,* and is legitimate prey for a neighboring trapper. See 2 *Property Ratione Soli,* Am.Jur., sec 12, at 699.

Appellant also asserts that the right of navigation includes the incidental use of the bottom. This is true where the use of the bottom is connected with navigation, such as walking as a trout fisherman does in a navigable stream, boating, standing on the bottom while bathing, casting an anchor from a boat in fishing, propelling a duck boat by poling against the bottom, walking on the ice if the river is frozen, etc. These have nothing in common with trapping because the latter involves the exercise of a property right in the land or the bottom.

The conservation department has authority to issue the license applied for.

NOTES

1. *The range of public uses. Munninghoff* raises the obvious follow-up question to *McIlroy*: Given public access to a waterway, how can the public use it? The nearly universal answer is that the public can use waterways for travel, fishing, swimming, and bathing. Rights to hunt (waterfowl hunting) are less often recognized, and trapping is rarely allowed. An expansive view of public rights, including hunting and "all recreation" uses, was embraced in

Southern Idaho Fish and Game Ass'n v. Picabo Livestock, Inc., 528 P.2d 1295 (Idaho 1974). A major exception is New York, in which fishing rights are limited to waterways subject to the ebb and flow of the tides. Compare *Douglaston Manor, Inc. v. Bahrakis,* 655 N.Y.S.2d 745 (1997) (rights to fish limited to tide-influenced waters) with *Adirondack League Club, Inc. v. Sierra Club,* 684 N.Y.S.2d 168 (1998) (all waterways navigable in fact are public highways open to travel and transport; recreational use establishes navigability).

2. *Private uses of non-navigable waters.* In a few jurisdictions, the public has limited rights to engage in recreational uses of waters deemed non-navigable generally but that are capable of being accessed by small water craft. In *Day v. Armstrong,* 362 P.2d 137 (Wyo. 1961), the Wyoming Supreme Court recognized public rights to engage in recreational travel but not fishing on *non-navigable* waters. In *Montana Coalition for Stream Access v. Curran,* 682 P.2d 163 (Mont. 1984), the Montana Supreme Court ruled that waterways were open for recreational use even when they were not considered navigable for other purposes. In *Conatser v. Johnson,* 194 P.3d 897 (Utah 2008), the court embraced the rule that all waterways were open for a full range of uses. That interpretation, however, was curtailed by the legislature the following year. Under the new statute, waterfowl hunting is allowed if the waterway is navigable, which means "useful for commerce" and with "a useful capacity as a public highway of transportation"; on the other hand, recreational floating, and fishing while floating (not standing in the river), are authorized on any water "that has sufficient width, depth, and flow to allow free passage of the chosen vessel at the time of floating." Ut. St. §§ 73–29–102, –201, –202.

3. *Who owns the muskrats?* A curious aspect of *Munninghoff* is the court's comment that muskrats raised by Munninghoff would remain his private property even when swimming in a navigable river, at least so long as they remain in the area licensed for the muskrat farm. The court analogizes the case to that of domestic waterfowl on the river, which would remain privately owned. But what about the rule of wildlife law that a wild animal is no longer owned when it is unconfined and has returned to something similar to its wild habitat? Is the rule that the court (in dictum) announces fair to public users of the river? How are they supposed to know which muskrats are owned and which are unowned? Doesn't the ruling effectively give the landowner an exclusive right to capture muskrats in a section of publicly owned water?

4. *Incidental land uses.* Another important issue raised in *Munninghoff* has to do with the scope of public rights to use adjacent land in the course of using the public waterway. The general rule is that public users can make incidental land use to the extent necessary to enjoy their public waterway rights. The scope of these incidental land uses has been highly contentious. Most states say that land use must be limited to activities necessary to get around obstacles. In New York, for instance, "the right to navigate carries with it the incidental privilege to make use, when absolutely

necessary, of the bed and banks, including the right to portage on riparian lands." *Adirondack League Club, Inc. v. Sierra Club*, 684 N.Y.S.2d 168, 173 (1998). Many states deal with the issue by statute. E.g., Id. St. § 36–1601 (where route is obstructed "members of the public may remove themselves and their boats, floats, canoes or other floating crafts from the stream and walk or portage such crafts around said obstruction re-entering the stream immediately below such obstruction at the nearest point where it is safe to do so"). The corresponding Utah statute requires that the land use be the "most direct," "least invasive," and "closest to the river." Ut. St. § 73–29–202. Louisiana law includes a more extensive right for the public to make use of privately owned banks, *Nevels v. States*, 665 So.2d 26 (La. App. 1995), but that state does not recognize the right to fish from boats on periodically accessible bayous. *Parm v. Shumate*, 513 F.3d 135, 142–45 (5th Cir. 2007).

CARNAHAN V. MORIAH PROPERTY OWNERS ASSOCIATION, INC.

Supreme Court of Indiana
716 N.E.2d 437 (1999)

SULLIVAN, J.

The Moriah Property Owners Association, Inc., which owns approximately 64% of a private lake, seeks to restrict watercraft use on it. The Carnahans, who own a portion of the lake, oppose the restrictions. They contend that they have a prescriptive easement for the recreational use of motorized watercraft on the entire lake. We hold that the Carnahans have failed to establish a prescriptive easement.

Background

Lake Julia is an approximately 22-acre lake located in Lake County. Prior to 1972, the lake and all the surrounding property were owned by Charles and Julia Drewry. In November of 1972, the Carnahans purchased a lot from the Drewrys, which was approximately one acre in size and included a portion of the lake bed. From the beginning, the Carnahans engaged in recreational activities including ice skating, fishing, swimming, and the use of various watercraft on portions of the entire lake. In the spring of 1973, the Carnahans placed a houseboat on the lake. They powered the houseboat around the lake, skied behind it, and lived on it intermittently until 1976 when they finished building a lakeside home. Thereafter, they used a ski boat on the lake until 1986, and wave runners and jet skis through the summer of 1993.

On July 26, 1984, the Carnahans purchased an adjacent one acre plot; approximately one-fifth of this new acreage constituted the lake bed. Beginning in 1987, the land around and under Lake Julia was surveyed and an engineering plan prepared which platted various lots comprising the Julia and Lake Additions to Lake County. On December 29, 1987, the

Carnahans acquired an additional adjacent 1.2 acres of land; approximately one-eighth of this new acreage included the lake bed. Our calculations suggest that at this point, the Carnahans owned just over half an acre (or 2.5%) of the total 22-acre lake bed.

On December 24, 1991, the current Moriah Property Owner's Association, Inc. ("Moriah") obtained the property rights to a majority of the lake bed including nearly all of the water above it suitable for the operation of watercraft. This property is now legally described as Lot 8, Moriah Addition to Lake County. Lot 8 is 15.6 acres, and 14.1 acres constitutes the lake. Our calculations suggest that this 14.1 acres comprises approximately 64% of the 22-acre lake bed.

In April 1992, Moriah prepared restrictive covenants which included rules intended for the safe use of that portion of Lake Julia described as Lot 8. The relevant restrictive covenant relating to the Carnahans' claimed prescriptive easement for the recreational use of watercraft on Lake Julia states as follows: "No motors are allowed on the lake except electric trolling motors powered by no more than two 12-volt batteries." (R. at 78.) In July 1992, the president of Moriah sent documents to the Carnahans including among other things the restrictive covenants for the use of Lot 8.

On May 21, 1993, the Carnahans filed this lawsuit to establish a prescriptive easement for the use of watercraft on Lake Julia and to quiet title in the easement; they also sought a declaratory judgment regarding their rights in relation to Moriah, and sought to enjoin any interference with their real property, easement, and riparian rights. . . .

I

The Carnahans contend that they have a prescriptive easement over an entire body of water. Prior Indiana decisions adjudicating riparian rights in the context of easements almost exclusively concern land access to the water itself or the construction and use of a dock. *See, e.g., Klotz v. Horn,* 558 N.E.2d 1096 (Ind.1990); . . . These decisions address the riparian rights of lakefront property owners whose land only abuts the water. This case is different and concerns the competing rights of property owners whose real estate is incidentally covered by a relatively small, private lake. Therefore, any decision we make concerning an easement or use right must coincide with our common law as it applies to property underlying an inland, nonnavigable lake.

"A private lake is a body of water on the surface of land within the exclusive dominion and control of the surrounding landowners." *Freiburger v. Fry,* 439 N.E.2d 169, 173 (Ind. App. 1982) (citing 1915–16 OP.Ind.Att'y Gen. 703; *Patton Park, Inc. v. Pollak,* 55 N.E.2d 328 (Ind. App. 1944)). Determinations of riparian rights of inland lakes are based upon whether a lake is navigable or nonnavigable. *Berger Farms, Inc. v.*

Estes, 662 N.E.2d 654, 656 (Ind. App. 1996) (citing *Bath v. Courts,* 459 N.E.2d 72, 75 (Ind. App. 1984)). A nonnavigable lake is one "enclosed and bordered by riparian landowners." *Id.* (citing *Bath,* 459 N.E.2d at 75 (citing in turn *Stoner v. Rice,* 22 N.E. 968 (Ind. 1889))).

This Court last determined the rights of a lake bed property owner in *Sanders v. De Rose,* 191 N.E. 331 (Ind. 1934). Sanders owned approximately twenty acres of land covered by a "non-navigable body of fresh water, known as Center Lake." *Id.* at 90, 191 N.E. at 331. De Rose was a non-property owner who gained access to the lake for fishing via the permission of another riparian owner, whose smaller portion of land both abutted and extended into Center Lake. In reversing the lower court and enjoining De Rose from fishing upon the waters of the lake overlying Sanders's property, this Court emphasized Sanders's rights with respect to other "owners of the bed of such lake." *Id.* at 333. It then set forth the common law rule as it applies to an inland, nonnavigable lake: "[E]ach owner has the right to the free and unmolested use and control of his portion of the lake bed and water thereon for boating and fishing." *Id.* . . .

II

Prescriptive easements are not favored in the law, *see* 25 Am.Jur.2d *Easements and Licenses* § 45, at 615 (1996 & Supp.1999), and in Indiana, the party claiming one must meet "stringent requirements," *Fleck v. Hann,* 658 N.E.2d 125, 128 (Ind. App. 1995) (reversing lower court decision finding prescriptive easement for use of lakefront pier, because testimony was conflicted as to "adverse" or "permissive" use, thus claimants failed to meet the "stringent requirements that an adverse user must prove to acquire a prescriptive easement"). In order to establish the existence of a prescriptive easement, the evidence must show an actual, hostile, open, notorious, continuous, uninterrupted adverse use for twenty years under a claim of right. *Greenco, Inc. v. May,* 506 N.E.2d 42, 45 (Ind.App.1987). "Each . . . element[ ] . . . must be established as a necessary, independent, ultimate fact, the burden of showing which is on the party asserting the prescriptive title, and the failure to find any one of such elements [is] fatal . . . , for such failure to find is construed as a finding against it." *Monarch Real Estate Co. v. Frye,* 133 N.E.156, 158 (Ind. App. 1921) (citing *Benedict v. Bushnell,* 117 N.E. 267 (Ind. App. 1917)).

Adverse use has been defined as a "use of the property as the owner himself would exercise, disregarding the claims of others entirely, asking permission from no one, and using the property under a claim of right." *Nowlin v. Whipple,* 22 N.E. 669, 670 (Ind. App. 1889). The concept of *adversity* was developed in the context of establishing use rights over static paths or roads that crossed the property of adjoining landowners. The Court of Appeals affirmed the trial court's conclusion as to adversity by citing a prototypical *path or road* case for the proposition that "[a]n unexplained use for 20 years is presumed to be adverse and sufficient to establish title by prescriptive easement." . . .

We agree with the reasoning in the *Mitchell, Fleck,* and *Reder* decisions that "an unexplained use for 20 years" of an obvious path or road for ingress and egress over the lands of another creates a rebuttable presumption that a use was adverse. However, we are unwilling to recognize such a presumption in favor of a party trying to establish a prescriptive easement for the recreational use of a body of water. This is because recreational use (especially of a body of water) is of a very different character from use of a path or road for ingress and egress over land. Recreational use (especially of water which leaves no telltale path or road) seems to us likely to be permissive in accordance with the widely held view in Indiana that if the owner of one land sees his neighbor also making use of it, under circumstances that in no way injures the [land] or interferes with [the landowner's] own use of it, [it] does not justify the inference that he is yielding to his neighbor's claim of right or that his neighbor is asserting any right; it signifies only that he is permitting his neighbor to use the [land]. *Monarch Real Estate Co.,* 133 N.E. at 159 (Ind. App. 1921) (quoting *Anthony v. Kennard Bldg. Co.,* 87 S.W. 921, 926 (Mo. 1905)). . . .

We thus conclude that claimants seeking to establish an easement based on the "recreational" use of another's property must make a special showing that those activities were in fact adverse; they will not be indulged a presumption to that effect. *Kessinger v. Matulevich,* 925 P.2d 864, 869 (Mont. 1996) ("Recreational use is insufficient to raise a presumption of adverse use.") (citing *Public Lands Access Ass'n v. Boone & Crockett Club Found., Inc.,* 856 P.2d 525, 528–29 (Mont. 1993)); *Ellis v. Municipal Reserve & Bond Co.,* 655 P.2d 204, 207 (Or. App. 1982) ("For the public to establish a public recreational easement through prescription, the proof must be clear and positive; vague and general testimony is insufficient.").

We have previously stated that "clear and convincing proof is a standard frequently imposed in civil cases where the wisdom of experience has demonstrated the need for greater certainty." . . . Therefore, we hold that a party seeking to establish a recreational prescriptive easement must show by clear and convincing evidence that their use was adverse. This holding we base on the need for greater certainty in determining the true character of a "recreational" land use, for the recreational use of a neighbor's land will oftentimes be perfectly consistent with that neighbor's (the servient titleholder's) title to the land. . . .

The trial court's findings do not address whether the Carnahans' recreational use of the lake was adverse to the Drewrys. They only track the Carnahans' periodic change in the use of recreational equipment over the years. (R. at 206–07; Findings of Fact Nos. 6–12.) Therefore, the findings of fact do not support the court's conclusion that the Carnahans' recreational activities constituted the "adverse seasonal use of Lake Julia." (R. at 210–11; Conclusion of Law No. 3.)

On the other hand, the record does contain ample evidence supporting the inference that the Carnahans' use of the lake was both non-confrontational and permissive in recognition of the Drewrys' authority as title holders to a majority of the lake bed. For example, Mr. Carnahan testified that Mr. Drewry "would wave" to them as they anchored their houseboat in "plain sight of his house," but that they kept the houseboat "in the middle" as opposed to the "south side of the lake" so as not "to bother anybody." (Suppl. R. at 378.) When asked why they retired their ski boat in 1986, Mr. Carnahan responded that they "didn't want to tick off the neighbors." *Id.* at 382. There are other examples of the Carnahans' non-adversarial use of the Lake, such as Mr. Carnahan's statement that it had "been under [his] driving force that if people were on the lake fishing, [the Carnahans] stayed off," *id.* at 407, and Mrs. Carnahan's statement that "[i]f there are children in the lake, we are either not out there or we are at the opposite end," *id.* at 101.

We find the evidence establishes that the Carnahans' use of Lake Julia was not adverse and was insufficient to overcome the special showing required with respect to establishing a recreational easement. . . .

NOTES

1. *The contrary "civil rule" of lakebed ownership.* A similar set of facts involving a non-navigable lake came to the Illinois Supreme Court in a 1988 case, *Beacham v. Lake Zurich Property Owners Association.* The lake covered 240 acres, and involved a plan by a landowner who owned "about 15% to 20% of the lake bed" to construct a commercial marina and to rent boats to the public for recreational use on the lake. The Illinois Supreme Court had never ruled on the surface-use rights of landowners around a non-navigable lake. It thus viewed the issue as one of first impression and felt free to craft a rule that it deemed most appropriate. The court's decision was to reject the common law rule, followed in *Carnahan,* and to apply the much different rule used in the continental European civil law system:

> Under the common law rule, the owner of a part of a lake bed has the right to the exclusive use and control of the waters above that property. This rule is a corollary of the traditional common law view that the ownership of a parcel of land entitles the owner to the exclusive use and enjoyment of anything above or below the

property. (See *Smoulter v. Boyd*, 58 A. 144 (Pa. 1904).) Courts following the common law principle have held that the owner of a part of a lake bed may exclude from the surface of the overlying water all other persons, including those who own other parts of the lake bed. . . .

In those States in which the civil law rule prevails, the owner of a part of a lake bed has a right to the reasonable use and enjoyment of the entire lake surface. (See *Duval v. Thomas*, 114 So.2d 791 (Fla. 1959); *Beach v. Hayner*, 173 N.W. 487 (Mich. 1919); *Johnson v. Seifert*, 100 N.W.2d 689 (Minn. 1960); *Snively v. Jaber* (1956), 296 P.2d 1015 (Wash. 1956).) Those courts rejecting the common law rule have noted the difficulties presented by attempts to establish and obey definite property lines (*Beach,* 173 N.W. at 488; *Snively,* 296 P.2d at 1019) and certain other impractical consequences of that rule, such as the erection of booms, fences, or barriers (*Duval,* 114 So.2d at 795). Moreover, application of the civil law approach promotes rather than hinders the recreational use and enjoyment of lakes. (*Duval,* 114 So.2d at 795; *Johnson,* 100 N.W.2d at 695.) We conclude that the arguments supporting the civil law rule warrant its adoption in Illinois. Restricting the use of a lake to the water overlying the owner's lake bed property can only frustrate the cooperative and mutually beneficial use of that important resource.

We, therefore, affirm the appellate court's holding that where there are multiple owners of the bed of a private, nonnavigable lake, such owners and their licensees have the right to the reasonable use and enjoyment of the surface waters of the entire lake provided they do not unduly interfere with the reasonable use of the waters by other owners and their licensees.

The question remains, however, whether the plaintiffs' use of the lake, including the renting of boats to members of the general public, is a reasonable one that does not unduly interfere with the reasonable use of the lake by other owners and their licensees. (See Comment, *Public Recreation on Nonnavigable Lakes and the Doctrine of Reasonable Use,* 55 Iowa L.Rev. 1064 (1970); see also Maloney & Plager, *Florida's Lakes: Problems in a Water Paradise,* 13 U.Fla.L.Rev. 1, 69–70 (1960) (discussing public use).) Because that question is not before us and remains for consideration by the trial court in the first instance, we express no view on it now.

Beacham v. Lake Zurich Property Owners Assn., 526 N.E.2d 154 (Ill. 1988).

2. *The two approaches.* Taken together, *Carnahan* and *Beacham* illustrate the two, much-different approaches that states use in defining the lake-use rights of owners of land beneath the surface of a *non-navigable* lake. Any member of the public can use the surface of a *navigable* lake or river so long as the person has lawful access to get to the water body. The common law treats land beneath non-navigable waterways the same as any other land

for purposes of trespass law: the landowner has the right to exclude subject to statutory rules and to presumptions in many regions that land is open to public use unless posted against entry. (Detailed posting requirements, as you might imagine, can be hard to follow in the case of submerged land.) The civil law rule treats surface use rights on the lake as an asset owned collectively by the owners of the underlying land.

By adopting the civil law rule, the Illinois court (and others taking the same approach) add a new legal issue calling for resolution in particular disputes. A partial owner of a lake surface can now make use of the entire surface, but only so long as the surface use is reasonable under the circumstances. How might a trial court facing the issue go about determining whether a pattern of lake-surface use is reasonable? The carrying capacity of the lake would seem relevant. How about the amount of underlying land that a person owns compared to the size of the lake as a whole? Other factors? Inevitably a trial court will have discretion, much as in determinations of reasonableness under water law and nuisance.

For recent rulings adhering to the common law approach, which remains dominant, see *Orr v. Mortvedt*, 735 N.W.2d 610 (Iowa 2007); *White's Mill Colony Inc. v. Williams*, 609 S.E.2d 811 (S.C. 2005).

3.   *Comparing the two approaches.* Many readers of *Beacham* are likely to think that the court reached the right decision. After all, its ruling allowed all landowners to use the entire lake surface. But keep in mind, when the people living around a non-navigable lake all get along, there is little need for law to define their respective use rights. Law is needed only when people do not get along; when they disagree about who can use the water in what way. One possible aim of the law could be to put the landowners in positions so that they are most likely to work out their problems, without going to court. Can we speculate on which legal approach—the common law or civil law—is more likely to achieve this goal?

Under the common law approach, landowners have an obvious incentive to get together and consent to shared use of the lake. If they do not, each owner is limited to the small water area above her land. Note that, when landowners do set up a property-owner or lake-management association, they can prescribe lake-use rules that are vastly more precise than the vague "reasonable use" rule applied in *Beacham* (and in *Thompson v. Enz*, 154 N.W.2d 473 (Mich. 1967), discussed in note 6, below). Note also another defect of the civil law approach: disputes must be taken to court for resolution, which means lengthy delays, expensive litigation, and unpredictable outcomes. Would it not be better to keep such disputes out of court, turning them over to tribunals of property owners? How complex are the legal and factual issues, and is the involvement of lawyers likely to help? On the other side, the common law approach does allow one or a few owners to frustrate a widely supported regime of lake use by refusing to go along. Does this undercut the virtue of the common law approach? What about the possibility of authorizing by statute some super-majority of landowners to set rules that would bind everyone? (Keep this question in mind when you consider, in a later chapter (pp. 400–425), the statutes enacted by states to govern underground pools of oil and gas, particularly compulsory or forced pooling and unitization statutes.)

4.   *Why unanimity in lake management?* In *Carnahan*, a clear majority of lakefront property owners apparently desired to restrict the use of motorboats on the relatively small lake. Through negotiations and voluntary agreements they were able to restrict uses of most of the lake but not all of it. Given that uses of the lake are inevitably interconnected, and given that the lake is essentially a single natural resource, not easily divided, should the law make it easier for surrounding landowners to establish a private management scheme? What about a law authorizing some super-majority of landowners to make rules governing the entire lake that would apply to everyone? What problems might arise with this approach, and could they be minimized?

5.   *Civil law, Scottish style.* Several scholars have called into question the historical accuracy of the names attached to these two legal approaches. See, e.g., Andrea B. Carroll, *Examining a Comparative Law Myth: Two Hundred Years of Riparian Misconception*, 80 Tul. L. Rev. 901 (2006). The approach known as the civil law rule entered Anglo-American law by way of the courts of Scotland, which developed the rule starting in the late eighteenth-century. Ancient Roman law—the root of the civil law— apparently embraced the rule today known as the common law approach. Centuries later English courts also embraced it. As for the Scottish approach, Scotland after the Act of Union forming Great Britain (1707) retained its own legal system, one that chiefly drew upon civil law systems of continental Europe and upon indigenous Celtic customs. Although the Scottish approach does not reflect ancient Roman law, it does bear resemblance to property norms of the Germanic peoples of Europe, norms that were more prone to recognize public or other shared land-use rights and that, together with Roman law, gave shape to the modern civil law. New labels for the approaches have been proposed to encourage courts to consider their relative merits without prejudice: the Roman versus Scottish rules; traditional versus modern rules; and exclusive dominion versus good neighbor rules. See Nicholas Harling, Note, *Non-Navigable Lakes and the Right to Exclude: The Common Misunderstanding of the Common Law Rule*, 1 Charleston L. Rev. 157 (2007).

The Scottish influence was apparently also evident in American trespass law, particularly in the South, on the issue of public rights to use the unenclosed countryside. See Grady McWhitney & Forest McDonald, *Celtic Origins of Southern Herding Practices*, 51 J. So. Hist. 165 (1985); see also C. Paul Rogers III, *Scots Law in Post-Revolutionary and Nineteenth-Century America: The Neglected Jurisprudence*, 8 L. & Hist. Rev. 205 (1990).

6.   *Extending the lake boundaries. Thompson v. Enz*, 154 N.W.2d 473 (Mich. 1967), involved a residential development along the edge of a lake in

which canals were dug into the adjacent land, thereby giving inland lot owners water access to the lake surface. Did they thereby gain legal rights to use the lake? The lake was apparently non-navigable (so the court implicitly assumed) and governed by the civil law rule (another implicit assumption), so rights to use the lake surface had to be based on upland ownership along the edge. The Michigan court ruled that the owners of the new back-lots, not formerly touching the lake, did not have any lake-use rights that came with their land. The court also concluded that the owners of the back-lots could not acquire lake-use rights by transfer from the people who owned the lots directly fronting on the former lake edge; these rights could not be severed from the land and transferred separately. The only way back-lot owners could use the lake surface was as guests of the people who owned land on the former lake edge. This could be done lawfully, the court said, but only subject to the requirement that the lake uses be reasonable under the circumstances. Thus, a trial court would need to decide, based on all the facts, whether the totality of surface uses by all back-lot owners was reasonable when these uses were attributed to the few lots that fronted on the old lake edge.

7. *Other landowner rights in lake surfaces.* Because riparian landowners have rather full rights to enjoy the waters that flow through or beside their lands, they have often recovered damages for various injuries to their nonconsumptive uses of the waters. See, e.g., *Springer v. Joseph Schlitz Brewing Co.*, 510 F.2d 468 (4th Cir. 1975) (a North Carolina riparian landowner can recover for pollution of river by upstream landowners, including an injunction); *Lee County v. Kiesel*, 705 So.2d 1013 (Fla. App. 1998) (a Florida landowner can recover for interference with its unobstructed view of the river caused by construction of a public bridge).

D. WATER THAT IS UNWANTED

BUTLER V. BRUNO
Supreme Court of Rhode Island
341 A.2d 735 (1975)

KELLEHER, J.

During the summer season, the litigants presently before us are next-door neighbors. The plaintiffs are husband and wife. They seek damages which result from the defendant's deflection of surface water from his property onto their premises. A nonjury trial was held before a justice of the Superior Court. At the conclusion of the presentation of all the testimony, the trial justice found for the defendant. The plaintiffs have appealed.

In 1961, the Butlers purchased a summer home. It is located in the Sand Hill Cove section of the town of Narragansett on Maple Avenue. There they have enjoyed many a pleasant and restful summer playing croquet and whiffle ball on the lawn, mowing the grass, and doing the usual things one is supposed to do in a season which one lyricist has described as a time when "the livin' is easy.' In 1969, Bruno purchased a number of undeveloped lots on Maple Avenue, one of which was contiguous with and ran along the easterly boundary of the Butler property.

Past and present residents of the area described the Bruno lot as having been a swamp or marshland before he began building on it. One witness told how when he went on the property to pick cattails he would have to wear rubbers because of the mud and water underfoot. There were witnesses who testified that the Bruno lot was lower in elevation than the surrounding lots and that consequently it served as a depository for the rainwater runoff coming from the adjoining easterly and northerly areas. The Butlers' property, they said, was at all times higher in elevation than the Bruno lot and was always dry.

Bruno began building activities in August 1970. He first spread 3 feet of gravel over the entire lot. This step was necessary because of the high-water table over his land and as a prerequisite of the State's approval of his proposed sewage disposal system. The home was built on top of the fill and by the spring of 1971 it was ready for occupancy. Bruno had a retaining wall built along the Butlers' property line. The wall, which was composed of asphalted wooden beams, was designed to hold the fill. The fill had been graded to taper toward the front and rear of the lot. However, Bruno failed to provide any drainage for the surface water that had previously flowed onto his land from the properties to the west of his lot.

The Butlers told the trial justice that once Bruno commenced filling in his land, their property took on the appearance of one massive puddle with the water flooding the rear portion of their premises for most of the year. Their sewerage system became inoperative as the sewage backed up into the house.

The trial justice found that before Bruno began building, the surface water had flowed from west to east and would gather on the Bruno lot. He also found that the additional 3 feet of fill and the construction of the retaining wall stopped the easterly flow of the surface water, causing it to flood the Butler property. The trial justice observed that if he were to rule that Bruno was liable to the Butlers, he would order the entry of a money judgment in their favor for $5,200. This sum was the figure used by a real estate expert in estimating the loss of value of the Butler property which was attributable to the flood.

At this juncture, the trial justice ruled that the Butlers' loss was *damnum absque injuria*, or in the vernacular, while the Butlers sustained damages, there could be no recovery because Bruno did not violate any recognized legal or equitable right. In making this observation, the trial justice commented on the paucity of precedent to guide him, and after examining the literature that has been written in this area of the law, accepted as the law of this state the so-called "common-enemy" doctrine as modified by the rule of "reasonable use." He thereupon held that although the Butlers had sustained damage, there would be no recovery since Bruno had used "reasonable care" in developing his property and he had not "unnecessarily injured" the Butlers.

We cannot fault the trial justice's attempt to decide what is or should be the surface water law of this jurisdiction. It is true that at the turn of the century this court, in deciding an issue different from the one now before us, assumed that the common-enemy doctrine was the law of Rhode Island. *Johnson v. White*, 58 A. 658 (R.I. 1904). We will, however, opt for another rule which shall be discussed after we first define the term surface water and discuss the various views which have been expressed by courts which have considered the rights of neighboring landowners and the damages resulting from the diverting of surface water.

As used in this opinion, the term surface water means the water from rains, springs, or melting snows which lies or flows on the surface of the earth but does not form part of a well-defined body of water or a natural watercourse. It does not lose its character as surface water merely because some of it may be absorbed by or soaked into the marshy or boggy ground where it collects. *Enderson v. Kelehan*, 32 N.W.2d 286 (Minn. 1948).

There are three basic rules which have been used to resolve the surface water disputes that have arisen in the United States.

The first is the common-enemy doctrine. The common-enemy doctrine is so named because at one time surface water was regarded as a common enemy with which each landowner had an unlimited legal privilege to deal as he pleased without regard to the consequences that might be suffered by his neighbor. This rule received judicial approbation in a time when the law held in high regard one's freedom to do with his land as he wished. One of the earliest cases to espouse this view was *Gannon v. Hargadon*, 92 Mass. (10 Allen) 106 (1865). New Jersey was the first jurisdiction to describe the rule by employing the phrase "common enemy." *Town of Union v. Durkes*, 38 N.J.L. 21 (1875). Several courts in adopting this rule have said that it encourages the development and improvement of real estate and clearly delineates the rights of all interested parties. Concededly, litigation is kept to a minimum because in its application no one's rights are invaded. However, the simplicity of the rule does create problems, for, as one commentator has expressed it: ". . . landowners are encouraged to engage in contests of hydraulic engineering in which might makes right, and breach of the peace is often inevitable."

Maloney & Plager, *Diffused Surface Water: Scourge or Bounty*, 8 Nat. Resources J. 73, 78 (1968).

The Butlers might have invoked the common-enemy rule. The engineer testified that they could have alleviated their drainage problems by raising the level of their land with fill. Such a step, the witness said, would cause the surface water to gather and accumulate on the land of the Butlers' westerly neighbor. Presumably, if the Butlers were to pursue this remedy, they, rather than Bruno, would be the defendants as the domino theory of litigation enveloped the Maple Avenue residents. One obvious drawback to the common-enemy approach is the risk that its adoption can encourage a proliferation of litigation and engender neighborhood ill will.

The second principle upon which some courts have relied in resolving surface water disputes is called the "civil-law" rule. The civil-law rule was first adopted in this country by Louisiana in 1812. *Orleans Navigation Co. v. New Orleans*, 2 Martin (O.S.) 214 (1812). It is said to have its roots in Roman Law and the Napoleonic Code. Annot., 59 A.L.R.2d 421, 429 § 5 (1958). The rule is usually expressed in terms of an easement of natural drainage so that the owner of the lower land must accept the surface water which naturally drains onto his land but the upper owner may do nothing to increase the flow. Expressed in a more precise manner, the rule is that "A person who interferes with the natural flow of surface water so as to cause an invasion of another's interests in the use and enjoyment of his land is subject to liability to the others." Kinyon & McClure, *Interferences with Surface Waters*, 24 Minn. L. Rev. 891 (1940). The civil-law rule has the virtue of predictability in that it tells a prospective purchaser or acquirer of a parcel of real estate just what is expected of him. If it is applied to the letter, the rule can impede the physical and economic development of a locality. Its application can cause an evidentiary problem as the courts seek to determine what was the exact course of the 'natural flow' of the surface water before the bulldozers arrived on the scene.

Both the common-enemy and the civil-law rules are encrusted with the verbiage that is usually associated with the law of real property. When they are used, one hears such terms as easements, the dominant estate, the servient estate, and servitudes, and the classicist has the opportunity to try his hand at translating such ponderous Latin phrases as *cujus est solum, ejus est usque ad coelum et ad infernos* ["To whomever the soil belongs, he owns also to the sky and to the depths"] or *aqua currit, et debet currere ut currere solebat* ["Water runs, and ought to run as it is accustomed to run"].

Because of the harsh and often inequitable consequences of a strict application of either rule, courts through the years have created numerous exceptions, distinctions, and permutations to alleviate otherwise unjust results. Sometimes these modifications have caused the two antithetical doctrines to produce the same results. Thus, although the basic common-enemy rule allows each owner a carte blanche to deal with unwanted surface water, courts have held that the owner may not discharge the unwanted water upon neighboring land by collecting it into a concentrated flow by artificial means and then discharging it, if by so doing he causes his neighbor injury. *E.g., Johnson v. White,* cited above. And although the basic civil rule held that no one may change the natural drainage flow, some courts have recognized that the upper owner may change the natural flow by collecting the water at one point thereby not increasing the amount of overall flow but causing greater volume at one point rather than another, so long as the increased flow is in a natural water course and injury is not too great to the lower land. *Stouder v. Dashner,* 49 N.W.2d 859 (Iowa 1951), and cases cited in Kinyon & McClure, cited above, at 921 *et seq.*

This convergence of the two theories has been aptly described as creating a situation in which ". . . the civil-law owner may never drain his land except by following the natural drainage, but the common-enemy owner may always drain his land except that he may not use artificial channels. The civil-law owner may never obstruct the natural flow of surface waters unless he acts reasonably, while the common-enemy owner may always obstruct the flow if he acts reasonably." Maloney & Plager, cited above, at 79.

A common modification of both rules holds that the landowner may change the flow of surface waters by either increasing or damming up the flow so long as he does so "in good faith" or "non-negligently" or "in a reasonable manner." *See, e.g., Chamberlain v. Ciaffoni,* 96 A.2d 140 (Pa. 1953); *Seventeen, Inc. v. Pilot Life Ins. Co.,* 205 S.E.2d 648 (Va. 1974), applying the modification to the common-enemy rule; and *Ratcliffe v. Indian Hill Acres, Inc.,* 113 N.E.2d 30 (Ohio App.1952), applying the modification to the civil-law rule. This is the modification to which the trial justice alluded and which he tacked onto the common-enemy rule.

The effect of these modifications is to bring disputes over surface water interference into the realm of modern tort concepts, and to depart from the rigid formulations of property law. . . .

Other courts, perhaps in recognition of the problems that have arisen by the application of the above two rules with all their modifications, have chosen a third doctrine. Instead of using the tort concepts as an overlay to mitigate the harsh results of the property law doctrine, they have instead created the standards for behavior entirely out of tort law, and abandoned the notions of servitude or absolute ownership.

Thus we come to the third surface water doctrine, which is generally known as the "rule of reasonable use." Under this rule, the property owner's liability turns on a determination of the reasonableness of his actions. The issue of reasonableness is a question of fact to be determined in each case upon the consideration of all the relevant circumstances. This approach was first employed in *Swett v. Cutts*, 50 N.H. 439, 446 (1870).

The New Jersey Supreme Court in adopting the rule of reasonable use expressed it in this manner:

> . . . each possessor is legally privileged to make a reasonable use of his land, even though the flow of surface waters is altered thereby and causes some harm to others, but incurs liability when his harmful interference with the flow of surface waters is unreasonable.

Armstrong v. Francis Corp., 120 A.2d 4, 8 (N.J. 1956).

The jurisdictions which have adopted this principle have set forth varying formulations of the test for determining liability. We find the clearest and most appropriate to be that adopted by Minnesota and expressed in *Enderson v. Kelehan,* cited above, where the court considered the following factors:

> (a) Is there a reasonable necessity for such drainage?

> (b) Has reasonable care been taken to avoid unnecessary injury to the land receiving the water?

> (c) Does the benefit accruing to the land drained reasonably outweigh the resulting harm?

> (d) When practicable, is the diversion accomplished by reasonably improving the normal and natural system of drainage, or if such a procedure is not practicable, has a reasonable and feasible artificial drainage system been installed?

At one time only two jurisdictions, New Hampshire and Minnesota, had adopted the reasonable-use rule. Since that time, however, at least nine other jurisdictions have embraced this view. In determining one's legal responsibility for the use of the surface water flowing across his land, we shall adopt the rule of reasonable use. One known advantage of the rule is its flexibility. It can be applied in situations unthought of in the day when surface water was truly considered to be the common enemy. Unlike the civil-law rule, it will not hamper land development, and in contrast to the common-enemy rule, the standard which we embrace today will permit a more equitable allocation of the costs of such improvements, for the owner improving his land must take into consideration the true cost of such development to the community.

Since the trial justice rested his decision on a theory that is completely at adds with the ultimate holding of this appeal, we must reverse and remand for further proceedings so that a new judgment which conforms to this opinion may be entered.

The plaintiffs' appeal is sustained, the judgment appealed from is vacated, and the case is remanded to the Superior Court.

JOSLIN, J. (dissenting)

The majority today hold that a landowner's liability for the diversion of surface water from his land to that of another hinges in each case upon a factual determination of whether in view of all the circumstances his conduct in the use and improvement of his property is reasonable or unreasonable, and they enunciate four guidelines to aid the factfinder in making that determination. Because I believe that the proposed factual test is no "rule" at all and that it fails to provide a landowner any reasonably certain standards governing the use of his land, I respectfully dissent.

NOTES

1. *The progress of the common law.* This is a somewhat unusual case in that the decision is based almost entirely on policy arguments, and the court undertook a rather overt, law-making role, as courts have often done when keeping the common law up to date. The court acknowledged that there is applicable precedent to resolve the dispute, but it just did not like the *common enemy* rule applied in the earlier cases, and rejected it in favor of a very different standard, *reasonable use.*

The court noted that states are divided in their treatment of drainage onto neighboring properties. The traditional common law approach is the *common enemy* doctrine, which views excess surface water as the "common enemy" of all landowners and, in its pure form, authorizes each landowner to drain surface water from her own land without any obligation toward neighboring property owners. The excess water then becomes the neighbors' problem, and they have the same right to drain it onto someone else's land, and so on. Presumably, the party with the lowest-lying land bears the brunt. The *civil law* rule in effect in Louisiana and a few other states, also known as the "natural flow" rule, holds that each landowner is obligated to accept the natural drainage from adjacent parcels, and must not alter the natural drainage from his own parcel in a way that adversely affects his neighbors. Strictly applied, the civil law rule appears to prohibit any alteration of surface flows, at least those that cross property lines; it could therefore stand as a major obstacle to land development. A third and more modern alternative is the *reasonable use* standard which has now been adopted by at least 14 states. It calls for a case-by-case determination of the reasonableness of any change to surface flows, considering such factors as the need for the change, whether the change was made in a reasonable manner, and whether the utility of the change outweighs the harms to neighboring property owners. What policy arguments did the court make for choosing the reasonable use rule over the other two principal alternatives? What policy arguments did the dissent make against adoption of the reasonable use rule? Which do you find more persuasive?

2.   *Clarity versus flexibility.* The dispute between the majority and dissent in this case mostly came down to competing assessments of whether property law is best served by clear rules, easy to apply, or instead by more vague, flexible rules that can be tailored to serve justice based on particular facts. The choice here can also be framed in a related way, as a choice between trying to avoid land-use conflicts *ex ante*, by defining rights precisely, and resolving the conflicts instead *ex post*, by taking into account all the relevant facts and circumstances. Here, the three methods of resolving surface drainage issues in fact reflect three of the major ways that the law can handle conflicts between neighboring landowners. A survey of those various methods appeared in chapter 1 at pages 24–25. *Butler* illustrates one of property law's chief trends over the past century, the move in various legal settings from clear rules of property to more vague, tort-like rules, typically framed in terms of reasonableness and requiring for resolution a more full, after-the-fact inquiry into the facts of a dispute.

3.   *Relationship to nuisance law.* In a footnote omitted from this excerpt, the *Butler* court noted that "the invasion of one's property by surface waters can be a nuisance, no different from an invasion by noise, noxious vapors, or the like" (citing *Sweet v. Conley*, 39 A. 326, 328 (R.I. 1898)). If inundating a neighbor's land with drainage water can be considered a private nuisance, then why do we need a special law of drainage? Why not simply handle legal disputes arising over drainage under general private nuisance principles? See, e.g., *Hocking v. City of Dodgeville*, 768 N.W.2d 552 (Wis. 2009) (applying "reasonable use" rule to determine the standard of care owed in a drainage dispute, and holding uphill owner not liable under theories of negligence and private nuisance because uphill owner had acted reasonably). In fact, the bodies of law in a given state are sometimes intertwined and overlapping, as the next opinion illustrates.

GRUNDY V. THURSTON COUNTY

Supreme Court of Washington
117 P.3d 1089 (2005)

IRELAND, J.

In this case, we consider whether a private nuisance claim brought by Evelyne Grundy, who alleges seawater damaged her property because her neighbors raised the height of their seawall, should be dismissed in light of the common enemy doctrine. We reverse the Court of Appeals dismissal of her private nuisance claim, and we hold that the common enemy doctrine does not apply to seawater.

Evelyne Grundy owns property on the west side of Johnson Point in Thurston County. She has lived there since 1981. Adjoining property at the end of the point was purchased by the Brack Family Trust (Bracks) about 10 years later. Although the properties were each protected by a seawall, the Bracks' wall was about 12 inches lower than Grundy's. Seawater from Puget Sound regularly flooded a portion of the Bracks' property during winter storms.

The Bracks extensively remodeled the single family residence located on their property and made other improvements. In 1997, they sandbagged along their seawall, and in the fall of 1998, they sought to raise the seawall surrounding their property by 16 to 18 inches. They obtained hydraulic project approval from the Department of Fish and Wildlife and a determination from Thurston County that they were not required to obtain a permit under the Shoreline Management Act of 1971, chapter 90.58 RCW. The stated purpose for raising the seawall was to prevent storm erosion and water intrusion. Grundy received no notice of the government action.

Seawater diverted by the Bracks' sandbags during winter storms in 1998–99 caused Grundy's property to be damaged by seawater for the first time. Water came within about 22 feet of Grundy's foundation and destroyed 1,200 square feet of vegetation. Grundy worried that more severe storms would cause water to enter her home through ground-level vents, destroying electrical and heating fixtures and undermining the structure.

Construction of the addition to the Bracks' seawall began in March 1999. Because the eastern portion was raised first, Grundy's view of the project was obscured until construction was almost complete.

Grundy filed a nuisance action against Thurston County and the Bracks in November 1999. She claimed Thurston County created a public nuisance by improperly exempting the Bracks' project from the permitting process. She also claimed the Bracks' seawall constituted a private nuisance because it made her property vulnerable to flooding. She sought abatement and attorney fees.

The Bracks moved for summary judgment, arguing that Grundy was not entitled to challenge Thurston County's decision because she did not timely seek review under the Land Use Petition Act, chapter 36.70C RCW. The Bracks also argued that Grundy could present no evidence that raising the seawall impacted her property.

[The trial court granted the Bracks' motion. By the time the case reached the Supreme Court the Grundy's had dropped their claim against the county of public nuisance. The case proceeded as a private nuisance action.]

"Nuisance is 'a substantial and unreasonable interference with the use and enjoyment of land.'" *Bodin v. City of Stanwood,* 901 P.2d 1065 n.2 (Wash. App. 1995) (quoting 1 William H. Rodgers, *Environmental Law* § 2.2, at 33 (1986)). Washington's law of nuisance is codified in chapter 7.48 RCW. Nuisance is broadly defined as "unlawfully doing an act, or omitting to perform a duty, which act or omission either annoys, injures or endangers the comfort, repose, health or safety of others . . . or in any way renders other persons insecure in life, or in the use of property." RCW 7.48.120. A nuisance "which affects equally the rights of an entire community or neighborhood" is a public nuisance. RCW 7.48.130. Among the enumerated public nuisances is "[t]o obstruct or impede, without legal authority, the passage of any river, harbor, or collection of water." RCW 7.48.140(3). Any nuisance that does not fit the statutory definition of a public nuisance is a private nuisance. RCW 7.48.150.

An actionable nuisance is "whatever is injurious to health or indecent or offensive to the senses, or an obstruction to the free use of property, so as to essentially interfere with the comfortable enjoyment of the life and property." RCW 7.48.010. Any person whose property is injuriously affected or whose personal enjoyment is lessened by a nuisance may sue for damages and for injunctive relief to abate the nuisance. RCW 7.48.020. . . .

The only issue properly before the appellate courts is Grundy's private nuisance action against the Bracks—and whether the common enemy doctrine applies to bar that action. The Court of Appeals held that the Bracks were "entitled to prevent damage to their property from the vagrant surface water once confined in Puget Sound, even when a neighbor may be injured by their defense." *Grundy,* 67 P.3d at 500. We disagree.

"In its strictest form, the common enemy doctrine allows landowners to dispose of unwanted surface water in any way they see fit, without liability for resulting damage to one's neighbor." *Currens v. Sleek,* 983 P.2d 626 (Wash. 1999). Washington courts first articulated the doctrine more than a century ago: "[S]urface water, caused by the falling of rain or the melting of snow, and that escaping from running streams and rivers, is regarded as an outlaw and a common enemy against which anyone may defend himself, even though by so doing injury may result to others." *Cass v. Dicks,* 44 P. 113 (Wash. 1896).

As the Court of Appeals points out, the *Cass* court specifically mentioned seawalls:

If a land-owner whose lands are exposed to inroads of the sea, or to inundations from adjacent creeks or rivers, erects sea-walls or dams, for the protection of his land, and by so doing causes the tide, the current, or the waves to flow against the land of his neighbor, and wash it away, or cover it with water, the land-owner so causing an injury to his neighbor is not responsible in damages to the latter, as he has done no wrong, having acted in self-defense, and having a right to protect his land and his crops from inundation.

44 P. 113 (quoting Edward P. Weeks, *The Doctrine of Damnum Absque Injuria Considered in Its Relation to the Law of Torts* 3, 4 (1879)). The same authority is later quoted in *Harvey v. Northern Pacific Railway Co.,* 116 P. 464 (Wash. 1911). But neither case concerned protection of land from the sea. Instead, the *Cass* and *Harvey* courts were presented with overflow from rivers. . . .

Further, we have specifically characterized surface water as follows:

The chief characteristic of surface water is its inability to maintain its identity and existence as a body of water. It is thus distinguished from water flowing in its natural course or collected into and forming a definite and identifiable body, such as a lake or pond.

Halverson v. Skagit County, 983 P.2d 643 (Wash. 1999). Storm-driven waves in Puget Sound remain part of a definite and identifiable body of water when splashing onto waterfront property. They do not satisfy the *Halverson* court's definition of surface water.

Washington courts have neither characterized storm-driven waves as surface water nor applied the common enemy doctrine to seawater. We decline to do so here. We hold that the common enemy doctrine does not apply to seawater, which does not meet our definition of surface water. We reverse the Court of Appeals decision in its entirety and remand this matter for trial on the merits of Grundy's private nuisance claim.

NOTES

1. *Nuisance and ecological interconnection.* Like the ruling in *Butler,* *Grundy* reflects a growing judicial dislike of the common-enemy approach to water management. In *Butler* the court changed the law applicable in the state. Here the court decided that the common-enemy approach did not apply to high waters from the ocean, even though it did apply, according to earlier state rulings, to similar high waters from rivers. The court does not give a full explanation as to why it decided not to extend the common-enemy rule to such ocean waters. Presumably, it had something to do with fears about the results: a landowner afflicted by flooding waters might simply build her wall higher, leading neighbors to do the same in an escalating conflict. Seawalls

do more than protect lands from encroachment. They disrupt natural wave patterns and, in doing so, can greatly alter natural process of eroding and depositing sand and gravel on beaches.

2. *Returning to the issue of reasonableness.* Note that, by ruling as it did, the Washington Supreme Court did not decide that the Bracks acted wrongly when they raised their seawall. It ruled only that Evelyne Grundy was entitled to her day in court to prove factually that the elevated seawall constituted a private nuisance. As we saw in chapter 2 (pp. 66–72), and as the court here explained, the plaintiff in such an action must show that the defendant's conduct has caused substantial harm and that the imposition of the harm under the circumstances was unreasonable. Thus, as in *Butler*, we see further evidence of the tendency by courts to embrace the normative standard of reasonableness to help resolve disputes among competing land and resource owners. What factors is a trial court likely to consider when evaluating the unreasonableness of the harm under the circumstances? Is it enough for the defendant to show that landowners for decades have built seawalls and raised them when needed?

E. THE PUBLIC TRUST DOCTRINE

We now take up the ancient framework and contemporary significance of public property law known as the public trust doctrine (PTD). Throughout its lengthy history, the PTD protected public access to submerged lands and navigable waters for the purposes of navigation, fishing, and commerce, and was originally focused on tidelands and the beds of navigable waters. The PTD also protects trust resources from substantial impairment, giving the PTD an environmental dimension in addition to its antimonopolistic emphasis.

The PTD is a significant component of natural resources law generally. Some courts and legislatures have expanded the protections of the PTD to wetlands, water rights, wildlife, parklands, beaches, groundwater, and perhaps even the atmosphere. The Hawaiian Constitution, for example, declares that all public natural resources are held in trust for the public. Haw. Const. art. XI, § 1. Moreover, a number of courts have recognized that the PTD protects those resources for purposes that extend beyond the traditional triad of navigation, fishing, and water-borne commerce, to include recreation, aesthetics, and ecological purposes. Flexible enough to evolve to meet the changing needs of society, the PTD remains grounded in the principles from which it originated.

The Institutes of Justinian described the basic concept of the public trust between citizen and sovereign as early as the sixth century:

> By the law of nature these things are common to all mankind—
> the air, running water, the sea, and consequently the shores of

the sea. No one, therefore, is forbidden to approach the seashore, provided that he respects habitations, monuments, and buildings [previously constructed]. . . .[2]

This ancient recognition of the public nature of the seashore emerged in English common law after the drafting of the Magna Charta in 1215. Sir Matthew Hale in the seventeenth century outlined the doctrine with respect to navigable waters and the sea coasts and defined a "public common of piscary":

> [Al]though the king is the owner of this great wast, and as a consequent of his propriety hath the primary right of fishing in the sea, and the creeks and arms thereof, yet the common people of England have regularly a liberty of fishing in the sea or creeks or arms thereof, as a public[ ] common of piscary, and may not without injury to their right be restrained of it, unless in such places or creeks or navigable rivers, where either the king or some particular subject hath gained a propriety exclusive of that common liberty.[3]

In the United States, the lands and waters owned by the English sovereign transferred to the newly created American states at the time of the Revolution. Early U.S. case law established that the ownership rights of the new states remained subject to these public rights and government fiduciary duties. *Martin v. Waddell's Lessee*, 41 U.S. 367, 413–14 (1842) ("[I]n the judgment of the court, the lands under the navigable waters passed to the grantee, as one of the royalties incident to the powers of government; and were to be held by him, in the same manner, and for the same purposes, that the navigable waters of England, and the soils under them, are held by the crown."). Subsequently admitted states acquired the same ownership and fiduciary duties under the so-called "equal footing" doctrine. *Pollard v. Hagan*, 44 U.S. 212 (1845). Thus, the states held title in trust for the public, forbidding monopolization of trust resources and recognizing future generations as among the trust's beneficiaries. See *Arizona Center for Law in the Public Interest v. Hassell*, 837 P.2d 158, 169 (Ariz. App. 1991).

Although the PTD is primarily a creature of common law, with contours varying from state to state, some states codified trust language in their constitutions and statutes. And some courts have interpreted declarations of public ownership or concerns for future generations as implicitly adopting the PTD. PTD cases frequently involve courts balancing private and public property rights. This chapter presents some

---

[2]   Institutes of Justinian, *Procemium*, § 2.1.1 (T. Sanders trans., 4th ed. 1867).

[3]   Matthew Hale, *De Jure Maris*, Harg. Law Tracts, *reprinted in* Stuart Moore, *A History of the Foreshore and the Law Relating Thereto* 377 (3rd ed. 1888).

of the foundational cases involving the PTD and briefly examines more recent cases along the PTD's emerging frontiers.

ILLINOIS CENTRAL RAILROAD CO. V. ILLINOIS

Supreme Court of the United States
146 U.S. 387 (1892)

[In 1869, the Illinois legislature passed a statute granting "all the right and title" of one square mile of submerged lands in Lake Michigan to Illinois Central Railroad to construct wharves, piers, docks, and other facilities in Chicago's harbor. The act placed nearly the whole of the submerged lands of the inner harbor in the power of the private company. In 1873, the legislature repealed the statute and revoked the grant. Ten years later, in 1883, the state attorney general filed suit against the railroad, alleging that the railroad's construction of improvements in Chicago's harbor was on submerged lands owned by the state. The railroad defended on the ground that the grant in the 1869 act was valid. The case reached the Supreme Court in 1892, producing the following opinion.]

FIELD, J.

* * *

The act . . . placed under the control of the railroad company . . . [the power] to delay indefinitely the improvement of the harbor, or to construct as many docks, piers, and wharves and other works as it might choose, and at such positions in the harbor as might suit its purposes, and permit any kind of business to be conducted thereon, and to lease them out on its own terms for indefinite periods. . . . A corporation created for one purpose, the construction and operation of a railroad between designated points, is by the act converted into a corporation to manage and practically control the harbor of Chicago, not simply for its own purpose as a railroad corporation, but for its own profit generally.

* * *

The question . . . is whether the legislature was competent to thus deprive the state of its ownership of the submerged lands in the harbor of Chicago, and of the consequent control of its waters; or, in other words, whether the railroad corporation can hold the lands and control the waters by the grant, against any future exercise of power over them by the state.

[T]he state holds the title to the lands under the navigable waters of Lake Michigan, within its limits, in the same manner that the state holds title to soils under tide water, by the common law . . . and that title necessarily carries with it control over the waters above them, whenever the lands are subjected to use. But it is a title different in character from that which the state holds in lands intended for sale. . . . It is a title held in trust for the people of the state, that they may enjoy the navigation of the waters, carry on commerce over them, and have liberty of fishing therein, freed from the obstruction or interference of private parties. The interest of the people in the navigation of the waters and in commerce over them may be improved in many instances by the erection of wharves, docks, and piers therein, for which purpose the state may grant parcels of the submerged lands; and, so long as their disposition is made for such purpose, no valid objections can be made to the grants. . . .

But that is a very different doctrine from the one which would sanction the abdication of the general control of the state over lands under the navigable waters of an entire harbor or bay, or of a sea or lake. Such abdication is not consistent with the exercise of that trust which requires the government of the state to preserve such waters for the use of the public. The trust devolving upon the state for the public, and which can only be discharged by the management and control of property in which the public has an interest, cannot be relinquished by a transfer of the property. The control of the state for the purposes of the trust can never be lost, except as to such parcels as are used in promoting the interests of the public therein, or can be disposed of without any substantial impairment of the public interest in the lands and waters remaining. It is only by observing the distinction between a grant of such parcels for the improvement of the public interest, or which when occupied do not substantially impair the public interest in the lands and waters remaining, and a grant of the whole property in which the public is interested, that the language of the adjudged cases can be reconciled. . . .

A grant of all the lands under the navigable waters of a state has never been adjudged to be within the legislative power; and any attempted grant of the kind would be held, if not absolutely void on its face, as subject to revocation. The state can no more abdicate its trust over property in which the whole people are interested, like navigable waters and soils under them, so as to leave them entirely under the use and control of private parties, except in the instance of parcels mentioned for the improvement of the navigation and use of the waters, or when parcels can be disposed of without impairment of the public interest in what remains, than it can abdicate its police powers in the administration of government and the preservation of the peace. In the administration of government the use of such powers may for a limited period be delegated to a municipality or other body, but there always remains with the state the right to revoke those powers and exercise them in a more direct manner, and one more conformable to its wishes. So with trusts connected with public property, or property of a special character, like lands under navigable waters; they cannot be placed entirely beyond the direction and control of the state.

* * *

The area of the submerged lands proposed to be ceded by the act in question to the railroad company embraces something more than 1,000 acres, being, as stated by counsel, more than three times the area of the outer harbor. . . . It is as large as that embraced by all the merchandise docks along the Thames at London; is much larger than that included in the famous docks and basins at Liverpool; is twice that of the port of Marseilles, and nearly, if not quite, equal to the pier area along the water front of the city of New York. And the arrivals and clearings of vessels at the port exceed in number those of New York, and are equal to those of New York and Boston combined. . . .

It is hardly conceivable that the legislature can divest the state of the control and management of this harbor, and vest it absolutely in a private corporation. Surely an act of the legislature transferring the title to its submerged lands and the power claimed by the railroad company to a foreign state or nation would be repudiated, without hesitation, as a gross perversion of the trust over the property under which it is held. So would a similar transfer to a corporation of another state. It would not be listened to that the control and management of the harbor of that great city—a subject of concern to the whole people of the state—should thus be placed elsewhere than in the state itself. All the objections which can be urged to such attempted transfer may be urged to a transfer to a private corporation like the railroad company in this case.

Any grant of the kind is necessarily revocable, and the exercise of the trust by which the property was held by the state can be resumed at any time. Undoubtedly there may be expenses incurred in improvements made under such a grant, which the state ought to pay; but, be that as it may, the power to resume the trust whenever the state judges best is, we think, incontrovertible. The position advanced by the railroad company in support of its claim to the ownership of the submerged lands . . . would place every harbor in the country at the mercy of a majority of the legislature of the state in which the harbor is situated.

We cannot, it is true, cite any authority where a grant of this kind has been held invalid, for we believe that no instance exists where the harbor of a great city and its commerce have been allowed to pass into the control of any private corporation. But the decisions are numerous which declare that such property is held by the state, by virtue of its sovereignty, in trust for the public. The ownership of the navigable waters of the harbor, and of the lands under them, is a subject of public concern to the whole people of the state. The trust with which they are held, therefore, is governmental, and cannot be alienated, except in those instances mentioned, of parcels used in the improvement of the interest thus held, or when parcels can be disposed of without detriment to the public interest in the lands and waters remaining[.]

This follows necessarily from the public character of the property, being held by the whole people for purposes in which the whole people are interested. As said by Chief Justice Taney in *Martin v. Waddell*, 41 U.S. 367, 410 (1842): "When the Revolution took place the people of each state became themselves sovereign, and in that character hold the absolute right to all their navigable waters, and the soils under them, for their own common use, subject only to the rights since surrendered by the constitution to the general government." In *Arnold v. Mundy*, 6 N.J.L. 1 (N.J. 1821), which is cited by this court in *Martin v. Waddell*, and spoken of by Chief Justice Taney as entitled to great weight, and in which the decision was made "with great deliberation and research," the supreme court of New Jersey comments upon the rights of the state in the bed of navigable waters, and, after observing that the power exercised by the state over the lands and waters is nothing more than what is called the "*jus regium*," the right of regulating, improving, and securing them for the benefit of every individual citizen, adds: "The sovereign power itself, therefore, cannot, consistently with the principles of the law of nature and the constitution of a well-ordered society, make a direct and absolute grant of the waters of the state, divesting all the citizens of their common right. It would be a grievance which never could be long borne by a free people." Necessarily must the control of the waters of a state over all lands under them pass when the lands are conveyed in fee to private parties, and are by them subjected to use.

* * *

The soil under navigable waters being held by the people of the state in trust for the common use and as a portion of their inherent sovereignty, any act of legislation concerning their use affects the public welfare. It is therefore appropriately within the exercise of the police power of the state.

In *Newton v. Commissioners*, 100 U.S. 548 (1879), it appeared that by an act passed by the legislature of Ohio in 1846 it was provided that . . . the county seat should be permanently established in [the town of Canfield.] . . . In 1874 the legislature passed an act for the removal of the county seat to another town. [C]itizens of Canfield [filed suit, seeking] an injunction against the contemplated removal. [The court held] there could be no contract and no irrepealable law upon governmental subjects, observing that legislative acts concerning public interests are necessarily public laws; that every succeeding legislature possesses the same jurisdiction and power as its predecessor; that the latter have the same power of repeal and modification which the former had of enactment . . .;

that all occupy in this respect a footing of perfect equality; that this is necessarily so, in the nature of things; that it is vital to the public welfare that each one should be able at all times to do whatever the varying circumstances and present exigencies attending the subject may require; and that a different result would be fraught with evil.

[This doctrine] must apply with greater force to the control of the soils and beds of navigable waters in the great public harbors held by the people in trust for their common use and of common right, as an incident to their sovereignty. The legislature could not give away nor sell the discretion of its successors in respect to matters, the government of which, from the very nature of things, must vary with varying circumstances. The legislation which may be needed one day for the harbor may be different from the legislation that may be required at another day[.] Every legislature must, at the time of its existence, exercise the power of the state in the execution of the trust devolved upon it. We hold, therefore, that any attempted cession of the ownership and control of the state in and over the submerged lands in Lake Michigan, by the act of April 16, 1869, was inoperative to affect, modify, or in any respect to control the sovereignty and dominion of the state over the lands, or its ownership thereof, and that any such attempted operation of the act was annulled by the repealing act of April 15, 1873, which to that extent was valid and effective. There can be no irrepealable contract in a conveyance of property by a grantor in disregard of a public trust, under which he was bound to hold and manage it.

NOTES

1. *Modern revival of the public trust doctrine.* Although rooted in ancient Roman law and inherited from English common law, the PTD emerged as a tool for environmental protection largely due to the remarkable work of scholar Joseph Sax. In his pioneering 1970 law review article, Sax outlined the history of the doctrine and, recognizing *Illinois Central* as "the lodestar" case, argued that the PTD provided a tool for democratization. Joseph Sax, *The Public Trust Doctrine in Natural Resource Law: Effective Judicial Intervention*, 68 Mich. L. Rev. 471 (1970). In contrast to the more common constitutional model protecting the fundamental rights of individuals, Sax identified the need for judicial review to protect the rights of the majority from an insular minority:

> [P]ublic trust law is not so much a substantive set of standards for dealing with the public domain as it is a technique by which courts may mend perceived imperfections in the legislative and administrative process. . . . [T]he public trust concept is, more than anything else, a medium for democratization. . . . Public trust problems are found whenever governmental regulation comes into question, and they occur in a wide range of situations in which diffuse public interests need protection against tightly organized

groups with clear and immediate goals. Thus, it seems that the delicate mixture of procedural and substantive protections which the courts have applied in conventional public trust cases would be equally applicable and equally appropriate in controversies involving air pollution, the dissemination of pesticides, the location of rights of way for utilities, and strip mining or wetland filling on private lands in a state where governmental permits are required.

Id. at 509, 556–57. Since the publication of Sax's influential article, the phrase "public trust doctrine" has appeared in at least 707 state court cases, 146 federal court cases, and more than 2,700 scholarly works.[4] Courts of foreign nations have also relied heavily on Sax's pioneering article. See, e.g., *M.C. Mehta v. Kamal Nath* (1997) 1 S.C.C. 388 (India); see below n. 9, p. 216.

2. *Limits on government alienation of trust property.* In discussing the public character of navigable waters and the submerged lands beneath them, the Supreme Court in *Illinois Central* relied on two early decisions arising from disputes over oyster harvesting in New Jersey. *Martin v. Waddell's Lessee*, 41 U.S. 367 (1842); *Arnold v. Mundy*, 6 N.J.L. 1 (N.J. 1821). Both *Illinois Central* and *Martin* quoted Chief Justice Andrew Kirkpatrick of the New Jersey Supreme Court from his decision in *Arnold v. Mundy* on the limits imposed on government ownership of trust lands:

> The sovereign power itself, therefore, cannot, consistently with the principles of the law of nature and the constitution of a well ordered society, make a direct and absolute grant of the waters of the state, divesting all the citizens of their common right. It would be a grievance which never could be long borne by a free people.

Id. at 78. Did the Court in *Illinois Central* suggest that a state can never convey trust property? What exceptions did the Court carve out for state alienation?

3. *Jus publicum vs. jus privatum.* Two years after *Illinois Central*, in *Shively v. Bowlby*, 152 U.S. 1 (1894), a case involving tidelands on the Oregon coast, the Court ruled that a federal pre-statehood grant of land to Shively did not include title to the tidelands and affirmed title in Bowlby, a state grantee of a post-statehood conveyance. The Court relied on *Arnold v. Mundy* and *Martin v. Waddell* for the proposition that the navigable waters and underlying lands "were intended to be a trust for the common use . . . for the benefit of the whole community, to be freely used by all for navigation and fishery." *Id.* at 16, quoting *Martin*, 41 U.S. at 413. Although the Court acknowledged that the federal government could privatize trust lands prior to statehood, it ruled that Congress had not done so in the Oregon Donation Act, limiting pre-statehood alienations to where "necessary . . . to perform international obligations," to improve commerce, "or to carry out other public purposes." *Id.* at 48. The opinion conceptually severed trust lands into *jus publicum* and *jus privatum*, for the purpose of indicating that public rights

---

[4] Westlaw search (Aug. 27, 2014).

were paramount to private rights and claimed that this dichotomous title was inherited from England:

> By the common law, both the title and the dominion of the sea, and of rivers and arms of the sea, where the tide ebbs and flows, and of all the lands below high-water mark, within the jurisdiction of the crown of England, are in the king. Such waters, and the lands which they cover, either at all times, or at least when the tide is in, are incapable of ordinary and private occupation, cultivation, and improvement; and their natural and primary uses are public in their nature, for highways of navigation and commerce, domestic and foreign, and for the purpose of fishing by all the king's subjects. Therefore the title, *jus privatum*, in such lands, as of waste and unoccupied lands, belongs to the king, as the sovereign; and the dominion thereof, jus publicum, is vested in him, as the representative of the nation and for the public benefit.

Id. at 11. As thus formulated, *jus publicum* had to do with the sovereign powers of government and the rights held by the public in various lands while *jus privatum* had to do with the proprietary or private powers that came with land ownership. According to Stuart Moore, writing late in the nineteenth century, English law was clear that private landowners who gained ownership of the foreshore by royal grant acquired only the *jus privatum*, and held their lands subject to the public use rights protected by the *jus publicum*. Stuart A. Moore, *A History of the Foreshore and the Law Relating Thereto* 652–55 (3d ed. 1888). The distinction continues to be used occasionally. See, e.g., *Arnold's Inn, Inc. v. Morgan,* 310 N.Y.S.2d 541 (N.Y. Sup. Ct., 1970); *McQueen v. South Carolina Coastal Council*, 580 S.E.2d 116 (S.C. 2003).

4. *Purposes of the public trust doctrine.* The traditional triad of public trust purposes—navigation, fishing, and commerce—has been supplemented in recent years with recreation and environmental purposes. The pathbreaking case was *Marks v. Whitney,* 491 P.2d 374, 380 (Cal. 1971) (announcing that public trust uses "are sufficiently flexible to encompass changing public needs," such as tidelands preservation for ecological purposes).

5. *The scope of the trust doctrine.* What resources, other than navigable waters and the submerged lands beneath them, would you describe as having a "public character" in which the "whole people are interested"? What about groundwater or the atmosphere? Dry sand beaches? Parklands? Does the type of use alter the analysis? For example, does a sunbather have the same right of access to the beach as a fisherman hauling in his nets? Although early cases focused on traditional uses of public trust resources—fishing, commerce, and navigation—more recent cases have recognized a broader range of activities protected by the trust including recreation, ecology, and even aesthetics. How can you link these varying resources and varying uses?

6. *The origins of the trust.* Did the trust the Court applied in *Illinois Central* originate in state or federal law? If state law, what state law did the Court cite? Most states apparently have interpreted *Illinois Central* as binding precedent, suggesting that the PTD is federal in nature (drawing on earlier rulings such as *Smith v. Maryland*, 59 U.S. (18 How.) 71, 74–75 (1855) (state has a "duty to preserve unimpaired those public uses for the [submerged] soil is held")). In *Idaho v. Coeur d'Alene Tribe*, 521 U.S. 261, 283–84 (1997), Justice Anthony Kennedy suggested the doctrine had constitutional underpinnings. Lands subject to it had "a unique status in the law" and "were infused with a public trust that the State itself is bound to respect":

> [A] State's title to these sovereign lands arises from the equal footing doctrine and is "conferred not by Congress but by the Constitution itself." . . . The principle which underlies the equal footing doctrine and the strong presumption of state ownership is that navigable waters uniquely implicate sovereign interests. The principle arises from ancient doctrines.

Justice Kennedy traced the doctrine of state ownership to the Magna Carta and the Institutes of Justinian in his analysis in *Coeur d'Alene Tribe*, and emphasized the public uses of river banks and the right to fish common to all persons. *Id.* at 284, quoting Henry de Bracton, 2 *De Legibus et Consuetudinibus Angliae* 40 (S. Thorne trans., 1968) ("All rivers and ports are public, so that the right to fish therein is common to all persons. The use of river banks, as of the river itself, is also public."). More recently, Kennedy distinguished state ownership of navigable waters and beds, which he grounded on *Pollard's* equal footing doctrine from a state's public trust doctrine, in *PPL Montana v. Montana*, 132 S.Ct. 1215, 1234–35 (2012):

> The public trust doctrine is of ancient origin. Its roots trace to Roman civil law and its principles can be found in the English common law on public navigation and fishing rights over tidal lands and in the state laws of this country. . . . Unlike the equal-footing doctrine, however, which is the constitutional foundation for the navigability rule of riverbed title, the public trust doctrine remains a matter of state law. . . . [T]he contours of that public trust do *not* depend upon the Constitution. Under accepted principles of federalism, the States retain residual power to determine the scope of the public trust over waters within their borders, while federal law determines riverbed title under the equal-footing doctrine. (Emphasis added.)

Although *PPL Montana* did not directly address whether a federal public trust exists (and did not contradict the language in *Coeur d'Alene Tribe* on the state's duty to respect the public trust), at least one federal decision has relied almost entirely on Kennedy's dictum to summarily dismiss claims alleging violations of the public trust by the federal government. See *Alec L. v. Jackson*, 863 F.Supp.2d 11 (D.D.C. 2012) (granting motion to dismiss plaintiffs' public trust claims for failure to state a federal question), aff'd, 561 F. Appx. 7 (D.C. Cir. 2014).

7.   *Public ownership of vs. public rights in submerged lands.* The equal footing navigability mentioned by Justice Kennedy is referred to as "title navigability" and is dependent on a demonstration of the commercial usefulness of a waterbody at the time of statehood. See *The Daniel Ball v. United States*, 77 U.S. 557, 563 (1870) (establishing the "navigable-in-fact" test to include those waters which are "used, or are susceptible of being used, in their ordinary condition, as highways for commerce, over which trade and travel are or may be conducted in the customary modes of trade and travel on water"). Navigability for public use, however, is not limited to commercial navigable waters at statehood, since the PTD does not apply only to state-owned lands. Recall the *jus publicum/privatum* distinction, discussed above. Many courts have adopted a more expansive view of navigability under state law, as evidenced by the ruling in *McIlroy*, considered earlier in the chapter.

The conceptual distinction between *jus publicum* and *jus privatum*, articulated in the *Shively* decision (n. 3, p. 185), has become an important vehicle for the recognition of public rights in private property as the following case illustrates.

GLASS V. GOECKEL
Supreme Court of Michigan
703 N.W.2d 58 (2005)

[Joan Glass claimed the right to walk along the shore of Lake Huron, one of the Great Lakes, due to the public trust doctrine. Littoral landowners, the Goeckels, argued that her walking along the beach was a trespass.]

CORRIGAN, J.

* * *

[W]e conclude that the public trust doctrine does protect [plaintiff's] right to walk along the shores of the Great Lakes. American law has long recognized that large bodies of navigable water, such as the oceans, are natural resources and thoroughfares that belong to the public. In our common-law tradition, the state, as sovereign, acts as trustee of public rights in these natural resources. Consequently, the state lacks the power to diminish those rights when conveying littoral property to private parties. This "public trust doctrine," as the United States Supreme Court stated in *Illinois Central R. Co. v. Illinois*, 146 U.S. 387, 435 (1892) (*Illinois Central I*), and as recognized by our Court in *Nedtweg v. Wallace*, 208 N.W. 51 (Mich. 1926), applies not only to the oceans, but also to the Great Lakes.

Pursuant to this longstanding doctrine, when the state (or entities that predated our state's admission to the Union) conveyed littoral property to private parties, that property remained subject to the public trust. In this case, the property now owned by defendants was originally conveyed subject to specific public trust rights in Lake Huron and its shores up to the ordinary high water mark. . . . Consequently, although defendants retain full rights of ownership in their littoral property, they hold these rights subject to the public trust.

We hold, therefore, that defendants cannot prevent plaintiff from enjoying the rights preserved by the public trust doctrine. Because walking along the lakeshore is inherent in the exercise of traditionally protected public rights of fishing, hunting, and navigation, our public trust doctrine permits pedestrian use of our Great Lakes, up to and including the land below the ordinary high water mark. Therefore, plaintiff, like any member of the public, enjoys the right to walk along the shore of Lake Huron on land lakeward of the ordinary high water mark. Accordingly, we reverse the judgment of the Court of Appeals and remand this case to the trial court for further proceedings consistent with this opinion.

* * *

Our public trust doctrine employs a term, "the ordinary high water mark," from the common law of the sea and applies it to our Great Lakes. While this term has an obvious meaning when applied to *tidal* waters with regularly recurring high and low tides, its application to nontidal waters like the Great Lakes is less apparent. . . . Notwithstanding some prior imprecision in its use, a term such as "ordinary high water mark" attempts to encapsulate the fact that water levels in the Great Lakes fluctuate. This fluctuation results in temporary exposure of land that may then remain exposed above where water currently lies. This land, although not immediately and presently submerged, falls within the ambit of the public trust because the lake has not permanently receded from that point and may yet again exert its influence up to that point. . . . Thus, the ordinary high water mark still has meaning as applied to the Great Lakes and marks the boundary of land, even if not instantaneously submerged, included within the public trust. . . .

* * *

III. The Public Trust Includes Walking Within Its Boundaries

We have established thus far that the private title of littoral landowners remains subject to the public trust beneath the ordinary high water mark. But plaintiff, as a member of the public, may walk below the ordinary high water mark only if that practice receives the protection of the public trust doctrine. We hold that walking along the shore, subject to regulation (as is any exercise of public rights in the public trust) falls within the scope of the public trust.

To reiterate, the public trust doctrine serves to protect resources—here the waters of the Great Lakes and their submerged lands—shared in common by the public. . . . As trustee, the state must preserve and protect specific public rights below the ordinary high water mark and may permit only those private uses that do not interfere with these traditional notions of the public trust. . . . Yet its status as trustee does not permit the state, through any of its branches of government, to secure to itself property rights held by littoral owners. . . .

We first note that neither party contests that walking falls within public rights traditionally protected under our public trust doctrine. Rather, they dispute where, not whether, plaintiff may walk: below the literal water's edge or below the ordinary high water mark. While the parties' agreement on this point cannot determine the scope of public rights, this agreement does indicate the existence of a common sense assumption: walking along the lakeshore is inherent in the exercise of traditionally protected public rights.

* * *

We can protect traditional public rights under our public trust doctrine only by simultaneously safeguarding activities inherent in the exercise of those rights. . . . Walking the lakeshore below the ordinary high water mark is just such an activity, because gaining access to the Great Lakes to hunt, fish, or boat required walking to reach the water. Consequently, the public has always held a right of passage in and along the lakes.

Even before our state joined the Union, the Northwest Ordinance of 1787, art. IV, protected our Great Lakes in trust: "The navigable waters leading into the Mississippi and St. Lawrence, and the carrying places between the same, shall be common highways and forever free. . . ." See Northwest Ordinance of 1787, art. IV. Given that we must protect the Great Lakes as "common highways," see *id.*, we acknowledge that our public trust doctrine permits pedestrian use—in and of itself—of our Great Lakes, up to and including the land below the ordinary high water mark.

NOTES

1. *Limited public rights.* Although the court in *Glass v. Goeckel* recognized pedestrian use under the public trust doctrine, its remedy was narrow, noting that the protection of traditional public trust uses required only the protection of activities inherent to those uses—including walking the lakeshore. At the close of its analysis, the court emphasized:

> We must conclude with two caveats. By no means does our public trust doctrine permit *every* use of the trust lands and waters. Rather, this doctrine protects only limited public rights, and it does not create an unlimited public right to access private land below the ordinary high water mark. . . . The public trust doctrine cannot serve to justify trespass on private property. Finally, any exercise of these traditional public rights remains subject to criminal or civil regulation by the Legislature.

Glass v. Goeckel, 703 N.W.2d at 75. Thus, the court struck a balance between private and public rights. Where does the regulatory authority of the legislature begin and end? Recall that the Supreme Court in *Illinois Central* concluded that the legislature overstepped the limits of its authority.

2. *An expanding scope of public rights.* What happens to private and public rights if the high water mark moves, as is likely in the future from rising seas due to climate change? Consider this excerpt from *McQueen v. South Carolina Coastal Council*, 580 S.E.2d 116 (S.C. 2003), where a landowner's oceanfront property became increasingly submerged (a likely recurring phenomenon in an era of sea-level rise). When the state barred him from filling his land to raise it above high tide, McQueen claimed the government had "taken" the land without compensation, but the court disagreed:

> Historically, [South Carolina] holds presumptive title to land below the high water mark. As stated by this Court in 1884, not only does the State hold title to this land in *jus privatum*, it holds it in *jus publicum*, in trust for the benefit of all the citizens of this State. . . .

> The State has the exclusive right to control land below the high water mark for the public benefit, and cannot permit activity that substantially impairs the public interest in marine life, water quality, or public access. The State's presumptive title applies to tidelands.

> Significantly, under South Carolina law, wetlands created by the encroachment of navigable tidal water belong to the State. Proof that land was highland at the time of grant and tidelands were subsequently created by the rising of tidal water cannot defeat the State's presumptive title to tidelands.

> As described above, each of McQueen's lots borders a man-made tidal canal. . . . [The] reversion to tidelands effected a restriction on McQueen's property rights inherent in the ownership of property bordering tidal water.

> The tidelands . . . are public trust property subject to control of the State. McQueen's ownership rights do not include the right to backfill or place bulkheads on public trust land and the State need not compensate him for the denial of permits to do what he cannot otherwise do. . . .

McQueen, 580 S.E.2d at 119–20. Note that this result makes a landowner's right to exclude dependent on the vagaries of nature: as tidal waters invade private land, the public gains access to that land. Can you see how the public trust doctrine might provide a defense to takings claims concerning what formerly were privately-owned uplands?

This issue also arose in a South Dakota dispute, *Parks v. Cooper*, 676 N.W.2d 823 (2004), involving the power of a landowner to exclude outsiders when a waterway expanded onto private land due to unusual rainfall. According to the court, all water within the state was owned by the public and managed by the state to promote public interests pursuant to a public trust. The public trust was not limited to lands beneath navigable waterways nor, in the case of waters, to waters located in navigable waterways. Because land titles were established at the time South Dakota entered the Union, the lands involved in the case remained privately owned. Nonetheless, the waters were subject to public trust limitations, which meant the state had both the power and duty to manage them for public use notwithstanding the private rights. It was up to the state legislature and appropriate state agencies in the first instance, the court concluded, to decide how to fulfill these trust duties. In so ruling, the South Dakota court noted that several Western states had reached contrary conclusions, limiting public waterway access under state law to waterways that were navigable when the respective states entered the Union.

NATIONAL AUDUBON SOCIETY v. SUPERIOR COURT OF ALPINE COUNTY

Supreme Court of California
658 P.2d 709 (1983)

[The Los Angeles Department of Water and Power was diverting water from non-navigable tributaries feeding Mono Lake under a water right granted by the state water resources control board. Mono Lake is a terminal saline lake east of Yosemite National Park providing important habitat to waterfowl on the Pacific Flyway. Environmentalists claimed that the diversions of fresh water from the lake's tributaries violated the state's public trust doctrine. After a lower court denied relief, they appealed to the California Supreme Court.]

BROUSSARD, J.

Mono Lake, the second largest lake in California, sits at the base of the Sierra Nevada escarpment near the eastern entrance to Yosemite National Park. The lake is saline; it contains no fish but supports a large population of brine shrimp which feed vast numbers of nesting and migratory birds. Islands in the lake protect a large breeding colony of California gulls, and the lake itself serves as a haven on the migration route for thousands of Northern Phalarope, Wilson's Phalarope, and

Eared Greve. Towers and spires of tufa on the north and south shores are matters of geological interest and a tourist attraction.

Although Mono Lake receives some water from rain and snow on the lake surface, historically most of its supply came from snowmelt in the Sierra Nevada. Five freshwater streams—Mill, Lee Vining, Walker, Parker and Rush Creeks—arise near the crest of the range and carry the annual runoff to the west shore of the lake. In 1940, however, the Division of Water Resources, the predecessor to the present California Water Resources Board, granted the Department of Water and Power of the City of Los Angeles (hereafter DWP) a permit to appropriate virtually the entire flow of four of the five streams flowing into the lake. DWP promptly constructed facilities to divert about half the flow of these streams into DWP's Owens Valley aqueduct. In 1970 DWP completed a second diversion tunnel, and since that time has taken virtually the entire flow of these streams.

As a result of these diversions, the level of the lake has dropped; the surface area has diminished by one-third; one of the two principal islands in the lake has become a peninsula, exposing the gull rookery there to coyotes and other predators and causing the gulls to abandon the former island. The ultimate effect of continued diversions is a matter of intense dispute, but there seems little doubt that both the scenic beauty and the ecological values of Mono Lake are imperiled.

Plaintiffs filed suit in the superior court to enjoin the DWP diversions on the theory that the shores, bed and waters of Mono Lake are protected by a public trust. . . .

This case brings together for the first time two systems of legal thought: the appropriative water rights system which since the days of the gold rush has dominated California water law, and the public trust doctrine which, after evolving as a shield for the protection of tidelands, now extends its protective scope to navigable lakes. Ever since we first recognized that the public trust protects environmental and recreational values (*Marks v. Whitney*, 491 P.2d 374 (Cal. 1971)), the two systems of legal thought have been on a collision course. Ralph W. Johnson, *Public Trust Protection for Stream Flows and Lake Levels*, 14 U.C. Davis L. Rev. 233 (1980). They meet in a unique and dramatic setting which highlights the clash of values. Mono Lake is a scenic and ecological treasure of national significance, imperiled by continued diversions of water; yet, the need of Los Angeles for water is apparent, its reliance on rights granted by the board evident, the cost of curtailing diversions substantial.

[T]he state's authority as sovereign to exercise a continuous supervision and control over the navigable waters of the state and the lands underlying those waters . . . applies to the waters tributary to Mono Lake and bars DWP or any other party from claiming a vested right to divert waters once it becomes clear that such diversions harm the interests protected by the public trust. . . . [However, t]he prosperity and habitability of much of this state requires the diversion of great quantities of water from its streams for purposes unconnected to any navigation, commerce, fishing, recreation, or ecological use relating to the source stream. The state must have the power to grant non-vested usufructuary rights to appropriate water even if diversions harm public trust uses. Approval of such diversion without considering public trust values, however, may result in needless destruction of those values. Accordingly, we believe that before state courts and agencies approve water diversions they should consider the effect of such diversions upon interests protected by the public trust, and attempt, so far as feasible, to avoid or minimize any harm to those interests.

The water rights enjoyed by DWP were granted, the diversion was commenced, and has continued to the present without any consideration of the impact upon the public trust. An objective study and reconsideration of the water rights in the Mono Basin is long overdue. The water law of California—which we conceive to be an integration including both the public trust doctrine and the board-administered appropriative rights system—permits such a reconsideration; the values underlying that integration require it.

* * *

1. *Background and history of the Mono Lake litigation.*

[The Court traced the background of the Mono Lake litigation, and observed that prior to its purchase of riparian rights in four of Mono Lake's tributaries, the DWP had diverted virtually all the waters of the Owens River and its tributaries to Los Angeles, transforming Owens Lake into an alkali flat. The city's rapid expansion prompted DWP to search for a new water source and the Mono Basin, located within 50 miles of the origin of the Owens River, could easily be integrated into the existing aqueduct. In 1940, the city applied to the Water Board for permits to appropriate water from the tributaries of Mono Lake.]

The board's decision states that "[i]t is indeed unfortunate that the City's proposed development will result in decreasing the aesthetic advantages of Mono Basin but *there is apparently nothing that this office can do to prevent it.* The use to which the City proposes to put the water under its Applications . . . is defined by the Water Commission Act as the highest to which water may be applied and to make available unappropriated water for this use the City has . . . acquired the littoral and riparian rights on Mono Lake and its tributaries. . . . This office therefore has *no alternative but to dismiss all protests based upon the possible lowering of the water level in Mono Lake and the effect that the diversion of water from these streams may have upon the aesthetic and recreational value of the Basin.*" (Div. Wat. Resources Dec. 7053 et al. (Apr. 11, 1940), at p. 26, italics added.)

* * *

Mono Lake has no outlets. The lake loses water only by evaporation and seepage. Natural salts do not evaporate with water, but are left behind. Prior to commencement of the DWP diversions, this naturally rising salinity was balanced by a constant and substantial supply of fresh water from the tributaries. Now, however, DWP diverts most of the fresh water inflow. The resultant imbalance between inflow and outflow not only diminishes the lake's size, but also drastically increases its salinity.

Plaintiffs predict that the lake's steadily increasing salinity, if unchecked, will wreck havoc throughout the local food chain. They contend that the lake's algae, and the brine shrimp and brine flies that feed on it, cannot survive the projected salinity increase. [P]laintiffs point to a 50 percent reduction in the shrimp hatch for the spring of 1980 and a startling 95 percent reduction for the spring of 1981. These reductions affirm experimental evidence indicating that brine shrimp populations diminish as the salinity of the water surrounding them increases.... DWP admits these substantial reductions, but blames them on factors other than salinity.

DWP's diversions also present several threats to the millions of local and migratory birds using the lake. First, since many species of birds feed on the lake's brine shrimp, any reduction in shrimp population allegedly caused by rising salinity endangers a major avian food source. The Task Force Report considered it "unlikely that any of Mono Lake's major bird species ... will persist at the lake if populations of invertebrates disappear." Second, the increasing salinity makes it more difficult for the birds to maintain osmotic equilibrium with their environment.

* * *

Plaintiffs allege that DWP's diversions adversely affect the human species and its activities as well. First, as the lake recedes, it has exposed more than 18,000 acres of lake bed composed of very fine silt which, once dry, easily becomes airborne in winds. This silt contains a high concentration of alkali and other minerals that irritate the mucous membranes and respiratory systems of humans and other animals....

[T]he lake's recession [also] diminishes its value as an economic, recreational, and scenic resource. Of course, there will be less lake to use and enjoy. The declining shrimp hatch depresses a local shrimping industry. The rings of dry lake bed are difficult to traverse on foot, and thus impair human access to the lake, and reduce the lake's substantial scenic value....

* * *

2. The Public Trust Doctrine in California.

"By the law of nature these things are common to mankind—the air, running water, the sea and consequently the shores of the sea." Institutes of Justinian 2.1.1. From this origin in Roman law, the English common law evolved the concept of the public trust, under which the sovereign owns "all of its navigable waterways and the lands lying beneath them 'as trustee of a public trust for the benefit of the people.' " *Colberg, Inc. v. State of California ex rel. Dept. Pub. Works*, 432 P.2d 3 (Cal. 1967). The State of California acquired title as trustee to such lands and waterways upon its admission to the union; from the earliest days its judicial decisions have recognized and enforced the trust obligation.

Three aspects of the public trust doctrine require consideration in this opinion: the purpose of the trust; the scope of the trust, particularly as it applies to the nonnavigable tributaries of a navigable lake; and the powers and duties of the state as trustee of the public trust. We discuss these questions in the order listed.

(a) The purpose of the public trust.

The objective of the public trust has evolved in tandem with the changing public perception of the values and uses of waterways. As we observed in *Marks v. Whitney*, 491 P.2d 374 (Cal. 1971), "[p]ublic trust easements [were] traditionally defined in terms of navigation, commerce and fisheries. They have been held to include the right to fish, hunt, bathe, swim, to use for boating and general recreation purposes the navigable waters of the state, and to use the bottom of the navigable waters for anchoring, standing, or other purposes." *Id.* at 380. We went on, however, to hold that the traditional triad of uses—navigation, commerce and fishing—did not limit the public interest in the trust res. In language of special importance to the present setting, we stated that "[t]he public uses to which tidelands are subject are sufficiently flexible to encompass changing public needs. In administering the trust the state is not burdened with an outmoded classification favoring one mode of utilization over another. There is a growing public recognition that one of the most important public uses of the tidelands—a use encompassed within the tidelands trust—is the preservation of those lands in their natural state, so that they may serve as ecological units for scientific study, as open space, and as environments which provide food and habitat for birds and marine life, and which favorably affect the scenery and climate of the area." *Id.*

Mono Lake is a navigable waterway. It supports a small local industry which harvests brine shrimp for sale as fish food, which endeavor probably qualifies the lake as a "fishery" under the traditional public trust cases. The principal values plaintiffs seek to protect, however, are recreational and ecological—the scenic views of the lake and its shore, the purity of the air, and the use of the lake for nesting and feeding by birds. Under *Marks v. Whitney*, it is clear that protection of these values is among the purposes of the public trust.

(b) The scope of the public trust.

Early English decisions generally assumed the public trust was limited to tidal waters and the lands exposed and covered by the daily tides; many American decisions, including the leading California cases, also concern tidelands. . . . It is, however, well settled in the United States generally and in California that the public trust is not limited by the reach of the tides, but encompasses all navigable lakes and streams. . . .[5]

Mono Lake is, as we have said, a navigable waterway. The beds, shores and waters of the lake are without question protected by the public trust. The streams diverted by DWP, however, are not themselves navigable. Accordingly, we must address in this case a question not discussed in any recent public trust case—whether the public trust limits conduct affecting nonnavigable tributaries to navigable waterways.

* * *

DWP points out that [*People v. Gold Run Ditch & Mining Co.*, 4 P. 1152 (Cal. 1884),] did not involve diversion of water, and that in [*People ex rel. Robarts v. Russ*, 64 P. 111 (Cal. 1901),] there had been no finding of impairment to navigation. But the principles recognized by those decisions apply fully to a case in which diversions from a nonnavigable tributary impair the public trust in a downstream river or lake. "If the public trust doctrine applies to constrain *fills* which destroy navigation and other public trust uses in navigable waters, it should equally apply to constrain the *extraction* of water that destroys navigation and other public interests. Both actions result in the same damage to the public interest." . . .

We conclude that the public trust doctrine, as recognized and developed in California decisions, protects navigable waters from harm caused by diversion of nonnavigable tributaries.

(c) Duties and powers of the state as trustee.

In the following review of the authority and obligations of the state as administrator of the public trust, the dominant theme is the state's sovereign power and duty to exercise continued supervision over the trust. One consequence, of importance to this and many other cases, is that parties acquiring rights in trust property generally hold those rights

---

[5] A waterway usable only for pleasure boating is nevertheless a navigable waterway and protected by the public trust.

subject to the trust, and can assert no vested right to use those rights in a manner harmful to the trust.

[I]n *Illinois Central Railroad Company v. Illinois*, 146 U.S. 387 (1892), . . . [t]he Supreme Court . . . explained that lands under navigable waters conveyed to private parties for wharves, docks, and other structures in furtherance of trust purposes could be granted free of the trust because the conveyance is consistent with the purpose of the trust. But the legislature, it held, did not have the power to convey the entire city waterfront free of trust, thus barring all future legislatures from protecting the public interest. . . . "In the administration of government the use of such powers may for a limited period be delegated to a municipality or other body, but there always remains with the State the right to revoke those powers and exercise them in a more direct manner, and one more conformable to its wishes. So with trusts connected with public property, or property of a special character, like lands under navigable waterways, they cannot be placed entirely beyond the direction and control of the State." *Id.* at 453–54.

* * *

[The state possesses continuing power over trust property] as administrator of the public trust, a power which extends to the revocation of previously granted rights or to the enforcement of the trust against lands long thought free of the trust (see *City of Berkeley v. Superior Court*, 606 P.2d 362 (Cal. 1980)). Except for those rare instances in which a grantee may acquire a right to use former trust property free of trust restrictions, the grantee holds subject to the trust, and while he may assert a vested right to the servient estate (the right of use subject to the trust) and to any improvements he erects, he can claim no vested right to bar recognition of the trust or state action to carry out its purposes.

[T]he public trust doctrine does not prevent the state from choosing between trust uses. . . . [However], no one could contend that the state could grant tidelands free of the trust merely because the grant served some public purpose, such as increasing tax revenues, or because the grantee might put the property to a commercial use.

Thus, the public trust is more than an affirmation of state power to use public property for public purposes. It is an affirmation of the duty of the state to protect the people's common heritage of streams, lakes, marshlands and tidelands, surrendering that right of protection only in rare cases when the abandonment of that right is consistent with the purposes of the trust.

* * *

4. The relationship between the Public Trust Doctrine and the California Water Rights System.

* * *

In our opinion, both the public trust doctrine and the water rights system embody important precepts which make the law more responsive to the diverse needs and interests involved in the planning and allocation of water resources. To embrace one system of thought and reject the other would lead to an unbalanced structure, one which would either decry as a breach of trust appropriations essential to the economic development of this state, or deny any duty to protect or even consider the values promoted by the public trust. Therefore, seeking an accommodation which will make use of the pertinent principles of both the public trust doctrine and the appropriative water rights system, and drawing upon the history of the public trust and the water rights system, the body of judicial precedent, and the views of expert commentators, we reach the following conclusions:

a. The state as sovereign retains continuing supervisory control over its navigable waters and the lands beneath those waters. This principle, fundamental to the concept of the public trust, applies to rights in flowing waters as well as to rights in tidelands and lakeshores; it prevents any party from acquiring a vested right to appropriate water in a manner harmful to the interests protected by the public trust.

b. As a matter of current and historical necessity, the Legislature, acting directly or through an authorized agency such as the Water Board, has the power to grant usufructuary licenses that will permit an appropriator to take water from flowing streams and use that water in a distant part of the state, even though this taking does not promote, and may unavoidably harm, the trust uses at the source stream. . . .

c. The state has an affirmative duty to take the public trust into account in the planning and allocation of water resources, and to protect public trust uses whenever feasible. . . . [T]he state must bear in mind its duty as trustee to consider the effect of the taking on the public trust, and to preserve, so far as consistent with the public interest, the uses protected by the trust.

NOTES

1. *The geographical scope of the public trust.* The California Supreme Court applied public trust principles to Mono Lake's non-navigable feeder streams as well as the navigable lake itself. Why?

2. *The scope of activities subject to the public trust.* The case did not involve the filling or alteration of tidelands or submerged lands, but instead the diversion of water out-of-basin under water rights granted long ago. Why did the court expand the scope of activities subject to the public trust?

3. *Unsettling private property rights.* Did *Mono Lake* upset expected private property rights? Are these expectations different from the private property rights of shoreside landowners in *Glass v. Goeckel*? Does this decision convince you that the public trust reflects changing public values? Or could the decision merely expand the description of pre-existing rights that the public has always possessed? See, e.g., David C. Slade, *The Public Trust Doctrine in Motion: Evolution of the Doctrine, 1997–2008*, at 47–48 (2008) (describing a state's public trust doctrine as grounded in the Tenth Amendment of the U.S. Constitution, the reserved powers doctrine, and therefore pre-dating the Fifth Amendment to the Constitution).

4. *The state's fiduciary duty.* The court ruled that the public trust is an affirmation of the state's duty to protect the public's common heritage in trust resources. What duty did the court impose on the state in this case? Did the court require the state to stop the diversions because protecting the lake was more important than Los Angeles' municipal water supply?

5. *The public trust and state water rights.* After the *Mono Lake* decision, some scholars predicted that other western states would apply the PTD to water rights. See, e.g., Michael C. Blumm & Thea Schwartz, Mono Lake *and the Evolving Public Trust in Western Water*, 37 Ariz. L. Rev. 701 (1995). But cases applying the PTD to water diversions have been sparse. The Idaho Supreme Court endorsed the application of the doctrine to water rights in *Kootenai Environmental Alliance v. Panhandle Yacht Club,* 671 P.2d 1085, 1094 (Idaho 1983), but the Idaho legislature subsequently declared that the doctrine did not apply to water rights. See Michael C. Blumm, Harrison C. Dunning & Scott W. Reed, *Renouncing the Public Trust Doctrine: An Assessment of the Validity of Idaho House Bill 794*, 24 Ecology L.Q. 461 (1997) (arguing that the statute exceeded governmental authority, although there have been no suits filed). When the Arizona legislature passed a similar statute, the Arizona Supreme Court struck down the law as inconsistent with the Arizona constitution's provisions on separation of powers and giving away public property. *San Carlos Apache Tribe v. Superior Court ex rel. County of Maricopa*, 972 P.2d 179 (Ariz. 1999). The court stated:

> The public trust doctrine is a constitutional limitation on legislative power to give away resources held by the state in trust for its people. See *Arizona Ctr. for Law in the Public Interest v. Hassell*, 837 P.2d 158, 166–68 (Ariz. Ct. App. 1991).... The legislature cannot order the courts to make the doctrine inapplicable to these or any proceedings.... The [l]egislature cannot by legislation destroy the constitutional limits on its authority....

Id. at 199.

The Hawaiian Supreme Court has ruled that the public trust burdens all of the state's waters—including groundwater—and described the trust as a dual mandate to protect the trust and to promote the reasonable and beneficial use of water resources:

> Under the public trust, the state has both the authority and duty to preserve the rights of present and future generations in the waters of the state. . . . [S]ee also *State v. Central Vt. Ry.*, 571 A.2d 1128 (Vt. 1989) ("[T]he state's power to supervise trust property in perpetuity is coupled with the ineluctable duty to exercise this power."), *cert. denied*, 495 U.S. 931 (1990). The continuing *authority* of the state over its water resources precludes any grant or assertion of vested rights to use water to the detriment of public trust purposes. . . . This authority empowers the state to revisit prior diversions and allocations, even those made with due consideration of their effect on the public trust. See *National Audubon*, 658 P.2d at 728.

In re Water Use Permit Applications ("Waiahole Ditch"), 9 P.3d 409, 453 (Haw. 2000). The court determined that because the Hawaiian constitution codified the public trust, it refused to merely "rubber stamp" agency or legislative action. Instead, the court applied a "close look" standard of review to determine whether agency action complied with the PTD.

The *Waiahole Ditch* court also ruled that the state's PTD required the application of "precautionary principles" to determine whether the state trustee provided adequate protections of trust water resources. *Id.* at 467. What does use of the principle of precaution mean to a decision maker? Requiring less than scientific proof before taking action?

6.   *The public trust and groundwater.* The Hawaiian Supreme Court is not the only court to conclude that the public trust doctrine extends to groundwater. See, e.g., *In re Omya Solid Waste Facility Final Certification*, Docket No. 96–6–10 (Vt. Envtl. Ct. Feb. 28, 2011); *Lake Beulah Mgmt. Dist. v. State Dept. of Natural Resources*, 799 N.W.2d 73 (Wisc. 2011); *Envtl. L. Foundation v. State Water Resources Control Bd.*, No. 34–2010–80000583 (Cal. Super. July 15, 2014). See generally Jack Tuholske, *Trusting the Public Trust: Application of the Public Trust Doctrine to Groundwater Resources*, 9 Vt. J. Envtl. L. 189 (2008) (discussing other states).

7.   *Moving beyond effects on navigable waters?* Mono Lake involved a significant expansion in the scope of the PTD in California, but it did not unmoor the doctrine from navigable waters. Why did the court conclude that the mountain feeder streams to Mono Lake are subject to the public trust? Is the doctrine concerned about the condition of the feeder streams or the condition of the lake? Notice that this case carried forth the emphasis on ecological values that the California Supreme Court expressed earlier in *Marks v. Whitney*, 491 P.2d 374 (Cal. 1971). The court made clear that the trust has among its purposes the protection of "the scenic views of the lake and its shore, the purity of the air, and the use of the lake for nesting and

feeding by birds." Assuming the court understood the ecological nexus between tributary streams and the lake, do you think it would also protect the lake from pollution (either waterborne or airborne, such as mercury)? Does it make sense to protect water levels of a water body but not the water *quality* of the water body? Natural resources law is notorious for artificially partitioning problems that are, in fact, inextricably connected as a matter of ecological function. Could the public trust provide a more integrated approach to management of a resource?

8.   *Is the PTD consistent with "first in time"?* The Los Angeles DWP, invoking the Western water law doctrine of temporal priority (first in time, first in right), argued that its 1940 priority date for its diversions insulated it from public trust interference. Why isn't the result of this case a violation of the "first in time, first in right" principle of Western water law? How did the court integrate public property (trust) rights into a system of private rights governed by prior appropriation?

9.   *No vested rights. Mono Lake* was especially controversial because, by emphasizing that no water rights could vest against the public trust, it undermined the security of private rights to divert water for irrigation, municipal, and other purposes. The opinion is in line with the many cases that apply the public trust retrospectively on privately owned tidelands. Collectively, these decisions underscore the antecedent and superior nature of public trust rights to private title or interests. At the same time, however, the doctrine in the water rights context operates as a doctrine of accommodation, similar to its role in delineating private and public rights in land parcels. See *Mono Lake*, above (seeking "an accommodation which will make use of the pertinent principles of both the public trust doctrine and the appropriative water rights system. . . ."). The effect of the decision was evident fairly quickly, as the court of appeal ruled, in *United States v. State Water Resources Control Bd.*, 227 Cal. Rptr. 161 (Cal. Ct. App. 1986), that the PTD enabled the state to modify water rights if necessary to preserve water quality.

10.   *Judicial decisionmaking in PTD cases.* Observe how the role of the court in this and other major public trust cases differs from the judicial posture in a statutory context. Statutory interpretation tends to focus on narrow and often quite technical issues of law. Courts give substantial deference to agencies and legislatures on matters of statutory law. By contrast, many of the leading public trust cases involve judicial decision-making in a very broad context. Public trust cases often require judges to create new principles of common law adapted to the issues at hand, using the reasoning of past cases to guide them. The court in *Mono Lake*, for example, observed that the case brought together "for the first time two systems of legal thought," the appropriative water rights system and the PTD. These two broad areas of law were headed on a collision course over issues such as those arising over Mono Lake and its tributaries. The court proceeded to craft a set of principles to reconcile and give effect to both legal doctrines, drawing

upon "the history of the public trust and the water rights system, the body of judicial precedent, and the views of expert commentators. . . ."

11. *The PTD and state statutes.* One important aspect of this case involved the relationship between the water board regulations governing appropriation (which implemented state constitutional provisions) and the trust. The DWP had argued that the constitutional provisions of reasonable and beneficial use, and the state water board's regulations implementing them, had "subsumed" the trust. The court squarely rejected this argument, finding that both the trust and the appropriation system form an integrated water rights management regime. The court's holding is instructive for other public trust cases, as most involve the interaction between statutory law and trust law. Government defendants characteristically assert that statutory regimes subsume the trust, but as the *Mono Lake* case (and the *Waiahole Ditch* case in note 5 above) shows, courts may conclude otherwise. Does this judicial inclination to protect the trust from being assimilated into statutes and regulations point to the fundamental role of the trust as providing a restraint on legislative power, as articulated by many of the cases in chapter 2?

12. *Fulfilling trust duties.* What must the state do to discharge its trust responsibility? Must it keep Mono Lake from drying up? The court suggested some fiduciary principles to guide water appropriation in accordance with trust values. First, it made clear that water management agencies have an "affirmative duty to 'take the public trust into account in the planning and allocation' of water resources" (and where this has not happened, agencies "ought to reconsider the allocation of the waters" in view of trust purposes). Second, the trust imposed on the state a duty of continuing supervision over waters with the authority (and, impliedly, the duty) to revoke permits that "may be incorrect in light of current knowledge or inconsistent with current needs." Third, although the state has the power to issue permits that do "not promote and may unavoidably harm, the trust uses at the source stream," the state also has the duty to "protect public trust uses whenever feasible" and "to preserve, so far as consistent with the public interest, the uses protected by the trust."

The Supreme Court of Pennsylvania also interpreted the PTD to include groundwater. As you read the following case, consider how the court frames the role of the public trust in reviewing legislative and agency action.

ROBINSON TOWNSHIP V. PENNSYLVANIA

Supreme Court of Pennsylvania
83 A.3d 901 (2013)

[In 2012, the Pennsylvania Legislature enacted amendments to the Oil and Gas Act (Act 13). The statute addressed permitting, funding, and fee collection for unconventional gas wells in the Marcellus Shale, a large subsurface natural gas reservoir. Extraction techniques used to recover the shale gas included hydraulic fracturing, or slick-water "fracking." Fracking involves pumping a mixture of sand, water, and chemicals at high pressure into the rock until the rock breaks, releasing the gas. Each well uses several million gallons of water. In addition to a standard regulatory permitting scheme, Act 13 prohibited local regulation of oil and gas operations, requiring statewide uniformity in local zoning ordinances concerning oil and gas resources. The Act included waivers of mandatory setbacks, which would have separated gas wells from sensitive water sources.

Several municipalities and individuals, along with an environmental organization, filed suit against the state, claiming that Act 13 violated the Pennsylvania constitution. A divided lower court enjoined the state from granting waivers of setbacks from certain types of state waters and allowed local governments to enforce existing zoning ordinances and adopt new ones despite Act 13, but the lower court rejected the argument that Act 13 violated the Environmental Rights Amendment of the Pennsylvania constitution.[6] All parties appealed to the Supreme Court, which, after determining that the citizens had standing and the issue was justiciable, struck down Act 13 as unconstitutional. Three members of the court thought the statute violated the Environmental Rights Amendment; another thought the statute violated substantive due process; two members dissented. Excerpts from the plurality opinion, authored by the Chief Justice of the court, follow.]

CASTILLE, C.J.

* * *

[A]lthough plenary, the General Assembly's police power is not absolute; this distinction matters. Legislative power is subject to restrictions enumerated in the Constitution and to limitations inherent in the form of government chosen by the people. . . . Specifically, ours is a government in which the people have delegated general powers to the General Assembly, but with the express exception of certain fundamental rights reserved to the people in Article I of our Constitution. . . .

Article I is the Commonwealth's Declaration of Rights, which delineates the terms of the social contract between government and the

---

[6] [*Editor's Note*: Pennsylvania's constitution includes an "Environmental Rights Amendment" that reads:

> The people have a right to clean air, pure water, and to the preservation of the natural, scenic, historic and esthetic values of the environment. Pennsylvania's public natural resources are the common property of all the people, including generations yet to come. As trustee of these resources, the Commonwealth shall conserve and maintain them for the benefit of all the people.

Pa. Const. art. I, § 27.]

people that are of such "general, great and essential" quality as to be ensconced as "inviolate." Pa. Const. art. I, pmbl. & § 25; see also Pa. Const. art. I, § 2 ("All power is inherent in the people, and all free governments are founded on their authority and instituted for their peace, safety and happiness."). . . . The Declaration of Rights assumes that the rights of the people articulated in Article I of our Constitution—vis-à-vis the government created by the people—are inherent in man's nature and preserved rather than created by the Pennsylvania Constitution. . . .

* * *

Initially, we note that the Environmental Rights Amendment accomplishes two primary goals, via prohibitory and non-prohibitory clauses: (1) the provision identifies protected rights, to prevent the state from acting in certain ways, and (2) the provision establishes a nascent framework for the Commonwealth to participate affirmatively in the development and enforcement of these rights. Section 27 is structured into three mandatory clauses that define rights and obligations to accomplish these twin purposes; and each clause mentions "the people."

A legal challenge pursuant to Section 27 may proceed upon alternate theories that either the government has infringed upon citizens' rights or the government has failed in its trustee obligations, or upon both theories, given that the two paradigms, while serving different purposes in the amendatory scheme, are also related and overlap to a significant degree. . . . Facing a claim premised upon Section 27 rights and obligations, the courts must conduct a principled analysis of whether the Environmental Rights Amendment has been violated.

* * *

According to the plain language of Section 27, the provision establishes two separate rights in the people of the Commonwealth. The first . . . is the declared "right" of citizens to clean air and pure water, and to the preservation of natural, scenic, historic and esthetic values of the environment. This clause affirms a limitation on the state's power to act contrary to this right. While the subject of the right certainly may be regulated by the Commonwealth, any regulation is "subordinate to the enjoyment of the right . . . [and] must be regulation purely, not destruction"; laws of the Commonwealth that unreasonably impair the right are unconstitutional.

The terms "clean air" and "pure water" leave no doubt as to the importance of these specific qualities of the environment for the proponents of the constitutional amendment and for the ratifying voters. Moreover, the constitutional provision directs the "preservation" of broadly defined values of the environment, a construct that necessarily emphasizes the importance of each value separately, but also implicates a holistic analytical approach to ensure both the protection from harm or damage and to ensure the maintenance and perpetuation of an environment of quality for the benefit of future generations.

Although the first clause . . . does not impose express duties on the political branches to enact specific affirmative measures to promote clean air, pure water, and the preservation of the different values of our environment, the right articulated is neither meaningless nor merely aspirational. The corollary of the people's Section 27 reservation of right to an environment of quality is an obligation on the government's behalf to refrain from unduly infringing upon or violating the right, including by legislative enactment or executive action. [E]ach branch of government [must] consider in advance . . . the environmental effect of any proposed action on the constitutionally protected features. The failure to obtain information regarding environmental effects does not excuse the constitutional obligation because the obligation exists *a priori* to any statute purporting to create a cause of action.

Moreover, as the citizens argue, the constitutional obligation binds all government, state or local, concurrently. . . .

* * *

Also apparent from the language of the constitutional provision are the substantive standards by which we decide a claim for violation of a right protected by the first clause of Section 27. The right to "clean air" and "pure water" sets plain conditions by which government must abide. We recognize that, as a practical matter, air and water quality have relative rather than absolute attributes. Furthermore, state and federal laws and regulations both govern "clean air" and "pure water" standards and, as with any other technical standards, the courts generally defer to agency expertise in making a factual determination whether the benchmarks were met. *Accord* 35 P.S. § 6026.102(4) (recognizing that General Assembly "has a duty" to implement Section 27 and devise environmental remediation standards). That is not to say, however, that courts can play no role in enforcing the substantive requirements articulated by the Environmental Rights Amendment in the context of an appropriate challenge. Courts are equipped and obliged to weigh parties' competing evidence and arguments, and to issue reasoned decisions regarding constitutional compliance by the other branches of government. The benchmark for decision is the express purpose of the Environmental Rights Amendment to be a bulwark against actual or likely degradation of, *inter alia,* our air and water quality. *Accord Montana Envtl. Info. Ctr. v. Dep't of Envtl. Quality,* 988 P.2d 1236, 1249 (Mont. 1999) (constitutional "inalienable . . . right to a clean and healthful environment" did not protect merely against type of environmental degradation "conclusively linked" to ill health or physical endangerment and animal death, but could be invoked to provide anticipatory and preventative protection against unreasonable degradation of natural resources).

Section 27 also separately requires the preservation of "natural, scenic, historic and esthetic values of the environment." Pa Const. art. I, § 27. By calling for the "preservation" of these broad environmental values, the Constitution again protects the people from governmental action that unreasonably causes actual or likely deterioration of these features. The Environmental Rights Amendment does not call for a stagnant landscape; nor, as we explain below, for the derailment of economic or social development; nor for a sacrifice of other fundamental values. But, when government acts, the action must, on balance, reasonably account for the environmental features of the affected locale, as further explained in this decision, if it is to pass constitutional muster. *Accord* John C. Dernbach, *Taking the Pennsylvania Constitution Seriously When It Protects the Environment: Part II—Environmental Rights and Public Trust*, 104 Dickinson L. Rev. 97, 17–20 (1999).

* * *

The second right reserved by Section 27 is the common ownership of the people, including future generations, of Pennsylvania's public natural resources. On its terms, the second clause . . . applies to a narrower category of "public" natural resources than the first clause of the provision. The drafters, however, left unqualified the phrase public natural resources, suggesting that the term fairly implicates relatively broad aspects of the environment, and is amenable to change over time to conform, for example, with the development of related legal and societal concerns. At present, the concept of public natural resources includes not only state-owned lands, waterways, and mineral reserves, but also resources that implicate the public interest, such as ambient air, surface and ground water, wild flora, and fauna (including fish) that are outside the scope of purely private property. See, e.g., 30 Pa. C.S. § 721 (fish: acquisition of property by Commonwealth); 34 Pa. C.S. § 103(a) (Commonwealth's ownership of game or wildlife); 71 P.S. § 1340.302(a) (acquisition and disposition of Commonwealth-owned forests). See also 35 P.S. §§ 691.1, 691.501, 691.503 (pollution of [state] waters, as broadly defined by act, is public nuisance; protection required); 35 P.S. § 1451 (public interest in quantity of water; authorizes immediate action by governor to conserve natural resources threatened by drought and forest fire); 35 P.S. §§ 4003, 4013 (violation of Air Pollution Control Act and related regulations, orders, permits is public nuisance); 35 P.S. §§ 4501, 4502 (immunity for shooting ranges in public nuisance suits for noise pollution; assumes noise pollution regulated at local level); *accord* Dernbach, 104 Dickinson L. Rev. at 10–11.

* * *

The third clause of Section 27 establishes the Commonwealth's duties with respect to Pennsylvania's commonly-owned public natural resources, which are both negative (*i.e.*, prohibitory) and affirmative (*i.e.*, implicating enactment of legislation and regulations). The provision establishes the public trust doctrine with respect to these natural resources (the corpus of the trust), and designates "the Commonwealth" as trustee and the people as the named beneficiaries. The terms of the trust are construed according to the intent of the settlor which, in this instance, is "the people." See *Estate of Sykes,* 383 A.2d 920, 921 (Pa. 1978) ("To ascertain this intent, a court examines the words of the instrument and, if necessary, the scheme of distribution, the circumstances surrounding execution of the [instrument] and other facts bearing on the question.").

"Trust" and "trustee" are terms of art that carried legal implications well developed at Pennsylvania law at the time the amendment was adopted. . . . The statement offered in the General Assembly in support of the amendment explained the distinction between the roles of proprietor and trustee in these terms:

> Under the proprietary theory, government deals at arms['] length with its citizens, measuring its gains by the balance sheet profits and appreciation it realizes from its resources operations. Under the trust theory, it deals with its citizens as a fiduciary, measuring its successes by the benefits it bestows upon all its citizens in their utilization of natural resources under law.

1970 Pa. Legislative Journal-House at 2273. See also *Nat'l Audubon Soc'y v. Superior Court,* 658 P.2d 709, 724 (Cal. 1983) ("[P]ublic trust is more than an affirmation of state power to use public property for public purposes. It is an affirmation of the duty of the state to protect the people's common heritage of streams, lakes, marshlands and tidelands, surrendering that right of protection only in rare cases when the abandonment of that right is consistent with the purposes of the trust."). The trust relationship does not contemplate a settlor placing blind faith in the uncontrolled discretion of a trustee; the settlor is entitled to maintain some control and flexibility, exercised by granting the trustee considerable discretion to accomplish the purposes of the trust. . . .

This environmental public trust was created by the people of Pennsylvania, as the common owners of the Commonwealth's public natural resources; . . . The Commonwealth is named trustee and, notably, duties and powers attendant to the trust are not vested exclusively in any single branch of Pennsylvania's government. The plain intent of the provision is to permit the checks and balances of government to operate in their usual fashion for the benefit of the people in order to accomplish the purposes of the trust. This includes local government. . . .

As trustee, the Commonwealth is a fiduciary obligated to comply with the terms of the trust and with standards governing a fiduciary's conduct. The explicit terms of the trust require the government to "conserve and maintain" the corpus of the trust. The plain meaning of the terms conserve and maintain implicates a duty to prevent and remedy the degradation, diminution, or depletion of our public natural resources. As a fiduciary, the Commonwealth has a duty to act toward the corpus of the trust—the public natural resources—with prudence, loyalty, and impartiality. . . .

As the parties here illustrate, two separate Commonwealth obligations are implicit in the nature of the trustee-beneficiary relationship. The first obligation arises from the prohibitory nature of the constitutional clause creating the trust, and is similar to other negative rights articulated in the Declaration of Rights. Stated otherwise, the Commonwealth has an obligation to refrain from performing its trustee duties respecting the environment unreasonably, including via legislative enactments or executive action. As trustee, the Commonwealth has a duty to refrain from permitting or encouraging the degradation, diminution, or depletion of public natural resources, whether such degradation, diminution, or depletion would occur through direct state action or indirectly, *e.g.*, because of the state's failure to restrain the actions of private parties. In this sense, the third clause of the Environmental Rights Amendment is complete because it establishes broad but concrete substantive parameters within which the Commonwealth may act. This Court perceives no impediment to citizen beneficiaries enforcing the constitutional prohibition in accordance with established principles of judicial review. . . .

The second obligation peculiar to the trustee is, as the Commonwealth recognizes, to act affirmatively to protect the environment, via legislative action. *Accord Geer v. Connecticut*, 161 U.S. 519, 534 (1896) (trusteeship for benefit of state's people implies legislative duty "to enact such laws as will best preserve the subject of the trust, and secure its beneficial use in the future to the people of the state"). The General Assembly has not shied from this duty; it has enacted environmental statutes. . . . As these statutes (and related regulations) illustrate, legislative enactments serve to define regulatory powers and duties, to describe prohibited conduct of private individuals and entities, to provide procedural safeguards, and to enunciate technical standards of environmental protection. These administrative details are appropriately addressed by legislation because, like other "great ordinances" in our Declaration of Rights, the generalized terms comprising the Environmental Rights Amendment do not articulate them. The call for complementary legislation, however, does not override the otherwise plain conferral of rights upon the people. . . .

Of course, the trust's express directions to conserve and maintain public natural resources do not require a freeze of the existing public natural resource stock; rather . . . the duties to conserve and maintain are tempered by legitimate development tending to improve upon the lot of Pennsylvania's citizenry, with the evident goal of promoting sustainable development. . . .

Within the public trust paradigm of Section 27, the beneficiaries of the trust are "all the people" of Pennsylvania, including generations yet to come. The trust's beneficiary designation has two obvious implications: first, the trustee has an obligation to deal impartially with all beneficiaries and, second, the trustee has an obligation to balance the interests of present and future beneficiaries. Dealing impartially with all beneficiaries means that the trustee must treat all equitably in light of the purposes of the trust. Here, the duty of impartiality implicates questions of access to and distribution of public natural resources, including consumable resources such as water, fish, and game. The second, cross-generational dimension of Section 27 reinforces the conservation imperative: future generations are among the beneficiaries entitled to equal access and distribution of the resources, thus, the trustee cannot be shortsighted. . . .

* * *

That Pennsylvania deliberately chose a course different from virtually all of its sister states speaks to the Commonwealth's experience of having the benefit of vast natural resources whose virtually unrestrained exploitation, while initially a boon to investors, industry, and citizens, led to destructive and lasting consequences not only for the environment but also for the citizens' quality of life. Later generations paid and continue to pay a tribute to early uncontrolled and unsustainable development financially, in health and quality of life consequences, and with the relegation to history books of valuable natural and esthetic aspects of our environmental inheritance. The drafters and the citizens of the Commonwealth who ratified the Environmental Rights Amendment, aware of this history, articulated the people's rights and the government's duties to the people in broad and flexible terms that would permit not only reactive but also anticipatory protection of the environment for the benefit of current and future generations. Moreover, public trustee duties were delegated concomitantly to all branches and levels of government in recognition that the quality of the environment is a task with both local and statewide implications, and to ensure that all government neither infringed upon the people's rights nor failed to act for the benefit of the people in this area crucial to the well-being of all Pennsylvanians.

[The plurality reviewed previous interpretations of the Environmental Rights Amendment, particularly *Payne v. Kassab,* 312 A.2d 86, 94 (Pa. Commw. Ct. 1973), *aff'd* 361 A.2d 263 (Pa. 1976), in which a lower court established a non-textual three-part balancing test that was employed by ensuing decisions to marginalize the constitutional text. The plurality determined that the balancing test was inappropriate except for challenges based on a failure to comply with statutory standards enacted to carry out the Environmental Rights Amendment.]

* * *

Reviewing the amended Act [13], few could seriously dispute how remarkable a revolution is worked by this legislation upon the existing zoning regimen in Pennsylvania, including residential zones. . . . The displacement of prior planning, and derivative expectations, regarding land use, zoning, and enjoyment of property is unprecedented.

* * *

[T]he citizens construe the Environmental Rights Amendment as protecting individual rights and devolving duties upon various actors within the political system; and they claim that breaches of those duties or encroachments upon those rights is, at a minimum, actionable. According to the citizens, this dispute is not about municipal power, statutory or otherwise, to develop local policy, but it is instead about compliance with constitutional duties. Unless the Declaration of Rights is to have no meaning, the citizens are correct.

* * *

The type of constitutional challenge presented today is as unprecedented in Pennsylvania as is the legislation that engendered it. But, the challenge is in response to history seeming to repeat itself: an industry, offering the very real prospect of jobs and other important economic benefits, seeks to exploit a Pennsylvania resource, to supply an energy source much in demand. The political branches have responded with a comprehensive scheme that accommodates the recovery of the resource. By any responsible account, the exploitation of the Marcellus Shale Formation will produce a detrimental effect on the environment, on the people, their children, and future generations, and potentially on the public purse, perhaps rivaling the environmental effects of coal extraction. The litigation response was not available in the nineteenth century, since there was no Environmental Rights Amendment. The response is available now.

The challenge here is premised upon that part of our organic charter that now explicitly guarantees the people's right to an environment of quality and the concomitant expressed reservation of a right to benefit from the Commonwealth's duty of management of our public natural resources. The challengers here are citizens—just like the citizenry that reserved the right in our charter. They are residents or members of local legislative and executive bodies, and several localities directly affected by natural gas development and extraction in the Marcellus Shale Formation. Contrary to the Commonwealth's characterization of the dispute, the citizens seek not to expand the authority of local government but to vindicate fundamental constitutional rights that, they say, have been compromised by a legislative determination that violates a public trust. The Commonwealth's efforts to minimize the import of this litigation by suggesting it is simply a dispute over public policy voiced by a disappointed minority requires a blindness to the reality here and to Pennsylvania history, including Pennsylvania constitutional history; and, the position ignores the reality that Act 13 has the potential to affect the reserved rights of every citizen of this Commonwealth now, and in the future. We will proceed now to the merits.

[The court ruled that Act 13's preemption of local regulations of oil and gas operations violated the Environmental Rights Amendment because the state had no authority to remove a local government's constitutionally imposed trust obligations. The court then considered Act 13's requirement that "all local ordinances" must "allow for the reasonable development of oil and gas resources," and concluded that also violated the constitutional trust for the following two reasons.]

* * *

We have explained that, among other fiduciary duties under Article I, Section 27, the General Assembly has the obligation to prevent degradation, diminution, and depletion of our public natural resources, which it may satisfy by enacting legislation that adequately restrains actions of private parties likely to cause harm to protected aspects of our environment. We are constrained to hold that [the statute] falls considerably short of meeting this obligation. . . .

Act 13 simply displaces development guidelines, guidelines which offer strict limitations on industrial uses in sensitive zoning districts; instead, Act 13 permits industrial oil and gas operations as a use "of right" in *every zoning district throughout the Commonwealth*, including in residential, commercial, and agricultural districts. [T]he provision compels exposure of otherwise protected areas to environmental and habitability costs associated with this particular industrial use. . . . The entirely new legal regime alters existing expectations of communities and property owners and substantially diminishes natural and esthetic values of the local environment, which contribute significantly to a quality of environmental life in Pennsylvania. . . .

A second difficulty arising from [the] requirement that local government permit industrial uses in all zoning districts is that some properties and communities will carry much heavier environmental and habitability burdens than others. This disparate effect is irreconcilable with the express command that the trustee will manage the corpus of the trust for the benefit of "all the people." Pa. Const. art. I, § 27. A trustee must treat all beneficiaries equitably in light of the purposes of the trust. . . . Act 13's blunt approach fails to account for this constitutional command at all. . . . Imposing statewide environmental and habitability standards appropriate for the heaviest of industrial areas in sensitive zoning districts lowers environmental and habitability protections for affected residents and property owners below the existing threshold and permits significant degradation of public natural resources. The outright ban on local regulation of oil and gas operations (such as ordinances seeking to conform development to local conditions) that would mitigate the effect, meanwhile, propagates serious detrimental and disparate effects on the corpus of the trust.

* * *

[The court also struck down state waivers of setback distances to protect streams and other water bodies because the statute lacked discernable standards, placed the burden of proof on the state to show harm, and marginalized public participation in approving permits.]

For these reasons, we are constrained to hold that the degradation of the corpus of the trust and the disparate impact on some citizens sanctioned by . . . Act 13 are incompatible with the express command of the Environmental Rights Amendment. We recognize the importance of this legislation, and do not question the intentions behind it; we recognize, too, the urgency with which the political branches believe they must act to secure the benefits of developing the unconventional natural gas industry. By any measure, this legislation is of sweeping import. But, in that urgency, it is apparent that . . . constitutional commands have been swept aside. Act 13's unauthorized use of the public trust assets is unprecedented and constitutionally infirm, even assuming that the trustee believes it is acting solely and in good faith to advance the economic interests of the beneficiaries.

NOTES

1. *The role of history.* Consider this additional excerpt from *Robinson Township*:

> We seared and scarred our once green and pleasant land with mining operations. We polluted our rivers and our streams with acid mine drainage, with industrial waste, with sewage. We poisoned our 'delicate, pleasant and wholesome' air with the smoke of steel mills and coke ovens and with the fumes of millions of automobiles. We smashed our highways through fertile fields and thriving city neighborhoods. We cut down our trees and erected eyesores along our roads. We uglified our land and we called it progress.

Robinson Township, 83 A.3d at 961 (quoting 1970 Pa. Legislative Journal-House at 2270). Should the economic and environmental history of Pennsylvania influence a court decision? For an examination of this case, see John C. Dernbach, James May & Kenneth Kristl, Robinson Township v. Commonwealth of Pennsylvania: *Examination and Implications*, Widener Law School Legal Studies Research Paper No. 14–10, available at http://ssrn.com/abstract=2412657.

2. *An environmental trust.* Notice that the right to a clean environment in clause 1 of Article I, section 27 of the Pennsylvania constitution is expressly tied to the trust language in clauses 2 (public natural resources are common property of the people, including future generations) and 3 (state as trustee must conserve and maintain trust assets for public beneficiaries).

3. *The public trust as part of the social contract.* Perhaps the most remarkable aspect of the plurality's decision is in the second paragraph in the excerpt above, where the opinion declared that the Article I list of citizen rights "delineates the terms of the social contract between the government and the people that are of such 'general, great, and essential' quality as to be ensconced as 'inviolate.'" Public trust rights are therefore "inherent in man's nature and preserved rather than created by the Pennsylvania Constitution." 83 A.3d at 947–48. Thus, although the *Robinson Township* decision is nominally an application (actually a disinterment) of section 27 of the Pennsylvania constitution, its recognition of the public trust as inherent in sovereignty may speak to courts in other jurisdictions.

4. *The role of the courts in enforcing the public trust.* The plurality opinion recognized that courts generally defer to the environmental standards set in statutes and regulations, but "[t]hat is not to say, however, that courts can play no role in enforcing the substantive requirements articulated in the Environmental Rights Amendment in the context of an appropriate challenge. Courts are equipped and obliged to weigh parties' competing evidence and arguments, and to issue reasoned decisions regarding constitutional compliance by the other branches of government."

Id. at 953. Notice also the plurality's reliance on the *Mono Lake* decision to emphasize the "duty of the state to protect the people's common heritage of [public trust resources]." *Id.* at 956.

5. *The scope of public trust resources.* The PTD continues to evolve as courts apply its principles to new types of resources and to new types of uses. *Robinson Township* concluded that the natural resources that implicated the public interest included "not only state-owned lands, waterways, and mineral reserves, but also . . . ambient air, surface and ground water, wild flora, and fauna. . . ." *Id.* at 955.

6. *Public trust equity.* Notice that the opinion concluded that Act 13 violated the public trust reflected in the Pennsylvania constitution because "some properties and communities will carry much heavier environmental and habitability burdens than others," a result inconsistent with the obligation of the trustee to manage trust resources for "all the people." *Id.* at 980. This interpretation seemed to suggest that the public trust doctrine contains a kind of implicit equal protection guarding against the assignment of disproportionate environmental burdens, which environmental justice advocates have claimed are commonplace. See, e.g., Clifford Ruchtschaffen, et al., *Environmental Justice: Law, Policy & Regulation* (2d ed. 2009).

7. *Intergenerational equity.* The plurality is also clear that the "beneficiaries of the trust are 'all the people' of Pennsylvania, including generations yet to come." 83 A.3d at 959. Edmund Burke, the great political philosopher of the late eighteenth century, described the social contract in generational terms, as: "a partnership not only between those who are living, but between those who are living, those who are dead, and those who are to be born. Each contract of each particular state is but a clause in the great primeval contract of eternal society. . . ." Edmund Burke, *Reflections on the Revolution in France* 108 (Macmillan ed., 1890). Burke proceeded to discuss intergenerational equity in terms of present estates and future interests, with surprising environmental overtones:

> [O]ne of the first and most leading principles on which the commonwealth and the laws are consecrated is [that] the temporary possessors and life-renters in it [should be mindful] of what is due to their posterity . . . [and] should not think it amongst their rights to cut off the entail or commit waste on the inheritance, by destroying at their pleasure the whole original fabric of their society; hazarding to leave to those who come after them a ruin instead of an habitation. . . .

Id. at 106. The *Waiahole Ditch* decision, discussed above in note 5 following the *Mono Lake* excerpt (pp. 200–201), also endorsed the obligation to protect future generations. 9 P.3d 409, 453 (Haw. 2000) ("Under the public trust, the state has both the authority and the duty to preserve the rights of present and future generations. . . .").

8. *The atmospheric trust.* An emerging strategy in support of the application of public trust principles to ambient air has gained momentum in recent years, led by the non-profit organization Our Children's Trust. This "atmospheric trust litigation" includes actions in all 50 states as well as a federal lawsuit, brought on behalf of youth plaintiffs who demand government action to bring atmospheric carbon concentrations below 350 parts per million in order to protect the climate for future generations. See, e.g., *Alec L. v. Jackson*, 863 F.Supp.2d 11 (D.D.C. 2012), aff'd 561 F. Appx. 7, 8 (D.C. Cir. 2014); *Svitak ex rel. Svitak v. State of Washington*, 178 Wash.App. 1020 (Wash. Ct. App. 2013); *Butler ex rel. Peshlakai v. Brewer*, 2013 WL 1091209 (Ariz. App. 2013). In all three of the cited cases, the courts declined to address the plaintiffs' claims. The D.C. District Court in *Alec L.* relied on the Supreme Court's *PPL Montana v. Montana* decision, 132 S.Ct. 1215, 1234–35 (2012), to conclude that no federal public trust exists. Alternatively, the court held—without in-depth analysis—that the Clean Air Act displaced any claim to the trust that plaintiffs may have. The courts in *Svitak* and *Butler*, both relying on the dismissal in *Alec L.*, similarly concluded that statutes addressing air pollution displace public trust claims at the state level.

In Texas, the campaign met with short-lived success. A lower court issued a decision concluding that public trust principles apply to the atmosphere. *Bonser-Lain v. Texas Commission on Environmental Quality*, No. D–1–GN–11–002194, 2012 WL 3164561 (Tex. 201st Dist. Aug. 2, 2012), but the Texas Court of Appeals vacated for lack of subject matter jurisdiction, 2014 WL 3702446. For some of the scholarship arguing that public trust assets include the air, see Mary Christina Wood, *Nature's Trust: Environmental Law for a New Ecological Age* (2014); Gerald Torres, *Who Owns the Sky?*, 19 Pace Envtl. L. Rev. 515 (2001).

9. *The public trust abroad.* In India and the Philippines, courts have issued decisions in public trust cases that conclude the trust arises from natural law rather than statutory or constitutional sources, and that the trust applies to all natural resources. See generally Michael C. Blumm & Mary Christina Wood, *The Public Trust Doctrine in Environmental and Natural Resources Law*, ch. 10 (2013) (also excerpting decisions from Uganda, Kenya, and Canada, as well as constitutional and statutory provisions in other countries). In *M.C. Mehta v. Kamal Nath* (1997) 1 S.C.C. 388 (India), the Supreme Court of India traced the ancient origins of the PTD and discussed the modern application of the trust that followed the publication of Professor Joseph Sax's law review article, 68 Mich. L. Rev. 471 (1970) (discussed above, n. 1, pp. 184–185), including references to the decisions in the *Illinois Central* and *Mono Lake* cases. The court concluded, "We see no reason why the public trust doctrine should not be expanded to include all ecosystems operating in our natural resources." *Id.* See also *Oposa v. Factoran, Jr.*, G.R. No. 101083 at 9, 12 (July 30, 1993) (Philippines) ("[T]hese basic rights need not even be written in the Constitution for they are assumed to exist from the inception of humankind. . . . It must . . . be

emphasized that the political question doctrine is no longer the insurmountable obstacle to the exercise of judicial power or the impenetrable shield that protects executive and legislative actions from judicial inquiry or review.").

Didn't the *Robinson Township* decision endorse the "natural law" approach of the *Mehta* and *Oposa* cases? Why would U.S. courts in the atmospheric trust cases be reluctant to discuss "natural law" as the origin for the public trust and be receptive to claims that alleged public trust violations present political questions more appropriately resolved by the legislative and executive branches? Did the courts in *Robinson Township* and *Mono Lake* consider the applicable statutory and regulatory regimes to displace the PTD?

F. WETLANDS

Wetlands, commonly referred to as swamps, bogs, and marshes, were once thought to be wastelands or worse: areas of mosquitos, foul odors, and disease. Consequently, wetlands were often drained or filled—more than half of America's original wetlands have been destroyed. But today, wetlands are widely recognized as critically important resources which help to regulate water flow, improve water quality, and reduce flood and storm damage. Moreover, because of their great ecological productivity—comparable to rain forests and coral reefs—wetlands provide important animal habitat and support hunting, fishing, and other recreational activities. They even help in atmospheric maintenance by storing carbon. U.S. Environmental Protection Agency, *America's Wetlands: Our Vital Link Between Land and Water* at 1–4 (n.d.).

Wetlands are areas periodically inundated frequently enough to produce wetland soils and promote wetland vegetation, so not every land which becomes submerged is a wetland. But because they exist at the land-water edge, wetlands are subject to developmental pressure for residential and commercial projects. Efforts to preserve and protect wetlands are consequently often seen as inhibiting valuable economic development and are at the center of numerous legal controversies.

Although many states do have regulations protecting at least some wetlands (more likely in coastal than inland areas), the principal regulatory program is a federal one, authorized by section 404 of the Clean Water Act, 33 U.S.C § 1344. Section 404 permits are issued by the U.S. Army Corps of Engineers (due to its historic regulation of navigation, dating back to 1824), and overseen by the U.S. Environmental Protection Agency (EPA). The Corps and EPA have had, at times, an uneasy relationship implementing the program. See, e.g., Michael C. Blumm & D. Bernard Zaleha, *Federal Wetlands Protection Under the Clean Water Act: Regulatory Ambivalence, Intergovernmental Tension, and a Call for Reform*, 60 U. Colo. L. Rev. 695 (1989). Some of the intergovernmental tension is due to the fact that unlike most regulatory programs, in section 404 one federal agency (EPA) has the authority not only to participate in the issuance of permit criteria but also to veto permits issued by another federal agency (the Corps).

One continuous source of section 404 controversy over the years has been the scope of the permit program, since the Clean Water Act clearly aimed to expand federal regulation beyond the Corps' traditional jurisdiction over waters that were navigable-in-fact. However, Congress was not clear concerning how expansive the new program was, defining navigable waters as "waters of the United States," 33 U.S.C. § 1362(7), which the statute's legislative history indicated extended to the full extent of federal authority under the Commerce Clause. S. Rep. No. 92–1236, at 144 (1972) ("The conferees fully intend that the term 'navigable waters' be given the broadest possible constitutional interpretation . . ."). However, as the cases below indicate, the Supreme Court has ignored this statement of congressional intent, focusing instead on the connection of wetlands to navigable waters as a prerequisite for federal jurisdiction. This narrow focus has limited the ability of the 404 program to protect many ecologically important wetlands.

UNITED STATES V. RIVERSIDE BAYVIEW HOMES, INC.
Supreme Court of the United States
474 U.S. 121 (1985)

[The Corps of Engineers sought to enjoin Riverside Bayview Homes from filling an 80-acre marshy lowland as part of a housing development. Although the land was a mile away from any navigable-in-fact water, the Corps claimed that the land was an "adjacent wetland," and therefore a "water of the United States" subject to Clean Water Act (CWA) jurisdiction. The district court agreed and enjoined Riverside Bayview, but the Sixth Circuit reversed, construing the Corps' regulation to exclude from the category of adjacent wetlands—and hence from "waters of the United States"—wetlands that were not subject to flooding by adjacent navigable waters at a frequency sufficient to support the growth of aquatic vegetation. The Sixth Circuit adopted this construction of the regulation because, in its view, a broader definition of wetlands might result in the taking of private property without just compensation. The court also expressed doubt that Congress, in granting the Corps jurisdiction to regulate the filling of "navigable waters," intended to allow regulation of wetlands that were not the result of flooding by navigable waters.]

WHITE, J.

* * *

We granted certiorari to consider the proper interpretation of the Corps' regulation defining "waters of the United States" and the scope of the Corps' jurisdiction under the Clean Water Act, both of which were called into question by the Sixth Circuit's ruling. 469 U.S. 1206 (1985). We now reverse.

II

The question whether the Corps of Engineers may demand that respondent obtain a permit before placing fill material on its property is primarily one of regulatory and statutory interpretation: we must determine whether respondent's property is an "adjacent wetland" within the meaning of the applicable regulation, and, if so, whether the Corps' jurisdiction over "navigable waters" gives it statutory authority to regulate discharges of fill material into such a wetland. . . .

* * *

[The Court ruled that the Sixth Circuit erred when it concluded that a narrow reading of the Corps' rule was necessary to avoid an unconstitutional taking problem. The fact that some limited individual properties might be "taken" by the permitting program was not enough to amount to a "serious takings problem," according to the Court.]

IV

A

An agency's construction of a statute it is charged with enforcing is entitled to deference if it is reasonable and not in conflict with the expressed intent of Congress. *Chevron U.S.A. Inc. v. Natural Resources Defense Council, Inc.,* 467 U.S. 837, 842–45 (1984). Accordingly, our review is limited to the question whether it is reasonable, in light of the language, policies, and legislative history of the Act for the Corps to exercise jurisdiction over wetlands adjacent to but not regularly flooded by rivers, streams, and other hydrographic features more conventionally identifiable as "waters."

On a purely linguistic level, it may appear unreasonable to classify "lands," wet or otherwise, as "waters." Such a simplistic response, however, does justice neither to the problem faced by the Corps in defining the scope of its authority under § 404(a) nor to the realities of the problem of water pollution that the Clean Water Act was intended to combat. In determining the limits of its power to regulate discharges under the Act, the Corps must necessarily choose some point at which water ends and land begins. Our common experience tells us that this is often no easy task: the transition from water to solid ground is not necessarily or even typically an abrupt one. Rather, between open waters and dry land may lie shallows, marshes, mudflats, swamps, bogs—in short, a huge array of areas that are not wholly aquatic but nevertheless fall far short of being dry land. Where on this continuum to find the limit of "waters" is far from obvious.

Faced with such a problem of defining the bounds of its regulatory authority, an agency may appropriately look to the legislative history and underlying policies of its statutory grants of authority. Neither of these sources provides unambiguous guidance for the Corps in this case, but together they do support the reasonableness of the Corps' approach of defining adjacent wetlands as "waters" within the meaning of § 404(a). Section 404 originated as part of the Federal Water Pollution Control Act Amendments of 1972, which constituted a comprehensive legislative attempt "to restore and maintain the chemical, physical, and biological integrity of the Nation's waters." CWA § 101, 33 U.S.C. § 1251. This objective incorporated a broad, systemic view of the goal of maintaining and improving water quality: as the House Report on the legislation put it, "the word 'integrity' . . . refers to a condition in which the natural structure and function of ecosystems is [are] maintained." H.R. Rep. No. 92–911, p. 76 (1972). Protection of aquatic ecosystems, Congress recognized, demanded broad federal authority to control pollution, for "[w]ater moves in hydrologic cycles and it is essential that discharge of pollutants be controlled at the source." S. Rep. No. 92–414, p. 77 (1972), U.S. Code Cong. & Admin. News 1972, pp. 3668, 3742.

In keeping with these views, Congress chose to define the waters covered by the Act broadly. Although the Act prohibits discharges into "navigable waters," see CWA §§ 301(a), 404(a), 502(12), 33 U.S.C. §§ 1311(a), 1344(a), 1362(12), the Act's definition of "navigable waters" as "the waters of the United States" makes it clear that the term "navigable" as used in the Act is of limited import. In adopting this definition of "navigable waters," Congress evidently intended to repudiate limits that had been placed on federal regulation by earlier water pollution control statutes and to exercise its powers under the Commerce Clause to regulate at least some waters that would not be deemed "navigable" under the classical understanding of that term. See S. Conf. Rep. No. 92–1236, p. 144 (1972); 118 Cong. Rec. 33756–33757 (1972) (statement of Rep. Dingell).

Of course, it is one thing to recognize that Congress intended to allow regulation of waters that might not satisfy traditional tests of navigability; it is another to assert that Congress intended to abandon traditional notions of "waters" and include in that term "wetlands" as well. Nonetheless, the evident breadth of congressional concern for protection of water quality and aquatic ecosystems suggests that it is reasonable for the Corps to interpret the term "waters" to encompass wetlands adjacent to waters as more conventionally defined. Following the lead of the Environmental Protection Agency, see 38 Fed. Reg. 10834 (1973), the Corps has determined that wetlands adjacent to navigable waters do as a general matter play a key role in protecting and enhancing water quality:

The regulation of activities that cause water pollution cannot rely on . . . artificial lines . . . but must focus on all waters that together form the entire aquatic system. Water moves in hydrologic cycles, and the pollution of this part of the aquatic system, regardless of whether it is above or below an ordinary high water mark, or mean high tide line, will affect the water quality of the other waters within that aquatic system.

For this reason, the landward limit of Federal jurisdiction under Section 404 must include any adjacent wetlands that form the border of or are in reasonable proximity to other waters of the United States, as these wetlands are part of this aquatic system." 42 Fed.Reg. 37128 (1977).

We cannot say that the Corps' conclusion that adjacent wetlands are inseparably bound up with the "waters" of the United States—based as it is on the Corps' and EPA's technical expertise—is unreasonable. In view of the breadth of federal regulatory authority contemplated by the Act itself and the inherent difficulties of defining precise bounds to regulable waters, the Corps' ecological judgment about the relationship between waters and their adjacent wetlands provides an adequate basis for a legal judgment that adjacent wetlands may be defined as waters under the Act.

This holds true even for wetlands that are not the result of flooding or permeation by water having its source in adjacent bodies of open water. The Corps has concluded that wetlands may affect the water quality of adjacent lakes, rivers, and streams even when the waters of those bodies do not actually inundate the wetlands. For example, wetlands that are not flooded by adjacent waters may still tend to drain into those waters. In such circumstances, the Corps has concluded that wetlands may serve to filter and purify water draining into adjacent bodies of water, see 33 CFR § 320.4(b)(2)(vii) (1985), and to slow the flow of surface runoff into lakes, rivers, and streams and thus prevent flooding and erosion, see §§ 320.4(b)(2)(iv) and (v). In addition, adjacent wetlands may "serve significant natural biological functions, including food chain production, general habitat, and nesting, spawning, rearing and resting sites for aquatic . . . species." § 320.4(b)(2)(i). In short, the Corps has concluded that wetlands adjacent to lakes, rivers, streams, and other bodies of water may function as integral parts of the aquatic environment even when the moisture creating the wetlands does not find its source in the adjacent bodies of water. Again, we cannot say that the Corps' judgment on these matters is unreasonable, and we therefore conclude that a definition of "waters of the United States" encompassing all wetlands adjacent to other bodies of water over which the Corps has jurisdiction is a permissible interpretation of the Act. Because respondent's property is part of a wetland that actually abuts on a navigable waterway, respondent was required to have a permit in this case.[7]

NOTES

1. *Striking down the Migratory Bird Rule.* In *Riverside Bayview,* the Supreme Court upheld the portion of the EPA and Corps' regulations that asserted jurisdiction over "adjacent wetlands," commenting that the word "navigable" in the CWA was of "limited import." 474 U.S. at 133. Left unanswered was the question of whether "isolated wetlands" fell within the Clean Water Act's jurisdictional scope. The regulations claimed jurisdiction over:

> [W]aters such as intrastate lakes, rivers, streams (including intermittent streams), mudflats, sandflats, wetlands, sloughs, prairie potholes, wet meadows, playa lakes, or natural ponds, the use, degradation or destruction of which could affect interstate or foreign commerce. . . .

33 C.F.R. § 328.3(a)(3) (2014).

The Corps later elaborated on this definition in its so-called "Migratory Bird Rule," asserting jurisdiction over intrastate waters which "are or would be used as habitat by birds protected by Migratory Bird Treaties; or . . . by other migratory birds which cross state lines; or . . . [by] endangered species. . . ." 51 Fed. Reg. 41,206, 41,217 (Nov. 13, 1986).

The Supreme Court took up the legality of these rules in *Solid Waste Agency of Northern Cook County (SWANCC) v. United States Army Corps of Engineers,* 531 U.S. 159 (2001). Chief Justice Rehnquist, writing for the five-member majority, reasoned that even if the term "navigable" was of limited import, it could not be read completely out of the statute. *Id.* at 172. Thus, because the Migratory Bird Rule gave the word "navigable" no independent significance, it exceeded the Corps' Clean Water Act authority. *Id.* at 174.

2. *SWANCC's regulatory gap.* One environmental law scholar noted that the effect of the *SWANCC* decision "may be the most devastating judicial opinion affecting the environment ever." William Funk, *The Court, the Clean Water Act, and the Constitution:* SWANCC *and Beyond,* 31 Envtl. L. Rep. 10741, 10741 (2001). Because of *SWANCC,* the federal government apparently lost the ability to regulate the dredging and filling of isolated wetlands, resources that are extremely important to migratory birds. As a

---

[7] Of course, it may well be that not every adjacent wetland is of great importance to the environment of adjoining bodies of water. But the existence of such cases does not seriously undermine the Corps' decision to define all adjacent wetlands as "waters." If it is reasonable for the Corps to conclude that in the majority of cases, adjacent wetlands have significant effects on water quality and the aquatic ecosystem, its definition can stand. That the definition may include some wetlands that are not significantly intertwined with the ecosystem of adjacent waterways is of little moment, for where it appears that a wetland covered by the Corps' definition is in fact lacking in importance to the aquatic environment—or where its importance is outweighed by other values—the Corps may always allow development of the wetland for other uses simply by issuing a permit. See 33 CFR § 320.4(b)(4) (1985).

result, the burden of protecting these important resources shifted to the states.

Still, in *U.S. v. Deaton*, 332 F.3d 698 (4th Cir. 2003), the court upheld the assertion of 404 jurisdiction over a discharge into a wetland adjacent to a roadside ditch with intermittent flow over 30 miles from the Chesapeake Bay. Interestingly, under the Corps' proposed regulations, discussed below on pp. 234–235, federal jurisdiction would require persistent, not intermittent, flows in ditches that cannot be built wholly on uplands and must contribute to the flow of traditionally navigable waters. See 79 Fed. Reg. 22,187, 22,268–69 (Apr. 21, 2014) (proposed 40 C.F.R. § 230.3(t)(3) and (4)).

States have taken different approaches to filling the regulatory gap concerning isolated wetlands. Ohio, for example, has created its own program requiring a state permit for such wetlands. Ohio Rev. Code Ann. § 6111.021 (2001). Like federal 404 permits, the Ohio isolated wetland permit requires applicants to consider practicable alternatives and to include mitigation in permits to reduce unavoidable adverse effects. *Id.* § 6111.023. Similarly, Wisconsin also passed legislation in the wake of *SWANCC* to protect isolated wetlands, while Minnesota and Michigan already had such legislation. See C. Victor Pyle, III, *Isolated Wetlands Jurisprudence Post-SWANCC and Resulting Federal and State Attempts to Fill the Void*, 11 S.E. Envtl. L.J. 91, 101–02 (2002).

In contrast to the approach of creating of a new permit requirement, other states have simply adapted existing programs to protect wetlands. In South Carolina, for example, the Department of Health and Environmental Control (DHEC) responded to the *SWANCC* ruling by extending existing coastal zone management authority to protect isolated wetlands. *Spectre, LLC v. S. Carolina Dep't of Health & Envt'l Control*, 688 S.E.2d 844 (S.C. 2010). In *Spectre*, the DHEC denied a stormwater permit to fill isolated wetlands to a local developer on the ground that the permit conflicted with the state's policies under the coastal zone management plan. *Id.* at 845–46. The South Carolina Supreme Court ruled that although the policy to protect isolated wetlands was not put into a regulation subject to public notice and comment, the legislature intended the coastal zone management plan policies to be enforceable. *Id.* at 851. Thus, at least some states, through legislation, administrative rules, and adaptation of existing programs, have taken steps to protect isolated wetlands left vulnerable by *SWANCC*. Many others have not.

3. *The "significant nexus" test.* The Court in *Riverside Bayview* commented in a footnote that "[i]f it is reasonable for the Corps to conclude that in the majority of cases, adjacent wetlands have *significant effects* on water quality and the aquatic ecosystem, its definition can stand." 474 U.S. at 135 n. 9 (emphasis added). The *SWANCC* Court was the first to use the term "significant nexus" to describe the finding of jurisdiction in *Riverside Bayview*. 531 U.S. at 167. However, *SWANCC* distinguished *Riverside Bayview* on the ground that adjacent wetlands, unlike isolated wetlands,

have a "significant nexus" to traditionally navigable waters. The Court's use of "significant nexus" as a potential test, possibly derived from *Riverside Bayview's* "significant effects" language in footnote 9, would prove to be quite important the next time the Court took up the question of CWA jurisdiction, in *Rapanos v. United States*, considered below.

4.   *Wetlands, takings, and the public trust doctrine.* In a celebrated case, the Wisconsin Supreme Court in 1972 ruled that a landowner's property rights did not include the right to fill wetlands adjacent to a navigable lake because "[a]n owner of land has no absolute and unlimited right to change the essential natural character of his land . . . for a purpose for which it was unsuited in its natural state and which injures the rights of others." *Just v. Marinette County*, 201 N.W.2d 761, 768 (Wisc. 1972) (suggesting that "destroying the natural character of a swamp or a wetland so as to make that location available for human habitation" was not a reasonable use, although it might be an economical one to a landowner). In *Zealy v. City of Waukesha*, 548 N.W.2d 528 (Wisc. 1996), the court cited *Just* in the course of upholding a rezoning of land that established a conservancy district protecting wetlands, despite a drastic decline in market value due to lost development rights. More recently, the same court in *Rock-Koshkonong Lake Dist. v. State Dep't of Natural Res.*, 833 N.W.2d 800 (Wisc. 2013), limited the scope of the state's public trust doctrine to navigable waters, interpreting the *Just* decision as a police power case. The exercise of the police power, the court emphasized, was limited by the constitution's takings clause, whereas the public trust doctrine is not. *Id.* at 824. What does this distinction between the police power and the public trust doctrine mean for wetlands protection in Wisconsin?

RAPANOS V. UNITED STATES

Supreme Court of the United States
547 U.S. 715 (2006)

[In these consolidated cases, the Court considered whether four wetlands, three belonging to the Rapanos and one belonging to the Carabells, were jurisdictional "waters of the United States" under the Clean Water Act (CWA), and thus subject to federal permit requirements. In 1989, John Rapanos filled three wetlands on his land for development. All of these wetlands had surface or drainage connections to navigable-in-fact waters of the United States. The Corps informed Rapanos that his saturated fields were "waters of the United States," the filling of which required a permit under section 404 of the CWA. The district court ruled that the wetlands were subject to the federal statute because they were "adjacent wetlands," similar to those involved in *Riverside Bayview*. The Sixth Circuit affirmed but on the ground that there was a hydrological connection between the wetlands and adjacent tributaries to navigable waters.

The other wetland, belonging to the Carabells, was separated from a man-made drainage ditch by a berm. Although the berm did not allow passage of water through it, there was occasional overflow into the ditch that drained into a navigable-in-fact water of the United States. The district court ruled that there was federal jurisdiction because the wetland was adjacent to navigable water and had a significant nexus to it. The Sixth Circuit again affirmed, holding that the Carabell wetland was "adjacent" to navigable waters.]

Justice Scalia announced the judgment of the Court and delivered an opinion, in which The Chief Justice [Roberts], Justice Thomas, and Justice Alito join.

[The plurality began with a scathing criticism of the Corps' expansion of regulatory authority under the CWA "without any change in the government statute." In particular, the plurality noted the immense cost in time and money for applicants to obtain permits and likened the Corps to an "enlightened despot."]

* * *

For a century prior to the CWA, we had interpreted the phrase "navigable waters of the United States" in the Act's predecessor statutes to refer to interstate waters that are "navigable in fact" or readily susceptible of being rendered so. *The Daniel Ball*, 77 U.S. 557, 563 (1870); see also *United States v. Appalachian Elec. Power Co.*, 311 U.S. 377, 406 (1940). . . .

The Corps' current regulations interpret "the waters of the United States" to include, in addition to traditional interstate navigable waters, 33 CFR § 328.3(a)(1) (2004), "[a]ll interstate waters including interstate wetlands," § 328.3(a)(2); "[a]ll other waters such as intrastate lakes, rivers, streams (including intermittent streams), mudflats, sandflats, wetlands, sloughs, prairie potholes, wet meadows, playa lakes, or natural ponds, the use, degradation or destruction of which could affect interstate or foreign commerce," § 328.3(a)(3); "[t]ributaries of [such] waters," § 328.3(a)(5); and "[w]etlands adjacent to [such] waters [and tributaries] (other than waters that are themselves wetlands)," § 328.3(a)(7). The regulation defines "adjacent" wetlands as those "bordering, contiguous [to], or neighboring" waters of the United States. § 328.3(c). It specifically provides that "[w]etlands separated from other waters of the United States by man-made dikes or barriers, natural river berms, beach dunes and the like are 'adjacent wetlands.' " *Id.*

* * *

Following our decision in *SWANCC*, the Corps did not significantly revise its theory of federal jurisdiction under § 1344(a). The Corps provided notice of a proposed rulemaking in light of *SWANCC*, 68 Fed. Reg. 1991 (2003), but ultimately did not amend its published regulations. Because *SWANCC* did not directly address tributaries, the Corps notified its field staff that they "should continue to assert jurisdiction over traditional navigable waters . . . and, generally speaking, their tributary systems (and adjacent wetlands)." 68 Fed. Reg. at 1998. In addition, because *SWANCC* did not overrule *Riverside Bayview,* the Corps continues to assert jurisdiction over waters "neighboring" traditional navigable waters and their tributaries. 68 Fed. Reg. at 1997 (quoting 33 CFR § 328.3(c) (2002)).

* * *

We need not decide the precise extent to which the qualifiers "navigable" and "of the United States" restrict the coverage of the Act. Whatever the scope of these qualifiers, the CWA authorizes federal jurisdiction only over "waters." 33 U.S.C. § 1362(7). The only natural definition of the term "waters," our prior and subsequent judicial constructions of it, clear evidence from other provisions of the statute, and this Court's canons of construction all confirm that "the waters of the United States" in § 1362(7) cannot bear the expansive meaning that the Corps would give it.

The Corps' expansive approach might be arguable if the CWA defined "navigable waters" as "water[s] of the United States." But "the waters of the United States" is something else. The use of the definite article ("the") and the plural number ("waters") shows plainly that § 1362(7) does not refer to water in general. In this form, "the waters" refers more narrowly to water "[a]s found in streams and bodies forming geographical features such as oceans, rivers, [and] lakes," or "the flowing or moving masses, as of waves or floods, making up such streams or bodies." Webster's New International Dictionary 2882 (2d ed. 1954) (hereinafter Webster's Second). On this definition, "the waters of the United States" include only relatively permanent, standing or flowing bodies of water. The definition refers to water as found in "streams," "oceans," "rivers," "lakes," and "bodies" of water "forming geographical features." *Id.* All of these terms connote continuously present, fixed bodies of water, as opposed to ordinarily dry channels through which water occasionally or intermittently flows. Even the least substantial of the definition's terms, namely, "streams," connotes a continuous flow of water in a permanent channel—especially when used in company with other terms such as "rivers," "lakes," and "oceans." None of these terms encompasses transitory puddles or ephemeral flows of water.

* * *

Our subsequent interpretation of the phrase "the waters of the United States" in the CWA likewise confirms this limitation of its scope. In *Riverside Bayview,* we stated that the phrase in the Act referred primarily to "rivers, streams, and other *hydrographic features more conventionally identifiable as 'waters'* " than the wetlands adjacent to such features. 474 U.S. at 131 (emphasis added). We thus echoed the dictionary definition of "waters" as referring to "streams and bodies *forming geographical features* such as oceans, rivers, [and] lakes." Webster's Second 2882 (emphasis added). Though we upheld in that case the inclusion of wetlands abutting such a "hydrographic featur[e]"— principally due to the difficulty of drawing any clear boundary between the two, see 474 U.S. at 132—nowhere did we suggest that "the waters of the United States" should be expanded to include, in their own right, entities other than "hydrographic features more conventionally identifiable as 'waters,' " *id.* at 131. Likewise, in both *Riverside Bayview* and *SWANCC*, we repeatedly described the "navigable waters" covered by the Act as "open water" and "open waters." See *Riverside Bayview,* at 132, and n. 8, 134; *SWANCC,* at 167, 172. Under no rational interpretation are typically dry channels described as "*open* waters."

* * *

[J]ust as we noted in *SWANCC*, the Corps' interpretation stretches the outer limits of Congress's commerce power and raises difficult questions about the ultimate scope of that power. See 531 U.S. at 173. (In developing the current regulations, the Corps consciously sought to extend its authority to the farthest reaches of the commerce power. See 42 Fed. Reg. 37,127 (1977).) Even if the term "the waters of the United States" were ambiguous as applied to channels that sometimes host ephemeral flows of water (which it is not), we would expect a clearer statement from Congress to authorize an agency theory of jurisdiction that presses the envelope of constitutional validity. See *Edward J. DeBartolo Corp. v. Florida Gulf Coast Building & Constr. Trades Council,* 485 U.S. 568, 575 (1988).

In sum, on its only plausible interpretation, the phrase "the waters of the United States" includes only those relatively permanent, standing or continuously flowing bodies of water "forming geographic features" that are described in ordinary parlance as "streams[,] . . . oceans, rivers, [and] lakes." See Webster's Second 2882. The phrase does not include channels through which water flows intermittently or ephemerally, or channels that periodically provide drainage for rainfall. The Corps' expansive interpretation of the "the waters of the United States" is thus not "based on a permissible construction of the statute." *Chevron U.S.A. Inc. v. Natural Resources Defense Council, Inc.,* 467 U.S. 837, 843 (1984).

IV

* * *

We . . . address in this Part whether a wetland may be considered "adjacent to" remote "waters of the United States," because of a mere hydrologic connection to them.

In *Riverside Bayview,* we noted the textual difficulty in including "wetlands" as a subset of "waters": "On a purely linguistic level, it may appear unreasonable to classify 'lands,' wet or otherwise, as 'waters.' " 474 U.S. at 132. We acknowledged, however, that there was an inherent ambiguity in drawing the boundaries of any "waters". . . .

* * *

Because of this inherent ambiguity, we deferred to the agency's inclusion of wetlands "actually abut[ting]" traditional navigable waters: "Faced with such a problem of defining the bounds of its regulatory authority," we held the agency could reasonably conclude that a wetland that "adjoin[ed]" waters of the United States is itself a part of those waters. *Id.* at 132, 135, and n. 9. The difficulty of delineating the boundary between water and land was central to our reasoning in the case: "In view of the breadth of federal regulatory authority contemplated by the Act itself and *the inherent difficulties of defining precise bounds to regulable waters,* the Corps' ecological judgment about the relationship between waters and their adjacent wetlands provides an adequate basis for a legal judgment that adjacent wetlands may be defined as waters under the Act." *Id.* at 134 (emphasis added).

When we characterized the holding of *Riverside Bayview* in *SWANCC,* we referred to the close connection between waters and the wetlands that they gradually blend into: "It was the *significant nexus* between the wetlands and 'navigable waters' that informed our reading of the CWA in *Riverside Bayview Homes.*" 531 U.S. at 167 (emphasis added). In particular, *SWANCC* rejected the notion that the ecological considerations upon which the Corps relied in *Riverside Bayview*—and upon which the dissent repeatedly relies today, . . .—provided an *independent* basis for including entities like "wetlands" (or "ephemeral streams") within the phrase "the waters of the United States." *SWANCC* found such ecological considerations irrelevant to the question whether physically isolated waters come within the Corps' jurisdiction. It thus confirmed that *Riverside Bayview* rested upon the inherent ambiguity in defining where water ends and abutting ("adjacent") wetlands begin, permitting the Corps' reliance on ecological considerations *only to resolve that ambiguity* in favor of treating all abutting wetlands as waters. Isolated ponds were not "waters of the United States" in their own right, see 531 U.S. at 167, and presented no boundary-drawing problem that would have justified the invocation of ecological factors to treat them as such.

Therefore, *only* those wetlands with a continuous surface connection to bodies that are "waters of the United States" in their own right, so that there is no clear demarcation between "waters" and wetlands, are "adjacent to" such waters and covered by the Act. Wetlands with only an intermittent, physically remote hydrologic connection to "waters of the United States" do not implicate the boundary-drawing problem of *Riverside Bayview,* and thus lack the necessary connection to covered waters that we described as a "significant nexus" in *SWANCC.* 531 U.S. at 167. Thus, establishing that wetlands such as those at the Rapanos and Carabell sites are covered by the Act requires two findings: first, that the adjacent channel contains a "wate[r] of the United States," (*i.e.,* a relatively permanent body of water connected to traditional interstate navigable waters); and second, that the wetland has a continuous surface connection with that water, making it difficult to determine where the "water" ends and the "wetland" begins.

* * *

KENNEDY, J., concurring in the judgment.

* * *

Contrary to the plurality's description, wetlands are not simply moist patches of earth. They are defined as "those areas that are inundated or saturated by surface or ground water at a frequency and duration sufficient to support, and that under normal circumstances do support, a prevalence of vegetation typically adapted for life in saturated soil conditions. Wetlands generally include swamps, marshes, bogs, and similar areas." § 328.3(b). The Corps' Wetlands Delineation Manual, including over 100 pages of technical guidance for Corps officers, interprets this definition of wetlands to require: (1) prevalence of plant species typically adapted to saturated soil conditions, determined in accordance with the United States Fish and Wildlife Service's National List of Plant Species that Occur in Wetlands; (2) hydric soil, meaning soil that is saturated, flooded, or ponded for sufficient time during the growing season to become anaerobic, or lacking in oxygen, in the upper part; and (3) wetland hydrology, a term generally requiring continuous inundation or saturation to the surface during at least five percent of the growing season in most years. . . . Under the Corps' regulations, wetlands are adjacent to tributaries, and thus covered by the Act, even if they are "separated from other waters of the United States by man-made dikes or barriers, natural river berms, beach dunes and the like." § 328.3(c).

* * *

The plurality's opinion begins from a correct premise. As the plurality points out, and as *Riverside Bayview* holds, in enacting the Clean Water Act Congress intended to regulate at least some waters that are not navigable in the traditional sense. *Riverside Bayview* at 133; see also *SWANCC* at 167. This conclusion is supported by "the evident breadth of congressional concern for protection of water quality and aquatic ecosystems." *Riverside Bayview* at 133; see also *Milwaukee v. Illinois,* 451 U.S. 304, 318 (1981) (describing the Act as "an all-encompassing program of water pollution regulation"). It is further compelled by statutory text, for the text is explicit in extending the coverage of the Act to some nonnavigable waters. In a provision allowing States to assume some regulatory functions of the Corps (an option Michigan has exercised), the Act limits States to issuing permits for:

> the discharge of dredged or fill material into the navigable waters (other than those waters which are presently used, or are susceptible to use in their natural condition or by reasonable improvement as a means to transport interstate or foreign commerce shoreward to their ordinary high water mark, including all waters which are subject to the ebb and flow of the tide shoreward to their ordinary high water mark, or mean higher high water mark on the west coast, including wetlands adjacent thereto) within its jurisdiction. 33 U.S.C. § 1344(g)(1).

Were there no Clean Water Act "navigable waters" apart from waters "presently used" or "susceptible to use" in interstate commerce, the "other than" clause, which begins the long parenthetical statement, would overtake the delegation of authority the provision makes at the outset. Congress, it follows, must have intended a broader meaning for navigable waters. The mention of wetlands in the "other than" clause, moreover, makes plain that at least some wetlands fall within the scope of the term "navigable waters." See *Riverside Bayview,* at 138–39, & n. 11.

From this reasonable beginning the plurality proceeds to impose two limitations on the Act; but these limitations, it is here submitted, are without support in the language and purposes of the Act or in our cases interpreting it. . . .

The plurality's first requirement—permanent standing water or continuous flow, at least for a period of "some months,"—makes little practical sense in a statute concerned with downstream water quality. The merest trickle, if continuous, would count as a "water" subject to federal regulation, while torrents thundering at irregular intervals through otherwise dry channels would not. Though the plurality seems to presume that such irregular flows are too insignificant to be of concern in a statute focused on "waters," that may not always be true. Areas in the western parts of the Nation provide some examples. The Los Angeles River, for instance, ordinarily carries only a trickle of water and often looks more like a dry roadway than a river. . . . Yet it periodically releases water volumes so powerful and destructive that it has been encased in concrete and steel over a length of some 50 miles. Though this particular waterway might satisfy the plurality's test, it is illustrative of what often-dry watercourses can become when rain waters flow. . . .

To be sure, Congress could draw a line to exclude irregular waterways, but nothing in the statute suggests it has done so. Quite the opposite, a full reading of the dictionary definition precludes the plurality's emphasis on permanence: The term "waters" may mean "flood or inundation," Webster's Second 2882, events that are impermanent by definition. Thus, although of course the Act's use of the adjective "navigable" indicates a focus on waterways rather than floods, Congress' use of "waters" instead of "water," does not necessarily carry the connotation of "relatively permanent, standing or flowing bodies of water". (And contrary to the plurality's suggestion, there is no indication in the dictionary that the "flood or inundation" definition is limited to poetry.) In any event, even granting the plurality's preferred definition— that "waters" means "water '[a]s found in streams and bodies forming geographical features such as oceans, rivers, [and] lakes,' " (quoting Webster's Second, at 2882)—the dissent is correct to observe that an intermittent flow can constitute a stream, in the sense of "[a] current or course of water or other fluid, flowing on the earth," (quoting Webster's Second at 2493), while it is flowing. . . . It follows that the Corps can reasonably interpret the Act to cover the paths of such impermanent streams.

* * *

The plurality's second limitation—exclusion of wetlands lacking a continuous surface connection to other jurisdictional waters—is also unpersuasive. To begin with, the plurality is wrong to suggest that wetlands are *indistinguishable* from waters to which they bear a surface connection. Even if the precise boundary may be imprecise, a bog or swamp is different from a river. The question is what circumstances permit a bog, swamp, or other nonnavigable wetland to constitute a "navigable water" under the Act—as § 1344(g)(1), if nothing else, indicates is sometimes possible. *Riverside Bayview* addressed that question and its answer is inconsistent with the plurality's theory. There, in upholding the Corps' authority to regulate "wetlands adjacent to other bodies of water over which the Corps has jurisdiction," the Court deemed it irrelevant whether "the moisture creating the wetlands . . . find[s] its source in the adjacent bodies of water." 474 U.S. at 135. The Court further observed that adjacency could serve as a valid basis for regulation even as to "wetlands that are not significantly intertwined with the ecosystem of adjacent waterways." *Id.* at 135, n. 9. "If it is reasonable," the Court explained, "for the Corps to conclude that in the majority of cases, adjacent wetlands have significant effects on water quality and the aquatic ecosystem, its definition can stand." *Id.*

* * *

Much the same evidence should permit the establishment of a significant nexus with navigable-in-fact waters, particularly if supplemented by further evidence about the significance of the tributaries to which the wetlands are connected. The Court of Appeals, however, though recognizing that under *SWANCC* such a nexus was required for jurisdiction, held that a significant nexus "can be satisfied by the presence of a hydrologic connection." 376 F.3d at 639. Absent some measure of the significance of the connection for downstream water quality, this standard was too uncertain. Under the analysis described earlier, mere hydrologic connection should not suffice in all cases; the connection may be too insubstantial for the hydrologic linkage to establish the required nexus with navigable waters as traditionally understood. In my view this case should be remanded so that the District Court may reconsider the evidence in light of the appropriate standard. See, e.g., *Pullman-Standard v. Swint,* 456 U.S. 273, 291 (1982) ("When an appellate court discerns that a district court has failed to make a finding because of an erroneous view of the law, the usual rule is that there should be a remand for further proceedings to permit the trial court to make the missing findings").

Carabell

[Justice Kennedy briefly described the evidence establishing that the Carabell wetland was adjacent to a tributary.]

* * *

The Court of Appeals, considering the *Carabell* case after its *Rapanos* decision, framed the inquiry in terms of whether hydrologic connection is required to establish a significant nexus. The court held that it is not, and that much of its holding is correct. Given the role wetlands play in pollutant filtering, flood control, and runoff storage, it may well be the absence of hydrologic connection (in the sense of interchange of waters) that shows the wetlands' significance for the aquatic system. In the administrative decision under review, however, the Corps based its jurisdiction solely on the wetlands' adjacency to the ditch opposite the berm on the property's edge. As explained earlier, mere adjacency to a tributary of this sort is insufficient; a similar ditch could just as well be located many miles from any navigable-in-fact water and carry only insubstantial flow toward it. A more specific inquiry, based on the significant nexus standard, is therefore necessary. Thus, a remand is again required to permit application of the appropriate legal standard. See, *e.g., INS v. Orlando Ventura,* 537 U.S. 12, 16 (2002) *(per curiam)* ("Generally speaking, a court of appeals should remand a case to an agency for decision of a matter that statutes place primarily in agency hands").

* * *

In these consolidated cases I would vacate the judgments of the Court of Appeals and remand for consideration whether the specific wetlands at issue possess a significant nexus with navigable waters.

* * *

NOTES

1.   *The* Rapanos *plurality.* Notice how closely the plurality opinion parsed the words of the statute in an apparent effort to ascertain congressional intent. The opinion made no mention of the statute's legislative history that suggested courts should interpret the statute's jurisdictional scope as broadly as constitutionally possible. See above pp. 217–218 (citing the legislative history). The antipathy of Justice Scalia, the author of the plurality, to legislative history is well known. See, e.g. Arthur Stock, *Justice Scalia's Use of Sources in Statutory and Constitutional Interpretation: How Congress Always Loses*, 1990 Duke L.J. 160, 161–71 (1990).

2.   *The Roberts concurrence.* Chief Justice Roberts wrote a concurrence in which he criticized the Corps for failing to undertake a rulemaking in the wake of the *SWANCC* decision and observing that the effect of the *Rapanos* opinion was likely to increase uncertainty about the jurisdictional reach of the Clean Water Act. 547 U.S. at 757–58. In 2014, the Corps and EPA seemed to follow the Chief Justice's suggestion by proposing new jurisdictional regulations. See note 6 below.

3.   *The* Rapanos *dissent.* A four-member dissent would have affirmed Clean Water Act jurisdiction over the contested wetlands as a reasonable interpretation of the term "waters of the United States" by the Corps. In a separate dissent, Justice Breyer thought that because the term is ambiguous, and because "Congress intended [the Corps] to make the complex technical judgments that lie at the heart of [*Rapanos*]," the Court ought to have deferred to the Corps under *Chevron* step two. *Id.* at 811–12.

4.   *The* Rapanos *environmental legacy.* One of the chief effects of the Supreme Court narrowing of the Clean Water Act's jurisdiction may be visited upon the Upper Midwest's so-called "prairie potholes"—wetlands that provide important habitat for migratory waterfowl—where millions of ducks, geese and migratory birds find sanctuary in shallow wetlands that stretch from Montana to portions of Minnesota and Iowa. According to a 2014 U.S. Fish and Wildlife Service report, wetlands in the region declined by an estimated 74,340 acres between 1997 and 2009—an average annual net loss of 6,200 acres. Roughly 75 percent of all North American waterfowl use the region for breeding and nesting, earning it the nickname of "America's duck factory," according to the report. U.S. Fish and Wildlife Serv., *Status and*

Trends of Prairie Wetlands in the United States 1997 to 2009, available at http://www.fws.gov/wetlands/Documents/Status-and-Trends-of-Prairie–Wetlands-in-the-United–States–1997–to–2009.pdf.

5. *The confused* Rapanos *legal legacy.* The plurality opinion in *Rapanos* created considerable confusion as to which test controls the Corps' jurisdiction over wetlands. The Seventh, Ninth, and Eleventh Circuits all found jurisdiction where Justice Kennedy's "significant nexus" test was met. *United States v. Gerke Excavating, Inc.,* 464 F.3d 723 (7th Cir. 2006); *Northern California River Watch v. City of Healdsburg,* 496 F.3d 993 (9th Cir. 2007); *United States v. Robison,* 505 F.3d 1208 (11th Cir. 2007). By contrast, the First, Third, and Eighth Circuits decided that there is federal jurisdiction if either the plurality's *or* Justice Kennedy's test is met. *United States v. Johnson,* 467 F.3d 56 (1st Cir. 2006); *United States v. Donovan,* 661 F.3d 174 (3rd Cir. 2011); *United States v. Bailey,* 571 F.3d 791 (8th Cir. 2009).

6. *The 2014 proposed regulations.* In 2008, the Corps issued a memorandum to clarify its jurisdiction in the wake of these increasingly muddied jurisprudential waters.[8] However, the guidance failed to produce much regulatory certainty. In his concurrence in *Sackett v. EPA*, 132 S.Ct. 1367, 1375 (2012), Justice Alito criticized the guidance, stating, "far from producing clarity and predictability, the agency's latest informal guidance advises property owners that many jurisdictional determinations concerning wetlands can only be made on a case-by-case basis by EPA field staff." Moreover, since it was a non-binding guidance document, courts continue to use the muddled *Rapanos* decision rather than the guidance to determine jurisdiction. See *Precon Dev. Corp., Inc. v. U.S. Army Corps of Engineers*, 633 F.3d 278 (4th Cir. 2011).

In response to the ongoing post-*Rapanos* uncertainty, EPA and the Corps proposed changes to their rule defining "waters of the United States." Definition of "Waters of the United States" Under the Clean Water Act, 79 Fed. Reg. 22,188 (proposed Apr. 21, 2014) (amending 33 C.F.R. pt. 328, 40 C.F.R. pt. 230). The proposed rule would attempt to increase regulatory certainty and decrease potential litigation by cutting down on the amount of time-consuming and costly case-by-case "significant nexus" determinations. *Id.* at 22,190. The rule would accomplish these goals by stating that all

---

[8]   In its guidance memo, the Corps essentially divided waters into three categories: 1) those over which it would always assert jurisdiction; 2) those over which it would not; and 3) those to which it would apply a case-by-case determination based on the significant nexus test. Clearly within CWA jurisdiction, according to the memo, are traditionally navigable waters and wetlands adjacent to them, relatively permanent non-navigable tributaries of navigable waters, and wetlands that directly abut such tributaries. On the other hand, swales, erosional features, and ditches not carrying a relatively permanent flow of water are not jurisdictional under the guidance, despite the fact that Justice Kennedy's significant nexus test would seem to allow jurisdiction under some circumstances. Finally, the Corps asserted jurisdiction on a case-by-case basis over non-permanent non-navigable tributaries and the wetlands adjacent to them, and wetlands adjacent (but not abutting) relatively permanent non-navigable tributaries. For these case-by-case determinations, the Corps stated it would apply a significant nexus test, determining if tributaries and wetlands "significantly affect the chemical, physical, and biological integrity of downstream navigable waters."

tributaries (including those that are tributary only to other tributaries) and all waters adjacent to them (whether they directly abut or not) have a significant nexus to navigable waters, and therefore are jurisdictional. *Id.* at 22,193. The rationale is that adjacent waters function in the aggregate with other adjacent waters and tributaries as a system that forms a significant nexus with downstream traditional navigable waters. *Id.* at 22,196.

The proposed rule would also clarify, for the first time, that "adjacent" means (by way of the definition of "neighboring") "within the riparian area or floodplain of [a navigable water or tributary], or waters with a surface or shallow subsurface hydrologic connection . . . to such a jurisdictional water." *Id.* at 22,207. Although "hydrologic connection" is not a new test, the floodplain concept is relatively new, and because the proposed rule would commit application of the term "floodplain" to the agency's best professional judgment, the agencies appear free to interpret that "floodplain" would mean the one-year floodplain, the 1,000-year floodplain, or anything in between.

In contrast to the categorical inclusion of adjacent wetlands within CWA jurisdiction, under the proposed rule, the Corps and EPA would continue to evaluate isolated wetlands on a case-by-case basis using the significant nexus test. *Id.* at 22,223. However, the proposed rule's use of the concept of aggregation could result in an expansion of jurisdiction to more isolated wetlands than were previously jurisdictional, since aggregation allows the Corps and EPA to evaluate the effect of a series of isolated wetlands instead of a single one. Groundwater would remain outside the scope of Clean Water Act jurisdiction under the proposed rule.

On September 9, 2014, the House of Representatives voted 262–152 to block EPA's proposed jurisdictional rule from taking effect (H.R. 5078), but the Senate adjourned without taking action. Less than a month after the House vote, EPA's Scientific Advisory Board backed the agency's assertion of jurisdiction over adjacent waters but criticized the proposed rule for not going far enough in asserting jurisdiction over isolated waters and groundwater. Anne Snider, *EPA Science Advisors Back Contentious Rule Proposal*, Energy & Environmental Policy News (Sept. 30, 2014).

7.   *404 individual permits.* Assuming the Corps has jurisdiction over a particular wetland, it may issue permits to allow discharges of dredged or fill materials on an individual or general (applied to a category of activities) basis. 33 U.S.C. § 1344(a).[9] In order to issue a permit, the Corps must determine that the permit: (a) is in the public interest, and (b) that the permit meets EPA guidelines under § 404(b)(1). 33 C.F.R § 320.4; 33 U.S.C. § 1344(b)(1).

a.   *The Corps' "public interest requirement."* The Corps imposed on itself a requirement that the "benefits which reasonably may be expected to

---

[9]   There is a statutory exception for "normal farming, silviculture, and ranching activities." 33 U.S.C. 1344(f)(1)(A), discussed in note 8 below. However, the exception does not apply to "deep ripping" activities to convert land to farmland. *Borden Ranch v. U.S. Army Corps of Engineers*, 261 F.3d 810 (9th Cir. 2001), *aff'd* 537 U.S. 99 (2002).

accrue from the proposal must be balanced against its reasonably foreseeable detriments." 33 C.F.R § 320.4(a)(1). The Corps' rule lists a number of factors it must take into account when evaluating whether a permit is in the public interest. *Id.* Further, the rule allows the Corps to look not only at direct effects of a project, but also its indirect and cumulative effects, giving the agency broad discretion to deny permits based on the public interest. *Gouger v. U.S. Army Corps of Engineers*, 779 F.Supp.2d 588, 614 (S.D. Tex. 2011).

b.   *EPA's 404(b)(1) guidelines.* Separate from the "public interest" requirement, the Corps must apply guidelines established by the EPA. 33 U.S.C. § 1344(b)(1); see 40 C.F.R. § 230.10. First, EPA requires a permit denial "if there is a practicable alternative" available that meets the primary purpose of the project and is "capable of being done" after taking cost into account. *Id.* § 230.10(a). If the project is not dependent on water, the regulation creates a rebuttable presumption that there is in fact a practicable alternative available. *Id.* § 230.10(a)(3). Second, the Corps may not issue a permit if it will violate a water quality standard or result in "jeopardy" or the destruction/adverse modification of critical habitat under the Endangered Species Act. *Id.* § 230.10(b). Third, "no discharge of dredged or fill material shall be permitted which will cause or contribute to significant degradation of the waters of the United States." *Id.* § 230.10(c). Finally, Corps permits must require that the permittee mitigate potential adverse effects of a project. *Id.* § 230.10(d) (see note 12 below on mitigation).

In 2014, a unanimous D.C. Circuit upheld EPA's authority under its § 404(b) authority to establish a special process to screen proposed mountaintop mining operations; the process identified mining operations likely to damage waterways and crafted permit terms that states could use, when authorizing the mining, to help protect water quality. The court decided that the guidance was not final agency action reviewable by courts until there was a permit denial. *Nat'l Mining Ass'n v. McCarthy,* 758 F.3d 243 (D.C. Cir. 2014).

c.   *EPA's veto authority.* Section 404(c) of the CWA gives EPA the authority to veto Corps-issued permits that would have "an unacceptable adverse effect on municipal water supplies, shellfish beds and fishery areas (including spawning and breeding areas), wildlife, or recreational areas." 33 U.S.C. § 1344(c). Although EPA has only exercised this veto power around a dozen times in forty years, it remains controversial. For example, a veto of a dam and reservoir in Virginia provoked a court challenge that produced two district court and two Fourth Circuit opinions, culminating in an affirmance of the EPA veto. *James City County, Va. v. EPA*, 12 F.3d 1330 (4th Cir. 1993) (upholding the permit on "unacceptable adverse environmental effects" grounds after earlier rejecting the veto due to a lack of evidence that the project proponent had no practicable alternatives).

A recent 404(c) case concerned when during the permit process EPA may exercise its veto authority. In West Virginia, the Corps issued a permit to a mining company (which EPA initially declined to veto) allowing a fill discharge into several streams as part of the company's mountaintop mining operation. In 2009, a full four years after the Corps issued the permit, EPA exercised its veto power, finding an unacceptable impact on downstream water quality. The district court decided that EPA lacked the authority to a veto a permit that the Corps had issued. *Mingo Logan Coal Co. Inc. v. U.S. EPA*, 850 F.Supp.2d 133, 134 (D.D.C. 2012), but the D.C. Circuit reversed, concluding that EPA's authority to retroactively veto permits was unambiguously authorized by the statute:

> Section 404 imposes no temporal limit on the Administrator's authority to withdraw the Corps's specification but instead expressly empowers him to prohibit, restrict or withdraw the specification *"whenever"* he makes a determination that the statutory "unacceptable adverse effect" will result. 33 U.S.C. § 1344(c) (emphasis added). Using the expansive conjunction "whenever," the Congress made plain its intent to grant the Administrator authority to prohibit/deny/restrict/withdraw a specification at *any* time. See 20 *Oxford English Dictionary* 210 (2d ed. 1989) (defining "whenever," used in "a qualifying (conditional) clause," as: "At whatever time, no matter when."). Thus, the unambiguous language of subsection 404(c) manifests the Congress's intent to confer on EPA a broad veto power extending beyond the permit issuance. This construction is further buttressed by subsection 404(c)'s authorization of a "withdrawal" which, as EPA notes, is "a term of retrospective application." EPA can *withdraw* a specification only after it has been made. See 20 *Oxford English Dictionary* 449 (2d ed. 1989) (defining "withdraw" as "[t]o take back or away (something that has been given, granted, allowed, possessed, enjoyed, or experienced)"). Moreover, because the Corps often specifies final disposal sites in the permit itself—at least it did here, see Spruce Mine Permit at 1 ("You are authorized to perform work in accordance with the terms and conditions *specified* below. . . .") (emphasis added)—EPA's power to withdraw can *only* be exercised post-permit. Mingo Logan's reading of the statute would eliminate EPA's express statutory right to withdraw a specification and thereby render subsection 404(c)'s parenthetical "withdrawal" language superfluous—a result to be avoided. See *Corley v. United States,* 556 U.S. 303, 314 (2009) (applying "one of the most basic interpretative canons, that a statute should be construed so that effect is given to all its provisions, so that no part will be inoperative or superfluous, void or insignificant").

*Mingo Logan v. U.S.E.P.A,*714 F.3d 608, 613 (D.C. Cir. 2013).

Although the *Mingo* court focused on retroactive veto power, it also stated that the word "whenever" imposes "no temporal limit," leaving open the question of whether EPA could also exercise its veto authority preemptively. The question of the validity of a preemptive veto is of particular importance concerning the Pebble Mine Project, an enormous proposed gold and copper mine in the Bristol Bay region of Alaska. On February 28, 2014, EPA announced it was initiating the process to veto the project, even though there has been no permit application filed yet for the project. U.S. Envtl. Prot. Agency, *Proposed Determination of the U.S. Environmental Protection Agency Region 10 Pursuant to Section 404(c) of the Clean Water Act: Pebble Deposit Area, Southwest Alaska* (July 2014), available at http://www2.epa.gov/sites/production/files/2014–07/documents/ pebble_pd_071714_final.pdf. If this 404(c) action is challenged, EPA will likely rely on the court's reasoning in *Mingo* to say that the lack of "temporal limit" extends to pre-permit projects, just as it does to post-permit projects.

8. *The "normal farming" exemption.* Section 404(f)(l)(A) of the Clean Water Act, 33 U.S.C. § 1344(f)(1)(A), exempts from permit requirements discharges associated with normal farming, silviculture, and ranching activities into waters of the United States, including wetlands. It has never been very clear how expansive an exemption Congress intended. In March 2014, EPA and the Corps issued an interpretive rule that listed fifty-five specific conservation measures that qualified for the exemption if executed to the standards set by the Department of Agriculture's Natural Resources Conservation Service, see Memorandum of Understanding, http://www2.epa. gov/sites/production/files/2014–03/documents/ interagency_mou_404f_ir_signed.pdf (Mar. 25, 2014). Because the list includes practices that currently do not require permits as well as those that do, it created widespread confusion and opposition among the regulated community, which was concerned that the federal agencies were narrowing the scope of the statutory exemption. Congress included the Agricultural Conservation Flexibility Act of 2014 (H.R 5071, 113th Congress) in its 2014 budget bill requiring EPA and the Corps to withdraw the guidance.

9. *404 general permits.* The 404 program encompasses thousands of small discharges, posing a challenge for overstrapped regulators. In order to accommodate the numbers, section 404(e) of the statute, 33 U.S.C. § 1344(e), authorizes the Corps to issue general permits on a nationwide (via regulation) or regional basis (through Corps district or regional offices) if they have minimal individual and cumulative adverse environmental effects. General permits can be issued for a period of no more than five years. Nationwide general permits, of which there are fifty, authorize roughly 50,000 nationwide reported activities annually, plus approximately 30,000 activities annually that do not require reporting. Nationwide permits may be revoked in a particular area by local Corps officials. See U.S. Army Corps of Engineers, *Fact Sheet on Nationwide Permit Reissuance* (Feb. 15, 2012), available at http://www.usace.army.mil/Portals/2/docs/civilworks/nwp/ NWP2012_factsheet_15feb2012.pdf.

10. *Administrative enforcement.* If EPA or the Corps determines that someone has violated the CWA, the agency has two options: (1) issue a compliance order, or (2) initiate a civil enforcement action under § 309(a)(3) of the statute. The compliance order had been a powerful tool for EPA until the Supreme Court decided in *Sackett v. EPA* that such orders are subject to

judicial review. 132 S.Ct. 1367 (2012). Until *Sackett*, if EPA determined that a person was in violation of CWA prohibitions, it could simply order compliance. The person then had to either comply with the order, or risk ruinous fines while waiting for EPA to bring an enforcement action. The Sacketts were faced with this conundrum when they filled part of their lot in preparation to build a house and chose to challenge the order as arbitrary and capricious under the Administrative Procedure Act's (APA) judicial review provision.

In evaluating whether pre-enforcement judicial review of compliance orders was available under the APA, the Court first held that the action was final, and that there were no other adequate remedies available in court (requirements of the APA provision). *Id.* at 1368–69. Next, the government advanced a series of arguments asserting that the CWA was meant to preclude judicial review under the APA. In a unanimous decision, the Supreme Court responded that:

> Nothing in the Clean Water Act *expressly* precludes judicial review under the APA or otherwise. But in determining "[w]hether and to what extent a particular statute precludes judicial review," we do not look "only [to] its express language." *Block v. Community Nutrition Institute*, 467 U.S. 340, 345 (1984). The APA, we have said, creates a "presumption favoring judicial review of administrative action," but as with most presumptions, this one "may be overcome by inferences of intent drawn from the statutory scheme as a whole." *Id.* at 349. The Government offers several reasons why the statutory scheme of the Clean Water Act precludes review.

> The Government first points to 33 U.S.C. § 1319(a)(3), which provides that, when the EPA "finds that any person is in violation" of certain portions of the Act, the agency "shall issue an order requiring such person to comply with [the Act], or . . . shall bring a civil action [to enforce the Act]." The Government argues that, because Congress gave the EPA the choice between a judicial proceeding and an administrative action, it would undermine the Act to allow judicial review of the latter. But that argument rests on the question-begging premise that the relevant difference between a compliance order and an enforcement proceeding is that only the latter is subject to judicial review. There are eminently sound reasons other than insulation from judicial review why compliance orders are useful. The Government itself suggests that they "provid[e] a means of notifying recipients of potential violations and . . . quickly resolving the issues through voluntary compliance." It is entirely consistent with this function to allow judicial review when the recipient does not choose "voluntary compliance." The Act does not guarantee the EPA that issuing a compliance order will always be the most effective choice.

* * *

Finally, the Government notes that Congress passed the Clean Water Act in large part to respond to the inefficiency of then-existing remedies for water pollution. Compliance orders, as noted above, can obtain quick remediation through voluntary compliance. The Government warns that the EPA is less likely to use the orders if they are subject to judicial review. That may be true—but it will be true for all agency actions subjected to judicial review. The APA's presumption of judicial review is a repudiation of the principle that efficiency of regulation conquers all. And there is no reason to think that the Clean Water Act was uniquely designed to enable the strong-arming of regulated parties into "voluntary compliance" without the opportunity for judicial review—even judicial review of the question whether the regulated party is within the EPA's jurisdiction. Compliance orders will remain an effective means of securing prompt voluntary compliance in those many cases where there is no substantial basis to question their validity.

* * *

We conclude that the compliance order in this case is final agency action for which there is no adequate remedy other than APA review, and that the Clean Water Act does not preclude that review. . . .

132 S.Ct. at 1372–74.

Since *Sackett*, EPA no longer has the power to issue compliance orders to directly "strong-arm" developers. However, one prominent Clean Water Act scholar has posited that a sternly worded warning letter may produce the same effect as an administrative compliance order. Craig N. Johnston, Sackett: *The Road Forward*, 42 Envtl. L. 993, 1006 (2012). These letters would not be "final agency action," so they would not be judicially reviewable. Moreover, if EPA did eventually issue a compliance order, the warning letters would help the EPA build a good administrative record, making it more difficult for a court to conclude that EPA's decision is arbitrary and capricious. *Id.* at 1007. Although these warning letters may be slightly less effective than compliance orders because they give EPA reduced leverage to directly force the hands of developers, they are certainly likely to be more effective than proceeding immediately to a civil enforcement action.

11. *Jurisdictional determinations.* Unlike compliance orders, several courts of appeal have decided that wetland jurisdictional determinations (by which the Corps asserts 404 regulation) are not final agency actions subject to judicial review because they allegedly do not affect legal rights or obligations or impose legal consequences. *Belle Co. v. U.S. Army Corps of Engineers*, 2014 WL 3746464 (5th Cir. July 30, 2014); *Fairbanks North Star Borough v. U.S. Army Corps of Engineers*, 543 F.3d 586 (9th Cir. 2008);

Commissioners of Public Works of City of Charleston v. U.S., 30 F.3d 129 (4th Cir. 1994).

12. *Mitigation and "no net loss" of wetlands.* The section 404(b) guidelines provide a "sequencing" of mitigation in 404 permitting. In other words, adverse effects of fills must first be avoided to the maximum extent practicable; then, remaining unavoidable impacts must be minimized; finally, adverse effects must be compensated to the extent appropriate and practicable. 40 C.F.R. § 230.91. In 2008, EPA promulgated a rule providing standards governing the application of compensatory mitigation that favors use of mitigation banks, in which a developer can purchase "credits" in the bank to compensate for losses after avoiding and minimizing efforts. 40 C.F.R. § 230.93(b)(2). Established wetland banks provide more certainty that the mitigation will be successful than permitee-responsible mitigation or so-called in-lieu fee mitigation because the latter often take place after the development. See U.S. Envtl. Prot. Agency, *Wetlands Compensatory Mitigation*, available at http://water.epa.gov/lawsregs/guidance/wetlands/upload/2003_05_30_wetlands_CMitigation.pdf.

Mitigation sequencing and standards for compensatory mitigation are important components in the federal policy of "no net loss" of wetlands, first established by the George H. W. Bush Administration in 1989 and continued by every administration since. See James Salzman & J.B. Ruhl, *"No Net Loss": Instrument Choice in Wetlands Protection* in *Moving to Markets in Environmental Regulation: Lessons from Twenty Years of Experience* (Jody Freeman & Charles D. Kolstad eds., 2007). However, there are substantial reasons to believe that no net loss is not being achieved. For example in U.S. Fish and Wildlife Serv., *Status and Trends of Wetlands in the Conterminous United States 2004 to 2009* (2011), available at http://www.fws.gov/wetlands/Documents/Status-and-Trends-of-Wetlands-in-the-Conterminous–United–States–2004–to–2009.pdf, the report concluded that in the five-year study period, there was a loss of over 62,000 acres of wetlands.

13. *Wetlands protection as regulatory takings.* As long ago as 1970, some courts recognized that regulatory protection of wetlands can result in a Fifth Amendment "taking" of private property. See *State v. Johnson*, 265 A.2d 711, 716 (Me. 1970). Two prominent examples are *Florida Rock Industries v. U.S.*, 18 F.3d 1560 (Fed. Cir. 1994), and *Loveladies Harbor, Inc. v. U.S.*, 28 F.3d 1171 (Fed. Cir. 1994).

In *Florida Rock*, the landowner sought to develop 98 acres of wetland property but was denied a section 404 permit to do so. 18 F.3d 1560. Judge Plager, writing for the Federal Circuit, decided that wetlands regulation can require just compensation if it has resulted in a "partial" taking and remanded the case back to the trial court to decide if the permit denial rose above "mere diminution of value" to the level of "partial taking." *Id.* at 1570.

The trial court ultimately applied the traditional *Penn Central* factors[10] to decide that the denial of the § 404 permit was a "partial taking," requiring just compensation. *Florida Rock Industries v. U.S.,* 45 Fed.Cl. 21, 43 (Fed. Cl. 1999).

In *Loveladies*, the landowner sought a permit to fill 11.5 wetland acres of what was originally a 250-acre parcel. Judge Plager again wrote for the Federal Circuit and decided that since most of the rest of the parcel had been sold before the enactment of the CWA, the court could confine its inquiry to the remaining 11.5 acres instead of the original 250 acres. *Loveladies,* 28 F.3d at 1182. Given this narrow focus of the size of the property at issue, the court concluded that the denial of a section 404 permit was a deprivation of "all economically beneficial use," and thus was a categorical "total" taking under the Supreme Court's decision in *Lucas*.[11] The final chapter of *Florida Rock* followed a similarly narrow inquiry. 45 Fed.Cl. 21. In that case, the Court of Federal Claims considered only 98 acres of a 1,560-acre parcel of land in deciding that the permit denial amounted to a taking. *Id* at 34.

NOTE ON THE RIVERS AND HARBORS ACT

In addition to the Clean Water Act, the Rivers and Harbors Act (RHA) also provides some protection for waters. Most importantly, section 10 of the RHA (1) bans the "creation of any obstruction not affirmatively authorized by Congress, to the navigable capacity of any of the waters of the United States," and (2) requires a permit in order to "excavate or fill, or in any manner to alter or modify the course, location, condition, or capacity of, any port, roadstead, haven, harbor, canal, lake, harbor or refuge, or inclosure within the limits of any breakwater, or of the channel of any navigable water of the United States." 33 U.S.C. § 403.

Although the statute provided no governing criteria for the issuance of RHA permits, Corps of Engineers' regulations require a project to satisfy a "public interest review," requiring a balancing of the "benefits which reasonably may be expected to accrue" against "reasonably foreseeable detriments." 33 C.F.R. § 320.4. Despite the fact that the RHA facially appears to be concerned about navigability, courts have consistently construed the Act broadly, and the Supreme Court validated the Corps' use of environmental factors in public interest review in *United States v. Alaska*, 503 U.S. 569 (1992). Perhaps because CWA section 404 permits and RHA section 10 permits are often necessary for the same project, the "public interest review" applies to both.

---

[10] *Penn Cent. Transp. Co. v. City of New York*, 438 U.S. 104, 124 (1978) (applying a three-factor balancing test: (1) the economic effect on the claimant; (2) the regulation's interference with investment-backed expectations; and (3) the character of the government action).

[11] *Lucas v. S. Carolina Coastal Council*, 505 U.S. 1003, 1019 (1992) (when a regulation deprives a landowner of "all economically beneficial use" of the property, there is a categorical "taking"). *Lucas*-type categorical takings are exceedingly rare, however, since most land retains some economic value, even after regulations restrict its use.

However, in contrast to the RHA's broad scope, the statute has a fairly narrow applicability in terms of the waters it covers. Corps regulations define "navigable waters" under the RHA to mean "those waters that are subject to the ebb and flow of the tide and/or are presently used, or have been used in the past, or may be susceptible for use to transport interstate or foreign commerce." 33. C.F.R. § 329.4. Thus, unlike the CWA, the RHA reaches only traditionally navigable waters.

NOTE ON THE NAVIGATION SERVITUDE

Although the Corps' exercise of authority under the RHA often results in value losses to landowners, the federal navigation servitude prevents landowners from claiming a Fifth Amendment taking. Under the Commerce Clause, Congress has the power to regulate all navigable waters. *Gibbons v. Ogden,* 22 U.S. 1 (1824). Due in part to this power, the Supreme Court has long held that because landowners have no property right to "the running water in a great navigable stream," there can be no taking. *United States v. Willow River Power Co.,* 324 U.S. 499, 509 (1945). In that case, the Willow River Power Company suffered economic losses because the government's actions on the river impaired the efficiency of the company's hydroelectric plant. The Supreme Court denied a takings claim, explaining, "[a landowner's use of navigable waters] constitute[s] a privilege or a convenience, enjoyed for many years, permissible so long as compatible with navigation interests, but it is not an interest protected by law when it becomes inconsistent with plans authorized by Congress for improvement of navigation." *Id.*

The Supreme Court also employed the navigation servitude in *U.S. v. Rands,* 389 U.S. 121, 124 (1967), denying a takings claim for loss of value to a riparian area as a result of changes to a navigable water. Justice White's opinion in *Rands* provided a description of the use and limits of navigation servitude in takings cases, explaining its expansion to riparian areas:

> The Commerce Clause confers a unique position upon the Government in connection with navigable waters. "The power to regulate commerce comprehends the control for that purpose, and to the extent necessary, of all the navigable waters of the United States. . . . For this purpose they are the public property of the nation, and subject to all the requisite legislation by Congress." This power to regulate navigation confers upon the United States a "dominant servitude," wh[ich] extends to the entire stream and the stream bed below ordinary high-water mark. The proper exercise of this power is not an invasion of any private property rights in the stream or the lands underlying it, for the damage sustained does not result from taking property from riparian owners within the meaning of the Fifth Amendment but from the lawful exercise of a power to which the interests of riparian owners have always been subject. Thus, without being constitutionally obligated to pay compensation, the United States may change the course of a navigable stream, or otherwise impair or destroy a riparian owner's

access to navigable waters, even though the market value of the riparian owner's land is substantially diminished.

The navigational servitude of the United States does not extend beyond the high-water mark. Consequently, when fast lands are taken by the Government, just compensation must be paid. But "just as the navigational privilege permits the Government to reduce the value of riparian lands by denying the riparian owner access to the stream without compensation for his loss, . . . it also permits the Government to disregard the value arising from this same fact of riparian location in compensating the owner when fast lands are appropriated."

Rands, 389 U.S. at 122–24.

Congress responded to *Rands* by enacting section 111 of the RHA, effectively reversing the decision by expressly providing for compensation of landowners. 33 U.S.C. § 595a (1970). The Supreme Court has also demonstrated reticence to recognize the navigation servitude as a "blanket exception" to the Fifth Amendment. *Kaiser Aetna v. U.S.*, 444 U.S. 164, 171–73 (1979) (just because a water is "navigable" does not automatically make it subject to the navigational servitude).

One limit on the navigation servitude as a defense to takings claims is that the Corps' actions must be at least in part motivated by navigation concerns. The RHA has long been used to promote not just navigational interests, but also environmental ones. *United States v. Alaska*, 503 U.S. 569, 581 (1992). However, so long as one of the purposes of the Corps is a bona fide interest in promoting navigation, the navigation servitude will be a defense to any takings claim. *Palm Beach Isles Associates v. United States*, 58 Fed.Cl. 657, 681 (Fed. Cl. 2003) *aff'd,* 122 F. App'x 517 (Fed. Cir. 2005) (although the primary reasons for a Corps permit denial were environmental, a takings claim failed because navigation was among the reasons for the denial).

NOTE ON NATURAL RESOURCES PROTECTION IN HYDROELECTRIC LICENSING UNDER THE FEDERAL POWER ACT

The Federal Power Act (FPA), 16 U.S.C. §§ 791 *et seq.*, was enacted to regulate private hydropower development of water resources. *Pac. Gas & Elec. Co. v. FERC*, 720 F.2d 78, 83 (D.C. Cir. 1983). The statute authorizes the Federal Energy Regulatory Commission (FERC, originally the Federal Power Commission), to issue non-federal hydropower licenses on navigable waters. 16 U.S.C. § 797 (2005). Unlike federal dams, non-federal dams are authorized for limited terms (usually 20 to 50 years) through FERC licenses, meaning they must periodically seek relicensing.

The Act contains three important provisions to protect natural resources, authorizing federal land and fishery managers to require certain conditions on licenses issued by FERC. First, section 4(e) allows federal land managers to issue conditions to protect reservations on which a hydropower project is located. *Id.* § 797(e). Second, section 18 authorizes federal fishery managers to issue conditions, called prescriptions, to protect fisheries. *Id.* § 811. Third, section 10(j), added in a 1986 amendment, authorizes resource agencies to issue conditions to provide adequate protection, mitigation, and enhancement of fish and wildlife affected by the project. *Id.* § 803(j). FERC must accept conditions promulgated under sections 4(e) and 18, but can reject section 10(j) conditions if FERC finds the condition to be inconsistent with the purposes and requirements of the FPA. *Escondido Mutual Water Co. v. La Jolla Band of Mission Indians*, 466 U.S. 765 (1984); *American Rivers v. FERC*, 201 F.3d 1186 (9th Cir. 1999). The Act was amended in 2005, adding procedures that allow licensees to challenge conditions in trial-type hearings and to propose alternative conditions. Energy Policy Act of 2005, Pub. L. No. 109–58, § 241, 119 Stat. 594 (Aug. 8, 2005). However, according to a recent Government Accountability Office report, these added procedures so far have not led to substantial changes in conditions promulgated by federal land managers or fish and wildlife agencies. U.S. Government Accountability Office, GAO–10–770, *Hydropower Relicensing: Stakeholders' Views on the Energy Policy Act Varied, but More Consistent Information Needed* (Aug. 2010).

In addition to providing affirmative protection for natural resources affected by dam construction and operations, these conditions and prescriptions also can lead to dam removal, particularly when FPA dams seek relicensing. See Michael C. Blumm & Andrew B. Erickson, *Dam Removal in the Pacific Northwest: Lessons for the Nation*, 42 Envtl. L. 1043 (2012) (also noting that section 401 of the Clean Water Act, 33 U.S.C § 1341, allowing states to certify federal projects as being consistent with state water quality standards, can produce the same effect, *id.* at 1062); see also *Public Utility Dist. No. 1 of Jefferson County v. Wash. Dept. of Ecology*, 511 U.S. 700, 722–23 (1994) (upholding state 401 conditions applied to a FERC-licensed project). The great expense of meeting the resource agencies' conditions and prescriptions (especially fish passageways) often convinces dam owners to agree to remove federally licensed dams. See 42 Envtl. L. at 1094–96.

CHAPTER 4

WILDLIFE

■ ■ ■

Wildlife law is one of the oldest bodies of natural resources law, reaching back to the earliest years of the Anglo-Norman legal system and indeed to Anglo-Saxon times. Early wildlife law mostly had to do with those particular species treated as game—that is, species used as food for people—as well as with pest species. Like any body of natural resources law, wildlife law included provisions that had the effect of allocating game animals to particular categories of people by prohibiting others from hunting or trapping them. In general, the King (or Queen) claimed ownership of all game species in England. In the case of a few particular species (whales, porpoises, swans), the King treated them as his personal property, wherever found, and strict rules prohibited others from taking or owning them without royal permission. Other game species were controlled by the crown with hunting rights to them allocated in various ways. Aside from cases involving criminal sanctions for poaching or trespassing on royal lands, most wildlife disputes that reached appellate courts had to do with fisheries, the most valuable form of wildlife in economic terms.

We begin our survey of contemporary wildlife law with the basic rule of capture—the means by which an individual can gain ownership of a wild animal. We then turn to the legal status of wildlife on private lands and the powers that landowners have over them, directly and indirectly. We consider the special rule of the state as trustee owner of wildlife on behalf of the people, before looking at specific topics relating to state wildlife agencies and their powers. We end with a brief survey of three major federal wildlife statutes, the Migratory Bird Treaty Act, the Lacey Act, and the Endangered Species Act. We leave for later chapters the laws governing wildlife on publicly owned lands and take only a brief look at the various special, wildlife-related powers of Indian tribes and tribal members.

A. CAPTURING ANIMALS AND THE DURATION OF PRIVATE RIGHTS

PIERSON V. POST

Supreme Court of New York
3 Cai. R. 175, 2 Am.Dec. 264 (1805)

This was an action of trespass on the case commenced in a justice's court, by the present defendant against the now plaintiff.

The declaration stated that Post, being in possession of certain dogs and hounds under his command, did, "upon a certain wild and uninhabited, unpossessed and waste land, called the beach, find and start one of those noxious beasts called a fox," and whilst there hunting, chasing and pursuing the same with his dogs and hounds, and when in view thereof, Pierson, well knowing the fox was so hunted and pursued, did, in the sight of Post, to prevent his catching the same, kill and carry it off. A verdict having been rendered for the plaintiff below, the defendant there sued out a *certiorari,* and now assigned for error, that the declaration and the matters therein contained were not sufficient in law to maintain an action.

TOMPKINS, J.

The question submitted by the counsel in this cause for our determination is, whether Lodowick Post, by the pursuit with his hounds in the manner alleged in his declaration, acquired such a right to, or property in, the fox, as will sustain an action against Pierson for killing and taking him away? The cause was argued with much ability by the counsel on both sides, and presents for our decision a novel and nice question. It is admitted that a fox is an animal *ferae naturae,* and that property in such animals is acquired by occupancy only. These admissions narrow the discussion to the simple question of what acts amount to occupancy, applied to acquiring right to wild animals?

If we have recourse to the ancient writers upon general principles of law, the judgment below is obviously erroneous. Justinian's Institutes, lib. 2 tit. 1 § 13. and Fleta, lib.3 c. 2 p. 175 adopt the principle, that pursuit alone vests no property or right in the huntsman; and that even pursuit, accompanied with wounding, is equally ineffectual for that purpose, unless the animal be actually taken. The same principle is recognised by Bracton, lib. 2 c. 1 p. 8. Puffendorf, lib. 4 c. 6 § 2. and 10. defines occupancy of beasts *ferae naturae,* to be the actual corporal possession of them, and Bynkershoek is cited as coinciding in this definition. It is indeed with hesitation that Puffendorf affirms that a wild beast mortally wounded, or greatly maimed, cannot be fairly intercepted by another, whilst the pursuit of the person inflicting the wound continues. The foregoing authorities are decisive to show that mere pursuit gave Post no legal right to the fox, but that he became the property of Pierson, who intercepted and killed him.

It therefore only remains to inquire whether there are any contrary principles, or authorities, to be found in other books, which ought to induce a different decision. Most of the cases which have occurred in England, relating to property in wild animals, have either been discussed and decided upon the principles of their positive statute regulations, or have arisen between the huntsman and the owner of the land upon which beasts *ferae naturae* have been apprehended; the former claiming them by title of occupancy, and the latter *ratione soli*. Little satisfactory aid can, therefore, be derived from the English reporters.

Barbeyrac, in his notes on Puffendorf, does not accede to the definition of occupancy by the latter, but, on the contrary, affirms, that actual bodily seizure is not, in all cases, necessary to constitute possession of wild animals. He does not, however, describe the acts which, according to his ideas, will amount to an appropriation of such animals to private use, so as to exclude the claims of all other persons, by title of occupancy, to the same animals; and he is far from averring that pursuit alone is sufficient for that purpose. To a certain extent, and as far as Barbeyrac appears to me to go, his objections to Puffendorf's definition of occupancy are reasonable and correct. That is to say, that actual bodily seizure is not indispensable to acquire right to, or possession of, wild beasts; but that, on the contrary, the mortal wounding of such beasts, by one not abandoning his pursuit, may, with the utmost propriety, be deemed possession of him; since, thereby, the pursuer manifests an unequivocal intention of appropriating the animal to his individual use, has deprived him of his natural liberty, and brought him within his certain control. So also, encompassing and securing such animals with nets and toils, or otherwise intercepting them in such a manner as to deprive them of their natural liberty, and render escape impossible, may justly be deemed to give possession of them to those persons who, by their industry and labour, have used such means of apprehending them. . . . The case now under consideration is one of mere pursuit, and presents no circumstances or acts which can bring it within the definition of occupancy by Puffendorf, or Grotius, or the ideas of Barbeyrac upon that subject.

The case cited from 11 *Mod.* 74–130. I think clearly distinguishable from the present; inasmuch as there the action was for maliciously hindering and disturbing the plaintiff in the exercise and enjoyment of a private franchise; and in the report of the same case, 3 Salk 9 Holt, Ch. J. states, that the ducks were in the plaintiff's decoy pond, and *so in his possession,* from which it is obvious the court laid much stress in their opinion upon the plaintiff's possession of the ducks, *ratione soli.*

We are the more readily inclined to confine possession or occupancy of beasts *ferae naturae,* within the limits prescribed by the learned authors above cited, for the sake of certainty, and preserving peace and order in society. If the first seeing, starting, or pursuing such animals, without having so wounded, circumvented or ensnared them, so as to deprive them of their natural liberty, and subject them to the control of their pursuer, should afford the basis of actions against others for intercepting and killing them, it would prove a fertile source of quarrels and litigation.

However uncourteous or unkind the conduct of *Pierson* towards *Post,* in this instance, may have been, yet his act was productive of no injury or damage for which a legal remedy can be applied. We are of opinion the judgment below was erroneous, and ought to be reversed.

LIVINGSTON, J.

My opinion differs from that of the court. . . .

Whether a person who, with his own hounds, starts and hunts a fox on waste and uninhabited ground, and is on the point of seizing his prey, acquires such an interest in the animal, as to have a right of action against another, who in view of the huntsman and his dogs in full pursuit, and with knowledge of the chase, shall kill and carry him away?

This is a knotty point, and should have been submitted to the arbitration of sportsmen, without poring over Justinian, Fleta, Bracton, Puffendorf, Locke, Barbeyrac, or Blackstone, all of whom have been cited; they would have had no difficulty in coming to a prompt and correct conclusion. In a court thus constituted, the skin and carcass of poor *reynard* would have been properly disposed of, and a precedent set, interfering with no usage or custom which the experience of ages has sanctioned, and which must be so well known to every votary of Diana. But the parties have referred the question to our judgment, and we must dispose of it as well as we can, from the partial lights we possess, leaving to a higher tribunal, the correction of any mistake which we may be so unfortunate as to make.

By the pleadings it is admitted that a fox is a "wild and noxious beast." Both parties have regarded him, as the law of nations does a pirate, *"hostem humani generis,"* and although *"de mortuis nil nisi bonum,"* be a maxim of our profession, the memory of the deceased has not been spared. His depredations on farmers and on barn yards, have not been forgotten; and to put him to death wherever found, is allowed to be meritorious, and of public benefit. Hence it follows, that our decision should have in view the greatest possible encouragement to the destruction of an animal, so cunning and ruthless in his career. But who would keep a pack of hounds; or what gentleman, at the sound of the horn, and at peep of day, would mount his steed, and for hours together, "*sub jove frigido,*" or a vertical sun, pursue the windings of this wily quadruped, if, just as night came on, and his stratagems and strength were nearly exhausted, a saucy intruder, who had not shared in the honours or labours of the chase, were permitted to come in at the death, and bear away in triumph the object of pursuit? Whatever Justinian may have thought of the matter, it must be recollected that his code was compiled many hundred years ago, and it would be very hard indeed, at the distance of so many centuries, not to have a right to establish a rule for ourselves. In his day, we read of no order of men who made it a business, in the language of the declaration in this cause, "with hounds and dogs to find, start, pursue, hunt, and chase," these animals, and that, too, without any other motive than the preservation of Roman poultry; if this diversion had been then in fashion, the lawyers who composed his institutes, would have taken care not to pass it by, without suitable encouragement. If anything, therefore, in the digests or pandects shall appear to militate against the defendant in error, who, on this occasion, was the foxhunter, we have only to say *tempora mutantur;* and if men themselves change with the times, why should not laws also undergo an alteration?

It may be expected, however, by the learned counsel, that more particular notice be taken of their authorities. I have examined them all, and feel great difficulty in determining, whether to acquire dominion over a thing, before in common, it be sufficient that we barely see it, or know where it is, or wish for it, or make a declaration of our will respecting it; or whether, in the case of wild beasts, setting a trap, or lying in wait, or starting, or pursuing, be enough; or if an actual wounding, or killing, or bodily tact and occupation be necessary. Writers on general law, who have favoured us with their speculations on these points, differ on them all; but, great as is the diversity of sentiment among them, some conclusion must be adopted on the question immediately before us. After mature deliberation, I embrace that of Barbeyrac, as the most rational, and least liable to objection. If at liberty, we might imitate the courtesy of a certain emperor, who, to avoid giving offence to the advocates of any of these different doctrines, adopted a middle course, and by ingenious distinctions, rendered it difficult to say (as often happens after a fierce and angry contest) to whom the palm of victory belonged. He ordained, that if a beast be followed with large dogs and hounds, he shall belong to the hunter, not to the chance occupant; and in like manner, if he be killed or wounded with a lance or sword; but if chased with beagles only, then he passed to the captor, not to the first pursuer. If slain with a dart, a sling, or a bow, he fell to the hunter, if still in chase, and not to him who might afterwards find and seize him.

Now, as we are without any municipal regulations of our own, and the pursuit here, for aught that appears on the case, being with dogs and hounds of imperial stature, we are at liberty to adopt one of the provisions just cited, which comports also with the learned conclusion of Barbeyrac, that property in animals *ferae naturae* may be acquired without bodily touch or manucaption, provided the pursuer be within reach, or have a *reasonable* prospect (which certainly existed here) of taking, what he has thus discovered an intention of converting to his own use.

When we reflect also that the interest of our husbandmen, the most useful of men in any community, will be advanced by the destruction of a beast so pernicious and incorrigible, we cannot greatly err, in saying, that a pursuit like the present, through waste and unoccupied lands, and which must inevitably and speedily have terminated in corporal possession, or bodily *seisin,* confers such a right to the object of it, as to make any one a wrongdoer, who shall interfere and shoulder the spoil. The justice's judgment ought, therefore, in my opinion, to be affirmed.

Judgment of reversal.

NOTES

1.   *What capture entails.* Both parties in *Pierson* took the legal stance that this dispute was about whether Post did or did not become owner of the fox. Whether Post gained ownership depended on whether his actions (and perhaps his mental state) were legally sufficient for him to become owner of the previously unowned fox. According to Justice Tompkins, what did Post need to do in order to gain property rights in the fox? In contrast, what does Justice Livingston in his dissent say was required to become owner? Read carefully the exact words that Tompkins and Livingston use to phrase what they each take to be the prevailing common law rule on hunting. Pay attention also to the policy rationales that each gives in support of their competing positions. On what policy grounds does Tompkins base his ruling? Does Livingston disagree on these points, or does he raise competing policy concerns? Might a judge today, looking at this issue fresh, take into account competing concerns—maybe even reasons why killing foxes is not a good idea?

The majority rule in *Pierson* has been dominant ever since. Physical capture or something equivalent to it is needed to gain ownership of an animal. Mortal wounding, as Tompkins noted in dicta, is typically enough, at least if the carcass is not abandoned. In the much-cited case of *State v. Shaw*, 65 N.E. 875 (Ohio 1902), the court concluded that fish caught in a trap net were adequately captured, even though there was a small route of exit for the fish. Special rules were developed by nineteenth century courts to deal with the particular cases of whales and hives of bees; both could be captured through means that gave notice of ownership to the world but sometimes did not involve actual physical control.

2.   *Unlawful capture.* As we shall see below, states are sovereign owners of all wildlife within their borders, holding title as trustees on behalf

of the people. This state ownership doctrine received a ringing endorsement by the United States Supreme Court in 1896, in the prominent case of *Geer v. Connecticut,* 161 U.S. 519 (1896). In its ruling, the Court surveyed English wildlife law in detail, emphasizing the long, unbroken power of government to regulate wildlife on behalf of the people. That sovereign power existed as "a trust for the benefit of the people, and not as a prerogative for the advantage of the government as distinct from the people, or for the benefit of private individuals as distinguished from the public good." This power passed from the English government to the original states upon Independence and to the new states upon their entry into the Union. One of the editors has argued that the "state ownership" of wildlife doctrine is actually part of the public trust doctrine, as discussed in chapter 3 (pp. 178–217), see Michael C. Blumm & Erika Doot, *Oregon's Public Trust Doctrine: Public Rights in Water, Wildlife, and Beaches*, 42 Envtl. L. 375, 401–07 (2012).

　　Geer was handed down during the era when states were enacting early forms of contemporary game laws and setting up agencies to administer them. The story is told in John F. Reiger, *American Sportsmen and the Origins of Conservation* (3d ed. 2001). As game laws became more widespread and enforcement increased (slowly in some states), courts had to decide the legal consequences of animal capture by a hunter who was unlicensed, took game out of season or otherwise violated game laws. After some hesitance they embraced the rule that no property rights were gained when the capture or possession of an animal violated a game law. See e.g., *James v. Wood*, 19 A. 160 (Me. 1889); *Jones v. Metcalf*, 119 A. 430 (Vt. 1923). The rule remains dominant. In *Fischer v. Knapp*, 332 N.W.2d 76 (N.D. 1983), for example, the court upheld the state seizure of foxes illegally dug out of a den. In *Wright v. Department of Natural Resources*, 562 S.E.2d 515 (Ga. App. 2002), the unlawful capture involved fencing a 30- to 40-acre pond that included alligators with room for them to reproduce; the capturer forfeited not just the original alligators but their offspring. The unlawful capture can involve a violation of any game-law provision. In *State* ex rel *Visser v. State Fish and Game Commission*, 437 P.2d 373 (Mont. 1968), the state confiscated an elk that was killed by a licensed hunter's unlicensed guide along with an elk for which a game tag was not properly filled out and attached. The court upheld the state confiscation, using that notion that the state owns the wildlife as a justification for state regulation of hunting.

　　Most cases involving this rule of law (that unlawful capture creates no property rights) relate to unlawful hunting. But not all: Sometime around 1988 Claire Bilida "rescued" an "orphaned raccoon," took the animal into captivity, and raised it as a pet for seven years. A police officer, responding to a security-alarm signal, noticed the penned raccoon and alerted the city animal control officer. When it was learned that Bilida lacked the required permit, the government seized the animal. Under a state law protecting against raccoon rabies, the raccoon was euthanized and tested for rabies because Bilida had fed it by hand. The raccoon had no rabies. Suing in federal court, Bilida claimed that the state deprived of her property without due process of law. The court concluded that Bilida had no property interest in the raccoon since it was captured and held in violation of state law. "Under Rhode Island law, 'wild game within a state belongs to the people in their collective sovereign capacity' and is not subject to 'private ownership except in so far as the people may elect to make it so.'" *Bilida v. McCleod*, 211 F.3d 166, 173 (1st Cir. 2000), *quoting State v. Kofines*, 80 A. 432, 440 (R.I. 1911).

3. *Duration of rights.* Rights in a wild animal captured alive come to an end when the animal regains its natural liberty in something like its natural habitat; that is, when it has returned to a place where people who see it are likely to assume it is native. An exception exists for animals that have a habit of returning (for instance, bees that return to a hive). *E.g., Manning v. Mitcherson*, 69 Ga. 447 (1882) (canary with habit of wandering). Occasionally an owner has retained ownership by proving that the animal was essentially tame. *E.g., Ulery v. Jones*, 81 Ill. 403 (1876) (bison "so tame and gentle as to render it no longer of a wild nature"). On what qualifies as adequate habitat, consider *Mullett v. Bradley*, 53 N.Y.S. 781 (N.Y. Sup. 1898) (sea lion returns to natural habitat when released into Atlantic Ocean, even though the species lives only in the Pacific). Over the generations, the species most often litigated, in terms of whether it has returned to the wild, is the oyster.

State game laws also impose restrictions on the duration of private rights in animals by prohibiting possession out of season, including possession of dead or even processed and frozen animals and animal parts. The validity of these laws was sustained by courts from the beginning. See e.g., *Magner v. State of Illinois*, 97 Ill. 320 (1881) (upholding ban on possession and selling game out season, even when the game was lawfully killed in season in an adjacent state).

4. *The many ways of allocating natural resources.* Every body of natural resources law features some rule that governs allocation of the resource. Often, as we have seen, a resource is considered part of the land where it is located, so that a person gains ownership of the resource by acquiring the land. In the case of discrete resources, such as a wild fox, the applicable law incorporates an allocation method—in this instance, by first-in-time capture. Both Tompkins and Livingston in the dispute agreed that first-in-time was the applicable rule. Their disagreement was about first-in-time to do what? To capture the animal physically? To pursue it vigorously with the intent and apparent ability to capture it?

The court in *Pierson* did not consider the possibility of other methods of allocating wild foxes found on public land open to public hunting. In fact, possible allocation methods are many. A resource can be simply offered for sale to the first one who purchases it. It can be allocated through an auction or by means of a lottery. Resources, as we shall see, are sometimes allocated based on public interest criteria, taking into account the social desirability of the proposed use and/or the traits of the various people who seek the resources. Resources have often been given to individuals or businesses as inducements to engage in certain behavior (e.g., land given for building a rail line through a region) or as a reward for service (e.g., land bounties for military veterans in the nineteenth century). Of course, corrupt allocation methods have long been much too familiar, whether allocation based on bribery or political or family influence. In the case of wildlife, the law could provide (as it basically does in Britain) that animals belong to the owner of land where they are located, but only so long as they remain there.

5. *Pros and cons of first occupancy.* What are the pros and cons of allocating resources based on a first-in-time basis as the law did in *Pierson*? One possibility, illustrated by the case, is that disputes can arise about who is first, as well as claims of improper interference in the race to capture (a possibility raised by the next case). Hoarding of a resource can also be a problem when people take more than they need and can use. A first-in-time rule can encourage people to exploit a resource too quickly, for fear that others will take it, a possibility illustrated in the first oil boom around 1900 when excessive production dropped oil prices to almost nothing. Simply having many people attempt to capture a resource (e.g., fish) can lead to great inefficiency when the resource could be fully harvested with far fewer harvesters and much less equipment.

One much-touted virtue of first-in-time is that it provides an incentive for people to act—to hunt with skill or to find valuable resources. Also, the act of capture gives at least some cause, morally speaking, to favor the capturer over other people who might also desire the resource but have done nothing to gain it. The act of capture does not *create* the resource in any sense and may not add much value to it. Thus, mere capture does not amount to the kind of moral justification that John Locke relied upon with his labor theory of private property. (Locke presumed that the item of property was so plentiful as to have no value in nature, and that the entire value of it was therefore due to the labor that the putative owner mixed with it. His theory, of course, is readily challenged on the ground that no natural resource is so plentiful as to have zero value.) Still, the one who captures the resource has done something, and competing claimants for the same resource, in contrast, might well have done nothing. When (as often) the resource starts off in communal hands, taxpayers might well feel cheated if the resource is allocated for free.

6. *The human drama and the bench. Pierson* is one of the most familiar, storied cases in all of property and natural resources law. It has fascinated generations of students and teachers in part because it seems so odd that two people would spend such time and effort fighting over a single dead fox. What's going on here? Both Pierson and Post, it turns out, were relatively young men, and the dispute was largely pursued by their families. Speculation long centered on the possibility that the lawsuit was part of an ongoing dispute between an English family and a Dutch family. Evidence uncovered more recently, however, suggests that the dispute had more to do with rights to use a town commons, on which the hunting apparently took

place. In any event, the court's ruling seems to conceal a great deal of human drama.

Pierson has also been of interest because the five members of the Supreme Court who heard the case were extraordinarily talented and destined for greatness. The majority author, Daniel Tompkins, later became Governor of New York and Vice President of the United States. Two years after this ruling, Brockholst Livingston joined the United States Supreme Court where he served until his death. Succeeding him on the Supreme Court was another member of the *Pierson* bench, Smith Thompson, who is remembered today for his ardent defense of the Cherokee Nation. Also on the bench was James Kent, later Chancellor of the State of New York and one of the first great authors of legal treatises, as well as Ambrose Spencer, later a powerful force in conservative New York politics.

Secondary writing on Pierson has expanded greatly in recent years with the discovery of new documentary evidence. Bethany R. Berger, *It's Not About the Fox: The Untold Story of* Pierson v. Post, 55 Duke L.J. 1089 (2006), considers evidence that the dispute had much to do with restricted rights to use town-owned land, where at least some of the events unfolded. Angela Fernandez, in *The Lost Record of* Pierson v. Post, *the Famous Fox Case*, 27 Law & Hist. Rev. 149 (2009), provides far more detail about the parties, the jurors, and the entire unusual proceeding. Andrea McDowell, in *Legal Fictions in* Pierson v. Post, 105 Mich. L. Rev. 735 (2007), adds material about foxes and fox hunting in the United States and England. She contends that Livingston knowingly (and perhaps humorously) distorted the underlying facts by suggesting that Post's aim in hunting was to rid the countryside of unwanted foxes and that the law shoulder favor him because he served the public interest. If in fact Post was simply interested in killing the fox as a pest, he presumably would have been pleased by Pierson's help, not upset.

7. *The precedent cited.* The exceptional quality of the bench and the equally exceptional energy exerted by the lawyers help explain the highly unusual legal citations in *Pierson*. The legal authors cited by Tompkins and Livingston were mostly seventeenth- and eighteenth-century writers from continental Europe, working in the "natural law" tradition of legal philosophy. These writings had no binding precedential value, in the United States or even in Britain. The New York court turned to them because, despite its research, it could not find even a single judicial precedent from Britain or America that dealt with similar facts. Lacking any relevant statutes or relevant case law, the court reached wider to find legal authors who wrote about the issue in more general terms.

The court gives us a good clue why the wild animal rulings that its research did uncover were not relevant to this dispute. Some rulings from England, the court tells us, were based on "positive statute regulations"—that is, on English statutes that did not apply in the United States. These rulings were plainly not relevant when, as in *Pierson*, no statute governed. Other rulings involved disputes between a hunter and the owner of the land where the hunt took place. In *Pierson*, no landowner showed up to make a claim, so these precedents were also not helpful. Notice that this dispute took place, in the court's words, on "wild and uninhabited, unpossessed and waste land." To the modern reader this sounds like the land was unowned. But that was perhaps not true. The words literally mean only that no owner was physically occupying and using the land; there could have been an absentee owner somewhere. (As noted, one historian claims that the hunting took place on a town commons in which specific town families, and not others, had use-rights.)

As for the natural law authors cited in the two opinions, and the reasons why the justices lavished such attention on the case (the ruling was handed down two years after the fox's death), *see* Angela Fernandez, Pierson v. Post: *A Great Debate, James Kent, and the Project of Building a Learned Law for New York State*, 34 Law & Soc. Inquiry 301 (2009); Charles Donahue, *Noodt, Titius, and the Natural Law School: The Occupation of Wild Animals and the Intersection of Property and Tort*, in J.A. Ankum, et al., eds., *Satura Roberto Feenstra* (1985).

KEEBLE V. HICKERINGILL

Queen's Bench
11 East 574, 103 Eng. Rep. 1127 (1701)

Action upon the case. Plaintiff [Samuel Keeble] declares that he was, 8th November in the second year of the queen, lawfully possessed of a close land called Minott's Meadow, *et de quodam vivario, vocato* a decoy pond, to which divers wildfowl used to resort and come: and the plaintiff had at his own costs and charges prepared and procured divers decoy ducks, nets, machines, and other engines for the decoying and taking of the wildfowl, and enjoyed the benefit in taking them: the defendant, knowing which, and intending to damnify the plaintiff in his vivary, and to fright and drive away the wildfowl used to resort thither, and deprive him of his profit, did, on the 8th of November, resort to the head of the said pond and vivary, and did discharge six guns laden with gunpowder, and with the noise and stink of the gunpowder did drive away the wildfowl then being in the pond: and on the 11th and 12th days of November the defendant, with design to damnify the plaintiff and fright away the wildfowl, did place himself with gun near the vivary, and there did discharge the said gun several times that was then charged with the gunpowder against the said decoy pond, whereby the wildfowl was frighted away, and did forsake the said pond. Upon not guilty pleaded a verdict was found for the plaintiff and 20 damages.

HOLT, C.J.

I am of opinion that this action doth lie. It seems to be new in its instance, but not new in the reason or principle of it. For 1st, this using or making a decoy is lawful. 2dly, this employment of his ground to that use is profitable to the plaintiff, as is the skill and management of that employment. As to the first, every man that hath a property may employ it for his pleasure and profit, as for alluring and procuring decoy ducks to come to his pond. To learn the trade of seducing other ducks to come here in order to be taken is not prohibited either by the law of the land or the moral law; but it is as lawful to use art to seduce them, to catch them, and destroy them for the use of mankind, as to kill and destroy wildfowl or tame cattle. Then when a man useth his art or his skill to take them, to see and dispose of for his profit; this is his trade; and he that hinders another in his trade or livelihood is liable to an action for so hindering him. . . . [W]here a violent or malicious act is done to a man's occupation, profession, or way of getting a livelihood; there an action lies in all cases. But if a man doth him damage by using the same employment; as if Mr. Hickeringill had set up another decoy on his own ground near the plaintiff's and that had spoiled the custom of the plaintiff, no action would lie because he had as much liberty to make and use a decoy as the plaintiff. This is like the case of 11 H. 4, 47. One schoolmaster sets up a new school to the damage of an antient school, and thereby the scholars are allured from the old school to come to his new. (The action there was held not to lie.) But suppose Mr. Hickeringill should lie in the way with his guns, and fright the boys from going to school, and their parents would let them go thither; sure that schoolmaster might have an action for the loss of his scholars. [ ] A man hath a market, to which he hath toll for horses sold: a man is bringing his horses to market to seel; a stranger hinders and obstructs him from going thither to the market; an action lies because it imports damage. . . . Now considering the nature of the case, it is not possible to declare of the number [of birds], that were frighted away; because the plaintiff had not possession of them, to count them. Where a man brings trespass for taking his goods, he must declare of the quantity, because he, by having had the possession, may know what he had, and therefore must know what he lost. . . . And when we do know that of long time in the kingdom these artificial contrivances of decoy ponds and decoy ducks have been used for enticing into those ponds wildfowl, in order to be taken for the profit of the owner of the pond, who is at the expense of servants, engines, and other management, whereby the markets of the nation may be furnished; there is great reason to give encouragement thereunto; that the people who are so instrumental by their skill and industry so to furnish the markets should reap the benefit and have their action. But in short, that which is the true reason, is, that this action is not brought to recover damage for the loss of the fowl, but for the disturbance. . . . So is the usual and common way of declaring.

NOTES

1.   *A property case?* Another classic judicial ruling, *Keeble* at first glance may seem to differ in outcome from *Pierson v. Post* and wildlife-

capture cases. According to the English court, the landowner enjoys legal protection while he is duck hunting even though he has not captured the ducks physically. But the ruling, of course, is not about the *ownership* of wild animals and how someone becomes owner. Instead, it is about the *protection* that a person enjoys while engaged in the process of capture. On the facts, what made Hickeringill's conduct wrongful? Was it his physical behavior alone? Was it his mental state (his apparent malice; his intent not to engage in lawful hunting but merely to drive the ducks away from the decoy)? Could he have gotten away with what he did by claiming that he was trying to hit the ducks but was simply a bad shot? As for Keeble, did he enjoy protection because he was a hunter or was it important also that he owned the land? Further, was it important that he lured and captured ducks as an economic activity; that he was a market hunter, not a recreational hunter? (On this, note the court's assertion: "Where a violent or malicious act is done to a man's occupation, profession, or way of getting a livelihood; there an action lies in all cases.")

An engaging, detailed look into the facts of this case, and duck hunting and duck decoys generally, is offered in A.W. Brian Simpson, *Leading Cases in the Common Law* 45–75 (1995). The decoy involved in *Keeble* was not simply a floating model duck. It was in fact a large structure of nets, screens, and channels, with live, clipped-wing ducks inside designed to attract other ducks. A decoy required substantial investment, worked only in a secluded, quiet area, and could cover multiple acres of water surface (one known decoy was 17 acres in size). Simpson notes that Edward Hickeringill—described by contemporaries as "a half crazy minister and controversial pamphleteer"—in fact was operating his own duck decoy a half-mile from Keeble's and that Hickergill's decoy was first in time. The court ordered several re-arguments of the case, which took years to resolve. Simpson, a noted legal historian, concludes from a study of the extended case file that Keeble won chiefly because he was engaged in a trade, not just recreational hunting, and because Hickeringill acted with malice. English courts after *Keeble* continued to struggle with duck disputes, mostly arising between decoy owners and market hunters who shot ducks from boats. Some rulings seemed to be based on the fairness of competition, but others protected decoy owners from market hunters in boats based on their priority in time. As for decoy hunting in the United States, the colorful story (mostly focused on Chesapeake Bay) is told in David & Jim Kimball, *The Market Hunter* (1969).

2. *Hunter harassment statutes.* Occasionally lawful hunters are disrupted in their hunting activities by citizen-activists who oppose hunting on moral grounds. When protests take place on private land, the owner can sometimes resolve the conflict by exercising property rights. On public lands the situation is more difficult. Nearly all states have addressed the issue—always favorably to the hunters, even though animal welfare supporters seem to outnumber them greatly—by enacting statutes that make it an offense to harass hunters engaged in the hunt. Typical of the statutes is Mississippi's:

No person shall intentionally:

(a) Interfere with or attempt to prevent the lawful taking of wildlife by another,

(b) Attempt to disturb wildlife, or attempt to affect their behavior with the intent to prevent their lawful taking by another; or

(c) Harass another person who is engaged in the lawful taking of wildlife or in the preparation for such taking.

Miss. Code Ann. § 49–7–147. Sanctions for violations vary by state, but may include criminal fines, imprisonment, civil damages, and injunctions.

A few state statutes have had provisions struck down as unconstitutional because the activities defined as harassment included simply speaking against hunting and trying to convince hunters not to hunt—classic exercises of free speech rights protected by the First Amendment of the Constitution. In a remarkable show of political clout, hunting groups have managed to get laws enacted even in states that have had not a single recorded instance of harassment. The statutes are considered critically in Jacqueline Tresl, *Shoot First, Talk Later: Holes in Freedom of Speech*, 8 Animal L. Rev. 177 (2002); Katherine Hessler, *Where Do We Draw the Line Between Harassment and Free Speech?: An Analysis of Hunter Harassment Law*, 3 Animal L. Rev. 129 (1997). The Illinois statute was partially invalidated on free speech grounds in *People v. Sanders*, 696 N.E.2d 1144 (Ill. 1998).

3. *Protections in the race to capture.* First-in-time allocation methods routinely pose the question: first in time to do what. As we shall see, the answer, in the case of water rights allocated by prior appropriation, was first to divert water and apply it to a beneficial use. In the case of hardrock mineral rights on federal lands, it was first to discover a valuable mineral deposit and locate a claim that included it. A second recurring issue in such allocation schemes has to do with the protection that a person needs to enjoy while engaged in the activity required to capture or appropriate the resource. *Keeble* and the hunter harassment statutes give an answer for the wildlife setting (clarified further by state game laws). In the case of hardrock mining law, mining prospectors enjoy a temporary right of occupancy in lands that are actually occupying when diligently searching for valuable minerals. We might generalize: Any resource scheme that employs first-in-time as the allocation method needs to be clear on "first-in-time to do what?" and on the level of protection enjoyed by those involved in the chase. As we shall see later, first-in-time disputes also raise questions about how to date a particular act of taking control of a resource when the activity involved takes an extended period of time to complete. Should it be dated from the first step in the process or later, when the process of taking control is complete? We will see the problem clearly when taking up the initial allocation of water rights under prior appropriation and learning about the relation-back doctrine (see chapter 6, pp. 474–479).

B. WILDLIFE AND PRIVATE LAND

RUTTEN V. WOOD
Supreme Court of North Dakota
57 N.W.2d 112 (1953)

SATHRE, J.

The plaintiff Raymond Rutten owns certain lands in Ramsey County, this State, adjoining both sides of a section line which is also a township line. The section line has been opened for travel and highway purposes pursuant to the laws of the State. During the hunting season of 1951 the plaintiff posted the land on both sides of the section line as provided by law. He brings this action to enjoin the defendant from hunting along said highway.

The complaint alleges in substance that the lands on each side of the section line referred to in the complaint are owned by the plaintiff; that the section line has been opened for highway purposes between plaintiff's two tracts of land for a width of two rods on each side of such line pursuant to statute and that the fee title to such land so used for highway purposes is in the plaintiff; that on the 17th day of October 1951 and at diverse other times the defendant entered upon said highway and parked his car along the right of way and hunted and shot geese flying across plaintiff's land and across the said highway; that such geese fell upon the plaintiff's land and that the defendant thereupon entered upon the plaintiff's fields to take such game; that the plaintiff has caused the lands referred to and described in the complaint to be posted against hunting thereon in accordance with the provisions of law; that the lands were so posted at the time the defendant entered upon said highway and said lands and hunted thereon . . .

He demands judgment enjoining the defendant from entering upon said highway for the purpose of hunting and from engaging in the hunting of game along said highway and from trespassing upon the lands of the plaintiff. . . .

The general rule as to the fee title to highways is stated in 25 Am.Jur. page 426, Highways, Section 132, as follows:

In the absence of a statute expressly providing for the acquisition of the fee, or of a deed from the owner expressly conveying the fee, when a highway is established by dedication or prescription, or by the direct action of the public authorities, the public acquires merely an easement of passage, the fee title remaining in the landowner.

This is the rule in this state. [Citations omitted.]

It is admitted that the plaintiff owns the land upon which the highway is located on both sides of the section line and that he posted 'no hunting' signs thereon as provided by law. The statutes of this state do not cover the precise question as to whether the public may legally hunt wild game upon the highways of the state.

Section 20–0119, NDRC 1943, provides that any person may enter upon legally posted land to recover game shot or killed on land where such person had a lawful right to hunt.

Section 20–0117, NDRC 1943 makes it a misdemeanor to hunt or pursue game or enter for the purpose of hunting or pursuing game upon any land belonging to another which has been legally posted, without first having obtained the permission of the person legally entitled to grant the same.

The general law as to the right to hunt on the highways is stated in 24 Am.Jur., Game and Game Laws, Section 5, page 377:

> Since the title to wild game within the boundaries of a state is vested in the people in their sovereign capacity, each of the inhabitants thereof may be said to have an equal right to kill such game. But this equal right is subject to at least two limitations. In the first place, the state may make regulations relative to the killing and marketing of game. Secondly, every landowner has an exclusive common-law right to kill or capture game on his own land, subject to the regulatory action of the state in the preservation of all game for the common use. This right is regarded at common law as property *ratione soli*, or in other words, as property by reason of the ownership of the soil. The state cannot, within constitutional limits, by the issuance of hunting licenses which purport to give a hunter the right to invade the private hunting grounds owned by another person, or by any other means, authorize one to enter another's premises, for the purpose of taking game, without the latter's permission.

This question was considered by the supreme court of Minnesota in the case of *L. Realty Co. v. Johnson*, 100 N.W. 94, 95 (Minn. 1904). We quote from the opinion:

> But we may safely assume that the killing of game belonging to the adjacent premises, and found temporarily in the highway, is in no manner connected with or incidental to the public right of passage and transportation. While true that the title to all wild game is in the state, and the owner of premises whereon it is located has only a qualified property interest therein, yet he has the right to exercise exclusive and absolute dominion over his property, and incidentally the unqualified right to control and protect the wild game thereon. In *Lamprey v. Danz*, [90 N.W. 578

(Minn. 1902),] the elementary rule on this subject was stated as follows: "Every person has exclusive dominion over the soil which he absolutely owns; hence such an owner of land has the exclusive right of hunting and fishing on his land, and the waters covering it." It necessarily follows that, in dedicating the highway in question to the public, respondent reserved to itself all of the other privileges and rights pertaining to the premises, which included the right to foster and protect, for its own use, the wild game thereon, and that such right and privilege were in no manner surrendered to the public in granting the easement. It also follows that the public, including appellant, in accepting the easement thus granted, acquired no right to kill or molest the game inhabiting the property while it was passing to and fro across the highway.

* * *

The judgment of the trial court was correct and is affirmed.

<h2 align="center">NOTES</h2>

1. *Hunting on private land.* The *Corbin* trespass case in chapter 2 introduced us to the rights of landowners today to exclude hunters. As *Corbin* illustrated, that right can be qualified; in that setting (Minnesota), by the legal right of hunters to enter private land to claim downed game even over the landowner's objection. *Rutten* give us another look. North Dakota law authorized landowners to exclude hunters if they posted their lands in accordance with detailed posting laws. Land not properly posted remained open to public use in accordance with longstanding custom. Here as in *Corbin* hunters had the right to retrieve game. The law on hunting access today is considered in Mark R. Sigmon, *Note, Hunting and Posting on Private Land in America*, 54 Duke L. J. 549 (2004).

2. *The trespassing hunter.* Hunters who trespass must release their captured game to the landowner if the landowner wants it. The rule in early America was different; the hunter could typically keep the animal and pay the small fine for the trespass (if there was one). American law changed in part as a result of the leading English ruling in *Blades v. Higgs*, 11 H.L. Cas. 621, 11 Eng. Rep. 1474 (H.L. 1865); the issue was sufficiently contentious and important to merit resolution by the House of Lords sitting as a judicial body. The English rule was adopted in Michigan in *Sterling v. Jackson*, 37 N.W. 845 (Mich. 1888), over a vigorous dissent by Justice Campbell who preferred to keep to the old rule, which was "untainted by feudalism and royal prerogative." 37 N.W. at 859. The English ruling gave the dead animal to the landowner because someone had to own it (it was no longer a wild animal) and the landowner was the obvious choice. A more common modern explanation was offered in *Rosenthal-Brown Fur Co. v. Jones-Frere Fur Co.*, 110 So. 630, 632 (La. 1926), where the court concluded that a trespassing

hunter "must account to [the land]owner for all the fruits of his unlawful exercise . . . this being in accord with the moral maxim of the law that 'no man ought to enrich himself at the expense of another.'" The rule also discourages trespass.

     3.   *Easement law and the issue of scope.* As noted in chapter 2 (pp. 72–107), many resource-use rights take the legal form of easements, which the law at one time called "incorporeal hereditaments" (meaning, interests in land that were nonpossessory (no exclusive right to possession) and that could pass to heirs and be transferred by will). The parties to an easement agreement have considerable flexibility in defining the easement as they see fit, at least if it is an *affirmative* easement (which allows the recipient of the easement to enter the land of easement grantor), rather than a *negative* easement (which restricts what the grantor can do on or with his land). Affirmative easements can take almost any form and give to the holder almost any combination of rights to enter the grantor's land (known as the *servient* estate) and do things there. What the easement holder can do, and when and where she can do it, is determined by the "scope" of the easement. The scope of an easement can be specified with great precision; or it can be left vague.

     In *Rutten*, the private land at issue was subject to an easement in favor of the state for a roadway. The legal dispute had to do with the precise scope of that public easement. The basic question was: Did the easement for a public road give to travelers on the road the right to shoot wild game? North Dakota law on the subject was vague; it merely specified that roadways in the state normally took the form of an easement rather than a fee interest, unless a fee interest was clearly specified. According to the court, the road was constructed on "an easement of passage." Travelers along the Oregon Trail a century earlier might well have needed the right to shoot game as an incident of passage, but highway travelers in the mid-twentieth century apparently do not. A contrary conclusion was reached by neighboring South Dakota in *Reis v. Miller*, 550 N.W.2d 78 (S.D. 1996), a ruling that stimulated legal conflict that continues (see *Benson v. State*, 710 N.W.2d 131 (S.D. 2006) (upholding constitutionality of statute that removed criminal sanction for hunting small game birds along public highways)).

     In many settings lawyers are called upon to draft private agreements that have the effect of creating natural resource use-rights—for instance, an agreement in which the holder of the right gains an easement to enter private land for hunting. Such an agreement needs to specify clearly the scope of the easement in terms of what hunting is allowed, when, where, by whom, using what methods, and so on. Recall the *Hunker* ruling in chapter two. It illustrated the importance, in such an agreement, of making clear whether the right granted in the easement is exclusive and what limits there are on the ability of the servient estate owner to change the land surface in ways that might diminish the value of the easement to the easement holder.

* * *

The following ruling gives more evidence of the Progressive-Era interest in game conservation, a movement led mostly by sportsmen concerned about declining game populations. Many of their efforts were aimed at eliminating market hunting of game and curtailing the plumage trade (feathers for women's hats). The conservation effort also included measures to reestablish populations of animals that had gone into decline.

BARRETT V. STATE
Court of Appeals of New York
116 N.E. 99 (1917)

ANDREWS, J.

At one time beaver were very numerous in this state. So important were they commercially that they were represented upon the seal of the New Netherlands and upon that of the colony as well as upon the seals of New Amsterdam and of New York. Because of their value, they were relentlessly killed, and by the year 1900 they were practically exterminated. But some 15 animals were left scattered through the southern portion of Franklin county. In that year the Legislature undertook to afford them complete protection, and there has been no open season for beaver since the enactment of chapter 20 of the Laws of 1900.

In 1904 it was further provided that:

"No person shall molest or disturb any wild beaver or the dams, houses, homes or abiding places of same." Laws 1904, c. 674, § 1.

This is still the law, although in 1912 the forest, fish, and game commission was authorized to permit protected animals which had become destructive to public or private property to be taken and disposed of. Laws 1912, c. 318.

By the act of 1904, $500 was appropriated for the purchase of wild beaver to restock the Adirondacks, and in 1906 $1,000 more was appropriated for the same purpose. The commission, after purchasing the animals, was authorized to liberate them. Under this authority 21 beaver have been purchased and freed by the commission. Of these 4 were placed upon Eagle creek, an inlet of the Fourth Lake of the Fulton Chain. There they seem to have remained and increased.

Beaver are naturally destructive to certain kinds of forest trees. During the fall and winter they live upon the bark of the twigs and smaller branches of poplar, birch, and alder. To obtain a supply they fell even trees of large size, cut the smaller branches into suitable lengths, and pull or float them to their houses. All this it must be assumed was known by the Legislature as early as 1900.

The claimants own a valuable tract of woodland upon Fourth Lake bounded in the rear by Eagle creek. Their land was held by them for building sites and was suitable for that purpose. Much of its attractiveness depended upon the forest grown upon it. In this forest were a number of poplar trees. In 1912 and during two or three years prior thereto 198 of these poplars were felled by beaver. Others were girdled and destroyed. The Court of Claims has found, upon evidence that fairly justifies the inference, that this destruction was caused by the four beaver liberated on Eagle creek and their descendants, and that by reason thereof the claimants have been damaged in the sum of $1,900. An award was made to them for that sum, and this award has been affirmed by the Appellate Division. To sustain it the respondents rely upon three propositions. It is said: First, that the state may not protect such an animal as the beaver which is known to be destructive; second, that the provision of the law of 1904 with regard to the molestation of beaver prohibits the claimants from protecting their property, and is therefore an unreasonable exercise of the police power; and, third, that the state was in actual physical possession of the beaver placed on Eagle creek, and that its act in freeing them, knowing their natural propensity to destroy trees, makes the state liable for the damage done by them.

We cannot agree with either of these propositions.

As to the first, the general right of the government to protect wild animals is too well established to be now called in question. Their ownership is in the state in its sovereign capacity, for the benefit of all the people. Their preservation is a matter of public interest. They are a species of natural wealth which without special protection would be destroyed. Everywhere and at all times governments have assumed the right to prescribe how and when they may be taken or killed. As early as 1705, New York passed such an act as to deer. Colonial Laws, vol. 1, p. 585. A series of statutes has followed protecting more or less completely game, birds, and fish.

> The protection and preservation of game has been secured by law in all civilized countries, and may be justified on many grounds. * * * The measures best adapted to this end are for the Legislature to determine, and courts cannot review its discretion. If the regulations operate, in any respect, unjustly or oppressively, the proper remedy must be applied by that body.

Phelps v. Racey, 60 N. Y. 10, 14 (1875).

Wherever protection is accorded, harm may be done to the individual. Deer or moose may browse on his crops; mink or skunks kill his chickens; robins eat his cherries. In certain cases the Legislature may be mistaken in its belief that more good than harm is occasioned. But this is clearly a matter which is confided to its discretion. It exercises a governmental function for the benefit of the public at large, and no one can complain of the incidental injuries that may result.

It is sought to draw a distinction between such animals and birds as have ordinarily received protection and beaver, on the ground that the latter are unusually destructive and that to preserve them is an unreasonable exercise of the power of the state.

The state may exercise the police power "wherever the public interests demand it, and in this particular a large discretion is necessary vested in the Legislature to determine, not only what the interest of the public require, but what measures are necessary for the protection of such interests. * * * To justify the state in thus interposing its authority in behalf of the public, it must appear, first, that the interests of the public generally, as distinguished from those of a particular class, require such interference; and, second, that the means are reasonably necessary for the accomplishment of the purpose, and not unduly oppressive upon individuals." *Lawton v. Steele*, 152 U. S. 133, 136 (1894).

The police power is not to be limited to guarding merely the physical or material interests of the citizen. His moral, intellectual, and spiritual needs may also be considered. The eagle is preserved, not for its use, but for its beauty.

The same thing may be said of the beaver. They are one of the most valuable of the fur-bearing animals of the state. They may be used for food. But apart from these considerations, their habits and customs, their curious instincts and intelligence, place them in a class by themselves. Observation of the animals at work or play is a source of never-failing interest and instruction. If they are to be preserved experience has taught us that protection is required. If they cause more damage than deer or moose, the degree of the mischief done by them is not so much greater or so different as to require the application of a special rule. If the preservation of the former does not unduly oppress individuals, neither does the latter. . . .

We therefore reach the conclusion that in protecting beaver the Legislature did not exceed its powers. Nor did it so do in prohibiting their molestation. It is possible that were the interpretation given by the respondents to this section right a different result might follow. If the claimants, finding beaver destroying their property, might not drive them away, then possibly their rights would be infringed. In *Aldrich v. Wright*, 53 N.H. 398 (1873), it was said in an elaborate opinion, although this question we do not decide, that a farmer might shoot mink even in the closed season should he find them threatening his geese.

But such an interpretation is too rigid and narrow. The claimants might have fenced their land without violation of the statute. They might have driven the beaver away, were they injuring their property. The prohibition against disturbing dams or houses built on or adjoining water courses is no greater or different exercise of power from that assumed by the Legislature when it prohibits the destruction of the nests and eggs of wild birds even when the latter are found upon private property.

The object is to protect the beaver. That object as we decide is within the power of the state. The destruction of dams and houses will result in driving away the beaver. The prohibition of such acts, being an apt means to the end desired, is not so unreasonable as to be beyond the legislative power.

We hold therefore that the acts referred to are constitutional. . . .

Somewhat different considerations apply to the act of the state in purchasing and liberating beaver. The attempt to introduce life into a new environment does not always result happily. The rabbit in Australia, the mongoose in the West Indies, have become pests. The English sparrow is no longer welcome. Certain of our most troublesome weeds are foreign flowers.

Yet governments have made such experiments in the belief that the public good would be promoted. Sometimes they have been mistaken. Again, the attempt has succeeded. The English pheasant is a valuable addition to our stock of birds. But whether a success or failure, the attempt is well within governmental powers.

If this is so with regard to foreign life, still more is it true with regard to animals native to the state, still existing here, when the intent is to increase the stock upon what the Constitution declares shall remain forever wild forest lands. If the state may provide for the increase of beaver by prohibiting their destruction, it is difficult to see why it may not attain the same result by removing colonies to a more favorable locality or by replacing those destroyed by fresh importations.

Nor are the cases cited by the respondents controlling. It is true that one who keeps wild animals in captivity must see to it at his peril that they do no damage to others. But it is not true that whenever an individual is liable for a certain act the state is liable for the same act. In liberating these beaver the state was acting as a government. As a trustee for the people and as their representative, it was doing what it thought best for the interests of the public at large. Under such circumstances, we cannot hold that the rule of such cases as those cited is applicable.

We reach the conclusion that no recovery can be had under this claim. . . .

NOTES

1.   *State ownership doctrine. Barrett* provides a typical expression of the state ownership doctrine in wildlife law, noted earlier. As in most such rulings, the doctrine is used to uphold state laws restricting the taking or harming of wildlife.

In a series of rulings leading up to and including *Hughes v. Oklahoma*, 441 U.S. 322 (1979), the United States Supreme Court cast doubt on the state ownership doctrine in the course of striking down state wildlife statutes that overtly discriminated against interstate commerce. The Supreme Court's comments, though, need to be understood in the specific context in which they were handed down, as courts have done (but many academic commentators in haste have not). Decisions since *Hughes* have interpreted the Court's rejecting of state-ownership reasoning as applicable only to laws that prohibit the sale of game outside the state or that in some other ways discriminate overtly against interstate commerce; we shall see this interpretation in the upcoming rulings in *Gillette* and *Simpson*. *E.g., State v. Fertterer*, 841 P.2d 467 (Mont. 1992); *O'Brien v. State*, 711 P.2d 1144 (Wyo. 1986). See Oliver A. Houck, *Why Do We Protect Endangered Species, and What Does That Say About Whether Restrictions on Private Property to Protect Them Constitute "Takings"?* 80 Iowa L. Rev. 297, 331 n. 77 (1995) ("The trust analogy announced in *Geer* was not overruled in *Hughes* and remains the most accurate expression of this state interest: Wildlife belongs to everyone and the state has a special authority, and obligation, to ensure its perpetuation."); Michael C. Blumm & Aurora Paulsen, *The Public Trust in Wildlife*, 2013 Utah L. Rev. 1437, 1488–1504 (documenting 47 state's claims to ownership of wildlife). Later in the chapter, we explore the meaning of this ownership and the confusion related to it caused by private game ranches, especially ranches featuring exotic species imported in captivity.

2.   *Bans on hunting on private land.* From time to time landowners have challenged limits on their ability to hunt on their private land, particularly when hunting is allowed on some lands and not on others. In an important early ruling, *Cawsey v. Brickey*, 144 P. 938 (Wash. 1914), the Washington Supreme Court upheld an order creating a game preserve that included land on which a private gun club had purchased exclusive hunting rights; the effect of the law was to render the hunting rights worthless. The law was challenged both as a taking of private property and as class legislation (that is, a law that treated landowners unequally). The court rejected both arguments:

> Do these provisions tend to deprive any one of property rights or vested privileges? We think not. Under the common law of England all property right in animals *ferae naturae* was in the sovereign for the use and benefit of the people. The killing, taking, and use of game was subject to absolute governmental control for the common good. This absolute power to control and regulate was vested in the colonial governments as a part of the common law. It passed with the title to game to the several states as an incident of their sovereignty, and was retained by the states for the use and benefit of the people of the states, subject only to any applicable provisions of the federal Constitution. [citations omitted] There is no private right in the citizen to take fish or game, except as either expressly

given or inferentially suffered by the state. *State v. Tice*, 125 P. 168 (Wash. 1912).

Section 21 of the Game Code provides:

"No person shall at any time or in any manner acquire any property in, or subject to his dominion or control, any of the game birds, game animals, or game fish, or any parts thereof, of the game birds, game animals or game fish herein mentioned, but they shall always and under all circumstances be and remain the property of the state." Laws of 1913, p. 365.

This is but declaratory of the common law. Whatever special or qualified rights or, more correctly speaking, privileges, a landowner may have as to game, while it is on his own land, though protected by the laws of trespass as against other persons, have no protection, because they have no existence, as against the state. . . .

Does the act here in question bear unequally on persons similarly situated so as to be obnoxious to the constitutional inhibition against class legislation? We think not. It is the universality of the operation of a law on all persons of the state similarly situated with reference to the subject-matter that determines its validity as a general and uniform law, not the extent of territory in which it operates. That its operation may not be at all times coextensive with the territorial limits of the state is usually an immaterial circumstance. *State ex rel. Lindsey v. Derbyshire*, 140 P. 540 (Wash. 1914). The owner of land which from its location and character is peculiarly suited for a game preserve is not situated similarly to other landowners with reference to the subject-matter and purpose of a law creating a preserve. The subject-matter and purpose is protection and preservation of game. It is so declared in the title of the act. One whose land is thus peculiarly suited to meet those purposes obviously occupies a different relation to the purpose of the law from that occupied by one whose land is not so suited. When, therefore, the state authorizes the setting apart of his land for a game preserve and deprives him and all others of the privilege of taking game thereon, the law operates equally on all persons similarly situated, and is a proper exercise of the police power.

Cawsey, 144 P. at 939–40.

In a more recent dispute, *Collopy v. Wildlife Commission, Dept. of Natural Resources,* 625 P.2d 994 (1981), the Colorado Supreme Court rejected a landowner's claim that his constitutionally grounded "right to hunt" on his private land was violated when the state banned goose hunting on his land while allowing it on nearby private lands. The landowner cited in support the two judicial rulings that have used "right to hunt" language to strike down statutes—*Alford v. Finch*, 155 So.2d 790 (Fla. 1963) and *Allen v. McClellan*, 405 P.2d 405 (N.M. 1965). The Colorado court decided to stick with what was the near universal rule that landowners had no right to hunt that was enforceable against the state:

> This constitutional claim is cognizable only if it is first acknowledged that a landowner's right to hunt on his own land is a "property right" under state law. We here decide that the right to hunt wild game upon one's own land is not a property right enforceable against the state under Art. II, Sec. 15 of the Colorado Constitution.
>
> Although the issue now before us was not unequivocally decided in *Maitland v. People*, [23 P.2d 116 (Colo. 1933)], this court there stated:
>
>> The right to kill game is a boon or privilege granted either expressly or impliedly, by the sovereign authority and is not a right inhering in any individual.
>
> *Maitland*, 23 P.2d at 117. Because *Maitland*, like the present case, dealt with a claim that the state had unconstitutionally taken a landowner's crops by forbidding him to kill game on his ranch, its characterization of the right to hunt game as a "boon or privilege" rather than an individual right suggests that this court has not heretofore classified property *ratione soli* as a distinct property right accompanying land ownership. *See also Game and Fish Commission v. Feast*, 402 P.2d 169 (1965).
>
> Moreover, *Maitland*'s characterization of the right to hunt as a privilege against the state rather than a property right comports with decisions in other jurisdictions which have rejected the argument that landowners enjoy a property right to take game on their own soil.

Collopy, 625 P.2d at 999–1000.

While courts have rejected efforts by landowners to assert rights to hunt to deflect state-law limits, they have been more receptive to arguments when the state's line drawing is either unauthorized (the agency has exceeded its delegated power—the *Allen* case) or arbitrary (the *Alford* case, it seems on the facts). It is also possible to present a regulatory takings argument when a ban on hunting leaves land with no other economic use. *See, e.g., Scofield v. Nebraska Dept. of Natural Resources*, 753 N.W.2d 345 (Neb. 2008).

3.   *A limited right to defend property.* Although they have failed in right-to-hunt arguments landowners have occasionally succeeded in using their property rights as shields when they have violated game laws by killing animals that cause serious property damage. When courts have allowed such defenses, they have typically required landowners to exhaust all nonlethal means of controlling the animals. See e.g., *Cross v. State*, 370 P.2d 371 (Wyo. 1962). In *State v. Vander Houwen,* 177 P.3d 93 (Wash. 2008), a landowner successfully raised a constitutional defense-of-property claim in a prosecution for killing harm-causing elk. To use the defense the defendant had to show

that the action was reasonably necessary given the failure of less lethal alternatives; when this was done, the burden shifted to the state to prove beyond a reasonable doubt that killing the elk was unjustified.

As populations of certain wildlife species have risen in recent decades (even as most species continue to face moderate or significant declines), many states have enacted statutes that authorize landowners to take action against nuisance wildlife and, less commonly, to receive money damages for wildlife-caused harm. These statutes are properly read along with state wildlife laws generally, which sometimes offer no protection for certain nuisance nongame species. One such statute was considered in *State v. Thompson*, 563 S.E.2d 325 (S.C. 2002) (rejecting landowner's defense-of-property claim to a game law violation when he could have received, but did not obtain, a state permit to capture harm-causing beaver). See Dale D. Goble & Eric T. Freyfogle, *Wildlife Law: Case and Materials* 225–32 (2d ed. 2010).

C. HUNTING RIGHTS OF INDIAN TRIBES

An important part of wildlife law addresses the special wildlife-related rights of many American Indian tribes, both on tribal reservations and off. These rights are recognized in treaties, with terms that vary considerably from treaty to treaty. Most litigation has arisen under treaties in which tribes relinquished lands to the federal government but retained specified rights to hunt or fish on them. These rights are protected by federal law and take precedence over any property rights in the land later acquired under federal or state law.

The following reading discusses the unique legal status of Indian tribes and the rules that govern treaty interpretation.

WILDLIFE LAW: TRIBES AND TREATIES
Eric T. Freyfogle & Dale D. Goble
Island Press, pp. 165–67 (2009)

Indian tribes occupy a legal status unlike any other entities in American law. They are not states, they are not foreign governments, nor are they like departments of the federal government. Their unique legal status has been the subject of various rulings by the United States Supreme Court, beginning in the nation's earliest years. As the Supreme Court has explained the roles of tribes it has talked also about the treaties between tribes and the United States: about where treaties stand in the legal hierarchy and how courts should interpret them.

Tribes and Treaties

The legal status of tribes was initially defined in 1831, when Chief Justice John Marshall took the position that they were neither states in the Union nor foreign governments. Instead, tribes were "domestic dependent nations," a term Marshall coined to avoid the practical consequences of recognizing the inherent sovereign powers of tribes. According to Marshall's framework, tribes resided in a "state of pupilage" to the federal government, a relationship that Marshall likened to that of a ward to his guardian. As for internal matters, the tribes were self-governing entities, which meant that state laws had no application on tribal lands.

The independence of tribal reservations from state law, as we shall see, is no longer so complete. Legal relationships have grown more complex. The basic framework, though, remains as Marshall described it. Recent rulings have described tribes as "unique aggregations possessing attributes of sovereignty over both their members and their territory." The tribes "have been implicitly divested of their sovereignty in certain respects by virtue of their dependent status," but they nonetheless enjoy "an historic immunity from state and local control" while retaining "any aspect of their historic sovereignty not inconsistent with the overriding interest of the National Government." Significantly, Indians have the right to make their own laws and be governed by them, a principle that requires "an accommodation between the interests of the Tribes and the Federal Government, on the one hand, and those of the State, on the other." Numerous rulings by the Supreme Court have fleshed out these broad principles.

Corresponding with this quasi-independent status of tribes is the duty of the federal government to exercise high standards of care in dealing with tribes and safeguarding their interests. The guardian-ward relationship, first expressed by John Marshall in 1831, has given rise over time to an extensive body of precedent. The federal government occupies the office of trustee with tribes as beneficiaries. As trustee, the government owes fiduciary duties to deal with tribes fairly and safeguard their interests; duties that sometimes obligate the federal government to bring lawsuits to safeguard tribal interests. The federal government cannot negotiate with them aggressively at arm's length as it would other entities. On various occasions, courts have found that the federal government has breached these trustee duties.

Treaties and Reservations of Rights

As the United States pushed its boundaries westward, it entered into numerous agreements with Indian tribes. It did so in recognition that the tribes possessed legal rights in their lands that the federal government was bound to respect. According to Chief Justice Marshall, writing in 1835, the "hunting grounds" of tribes "were as much in their actual possession as the cleared fields of the whites; and their rights to its exclusive enjoyment in their own way and for their own purposes were as much respected, until they abandoned them, made a cession to the government, or an authorized sale to individuals." Thus, as tribes entered into treaties they did not *acquire* property rights in land from the federal government. Instead, the tribes retained or *reserved* rights that they already possessed. Although the lands that they reserved became part of the United States and of the individual states, tribal property rights were not created under federal or state law.

Almost since the beginning, courts have been sensitive to the challenges tribes faced when negotiating with the United States. The treaties that memorialized these negotiations were written in English and communication problems were vast. Tribes often experienced understandable difficulties traversing the legal and cultural gaps. In response to these problems and by way of leveling the playing field, courts have long interpreted treaties using canons of construction that strongly favor tribes. Repeatedly they have stated that treaties are liberally construed in favor of the tribes. Ambiguities are interpreted in their favor. In addition, courts interpret treaties as Indians at the time would have understood them, not according to the understandings of contemporary federal agents (and much less the interpretations readers today might give them).

These interpretive principles apply not just to ambiguities in what is written but to the larger transactions of which treaties were a part. For instance, courts interpreting treaties have considered the larger factual contexts of particular treaty negotiations—including the often weak bargaining position of the tribes—to decide that treaties reserved rights to harvest wildlife, even though the reservations were not clearly expressly in the written document. They have given particular weight to the fact that hunting and fishing rights were so vital to many tribes that the tribes would never have signed a treated relinquishing the rights. This reality has led courts to interpret treaties as reserving such harvesting rights even when not expressly mentioned.

Once treaties are interpreted to reserve particular tribal rights, courts are reluctant to conclude that later federal actions have curtailed or limited these rights or powers. Any federal action that might arguably abridge them is construed narrowly to minimize any reduction of tribal rights and autonomy.

Dissimilar Rights

As a consequence of these many treaties, members of Indian tribes typically have legal rights that non-Indians do not possess. As the Supreme Court has noted, however, treaty rights to hunt and fish are "servitudes".... There rights thus are a type of property entitlement. They therefore have a sound legal basis and do not violate any constitutional principles requiring equal protection of laws.

STATE V. STASSO
Supreme Court of Montana
563 P.2d 562 (1977)

HARRISON, J.

Defendant Lasso Stasso, a duly enrolled member of the Confederated Salish and Kootenai Indian Tribes, was convicted in justice court, Thompson Falls, Montana, of a violation of the game laws of Montana. The specific charge was killing a deer out of season. This conviction was appealed to the district court and was set aside and the charges dismissed. The state appeals.

These facts were stipulated by the parties:

1. Defendant, Lasso Stasso, is a duly enrolled member of the Confederated Salish and Kootenai Tribes of the Flathead Reservation, Montana. The Confederated Tribes were parties to the Treaty of Hell Gate of July 16, 1885, 12 Stat. 975, with the United States.

2. Defendant shot and killed a deer on August 24, 1972, in the general vicinity of White Pine Creek, Sanders County, Montana. At the time of the incident the season was closed for hunting deer, pursuant to Montana law.

3. That the location is outside the boundaries of the Flathead Reservation, as established by Article II of the Treaty of Hell Gate of July 16, 1855, but within National Forest Service lands which have never been patented to any private person.

The state relied solely on the stipulated facts. Defendant, however, presented the testimony of an expert witness and exhibits clearly outlining the aboriginal hunting territory of the Confederated Salish and Kootenai Tribes. The evidence indicated the deer was taken within this aboriginal hunting territory, but without the confines of the present day Flathead Reservation.

The district court found the lands upon which the offense occurred were open and unclaimed lands under the Treaty of Hell Gate and provisions of the treaty are superior to any reserved power of the state and therefore exempt from state regulation. The complaint was dismissed for failure to state the commission of a public offense.

The issue to be decided is whether present day members of the Confederated Salish and Kootenai Tribes have a right to hunt free from the regulation of Montana game laws, on "open and unclaimed lands" by virtue of Article II of the Treaty of Hell Gate. In determining this issue, we first consider whether Forest Service land may be included within the meaning of "open and unclaimed lands."

The concept of aboriginal title to lands historically occupied by American Indians is recognized in *Sac and Fox Tribe v. United States*, 383 F.2d 991, 997, 179 Ct.Cl. 8 (1967), *cert. denied*, 389 U.S. 900 (1967), where the court stated:

> * * * the right of sovereignty over discovered land was always subject to the right of use and occupancy and enjoyment of the land by Indians living on the land. This right of use and occupancy by Indians came to be known as "Indian title." It is sometimes called "original title" or "aboriginal title."

Hunting and fishing rights are part and parcel with aboriginal title. *State v. Coffee*, 556 P.2d 1185 (1976).

Aboriginal title is founded on the concept that Indian occupancy and use of the land prehistorically predated the present sovereign. This being so, we examine the terms by which the Indians ended their land to the United States to determine to what extent Indian hunting rights on that land remain unextinguished.

The parties stipulated the Confederated Salish and Kootenai Tribes, of which the defendant is a member, were parties to the Treaty of Hell Gate. This treaty was executed on July 16, 1855 at Hell Gate in the Bitter Root Valley. Isaac I. Stevens, governor and superintendent of Indian affairs for the Territory of Washington, represented the United States. Representative chiefs, headmen, and delegates of the Flathead, Kootenai, and Upper Pend d'Oreilles Indian Tribes signed for them.

Through the provisions of Article I of this treaty, the Indians ceded all their lands to the United States:

> ARTICLE I. The said confederated tribes of Indians hereby cede, relinquish, and convey to the United States all their right, title, and interest in all to the country occupied or claimed by them, bounded and described as follows * * *.

The treaty further provided that in exchange for the cession of their lands the Indians were to receive a reservation and monetary compensation. In addition Article III of the Treaty provided the Indians were to receive:

> The exclusive right of taking fish in all the streams running through or bordering said reservation is further secured to said Indians; as also the right of taking fish at the usual and accustomed places, in common with citizens of the Territory, and of erecting temporary buildings for curing; together with the privilege of **hunting, gathering roots and berries, and pasturing their horses and cattle upon open and unclaimed land.** (Emphasis added). . . .

The application of the provisions of the Treaty of Hell Gate to a fact situation such as the instant case is a matter of first impression in this jurisdiction. It is clear however that the provisions of the treaty must be considered as a reservation by the Indians, rather than a grant by the federal government. Therefore, the Indians, at the time of the treaty, reserved the right to hunt on open and unclaimed lands outside their present day reservation, but within their aboriginal hunting territory. The determination remaining to be made is-to what extent does this reservation of right remain unextinguished?

Idaho courts have decided the instant question in that jurisdiction. In view of the striking similarities of the fact pattern of the Idaho cases with the instant case, these cases will be discussed here.

State v. Arthur, 261 P.2d 135, 143 (Idaho 1953), involved an attempt by the state of Idaho to enforce its hunting laws against a member of the Nez Perce Tribe who killed a deer out of season on National Forest land. The incident occurred outside the boundaries of the reservation, but within the area ceded to the federal government by the Tribe. The treaty provisions involved in Arthur were identical to Article III of the Treaty of Hell Gate. The Supreme Court of Idaho rejected the state's attempt to enforce the hunting laws upon the Indian-defendant:

> We are not here concerned with the wisdom of the provisions of the treaty under present conditions nor with the advisability of imposing upon the Indians certain regulatory obligations in the interest of conserving wild life; that is for the Federal Government, the affected tribe, and perhaps the State of Idaho to resolve under appropriate negotiations; our concern here is only with reference to protecting the rights of the Indians which they reserved under the Treaty of 1855 to hunt upon open and unclaimed land without limitation, restriction or burden. "We hold that the rights reserved by the Nez Perce Indians in 1855, which have never passed from them to hunt upon open and unclaimed land still exist unimpaired and that they are entitled to hunt at any time of the year in any of the lands ceded to the federal government though such lands are outside the boundary of their reservation. * * * "

State v. Tinno, 497 P.2d 1386, 1391 (Idaho 1972), is in accord with *Arthur*. In *Tinno* a member of the Shoshone-Bannock Tribes was charged with taking a chinook salmon with a spear in violation of Idaho fishing regulations. The Idaho Supreme Court found the Tribes' treaty gave the right to hunt and fish on unoccupied lands of the United States even though fishing was not specifically mentioned in the language of the treaty. . . .

State v. Coffee, 556 P.2d 1185 (Idaho 1976), was decided in November 1976. In *Coffee* a member of the Kootenai Tribe was charged with the killing of two deer out of season on private property. The Idaho Supreme Court affirmed the district court conviction on the grounds the Tribe's aboriginal hunting right only applied to open and unclaimed lands and not to lands owned by private parties.

We find the Idaho cases interpreting Indian treaties containing language dealing with Indian hunting rights common to the Treaty of Hell Gate persuasive in the instant case. Article III of the Treaty of Hell Gate reserves for present day members of the tribes signing that document the right to hunt game animals free from state regulation on lands ceded by the tribes to the federal government. However, it is clear this right is limited to land which is open and unclaimed at the time of the incident. Land owned or occupied by private parties is in no way open and unclaimed within the contemplation of this treaty.

In *State v. Arthur,* 261 P.2d 135, 141 (Idaho 1953), the term "open and unclaimed lands" was interpreted as:

> * * * lands as were not settled and occupied by the whites under possessory rights or patent or otherwise appropriated to private ownership and was not intended to nor did it exclude lands title to which rested in the federal government * * *.

We find this definition persuasive in light of the fact that the treaty interpreted in Arthur was identical to the Treaty of Hell Gate.

We find the National Forest lands involved herein are open and unclaimed lands. *State v. Arthur*, cited above; *Confederated Tribes of Umatilla Indian Res. v. Maison*, 262 F.Supp. 871 (D. Or. 1966), *affirmed in Holcomb v. Confederated Tribes of Umatilla Indian Res.*, 382 F.2d 1013 (9th Cir. 1967).

The judgment of the district court is affirmed.

NOTES

1.   *A free-standing right to hunt.* The defendant in this criminal case was exercising a right to hunt that allows hunting in violation of state game laws. What are the elements or contours of this right to use open and unclaimed lands? Who seems to possess the land-use right and how long does it apparently last? More basically, to what law would we look in resolving questions about the scope of the right?

Since this ruling, other courts have followed the lead of the Idaho decisions discussed in *Stasso*, agreeing that lands are not "open and unclaimed" if they have passed into private hands. See e.g., *State v. Watters,* 156 P.3d 145 (Or. Ct. App. 2007). Disputes have been frequent because the language covering fishing and hunting rights used in the treaty in *Stasso* was also in many other treaties with Indian tribes in the Pacific Northwest.

Note that the *fishing* rights reserved in this treaty—"the right of taking fish at the usual and accustomed places, in common with citizens of the Territory"—are not limited to places that remain open and unclaimed. These fishing rights remain valid even when title to the underlying land passes into private hands. *Seufert Brothers Co. v. United States*, 249 U.S. 194 (1919); *United States v. Winans*, 198 U.S. 371 (1905). Moreover, the language "in common with citizens of the Territory" does not mean that Indians can be treated like all other citizens. *Washington v. Washington State Commercial Passenger Fishing Vessel Assn.*, 443 U.S. 658 (1979). For an examination of tribal treaty fishing rights as property rights, see Michael C. Blumm & Brett M. Swift, *The Indian Treaty Piscary Profit and Habitat Protection in the Pacific Northwest: A Property Rights Approach*, 69 U. Colo. L. Rev. 407 (1998). A federal court has ruled that state actions greatly reducing salmon populations can violate treaty rights, *United States v. Washington*, 2007 WL 2437166 (W.D. Wash. Aug. 22, 2007) (concerning the construction and poor maintenance of state road culverts). See Michael C. Blumm & Jane G. Steadman, *Indian Treaty Fishing Rights and Habitat Protection: the Martinez Decision Supplies a Resounding Judicial Reaffirmation*, 49 Nat. Res. J. 653 (2009) (discussing the culverts decision). In March 2013, the district court ordered the state of Washington to provide fish passage at some 180 culverts by 2016, and at all 817 by 2030. The state, estimating a total cost of $2.4 billion, has appealed that decision and the 2007 decision to the Ninth Circuit.

2.   *Rights within the tribe.* The rights to fish and hunt reserved under these various treaties (and others like them, covering tribes elsewhere) were reserved by the tribes as such. Within the tribes, however, these rights were sometimes held by individual families and not just retained for collective use. In *Whitefoot v. United States*, 293 F.2d 658 (Ct. Cl. 1961), Yakima tribal member Minnie Whitefoot sought compensation from the federal government for the loss of her six "usual and accustomed fishing stations" when the fishing spots were inundated by a new reservoir on the Columbia River. The federal government condemned the fishing spots as part of its acquisition of land for the reservoir and paid $15 million specifically for the fishing spots. That money was paid, however, to the Yakima Nation, which distributed it in equal shares to all tribal members without regard for which individuals and families controlled the spots. The Court of Claims concluded that Whitefoot had no claim against the United States once the federal government had paid full value for the land. "The use of accustomed fishing places, whether on or off the reservation, is a tribal matter for adjustment by the tribe." For more on Indian hunting and fishing rights, see Judith V. Royster, Michael C. Blumm & Elizabeth Ann Kronk, *Native American Natural Resources Law: Cases and Materials*, ch. 9 (3rd ed. 2013) (referring to these rights as "usufuctuary rights").

3. *Individual fishing quotas.* Efforts to reverse declines in coastal ocean fisheries have often involved attempts to control overfishing by crafting specific use rights and allocating them in some way to competing fishing interests. Some have taken the form of individual fishing quotas or individual take quotas. Lawmakers face obvious challenges when crafting the terms of such rights. The rights must specify the number of fish that can be caught and processes for adjusting that number; the duration of the rights; their transferability; the types of equipment that can be used; seasons of capture, and much more. The knotty challenges of defining such rights—too often overlooked in debates about the merits of the approach—are considered in Katrina M. Wyman, *The Property Rights Challenge in Marine Fisheries*, 50 Ariz. L. Rev. 511 (2008).

D. STATE POWERS AND DUTIES

As we have seen (pp. 252–254, 265–272) states have broad powers to regulate the taking of wildlife on private as well as public lands and can define as they see fit the property rights that private actors gain in wildlife lawfully captured. Courts upholding these powers often refer to the state's ownership of the wildlife, not so much as the source of the regulatory power (that is inherent in state sovereignty), but by way of highlighting the legitimacy of a state's concern about the welfare of wildlife species and populations. The state's own wildlife not as they own other types of property but in a special trust capacity, managing the wildlife on behalf of the people of the state who are the beneficiaries of the trust and, accordingly, beneficial owners of the wildlife. Countless courts have recognized this special legal arrangement. Few of them, however, have clarified the content of this trust, in terms of the special powers it might confer on states and the duties that states might bear by virtue of their obligations as trustee.

WASHINGTON V. GILLETTE

Court of Appeals of Washington
621 P.2d 764 (1980)

REED, C.J.

Defendants Cyril and Sharon Gillette appeal a verdict and judgment awarding damages to the Washington State Department of Fisheries for loss of salmon caused when the Gillettes reconstructed the bank of a stream bordering their property. Defendants challenge the Department of Fisheries' capacity and standing to bring this action, the sufficiency of the evidence of damages, and the court's instructions on the measure of damages. They also raise several evidentiary questions. We hold the Department has both the capacity and standing to bring the action and has shown itself entitled to recover. We find no error in regard to the evidentiary issues and therefore affirm the judgment of the trial court.

Defendants live on farm property bordering Cedar Creek, a salmon spawning stream in Clark County. Seasonal flooding of the creek left unwanted deposits of soil and gravel in Gillettes' adjoining pasture. In the spring of 1976, the flooding washed away so much of the bank that a utility pole was left dangling unsupported along the edge of the creek. Mr. Gillette appealed to the local Public Utility District for assistance in resetting the pole. Although P.U.D. officials did not help, they evidently suggested the Gillettes reconstruct the bank themselves. Accordingly, one of Gillettes' employees, Ricky Smith, was directed to rebuild the bank. Gillette and the employee testified the reconstruction took place in September 1976. Smith testified that, using a caterpillar tractor with an attached blade, he drove back and forth through the stream and pushed material from the creek bed and the adjacent field into the bank. The dike thus created rose as much as 20 feet above the creek.

RCW 75.20.100 provides that anyone wishing to construct a hydraulic project that will interfere with any river or stream bed must obtain written approval from both the Director of Fisheries and the Director of Game. The statute's purpose is to ensure that such projects include adequate protection for the fish life involved. Violation of the statute is a gross misdemeanor. Being unaware of the statute's requirements, the Gillettes did not obtain the necessary hydraulics project permit.

Representatives of both the Department of Game and the Department of Fisheries responded to reports of the construction and inspected the scene. The Department of Fisheries then filed this action in negligence for damages for the loss to the salmon fishery caused by the project. At the close of the evidence, the court granted Fisheries a directed verdict on the issue of liability. The jury thus considered only proximate cause and damage issues and awarded the State $3,150. Defendants appeal.

Capacity and Standing

[The court first upheld the capacity of the state Department of Fisheries to bring the action for damages to the state's fishery, noting in part that "the people of the state of Washington are the real parties in interest to this action."]

The second prong of defendants' argument opposing Department of Fisheries' standing raises a more significant question. Does the Department of Fisheries, or the State of Washington for that matter, have standing to bring a civil action for damage to fish, absent specific legislative authorization? Although no Washington cases have addressed this question, and other jurisdictions have divided on the issue, we believe our statutes and court decisions provide the guidance necessary for its resolution.

First, the legislature has specifically charged the Department of Fisheries with the duty

> to preserve, protect, perpetuate and manage the food fish and shellfish in the waters of the state. . . (T)he department shall seek to maintain the economic well-being and stability of the commercial fishing industry in the state of Washington.

RCW 75.08.012. Our courts have long recognized the rule that

> when a statute contains a grant of authority to achieve a lawful objective there is included in the grant by implication the doing of such acts as are reasonably necessary to properly attain such objective. . . .

Second, the state's proprietary interest in animals *ferae naturae* dates at least from the common law of England. See 2 W. Blackstone, Commentaries 403 (1803). Our courts have incorporated this concept in cases upholding the state's authority to regulate fish and game. *State Department of Fisheries v. Chelan County P.U.D. 1*, 588 P.2d 1146 (Wash. 1979) and cases cited therein. Washington courts have emphasized that the food fish of the state are the sole property of the people and that the state, acting for the people, is dealing with its own property, "over which its control is as absolute as that of any other owner over his property." *State ex rel. Bacich v. Huse*, 59 P.2d 1101 (Wash. 1936). See, e. g., *Judd v. Bernard*, 304 P.2d 1046 (Wash. 1956); *accord, State ex rel. Campbell v. Case*, 47 P.2d 24 (Wash. 1935). See also *State v. Cramer*, 8 P.2d 1004 (Wash. 1932) ("The fish were the property of (the state) until such time as they were lawfully reduced to possession (of individual)"). In addition to recognizing the state's proprietary interest in its fish, our courts have also held that the state holds its title as trustee for the common good. *State ex rel. Bacich v. Huse*, cited above.

In bringing this action, the Department of Fisheries specifically relied on its capacity as trustee and its responsibilities under RCW Title 75 to protect the state's fisheries. Violation of a statute is negligence per se and an individual in the class protected by the statute has a cause of action for damages proximately caused by the violation. *Currie v. Union Oil Co.*, 307 P.2d 1056 (Wash. 1957); *Engelker v. Seattle Elec. Co.*, 96 P. 1039 (Wash. 1908). Defendants admit they violated RCW 75.20.100, which is designed to protect society's interest in preserving the fishery and fish habitat. Representing the people of the state the owners of the property destroyed by violation of the statute the Department of Fisheries thus has a right of action for damages. In addition, the state, through the Department, has the fiduciary obligation of any trustee to seek damages for injury to the object of its trust. We note in passing that if the state were denied a right of recovery for the damage which the jury found this construction did to the state's fishery, no one would have standing to recover for the injury. *Department of Environmental Protection v. Jersey Central Power & Light Co.*, 336 A.2d 750, 759 (N.J. Super. Ct. App. Div. 1975), *rev'd on other grounds*, 351 A.2d 337 (N.J. 1976) (questionable whether, absent special interest, anyone but state is proper party to sue for damages to environment); 35 Am.Jur.2d Fish and Games 22 (1967). We therefore hold that where the violation of a statute designed to protect the state's property causes injury to that property, the state or a responsible executive agency of the state has standing to seek compensation for the injury.

Damage Arguments

Addressing defendants' damage arguments, we turn first to their challenge to the sufficiency of the evidence that their activities caused any damage to fish at all. . . .

From the record, we glean the following summary of testimony which the jury was entitled to believe. Prior to the construction, the stream bed at the site was "one of the better spawning areas." Salmon spawning peaks in late October. There was no sign of construction as late as October 15. On October 25, fishermen noticed muddy water downstream from the site. The next day they visited the site and saw carcasses and dried salmon eggs in fresh tractor tracks on the Gillette bank. They also saw salmon trying to spawn in the area. The stream bottom appeared mushy and lacked the gravel necessary for nesting sites. Based on the number of salmon redds (nests) in the half-mile below the construction site, there should have been 30 redds in the affected area. Fisheries Department specialists saw no redds at all on December 1. The Department's expert witnesses concluded spawning had probably occurred in the area. Core samples taken in January indicated the stream bed had a percentage of fine materials significantly higher than would permit incubating salmon to survive. If salmon had spawned in the area before construction, most of the nests would have been destroyed. Any remaining eggs would have a poor chance of surviving. Spawning attempted after construction would have been unsuccessful because of the lack of gravel and the high percentage of silt. Fry counts in the spring of 1977 showed virtually no fry in the construction area, the counts being the second lowest of any stream in Southwest Washington. Thus, even accepting Gillettes' contention that the construction occurred in September, the jury had before it sufficient circumstantial evidence from which it could find actual damage. A reviewing court will not disturb a jury verdict supported by substantial evidence. *Hernandez v. Western Farmers Ass'n*, 456 P.2d 1020 (Wash. 1969).

Defendants next challenge the trial court's adoption in its instructions of the measure of damages theory presented by the Department of Fisheries. The only evidence regarding the value of the fish lost derived from the testimony of Donald McIsaac, a biostatistician and fish production specialist from the Department of Fisheries. Working from the testimony of other witnesses as to the number of nests which should have been in the construction area, Mr. McIsaac referred to studies showing number of eggs per nest and survival rates to predict the number of fish which would have survived to be caught. He concluded that the state's fishery lost 606 adult fish as a result of defendants' construction project.

According to his testimony, as summarized in the statement of facts, the value of these fish was basically the market value of the fish, which was the net economic value of the salmon to the public fishery. (H)e defined net economic value . . . as essentially the amount of value or profits society made from the catch of the fish.

For the sports fishery, this figure was derived from a 1976 study adjusted for inflation and included the amount people would spend for the opportunity to catch fish. For the commercial fishery, Mr. McIsaac multiplied the ex-vessel price paid by a commercial processor by a factor of 2.1 to "reflect additional value to society for wages and income generated by further processing of fish." Under this theory, the value of the destroyed fish was $9,431.78. On cross examination, Mr. McIsaac admitted the ex-vessel price for all the fish would be $3,859.10. As indicated, the jury's award was $3,150.

Defendants challenge this measure of damages as too remote and speculative to provide a basis for recovery. Defendants, however, do not challenge the technical validity of the basis of Mr. McIsaac's valuation theory. Nor did they present evidence other than Mr. McIsaac's cross examination testimony as to any other theory for measuring damages to society. This court declines to assess the technical validity of a theory which was presented by expert testimony, a matter generally within the trial court's discretion. See *Myers v. Harter*, 459 P.2d 25 (Wash. 1969). In any event, we are reluctant to immunize a defendant once damage has been shown merely because "the extent or amount thereof cannot be ascertained with mathematical precision, provided the evidence is sufficient to afford a reasonable basis for estimating loss." *Jacqueline's Washington, Inc. v. Mercantile Stores Co.*, 498 P.2d 870 (Wash. 1972); accord, *Lundgren v. Whitney's, Inc.*, 614 P.2d 1272 (Wash. 1980). Here, defendants do not deny their activity disrupted the bed of a salmon spawning stream. The Department presented ample evidence to justify a finding that damage did occur as a result of defendants' project. On this record, we believe Mr. McIsaac's testimony on direct and cross examination provided the jury with the requisite reasonable basis for estimating the loss.

Affirmed.

NOTES

1. *The power (and duty?) to recover damages. Gillette* is typical of rulings that recognize the power of states to recover monetary damages for harm to wildlife in their capacity as trustee owners. Two early rulings held otherwise, but the tide turned in the early 1970s with rulings such as *State v. City of Bowling Green*, 313 N.E.2d 409 (Ohio 1974). An important issue in such cases has to do with the value of the wildlife that are killed or otherwise harmed. How did the court in *Gillette* address the valuation issue? Are there other value methodologies that might be used instead, perhaps related to the costs of creating suitable habitat for a species to replace habitat that has been degraded?

Note that the court stated that the wildlife trust goes beyond the matter of state powers. The state, the court opined, "has the fiduciary obligation of any trustee to seek damages for injury to the object of its trust." If the state as trustee is, in fact, in a role similar to other trustees, it must protect the corpus of the trust (the wildlife), not just seek damages after it has been destroyed.

Under standard trust law, the beneficiaries of a trust can seek relief against a trustee who fails to abide by the duties imposed by the terms of the trust. Few cases have considered the ability of private citizens to seek to enforce the wildlife trust. A prominent case was *Center for Biological Diversity, Inc. v. FPL Group, Inc.*, 166 Cal.App.4th 1349 (2008), in which a not-for-profit conservation group sought to challenge owners and operators of wind turbines, arguing that the bird deaths caused by the turbines violated the terms of the wildlife trust. The court agreed that the trust imposed affirmative duties to protect trust property, and agreed further that citizens had the power to enforce the trust. An action to enforce the trust, however, had to be brought against the state as trustee, not against private actors whose conduct harmed trust property. The trust doctrine is considered in some detail in Michael C. Blumm & Aurora Paulsen, *The Public Trust in Wildlife*, 2013 Utah L. Rev. 1437 (including a survey of all states' claims to ownership of wildlife).

2. *A public right to view wildlife?* If we take seriously the idea that the state owns wildlife on behalf of the people (and with trust duties to protect them, as courts have regularly asserted), could a member of the public claim that the public's ownership of wildlife should include an ancillary right to enter private land to view the wildlife—perhaps so long as there is no interference with the landowner's activities? Should not a person's co-ownership of wild animals include some minimal ability to enjoy them, particularly if they reside only on private land? If not, why not, at least when the private landowner is not being physically disturbed by the entry? On this issue, consider the ruling in chapter one in *Park County* (p. 29), applying Colorado law that empowered owners of discrete water rights to cross private land to gain access to the water and to divert the water through natural channels, all without the permission of the owner of the land being crossed.

The idea of state ownership has come under strain by the rising popularity of private wildlife reserves, some set up for private hunting, others for purposes of conserving wildlife species and providing homes for animals unable to live in the wild. The questions posed by these reserves echo longstanding uncertainties about which animals are considered wild (publicly owned) and which are domesticated (privately owned).

The following opinion arose out of these uncertainties. As you read it, pay particular attention to the opening paragraphs, which supply the background of this longstanding dispute. The earlier incarnation of the dispute, leading to the *Couch* ruling that the court discusses, prompted the state legislature to get involved in clarifying the legal status of the exotic species. The state statute, however, seemed ambiguous, at least to the owners of the exotic wildlife. They brought this action seeking clarification, asking the lower court to provide answers to seven questions. In its ruling, the court answers the first two of them. The other five are set forth in a footnote. As you read the opinion, consider how the court would likely have answered the other five questions. What prompted the plaintiffs to ask these questions, and what answers were they likely hoping the court would give to them?

SIMPSON V. DEPARTMENT OF FISH AND WILDLIFE

Court of Appeals of Oregon
255 P.3d 565 (2011)

ROSENBLUM, J.

ORS 498.002(1) provides, in part, that "[w]ildlife is the property of the state." Petitioners own game ranches in Oregon. Most of their animals are defined by administrative rule as "wildlife." Petitioners sought a declaratory ruling from the Department of Fish and Wildlife (ODFW) as to whether their animals are the "property of the state" under ORS 498.002(1). ODFW ruled that the state does not own or have any proprietary or possessory interest in petitioners' animals. Petitioners seek judicial review, arguing that ODFW erred in failing to declare that their animals are the property of the state and that the agency's ruling as to the state's interest in their animals is not supported by ORS 498.002(1). On review for errors of law, ORS 183.480, ORS 183.482, we modify the ruling to declare expressly that petitioners' animals are the "property of the state," as that phrase is used in ORS 498.002(1), and otherwise affirm.

This case arose out of actions bearing on the meaning of "wildlife" by all three branches of the state government. In 2006, in *State v. Couch,* 147 P.3d 322 (Or. 2006), the Supreme Court construed that term as it was then defined in ORS 496.004(19) (2005): " 'Wildlife' means fish, shellfish, wild birds, amphibians and reptiles, feral swine as defined by State Department of Agriculture rule and other wild mammals." The question before the court was whether nonindigenous species of deer owned and held in captivity constituted "wildlife." The court concluded that mammals constitute wildlife only if they are "wild"—that is, if they "exist untamed and undomesticated in a state of nature * * *." *Couch,* 147 at 327.

In 2007, the Legislative Assembly, in response to *Couch,* amended ORS 496.004(19), granting the State Fish and Wildlife Commission authority to define "wild birds" and "wild mammals": " 'Wildlife' means fish, shellfish, amphibians and reptiles, feral swine as defined by State Department of Agriculture rule, wild birds as defined by commission rule and other wild mammals as defined by commission rule." Or. Laws 2007, ch. 523, § 1; *see also* Staff Measure Summary, House Committee on Agriculture and Natural Resources, S.B. 804, May 15, 2007 (noting that *Couch* had "narrowed the Commission's authority to regulate wildlife" and that the amendment was intended to "reinstat[e] its ability to regulate wildlife as it had done historically prior to the Supreme Court decision").

After the amendment to ORS 496.004(19) became effective, the commission promulgated OAR 635–057–0000, defining "wild mammals" and "wild birds." The rule expressly states that its purpose is to "clarify the scope of the term 'wildlife' " and that its intent is to "include as 'wild mammals' and 'wild birds' all species which, if viewed globally, typically exist in a wild state." Thus, rather than identifying particular species that constitute wild mammals or wild birds, the rule provides that those terms means *all* mammals and birds, respectively, *except* those species specifically identified in the rule. The species that are excepted from the definitions are those that one might expect to be kept as farm animals or pets, such as cattle, sheep, dogs, cats, chickens, and parakeets.

After the commission promulgated OAR 635–057–0000, petitioners filed a petition seeking a declaratory ruling from ODFW, which administers the commission's rules, regarding the application of ORS 496.004(19), OAR 635–057–0000, and ORS 498.002(1), which provides, in part, "Wildlife is the property of the state." For purposes of obtaining the declaration, petitioners stipulated that they hold in captivity in Oregon and have a property interest in elk, fallow deer, ibex, bison, water buffalo, Barbary sheep, and Russian boars. They also stipulated that all of the animals were purchased from licensed holders in Oregon, legally imported from out of state, or born in captivity in petitioners' facilities in Oregon. Petitioners asked ODFW to answer seven questions, two of which are at issue on judicial review: "Are [petitioners'] animals 'wildlife' under ORS 496.004(19)?" and "Are [petitioners'] animals the property of the state under ORS 498.002(1)?" The remaining five questions related to the consequences of their animals being recategorized as "wildlife" on petitioners' rights with respect to their animals.[1]

[The petitioners in this unusual action remained confused about the meaning of the state statute declaring that all wildlife was owned by the state. They brought this action, as the court has explained, mostly to get clarification of the meaning of the statute. The question, as they phrased it, was: did or did not the state own the wildlife? As the appellate court explains in the following paragraphs, the question did not admit of a simple yes or no answer.]

To determine the meaning of a statutory term ["property"], we look to the words of the statute in context and, if necessary, to the legislative history and other interpretive aids. *State v. Gaines,* 206 P.3d 1042, 1050–51 (Or. 2009). When particular terms are not statutorily defined, we give them their plain, natural, and ordinary meaning unless the context indicates that the legislature intended some other meaning. *State v. Cunningham,* 985 P.2d 827, 830–31 (Or. Ct. App. 1999). . . .

The preexisting common-law and statutory framework in which ORS 498.002(1) was enacted indicates that "property," as used in that statute, is not intended to convey that the state has exclusive and perpetual ownership rights in all wildlife. As we explained in our opinion in *Couch,* common-law principles concerning property rights in wildlife stem from the laws of ancient Rome. 103 P.3d at 676. "The Romans classified animals as either *ferae naturae* (of a wild nature) or *domitae naturae* (literally, 'accustomed to the house,' *i.e.,* domesticated)." *Id.* Wild animals were viewed as being held in common by the people. *Id.* at 677. That understanding formed the framework for English common-law game laws. *Id.* at 676. However, the notion that wild animals were held in common by the people became transformed. *Id.* at 677. According to Blackstone, wild animals "belonged not to the people in common but to the King." *Id.*

---

[1] The remaining five questions were as follows:

"3. May [petitioners] be prohibited, as a violation of the wildlife laws or of any rule promulgated pursuant thereto, from angling for, taking, hunting, trapping or possessing, or assisting another in angling for, taking, hunting, trapping or possessing, their animals under ORS 498.002(1)?

"4. May [petitioners] be prohibited, as a violation of the wildlife laws or of any rule promulgated pursuant thereto, from purchasing, selling, exchanging, or offering to purchase, sell, or exchange their animals under ORS 498.022?

"5. May [petitioners] be prohibited, as a violation of the wildlife laws or of any rule promulgated pursuant thereto, from removing from its natural habitat or acquiring and holding in captivity their animals under ORS 497.308(1)?

"6. Are [petitioners] required to obtain a wildlife propagation license in order to engage in the business of propagating game mammals for sale under ORS 497.228?

"7. Are [petitioners] subject to any requirements prescribed by the Commission for the care, inspection, transportation, sale, taking, or other disposition, or regarding record keeping or other reporting procedures as to game mammals under ORS 497.228?"

The view that property rights in wild animals lie in the sovereign was adopted in America, including by the Oregon Supreme Court. *Id.* In *State v. Hume,* 95 P. 808, 810 (Or. 1908), the court stated,

"It is a generally recognized principle that migratory fish in the navigable waters of a state, like game within its borders, are classed as animals *ferae naturae,* the title to which, so far as that claim is capable of being asserted before possession is obtained, is held by the state, in its sovereign capacity in trust for all its citizens[.]"

The court explained that the state's "assumed ownership" gave the state authority to regulate the treatment and taking of wildlife. *Id.* ("[A]s an incident of the assumed ownership, the legislative assembly may enact such laws as tend to protect the species from injury by human means and from extinction by exhaustive methods of capture[.]"); *see also State v. Pulos,* 129 P. 128 (Or. 1913) ("[It is a] well-known principle that title to wild game is in the State, and that no person has an absolute property right in game or fish while in a state of nature and at large; that the taking of them is not a right, but is a privilege, which may be restricted, prohibited, or conditioned, as the law-making power may see fit.").

In *Monroe v. Withycombe,* 165 P. 227, 229 (Or. 1917), another case involving wild fish, the court expressly stated that the state's sovereign title to animals *ferae naturae* is not a proprietary interest. The court stated that fish are "classified as *ferae naturae,* and while in a state of freedom their ownership, so far as a right of property can be asserted, is in the state, not as a proprietor, but in its sovereign capacity for the benefit of and in trust for its people in common." *Id.* at 229.

Until 1921, the state's property interest in wildlife was not codified. Statutes prohibited hunting, taking, or possessing various animals, but none declared that any wildlife was the property of the state. *See* The Codes and General Laws of Oregon, ch VIII, title II, §§ 1930–1951 (Hill 2d ed 1892). In 1921, the legislature enacted Oregon Code section 39–201, which provided,

"No person shall at any time or in any manner acquire property in, or subject to his dominion or control, any of the wild game animals, fur-bearing animals, game birds, nongame birds or game fish, or any part thereof, of the state of Oregon, but they shall always and under all circumstances be and remain the property of the state, except that by killing, catching or taking the same in the manner and for the purpose herein authorized and during the period not herein prohibited, the same may be used by any person at the time, and in the manner, and for the purpose herein expressly provided. Any person hunting or trapping for or having in possession any game animals, fur-bearing animals, game birds, nongame birds, or game fish, at any time in any manner shall be deemed to consent that the title shall be and remain in the state for the purpose of regulating the use and disposition of the same, and such possession shall be deemed the consent of such person aforesaid, whether said animals, birds or fish were taken within or without the state."

Oregon Code, title XXXIX, ch. II, § 39–201 (1930). Although that statute declared that the specified wild animals "shall always and under all circumstances be and remain the property of the state" and that "[n]o person shall at any time or in any manner acquire property in, or subject [such animals] to his dominion or control," those declarations were qualified by the provision that "title shall be and remain in the state *for the purpose of regulating the use and disposition of the same * * *.*" (Emphasis added.) Thus, the statute remained consistent with the common-law view of the state's property interest in wildlife.

In 1933, the statute was amended to add a provision that "any trophy or game animal or bird sold pursuant to a permit of the state game commission shall become the property of the person buying same," Or. Laws 1933, ch. 174, § 9, further indicating that the state's property interest in wildlife was not absolute.

Our understanding of section 39–201 is confirmed by *Fields v. Wilson,* 207 P.2d 153 (Or. 1949), a case involving a challenge to a program giving certain individuals exclusive rights to trap beaver. In it, the court quoted *Monroe* in stating that "[b]eaver are animals *ferae naturae,* 'and while in a state of freedom their ownership, so far as a right of property can be asserted, is in the state, not as a proprietor, but in its sovereign capacity for the benefit of and in trust for its people in common.'" *Id.* at 156 (quoting *Monroe,* 165 P. at 229). . . .

A year later, the court revisited the distinction between sovereign and proprietary ownership of wildlife in *Anthony et al. v. Veatch et al.,* 220 P.2d 493 (Or. 1950), *cert. dismissed,* 340 U.S. 923 (1951), another case involving salmon. . . . [In its opinion,] the court reiterated that the state's property interest in wildlife is sovereign, not proprietary.

OCLA section 82–201 was recodified as ORS 498.005 in 1953. The statute remained substantively the same until it was repealed in 1973. *See* Or. Laws 1973, ch. 723, § 130. That year, the legislature repealed that statute and enacted ORS 498.002 as follows: "Wildlife is the property of the state. No person shall angle for, hunt, trap or possess, or assist another in angling for, taking, hunting, trapping or possessing any wildlife in violation of the wildlife laws or of any rule promulgated pursuant thereto." *See* Or. Laws 1973, ch. 723, § 73. The new statute was enacted as part of an overhaul of the wildlife laws. Although the wording of ORS 498.002 is quite different from that of *former* ORS 498.005, nothing in the new wildlife laws indicates that the legislature intended to alter the understanding of the state's property interest in wildlife. The legislative history confirms that the legislature did not intend a substantive change. . . .

It follows that, under ORS 498.002(1), "property" continues to have the same meaning that it had in *former* ORS 498.005. That is, the state's property interest in wildlife is sovereign, not proprietary. It follows, as the presiding officer stated, that "the state's property interest in wildlife under ORS 498.002(1) is not a proprietary or possessory interest that amounts to ownership, as ownership is commonly understood." As we explained in *Couch,* "the idea that the state 'owns' wild game is a legal fiction." 103 P.3d at 677 n. 5.

In summary, we modify ODFW's ruling only to declare expressly what is implicit in the ruling: that petitioners' animals are the "property of the state," as that phrase is used in ORS 498.002(1). We affirm what is express in the ruling: that the state's property interest in petitioners' animals is not proprietary or possessory, and that the state does not own petitioners' animals in the common sense of "ownership."

Declaratory ruling modified to declare that petitioners' animals are the "property of the state" for purposes of ORS 498.002(1); otherwise affirmed.

NOTES

1. *Exotic animals and the law.* As the court in *Simpson* concluded, Oregon owns exotic animals in the state to the same extent that it owns wild animals that are native to the state. (The law treats the bison differently because it is raised as a domestic animal for food.) The court's reasoning distinguishes between sovereign and proprietary ownership rights. If the state's ownership does not include the typical elements of property rights, what does it include? Or to pose this question in a related way, how would the court in *Simpson* answer questions three through seven posed by the plaintiffs in the litigation?

The outcome in this case reflects the clear majority rule among states. Exotic animals are treated as wild under state law, with the state having the same powers and duties related to these animals as it does toward native wildlife. As noted right before this case, lawmakers have long struggled to distinguish between wild animals and domesticated ones, and in some legal settings between wild animals and tame animals, as well as (as we shall see in the next case) between game species and nongame species. In an early ruling the New York high court concluded that deer raised in captivity for slaughter and shipment to markets in New York were not covered by the state's game laws, even though the deer roamed in a private deer park of approximately 2,400 acres. *Dieterich v. Fargo,* 87 N.E. 518 (N.Y. 1909). Similarly, the court in *Jones v. State,* 45 S.W.2d 612 (Tex. Crim. App. 1931) reversed a conviction for violating state fishing regulations in the case of fish removed from a private pond. In *State v. Mierz,* 901 P.2d 286 (Wash. 1995), the court ruled that coyotes are wild animals, even though taken into captivity and treated as pets.

On the challenges of this line-drawing, and the many answers the law has given, see Dale D. Goble & Eric T. Freyfogle, *Wildlife Law: Cases and Materials* 18–21, 182–94 (2d ed. 2010).

2.   *The open property-related issues. Simpson* had to do with the powers and duties of the state in relation to the proprietary rights of landowners and animal owners. As for the property rights of the private parties, they remain unclear in settings involving game reserves. Few states have resolved the issues, by statute, regulation, or case law. A captive wild animal is no longer owned when it escapes to something like its native habitat. How does this rule apply on game reserves when animals are released? Should the answer depend on whether the land is fenced, the size of the enclosure, and whether a species has the power and inclination to move over long distances?

At first glance, game-reserve owners might want to retain property rights in these animals so as to enjoy with respect to them the various protections of property owners. But they need to realize that with ownership comes heightened responsibilities, for visitors on the land who might be injured by the animals (including trespassers) and for harm caused when the animals escape. (Tort issues are covered below.) Cruelty-to-animal statutes, as we will see, typically cover animals that are owned and not those that are wild (with cruelty including a failure to provide food and shelter). Further, animals that are owned are possessed, and owners could thus run afoul of statutes that prohibit possession of game species out of season. Then there is the initial issue of capture: When a landowner encloses a large area that includes wild animals, have those animals been captured and, if so, does their capture violate game laws setting hunting seasons and bag limits? These latter issues also arise simply when wild animals are brought into the state in captivity. For the most part, state laws have few clear answers to these questions.

3.   *Tort liability.* In general, owners of animals are responsible for them and face tort liability if the animals cause personal injury or property damage. In the case of domesticated animals, liability typically requires a showing of negligence by the owner although fencing laws sometimes impose strict liability for damage to fences. The same rule has been applied on occasion to wild animals that have become tame, so that the owner might sensibly treat an animal as domesticated rather than wild. In the case of wild animals, particularly those that are inherently dangerous, courts have typically applied strict liability, which means the owner is liable for resulting harm unless the injured plaintiff in some way assumed the risk. That fact pattern and the applicable law appear in *Irvine v. Rare Feline Breeding Center, Inc.,* 685 N.E. 2d 120 (Ind. App. 1997) (possibly intoxicated and

reckless plaintiff is injured when he puts his arm into cage of male tiger to pet it).

Strict liability also applies when wild animals escape unless they have fully regained their liberty in a natural habitat. See, e.g., *Smith v. Jalbert*, 221 N.E.2d 744 (Mass. 1966) (zebra on streets of West Springfield, Massachusetts); *Candler v. Smith*, 179 S.E. 395 (Ga. App. 1935) (baboon that escaped from zoo and entered private car and attacked girl). Property-damage cases involving escaped animals are far fewer than personal injury cases; in the property setting the same liability rule largely applies either directly or by the willingness of courts to conclude that an animal owner has acted negligently whenever animals can escape. An early case, still important, is *King v. Blue Mountain Forest Association*, 123 A.2d 151 (N.H. 1956), dealing with damages to crops and farmlands caused by Prussian wild boars that escaped and reproduced.

On the other hand, private landowners typically have no responsibility for harm caused by wild animals on their lands, even for a failure to warn of dangers, unless they have somehow augmented the danger or concealed it. This rule applies to wildlife-caused harms both outdoors and indoors and can include animals once captive that have returned to the wild. *E.g.*, *Brunelle v. Signore*, 215 Cal.App.3d 122 (1989) (plaintiff bitten by brown recluse spider in defendant's living room); *Robison v. Gantt*, 673 So.2d 441 (Ala. Civ. App. 1995) (water moccasin at swimming pool); *St. Joseph's Hospital v. Cowart*, 891 So.2d 1039 (Fla. App. 2004) (spider bite in hospital); *Palumbo v. Game & Fresh Water Fish Commn.*, 487 So.2d 352 (Fla. App. 1986) (alligators).

4. *Canned hunts and game ranches.* Various states have enacted statutes regulating game ranches, sometimes prohibiting importation and possession of exotic animals. One motive is to reduce the chance that exotic animals will spread diseases to domestic livestock. Another is the belief that the hunting of confined animals is not sporting, particularly when enclosures are small relative to the animals' natural habitats. These laws build on generations of game laws that restrict hunting practices viewed as unsporting. One of the longstanding aims of wildlife law has been to promote sportsmanship and sound hunting ethics. The wildlife reserve issue is considered in Alyssa Falk, *As Easy as Shooting Fish in a Barrel? Why Private Game Reserves Offer a Chance to Save the Sport of Hunting and Conservation Practices*, 2015 Univ. Ill. L. Rev. (forthcoming).

5. *State ownership and dead animals.* States routinely prohibit possession of game animals out of season or without appropriate permits. These rules apply whether or not the possessor is the one who killed the animal, in part because game-law enforcers have little ability to prove who caused the death of any animal. A different result was reached in a recent Minnesota case, based on the exact language of a statute similar to the one interpreted in *Simpson*. A farmer found a bear carcass on his land. He took it to a taxidermist and had his lawyer notify the state Department of Natural Resources. Conservation officers seized the carcass because the farmer had

allegedly taken possession of the animal in violation of fish and game laws. The farmer sought to recover the bear on the ground it was no longer a wild animal when he took it into possession and thus not subject to state game laws. The court held that state fish and game laws did not apply because they defined wild animals as "all living creatures, not human, wild by nature." Because the bear was not "living" when found the farmer gained a valid property interest by taking possession of it. Based on the clarity of the statutory language the court rejected arguments made by the state that its game laws needed to apply to dead animals (as they typically do) in order for the state to enforce its game laws effectively. *Swenson v. Holsten*, 783 N.W.2d 580 (Minn. App. 2010).

States typically manage wildlife through administrative departments or agencies set up for the purpose. Their main focus is on game animals and the rules governing hunting and fishing, but their duties can and often do extend to nongame species as well. Like any agency, they must exercise only those powers delegated to them, and cannot regulate outside their jurisdiction. Cases about agency power often arise. Legislatures sometimes reserve for themselves the power to make decisions on controversial issues, such as the one involved in the next case. Jurisdictional issues arise also because fish and game departments often find it useful to regulate aspects of hunting and fishing without having the express power to do so (for instance, to require hunters to wear fluorescent orange clothing, *Armstrong v. State*, 958 P.2d 1010 (Wash. App. 1998) (holding agency did possess this power)).

WISCONSIN CITIZENS CONCERNED FOR CRANES AND DOVES V. DEPARTMENT OF NATURAL RESOURCES

Supreme Court of Wisconsin
677 N.W.2d 612 (2004)

WILCOX, J.

The issue on appeal is whether the legislature has granted the DNR authority to set an open season for mourning doves. We have also asked the parties to address what impact, if any, the recently adopted "Right to Hunt" amendment to the Wisconsin Constitution has on the outcome of this case. Wis. Const. art. I, § 26. For the reasons discussed below, we . . . hold that the DNR has express authority under Wis. Stat. § 29.014(1) (1999–2000) to adopt § NR 10.01(1)(h) because the legislature has granted broad authority to the DNR to set open and closed seasons for "game" under § 29.014(1) and mourning doves fall within the unambiguous definition of "game" contained therein.

The facts of this case are few and undisputed. On May 1, 2001, pursuant to § 29.014(1), the DNR adopted § NR 10.01(1)(h), which established an open season for mourning doves in Wisconsin from September 1 through October 30 and set daily bag and possession limits. On June 19, 2001, Wisconsin Citizens Concerned for Cranes and Doves, John Wieneke, and Pat Fisher (collectively "WCCCD") commenced an action under Wis. Stat. § 227.40, seeking a declaration that the DNR exceeded its authority in promulgating the dove hunting rule and an injunction prohibiting the DNR from enforcing the rule. The U.S. Sportsmen's Alliance Foundation (Alliance) intervened on behalf of the DNR. . . .

The central issue in this case is the validity of § NR 10.01(1)(h). A court may declare an administrative rule invalid "if it finds that it violates constitutional provisions or exceeds the statutory authority of the agency or was promulgated without compliance with statutory rule-making procedures." Wis. Stat. § 227.40(4)(a). WCCCD alleges that § NR 10.01(1)(h) exceeds the statutory authority of the DNR.

The nature and scope of an agency's powers are issues of statutory interpretation. *GTE North Inc. v. PSC,* 500 N.W.2d 284, 286 (Wis. 1993). When interpreting a statute, our goal is to discern the intent of the legislature, which we derive primarily by looking at the plain meaning of the statute. *Kitten v. DWD,* 644 N.W.2d 649, 656 (Wis. 2002). *See also Columbus Park Hous. Corp. v. City of Kenosha,* 671 N.W.2d 633, 637 (Wis. 2003). The language of a statute is read in the context in which it appears in relation to the entire statute so as to avoid an absurd result. *Landis v. Physicians Ins. Co. of Wis.,* 628 N.W.2d 893, 898 (Wis. 2001). . . .

[The court further noted that, when deciding whether an agency had exceeded its statutory authority, the agency's interpretation of its authority was not entitled to any deference; courts reviewed the legal issue de novo.]

In determining whether an administrative agency exceeded the scope of its authority in promulgating a rule, we must examine the enabling statute to ascertain whether the statute grants express or implied authorization for the rule. *Wis. Hosp. Ass'n v. Natural Res. Bd.,* 457 N.W.2d 879, 886 (Wis. Ct. App. 1990). It is axiomatic that because the legislature creates administrative agencies as part of the executive branch, such agencies have "only those powers which are expressly conferred or which are necessarily implied by the statutes under which it operates." *Kimberly-Clark Corp. v. PSC,* 329 N.W.2d 143, 146 (Wis. 1983). *See also DOR v. Hogan,* 543 N.W.2d 825, 835 (Wis. Ct. App. 1995). Therefore, an agency's enabling statute is to be strictly construed. *Id.* We resolve any reasonable doubt pertaining to an agency's implied powers against the agency. *Kimberly-Clark Corp.,* 329 N.W.2d at 146–47. . . .

It is well established that "wild animals, including migratory birds, within the state, so far as it can be said such animals and birds are the subject of ownership, are owned by the state in its sovereign capacity in trust for the benefit of the people of the state[.]" *State v. Herwig,* 117 N.W.2d 335, 337 (Wis. 1962). Pursuant to Wis. Stat. § 227.11(2)(d), "an agency may promulgate rules implementing or interpreting a statute that it will enforce or administer...." The DNR claims authority under § 29.014(1) to promulgate the dove hunting rule.

Section 29.014(1) provides:

> The department shall establish and maintain open and closed seasons for fish and game and any bag limits, size limits, rest days and conditions governing the taking of fish and game that will conserve the fish and game supply and ensure the citizens of this state continued opportunities for good fishing, hunting and trapping.

Wis. Stat. § 29.014(1). As noted *supra,* § NR 10.01(1)(h) established an open season for mourning doves in Wisconsin from September 1 through October 30 and set daily bag and possession limits.

[T]his case turns on whether mourning doves are "game" within the purview of § 29.014(1). Section 29.001(33) defines "game" as follows: " 'Game' includes all varieties of wild mammals or birds." The DNR argues that mourning doves clearly fall within the unambiguous definition of the term "game" in § 29.001(33), such that § 29.014(1) confers authority on the DNR to sanction an open hunting season for mourning doves.

In contrast, WCCCD argues that the term "game" is ambiguous when it is considered within the entire context of chapter 29. Specifically, WCCCD argues that "game" is readily susceptible to more than one meaning when read in conjunction with the terms "game birds" and "nongame species." WCCCD argues, and the DNR concedes, that mourning doves are not "game birds," but do fall under the category "nongame species."

WCCCD asserts that a reasonable mind could conclude that mourning doves cannot be "game" and at the same time not fall under the definition of "game birds," such that they are a "nongame species." Thus, utilizing various canons of statutory construction, WCCCD argues that the term "game" in § 29.014(1) encompasses only what it characterizes as the defined subcategories of "game birds," "game fish," or "game animals," such that under § 29.014(1), the DNR may authorize open seasons only for those defined subcategories and may not authorize the hunting of "nongame species." WCCCD claims that as "nongame species," mourning doves fall under the more specific statutory provision, Wis. Stat. § 29.039(1), which according to WCCCD, does not authorize the DNR to allow hunting of "nongame species."

WCCCD emphasizes that in 1971 the legislature designated the mourning dove as the state symbol of peace and removed mourning doves from the definition of "game birds." Ch. 129, Laws of 1971 (amending Wis. Stat. § 1.10 and Wis. Stat. § 29.01(3)(d)). WCCCD argues that this enactment indicates the intent of the legislature "that the symbol of peace not be subjected to destruction by the hunter's gun." Pet'r Br. at 26. WCCCD zealously proclaims:

> The mourning dove is an official state symbol that reflects a philosophical concept, the pursuit of peace, and which was recognized officially in the context of an acrimonious and unpopular war. That this state symbol represents such a philosophical concept differentiates and distinguishes the dove from various other state symbols, and supports the contention that the Legislature intended that this gentle bird be accorded special status.

Pet'r Br. at 27–28.

Despite WCCCD's impassioned argument, we find several flaws with its reasoning. First, the legislature has specifically chosen to provide a definition for the terms "game," "nongame species," and "game birds." "Game" is defined in § 29.001(33) to include "all varieties of wild mammals or birds." Mourning doves clearly fall within the definition of "game" that the legislature provided. The legislature has also specifically chosen to define the term "nongame species": " 'Nongame species' means any species of wild animal not classified as a game fish, game animal, game bird or fur-bearing animal." Wis. Stat. § 29.001(60). Mourning doves clearly fall within this definition as well because they are not "game birds," as defined in Wis. Stat. § 29.001(39). . . .

WCCCD's argument that mourning doves cannot logically be both "game" and a "nongame species" fails because it erroneously relies on the ordinary meaning of these terms and their supposed contextual ambiguity, ignoring the definition the legislature has specifically chosen to provide for those terms in chapter 29. *See id.* Notably, the legislature defined "nongame species" in relation to "game birds," specifically excluding the latter from the definition of the former. Wis. Stat. § 29.001(60). However, the legislature chose to define "game" broadly in § 29.001(33). WCCCD would essentially have us define "game" as "all varieties of wild mammals or birds *except those that have been designated as " 'nongame species.' "* We decline to rewrite the statute in such a fashion, as the legislature did not define "game" and "nongame species" as mutually exclusive terms. The legislature could have defined "game" as composed of "game birds," "game fish," and "game animals," for purposes of § 29.014(1), but chose not to do so. The provided legislative definition of "game" is clear and unambiguous: "all varieties of wild mammals or birds." The presence of the terms "nongame species" and "game birds" within chapter 29 does not render the term "game" ambiguous.

This court has previously recognized that the DNR has broad authority as custodian of Wisconsin's wildlife to enact regulations that maintain a balance between conserving and exploiting the state's wildlife. *Barnes v. DNR,* 516 N.W.2d 730, 737 (Wis. 1994). The legislature has expressly granted the DNR broad regulatory authority to "establish and maintain open and closed seasons for fish and game . . . and conditions governing the taking of fish and game that will conserve the fish and game supply and ensure the citizens of this state continued opportunities for good fishing, hunting, and trapping." Wis. Stat. § 29.014(1).

The legislature did not limit that authority to set open seasons only for "game birds," "game fish," and "game animals" under § 29.014(1). Likewise, § 29.014(1) does not prohibit the DNR from authorizing an open season for "nongame species." Indeed, the only limitation upon the DNR's authority contained within § 29.014(1) is that any open season for "game" and the conditions therefor must conserve the game supply and provide continued opportunities for the citizens of this state to hunt. Regardless of the fact that mourning doves are no longer on the list of "game birds," § 29.014(1) does not refer to "game birds"; it refers to "game." . . .

Having determined that § 29.014(1) confers upon the DNR express authority to establish an open season for mourning doves, we next examine whether that authority is in any way affected by the newly enacted "Right to Hunt" amendment to the Wisconsin Constitution. Article I, Section 26 of the Wisconsin Constitution, as adopted by the citizens of this state in April of 2003, provides: "The people have the right to fish, hunt, trap, and take game subject only to reasonable restrictions as prescribed by law." Wis. Const. art. I, § 26. We interpret provisions of the Wisconsin Constitution de novo, examining three primary sources to determine a provision's meaning:

> the plain meaning of the words in the context used; the constitutional debates and the practices in existence at the time of the writing of the constitution; and the earliest interpretation of the provision by the legislature as manifested in the first law passed following adoption.

State v. Cole, 665 N.W.2d 328, 333 (Wis. 2003) (quoting *Thompson v. Craney,* 546 N.W.2d 123, 127 (Wis. 1996)).

An examination of the plain language of Article I, Section 26 of the Wisconsin Constitution reveals that the 2003 constitution amendment was intended to codify the common law right to hunt that existed prior to its adoption. In *State v. Nergaard,* 102 N.W. 899 (Wis. 1905), this court declared that the citizens of the state have a common law right to hunt and fish game as they see fit in the absence of state regulations, so long as they do not infringe private rights. This court described the right as follows:

> [T]he state has the right, in the exercise of its police power, to make all reasonable regulations for the preservation of fish and game within its limits. It may ordain closed seasons; it may prescribe the manner of taking, the times of taking, and the amount to be taken within a given time, as it may deem best for the purpose of preserving and perpetuating the general stock. In the absence of legislation the citizen may doubtless pursue, take, and dispose of fish and game as he sees fit and without restraint, so long as he violates no private rights; but when the state steps in and makes proper police regulations, the citizen takes his right of fishing or fowling hampered by such regulations; in other words, his right is the right which the state leaves to him, no more and no less.

Id. at 901.

The language of the 2003 constitutional amendment closely parallels the language in *Nergaard,* providing that the people of this state have the right to take game, subject to reasonable regulations. The 2003 amendment does not impose any limitation upon the power of the state or DNR to regulate hunting, other than that any restrictions on hunting must be reasonable. However, the WCCCD has not alleged that § NR 10.01(1)(h) is unreasonable. Therefore, the 2003 constitutional amendment does not affect our analysis of the DNR's authority in this case.

However, we do note that the fact that citizens of this state enjoy the right to hunt in the absence of reasonable regulations does not necessarily mean that it is "open season" on any species of birds not regulated by the DNR. Wisconsin Admin. Code § NR 10.02 currently provides that certain enumerated species are protected and may not be taken without authorization by the DNR. Specifically, Wis. Admin. Code § NR 10.02(8) (Nov., 2003) provides that "[a]ny other wild bird not specified in this chapter[ ]" may not be taken absent express authorization by the DNR. Therefore, under § NR 10.02(8), the DNR must engage in rule-making and expressly authorize the taking of any species of wild bird that is not currently regulated. If the DNR elects to do so, it is obviously restrained by its own rule-making procedures, federal law governing migratory birds, and federal and state law relating to endangered or threatened species. . . .

The decision of the court of appeals is affirmed.

NOTES

1.   *Agency powers and their statutory and constitutional limits.* The *WCCCD* ruling provides a sound introduction to the powers of administrative agencies, and how courts go about deciding whether a particular action by an agency is within its statutory powers. Given the court's ruling, is the state agency in any way limited in its ability to declare open hunting seasons on birds or wild mammals? Could it authorize the hunting of, for instance, robins and bluebirds? (On that issue, consider the next principal case under the federal Migratory Bird Treaty Act.) What about a hunting or trapping season on feral housecats? As for the state constitutional provision that the court discusses, what legal effect, if any, does it seem to have? If it has no effect, has the court fairly interpreted it?

2.   *The clash over hunting.* The mourning dove has become a flashpoint of conflict between hunting groups, which view the bird as appropriate game (although rarely for food), and animal welfare groups that deem it a songbird and thus deserving of protection. Doves are fast moving and take off quickly; they are thus challenging for hunters to hit. While animal welfare groups often side with the dove, environmental groups lean the other way (although often reluctant to say anything publicly for fear of upsetting members concerned about animal welfare). The mourning dove is an abundant species and hunting pressure, in those states where allowed, has no noticeable effect on bird populations. Hunting them may be ecologically preferable to hunting other, traditional game birds (quail, grouse, pheasants), which reproduce more slowly (many are density dependent) and have vastly lower populations, chiefly due to habitat loss. Environmental organizations typically favor the hunting of species that are abundant, if not overabundant, over those that are scarce.

Animal welfare groups sometimes gain legislative protection for species. However, they often must still fight state fish and game agencies, typically staffed by officials favoring hunting and fishing, to ensure that statutes are adequately respected. For an illustration of the conflict, see *Mass. Society for the Prevention of Cruelty to Animals v. Division of Fisheries and Wildlife*, 651 N.E.2d 388 (Mass. 1995) (state agency has the authority to authorize trapping using "padded" leg traps despite state statute prohibiting the use of "any steel jaw leghold trap on land"). In the case of many state regulatory agencies, their membership requirements, set by statute, largely exclude citizens opposed to hunting and fishing. *See, e.g., Humane Society v. New Jersey State Fish and Game Council*, 362 A.2d 20 (N.J. 1976) (upholding, against constitutional challenge, a state statute establishing an eleven-member fish and game council composed of three farmers, six sportsmen recommended by the state federation of sportsmen's clubs, and two commercial fishermen).

Hunting interests have pushed back, fearful that rising animal welfare sentiment could lead to reductions in hunting. See, for example, Utah Const. Art. VI, sec. 1(2)(a)(ii) (voter approved constitutional amendment stating that any law "to allow, limit, or prohibit the taking of wildlife or the season for or method of taking wildlife" must be approved by a two-thirds majority, while a simple majority was sufficient for all other laws).

Hunting interests have also successfully pushed constitutional amendments of the type discussed in *WCCCD,* proclaiming a right to hunt but without curtailing agency powers to regulate hunting. The irony of such provisions is that they have little to do with what citizens at the time of America's founding meant by their right to hunt—the right to hunt on all unenclosed land and to fish on all boatable waters without needing permission of the landowner. (Vermont's constitution still contains such a constitutional right; representatives from Pennsylvania sought to include it in the federal bill of rights.) As one early court explained, the English rule—allowing landowners to exclude public hunters—was "founded upon a tender solicitude for the amusement and property of the aristocracy of England." *State v. Campbell,* 1 T.U.P.C. 166, 167–68 (Ga. 1808). The sentiment did not die, even as states slowly began expanding the powers of landowners to exclude. See e.g., *Sterling v. Jackson,* 37 N.W. 845, 855–56 (Mich. 1888) (Morse, J., dissenting) ("Our fish and game laws have not been passed for the express benefit of clubs of wealthy sportsmen, who can afford to buy up or lease all the land along the navigable streams and lakes of this state, and thus shut out the poor man who loves the rod or gun as well as they do, and who, in the spirit of our institutions, has a common right with them in the 'fowl of the air and the fish of the sea.' ")

3. *Federal constitutional limits on agency action.* A variety of federal constitutional claims have been pressed against the actions of fish and game agencies. An occasional case raises issues about free speech and the free exercise of religions (e.g., a challenge by an Amish hunter to hunter-orange clothing requirements, based on religion clauses, *State v. Bontrager,* 683 N.E.2d 126 (Ohio App. 1996)). More common are equal-protection claims involving game laws that open some areas for hunting and not others (almost all unsuccessful), and arguments that bans on hunting on private land amount to unlawful takings (also almost all unsuccessful). Predictably, the recent expansion of the second amendment right to bear arms has produced litigation. *Hunters United for Sunday Hunting v. Pa. Game Comm'n.,* 2014 WL 2770228 (M.D. Pa. June 8, 2014) (rejecting challenge to partial ban on Sunday hunting, concluding that the second amendment did not protect recreational hunting).

Most common among constitutional challenges are preemption arguments—that state regulation has been preempted by federal law—and the many claims that states in their licensing and fee structures unduly favor resident hunters and fishers from nonresidents. The latter cases typically are brought under the dormant commerce clause and the privileges and immunities clause (article IV, sec. 2, cl. 1) of the federal constitution. In brief, states have broad powers to discriminate in the case of recreational hunting and fishing—under the privileges and immunities clause because it does not apply to recreational activities and under the dormant commerce clause because Congress has expressly authorized it by statute. Discrimination in the case of commercial fishing and hunting is more suspect and is almost always contrary to the dormant commerce clause when it is overt. States can freely ban the importation of particular species if they prohibit ownership of them within the state. They can similarly prohibit sale of a species but not if they allow it within the state and only prohibit interstate sales. The constitutional framework of wildlife law—covering these issues as well as the matter of federal powers generally—is surveyed in Eric T. Freyfogle & Dale D. Goble, *Wildlife Law: A Primer* 108–34 (2009).

4. *Cruelty to wild animals.* One of the intriguing, incipient trends in wildlife law today is the extension of longstanding laws banning cruelty to animals to wild animals. Early anti-cruelty statutes typically protected only beasts of burden (oxen, horses, mules) from excessive beating by their owners. Only in the twentieth century did statutes typically begin extending legal protection to other categories of domesticated animals such as dogs and cats. In recent years, various legislatures have revised their statutes to extend their reach to certain animals in the wild, often, though, without considering how the statutes fit together with hunting and fishing laws. Consider, as an example, the case of *Boushehry v. State*, 648 N.E.2d 1174 (Ind. App. 1995). Two men were engaged in construction work at a subdivision site. During a work break one of the men took a rifle from his car and shot two geese on a vacant lot. One of the geese died instantly. The other was wounded, and one of them slit the goose's throat. The men kept the geese to eat. Both were charged with violating the state cruelty-to-animals statute, which penalized anyone who intentionally "tortures, beats or mutilates a vertebrate animal resulting in serious injury of death" or who "kills a vertebrate animal without the authority of the owner of the animal." The court ruled that the statute was violated by slitting the throat of the wounded goose; it was not violated in the case of the goose killed by the gunshot. A dissenting judge voted to acquit on the ground that the wounded goose was humanely killed to end its suffering.

Note that this Indiana statute promotes two quite different aims. The second part simply protects the property rights of an animal owner; it adds criminal penalties to actions that would trigger civil suits in trespass for harm to personal property. The first part of the statute, in contrast, aims to promote animal welfare by protecting the animals themselves (vertebrates, that is), from actions by owners as well as nonowners. We can rightly view this first provision, however, also as a property law, in that it helps define the rights of ownership. The statute limits the property rights a person may maintain in vertebrate animals by constraining how the owner can discipline or kill them. On the facts in *Boushehry*, both men were guilty of violating game laws by hunting geese out of season. Such offenses, though, are often treated lightly or not prosecuted at all. Violations of animal cruelty statutes are, these days, viewed more seriously and carry higher penalties.

E. FEDERAL WILDLIFE STATUTES

Although most wildlife law arises at the state level—with some supplementation by local governments, particularly bans on possessing many species in urban areas—several important components of wildlife law originate at the federal level. One of them is the Migratory Bird Treaty Act, which broadly protects all migratory bird species in the United States as a means of implementing treaties with other countries covering these species. The Act is unusual in that it begins by prohibiting all actions that kill or harm migratory birds, and then authorizes the Secretary of the Interior to issue regulations that permit hunting, wildlife control, and other measures. State game laws authorizing the hunting of such birds must comply with these federal regulations. The statute applies to nests and bird parts and governs possession, sale, shipment, and so on. Further, as the following case illustrates, the list of protected species is quite long, covering many species that birders would not deem migratory. Birds enjoy far greater legal protection than any other wildlife family, with even greater protections extended to such charismatic species as bald and golden eagles.

UNITED STATES V. DARST

United States District Court, District of Kansas
726 F.Supp. 286 (1989)

CROW, D.J.

The case comes before the court on the defendant's appeal of his conviction of taking migratory birds, in particular great horned owls, in violation of 16 U.S.C. § 703 and 50 C.F.R. § 21.11. . . .

On October 1, 1988, Jerry Almquist, a conservation officer with the State of Kansas, visited the defendant's residence and observed a great horned owl in a leg trap. Mr. Almquist told defendant that taking or killing great horned owls is illegal and that he should call Mr. Case Vendel, a federal game officer, to inquire about a permit for trapping owls if they were killing his chickens. On February 20, 1989, Mr. Almquist returned to defendant's residence and saw another great horned owl trapped on a different pole. Defendant informed Mr. Almquist that he had set four traps on four different poles in order to protect his chickens and that the federal agent was never contacted about a permit.

Defendant represented himself at the trial held on May 12, 1989. He admitted in his testimony that he trapped and killed the great horned owls on both occasions and that he had not contacted federal agent Vendel nor obtained a permit from him. Defendant stated that his authority for killing the owls came from his constitutional right to defend his property.

The Magistrate found defendant guilty and fined him $125 and assessed costs of $25. Defendant appeals on the following legal issues: (a) whether the great horned owl is a properly designated migratory bird; (b) whether the statute is unconstitutionally broad for including as violations the defendant's actions taken in defense of his property; and (c) whether 16 U.S.C. § 703 is unconstitutionally vague in that the term, "migratory bird," is not adequately defined except by regulation, 50 C.F.R. § 10.13, which is excessively broad.

The Migratory Bird Treaty Act (MBTA), 16 U.S.C. § 703 *et seq.*, was passed in 1918 to give force and effect to a 1916 treaty between the United States and Great Britain entered "for the protection of migratory birds." The Supreme Court upheld the constitutionality of the MBTA in 1920. *Missouri v. Holland,* 252 U.S. 416 (1920). The MBTA was later expanded to include conventions for the protection of birds entered by the United States with the countries of Mexico and Japan. The convention with Mexico provides that other migratory birds may be added later upon the agreement of the Presidents of both countries. *United States v. Richards,* 583 F.2d 491, 493 (10th Cir. 1978); *United States v. Blanket,* 391 F.Supp. 15, 18 (W.D. Okla. 1975). The protected migratory birds are listed in 50 C.F.R. § 10.13 which "does not enlarge or purport to enlarge the Conventions or extend the scope of the Act to any bird not included in the Conventions." *Blanket,* 391 F.Supp. at 19. Among the list of protected birds is the great horned owl.

Defendant first contends that the great horned owl is not a migratory bird and, therefore, he did not know it was protected under the MBTA. This contention is also tied into defendant's other issue of whether 16 U.S.C. § 703 is unconstitutionally vague in not defining a migratory bird except by regulation. It would be proper for this court to decline consideration of these issues as they were not properly presented to the trial court. *See United States v. Mebane,* 839 F.2d 230, 232 (4th Cir. 1988). In fact, the record shows plaintiff argued only before the Magistrate that the great horned owl, was a "protected" bird but was not an endangered species. (Tr. 50). This oral argument obviously has no relevance to the MBTA.

The Secretary of Interior is authorized by 16 U.S.C. § 704 to promulgate regulations regarding who may take or possess migratory birds and under what circumstances. Section 703 is prefaced with correlating language, as follows: "[u]nless and except as permitted by regulations made as hereinafter provided. . . ." By reading § 703 in conjunction with § 704, a person is adequately alerted that applicable regulations specify what conduct is prohibited and what migratory birds are protected. Neither the MBTA nor its attendant regulations are so vague that a person of ordinary intelligence would not reasonably know what conduct is prohibited under these provisions. *See United States v. Brandt,* 717 F.2d 955, 957 (6th Cir. 1983).

A defendant in a criminal case cannot collaterally attack the Secretary's determination that a given species of birds needs protection, as long as the regulation promulgated to that end is facially valid. *United States v. Gigstead,* 528 F.2d 314, 317 (8th Cir. 1976). The term, "migratory bird," is defined in 50 C.F.R. § 10.12 as any bird which belongs to a species listed in § 10.13. The court has not been provided any reason to question the listing of the great horned owl in § 10.13 as the proper designation of a species protected by the terms of the controlling treaties. Defendant's legal issues (a) and (c) are without merit.

Defendant argues that the statutes and regulations are unconstitutional if they penalize someone for killing protected wildlife when the killing is otherwise justified under circumstances of defense of property. Defendant relies upon the general rule stated at 35 Am.Jur.2d Fish and Game § 37 (1967), that "a statute forbidding the killing of game under penalty does not apply to a killing which is necessary for the defense of person or property." The defendant also discusses several of the state court decisions cited in 35 Am.Jur.2d § 37 for support of the above general rule.

Defendant's argument is essentially that his right to defend his property is absolute and cannot be subjected to any governmental regulation. First, defendant has not cited any authority for a federal constitutional right, absolute or not, to defend his property from federally protected wildlife. The Ninth Circuit has recently held that the U.S. Constitution does not expressly or implicitly recognize a right to kill federally protected wildlife in defense of property. *Christy v. Hodel,* 857 F.2d 1324, 1329–1330 (9th Cir. 1988), *cert. denied,* 490 U.S. 1114 (1989). *See generally Mountain States Legal Foundation v. Hodel,* 799 F.2d 1423, 1428 (10th Cir. 1986) (en banc), *cert. denied,* 480 U.S. 951 (1987). (No case recognizing such a right under the U.S. Constitution). Second, defendant has not attacked the congressional authority for enacting provisions which protect certain species of birds and for allowing regulations which balance the interests of landowners against the public interest in wildlife. The regulations at issue do not forbid all manners of defending one's property against destruction from federally protected wildlife. Rather than allowing landowners alone to decide whether a killing of protected wildlife is necessary, the regulations require landowners to seek the assistance of a governmental official who is expected to act in the public interest. *See Christy v. Hodel,* 857 F.2d at 1321; *State v. Webber,* 736 P.2d 220, 221–22 (Or. Ct. App. 1987). In the absence of a showing that these regulations constitute an unreasonable restraint, defendant's defense of property argument fails. *See Webber,* 736 P.2d 220. Defendant has no unconditional or absolute right to kill federally protected birds in defense of his property.

The Magistrate's finding is supported by the evidence, and the defendant's legal issues are without merit.

It is therefore ordered that defendant's conviction is affirmed.

NOTES

1. *What is a migratory bird?* At the heart of this dispute is the question: is a great horned owl—a year-round resident of Kansas—a migratory bird within the meaning of the federal statute? The court answered by saying that a bird is migratory if it is on the list published by the U.S. Fish and Wildlife Service, and that a criminal defendant cannot, in the criminal action, challenge the inclusion of a species on the list. Can we discern from the opinion when and on what basis a private party might challenge the federal agency's decision to include a particular species?

In practice, nearly all bird species in North America are included on the Fish and Wildlife list, and included by families rather than species by species. The list is far more extensive (nearly 1000 species) than the list of birds that birders would consider migratory; indeed, it includes almost all birds that are able to fly more than short distances, whether or not they change locations on a seasonal basis. The primary exclusions (along with upland game birds that do little flying) are species not native to North America, including, most prominently, the house (English) sparrow and the European starling. Among these nonnative species is the mute swan, beloved and defended by many but disliked by others because of its aggressive behavior toward other birds. Also unprotected are parrots, parakeets, cockatiels, and similar birds that have escaped from or been released by owners. Of the more than 100 nonnative species that have no protection, some 17 (including the house sparrow, starling, and rapidly expanding mute swan) have established self-sustaining populations in the United States.

2. *The reach of the MBTA.* The federal act contains detailed provisions regulating takings of migratory birds, and violators of the detailed rules are often prosecuted under the Act in federal court for what would otherwise be a violation of state hunting laws. *E.g., United States v. Morgan,* 311 F.3d 611 (5th Cir. 2002) (upholding conviction for possessing too many game birds; hunter's excuse was that his "poorly trained" bird dog brought him six ducks shot by other hunters as well as his own two). One highly regulated area has to do with ducks raised in captivity and either slaughtered for sale as food or released onto private hunting grounds. (The rules generally state that captive-raised ducks released for hunting can be hunted only on the same terms as wild ducks, with an exception for mallards released on shooting preserves licensed by the state.) Particularly contentious have been cases in which landowners have been charged with violating the MBTA because their land-use activities (often polluting activities) cause the inadvertent death of

protected birds. Finally, regulators have struggled for years with the details of the ban on hunting over bait, trying to make clear what substances are considered bait, what acts are considered hunting, and when farm crops left in the field are covered. The statute is surveyed in Eric T. Freyfogle & Dale D. Goble, *Wildlife Law: A Primer* 191–202 (2009).

———

Another major federal wildlife statute is the Lacey Act, the first effort by Congress to get involved in wildlife conservation. The following excerpt summarizes the Act, which got federal law enforcement agencies involved in helping states enforce their game laws, particularly against violators who crossed state lines. The Act continues to do little more than provide federal penalties and federal enforcement for actions that violate some other wildlife law—federal, state, tribal, or foreign. The Act itself imposes few direct limits on private parties. But the federal involvement is critical, particularly when federal penalties are noticeably more severe than the corresponding penalties imposed for the underlying violation and when enforcement efforts need to cross state lines.

WILDLIFE LAW: THE LACEY ACT
Eric T. Freyfogle & Dale D. Goble
Island Press, pp. 185–202 (2009)

The Lacey Act

The federal government got involved in wildlife conservation nationally in 1900 when it enacted the Lacey Act, a statute aimed at the nagging problem of game law violators who conducted business across state lines, frustrating state enforcement efforts. As originally written the statute required people transporting wild animals or animal parts across state lines to label their packages clearly so that law enforcement officers could determine what they contain. The labeling provisions were designed to reinforce the statute's prohibitions against transporting wild animals or animal parts that had been taken or possessed in violation of state law. Over the next eight decades the statute was broadened to encompass a wider variety of wild species and a greater variety of laws, including Indian tribal laws, foreign laws, and international treaties in addition to violations of state laws. The statute's scope gained breadth but prosecutions under it remained few. Maximum penalties were relatively low. Also, felony prosecutions were difficult because of the heavy burden imposed on prosecutors to prove the defendant's actual knowledge and specific intent to gain a conviction.

The Lacey Act was extensively revised in 1981. Congress clarified and reorganized the statute's provisions, increased the maximum penalties, and reduced what prosecutors had to prove. These changes made the Act a much stronger conservation tool. Prosecutions have become more common.

The central element of the Lacey Act is section 3372(a), which prohibits anyone from handling wildlife in various ways if the wildlife was "taken, possessed, transported, or sold in violation" of a variety of wildlife laws or regulations. A violation of the Lacey Act, that is, includes two elements. First, there must be an initial violation of some other wildlife law (the "predicate offense"). Then, the wildlife involved, dead or alive and in whole or in part, must be handled in one of the ways specifically listed in the statute.

As for the initial violation of another wildlife law, that law can be state law, Indian tribal law, foreign law, a federal treaty or even another federal statute. Without the violation of some other law, however, there is no violation of the Lacey Act. (As noted below, this is not true in the case of the Lacey Act's rules on marking wildlife and filling out wildlife declarations; also, since 2003 the Lacey Act has directly protected certain big cats.)

If the underlying statute or regulation that has been violated is either a *federal* law or *Indian tribal* law, then any person who imports, exports, sells, receives, acquires or purchases the wildlife violates the statute. If instead the underlying statute or regulation is either a *state* law or a *foreign* law, then the Lacey Act is violated when such a person engages in one of the same actions "in interstate or foreign commerce." Thus, violations of the Lacey Act are somewhat harder to prove when the underlying law that has been violated is a state or foreign law. In those instances, the person accused of violating the Lacey Act must "import, export, transport, sell, receive, acquire or purchase" the wildlife in a transaction that is somehow linked to commerce among the states or among nations, which generally requires that the person or the wildlife crossed a state or international boundary.

The Lacey Act, like most modern federal statutes, contains its own definitions of the terms used. Two of the definitions are particularly important. The Act applies to all fish or wildlife. That category includes all wild animals, dead or alive, "whether or not bred, hatched, or born in captivity." It also includes "any part, product, egg, or offspring thereof." Thus, the Act applies to captive animals, not just those taken from the wild. Thus, a federal court ruling from Oklahoma in 2006, *U.S. v. Condict*, 2006 WL 1793235 (E.D. Okla. June 27, 2006), applied the statute to "farm raised domesticated deer." The definition of "transport" is also significant because it includes not just moving a wild animal but delivering or receiving it "for the purpose of movement, conveyance, carriage, or shipment." A person or business can therefore violate the Act merely by turning wildlife over to a shipping agent or by receiving an item for shipment or other transport, without ever personally moving the wild animal any distance. Transport, in short, can take place without any motion.

Recent prosecutions illustrate how the two parts of a Lacey Act violation fit together. In a 2004 prosecution in Nebraska, a hunter was found guilty of shooting and killing a deer (two separate violations) in a closed portion of a national wildlife refuge, in violation of the federal law governing the refuge. The hunter then removed the deer from the refuge and took it home. The violation of the refuge rules provided the underlying illegal act. The removal from the refuge satisfied the requirement of transport. Since the predicate violation was of a federal law, there was no need to prove that the transport crosses a state or international boundary.

A similar federal court case from 2001 involved a hunter who killed an elk on Ute tribal lands. The taking of the elk violated several tribal laws—it was out of season and after dark (hunting was allowed only in daylight); the hunter had no permit; the hunter was not a tribal member; and the elk was not tagged. Again, by taking the animal home to eat it the hunter engaged in transport. As with violations of federal law, violations of tribal laws do not require that the transport cross state or national boundaries. . . .

Lacey Act violations based on underlying state laws formed the basis of a 2004 federal appellate ruling from Tennessee, *U.S. v. Hale*, 113 Fed.Appx. 108 (6th Cir. 2004). A Tennessee couple operated a caviar business using the roe of paddlefish. They routinely and knowingly bought the roe from fisherman who had taken paddlefish out of season. They then sold the caviar in Kentucky as well as Tennessee. Their Lacey Act convictions were upheld because the caviar was transported into Kentucky. Similarly, in a case from Oklahoma in 2001 a federal appellate court upheld the conviction of a man who lured elk from a national wildlife refuge on to his own fenced land and then advertised in Texas for hunters to shoot them. A hunter did so (in a penned area of only 15 acres where the "hunt" took 10 minutes) and then returned to Texas with the carcass. The landowner violated Oklahoma law by failing to obtain various permits. The interstate advertising, along with the sale of the "hunting" experience, provided an adequate connection to interstate commerce. In its ruling the court made clear that the state law being violated did not have to be a wildlife conservation law; it could be a revenue-generating licensing law.

A closer case involved a North Carolina resident who purchased rockfish that had been taken illegally in Virginia. The man intended to market the fish in New York or Maryland, and sold it to a North Carolina company that he knew would transport the fish to those markets. His conviction was upheld because he "knew that the rockfish would be shipped in interstate commerce and he took steps that began their travel to interstate markets."

This brings us to the final federal statute that we shall take up. (Among those not covered here is the important federal statute dealing with ocean fisheries and laws covering marine mammals.) The Endangered Species Act is perhaps the best known federal wildlife statute, and the one that has engendered the most civil litigation. (Criminal prosecutions for violating it have been quite rare; nothing like the caseload under the Migratory Bird Treaty Act and the Lacey Act.)

The Endangered Species Act has the reputation of being a strong, firm protection for species that have been listed as either endangered or threatened. But as the following overview explains, that reputation is by no means earned. (It is firm only when a single proposed activity would eliminate the only known population of a listed species—an exceedingly rare occurrence.) As you read the excerpt, get clear on the various ways that the statute seeks to protect listed species and on whose activities are covered by the statute. The ESA ruling that follows the excerpt provides a good illustration of how nearly all of these protections can play roles in a single factual dispute.

WILDLIFE LAW: ESA OVERVIEW
Eric T. Freyfogle & Dale D. Goble
Island Press, pp. 236–38 (2009)

Overview

The ESA is triggered by the listing of a species as either endangered or threatened. Most frequently, this is a result of a petition filed by one or more citizens requesting the listing and providing biological evidence that the species is at risk of extinction. The act specifies that decisions about listing are to be made using the best available scientific data available and that the listing agency cannot take account of the economic, social, and political consequences that might come from the classification.

Species that face the most severe dangers are listed as endangered; those facing less severe dangers are listed as threatened. Although most of the ESA's protections apply only to listed species, some protections extend to species that are proposed for listing and even to those that are candidates for study. Indeed, a major trend in the scope of the ESA over the years has been to find ways to protect species before they reach the brink of extinction and listing becomes necessary.

Once a species gains the dubious honor of being listed, it is covered by two types of statutory provisions. The first are intended to prevent the species' extinction; the second to increase its numbers to the point where it has been recovered and can be delisted.

There are two important extinction-prevention provisions. The first is the ESA's broadly phrased prohibition against taking or harming an endangered species. The prohibition applies not only to intentional and unintentional harms but also to certain types of habitat modification. Although this statutory provision is stated as an absolute prohibition on taking a listed species, various permit programs nonetheless allow citizens and agencies to engage in activities that incidentally harm species.

A second extinction prevention requirement applies to activities undertaken or permitted by the federal government. No such federal action (including issuance of a federal permit) can take place if it will either jeopardize the continued existence of the species or adversely modify the species' critical habitat. This prohibition is supplemented by an inter-agency consultation process. Before undertaking an action that could harm a species a federal agency must consult with the USFWS to clarify the possible harms to the species and figure out whether less harmful options are available.

These extinction-prevention provisions are intended to stop a species' downward slide. The acts recovery provisions are designed to go further, to increase the numbers and distribution of a listed species to the point at which it is no longer at risk and thus can be delisted. Recovery, a synonym for "conservation," means improving a species status so that it no longer requires protection under the ESA. Typically, this requires increasing the population of a species, not simply eliminating current threats. Often it requires expanding the range that a species inhabits, and promoting multiple, independently viable populations of the species, so as to reduce the chance that an ecological disturbance affecting one population will wipe out the entire species. It is not enough, in short, to halt a species' decline, at least if a species has descended to the status of threatened or endangered.

The recovery process begins when the listing agency prepares a plan for the recovery of the species. The plan, as we will see, is intended to guide other federal agencies in fulfilling their affirmative obligations to help recover listed species.

These are the Act's main legal provisions: the prohibition on taking or harming species; the ban on jeopardizing the species or adversely modifying critical habitat; and the recovery plan. These provisions are supplemented by additional rules restricting imports, exports, and sales of listed species, dead or alive, including animal parts. On balance, the acts greatest success has been in slowing the tide of extinction. On the other hand, few species have recovered to the point where agencies can remove them from the lists. Delistings have mostly been species that were being harmed by direct or indirect takes (for example, by hunters or toxic chemicals), which were relatively easy to stop. Recovery has been more rare and prospects are much dimmer for species that have declined due to habitat loss, particularly widespread land-use practices. The ESA has proven ineffective in protecting habitat for species that require wide ranges.

By reputation, the Endangered Species Act is commonly viewed as a powerful or absolute statute, one that elevates species protection above competing interests. The reality is very different, particularly, again, in the case of habitat alteration. The statute's seemingly absolute prohibitions are subject to permit provisions that make them far more flexible and, as a result, provide much weaker protection. In addition, enforcement is often spotty

One final, key point: for more than three decades, endangered species protection has generated heated controversy. Pressures to gut the Endangered Species Act have been nearly constant, along with (on the other side) recurring proposals to give the act more teeth and expand its coverage. Perhaps because of these conflicting pressures, the Act has not been amended in twenty years. Political opposition has been strong enough to keep the Fish and Wildlife Service (and National Marine Fisheries Service) from having enough money to carry out their many duties. Most controversial have been the efforts the agencies make to list new species and to designate habitat that is critical to their recovery. Congress has repeatedly imposed tight financial limits on the money the agencies can spend for these purposes. (For a time Congress even insisted that the Fish and Wildlife Service spend literally no money on listing, including money donated for the purpose by private parties!) When budgets are tight, the Fish and Wildlife Service lists fewer species and designates less critical habitat. As that happens, year after year, the ESA becomes less of an obstacle to business as usual in America while the nation's rare species continue to decline.

Tight budgets, it seems, are an enduring reality. Necessarily, agencies must make tough choices on how to spend their money. Citizens groups often chime in, challenging spending priorities. Prompted by disgruntled citizen groups, courts have repeatedly ordered the Fish and Wildlife Service to spend money on specific tasks mandated by law, even when the agency believes its limited resources would yield greater conservation benefits if applied elsewhere. Low budgets, in fact, increase the work and effectively waste resources. Agencies must regularly take time to explain why they have not accomplished more. They must regularly defend litigation that arises simply because they have not met deadlines: because they have not, for instance, completed required five-year reviews of listed species; designated critical habitat; or studied candidate species fast enough. The reality is that many ESA regulations exist solely to deal with funding shortfalls and to juggle competing responsibilities. When tight budgets and litigation by divergent interested groups meet an administration that is openly hostile to the ESA's objectives, the result is stalemate.

The following judicial ruling applies these various provisions of the Endangered Species Act. The dispute had to do with a large, private project, a pipeline some 678 miles in length. The pipeline was being built by a private company, Ruby Pipeline. Private parties are subject to the "no take" mandate of section 9 of the ESA. That mandate is absolute, in that it prohibits taking even one animal of a listed species. Ruby's project clearly was going to do that. To construct the pipeline, Ruby needed permission from two elements of the federal government—FERC (a license for the pipeline), and the BLM (permission to use BLM land for parts of the pipeline). Because these federal agencies had to approve the project, it was transformed from a strictly private property to a federal one. This meant that section 7 of the ESA also came into play. Section 7 applies only to federal actions, including, as in this instance, actions that can go forward only with federal permits. Section 7 added further requirements for the pipeline project.

As we shall see, the dispute ended up implicating all the elements of section 7: the "no jeopardy" requirement, the ban on adversely modifying critical habitat, and the consultation requirement. FERC and the BLM believed they had complied with section 7, and their belief was backed by an opinion to that effect from the Fish and Wildlife Service (FWS). Attached to that FWS opinion was an "incidental take statement," which authorized Ruby, as it constructed the pipeline, to kill (take) individual protected animals as an incidental consequence of the pipeline construction. Once it had this incidental take statement, Ruby could go ahead with the construction without worrying about the section 9 ban on taking.

As you read the opinion, pay attention to the four major players—Ruby, FERC, BLM, and FWS. It is essential to get clear on the roles of each. The case ultimately has to do with the processes of decision-making, not whether the pipeline did or did not violate the substantive standards of section 7 (the no-jeopardy standard and no-modification-of-critical habitat standard). In that regard, it is typical of ESA cases. Environmental plaintiffs succeed far more often challenging the processes used in decision-making than in challenging the agency's scientific opinion.

CENTER FOR BIOLOGICAL DIVERSITY V.
UNITED STATES BUREAU OF LAND MANAGEMENT

Ninth Circuit Court of Appeals
698 F.3d 1101 (2012)

BERZON, C.J.

Our case concerns a decision by the Bureau of Land Management ("BLM") to authorize the Ruby Pipeline Project ("Project"). The Project involves the construction, operation, and maintenance of a 42-inch-diameter natural gas pipeline extending from Wyoming to Oregon, over 678 miles. The right-of-way for the pipeline encompasses approximately 2,291 acres of federal lands and crosses 209 rivers and streams that support federally endangered and threatened fish species. According to a Biological Opinion ("the Biological Opinion" or "the Opinion") formulated by the Fish and Wildlife Service ("FWS"), the project "would adversely affect" nine of those species and five designated critical habitats. The FWS nonetheless concluded that the project "would not jeopardize these species or adversely modify their critical habitat." The propriety of the FWS's "no jeopardy" conclusion, and the BLM's reliance on that conclusion in issuing its Record of Decision, are at the heart of this case.

This opinion addresses those challenges to the Project that petitioners Center for Biological Diversity, Defenders of Wildlife *et al.*, and Summit Lake Paiute Tribe have raised under the Endangered Species Act ("ESA"), 16 U.S.C. § 1531 *et seq.* Specifically, we resolve petitioners' claims that the Biological Opinion and its accompanying Incidental Take Statement were arbitrary and capricious because: (1) the Biological Opinion's "no jeopardy" and "no adverse modification" determinations relied on protective measures set forth in a conservation plan not enforceable under the ESA; (2) the Biological Opinion did not take into account the potential impacts of withdrawing 337.8 million gallons of groundwater from sixty-four wells along the pipeline; (3) the Incidental Take Statement miscalculated the number of fish to be killed, by using a "dry-ditch construction method" for water crossings; and (4) the Incidental Take Statement placed no limit on the number of "eggs and fry" of threatened Lahontan cutthroat trout to be taken during construction.

We agree with the first two contentions and so set aside the Biological Opinion as arbitrary and capricious. We also set aside the Record of Decision, as it relied on the invalid Biological Opinion.

I. *Background*

A. *Statutory Scheme*

The Endangered Species Act is a comprehensive scheme with the "broad purpose" of protecting endangered and threatened species. *Babbitt v. Sweet Home Chapter of Comtys. for a Great Or.,* 515 U.S. 687, 698 (1995); *see Tenn. Valley Auth. v. Hill,* 437 U.S. 153, 180 (1978). Two interlocking provisions of the Act are of particular significance here: section 9, which prohibits the "take"[2] of any member of an endangered or threatened species, 16 U.S.C. § 1538(a)(1)(B), and section 7, which imposes upon federal agencies an "affirmative duty to prevent violations of section 9," *Ariz. Cattle Growers' Ass'n v. U.S. Fish & Wildlife,* 273 F.3d 1229, 1238 (9th Cir. 2001) (citing 16 U.S.C. § 1536(a)(2)).

Under Section 7, a federal agency must "insure that any action authorized, funded, or carried out by such agency . . . is not likely to jeopardize the continued existence of any endangered species or threatened species or result in the destruction or adverse modification of [critical] habitat of such species." 16 U.S.C. § 1536(a)(2).[3] To facilitate compliance with this substantive requirement, section 7 and its implementing regulations also impose specific procedural duties upon federal agencies: Before beginning any "major construction activities," agencies must prepare a "biological assessment" to determine whether listed species or critical habitat "are likely to be adversely affected" by the proposed action. 50 C.F.R. § 402.12 (2012). If so, the action agency must formally consult with the appropriate wildlife agency, in this case the FWS, before undertaking the action. 50 C.F.R. § 402.14; *see Karuk Tribe of Cal. v. U.S. Forest Serv.,* 681 F.3d 1006, 1020 (9th Cir. 2012) (en banc); *Sierra Club v. Babbitt,* 65 F.3d 1502, 1505 (9th Cir. 1995).

During the formal consultation process, the FWS must "[f]ormulate its biological opinion as to whether the action, taken together with cumulative effects, is likely to jeopardize the continued existence of listed species or result in the destruction or adverse modification of critical habitat." 50 C.F.R. § 402.14(g)(4). If the FWS concludes that jeopardy or adverse modification is likely, then any take resulting from the proposed action is subject to section 9 liability (unless that take is authorized by other provisions of the Act not relevant here). *See Sierra Club v. Babbitt,* 65 F.3d at 1505; *Defenders of Wildlife v. EPA,* 420 F.3d 946, 966 (9th Cir. 2005), *rev'd on other grounds, Nat'l Ass'n of Home Builders v. Defenders of Wildlife,* 551 U.S. 644 (2007). Although a federal agency or project applicant is "technically free to disregard the Biological Opinion and proceed with its proposed action, . . . it does so at its own peril (and that of its employees), for 'any person' who knowingly 'takes' [a member of] an

---

[2] "The term 'take' means to harass, harm, pursue, hunt, shoot, wound, kill, trap, capture, or collect, or to attempt to engage in any such conduct." 16 U.S.C. § 1532(19).

[3] The ESA defines "critical habitat" as: (i) areas occupied by the species, at the time the species is "listed" as endangered or threatened under the Act, that contain "those physical or biological features (I) essential to the conservation of the species and (II) which may require special management considerations or protection;" and (ii) areas not occupied by the species at the time of listing that are determined by the Secretary of the Interior to be "essential for the conservation of the species." 16 U.S.C. § 1532(5)(A).

endangered or threatened species is subject to substantial civil and criminal penalties, including imprisonment." *Bennett v. Spear,* 520 U.S. 154, 170 (1997); *see also San Luis & Delta-Mendota Water Auth. v. Salazar,* 638 F.3d 1163, 1170 (9th Cir. 2011) ("[T]he determinative or coercive effect of a Biological Opinion stems directly from the Service's power to enforce the no-take provision in ESA § 9. . . .").

If, on the other hand, the FWS concludes in its biological opinion that *no* jeopardy or adverse modification is likely, but that the project is likely to result only in the "incidental take"[4] of members of listed species, then the FWS will provide, along with its biological opinion, an incidental take statement authorizing such takings. 50 C.F.R. § 402.14(i). An incidental take statement must:

> (1) specify the impact [i.e., the amount or extent] of the incidental taking on the species; (2) specify the "reasonable and prudent measures" that the FWS considers necessary or appropriate to minimize such impact; [and] (3) set forth "terms and conditions" with which the action agency must comply to implement the reasonable and prudent measures. . . .

Or. Natural Res. Council v. Allen, 476 F.3d 1031, 1034 (9th Cir. 2007) (quoting 16 U.S.C. § 1536(b)(4); 50 C.F.R. § 402.14(i)). "Significantly, the Incidental Take Statement functions as a safe harbor provision immunizing persons from Section 9 liability and penalties for takings committed during activities that are otherwise lawful and in compliance with its terms and conditions." *Ariz. Cattle Growers' Ass'n,* 273 F.3d at 1239 (citing 16 U.S.C. § 1536(o)).

ESA regulations further require federal agencies and project applicants to "monitor the impacts of incidental take" by "report[ing] the progress of the action and its impact on the species" to the FWS. 50 C.F.R. § 402.14(i)(3). If the amount or extent of incidental taking is exceeded, the action agency "must immediately reinitiate consultation with the FWS." *Allen,* 476 F.3d at 1034–35 (citing 50 C.F.R. §§ 402.14(i)(4), 402.16(a)). The action agency must also reinitiate consultation if the proposed action "is subsequently modified in a manner that causes an effect to the listed species or critical habitat that was not considered in the biological opinion." 50 C.F.R. § 402.16(c); *see also Defenders of Wildlife v. Flowers,* 414 F.3d 1066, 1070 (9th Cir. 2005). When reinitiation of consultation is required, the original biological opinion loses its validity, as does its accompanying incidental take statement, which then no longer shields the action agency from penalties for takings. *See Allen,* 476 F.3d at 1037; U.S. Fish & Wildlife Serv. & Nat.

---

[4] "Incidental take refers to takings that result from, but are not the purpose of, carrying out an otherwise lawful activity conducted by the Federal agency or applicant." 50 C.F.R. § 402.02.

Marine Fisheries Serv., *Endangered Species Consultation Handbook: Procedures for Conducting Consultation and Conference Activities under Section 7 of the Endangered Species Act* 4–23 (1998) [hereinafter *ESA Handbook*].

B. *The Ruby Pipeline Project:*
Formal Consultation and the Biological Opinion

In January 2009, Respondent-Intervenor Ruby Pipeline L.L.C. ("Ruby") filed a formal application with the Federal Energy Regulatory Commission (FERC) seeking a Certificate of Public Convenience and Necessity ("Certificate"), *see* 15 U.S.C. § 717f(c)(1)(A), authorizing the Project. After Ruby and FERC had agreed on the rough scope of the project, FERC requested consultation with the FWS about the proposed license.

FWS's resulting Biological Opinion focused on nine listed species it determined the Project "would adversely affect," as well as the 209 bodies of water the Project would cross that either fall within or connect to the listed species' critical habitats. Five of the species—Lahontan cutthroat trout, Warner sucker, Lost River Sucker, shortnose sucker, and Modoc sucker—inhabit waters in Nevada, Oregon, or both. The other four species—Colorado pikeminnow, humpback chub, razorback sucker, and bonytail chub—live in the Colorado River system. The FWS determined that the first group of species, the Nevada/Oregon group, would be adversely affected by the Project's stream crossings, while the second group, those in the Colorado River system, would be adversely affected by the use and depletion of ground and surface water during construction.

Crucially, the Biological Opinion factored into its jeopardy determination several "voluntary" conservation actions Ruby had indicated it would facilitate implementing, which the Opinion identified as "reasonably certain to occur." The Opinion explained that these actions, set forth in an Endangered Species Conservation Action Plan (sometimes "CAP"), were "to be implemented by Ruby in the future," "would be beneficial to listed fishes and their habitats, and . . . [would] eventually contribute to the conservation and recovery of these fishes." Whether the Biological Opinion properly relied upon the Conservation Action Plan as mitigating the adverse effects of the Project is the central issue in this case.

Although it recognized that the Project would adversely affect the nine listed species, the Biological Opinion ultimately concluded that the Project was "not likely to jeopardize the continued existence" of these species or "adversely modify or destroy designated critical habitat." The FWS therefore provided an Incidental Take Statement authorizing "mortality to Lahontan cutthroat trout, Warner sucker, Modoc sucker, Lost River sucker, and shortnose sucker," provided the specified terms and conditions were met. It also "exempt[ed from section 9 liability] all take in the form of harm that would occur from the Project's removal of 49.5 acre-feet of water" from the Colorado River Basin.

II. *Discussion*

The Administrative Procedure Act ("APA") governs our review of agency decisions under the ESA. *Karuk Tribe,* 681 F.3d at 1017. Under the APA, an agency action is valid unless it is " 'arbitrary, capricious, an abuse of discretion, or otherwise not in accordance with law.' " *Id.* (quoting 5 U.S.C. § 706(2)(A)). . . .

A. *The Conservation Action Plan*

The petitioners' central argument is that the Biological Opinion was arbitrary and capricious because it relied in part on the projected beneficial effects of the Conservation Action Plan for its conclusion that the Project would not jeopardize the nine listed fish species or adversely affect critical habitat. The Conservation Action Plan measures are unenforceable under the procedures established by the ESA, petitioners maintain, but should be, and so cannot be relied upon in assessing the likely impact of the project on listed species. Unless the Conservation Action Plan is binding under the ESA, the FWS will be unable to use the ESA's "strict civil and criminal penalties," *Gifford Pinchot Task Force v. U.S. Fish & Wildlife Serv.,* 378 F.3d 1059, 1063 (9th Cir. 2004), to ensure that the plan is implemented. We agree that the Opinion's reliance on the CAP is inconsistent with the statutory scheme, and that the Opinion is therefore invalid.

1. *Background*

a. *Development and Features of the Conservation Action Plan*

[The court in this section of its opinion explained the origins and elements of the plan (the CAP) developed to diminish the ill effects of the pipeline project on the listed species and their critical habitats. The plan originated with the FWS, which proposed that it be included in the pipeline proposal. If FERC had agreed, the CAP would have been considered in the section 7 consultation process. FERC objected to including the CAP within the scope of the project, so the CAP was rewritten to be a separate, freestanding commitment that Ruby would make in the form of a Letter. That Letter, and the plan attached to it (the CAP), was submitted to the BLM and relied upon when the BLM gave permission to cross BLM lands. It was also submitted to FERC to gain its permission to construct and operate the pipeline.]

To the Letter was attached a list of, among other things, twelve fish-specific conservation measures; the Letter referred to the attachment as "Ruby's Endangered Species Act Conservation Action Plan." The listed conservation measures, if completed, were to benefit each of the nine listed species that, according to the Biological Opinion, the Project would adversely affect. Included were the construction of a fish migration barrier to protect Lahontan cutthroat trout from invasive non-native trout; improvements to a road adjacent to Modoc sucker spawning and rearing habitat; research and monitoring of Warner sucker populations; and restoration of native riparian vegetation along select tributaries in the Green River Basin, to decrease water loss that could adversely impact the endangered Colorado River fishes.

Ruby committed to funding fully only seven of the twelve Conservation Action Plan measures. For the remaining five measures, Ruby agreed to contribute partial funding, with the remaining funds to be "acquired via cost-share." For four of those five projects, Ruby's partial contribution would amount to twenty-five percent of the costs; the remaining seventy-five percent would be "obtained from other sources." For the remaining partially-funded project, Ruby would pay $150,000, leaving an unspecified amount of "remaining funds" to be acquired elsewhere. The Letter of Commitment indicated that it would be the FWS's responsibility to obtain cost-share funding. Ruby agreed, if the FWS were unable to do so, to "pay any reasonable costs, *as determined by Ruby in its sole discretion* . . . to ensure the identified conservation action is completed." (Emphasis added.) . . .

To the degree there are funding commitments, the CAP measures are, however, in some measure enforceable, albeit not through the ESA's mechanisms. The Action Plan was incorporated into both the FERC Certificate and the BLM's Record of Decision, each of which provides for discretionary agency enforcement. [The court went on to explain that both the BLM and FERC could impose "stiff consequences" if Ruby failed to comply with its plan, but noted also that enforcement was optional with these agencies and that the FWS had no role in it.]

b.   *The Biological Opinion's Reliance on the Conservation Action Plan*

The Biological Opinion relied in part on the Conservation Action Plan to conclude that the Project would not jeopardize the continued existence of the nine listed fish or adversely modify critical habitat. Specifically, the Biological Opinion's jeopardy analysis referenced the Conservation Action Plan measures in its review of the Project's anticipated "cumulative effects," that is, the "effects of future [non-Federal] activities . . . that are reasonably certain to occur within the action area" of the Project. . . .

2.   *Analysis*

The pivotal question is whether the FWS was permitted to consider the CAP measures when determining whether the Project would jeopardize listed species or adversely modify critical habitat. An agency action is arbitrary and capricious when the agency "relie[s] on factors which Congress has not intended it to consider." *Pac. Coast Fed'n of Fishermen's Ass'ns,* 265 F.3d at 1034 (quoting *Motor Vehicle Mfrs. Ass'n,* 463 U.S. at 43). Because the Plan should properly have been part of the project itself, the FWS should not have treated its anticipated benefits as background cumulative effects and used them as a basis for determining the likely effects of the Project. Doing so rendered the Plan unenforceable under the ESA, depriving FWS of the power to ensure that the measures were actually carried out.

[As the court explained, the effects of the action being proposed by the "action agency" (in this instance, FERC, acting on its behalf and for the BLM) included the effects of "interrelated actions" that were part of the proposed action and dependent on it for their justification. These interrelated effects did *not* include the consequences of unrelated private or state activities that were likely to be taking place in the same geographic region at the same time as the proposed federal action. The FWS treated the CAP as an unrelated, nonfederal action, and thus as one of the "cumulative effects," rather than an interrelated effect. By doing so, it excluded the CAP from the scope of the proposed project and from its anticipated effects. As a consequence, the section 7 consultation under the ESA did not include a careful look at the CAP. Instead, the anticipated benefits of implementing the CAP were included when determining what the overall consequences would be of the proposal project (that is, of the pipeline). The effect of considering the CAP in this manner was to diminish the anticipated harms of the project, and thus make it more likely that it would not jeopardize the listed species or adversely modify critical habitat.

The court then proceeded to explain that, when the CAP was treated as part of the "cumulative effects," rather than as part of the proposed project, the terms of the CAP were not enforceable under the ESA, either by the FWS or through citizen suits. Although the CAP would still be enforceable by the BLM and FERC, their enforcement powers did not include criminal penalties and the statutory schemes governing them did not authorize citizen enforcement suits.]

In sum, miscategorizing mitigation measures as "cumulative effects" rather than conservation measures incorporated in the proposed project profoundly affects the ESA scheme. Any such miscategorization sidetracks the FWS, the primary ESA enforcement agency; precludes reopening the consultation process when promised conservation measures do not occur; and eliminates the possibility of criminal penalties and exposure to citizen suit enforcement incorporated in the ESA to assure that listed species are protected. . . .

We now hold [that] a conservation agreement entered into by the action agency to mitigate the impact of a contemplated action on listed species must be enforceable *under the ESA* to factor into the FWS's "biological opinion as to whether [an] action, taken together with cumulative effects, is likely to jeopardize the continued existence of listed species or result in the destruction or adverse modification of critical habitat." 50 C.F.R. § 402.14(g)(4). . . .

c. *Categorizing the Conservation Action Plan Measures*

Our question, then, is whether the CAP measures in this case were properly categorized as background "cumulative effects" or whether, instead, they should have been treated as part of the proposed project, reviewed as such in the Biological Opinion, and, if accepted as adequate, enforceable under the ESA if not carried out. We conclude that the CAP— entered into by FERC, the federal government action agency—does not meet the criteria for background "cumulative effects" and should only have been taken into account in the Biological Opinion if incorporated as part of the proposed project. . . .

The Biological Opinion . . . unreasonably relied on the Conservation Action Plan measures as "cumulative effects" and took them into account in the jeopardy determination, when reliance on them would have been proper only if they were included as part of the project and so subject to the ESA's consultation and enforcement provisions. As the Opinion is therefore arbitrary and capricious, it must be set aside.

B. *Withdrawals of Groundwater*

Petitioners also contend that the Biological Opinion was arbitrary and capricious because, in reaching incidental take conclusions for listed fish species, it did not consider the potential effects of withdrawing 337.8 million gallons of groundwater from sixty-four wells along the length of the pipeline. We agree.

[On this issue the court proceeded to survey the considerable scientific data available to the FWS and the BLM dealing with the possible ill effects on the listed species of the anticipated groundwater withdrawals. The legal issue was whether these withdrawals "may affect" the listed species or their critical habitat. If they would, then they became "relevant factors" and the consultation and resulting Biological Opinion needed to take them into account.]

2. *Discussion*

* * *

To determine whether the groundwater withdrawals were a "relevant factor" that should have been analyzed in the Biological Opinion, we begin with the ESA regulations. Section 402.14 of those regulations states that "[e]ach federal agency shall review its actions at the earliest possible time to determine whether any action may affect listed species or critical habitat." 50 C.F.R. § 402.14(a) (emphasis added). Where actions "may affect" listed species, "the burden is on the Federal agency to show the absence of likely, adverse effects to listed species or critical habitat as a result of its proposed action in order to be excepted from the formal consultation obligation." 51 Fed.Reg. 19926, 19949 (June 3, 1986). Otherwise, formal consultation must proceed, and the FWS must formulate a Biological Opinion that, among other things, includes "[a] detailed discussion of the effects of the action on listed species or critical habitat." 50 C.F.R. § 402.14(h)(2).

We have previously held that the " 'may affect' standard 'must be set sufficiently low to allow Federal agencies to satisfy their duty to insure under section 7(a)(2) [that species are not jeopardized].' " *Flowers,* 414 F.3d at 1072 (quoting 51 Fed.Reg. at 19,949) (internal quotation marks omitted) (alteration in original). "*Any possible effect, whether beneficial, benign, adverse, or of an undetermined character,* triggers the formal consultation requirement." *Id.* (internal quotation marks omitted) (emphasis in original); *accord Cal. Wilderness Coal. v. U.S. Dep't of Energy,* 631 F.3d 1072, 1106 (9th Cir. 2011). Thus, while petitioners bear the burden of showing that the groundwater withdrawals "may affect" listed species or critical habitat, the burden is not a heavy one. Essentially, petitioners need to show only that an effect on listed species or critical habitat is plausible.

The government first argues that groundwater withdrawals would have no discernible impact on listed fish species because "[t]hose species do not live in ground water—they live in rivers and streams." That explanation is specious. Obviously, fish do not live underground. But, as the government recognizes, "groundwater and surface water are 'physically interrelated as integral parts of the hydrologic cycle.' " Indeed, "[i]n most areas, the surface-and ground-water systems are intimately linked," U.S. Geological Survey, U.S. Dep't of the Interior, *Fact Sheet No. 103–03, Ground-Water Depletion Across the Nation* 2 (2003), and withdrawing groundwater from nearby surface waters "can diminish the available surface-water supply by capturing some of the ground-water flow that otherwise would have discharged to surface water," Thomas C. Winter et al., U.S. Geological Survey, U.S. Dep't of the Interior, Circular No. 1139, *Ground Water and Surface Water: A Single Resource* 12 (1998). . . .

Anticipating this conclusion, the government alternatively argues that "the groundwater depletions contemplated by this Project are simply too small to have any discernible effect on the surface water flows to which they are connected." Asserting that "the relationship of groundwater flows to surface water flows is not one-to-one," the government maintains that "[a]lthough 337.8 million gallons of groundwater depletion might sound significant to those outside the field, in the context of ESA consultation it is not, when the depletion will occur as a one-season event spread between 6[4] separate locations along the Pipeline route. . . ."

The record, however, indicates that this assertion is not self-evident even to those *not* "outside the field." The Final Environmental Impact Statement noted that "[t]he use of . . . groundwater for hydrostatic testing, dust abatement, and vehicle washing *could* directly or indirectly affect surface water volumes." (Emphasis added.) It also characterizes the volume of groundwater to be withdrawn as "considerable," especially considering that "the project is located in a region of the country where water resources are limited." In addition, a draft of the Biological Assessment revealed comments by FWS staff advocating the "use of high pressure air in place of water to test the pipeline in order to avoid adverse effects to LCT [Lahontan cutthroat trout] through water depletion from *both* surface *and* groundwater sources" (Emphasis added.) Moreover, contrary to the government's intimation that the groundwater withdrawals were individually small, over 40 million gallons of groundwater was to be withdrawn from a single source. In comparison, the largest withdrawal of surface water from any single source would amount to just over 16 million gallons. The record therefore provides a basis for inferring that even if surface water levels do not vary on a one-to-one ratio in response to fluctuating groundwater levels, the groundwater withdrawals at the level contemplated are not, as the government now maintains, *de minimis*, and so "may affect" listed fish species. . . .

In sum, groundwater withdrawals constituted a "relevant factor" to determining whether the Project would result in jeopardy to listed fish species or adverse modification of those species' critical habitat. *See Pac. Coast Fed'n of Fishermen's Ass'ns v. Nat'l Marine Fisheries Serv.*, 265 F.3d 1028, 1034 (9th Cir. 2001). The FWS therefore acted unreasonably when it did not discuss the potential impacts of groundwater withdrawals on the listed species occupying the Project's action areas in Nevada and Oregon, or, alternatively, explain why the withdrawals would not likely have such impacts. The Biological Opinion was therefore arbitrary and capricious in failing to "examine the relevant data and articulate a satisfactory explanation for its action including a 'rational connection between the facts found and the choice made' " in remaining silent on the potential impact of the Project's proposed groundwater withdrawals. *See Motor Vehicle Mfrs. Ass'n v. State Farm Mut. Auto. Ins. Co.*, 463 U.S. 29, 43 (1983) (quoting *Burlington Truck Lines v. United States,* 371 U.S. 156, 168 (1962)); *see also Allen,* 476 F.3d at 1041.

[In other sections of its lengthy opinion, the court ruled that the FWS did not act arbitrarily and capriciously when it relied on an earlier biological opinion to calculate the number of listed fish that might be "incidentally taken" when the pipeline was constructed across the various rivers and streams. It also ruled for the FWS as to whether its biological opinion was flawed because it did not set forth precise numeric limits on the incidental take of fish "eggs and fry" of the threatened Lahontan cutthroat trout near eighteen water crossings. In the court's view, numeric limits were impracticable, for reasons that were sufficiently obvious to require no apparent explanation.]

E. The BLM's Reliance on the Biological Opinion

Finally, the petitioners maintain that the BLM's Record of Decision must be set aside because it relied on the FWS's flawed Biological Opinion. Section 7 of the ESA imposes a substantive duty on the BLM to ensure that its actions are not likely to jeopardize the continued existence of the listed fish or result in destruction or adverse modification of critical habitat. *See* 16 U.S.C. § 1536(a)(2). " 'Arbitrarily and capriciously relying on a faulty Biological Opinion violates this duty.' " *Wild Fish Conservancy v. Salazar,* 628 F.3d 513, 532 (9th Cir. 2010) (quoting *Defenders of Wildlife v. EPA,* 420 F.3d at 976). In particular, an agency cannot meet its section 7 obligations by relying on a Biological Opinion that is legally flawed or by failing to discuss information that would undercut the opinion's conclusions. *See id.*

The Biological Opinion here was both legally flawed—because it relied in large part on the beneficial effects of the Conservation Action Plan measures as "cumulative effects" to reach its "no jeopardy" and "no adverse modification" determinations—and inadequate with regard to evaluating the potential impacts of the Project's groundwater withdrawals. Accordingly, the BLM violated its substantive duty to ensure that its authorization of the Project would not jeopardize the survival of the nine listed fish or adversely modify the species' critical habitat.

* * *

For the foregoing reasons, we vacate the FWS's Biological Opinion and remand for the agency to formulate a revised Biological Opinion that: (1) addresses the impacts, if any, of Ruby's groundwater withdrawals on listed fish species and critical habitat; and (2) categorizes and treats the Conservation Action Plan measures as "interrelated actions" or excludes any reliance on their beneficial effects in making a revised jeopardy and adverse modification. We otherwise deny the petition as to the issues discussed in this opinion. We also vacate and remand the BLM's Record of Decision.

Vacated and remanded.

NOTES

1.   *The parties and the ESA protections.* As the court explained, Ruby Pipeline worked with three federal agencies—FERC, the BLM, and the FWS—to gain the two permissions it needed to construct the pipeline (the FERC license and BLM land-use permission). These federal permissions required the agencies (with FERC taking the lead) to consult with the FWS and obtain, from the FWS, a "biological opinion" stating that the pipeline would not violate the two substantive provisions of section 7. The FWS gave that desired opinion, attaching to it an incidental take statement (ITS) that authorized activities which killed protected animals, activities that would otherwise have violated the section 9 ban on takings. The environmental groups that brought the case likely participated in these activities from a relatively early stage, and likely supplied some scientific information to the FWS to use in its biological opinion. In any event, they challenged the biological opinion, claiming that it was faulty in several major respects. They urged FERC and BLM not to rely upon it to justify approving the pipeline project. The defect in the biological opinion also meant that the incidental take statement was invalid. That in turn meant that Ruby Pipeline was subject to the full restrictions of section 9, which it violated.

As you study the case, get clear on all of these points—the procedural steps and the substantive ESA protections. They are all tightly intertwined. Also get clear on the relative roles and legal responsibilities of the various agencies.

2.   *The fine-tuned process.* The key to appreciating this complex case is to understand the section 7 consultation process, step by step.

a.   The first step is taken by the "action agency," when it contemplates undertaking an action that might harm a species. If the contemplated activity is sufficiently significant, the agency needs to undertake a "biological assessment" to see if the activity might adversely affect the species. If there are no adverse effects, consultation is needed. If there are adverse effects, consultation is mandatory. As the court described this first step, it might seem as if the action agency does this work in isolation. In fact, action agencies often solicit information from the FWS about the presence of any protected species in the geographic area of the proposed activity, and they sometimes also ask for FWS help in making the initial biological assessment. According to the court, when is a federal action sufficiently significant to require a biological assessment, and what precise standard applies in the assessment; that is, how much evidence of possible harm is needed to trigger the obligation to proceed with formal consultation? In the view of FERC, what parts of the pipeline project required formal consultation, and what parts did not?

At this early stage, many action agencies will consider modifying their project plans (with FWS help), so that they are able to avoid the cost and delay of formal consultation. This kind of early interaction is termed informal consultation; it can occur behind the scenes with no public disclosure.

b.   Formal consultation considers the effects of the proposed project. To do that, it is necessary to identify what the project entails. That determination may sound easy, but it typically is not. It becomes particularly challenging when the proposed activity will stimulate other activities in the same geographic area, activities that are not really part of the project but that would not take place without the project. Such activities are termed "interrelated actions" and, as the court noted, they are part of the project, and thus considered by FWS when deciding whether the project is consistent with the two key substantive protections of section 7(a)(2).

The assessment of a project's effects requires a before-and-after inquiry: what is the situation on the land before the project starts, and what will the land look like after the project is fully finished and all of the interrelated actions have taken place? That inquiry requires looking forward in time, never an easy task. The forward look is more complex because the landscape is likely to be changing due to activities by other parties, by private actors and state and local governments. FWS thus has to consider how the activity that it is studying will fit together with these other likely, nonfederal actions that are also taking place. The effects of these other activities need to be taken into account to decide whether the proposed federal action will comply with 7(a)(2). It is the cumulative effect of all these activities—federal, state, private—that will decide the fate of the listed species.

In the end, though, FWS only exercises control over the federal project brought to it for review. If the agency recommends changes to reduce the harm to a listed species, the changes have to relate to the project itself. Similarly, its biological opinion can be contingent only on the successful carrying out of the project, not on whether nonfederal actors have undertaken their own anticipated activities.

c.   As the court explained, the various actors in combination prepared a Conservation Action Plan (CAP)—a set of actions that Ruby intended to carry out that would reduce the ill effects of the pipeline project. By reducing the ill effects, the conservation work described in the plan would increase the probability that FWS would issue a "no-jeopardy" biological opinion; that was the whole point of the plan. And it worked: the FWS considered the good consequences of the conservation plan, took them into account, and decided that the pipeline project with the CAP would not violate 7(a)(2). It worked, that is, until this lawsuit came along to challenge the consultation process.

d.   This brings us to the key issue in the case: Was the CAP an "interrelated action" of the federal project, so that it was considered part of the project, or was it instead an unrelated private activity that made up part of the "cumulative effects" that were considered in the before-and-after assessment of the project's consequences but not considered to be part of the project itself? On this point, review the court's reasoning carefully. Exactly why does it decide that the CAP was properly considered an interrelated action, not merely an unrelated action that contributed to the cumulative effects? What were the precise legal effects of this categorization? Why did the error by the federal agencies result in the invalidation of the FWS biological opinion (its no-jeopardy ruling)?

e.   Notice what the court said about an action agency's duty to reinitiate consultation with the FWS concerning a project after the conclusion of initial consultation. What legal standard seems to apply to this duty (that is, when is further consultation required)? And what are the legal consequences of reinitiating consultation, in terms of the original biological opinion and the incidental take statement attached to it?

f.   Finally, note what the court said about the legal effects of a biological opinion and who, ultimately, is responsible for ensuring compliance with the substantive protections of section 7. If FWS issues a no-jeopardy ruling, is the action agency then insulated from any claim that it has violated section 7? (In this case the answer, plainly, is no, but what if the no-jeopardy ruling emerged from a process that was not defective?) What about the converse, the situation in which the FWS issues a jeopardy ruling? Could an action agency disagree and charge ahead with its proposed project?

3.   *Different agency cultures and aims.* Beneath the surface of this ruling (and here and there on the surface) is the court's sense that different federal agencies have different cultures and missions, so that it makes a difference which agency is responsible for making decisions. The court clearly views the FWS as having the greatest expertise on wildlife issues. FWS is also more likely, the court assumes, to exercise its discretionary enforcement powers to protect wildlife. FERC and the BLM, in contrast, have other aims. While they may be concerned about wildlife, they are more likely, the court assumes, to trade off wildlife protection against other, economic development goals. It is thus critical for the court that FWS have the power to enforce the CAP in this case; it is not enough that FERC and BLM can enforce it. Further, the remedies for nonperformance are important for the court. Only the FWS can bring criminal enforcement actions, and only under the ESA, the court explained, can citizens file suit to compel agency action.

4.   *The continuous efforts to avoid legal action.* The facts of this dispute illustrate one of several ways that federal agencies and private actors are prompted to take steps voluntarily so that they can avoid particular legal requirements with consequences they would rather avoid. Here, Ruby and the federal agencies developed a voluntary CAP so as to avoid an unwanted jeopardy ruling from the FWS. This kind of avoidance behavior appears at all stages of ESA implementation:

a.   *Avoid listing.* Steps are often taken by federal agencies and other actors to protect and enhance the prospects of an imperiled species, so that it does not need to be listed as a threatened or endangered species under the ESA. The decision to list a species is made by the FWS based on the degree of peril that a species faces, taking into account all relevant factors, including habitat loss, overharvesting, disease, predation, and other "natural or manmade factors affecting" the continued existence of the species. (Section 4(a), (b)) That decision can also take into account conservation measures that are in place to protect the species. When conservation measures are implemented, the peril facing the species may be less, perhaps enough so that the species need not be listed. Such conservation measures, to be considered, must be enforceable or otherwise nearly certain to be carried out. FWS has various programs under which landowners and others can enter into agreements to care for species in an effort to keep them from being listed. For a critical discussion of how FWS has avoided confronting climate change in its listing decisions, see Michael C. Blumm & Kya B. Marienfeld, *Endangered Species Act Listings and Climate Change: Avoiding the Elephant in the Room,* 20 Animal L. 277 (2014) (discussing the pika, the polar bear, the wolverine, and the Gunnison sage-grouse) (article is part of a symposium on the 40th anniversary of the ESA).

      b.   *Avoiding consultation and jeopardy rulings.* As noted above, federal agencies often revise the elements of proposed activities so as to avoid having to undertake formal consultation with the FWS about them, often working informally with the FWS to achieve this outcome. If consultation is necessary, the action agency can work further with the FWS to modify plans so as to ensure a no-jeopardy ruling. Quite often that result is reached without the need for a formal biological opinion when the action agency does not need an incidental-take statement. If the agency project could take a protected animal, the agency may then push ahead to obtain the formal opinion with its attached incidental-take statement.

      c.   *Avoiding the no-take rule and habitat conservation planning.* The pipeline in this dispute involved a construction activity that altered the habitat of listed species in ways that harmed them. Habitat modification amounts to an unlawful taking of species under section 9 unless (i) the taking is incidental to a project with different aims, and (ii) the actor has gained permission to engage incidental takes. Here, Ruby received indirect permission for incidental takes in the statement attached to the FWS biological opinion. The ESA contains other means by which private actors can obtain such permission. Under section 10(a)(1)(A), the FWS can issue incidental take permits to private parties when doing so would enhance the conservation of a species. These are sometimes issued when landowners agree to take certain conservation steps voluntarily as part of a pattern of land use that has the effect of incidentally taking members of a species. Again, the aim is to avoid more full-blown legal steps, in this instance the preparation of a formal habitat conservation plan, with public comment (see below), which can be challenged in court by conservation interests dissatisfied with it.

      5.   *Other ESA issues.* Although the ruling above introduces all of the major ESA protections and the 7(a)(2) consultation process, it does not touch upon a number of other key issues that regularly arise in ESA litigation.

      a.   *Listing.* The ESA protects species that have been listed as either threatened or endangered (with a few protections applying to candidates proposed for listing). (A "species" is defined so as to include subspecies and "distinct population segment" of a vertebrate animal, with much litigation over when a geographically separate animal population qualifies as a distinct population segment.) Listing must be based on scientific data and taking into account all of the factors bearing on a species' prospects for survival. Citizens can petition FWS to list a species, and FWS faces time deadlines for taking action, at least if a petition contains enough scientific information to demonstrate that listing may be warranted. (A petition lacking adequate scientific documentation can be rejected.) The FWS lacks adequate staff to follow up on all petitions expeditiously, so it regularly misses mandatory deadlines, leading to litigation and court orders. The agency routinely explains its delays by saying that the listing of a particular species might be warranted but the agency cannot say so with any finality because it is too busy working on other matters. The funds FWS has available to use in listing typically come from the same pot as funds used to do other work. FWS has often preferred to spend its resources listing more species on the ground that listing brings the most conservation benefit for the money. However, FWS is often forced to spend resources on other efforts, such as designating critical habitat and responding to petitions to remove a species from the list. Perhaps most annoying for the agency is when it must spend resources that could be used to list species to defend itself in court against lawsuits complaining about its delays in listing.

b. *Designating and protecting "critical habitat."* A key part of the process of conserving a species (that is, bringing about recovery so that protection under the ESA is no longer needed) is the identification and protection of the habitat it requires. The ESA requires (in section 4(a)(3)) FWS to designate the critical habitat of a species at the time the species is listed, "to the maximum extent prudent and determinable." The statute defines critical habitat as the specific areas occupied by the species "on which are found those physical or biological features" that are essential for its conservation and that "may require special management considerations or protection." Critical habitat may also include areas that the species does not currently occupy if FWS decides that those areas are essential to conservation of the species.

Although the designation of critical habitat begins with biological science and the needs of the listed species, the process goes well beyond science. Section 4(b)(2) of the ESA instructs FWS to consider all effects of the habitat designation, including economic and social effects and (in a more recent statutory amendment) effects on national security. FWS "may exclude" habitat that would otherwise be critical upon a finding that the overall benefits of excluding the area from habitat designation exceed the benefits of designation, unless the failure to designate the habitat "will result in the extinction of the species concerned."

The process of designating critical habitat raises a number of difficult issues. Habitat need not be designated if it is not determinable; that is, if FWS lacks sufficient scientific knowledge to make the designation. The issue in such cases usually is one of resource availability rather than impossibility of performing the task. The "not determinable" explanation justifies only a one-year delay. At the end of that time, FWS must designate habitat based on the available information. Designation can also be avoided if it would not be "prudent." The FWS has used this justification when designation of habitat for a given species (done in publicly available maps) could increase illegal taking of the species by informing potential takers of the species' location (a particular problem with respect to endangered flowering plants and butterflies). Finally, the agency may withhold designation when it "would not be beneficial to the species," a rationale cited when habitat is already protected—for instance, when it is located in national parks, wilderness areas, or wildlife refuges—or a species is at risk for reasons not related to habitat loss.

Critical habitat is important because the section 7 protection prohibits its adverse modification. Left unclear is when a modification is sufficiently material to violate the statute. For many years FWS took the view that modification was unlawful only when it was so severe as to put the species in jeopardy. That interpretation was plainly wrong, and courts in time said so. The issue lingers.

c. *Private lands and habitat conservation planning.* As noted, a landowner can violate the section 9 ban on takings by modifying the habitat of a listed species in ways that actually kill or harm living animals. To avoid violation, the landowner needs to obtain a permit that allows takings that are incidental to some legitimate land use (forestry, for instance). When their activities become federal actions due to the need for a federal permit—as in the above dispute—the private party can gain an incidental take statement by means of the section 7 consultation process.

For private action that is not covered by section 7, the actor needs an incidental take permit in some other way. One way is to enter into a conservation agreement (explained in note 4.c., above). The other method is to prepare and gain approval (under section 10(a)(1)(B)) of a habitat conservation plan (HCP) that sets forth in detail 1) the effect that the proposed action will have on the species; 2) the steps that will be taken to "minimize and mitigate" such adverse effects; 3) the funding that will be available to implement these steps; 4) alternative actions that the applicant considered, and why the alternatives were rejected; and 5) "such other measures that the Secretary may require as being necessary or appropriate for purposes of the plan."

Once it is prepared, FWS reviews the HCP and makes it available for public review and comment. FWS can approve the plan if it finds that 1) the taking will be incidental; 2) the applicant will minimize and mitigate the effects of the taking "to the maximum extent practicable"; 3) the plan is adequately and securely funded; and 4) the taking "will not appreciably reduce the likelihood of the survival and recovery of the species in the wild." Before approving the plan, the agency can insist on receiving "other assurances" that the plan will be implemented. If the plan is approved, the agency issues an incidental take permit.

Litigation over habitat conservation plans and incidental take permits has focused on the requirements for the plans and on the standards used by the FWS in reviewing them. Central to many controversies is whether the plan will actually reduce harm "to the maximum extent practicable" and whether the HCP will be carried out over its full lifetime, which is sometimes in perpetuity. Particularly contentious are cases in which the HCP requires continued funding, and the funding source is arguably insecure; for example, when dependent upon the continued sale of lots in an expanding subdivision or upon continued funding by a governmental entity that allocates money annually. Additional complexity occurs when conservation plans cover multiple listed species and include provisions protecting unlisted species in the hope that listing of them will not become necessary.

CHAPTER 5

SUBSURFACE RESOURCES

■ ■ ■

As this book illustrates, the management of natural resources on private property is fraught with legal challenges—those arising between and among neighboring property owners and between property owners and federal, state, or local regulators. Yet most of these challenges take place on one horizontal plane—that is, the surface of property. The surface estate, however, is only one plane where property conflicts are likely to occur, and it is actually nested between two other estates in a vertical property rights structure. One of those estates, as discussed in Chapter 10, implicates the right to use airspace above one's property. The other estate, the subject of this chapter, implicates the right to own, preserve, or use subsurface resources.

The ownership, use, and management of minerals, oil and gas, subsurface storage space, caves, underground aquifers, and other subsurface resources gives rise to a host of legal questions. Which natural resources are parts of the land and which are available instead for separate acquisition? Should we answer this question using an abstract, easily understood ideal of land ownership, or does it make more sense to consider each resource separately, paying attention to its physical attributes and to the practical challenges of putting the resource to effective use? How do we balance the competing interests of subsurface resource owners and overlying surface owners, given the inevitable conflicts between them? What happens when technological advances change the nature and uses of subsurface resources, such as in the case of carbon capture and storage as a tool to combat climate change? How does (and should) the law adapt to accommodate such advances in a way that still preserves the rights of the various surface and subsurface owners?

Although these questions address just a handful of issues related to subsurface resources, such inquiries are becoming increasingly important. Markets have shifted in recent years, ushering in a boom of natural gas production across the United States. Natural gas fracturing ("fracking") operations are occurring at the surface of regions of the U.S. where they have never before occurred, giving rise to conflicts between surface owners and subsurface owners. Surface owners who own the rights to the gas may wish to develop those resources but may face resistance from nearby landowners, who are concerned about health impacts on water quality, aesthetics of surface estates, or a number of other issues. Similarly, subsurface properties long drained of oil and gas are now candidates for storage of both fossil fuel products and carbon captured to combat climate change. These examples illustrate that subsurface natural resources are as dynamic as those on the overlying surface estate, and so are the legal issues associated with them.

In chapter 1, we took a first look at subsurface rights in *Hicks v. Bell,* a California gold rush ruling that explained the common law approach to minerals. In England the valuable minerals were gold and silver, and they belonged to the King. Although *Hicks* embraced this legal position, as did some other early rulings, it was rather quickly abandoned in favor of the now-dominant rule that subsurface minerals—at least those that stay in place—belong to the surface landowner. In the same chapter, we saw in the *Park County* ruling that water beneath the ground is often not owned by the surface landowner, and that the surface landowner might have no legal right to object if someone else stores water beneath her land. As these two initial cases reflect, surface landowners have extensive but far from unlimited control over the subsurface. Their control diminishes further when specific subsurface minerals, or subsurface use rights, are severed from surface ownership and placed into separate hands.

In the first of this chapter's four subparts, we look at the subsurface rights of landowners (putting to one side, to consider in the next chapter, the special case of subsurface water). In the second part, we take up issues relating to the severance of mineral rights from the land surface, highlighting uncertainties as to which minerals have been severed and the ensuing issues about the rights of mineral owners to use the land surface and the subsurface to exploit their minerals. The chapter's third part explores the basics of oil and gas production and leasing, looking quickly at common regulatory schemes and at some of the central terms of oil and gas leases. The chapter ends with a case study of conflict between mineral extraction and the protection of surface natural resources—in this case wetlands and the rich biotic life that inhabits them.

A. SUBSURFACE PROPERTY RIGHTS

Eᴅᴡᴀʀᴅs ᴠ. Sɪᴍs
Kentucky Court of Appeals
24 S.W.2d 619 (1929)

Sᴛᴀɴʟᴇʏ, C.

This case presents a novel question. [The facts that follow are excerpted from a subsequent opinion in this same dispute, set forth below.]

[Around 1909] L.P. Edwards discovered a cave under land belonging to him and his wife, Sally Edwards. The entrance to the cave is on the Edwards land. Edwards named it the "Great Onyx Cave," no doubt because of the rock crystal formations within it which are known as onyx. This cave is located in the cavernous area of Kentucky, and is only about three miles distant from the world-famous Mammoth Cave. Its proximity to Mammoth Cave, which for many years has had an international reputation as an underground wonder, as well as its beautiful formations, led Edwards to embark upon a program of advertising and exploitation for the purpose of bringing visitors to his cave. Circulars were printed and distributed, signs were erected along the roads, persons were employed and stationed along the highways to solicit the patronage of passing travelers, and thus the fame of the Great Onyx Cave spread from year to year, until eventually, and before the beginning of the present litigation, it was a well-known and well-patronized cave. Edwards built a hotel near the mouth of the cave to care for travelers. He improved and widened the footpaths and avenues in the cave, and ultimately secured a stream of tourists who paid entrance fees sufficient not only to cover the cost of operation, but also to yield a substantial revenue in addition thereto. The authorities in charge of the development of the Mammoth Cave area as a national park undertook to secure the Great Onyx Cave through condemnation proceedings, and in that suit the value of the cave was fixed by a jury at $396,000. In April, 1928, F.P. Lee, an adjoining landowner, filed this suit against Edwards and the heirs of Sally Edwards, claiming that a portion of the cave was under his land, and praying for damages, for an accounting of the profits which resulted from the operation of the cave, and for an injunction prohibiting Edwards and his associates from further trespassing upon or exhibiting any part of the cave under Lee's land. At the inception of this litigation, Lee undertook to procure a survey of the cave in order that it might be determined what portion of it was on his land. The chancellor ordered that a survey be made, and Edwards prosecuted an appeal from that order to this court. The appeal was dismissed because it was not from a final judgment. *Edwards v. Lee*, 19 S.W.2d 992 (Ky. Ct. App. 1929). . . .]

[Edwards then filed a separate suit, asking the appellate court to issue a writ of prohibition, preventing the underground survey from taking place. The chief issue in this new case was whether Edwards, as owner of the cave entrance, would be harmed by having a survey come upon his land to conduct the survey. That issue in turn depended upon the relative property rights of the parties in the cave.]

There is but little authority of particular and special application to caves and cave rights. In few places, if any, can be found similar works of nature of such grandeur and of such unique and marvelous character as to give to caves a commercial value sufficient to cause litigation as those peculiar to Edmonson and other counties in Kentucky. The reader will find of interest the address on "The Legal Story of Mammoth Cave" by Hon. John B. Rodes, of Bowling Green, before the 1929 Session of the Kentucky State Bar Association, published in its proceedings. In *Cox v. Colossal Cavern Co.*, 276 S.W. 540 (Ky. Ct. App. 1925), the subject of cave rights was considered, and this court held there may be a severance of the estate in the property, that is, that one may own the surface and another the cave rights, the conditions being quite similar to but not exactly like those of mineral lands. But there is no such severance involved in this case, as it appears that the defendants are the owners of the land and have in it an absolute right.

Cujus est solum, ejus est usque ad coelum ad infernos (to whomsoever the soil belongs, he owns also to the sky and to the depths), is an old maxim and rule. It is that the owner of realty, unless there has been a division of the estate, is entitled to the free and unfettered control of his own land above, upon, and beneath the surface. So whatever is in a direct line between the surface of the land and the center of the earth belongs to the owner of the surface. Ordinarily that ownership cannot be interfered with or infringed by third persons. There are, however, certain limitations on the right of enjoyment of possession of all property, such as its use to the detriment or interference with a neighbor and burdens which it must bear in common with property of a like kind.

With this doctrine of ownership in mind, we approach the question as to whether a court of equity has a transcendent power to invade that right through its agents for the purpose of ascertaining the truth of a matter before it, which fact thus disclosed will determine certainly whether or not the owner is trespassing upon his neighbor's property. Our attention has not been called to any domestic case, nor have we found one, in which the question was determined either directly or by analogy. It seems to the court, however, that there can be little differentiation, so far as the matter now before us is concerned, between caves and mines. And as declared in 40 C. J. 947: "A court of equity, however, has the inherent power, independent of statute, to compel a mine owner to permit an inspection of his works at the suit of a party who can show reasonable ground for suspicion that his lands are being trespassed upon through them, and may issue an injunction to permit such inspection." . . .

We can see no difference in principle between the invasion of a mine on adjoining property to ascertain whether or not the minerals are being extracted from under the applicant's property and an inspection of this respondent's property through his cave to ascertain whether or not he is trespassing under this applicant's property.

It appears that before making this order the court had before him surveys of the surface of both properties and the conflicting opinions of witnesses as to whether or not the Great Onyx Cave extended under the surface of the plaintiff's land. This opinion evidence was of comparatively little value, and as the chancellor (now respondent) suggested, the controversy can be quickly and accurately settled by surveying the cave; and "if defendants are correct in their contention this survey will establish it beyond all doubt and their title to this cave will be forever quieted. If the survey shows the Great Onyx Cave extends under the lands of plaintiffs, defendants should be glad to know this fact and should be just as glad to cease trespassing upon plaintiff's lands, if they are in fact doing so." The peculiar nature of these conditions, it seems to us, makes it imperative and necessary in the administration of justice that the survey should have been ordered and should be made. . . .

The writ of prohibition is therefore denied.

LOGAN, J. (dissenting).

The majority opinion allows that to be done which will prove of incalculable injury to Edwards without benefiting Lee, who is asking that this injury be done. I must dissent from the majority opinion. . . . It deprives Edwards of rights which are valuable, and perhaps destroys the value of his property, upon the motion of one who may have no interest in that which it takes away, and who could not subject it to his dominion or make any use of it. . . .

It sounds well in the majority opinion to tritely say that he who owns the surface of real estate, without reservation, owns from the center of the earth to the outmost sentinel of the solar system. The age-old statement, adhered to in the majority opinion as the law, in truth and fact, is not true now and never has been. I can subscribe to no doctrine which makes the owner of the surface also the owner of the atmosphere filling illimitable space. Neither can I subscribe to the doctrine that he who owns the surface is also the owner of the vacant spaces in the bowels of the earth.

The rule should be that he who owns the surface is the owner of everything that may be taken from the earth and used for his profit or happiness. Anything which he may take is thereby subjected to his dominion, and it may be well said that it belongs to him. I concede the soundness of that rule, which is supported by the cases cited in the majority opinion; but they have no application to the question before the court in this case. They relate mainly to mining rights; that is, to substances under the surface which the owner may subject to his dominion. But no man can bring up from the depths of the earth the Stygian darkness and make it serve his purposes; neither can he subject to his dominion the bottom of the ways in the caves on which visitors tread, and for these reasons the owner of the surface has no right in such a cave which the law should, or can, protect because he has nothing of value therein, unless, perchance, he owns an entrance into it and has subjected the subterranean passages to his dominion.

A cave or cavern should belong absolutely to him who owns its entrance, and this ownership should extend even to its utmost reaches if he has explored and connected these reaches with the entrance. When the surface owner has discovered a cave and prepared it for purposes of exhibition, no one ought to be allowed to disturb him in his dominion over that which he has conquered and subjected to his uses.

* * *

In the light of these unannounced principles which ought to be the law in this modern age, let us give thought to the petitioner Edwards, his rights and his predicament, if that is done to him which the circuit judge has directed to be done. Edwards owns this cave through right of discovery, exploration, development, advertising, exhibition, and conquest. Men fought their way through the eternal darkness, into the mysterious and abysmal depths of the bowels of a groaning world to discover the theretofore unseen splendors of unknown natural scenic wonders. They were conquerors of fear, although now and then one of them, as did Floyd Collins, paid with his life, for his hardihood in adventuring into the regions where Charon with his boat had never before seen any but the spirits of the departed. They let themselves down by flimsy ropes into pits that seemed bottomless; they clung to scanty handholds as they skirted the brinks of precipices while the flickering flare of their flaming flambeaux disclosed no bottom to the yawning gulf beneath them; they waded through rushing torrents, not knowing what awaited them on the farther side; they climbed slippery steeps to find other levels; they wounded their bodies on stalagmites and stalactites and other curious and weird formations; they found chambers, star-studded and filled with scintillating light reflected by a phantasmagoria revealing fancied phantoms, and tapestry woven by the toiling gods in the dominion of Erebus; hunger and thirst, danger and deprivation could not stop them. Through days, weeks, months, and years—ever linking chamber with chamber, disclosing an underground land of enchantment, they continued their explorations; through the years they toiled connecting these wonders with the outside world through the entrance on the land of Edwards which he had discovered; through the years they toiled finding safe ways for those who might come to view what they had found and placed their seal upon. They knew nothing, and cared less, of who owned the surface above; they were in another world where no law forbade their footsteps. They created an underground kingdom where Gulliver's people may have lived or where Ayesha may have found the revolving column of fire in which to bathe meant eternal youth.

When the wonders were unfolded and the ways were made safe, then Edwards patiently, and again through the years, commenced the advertisement of his cave. First came one to see, then another, then two together, then small groups, then small crowds, then large crowds, and then the multitudes. Edwards had seen his faith justified. The cave was his because he had made it what it was, and without what he had done it was nothing of value. The value is not in the black vacuum that the uninitiated call a cave. That which Edwards owns is something intangible and indefinable. It is his vision translated into a reality.

Then came the horse leach's daughters crying: "Give me," "give me." Then came the "surface men" crying, "I think this cave may run under my lands." They do not know they only "guess," but they seek to discover the secrets of Edwards so that they may harass him and take from him that which he has made his own. They have come to a court of equity and have asked that Edwards be forced to open his doors and his ways to them so that they may go in and despoil him; that they may lay his secrets bare so that others may follow their example and dig into the wonders which Edwards has made his own. What may be the result if they stop his ways? They destroy the cave, because those who visit it are they who give it value, and none will visit it when the ways are barred so that it may not be exhibited as a whole.

For these reasons I dissent from the majority opinion.

[The trial court ordered the survey of the cave, which in time led to the following appellate ruling concerning Lee's request for compensation for the trespass.]

EDWARDS V. LEE'S ADMINISTRATOR

Kentucky Court of Appeals
96 S.W.2d 1028 (1936)

STITES, J.

This is an appeal from a judgment of the Edmonson circuit court sitting in equity. Appellants argue but two points in this court: (1) That the court below applied an improper measure of damages; and (2) even if the measure of damages was correct, the amount was erroneously computed. . . .

A tremendous amount of proof was taken on each side concerning the title of Lee to the land claimed by him; how much, if any, of the cave is under the land of Lee; the length of the exhibited portion of the cave and the amount thereof under the land of Lee; the net earnings of the cave for the years involved; the location of the principal points of interest in the cave and whether they were under the lands of Edwards or of Lee; and whether or not Edwards and his associates had knowledge of the fact that they were trespassing on Lee's property. . . . [On remand, the trial judge determined that approximately one-third of the cave lay beneath Lee's land. Rather than compensate Lee only for the nominal injury he suffered, the judge awarded him one-third of the net proceeds of the cave operation, plus interest. It also enjoined future trespasses.]

Appellants, in their attack here on the measure of damages and its application to the facts adduced, urge: (1) That the appellees had simply a hole in the ground, about 360 feet below the surface, which they could not use and which they could not even enter except by going through the mouth of the cave on Edwards' property; (2) the cave was of no practical use to appellees without an entrance, and there was no one except the appellants on whom they might confer a right of beneficial use; (3) Lee's portion of the cave had no rental value; (4) appellees were not ousted of the physical occupation or use of the property because they did not and could not occupy it; (5) the property has not in any way been injured by the use to which it has been put by appellants . . .

Appellees, on the other hand, argue that this was admittedly a case of willful trespass; that it is not analogous to a situation where a trespasser simply walks across the land of another, for here the trespasser actually used the property of Lee to make a profit for himself; that even if nothing tangible was taken or disturbed in the various trips through Lee's portion of the cave, nevertheless there was a taking of esthetic enjoyment which, under ordinary circumstances, would justify a recovery of the reasonable rental value for the use of the cave . . .

Appellees brought this suit in equity, and seek an accounting of the profits realized from the operation of the cave, as well as an injunction against future trespass. In substance, therefore, their action is ex contractu ["from a contract"] and not, as appellants contend, simply an action for damages arising from a tort. Ordinarily, the measure of recovery in assumpsit [breach of contract] for the taking and selling of personal property is the value received by the wrongdoer. On the other hand, where the action is based upon a trespass to land, the recovery has almost invariably been measured by the reasonable rental value of the property. *Profile Cotton Mills v. Calhoun Water Co.*, 85 So. 284 (Ala. 1920).

Strictly speaking, a count for "use and occupation" does not fit the facts before us because, while there has been a recurring use, there has been no continuous occupation of the cave such as might arise from the planting of a crop or the tenancy of a house. Each trespass was a distinct usurpation of the appellees' title and interruption of their right to undisturbed possession. But, even if we apply the analogy of the crop cases or the wayleave cases [*Phillips v. Homfray*, 24 Ch. Div. 439 (1883); *Whithem v. Westminster Co.*, 12 Times L.R. 318; *Carmichael v. Old Straight Creek Coal Corporation*, 22 S.W.2d 572 (Ky. Ct. App. 1929)], it is apparent that rental value has been adopted, either consciously or unconsciously, as a convenient yardstick by which to measure the proportion of profit derived by the trespasser directly from the use of the land itself [9 R.C.L. 942]. In other words, rental value ordinarily indicates the amount of profit realized directly from the land as land, aside from all collateral contracts.

* * *

Clearly, the unjust enrichment of the wrongdoer is the gist of the right to bring an action ex contractu. Rental value is merely the most convenient and logical means for ascertaining what proportion of the benefits received may be attributed to the use of the real estate. . . .

Similarly, in illumination of this conclusion, there is a line of cases holding that the plaintiff may at common law bring an action against a trespasser for the recovery of "mesne profits" following the successful termination of an action of ejectment. . . . For example, *see Capital Garage Co. v. Powell*, 127 A. 375 (Vt. 1925). Here again, the real basis of recovery is the profits received, rather than rent. . . .

Finally, in the current proposed final draft of the Restatement of Restitution and Unjust Enrichment (March 4, 1936), Part I, § 136, it is stated:

> "A person who tortiously uses a trade name, trade secret, profit a prendre, or other similar interest of another, is under a duty of restitution for the value of the benefit thereby received." . . .

Whether we consider the similarity of the case at bar to (1) the ordinary actions in assumpsit to recover for the use and occupation of real estate, or (2) the common-law action for mesne profits, or (3) the action to recover for the tortious use of a trade-name or other similar right, we are led inevitably to the conclusion that the measure of recovery in this case must be the benefits, or net profits, received by the appellants from the use of the property of the appellees. The philosophy of all these decisions is that a wrongdoer shall not be permitted to make a profit from his own wrong. . . .

THOMAS, J. (concurring).

I concur in the ultimate conclusion reached by my brethren as expressed in the majority opinion, but I differ widely from the reasoning employed therein as a basis for reaching it. . . .

The opinion states the facts, and correctly concludes that "the case is sui generis." It then adds: "Counsel have been unable to give us much assistance in the way of previous decisions of this or other courts. We are left to fundamental principles and analogies." Those excerpts therefrom are undoubtedly true, and some principle must be found by which (1) the involved property (the cave) may be rendered profitable to each of its several owners, and (2) that it may be kept open in its entirety; not only for the purpose of making each owner's portion profitable to him, and all others having proprietary rights therein, but also that the patronizing public might not be deprived of the educational and other benefits to be deprived from visiting the nature made wonder throughout its length, without any obstructing walls by separate segment owners, which under the theory of the opinion they would undoubtedly have the right to construct, provided they could gain entrance into the cave for that purpose.

It is because of the recognition of such segment ownership, as recognized and applied by the opinion, with its following consequences, that has led me to adopt the views hereinafter expressed, and which I am confident will be found to be not only the more practical, but also an assured guarantee is thereby furnished against the possible obstructions, already mentioned, and other potential consequences that lurk in the theory approved and adopted by the court's opinion. . . .

[Thomas urged that the proper measure of damages was not profits from the cave operation, but instead the reasonable rental value of the cave portion owned by Lee. The trespasser's profit was the appropriate measure, he asserted, only when the profit was equal in value to some physical thing that had been severed from the land.] In all such cases where the trespassing act is willfully done, the measure of recovery of the one trespassed upon is the net value of the substance taken away from the corpus of his property. On the other hand, where no corpus is abstracted and taken away, but only a mere use of the property, with the corpus left intact upon the cessation of the use, the measure of recovery is the reasonable rental value of the property.

I have yet to meet with a case where A would be made to account to B for all of the agricultural profits grown by A on B's land while the grower was an undoubted trespasser. The measure would be the damages that A did to B's land (all of which he would leave intact after the trespassing act ceased) and which is practically universally determined as being the rental value of the land for the use to which it was put. . . .

My theory is this: That the cave in this sui generis case should be treated as a unit of property throughout its entire exhibitable length, including the augmentations of prongs or branches, and that it should be adjudged as owned jointly by all of the surface owners above it, in proportion that the length of their surface ownership bears to the entire length of such exhibitable portion. I realize that herein lies the departure (but which I think is justified from the exigencies of the case) from the ancient rule of, "*Cujus est solum, ejus est usque ad coelum et ad infernos* (to whomsoever the soil belongs, he owns also to the sky and to the depths.)" That maxim literally followed would segmentize ownership both above and below the surface corresponding to boundaries of the latter; and it is the denying of that effect, as applied to property of the nature of a cave, that constitutes the departure from, or exception to the rule that I advocate; whilst the majority opinion not only discards that theory, but advocates other departures equally if not more drastic, and which are necessarily followed by much more impractical and destructive consequences. The same departure has already been made by all courts before which the question has arisen, with reference to ownership "to the sky" by the owner of the surface, in determining aerial navigation rights, and which departure was forced by the necessities of the case. I, therefore, can conceive of no objection to extending it in the opposite direction when the same necessities demand it.

* * *

The theory of joint ownership which I conclude is the correct one to adopt and apply under the exigencies of this case does not conflict with the maxim supra that the surface owner also owns to the "depths below," except that it applies his ownership—not to the particular segment underlying his surface rights—but to the aliquot part of the entire attractive vacuum made by nature, called "a cave," and that the extent of his joint ownership in the entire property is measured by his surface rights. . . .

For the reasons stated, I concur in the result of the majority opinion, but disagree with the principles or theory upon which it is based.

NOTES

1. *The three approaches to cave ownership.* The Edwards/Onyx Cave litigation is a classic in natural resources (and property) law, in part because of the three ownership approaches proposed by the various judges. As you identify and clarify the three competing approaches, considering their relative merits and demerits, it is useful to keep the following points in mind.

First, to use the cave at all, people need access to it, which means crossing someone's private land to get to the entrance. A share in the cave is far less valuable without an ability to make use of it. How do the various approaches handle this practical need?

Second, when the overlying landowners all get along and can work things out themselves, law is hardly needed. Law is most important when the owners do not get along. Thus, in testing the relative appeal of the three approaches we need to imagine the case in which the owners have strong disagreements. How do the various approaches handle these disagreements? What legal remedies does a disgruntled person likely possess?

Finally, as you consider the options do not look merely to the relative rights of the parties as established by law. Think also of how the landowners are likely to act, given their legal rights, once the rights are established by the court. What negotiations might take place? And what will happen if the negotiations break down?

2. *Shared governance: caves.* One problem that arises with the joint ownership option is the need to decide what rights group members have to get to the cave entrance. That problem is avoided, of course, when the owner of the entrance owns the entire cave. (But how sensible is the entrance-owner-owns-all approach when there are multiple entrances, or when a surface owner cuts a new entrance? Are these problems tractable?)

Although Justice Thomas in the second case refers to joint ownership, presumably he has in mind not joint tenancy (with its rights of survivorship) but something like tenancy in common. Recall from your study of basic property the main elements of that form of concurrent ownership: each co-owner in tenancy in common possesses the right to use the whole of the property (the entire cave) consistent with the rights of the others to do the same. Moreover, each of them can sell his or her share without getting permission from the other owners. Could the various co-tenants under Thomas's approach each set up cave tour companies and then compete with one another? And what if one landowner simply does not want the cave used, perhaps preferring to leave resident bats in peace?

Recall that each tenant in common also has the right at any time to seek partition of the property, usually with no questions asked. Would a court likely favor partition of the cave in kind (leading, presumably, to something like the majority's approach of fragmented physical ownership), or would it instead order the cave sold and then divide the money? If the latter, could anyone other than the owner of the entrance reasonably bid on it? Finally, what might Justice Thomas say about the ownership of valuable minerals found in a jointly owned cave? Would the joint ownership extend to the minerals, or would it cover only recreational uses of the cave?

3. *Cujus est solum . . .* Like essentially all legal maxims, this one is subject to many exceptions, so much so that one is prompted to ask: was it really the reason for the court's ruling or instead a convenient phrase to

deploy in justifying a conclusion reached on other grounds? Is there benefit in having a maxim such as this? Is it merely an elevation of abstraction over sound, practical reasoning, or is there something to be said for a rule of ownership that everyone can readily grasp? The influence of such maxims gained ground in the common law over the centuries, reaching a peak at the end of the nineteenth century (the zenith of abstract thinking about property ownership). Since then courts have viewed them with greater suspicion, using them when helpful, ignoring or even vilifying them when not.

As for the maxim that a landowner owns to the center of the Earth, it apparently was interjected into Anglo-American law by legal treatise writer William Blackstone in the eighteenth century. English precedents seemed to protect landowner interests only near the surface. As John Sprankling explained in a recent detailed survey of subsurface property rights, American courts quoted the maxim repeatedly in cases having nothing to do with subsurface activities, so that "by the end of the nineteenth century, frequent repetition had transformed Blackstone's naked assertion into a supposed rule of American law." John G. Sprankling, *Owning the Center of the Earth*, 55 U.C.L.A. L. Rev. 979, 983 (2008) (noting that the idea first entered U.S. law— as obvious dictum—in a dispute over items found four feet beneath the land surface).

In a decision authorizing airplanes to fly over private land without worry of trespass the U.S. Supreme Court summarily brushed the legal expression aside: *cujus est solum*, it asserted, "has no place in the modern world." *United States v. Causby*, 328 U.S. 256, 260–61 (1946) (per Justice Douglas). A recent ruling by the Texas Supreme Court mimicked the sentiment: "Lord Coke, who pronounced the maxim, did not consider the possibility of airplanes. But neither did he imagine oil wells. The law of trespass need no more be the same two miles below the surface than two miles above." *Coastal Oil & Gas Corp. v. Garza Energy Trust*, 268 S.W.3d 1, 11 (Tex. 2008). The Texas ruling reiterated sentiment from another major oil-producing state, Louisiana, in *Nunez v. Waincoco Oil & Gas,* 488 So.2d 955 (La. 1986), which similarly set aside subsurface landowner rights in the context of regulated oil production. A more clear rejection of the maxim came in *Chance v. BP Chemicals, Inc.*, 670 N.E.2d 985, 992 (Ohio 1996), where the court refused to find a trespass based on migrating chemicals a half-mile beneath the surface, ruling that landowners could exclude only those invasions "that actually interfere with [their] reasonable and foreseeable use of the subsurface." Oil- and gas-related rulings are considered in Owen L. Anderson, *Subsurface 'Trespass': A Man's Subsurface Is Not His Castle*, 49 Washburn L. J. 247 (2010). We return to this issue below.

4.   *The labor theory of property ownership.* Justice Logan's peroration on the bravery and fortitude of spelunkers contains strong echoes of John Locke's seventeenth-century labor theory of private ownership. The labor theory (which was well known before Locke) justified private property on the ground that its value was created by the owner. To recognize private property was thus to give to the owner what he created by his labor. Here, the labor

lay not in creating the cave (nature gets credit for that) but instead in preparing it for use and establishing a popular cave-exploration business. Is it fair for other landowners to claim part of this labor, which no doubt accounted for much of the cave's earnings? Would it be for them an unearned economic windfall?

5. *Measuring damages for misuse of resources.* The most important legal decision made by Lee's lawyer was to recognize that Lee would win virtually nothing if he merely brought a typical trespass suit and asked for damages caused by the trespass. Lee did not even know that the trespass was occurring. At the time of the case he had suffered no injury because of it since he had no access to the cave and no way of using it or even checking it for damages. Had Lee asked for trespass damages, he might well have received an award of $1. Alert to the problem and aware of the existence of alternative remedies, the lawyer decided to waive the tort and to sue in assumpsit, a remedy based on (in this case) a fictional, presumed contract between the parties. The appropriate measure of recovery thus had nothing to do with the injury suffered by Lee. It was instead the amount that Edwards owed under the fictional contract. What the judges could not agree upon was the measure of damages. Was it the rental value of the land used, or was it instead the net profits earned by the trespasser as a result of the trespass?

Do you find persuasive the observation made by the concurrence in *Lee's Administrator* that "I have yet to meet with a case where A would be made to account to B for all of the agricultural profits grown by A on B's land while the grower was an undoubted trespasser"? According to many courts, rental value and net profits of the trespasser ought to be the same, but the Kentucky court thought otherwise. Assumpsit and other restitutionary remedies often prove useful to plaintiffs in cases involving misuses of natural resources, particularly when the misuse of the land involves no physical taking from the land and no physical injury to it.

6. *Measuring damages for wrongful drilling.* In light of the Onyx Cave litigation, what measure of monetary recovery should a landowner receive if someone unlawfully drills a well on his land and the well turns up dry, thus providing evidence that no oil underlies the land? The issue arose in *Humble Oil & Refining Co. v. Kishi*, 276 S.W. 190 (Tex. App 1925), when the lessee oil company entered the plaintiffs land under a lease that had expired. The plaintiff's 50-acre tract was adjacent to land with a producing oil well. Because of the prospects of finding oil on it, the land had a leasehold value of $1,000 per acre. The trial court awarded trespass damages of only $1, on the ground that the amount of damages was uncertain and not susceptible of proof. But the Texas Court of Appeals reversed, ruling that the plaintiff's injury was $1,000 per acre, since the plaintiff's land declined in value by this amount due to the dry hole. This was the market value of the leasehold interest that Humble Oil effectively took, and the court held that it was appropriate that Humble Oil pay for the loss in market value. Compare *Martel v. Hall Oil Co.*, 253 P. 862 (Wyo. 1927) (awarding no damages on similar facts because the trespasser merely made the truth known that the

plaintiff's land lacked oil; the plaintiff was merely denied the ability to sell worthless mineral rights to an unsuspecting buyer).

7. *Right to exclude: mining in early Virginia.* Locke's labor theory of property came together with ideas of individual liberty and with memories of the king's rights in valuable mines in an early Virginia statute dealing with mining. The statute authorized any citizen to enter the unenclosed rural land of another person, in the company of a justice of the peace, and to prospect for minerals. Any minerals found became the property of the finder, who also gained rights to extract the minerals subject only to a requirement that the mine owner compensate the surface owner for damage to the land surface. The statute was one of many indications that early America gave only limited recognition to the landowner's desire to control access to rural, unenclosed lands (an issue taken up in chapter 2) and was also an indication of the desire of early America to put the continent's natural resources to best use. Ideas about property ownership and the right to property in the late eighteenth century are surveyed in Eric T. Freyfogle, *The Land We Share: Private Property and the Common Good* 50–63 (2003).

ELLIFF V. TEXON DRILLING CO.

Supreme Court of Texas
210 S.W.2d 558 (1948)

FOLLEY, J.

[This action was brought by the Elliffs, seeking money damages for the harms they suffered as landowners when an oil well operated by Texon Drilling on land adjacent to theirs had a "blowout." The Elliffs' land was also leased to an oil company; under the lease the Elliffs received a standard one-eighth royalty based on product from their well. (Under approximately half of their land, the Eliffs shared the mineral rights equally with another party, so that the royalty of the Elliffs on that part of their land was actually a one-sixteenth interest.) The Elliffs' land covered approximately half of the land surface above a "huge reservoir" of gas. On the other half of the land, Texon. a lessee, drilled an "offset well," which is to say that the lessee installed the well to produce oil and gas that would have otherwise simply migrated to the well on the Elliffs' land and been extracted by the Elliffs and their lessee.]

Prior to November 1936, respondents [Texon Drilling Co.] were engaged in the drilling of Driscoll-Sevier No. 2 as an offset well at a location 466 feet east of [the Elliffs'] east line. On the date stated, when respondents had reached a depth of approximately 6838 feet, the well blew out, caught fire and cratered. Attempts to control it were unsuccessful, and huge quantities of gas, distillate and some oil were blown into the air, dissipating large quantities from the reservoir into which the offset well was drilled. When the Driscoll-Sevier No. 2 well blew out, the fissure or opening in the ground around the well gradually increased until it enveloped and destroyed Eliff No. 1. The latter well also blew out, cratered, caught fire and burned for several years. Two water wells on petitioners' land became involved in the cratering and each of them blew out. Certain damages also resulted to the surface of petitioners' lands and to their cattle thereon. The cratering process and the eruption continued until large quantities of gas and distillate were drained from under petitioners' land and escaped into the air, all of which was alleged to be the direct and proximate result of the negligence of respondents in permitting their well to blow out. . . .

The jury found that respondents were negligent in failing to use drilling mud of sufficient weight in drilling their well, and that such negligence was the proximate cause of the well blowing out. It also found that petitioners had suffered $4,620.00 damage to sixty acres of the surface, and $1,350.00 for the loss of 27 head of cattle. The damages for the gas and distillate wasted "from and under" the lands of petitioners, due to respondents' negligence, was fixed by the jury at $78,580.46 for the gas, and $69,967.73 for the distillate. . . .

. . . . [O]ur attention will be confined to the sole question as to whether the law of capture absolves respondents of any liability for the negligent waste or destruction of petitioners' gas and distillate, though substantially all of such waste or destruction occurred after the minerals had been drained from beneath petitioners' lands.

We do not regard as authoritative the three decisions by the Supreme Court of Louisiana to the effect that an adjoining owner is without right of action for gas wasted from the common pool by his neighbor, because in that state only qualified ownership of oil and gas is recognized, no absolute ownership of minerals in place exists, and the unqualified rule is that under the law of capture the minerals belong exclusively to the one that produces them. . . .

In Texas, and in other jurisdictions, a different rule exists as to ownership. In our state the landowner is regarded as having absolute title in severalty to the oil and gas in place beneath his land. The only qualification of that rule of ownership is that it must be considered in connection with the law of capture and is subject to police regulations. . . .

The conflict in the decisions of the various states with reference to the character of ownership is traceable to some extent to the divergent views entertained by the courts, particularly in the earlier cases, as to the nature and migratory character of oil and gas in the soil. In the absence of common law precedent, and owing to the lack of scientific information as to the movement of these minerals, some of the courts have sought by analogy to compare oil and gas to other types of property such as wild animals, birds, subterranean waters, and other migratory things, with reference to which the common law had established rules denying any character of ownership prior to capture. However, as was said by Professor A. W. Walker, Jr., of the School of Law of the University of Texas: "There is no oil or gas producing state today which follows the wild-animal analogy to its logical conclusion that the landowner has no property interest in the oil and gas in place." 16 Tex. L. Rev. 371.

In the light of modern scientific knowledge these early analogies have been disproven, and courts generally have come to recognize that oil and gas, as commonly found in underground reservoirs, are securely entrapped in a static condition in the original pool, and, ordinarily, so remain until disturbed by penetrations from the surface. It is further established, nevertheless, that these minerals will migrate across property lines towards any low pressure area created by production from the common pool. This migratory character of oil and gas has given rise to the so-called rule or law of capture. That rule simply is that the owner of a tract of land acquires title to the oil or gas which he produces from wells on his land, though part of the oil or gas may have migrated from adjoining lands. He may thus appropriate the oil and gas that have flowed from adjacent lands without the consent of the owner of those lands, and without incurring liability to him for drainage. The nonliability is based upon the theory that after the drainage the title or property interest of the former owner is gone. This rule, at first blush, would seem to conflict with the view of absolute ownership of the minerals in place, but it was otherwise decided in the early case of *Stephens County v. Mid-Kansas Oil & Gas Co.*, 254 S.W. 290 (Tex. 1923). Mr. Justice Greenwood there stated:

> The objection lacks substantial foundation that gas or oil in a certain tract of land cannot be owned in place, because subject to appropriation, without the consent of the owner of the tract, through drainage from wells on adjacent lands. If the owners of adjacent lands have the right to appropriate, without liability, the gas and oil underlying their neighbor's land, then their neighbor has the correlative right to appropriate, through like methods of drainage, the gas and oil underlying the tracts adjacent to his own.

Thus it is seen that, notwithstanding the fact that oil and gas beneath the surface are subject both to capture and administrative regulation, the fundamental rule of absolute ownership of the minerals in place is not affected in our state. In recognition of such ownership, our courts, in decisions involving well-spacing regulations of our Railroad Commission, have frequently announced the sound view that each landowner should be afforded the opportunity to produce his fair share of the recoverable oil and gas beneath his land, which is but another way of recognizing the existence of correlative rights between the various landowners over a common reservoir of oil or gas.

It must be conceded that under the law of capture there is no liability for reasonable and legitimate drainage from the common pool. The landowner is privileged to sink as many wells as he desires upon his tract of land and extract therefrom and appropriate all the oil and gas that he may produce, so long as he operates within the spirit and purpose of conservation statutes and orders of the Railroad Commission. These laws and regulations are designed to afford each owner a reasonable opportunity to produce his proportionate part of the oil and gas from the entire pool and to prevent operating practices injurious to the common reservoir. In this manner, if all operators exercise the same degree of skill and diligence, each owner will recover in most instances his fair share of the oil and gas. This reasonable opportunity to produce his fair share of the oil and gas is the landowner's common law right under our theory of absolute ownership of the minerals in place. But from the very nature of this theory the right of each land holder is qualified, and is limited to legitimate operations. Each owner whose land overlies the basin has a like interest, and each must of necessity exercise his right with some regard to the rights of others. No owner should be permitted to carry on his operations in reckless or lawless irresponsibility, but must submit to such limitations as are necessary to enable each to get his own.

While we are cognizant of the fact that there is a certain amount of reasonable and necessary waste incident to the production of oil and gas to which the non-liability rule must also apply, we do not think this immunity should be extended so as to include the negligent waste or destruction of the oil and gas. . . .

In common with others who are familiar with the nature of oil and gas and the risks involved in their production, the respondents had knowledge that a failure to use due care in drilling their well might result in a blowout with the consequent waste and dissipation of the oil, gas and distillate from the common reservoir. In the conduct of one's business or in the use and exploitation of one's property, the law imposes upon all persons the duty to exercise ordinary care to avoid injury or damage to the property of others. Thus under the common law, and independent of the conservation statutes, the respondents were legally bound to use due care to avoid the negligent waste or destruction of the minerals imbedded in petitioners' oil and gasbearing strata. This common-law duty the respondents failed to discharge. . . .

NOTES

1.   *Ownership-in-place and exclusive-right-to-take.* The *cujus est solum* (aka *ad coelum*) principle highlighted in the two *Edwards* cases ("to whomsoever the soil belongs, he owns also to the sky and to the depths") supplied courts with only vague guidance when it came to "fugitive resources" such as oil and gas, ones that do not stay neatly fixed below the surface. A

well on one tract of land typically draws oil and gas from beneath neighboring lands. How is a court to determine who owns specific amounts of oil and gas? Shifting to a rule of capture seemed to be the answer. Under this rule, property owners who reduce oil or gas to possession at the surface gain title to it. As the Pennsylvania Supreme Court noted in the context of natural gas,

> Possession of the land, therefore, is not necessarily possession of the gas. If an adjoining, or even a distant, owner drills his own land, and taps your gas, so that it comes into his well and under his control it is no longer yours, but his. . . . [T]he one who controls the gas—has it in his grasp, so to speak—is the one who has possession in the legal as well as the ordinary sense of the word.

Westmoreland & Cambria Nat. Gas Co. v. DeWitt, 18 A. 724 (Pa. 1889).

There are two basic approaches to the rule of capture: the "ownership-in-place" theory and the "exclusive-right-to-take" theory. Under ownership-in-place a landowner holds title to oil and gas resources underneath the surface estate, but loses title to them if they migrate under another surface estate. The exclusive-right-to-take theory, which the *Elliff* court called "qualified ownership of oil and gas," posits that no one holds title to oil or gas resources underground but that property owners gain title to it by pumping it from the ground and capturing it. This is the approach followed in Louisiana. One of the primary differences between the two approaches, as *Elliff* illustrated, is that, under the exclusive-right-to-take approach, a person who "wastes" oil or gas at the surface is not liable to other surface estate owners overlying the hydrocarbon field. *See, e.g., McCoy v. Arkansas Natural Gas Co.*, 165 So. 632 (La. 1936); *McCoy v. Arkansas Natural Gas Co.*, 143 So. 383 (La. 1932); *Louisiana Gas & Fuel Co. v. White Bros.*, 103 So. 23 (La. 1925).

As *Elliff* explained, Texas embraces the ownership-in-place rule. Under it, one owner's underlying oil and gas can be captured by a neighbor, but only if the capture takes place in a reasonable, non-wasteful way. Waste entails not legitimate capture but the wrongful taking of oil and gas owned by a neighbor.

At first glance, these two rules of ownership seem far apart—one says landownership includes oil and gas, the other says it does not. But given the rule of capture, the two approaches actually differ very little. Indeed, the fact pattern of *Elliff* illustrates one of the few ways that the rules can lead to different legal outcomes.

2. *The defects of capture, fair share, and correlative rights.* Texas continues to adhere to the ownership-in-place rule but defines that ownership in a way that sounds very much like the rule in exclusive-right-to-take jurisdictions:

> While a mineral rights owner has a real interest in oil and gas in place, "this right does not extend to *specific* oil and gas beneath the property"; ownership must "be considered in connection with the

law of capture, which is recognized as a property right"—as well. The minerals owner is entitled, not to the molecules actually residing below the surface, but to "a fair chance to recover the oil and gas in or under his land, *or* their equivalents in kind."

Coastal Oil & Gas Corp. v. Garza Energy Trust, 268 S.W.3d 1, 15 (Tex. 2008) (citations omitted; more on this important ruling below).

On this issue, note the court's statements in *Elliff* that the essence of each landowner's property right is the reasonable opportunity to produce his "fair share of the recoverable oil and gas beneath his land." This language of "fair share," the court tells us, was "but another way of recognizing the existence of correlative rights between the various landowners over a common reservoir of oil and gas." In a correlative rights scheme, each owner can claim only a pro rata share of a resource and is guilty of taking the property of another should she extract more than her fair share. This line of thinking seems to conflict with the rule of capture in which those who act fast get the most. And it does, for good reasons.

Ownership-in-place and exclusive-right-to-take differ with regard to wasteful pumping of oil and gas—as we have just seen—but they share the chief defects of the rule of capture. Under both, landowners are prompted to act quickly, seizing as much oil as they can for fear that other landowners will take it. With the resource essentially uncontrolled, no one has the power to delay all production until oil prices are higher.

Other problems have to do with the geologic realities of oil production. When oil is removed quickly, more of it remains in place; a slower, steadier rate of withdrawal can produce more oil. Also, wells too close together can interfere with one another, and it is wasteful to have a large number of wells in a field when one or a few wells in time can extract all of the oil. These realities led to cooperation within the oil business and to the establishment of regulatory agencies that control such matters as well spacing, well construction, and rates of withdrawal. They also produced even greater alterations of common law property rights by way of pooling and unitization arrangements, which place landowners into collective pumping groups. These collective pumping efforts can force landowners to participate over their objections.

When the Texas Supreme Court began considering these new regulatory systems (in Texas, promulgated, for historical reasons, by the Railroad Commission), it could see the necessity for them. A rule of capture, limited only by a duty to avoid excessive waste, was itself wasteful, and the court saw a need to revise it. Far better results came when landowners above a reservoir worked in concert to exploit it. Cooperation in turn seemed more legitimate and constitutionally permissible when courts defined the property rights of landowners, not in terms of the maximum petroleum each could extract in an all-out race, but instead in terms of their respective fair shares of the underlying pool. The Texas court could have redefined landowner rights more fundamentally, so that each surface owner held title to a specific share of the underlying oil and gas with no right to capture oil and gas from beneath neighboring lands. Instead it took an intermediate stance: What each landowner actually possessed was the "reasonable opportunity" to capture her fair share. If an owner had a reasonable opportunity to capture but did not use it, her oil could be captured and kept by neighbors. This intermediate stance, although retaining a modified version of the rule of capture, made it seem more legitimate for a state agency to regulate capture efforts in an oil and gas field by, for instance, limiting production by individual wells and requiring that revenues from wells be shared among overlying landowners. As we will see in a later case, regulatory agencies can issue proration orders to well operators, limiting them to fair-share extraction and penalizing them if they take too much.

3. *Royalty interests in minerals.* The royalty arrangement in *Elliff* is typical of oil and gas leases. The surface owner today commonly receives as compensation a one-sixth royalty on the oil and gas produced. (The Elliffs received a one-eighth royalty, then more common, and half that on their co-owned land.) Royalty interests are often highly fragmented. In addition to royalties, surface owners commonly receive a single, up-front cash payment to execute the lease. This payment is termed a "bonus" because it is a payment in addition to royalties. Owners retain bonus payments even if the well produces no oil or gas and even if no test well is ever drilled. Bonus payments vary greatly in amount, far more than royalty terms. Leases also typically include various other payments to landowners to cover time periods when no royalties are earned (for instance, when drilling is delayed or a producing well is temporarily shut down).

ANDERSON V. BEECH AIRCRAFT CORPORATION

Supreme Court of Kansas
699 P.2d 1023 (1985)

PRAGER, J.

This is an action brought by the owners of a tract of land and the lessee under an oil and gas lease against Beech Aircraft Corporation to quiet title, to recover damages for slander of title and trespass, and for an accounting. The basic dispute is over the ownership of non-native gas [*i.e.,* gas that was originally pumped from some other location] injected by Beech Aircraft into an underground reservoir used by Beech for gas storage for many years and which gas the plaintiffs now seek to produce. Plaintiffs are Lowell L. Anderson and Aileen R. Anderson, the landowners, and Avanti Petroleum, Inc., the lessee under an oil and gas lease on the Anderson property. . . .

[T]he issue raised on this appeal, simply stated, is as follows: Do the owners of land and of an oil and gas lease have the right to produce as their own non-native gas from their land, which gas has previously been purchased, injected, and stored in a common reservoir by another landowner having no license, permit, or lease covering the land from which the non-native gas is produced?. . . .

Today, natural gas is being stored in underground reservoirs in most of the gas producing states. This tremendous increase in gas storage was the result of the increased demand for, and popularity of, natural gas as a consumer fuel. The demand for natural gas far exceeded the supply, and pipelines proved incapable of supplying peak consumer demands which were mainly caused by cold weather. During periods of lesser demand, the pipelines could transport more than enough gas. Above ground storage of gas was impossible. It simply was not economically feasible to fabricate containers large enough to serve all consumers. Experience proved that the problem of meeting peak consumer demands for natural gas could be solved only by the use of underground storage of gas. It became obvious that depleted oil and gas fields could be effectively converted into vast storage containers. However, suitable formations for underground storage of natural gas do not exist in all states. A formation must possess a high degree of porosity in order to accommodate large quantities of gas and must also possess a high degree of permeability to allow the gas to be injected and withdrawn rapidly. In addition to these basic requirements, the formation must be sufficiently sealed geologically to prevent migration of the injected gas.

With the underground storage of natural gas, there developed many legal problems involving the interrelationship between a gas company or a storage operator and the owners of land or mineral interests included within the storage reservoirs. [Here the court mentioned several recurring legal issues: Who owned the gas that was injected into the ground? Who had rights to use underground formations for the purposes of storage? And, to the extent that rights were held by the surface owner, what happens when the surface owner has sold or lease mineral rights under his land to someone else: do the surface owner's right pass to the owner or less or the minerals, or do they remain with the owner of the land surface? Notice that this law suit was brought jointly by the surface owner and the lessee of oil and gas under the land; presumably they agreed to sort out their relative rights later if they won the case.]

The specific issue presented in this case is truly one of first impression in Kansas. As far as natural gas is concerned, Kansas has long recognized the law of capture, holding that natural gas in the ground is part of the real estate until it is actually produced and severed. At that point, it becomes personalty. *Burden v. Gypsy Oil Co.,* 40 P.2d 463 (Kan. 1935); *Gas Co. v. Neosho County,* 89 P. 750 (Kan. 1907); *In re Estate of Sellens,* 637 P.2d 483 (Kan. App. 1981), *rev. denied* 230 Kan. 818 (1982).

As underground reservoirs for natural gas have become more common, the issue of title to the stored gas has been presented to the courts. The issue of title was first addressed in *Hammonds v. Central Kentucky Natural Gas* Co., 75 S.W.2d 204 (Ky. 1934). In *Hammonds,* the gas company depleted an underground reservoir underlying approximately 15,000 acres and subsequently injected gas from distant wells into the reservoir for storage purposes. Della Hammonds owned 54 acres within the boundary of the reservoir which was never leased to the gas company. It was undisputed the reservoir lay under the Hammonds property. Della Hammonds sued the gas company for trespass and sought to recover damages for use and occupation of the reservoir underlying her property. The lower court held for the gas company and Hammonds appealed. The Kentucky Court of Appeals affirmed. But Hammonds won the victory in the long run. The Kentucky court initially discussed the doctrine of capture, declaring that "oil and gas are not the property of any one until reduced to actual possession by extraction, although by virtue of his proprietorship the owner of the surface, or his grantee of the severed mineral estate, has the exclusive right of seeking to acquire and of appropriating the oil and gas directly beneath." 255 Ky. at 688, 75 S.W.2d 204. The court also recognized the nature of oil and gas as being fugitive and migratory, having the power and tendency to escape without the volition of its owner. The court analogized oil and gas to wild animals or animals *ferae naturale.* It noted that ownership in birds and wild animals becomes vested in the person capturing or reducing them to possession. However, when restored to their natural wild and free state, the dominion and individual proprietorship of any person over them is at an end and they resume their status as common property. The court also considered cases involving subterranean and percolating water where it has been held that, once the water is restored to the earth or to the running stream, a prior possessor's exclusive, individual title is lost. The court concluded in *Hammonds* that, if non-native injected gas wanders into the land of an adjoining landowner, the gas company is not liable for trespass as the gas company no longer owns the gas. See also *Central Kentucky Natural Gas Co. v. Smallwood,* 252 S.W.2d 866 (Ky. 1952).

The *Hammonds* doctrine was recognized by a Pennsylvania trial court in *Protz v. Peoples Natural Gas Co.,* 93 Pitts. Leg. J. 239, *aff'd,* 94 Pitts. Leg. J. 139 (1945). [The discussion of this case, and other precedents embracing the same rule as *Hammonds,* has been omitted.]

The non-ownership theory which was adopted in *Hammonds* has been criticized by writers in the field. One writer argued that the theory expressed in the *Hammonds* decision is illogical and invalid for the reason that once man has reduced natural gas to possession, and processed and transported it to the storage area, the gas in no way resembles gas in its native state. Smith, *Rights and Liabilities on Subsurface Operations,* Southwestern Legal Foundation, Eighth Annual

Institute on Oil and Gas Law and Taxation 1, 25–6 (1957). Several courts have refused to follow the rationale set forth in *Hammonds*.

In *White v. New York State Natural Gas Corporation*, 190 F.Supp. 342 (W.D. Pa. 1960), . . . the issue was whether title to natural gas, once having been reduced to possession, was lost by the injection of such gas into a natural underground reservoir for storage purposes. The Pennsylvania federal district court rejected the mineral *ferae naturae* concept, stating the application of that theory was limited to the original capture of native gas and oil. The court predicted the Supreme Court of Pennsylvania would hold that title to natural gas, once having been reduced to possession, is not lost by the injection of such gas into a natural underground reservoir for storage purposes, and entered judgment in favor of the defendant. [Discussion of several similar precedents also omitted.]

In addition to these court decisions, there have been statutes enacted in various states to regulate the underground storage of natural gas. These statutes vary widely in their provisions. The Washington (Wash.Rev.Code Ann. § 80.40.050 [1985 Supp.]), Georgia (Ga.Code Ann. § 46–4–57 *et seq.* [1982]), Louisiana (La.Rev.Stat.Ann. § 30:22 [West 1975]), and Colorado (Colo.Rev.Stat. 34–64–101 *et seq.* [1984]) statutes provide for the condemnation of underground reservoirs for the storage of natural gas. Those state statutes provide that the injected gas shall remain the property of the injector but preserve the rights of owners to drill through the underground reservoir. The Missouri statute (Mo.Ann.Stat. § 393.500 [Vernon 1985 Supp.]), and the Oklahoma statute (Okla.Stat.Ann. tit. 52 § 36.6 [West 1969]) provide that the gas remains the property of the injector, *but such rule is not applied to a person whose land is not acquired.* In the latter instance, it appears that both Missouri and Oklahoma have adopted the rule that such injected gas becomes subject to the law of capture if it migrates from the contained area. The New Mexico act (N.M.Stat.Ann. § 70–6–8 [1978]) also contains the exceptions presented in the Missouri and Oklahoma statutes. These various statutes are cited in order to show the wide variations in the legislative policy governing the creation of underground gas storage facilities and the condemnation of land for that purpose.

With this background in mind, we turn now to the statutory scheme adopted in Kansas. As noted previously, in *Strain v. Cities Service Gas Co.*, 83 P.2d 124 (Kan. 1938), this court held that a natural gas public utility did not have the power to condemn property in order to create an underground gas storage area. After the decision in *Strain,* there was nothing to change the law of Kansas until 1951 when the legislature enacted K.S.A. 55–1201 *et seq.*, which regulates the underground storage of gas. [The 1951 statute sought to promote underground gas storage and authorized public utilities to exercise eminent domain to obtain subsurface storage rights when the propriety of doing so was certified by a state commission.]

K.S.A. 55–1205 provides the procedure by which a natural gas public utility, having first obtained a certificate from the commission, shall exercise the right of eminent domain for the purpose of acquiring property for the underground storage of natural gas. K.S.A. 55–1207, which was enacted in 1961, provides for the leasing of state-owned land for the underground storage of natural gas.

From our analysis of the Kansas statutory scheme as contained in K.S.A. 55–1201 *et seq.,* it is clear that the expressed intention of the legislature is that the condemnation of property for the underground storage of natural gas is restricted to natural gas public utilities. Furthermore, it is clear that under the legislative scheme, before an underground gas storage area may be established, a certificate must be obtained from the Kansas Corporation Commission containing the findings set forth in K.S.A. 55–1204, after a public hearing with reasonable notice to interested parties.

In determining the issue presented in this case, this court has the obligation to consider more than the relative merits and demerits of the wild animal theory adopted in *Hammonds* and rejected in some of the cases. This court has the further duty to carry out the legislative intent as expressed in K.S.A. 55–1201 *et seq.* We have concluded that, in order to carry out the legislative intent and to adopt a rule which will be fairest and most beneficial to the people of this state, in a factual situation such as is presented in this case, where the landowner, Beech Aircraft Corporation, is not a natural gas public utility and has attempted to create an underground storage reservoir under the property of an adjoining landowner without acquiring by contract the right to do so, the law of capture should be applied to any non-native gas which is purchased elsewhere and injected into the common pool for storage. We thus hold that Beech Aircraft lost its ownership of the stored gas after injecting it into the reservoir in this case.

In arriving at this conclusion, we have considered the undesirable consequences of the position which Beech Aircraft has asserted in this case. Beech Aircraft contends that it has the right to store gas under the land of an adjoining landowner without obtaining a permit, license, or rights afforded by condemnation, and without paying any rentals or other compensation. In our judgment, the adoption of such a rule would result in extensive litigation between adjoining property owners in the oil and gas areas of this state. For example, if there is gas production near a storage reservoir on land without license for gas storage, there is a bound to be litigation to determine how much of the gas being produced is native and how much is stored gas, what damages are owed to what adjacent landowner for the storage of unauthorized gas, and who is entitled to what share of the gas produced. . . .

For the reasons set forth above, we hold that the trial court correctly determined that, under the circumstances of this case, where a natural gas public utility was not involved, where no certificate authorizing an underground storage facility had been issued by the Kansas Corporation Commission, and where the defendant had used the property of an adjoining landowner for gas storage without authorization or consent, the defendant, as the owner of non-native natural gas, lost title thereto when it injected non-native gas into the underground area and the gas was then produced from the common reservoir located under the adjacent property.

NOTES

1. *Procedure.* This case provides a good opportunity to examine the legal remedies available to land and resource owners to clarify and protect their legal rights. One of the Andersons' causes of action in this case was an action to *quiet title.* This is an equitable action brought by a person claiming an existing interest in a parcel of land against one or more other claimants of rights in the same land. In it, a court is called upon to sort out the various conflicting claims and to declare who owns what, producing a ruling that can then be recorded. A successful action "quiets" the title by ending disputes about it. *Slander of title* is a legal action brought by someone claiming an ownership interest in land who contends that someone else has falsely and maliciously made a statement or taken an action (*e.g.*, recording a document; entering into a lease) that casts doubt on the plaintiff's title. It is similar to the business tort of product disparagement. An *accounting* is an action (originally at law, now more likely in equity) seeking to compel the rendering of an account (of money or property) by a person under a legal duty to account. It typically arises out of a contract, express or implied, or based on co-ownership of property. All three types of actions have been, to one degree or another, given statutory form, often in codes of civil procedure.

In this dispute, the Andersons (and their lessee) were challenging the legal right of Beech Aircraft to store gas under their land, a right which Beech Aircraft claimed. The Andersons' request to quiet title was thus a request to have the court declare that Beech Aircraft had no legal right to use the Andersons' land, thereby quieting their title to the land. Beech Aircraft's claim to have such a right also arguably slandered the title of the Andersons by contending that their rights were thus impaired. As for the accounting, the Andersons claimed that Beech Aircraft, by storing gas under the land, was trespassing on the land, and in a way profitable for Beech Aircraft—even though it caused no harm to the Andersons. A landowner in a trespass action typically asks for money damages for the harm caused by the trespass. Sometimes, though—as we saw in the Kentucky cave cases (pp. 335-47)—a trespass enables the trespasser to generate earnings; earnings that are illicit due to the wrongful trespass. In such instances the landowner suing in trespass can "waive" the tort of trespass and ask the court instead for a judgment requiring the defendant to pay to the plaintiff landowner the profits earned as a result of the wrongful trespass.

2. *Real property, personal property, and the wild animal analogy.* As a practical matter, the *Beech Aircraft* case was a fight over (i) the ownership of gas pumped into the ground, and (ii) legal rights to store gas or to charge rent to allow someone else to store the gas. The latter issue was clearly an issue about real property—the property rights in the subsurface. The former issue was, at least from the perspective of Beech Aircraft, a personal property action. The natural gas, once taken from the ground, became the personal property of its owner. Beech Aircraft claimed that, when it pumped the gas into the ground, it remained its property. Had the Andersons started taking the gas, Beech Aircraft would have brought an action to recover the value of its personal property—either trespass to chattels (personal property) or an action in (trover and) conversion—if, that is, it still owned the gas.

The Kentucky case in *Hammonds*, discussed in *Beech Aircraft*, was nationally prominent in part for its use of a seemingly odd analogy, the one comparing oil and gas with wild animals. A person who lawfully captures a wild animal becomes owner of it, but ownership rights continue only so long as the animal remains under control and has not escaped back to something like its natural habitat. In *Hammonds*, the court viewed gas as akin to wild animals in that gas, like animals, did not respect property boundaries and gas, like animals, was unowned until capture. To the court, it made sense that, when the company released the gas into the ground, the legal effect was the same as when a wild animal returned to its native habitat: the private property rights came to an end when the owners released the natural resource into the commons.

Mrs. Hammonds filed suit in trespass to recover the rental value of her subsurface space. She lost because, in the court's view, the gas pumped back into the ground was not owned by the defendant (or anyone else), so the defendant could not be charged rent for storing the gas. As the court here noted, Mrs. Hammonds won the case (despite losing on her trespass claim) largely because she had a legal right after the ruling to sink a well and extract the gas without violating any property rights of Central Kentucky Gas.

The court in *Beech Aircraft* noted that Kansas, unlike Kentucky, follows an ownership in place rule, and the court discussed criticisms of the wild animal analogy. Yet the court still reached the same result as in *Hammonds*—gas, once released into the ground, is no longer owned by the person who injected it. In *Hammonds* no one owned the re-injected gas. Kansas, presumably, would recognize the surface landowner as owner of the re-injected gas. Why did the Kansas court reach this result? More specifically, what policy concerns pushed the court to resolve the dispute as it did? (On this question, consider this issue: If Beech Aircraft still owned the nonnative gas inserted into the ground, and its actions involved a trespass, would the court have enjoined the trespass—forcing Beech Aircraft to remove the gas— or it would it instead have merely awarded damages?)

As the *Beech Aircraft* court observed, the wild animal analogy is of questionable relevance. The general rule in personal property law is that an owner of personal property continues to own the item unless transferred or abandoned. Property rights do not end simply because an owner does not, at a given moment, have possession of the item. Many courts have said that, once gas is pumped from the ground and becomes someone's personal property, it remains personal property even when returned to the ground. If that is true, the owner of the gas would need to make arrangements to store the gas or be liable for trespass.

3.   *Shared governance: underground oil and gas storage.* It is easy to see that an underground formation, suitable for storing gas, is just as much a common-pool resource as the gas itself (and as the cave in the Kentucky cases). Even more than other common-pool resources, however, an underground formation requires collectively managed use. Because gas freely moves around within the formation, no one can make use of just part of it, nor can two people use the formation (as they could a fishery or even a cave) without having their gas intermingle (though some types of gas are physically distinguishable). Some sort of collective management is thus essential. Ideally, the overlying landowners could get together and work cooperatively for mutual gain. Often, governments must intervene either to facilitate cooperative private action or undertake the overall planning itself. In *Beech Aircraft*, we see that the Kansas legislature did intervene in subsurface storage disputes to authorize natural gas public utilities to obtain certificates authorizing subsurface storage, and then to use eminent domain to obtain storage rights from uncooperative surface owners. The statute did not authorize other private actors to do the same (such as businesses that were not natural gas utilities). This meant that Beech Aircraft could gain rights to store its gas only if it could negotiate storage rights from all overlying landowners—which is to say, subsurface storage could take place only with the unanimous consent of the overlying landowners. Such a unanimity rule can pose a serious roadblock for those who seek to use a common pool resource, and it often means that the resource goes unused (an outcome that could, of course, be welcome or unwelcome).

4.   *Subsurface injections.* Many court rulings in recent years have considered the legal consequences of injecting substances deep into the ground. When they are sufficiently deep that they have no adverse effect on surface landowners, should the landowners have the legal power to complain? Consider the following Texas rulings:

In *Railroad Commission of Texas v. Manziel*, 361 S.W.2d 560 (Tex. 1962), the Texas Supreme Court concluded that a landowner could not sue to halt a prospective trespass when saltwater was pumped into the ground in an effort to increase oil extraction, at least when the pumping was approved by the state regulatory agency (the Railroad Commission). "The technical rules of trespass have no place," the court reasoned, "in the consideration of the validity of the orders of the Commission." 361 S.W.2d at 568–69. Importantly, the court did not rule that a landowner harmed by such an invasion would have no remedy for damages.

In *Coastal Oil & Gas Corp. v. Garza Energy Trust*, 268 S.W.3d 1 (Tex. 2008), the court considered the application of trespass law to hydraulic fracturing, in which a landowner pumps fluid and small particles (proppants) into the ground under high pressure, creating cracks and forcing the particles into the cracks to keep them open while gas escapes. At issue was whether such fracking amounted to trespass when the fluid and particles entered neighboring land. The suit was an unusual one procedurally, filed by owners of mineral rights who had leased their rights and who thus did not, themselves, have a right to immediate possession (holding only royalty interests and reversionary rights). The court ruled that such plaintiffs, having no right to possess the subsurface, could obtain relief for a trespass only upon showing actual harm. On the facts, the plaintiffs could not show such harm. Because the rule of capture applied, the neighbor doing the fracking had the right to extract the gas. As for the invasion by the fracking solution and the proppants, they caused no actual injury to the surface landowner. The court left for a later day the question whether a plaintiff who owned mineral rights (and thus who did possess the subsurface) could successfully sue in trespass with no showing of actual harm.

Three justices in *Garza Energy* argued that it was improper to apply the rule of capture (as the majority did) without deciding first whether the fracking amounted to a trespass. If fracking did involve trespass, the oil and gas capture was wrongful because a landowner has the right to capture from beneath neighboring land only when acting lawfully (the rule in *Elliff*). A concurring justice was prepared to rule immediately that fracking did not involve any trespass: "Orthodox trespass principles that govern surface invasions seem to me to have dwindling relevance, particularly as exploration techniques grow ever sophisticated. . . . The interplay of common-law trespass and oil and gas law must be shaped by concern for the public good." 268 S.W.3d at 29, 34 (Willett, J., concurring).

A recent federal district court ruling rejected the reasoning of *Coastal Oil,* concluding that, under West Virginia law, fracking did involve a subsurface trespass, even though occurring thousands of feet beneath the land surface. *Stone v. Chesapeake Appalachia, LLC,* 2013 WL 2097397 (N.D. W.Va. 2013).

Finally, in *FPL Farming Ltd. v. Environmental Processing Systems,* 351 S.W.3d 306 (Tex. 2011), the Texas court considered the case of a well that injected wastewater approximately a mile and half beneath the surface. Citing *Manziel* and *Garza Energy*, the lower court concluded that no trespass occurred, since state law and an ensuing permit authorized the injection well. On appeal, the court did not resolve the trespass issue, holding only that the permit issued by the state did not insulate the well operator from trespass liability.

5.   *Carbon capture and storage.* Efforts to expand carbon capture and storage (CCS) have taken off in recent years as policy-makers explore technological advances to assist in mitigating the buildup of greenhouse gases in the atmosphere. *See* International Energy Agency, *Carbon Capture and Storage*, http://www.iea.org/topics/ccs/. The issue and its largely unresolved legal implications are thoughtfully considered in the context of subsurface activities in two articles by Alexandra B. Klass & Elizabeth J. Wilson, *Climate Change, Carbon Sequestration, and Property Rights*, 2010 U. Ill. L. Rev. 363; and *Climate Change and Carbon Sequestration: Assessing a Liability Regime for Long-Term Storage of Carbon Dioxide*, 58 Emory L. J. 103 (2008) (considering environmental and tort liability); and also in Will Reisinger, Nolan Moser, Trent A. Dougherty & James D. Madeiros, *Reconciling King Coal and Climate Change: A Regulatory Framework for Carbon Capture and Storage*, 11 Vt. J. of Env. L. 1 (2009).

6.   *Storing water.* Recall the *Park County* ruling considered in chapter 1 (p. 29). In it, the Colorado Supreme Court concluded that a water owner could store water beneath the ground—and retain ownership of it—without permission of the surface landowner. The arrangement did not violate the surface owner's property rights for the simple reason that, under Colorado land law, the surface owner did not control use of the subsurface storage space. The same issue arose in *Central Nebraska Public Power and Irrigation District v. Abrahamson,* 413 N.W.2d 290 (Neb. 1987), where the court considered the validity of a state statute that authorized a state agency to grant subsurface storage rights to water rights holders. The court concluded that the statute did not amount to an unconstitutional taking of the property rights of surface landowners by authorizing water storage without their permission or payment. According to the court, the landowners could not demonstrate a taking because the subsurface storage did not interfere with their own property uses and did not diminish their own groundwater rights. The court noted that the water-use project that included the subsurface storage would benefit the region economically and would help preserve many beneficial uses of water. The court did not consider whether the legal landscape might change if and when surface landowners came up with economically productive ways to use their subsurface spaces—for instance, to store natural gas. Aquifer storage of gas is common in the American Midwest.

A somewhat similar approach to water storage was taken in *Central and West Basin Water Replenishment District v. So. Cal. Water Co.*, 109 Cal.App.4th 891 (2003). The Central Basin in Los Angeles County underlies approximately 277 square miles of land. At the time of the case, rights to extract groundwater from the basin were held by 148 pumpers. The pumpers claimed that they collectively controlled the unused storage capacity of the basin (totaling approximately 645,700 acre feet of storage), as part of their acknowledged legal rights to take water from it. (That is, they argued that the storage right was ancillary to their water extraction rights.) The court held: (i) the right to store water is a separate and distinct right from the right to extract groundwater, even when (as here) groundwater pumpers possess limited rights to leave water in the ground from year to year, thus giving them limited storage rights; (ii) the Central Basin is a public resource that, like other water resources, must be used in the public interest; (iii) allowing the 148 pumpers to control the storage space, even though many of them were public utilities, did not adequately protect the public interest and respect the legislature's expressed priority for domestic water uses, and (iv) the express authority of the state-created Water Replenishment District to store water in the Basin and to manage and control water for persons within the district gave the district the power to control storage in the basin. Significantly, no litigant made any claim that rights to control the basin were vested in overlying landowners. As a matter of state property law, landowners did not own or control subsurface cavities useful for water storage.

B. SEVERING THE MINERALS

A common question arising in subsurface resource conflicts has to do with the scope of a particular reservation of mineral rights. In many settings, ownership of some or all subsurface minerals is severed from ownership rights in the surface. When that happens, what minerals are included in the reservation, and which ones instead remain owned by the surface landowner?

In some settings (such as the first case below), severance of this type is done by a statute or regulation. When that happens, the scope of the mineral interest presents an issue of *law*: What did the drafters of the statute or regulation mean to include within the mineral estate given the language that they used? More often, the severance of the mineral estate from the surface estate is done by means of a privately written document, through a deed, easement agreement, lease, license or the like. Again, when this occurs, what minerals are included in the mineral estate, and which ones still belong to the surface owner? In the latter type of dispute, a court will begin with the language of the written document. But private writings are often ambiguous and incomplete, and the parties who signed the document are often long dead. Many times a subsurface material becomes valuable, and thus desirable, only long after a particular document was written. How do courts resolve these ambiguities?

As you read the following materials, keep two issues at the forefront. One has to do with the principles or techniques courts use as they undertake their interpretive work. What presumptions do they make? To what extent do they use dictionary definitions or perhaps scientific or technical definitions? To what extent do they look to external facts and circumstances? The second issue is just as vital. To what extent do courts treat these questions as ones of *fact*, based on the intentions of the drafters or parties, and to what extent do they treat the questions as matters of *law*?

Particularly when courts interpret private agreements, we might expect judges to say that their questions are ones of fact; after all, that is the guiding principle of contract interpretation. But as we shall see, additional considerations come into play when courts interpret land titles. In this setting, disputes often arise years later, and between parties who were not involved in the original document drafting. Documents are recorded on land titles, and various outsiders have legitimate reasons to want to know, in the case of a tract of land, who owns what (mortgage lenders, for instance, and mineral development companies looking to acquire mineral rights).

The whole land-title system begins to break down when a person reading a deed or easement agreement in the public records cannot determine its meaning from the language alone. The need for clarity in land titles—the need for particular words to have reliable, known meanings—pushes courts to treat interpretive questions as matters of law rather than of fact. But when they do that, they can sometimes reach conclusions different from what the original parties had in mind when they signed their document. As you keep this issue in mind, consider the possibility that courts might in fact blend these two positions: treating the meaning of a word mostly as a matter of law but leaving open the possibility that factual evidence in a given case might lead to a different interpretive conclusion. Keep alert to the possibility also that courts will pay attention to public interest considerations. They may, for instance, favor an interpretation that promotes the efficient exploitation of resources over an alternative interpretation that makes resources harder to use.

AMOCO PRODUCTION COMPANY V. SOUTHERN UTE INDIAN TRIBE

Supreme Court of the United States
526 U.S. 865 (1999)

KENNEDY, J.

Land patents issued pursuant to the Coal Lands Acts of 1909 and 1910 conveyed to the patentee the land and everything in it, except the "coal," which was reserved to the United States. The United States Court of Appeals for the Tenth Circuit determined that the reservation of "coal" includes gas found within the coal formation, commonly referred to as coalbed methane gas (CBM gas). We granted certiorari and now reverse.

I.

During the second half of the 19th century, Congress sought to encourage the settlement of the West by providing land in fee simple absolute to homesteaders who entered and cultivated tracts of a designated size for a period of years. Public lands classified as valuable for coal were exempted from entry under the general land-grant statutes and instead were made available for purchase under the 1864 Coal Lands Act, ch. 205, § 1, 13 Stat. 343, and the 1873 Coal Lands Act, ch. 279, § 1, 17 Stat. 607, which set a maximum limit of 160 acres on individual entry and minimum prices of $10 to $20 an acre. Lands purchased under these early Coal Lands Acts—like lands patented under the Homestead Acts— were conveyed to the entryman in fee simple absolute, with no reservation of any part of the coal or mineral estate to the United States. The coal mined from the lands purchased under the Coal Lands Acts and from other reserves fueled the Industrial Revolution.

At the turn of the 20th century, however, a coal famine struck the West. At the same time, evidence of widespread fraud in the administration of federal coal lands came to light. Lacking the resources to make an independent assessment of the coal content of each individual land tract, the Department of the Interior in classifying public lands had relied for the most part on the affidavits of entrymen. Railroads and other coal interests had exploited the system to avoid paying for coal lands and to evade acreage restrictions by convincing individuals to falsify affidavits, acquire lands for homesteading, and then turn the land over to them.

In 1906, President Theodore Roosevelt responded to the perceived crisis by withdrawing 64 million acres of public land thought to contain coal from disposition under the public land laws. As a result, even homesteaders who had entered and worked the land in good faith lost the opportunity to make it their own unless they could prove to the land office that the land was not valuable for coal.

President Roosevelt's order outraged homesteaders and western interests, and Congress struggled for the next three years to construct a compromise that would reconcile the competing interests of protecting settlers and managing federal coal lands for the public good. President Roosevelt and others urged Congress to begin issuing limited patents that would sever the surface and mineral estates and allow for separate disposal of each. Although various bills were introduced in Congress that would have severed the estates-some of which would have reserved "natural gas" as well as "coal" to the United States-none was enacted.

Finally, Congress passed the 1909 Act, which authorized the Federal Government, for the first time, to issue limited land patents. In contrast to the broad reservations of mineral rights proposed in the failed bills, however, the 1909 Act provided for only a narrow reservation. The 1909 Act authorized issuance of patents to individuals who had already made good-faith agricultural entries onto tracts later identified as coal lands, but the issuance was to be subject to "a reservation to the United States of all coal in said lands, and the right to prospect for, mine, and remove the same." The 1909 Act also permitted the patentee to "mine coal for use on the land for domestic purposes prior to the disposal by the United States of the coal deposit." A similar Act in 1910 opened the remaining coal lands to new entry under the homestead laws, subject to the same reservation of coal to the United States.

Among the lands patented to settlers under the 1909 and 1910 Acts were former reservation lands of the Southern Ute Indian Tribe, which the Tribe had ceded to the United States in 1880 in return for certain allotted lands provided for their settlement. In 1938, the United States restored to the Tribe, in trust, title to the ceded reservation lands still owned by the United States, including the reserved coal in lands patented under the 1909 and 1910 Acts. As a result, the Tribe now has equitable title to the coal in lands within its reservation settled by homesteaders under the 1909 and 1910 Acts.

We are advised that over 20 million acres of land were patented under the 1909 and 1910 Acts and that the lands-including those lands in which the Tribe owns the coal-contain large quantities of CBM gas. At the time the Acts were passed, CBM gas had long been considered a dangerous waste product of coal mining. By the 1970's, however, it was apparent that CBM gas could be a significant energy resource . . . and, in the shadow of the Arab oil embargo, the Federal Government began to encourage the immediate production of CBM gas through grants and substantial tax credits.

Commercial development of CBM gas was hampered, however, by uncertainty over its ownership. "In order to expedite the development of this energy source," the Solicitor of the Department of the Interior issued a 1981 opinion concluding that the reservation of coal to the United States in the 1909 and 1910 Acts did not encompass CBM gas. In reliance on the Solicitor's 1981 opinion, oil and gas companies entered into leases to produce CBM gas with individual landowners holding title under 1909 and 1910 Act patents to some 200,000 acres in which the Tribe owns the coal.

In 1991, the Tribe brought suit in Federal District Court against petitioners, the royalty owners and producers under the oil and gas leases covering that land, and the federal agencies and officials responsible for the administration of lands held in trust for the Tribe. The Tribe sought, inter alia, a declaration that Congress' reservation of coal in the 1909 and

1910 Acts extended to CBM gas, so that the Tribe—not the successors in interest of the land patentees—owned the CBM gas.

The District Court granted summary judgment for the defendants, holding that the plain meaning of "coal" is the "solid rock substance" used as fuel, which does not include CBM gas. On appeal, a panel of the Court of Appeals reversed. The court then granted rehearing en banc on the question whether the term "coal" in the 1909 and 1910 Acts "unambiguously excludes or includes CBM." Over a dissenting opinion by Judge Tacha, joined by two other judges, the en banc court agreed with the panel. The court held that the term "coal" was ambiguous. It invoked the interpretive canon that ambiguities in land grants should be resolved in favor of the sovereign and concluded that the coal reservation encompassed CBM gas.

The United States did not petition for, or participate in, the rehearing en banc. Instead, it filed a supplemental brief explaining that the Solicitor of the Interior was reconsidering the 1981 Solicitor's opinion in light of the panel's decision. On the day the federal respondents' response to petitioners' certiorari petition was due the Solicitor of the Interior withdrew the 1981 opinion in a one-line order. The federal respondents now support the Tribe's position that CBM gas is coal reserved by the 1909 and 1910 Acts.

[The Court began by discussing the "chemistry and composition" of coal, noting that the rock's formation generates methane and other gases, some of which is retained in the coal—that is, coal bed methane].

While the modern science of coal provides a useful backdrop for our discussion and is consistent with our ultimate disposition, it does not answer the question presented to us. The question is not whether, given what scientists know today, it makes sense to regard CBM gas as a constituent of coal but whether Congress so regarded it in 1909 and 1910. In interpreting statutory mineral reservations like the one at issue here, we have emphasized that Congress "was dealing with a practical subject in a practical way" and that it intended the terms of the reservation to be understood in "their ordinary and popular sense." *Burke v. Southern Pacific R. Co.*, 234 U.S. 669, 679 (1914) (rejecting "scientific test" for determining whether a reservation of "mineral lands" included "petroleum lands"). We are persuaded that the common conception of coal at the time Congress passed the 1909 and 1910 Acts was the solid rock substance that was the country's primary energy resource.

[The Court next looked at dictionary definitions of coal, which ultimately defined it as a solid fuel resource. The Court then compared those definitions with dictionary definitions of coal bed methane, most often defined as a gas "given off" by coal. The Court determined that these definitions demonstrate that in 1909 and 1910 coal and CBM gas would not have been considered the same resource].

* * *

As a practical matter, moreover, it is clear that, by reserving coal in the 1909 and 1910 Act patents, Congress intended to reserve only the solid rock fuel that was mined, shipped throughout the country, and then burned to power the Nation's railroads, ships, and factories. In contrast to natural gas, which was not yet an important source of fuel at the turn of the century, coal was the primary energy for the Industrial Revolution.

As the history recounted in Part I, above, establishes, Congress passed the 1909 and 1910 Acts to address concerns over the short supply, mismanagement, and fraudulent acquisition of this solid rock fuel resource. Rejecting broader proposals, Congress chose a narrow reservation of the resource that would address the exigencies of the crisis at hand without unduly burdening the rights of homesteaders or impeding the settlement of the West.

It is evident that Congress viewed CBM gas not as part of the solid fuel resource it was attempting to conserve and manage but as a dangerous waste product, which escaped from coal as the coal was mined. Congress was well aware by 1909 that the natural gas found in coal formations was released during coal mining and posed a serious threat to mine safety. Explosions in coal mines sparked by CBM gas occurred with distressing frequency in the late 19th and early 20th centuries. . . .

That CBM gas was considered a dangerous waste product which escaped from coal, rather than part of the valuable coal fuel itself, is also confirmed by the fact that coal companies venting the gas to prevent its accumulation in the mines made no attempt to capture or preserve it. The more gas that escaped from the coal once it was brought to the surface, the better it was for the mining companies because it decreased the risk of a dangerous gas buildup during transport and storage.

* * *

[T]he question before us is not whether Congress would have thought that CBM gas had some fuel value, but whether Congress considered it part of the coal fuel. When it enacted the 1909 and 1910 Acts, Congress did not reserve all minerals or energy resources in the lands. It reserved only coal, and then only in lands that were specifically identified as valuable for coal. It chose not to reserve oil, natural gas, or any other known or potential energy resources.

The limited nature of the 1909 and 1910 Act reservations is confirmed by subsequent congressional enactments. When Congress wanted to reserve gas rights that might yield valuable fuel, it did so in explicit terms. In 1912, for example, Congress enacted a statute that reserved "oil and gas" in Utah lands. In addition, both the 1912 Act and a later Act passed in 1914 continued the tradition begun in the 1909 and 1910 Acts of reserving only those minerals enumerated in the statute. It was not until 1916 that Congress passed a public lands Act containing a general reservation of valuable minerals in the lands.

* * *

[E]ven were we to construe the coal reservation to encompass CBM gas, a split estate would result. The United States concedes (and the Tribe does not dispute) that once the gas originating in the coal formation migrates to surrounding rock formations it belongs to the natural gas, rather than the coal, estate. Natural gas from other sources may also exist in the lands at issue. Including the CBM gas in the coal reservation would, therefore, create a split gas estate that would be at least as difficult to administer as a split coal/CBM gas estate. . . .

Because we conclude that the most natural interpretation of "coal" as used in the 1909 and 1910 Acts does not encompass CBM gas, we need not consider the applicability of the canon that ambiguities in land grants are construed in favor of the sovereign or the competing canons relied on by petitioners.

The judgment of the Court of Appeals is reversed.

GINSBURG, J., dissenting

I would affirm the judgment below substantially for the reasons stated by the Court of Appeals and the federal respondents. As the Court recognizes, in 1909 and 1910 coalbed methane gas (CBM) was a liability. Congress did not contemplate that the surface owner would be responsible for it. More likely, Congress would have assumed that the coal owner had dominion over, and attendant responsibility for, CBM. I do not find it clear that Congress understood dominion would shift if and when the liability became an asset. I would therefore apply the canon that ambiguities in land grants are construed in favor of the sovereign.

NOTES

1. *The meaning of a single word.* The facts of this dispute ultimately were simple, and the legal issue came down to the meaning of a single word. Some 20 million acres of land were patented to private owners under the Coal Lands Acts of 1909 and 1910. The federal government retained ownership of the subsurface coal. In time these coals rights were turned over to the Southern Ute Indian Tribe. Did the tribe's rights to coal under these lands include the coalbed methane gas (CBM) contained in the coal, or was the CBM one of the resources owned by the surface owner? That issue required the Supreme Court to interpret what the word "coal" meant in these two

statutes (which contained essentially identical language). Did coal include the gas embedded in it?—gas that, at the time Congress drafted the statutes, was viewed as noxious and undesirable? The Solicitor General had long said it did not, but during this litigation he shifted the government's interpretation to support the tribe's view that it did.

The court's conclusion—that coal does not include CBM—is legally valid only for deeds issued under these two statutes. The word coal in a different legal setting—under a different statute or in a privately written agreement— may have a different meaning. An interpretation that does apply more broadly includes the Court's comments about how to construe such language in a statute or regulation. What principles of interpretation apply, and to what extent do pragmatic considerations come into play?

How did the Court go about interpreting the statutes? It made clear that the word coal must be given the meaning it had for Congress when the statutes were written in 1909 and 1910. What else did the opinion set forth as interpretive principles? To what extent was the Court influenced by the fact that CBM at the time was a noxious waste product, not a potential fuel? Note that the Court emphasized, by way of interpreting the intent of Congress, that Congress considered and rejected the idea of reserving more minerals when these lands were patented. In short, Congress considered but rejected the idea of reserving oil and gas as well as coal. That action by Congress, the Court noted, implied that Congress had in mind a quite-narrow reservation of mineral rights.

2. *Split mineral estates.* What about the practical difficulties that would have arisen had the Court agreed with the tribe and concluded that CBM was indeed reserved by the United States? The Court noted that CBM gas associated with the coal could leach out and intermingle with other sources of natural gas in the ground. As it did so, CBM would then become natural gas, as the term was legally understood, and thus be owned by the surface owner. The tribe's legal position, thus, would have required careful monitoring to determine which gas was CBM (and owned by the tribe), and which was natural gas owned by the surface owner. On the other hand, the Court's outcome hardly avoids such problems and indeed could create serious environmental problems. If a coal company extracting coal does not own the CBM, then why should it take steps to control it and put it to use? (Environmental regulation, of course, could come into play.) Note that Court did not claim that the distinction it drew (between solid coal and all gas) will be any easier to implement, only that it will be no harder. For more information on the issue of coalbed methane and mineral reservations, *see* Elizabeth A. McClanahan, Jill M. Harrison, John K. Byrum, Jr. & Lisa W. Seaborn, *Title Issues: Beyond* Amoco v. Southern Ute, *Regulation and Development of Coalbed Methane*, (Rocky Mt. Min. L. Found. Paper, 2002–4, Nov. 14–15, 2002).

In the following ruling, we turn to the interpretive challenges raised by privately written instruments. In this setting the law again emphasizes the intentions of the drafters. Here, though, the drafters are private parties, not Congress or other lawmakers. When interpreting a statute such as the Coal Acts, the interpretive question is clearly one of law. When it comes to private agreements, however, the meaning of an instrument is typically a question of fact. But as we shall see, there are important policy reasons why courts, even in the private setting, may interpret key words as a matter of law. Even when courts contend that they are ruling based on private intent and on an assessment of the facts, we need to be alert to the possibility that they will often favor particular, settled interpretations of key words (e.g., "minerals") so as to enhance predictability in land titles—long considered a desirable goal as a way to facilitate transactions and resource exploitation.

BUTLER V. CHARLES POWERS ESTATE

Supreme Court of Pennsylvania
65 A.3d 885 (2013)

BAER, J.

We granted allowance of appeal to consider whether a deed executed in 1881, which reserved to the grantor the subsurface and removal rights of "one-half [of] the minerals and Petroleum Oils" contained beneath the subject property, includes within the reservation any natural gas contained within the shale formation beneath the subject land known as the Marcellus Shale Formation. The trial court in this matter, relying on the 1882 decision of this Court in *Dunham & Shortt v. Kirkpatrick*, 101 Pa. 36 (Pa. 1882), and its progeny held that because the deed reservation did not specifically reference natural gas, any natural gas found within the Marcellus Shale beneath the subject land was not intended by the executing parties to the deed to be encompassed within the reservation. The Superior Court reversed that decision and remanded the case with instructions to the trial court to hold an evidentiary hearing complete with expert, scientific testimony to examine whether: (1) the gas contained within the Marcellus Shale is "conventional natural gas"; (2) Marcellus shale is a "mineral"; and (3) the entity that owns the rights to the shale found beneath the property also owns the rights to the gas contained within that shale. For the reasons that follow, we respectfully hold that the Superior Court erred in ordering the remand for an evidentiary hearing and reinstate the order of the trial court.

I.

Appellants in this matter, John and Mary Josephine Butler, own 244 acres of land in Susquehanna County. Appellants' predecessors in title obtained the land in fee simple by deed in 1881 from Charles Powers. The deed contained the following reservation:

> [O]ne-half the minerals and Petroleum Oils to said Charles Powers his heirs and assigns forever together with all and singular the buildings, water courses, ways, waters, water courses, rights, liberties, privileges, hereditaments, and appurtenances, whatsoever there unto belonging or in any wise appertaining and the reversions and remainders rents issues and profits thereof; And also all the estate right, title interest property claimed and demand whatsoever there unto belonging or in any wise appertaining in law equity or otherwise however of in to or out of the same.

[The Butlers filed a quiet title action seeking a judicial declaration that natural gas in the Marcellus Shale was covered by their reserved rights to the "minerals and Petroleum Oils" under the land at issue. Representatives of the Powers Estate countered, claiming that this reservation did not include gas, citing the state supreme court ruling in *Highland v. Commonwealth*, 161 A.2d 390 (Pa. 1960). The trial court agreed with the Estate, noting that, in Pennsylvania under its "*Dunham* Rule," the term minerals as a matter of law did not include gas unless the gas was expressly mentioned in an instrument. The appellate court disagreed, drawing not upon the *Dunham* Rule but instead upon a 1983 decision, *United States Steel Corporation v. Hoge*, 468 A.2d 1380 (Pa. 1983) (*Hoge II*). There, the state supreme court had held that coalbed methane gas was covered by a deed reservation of coal; the gas present in the coal, the court said in *Hoge II*, must necessarily belong to the owner of the coal. The appellate court (known as the Superior Court) extended this reasoning: any natural gas found in shale, it concluded, would belong to the owner of the shale. The Butlers thus owned the gas *if* their reservation of minerals included the shale. It was unclear if the Butlers did own the shale. For that reason, the Superior Court proposed to send the case back to the trial court to determine ownership of the shale.]

II.

A.   *The Dunham Rule and its Progeny*

Before delving into the parties' arguments, we find it prudent to recount the history of the *Dunham* Rule to facilitate a full understanding of the issues before us. While *Dunham* was decided in 1882, the doctrine for which that case has become well-known has its genesis in the 1836 decision of *Gibson v. Tyson*, 5 Watts 34 (Pa. 1836). In *Gibson*, a deed reserved to the grantor of land "all minerals or magnesia of any kind" contained beneath the property. The Court was tasked with determining whether chrome (also known as chromate of iron) should be encompassed within the "all minerals" portion of the reservation. The Court noted that "the first, and indeed the only matter then is, to ascertain, if possible, what the parties intended and gave their assent to by making the agreement in question." In determining the parties' intent, the court continued, to people "entirely destitute of scientific knowledge in regard to such things . . . [to] the bulk of mankind, . . . [n]othing is thought by [minerals] to be such unless it be of a metallic nature, such as gold, silver, iron, copper, lead, [etc.]. . . ." Reluctantly, the Court determined that chrome would be considered by "the bulk of mankind" as a mineral because it was commonly thought to be of a metallic nature, akin to gold or silver, as demonstrated by parol evidence introduced before the trial court. Thus, the Court held the reservation specifying minerals included chrome based upon a common usage understanding, as opposed to any scientific basis.

* * *

With the notion that the common-man comprehension of terms included in contracts should be used, this Court in *Dunham* examined an 1870 deed, which reserved to the grantor "all the timber suitable for sawing; also all minerals," to determine whether the reservation included oil within the term "all minerals." The Court first noted the reluctance of the *Gibson* Court to find chrome a mineral absent parol evidence; thus, it queried whether oil, which unquestionably was regarded "by science and law" as a mineral solely because of its inorganic character, should likewise be considered a mineral to laypersons. To answer this question, this Court considered whether the deed should be viewed through the lenses of "scientists; or as business men, using the language governed by the ideas of every-day life?"

The Court followed the lead of *Gibson* and *Moore* and held that a common understanding of the word "minerals" should be used. The Court resolved that, should the scientific construction of the term mineral, i.e., anything inorganic, be used, the term would be as "extensive as the grant, hence work[ing] its own destruction." Accordingly, using the common understanding of mankind, the court determined that oil is not a mineral pursuant to the framework laid by the *Gibson* Court that minerals are of a metallic nature. Thus, for the deed reservation to include oil, it must specifically be included within the clause.

[The court proceeded to review in detail three further rulings reiterating and applying the *Dunham* Rule, noting that the Rule was consistently applied in Pennsylvania even as other statutes followed a different interpretive path. In the rulings it discussed—*Silver v. Bush*, 62 A. 832 (Pa. 1906); *Preston v. S. Penn Oil Co.*, 86 A. 203 (Pa. 1913); *Bundy v. Myers*, 94 A.2d 724 (Pa. 1953)—the court emphasized that the term minerals in the common mind typically meant metals, thus excluding gas. It also emphasized that the *Dunham* Rule had become a firmly established rule of law long relied upon by title searchers and other private parties. The court's review of its prior rulings concluded with a look at *Highland*:]

Our extensive examination of the *Dunham* Rule concluded in 1960 in *Highland v. Commonwealth*, 161 A.2d 390 (Pa. 1960). *Highland* concerned the grant of several tracts of land by several different deeds, some of which only reserved the subsurface rights to "coal, coal oil, fire clay and other minerals of every kind and character," while other deeds expressly contained reservations for natural gas. Citing to the litany of cases already discussed above, the *Highland* Court put into plain and simple terms what over one hundred years of case law had combined to say:

> If, in connection with a conveyance of land, there is a reservation or an exception of 'minerals' without any specific mention of natural gas or oil, a presumption, rebuttable in nature, arises that the word 'minerals' was not intended by the parties to include natural gas or oil. [. . .] To rebut the presumption [. . .] there must be clear and convincing evidence that the parties intended to include natural gas or oil within [minerals].

Id. at 398–99.

The Court did so while recognizing, as did its predecessors, that mankind generally divided all known matter into three categories—animal, vegetable, and mineral—and that petroleum and natural gas are unquestionably minerals under that broad categorization. Nonetheless, we reaffirmed that for deed reservations we must assume, absent evidence to the contrary, that mineral is a term of "general language, and presumably is intended in the ordinary popular sense which it bears among English speaking people," i.e., metallic substances and not oil and gas. Thus, the *Dunham* Rule, a well-established and relied upon rule of property, continues to bind all situations in which a deed reservation does not expressly include oil or natural gas within the reservation. Indeed, such a conclusion was demanded by the long-standing jurisprudence of this Commonwealth concerning property law: "A rule of property long acquiesced in should not be overthrown except for compelling reasons of public policy or the imperative demands of justice." *Id.* at 399 n. 5.

B. *United States Steel Corp. v. Hoge*

As noted, the Superior Court in this case found the *Dunham* progeny did not end the analysis because of *Hoge II*. Thus, we turn next to that decision. In the late 1970s, a question was raised concerning so-called "coalbed gas," which is a combination of methane, ethane, propane and other gases. Within the coal mining and natural gas industries, coalbed gas, which is found within crevices and empty pockets in coal seams and commonly known among miners as "firedamp," bears "little if any distinction [from] the gas found in oil-and-gas-bearing sands (natural gas)." *U.S. Steel Corp. v. Hoge*, 450 A.2d 162, 173 n. 16 (Pa. Super. Ct. 1982) (*Hoge I*). As detailed below, the *Hoge* case examined the ownership of coalbed gas.

[This dispute involved the interpretation of deeds in which U.S. Steel retained all coal and "the right of ventilation and drainage and the access to the mines for men and materials." The landowners retained, however, "the right to drill and operate through said coal for oil and gas without being held liable for any damages." The issue posed: did the reservation of coal include coalbed methane? Without discussing the *Dunham* Rule, the Court in *Hoge II* concluded that it did, reasoning that gas contained in the coal was part of the coal and went with it. The surface owner expressly retained the right to drill for gas and oil. In the court's view, however, it "strain[ed] credulity" to think that the surface owner would want to retain ownership of something then deemed a dangerous waste substance.]

III.

Based on the foregoing, we now turn to the parties' primary arguments in this case. [The Powers Estate], advocating for the reversal of the Superior Court's remand order and reinstatement of the trial court's judgment, rely exclusively on the *Dunham* Rule and its consistent application for over one hundred years that natural gas is not included within a deed reservation without either (1) being explicitly contemplated within the reservation; or (2) clear and convincing parol evidence that the parties intended for natural gas to be included within the deed reservation, despite only a general reservation of minerals. . . . [The Butlers, in contrast, relied upon *Hoge II,* claiming that their reserved rights included the shale and that the natural gas in it therefore belonged to them. After surveying the parties' arguments, the Court offered its analysis:]

* * *

First, as has been related herein, this Court has never explicitly questioned the vitality of the *Dunham* Rule. Like the *Silver* Court did in 1906, we recognize that the *Dunham* Rule has now been an unaltered, unwavering rule of property law for 131 years; indeed its origins actually date back to the *Gibson* decision, placing the rule's age at 177 years. As noted by this Court in *Highland*, "[a] rule of property long acquiesced in should not be overthrown except for compelling reasons of public policy or the imperative demands of justice." In our view, neither the Superior Court nor Appellees have provided any justification for overruling or limiting the *Dunham* Rule and its longstanding progeny that have formed the bedrock for innumerable private, real property transactions for nearly two centuries.

* * *

We next examine whether the *Dunham* Rule applies to this appeal, and, readily hold that it does. At the outset, we note the obvious: the term "natural gas" is contained nowhere in the plain language of the deed reservation. Under the *Dunham* Rule, then, the burden is on Appellees to plead and prove, by clear and convincing parol evidence, that the intent of the parties when executing the deed in 1881 was to include natural gas within the reservation. . . . The *Dunham* Rule is clear, dating back to *Gibson*, that the common, layperson understanding of what is and is not a mineral is the only acceptable construction of a private deed. Notwithstanding different interpretations proffered by other jurisdictions, the rule in Pennsylvania is that natural gas and oil simply are not minerals because they are not of a metallic nature, as the common person would understand minerals.

* * *

Finally, we disagree with the Superior Court that because the natural gas at issue in this case is contained within the Marcellus Shale, the *Hoge II* decision and its statement that "such gas as is present in coal must necessarily belong to the owner of the coal" become relevant or controlling. First, . . . we reject any insinuation by Appellee that *Hoge II* limited or overruled the *Dunham* Rule by stating that "gas is a mineral." The *Hoge II* Court made this statement without discussing the *Dunham* Rule, and therefore we find no merit to any averment that *Hoge II sub silentio* abrogated the *Dunham* Rule.

Concerning the *Hoge II* decision itself, the deed reservation at issue there concerned coal rights and the related right of ventilation of coalbed gas. This distinction between *Hoge II*, the *Dunham* line of cases, and the instant appeal is critical for several reasons. First, the right of ventilation would only apply to coalbed gas because of its extremely dangerous and volatile nature. Related thereto, coalbed gas was not commercially viable at the time the deed reservation in *Hoge II* was executed due to its explosive characteristics. Second, the *Hoge II* Court inherently made a legal distinction between coalbed gas and natural gas, despite recognizing the chemical similarities between the two, by upholding the landowners' right to drill through the coal seam to obtain natural gas. To this end, Appellees in the appeal *sub judice* forward no argument that the Marcellus shale natural gas is different than natural gas commonly found in sand deposits. Indeed, Appellants and their amici explicitly note that Marcellus shale natural gas is merely natural gas that has become trapped within the Marcellus Shale, rather than rising to the more permeable sand formations below the surface.

Lastly, the situs of Marcellus shale natural gas and the methods needed and utilized to extract that gas do not support deviation from a *Dunham* analysis. While we recognize that hydrofracturing methods are employed to obtain both coalbed gas and Marcellus shale natural gas, the basis of the *Dunham* Rule lies in the common understanding of the substance itself, not the means used to bring those substances to the surface. We therefore find no merit in any contention that because Marcellus shale natural gas is contained within shale rock, regardless of whether shale rock is or is not be a mineral, such consequentially renders the natural gas therein a mineral. Accordingly, we find no reason to apply *Hoge II* to this appeal, and, thus, no need to remand this case for fact-finding.

* * *

. . . . Accordingly, we reverse the order of the Superior Court and reinstate the order of the Susquehanna County Court of Common Pleas sustaining Appellants' preliminary objection.

NOTES

1. *The challenge of determining private intent.* In this 2013 ruling, the Pennsylvania Supreme Court interpreted words in a document written and executed by private parties in 1881, some 132 years earlier. As best we can tell, the court had no evidence to use in discerning the parties' intentions other than the language of the document itself and a general knowledge of the state of affairs in Pennsylvania in 1881. The court had no special knowledge about what these parties actually intended. It was left to guess what ordinary people of that time and place might have intended when they used these words. As we shall see, sometimes courts rely on the specific facts of a transaction in their efforts to discern private intent. It can make a difference, for instance, whether mineral extraction is already taking place on the land covered by the document. It can make a difference if a particular mineral is already known to exist under the land, or whether it might be visible from the land surface (e.g., exposed limestone). A court could pay attention to then-existing surface uses of the land, perhaps assuming that a surface owner who sells off minerals would not intend to give the mineral estate owner the legal power to disrupt her surface land uses. As we imagine various sets of facts, we can likely come up with many possible circumstances that could shed light on the parties' intentions.

Imagine what would happen if one party to a dispute like this one—a dispute over a deed more than a century old—showed up in court with private letters written by one of the document signers, or even a personal diary, in which the person commented on the transaction in a way that shed light on the person's actual intent. The court here certainly left open the possibility that clear evidence, even evidence completely off the public record, could be used to produce an interpretation far different than the one that would be reached without the external evidence. If that happened, a deed on the public record could have a meaning far different from what outsiders would assume simply by reading the document itself. It is easy to see why the court took the position it did; after all, the private parties were at liberty to structure their transaction as they saw fit, and the court's task is to carry out their intentions. Still, the cost of doing so can be high. Deeds on the public record might not mean what they seem to mean.

2. *What does the "common man" think is a mineral . . . and does it matter?* As did the Supreme Court in *Amoco*, above, the *Butler* court made clear that, in the absence of specific evidence of private intent, it would interpret the word mineral by looking to what a common man *at the time of the deed* would have considered a mineral. What such a common man then would have thought is, in the first instance, a question of historical fact. But the court had already determined that fact in various earlier rulings, and it seemed disinclined to let anyone today reopen the question. To the common man of the 1880s the term minerals did not include natural gas. This conclusion, we would say, remains a conclusion of fact after all these years, not one of law. But given the court's consistent adherence to the interpretation, it has become over time just as settled as any interpretation of law: an interpretation upon which title searchers and others can rely. The court thus seems to have accomplished two goals that often do not go together: It adequately deferred to private intent, thus honoring the liberty of the contracting parties, while also reaching a stable, predictable result that keeps land titles secure.

But what about the possibility that the "common-man comprehension" of the 1880s was not in fact a stable one over time? Is it right to assume that an interpretation common in the 1880s was still common in, for instance, the 1930s or 1960s? Given the choice between scientific, commercial or "ordinary" understandings of minerals, is it wise to base property rights embedded within property conveyances or reservations on "popular estimations" rather than scientific understanding? In more modern times—when scientific processes and analysis are so deeply engrained within daily life—might a party drafting a grant presume that a court would construe ambiguities in descriptions of a mineral estate scientifically?

3. *Hoge II and the* Dunham *Rule.* In *Butler*, the Pennsylvania court labored at length to get around its earlier decision in *Hoge II*, a ruling that the parties, and the lower court, viewed as quite different from the *Dunham* Rule. But how different were they? In *Hoge II*, the owner of the coal had the express right to vent the coalbed gas—that is, to dispose of it in the course of its coal mining. None of the *Dunham* Rule cases included any similar provision bearing on the actual intentions of the parties involved concerning the control of natural gas. The *Butler* court thus might have reconciled the cases by saying that *Hoge II* involved a rare instance in which the extra evidence (here, the language on venting) took the deeds outside the general rule of *Dunham*.

4. *Coal with or without coalbed methane.* Recall that the *Amoco* Court, above, ruled that coalbed methane did not go along with the coal in the reservation. The *Hoge II* court, however, found that coalbed methane did go along with the reserved coal. Are the cases simply inconsistent?

We can approach this question by noting that *Amoco* involved a statute, while *Hoge II* involved private agreements; that is, one case posed a question purely of law, the other a question chiefly of fact. This distinction, though, does not seem that weighty, given that in both settings the court's task was to figure out what the relevant drafters intended—Congress in one instance, the private actors in another. And, as they performed their interpretive work, both courts paid attention to common understandings of the era when the documents were written.

Another way to reconcile the cases is to pay attention to the particular facts. In the case of *Amoco*, only the intention of Congress was relevant; there was no second party involved. Congress sought to retain the coal for one and only one reason: because it was valuable. Given the focus on value, Congress had no reason to want to reserve the CBM, which was not just valueless but harmful (at least at the time). Why would it want to retain an explosive gas? In *Hoge II*, the situation was somewhat different: the landowners conveyed minerals beneath their lands to various coal companies. From their perspective, why would they want to retain title to the hazardous gas embedded in the coal? It was of no value to them, and they might well have wanted the coal companies to deal with it safely. From this perspective, it makes sense to assume that the surface landowners were happy to get rid of the gas.

5. *Interpreting deeds as a matter of law.* The *Dunham* Rule in Pennsylvania seems to operate as a rule of law, even as courts remain open to the remote chance that external facts in a given setting might lead to a different interpretation. This outcome is often encountered in mining law generally. As another illustration, consider the ruling in *Save Our Little Vermillion Environment, Inc. v. Illinois Cement Co.*, 725 N.E.2d 386 (Ill. App. 2000). Did a deed that conveyed "coal and other minerals" on and under a tract of land cover limestone or, instead, did the limestone remain part of the surface estate? The court stated that it would base its decision upon "the language of the grant or reservation, the surrounding circumstances, and the intention of the grantor if it can be ascertained." The issue, that is, was plainly and purely a matter of fact.

But the court determined that the grant was ambiguous, and that no external evidence shed light on the parties' actual intentions. It therefore concluded that the term "other minerals" in fact did not include limestone, leading to the seemingly anomalous result that the mineral estate owner had to stand back and watch while the surface owner engaged in mining. In reaching its conclusion, the court emphasized that every other American court to consider the issue had reached the same result; in no dispute did "minerals" include limestone. This uniform pattern of rulings suggests that this interpretive stance, like the *Dunham* Rule in Pennsylvania, has become for all practical purposes a conclusion of law.

GEOTHERMAL KINETICS, INC. V. UNION OIL COMPANY OF CALIFORNIA

California Court of Appeal
75 Cal.App.3d 56 (1977)

SCOTT, J.

The issue presented here is whether geothermal resources belong to the owner of the mineral estate or the owner of the surface estate. We conclude that the general grant of minerals in, on or under the property includes a grant of geothermal resources, including steam therefrom.

[Geothermal Kinetics held title under a 1951 deed to "all minerals in, on or under" a 408-acre tract of land located in an area of Sonoma County known as "The Geysers." Union Oil owned the surface rights. In 1973, Geothermal Kinetics drilled a geothermal well on the property at a cost of approximately $400,000. The trial court ruled that the mineral estate of Geothermal gave it rights to the geothermal resources.]

I.

Appellants' [Union Oil and others] primary contention is that geothermal energy is not a mineral; they argue that the resource is not steam, rocks or the underground reservoir but the heat transported to the surface by means of steam. A mineral, appellants claim, must have physical substance and heat is merely a property of a physical substance. In support of this contention, appellants cite several definitions of "mineral" containing reference to "substance." . . .

Respondent contends that since the parties did not specify particular minerals that were intended to be within the scope of the grant nor include any limitations on it, the grant conveyed the broadest possible estate. It urges that the "grant is to be interpreted in favor of the grantee." (Civ.Code, § 1069.) Respondent urges that we not adopt a mechanistic approach based upon textbook definitions of the term mineral; instead we should adopt a "functional" approach which focuses upon the purposes and expectations generally attendant to mineral estates and surface estates. Since normally the owner of the mineral estate seeks to extract valuable resources from the earth, whereas the surface owner generally desires to utilize land and such resources as are necessary for his enjoyment of the land, the geothermal resources should follow the mineral estate. We agree with respondent's contention.

II.

Geothermal resources have been used commercially for several centuries, including their use to generate electricity in the early 1900s. In the United States, exploration and utilization of such resources has occurred generally in the western part of the nation, particularly in California. Commercial development of The Geysers area near Santa Rosa began in 1955 with the successful drilling of four wells. In 1960, Pacific Gas & Electric Company opened an electrical generating plant at The Geysers using the geothermal steam to power the generating turbines. Geothermal steam from respondent's well is piped to the P.G. & E. plant located about a mile away.

Geothermal energy is a naturally occurring phenomenon whose origin is the heat of the interior of the earth. The geothermal resources of The Geysers is apparently due to a layer of molten or semi-molten rock, called "magma," which has risen from the interior of the earth to a depth of 20,000 to 30,000 feet. Above this mass of magma, which constitutes the basic heat source for the area, are protuberances of magma called "plugs" or "stocks," which may rise within 10,000 to 15,000 feet of the surface of the earth. This intrusion of hot magma expells gases and liquids which combine with ancient water trapped in the surrounding sediment to form a geothermal fluid or brine. This fluid converts to steam which circulates in a sedimentary formation and transports mineral and heat from the magma toward the surface. Convection currents cause water to rise and cool, forming a mineral shell of silica and calcium carbonate which seals off the magma intrusion from the surface. This shell is approximately 1000 feet thick in the area of respondent's well. Immediately below this silicacarbonate seal is circulating geothermal steam and other gases; below these gases is boiling brine.

The seal over the steam reservoir permits only a small amount of ground water to penetrate. The amount of this ground water is insignificant compared to the volume of geothermal steam and brine; its penetration of the seal does not serve to materially deplete the general supply of ground water available for surface use. Hence, the ground water system and the geothermal steam reservoir are separate and distinct. Some geothermal steam escapes from the reservoir to the earth's surface through cracks in the silicacarbonate seal.

At The Geysers wells drilled through the silicacarbonate seal bring geothermal steam to the surface. Respondent's well is approximately 7,200 feet deep. The extracted hot steam, which contains minerals, powers steam turbines to produce commercially valuable electric power. The minerals in the condensed steam are generally toxic, requiring the reinjection of this water back below the silicacarbonate seal. Purification of the condensed steam so as to render it safe for agricultural or domestic purposes is not economically feasible. Geothermal resources are not necessary or useful to surface owners, other than as a source of electricity. The utilization of geothermal resources does not substantially destroy the surface of the land. The production of the energy from geothermal energy is analogous to the production of energy from such other minerals as coal, oil and natural gas in that substances containing or capable of producing heat are removed from beneath the earth. In fact, the wells used for the extraction of the steam are similar to oil and gas wells.

III.

In the construction of a grant or reservation of an interest in real property, a court seeks to determine the intent of the parties, giving effect to a particular intent over a general intent. (Civ.Code, §§ 1066, 1636; Code Civ.Proc. § 1859.) In the present case, the 1951 grant of mineral rights makes no specific mention of geothermal resources; hence, the general intent of the parties must be ascertained. In the absence of an expressed specific intent, several courts have sought to determine the general intent of the parties in construing the word "mineral" in a deed, rather than resort to attempts at rigid definition. (*See United States v. Union Oil Co. of California*, 549 F.2d 1271, 1274 n. 7 (9th Cir. 1977); *Northern Natural Gas Co. v. Grounds*, 441 F.2d 704, 714 (10th Cir. 1971), *cert. denied*, 404 U.S. 951 (1971); *Acker v. Guinn*, 464 S.W.2d 348, 352 (Tex. 1971).)

Initially, we observe that "as a general rule a grant or reservation of all minerals includes all minerals found on the premises whether or not known to exist." (*Renshaw v. Happy Valley Water Co.*, 250 P.2d 612, 615 (Cal. App. 1952).) Thus, the fact that the presence of geothermal resources may not have been known to one or both parties to the 1951 conveyance is of no consequence.

Generally, the parties to a conveyance of a mineral estate expect that the enjoyment of this interest will not involve destruction of the surface. In *Acker v. Guinn*, 464 S.W.2d 348, 351 (Tex. 1971), the deed of "oil, gas and other minerals in and under" the property did not convey an interest in the iron ore. The court observed that the parties to a mineral lease or deed usually think of the mineral estate as including valuable substances that are removed from the ground by means of wells or mine shafts, but "a grant . . . of minerals . . . should not be construed to include a substance that must be removed by methods that will, in effect, consume or deplete the surface estate." (at p. 352.)

Here, the trial court found that the exploitation of geothermal resources does not substantially destroy the surface of the property. . . .

The parties to the 1951 grant had a general intention to convey those commercially valuable, underground, physical resources of the property. They expected that the enjoyment of this interest would not destroy the surface estate and would involve resources distinct from the surface soil. In the absence of any expressed specific intent to the contrary, the scope of the mineral estate, as indicated by the parties' general intentions and expectations, includes the geothermal resources underlying the property.

In *United States v. Union Oil Co. of California*, 549 F.2d 1271 (9th Cir. 1977), the court, dealing with other property in The Geysers area, interprets mineral reservations of "all the coal and other minerals" in patents issued under the Stock-Raising Homestead Act of 1916 to include geothermal resources underneath the patented land (at 1273). Although the basis for the holding is partly the Congressional intent to retain government control over energy resources, the court stated that "the words of the mineral reservation in the Stock-Raising Homestead Act clearly are capable of bearing a meaning that encompasses geothermal resources" (at 1274).

* * *

Several courts have held that the grant or reservation of a mineral estate does not include rights to surface or subsurface water. (*See Fleming Foundation v. Texaco*, 337 S.W.2d 846 (Tex. App. 1960); *Mack Oil Co. v. Laurence*, 389 P.2d 955 (Okla. 1964).) However, such cases concern water that is part of the normal ground water system. As the trial court found, the water and steam components of geothermal resources are part of a separate water system cut off from these surface and subsurface waters by a thick mineral cap. Only insignificant amounts of ground water enter the geothermal water system. Unlike the surface and subsurface waters, the origin of geothermal water is not rainfall, but water present at the time of the formation of the geologic structure. Because rainfall does not replenish geothermal water, it is a depletable deposit.

* * *

Examining both the broad purpose of the 1951 conveyance of the mineral estate and the expected manner of enjoyment of this property interest, it appears that the rights to the geothermal resources are part of the grant. A principal purpose of this conveyance was to transfer those underground physical resources which have commercial value and are not necessary for the enjoyment of the surface estate. The trial court correctly determined that the mineral grant herein conveyed to respondent the right to the geothermal resources located in, on or under the property in question.

Judgment is affirmed.

NOTES

1. *Another interpretive approach.* How did the *Geothermal Kinetics* court go about its interpretive work, and how do the interpretive principles it employed compare with what we saw in *Amoco* and *Butler*? This dispute, like

the one in *Butler*, had to do with the meaning of a private agreement, and the court announced that it aimed to implement the intentions of the parties. Did it actually do so? Did it arrive at a result tailored to the facts and circumstances of the case? Or has it, like other courts, reached a conclusion approaching the solidity and reliability of a rule of law?

As you trace the court's reasoning, note its willingness to push aside the knowledge of the parties about which resources might be present. It does not expressly ignore the related question about the parties' knowledge concerning value. If we do not care what the parties knew about resources, perhaps we can also ignore their knowledge of economics. Might we sense, reading this, that the court was perhaps less interested in actual intention than it claimed to be? Note also the court's distinction between particular intent and general intent. The court seemed to say that we have no knowledge of particular intent—that is, the intent of the original parties at the time of deed drafting. As for general intent, whose intent did the court have in mind? Or did general intent really refer to presumptions that the court itself was inclined to embrace, drawing (as here) on the practices of other courts elsewhere?

2. *The "functional approach" to interpretation and the surface–subsurface distinction.* Ultimately, the California court embraced what it termed a functional approach to deed interpretation: "Normally the owner of the mineral estate seeks to extract valuable resources from the earth," the court tells us, "whereas the surface owner generally desires to utilize land and such resources as are necessary for his enjoyment of the land." This sounds rather like the common-man comprehension used in *Butler*. But of course the focus was much different: *Butler* used the common-man perspective to give meaning to a particular word: What did the word mean to an ordinary person? Here the court asked and answered a much different question: How would ordinary parties to such a transaction have thought that they were dividing up the tract of land? What purpose did the mineral claimant have in mind, and what was the purpose of the surface owner? The court gave an answer that did not seem particularly linked to the time and place of this transaction or to any facts relating to it. Its answer, indeed, seemed almost timeless.

3. *The Texas experience, before and after* Geothermal Kinetics. At bottom, the court in *Geothermal Kinetics* drew a line between the subsurface and the surface. The mineral estate owner enjoys everything beneath the ground if it can be extracted without material disruption of the surface; the surface-owner gets to use the surface. In support of its position, the court cited the Texas Supreme Court opinion in *Acker v. Guinn*, 464 S.W.2d 348 (Tex. 1971). In that nationally prominent ruling, the Texas court announced it was giving up on its longstanding effort to determine what parties to a mineral deed did or did not intend; such an inquiry, it said, was simply too unreliable. Instead, it embraced as a matter of law what quickly became known as the surface-destruction test. Whether a particular subsurface material is a mineral depended on whether it could be removed without destroying the surface; if it could be removed without destruction, it was a

mineral. In *Acker*, the court ruled that iron ore was not a mineral as a matter of law because its removal would have destroyed the surface. As they applied the surface-destruction test over the ensuing decade, Texas courts seemed to pay attention also to whether a particular substance did or did not lie on or near the surface of the land, so that removal of it could be undertaken by open pit or strip mining. This was the state of Texas law at the time of *Geothermal Kinetics*.

Before long, the Texas court realized that its new test also was not workable. It was odd enough in *Acker* to say that valuable iron ore was not a mineral. Even harder cases soon arose, involving uranium, which could only be extracted with substantial harm to the surface. How could uranium not be a mineral? In *Moser v. United States Steel Corp.*, 676 S.W.2d 99 (Tex. 1984), the court shifted directions again, embracing an "ordinary and natural meaning" test but applying it, seemingly, as a matter of law. Uranium, it held, was a mineral as a matter of law, even when removal required surface destruction. Even as it embraced its new approach, though, the court realized it could not upset longstanding expectations, specifically stating that its prior rulings, finding particular resources to be non-minerals as matters of *law* (building stone, limestone, surface shale, water, sand, gravel, near-surface coal and iron ore) would remain valid and the resources non-minerals. It also limited its decision to deeds executed after June 8, 1983.

4. *Is water a mineral?* The *Geothermal Kinetics* court noted that "several courts have held that the grant or reservation of a mineral estate does not include rights to surface or subsurface water," but distinguished those cases on the grounds that "the water and steam components of geothermal resources are part of a separate water system cut off from these surface and subsurface waters by a thick mineral cap." Do you find this argument persuasive? What if a state explicitly considers water a mineral? The Louisiana Mineral Code states:

> The provisions of this Code are applicable to all forms of minerals, including oil and gas. They are also applicable to rights to explore for or mine or remove from land the soil itself, gravel, shells, *subterranean water*, or other substances occurring naturally in or as a part of the soil or geological formations on or underlying the land.

La. R.S. § 31:4, enacted by Acts 1974, No. 50, § 1, eff. Jan. 1, 1975 (emphasis added). In addition, Article 6 of the Louisiana Mineral Code makes clear that ownership of land does not include ownership of minerals, but rather gives the landowner exclusive right to "explore and develop his property for the production of such minerals and to reduce them to possession and ownership." La. R.S. § 31:6, enacted by Acts 1974, No. 50, § 1, eff. Jan. 1, 1975. In reality, given the dearth of judicial interpretation of this provision in the context of Louisiana groundwater, the question of how transferable the jurisprudence on traditional minerals, such as oil and gas, is for water remains unclear. What if a surface estate owner is engaged in agricultural operations requiring the pumping of a lot of water—could a mineral estate owner who received an estate including all "minerals" claim ownership of the water?

5. *Geothermal energy development.* The state of California has a geothermal grant and loan program "to promote the development of new or existing geothermal resources and technologies." *See* California Energy Commission, Geothermal Grant and Loan Program, http://www.energy.ca. gov/geothermal/grda.html. For more information on the development of geothermal resources *see* John W. Lund, *Characteristics, Development, and Utilization of Geothermal Resources*, Geo-Heat Center Bulletin (Or. Inst. of Tech. June 2007), *available at* http://geoheat.oit.edu/pdf/tp126.pdf; Daniel J. Fleischmann, *An Assessment of Geothermal Resource Development Needs in the Western United States*, Geothermal Energy Association, http://www.geo-energy.org/reports/States%20Guide.pdf.

HUNT OIL COMPANY V. KERBAUGH
Supreme Court of North Dakota
283 N.W.2d 131 (1979)

SAND, J.

Ivan and Shirley Kerbaugh appealed from an order of the district court enjoining them from interfering with geophysical explorations carried on over their property by the plaintiffs, Hunt Oil Co. and Williams Oil Co. The Kerbaughs asserted the oil companies do not have an unlimited right to conduct seismic exploration over their property and also that the record in this case was inadequate to grant the oil companies injunctive relief. We conditionally affirm.

This case involves geophysical exploration for oil and gas over approximately 1000 acres of land located in Williams County and owned by the Kerbaughs. The Kerbaughs acquired about 480 acres of this land in 1966 by way of a warranty deed which reserved in the grantor ". . . ALL of the minerals, including oil and gas, in and under or that may be produced and saved from said lands, together with the right of ingress and egress." The Kerbaughs own the remaining land under a 1972 contract for deed which also reserved in the grantor all the minerals under the land, together "with such easement for ingress, egress and use of the surface which may be incidental or necessary to use such rights."

The owners of the mineral estates in this case leased their oil and gas interests to Edward Mike Davis for a period of five years in 1974 and 1975, respectively.[1] Davis then conducted seismic exploration over the property in the early part of 1976. Ivan Kerbaugh testified that after the

---

[1] The lease to Davis of the first tract of land was a form lease which provided: "Lessee shall pay for damages caused by his operation to growing crops on said lands." The leases covering the remaining lands were on what appear to be identical forms, although the above provision was altered to read: "Lessee shall pay for damages caused by his operation to growing crops on said lands. & all surface & underground water."

1976 seismic activity, the flow from a spring which supplied water to his home and livestock, gradually decreased until it stopped in November 1976. Kerbaugh said he restored the flow of the spring, although at a reduced rate, at his own expense. Ivan also testified, that as a result of the 1976 exploration, open holes were left in his property, along with various types of debris.

In 1977, Davis assigned the oil and gas leases to Williams Exploration Co., who subsequently assigned a share of the same leases to Hunt Oil Co. The following summer the oil companies contracted with Pacific West Exploration Co. to conduct seismic exploration activities over certain lands in Williams County, including the Kerbaugh property. Pacific West Exploration contacted Ivan Kerbaugh for permission to conduct the exploration, offering to pay $50 per hole plus additional amounts for damages to growing crops. Kerbaugh rejected the offer and counteroffered with a request of $200 per hole, plus $1 per rod of tracks on the land, a commitment to cement shut any holes, and a guarantee of continued water supply. Although Kerbaugh later reduced his requests, they were rejected by Pacific.

When surveying for the exploration started, Kerbaugh requested the surveyors to leave until an agreement was reached as to compensation for damages to his surface rights. The oil companies then filed a summons and complaint seeking temporary and permanent injunctive relief restraining the Kerbaughs from interfering with the oil companies in the exercise of their rights under the oil and gas lease. [The trial court issued a temporary injunction and Pacific West Exploration then commenced the seismic activities. Later the trial court issued a permanent injunction against the Kerbaughs.]

The Kerbaughs argued the oil companies did not have an unlimited right to conduct seismic exploration over the Kerbaugh property. This court in *Christman v. Emineth*, 212 N.W.2d 543, 550 (N.D. 1973), adopted the general rule set forth in 58 C.J.S. Mines and Minerals § 159b as to the implied rights of the mineral estate owner:

> * * * unless the language of the conveyance repels such a construction, as a general rule a grant of mines or minerals gives to the owner of the minerals the incidental right of entering, occupying, and making such use of the surface lands as is reasonably necessary in exploring, mining, removing, and marketing the minerals * * *. The incidental right of entering, occupying, and making such use of the surface lands as is reasonably necessary exists in the case of a reservation of mineral rights as well as a grant.

We have also considered the rights of the lessee under the usual oil and gas lease. In *Feland v. Placid Oil Co.*, 171 N.W.2d 829, 834 (N.D. 1969), Chief Justice Teigen, speaking for the court, stated:

> Under a usual oil and gas lease, the lessee, in developing the leased premises, is entitled to use of the land reasonably necessary in producing the oil. . . .

> Whether the express uses are set out or not, the mere granting of the lease creates and vests in the lessee the dominant estate in the surface of the land for the purposes of the lease; by implication it grants the lessee the use of the surface to the extent necessary to a full enjoyment of the grant. Without such use, the mineral estate obtained under the lease would be worthless. . . . *Texaco, Inc. v. Faris*, 413 S.W.2d 147, 149 (Tex. Civ. App. 1967).

The above cases recognize the well-settled rule that where the mineral estate is severed from the surface estate, the mineral estate is dominant. See Annot., 53 A.L.R.3d 16; 4 Summers, *Oil and Gas*, § 652; 58 C.J.S. *Mines and Minerals* § 159b. The mineral estate is dominant in that the law implies, where it is not granted, a legitimate area within which mineral ownership of necessity carries with it inherent surface rights to find and develop the minerals, which rights must and do involve the surface estate. Without such rights the mineral estate would be meaningless and worthless. Thus, the surface estate is servient in the sense it is charged with the servitude for those essential rights of the mineral estate.

In the absence of other rights expressly granted or reserved, the rights of the owner of the mineral estate are limited to so much of the surface and such use thereof as are reasonably necessary to explore, develop, and transport the minerals. See *Union Producing Co. v. Pittman*, 146 So.2d 553 (Miss. 1962); 58 C.J.S. *Mines and Minerals* § 159c; Annot., 53 A.L.R.3d 16 § 3(a). In addition to, or underlying the question of what constitutes reasonable use of the surface in the development of oil and gas rights, is the concept that the owner of the mineral estate must have due regard for the rights of the surface owner and is required to exercise that degree of care and use which is a just consideration for the rights of the surface owner. *Getty Oil Co. v. Jones*, 470 S.W.2d 618, 621 (Tex. 1971). *Union Producing Co. v. Pittman*, above; 58 C.J.S. *Mines and Minerals* § 159c; Annot., 59 A.L.R.3d 16 § 3(c). Therefore, the mineral estate owner has no right to use more of, or do more to, the surface estate than is reasonably necessary to explore, develop, and transport the minerals. *Union Producing Co. v. Pittman*, above; 58 C.J.S. Mines and Minerals § 159c. Nor does the mineral estate owner have the right to negligently or wantonly use the surface owner's estate.[2] See *Union Producing Co. v. Pittman*, above; 4 Summers, *Oil and Gas*, § 652.

The requirement that due regard be given to the rights of the surface owner, defines, to a certain extent, a consideration in determining if the mineral owner's use of the surface is reasonably necessary. In *Getty Oil Co. v. Jones*, above, the Texas Supreme Court set forth what has become known as the "accommodation doctrine":

> There may be only one manner of use of the surface whereby the minerals can be produced. The lessee has the right to pursue this use, regardless of surface damage. (Citations omitted.) And there may be necessitous temporary use governed by the same principle. But under the circumstances indicated here; i. e., where there is an existing use by the surface owner which would otherwise be precluded or impaired, and where under the established practices in the industry there are alternatives available to the lessee whereby the minerals can be recovered, the rules of reasonable usage of the surface may require the adoption of an alternative by the lessee. 470 S.W.2d at 622.

The Utah Supreme Court adopted the opinion of the Texas court in *Flying Diamond Corporation v. Rust*, 551 P.2d 509 (Utah 1976), where it said, at 511:

> . . . wherever there exist separate ownerships of interests in the same land, each should have the right to the use and enjoyment of his interest in the property to the highest degree possible not inconsistent with the rights of the other. We do not mean to be understood as saying that such a lessee must use any possible

---

[2] This case does not present, nor does this opinion decide, the issue of whether or not the owner or lessee of the mineral estate is liable for damages arising from the reasonably necessary use of the surface incident to the exploration, development, and transportation of the minerals. The authorities which have considered the issue appear to be in agreement that such damages are *Damnum absque injuria* and no recovery can be had against the mineral estate owner or lessee. See, *Getty Oil Co. v. Jones*, above; Frankfort Oil Co. v. Abrams, 413 P.2d 190 (Colo. 1966); *Union Producing Co. v. Pittman*, above; 4 Summers, *Oil and Gas*, § 652; Browder, *The Dominant Oil and Gas Estate Master or Servant of the Servient Estate*, 17 S.W.L.J. 25 (1963). This conclusion seems to rest on a principle that injury necessarily inflicted in the exercise of a lawful right does not create a liability, but rather, the injury must be the direct result of the commission of a wrong. See 10A *Thompson on Real Property* (1957 Replacement) § 5325. We question, however, the social desirability of a rule which potentially allows the damage or destruction of a surface estate equal or greater in value than the value of the mineral being extracted.

Future mineral exploration and development can be expected to expand as our demands for energy sources grow. Equity requires a closer examination of whether or not the cost of surface damage and destruction arising from mineral development should be borne by the owner of a severed surface estate or by the developer and consumer of the minerals. Although we do not doubt the mineral estate owner's right to use the surface estate to explore, develop and transport the minerals, we specifically do not decide if the right of reasonable use also implies the right to damage and destroy without compensation. But cf., *Bell v. Cardinal Drilling Co.*, 85 N.W.2d 246 (N.D.1957). (Under the terms of the oil and gas lease, lessee had the right to use so much of the land as was reasonably necessary in the operation of drilling the test well.)

alternative. But he is obliged to pursue one which is reasonable and practical under the circumstances.

We join with the Utah court in adopting the accommodation doctrine set forth in *Getty*:

> The reasonableness of a surface use by the lessee is to be determined by a consideration of the circumstances of both and, as stated, the surface owner is under the burden of establishing the unreasonableness of the lessee's surface use in this light. The reasonableness of the method and manner of using the dominant mineral estate may be measured by what are usual, customary and reasonable practices in the industry under like circumstances of time, place and servient estate uses. . . . (I)f the manner of use selected by the dominant mineral lessee is the only reasonable, usual and customary method that is available for developing and producing the minerals on the particular land then the owner of the servient estate must yield. However, if there are other usual, customary and reasonable methods practiced in the industry on similar lands put to similar uses which would not interfere with the existing uses being made by the servient surface owner, it could be unreasonable for the lessee to employ an interfering method or manner of use. These (conditions) involve questions to be resolved by the trier of the facts. 470 S.W.2d at 627–628.

In this case the Kerbaughs sought to prevent the oil companies from conducting seismic exploration activities on their property. The oil companies, on the other hand, sought an injunction prohibiting the Kerbaughs from interfering with such exploration.

The Kerbaughs, in support of their argument for denial of injunctive relief, offered affidavits and testimony indicating the damages they had sustained as the result of prior seismic exploration; that the present seismic activity was causing damage to their grain crop, pasture, and other farmland; and that they fear additional damage to property from further seismic activity.

Whether or not the use of the surface estate by the mineral estate owner is reasonably necessary is a question of fact for the trier of facts. *Slope County Board of County Commissioners v. Consolidation Coal Co.*, 277 N.W.2d 124 (N.D. 1979); *Getty Oil Co. v. Jones,* above. In addition, the burden of proof in such a determination is upon the servient estate owner. *Getty Oil Co. v. Jones*, above.

The Kerbaughs presented evidence establishing the damage to their property that arose or was likely to arise as a result of seismic activity. They offered, however, no evidence of reasonable alternatives available to the oil companies to explore the properties. They offered no evidence that the same information could be obtained from the prior geophysical exploration; they offered no evidence that the same information could be obtained without transversing over cropland; and the record does not indicate that they offered evidence that the tests could be conducted in another manner which would cause less damage to the Kerbaughs. Although the Kerbaughs did offer evidence suggesting some damage could have been avoided by having the oil companies conduct the operations a few weeks later, the affidavits filed by the oil companies indicate this was not a reasonable alternative. On the basis of the evidence presented by the parties, the Kerbaughs failed to meet their burden of proof that the proposed activities of the oil companies were not reasonably necessary for the exploration of the leased mineral estate. Accordingly, the conclusion by the district court that the oil companies were entitled to injunctive relief was not in error.

It is important to note that the Texas Supreme Court in *Getty* concluded the accommodation doctrine is not a balancing type test weighing the harm or inconvenience to the owner of one type of interest against the benefit to the other. Rather the court said the test is the availability of alternative non-conflicting uses of the two types of owners. Inconvenience to the surface owner is not the controlling element where no reasonable alternatives are available to the mineral owner or lessee. The surface owner must show that under the circumstances, the use of the surface under attack is not reasonably necessary. *Getty Oil Co. v. Jones*, above, at 623.

We agree a pure balancing test is not involved under the accommodation doctrine where no reasonable alternatives are available. Where alternatives do exist, however, the concepts of due regard and reasonable necessity do require a weighing of the different alternatives against the inconveniences to the surface owner. Therefore, once alternatives are shown to exist a balancing of the mineral and surface owner's interest does occur.

* * *

The order of the district court is affirmed.

NOTES

1. *Reasonably necessary surface uses.* The *Kerbaugh* court sets forth the general rules about the relative rights of the surface landowner and the mineral lessee. The mineral lessee's rights are dominant to the extent that the lessee needs to use the surface for mining purposes, at least so long as the surface use is reasonably necessary. What is reasonably necessary in a given situation will depend greatly upon the facts. According to the court, the issue is one of fact, and thus is for resolution by the jury or other fact-finder. What is reasonably necessary in one case may not be necessary in another. The

standard, as we've seen in other settings, is a vague one—hardly more than a general idea rather than a clear standard.

2. *Accommodation: mineral lessees and the virtue of vagueness.* *Kerbaugh* has been a visible, influential ruling in oil and gas law, embracing and extending the accommodation doctrine prominently announced by the Texas Supreme Court in the *Getty Oil* case. The accommodation doctrine is plainly a variant or refinement of the "reasonably necessary" test that has long applied. What exactly are the elements of this new accommodation doctrine? When does it require a lessee to make changes in surface-use practices so as to avoid unnecessarily harming existing surface uses? As the court made clear, a lessee is not obligated to implement exceptional oil-production methods. It must only consider and, if feasible, adopt other "usual, customary and reasonable methods practiced in the industry on similar lands put to similar uses." A lessee must give only "due regard" for the rights of the surface owner. Note that the doctrine seems to apply only in the case of surface uses by the landowner that are pre-existing, not those that the surface owner begins later. Also important is the fact that the surface owner has the burden of showing that reasonable accommodation was possible.

A marked characteristic of the accommodation doctrine is its vagueness. Is this a defect in the rule, or might it be somewhat of a virtue? Vagueness affects both sides of a transaction, in that neither side knows where it stands, and both might be prone to compromise due to the uncertainty. Might the vagueness of the doctrine make it more effective in getting surface owners and mineral lessees to talk to one another; that is, can we think of it not as a substantive limit on the rights of miners but more as a process method of stimulating resource-users to try to get along and accommodate each other?

3. *Paying for surface damages.* The *Kerbaugh* court went out of its way, in a footnote, to consider whether state law ought to change to require mineral lessees to pay for the surface damage that they cause. The issue is a complex one, often (although not always) covered in the applicable mineral lease. In general, in recent decades, legislatures (and, less often, courts) have shown increasing willingness to compel lessees and other mineral rights holders to pay for surface damage. Statutes in several states protect agricultural and ranching activities from disruption by oil and gas activities. Surface damage does not include simply the rental value of using the surface; lessees can use the surface as a matter of right. Nor does the new liability rule give to surface owners any right to deny the surface use; the lessee can use the surface as of right. The sole duty is to pay for physical damage or in some other way to make amends.

4. *A hard-rock mining equivalent, and rights to use the subsurface.* The *Kerbaugh* court had no need to consider one important limit on the surface use rights of mineral owners, and that is the requirement that they use the surface only in connection with mineral activities taking place on that land. Mineral developers are not permitted to use the surface of one land tract to support activities taking place elsewhere unless that right has been expressly

reserved in the governing deed. Many of the same issues arise in the case of hardrock mining, having to do with both surface-land uses and uses of the subsurface. (For one federal lands example, see *United States v. Curtis-Nevada Mines, Inc.*, 611 F.2d 1277 (9th Cir. 1980), discussed in chapter 8, p. 701 (conflict between an alleged miner and recreationalists)). In what ways can a miner use the land surface, and what about subsurface shafts that cross under several land parcels? A further issue, more common in hardrock mining (although not unknown in oil and gas), relates to land subsidence. Can a miner engage in activities that cause subsidence as of right, and if so is the miner liable monetarily for the injury suffered by the surface owner?

The Illinois Supreme Court addressed such questions in *Jilek v. Chicago, Wilmington & Franklin Coal Co.*, 47 N.E.2d 96 (Ill. 1943). The case involved a deed that purported to convey in place "all the coal, oil, gas, and other minerals in or underlying" certain land. The deed specifically included:

> the rights to mine and remove all the coal and other minerals underlying said land without any liability for surface subsidence caused by mining out of the coal or other minerals and from not leaving pillars or artificial supports under said land and the further right to make underground passages or entries though, to and from other mines and lands adjacent thereto, and with the right to the perpetual use of the same for mining purposes. It is also covenanted and agreed that the grantee herein, his heirs and assigns shall have the right to take and use as much of the surface of the said land as may be deemed necessary [including land for] necessary roadways and railroad tracks . . .

The grantee under the deed, years later, sought to extract oil and gas from the land, and questions arose as to whether the granter under the deed had rights to use the surface and subsurface for that purpose. The question was particularly challenging because the deed language focused chiefly on coal mining. To answer the questions, the court reviewed the basics of mineral rights:

> There appears to be little doubt when the mineral estate is severed from the surface estate that with the mineral estate all means to attain it are also granted for the purpose of enjoying it. This is because it is presumed the grantor intended to convey, and the grantee expected to receive, the full benefit of the mineral estate, and therefore the grantor not only conveyed the thing specifically described, but all other rights and privileges necessary to the enjoyment of the thing granted. . . .

> It is said, however, by appellants, that the rule that the expression of a particular subject implies the exclusion of subjects not enumerated is applicable here, because the specific reservation in the conveyance granting the mineral interest of (a) the right of subsidence without damage; (b) the use of passage ways and entries to move coal from other land; and (c) the right to take surface land

for other mining purposes at a certain price, excludes any right to enter the mineral estate from the surface, which might otherwise be implied. If the rights reserved in the mineral deed were, in fact, opposed to the implied right to enter upon the land for the purpose of drilling and exploring for oil, there would be force to this suggestion. However, the rights just enumerated in the mineral deed are not ones which are implied by a grant of the mineral estate. The law requires the owner of the mineral estate to extract minerals without damaging the surface, and, unless there is a specific exemption of liability, the owner of the surface can recover for damages caused by sinking or subsidence caused by mining. *Wilms v. Jess*, 94 Ill. 464 (Ill. 1880); *Lloyd v. Catlin Coal Co.*, 71 N.E. 335 (Ill. 1904).

It requires no citation of authority to sustain the proposition that the surface of the land could not be covered with railway tracks, reservoirs, structures and manufacturing equipment upon the bare license to enter the mineral estate for the purpose of removing the mineral therefrom. These rights necessarily must be covered by an express contract or covenant or they will not exist, and are therefore rights in addition to the implied right to enter, and an extension thereof and not in opposition thereto. . . .

47 N.E.2d at 97, 100–01.

Jilek is particularly useful concerning the incidental rights acquired by a purchaser or lessee of mineral rights. Under Illinois law, a mineral lease includes automatically, along with the minerals, certain rights to use the surface and subsurface. Other rights are not conveyed, and the purchaser or lessee who desires them must negotiate for them and include them expressly in the appropriate documents of conveyance. The grantee in *Jilek* clearly understood Illinois law on the subject and made sure that the additional desired incidental rights (to cause subsidence, for instance) were expressly conveyed by the deed.

    5.   *Water needed for mining.* The conveyance or reservation of mineral interests implicitly includes not just rights to use the land surface and subsurface generally but also rights to use other particular resources on the land as reasonably needed to exploit the minerals. Mining companies that used timbers to support mining shafts could cut timber from the surface and use it, without the surface owner's permission or payment of damages. The same general rule applies to use of water that is accessible from the land surface and that the surface landowner has rights to use. The issue of water usage reached the Texas Supreme Court in *Sun Oil Company v. Whitaker*, 483 S.W.2d 808 (Tex. 1972). Sun Oil had extracted all the oil it could from the land involved using primary production methods. It then gained regulatory approval to inject 100,000 gallons of fresh water per day into the ground to maintain pressure and sustain oil production. The water withdrawals interfered with the surface owners' irrigated farming. The Court approached

the issue by surveying the general principles governing the powers of mineral owners:

> The oil and gas lessee's estate is the dominant estate and the lessee has an implied grant, absent an express provision for payment, of free use of such part and so much of the premises as is reasonably necessary to effectuate the purposes of the lease, having due regard for the rights of the owner of the surface estate. The rights implied from the grant are implied by law in all conveyances of the mineral estate and, absent an express limitation thereon, are not to be altered by evidence that the parties to a particular instrument of conveyance did not intend the legal consequences of the grant.

> The implied grant of reasonable use extends to and includes the right to use water from the leased premises in such amount as may be reasonably necessary to carry out the lessee's operations under the lease. . . .

> Courts have held water-flood projects to be reasonably necessary operations under oil and gas leases. As stated in *Holt v. Southwest Antioch Sand Unit*, 292 P.2d 998 (Okla. 1956) at page 1000:

>> It would be difficult to conceive of a use of the water more essentially a part of the operation of mining and removing the petroleum minerals from under said land.

> In *Carter Oil Co. v. Dees*, 92 N.E.2d 519 (Ill. App. 1950), though the lease was silent as to a gas re-pressuring method of secondary recovery, the Court held that the lessee in using reasonable diligence under the lease could adopt such method. Sun has an implied right to water-flood because the water-flood operation is reasonably necessary to carry out the purposes of the lease. The reasonableness of Sun's water-flood operation stands uncontradicted in this record. Its use of Ogallala water for injection was approved by the Railroad Commission. The stipulations are conclusive under this record that the use of Ogallala water was reasonably necessary to effectuate the purposes of the lease.

The majority's conclusion drew an extended dissent from four members of the court:

> . . . . I adhere to that portion of the majority opinion which restates the general rule that, unless otherwise provided by contractual provisions, an oil and gas lessee has an implied right or easement to make such use of underground water as may be reasonably necessary for ordinary and customary primary drilling and producing operations. However, I completely disagree with the majority's extension of this 'implied easement' doctrine so as to permit Sun also to take, consume and deplete an enormously greater quantity of water for a vastly different re-pressuring and secondary recovery process in the face of jury findings that the

parties to the lease did not contemplate or mutually intend such use; that it would materially affect the supply which the surface owner could produce by wells for irrigation of the surface; that such use was not reasonably necessary; and that it will substantially reduce the value of the surface for agricultural purposes.

The majority fails to consider the vital distinction between the occupancy and use of the surface, including water, for ordinary drilling and production operations which do not substantially consume, diminish or destroy the surface estate and the relatively new, extraordinary and far more extensive taking of fresh water for injection into oil sands in a manner which substantially destroys and diminishes the surface estate. Water flooding is not an ordinary primary production method; it is an extraordinary and extraneous medium usually employed after ordinary primary operations have terminated.

Sun Oil, cited above, 483 S.W.2d at 810–14.

TEXACO V. SHORT
United States Supreme Court
454 U.S. 516 (1982)

STEVENS, J.

In 1971 the Indiana Legislature enacted a statute providing that a severed mineral interest that is not used for a period of 20 years automatically lapses and reverts to the current surface owner of the property, unless the mineral owner files a statement of claim in the local county recorder's office. The Indiana Supreme Court rejected a challenge to the constitutionality of the statute. Ind., 406 N.E.2d 625 (Ind. 1980). We noted probable jurisdiction, 450 U.S. 993 and now affirm.

As the Indiana Supreme Court explained, the Mineral Lapse Act "puts an end to interests in coal, oil, gas or other minerals which have not been used for twenty years." The statute provides that the unused interest shall be "extinguished" and that its "ownership shall revert to the then owner of the interest out of which it was carved." The statute, which became effective on September 2, 1971, contained a 2-year grace period in which owners of mineral interests that were then unused and subject to lapse could preserve those interests by filing a claim in the recorder's office.

The "use" of a mineral interest that is sufficient to preclude its extinction includes the actual or attempted production of minerals, the payment of rents or royalties, and any payment of taxes; a mineral owner may also protect his interest by filing a statement of claim with the local recorder of deeds. The statute contains one exception to this general rule: if an owner of 10 or more interests in the same county files a statement of claim that inadvertently omits some of those interests, the omitted interests may be preserved by a supplemental filing made within 60 days of receiving actual notice of the lapse.

The statute does not require that any specific notice be given to a mineral owner prior to a statutory lapse of a mineral estate. The Act does set forth a procedure, however, by which a surface owner who has succeeded to the ownership of a mineral estate pursuant to the statute may give notice that the mineral interest has lapsed. . . .

At all stages of the proceedings, appellants [whose mineral rights lapsed under the statute] challenged the constitutionality of the Dormant Mineral Interests Act. Appellants claimed that the lack of prior notice of the lapse of their mineral rights deprived them of property without due process of law, that the statute effected a taking of private property for public use without just compensation, and that the exception contained in the Act for owners of 10 or more mineral interests denied them the equal protection of the law; appellants based these arguments on the Fourteenth Amendment of the United States Constitution. Appellants also contended that the statute constituted an impairment of contracts in violation of Art. 1, § 10, of the Constitution.[3] The state trial court held that the statute deprived appellants of property without due process of law, and effected a taking of property without just compensation.

On appeal, the Indiana Supreme Court reversed. The court first explained the purpose of the Mineral Lapse Act:

> "The Act reflects the legislative belief that the existence of a mineral interest about which there has been no display of activity or interest by the owners thereof for a period of twenty years or more is mischievous and contrary to the economic interests and welfare of the public. The existence of such stale and abandoned interests creates uncertainties in titles and constitutes an impediment to the development of the mineral interests that may be present and to the development of the surface rights as well. The Act removes this impediment by returning the severed mineral estate to the surface rights owner. There is a decided public interest to be served when this occurs. The extinguishment of such an interest makes the entire productive potential of the property again available for human use." Ind., 406 N.E.2d at 627.

The court rejected the argument that a lapse of a vested mineral interest could not occur without affording the mineral owner prior notice and an opportunity to be heard. The court noted that "[p]rior to any extinguishment the owner of an interest will have had notice by reason of

---

[3] "No State shall . . . pass any Bill of Attainder, ex post facto law, or Law impairing the Obligations of Contracts, or grant any Title of Nobility."

the enactment itself of the conditions which would give rise to an extinguishment and at a minimum a two-year opportunity to prevent those conditions from occurring by filing a statement of claim." The Indiana Supreme Court also rejected the argument that the statute effected a taking without just compensation. . . .

Appellants raise several specific challenges to the constitutionality of the Mineral Lapse Act. Before addressing these arguments, however, it is appropriate to consider whether the State has the power to provide that property rights of this character shall be extinguished if their owners do not take the affirmative action required by the State.

In *Board of Regents v. Roth*, 408 U.S. 564, 577 (1972), the Court stated:

> Property interests, of course, are not created by the Constitution. Rather, they are created and their dimensions are defined by existing rules or understandings that stem from an independent source such as state law—rules or understandings that secure certain benefits and that support claims of entitlement to those benefits.

The State of Indiana has defined a severed mineral estate as a "vested property interest," entitled to "the same protection as are fee simple titles." Through its Dormant Mineral Interests Act, however, the State has declared that this property interest is of less than absolute duration; retention is conditioned on the performance of at least one of the actions required by the Act. We have no doubt that, just as a State may create a property interest that is entitled to constitutional protection, the State has the power to condition the permanent retention of that property right on the performance of reasonable conditions that indicate a present intention to retain the interest.

From an early time, this Court has recognized that States have the power to permit unused or abandoned interests in property to revert to another after the passage of time. In *Hawkins v. Barney's Lessee*, 30 U.S. 457 (1831), the Court upheld a Kentucky statute that prevented a landowner from recovering property on which the defendant had resided for more than seven years under a claim of right. The Court stated:

> "Such laws have frequently passed in review before this Court; and occasions have occurred, in which they have been particularly noticed as laws not to be impeached on the ground of violating private right. What right has any one to complain, when a reasonable time has been given him, if he has not been vigilant in asserting his rights?"

Id., at 466.

Similarly, in *Wilson v. Iseminger*, 185 U.S. 55 (1902), the Court upheld a Pennsylvania statute that provided for the extinguishment of a reserved interest in ground rent if the owner collected no rent and made no demand for payment for a period of 21 years. Though the effect of the Pennsylvania statute was to extinguish a fee simple estate of permanent duration, the Court held that the legislation was valid.

In these early cases, the Court often emphasized that the statutory "extinguishment" properly could be viewed as the withdrawal of a remedy rather than the destruction of a right. We have subsequently made clear, however, that, when the practical consequences of extinguishing a right are identical to the consequences of eliminating a remedy, the constitutional analysis is the same. *El Paso v. Simmons*, 379 U.S. 497, 506–507 (1965). The extinguishment of the property owners' "remedy" in *Hawkins* and *Iseminger* placed them in precisely the same position as that held by the mineral owners in the instant cases after their interests had lapsed. . . .

These decisions clearly establish that the State of Indiana has the power to enact the kind of legislation at issue. In each case, the Court upheld the power of the State to condition the retention of a property right upon the performance of an act within a limited period of time. In each instance, as a result of the failure of the property owner to perform the statutory condition, an interest in fee was deemed as a matter of law to be abandoned and to lapse.

In ruling that private property may be deemed to be abandoned and to lapse upon the failure of its owner to take reasonable actions imposed by law, this Court has never required the State to compensate the owner for the consequences of his own neglect. We have concluded that the State may treat a mineral interest that has not been used for 20 years and for which no statement of claim has been filed as abandoned; it follows that, after abandonment, the former owner retains no interest for which he may claim compensation. It is the owner's failure to make any use of the property—and not the action of the State—that causes the lapse of the property right; there is no "taking" that requires compensation. The requirement that an owner of a property interest that has not been used for 20 years must come forward and file a current statement of claim is not itself a "taking." . . .

[The Court also rejected the appellants' claims that the state improperly impaired contracts, and that they were denied due process because they were not given personal advance notice that their mineral rights were about to lapse.]

NOTES

1.   *Cleaning-up land titles.* A grave practical problem arises when mineral rights in a parcel of land are fragmented among many owners, and it is difficult, if not impossible, for a potential purchaser or lessee to track down all the owners to negotiate a deal. The problem is most severe when mineral rights are severed from the land surface and separately owned by a person who does not use them. That person dies, perhaps forgetting about the mineral rights. Another generation comes along, and perhaps another after that, with mineral rights increasingly fragmented among heirs who may be entirely unaware of them. Mining companies often hire genealogists or private investigators to track down missing heirs, so that they can buy or lease mineral rights. The Indiana statute upheld in *Texaco v. Short* aimed to help with the problem. Many states have such statutes, with a wide variety of differences among them in terms of which mineral interests are covered and which actions are sufficient to sustain the interests.

2.   *Regulation or redefinition?* Notice that the Supreme Court chiefly treated the new statute as if it were a regulation of mineral rights. But could we not view it as simply a redefinition of the property rights that a person holds in minerals (as the court seems to do in parts of the opinion)? State law defines private rights in minerals, and such rights extend only so far as state law provides. Has not Indiana merely exercised its right to recalibrate the duration of private rights in minerals? Just as the state can redefine the rights a landowner has to use property and to protect against interferences, should it also be able to redefine the duration of private rights, making them less than perpetual?

C. OIL AND GAS PRODUCTION

Much of the field of oil and gas law has to do with the contractual relationships governing oil and gas production by lessees. It also has to do with the regulation (mostly by states) of oil drilling and production, undertaken for various purposes including, primarily, the promotion of economic efficiency and fairness among landowners. The following ruling introduces many key elements of this important body of regulatory law.

WRONSKI V. SUN OIL COMPANY
Michigan Court of Appeals
279 N.W.2d 564 (1979)

HOLBROOK, J.

Plaintiffs are the owners of 200 acres of land and the attendant mineral rights located in St. Clair County: Plaintiffs Koziara own two twenty-acre tracts (Tracts 1 & 2) and one forty-acre tract (Tract 6). Plaintiffs Wronski own an eighty-acre tract (Tract 7) and a forty-acre tract (Tract 13). These properties overlie the Columbus Section 3 Saline-

Niagaran Formation Pool, and Tracts 2, 6 and 7 have producing oil wells. Tracts 6 and 7 are under lease to defendant Sun Oil Company.

The Supervisor of Wells, Michigan Department of Natural Resources, pursuant to the authority granted him by 1939 P.A. 61, as amended, established twenty-acre drilling units for the Columbus 3 pool, and provided for a uniform well spacing pattern. The purpose of this order was to "prevent waste, protect correlative rights and provide for orderly development of the pool". The Supervisor, by a proration order effective February 1, 1970, further limited production in the Columbus 3 pool to a maximum of 75 barrels of oil per day per well. This order remained in effect until June 30, 1974, when Columbus 3 was unitized.

Defendant Sun Oil leases property from H. H. Winn (Tract 9) and from H. H. Winn, *et al.* (Tract 12). Sun Oil has drilled several wells on these tracts in compliance with the uniform well spacing pattern, including well 1–C on Tract 9 and wells 3 and 6 on Tract 12. These three wells were operating during the effective date of the proration order and were subject to its terms. Plaintiffs contend that Sun Oil illegally overproduced more than 180,000 barrels of oil from these three wells, and that the illegally overproduced oil was drained from beneath plaintiffs' lands. They sought rescission *ab initio* of their oil and gas leases with Sun Oil coupled with an accounting, or in the alternative both compensatory and exemplary damages.

After a bench trial the court found that Sun Oil had intentionally and illegally overproduced 150,000 barrels of oil, and that 50,000 barrels of this oil had been drained from plaintiffs' property. The court held that this overproduction and drainage constituted tortious breaches of Sun Oil's contractual obligations under the oil and gas leases entered into with plaintiffs, as well as violating plaintiffs' common-law rights to the oil beneath their property. . . .

The Court determines on the basis of all the testimony and evidence in this case and after considering the matters stated above, that it would be reasonable and proper to assess exemplary damages against Defendant Sun Oil Company in the amount of Fifty (50%) per cent of the compensatory damages previously awarded to the Plaintiffs. . . .

The trial court found that Sun Oil's actions were intentional tortious breaches of its contractual obligation to both plaintiffs under their respective oil and gas leases. It found breaches of the implied covenant to prevent drainage as well as a failure to comply with the orders of the Supervisor of Wells as required by the provisions of the lease. It also found that:

> Sun Oil Company has violated the common law rights of Plaintiffs Wronski and Koziara by illegally, unlawfully and secretly draining valuable oil from beneath their properties.

The nature of Sun Oil's violation, while not clearly stated by the trial court, was a claim for the conversion of oil.

"Conversion is any distinct act of dominion wrongfully exerted over another's personal property in denial of or inconsistent with his rights therein." *Thomas v. Tracy Motor Sales Inc.*, 104 N.W.2d 360, 362 (Mich. 1960), quoting *Nelson & Witt v. Texas Co.*, 239 N.W. 289 (Mich. 1931).

We only address the finding regarding conversion as it is dispositive of the questions in this appeal.

In Michigan we adhere to the ownership-in-place theory. *Attorney General v. Pere Marquette R. Co.*, 248 N.W. 860 (Mich. 1933). Under this theory "the nature of the interest of the landowner in oil and gas contained in his land is the same as his interest in solid minerals". Williams & Meyers, *Oil and Gas Law*, s 203.3, at 44. Solid minerals are a part of the land in or beneath which they are located, *Mark v. Bradford*, 23 N.W.2d 201 (Mich. 1946), and as a consequence the owner of land is also the owner of the oil and gas in or beneath it.

Oil and gas, unlike other minerals, do not remain constantly in place in the ground, but may migrate across property lines. Because of this migratory tendency the rule of capture evolved. This rule provides:

"The owner of a tract of land acquires title to the oil and gas which he produces from wells drilled thereon, though it may be proved that part of such oil or gas migrated from adjoining lands. Under this rule, absent some state regulation of drilling practices, a landowner . . . is not liable to adjacent landowners whose lands are drained as a result of such operations. . . . The remedy of the injured landowner under such circumstances has generally been said to be that of self-help "go and do likewise"." Williams & Meyers, above, § 204.4, at 55–57 (emphasis supplied.)

This rule of capture was a harsh rule that could work to deprive an owner of oil and gas underneath his land. To mitigate the harshness of this rule and to protect the landowners' property rights in the oil and gas beneath his land, the "fair share" principle emerged. As early as 1931, the Board of Directors of the American Petroleum Institute expressed this principle by declaring a policy: "that it endorses, and believes the petroleum industry endorses the principle that each owner of the surface is entitled only to his equitable and ratable share of the recoverable oil and gas energy in the common pool in the proportion which the recoverable reserves underlying his land bears to the recoverable reserves in the pool." Graham, *Fair Share or Fair Game? Great Principle, Good Technology But Pitfalls in Practice*, 8 Nat.Res.Law. 61, 64–65 (1975).

The API clarified the principle in 1942 by saying: "Within reasonable limits, each operator should have an opportunity equal to that afforded other operators to recover the equivalent of the amount of recoverable oil (and gas) underlying his property. The aim should be to prevent reasonably avoidable drainage of oil and gas across property lines that is not offset by counter drainage." Id. at 65.

This fair-share rule does not do away with the rule of capture, but rather acts to place limits on its proper application.

Texas has adopted both the ownership-in-place doctrine and the fair-share principle. Its courts have addressed the interrelationship between these two principles and the rule of capture.

It must be conceded that under the law of capture there is no liability for reasonable and legitimate drainage from the common pool. The landowner is privileged to sink as many wells as he desires upon his tract of land and extract therefrom and appropriate all the oil and gas that he may produce, so long as he operates within the spirit and purpose of conservation statutes and orders of the Railroad Commission. These laws and regulations are designed to afford each owner a reasonable opportunity to produce his proportionate part of the oil and gas from the entire pool and to prevent operating practices injurious to the common reservoir. In this manner, if all operators exercise the same degree of skill and diligence, each owner will recover in most instances his fair share of the oil and gas. This reasonable opportunity to produce his fair share of the oil and gas is the landowner's common law right under our theory of absolute ownership of the minerals in place. But from the very nature of this theory the right of each land holder is qualified, and is limited to legitimate operations.

Elliff v. Texon Drilling Co., 210 S.W.2d 558, 562 (Tex. 1948).

The rule of capture is thus modified to exclude operations that are in violation of valid conservation orders.

Michigan recognizes the fair-share principle and its subsequent modifications of the rule of capture. When an adjacent landowner drilled an oil well too close to a property line the Supreme Court said that this: "(D)eprived plaintiff of the opportunity of claiming and taking the oil that was rightfully hers; and defendants must respond in damages for such conversion." *Ross v. Damm*, 270 N.W. 722, 725 (Mich. 1936).

The Supervisor of Wells Act also incorporated the fair share principle into Section 13. This section concerns proration orders and states in part that:

> The rules, regulations, or orders of the supervisor shall, so far as it is practicable to do so, afford the owner of each property in a pool The opportunity to produce his just and equitable share of the oil and gas in the pool, being an amount, so far as can be practicably determined and obtained without waste, and without reducing the bottom hole pressure materially below the average for the pool, substantially in the proportion that the quantity of the recoverable oil and gas under such property bears to the total recoverable oil and gas in the pool, and for this purpose to use his just and equitable share of the reservoir energy.

M.C.L. § 319.13; M.S.A. § 13.139(13).

This right to have a reasonable opportunity to produce one's just and equitable share of oil in a pool is the common-law right that the trial court found Sun Oil violated. Under the authority of *Ross v. Damm*, above, if it can be said that Sun Oil's overproduction deprived plaintiffs of the opportunity to claim and take the oil under their respective properties, then Sun Oil will be liable for a conversion.

Production in the Columbus 3 field was restricted to 75 barrels of oil per well per day. Compulsory pooling was also in effect, limiting the number of oil wells to one per twenty acres, and specifying their location. The purpose behind proration is that the order itself, if obeyed, will protect landowners from drainage and allow each to produce their fair share. A violation of the proration order, especially a secret violation, allows the violator to take more than his fair share and leaves the other landowners unable to protect their rights unless they also violate the proration order. We therefore hold that any violation of a proration order constitutes conversion of oil from the pool, and subjects the violator to liability to all the owners of interests in the pool for conversion of the illegally-obtained oil. See *Bolton v. Coates*, 533 S.W.2d 914 (Tex. 1975), *Ortiz Oil Co. v. Geyer*, 159 S.W.2d 494 (Tex. 1942). . . .

The rule as to the amount of damages for a conversion of oil was established in Michigan in *Robinson v. Gordon Oil Co.*, 253 N.W. 218 (Mich. 1934). The Court stated:

> The general rule in the United States in actions for the conversion of oil, as in the case of conversion of minerals and other natural products of the soil is that, although a wilful trespasser is liable for the enhanced value of the oil at the time of conversion without deduction for expenses or for improvements by labor, an innocent trespasser is liable only for the value of the oil undisturbed; that is, he is entitled to set off the reasonable cost of production. (Citations omitted.)

Robinson, 253 N.W. at 219.

This rule sets the liability of the convertor as the enhanced value of the oil at the time of conversion, but then subdivides this liability into two subrules depending upon the nature of the conversion. These two subrules are a "mild" rule which applies to innocent or nonwilful conversion and a "harsh" rule which applies to bad faith or wilful conversions. [The court decided that the "harsh" rule was appropriate on the facts of this case. It also decided that, because of the application of the harsh rule, it was wrong for the trial court also to assess exemplary damages.]

NOTES

1. *Oil and gas production today.* *Wronski* offers a look at how oil production is managed today in larger fields with multiple overlying landowners. The Michigan court, as we see, drew heavily upon Texas jurisprudence, deferring to a state that has far more experience in the field and much more developed case law. The Michigan court relied upon the *Elliff* ruling, with which we started the chapter (p. 347), and its comments about the nature of a landowner's rights to oil and gas. Each owner, we are told (as in *Elliff*), has a property right to a reasonable opportunity to produce a just and equitable share of oil in a pool. Loosely speaking, that means each landowner owns a pro-rata share of the oil, but subject to the duty to make timely use of the opportunity to extract it. A landowner who sits back while others draw down the pool has no remedy.

The court referred to the main types of regulatory rules that limit what landowners can do (aside from technical rules about constructing wells, pipelines, and the like). The minimum land size for a well, we are told, is 20 acres. In fact, states typically offer variances to accommodate particular needs and offer ways for owners of smaller tracts to pool their lands to get up to the minimum required drilling-unit size. States impose set-back requirements, so that landowners do not put their wells too close to property lines, and impose additional requirements that wells be certain distances apart (well-spacing rules), although these rules often allow variances, particularly when a landowner otherwise risks having too much of his underlying oil and gas drained by a neighbor. To control the pace at which oil and gas is removed from a field, in part to sustain the underlying pressure, regulatory agencies often, as here, impose strict orders on how much oil can be produced in each well. These are termed proration orders. In *Wronski*, the state limited the various wells to 75 barrels per day. Sun Oil's overproduction of 150,000 barrels was thus hardly a slight error and plainly was done intentionally.

2. *Making fair shares specific.* Notice how the court viewed the proration orders in the dispute as much more than regulatory limits that, if violated, would subject a well owner to fines or other penalties. The proration order, the court remarked, gave specific meaning to the property rights of each landowner. When a proration order is in place, one landowner cannot

take out more oil than that without wrongfully converting property owned by other surface landowners. Presumably, had not the fair-share proration order been in effect, the plaintiffs would have had a much tougher job arguing that their fair share had been partially taken by Sun Oil.

3. *The duties of lessees.* This dispute is particularly intriguing because the wrong-doer in the case, Sun Oil, was the lessee of the plaintiffs and was properly extracting oil from the plaintiffs' land. Sun Oil's wrongdoing took place on other lands that it leased from other surface landowners. In their suit, the plaintiffs alleged three causes of action, two of them based on the contractual relationship between themselves and Sun Oil. The trial court saw merit in all three claims and sided with the plaintiffs on all of them. The appellate court ruled for the plaintiffs on the third claim and, having done so, did not bother to comment on the other two.

The first claim was simply a generalized claim that Sun Oil breached its lease agreements with the plaintiffs. No doubt this claim was more particularized, but the appellate court, seeing no need to address it, left out the details. The second claim was that Sun Oil, as lessee for the plaintiffs, breached its implied covenants in these leases to prevent drainage of oil from the plaintiff's lands. This covenant exists in all oil and gas leases by implication (that is, without being expressly included), unless the parties deliberately choose to exclude it. It is a wide-ranging covenant (promise) by the lessee to look after the lessor's oil and gas and take whatever steps might be needed to ensure that neighbors do not end up taking too much of it. Efforts to halt drainage can include installing an offset well and enrolling property in drilling units and unitization schemes, all to make sure that an owner is not losing out. The danger for the lessor, as here, is that the lessee is unlikely to take these steps to protect against drainage unless pressed to do so. If Sun Oil is operating all the wells in an area under various leases, it may make little difference to it whether oil is produced from one well on one tract rather than another well on another tract. Sun Oil may make the same amount of money from the production, and pay the same royalty. The danger is worsened if Sun Oil pays differing royalties under differing leases or otherwise has a financial incentive to produce from one well rather than another. We will see more about the duties of lessees in the next case.

The appellate court in *Wronski*, as noted, decided not to rule based on either of these contract-based theories. Instead, it proceeded directly to the property rights of the plaintiffs—the issue in the plaintiffs' third cause of action. The court expressed its holding plainly: "We therefore hold that any violation of a proration order constitutes conversion of oil from the pool, and subjects the violator to liability to all the owners of interests in the pool for conversion of the illegally-obtained oil." Put otherwise, an oil company that violates a proration order is wrongfully taking the personal property (oil) from neighboring lands and is obligated to pay for it at its full value.

Note that this ruling by the court was of vastly broader applicability than a ruling would have been if based on one of the first two causes of action. The first cause of action protected only landowners in essentially the same situation as the plaintiffs here—when the landowner's lessee was also the oil company engaging in unlawful overproduction. The second cause of action would likely protect more landowners, but it is more difficult to prove an unreasonable failure to prevent drainage. And in any event, that action also could be brought only against the plaintiff's lessee, which need not be the party engaged in overproduction. What landowners most need—and what the court gave them,—was the legal right to sue directly the oil company doing the overproduction, whether or not it was also the landowners' lessee. And they needed a right that was easily enforced. Here the proration order was set at 75 barrels per day. An oil company producing more than that is guilty of wrongfully taking property.

4.   *Calculating damages.* Finally, notice how the court handled the issue of damages. It did so in the way often used by courts when oil and gas is improperly taken: if the taking is innocent and in *good faith* (although still wrongful), the oil company engaged in overproduction is liable for the full value of the oil and gas wrongly taken after offsetting its production costs. An *intentional* wrongdoer, such as Sun Oil, has to pay the full wellhead value of the oil without any reduction for the expenses it incurred in producing it. And the dollar value is, of course, not at all a one-sixth royalty: it is the full value of the oil. For Sun Oil this was an expensive mistake, expensive enough for the court to decide that punitive damages did not need to be added.

5.   *Another approach to fair share.* Mining scientists and engineers are increasingly able to estimate the exact amount of oil and gas in a pool, thus making it possible to allocate fair shares among landowners in terms of overall quantities of oil and gas, not merely daily rates of extraction. This knowledge raises the possibility of a further legal step away from the rule of capture. Why not define landowner rights in terms of specific quantities of oil and gas in the ground, leaving landowners then free to extract the resources when and as they want, without worry that they will lose their reasonable opportunity to extract it by waiting too long. An owner who did not want to extract could sell her rights to someone else in a one-time transaction and not worry about the complications of leasing, royalty monitoring, and so on.

A precedent for this kind of fair-share allocation is offered by certain fisheries in which the individual fishers hold individual transferable quotas (ITQs), a form of private property rights. A fisher with a harvest quote can exercise an ITQ or trade it to other fishers. Similar arrangements sometimes exist within irrigation districts run by irrigators. The water rights of the individual irrigators who are members of the district are often defined by specific quantities that the holders can either exercise or lease to other irrigators who seek more water. One of the benefits of such systems is that they can make more efficient use of the tools and equipment used in the resource harvesting. If an oil well needs to be shut down for some reason, a landowner with a transferable right can lease it to another pumper until the well is back in operation.

DANNE V. TEXACO EXPLORATION AND PRODUCTION
Oklahoma Court of Appeals
883 P.2d 210 (1994)

BOUDREAU, P.J.

Herbert J. Danne, Richard Danne, Arthur Danne, Florence Wetting, Eloise M. Flint, and William F. Lohmeyer Living Trust, Plaintiffs (lessors), brought this action to cancel oil and gas leases in section 35–17N–8W, Kingfisher County, Oklahoma, leased to Texaco, Inc., Defendant (lessee). Texaco appeals a trial court judgment in favor of all lessors terminating the leases for failure to produce in paying quantities and for failure to exercise due diligence to market the product. Four questions are presented on appeal: (1) whether a lease can expire automatically, according to its own terms, in the secondary lease term; (2) whether a lease can expire automatically for failure to pay shut-in royalties in a timely fashion; (3) whether the acceptance of shut-in royalty and royalty payments estops a lessor from asserting that a lease is terminated; and (4) whether a lessee violates the implied covenant to market by failing to produce gas for over four years from a well that is capable of production.

Factual History

[The case chiefly involved three leases, all of which pertained to a single drilling and spacing unit—which meant that a single well produced gas on behalf of all of the landowner-lessors. A producing gas well was opened, and the three leases covering it were all extended beyond their primary terms into the secondary terms as production continued. For over four years, however, the lessee (Texaco) halted production, and then resumed.

[The leases contained a shut-in royalty clause, under which Texaco had to make annual royalty payments to keep the leases from terminating. Texaco tendered the royalties only at the end of the four-year period. Lessor Danne refused the payments; lessors Lohmeyer and Flint accepted them. When product resumed, Danne refused production royalty payments while Lohmeyer and Flint accepted them. All three lessors then sought to cancel the lease due to the four-year gap in production. Danne argued that the leases terminated automatically due to the cessation. Lohmeyer and Flint argued the same, and also claimed that the acceptance of payments did not revive the leases. The court began its analysis by asking whether the leases ended automatically due to the halt in production, or whether instead the lessors had to take affirmative action to terminate the leases—a distinction that will be familiar to students of the law of estates in land and future interests.]

Automatic Termination of a Lease
for Failure to Satisfy the Habendum Clause

Lessors assert, and the trial court agreed, that Texaco's lease terminated automatically, according to the terms of its habendum clause [the lease clause defining the lessee's interest—eds.], for failure to produce gas in paying quantities. The question of automatic lease termination is significant in this action; if automatic termination can occur, no action of the lessors (even acceptance of royalty benefits) will have the effect of maintaining the lease in full force and effect. Since the facts relating to the terms of these leases are stipulated, the issue presented is one of law. . . .

We first consider the habendum clauses in the Danne, Lohmeyer, and Flint leases. Each states: "It is agreed that this lease shall remain in force for a period of ___ years from date (herein called primary term) and *as long thereafter* as oil or gas, or either of them, is produced from said land by the lessee" (Emphasis added). In Oklahoma, "[t]he term 'produced,' when used in a 'thereafter' provision of the habendum clause, denotes in law production in paying quantities." *Stewart v. Amerada Hess Corp.,* 604 P.2d 854, 857 (Okla. 1979). *See also Pack v. Santa Fe Minerals, A Div. of Santa Fe Int'l Corp.,* 869 P.2d 323, 326 (Okla. 1994) (a typical habendum clause which extends the lease past its primary term as long as oil or gas is produced is interpreted to mean "produced in paying quantities").

Most jurisdictions view habendum clauses using a "thereafter" provision as "conveying an interest subject to a special limitation rather than as conveying an interest subject to a condition, power of termination or right of re-entry." 3 Howard R. Williams, *Oil and Gas Law* § 604 (1991). In these jurisdictions, the habendum clause may be likened to a determinable estate, which automatically ends upon the happening of a condition, with no action required by the grantor. Oklahoma does not, however, take the view that habendum clauses are special limitations; rather, Oklahoma views the habendum clause as an estate on condition subsequent creating only a right of entry in the grantor. With such an estate, the grantor must bring an action to cause forfeiture of the estate. For example, in *Stewart,* the court held that "[t]he occurrence of the limiting event or condition *does not automatically effect an end to the right."* *Stewart,* 604 P.2d at 858 (emphasis added). The court further commented that:

> Our law is firmly settled that the result in each case [with regard to cessation of production] must depend upon the circumstances that surround cessation. Our view is no doubt influenced in part by the strong policy of our statutory law against forfeiture of estates. The terms of 23 O.S.1971 § 2 clearly

mandate that courts avoid the effect of forfeiture by giving due consideration to compelling equitable circumstances.

Id. This view was confirmed in a recent decision where mineral owners brought an action to cancel a lease for failure to produce in paying quantities during a temporary shut in of gas. The court held that "under *no* circumstances will cessation of production in paying quantities *ipso facto* deprive the lessee of his extended-term estate." *Pack,* 869 P.2d at 327 (quoting *Stewart,* 604 P.2d at 858) (emphasis original).

The view of the Supreme Court in *Pack* is fully consistent with previous Oklahoma law regarding habendum clauses, but may appear confusing because Oklahoma has also recognized automatic termination of oil and gas leases in some circumstances. However, an examination of the cases indicates that, for the purposes of lease termination, Oklahoma makes a distinction between clauses of the primary term and clauses of the secondary term of the lease *See Duer v. Hoover & Bracken Energies, Inc.,* 753 P.2d 395, 398 (Okla. Ct. App. 1986). . . .

In the primary term, before hydrocarbons are discovered, the lessee has the right to explore for a fixed period of time. If he fails to discover hydrocarbons within the enumerated period, he must either buy more time (through payment of something like a delay rental) or lose the lease when the term has expired. When the time runs out on the primary term, the estate is not forfeited, it simply ceases to exist by its own terms, a simple terminable estate. Automatic termination of the lease at this stage of exploration does not divest the lessee of valuable assets, since no assets have yet been proved. *See Duer,* 753 P.2d at 398; *Petroleum Eng'rs,* 350 P.2d at 604; *Ellison,* 244 P.2d at 835.

Occurrences of limiting conditions in the secondary lease term are treated differently. The habendum clause enumerates the conditions of continuation of the lease from the primary fixed term into a secondary term of indefinite duration. It directs continuation of the lease so long as production is maintained for the mutual benefit of the lessee and lessor. No automatic termination of the lessee's estate can be tolerated at this stage in the life of the lease, because the lessee has proved a valuable asset and has established a right to develop that asset. The interest the lessee has, after drilling and proving hydrocarbons, can be likened to a vested estate, the loss of which can only be effected through an action for forfeiture. Consequently, at law, the lessee in the secondary term must be given a reasonable opportunity to develop the asset without unreasonable fear of forfeiture.

Therefore, in the case at bar, since production from the Helen Danne No. 1 well has moved the lease into its secondary term, we hold that Texaco's lease cannot be terminated automatically.

II

Automatic Termination of Lease for Failure to Make Timely Payment of Shut-in Royalties

Texaco tendered shut-in royalties to lessors Lohmeyer and Flint four years after the Helen Danne No. 1 well was shut in. The terms of their leases require that shut-in royalties be paid annually to the lessors when a producing well is shut in. . . . By tendering payments four years after the well was shut in, Texaco failed to make timely payment of the shut-in royalties as directed by the terms of the lease. Lessors cite a recent Oklahoma Court of Appeals, Division 3, case as a similar fact situation where the court of appeals affirmed a trial court grant of judgment, in part, on the grounds that "the lease expired under its own terms for failure to pay shut-in royalties in the manner provided by the lease." *Christian v. Texaco,* Appeal No. 79,590 (Okla. Ct. App., June 22, 1993, unpublished opinion). To the extent that lessors rely on *Christian* for the proposition that failure to pay shut-in royalties results in automatic lease termination, we believe they are misguided. Unless a lease clearly provides for forfeiture of the lessee's estate upon failure to make timely payment, the lessor's grounds for relief lay only in contract law. [citations omitted] Similarly, in a case where a lessee failed to pay shut-in royalties promptly the court held that "failure to pay shut-in royalties in and of itself does not operate to cause a termination of the lease." *Pack,* 869 P.2d at 330. We therefore hold that Texaco's failure to timely tender shut-in royalties does not cause automatic forfeiture of Texaco's lease, because the Lohmeyer and Flint leases do not expressly state that such forfeiture is mandated.

III

Estoppel by Acceptance of Benefits

It has been held in Oklahoma that acceptance of royalties does not estop the lessor from asserting lease cancellation, if the lease has already automatically expired, by its own terms, prior to acceptance of royalties. *Woodruff v. Brady,* 72 P.2d 709, 711–12 (Okla. 1937). "[I]f a lessee should continue to make royalty payments to the lessor after the lease has terminated according to its own terms, the receipt of such payments will not work an estoppel against the lessor, and such lessor may nevertheless assert that the lease has terminated." 3 E. Kuntz, *Oil and Gas* § 43.2 (1989).

When a lease does not expire automatically, however, the lessor's acceptance of benefits may estop the lessor from asserting lease termination. Even in a case where an express covenant to drill wells was breached by the lessee, the lessor has been estopped from asserting termination of the lease on grounds of acceptance of royalties from lessee. *Anderson v. Talley,* 187 P.2d 206 (Okla. 1947). The court ruled that "[b]y the receipt of the [royalty] payments, the lessor clearly and definitely recognized the existence of the lease long after the breach. We conclude the lessor waived the breach of the lease which the lessees had committed and that plaintiff is not entitled to cancellation of the lease therefor." *Id.* 187 P.2d at 208.

Similarly, the court has held that it is "[a] long recognized rule . . . that acquiescence in a lease and acceptance of royalty constitutes waiver of any objection the lessor could have taken regarding alteration and estops the lessor from denying the lessee's title." [citations omitted]

It is undisputed that Texaco tendered and lessors, Lohmeyer and Flint, accepted shut-in royalties dated June 3, 1991 (for the period April 14, 1989, to April 13, 1992) and also accepted shut-in royalties dated February 21, 1992 (for annual shut-in royalties dated April 18, 1992). Lohmeyer and Flint also accepted monthly production royalty checks from Texaco from February 24, 1992, to January 23, 1993. Since these leases were held by production in the secondary term, these leases could not expire automatically by their terms; rather, they could only terminate through an action against Texaco. However, before bringing such action, Lohmeyer and Flint accepted the benefits of shut-in royalties tendered expressly for the purpose of continuing the lease in the absence of production. Lohmeyer and Flint also accepted production royalties both before and after this law suit was filed. We find that the conduct of Lohmeyer and Flint affirmed the existence of their leases with Texaco and that they are now estopped from denying Texaco's claim of title. We, therefore, reverse the trial court's grant of lease cancellation to Lohmeyer and Flint.

IV

Termination of the Lease for Failure to Produce in
Paying Quantities and Breach of Implied Covenant to Market

Since lessor Danne did not accept benefits in the form of royalties from Texaco after the Helen Danne No. 1 well was shut-in, Danne is not estopped from asserting cancellation of the lease for failure to produce in paying quantities or for failure to exercise due diligence to market the product. It is, therefore, necessary to further consider these issues.

Though we have held that a lease cannot terminate automatically in the secondary term of the lease, this holding should not be construed to imply that failure to satisfy the terms of the habendum clause can never result in forfeiture of the lease. Rather, such forfeiture can result if an action is brought and it is demonstrated that the lessee either failed to produce in paying quantities or failed to market the product with due diligence in breach of the implied covenant to market the product.

In the case at bar, lessors contend that the Helen Danne No. 1 well's capability of producing in paying quantities cannot satisfy the terms of a "thereafter" habendum clause. This issue has been previously considered in Oklahoma in a case where a discovery was made in the primary term of the lease, but a market had not yet been found for the product before expiration of the primary term. *McVicker v. Horn, Robinson & Nathan,* 322 P.2d 410 (Okla. 1958). The court in *McVicker* held that with the exercise of due diligence, capability to produce could hold the lease into the secondary term within the meaning of production in the habendum clause. *Id.* The court, however, limited this holding by stating that "[o]il and gas lessees should not be allowed to hold their leases indefinitely, while no product therefrom is being marketed and diligent efforts are not being made to accomplish this." *Id.* at 416. . . .

Most persuasively, in a fact situation nearly identical to the case at bar, where the lessors attempted a lease cancellation because a well that was capable of production had been shut in, the supreme court clarified that capability of production satisfies the terms of the habendum clause. *James Energy Co. v. HCG Energy Corp.,* 847 P.2d 333, 339 (Okla. 1992). The plaintiffs admitted that the well was capable of producing in paying quantities. Therefore, the court held that the leases were held by production and did not expire by their own terms. *Id.* We, therefore, hold that a well that is capable of production in the secondary term of the lease can satisfy the requirement of "production" in a "thereafter" habendum clause, subject to satisfaction of other covenants in the lease.

Capability of production alone, however, without a significant attempt to market the product, will not suffice to hold the lease because there is a covenant to market the product with due diligence implied in each oil and gas lease. *See Pack,* 869 P.2d at 330 ("typical oil and gas leases contain an implied covenant to market oil and gas from the subject wells"). The efforts to secure a market for production must be assessed according to the facts and circumstances of each case. *See Flag Oil Corp. of Delaware v. King Resources Co.,* 494 P.2d 322, 325 (Okla. 1972) ("[I]n the absence of . . . an express requirement [to market the product], the lessee's duty to market is based on an implied covenant. . . . [T]he diligence of the lessee's efforts, and the reasonable probability of their [*sic*] success, are factors to be taken into consideration in determining what constitutes a 'reasonable time' under this rule.") An action for lease cancellation, brought for failure to market the product with due diligence, is an action of equitable cognizance, and we will affirm the judgment of the trial court unless it is clearly against the weight of the evidence. *Barby v. Singer,* 648 P.2d 14, 17 (Okla. 1982).

Texaco operates a well that is capable of production, but was shut in for over four years. Texaco asserts that the well was shut in by mistake, but acknowledges that during the first two years of shut in, Phillips had a gas meter at the well and could have taken the gas at spot-market prices. Under these facts and circumstances, the trial court took the view that Texaco failed to exercise due diligence to market the product to a readily-available gas purchaser. The trial court's view is neither inconsistent with the facts presented, nor unsupported by previous decisions.

. . . Absent any clear evidence undermining the trial court's view that Texaco lacked sufficient cause to justify the shut in, and absent circumstances estopping the claim of lease cancellation (such as affect lessors Lohmeyer and Flint), the trial court's view that this lease is terminated for failure to market the product with due diligence must be upheld. We therefore affirm the trial court's grant of lease cancellation to lessor Danne.

Conclusion

In summary, we hold that a lease cannot terminate automatically for lessee's failure to produce in paying quantities within the meaning of the habendum clause or to make timely payment of shut-in royalties. In the secondary term of the lease, when the lease is capable of production, an action for lease termination must be brought in order to cause forfeiture of the lessee's estate. Because Lohmeyer and Flint accepted benefits from Texaco before bringing such action, they are now estopped from denying Texaco's title. We, therefore, reverse the trial court's grant of lease termination to Lohmeyer and Flint. Danne, however, has accepted no benefits from Texaco since bringing this action and is thus not estopped from denying Texaco's title.

Though we hold that, in the secondary term, a well that is capable of production can hold the lease within the meaning of the habendum clause, we find that the weight of evidence supports the trial court's holding that Texaco failed to act with due diligence to market the product. We therefore affirm the trial court's grant of lease cancellation to Danne on grounds that Texaco forfeited the lease for breach of the implied covenant to market.

NOTES

1.   *Oil and gas leases.* The *Danne* decision provides a good overview of the various lease provisions commonly used in the oil and gas industry to specify the duration of private rights. It may prove useful to identify all of them, and then go through the list with the following question in mind: Which provisions are included to protect or promote the interests of the landowner, and which are included instead to protect or aid the lessee-producer? Is the ultimate effect, considering all the provisions, a fair balance between the two parties or does the law (as one might guess) unduly favor oil companies over landowners?

The particular rules of law set forth in *Danne* invite questions. As the court explained, the typical oil and gas lease extends for a particular number of years (5 or 10, but with considerable variation), known as the primary term. If either oil or gas is found and a well capable of production is installed by the end of this primary period, the lease does not automatically end. Instead, it continues in duration as long as oil and gas is "produced" in paying quantities. (More on that below.) If production ceases, the lease either automatically ends (the dominant rule), or the lessor has the legal power to go to court to seek an order of termination (the Oklahoma and minority rule). Under many leases, a lessee who fails to produce can keep a lease going by paying set dollar amounts per year as shut-in royalties. Texaco had the legal right to do that but seems to have forgotten to send in the checks.

Before turning to further implied provisions in standard leases, it is useful to consider Oklahoma law on the duration of leases. If a lessee does not produce by the end of the primary term, the lease automatically ends, the court tells us. But if production stops during the secondary term, it does *not* end automatically; the landowner must take legal action. We might wonder what explains the difference. Here, Texaco failed not only to produce gas for four years but to make timely payments. One likely explanation for this difference is that a primary term typically ends because the lessee has done nothing, not even try a test well. The lessee then only loses the up-front bonus paid for the lease (often taken on speculation) and any delay rentals that might have been paid during the primary term.

But in the secondary term the lessee is likely to have drilled a well and spent considerable money developing it. There is much more to lose, and a court might rightly say the lessee needs to have time to correct mistakes. As for that, notice what the court says about accepting late payments from a lessee; the landowner/lessor who does so is thereafter estopped to complain about what the lessee has done. This is true, apparently, even if the lessor is unaware of the legal consequences of accepting a check sent through the mail. (On this issue, compare *Freeman v. Magnolia Petroleum Co.*, 171 S.W.2d 339 (Tex. 1943) (failure to pay shut-in royalty on time results in automatic termination of lease).)

2. *What is production?* A critical issue in many leases that link lease continuance to production has to do with the definition of production. As this case highlights, the definition is not always obvious. Here, the ability to produce oil or gas, matched with marketing efforts, is enough. Nearly all states take the view that production must be in "paying quantities" in order to qualify. A leading court defined this phrase as follows:

> The term "paying quantities" involves not only the amount of production, but also the ability to market the product (gas) at a profit. Whether there is a reasonable basis for the expectation of profitable returns from the well is the test. If the quantity be sufficient to warrant the use of the gas in the market, and the income therefrom is in excess of the actual marketing cost, and

operating costs, the production satisfies the term "in paying quantities."

Clifton v. Koontz, 325 S.W.2d 684 (Tex. 1959). When deciding profit for this purpose, the calculation looks only at marginal costs. The initial costs of drilling and equipping the well are not considered, since these are sunk costs that do not affect decisions about whether to continue production. Complications arise as to overriding royalties (sometimes included in expenses, sometimes not) and as to the cost of plugging wells and other "clean up" expenses. A further issue that has nagged courts has to do with depreciation on well equipment. The tendency is to exclude depreciation on original drilling costs but to include depreciation on production-related equipment that diminishes in value through continued use. See e.g., *Stewart v. Amerada Hess Corp.,* 604 P.2d 854 (Okla. 1979).

3. *The duty to market, and marketing in lieu of production.* As the court explained, the standard oil and gas lease includes not just a duty to develop (and, may include, even earlier a duty to drill a test well) and the duty to prevent drainage (discussed in the last case) but also a duty (that is, a covenant or a promise by the lessee) to exercise due diligence in marketing. The court did not really explain what this duty entailed. How much effort is needed to qualify as due diligence? Here, it appeared that Texaco's well was connected to a pipeline, and the company could have sold its product at any time on the "spot" market (that is, receiving whatever the daily price is, instead of a price established by a longer-term contract). Lack of production for four years, particularly given the lessee's ready ability to sell on the spot market for much of the time, was adequate evidence to support the trial court's finding of lack of due diligence.

Perhaps the biggest surprise in this opinion was the court's conclusion that a gas well produces gas in paying quantities, even when shut in, so long as the lessee is making reasonable efforts to find someone to buy the gas. (On this issue, it helps to know that above-ground storage of gas is costly and dangerous. Gas is therefore usually not produced from a well unless a buyer is willing to take the gas immediately.) A landowner waiting for royalty checks might well be surprised and dismayed to hear this! What policy considerations might explain this rule? Note that the rule operates in tandem with the covenant, implied in all leases, that the lessee must make reasonable efforts to market the gas. The effect of the two provisions is to retain a use-it-or-lose it element in the lease (the lessee must either produce or actively market), while at the same time acknowledging that production might sometimes halt due to the lack of a buyer.

4. *A hardrock mining analogy.* In *Vulcan Materials Co. v. Holzhauer,* 599 N.E.2d 449 (Ill. App. 1992), a lease covering a rock quarry obligated the lessee to "proceed to mine and quarry the sand, gravel, and/or limestone there contained in a good and economical manner so as to take out the greatest amount of sand, gravel or limestone . . . Lessee shall work and mine said premises as aforesaid as steadily and continuously as the market . . . and

the weather will permit." The lease called for royalty payments based on the tonnage and selling prices of substances removed and also provided for minimum royalties of $5,000 per quarter. If the lessee "abandoned" the premises for one year, the lessor could cancel the lease. After mining the site for several years, the lessee ceased mining for ten years, while paying the minimum royalty. At that point, the lessee announced a plan to resume mining. The lessor promptly canceled the lease on abandonment grounds, but then accepted a further check for the minimum royalty. The Illinois Court of Appeals ruled that acceptance of the royalties over the ten-year period had no effect on the lessor's rights. The lessor, however, waived his right to cancel the lease when he accepted a further royalty payment after sending notice of termination.

KIDD V. JARVIS DRILLING, INC.

Tennessee Court of Appeals
2006 WL 344755 (2006)

KOCH, J.

This appeal arises from a dispute between an oil drilling company and a group of Scott County property owners regarding the company's plans to recover oil from the currently non-producing West Oneida Field. After the Tennessee Oil and Gas Board approved the company's unitization and secondary recovery plans, the property owners filed a petition in the Chancery Court for Davidson County seeking judicial review of the Board's decision. . . .

I.

The West Oneida Field, located on the Fort Payne reservoir in Northeast Tennessee, was discovered in 1943. The first oil well was drilled in September 1969, and in 1979, the peak oil rate reached 1,720 barrels per day. By 1974, there were 51 producing oil wells and 13 natural gas wells on the field. By 1997, the number of oil wells had increased to 62, and the number of natural gas wells to 15. A majority of the producing wells were operated by Jarvis Drilling, Inc. (Jarvis Drilling), a Kentucky corporation that had possessed an ownership interest in the field since 1977.

By December 1996, the West Oneida Field had produced 1,452,355 barrels of oil or 12.9% of the estimated amount of oil originally in the field. However, production had fallen off significantly because of the release over the years of the natural gas that had provided the energy needed to extract the oil. Jarvis Drilling retained experts to assess the amount of oil remaining in the field and to recommend economically feasible alternatives for extracting the remaining oil. In December 1997, these experts reported that another 1,493,000 barrels of oil could be recovered from the West Oneida Field over twenty years using an enhanced secondary recovery process. The process recommended by the experts entailed injecting natural gas back into the field to increase the pressure in the reservoir. The experts anticipated that the re-pressurization of the field would drive the remaining oil to the downdip oil wells.

Accordingly, Jarvis Drilling set about to devise a financially viable secondary recovery plan to extract more oil from the West Oneida Field. Its plan had two key components. The first component was the unitization of the West Oneida Field.[4] The second component was the use of the field to store natural gas owned by others for a fee. This natural gas, referred to as "working gas," would aid in the re-pressurization of the field and would be an additional source of income that would make the secondary recovery plan financially viable.

In April 2001, Jarvis Drilling filed a petition with the Tennessee Oil and Gas Board (Board) seeking the unitization of the West Oneida Field in accordance with Tenn. Comp. R. & Regs. 1040–5–1–.01 (1999). Jarvis Drilling also sought the Board's approval of its "pressure maintenance and secondary recovery project" under Tenn. Comp. R. & Regs. 1040–4–9–.03 (1999). . . .

The Board notified all affected persons of Jarvis Drilling's petition and of a contested case hearing set for June 10, 2002. This hearing was held in Nashville and was attended by representatives of Jarvis Drilling and several property owners and their lawyer who objected to the unitization plan. Jarvis Drilling presented a great deal of evidence regarding the technical details of its secondary recovery plan. It also presented evidence that 95.45% of the persons affected by its proposal had approved its secondary recovery project. The dissenting property owners, in turn, voiced their objections to unitization and gas storage. These objections were based on the property owners' belief that the proposed unitization plan did not compensate them adequately for their interests and that the plan, if implemented, would prevent them from obtaining natural gas from the field for personal use. On November 12, 2002, the Board filed a final order approving the unitization plan as well as the pressure maintenance and secondary recovery project. . . .

II.

. . . . The Board has promulgated rules defining the conditions that must be met before it will exercise its power under Tenn.Code Ann. § 60–1–202(a)(4)(M) to force unitization of a field. Unitization may be required

---

[4] Unitization is an industry term for operating multiple tracts of land as a single tract for the purpose of producing oil or gas. Tenn. Comp. R. & Regs. 1040–1–1–.01 (1999) defines a "pooled unit" as "two or more tracts of land, of which their ownership may be different, that are consolidated and operated as a single tract for production of oil and/or gas, either by voluntary agreement between the owners thereof, or by exercising of the authority of the Board under the statute."

only after the Board has determined that unitization (1) is necessary to conserve the State's natural resources, (2) will prevent waste of oil and gas and the drilling of unnecessary wells, (3) will appreciably increase the ultimate recovery of oil and gas from the affected pool, (4) is economically feasible, and (5) will protect the correlative rights of both landowners and owners of mineral rights. Tenn. Comp. R. & Regs. 1040–5–1–.01(1)(a) (1999). The Board must also see to it that the proposed unitization plan assures that the owners of the separate tracts receive their just and equitable share of the recoverable oil or gas in the unit, Tenn. Comp. R. & Regs. 1040–5–1–.01(1)(b), and that the cost of production is proportionately allocated among the separately owned tracts. Tenn. Comp. R. & Regs. 0140–5–1–.01(1)(d).

Projects involving subterranean natural gas storage must be approved by the Board following a public hearing. Tenn. Comp. R. & Regs. 1040–4–8–.01 (1999). The rules regarding subterranean natural gas storage differentiate between reservoirs "capable of producing oil and gas in paying quantities" and reservoirs that cannot. With regard to reservoirs that are capable of producing oil and gas in paying quantities, the rule provides that the Board may not approve a subterranean gas storage project unless "all owners in such underground reservoir shall have agreed thereto in writing." Tenn. Comp. R. & Regs. 1040–4–8–.01(1),–01(2). . . .

III.

. . . The property owners insist that the Board lacks authority to force unitization for the purpose of subterranean natural gas storage for two reasons. First, they argue that the Board's enabling statutes do not expressly empower the Board to require unit operations for subterranean natural gas storage. Second, they assert that, even if the Board has the authority to approve unit operations for natural gas storage, its regulations do not permit subterranean gas storage without the unanimous written approval of all owners in interest. The property owners are mistaken on both counts. . . .

B.

The Board has unquestioned statutory authority to approve and regulate secondary recovery projects. Tenn. Code Ann. § 60–1–202(a)(4)(K). While neither the statutes nor the Board's rules define "secondary recovery project," the term is commonly used in the industry to refer to the enhanced methods used to recover additional oil or to prolong the production of oil in fields where the primary production has run its course. The purpose of a secondary recovery project is to restore the pressure in the reservoir by mechanisms such as gas reinjection.

One of the Board's obligations is to prevent the waste of Tennessee's non-renewable oil and natural gas resources. Secondary recovery projects prevent waste by prolonging the economic life of older oil fields and by increasing the quantity of oil ultimately recovered from the reservoir. In a similar manner, unit operations also prevent waste by increasing the amount of oil produced in a particular field.

The Board's rules explicitly envision that field unitization may be a part of a secondary recovery project. Tenn. Comp. R. & Regs. 1040–4–9–.04 states that a unitization plan must be approved before approving a secondary recovery project when the common source of supply is not limited to a single lease. Thus, the Board's statutes and rules clearly permit the Board to impose unitization on an oil field for the purpose of operating a secondary recovery project.

The property owners assert that even if the Board has the power to approve forced unitization as part of the secondary recovery project, it does not have the power to permit the unit operator to engage in the subterranean gas storage business as part of the operation of a secondary recovery project. The enabling statutes and the rules do not support this argument.

Restoring the pressure in an oil field is accomplished by injecting natural gas back into the field. The unit operator may obtain the required natural gas in one of two ways. It may purchase the natural gas, or it may charge others to store their natural gas in the oil field. The net effect is the same whether the operator buys the natural gas or charges others to store the gas—the field is re-pressurized, and additional oil that would not otherwise be recovered is produced. Accordingly, the Board's broad statutory authority to regulate secondary recovery projects includes the authority to authorize subterranean gas storage as part of a secondary recovery project.

C.

Using a reservoir for subterranean gas storage may be part of a secondary recovery project. However, if the operator of a secondary recovery project intends to include subterranean gas storage as part of the secondary recovery project, then the operator must also comply with the Board's requirements for subterranean gas storage. The property owners insist that Jarvis Drilling cannot comply with these requirements because all the affected owners have not consented to the subterranean storage of natural gas in the West Oneida Field.

The property owners have misconstrued Tenn. Comp. R. & Regs. 1040–4–8–.01(1). This rule requires unanimous written agreement by all the owners of the underground reservoir only when the reservoir involved is "capable of producing oil and gas in paying quantities." The evidence before the Board demonstrates convincingly that the West Oneida Field is no longer capable of producing oil and gas in paying quantities. Therefore, Jarvis Drilling was not required to obtain the written consent of all owners before obtaining the Board's approval to use the West Oneida Field for subterranean gas storage. . . .

IV.

As a final matter, the property owners assert that the Board erred by approving Jarvis Drilling's unitization plan for the West Oneida Field because (1) the proposed unitization plan is not economically feasible, (2) the proposed unitization agreement is not fair and equitable, and (3) the dissenting property owners cannot be charged for the cost of gas storage. We have determined that each of these arguments are misplaced.

Unitization plans must be economically feasible. Tenn. Comp. R. & Regs. 1040–5–1–.01(1)(a). The property owners, separating the proposed unitization plan from its gas storage component, insist that unitization of the West Oneida Field is not economically feasible because it would not be profitable without gas storage income. While the property owners are correct that the gas storage income is necessary to the economic feasibility of the project, they are incorrect when they argue that the secondary recovery project and the gas storage proposal should be considered separately. Subterranean gas storage is an integral part of the secondary recovery project because it is one of the ways that Jarvis Drilling plans to re-pressurize the West Oneida Field. Secondary recovery will not be possible without re-pressurization, and re-pressurization will necessitate injecting natural gas into the reservoir. Insofar as re-pressurization is concerned, it matters not how Jarvis Drilling obtains the natural gas. Accordingly, the Board acted properly when it considered the economic feasibility of Jarvis Drilling's unitization plan in light of the revenue Jarvis Drilling anticipated from natural gas storage.

Unitization plans must protect the correlative rights of the affected parties and must be just and equitable. Tenn. Comp. R. & Regs. 1040–5–1–.01(1)(a), (b). The property owners take issue with eight provisions in Jarvis Drilling's proposed unitization agreement and insist that the Board erred by approving the proposed agreement without separately considering the fairness of each provision in the agreement. We find no authority for requiring the Board to review each provision in a proposed unitization agreement, and, therefore, we decline to find that the Board erred by considering the entire agreement in light of the parties' testimony regarding its fairness.

An overwhelming number of affected property owners must have found the terms of the proposed unitization agreement to be just and equitable because they consented to it. In light of the overwhelming acceptance of the agreement, the dissenting property owners faced an uphill struggle to demonstrate to the Board how the proposed agreement was not just and equitable. Their evidence focused on their skepticism that they would receive any of the revenue from the secondary recovery project, their belief that they might have received more if Jarvis Drilling were required to negotiate with them individually, and their concern that they would no longer be permitted to use natural gas from the West Oneida Field for their personal use. The record reflects that the Board factored these concerns into its deliberations and then determined, based on its expertise, that the proposed unitization agreement was consistent with industry standards and that it was just and equitable. We will not second-guess the Board.

Finally, the dissenting property owners insist that the Board erred by approving a provision requiring that part of the costs of the natural gas storage portion of the secondary recovery project be deducted from their proceeds. They insist that the Board does not have the authority to require them to share in the costs of a subterranean gas storage program. We disagree because the gas storage program is an integral part of the secondary recovery project. The Board's rules expressly require affected property owners to pay their pro-rata share of the costs of the secondary recovery project.

Unit operations and secondary recovery projects are intended to benefit all affected owners by increasing the amount of oil recovered from a field. The Board's rules reflect a policy that owners who benefit from these projects must pay their fair share of the expenses reasonably incurred to extract the oil. These rules are intended to dissuade dissenting property owners from becoming "free riders."[5] They require property owners either to pay their pro-rata share of the costs of the project or to have between 150% and 350% of these costs deducted from their share of the proceeds. Tenn. Comp. R. & Regs. 1040–4–9–.07, 1040–5–1–.01(d).

The fact that Jarvis Drilling's proposal for the West Oneida Field contains a subterranean gas storage component does not transform the project into anything other than a secondary recovery project. Accordingly, Tenn. Comp. R. & Regs. 1040–4–9–.07 applies, and the Board, in its discretion, had the power to set the surcharge on dissenting property owners who declined to pay their pro-rata share of the costs of the secondary recovery project anywhere between 150% and 200% of their share of the actual costs. Based on the evidence, the Board determined that the surcharge to dissenting owners who did not contribute their pro-rata share of the production costs would be 200%. The record provides no legal or factual basis to disagree with this decision. . . .

---

[5]   In the parlance of economics, a "free rider" is a person who chooses to receive the benefits of a good or service without paying for it. Free riders are persons who take more than their fair share of benefits, or who do not shoulder their fair share of the costs of their use of a resource.

NOTES

1. *Pooling and unitization.* From an early point in the nation's experience with oil and gas production, it became clear that landowners stood to gain if they could coordinate their exploitation activities. Fewer wells would be needed to extract the minerals from a reservoir, and carefully controlled extraction could remove more minerals overall. Coordination was even more important when it came to undertaking secondary recovery operations, which entail injecting a substance into an underground formation to lift the oil and gas or otherwise make it easier to extract. In this case, natural gas was being injected to pressurize the formation. Incidentally, the storage is valuable to the owner of the gas, who is paying for it, and making the entire operation economically feasible.

Due to well-spacing and minimum drilling-size requirements many individual landowners often cannot drill because their land parcels are too small. Only if several landowners cooperate can drilling go on. The coordination of land parcels under such requirements is commonly called *pooling*. In many states a landowner can be compelled to engage in pooling involuntarily. Secondary and tertiary operations that cover entire fields are commonly called *unitization*, which in many states can also take place involuntarily. Note the standards that Tennessee law sets for the approval of involuntary unitization. The statute appears to protect landowner rights strictly, but it fails to do so in important ways. Most plainly, a landowner no longer has the right to say no; the statute effectively allows the use of private property over the landowner's objection (that is, it authorizes private condemnation). Beyond that, pooling and unitization effectively alter the rule of capture as among members of a pool or unit. The members share revenues on a correlative basis, taking into account (but not necessarily strictly following) the relative acreages that people own. With production undertaken jointly, landowners also lose control over the timing of production. Do the statutory requirements seem sufficient to protect landowner interests? Are they all necessary?

2. *Joint management.* In the case of pooling and unitization, the goals of landowners are largely the same—to maximize income from production while reducing risk. It is therefore understandable that mandatory pooling and unitization statutes gained legislative support, even though they involved major revisions of private property rights as commonly understood. Petroleum pools and units also do not typically encounter anything like the kind of sharp management disagreements that we might expect in the case, for instance, of the Great Onyx Cave that was the subject of the Kentucky litigation early in this chapter, or with a non-navigable lake that owners might want to use for widely varied purposes. Still, the pooling and unitization cases provide important legal precedents for compulsory resource management in the United States, sometimes on a wide spatial scale. The law in effect treats natural resources as jointly owned by the overlying landowners and authorizes the creation of private management entities to control the resource. Although landowners representing a majority or

supermajority of interests must support (and usually initiate) the planned pooling or unitization, minority landowners can no longer veto their efforts.

3. *Holdouts and free riders.* Forced participation in resource management makes the greatest sense in two rather similar factual settings. One case involves a resource that is effectively co-owned (like the underground storage capacity of a gas field), a resource that no one can use unless all owners consent. A single hold-out could halt the operation. Related to this is the situation in which expenditures to develop a resource benefit all landowners, whether or not they have contributed to it. When a well pumps oil from a shared reservoir, and all overlying landowners share in the royalties—whether or not they have contributed to the costs of production—a free rider situation arises. That is, a landowner can refuse to contribute to production costs while still enjoying the benefits—unless the law either denies the landowner the benefit or compels the landowner to contribute involuntarily. In the case of an open-access fishery, all gillnet fishers benefit from snag removal, even when only a few of them exert the effort to perform the chore.

In many oil and gas settings, landowners today cannot be compelled to contribute to exploratory drilling costs, even though they will participate in resulting royalties. They can stand aside as free riders. Typically, though, their shares of production costs are subtracted from any royalties that they receive. Also, they may be forced to pay extra costs (often a double share) because they did not incur the risk of a dry hole. Holdout and free-rider problems arise frequently in natural resources law. Eminent domain has often been used to remedy these problems, although as we saw in chapter 2, the "public use" requirement might now stand as a more formidable obstacle to its continued use (pp. 111–123).

4. *Why unanimity?* In the case of resources such as oil and gas, which are best exploited on a scale that often transcends property boundaries, why do we typically begin with the assumption that joint operations require the unanimous consent of all affected landowners? Why do we give individual landowners the legal power to remain holdouts, thereby halting an activity supported by a majority of their neighbors?

Consider the common case of the residential subdivision with a homeowners association. The association might manage common areas that are co-owned by the residents, and it might also regulate land uses, even in detail. These associations are legally valid because they are supported by restrictive covenants, which a developer imposed before subdividing the land and selling the lots. Under present law, covenants cannot be imposed after lots are sold unless each landowner consents to them. In the case of developer-imposed covenants, by purchasing their lots with knowledge of the association and its powers, individual lot owners consent to them. But how free is this consent, particularly in geographic regions in which essentially all homes are covered by them? And if buying a home amounts to consent to a homeowners' association, could we similarly say that a landowner consents by continuing to own a lot that is subject to a newly created association? That is, might we say that a landowner has the ability to escape control by a new homeowners' association only by selling her home and departing? Is this option to escape an adequate level of landowner autonomy?

Consider as a further comparison the typical governmental body. Under many state statutes, a majority of residents in a region can create a new taxing authority empowered to acquire and operate parks or forest preserves or to perform other functions. Landowners need not support the new institutions unanimously. Individual landowners can dissent only by exiting (moving out of the jurisdiction). Why might we allow for the creation of such government bodies, without unanimity, while requiring that landowners unanimously consent to restrictive covenants that create a private homeowners' association? Keep in mind that homeowners are also subject to the regulatory actions of local government whether or not they consent to them. Is it an adequate response to say that government bodies are subject to constitutional limitations while private bodies, such as homeowners' associations, are not?

D. SUBSURFACE-SURFACE CONFLICTS— EBENEZER SWAMP CASE STUDY[6]

To conclude this chapter, we consider the complexity of subsurface property rights by means of a case study. As you review it, think about the relative interests of the property owners in the use of theirproperty. Most of the cases we have reviewed thus far have dealt with vertical conflicts between surface and subsurface estate holders, or horizontal conflicts between adjacent subsurface estate holders. This case study, however, presents a different scenario—a diagonal conflict where one party's use of its subsurface estate damages an adjacent property owner's use of the surface.

> Ebenezer Swamp (officially known as Ebenezer Wetlands Ecological Preserve—the "Preserve"), is a wetland situated just outside the city of Montevallo, Alabama and owned by the University of Montevallo. The Preserve consists of approximately 120 acres of wooded wetlands and is home to numerous species of plants and animals, nine of which are considered imperiled, threatened or endangered. Ebenezer Swamp forms a portion of the headwaters for the ecologically diverse and environmentally sensitive Cahaba River Watershed. The Cahaba is the longest remaining free-flowing river in the state of Alabama, has more species of fish per mile than any river in North America, and is one of eight river biodiversity hotspots in the U.S.

---

[6]   Portions of this section are excerpted from earlier drafts of Blake Hudson & Michael Hardig, *Isolated Wetland Commons and the* Constitution, 2014 BYU L. Rev. (forthcoming 2014).

In 1998, the University gained title to much of the property within the boundary of the swamp via a grant stating that the property should be "held in perpetuity by the Grantee and used by the Grantee and the University of Montevallo in connection with its academic mission and program; and maintained in its natural state to the greatest extent reasonably possible. . . ." Amended Complaint at 12–13, *University of Montevallo Foundation v. Middle Tennessee Land Development Co., LLC* (Circuit Court of Shelby County, Alabama 2005) (CV–05–624). To date, the University of Montevallo has pursued a policy of encouraging public use by increasing public access, including the construction of approximately 1,000 feet of ADA-compliant boardwalk through a portion of the Preserve which is outfitted with seventeen interpretive plaques, benches, and viewing areas. Public restrooms and an outdoor classroom have been added. These projects have been supported in part through the procurement of federal appropriations. The Ebenezer Swamp boardwalk is accessible to all visitors seven days a week, from dawn until dusk and without need of reservation or scheduling, for self-guided tours. The University of Montevallo provides scheduled guided tours to civic groups, school groups, clubs, and private groups as requested, free of charge. Ebenezer Swamp continues to serve as a fieldtrip destination for local colleges and universities and has served as resource in various research projects over the years, for students in a variety of disciplines, such as Art, Biology, Business, and Mass Communication.

An important physical attribute of this species-rich ecosystem is that it is aquifer and rain-fed, rather than being continuously fed by surface streams or other "navigable waters," as that term has been interpreted under recent U.S. Supreme Court Clean Water Act jurisprudence (*see Solid Waste Agency of Northern Cook County (SWANCC) v. U.S. Army Corps of Engineers*, 531 U.S. 159 (2001) and *Rapanos v. United States*, 547 U.S. 715 (2006)). The combination of groundwater inputs from numerous springs in the area and surface water input after rainfall events is what permits the establishment of a mature upland hardwood swamp wetlands like Ebenezer Swamp. This physical attribute, therefore, has significant legal implications, as described below.

In the early part of 2005 the University of Montevallo became aware of the efforts of an entity doing business as The Middle Tennessee Land Development Co., LLC to acquire the title to approximately 412 acres in the vicinity of Ebenezer Swamp, upon which they intended to develop a 239 acre quarry operation. Their intent was to quarry the Newala Limestone beneath this portion of the valley, an operation that they estimated would require 40 years and would extract $400 million worth of resources. The proposed quarry would have been located approximately 900 feet upstream from Ebenezer Swamp. Currently, there are eight active limestone/dolomite quarries in operation within the immediate area of western Shelby County and Ebenezer Swamp. An acquired familiarity with the effects of these local quarry operations gave the University of Montevallo good reason to be concerned about the likely adverse effects of the proposed quarry on Ebenezer Swamp. The University of Montevallo was much informed by the work of Warren on sinkhole occurrence in Shelby County and the personal observations of key personnel. *See* W.M. Warren, *Sinkhole occurrence in western Shelby County, Alabam*a (Circular 101, Geological Survey of Alabama, Water Resources Div. 1976).

The University's principal concern was the effects that the quarrying operation would have on the amount of groundwater available to sustain Ebenezer Swamp. Without virtually continuous pumping, these quarries would quickly fill with water from the aquifer. Consequently, the quarries must be dewatered. One such quarry, approximately 4 miles southeast of Ebenezer Swamp, in the area of Dry Valley, is being dewatered for limestone quarrying operations. Sinkholes began developing in Dry Valley during 1964 and the rate of formation and affected area has been steadily increasing since. It is estimated that more than 1,000 sinkholes and related features have occurred in the approximately 10 square miles affected by the water-table decline. Additionally, once-perennial springs that historically fed lower Spring Creek have stopped flowing as a result of the dewatering operation and depressed water table.

In 2001 lower Spring Creek went dry during a prolonged period of drought, despite the fact that water continued to flow from Ebenezer Swamp on upper Spring Creek. The most-probable explanation for this development is that reduced surface flow associated with drought, combined with a lowering of the water table due to dewatering in the adjacent Dry Valley quarries, lowered the stream surface to a point where it flowed in the bedrock beneath the stream bottom. Many specimens of fish perished when the stream "dried" up. This condition persisted until the first major rains of the year, a short time after which the stream surface rose above the stream bottom and flow returned to normal. This episode is symptomatic of the effects of water table alterations on wetlands, and demonstrates the complex hydrology that affects important national waterways regardless of the "navigability" of the water.

Significant resistance to the proposed quarry, by local residents, two municipalities and by the University of Montevallo, developed quickly. The former president of the University of Montevallo held a meeting involving the mayors of Calera, Montevallo, and Alabaster, to discuss appropriate actions of resistance. While the mayor of Calera was not inclined to participate, the mayors of Montevallo and Alabaster were unanimous in their opposition to the proposed development. The mayor of Alabaster proposed raising administrative challenges to the Alabama Department of Environmental Management (ADEM) permitting process based on a lack of due diligence on their part, and organizing public meetings to inform and engage the local populace. The administrative challenges ultimately proved fruitless, but the public meetings were very effective for distributing relevant information and in promoting a grass-roots organization that coordinated letter writing campaigns targeted at ADEM and state officials. The University of Montevallo decided for their part to seek a legal injunction through the court system, on the grounds that the quarry operation would ruin the ecological and educational value of Ebenezer Swamp.

The basis of the University's lawsuit was that the groundwater connections between the quarry site and Ebenezer Swamp are so extensive that the quarry's operation upstream and within the swamp's source water area would ensure degradation, and eventual destruction, of the swamp. To support that argument, the University of Montevallo hired the services of P.E. LaMoreaux and Associates, Inc. (PELA) to perform a hydrogeologic investigation. *See* Lois D. George, Bashir A. Memon & Michael R. Burston, *The Hydrogeology of Ebenezer Swamp and Vicinity-Preservation of a Ground-Water Dependent Ecosystem* (P.E. LaMoreaux & Assoc, 2005) (on file with authors). Principals of PELA reviewed published information, performed site reconnaissance visits to both Ebenezer Swamp and the proposed quarry site, examined drilling logs from an earlier study of the quarry site, performed additional drilling and geophysical logging on the quarry site, and modeled predicted drawdowns on the water table that would be caused by dewatering at the quarry site. University of Montevallo personnel spent much of the summer of 2005 finding and documenting the numerous (>80) springs and seeps located within the Ebenezer Swamp boundary. The case of University of Montevallo, et al. (Plaintiff) v Middle Tennessee Land

Development Co., LLC (Defendant) was tried in the Circuit Court of Shelby County, Alabama, in 2006.

It its complaint, the University claimed "devastating and irreparable impact" were the quarry to be developed, based primarily upon: the loss of an education and research resource for students at all levels of education and the general citizenry; loss of recruitment of prospective students; loss of good will within the local and regional community, which expected the University to exercise care of the resource; loss of investments in the enhancement of the Preserve; and harm to the University's reputation for having failed to hold in perpetuity and maintain the Preserve in its natural state, as it was entrusted to do. The University's legal claims were based, first, on unreasonable use of groundwater, second, on nuisance, and third, on a theory of public trust. All of these, of course, are state common law claims, because University lawyers believed that the preserve was isolated enough from traditional navigable waters that the University would have no federal Clean Water Act claim for the draining of the wetland by a neighboring property owner (especially given recent interpretations of the term "navigable waters" in the recent *SWANCC* and *Rapanos* cases, noted above).

Regarding the claim of unreasonable use of water, the University established that the Preserve and Middle Tennessee shared the aquifer below the respective properties. They argued that the use of water by Middle Tennessee was per se unreasonable since the primary reason the water was being pumped from the aquifer was because it was a "barrier to the extraction of the minerals, and is thus wasted rather than being used." Amended Complaint at 26, *University of Montevallo Foundation v. Middle Tennessee Land Development Co., LLC* (Circuit Court of Shelby County, Alabama 2005) (CV–05–624); *See Martin v. City of Linden*, 667 So. 2d 732 (Ala. 1995); *Waters* (78 Am. Jur. 2d pp. 550–51—"there is no right to draw water from a common underground reservoir merely for the purpose of wasting it to the injury of other landowners having an equal right to and means of access thereto."). The University further argued that as owner of the land it was also the owner of the groundwater underlying the land under Alabama law, and therefore could bring a claim for damages to it. The complaint alleged that the Preserve is "totally dependent upon the groundwater in the aquifer which underlies it. The wetlands are formed by the nature-provided mineral and chemical composition of the groundwater in the aquifer." Amended Complaint at 22, *University of Montevallo Foundation v. Middle Tennessee Land Development Co., LLC* (Circuit Court of Shelby County, Alabama 2005) (CV–05–624). The complaint further argued that if the water was removed from the aquifer under the Preserve through pumping for mining limestone, the Preserve could never be restored.

As for nuisance, the University argued that not only would the mining's effects on the water table damage the Preserve, but that the removal of soil and vegetation overlying the mine would lead to erosion that would contaminate the waters of the Preserve, negatively impacting fish and plant species, and would also remove an important water purification mechanism leading to increased contaminants and pollutants in both the aquifer and the surface water. Sinkholes developing in areas not mined would also threaten the Preserve. Dust created by quarrying operations would clog pores in the surface and thereby diminish the recharge rate for the aquifer, choke vegetation at the Preserve, leach into the soil causing further vegetation death, and remove food sources for the fauna there. Finally, the University claimed that discharged wastewater would ultimately make its way into the Preserve, and that blasting during the mining process would loosen soils, divert surface and groundwater, and interfere with biological life cycle processes.

While a typical nuisance in Alabama is considered an action which "works hurt, inconvenience, or damage" to a property owner's property, the injury here had not yet occurred. The University, therefore, relied upon the doctrine of "anticipatory nuisance," which is described in the Alabama Code as "Injunction Before Completion." Alabama Code § 6–5–125, 1975. The code states that "where the consequences of a nuisance about to be erected or commenced will be irreparable in damages and such consequences are not merely possible but to a reasonable degree certain, a court may interfere to arrest a nuisance before it is completed." The University claimed that the quarrying operation would constitute both a public and private nuisance—private because of the damages to the University's property, and public because it would injure a wide range of citizens, including present and future students.

Finally, on the claim of public trust, the University cited cases from other states supporting the conclusion that wetland resources like Ebenezer Preserve were subject to public trust protections. *Illinois Central Railroad Co. v. State of Illinois*, 146 U.S. 387 (1892); *Robbins v. Department of Public Works*, 244 N.E.2d 577, 578 (Mass. 1969) (prohibiting highway construction which would have replaced "wetlands of considerable natural beauty with a large capacity for the storage of water during flood seasons and [which] are often used for nature study and recreation."). The theory was that donation of the tract for preservation in perpetuity, to be maintained in a natural state, indicated that the University was to act as a trustee over the Preserve, and presumably since the University was an organ of the state, this duty extended to the state.

Based upon these three claims, the University sought a declaratory judgment and preliminary and permanent injunctive relief against Middle Tennessee Land Company. Trial was held in August and September 2006.

Below is the order deciding the claims brought by the University against Middle Tennessee.

UNIVERSITY OF MONTEVALLO V. MIDDLE TENNESSEE LAND DEVELOPMENT CO.
Circuit Court of Shelby County, AL
Case No.: CV 2005–624 (2006)

HARRINGTON, J.

This cause came before the Court for trial on Plaintiffs' complaint seeking declaratory and injunctive relief against Defendant's proposed quarry operation. . . .

The Preserve is utilized by the University of Montevallo for educational and research purposes. The use and benefit of the Preserve is afforded the university in accordance with the foundation's purpose of supporting the university in its educational endeavors. Pursuant to an executory real estate sales contract, defendant Middle Tennessee Land Development Company, LLC has an interest in some 230 acres of land commonly known as the Nolen property. Once acquired, Middle Tennessee intends to utilize the property for limestone quarrying operations. Plaintiffs contend that the operation of a quarry would irreparably harm the Preserve by depleting or contaminating groundwater, and that the operation would constitute a nuisance. The factual bases for these claims are virtually identical.

It is undisputed that a lawful operation of a rock quarry on the proposed site is permissible, as the present use of the land is not restricted by zoning or any other land use constraint. Plaintiffs do not contend that a lawful quarry operation would constitute a nuisance per se, and are not required to prove a nuisance per se as a requirement for obtaining injunctive relief. *Parker v. Ashford*, 661 So.2d 213, 218 (Ala. 1995). The plaintiffs must, nevertheless, prove that the quarry operation will constitute a nuisance; that injunctive relief is necessary to prevent irreparable injury; and that Plaintiffs have no adequate remedy at law. *Gulf House Association, Inc. v. The Town of Gulf Shores*, 484 So.2d 1061, 1064 (Ala. 1985).

"A 'nuisance' is anything that works hurt, inconvenience or damages to another. The fact that the act done may otherwise be lawful does not keep it from being a nuisance. The inconvenience complained of must not be fanciful or such as would affect only one of a fastidious taste, but it should be such as would affect an ordinary reasonable man." § 6–5–120 Ala. Code (1975). "Where the consequences of a nuisance about to be erected or commenced will be irreparable in damages and such consequences are not merely possible but to a reasonable degree certain, a court may interfere to arrest a nuisance before it is completed." § 6–5–125 Ala. Code (1975).

In the case at bar Plaintiffs claim that the quarry operation will, by depletion, disruption or degradation, unreasonably interfere with the groundwater which is essential to the Preserve's continued existence in its present state. Nuisance is also the controlling legal theory "in the context of property damage caused by a continuing activity involving the use of underground water. See *Harper v. Regency Development, Co.*, 399 So.2d 248, 253 (Ala. 1981); *Martin v. City of Linden*, 667 So.2d 732, 738 (Ala. 1995). This principle was established in the case of *Henderson v. Wade Sand & Gravel Co.*, 388 So.2d 900 (Ala. 1980). In that case, the

> Court reversed a judgment entered on a directed verdict for a quarry, whose incidental pumping activities had drained the groundwater from under the plaintiffs' land, opening sinkholes and causing the plaintiffs' houses to sink and break up. . . . [The] Court in Henderson found that the quarry owner's diversion of the groundwater, incidental to the use of the owner's land, interfered with the plaintiff's use. . . . Henderson concerned the interference with a plaintiff's use (for consumption or subterranean support) of groundwater by a defendant's diversion of that water incidental to use of his own land . . .

Martin v. City of Linden, 667 So.2d 732, 738 (Ala. 1995) (emphasis in original).

It has long been held that the granting of anticipatory injunctive relief "is one of the extraordinary powers of the court, and should be cautiously and sparingly exercised." *St. James' Church v. Arrington*, 36 Ala. 546, 548 (1860). The granting of such relief is, however, authorized by statute in § 6–5–125 of the *Code of Alabama*. The obtainment of anticipatory injunctive relief requires the plaintiffs in the case to prove "to a reasonable degree certain" that the consequences of the defendant's proposed quarry operation "will be irreparable in damages." § 6–5–125 Ala. Code (1975).

If it is impossible, before the construction of a project has been completed and the project is operating, for a court to ascertain whether it will or will not constitute a nuisance, or if reasonable doubt exists as to the probable effect of the proposed project, then a court will not intervene until the project is completed and can be tested by actual use. That is, if from the facts it appears that the injury or harm alleged by the persons seeking an injunction is uncertain or speculative; that the use of the project is only possibly productive of injury; or that the public benefit to be served by the project may outweigh the inconvenience caused to the plaintiffs, then the court must refuse the injunction and await the completion and operation of the project to determine whether the project is a nuisance. See, e.g., *Jackson v. Downey*, 42 So.2d 246 (Ala. 1949).

However, "[w]here the consequences of a nuisance about to be erected or commenced will be irreparable in damages and such consequences are not merely possible but to a reasonable degree certain, a court may interfere to arrest a nuisance before it is completed." Ala.Code 1975, Section 6–5–125; see *Rouse & Smith v. Martin & Flowers*, 75 Ala. 510 (1883). . . . An activity that is lawful in its nature and that is not a nuisance in one locality may be or become a nuisance when erected and maintained in certain other localities, depending on the particular location of the activity and the way it is managed or operated, See *Nevins v. McGavock*, 106 So. 597 (Ala. 1925). In determining whether an activity is or has become a nuisance, a court must consider its effect upon an ordinary reasonable person—i.e., a person of ordinary sensibilities; it is not sufficient that it would be considered harmful or inconvenient by a person of fastidious tastes or sensibilities. See, e.g., *First Avenue Coal & Lumber Co, v. Johnston*, 54 So. 598 (Ala. 1911).

Parker v. Ashford, 661 So.2d 213, 217–18 (Ala. 1995).

In the case at bar the question for the Court's determination is a simple one; can the University's Ebenezer Wetlands Preserve co-exist with Middle Tennessee's rock quarry operation? The answer presents difficult questions of law and fact and a balancing of valid and legitimate competing interests. The initial guiding principle must be that a property owner has a right to utilize his property for any lawful purpose as he sees fit. Were this the only consideration, Middle Tennessee would have an unfettered right to commence quarry operations. Instead, that right is tempered by statute, and by common law and equitable principles, each of which have been addressed by the parties through the evidence proffered at trial.

In support of their respective positions each party presented detailed expert testimony from renowned hydrogeologists with impeccable credentials. The experts are highly qualified with experience and expertise in the issues presented by this case. The opinion testimony of these experts is supported by onsite inspection, test data, historical data, government publications, mathematical analysis, anecdotal evidence, photographic evidence, governmental maps and charts, scientific literature and the like.

The opinions proffered and the ultimate conclusions reached by experts of such caliber should be given considerable weight and consideration. In this case, however, the experts cannot even agree on the basic science to be applied. The result is that Plaintiffs' experts conclude that the commencement of quarrying operations will have a doomsday effect, causing the immediate and cataclysmic demise of the Ebenezer Swamp. The testimony of Defendant's expert is in direct opposition, postulating that the 80 acre, 320 foot deep quarry operation may even be beneficial to the hydrology of the swamp. As a result of these diametrically opposed conclusions, and because the experts proffered by the parties were such fierce advocates for their respective clients, the court is faced with the challenge of resolving the vast conflicts in the expert testimony. In so doing the court must rely upon the appropriate applied science, and upon the reasonable interpretations of the available data collated through reliable testing procedures.

As the expert testimony demonstrates, the science and the application of the available scientific data are subject to diverse interpretations. As a general principle, science is predicated upon reproducible physical observations and controlled experiments. The ultimate scientific questions in this case, however, cannot be resolved from a reproducible observation or an experiment, as the definitive answer to the question before this court can only be determined to an absolute certainty by commencement of the quarrying operation. No truly reproducible observations or experiments can be performed beforehand, as these unique circumstances cannot be replicated by laboratory experiments. Moreover, it would be virtually physically and financially impossible to gather additional test data sufficient to significantly improve the scientific analyses proffered by the parties. This case must, therefore, be resolved by proper application of the reliable data currently available.

Based upon its review of the evidence presented, the court has determined both the appropriate science and the reliable data to be utilized in its analysis of the case. The court's findings of fact and conclusions of law were set forth in detail by pronouncement made in open court on August 31, 2006, The court hereby adopts these findings of fact and conclusions of law which are incorporated by reference as if fully set out herein.

Accordingly, it is ORDERED that judgment be, and it hereby is, entered in favor of Plaintiffs and against Defendant, and that pursuant to said judgment Defendant is enjoined from commencing its proposed quarry operation for so long as the existing ecological system of the Ebenezer Wetlands Preserve remains inviolate and the University of Montevallo continues to utilize the Preserve for educational and research purposes, or until further order of this court. In the event that this injunction should be lifted at some future time, all issues pertaining to operational requirements and restrictions are reserved.

NOTES

1. *Divining the court's analysis.* The court gave short shrift to the facts of the conflict in its written legal analysis by incorporating by reference the arguments made in open court. Based upon the case study's introduction, what facts do you think supported a finding of anticipatory nuisance in this case? Alabama's codification of anticipatory nuisance, which "requires the plaintiffs in the case to prove 'to a reasonable degree certain' that the consequences of the defendant's proposed quarry operation 'will be irreparable in damages,'" is a typical exposition of the doctrine. Anticipatory nuisance is one of the most difficult common law property claims for a plaintiff to prove successfully. The burden is much more than the burden implicated by a standard nuisance claim—where one must prove that A's use of her property is unreasonably interfering with B's use and enjoyment of property—more or less a "preponderance of the evidence" standard. Anticipatory nuisance, on the other hand, may be more akin to the "beyond a reasonable doubt" standard in criminal law when considering where it lies on the burden of proof spectrum.

The court stated that deciding the case "presents difficult questions of law and fact and a balancing of valid and legitimate competing interests." What facts do you think most support the court's ruling? The ecological value of the swamp? The educational mission it supports? The purposes supporting the contractual grant of the swamp to the university? How does the claim that the limestone quarry would result in $400 million worth of resources over forty years play into the analysis? Do the relative costs and benefits matter, or is it only that A's use of property harms B?

What testimony from scientific experts would support a ruling for the plaintiff? For the defendant? What should a court do when "the experts cannot even agree on the basic science to be applied?" The court noted that the completely opposite positions of the experts required the court to "rely upon the appropriate applied science, and upon the reasonable interpretations of the available data collated through reliable testing procedures."

2. *Is anticipatory nuisance sufficient?* How do you think these types of diagonal conflicts should be resolved? What if the neighbor had not been a university that was paying close attention to an adjacent property owner's proposed activities or otherwise did not have the resources to challenge those activities in court? Is there a role for regulation to play in balancing the interests in these various resources? Is that a regulatory role best reserved for the local, state, or federal government?

3. *Importance of wetlands: redux.* Wetlands—including isolated wetlands, many of which now seem outside the ambit of federal regulatory authority under the Clean Water Act—provide a number of important ecosystem services. See chapter 3, pp. 217–245. Wetlands reduce damages associated with flooding, protecting property owners, industries and other developments, and ecosystems downstream; they facilitate groundwater recharge and discharge, acting as sponges that slowly absorb and release water from and into the soil; they perform important erosion control services and water quality control services, filtering out nutrients like nitrogen, phosphorus, and organic pollutants. They can reduce the costs of developing human-built structures in the form of municipal water treatment systems.

Wetlands also provide recreational opportunities and crucial habitat for a diverse number of economic and non-economic species. One-third of species threatened or endangered in the U.S. depend on wetlands generally, and many of those are found solely in isolated wetland habitats. Raissa Marks, Wildllfe Habitat Council, Natural Resources Conservation Service, *Ecologically Isolated Wetlands* 4 (October 2006). A fifty-state study in 2005 concluded that isolated wetlands supported 274 at-risk plant and animal species, many of which were endemic to isolated wetland habitats. Karen Cappiella & Lisa Fraley-McNeal, Center for Watershed Protection, *The Importance of Protecting Vulnerable Streams and Wetlands at the Local Level*, 11 (August 2007). One study determined that twenty species of amphibians in the state of South Carolina would become extinct if all isolated wetlands were lost. Southern Environmental Law Center (SELC). *At Risk: South Carolina's "Isolated" Wetlands 2003–2004.* (2004). Finally, wetlands store vast quantities of carbon and can "contribute to amelioration of climate change impacts." Loren M. Smith, Ned H. Euliss Jr., & David A. Haukos, *Are Isolated Wetlands Isolated?*, 33 Nat'l Wetlands Newsletter 26, 27 (2011) (citing Ned. H. Euliss Jr. et al., *North American Prairie Wetlands Are Important Non-Forested Land-Based Carbon Storage Sites*, 361 Sci. Total Env't 179–88 (2006)).

Isolated wetlands in particular are threatened by agriculture, forestry and mining activities, and general land development for commercial, residential, and other purposes. Over the last century, development has claimed over half of all wetlands in North America. David Moreno-Mateos et al., *Structural and Functional Loss in Restored Wetland Ecosystems*, 10 PLOS Biology 1, 1 (2012), *available at* http://www.plosbiology.org/article/info %3Adoi%2F10.1371%2Fjournal.pbio.1001247. The states of Arkansas, California, Connecticut, Illinois, Indiana, Iowa, Kentucky, Maryland,

Missouri, and Ohio have lost 70% or more of their original wetland acreage. Marks, cited above, at 2. Iowa has lost 95% of its wetlands, Minnesota 53%, South Dakota 35%, and North Dakota 60%. National Wildlife Federation & Natural Resources Defense Council, *Wetlands at Risk—Imperiled Treasures*, 10 (2002). These wetland losses have created dramatic habitat fragmentation, isolating many wetlands from surrounding waters, which negatively impacts the services they are able to provide—and especially the provision of biodiversity habitat.

Given that many wetlands around the nation are aquifer-fed, how might the various uses of subsurface estates described in this chapter threaten these resources? How might the various conflicts described above be resolved if a neighboring surface estate wetland is threatened by the proposed subsurface activity?

CHAPTER 6

WATER LAW

■ ■ ■

Because of its importance to human health and well-being and its centrality to other natural resources uses, water is probably the most important natural resource. Water law consequently concerns itself with rights to use water, including consuming it for domestic and agricultural use. Two distinct water law regimes dominate surface water rights in the U.S.–riparian rights in the eastern states; prior appropriation in the western states. Some states have mixed versions of the two. Riparian rights were inherited from England and are ancillary to land ownership. That is, owners of shorelands (so-called riparian lands) have water rights; owners of land not bordering on waterbodies have no riparian rights. Riparian rights give landowners a right to use water reasonably, considering other neighboring uses by riparians and factors such as the amount and quality of the water available and the relative values of the competing water uses. In recent years, some riparian jurisdictions have modified riparian rights by statute, creating a "regulated riparianism" in which riparian users must obtain state permits before initiating new uses and are subject to periodic reevaluation in accordance with notions of the public interest.

In the arid western U.S. (beginning roughly with the 100th meridian—or central Kansas and Nebraska), water rights were disassociated from land ownership, no doubt due in part to the fact that the largest landowner in the West is the federal government. Unlike the landowner-centered water law of the East, the dominant rule of the West is based on temporal priority—the first to capture water and appropriate it to "beneficial use" received the paramount right in the form of priority date that would trump later established rights. This "prior appropriation" system of water law rewards old uses (likely to be the least efficient uses) and has little in common with riparian rights. Historically, it required that water be diverted from streams to establish a water right—a classic rule of capture—and the right could be lost through non-use. This "use-it-or-lose-it" doctrine is completely foreign to riparian rights, which are incidents of a landowner's fee simple. Moreover, the historical rule that required a diversion of water to obtain a water right led to many western streams drying up during the summer irrigation season.

A third system of water rights is employed concerning federal lands, at least those that have been reserved for particular purposes, like conservation, defense, or homelands for Indian tribes. Under the so-called "reserved rights" doctrine, federal water rights are "reserved" from state systems of water allocation. In the West, reserved rights receive a priority date as of the date of the land reservation, not the date of any water diversion, and those reservation dates are often quite old (or "senior" in the language of prior appropriation law). Therefore, they can cast a large shadow of uncertainty over Western states' prior appropriation systems, particularly since the amount of water rights reserved—that which is "necessary to fulfill the purposes of the reservation"—is usually unclear. Consequently, federal reserved water rights are quite controversial in the arid West, raising fundamental federalism and environmental issues. Reserved rights have not been applied in riparian jurisdictions, although there is no good conceptual reason why they should not be.

To make matters even more complex, rights to subsurface water (groundwater) do not parallel surface water right regimes. The dominant system is called the American reasonable use rule, but it is not the reasonable use rule of surface riparian rights. Instead, it allows a landowner to capture water lying underneath her land and use all that she can on the land she owns overlying the water, a rule that presumably helps conserve the underlying aquifer through seepage. Some western states have rejected the American reasonable use rule in favor of prior appropriation, which can lead to an integrated system of surface and groundwater systems. Another alternative—the rule of capture—was inherited from England but has been largely supplanted as wasteful, since it allows the overlying surface owner to own all that she captures without having to use it on the overlying land. However, the Texas Supreme Court—almost alone among the states—recently reaffirmed the rule of capture in Texas (commonly termed the absolute ownership rule). A final alternative, called the correlative rights doctrine, resembles surface riparian rights in that it recognizes rights based on a variety of factors, such as the amount of overlying land, the date of use, and the relative values of the competing uses. It is also a decided minority rule, applying only in California and Nebraska, probably because of the difficulty of assembling information on the amounts of water underlying various surface tracts of land.

This chapter considers all of these systems of establishing private and public rights in water, beginning with the various surface water regimes.

A. RIPARIAN RIGHTS

As mentioned above, the riparian rights systems of the East are based on reasonable use. However, this rule took some generations to emerge in early America. The beginning point, it appears, was one that required landowners to use water only in ways that did not noticeably alter the water flow or degrade it if doing so would harm another water user. The rule tended to favor the first water user on a river and to discourage a later one, even when the latter's use of water was more valuable socially and economically. One problem under the new reasonable use rule was how to apportion water among reasonable uses when there was not enough water to satisfy everyone.

EVANS V. MERRIWEATHER
Supreme Court of Illinois
3 Scam. 492 (1842)

[Merriweather, a downstream mill owner, filed suit against Evans, an upstream mill owner, for obstructing and diverting a watercourse, actions that prevented the downstream mill from operating during a drought. The lower court found for Merriweather, awarding him $150 in damages due to Evans' damming and diversion. Evans appealed.]

LOCKWOOD, J.

* * * [T]he question is presented, as to what extent riparian proprietors, upon a stream not navigable, can use the water of such stream?

* * * Each riparian proprietor is bound to make such a use of running water as to do as little injury to those below him as is consistent with a valuable benefit to himself. The use must be a reasonable one. Now the question fairly arises, is that a reasonable use of running water by the upper proprietor, by which the fluid itself is entirely consumed? To answer this question satisfactorily, it is proper to consider the wants of man in regard to the element of water. These wants are either natural or artificial. Natural are such as are absolutely necessary to be supplied, in order to his existence. Artificial, such only as, by supplying them, his comfort and prosperity are increased. To quench thirst, and for household purposes, water is absolutely indispensable. In civilized life, water for cattle is also necessary. These wants must be supplied, or both man and beast will perish.

The supply of man's artificial wants is not essential to his existence; it is not indispensable; he could live if water was not employed in irrigating lands, or in propelling his machinery. In countries differently situated from ours, with a hot and arid climate, water doubtless is absolutely indispensable to the cultivation of the soil, and in them, water for irrigation would be a natural want. Here it might increase the products of the soil, but it is by no means essential, and cannot, therefore, be considered a natural want of man. So of manufactures, they promote the prosperity and comfort of mankind, but cannot be considered absolutely necessary to his existence; nor need the machinery which he employs be set in motion by steam.

From these premises would result this conclusion: that an individual owning a spring on his land, from which water flows in a current through his neighbor's land, would have the right to use the whole of it, if necessary to satisfy his natural wants. He may consume all the water for his domestic purposes, including water for his stock. If he desires to use it for irrigation or manufactures, and there be a lower proprietor to whom its use is essential to supply his natural wants, or for his stock, he must use the water so as to leave enough for such lower proprietor. Where the stream is small, and does not supply water more than sufficient to answer the natural wants of the different proprietors living on it, none of the proprietors can use the water for either irrigation or manufactures. So far, then, as natural wants are concerned, there is no difficulty in furnishing a rule by which riparian proprietors may use flowing water to supply such natural wants. Each proprietor in his turn may, if necessary, consume all the water for these purposes. But where the water is not wanted to supply natural wants and there is not sufficient for each proprietor living on the stream, to carry on his manufacturing purposes, how shall the water be divided? We have seen that, without a contract or grant, neither has a right to use all the water; all have a right to participate in its benefits. Where all have a right to participate in a common benefit, and none can have an exclusive enjoyment, no rule, from the very nature of the case, can be laid down, as to how much each may use without infringing upon the rights of others. In such cases, the question must be left to the judgment of the jury, whether the party complained of has used, under all the circumstances, more than his just proportion.

It appears, from the facts agreed on, that Evans obstructed the water by a dam, and diverted the whole into his well. This diversion, according to all the cases, both English and American, was clearly illegal. For this diversion, an action will lie. . . .

For these reasons I am of opinion that the judgment ought to be affirmed, with costs.

Judgment affirmed.

NOTES

1. *Preferences among reasonable uses.* The *Evans v. Merriweather* decision, quite influential in other jurisdictions, established a hierarchy among reasonable uses, preferring "natural wants," such as domestic and stockwatering, to irrigation and manufacturing uses. Notice that the court suggested that in more arid climates than Illinois, where water is "absolutely indispensable to the cultivation of the soil . . . water for irrigation would be a

natural want." Note that the Illinois Supreme Court refused to articulate a rule that would establish priorities among reasonable uses not serving "natural wants." The court simply left that issue to the fact finder to decide whether a riparian user has "under all the circumstances, [used] more than his just proportion." Under this interpretation of riparianism, one's rights remain indeterminate until adjudicated.

2. *From natural flow to reasonable use.* In its original form, riparian rights allowed landowners to make only modest uses of water. They could use it for "domestic purposes"—household drinking and watering barnyard animals. All other uses were subject to the strict-sounding limit that the use cause no alteration of the water's natural flow, either in terms of quantity or quality, at least if the alteration would harm anyone downstream. The rule was stated in an early, influential New Jersey decision, *Merritt v. Parker*, 1 N.J.L. 460, 463 (N.J. 1795):

> In general, it may be observed, when a man purchases a piece of land, through which a natural water-course flows, he has a right to make use of it in its natural state, but not to stop or divert it to the prejudice of another. *Aqua currit, et debet currere,* [more fully, *aqua currit et debet currere ut currere solebat*; that is: water runs and ought to run as it is wont to run—Eds.] is the language of the law. The water flows in its natural channel, and ought always to be permitted to run there, so that all, through whose land it pursues its natural course, may continue to enjoy the privilege of using it for their own purposes. It cannot legally be diverted from its course without the consent of all who have an interest in it. If it should be turned into another channel, or stopped, and this illegal step should be persisted in, I should think a jury right in giving almost any valuation which the party thus injured should think proper to affix to it. This principle lies at the bottom of all the cases which I have met with, and it is so perfectly reasonable in itself, and at the same time so firmly settled as a doctrine of the law, that it should never be abandoned or departed from.

This rule was designed to protect family homesteads and other agrarian uses. It also protected fish and other aquatic life, and thus the people whose livelihoods depended upon them. And the rule embodied the then-strong belief that the key element of private property was the right to halt any interferences with what one was doing; the essence of a property right was not any right to engage in intensive uses of the thing owned, despite harms imposed on others. The natural-flow rule, though, stood as a serious obstacle in the path of industrial development. How was a riparian landowner to construct a dam and water wheel to create waterpower to run a new textile mill? And what about the pollution that the textile mill inevitably caused? Could a downstream landowner go to court and get the mill shut down, regardless of economic and other community benefits? The legal answer appeared to be yes—and, given the times, it was the wrong answer both politically and culturally. The natural-flow approach in practice also tended

to favor the first user in time—given that it was the second user who created
the harm—which meant that the law vested monopolistic power in the first
user of the water.

Disliking this anti-developmental answer, courts and other lawmakers
changed the law fundamentally. In their conservative writing style, courts
continued to repeat the natural flow language—each landowner was entitled
to it. But slipped in was a major qualification: an owner's right to the natural
flow was now subject to the right of upstream owners to make "reasonable
use" of the water, even when that use altered the natural flow in quantity or
quality. For example, in *Tyler v. Wilkinson,* 24 F. Cas. 472 (C.C.D. R.I. 1827),
Justice Story, riding circuit, used both natural flow and reasonable use
language but indicated that some diminution in natural flow was permissible
so long as it was "not positively and sensibly injurious." *Id.* at 474. The effect
of this shift was profound. Landowners could now use the water more
intensively but, as a result, they lost much of their legal right to complain
when other users caused them harm. This legal shift reconfigured landowner
rights, increasing one stick in the bundle of rights (the right to use
intensively) while pruning another stick (the right to protection against
interferences). This same shift—to allow more intensive resource uses, at the
expense of protections against harm—happened in many areas of natural
resources law during the nineteenth century.

3.   *The effect of reasonable use.* The effect of adopting a reasonable use
standard—one that did not give priority to the first users—was that a
riparian proprietor no longer enjoyed an unobstructed use of water in its
natural flow. Thus, the prior erection of a mill upon a stream, and use of its
waters by the mill, did not give the mill owner exclusive use of the water
(monopolistic power), unobstructed by the subsequent erection of other mills
on the same stream. Although the first mill owner may be somewhat injured,
the courts considered the effect to be *damnum absque injuria*, or loss without
legal injury, provided that the upstream mill owner did not divert water out
of the stream or waste the water in the stream. For a discussion of the
judicial role in the evolution from natural flow to reasonable use, see Morton
J. Horwitz, *The Transformation of American Law, 1780–1860*, at 37–38
(1977), discussing *Palmer v. Mulligan,* 3 Cai. R. 307 (N.Y. Sup. Ct. 1805); and
Platt v. Johnson, 15 Johns. 213 (N.Y. 1818), as introducing into American law
"the entirely novel view that an explicit consideration of the relative
efficiencies of conflicting property uses should be the paramount test of what
constitutes legally justifiable injury." The rise of reasonable use coincided
with a six-fold increase in the capacity of cotton mills between 1820 and 1831.
Horwitz, at 40.

On the other hand, use of such a multi-faceted, contextual rule such as
reasonable use makes it difficult to know in advance the scope of one's water
rights. This uncertainty can lead riparian owners to turn to litigation to
clarify their rights, imposing high transaction costs on the parties. A flexible
rule, reflecting contemporarily felt necessities, is much more costly to

administer than a bright-line, clear rule. The question is: are those costs of administration worth the social benefits of a flexible rule?

4. *Reasonable use and pollution.* In *Snow v. Parsons,* 28 Vt. 459 (1856), Parsons, the owner of a downstream mill, which was constructed first, complained of an upstream tannery that was depositing wood refuse (a byproduct of the tanning process) into the stream, causing a malfunction of a new waterwheel at the downstream mill. A lower court ruled in favor of the downstream mill owner. The Vermont Supreme Court reversed, ruling that the reasonableness of the pollution was a question of fact. If it was true that there was no reasonable alternative to the tannery's dumping of refuse, it would not be unreasonable to use the stream to carry away the refuse despite the resulting harm. A riparian owner had to be able to make use of a stream in a manner so as to make the land useful to himself, even if it causes "inconveniences" downstream.

5. *Using water on non-riparian lands.* Classical riparian rights law limited the use of water to riparian (shoreland) lands, a limitation with some environmental implications: water uses on riparian lands would more likely lead to return-flows to the stream, keeping it from drying up during periods of heavy use. Over time courts gradually relaxed this place-of-use limitation. The following case was among the leading decisions.

STRATTON V. MT. HERMON BOYS' SCHOOL

Supreme Judicial Court of Massachusetts
103 N.E. 87 (1913)

[Stratton, the owner of a mill on a small stream, sued the school, an upper riparian, for wrongful diversion of water. The school owned riparian land, on which it constructed a pumping station. From there it diverted about 600,000 gallons of water per day to lands it owned that were not riparian to the stream, and in fact located a mile away in a different watershed. The purpose was to accommodate an expanding school population—from 363 in 1908 to 525 in 1911. Stratton sued, claiming an unlawful non-riparian use. The diversion, he claimed, "caused a substantial diminution in the volume of water which otherwise in the natural flow of the stream would have come" to Stratton's mill, thereby reducing his water power. The school defended on the premise that it had not diverted an unreasonable amount of water. The lower court agreed with Stratton, and the school appealed.]

RUGG, C.J.

* * *

[The boy's school] requested the court to rule in effect that diversion of water to another nonriparian estate owned by it was not conclusive evidence that the defendant was liable, but that the only question was whether it had taken an unreasonable quantity of water under all the circumstances. This request was denied and the instruction given that the defendant's right was confined to a reasonable use of the water for the benefit of its land adjoining the water course, and of persons properly using such land, and did not extend to taking it for use upon other premises, and that if there was such use the plaintiff was entitled to recover at least nominal damages even though he had sustained no actual loss. The exceptions raise the question as to the soundness of the request and of the instruction given.

The common-law rights and obligations of riparian owners upon streams are not open to doubt. Although the right to flowing water is incident to the title to land, there is no right of property in such water in the sense that it can be the subject of exclusive appropriation and dominion. The only property interest in it is usufructuary. The right of each riparian owner is to have the natural flow of the stream come to his land and to make a reasonable and just use of it as it flows through his land, subject, however, to the like right of each upper proprietor to make a reasonable and just use of the water on its course through his land and subject further to the obligation to lower proprietors to permit the water to pass away from his estate unaffected except by such consequences as follow from reasonable and just use by him. This general principle, simple in statement, often gives rise to difficulties in its application. What is a reasonable and just use of flowing water is dependent upon the state of civilization, the development of the mechanical and engineering art, climatic conditions, the customs of the neighborhood and the other varying circumstances of each case. To some extent often the amount and character of the flow may be modified by such use, for which, even though injurious to other proprietors, no action lies. A stream may be so small that its entire flow may be abstracted by the ordinary domestic uses of a farmer. Its bed may be so steep that its reasonable utilization for the generation of power requires its impounding in numerous reservoirs. But whatever the condition, each riparian owner must conduct his operations reasonably in view of like rights and obligations in the owners above and below him. The right of no one is absolute but is qualified by the existence of the same right in all others similarly situated. The use of the water flowing in a stream is common to all riparian owners and each must exercise this common right so as not essentially to interfere with an equally beneficial enjoyment of the common right by his fellow riparian owners.

* * *

In the main, the use by a riparian owner by virtue of his right as such must be within the watershed of the stream, or at least that the current of the stream shall be returned to its original bed before leaving the land of the user. This is implied in the term "riparian." It arises from the natural incidents of running water. A brook or river, so far as concerns surface indications, is inseparably connected with its watershed and owes the volume of current to its area. A definite and fixed channel is a part of the conception of a water course. To divert a substantial portion of its flow is the creation of a new and different channel, which to that extent defeats the reasonable and natural expectations of the owners lower down on the old channel. Abstraction for use elsewhere not only diminishes the flow of the parent stream but also increases that which drains the watershed into which the diversion is made, and may injure thereby riparian rights upon it. Damage thus may be occasioned in a double aspect. The precise point whether riparian rights include diversion in reasonable quantities for a proper use on property outside the watershed has never been decided in this commonwealth.

* * *

There are numerous expressions to the effect that the rights of riparian ownership extend only to use upon and in connection with an estate which adjoins the stream and cannot be stretched to include uses reasonable in themselves, but upon and in connection with nonriparian estates. See, for example, Lord Cairns in *Swindon Water Works Co. v. Wilts & Berks Canal Navigation* Co., L. R. 7 H. L. 697, 704, 705. But see, to the contrary, *Gillis v. Chase*, 31 A. 18 (N.H. 1892), and *Lawrie v. Silsby*, 56 Atl. 1106 (Vt. 1904); s.c., 74 Atl. 94 (Vt. 1909). These principles, however, are subject to the modification that the diversion, if for a use reasonable in itself, must cause actual perceptible damage to the present or potential enjoyment of the property of the lower riparian proprietor before a cause of action arises in his favor. This was settled after an elaborate discussion by Chief Justice Shaw in *Elliot v. Fitchburg R.R.*, 64 Mass. 191 (1852), a case where an upper riparian proprietor granted to the defendant railroad corporation a right to erect a dam across a stream and conduct water to its depot not on a riparian estate for use in furnishing their locomotive steam engines with water. The plaintiff, a lower riparian proprietor, was denied the right to recover nominal damages in the absence of proof of actual damages, although the principle was fully recognized that an action would lie for any encroachment upon the substantial rights of the lower owner though causing no present damage. See *Anderson v. Cincinnati Southern R. R.*, 5 S.W. 49 (Ky. 1887). In reason, there seems to be no distinction between diversion of water from a stream for use in the locomotive engines of a railroad, which of necessity consume the water by evaporation on their journeys without perceptible return to any stream, and the diversion of water for any other legitimate use outside the watershed and upon nonriparian land.

* * *

The governing principle of law in a case like the present is this: A proprietor may make any reasonable use of the water of the stream in connection with his riparian estate and for lawful purposes within the watershed, provided he leave the current diminished by no more than is reasonable, having regard for the like right to enjoy the common property by other riparian owners. If he diverts out of the watershed or upon a disconnected estate the only question is whether there is actual injury to the lower estate for any present or future reasonable use. The diversion alone without evidence of such damage does not warrant a recovery even of nominal damages.

The charge of the court below was not in conformity to this principle. It would have permitted the recovery of nominal damages, in any event, quite apart from the possibility of real injury to the plaintiff. But the defendant has suffered no harm by this error. The verdict of the jury was for substantial damages[,] and there was ample evidence to support such a conclusion. Exceptions overruled.

NOTES

1. *Place of use.* Under the rule of riparian rights, the right to use surface water is an attribute of owning land over which or adjacent to which the water flows. The water comes with land, as part of the package, when an owner acquires the land. It thus seems logical that the landowner may only use the water on the riparian tract of land itself, not elsewhere. Yet such a rule raises obvious questions. What is the riparian tract? Can a landowner expand it by acquiring adjacent land? (Yes, say nearly all states except California.) If a riparian tract is divided so that one part no longer touches the water, do the water rights on that portion end? (Yes.) Also, is it entirely impermissible to use water offsite of a riparian tract, or is the law here more of a liability rule: the water can be used elsewhere so long as the use harms no other lawful water user? How does the court in *Stratton* resolve this last issue? Does its holding adequately protect other riparian owners on the river? Does it take into account the legitimate interests of public users of the waterway?

2. *The watershed limit.* Along with the rule that water be used on the riparian tract is the court's concern in *Stratton* about using water within the watershed. A watershed (or, more aptly, a catchment basin) is an area of land that drains into a single waterway. Watersheds, of course, come in various sizes, with smaller ones often nested within larger ones. This physical reality creates problems when it comes to applying a watershed limit on place of use. What is the relevant watershed? Can a water user in Missouri, for instance, claim that the watershed rule is impossible to violate since all waters in the state flow into the Mississippi River? How should we define watershed for this purpose, taking into account (as we should, no doubt) the reason for the rule? And might our answer depend upon the identity and locations of the disputants in a particular case (that is, might the relevant watershed be determined by the location of the downstream user who is complaining)? In

any event, what is the point of the watershed rule, and why not just phrase the place of use limit in terms of the riparian tract?

3. *Water law and industrialization.* Note the facts of the principal precedent relied upon in *Stratton,* the opinion of the great Massachusetts jurist Lemuel Shaw in *Elliot v. Fitchburg Railroad,* 64 Mass. 191 (1852). In that case, a steam railroad needed water to run its boilers. It took on more water at particular stops, and then consumed the water as it chugged down the tracks. Obviously, the water was not consumed on the riparian tract from which it came; it was mostly taken away and used elsewhere. The obvious problem: How was a railroad to get the water it needed in a state with a strict place-of-use rule? (As we will see, a similar place-of-use rule applies in the case of groundwater.) Could a railroad comply with this rule by arguing that it "used" the riparian water when it put the water into the train boilers, rather than when it turned the water into steam (although in *Elliot* even the train depot was off the riparian tract)? Justice Shaw chose to modify the strict riparian place-of-use rule rather than allow the law to impede industrialization.

Strict place-of-use rules governing riparian rights would have meant that the nation's new water-using industrial activities had to be conducted on riparian tracts and within the watershed. If an industry used the water elsewhere, it risked the possibility that its water use would be ended by some other water user who could show actual harm. This was plainly a problem for states that wanted to promote industrial development. Somehow, water law needed to change to allow water use by industries not located on riparian tracts. Many courts did so in the way that Massachusetts Supreme Judicial Court did, by authorizing off-tract uses subject to a no-harm rule. This particular shift in water law was one of many ways that nineteenth-century property law changed to accommodate industrial growth in America—a trend, already noted, that authorized more intensive land and resource uses. The larger story is sketched in J. Willard Hurst, *Law and the Conditions of Freedom in the Nineteenth Century United States* 6–7 (1956); Morton J. Horwitz, *The Transformation of American Law, 1780–1860,* at 31–62 (1977). A perceptive study that pays attention to the ways railroads influenced the common law is Howard Schweber, *The Creation of American Law, 1850–1880: Technology, Politics, and the Construction of Citizenship* (2004).

4. *What about the public?* Under the rule of law embraced in *Stratton,* the boys' school can use water in a distant location so long as no downstream riparian is harmed in an actual or likely future water use. Does this mean that the last landowner on a river can drain the river dry because there is no one downstream to complain? And what about members of the public who might use the river for boating or fishing, or who are concerned about its ecological condition? Should harm to their interests in the river allow them to challenge water uses that are off tract or out of the watershed?

If we adhere strictly to the reasoning in *Stratton,* it appears that only riparian landowners have water rights, and only holders of such rights can complain about what other water users are doing. The public has little or no role. Is the public interest in cases like this limited to public nuisance actions?

PYLE V. GILBERT
Supreme Court of Georgia
265 S.E.2d 584 (1980)

[The Gilberts, owners of a 140-year-old water-powered gristmill on a non-navigable watercourse, filed suit against various upper riparian landowners who diverted water for irrigation both on and off the riparian tracts. The Gilberts alleged that the diversion of water was both a nuisance and a trespass and sought injunctive relief. The defendants maintained that the diversions were justified because they were reasonable uses. The lower court decided in favor of the Gilberts, and the defendants appealed.]

HILL, J.

* * *

[The court summarized the historical development of Georgia water law. The state adopted a version of the reasonable use doctrine of riparian rights in 1848. Under it a riparian owner could use water but in doing so had to avoid "material injury" to other water users. In 1863, while Georgia was part of the Confederate States of America, the legislature added provisions that seemed to ban any water diversions, and any pollution of a nonnavigable waterway, that harmed a downstream users. Otherwise, each owner was entitled to the "natural flow" of the river subject to the reasonable use of the water by other riparian owners.]

Georgia's law of riparian rights is a natural flow theory modified by a reasonable use provision. Kates, *Georgia Water Law* 63 (1969); Agnor, *Riparian Rights in Georgia*, 18 Ga.B.J. 401, 403 (1956). The reasons for the rule and its contradictory reasonable use provision were well stated by the court in *Price v. High Shoals Mfg. Co.*, 64 S.E. 87, 88 (Ga. 1909): "Under a proper construction (of the pertinent Code sections), every riparian owner is entitled to a reasonable use of the water in the stream. If the general rule that each riparian owner could not in any way interrupt or diminish the flow of the stream were strictly followed, the water would be of but little practical use to any proprietor, and the enforcement of such rule would deny, rather than grant, the use thereof. Every riparian owner is entitled to a reasonable use of the water. Every such proprietor is also entitled to have the stream pass over his land according to its natural flow, subject to such disturbances, interruptions, and diminutions as may be necessary and unavoidable on account of the reasonable and proper use of it by other riparian proprietors. Riparian proprietors have a common right in the waters of the stream, and the necessities of the business of one cannot be the standard of the rights of another, but each is entitled to a reasonable use of the water with respect to the rights of others."

In this case, the trial court found that irrigation with modern equipment was a "diversion" which is entirely prohibited by Georgia law, Code §§ 85–1301, 105–1407; *i.e.*, the trial court found that irrigation with modern equipment constituted a trespass as a matter of law. We disagree. The use of water for agricultural purposes was recognized as a reasonable use along with domestic use in the first reported Georgia case on riparian rights. *Hendrick v. Cook*, 4 Ga. 241 (1848).

The first question, then, is whether the use of water for irrigation is a diversion under our laws and thus is prohibited. We find that it is not. . . . In prohibiting "diversion", Code §§ 85–1301, 105–1407, we do not find that the General Assembly intended to prevent the use of riparian water for irrigation, even though irrigation is accomplished by removing water from its natural watercourse. Rather we think the General Assembly intended to prohibit the diversion of water from a watercourse for other purposes, such as to drain one's own property (see Goodrich v. Ga. R. & Bkg. Co., 41 S.E. 659 (Ga. 1902)) or to create a new watercourse on the diverter's property (see McNabb v. Houser, 156 S.E. 595 (Ga. 1930)). That this latter use would have been of some concern to the General Assembly is evidenced by the adoption of the natural flow theory, which recognizes that the mere presence of a watercourse on one's property generally enhances it. Rest. Torts 2d, Chapter 41, Topic 3, Introductory Note, at 212.

* * *

In sum, we find that the right of the lower riparian to receive the natural flow of the water without diversion or diminution is subject to the right of the upper riparian to its reasonable use (*Rome R. Co. v. Loeb*, 80 S.E. 785 (Ga. 1913)), for agricultural purposes, including irrigation. [The court further concluded that the issue of reasonableness was one of fact, not of law. It then went on to consider the use water off the riparian tract, either by a riparian landowner or by a water user who acquired water from a riparian owner. The court noted that a 1932 ruling limited water uses to the riparian tract, while a 1936 ruling, without discussing the 1932 ruling, came to a contrary conclusion.]

* * *

A major study of Georgia water law concluded that "Another disadvantage of this doctrine is that it permits the use of stream water only in connection with riparian land." Institute of Law and Government, University of Georgia Law School, *A Study of the Riparian and Prior Appropriation Doctrines of Water Law* 104 (1955). Likewise, the American

Law Institute now recommends allowing use of water by riparian owners on non-riparian land, Rest. Torts 2d § 855, as well as allowing non-riparian owners to acquire a right to use water from riparian owners. Id. § 856(2), (see also 7 Clark, *Waters and Water Rights*, § 614.1 at 71–72 (1976)). The Restatement relies on two principles: that riparian rights are property rights and as such could normally be transferred, and that water law should be utilitarian and allow the best use of the water. *Id.* § 855, comment b. Also, the Institute considers the acquisition of water rights by condemnation a "grant of riparian right." *Id.* comment c.

* * *

We agree with the American Law Institute that the right to use water on non-riparian land should be permitted and if that right can be acquired by condemnation, it can also be acquired by grant. Thus we find that the right to the reasonable use of water in a non-navigable watercourse on non-riparian land can be acquired by grant from a riparian owner. . . .

Judgment reversed.

NOTES

1. *Place of use in Georgia.* How does *Pyle v. Gilbert* differ from *Stratton* in terms of the riparian landowner's ability to use water off the riparian tract and outside the watershed? (Hint: quite a bit.) What does the court say about severing water rights from the land for sale as separate resources? If we freely allow uses of water away from riparian tracts, subject only to the reasonable use limit, how successful will the law be in avoiding overuse of the river? Also, if water can be used anywhere, subject only to a reasonable use limit, why then do we retain the allocation rule that allows only riparians to withdraw water? Why not say that anyone with access to a water body can make reasonable use of it? Why is it that riparian landowners should own all of the surface water rights if their water rights are not directly linked to and limited by the use of their lands?

2. *Pyle refined.* In a 2010 ruling, the Georgia Supreme Court qualified some of its language in *Pyle*. Some readers of *Pyle* concluded that irrigation as a use of water was equal in social importance to domestic water uses and shared top priority with them. In *Tunison v. Harper*, 690 S.E.2d 819 (Ga. 2010), the court expressly rejected this reading. Strictly domestic uses of water were the highest priority; all other uses occupied a lower plane.

3. *Reasonable use and the Restatement (Second) of Torts.* As they have done in the case of nuisance law, various courts have turned for guidance when determining reasonableness to the Restatement (Second) of Torts (1979), which contains the following provision:

§ 850A.   Reasonableness Of The Use Of Water

The determination of the reasonableness of a use of water depends upon a consideration of the interests of the riparian proprietor making the use, of any riparian proprietor harmed by it and of society as a whole. Factors that affect the determination include the following:

(a)   The purpose of the use,

(b)   the suitability of the use to the watercourse or lake,

(c)   the economic value of the use,

(d)   the social value of the use,

(e)   the extent and amount of the harm it causes,

(f)   the practicality of avoiding the harm by adjusting the use or method of use of one proprietor or the other,

(g)   the practicality of adjusting the quantity of water used by each proprietor,

(h)   the protection of existing values of water uses, land, investments and enterprises and

(i)   the justice of requiring the user causing harm to bear the loss.

This list of relevant factors is, of course, extensive, and invites a court to undertake pretty much an all-things-considered assessment of the propriety and wisdom of a particular water use. This, plainly, is a vague standard, giving great discretion to a jury or judge.

On the issue of place of use, the Restatement authorizes off-tract uses so long as they are, under all circumstances, reasonable. Section 855 of the Restatement, which authorizes off-tract uses, includes the following comment:

The fact that a use by a riparian proprietor is made on nonriparian land is thus an additional factor to be considered in determining the reasonableness of the use. If it is otherwise reasonable under the rule of § 850A because it is made for a beneficial purpose, is suitable to the water body and has social and economic value, a nonriparian use that can be accommodated with riparian uses and causes no substantial harm to them can be reasonable despite its nonriparian character. On the other hand, it may be unreasonable for a riparian to take a quantity of water that is disproportionate to the size of the riparian tract and carry it away from the stream, especially if other riparian demands on the stream are high and other riparian are likely to be harmed.

B. REGULATED RIPARIANISM

As demands for uses of water have intensified, about half of the eastern states have instituted permit systems modifying traditional riparian rights systems. The effect was to transition from a common law system of private rights to a regulatory system with greater public control. This shift to a complex system of administrative law often occurred incrementally, rather than from a conscious design to revolutionize water law. Consequently, there remains some disagreement as to whether there has emerged a system of regulated riparianism that is truly distinct from traditional riparian rights. See Joseph W. Dellapenna, *Adapting Riparian Rights to the Twenty-First Century*, 106 W. Va. L. Rev. 539 (2004) (discussing 18 states that have enacted regulated riparian systems); see also Joseph W. Dellapenna, *The Regulated Riparian Version of the ASCE Model Water Code: The Third Way to Allocate Water,* 30 J. Am. Water Res. Ass'n 197 (1994).

One important issue that all statutory modifications of riparianism must confront is how to treat pre-existing riparian rights. That was an issue in the following Florida case.

SOUTHWEST FLORIDA WATER MANAGEMENT DISTRICT V. CHARLOTTE COUNTY

District Court of Appeal of Florida
774 So.2d 903 (2001)

[Several Florida counties and a citrus company challenged various rules governing water use permits proposed by the Southwest Florida Water Management District. An administrative law judge heard their claims and invalidated several of the rules. Both parties appealed. In its ruling, the court explained how the state's "regulated" riparian rights system replaced its earlier, common law of riparian rights. Starting with the 1972 statute riparian water users were required to obtain water use permits. Then-existing water users obtained permits under a more relaxed standard, but as the court's ruling explains these water users, like new users, were obligated to seek renewal of their rights when their initial permits expired, suggesting that their rights were less than vested. The 1972 statute prescribed standards governing all water uses and provided mechanisms for water districts to set more detailed rules for sensitive water areas. This dispute included challenges to detailed rules proposed for Southwest Florida. It also questioned whether pre-1972 water users, when they sought renewal of their permits, were subject to the same renewal standards as other permit holders.]

DANAHY, J.

* * *

Prior to the Florida Water Resources Act of 1972, which is codified in chapter 373, Florida Statutes, water rights were governed under Florida common law by the reasonable use rule. The Florida Water Resources Act brought Florida from a common law system to a statutory permitting system and was patterned, in large part, upon *A Model Water Code,* a legislative proposal drafted by law professors at the University of Florida. See Erik Swenson, *Public Trust Doctrine and Groundwater Rights*, 53 U. Miami L. Rev. 363 (1999).

* * *

Section 373.223(1), Florida Statutes (1995), states that to obtain a [water use permit], the applicant must establish that the proposed use of water: (a) is reasonable-beneficial; (b) will not interfere with any presently existing legal water use; and (c) is consistent with the public interest. Section 373.113, Florida Statutes (1995), states that in administering the provisions of chapter 373 a governing board of a water management district "shall adopt, promulgate, and enforce such regulations as may be reasonably necessary to effectuate its powers, duties, and functions pursuant to the provisions of chapter 120." *See also* § 373.044, Fla.Stat. (1995). Section 373.219(1), Florida Statutes (1995), gives the water management districts the power to require permits for the consumptive use of water and to impose such reasonable conditions as are necessary to ensure "that such use is consistent with the overall objectives of the district or department." Thus, the [Southwest Florida Water Management] District may adopt reasonable rules in connection with its water use permitting duties in implementing the three-prong test under section 373.223(1). [The court further explained that, under the state statute, such district rules were subject to review by the state Department of Environmental Protection (DEP); indeed, the DEP had the exclusive authority to review such rules to ensure that they complied with state standards.]

[The Southwest District, in its draft rules governing water use permits, implemented the three-prong general standard of section 373.223(1) (summarized above), by setting forth the following fourteen criteria that an applicant for a permit needed to satisfy:]

(1) In order to obtain a Water Use Permit, an Applicant must demonstrate that the water use is reasonable and beneficial, is in the public interest, and will not interfere with any existing legal use of water, by providing reasonable assurances, on both an individual and a cumulative basis, that the water use:

(a) Is necessary to fulfill a certain reasonable demand;

(b) Will not cause quantity or quality changes which adversely impact the water resources, including both surface and ground waters;

(c) Will not cause adverse environmental impacts to wetlands, lakes, streams, estuaries, fish and wildlife or other natural resources;

(d) Will not cause water levels or rates of flow to deviate from the ranges set forth in Chapter 40D 8;

(e) Will utilize the lowest water quality the Applicant has the ability to use;

(f) Will not significantly induce saline water intrusion;

(g) Will not cause pollution of the aquifer;

(h) Will not adversely impact offsite land uses existing at the time of the application;

(i) Will not adversely impact an existing legal withdrawal;

(j) Will utilize local water resources to the greatest extent practicable;

(k) Will incorporate water conservation measures;

(*l*) Will incorporate reuse measures to the greatest extent practicable;

(m) Will not cause water to go to waste; and

(n) Will not otherwise be harmful to the water resources within the District.

[The counties and the company challenged this draft rule and various others proposed by the District as inconsistent with the state statute and because, they asserted, the powers given by statute to the Department of Environmental Protection had been improperly delegated to the District. The court disagreed. It noted that the DEP retained authority—exclusive authority—to review district rules for compliance with the statute. Having upheld the new 14-point permit issuance standard, the court then turned to the issue of the statute's effect on common law riparian rights, in particular to the question whether permit holders who received their permits based on pre-1972 water uses had to comply with the new permit standards when they sought renewals of their permits One county (Pinellas) claimed that it should be entitled to a permit renewal without being judged under the 14-point standard.]

As noted, prior to the Act, water rights were governed under the common law reasonable use rule. The Act replaced the common law with a statutory permitting system. Section 373.226(1) notes that all existing water uses, unless exempted, may be continued only with a permit. Section 373.226(2) states that the "governing board [of a water management district] or [DEP] shall issue an initial permit for the continuation of all uses in existence before the effective date of implementation of this part if the existing use is a reasonable-beneficial use . . . and is allowable under the common law of this state." Section 373.226(3) states that an application for a permit under subsection (2) must be made within two years from the date of the implementation of the regulations described in the Act or the use would be deemed abandoned.

Section 373.229, which governs the WUP [water use permit] application procedure, including what information must be included in the application itself, has been in existence in substantially the same form since the date of the Act. Section 373.239, which has also been in existence since the date of the Act, governs modifications and renewals of WUPs. Section 373.239(3) states that "[a]ll permit renewal applications shall be treated under this part in the same manner as the initial permit application." Pinellas argues that when read *in pari materia* with part II of chapter 373, section 373.239(3) contemplates that the two-prong test of section 373.226(2) [requiring only that a water use be reasonable-beneficial and allowed under the common law] continues to apply to applicants seeking to renew permits for water uses in existence prior to the District's implementation of the water use permitting system described in part II of the chapter.

The ALJ found that "[t]here appears to be no continuing rule in the statutory scheme for the two-prong test of section 373.226(2) two years after the effective date of the implementation of a consumptive use permitting program by the District. Reference in section 373.226 to whether a use was 'allowable under the common law of the state' tends to confirm that this two-prong test was a one-time transitional procedure for converting common law uses to permitted uses." The ALJ went on to find that "if the legislature had intended to create a favored position for the renewal of uses that predated the permitting program, that intent would have been more explicitly spelled out. The authors of the Model Water Code specifically contemplated and rejected such a preference. See Commentary to Model Water Code, at 183. There is no clear indication that the Florida Legislature intended to adopt a renewal process for common law uses that is directly contrary to the position of the authors of the Model Water Code." The ALJ further found that "[i]n adopting the Florida Water Resources Act, the legislature clearly intended to supplant the common law allocation system. Consistent with this goal, the purposes of chapter 373 are best served by making all applicants subject to the three-prong test on permit renewal, regardless of whether the use predated the origination of the permitting program. No statutory purpose is served by the continuing vestiges of the common law allocation system."

We agree with the ALJ's determination that the legislature did not intend to allow vested common law water rights to exist ad infinitum alongside a statutory-permitting system, and we also agree with his interpretation of the two-prong test of section 373.226(2) "as simply a transitional tool for implementation of the Florida Water Resources Act."

* * *

NOTES

1. *Transitioning to a regulatory system.* The Florida Supreme Court interpreted the 1972 statute to impose a fairly quick transition from a privately enforced common law liability system of riparian rights to a regulatory system controlled by administrative agencies. This transition necessarily involved a significant redefinition of the property rights of riparian landowners. Before the statute, each landowner could make reasonable use of surface water flowing over or alongside her land. After the statute, water uses required permits, and permit applications could be turned down. As the notes below explore, the rules governing water-use conflicts also changed. The 1972 statute continued to use the language of reasonable use, but that governing standard—particularly as refined by specific water districts—took on quite a different meaning. As it did so, the contours of a riparian owner's water-use right shifted considerably, in ways that benefited some water users but harmed others. The transition, of course, raised constitutional issues. But only a rare riparian landowner could likely present a substantial claim that the statute (including its implementing regulations) involved a taking of private property without the payment of just compensation under the leading rulings of the U.S. Supreme Court.

2. *Redefining reasonable use.* Central to Florida's version of regulated riparian rights is its new definition of reasonable use. The statute, as the court explained, says that water use permits can be granted for water uses that are reasonable/beneficial, that will not interfere with any presently existing legal water use, and that are consistent with the public interest. How much of a change to the common law does this language involve? The answer would likely vary a fair amount from state to state, based on variations in the common law. But the language plainly gives stronger protection than the common law did to existing water uses. Under the common law, all riparians share a waterway, and a riparian who is late in putting water to use is not, at least in theory, disadvantaged in a dispute with preexisting water users. But to say (as the statute does) that a new water use cannot "interfere" with an existing one is to suggest that priority in time now has greater importance than sharing among riparians.

We should note also the requirement that a water use must be in the public interest. Under the common law riparian rights system, the law divides water among riparian landowners: they are the only ones who can use it, and thus the only people who could be legally harmed by a given water use. Although common law authority on the issue is scant, it appears that only a riparian who is disrupted in her use of water can challenge another water use as unreasonable, and it is unreasonable only when and because it interferes with the riparian-plaintiff's water use. There is no independent common law requirement that a water use promote the public interest. That issue would be relevant only when competing riparians are fighting for the same water.

In the dispute above, of course, the Southwest Florida Water Management District took this simple (but meaningful) three-prong statutory test and expanded it substantially, into a detailed, fourteen-part test. The fourteen factors are worth studying with some care because they reflect quite a wide variety of policy concerns about water use practices, reaching far beyond disputes between two competing water users. It would be worthwhile to list all of the underlying concerns reflected in this complex standard, some designed to protect existing water (and land) uses, others more clearly environmental, still others aimed at promoting perceived economic efficiency and maximum public benefit. This Florida fourteen-point standard is usefully compared with the definition of reasonableness set forth in Section 850A of the Restatement (Second) of Torts, quoted in note 3 after the *Pyle* ruling. The Florida statute shows much more particularized concern over environmental issues. How else do they differ, and what policy motives likely account for the differences? As you contemplate this question, a key issue to consider is, how much weight do these contrasting definitions give to *priority in time* as a factor used to resolve conflicts among competing water uses? To the extent that the standards employ a "do-no-harm" test for water users, can we imagine the problems that will arise in resolving issues of causation (covered at length in chapter two)? Do lawmakers seem to assume that, in a dispute between two water uses, the second-in-time to begin use is the one that has caused the problem?

3. *The rise of administrative discretion.* Permit systems usually assign to an administrative agency the chore of determining what constitutes a reasonable use. Creating a system dependent on administrative agency discretion was unsuccessfully challenged in the principal case on non-delegation grounds. See also *Hudson River Fisherman's Ass'n v. Williams*, 139 A.D.2d 234 (N.Y. App. Div. 1988), which also upheld broad discretion on the part of the New York water agency to set the terms of a water storage permit. *Id.* at 240. Deference to agency interpretations of ambiguous statutory provisions the agency administers and to agency exercises of discretion is well established in the federal system. See *Chevron U.S.A. v. Natural Resources Defense Council,* 467 U.S. 837 (1984) (deference to legal interpretations); Antonin Scalia, *Judicial Deference to Administrative Interpretations of Law,* 1989 Duke L.J. 511 (1989); Am. Bar Ass'n, *A Guide to Judicial and Political Review of Federal Agencies* (2005).

4. *Term permits and The Model Water Code.* Another significant change made by the Florida statute was to eliminate perpetual water rights and to substitute instead use rights with definite ending dates. One of the key elements of any resource use right is its duration, and most rights have

time limits to them either built in or operating on the outside. An easement may last only so long as it is needed to carry out its intended purpose. Many resource rights, prior appropriation water rights included, are subject to forfeiture and abandonment rules. Such rules are part of a larger suite of legal provisions based on the idea of "use it or lose it." As we saw in chapter 5, oil and gas leases that enter the second lease term typically last only so long as oil or gas are produced. Unpatented mining claims on federal lands endure only if owners undertake at least the minimum needed annual assessment work. The effect of such rules is to get rid of resource rights that are no longer useful; they disappear, thereby clearing the land title (and often giving surface landowners more freedom of action). In the case of publicly owned resources, water in particular, a term-permit system allows government water agencies to regain control of the resource periodically and reallocate it to a use that is perhaps more socially valuable.

The Regulated Riparian Model Water Code, adopted by the American Society of Civil Engineers in 1996, called for term permits of no longer than 20 years unless a longer term was necessary to retire the debt associated with public facilities (not to exceed 50 years), although it did allow for permit renewals. The commentary explained that term permits would allow the state to reallocate waters to more reasonable uses and to revise permit terms and conditions to reflect changing circumstances. Am. Soc'y Civil Eng'rs, *Regulated Riparian Model Water Code* § 7R–1–02 (2004).

C. PRIOR APPROPRIATION

The landowner system of riparian water rights, inherited from England, worked well in the eastern U.S. Rainfall was plentiful, making conflicts over consumptive use rare, and irrigation was not necessary to grow crops. But rainfall was not plentiful beyond the 100th meridian, and a landowner-centered doctrine would have left control of the region's water resources largely in the hands of the federal government. Moreover, riparian rights would leave considerable uncertainty as to the scope of consumptive water use that would have to be resolved *post hoc* by triers of fact like courts. None of this was acceptable in the West, which sought certain water rights and rapid development for mining and irrigation.

The upshot was the creation of an entirely indigenous type of water law, based not on land ownership, but on first beneficial use. Temporal priority of use may have been a factor in riparianism's reasonable-use decisionmaking, but in the new western system, priority of use became determinative of priority of right. This "first-in-time" system seemed to provide certainty in the water-short West, making it attractive to the miners and the judges who reviewed their conflicts.

The initial case recognizing first-in-time as determinative in water rights disputes was *Irwin v. Phillips*, 5 Cal. 140 (1855), which involved two public land miners during the California Gold Rush. Irwin developed his mine first, diverting water for his off-stream use. Phillips staked a mine claim later downstream of Irwin's claim. When there was insufficient water for both, Phillips filed suit, claiming that Irwin's diversion violated natural flow riparianism. The California Supreme Court rejected Phillips' claim, adopting the temporal priority system first developed in the mining camps, stating that "[c]ourts are bound to take notice of the political and social condition of the country, which they judicially rule" *id.* at 146, thus ratifying the first-in-time rule of the mining camps. Neither claimant was actually a riparian owner, since both were mining on federal public lands. Because neither party possessed riparian rights, the court's ruling did not suggest that its first-in-time system displaced them. Indeed, in a later ruling the California court concluded not just that riparian rights survived but that they were superior to water rights acquired based on priority in time. In the meantime, however, first-in-time priority spread to other jurisdictions, which applied the doctrine much more broadly, including the influential Colorado decision below.

COFFIN V. LEFT HAND DITCH COMPANY

Supreme Court of Colorado
6 Colo. 443 (1882)

[The Left Hand Ditch Company, serving a variety of ranch and farm irrigators, diverted water from the South Fork of the St. Vrain Creek, and from there by ditch far outside the watershed. Coffin was a riparian owner along the St. Vrain, downstream of the Left Hand diversion, who "naturally irrigated" from the creek, probably by flood irrigation. In 1879, there was a drought with insufficient water in the creek to satisfy both Left Hand and Coffin. Coffin took matters into his own hands, tearing out Left Hand's diversion works. Left Hand filed suit seeking damages for the trespass and an injunction to prevent repetitions in the future. The lower court found for Left Hand based on its earlier actual appropriation of the water, rejecting Coffin's claim of superior rights based on riparian landownership. The court also rejected Coffin's claim that the Left Hand Ditch diversion was wrongful because it sent the water to a different watershed. Coffin appealed.]

HELM, J.

* * *

It is contended by counsel for appellants that the common law principles of riparian proprietorship prevailed in Colorado until 1876, [when] the doctrine of priority of right to water by priority of appropriation thereof was first recognized and adopted in the constitution. But we think the latter doctrine has existed from the date of the earliest appropriations of water within the boundaries of the state.

The climate is dry, and the soil, when moistened only by the usual rainfall, is arid and unproductive; except in a few favored sections, artificial irrigation for agriculture is an absolute necessity. Water in the various streams thus acquires a value unknown in moister climates. Instead of being a mere incident to the soil, it rises, when appropriated, to the dignity of a distinct usufructuary estate, or right of property. It has always been the policy of the national, as well as the territorial and state governments, to encourage the diversion and use of water in this country for agriculture; and vast expenditures of time and money have been made in reclaiming and fertilizing by irrigation portions of our unproductive territory. Houses have been built, and permanent improvements made; the soil has been cultivated, and thousands of acres have been rendered immensely valuable, with the understanding that appropriations of water would be protected. Deny the doctrine of priority or superiority of right by priority of appropriation, and a great part of the value of all this property is at once destroyed.

The right to water in this country, by priority of appropriation thereof, we think it is, and has always been, the duty of the national and state governments to protect. The right itself, and the obligation to protect it, existed prior to legislation on the subject of irrigation. It is entitled to protection as well after patent to a third party of the land over which the natural stream flows, as when such land is a part of the public domain; and it is immaterial whether or not it be mentioned in the patent and expressly excluded from the grant.

The act of congress protecting in patents such right in water appropriated, when recognized by local customs and laws, "was rather a voluntary recognition of a pre-existing right of possession, constituting a valid claim to its continued use, than the establishment of a new one." *Broder v. Natoma W. & M. Co.*, 101 U.S. 274 (1879).

We conclude, then, that the common law doctrine giving the riparian owner a right to the flow of water in its natural channel upon and over his lands, even though he makes no beneficial use thereof, is inapplicable to Colorado. Imperative necessity, unknown to the countries which gave it birth, compels the recognition of another doctrine in conflict therewith. And we hold that, in the absence of express statutes to the contrary, the first appropriator of water from a natural stream for a beneficial purpose has, with the qualifications contained in the constitution, a prior right thereto, to the extent of such appropriation. See *Schilling v. Rominger*, 4 Colo. 100, 103 (1878).

* * *

It is urged, however, that even if the doctrine of priority or superiority of right by priority of appropriation be conceded, appellee in this case is not benefited thereby. Appellants claim that they have a better right to the water because their lands lie along the margin and in the neighborhood of the St. Vrain. They assert that, as against them, appellee's diversion of said water to irrigate lands adjacent to Left Hand creek, though prior in time, is unlawful.

In the absence of legislation to the contrary, we think that the right to water acquired by priority of appropriation thereof is not in any way dependent upon the locus of its application to the beneficial use designed. And the disastrous consequences of our adoption of the rule contended for, forbid our giving such a construction to the statutes as will concede the same, if they will properly bear a more reasonable and equitable one.

The doctrine of priority of right by priority of appropriation for agriculture is evoked, as we have seen, by the imperative necessity for artificial irrigation of the soil. And it would be an ungenerous and inequitable rule that would deprive one of its benefit simply because he has, by large expenditure of time and money, carried the water from one stream over an intervening watershed and cultivated land in the valley of another. It might be utterly impossible, owing to the topography of the country, to get water upon his farm from the adjacent stream; or if possible, it might be impracticable on account of the distance from the point where the diversion must take place and the attendant expense; or the quantity of water in such stream might be entirely insufficient to supply his wants. It sometimes happens that the most fertile soil is found along the margin or in the neighborhood of the small rivulet, and sandy and barren land beside the larger stream. To apply the rule contended for would prevent the useful and profitable cultivation of the productive soil, and sanction the waste of water upon the more sterile lands.

* * *

Affirmed.

NOTES

1. *Dividing water from land. Coffin v. Left Hand Ditch* was a milestone in natural resources law. The effect of the ruling was to sever water from the land and make it available as a discrete resource. For various reasons, practical and political, the court decided that water law needed to change. By changing the law, the court changed the bundle of rights that landowners obtained. As it engaged in this lawmaking, the court maintained—as courts often do—that it was merely applying the law that already existed. But we should not be misled. Like other states, Colorado adopted the common law not later than when it entered the Union, riparian rights included. In *Coffin* the court exercised its power to tailor the common law to local circumstances. The effect of shifting to prior appropriation was to strip riparian landowners of their water rights—an extraordinary change in an arid land, and one that courts in other jurisdictions would later view as an

unconstitutional interference with private rights. See, e.g., *Lux v. Haggin*, 4 P. 919, 10 P. 674 (Cal. 1886) (recognizing both riparian and prior appropriation rights in California; see note 4 below).

2. *Why the change?* What prompted the court to decide that riparian rights were ill-suited to circumstances in Colorado? We need to read the case carefully to answer this question, but we can surmise some problems based upon *Stratton* and *Pyle*. The riparian rights place-of-use limit was apparently a large problem in both of its forms—its limits to the riparian tract and to the watershed of origin. Another problem was the requirement to protect a river's natural flow (although this limit had largely faded by the time of *Coffin*). Especially in a booming mining region in arid country, it was impractical to require water users to maintain the natural streamflow or to limit rights-holders to owners of streamside land. And so the Colorado court discarded riparian rights as the governing legal rule. Might the court have done otherwise—maintaining riparian rights—if the riparian rights law that then prevailed had looked something like the more flexible version applied a century later in *Pyle* (which countenanced a major out-of-basin diversion)? In other words, could Colorado have responded to perceived water problems by modifying riparian rights, allowing more intensive water uses and relaxing place-of-use limits, rather than abandoning the doctrine wholesale?

In a provocative study of the origins of prior appropriation in Colorado, David Schorr has argued that courts consciously interpreted water law to promote widespread use by as many users as possible, avoiding monopoly and promoting productive use at the same time. He linked this philosophy to longstanding national agrarian traditions, including an anti-monopoly sentiment that resisted restricting water rights to those few landowners with riparian lands. David B. Schorr, *The Colorado Doctrine: Water Rights, Corporations, and Distributive Justice on the American Frontier* (2013).

3. *Choosing a water rights system.* As noted immediately before *Coffin* (pp. 460–461), the prior appropriation system began life in California as a way of allocating water rights on federally owned land, a setting in which neither claimant possessed riparian rights. A few years after *Coffin*, the California Supreme Court was urged in a major case to abandon riparian rights and shift entirely to prior appropriation, as Colorado had done. The California court rejected the idea in *Lux v. Haggin*, 4 P. 919, 10 P. 674 (Cal. 1886) (still the court's longest decision), thereby retaining riparian rights and making them superior in claim to all prior appropriation rights, regardless of date of original appropriation. The result was to recognize both kinds of water rights, creating a form of legal and economic confusion that lingers to this day. An ensuing state constitutional amendment subjected both prior appropriation and riparian rights to a reasonableness standard (see discussion of the *Joslin* case, below at pp. 529–535).

As for water on federal lands, the federal government could have, if it had chosen, crafted a water allocation system applicable on such lands, just as it has developed resource-use systems for other natural resources on the lands (minerals, oil and gas, timber, forage). Instead, it stood aside while states applied their own water allocation systems, intervening (as we will see below) only to take control of water when it was needed to support federal activities on specific parcels of federal land that were reserved for specific federal purposes. This dominant role for the states in managing and allocating water on federal lands was confirmed by the U.S. Supreme Court in *United States v. Rio Grande Dam & Irrigation Co.*, 174 U.S. 690, 702–03 (1899). The federal government would not stand in the way of states choosing their own water allocation system: "[A]s to every stream within its dominion a State may change this common-law rule, and permit the appropriation of the flowing waters for such purposes as it deems wise."

4. *Comparing surface water right systems.* The following chart compares the elements of the various surface-water regimes, including the federal reserved water rights doctrine taken up later:

Comparing Surface-Water Right Systems

	Riparian Rights	Prior Appropriation	Reserved Rights*
Land-based?	Yes—part of the fee	No—water is severed from land	Yes—attaches to reserved federal lands at time of land reservation
Measure of the right	Reasonable use	Beneficial use without waste	Sufficient for purposes of the land reservation
Temporal priority important?	Nominally no but often used as tie-breaker	Yes	Yes—at least in the West
Use or lose it?	No	Yes	No
Place of use	Riparian lands**	None initially, but water right then attaches to land	Mostly on the land reserved
Transferability?	Transfers with the riparian land	Yes—but limited by "no injury" rule	When Congress authorizes

---

*   Federal reserved water rights are considered below (pp. 574–588). They are rights that attach to federally owned lands when the lands are removed from the public domain and set aside (reserved) to fulfill particular federal purposes. Because federal water-rights disputes almost always arise in prior appropriation jurisdictions, federal rights are typically described as appropriative-type rights that date from the date of the land reservation; they are thus inferior to then-existing appropriative rights but senior to all water rights acquired later.

**   In some states, a riparian landowner may use water on non-riparian lands so long as there is no injury to other riparian uses; in a few states (as in *Pyle*) she can use the water off tract for any reasonable use and can allow others to use the water.

	Riparian Rights	Prior Appropriation	Reserved Rights*
Shortages shared?	Yes	No; imposed on junior users	No, imposed on junior users (in West)

5.   *At what cost?* The facts of *Coffin* point out the need for greater legal flexibility in water use than the riparian rights doctrine originally allowed. Change of some sort was plainly required to accommodate social policies favoring widespread use and irrigating arable lands (which were not always riparian lands). But what costs were involved in the shift from riparian rights to prior appropriation? On this question, consider the effects of transporting water for use miles from the source and outside the watershed. What effects might long-distance water transport have on the ecological functioning and biodiversity of the various waterways involved? Consider also the efficiency of such transport. How much water would be lost along the way? Note that the competing water users in *Coffin* were both irrigators growing crops. As applied here, the first-in-time rule gave the water to the irrigator located a considerable distance from the river (the Left Hand Ditch Company), instead of to the irrigator who was located along the banks of St. Vrain Creek itself. How sensible is this water use pattern? And what if half of the water diverted from the St. Vrain was lost while transporting the water to the distant, first-in-time irrigation project? Should this inefficiency not be relevant in deciding who gets the water? We return to the issue below.

6.   *Blood, water, and the role of self-help.* Notice that Coffin was an unsympathetic plaintiff because he took it upon himself to destroy Left Hand's irrigation works. Resort to self-help was also an issue in *Power v. People*, 28 P. 1121 (Colo. 1892), in which Charles Baer was diverting water through a ditch on Mark Power's ranch when Power shot and killed him. The court instructed the jury that the fact that Baer may have wrongfully operated the ditch did not justify murder. The Colorado Supreme Court upheld the instruction and the conviction, stating, "Human blood is more precious than water, even in this thirsty land." *Id.* at 1124.

7.   *What water?* By severing property rights in water from the land, the Colorado Supreme Court created for itself various legal problems that did not exist under riparian rights. One problem, which the court would be forced to consider repeatedly over the years, was the need to divide up the hydrologic system. Water, of course, moves in circular flows, beginning as rain, flowing over or percolating through the ground, perhaps reaching the sea, but in any event returning through evaporation and transpiration to the sky. When a drop of rain hits the ground, at what point does it enter the river system so that it becomes subject to the first-in-time rule? Surely if the rain is immediately soaked up by plants on a person's land, the landowner has done nothing wrong. But can the landowner also collect rainwater in a cistern and use it, on the theory that he is using rainwater, not water taken from a river? And what about water that flows out of a natural spring on the land? Is this

water part of the land, on the theory that it is not yet river water, or is it instead subject to the superior rights of some downstream appropriator the moment it comes from the ground? The possible conflicts are almost countless in terms of their factual permutations, as the following decision illustrates.

SOUTHEASTERN COLORADO WATER CONSERVANCY DIST. V. SHELTON FARMS

Supreme Court of Colorado
529 P.2d 1321 (1974)

[Shelton Farms claimed an appropriation water right on the over-appropriated Arkansas River, free of any "call" of senior water rights, because it enhanced the river flow by removing phreatophytes (water-loving trees, like salt cedar) and cottonwoods along the banks of the river and filling in a wetland. The district court awarded Shelton a water right in the water saved, reasoning that the water would not be in the river without Shelton's work. The water district appealed.]

DAY, J.

* * *

To comprehend the importance of this lawsuit, it is necessary to understand the Arkansas River and its tributaries.

In 1863 there were virtually no "water-loving" trees along the banks of the river. Their growth was prevented when the great roaming buffalo herds ate the saplings, and the native Indians used most of the timber. In the next 40 years both the buffalo and the Indians were decimated. Phreatophytes (water consuming plants) and cottonwood began to appear along the Arkansas. After the great Pueblo flood of 1921 the river bottom became thickly infested with tamarisk or salt cedar, a highly phreatophytic growth.

Since 1863[,] all surface flow of the river has been put to beneficial use, until today the Arkansas is greatly over-appropriated. There is not enough flow to satisfy decreed water rights. The phreatophytes have hindered the situation, for they have consumed large quantities of subsurface water which would otherwise have flowed in the stream and been available for decreed use.

In 1940, appellee Shelton bought 500 acres of land on the Arkansas River. Since then, he has cleared two land areas of phreatophytes, and filled in a third marshy area. Shelton claimed he had saved approximately 442 acre-feet of water per year, previously consumed by phreatophytes or lost to evaporation, which is now available for beneficial use. Shelton had 8 previously decreed wells. He asked for the right to augment his previous water rights with the salvaged water, to use during those times when pumping is curtailed by the State Engineer.

The objectors Southeastern Water Conservancy District, and others, moved to dismiss the augmentation application. The motion was denied and trial was held. The lower court awarded Shelton 181.72 acre-feet of water, free from the call of the river. The lower court analogized to the law of accretion, stating that the capture and use by another of water which ordinarily would be lost is not detrimental to prior holders.

* * *

II

The fact[s] . . . are not disputed. Before this Court is totally a question of law. The issue can be stated very simply: May one who cuts down water-consuming vegetation obtain a decree for an equivalent amount of water for his own beneficial use free from the call of the river?

Appellees state that the Water Right Determination and Administration Act (the Act), 1969 Perm.Supp., C.R.S.1963, 148–21–1 *et seq.*, permits augmentation or substitution of water captured. Those are flexible terms. Thus, appellees feel that the source of water so provided— whether developed or salvaged—is immaterial, so long as prior vested rights are not injured. They insist that but for their actions the salvaged water would have been available to no one, so now they may receive a water right free from the call of prior appropriators, who are in no way harmed. Appellees conclude that their actions provide maximum utilization of water, protect vested rights, and encourage conservation and waste reduction in the water-scarce Arkansas River Valley.

Also appearing here is the Colorado Water Protection and Development Association, which has filed an amicus brief in support of both judgments below. The Association is presently developing and implementing a plan for augmentation, similar to Shelton's to permit its member wells to continue pumping, allegedly without injury to vested senior rights on the river.

The objectors assert that the lower court's resolution of the issue does violence to Colorado's firm appropriation doctrine of "first in time—first in right" on which the priority of previous decrees is bottomed. They point out that the existing case law in Colorado, which was not changed by statute, limits the doctrine of "free from call" to waters which are *truly developed and were never part of the river system.* They argue that appellees' claims were not for developed water, and thus must come under the mandates of the priority system. Furthermore, a priority date free from the call of the river will impinge the entire scheme of adjudication of water decrees as required by the Act.

There is no legal precedent squarely in point for either denying or approving these claims. The answer requires consideration of judicial precedent relating to "developed" and "salvaged" water, as well as consideration of the provisions of the Water Act. Also squarely before us is the equally serious question of whether the granting of such an unique water right will encourage denuding river banks everywhere of trees and shrubs which, like the vegetation destroyed in these cases, also consume the river water.

III

We first consider existing case law. There is no question that one who merely clears out a channel, lines it with concrete or otherwise hastens the flow of water, without adding to the existing water, is not entitled to a decree.

* * * A thorough research by all parties, including the amicus, shows no Colorado case where a person has been granted a water right free from the call of the river for water which has always been tributary to a stream. If it is shown that the water would ultimately return to the river, it is said to be part and parcel thereof, and senior consumers are entitled to use it according to their decreed priorities. . . .

Thus, this case law draws a distinction between "developed" and "salvaged" water. Both terms are words of art. Developed implies *new* waters not previously part of the river system. These waters are free from the river call, and are not junior to prior decrees. Salvaged water implies waters in the river or its tributaries (including the aquifer) which ordinarily would go to waste, but somehow are made available for beneficial use. Salvaged waters are subject to call by prior appropriators. We cannot airily waive aside the traditional language of the river, and draw no distinctions between developed and salvaged water. To do so would be to wreak havoc with our water law. Those terms, and others, evolved specifically to tread softly in this state where water is so precious.

The roots of phreatophytes are like a pump. The trees, which did not have to go to court or seek any right, merely "sucked up" the water from prior appropriators. Appellees now take the water from the trees. Therefore, appellees also are continuing to take from the appropriators, but seek a court decree to approve it. They added nothing new; what was there was merely released and put to a different use. To grant appellees an unconditional water right therefor would be a windfall which cannot be allowed, for thirsty men cannot step into the shoes of a "water thief" (the phreatophytes). Senior appropriators were powerless to move on the land of others and destroy the "thief"—the trees and phreatophytes— before they took firm root. They are helpless now to move in and destroy them to fulfill their own decrees. The property (the water) must return from whence it comes—the river—and thereon down the line to those the river feeds in turn.

IV

Each appellee decree was assigned an historical priority date. However, each decree was nevertheless to be free from the call of the river. In other words, despite a paper date the decree was to be outside the priority system, in derogation of the "first in time—first in right" water theory normally followed in Colorado.

Appellees argue that there is no injury to prior appropriators by this unusual practice. They assert that the water was unavailable for use anyway, so to grant it to another harms no one, yet benefits the policies of maximum utilization and beneficial conservation. Objectors counter that any decree so granted would found a new system of "last in time—first in right," and make administration of the priority system of the Act impossible.

Appellees would substitute the priority doctrine with a lack of injury doctrine. In *Fellhauer v. People*, [447 P.2d 986 (Colo. 1968)], we spoke of the future of water law:

> . . . It is implicit . . . that, along with *vested rights*, there shall be *maximum utilization* of the water of this state. As administration of water approaches its second century the curtain is opening upon the new drama of *maximum utilization* and how constitutionally that doctrine can be integrated into the law of *vested rights*. We have known for a long time that the doctrine was lurking in the backstage shadows as a result of the accepted, though oft violated, principle that the right to water does not give the right to waste it. (Emphasis in original.)

The Colorado legislature responded to the *Fellhauer* decision and its twin mandates of protecting vested rights and achieving maximum utilization by enacting various amendments to the 1963 Water Right Determination and Administration Act. 1969 Perm.Supp., C.R.S.1963, 148–21–2(1) is a declaration of policy that all waters in Colorado have been

> . . . declared to be the property of the public. . . . As incident thereto, it shall be the policy of this state to integrate the appropriation, use and administration of underground water tributary to a stream with the use of surface water, in such a way as to maximize the beneficial use of all of the waters of this state.

Section 148–21–2(2) further states that

> "(a) . . . it is hereby declared to be the further policy of the state of Colorado that in the determination of water rights, uses and administration of water the following principles shall apply:

"(b) *Water rights and uses heretofore vested* in any person by virtue of previous or existing laws, including an appropriation from a well, *shall be protected* subject to the provisions of this article.

"(c) The existing use of ground water, either independently or in conjunction with surface rights, shall be recognized to the fullest extent possible, *subject to the preservation of other existing vested rights*. . . . (Emphasis added.)

* * *

We do not read into the enactment of the post-*Fellhauer* amendments carte blanche authority to substitute water consumption and raise it to a preferential right.

Beyond question, the Arkansas River is over-appropriated. Water promised has not been water delivered, for there is simply not enough to go around. Thus, the question is not whether prior appropriators are injured *today* by appellees' actions. The injury occurred *long ago*, when the water-consuming trees robbed consumers of water which would have naturally flowed for their use. The harm was real and enormous. The logical implication of the injury standard is that *until senior consumers have been saturated to fulfillment*, any displacement of water from the time and place of their need is harmful to them.

Perhaps most important is the mandate of 1971 Perm.Supp., C.R.S. 1963, 148–21–22. This sets up the priority system of "first in time—first in right" in Colorado:

. . . the priority date awarded for water rights . . . adjudged and decreed on applications for a determination of the amount and priority thereof . . . during each calendar year shall establish the relative priority among other water rights . . . awarded on such applications filed in that calendar year; *but such water rights . . . shall be junior to all water rights . . . awarded on such applications filed in any previous calendar year*. . . . (Emphasis added.)

This section cannot be ignored, as it is part of the same overall Act. There is nothing in the plain language of the statute to exempt appellees' plans from the priority date system. Thus, we hold that all water decrees of any kind are bound to the call of the river, subject to any specific exemptions found within the law. To hold any other way would be to weaken the priority system, and create a super class of water rights never before in existence.

We arrive at the instant decision with reluctance, as we are loathe to stifle creativity in finding new water supplies, and do wish not to discourage maximized beneficial use of Colorado's water. But there are questions of policy to consider. If new waters can be had by appellees' method, without legislative supervision, there will be perhaps thousands of such super decrees on all the rivers of the state. S. E. Reynolds, State Engineer of New Mexico for many years, pointed out the dangers inherent in this procedure:

> ... If one ignores the technical difficulty of determining the amount of water salvaged, this proposal, at first blush, might seem reasonable and in the interest of the best use of water and related land resources.

> * * *

> On closer scrutiny, it appears that if the water supply of prior existing rights is lost to encroaching phreatophytes and then taken by individuals eradicating the plants the result would be chaos. The doctrine of prior appropriation as we know it would fall—the phreatophytes and then the individual salvaging water would have the best right. Furthermore, if individuals salvaging public water lost to encroaching phreatophytes were permitted to create new water rights where there is no new water, the price of salt cedar jungles would rise sharply. And we could expect to see a thriving, if clandestine, business in salt cedar seed and phreatophyte cultivation.

> If these decrees were affirmed, the use of a power saw or a bulldozer would generate a better water right than the earliest ditch on the river. The planting and harvesting of trees to create water rights superior to the oldest decrees on the Arkansas would result in a harvest of pandemonium. Furthermore, one must be concerned that once all plant life disappears, the soil on the banks of the river will slip away, causing irreparable erosion.

> * * *

> We believe that in this situation unrestrained self-help to a previously untapped water supply would result in a barren wasteland. While we admire the industry and ingenuity of appellees, we cannot condone the removal of water on an *ad hoc*, farm by farm basis. The withdrawal of water must be orderly, and to be orderly it must come under the priority system.

> * * *

> Judgments reversed and cause remanded to the trial court with directions to vacate the decrees.

NOTES

1.   *The call of the river.* For water lawyers, the "call of the river" means something quite different from what it meant to Huckleberry Finn. The first-in-time system can work only if an earlier water user who is short of water can look upstream and demand that lower priority water users halt their uses, to the extent physically necessary for the senior water user to get water. (As we will see later, this legal arrangement can be quite inefficient if substantial water is lost getting the water down river to the senior user.) The demands of senior users form the river's call. When water in a river is fully appropriated, someone who wants to use water either needs to acquire it from an existing user or find water that is not yet subject to the river's call, leading to litigation such as this one.

2.   *Salvaged water vs. developed water.* Note the court's distinction between efforts landowners make to save water from loss (as by lining irrigation ditches) and efforts that actually add new water to a river system (as by importing water from another river system or finding water that would never make it to the river). Is this distinction adequate to resolve all controversies? You should pay particular attention to the examples that the court gives of developed water; this list is nearly exhaustive, rather than illustrative.

3.   *Ecological considerations.* One concern motivating the court's holding was its worry about encouraging landowners to destroy streamside vegetation. Such vegetation plays critical ecological roles in riparian ecosystems, sometimes providing habitat for endangered species. According to the majority, both water and land are important, and "the elements of water and land must be used in harmony to the maximum *feasible* use of both." If we took this idea seriously, how might it influence the ways we define "permissible" water uses? Traditionally (as we will see), the beneficial nature of a water use was determined in the abstract, based on the type of use (for irrigation, industry, drinking, etc.) with only minimal concerns about water-use efficiency and essentially no concern at all about the ecological disruption of diverting and consuming the water. As for the trees themselves, should the law take into account whether the trees are "native" to the region—that is, whether they existed there when buffalo roamed freely—or is it enough to note their highly-valued roles in the altered riparian ecosystems of today?

4.   *Conserved water.* The *Shelton Farms* court was wary that granting senior rights for this sort of created or salvaged water would threaten the stability of the prior appropriation system, claiming that "the doctrine of prior appropriation as we know it would fall," producing a "clandestine business in salt cedar seed and phreatophyte cultivation" and lead to "unrestrained self-help" in the eradication of plant life on the banks which would "result in a barren wasteland." However, other states, such as Oregon, allow appropriative rights in conserved water. Oregon permits an applicant to keep up to 75 percent of the water she conserves. See O.R.S. § 537.470(3)

(2003): "After determining the quantity of conserved water, if any, required to mitigate the effects on other water rights, the commission shall allocate 25 percent of the remaining conserved water to the state and 75 percent to the applicant."

5. *Dividing water from land by law.* Aside from the above points, *Shelton Farms* is a vivid illustration of the problems that arise whenever lawmakers decide to sever one natural "resource" from the land and allocate it separately to someone other than the landowner. No matter what the natural resource, practical problems arise in drawing the line between the rights of the landowner and the rights of the owner of the discrete resource. Nature does not come in neat bundles; one valuable resource is ecologically connected to everything around it. Water lawyers for decades have complained about the law's tendency to come up with different rules governing surface water and groundwater, as if the hydrological cycle did not exist. The same issue comes up in other settings, for nature's parts are inevitably interdependent. *Shelton Farms* reminds us that plants soak up water. Water is also lost to evaporation and seepage. At the same time, shade trees along rivers can keep water temperatures down, aiding aquatic life and reducing evaporation. One way, then, to think about *Shelton Farms* is as a case that articulates the rights of landowners to water on their lands, even in a prior appropriation jurisdiction. According to the court, for instance, a landowner who "finds" water not part of a river system gets to keep it, just as the landowner can usually capture rainfall and keep it. To see this dividing line—between the rights of the landowner and the rights of the owner of the discrete resource—is to identify one of the main functions of natural resources law: it draws this vital line, clarifying the rights of the resource owner, thereby specifying the limits as to what a landowner owns.

Temporal priority is of course the *sine qua non* of the prior appropriation doctrine. But just what counts as first-in-time?

OPHIR SILVER MINING CO. V. CARPENTER

Supreme Court of Nevada
4 Nev. 534 (1869)

[In another foundation case, Ophir claimed that Carpenter interfered with its senior water right; Carpenter defended on the ground that he, not Ophir, held the senior water right. Ophir's predecessor began constructing its diversion in 1859, finishing in 1860; defendant's predecessor—Rose—began his ditch earlier, in 1858, and actual diverted water through it in 1859. Rose began a major expansion of this ditch (planned all along, it was said) starting 1862 and concluding in 1865, at which point his water diversion increased approximately ten-fold. Rose claimed an 1858 priority date for all of its water under the so-called "relation back" doctrine, which allows a claimant to date a diversion from the beginning of work on it so long as the claimant "diligently pursues" the project to completion. Carpenter countered by claiming that Ophir held two water rights, not one; an early water right for its 1859 actual diversion and a second water right, later in time than Carpenter's, covering the additional flow in the expanded ditch.]

LEWIS, C.J.

* * *

As we have already stated, we concede the fact, for the present, that Rose designed, when he constructed his ditch in the year 1858, to enlarge it to the capacity of the present ditch, and if he has shown that the design thus conceived was prosecuted with a reasonable degree of diligence until its completion, then the defendant's right to that quantity of water now claimed by them will relate back to the spring of 1858, and thus antedate the plaintiff's right eighteen months or two years, thereby giving them the superior right. But in our opinion the evidence shows an utter failure on the part of Rose to prosecute his original design with that diligence which the law requires.

The manner in which this work was prosecuted we gather from the testimony of Rose himself. In the year 1858 the ditch was constructed, and a great deal of work was necessarily done. In the succeeding year also a considerable amount of work was done in cleaning out the ditch and enlarging it in some places. Sometime in the summer of this year the ditch was completed to such an extent that a small quantity of water was run through it to Dayton. It is very doubtful whether any work was done this year towards a systematic enlargement of the ditch for the purpose of increasing its general capacity. Rose himself thus describes the work done: "I was trying to get more water through; so wherever earth or rock slid in from the sides of the ditch, all the men hired by the day were instructed to dig or throw it out, and to throw out all the loose dirt or gravel that was not worked out by the water running through." However this may be, it is certain that in the succeeding year, that is in 1860, nothing whatever was done towards enlargement. Indeed the only thing done during the entire year was the employment of two men, who were engaged for a few days in throwing out rock from the ditch. This is all the work that was done between the fall of 1859 and the month of May, A. D. 1861, a period of more than eighteen months. As counsel for appellant very aptly remarked, "Rose during this time gave to other pursuits his time and industry, and to the vast enterprise of securing all the waters of the Carson [R]iver, only a diligent contemplation."

The year 1861 is little less barren of results. A few men were employed for a period of three months only, who, Rose says, were engaged in cleaning out and enlarging the ditch. From the fall of 1861 to the summer of 1862 nothing appears to have been done. In the summer from three to twenty men were employed, and continued work for about five months. But it is not pretended that they were employed at enlarging, but only cleaning out the ditch. Rose testifies that he did not know that it was enlarged at all that year; that the heavy rains during the winter had filled it up in many places; that he had it all cleaned out. In September of this year the contract between Rose and Shanklin and McConnell was entered into, and during the years 1863 and 1864 the work progressed, and the present ditch of the defendants was completed.

Thus, it appears, that from the fall of 1859 to the summer of 1862, a period of over two years and a half, work was done upon the ditch for about three months only; that was during the year 1861, when Rose testifies that from seventeen to twenty men were employed. During this period of inactivity on the part of Rose, the grantors of the plaintiff prosecuted their work vigorously, and finished their ditch to its present capacity in the year 1860. These facts, it is argued on behalf of defendants, show such diligence on the part of their grantor in the prosecution of his original design as to make their right to the quantity of water now diverted by them relate to the time when Rose in the year 1858 did the first act towards appropriation. We are constrained to differ from counsel upon this proposition.

In our judgment those facts exhibit an utter want of diligence in the prosecution of the design which it is claimed was undertaken by Rose. If the labor of twenty men for three or four months, in a period of two years and a half, constitutes diligence in the prosecution of such a vast enterprise as this, it is difficult, if not impossible, to designate the entire want of diligence. The manner in which this work was prosecuted certainly does not accord with what is generally understood to be reasonable diligence. Diligence is defined to be the "steady application to business of any kind, constant effort to accomplish any undertaking." The law does not require any unusual or extraordinary efforts, but only that which is usual, ordinary, and reasonable. The diligence required in cases of this kind is that constancy or steadiness of purpose or labor which is usual with men engaged in like enterprises, and who desire a speedy accomplishment of their designs. Such assiduity in the prosecution of the enterprise as will manifest to the world a *bona fide* intention to complete it within a reasonable time. It is the doing of an act, or series of acts, with all practical expedition, with no delay, except such as may be incident to the work itself.

The law, then, required the grantors of the defendants to prosecute the work necessary to an execution of the design with all practical expedition. But the evidence clearly shows that this was not done. The ditch was of the same general size, and the flumes of the same capacity, at the time when Shanklin and McConnell commenced work, as they were in the spring of 1859. As no great effort is made necessary, so no unreasonable dilatoriness or delay is tolerated. But it is unnecessary for us to determine what would be deemed reasonable diligence on the part of the grantors of the defendants in this case; it is enough to say that the doing of five or six days' work during a period of sixteen months, that is from the fall of 1859 to the month of May, 1861, and only three months' labor during a period of two years and a half, does not exhibit that diligence which the law requires. The weather would not have prevented work upon this ditch ordinarily more than three or four months in the year, hence labor upon it could probably have been prosecuted during eight or nine months out of every twelve. Here, however, there was a period of thirty months, when only about three months' work was done, or one month out of every ten. Rose during this time may have dreamed of his canal completed, seen it with his mind's eye yielding him a great revenue; he may have indulged the hope of providential interposition in his favor; but this cannot be called a diligent prosecution of his enterprise. Surely he could hardly have expected to complete it during his natural life by such efforts as were made through this period.

It is, however, claimed on behalf of the defendants that all the work was done at this time which under the circumstances could be done, and that the law requires no more. Rose's illness for a short time early in the year 1860; his want of means, and considerations of economy, are suggested as circumstances to be considered in determining whether the enterprise was prosecuted with reasonable diligence. Rose testifies that in the spring of the year 1860 he was sick. But it is not shown that that should necessarily interfere with the prosecution of the work. For aught that appears in the record it could have proceeded notwithstanding his illness. If it were admitted, however, that his illness constituted a valid excuse for a want of diligence, it would only excuse it whilst such illness continued, which was only for a short time in the early part of 1860. But we are inclined to believe that his illness is not a circumstance which can be taken into consideration at all. Like the pecuniary condition of a person, it is not one of those matters incident to the enterprise, but rather to the person. The only matters in cases of this kind which can be taken into consideration are such as would affect any person who might be engaged in the same undertaking, such as the state of the weather, the difficulty of obtaining laborers, or something of that character. It would be a most dangerous doctrine to hold that ill-health or pecuniary inability of a claimant of a water privilege will dispense with the necessity of actual appropriation within a reasonable time or the diligence which is usually required in the prosecution of the work necessary for the purpose. . . .

We conclude, therefore, that Rose and his associates did not prosecute the work upon their ditch with that diligence which the law required, and so their right to any quantity of water, beyond what could be taken through the old ditch, is subordinate and subject to the rights of the plaintiff.

* * *

NOTES

1. *First to do what?* According to *Ophir,* what does a putative appropriator have to do in order to gain a property interest in water? An initial need, of course, is to find water that is not already claimed. But what else in physical terms? This question—first to do what?—routinely arises in any resource setting in which a resource is allocated or made available on a first-in-time basis. In the context of a wild game animal, it is made available to the first one to capture it. That rule, as we saw in chapter 4, seems easy enough, but it can get tricky. What does capture entail? The dispute in *Pierson v. Post* (p. 248) presented the question squarely: first to take physical possession, the majority concluded; for Judge Livingston it was first to start the animal and follow it in hot pursuit with the intent and apparent ability to capture it. We shall see in a later chapter another illustration, the case of mineral rights on federal lands under the Mining Law of 1872 (chapter 8, pp. 690 et seq.). The answer in that setting is: first to discover a valuable mineral deposit and properly locate a mining claim that includes it.

First in time, as we have noted, is simply one of many possible resource allocation methods. In the case of common law riparian rights, the right to use water is included in the package of landowner rights and allocated along with the land and in the same manner. In the instance of regulated riparian rights, the allocation method, as we have just seen, is a more complex one, taking into account public interest, riparian landownership and priority in time. One virtue of first in time, particularly in settings such as the early mining camps, is that the allocation method does not require a governmental presence to run it. Private parties can handle matters on their own except when specific disputes arise.

2. *The relation-back doctrine. Ophir* is chiefly about the relation-back doctrine, which allows an appropriator completing an appropriation with due diligence to obtain a priority date as of the date that work on the diversion began. The diversion work must be fully completed, and water actually applied to a beneficial use, to trigger the relation-back doctrine. In operation the doctrine protects large water-diversion projects from interference by water diverters who begin their diversions later but finish them first. An appropriator can take advantage of this relation-back rule, the court tells us, only by using due diligence in completing the project. What, though, is due diligence in a setting such as this? More aptly, what excuses can an appropriator employ to explain delays in completing a project?

Today, appropriators must first obtain permits to initiate a water use, but the relation-back rule of due-diligence still applies. A water right only ripens into a lasting form of private property when all the elements of appropriation are met. Presumably, if a person's due diligence is interrupted by a competing claimant, the person has an excuse for not completing work in a timely manner.

The relation-back doctrine has particular importance in the case of municipal water supply projects, which often take years to complete and are subject to the vagaries of the public funding process. Sometimes, it can take decades to finish a municipal project. For example, the second aqueduct carrying water from the Mono Lake Basin in northern California to Los Angeles took decades to complete. The California courts nonetheless assumed that the aqueduct, finally completed in the 1970s, had a 1940 priority date.

3. *Use-it-or-lose-it.* A cardinal tenet of prior appropriation law is that the water right lasts only as long as it is used. Recall that the origins of the doctrine in Colorado lie in fostering widespread use of water and preventing monopolies by landowners. See Shorr, *The Colorado Doctrine*, discussed above, p. 464. Thus, one who fails to use the water for beneficial use loses the water right through abandonment. The following case considers an abandonment claim.

WHEATLAND IRRIGATION DISTRICT V. LARAMIE RIVERS CO.

Supreme Court of Wyoming
659 P.2d 561 (1983)

[Wheatland Irrigation District filed a petition with the state water agency (the Board of Control) seeking a declaration that the appellee Laramie Rivers Company had abandoned most of its longstanding rights to store water in its Lake Hattie Reservoir near Laramie, Wyoming. According to Wheatland, Laramie Rivers abandoned rights to store 41,100 acre feet of water from its original permitted storage right of 68,500 acre feet because, for five consecutive years, it never stored more than 27,400 acre feet; it failed, that is, to make beneficial use of a major portion of its storage right and thus ran afoul of the state statute that declared water rights forfeited when not put to beneficial use for that time period. The state agency denied the petition, even though more than five years of nonuse had elapsed, reasoning that Laramie Rivers had begun substantial repair work on the reservoir before the filing of the abandonment petition. Wheatland appealed.]

ROSE, J.

* * *

The record in this case shows that a restriction to 27,400 feet of storage has been in effect at Lake Hattie since April 5, 1972 when it was imposed by the State Engineer because of infirmities in the dam. In March of 1980, the state of Wyoming approved a loan to Laramie Rivers so that the dam could be repaired, after which, on May 16, 1980, Laramie

Rivers publicly announced its intentions with respect to dam repair and future water storage plans. This was the first Wheatland knew of Laramie Rivers' loan approval and dam improvement plans. One week later, on May 23, the abandonment petition was filed. Two days before the filing of the petition, soil compaction tests had been made and the construction company hired for the repair work was placing fill and proceeding with the construction. By July 7, 1980 the work was substantially complete.

According to the record that is available to this court, the Laramie Rivers Company had not stored water in Lake Hattie, and had not beneficially used any water therefrom in excess of the 27,400 acre-foot limitation from April, 1972 until the time the petition for abandonment was filed on May 23, 1980. In fact, no water was stored or beneficially used above the limitation up to the time of hearing before the Board of Control on February 17, 18 and 19, 1981, nor had any water been stored or used above the limitation when the parties were before the district court on July 1, 1982.

* * *

These things being so, we must look to the statute to see whether or not the Board of Control was possessed of the authority to deny Wheatland's petition for partial abandonment on the ground that, at the time of its filing, "substantial work had been undertaken to repair the dam," (citation omitted) and therefore the petition was not "promptly asserted" (citation omitted).

The Law

Statutory Construction

* * *

There are no innuendos or double entendres to be found in § 41–3–401(a). The intention of the legislature is there expressed in plain English, leaving no room whatever for our seeking out any rules of statutory construction except those which direct us to apply the statute according to the plain, ordinary meaning of the words to be found therein. *Board of County Commissioners of the County of Campbell v. Ridenour,* 623 P.2d 1174 (Wyo. 1981), *reh. denied* 627 P.2d 163 (Wyo. 1981).

What does the statute say? It says that where the holder of an appropriation of water for a reservoir water source *"fails . . . to use the water therefrom for the beneficial purposes for which it was appropriated . . ."* for a period of five successive years, *"he is considered as having abandoned the water right and shall forfeit all water rights and privileges appurtenant thereto"* (emphasis added).

* * *

The Board denied the petition on the grounds that contestee, Laramie Rivers, had undertaken "substantial work" (citation omitted) to repair the dam when the petition was filed and therefore it was not asserted "promptly." (Citation omitted.) But where in the statute can language be found which permits the Board such leeway as will countenance this holding? It simply is not there. The only thing that will save the contestee from the harshness of the abandonment statute's dictate is for Laramie Rivers to be able to show—once nonuse for the statutory period has been established by the contestant—that the water in contest here was not available for application to a beneficial use within the five-year period contemplated by the statute. See § 41–3–401(b), W.S.1977. *State Board of Control v. Johnson Ranches, Inc.*, 605 P.2d 367 (Wyo. 1980).

* * *

We subscribe to the rule . . . that § 41–3–401(a) requires forfeiture to be declared where the nonuse is shown for the statutory period and the only use which will rescue contestees from the gnashing teeth of that statute is *the use of the water* . . . for the beneficial purposes for which it was appropriated. . . . Undertaking repairs before filing a petition does not prevent forfeiture. Only the use of the water will prevent a forfeiture. § 41–3–401(a), W.S.1977.

* * *

Conclusion

We hold that the Wheatland Irrigation District's petition was timely filed, and the Board of Control may not, as was done in this case, circumvent the clear language of § 41–3–401(a), which provides that a forfeiture may only be avoided by application of water to beneficial use. . . .

* * *

NOTES

1. *Why forfeiture?* According to the facts, Laramie Rivers partially drained its reservoir because it had to. The reservoir was unsafe; repairs were needed. Before making repairs, inspections were needed, engineering work had to take place, and owners needed to arrange financing. All of this can take time. Why does the law impose such a strict, five-year time requirement for getting the work done and refilling the reservoir? Can we imagine a different rule—some sort of flexible, due-diligence rule like the relation-back doctrine we considered in *Ophir*? What are the pros and cons of a forfeiture rule that has a strict deadline?

To answer that question, we presumably need to dig even deeper. Why do we have forfeiture rules to begin with? Presumably, Wheatland Irrigation District as a junior appropriator stands to gain if Laramie Rivers has abandoned its storage permit. Could the law simply allow the parties to work things out through negotiation? Does the forfeiture rule in operation promote the most efficient and socially beneficial use of water? The underlying idea is a use-it-or-lose-it rule, intended to get people to use their resources. But why force a resource-owner to use a resource if use under the circumstances makes little sense? Can't a use-it-or-lose-it mentality sometimes promote wasteful practices by resource users who want to avoid losing their rights? For instance, why press an irrigator to use more water during unusually wet years, just to avoid any possibility of forfeiture?

2. *A literal application of law?* The Wyoming court chastised the Board of Control for failing to apply the state forfeiture statute in accordance with its literal terms. But did not the court do the same thing? The Board of Control concluded that Laramie Rivers deserved protection from forfeiture so long as it began repairing the reservoir before any junior water user filed a petition of forfeiture. The court disagreed, viewing this legal conclusion as inconsistent with seemingly automatic rule of forfeiture after five years. But the court then proceeded to announce that Laramie Rivers could avoid forfeiture if it resumed actual beneficial use of the water before a petition was filed. The language on this possibility is dictum, given that Laramie Rivers did not resume beneficial use. But where did the court get this rule of law? If forfeiture is automatic (as the court stated when it chastised the Board), then how can Laramie Rivers regain its old water right by resuming its beneficial use? That is, do we have here a distinction between forfeiture that is automatic (akin to a determinable fee), and forfeiture that occurs only if and when a junior water user acts affirmatively to terminate the unused water right (akin to a fee simple subject to a condition subsequent)?

Putting to one side the statutory language, which of these approaches would be better? Is it wise to have a right that terminates on its own, without any legal action, or is it better to require that a junior user step forward and take legal action to declare a forfeiture? In the case of a large water right of considerable value, a legal action might make sense. But what about a rather modest water right, not worth enough economically to justify legal expenses? Keep in mind, as you consider this issue, the reality that many water disputes are not as publicly visible as this one. Presumably, any person could see that Laramie Rivers had largely drained its reservoir and was not fully using its storage permit. But what about water uses that are more private? How is another water user supposed to know that an irrigator has used only three-quarters of his water right for a period in excess of five years? Going further, would it be possible under this ruling for a person to try to revive a water right that has not been used for 50 or even 100 years, just by quietly resuming beneficial use before anyone takes legal action?

3. *The costs of uncertainty.* As you consider this case, pay attention to the awkward positions of the two parties in light of the court's ruling.

Laramie Rivers wanted to repair its reservoir but the five-year period had run. Should it risk beginning repair work if, at any moment prior to completion, a junior user could file a petition of forfeiture? On the other hand, if you represented Wheatland Irrigation, would you think it worth the effort and money to file a forfeiture action if it seemed highly unlikely that Laramie Rivers would ever try to repair the reservoir? Why incur the legal costs? Might both sides (and everyone else) be better off with a mechanical rule of automatic forfeiture after five years?

4. *Use in the wrong place.* When we think of nonuse, we typically think about a complete failure to use a resource. But what if the resource is used, but in the wrong way or in the wrong place? In *Hannigan v. Hinton*, 97 P.3d 1256 (Or. App. 2004), the Oregon Water Resources Department cancelled a water right on the ground that the rights holder used the water in an unauthorized place. Use in the wrong place, the Department ruled, amounted to nonuse within the forfeiture statute, just as did use of the water for an impermissible purpose. On appeal, the court agreed:

> As we have already noted, ORS 540.610(1) provides that "[b]eneficial use shall be the basis, the measure and the limit of all rights to the use of water * * *." Rights are forfeited when the certificate holder "fails to *use* all or part of the water appropriated for a period of five successive years." *Id.* (emphasis added). Accordingly, our task is to determine whether use of water on land other than that specified in the certificate constitutes "use" for purposes of ORS 540.610.

> In *Hennings v. Water Resources Dept.,* 50 Or.App. 121, 124, 622 P.2d 333 (1981), we held that water use for a *purpose* other than that set forth in the certificate did not constitute "use" that could avoid forfeiture of water rights under a prior version of ORS 540.610. The petitioner in *Hennings* had used the water to wet ground for plowing but not for "irrigation" as designated in the certificate. 50 Or.App. at 123–24, 622 P.2d 333. We noted that "[t]he statutory scheme as a whole illustrates that the use contemplated must be that of the perfected water right and not some other use." *Id.* at 124, 622 P.2d 333. . . .

> By contrast, in *Russell-Smith v. Water Resources Dept.,* 152 Or.App. 88, 96, 952 P.2d 104, *rev den,* 327 Or. 173, 966 P.2d 217 (1998), we held that the same forfeiture penalty does not apply to unauthorized changes in *point of diversion;* rather, such actions are subject only to injunctive relief, or civil or criminal penalties. *Id.* at 98, 952 P.2d 104. Our conclusion was based on the recognition that Oregon water rights law treats "use" and "point of diversion" as distinct concepts and the forfeiture statute is addressed only to "use." *See id.* at 96, 952 P.2d 104. In *Russell–Smith,* we distinguished our application of the forfeiture statute in *Hennings* on the ground that the "type of use" at issue in *Hennings* was a component of "use."

Id. at 97–98, 952 P.2d 104.

We conclude that "place of use" likewise is a component of "use" for purposes of forfeiture. As discussed with regard to "type of use" in *Hennings,* the statutory scheme as a whole illustrates that the place of use contemplated must be that of the perfected water right and not some other place of use. *Cf. Hennings,* 622 P.2d 333. A critical part of that statutory scheme is ORS 540.510(1), which provides, in part:

> Except as provided in subsections (2) to (8) of this section, all water used in this state for any purpose shall remain appurtenant to the premises upon which it is used and no change in use or place of use of any water for any purpose may be made without compliance with the provisions of ORS 540.520 and 540.530.

Water rights are appurtenant to specific parcels of land; the right to use water is tied to the location on which the water right was perfected ("the premises upon which it is used"), which necessarily is also the location named in the water right certificate. . . .

* * *

Waste is the antithesis of "use." *In re Waters of Deschutes River,* 286 P. 563, 577 (Or. 1930), *on reh'g,* 294 P. 1049 (Or. 1930), *appeal dismissed,* 290 U.S. 590 (1933) ("wasteful application of water, even though a useful project, * * * is not included in the term 'use' as contemplated by the law of waters"); *Hennings v. Water Resources Dept.,* 622 P.2d 333, 335 (Or. App. 1998) ("unreasonable waste of all or part of the water constitutes 'non-beneficial use' "). Accordingly, unless the statutory procedure for change of place of use is followed, failure to use a water right for five successive years in the certificated place of use constitutes nonuse and results in forfeiture of the right under ORS 540.610.

5. *The centrality of beneficial use.* The Oregon court emphasized the importance of the concept of "beneficial use" to prior appropriation law. It is often said that beneficial use is both the basis and the measure of a western water right, meaning that without a beneficial use, there is no protectable water right, and that the scope of the protectable right is the amount necessary to provide the beneficial use. See generally Janet C. Neuman, *Beneficial Use, Waste, and Forfeiture: The Inefficient Search for Efficiency in Western Water Use,* 28 Envtl. L. 919 (1998) (maintaining that beneficial use is an inadequate means of ensuring efficiency in modern water law and suggesting reforms).

The following case provides a veritable treatise on this defining element of a prior appropriation right from a jurist with a deep background in western water law. The case below and the following one examine the meaning of the beneficial use requirement and explore the role of beneficial use in providing protections of rights holders against conflicting water users, including limits on overuse of the water resource.

EMPIRE LODGE HOMEOWNERS' ASS'N V. MOYER
Supreme Court of Colorado
39 P.3d 1139 (2001)

[The Moyers, possessors of a decreed water right, challenged Empire Lodge, a junior user, which was filling two ponds for fishing and recreation in a residential subdivision. The water court (a specialized trial court in Colorado) upheld the Moyers' more senior claim, and Empire appealed. In the course of affirming the water court, the Colorado Supreme Court made the following observations.]

HOBBS, J.

* * *

Prior appropriation water law is a property rights-based allocation and administration system that promotes multiple use of a finite resource for beneficial purposes. Accordingly, it fosters optimum use, efficient water management, and priority administration. See *Santa Fe Trail Ranches Prop. Owners Ass'n v. Simpson*, 990 P.2d 46, 54 (Colo. 1999). The objective of the water law system is to guarantee security, assure reliability, and cultivate flexibility in the public and private use of this scarce and valuable resource. Security resides in the system's ability to identify and obtain protection for the right of water use. Reliability springs from the system's assurance that the right of water use will continue to be recognized and enforced over time. Flexibility emanates from the fact that the right of water use can be changed, subject to quantification of the appropriation's historic beneficial consumptive use and prevention of injury to other water rights.

Colorado's prior appropriation system centers on three fundamental principles: (1) that waters of the natural stream, including surface water and groundwater tributary thereto, are a public resource subject to the establishment of public agency or private use rights in unappropriated water for beneficial purposes; (2) that water courts adjudicate the water rights and their priorities; and (3) that the State Engineer, Division Engineers, and Water Commissioners administer the waters of the natural stream in accordance with the judicial decrees and statutory provisions governing administration. *Santa Fe Trail Ranches*, 990 P.2d at 53–54, 58.

* * *

The property right we recognize as a Colorado water right is a right to use beneficially a specified amount of water, from the available supply of surface water or tributary groundwater, that can be captured, possessed, and controlled in priority under a decree, to the exclusion of all others not then in priority under a decreed water right. *Santa Fe Trail Ranches*, 990 P.2d at 53. "Water right" means a right to use in accordance with its priority a certain portion of the waters of the state by reason of the appropriation of the same. § 37–92–103(12), 10 C.R.S. (2001). A water right is created when a person appropriates or initiates an appropriation of unappropriated water of a natural stream of the state. *Shirola v. Turkey Canon Ranch Ltd. Liab. Co.*, 937 P.2d 739, 748 (Colo. 1997).

A right to use water of the natural stream arises from placing the unappropriated water to beneficial use; a conditional water right holds a place in the priority system to which the water right antedates in the event the appropriator places the unappropriated water to beneficial use. *Dallas Creek Water Co. v. Huey*, 933 P.2d 27, 35 (Colo. 1997). Conditional water rights are subject to a requirement of reasonable diligence in actualizing the intended appropriation, and the applicant must file a diligence application six years after the entry of the prior conditional decree or diligence decree for an examination of reasonable diligence in completing the appropriation. § 37–92–304(4)(a)(I) & (III), 10 C.R.S. (2001); *Mun. Subdist. v. Chevron Shale Oil Co.*, 986 P.2d 918, 921 (Colo. 1999). A decree for an absolute water right confirms that an appropriative right has vested and identifies the right's priority and amount. *Williams v. Midway Ranches Prop. Owners Ass'n*, 938 P.2d 515, 521 (Colo. 1997).

Appropriation of natural stream waters is subject to administration in priority in accordance with judicial decrees determining the existence of water rights. *Aspen Wilderness Workshop, Inc. v. Hines Highlands Ltd. P'ship*, 929 P.2d 718, 724 (Colo. 1996). A water right adjudication is a proceeding to determine the respective priorities of water rights on the stream system for purposes of administration. *City of Lafayette v. New Anderson Ditch Co.*, 962 P.2d 955, 960 (Colo. 1998). Direct flow water rights and storage water rights are entitled to administration based on their priority, regardless of the type of beneficial use for which the appropriation was made. *People ex rel. Park Reservoir Co. v. Hinderlider*, 57 P.2d 894, 898–99 (Colo. 1936) (Butler, J., concurring). The applicant for issuance of a conditional decree bears the burden of demonstrating that there is unappropriated water available for the appropriation, taking into account the historic exercise of decreed water rights. *Bd. of County Comm'rs v. Crystal Creek Homeowners' Ass'n*, 14 P.3d 325, 333 (Colo. 2000). In order to perfect the conditional right and obtain an absolute decree, the applicant must have: (1) captured, possessed, and controlled unappropriated water; and (2) placed the water to beneficial use. *City of Lafayette*, 962 P.2d at 961.

Water rights are decreed to structures and points of diversion. *Dallas Creek Water Co.*, 933 P.2d at 38. But see *Colo. River Water Conservation*

Dist. v. Colo. Water Conservation Bd., 594 P.2d 570, 574 (Colo. 1979) (establishing that, instead of identifying diversion points and structures, instream flow or lake level water rights identify stream segments or lakes for preservation of the environment to a reasonable degree). Priority, location of diversion at the source of supply, and amount of water for application to beneficial uses are the essential elements of the appropriative water right. *People ex rel. Simpson v. Highland Irrigation Co.*, 917 P.2d 1242, 1252 n. 17 (Colo. 1996).

* * *

NOTES

1. *Goals of prior appropriation.* This excerpt (written by Justice Hobbs, who also wrote the 2002 opinion in *Park County* ruling in chapter 1, p. 29) presents the Colorado water law regime as a coherent, well-functioning whole. We have reason to wonder, though, whether the regime is not being oversold withits limits and internal conflicts hidden from view.

In the first paragraph, Hobbs identifies the three goals of the system: security, reliability, and flexibility. We might wonder whether security and flexibility sometimes clash: security might well be greatest in a system that is highly inflexible. In the next paragraph we learn that water is "a public resource" yet is subject to "private use rights." Again, do we have a tension here that is glossed over? And is this related to the tension between secure private rights and the requirement that all water uses be beneficial? According to Hobbs, temporal priority is critical when shortages develop and not all water users can get water. Yet we cannot be sure, can we, that the most senior uses will be the ones that promote the goal of "optimum use"? What if a junior water rights holder is engaged in a far more socially valuable water use than a senior one? Doesn't the temporal priority system in such a case interfere with optimum use?

2. *Water courts and conditional water rights.* Colorado is unusual in that it has special water courts to adjudicate water rights claims and issue decrees specifying the terms of valid rights. In other states, this work is typically done by a state agency. Colorado also has a special "conditional water rights" category that allows a water user to lay claim to a water flow without actually applying it to a beneficial use. The water claimant must return to court from time to time to demonstrate that it is moving ahead with its diversion project with "reasonable diligence." If a claimant fails to use reasonable diligence, its conditional water right can end.

STATE DEPARTMENT OF ECOLOGY v. GRIMES

Supreme Court of Washington
852 P.2d 1044 (1993)

[The state Department of Ecology initiated, in superior court, a general adjudication to clarify all existing rights to divert, withdraw, or otherwise use the surface and ground waters of the Marshall Lake Basin. Grimes submitted five water rights claims, one of which was for an instantaneous flow rate of 3 cfs for irrigation and a storage right of 1,520 acre-feet in the Marshall Lake reservoir. The referee recommended only 1.5 cfs for irrigation and only 183 acre-feet, plus 737 acre-feet for evaporation loss, for a total storage right of 920 acre-feet. Grimes appealed. The Washington Supreme Court accepted direct review to clarify the meaning of "reasonable use" of water as an element of "beneficial use" under state statutes.]

SMITH, J.

* * *

General Adjudication

A general adjudication is a special form of quiet title action to determine all existing rights to the use of water from a specific body of water. In Washington, the adjudication procedure is set forth in RCW 90.03.110 *et seq.* The provisions for adjudication in the Water Code, RCW 90.03.110–.245, may not be used to lessen, enlarge or modify existing water rights. An adjudication of water rights is only for the purpose of determining and confirming those rights. The surface water rights of the Grimes in this case are pre-1917 rights, established 11 years before adoption of the Water Code of 1917 and 65 years before adoption of the Water Resources Act of 1971. Subsequent amendments to the 1917 Water Code have clearly stated that nothing in the act "shall affect or operate to impair any existing water rights." To confirm existing rights, the referee must determine two primary elements of a water right: (1) the amount of water that has been put to beneficial use and (2) the priority of water rights relative to each other.

* * *

The Doctrine of Prior Appropriation

The law of prior appropriation was established in this state by the Territorial Legislature in 1873 and recognized by this court in 1897. This court in *Neubert v. Yakima-Tieton Irrig. Dist.* said that "[t]he appropriated water right is perpetual and operates to the exclusion of subsequent claimants." In that case we said appropriative water rights require that:

Once appropriated, the right to use a given quantity of water becomes appurtenant to the land. The appropriated water right is perpetual and operates to the exclusion of subsequent claimants.

The key to determining the extent of plaintiffs' vested water rights is the concept of "beneficial use". . . . An appropriated water right is established and maintained by the purposeful application of a given quantity of water to a beneficial use upon the land. (Citations omitted.) *Neubert,* 814 P.2d 199, 201–02 (Wash. 1991).

Beneficial use refers to the quantity of water diverted by the appropriator, not to its availability in the source of supply. "The underlying reason for all this constitutional, legislative and judicial emphasis on beneficial use of water lies in the relation of available water resources to the ever-increasing demands made upon them."

"Beneficial use" is a term of art in water law, and encompasses two principal elements of a water right. [ ] First, it refers to the purposes, or type of activities, for which water may be used. Use of water for the purposes of irrigated agriculture is a beneficial use. The Grimes' use of water to irrigate alfalfa fields is not at issue in this case.

Second, beneficial use determines the measure of a water right. The owner of a water right is entitled to the amount of water necessary for the purpose to which it has been put, provided that purpose constitutes a beneficial use. To determine the amount of water necessary for a beneficial use, courts have developed the principle of "reasonable use." Reasonable use of water is determined by analysis of the factors of water duty and waste.

In his findings establishing the measure of the Grimes' water right, the referee stated that:

[A] valid right for irrigation purposes only exists for the benefit of these claimants and such right is derived from the original 1906 Linsley notice. It is, therefore, recommended that a right be confirmed to these defendants, with a July 13, 1906 priority for the irrigation of 73 acres from Marshall Lake. Quantification of the amount of water to which this right is entitled creates somewhat of a problem in that there has been no direct testimony regarding the amount of water placed to beneficial use other than a reference in the state's investigatory report that 56 sprinklers are utilized in the system. . . . Therefore, the Referee will allow the standard duty of water which would be 1.2 cubic feet per second plus an additional 25 percent for transportation loss, thus making an aggregate amount of 1.5 cubic feet per second identified with this right. . . .

A second element concerning this right is the amount of storage of water to which these claimants are entitled. . . . [T]hese waters also have recreational benefits, not only to the riparian owners around the lake but also to the general public through the use of resort facilities located on the lake. . . . Therefore, the Referee recommends that a related but separate right be confirmed to these defendants for the storage of 920 acre-feet in Marshall Lake for irrigation and recreation purposes. The priority shall be fixed as of July 13, 1906. The period during which waters may be stored shall be identified as those periods of the year which do not include the April 1 to October 31 irrigation season.

The Grimes' challenge the referee's "consideration of the evidence" and his application of the law in making these findings. We first consider the evidence used by the referee in establishing the factors of water duty and waste. We then consider the test of "reasonable efficiency" employed by the referee, and adopted by the Superior Court, to evaluate these factors.

Water Duty

"[Water duty] [is] that measure of water, which, by careful management and use, without wastage, is reasonably required to be applied to any given tract of land for such period of time as may be adequate to produce therefrom a maximum amount of such crops as ordinarily are grown thereon. It is not a hard and fast unit of measurement, but is variable according to conditions."

The referee based his determination of the volume of water necessary for irrigation in the Marshall Lake basin on a Washington State University Research Bulletin entitled "Irrigation Requirements for Washington—Estimates and Methodology," and on the expert testimony of Jim Lyerla, the District Supervisor for seven Eastern Washington counties, including Pend Oreille County, in the Water Resources Program of the Department of Ecology. Mr. Lyerla testified that as a part of his work in assigning water quantities to new water permittees, he relied on the Irrigation Report to determine the "water duty" for a proposed use of water. The Irrigation Report provides information for water requirements for specific crops, given in inches per acre per irrigation season, in 40 locations around the state, including Newport, Washington, 5 miles south of Marshall Lake.

Based on the testimony of Mr. Lyerla and the Irrigation Report, the referee determined that an irrigated alfalfa crop grown in the Marshall Lake area requires 21 inches or 1.75 acre feet of water per acre during the irrigation season. The referee then applied an efficiency factor and increased this water duty to 2.5 acre feet per acre per year.

* * *

The referee also observed that "the use of water under all irrigation rights is, however, limited to the amount of water that can be beneficially applied to that number of acres identified in the water right." The referee did not indiscriminately award this water duty to any claim for an irrigation right, but required claimants to prove the number of acres historically irrigated.

In water rights adjudications, the establishment of a water duty must not be disturbed in "the absence of very conclusive evidence contrary to the . . . adjudication, showing arbitrariness on [the] part [of the adjudicator]. . . ." The referee's determination of a generic water duty for irrigation of alfalfa in the Marshall Lake basin is supported by a preponderance of the evidence and will not be disturbed by this court.

Waste

From an early date, courts announced the rule that no appropriation of water was valid where the water simply went to waste. Those courts held that the appropriator who diverted more than was needed for the appropriator's actual requirements and allowed the excess to go to waste acquired no right to the excess. A particular use must not only be of benefit to the appropriator, but it must also be a reasonable and economical use of the water in view of other present and future demands upon the source of supply. The difference between absolute waste and economical use has been said to be one of degree only.

Appellant Clarence E. Grimes acknowledged in his testimony that his existing irrigation system required a water flow of up to 3 cubic feet per second in order to deliver 1 cubic foot per second to the field, and that this system was highly inefficient, causing one-half to two-thirds loss of water. Mr. Grimes also testified that uncertainties and ongoing litigation concerning the stability and safety of the irrigation dam had prevented continuous irrigation of his alfalfa acreage. Other claimants testified concerning their use of the water claimed.

While an appropriator's use of water must be reasonably efficient, absolute efficiency is not required. The referee determined that, pursuant to RCW 90.14.160, the uncertainties concerning the irrigation dam constituted sufficient cause not to find a complete abandonment of the Grimeses' water right. He resolved the conflicting testimony by limiting the irrigable acreage to the 73 acres recommended by Ecology. Relying on a standard efficiency factor for irrigation sprinkler systems found in the irrigation report, he confirmed in the Grimeses a water right with one-fourth conveyance loss for a total of 1.5 cubic feet per second. There was at least sufficient evidence for the referee to determine the maximum acreage to which the Grimeses' water right applied, and in limiting the allowable loss for system inefficiency in establishing their instantaneous flow.

The Reasonable Efficiency Test

In limiting the Grimes' vested water right, the referee balanced several factors, including the water duty for the geographical area and crop under irrigation, the claimants' actual diversion, and sound irrigation practices. In his report, the referee described his method of calculating the Grimes' water right as a "reasonable efficiency" test.

Amici curiae argue that this test is contrary to judicial decisions which have recognized that the standard of reasonable beneficial use of water for irrigation is limited to consideration of the use of the established means of diversion and application according to the reasonable custom of the locality. Respondent Ecology argues that the 3-part "reasonable efficiency" test cited by the referee provides "the balance sought by the courts between the competing needs of efficiency and maximum utilization of the water, and the existing physical and economic limitations in each situation." Ecology asserts that local custom in irrigation practices is but one of several factors the court must consider in deciding whether a given use of water is reasonable, and, therefore, beneficial.

While the referee stated that he relied on this test, and while he did in fact consider some of its elements, he did not actually utilize the test in its entirety. Therefore, we will review the factors he did consider to determine whether his analysis remained within the boundaries of prior appropriation law.

* * *

Decisions of courts throughout the western states provide a basis for defining "reasonable efficiency" with respect to irrigation practices. While customary irrigation practices common to the locality are a factor for consideration, they do not justify waste of water. . . . Local custom and the relative efficiency of irrigation systems in common use are important elements, but must be considered in connection with other statutorily mandated factors, such as the costs and benefits of improvements to irrigation systems, including the use of public and private funds to facilitate improvements.

In limiting the Grimeses' water use by a requirement of reasonable efficiency, the referee properly considered the irrigation report, the Grimeses' actual water use, and their existing irrigation system. The referee alluded to a test incorporating factors that consider impacts to the water source and its flora and fauna. While consideration of these impacts is consonant with the State's obligations under RCW 90.03.005 and 90.54.010(1)(a) and (2), these factors cannot operate to impair existing water rights. Other laws may, however, operate to define existing rights in light of environmental values.

[The court proceeded to review the work of the referee, ultimately concluding that, although the referee endorsed a "reasonable efficiency" test, he did not actually employ the test when curtailing the water right of the Grimes.]

Adjudication proceedings cannot be used "to lessen, enlarge, or modify the existing rights of any riparian owner, or any existing right acquired by appropriation, or otherwise." The suggested test would be contrary to the vested rights of water users. "It has long been settled in this state that property owners have a vested interest in their water rights to the extent that the water is beneficially used on the land." Included in the vested rights is the right to diversion, delivery and application "according to the usual methods of artificial irrigation employed in the vicinity where such land is situated." The Legislature sets a standard clearly contradictory to the suggested test in RCW 90.03.040, which relates to eminent domain over water rights. The test is contrary also to long established principles of Western water law.

While we reject use of the specific test suggested by the referee, we affirm because (1) there is no indication in the record that he in fact applied the factors stated in the "test", and (2) he applied the actual beneficial use made by Grimes, taking into account the actual needs and use and the methods of delivery and application in the vicinity. The adjudication and confirmation of a water right in an amount less than claimed by Grimes does not result from application of the so-called test. Rather, as the referee makes clear:

> Quantification of the amount of water to which this right is entitled creates somewhat of a problem in that there has been no direct testimony regarding the amount of water placed to beneficial use other than a reference in the state's investigatory report that 56 sprinklers are utilized in the system.

In the absence of such proof, the referee nevertheless confirmed the right by using a normal duty of water for the type of crops raised and specifically added 25 percent for transportation loss. Making the best of inadequate proof by the claimant, it appears from the record that the referee applied the usual methods of irrigation employed in the vicinity where the Grimes' land is located.

[The court also denied the Grimes' claim that their water right was taken by the state: "[T]he concept of 'beneficial use', as developed in the common law . . . operates as a permissible limitation on water rights. . . . [The] Grimes were entitled to 'divert or withdraw' the subject water. However, the . . . finding [that they failed] to beneficially use all of the waters diverted" divested their interest in the water.]

* * *

NOTES

1.   *The elements of a private water right. Grimes* and *Empire Lodge* set forth the basic elements of a discrete water right under prior appropriation law. A water right is limited by actual use and further limited by the requirement that the water use be beneficial. Note carefully the various elements that make up the beneficial use limit on a water right in Washington:

a.   First, we are told, the term relates to the *type of use*—in this case, agriculture. Apparently, no one in the litigation claimed that the use of water to irrigate alfalfa (a hay crop) was not beneficial. In arid and semi-arid parts of the West, the vast bulk of all water is used for agriculture, much of it for low-valued crops such as alfalfa. The economic value of such uses is trivial compared with the value of water devoted to municipal and many industrial uses. Agricultural water uses vary greatly among themselves in terms of the economic value produced by the water use. Is it sensible for lawmakers to continue to sweep all agricultural uses into a single category and label them all beneficial, or has the time come to look at individual agricultural activities more closely and decide which ones are beneficial? Is it beneficial to use water to grow corn or cotton, both of which are overabundant in the nation? To answer this question we need to grapple with another one: is beneficial use determined by looking at the type of activity overall (growing corn, which is certainly beneficial) or instead do we examine particular land uses as instances of producers at the margin (that is, asking whether the extra amount of corn or hay produced by irrigators is beneficial, given the massive supply that comes from landowners who do not have to irrigate)?

b.   Beneficial use, we are told, also refers to the *amount of water* "necessary" for the particular purpose. The amount necessary is limited by the idea of reasonable use, which in the case of irrigation is based on the "water duty" and the prohibition on "waste." How does the court define these two terms? Note that, in the case of water duty, the court looks to expert opinion as to the amount of water that ought to be necessary, not to the amount that the landowner actually used. As for waste, the court defines it based on the "reasonable and economical use of the water in view of other present and future demands upon the source of supply." Does this language propose a comparison among various possible uses of the same water? The language seems to suggest that it does, but we see no evidence of the court actually paying attention to other possible uses of this particular water. What factors does the court ultimately view as relevant, and how restrictive are they? How much deference does it give to local custom?

2.   *Beneficial use and recreation and aesthetics.* In *Empire Water & Power Co. v. Cascade Town Co.*, 205 F. 123, 129 (8th Cir. 1913), Cascade Town, a Colorado summer vacation resort, successfully defended its water uses against a claim by a hydroelectric power company that recreation and aesthetics were not beneficial. By building and operating a resort town, Cascade Town had effectively appropriated the waters to sustain the lush vegetation and landscape. The court decided that recreation was within beneficial use; however, Cascade Town did not have an exclusive right to all the waters of the stream without any diminution.

3.   *General adjudications and the need to prove up.* *Grimes* involved a special type of water litigation known as a general (or "whole-stream") adjudication, which is a proceeding in which all parties claiming water from a particular water source are obligated to show up in court and prove their water rights. It is a day of reckoning for users who have shaky titles or who otherwise are claiming more water than they deserve based upon actual beneficial use. So long as a water use goes unchallenged, a user need not prove what she really owns. General adjudications can become extremely complex and consume years of time, particularly when they involve dozens or hundreds of water users and when junior users, anxious to move up in priority, are intent on challenging the factual claims made by senior users.

4.   *The reasonable efficiency test.* A contentious issue in *Grimes* was whether a water user was obligated to use reasonable efficiency in the methods of water use. Why did this issue arouse the passions of the amici in the case, and what was their objection to it? Is there something inherently dangerous about the idea that the law might require water users to pass such a test? The court makes clear that Washington law contains no such test, and thus water users need not abide by it. But why is this so?

5.   *The issue in the closet.* Lurking behind the scenes in *Grimes* was an issue that the court seemed unwilling to express and address directly: Is beneficial use an evolving requirement that applies to existing water users as well as to newly initiated uses? Put otherwise, might a water use qualify as beneficial when it is begun, but later fail the test as the standard of beneficial use changes? If beneficial use is at all like the do-no-harm, reasonable use tests that we have seen applied to landed property rights, the question is easy to answer: yes, the test does change over time, and yes, property owners need to abide by it or risk having their property uses halted. Note that in some ways, the test as applied in *Grimes* clearly does evolve over time. The definition of waste clearly looks to current irrigation methods, not irrigation methods used when the appellants' water uses began in 1906. But what about the type of water use? Might a water use that seems socially useful at one time become socially wasteful a century later? Then, too, we have the court's express statement that waste is linked to "other present and future

demands upon the source of supply." Can this factor receive weight without forcing water users to change their ways over time?

IMPERIAL IRRIGATION DIST. V. STATE WATER RESOURCES CONTROL BOARD

California Court of Appeal
225 Cal. App. 3d 548 (1990)

[In 1980, a property owner asked the State Water Resources Control Board (Board) to investigate the alleged misuse of water by the Imperial Irrigation District (IID), a massive water user, misuse that resulted in a rise in the water level of the Salton Sea and consequent flooding of the owner's land. The factual record made clear that "very large quantities of water . . . were being lost," including some 53,000 to 135,000 acre feet lost through 'canal spill' and some 312,000 to 559,000 acre feet lost through mismanagement of tailwater. After conducting a hearing, the state board concluded in a 1984 decision (Decision 1600) that the water use practices of IID and its customers were wasteful. It ordered IID to prepare and implement a water conservation plan. IID appealed.]

FROELICH, J.

* * *

[The court initially addressed the power of the State Board to take action against the IID (as it did) in an administrative action, based on its own initiative and investigation. According to the IID, the Board's jurisdiction was limited to the resolution of water-use controversies brought to it by outside parties. The court sided with the Board, concluding that the Board could initiate administrative actions on its own and issue appropriate rulings.]

* * *

(b) *Interference With Vested Rights*

Water used by IID and its customers is diverted from the Colorado River. Diversion instrumentalities, including dams, power plants and the All-American Canal, which brings water from the river to the Imperial Valley, were authorized by the Boulder Canyon Project Act, enacted December 21, 1928. (43 U.S.C. §§ 617 *et seq.*) The Boulder Canyon Project Act vested in the Secretary of the Interior the power to enter into contracts for the delivery and allocation of water to users in the southwestern United States. The several interested states were unable to come to an agreement as to water allocation, and their entitlements were finally resolved by the United States Supreme Court in 1963. (*Arizona v. California*, 373 U.S. 546 (1963).) Allocation of Colorado River water among users in Southern California was achieved through mutual agreement, however. The agreement, termed the "California Seven—Party Agreement," was executed on August 18, 1931, and remains in effect. Amount of entitlement and priority of distribution to IID are established in this agreement.

IID's water rights, therefore, are the result of federal statute, U.S. Supreme Court decision, and a seven-party agreement allocating water among Southern California users. Water rights within the state of California traditionally were derived from riparian rights or entitlement based upon prior appropriation. (See historical discussion in *United States v. State Water Resources Control Bd.*, 182 Cal.App.3d 82, 100–02 (1986).) It is conceivable that IID's water rights, based as they are upon a unique blend of statutory and contractual origins, could be characterized as somehow more stable or securely vested than water rights from traditional sources. IID does not, however, make this claim. It simply contends that a right to use water, no matter how derived, once vested, becomes a property right which cannot be undermined without due compensation.

Illustrative of IID's broad contention is the following quote from *United States v. State Water Resources Control Bd.*, 182 Cal.App.3d at 101: "It is . . . axiomatic that once rights to use water are acquired, they become vested property rights. As such, they cannot be infringed by others or taken by governmental action without due process and just compensation." The essence of IID's contention, therefore, is that the Board was without power to deprive IID of its discretionary power of determination of water use without providing compensation (which the Board admittedly has no power to provide).

As a preliminary matter we should note exactly what the Board did require of IID. The principal mandate contained in the Board Decision was an injunction that IID develop and present a water conservation plan. The trial court in its memorandum of decision noted that "except for requiring the District to repair defective tailwater structures, Decision 1600 itself requires no specific conservation measures, nor does it compel IID to sell, transfer, or otherwise convey water to the Metropolitan Water District or any other party. Decision 1600 simply requires the District to prepare plans to remedy its misuse of water, while retaining jurisdiction to review the adequacy of IID's plans."

We are unable, however, to agree that Decision 1600 did not substantially erode IID's otherwise virtually complete control over its water use. IID was required within a period of eight months to submit a plan for reservoir construction and to affirm its intent to construct one reservoir per year. Once a general plan of water conservation was achieved, IID was required to submit progress reports every six months "until the objectives have been achieved." The board reserved jurisdiction to monitor IID progress and to "take such other action" as might be required to assure compliance with an approved plan. There can be no doubt that the Board's intrusion into IID's previously untrammeled administration of the use of water in its district was substantial. As often stated in water law cases, "what is meant by a water right is the right to *use* the water. . . ." (*Id.* at 100.) While the Board's decision in no way interfered with IID's contractual and statutory entitlement to Colorado River water, it most certainly presaged an interference with IID's utilization of that water once it traversed the All-American Canal.

Our conclusion that the Board Decision substantially impacted the practical use and administration by IID of its water does not, however, result in our acceptance of IID's contention of unconstitutional interference with "vested" rights. Historic concepts of water "rights" in California were dramatically altered by the adoption in 1928 of the above referenced constitutional amendment. (*Id.* at 105–06.) Our Supreme Court, in *Gin S. Chow v. City of Santa Barbara*, 22 P.2d 5 (Cal. 1933), acknowledged that the new provision altered previously vested rights. "As already observed the amendment purports only to regulate the use and enjoyment of a property right for the public benefit, for which reason the vested right theory cannot stand in the way of the operation of the amendment as a police measure. A vested right cannot be asserted against it because of conditions once obtaining. It has been long established that all property is held subject to the reasonable exercise of the police power and that constitutional provisions declaring that property shall not be taken without due process of law have no application in such cases." (*Id.* at 17.)

* * *

Put simply, IID does not have the vested rights which it alleges. It has only vested rights to the "reasonable" use of water. It has no right to waste or misuse water. The interference by the Board with IID's misuse (this finding of fact by the Board being accepted for purposes of the present issue) does not constitute a transgression on a vested right.

(c) *Violation of Separation of Powers Doctrine*

[The court concluded that the Board did not violate the separation of powers doctrine by directing IID (itself a government body) to construct capital improvements, adopt new water use regulations, and probably assess additional charges to its users. According to the court, these were not discretionary, legislative-type decisions of a type inappropriate for a state administrative agency.]

* * *

Conclusion and Disposition

* * *

We note from IID's brief that it has "engaged for three decades in costly and critical litigation about its water rights." It asks that we reverse all the lengthy deliberations that have preceded our hearing and requests even again an "opportunity to more extensively brief the issue."

All things must end, even in the field of water law. It is time to recognize that this law is in flux and that its evolution has passed beyond traditional concepts of vested and immutable rights. In his review of our Supreme Court's recent water rights decision in *In re Water of Hallett Creek Stream System*, 749 P.2d 324 (Cal. 1988), Professor Freyfogle explains that California is engaged in an evolving process of governmental redefinition of water rights. He concludes that "California has regained for the public much of the power to prescribe water use practices, to limit waste, and to sanction water transfers." He asserts that the concept that "water use entitlements are clearly and permanently defined," and are "neutral [and] rule-driven," is a pretense to be discarded. It is a fundamental truth, he writes, that "everything is in the process of changing or becoming" in water law.

In affirming this specific instance of far-reaching change, imposed upon traditional uses by what some claim to be revolutionary exercise of adjudicatory power, we but recognize this evolutionary process, and urge reception and recognition of same upon those whose work in the practical administration of water distribution makes such change understandably difficult to accept.

NOTES

1. *Issue of law or fact?* A highly practical consideration in litigation involving the beneficial-use and reasonable-use limits of water law is whether they are issues of fact, issues of law, or some mixture of both. The answer to this question can greatly affect how much deference a trial court finding receives when it is subject to appellate review. The issue arose in *In re Drainage Area of Utah Lake v. Pinecrest Pipeline*, 98 P.3d 1 (Utah 2004). The court analyzed beneficial use, as a trial court determination, under the three-part test it had announced in a 1998 ruling, *State v. Pena*, 869 P.2d 932 (Utah 1994). As it applied the *Pena* three-factor test to determine how much deference was due to a trial-court ruling, the court also commented on the nature of the beneficial-use limit:

> We begin with the first *Pena* consideration, which requires us to evaluate the complexity and variety of possible factual issues. In this regard, we note that beneficial use determinations rely heavily on the facts and circumstances of each case, with the underlying facts varying significantly in each dispute. This variety of factual

scenarios supports a broad, rather than narrow, grant of discretion to the finder of fact. See *Dep't of Human Servs. ex rel. Parker v. Irizarry*, 945 P.2d 676, 678 (Utah 1997) ("The variety of fact-intensive circumstances involved [in equitable estoppel cases] weighs heavily against lightly substituting our judgment for that of the trial court. Therefore, we properly grant the trial court's decision a fair degree of deference when we review the mixed question of whether the requirements of the law of estoppel have been satisfied in any given factual situation."); *Kohler v. Martin*, 916 P.2d 910, 912 (Utah Ct. App. 1996) ("When the decisions are more fact-dependent, or when the credibility of the witnesses has a strong bearing on the decision, broader discretion is generally granted to the trial court.").

In addition, we note that the concept of beneficial use is not static. Rather, it is susceptible to change over time in response to changes in science and values associated with water use. Janet C. Neuman, *Beneficial Use, Waste, and Forfeiture: The Inefficient Search for Efficiency in Western Water Use*, 28 Envtl. L. 919, 942 (1998) ("What is a beneficial use, of course, depends upon the facts and circumstances of each case. What may be a reasonable beneficial use, where water is present in excess of all needs, would not be a reasonable beneficial use in an area of great scarcity and great need. What is a beneficial use at one time may, because of changed conditions, become a waste of water at a later time." (quoting *Imperial Irrigation Dist. v. State Water Res. Control Bd.*, 225 Cal.App.3d 548 (1990))); Neuman, at 946 ("Beneficial use is a somewhat flexible concept, changing over time to accommodate developments in thinking about water use, such as changes in science and values."). Accordingly, beneficial use "must remain a flexible and workable doctrine." *Jeffs v. Stubbs*, 970 P.2d 1234, 1245 (Utah 1998) (applying the *Pena* considerations to unjust enrichment rulings and granting trial court's broad discretion).

The second *Pena* consideration requires us to evaluate the relative novelty of the applicable legal principle. In examining this consideration, we note that the doctrine of beneficial use has roots dating back to the turn of the last century. See Neuman, 28 Envtl. L. at 920–21. However, our cases and statutes addressing beneficial use have generally used the term without defining it and have failed to identify any standard factors to be considered in evaluating whether a particular use is beneficial. Stated in terms of the *Pena* metaphor, trial judges in this state confront a pasture that has yet to be narrowly fenced in individual determinations of beneficial use. See *Pena*, 869 P.2d at 937–38 (analogizing the extent of a trial judge's discretion to a pasture that diminishes in size as it is "fenced" by existing laws and clarifications by appellate courts). Consequently, this consideration also supports a relatively broad grant of discretion to the trial court. See *Carrier v. Pro-Tech Restoration*, 944 P.2d 346, 352 (Utah 1997) (granting limited discretion to a trial court's rule 47(c) decisions because, in part, this court had already "fenced off many scenarios that might arise in such cases," and few possible scenarios remained).

The third *Pena* consideration emphasizes the special ability of trial courts to weigh contradictory evidence from witnesses, assess credibility and demeanor, and make factual findings. 869 P.2d at 939; *Jeffs*, 970 P.2d at 1245. As previously mentioned, beneficial use determinations are generally dependent on the trial court's findings of fact. The same is true in the case now before us, and this consideration thus weighs in favor of our granting broad discretion to the trial judge in determining whether BCWDC put its water to beneficial use.

While the first three *Pena* considerations suggest that the trial court's determination of beneficial use is entitled to broad discretion, we must also consider whether any countervailing policy reason dictates a contrary result. Such a policy reason exists in this case. We have repeatedly recognized the importance of insuring that the waters of our state are put to beneficial use. See, e.g., *Eskelsen v. Town of Perry*, 819 P.2d 770, 775–76 (Utah 1991) ("[T]he state is . . . vitally interested in seeing that none of the waters are allowed to run to waste or go without being applied to a beneficial use for any great number of years."); *Wayman v. Murray City Corp.*, 458 P.2d 861, 863 (Utah 1969) ("Because of the vital importance of water in this arid region both our statutory and decisional law have been fashioned in recognition of the desirability and of the necessity of insuring the highest possible development and of the most continuous beneficial use of all available water with as little waste as possible.").

In view of the importance of beneficial use determinations in this state, we hold that the discretion afforded to the trial court should be somewhat narrowed. In *Pena*, we described a "spectrum of discretion . . . running from 'de novo' on the one hand to 'broad discretion' on the other." 869 P.2d at 937. In beneficial use determinations, the appropriate degree of deference to the trial court falls somewhere between the two ends of the spectrum. Accordingly, in reviewing the trial court's ruling on beneficial use, we will afford the trial court significant, though not broad, discretion.

2.   *Redefining beneficial use.* Consider the following suggestion made some years ago for a reinterpretation of beneficial use by one of the casebook authors:

[W]e need to get serious about the long-standing yet ineffectual requirement that all water uses be beneficial. As too often now applied, beneficial use is out of date, not the least because it ignores water quality.

Beneficial use too often means beneficial based on circumstances in effect in the late nineteenth century when almost any type of mining, agricultural, or commercial use of water seemed beneficial, without regard for environmental consequence or foreseeable shortages. Beneficial use as it stands today is an affront to attentive citizens who know stupidity when they see it, who know, for instance, that no public benefit arises when a river is fully drained so its waters might flow luxuriously through unlined, open ditches onto desert soil to grow surplus cotton and pollute the water severely. People know better than this, and if the law does not soon learn better, the clamor for change will become more angry and disruptive.

Beneficial use must expressly come to mean beneficial by the standards of *today's* culture, not by the standards of some culture long-eclipsed by changing values and circumstances. It must come to mean beneficial to the *community*, not just to the individual user, particularly a user whose calculation of gain ignores resulting ecological harms. Bank robbery, after all, is beneficial to the robber.

Eric T. Freyfogle, *Water Rights and the Common Wealth*, 26 Envtl. L. 27, 42 (1996). See also Steven J. Shupe, *Waste in Western Water Law: A Blueprint for Change*, 61 Or. L. Rev. 483, 492 (1982) (suggesting a five-part redefinition of beneficial use, at least in the case of irrigated agriculture: 1) judicial recognition that the protectable water right is the right to accrue benefits from watering crops; 2) with new technologies that allow more efficient conveyance and application of water, the use of old, water-intensive practices becomes a privilege rather than part of the vested right; 3) when local supplies become fully appropriated, the privilege is lost and use of the excess water becomes waste; 4) once the statutory forfeiture period has run, the wasted portion reverts to the state; and 5) courts and agencies should determine how much has been forfeited as waste and allow diversion of only as much water as is reasonably needed under modern practices).

3. *Dynamic right vs. redefinition vs. taking.* How can we best describe in functional terms what the state water board is doing in this case? IID took the view that the board was depriving it of a secure property right by insisting that it change its water use practices, in ways that would save water (enough water, we might note, to meet the household needs of some 2 million people!). How else might we characterize the board's actions?

One possibility is to say that the board is redefining the property right, exercising a function that common law courts exercised for generations. Just as courts kept the common law up to date by tinkering with the elements of private rights, so too the board is performing that function in the case of private rights in water.

Another possibility is to say that the property right that IID possessed had a dynamic element built into it. The property right limited uses of water to those that were both reasonable and beneficial. As we saw in chapter 2, we can apply such vague terms only by looking to the ideas and values that prevail in the present. The law has long defined private rights in terms of reasonable use, and reasonable use has always drawn its content by looking to circumstances and understandings at the time of the adjudication. Thus, whether a water right is reasonable in 1990 is properly determined in light of values and understandings widely shared in 1990, not values and understandings that prevailed generations ago. This perspective is well entrenched in property law generally. Is there a reason why a different understanding should prevail in the case of water rights? Does the fact that water rights are defined precisely, and often quite narrowly in terms of place and nature of use, give cause to adopt a different understanding?

4. *Is a more moderate remedy needed?* The beneficial-use limit is, of course, a specific application of the reasonable-use principle that applies to private property generally. Yet, as courts explain, water is no ordinary resource. It is exceptionally important in parts of the country that are arid or semi-arid. All life depends on it. There is thus a greater social interest in ensuring that water is not wasted or applied to uses that are less then socially optimal. In the case of most resources, we rely upon the market to shift the resources to more highly valued uses. In the case of water, however, the market is less able to bring about such shifts. The problem is that the water rights of one person are often tightly squeezed into a water-use regime in such a way that a user cannot readily make changes in either the place or nature of a water use without harming other people. When water is very short in supply, a water user may have only limited ability to shift water to a new use. The problem is heightened when the new use will take place elsewhere and when it involves diverting water from another location along the river. Changing the place and nature of a water use can greatly affect other water users and can easily and wrongfully interfere with their rights.

What happens, then, when a court (or, as in the above case, a state agency) decides that a given water use is wasteful or otherwise not beneficial? What happens to the water right? Under the literal elements of water law, a water user has no right to use water in a non-beneficial way (or, in California, a non-reasonable way). A non-beneficial water use can therefore be halted immediately. In addition, a water rights holder who goes five years without using water beneficially (the time period varies among states) can lose it under forfeiture statutes or common law abandonment (as we saw in *Wheatland Irrigation*, p. 479). Note that in this case, however, the state agency was vastly more lenient toward IID. It could have asserted aggressively that IID had already lost its rights in the water it was wasting. Instead, the agency merely demanded that IID come up with a conservation plan. On the surface the Board might seem to have acted boldly, but in fact it pulled its punches—it questioned the reasonableness of the water use, but then did not propose to impose the harsh penalty of forfeiture that normally goes along with that conclusion.

Why might the Board have acted so cautiously? Political realities, no doubt, were important, plus the Board likely wanted IID to have time to make needed changes. Might these considerations, though, apply in the case of many other water disputes? Courts have been highly reluctant to conclude that particular water uses are unreasonable or non-beneficial, perhaps because the penalty of forfeiture is so harsh. Would they be more likely to do so if a less harsh remedy were available—if they could, for instance, do something akin to what the Board did with IID? Courts might challenge inefficient water uses more regularly if they could, by way of remedy, give the water rights holder a certain period of time in which to improve the water use to make it lawful or sell the water to someone who can use it properly.

STATE EX REL. CARY V. COCHRAN
Supreme Court of Nebraska
292 N.W. 239 (1940)

[Kearney Canal irrigators and the Central Power Company, the owners of the most senior water rights in the Platte River Basin, filed suit against the State of Nebraska. They alleged that the state violated their water rights by allowing junior appropriators located far upstream to divert water for irrigation and storage, leaving them without adequate water fill their more senior rights. The lower court refused the request of the senior appropriators for a directive ordering the state to respect temporal priority, and they appealed.]

CARTER, J.

* * *

[The court noted that the plaintiff irrigators and canal company held the senior right to divert 162 cubic feet of water per second (cfs or "second feet"), and that these rights were earlier in time than those of the upstream appropriators whose diversions were being challenged. The court then considered the river system itself and the substantial loss of water that occurred as water flowed across the state, slowly getting to the downstream diversion point of the senior appropriators.]

The North Platte River is a nonnavigable stream which has its source in the mountains of Colorado and flows across a part of Wyoming and Nebraska to a point approximately 200 miles from the Wyoming-Nebraska line, where it joins the South Platte river to form the Platte river. The present case involves the administration of irrigation and power rights on the North Platte and Platte rivers from the Wyoming-Nebraska line to the headgate of the Kearney canal located 13 miles west of Kearney, Nebraska. The water discharged into the Platte river from the South Platte river also has its place in the problem before us, but it does not appear to have been treated as of major importance by the parties in the present suit. The North Platte and Platte rivers will therefore be treated as the primary subject of the litigation. For the purposes of this suit, the upper end of the river is at the Wyoming-Nebraska line and the lower end at the headgate of the Kearney canal, it being the last point of diversion for irrigation and power purposes on the river.

* * *

The flow of the river even in the summer months is affected by the amount of snow falling in the mountains of Colorado within its drainage basin. The river passes through parts of Colorado and Wyoming, both of which states require irrigation water in excess of the available supply. Storage and control dams under the control of the federal government also exist along the river west of the point where the river enters Nebraska. Water rights, both senior and junior to existing rights and priorities in Nebraska, coupled with the uncertainty of their accurate administration, add to the indefiniteness of the amount of water that passes at any given time across the state line and under the control of the administrative officers of this state.

Losses from evaporation and transpiration are heavy, due to the wide and shallow character of the river. Changes of temperature and varying types of wind add to the uncertainty of the losses resulting from these changing conditions. Losses from percolation vary along the various sectors of the river. The evidence shows that the river valley from the Wyoming-Nebraska line to North Platte or thereabouts is underlaid with impervious formations which do not permit losses of subterranean waters into other watersheds. At some unknown point between North Platte and Gothenburg, the river cuts through the impervious formations and runs into the sheets of sand and gravel with which the territory is underlaid. Losses begin to occur at this point due to the percolation of river water through this sand and gravel formation, in a southeasterly direction into the basin of the Republican River. . . .

Experts with experience on the river estimate that the loss in delivering water from North Platte to the headgate of the Kearney canal with a wet river bed amounts to three times the amount of delivery, and with a dry river bed that it is almost impossible to get water through without a flood or a large sustained flow. In other words, it requires approximately 700 second-feet of water at North Platte to deliver 162 second-feet at the headgate of the Kearney canal when the river bed is wet. The underlying sand and gravel beds thicken as the river moves east. With the bed of the river on the surface of these sand and gravel deposits, it requires a huge amount of water to recharge the river channel and surrounding water table after the river bed once becomes dry. Until the water table is built up to the surface of the river bed, the river channel will not support a continuous flow. . . . The evidence bears out the statement that the Platte river east of Gothenburg is a very inefficient carrier of water. In addition to the subterranean losses noted, the river spreads out, causing a broad surface of water and channel bed to be subjected to large evaporation losses. . . .

Appropriations of water are made throughout the length of the river. The priority dates of these appropriations have no relation whatever to their location on the stream. Hence, very early appropriations may be found at the upper and lower ends of the stream, while very late appropriations are likewise found at both ends. In times of water shortage, the later appropriators are the first to be deprived of water. The closing of canals in accordance with the inverse order of their priority dates necessarily requires certain canals to close their headgates all along the stream at the same time. Water moves down the stream at approximately 25 miles per day with the result that it requires approximately ten days to deliver water from the state line to the Kearney headgate under normal conditions. The resulting lag therefore becomes an important factor to be considered. During the lag period, conditions over which the administrator of the river has no control may change or disrupt all calculations. Excessive heat, continued drought, and unusual winds may greatly reduce estimated quantities of river-flow, or, on the other hand, low temperatures, rains and floods in the lower river basin may relieve immediate demands These elements of uncertainty must be considered in protecting the rights of all on the stream. The position of relators at the lower end of the stream is in itself a recognized condition, and while they have the second oldest priority on the river, it is inescapable that their location subjects them to unfavorable conditions which are practically impossible to eliminate.

It must also be borne in mind that the amount of flow in the river at any given time during the irrigation season is nothing more than an estimate based on spot measurements. Accurate figures are not obtainable until several weeks after the immediate problem has been determined. The best available basis for the determination of the facts therefore is often very uncertain. The effect of the use of the river as a carrier of storage water also enters into the calculations. The best estimates of the administrator are often affected by unlawful diversions by junior appropriators, injunctions and restraining orders issued by the courts, errors of judgment by the administrator and his subordinates, dilatory compliance with closing orders, and inaccurate reports of rains, floods and weather conditions generally. All of the factors . . . mentioned [above] contribute to the uncertainty of an efficient and accurate distribution of water in accordance with adjudicated appropriations in the order of their priority.

The use of water for irrigation in this state is a natural want. The inadequacy of supply to meet the demands of the public requires strict administration to prevent waste. It is therefore the policy of the law that junior appropriators may use available water within the limits of their own appropriations so long as the rights of senior appropriators are not injured or damaged. And so, in the instant case, junior appropriators may lawfully apply water to their lands within the limits of their adjudicated appropriations until the Kearney canal fails to receive its full appropriation of 162 second-feet. Until the senior appropriator is injured, there is the ever-present possibility of changed weather conditions, precipitation, or other sources of water supply which might alleviate the situation and supply the needs of the Kearney canal. To pursue any other rule would greatly add to the loss by waste of the public waters of this state. We conclude therefore that the use of water by a junior appropriator does not become adverse to or injure a senior appropriator until it results in a deprivation of his allotted amount, or some part thereof. This rule is supported, we think, by our decisions as well as the decisions of other states.

The real question to be decided, however, is the determination of the duty imposed upon the officers of the state in administering the waters of the stream when the available supply of water at the headgate of the Kearney canal is reduced to an amount less than the 162 second-feet to which the relators are entitled. The rights of relators to the use of this water as against all appropriators subsequent to September 10, 1882, cannot be questioned. It is the duty of the administrative officers of the state to recognize this right and to give force to relators' priority. This requires that junior appropriators be restrained from taking water from the stream so long as such water can be delivered in usable quantities at the headgate of the Kearney canal. If it appear[s] that all the available water in the stream would be lost before its arrival at the headgate of the Kearney canal, it would, of course, be an unjustified waste of water to attempt delivery. Whether a definite quantity of water passing a given point on the stream would, if not diverted or interrupted in its course, reach the headgate of the Kearney canal in a usable quantity creates a very complicated question of fact. It therefore is the duty of the administrative officers of the state to determine from all available means, including the factors hereinbefore discussed, whether or not a usable quantity of water can be delivered at the headgate of the Kearney canal. It necessarily follows that this finding of fact must be determined in the first instance by the officers charged with the administration of the stream. . . .

After determination that a given quantity of water passing a certain point on the river would not, even if uninterrupted, reach the headgate of the Kearney canal in usable quantities, the administrative officers of the state may lawfully permit junior appropriators to divert it for irrigation purposes. This results oft times in having junior appropriators receiving a head of water at a time when an appropriator farther downstream is getting none, though he is prior in time. Such situations are not therefore conclusive evidence of unlawful diversions.

Amici curiae urge that the doctrine of reasonable use is in force in this state and that it should be applied to the case at bar. We recognize the principle that the public has an interest in the public waters of the state and it is the use thereof only that may be appropriated. Even though an adjudicated appropriation may be vested, it may be subjected to regulation and control by the state by virtue of its police power. It may likewise be circumscribed to the extent that a limited diversion for a specified purpose will not permit of an undue interference with the rights of other appropriators on the stream. But we cannot agree that the doctrine of reasonable use can be applied in a case where delivery of a usable quantity of water can be made, although the losses suffered in so doing are great. To permit the officers of the state the right to say whether prospective losses would or would not justify the delivery of usable quantities of water would clothe such officers with a discretion incompatible with the vested interests of the relators, and destroy the very purpose of the doctrine of appropriation existent in this state. When upstream appropriators applied for and received adjudicated priorities, they did so with the knowledge that there was an earlier appropriator at the lower end of the stream whose rights had to be recognized. When the relators applied for and received their adjudications, they are likewise presumed to have known that other appropriators would obtain inferior rights above them that would have to be recognized. Each is required to respect the vested rights of the others, even though some hardships may be thereby imposed. We therefore hold that the doctrine of reasonable use does not extend so far as to authorize the administrator of the waters of the stream to refrain from delivering a usable quantity of water to a senior appropriator because it might appear to him that excessive losses would result. The duty of the administrator, in administering the waters of the stream by virtue of the police power of the state, is to enforce existing priorities, not to determine, change or amend them. . . .

* * *

[The court held that, while the senior appropriators were entitled to the water, the trial court properly denied relief because they were too slow in filing their request for mandamus.]

NOTES

1. *A wasteful protection?* To understand this case we need to examine the facts closely, especially the numbers. How much water had to stay in the

river in order to supply water to the senior user? What happened to the water that did not make it down to the senior user? Was this water essentially wasted? (In answering this question, pay attention to the court's comments on the hydrologic functioning of the river and associated groundwater.) If you were concerned mostly about the ecological health of the river, what might you say about this ruling?

We also need to note carefully the timing of the senior user's ability to shut down an upstream junior user. What legal rule does the court announce, and does the rule fully protect the senior user? Has the court in some small way reduced the protection enjoyed by senior users?

2. *Water quality.* Senior water users are protected not just from diversions by junior users, but also by degradations in water quality. Consider *Farmers Irrigation v. Game and Fish Commission*, 369 P.2d 557 (Colo. 1962). Farmers operated an extensive ditch and reservoir system on East Rifle Creek, used for domestic and irrigation purposes. In 1954, the state Game and Fish Commission constructed a fish hatchery on the creek. According to the plaintiffs, the state diverted practically all of the water of East Rifle Creek from its natural channel and into the fish hatchery, and into associated divisions and ponds. The state, in its operations, placed large quantities of ground liver, flesh, and similar substances and other protein matter used for fish feed in the water diverted into and through the hatchery. The feed became putrid and caused the odor of the water to become offensive. It likewise caused the water to become unwholesome and unfit for domestic use.

As a result of the pollution, the court concluded, "the water diverted by the Farmers Irrigation Company for use and benefit of its stockholders has acquired a bad and offensive odor and has become noxious, offensive, and unfit for human consumption [so] that plaintiffs are now unable to use said water for domestic purposes because of the unwholesome matter placed therein by defendants; that plaintiffs have no other source of supply for domestic uses and are compelled to haul water a considerable distance for such uses. . . ." *Id.* at 558. The court held that the state hatchery, by seriously polluting the water, damaged the plaintiffs' property rights. The state action amounted to an unconstitutional taking of private property without the payment of just compensation.

3. *The "no injury" rule for water right transfers.* Another basic element of prior appropriation law is the ability to transfer water rights to others, including willing buyers. Problems can ensue if the purchaser wants to use the water in a different way or at a different location. Water uses generate distinct patterns of return flows, and a change in the nature or place of use can greatly affect downstream users. These third-party effects can make water transfers highly contentious. But transfers are necessary if vested water rights are to move from old, inefficient uses (certain types of irrigated agriculture) to new, more highly-valued uses (e.g., municipal water supply). A prominent limit on water transfers is the rule that they may not impose

material injury on other water users, even junior users. The following decision highlights some of the complexities of this so-called "no injury" rule.

GREEN V. CHAFFEE DITCH COMPANY
Supreme Court of Colorado
371 P.2d 775 (1962)

[Morrison and Hoffman claimed rights to 16 cubic feet per second (cfs), about half the flow of Cache La Poudre River. They proposed to sell 8 cfs to the City of Fort Collins, which planned to change the point of water diversion some thirteen miles upstream. The plan drew numerous protests by other water users. The trial court concluded that Morrison and Hoffman had a much smaller water right than they claimed—only the water that Morrison and Hoffman were actually diverting and beneficially using—and that they could transfer only a portion of that water right to Fort Collins. On appeal the Colorado Supreme Court affirmed.]

MOORE, J.

* * *

The trial court entered findings which, in pertinent part, contain the following:

"That the land owned by said petitioners, Milton Coy Hoffman and Lydia Hoffman Morrison, irrigated by said water is seventy-two acres along the river bottom, the Cache La Poudre River dividing said land. That the top soil is a sandy loam and varies in thickness from about five feet to a few inches and is underlain with coarse gravel, which in some places comes to the surface. That because of the soil conditions and the proximity to the river, all water applied to said land, not consumed by plant life and evaporation, returns to the river within a very short time and again becomes a part of the river and available to other appropriators. That the amount of water necessarily consumed by plant life to produce a maximum crop, in addition to natural rainfall, is 15 inches of water or one and one-fourth acre feet of water for each acre irrigated, thus requiring 90 acre feet of water each year for the proper irrigation of said land. That the efficiency of water on this particular land is 25%, requiring the application to this land of 360 acre feet of water during each irrigating season to produce maximum crops. That in addition to the 90 acre feet of water consumed on this land, five acre feet are lost by evaporation and seepage while the water is in transit from the headgate of the Coy Ditch to the Hoffman-Morrison farm, making a total consumptive use of 95 acre feet of water each year. That the only domestic use of this water has been a small amount for the watering of livestock. That the irrigating season on this land has been from April 15th to October 15th of each year.

"That the City of Fort Collins, during the period from April 15th and October 15th of each year has an average return flow through its sewage disposal plant, storm sewers and other sources of 50% of the water taken in at its intake pipeline.

"That for many years last past, and ever since the entry of the original adjudication Decree, the petitioners Milton Coy Hoffman and Lydia Hoffman Morrison and their predecessors in title and interest have never beneficially used at any one time more than eight cubic feet of water per second of time for the irrigation of the lands now owned by them. Any diversions by petitioners or others in excess of that amount were a subterfuge and not made in good faith.

"That any diversion of water from said priority from October 16th of any year to April 14th, inclusive, of the following year, except for livestock purposes, would injuriously affect the storage rights of protestants, or some one or more of them, as they have historically depended upon the filling of their storage decrees during said time."

The court decreed inter alia that:

"No diversion from Priority No. 13 awarded to the Coy Ditch can be transferred without injury to junior appropriators, except under the conditions herein set forth, and any transfer of water, heretofore beneficially used, must be upon condition that the land heretofore irrigated must be forever deprived of irrigation water from this Decree, and cannot be a transfer of water not needed or beneficially used.

"That there can be diverted from the headgate of the Coy Ditch to the headgate of the City of Fort Collins pipeline without injury to the protestants, that amount of water which, when the return flow from the City sewage plant and other sources is considered, permits the City to consumptively use 95 acre feet of water during the irrigating season. Therefore, under the foregoing findings, the City should be permitted to divert 190 acre feet of water during each irrigation season under the conditions that the City at no time shall divert more than eight cubic feet of water per second of time. . . .

"Since all diversions by petitioners and their predecessors in excess of eight cubic feet of water per second of time were a subterfuge and not in good faith, and since not more than eight cubic feet of water per second of time could be beneficially used, all water in excess of said eight cubic feet of water per second of time has been totally and completely abandoned.

"Junior appropriators, who appropriated this excess water have a vested right to have the conditions on the river remain as they were when their appropriations were made.

"The Court is aware that as the City of Fort Collins continues to grow, additional water will be needed for its inhabitants. However, need is not the matter to be considered in a change of point of diversion. The element to be considered under the statutes is injury to junior appropriators. No change may be allowed unless injury can be obviated by the imposition of conditions. In this case, the conditions listed are essential to protect junior appropriators against substantial injury.

"To prevent injury to junior appropriators, no call for water under said priority may be made at the new point of diversion during any period from October 16th to April 14th, inclusive. No call for water under said priority for use on the farm lands of petitioners or elsewhere may be made, except allowed at the new point of diversion, except water for livestock purposes from October 16th to April 14th, inclusive. If any one or more of said conditions is not imposed there will be injury to junior appropriators on the river, and this is the controlling factor."

There is competent evidence in the record before us to sustain all the findings of fact entered by the trial court. . . . [The court specifically emphasized that Morrison and Hoffman had never diverted more than 8 cfs, and that a paper right to a larger diversion had no legal effect when the larger amount of water had not been diverted and applied to an actual beneficial use. The court emphasized that the amount of the paper right in excess of 8 cfs had not been abandoned; it had never come into existence because it had never been put to use. The court then proceeded to explain the general rule governing the change of a point of diversion for a water right. Such a change could be made, but only when and to the extent that the change did not harm any other water user, whether junior or senior. It quoted from its earlier ruling in *Farmers Highline Canal and Reservoir Company v. City of Golden*, 272 P.2d 629 (Colo. 1954), which involved a similar application for change in the point of diversion of water:]

> (2) 'It is recognized that water is a property right, subject to sale and conveyance, and that under proper conditions not only may the point of diversion be changed, but likewise the manner of use. It further is recognized that such change may be permitted, by proper court decree, only in such instances as it is specifically shown that the rights of other users from the same source are not injuriously affected by such change, and that the burden of proof thereof rests upon petitioner.

* * *

> (3) 'There is absolutely no question that a decreed water right is valuable property; that it may be used, its use changed, its point of diversion relocated; . . . provided that no adverse effect be

suffered by other users from the same stream, particularly those holding junior priorities.

(4) 'Equally well established, as we have repeatedly held, is the principle that junior appropriators have vested rights in the continuation of stream conditions as they existed at the time of their respective appropriations, and that subsequent to such appropriations they may successfully resist all proposed changes in points of diversion and use of water from that source which in any way materially injuries or adversely affects their rights.

* * *

We conclude that the trial court determined the issues in the instant case in a manner consistent with the foregoing principles, and find no error requiring a reversal of the judgment. There was no abuse of discretion in the assessment of costs.

The judgment accordingly is affirmed.

NOTES

1.   *Interlocking rights. Green* is a splendid decision in terms of the vivid illustration it gives of interlocking water rights and of the way the law looks to actual water-use practices to define the extent of private rights. Hoffman and Morrison, the court tells us, own only the right to use the precise amount of water that they have been using consistently over the years. And their right is limited by all the particulars of their pattern of use. They can only use the water during the precise times when they have been using it (here, during the irrigation season of April 15 to October 15). They cannot at any time divert more water than they have diverted in the past (here, a maximum of 8 cfs). And the total diversions during the year cannot exceed the amount they have been diverting annually (here, a total of 365 acre-feet per year of which 5 were lost in transit and 360 used to produce maximum crops). It is the actual pattern of beneficial use that sets the terms of a water right, not the number written on a decree or permit.

The reason why water rights are so carefully limited is to protect the junior users on the river who rely upon this pattern of use to establish their own water uses. Note the general rule that the court announces: "Junior appropriators who appropriated this excess water have a vested right to have the conditions on the river remain as they were when their appropriations were made." This is a bedrock principle of prior appropriation law, and has both high benefits and high costs. The main benefit of protecting the expectations of junior users is that these users can begin their water-using activities with a fairly high degree of confidence that they will have water available (natural fluctuations aside, of course. The rule, that is, encourages junior users to take advantage of return flows, and thus encourages the full, multiple use of water before it finally ends up in the ocean. The downside is that it makes water uses rather inflexible. To protect the junior users is to restrict greatly the ability of senior users to alter where and how they use their water flows. They can make changes in the nature and place of their water uses and their points of diversion only so long as the changes cause no harm to anyone else.

Pay attention to how this do-no-harm rule plays out on the facts of this case. (It may help to draw a picture of the river and to go over the court's arithmetic calculations.) The court decides that Hoffman and Morrison have been consuming 95 acre-feet of water per year (with the rest—270 acre-feet—returning to the river). That water is lost to the river, and thus is not available for use by water users downstream. If Hoffman and Morrison transferred 95 acre-feet to Fort Collins and halted their own irrigation uses, no one downstream would be worse off. But note that Fort Collins does not consume all of the water that it diverts. About half of its diverted water returns to the river and is available for downstream users. When the court takes this return flow into account, it concludes that Fort Collins can divert a total of 190 acre-feet without causing any harm to any other water users. So far as we can tell, it makes little difference that Fort Collins plans to divert the water from a *location* thirteen miles upstream. Had intervening water users been harmed by the switch in location, we presumably would have heard about it.

2. *The dangers and inefficiencies of water transfers.* One of the dangers for a water user in stepping forward to propose a water transfer is that the transfer process draws scrutiny to the user's actual pattern of behavior. Has the use consistently been beneficial? Has there been a gap in use that can raise claims of forfeiture? What exactly are the limits on water-use practices, and how much of a water right has been lost through nonuse? Many water users would rather not have these questions asked, and are therefore reluctant to consider water transfers. The effect is to inhibit water markets. But what can be done about this situation, short of changing the legal protections enjoyed by junior users?

Consider also the economic effect of the transfer rules. Hoffman and Morrison were diverting 365 acre-feet of water per year. They were able to transfer to Fort Collins only the right to divert 190 acre-feet per year. Any right to divert more than that quantity was lost. This transaction will make economic sense to the parties, then, only if the 190 acre-feet is worth more to Fort Collins than the 365 acre-feet to Hoffman and Morrison. If the water is worth, on a per-acre-foot basis, only 50 percent more to Fort Collins than to Hoffman and Morrison, the transfer would not take place. Indeed, given the high transaction costs involved in these transfers, the transfer is likely to occur only if the water to Fort Collins is worth at least three or four times more than it is to Hoffman and Morrison. Water transfers, that is, do not move water to slightly more valuable uses. They move water only to water uses that are considerably more valuable. In economic terms, the market is decidedly inefficient.

One way to describe this situation is to highlight the tension between protecting junior users and promoting a well-functioning market. The law can do one or the other, but cannot do both. Protecting junior users promotes the full use of water before it gets to the ocean. Promoting the market, on the other side, leaves junior users at great risk but allows for more ready transfers of senior water rights to higher and better uses. This tradeoff is at the heart of the water predicament today in arid parts of the American West. Market advocates call for "streamlining" transfers so as to facilitate markets. Too often, they shortchange the cost of doing that—diminished protections for junior water users.

Imagine if Hoffman and Morrison were allowed to transfer to Fort Collins the full amount of water that they wanted to transfer—8 cubic feet per second year round. The harm to downstream users could have been considerable as Fort Collins diverted far more water than Hoffman and Morrison ever did. (The harm would have been even greater if Hoffman and Morrison had continued their own water diversion, as they proposed.) To give Hoffman and Morrison that right would be to redefine radically the property rights of downstream junior users in ways sharply harmful to them. On the other side, defenders of the current, protective regime can sometimes fail to see its high costs. Current water uses are hard to change when junior users are fully protected. The system overall experiences gridlock. Water is devoted to low-valued uses while higher-valued needs go unmet. For an argument that prior appropriation law should change to facilitate transfers by reducing the security enjoyed by downstream users, see Stephen F. Williams, *A Market-Based Approach to Water Rights: Evaluating Colorado's Water System*, in *Tradition, Innovation and Conflict: Perspectives on Colorado Water Law* (Lawrence J. MacDonnell ed., 1986) (article by a current senior federal circuit court judge suggesting that the existing "no injury" rule constitutes a windfall to downstream users). Compare Joseph W. Dellapenna, *The Importance of Getting Names Right: The Myth of Markets for Water*, 25 Wm. & Mary Envtl. L. & Pol'y Rev. 317 (2000) (suggesting that the "no injury" rule prevents water transfers which could produce loss of downstream users' property rights).

BONHAM v. MORGAN
Supreme Court of Utah
788 P.2d 497 (1989)

[The holders of certain water rights (the Salt Lake County Conservancy District and the Draper Irrigation Company) filed with the state engineer an application to change where and how they were diverting and using their water. They obtained preliminary approval to make the changes, and proceeded to do so. Bonham, who was not a water-rights user, intervened to challenge the changes, claiming that the changes caused substantial flooding and damage to his land and to nearby property planned for a public park. The state engineer concluded that he could not take Bonham's claims into account in his final ruling on the application; he could only consider, he asserted, claims of harm based on impairment of other water rights and Bonham did not hold a water right. Bonham appealed.]

PER CURIAM.

* * *

Utah Code Ann. § 73–3–3 (1980) [the statute governing changes in water uses], at the time the state engineer rendered his decision, read in pertinent part:

> Any person entitled to the use of water may change the place of diversion or use and may use the water for other purposes than those for which it was originally appropriated, but no such change shall be made if it impairs any vested right without just compensation. Such changes may be permanent or temporary. Changes for an indefinite length of time with an intention to relinquish the original point of diversion, place or purpose of use are defined as *permanent changes. Temporary changes* include and are limited to all changes for definitely fixed periods of not exceeding one year. Both permanent and temporary changes of point of diversion, place or purpose of use of water including water involved in general adjudication or other suits, shall be made in the manner provided herein and not otherwise.

> No permanent change shall be made except on the approval of an application therefor by the state engineer. . . . *The procedure in the state engineer's office and rights and duties of the applicants with respect to applications for permanent changes of point of diversion, place or purpose of use shall be the same as provided in this title for applications to appropriate water*; but the state engineer may, in connection with applications for permanent change involving only a change in point of diversion of 660 feet or less, waive the necessity for publishing notice of such applications. No temporary change shall be made except upon an application filed in duplicate with the state engineer. . . . The state engineer shall make an investigation and *if such temporary change does not impair any vested rights of others he shall make an order authorizing the change.* (Emphasis added.)

Section 73–3–8 (1985) [the statute governing issuance of permits for new appropriations], at the time the state engineer rendered his decision, read in pertinent part:

> (1) It shall be the duty of the state engineer to approve an application if: (a) there is unappropriated water in the proposed source; (b) the proposed use will not impair existing rights or

interfere with the more beneficial use of the water; (c) the proposed plan is physically and economically feasible, unless the application is filed by the United States Bureau of Reclamation, and would not prove detrimental to the public welfare; (d) the applicant has the financial ability to complete the proposed works; and (e) the application was filed in good faith and not for purposes of speculation or monopoly. *If the state engineer, because of information in his possession obtained either by his own investigation or otherwise, has reason to believe that an application to appropriate water will interfere with its more beneficial use for irrigation, domestic or culinary, stock watering, power or mining development or manufacturing, or will unreasonably affect public recreation or the natural stream environment, or will prove detrimental to the public welfare, it is his duty to withhold his approval or rejection of the application until he has investigated the matter. If an application does not meet the requirements of this section, it shall be rejected.* (Emphasis added.)

* * *

We agree with the position taken by plaintiffs and the NPCA that both statutory purposes and a reasonable textual interpretation of water allocation statutes support the application of appropriation criteria to permanent change applications. The language critical to our determination was added to section 100–3–3, R.S. Utah 1933, in 1937. The amendment removed provisions addressing notice requirements and added for the first time language defining permanent and temporary changes. After setting out procedures relating to applications for permanent changes, the 1937 amendment continued:

> The procedure in the state engineer's office and the rights and duties of the applicant with respect to application for permanent changes of point of diversion, place, or purpose of use shall be the same as provided in this title for applications to appropriate water. (Emphasis added.)

The remaining amendments to section 100–3–3 dealt with procedures relating to temporary changes, criteria for rejecting applications for both permanent and temporary changes, procedures with respect to types of changes, and finality of the state engineer's decision and penalties for changes without following statutory prescriptions. In essence, the substantive provisions enacted in 1937 remain unchanged to date.

The appropriations statute, section 100–3–8, R.S. Utah 1933, to which the amendment made cross-reference, contained then, as section 73–3–8 does now, a specification on the duties of the state engineer when acting on appropriation applications. These were to be granted if, and only if, they did not interfere with more beneficial use, public recreation, the natural stream environment, or the public welfare, as more specifically set out in the statute. In contrast to the cross-reference between *permanent change* applications and appropriations, the 1937 amendments prescribed different and very summary procedures for *temporary changes,* under which the state engineer "shall make an investigation and *if such temporary change does not impair any vested rights of others, he shall make an order authorizing the change.*" From these contrasting references and procedures, we draw the rational inference that in temporary change applications the review criteria (now contained in section 73–3–8) did not apply, but in considerations of permanent change applications they did. . . .

* * *

Even were we convinced, which we are not, by the state engineer's argument that the "procedure in the state engineer's office" in section 73–3–3 refers only to his ministerial duties, the lack of precision in the cross-reference is of little avail to the state engineer. The further mention in that section of the "rights and duties" of the applicants and the reference to section 73–3–8 are sufficient by themselves to show that the legislature meant to require more than similar procedures alone. The only reasonable meaning to read into section 73–3–3 is that the state engineer must investigate and reject the application for either appropriation or permanent change of use or place of use if approval would interfere with more beneficial use, public recreation, the natural stream environment, or the public welfare. It is unreasonable to assume that the legislature would require the state engineer to investigate matters of public concern in water appropriations and yet restrict him from undertaking those duties in permanent change applications. Carried to its logical conclusion, such an interpretation would eviscerate the duties of the state engineer under section 73–3–8 and allow an applicant to accomplish in a two-step process what the statute proscribes in a one-step process. For all that an applicant would need to do to achieve a disapproved purpose under section 73–3–8 would be to appropriate for an approved purpose and then to file a change application under section 73–3–3.

* * *

We hold that the state engineer is required to undertake the same investigation in permanent change applications that the statute mandates in applications for water appropriations and that plaintiffs are aggrieved persons who have standing to sue him pursuant to Utah Code Ann. § 73–3–14 (1980) for a review of his decision approving the subject change application. The summary judgment in favor of the state engineer is vacated, and plaintiffs' complaint against him reinstated for trial on the merits.

NOTES

1. *Broader protections, and more gridlock?* In Utah, as in most western states, changes in the nature and place of a water use (very minor changes aside) typically require approval in an administrative or even judicial proceeding. Anyone who would suffer legal injury from the change can step forward to block it, in whole or in part. Note the extensive review that Utah provides. The change can be made only if it will not impair existing rights, interfere with the "more beneficial" use of water or prove detrimental to the public welfare. The statute proceeds to mention protection for public recreation and natural stream conditions. In combination, the statutory provisions would seem to embrace a strict do-no-harm rule, barring any material changes in water use practices that could cause noticeable harm of any sort, including (as here) harm to landowners who are not themselves water users. As you consider the statute, you might imagine the difficulties that would arise from applying it. How much diminution in a water flow would be enough to interfere with public recreation? And what rivers display anything close to "natural stream conditions"?

Has the Utah statute perhaps gone too far in limiting transfers, given the resulting difficulties water owners will have selling to new, possibly more valuable uses? Would it make better sense to allow transfers to take place while requiring the transferee to pay damages to anyone specifically harmed by the transfer—without allowing the injured party to halt the transaction? (A thoughtful proposal to that effect is offered in Megan Hennessey, *Note, Colorado River Water Rights: Property Rights in Transition*, 71 U. Chi. L. Rev. 1661 (2004).) Perhaps most significantly, can we fault lawmakers for not taking a broader view of the situation? What about a water transfer that produces a more desirable water use pattern overall, even though it causes some harm? Would it make more sense to have courts undertake an overall, before-versus-after comparison, to decide whether the transfer makes good sense as a whole, despite the ensuing harm?

2. *Permanent versus temporary changes.* Note the different, easier rules that govern when a water user seeks to make a temporary change in water use practices. The easier rules do pose dangers to public interests, but the possible benefits are evident. A water user who can temporarily avoid using water is given an easier way to make it available to someone else. Overall water uses are more efficient, and the water owner does not have to worry about losing the water right through abandonment or forfeiture. Temporary changes also facilitate deal-making to address times of drought. One water user can temporarily sell water to another as a way to address a water emergency.

3. *Public interest allocation and restrictions on transfer.* A comment made by the court in *Bonham* highlights a problem that we have seen before.

The court explained that a transfer of water to a new use needs to comply with the criteria for initial water appropriation, because if it did not, a water user then could circumvent the limits on original appropriation. "For all the applicant would need to do to achieve a disapproved [water use], would be to appropriate for an approved purpose and then to file a change of application." Put simply, if lawmakers want water used in particular ways, they need to limit transfers of the water to make sure that new uses of it (by the same or another owner) are consistent with the same use limits. Phrased more broadly, when allocation of a natural resource is based on public-interest criteria, the same criteria have to be applied later, when the resource is transferred, to avoid giving resource users a two-step process for devoting the resource to a disapproved use. When subsequent transfers are limited in this way, though, markets are impaired and reallocation becomes harder. The market works on the assumption that resources should go to the highest bidder—an allocation system quite contrary to allocation based on merit or public interest.

4.   *Farm water for farmers alone.* A Washington state statute, the Family Farm Water Act, gave farmers a special opportunity to gain water for use on "family farms." The statute allowed some flexibility in shifting irrigation water to other agricultural uses and to certain uses in "urbanizing areas" consistent with "adopted land use plans." A court held that, given the clear public-interest limits imposed by the statute, a family farmer could not lease his water rights for 50 years to City of West Richland because the city's use did not qualify for the special treatment accorded family farms. *City of West Richland v. Department of Ecology*, 103 P.3d 818 (Wash. Ct. App. 2004).

5.   *Interstate commerce in water.* Although a state can impose severe restrictions on where water can be used and on water transfers—prohibiting them entirely if it wants—it faces constitutional limits when it defines transfer options in ways that discriminate against interstate commerce. In *Sporhase v. Nebraska ex rel. Douglas*, 458 U.S. 941 (1982), the Supreme Court struck down, as a violation of the dormant commerce clause, a Nebraska statute that authorized the transport of groundwater to another state only if that state similarly allowed the export of its own water into Nebraska. The Court recognized that Nebraska might preserve its water for use by state residents as a way of dealing with scarcity and promoting conservation. The challenged provision, however, was not carefully tailored to promote conservation: it authorized export of water in a discriminatory way.

The above two cases and accompanying notes explain the basic rules on water transfers in prior appropriation jurisdictions. Transfers are possible but transaction costs are high. Moreover, the basic do-no-harm rule operates in many jurisdictions to ban water transfers except to the extent of a water user's consumptive use. Water that is used consumptively is entirely lost to a river system and thus can be diverted for use elsewhere, for any purpose, without causing harm to the river system of origin and to downstream water users. But when water owners desire to transfer more of their water, problems arise—as we have seen. The law tends to limit transfers in the interest of protecting junior users and thus the stability of the entire water-use regime. But how, then, are we to facilitate shifts of water to higher-valued uses, particularly to urban uses where thirsty water users are willing and easily able to compensate agricultural users?

One possible answer to this problem is for states to redefine reasonable and beneficial water use so as to prohibit water uses that no longer make economic and social sense. If urban areas need water (as they do), and if lawmakers view municipal water uses as high in social priority (as they do), then why should massive amounts of water be used for low-valued agricultural purposes, particularly to irrigate crops (such as corn and cotton) that are overabundant, to pasture livestock (also abundant), and to produce hay (of little value except in local markets)? And why should irrigators be allowed to continue using irrigation methods that are vastly less efficient than technological options that are readily available and widely used outside the United States?

What if a court, legislature, or regulatory agency decided that a water use was not reasonable or beneficial because it involved irrigating low-valued crops or entailed the use of inefficient distribution systems— as the California State Water Resources Control Board did in the Imperial Irrigation District dispute? What would the effect of such a ruling be, particularly if the irrigators affected by it were given a period of time in which to shift to a more beneficial use or to sell the water to someone else? Could a new definition of reasonable and beneficial use not only curtail socially undesirable water uses but stimulate a more active market in water rights? Alternatively, should we move in precisely the opposite direction, getting rid of the beneficial use limit and doing all we can to stimulate markets, as suggested by Judge Williams (p. 515)? Is that option, however disruptive to junior users in the short run, more likely (given American culture) to bring long-term benefits? (As you assess these questions, you might consider how the public trust doctrine and public trust values (considered in chapter 3) might come into play.)

The prior appropriation doctrine largely began life as a simple rule of capture: a diverter of water obtained a vested property right in the use of water if the water was put to beneficial use (e.g., mining, irrigation, municipal use). This taker-centered rule worked well to spread water rights among the many and avoid monopolization by the few (i.e., riparian landowners), as long as water supplies were plentiful. But in the water-short West, river systems were quickly overappropriated. As overall water shortages increased, it became important that remaining water supplies go to the highest valued uses, not just to any beneficial use. Many states have reacted by modifying their water codes to require that all new water uses satisfy specified public-interest criteria. These statutory changes have transformed what was a taker-centered property rights system into an administrative law system subject to the discretion of government officials.

The following case considers the effect of public interest factors on a new appropriation.

SHOKAL V. DUNN
Supreme Court of Idaho
707 P.2d 441 (1985)

[A trout company applied for a permit to appropriate 100 cfs of water from Billingsley Creek near Hagerman, Idaho, for a trout farm. Many local residents, property owners, and water users objected. The state department of water resources nonetheless issued the permit and some of the protestants filed suit. The lower court reversed the agency, questioning whether the project satisfied state statutes having to do with the financial capacity of the company and "the local public interest." The company appealed.]

BISTLINE, J.

* * *

II. *Financing*

Judge Smith held that the Director of Water Resources used an incorrect standard with regard to financing of projects in conjunction with a permit application. I.C. § 42–203A requires the Director to consider as one of several factors the financial resources of the applicant when deciding whether or not to issue a permit. In the instant case the Director, at the first hearing on the matter, determined the applicant had sufficient financial resources. Judge Schroeder [Judge Schroeder was the district judge who originally heard the case; an appeal was filed with "the district court, this time before the Honorable W.E. Smith, 707 P2d. at 444—Eds.] disagreed and held the Director's decision was clearly erroneous: "A finding of financial ability to complete a $265,000 to $270,000 project on a $4,500 base is 'clearly erroneous' within the meaning of I.C. 67–515." Judge Schroeder concluded "there is a clear lack of evidence to support the finding of financial ability" and remanded the case to Water Resources for further hearing.

On remand, the Director determined the applicants did have sufficient financial resources. The Director stated:

The financial ability criterion of I.C. 42–203[A] should not be interpreted as requiring the applicant, at the time of the hearings on the protested application, to have enough cash available to immediately complete the project. The applicant must show that he can obtain the necessary financing to complete the project within five years. At the hearing, the applicant must prove that it is reasonably probable that he can obtain the necessary financing to complete the project within the time constraint of the permit and the Idaho Code.

The Director then stated in Conclusion of Law No. 4: "At a hearing on a protested application, the applicant must prove that it is reasonably probable that he can obtain the necessary financing to complete the project within the time constraints of the permit and the Idaho Code." The Director concluded that the applicant, Trout Co., made the necessary evidentiary showing and had established its financial ability to complete the project. On the second appeal to the district court, Judge Smith disagreed with the Director's analysis.

Judge Smith objected to the "reasonably probable" standard used by the Director. He also concluded that the evidence in the case clearly did not support the Director's conclusions. [As Judge Smith interpreted the Idaho statute, "an applicant was bound to show at the hearing that he then and there had the financial resources to complete the project within the time allotted—not to exceed five (5) years." Using this interpretation the Judge found the Director's actions clearly erroneous.]

* * *

We believe Judge Smith was incorrect in his interpretation of the financial showing an applicant must make to comply with I.C. § 42–203A. Judge Smith's requirement that applicants show that they "then and there" have the financial resources is far too restrictive; such a standard may have an excessively chilling effect on water and land development in this state. The ultimate question under the financial resources requirement of I.C. § 42–203A is this: who should bear the risk of failure. Under the district court's "then and there" standard any risk of failure is eliminated at the permit application stage. Yet, opportunities for development of the water resources of the state also are eliminated for those who may not have the cash in the bank, but may be able to secure sufficient resources during the five-year time limitation imposed by I.C. § 42–204 to put the water to beneficial use. The "then and there" standard, while admirably encouraging pecuniary caution, goes beyond a reasonable reading of the statutory requirement of "sufficient financial resources." I.C. § 42–203A(5)(d).

The "reasonably probable" standard used by Water Resources shifts the risk of failure and shows that the state is more willing to take a risk by providing individuals with the opportunity to put water to beneficial use. It indicates a willingness on the part of the state to take a chance that a proposed water use with sound prospects of financing will become a successful venture, thereby benefiting both the water user and the state. We believe this to be a more appropriate standard for the financial resources requirement of I.C. § 42–203A. The water resources of this state are not so limited that they must be safeguarded with permits issued *only* when the applicant has secured all necessary financing prior to the water appropriation permit application. At the same time, the applicant must make a showing that it is reasonably probable he or she will obtain the necessary financing within five years. The extent of the applicant's own investment is a strong factor to be considered.

The financial resources requirement, added in 1935, was clearly intended to prevent the tying up of our water resources by persons unable to complete a project because of financial limitations. The financial requirement provision was added at a time when unscrupulous promoters were obtaining permits and lulling unsuspecting investors into purchasing worthless securities on worthless projects. The legislature has provided Water Resources with the authority to weed out the financially insufficient applications. I.C. § 42–203A. We believe a showing by the applicant that it is "reasonably probable" that financing can be secured to complete the project within five years serves the purpose of screening out undeserving projects without being destructive of growth and development in the state.

* * *

III. *The Local Public Interest*

Since Water Resources' decisions on financing are reinstated, the only matters for the agency to consider on remand are those which relate generally to the local public interest. I.C. § 42–203A(5)(e). We turn first to the interpretation of this provision, a question of first impression before this Court.

A. *Defining the Local Public Interest*

Under I.C. § 42–203A(5)(e), if an applicant's appropriation of water "will conflict with the local public interest, where the local public interest is defined as the affairs of the people in the area directly affected by the proposed use," then the Director "may reject such application and refuse issuance of a permit therefor, or may partially approve and grant a permit for a smaller quantity of water than applied for, or may grant a permit upon conditions."

The Utah Supreme Court interpreted a similar provision to authorize the State Engineer "to reject or limit the priority of plaintiff's application [for a permit to appropriate water for a power project] in the interest of the public welfare." *Tanner v. Bacon,* 136 P.2d 957, 964 (Utah 1943); see also *People v. Shirokow,* 605 P.2d 859, 866 (Cal. 1980) (In the public interest, the Water Board may impose the condition that the applicant salvage the water required for his or her project.); *East Bay Municipal Utility District v. Department of Public Works,* 35 P.2d 1027, 1029 (Cal. 1934) ("Where the facts justify the action, the water authority should be allowed to impose [on an application to appropriate water for a power project], in the public interest, the restrictions and conditions provided for in the act," or to reject the application "in its entirety."). Both the Utah and California Supreme Courts have upheld state water agencies which had granted appropriations subject to future appropriations for uses of greater importance—in effect prioritizing among uses according to the public interest. *Tanner,* 136 P.2d at 962–64; *East Bay,* 35 P.2d at 1027–30 (Both cases approved making appropriations for power subject to future appropriations for agricultural or municipal purposes.). The Director of Water Resources has the same considerable flexibility and authority, which he has already implemented in earlier proceedings in this matter, to protect the public interest.

Indeed, I.C. § 42–203A places upon the Director the affirmative *duty* to assess and protect the public interest. In assessing the duty of the state water board imposed by California's "public interest" provision, the California Supreme Court declared, "If the board determines a particular use is not in furtherance of the greatest public benefit, on balance the public interest must prevail." *Shirokow,* 605 P.2d at 866; *accord, Tanner,* 136 P.2d at 962 (The State has "the *duty* to control the appropriation of the public waters in a manner that will be for the best interests of the public.") (emphasis added).

The authority and duty of the Director to protect the public interest spring naturally from the statute; the more difficult task for us is to define "the local public interest." Public interest provisions appear frequently in the statutes of the prior appropriation states of the West, but are explicated rarely. See, e.g., Cal. Water Code § 1253; see generally 1 R. Clark, ed., *Waters and Water Rights,* § 29.3 (1967). I.C. § 42–203A provides little guidance. Fortunately, however, the legislature did provide guidance in a related statute, I.C. § 42–1501. We also derive assistance from our sister states and from the academic community.

In I.C. § 42–1501, the legislature declared it "in the public interest" that:

> the streams of this state and their environments be protected against loss of water supply to preserve the minimum stream flows required for the protection of fish and wildlife habitat, aquatic life, recreation, aesthetic beauty, transportation and navigation values, and water quality.

* * *

Several other public interest elements, though obvious, deserve specific mention. These are: assuring minimum stream flows, as specifically provided in I.C. § 42–1501, discouraging waste, and encouraging conservation. See *Shirokow,* 605 P.2d at 866 (The California Supreme Court found water salvage to be sufficiently in the public interest to require it of a permittee.).

The above-mentioned elements of the public interest are not intended to be a comprehensive list. As observed long ago by the New Mexico Supreme Court, the "public interest" should be read broadly in order to "secure the greatest possible benefit from [the public waters] for the public." *Young & Norton v. Hinderlider,* 110 P. 1045, 1050 (N.M. 1910). . . .

Of course, not every appropriation will impact every one of the above elements. Nor will the elements have equal weight in every situation. The relevant elements and their relative weights will vary with local needs, circumstances, and interests. For example, in an area heavily dependent on recreation and tourism or specifically devoted to preservation in its natural state, Water Resources may give great consideration to the aesthetic and environmental ramifications of granting a permit which calls for substantial modification of the landscape or the stream.

Those applying for permits and those challenging the application bear the burden of demonstrating which elements of the public interest are impacted and to what degree. . . .

However, the burden of proof in all cases as to where the public interest lies, as Judge Schroeder also correctly noted, rests with the applicant:

> [I]t is not [the] protestant's burden of proof to establish that the project is not in the local public interest. The burden of proof is upon the applicant to show that the project is either in the local public interest or that there are factors that overweigh the local public interest in favor of the project.

The determination of what elements of the public interest are impacted, and what the public interest requires, is committed to Water Resources' sound discretion. See 1 R. Clark, ed., *Waters and Water Rights* § 29.3, 170 (1967).

In light of the preceding discussion, the district court admirably established some of the public interest elements which Water Resources must consider in this case. Judge Schroeder observed:

> First, as previously outlined, if the Department gives weight to the economic benefits of the project, it should also give

The use of water for irrigation in this state is a natural want. The inadequacy of supply to meet the demands of the public requires strict administration to prevent waste. It is therefore the policy of the law that junior appropriators may use available water within the limits of their own appropriations so long as the rights of senior appropriators are not injured or damaged. And so, in the instant case, junior appropriators may lawfully apply water to their lands within the limits of their adjudicated appropriations until the Kearney canal fails to receive its full appropriation of 162 second-feet. Until the senior appropriator is injured, there is the ever-present possibility of changed weather conditions, precipitation, or other sources of water supply which might alleviate the situation and supply the needs of the Kearney canal. To pursue any other rule would greatly add to the loss by waste of the public waters of this state. We conclude therefore that the use of water by a junior appropriator does not become adverse to or injure a senior appropriator until it results in a deprivation of his allotted amount, or some part thereof. This rule is supported, we think, by our decisions as well as the decisions of other states.

The real question to be decided, however, is the determination of the duty imposed upon the officers of the state in administering the waters of the stream when the available supply of water at the headgate of the Kearney canal is reduced to an amount less than the 162 second-feet to which the relators are entitled. The rights of relators to the use of this water as against all appropriators subsequent to September 10, 1882, cannot be questioned. It is the duty of the administrative officers of the state to recognize this right and to give force to relators' priority. This requires that junior appropriators be restrained from taking water from the stream so long as such water can be delivered in usable quantities at the headgate of the Kearney canal. If it appear[s] that all the available water in the stream would be lost before its arrival at the headgate of the Kearney canal, it would, of course, be an unjustified waste of water to attempt delivery. Whether a definite quantity of water passing a given point on the stream would, if not diverted or interrupted in its course, reach the headgate of the Kearney canal in a usable quantity creates a very complicated question of fact. It therefore is the duty of the administrative officers of the state to determine from all available means, including the factors hereinbefore discussed, whether or not a usable quantity of water can be delivered at the headgate of the Kearney canal. It necessarily follows that this finding of fact must be determined in the first instance by the officers charged with the administration of the stream. . . .

After determination that a given quantity of water passing a certain point on the river would not, even if uninterrupted, reach the headgate of the Kearney canal in usable quantities, the administrative officers of the state may lawfully permit junior appropriators to divert it for irrigation purposes. This results oft times in having junior appropriators receiving a head of water at a time when an appropriator farther downstream is getting none, though he is prior in time. Such situations are not therefore conclusive evidence of unlawful diversions.

Amici curiae urge that the doctrine of reasonable use is in force in this state and that it should be applied to the case at bar. We recognize the principle that the public has an interest in the public waters of the state and it is the use thereof only that may be appropriated. Even though an adjudicated appropriation may be vested, it may be subjected to regulation and control by the state by virtue of its police power. It may likewise be circumscribed to the extent that a limited diversion for a specified purpose will not permit of an undue interference with the rights of other appropriators on the stream. But we cannot agree that the doctrine of reasonable use can be applied in a case where delivery of a usable quantity of water can be made, although the losses suffered in so doing are great. To permit the officers of the state the right to say whether prospective losses would or would not justify the delivery of usable quantities of water would clothe such officers with a discretion incompatible with the vested interests of the relators, and destroy the very purpose of the doctrine of appropriation existent in this state. When upstream appropriators applied for and received adjudicated priorities, they did so with the knowledge that there was an earlier appropriator at the lower end of the stream whose rights had to be recognized. When the relators applied for and received their adjudications, they are likewise presumed to have known that other appropriators would obtain inferior rights above them that would have to be recognized. Each is required to respect the vested rights of the others, even though some hardships may be thereby imposed. We therefore hold that the doctrine of reasonable use does not extend so far as to authorize the administrator of the waters of the stream to refrain from delivering a usable quantity of water to a senior appropriator because it might appear to him that excessive losses would result. The duty of the administrator, in administering the waters of the stream by virtue of the police power of the state, is to enforce existing priorities, not to determine, change or amend them. . . .

* * *

[The court held that, while the senior appropriators were entitled to the water, the trial court properly denied relief because they were too slow in filing their request for mandamus.]

NOTES

1. *A wasteful protection?* To understand this case we need to examine the facts closely, especially the numbers. How much water had to stay in the

consideration to the economic detriments. The effect of the project on water quality should be considered. It is not clear to what extent that was done in this case. The effect of the project on alternative uses of the watercourse should be considered— e.g., the impact on recreational and scenic uses. The effect on vegetation, wildlife, and other fish should be considered. This is not a catalogue of all factors that may relate to the public interest element, but is a suggestion of factors to be weighed in determining whether the project will or will not be in the public interest.

* * *

3. *Health Hazard*

Judge Smith opined that the law will not allow Billingsley Creek to become a nuisance or a health hazard, adding also that "a permit cannot issue which would allow construction of a project contrary to the authority of the Board of Health in policing water for pollution." Hence, Judge Smith concluded that the Director had authority to consider whether the design of any particular facility will meet all environmental requirements.

We believe this to be a correct assessment of the law, but add a word of caution regarding the differing functions of Water Resources and the Department of Health and Welfare. Water Resources must oversee the water resources of the state, insuring that those who have permits and licenses to appropriate water use the water in accordance with the conditions of the permits and licenses and the limits of the law. It is not the primary job of Water Resources to protect the health and welfare of Idaho's citizens and visitors—that role is vested in the Department of Health and Welfare, including compliance with the water quality regulations and monitoring effluent discharge in our state's waterways. Nevertheless, although these agencies may have separate functions, Water Resources is precluded from issuing a permit for a water appropriation project which, when completed, would violate the water quality standards of the Department of Health and Welfare. It makes no sense whatsoever for Water Resources to blindly grant permit requests without regard to water quality regulations. Hence, Water Resources should condition the issuance of a permit on a showing by the applicant that a proposed facility will meet the mandatory water quality standards.

* * *

The decision of the district court is reversed in part, affirmed in part, and remanded for further proceedings. . . .

NOTES

1. *Reasonable use: conflict with first-in-time?* Idaho supposedly still embraces the prior appropriation system of water allocation, in which water goes to the first person to divert it. But how relevant is priority in time anymore—at least with respect to future appropriations—when the public interest review is as strict as it seems to be in *Shokal?* Isn't allocation based on public interest really quite different from allocation based simply on first-in-time? In the extreme, could a state water agency after *Shokal* decide how remaining unappropriated water ought to be used, and then make the water available only for that use? Wouldn't this amount to a complete abandonment of priority in time?

What should be clear here is that first-in-time is a quite different method of allocating a resource than allocation by public interest. The two methods can be combined in various ways, which Idaho apparently does (by giving the water to the first applicant meeting public interest standards). But we should not overlook the distinct tradeoff involved here. The more we emphasize public interest, the less we emphasize priority in time.

2. *Which public? Which interest?* According to the court, how does Idaho law go about identifying the public interest? Don't members of the public in reality have widely differing ideas about how water might best be used? Surely it is one thing to compile a lengthy list of relevant public-interest factors, and quite another to resolve conflicts among them and set priorities. In any event, won't the public interest shift over time, so that a water use that makes sense today could later seem less appealing? Is this a resource setting in which we should allow market mechanisms to govern, given the market's ability to shift resources to the use that brings the most money for the owner? Or are the indirect effects and ecological implications of water uses so great that market mechanisms are inevitably flawed?

3. *The public trust doctrine and water rights.* The requirement that Water Resources protect the public interest is related to the larger doctrine of the public trust, which Justice Huntley comprehensively discussed in *Kootenai Environmental Alliance v. Panhandle Yacht Club, Inc.,* 671 P.2d 1085 (Idaho 1983). The state holds all waters in trust for the benefit of the public, and "does not have the power to abdicate its role as trustee in favor of private parties." *Id.* at 1088. Any grant to use the state's waters is "subject to the trust and to action by the state necessary to fulfill its trust responsibilities." *Id.* at 1094. Trust interests include property values, "navigation, fish and wildlife habitat, aquatic life, recreation, aesthetic beauty and water quality." *Id.* at 1095. Reviewing courts must "take a 'close look' at the action [of the legislature or of agencies such as Water Resources] to determine if it complies with the public trust doctrine and [should] not act merely as a rubber stamp for agency or legislative action." *Id.* at 1092. Justice Huntley concluded, "The public trust doctrine at all times forms the outer boundaries of permissible government action with respect to public trust resources." *Id.* at 1095.

The Idaho legislature responded to the *Kootenai* decision by declaring the public trust doctrine inapplicable to water allocation in the state. See Michael C. Blumm, Harrison C. Dunning & Scott W. Reed, *Renouncing the Public Trust Doctrine: An Assessment of the Validity of Idaho House Bill 794*, 24 Ecology L.Q. 461 (1997). However, California and Hawaii both apply the public trust doctrine to water rights. *Nat'l Audubon Soc'y v. Superior Court*, 658 P.2d 709 (Cal. 1983); *In re Water Use Permit Applications*, 9 P.3d 409 (Haw. 2000) (applying the trust doctrine to groundwater). See pp. 192, 201, above.

4. *California Doctrine states.* As mentioned previously, in *Lux v. Haggin*, 4 P. 919, 10 P. 674 (1886), the California Supreme Court refused to interpret its endorsement of the prior appropriation system in *Irwin v. Phillips,* 5 Cal. 140 (1855), to eliminate riparian rights in the state, as the Colorado Supreme Court did in *Coffin v. Left Hand Ditch,* 6 Colo. 443 (1882) (p. 461). In addition to California, several other states, including Nebraska and Oklahoma, recognize both prior appropriation and riparian rights. The upshot in so-called "California Doctrine" states is an uneasy relationship between prior appropriation and riparian rights. Some of the difficulties are highlighted in the following decision.

JOSLIN V. MARIN MUNICIPAL WATER DISTRICT
Supreme Court of California
429 P.2d 889 (1967)

[Riparian landowners adjacent to Nicasio Creek in Marin County filed suit, alleging that the normal flow of the creek deposited rock, sand, and gravel on their land essential to their rock and gravel business. The water district's new dam, they contended, deprived them of this gravel flow. They sought nearly $300,000 in damages for the resulting harm. The lower court rejected the claim, and the landowners appealed. The supreme court framed the issue as when and whether an upstream *appropriator* (the water district) was liable to a downstream *riparian* who was making use of the water.]

SULLIVAN, J.

* * *

To bring this appeal into focus, we must first briefly review the growth and development of California water law. In its first stage which began with the "gold rush," this law dealt mainly with those who diverted water from streams in the public domain for mining purposes and sought to adjudicate the competing claims of the parties using such water on the basis of a principle of prior appropriation. Subsequently with the increasing importance of agriculture over mining, the courts became more involved with riparian rights. This doctrine which had its genesis in the common law of England initially was made to rest in California on the basic principle "that the riparian proprietor is entitled to the full flow of the stream, reduced only by the proper riparian uses which may be made of the water by proprietors above him." (*Miller & Lux v. Enterprise Canal & Land Co.*, 147 P. 567, 578 (Cal. 1915); see *Lux v. Haggin*, 4 P. 919, 10 P. 674 (Cal. 1886); *Herminghaus v. Southern California Edison Co.*, 252 P. 607 (Cal. 1926).) Such riparian rights extended to "the entire flow of the waters of [a] river, considering the same with its seasonal accretions as the usual and ordinary flow of said stream during each and every year." (*Herminghaus*, 252 P. at 611.)

It was inevitable that the claims of appropriators and riparian owners would collide and that the legal principles upon which they were asserted would appear to be in conflict. Reconciling these principles, this court in the leading case of *Lux v. Haggin*, 4 P. 919, 10 P. 674 (Cal. 1886) declared "that the rights of the riparian owners to the use of the waters of the abutting stream were paramount to the rights of any other persons thereto; that such rights were parcel of the land and that any diminution of the stream against the will of the riparian owner by other persons was an actionable injury. The question was settled by that case and the riparian right has never since been disputed." As a result the principle emerged that an upstream appropriator could not deprive a downstream riparian owner of his right to the use of the full flow of a stream, even though only a small percentage of the flow was utilized to benefit the lands of the downstream riparian.

Thereafter, and in apparent response to the *Herminghaus* decision (see *Gin S. Chow v. City of Santa Barbara*, 22 P.2d 5 (Cal. 1933)), the California Constitution was amended in 1928. (Art. XIV, § 3.) The amendment was generally construed as applying a rule of reasonable use "to all water rights enjoyed or asserted in this state, whether the same be grounded on the riparian right or the right, analogous to the riparian right, of the overlying land owner, or the percolating water right, or the appropriative right." *Peabody v. City of Vallejo*, 40 P.2d 486, 499 (Cal. 1935). Thus the rule of reasonableness of use as a measure of the water right which had theretofore been applied as between other contesting claimants but had been denied application as between riparian owners and appropriators was finally extended to include the latter.

As epitomized in *Peabody*, the amendment is said to declare: "1. The right to the use of water is limited to such water as shall be reasonably required for the beneficial use to be served. 2. Such right does not extend to the waste of water. 3. Such right does not extend to unreasonable use or unreasonable method of use or unreasonable method of diversion of water. 4. Riparian rights attach to, but to no more than so much of the flow as may be required or used consistently with this section of the Constitution." (40 P.2d at 491.)

It has been long and clearly settled in California that the effect of the passage of article XIV, section 3, "has been to modify the long-standing riparian doctrine . . . and to apply, by constitutional mandate the doctrine of reasonable use between riparian owners and appropriators, and between overlying owners and appropriators. The right to the waste of water is not now included in the riparian right." *Peabody*, 40 P.2d at 492. What is a reasonable use or method of use of water is a question of fact to be determined according to the circumstances in each particular case. *Gin S. Chow*, 22 P.2d at 18.

In *Peabody*, several lower riparian owners sought to enjoin the City of Vallejo, as an appropriator, from storing the waters of a creek by the construction of a dam and thereafter diverting them to municipal uses. Peabody, one of the plaintiffs, asserted a right to have all the waters flow without interruption since by normally overflowing his land they not only deposited silt thereon but also washed out salt deposits on portions of the land. The court held that "[t]his asserted right does not inhere in the riparian right at common law, and as a natural right cannot be asserted as against the police power of the state in the conservation of its waters. This asserted right involves an unreasonable use or an unreasonable method of use or an unreasonable method of diversion of water as contemplated by the Constitution." *Peabody*, 40 P.2d at 492.

Although, as we have said, what is a reasonable use of water depends on the circumstances of each case, such an inquiry cannot be resolved *in vacuo* isolated from state-wide considerations of transcendent importance. Paramount among these we see the ever increasing need for the conservation of water in this state, an inescapable reality of life quite apart from its express recognition in the 1928 amendment. On the other hand, unlike the unanimous policy pronouncements relative to the use and conservation of natural waters, we are aware of none relative to the supply and availability of sand, gravel and rock in commercial quantities. Plaintiffs do not urge that the general welfare or public interest requires that particular or exceptional measures be employed to insure that such natural resources be made generally available and should therefore be carefully conserved.

Is it "reasonable" then, that the riches of our streams, which we are charged with conserving in the great public interest, are to be dissipated in the amassing of mere sand and gravel which for aught that appears subserves *no* public policy? We cannot deem such a use to be in accord with the constitutional mandate that our limited water resources be put only to those beneficial uses "to the fullest extent of which they are capable," that "waste or unreasonable use" be prevented, and that conservation be exercised "in the interest of the people and for the public welfare." (Cal. Const., art. XIV, § 3.) We are satisfied that in the instant case the use of such waters as an agent to expose or to carry and deposit sand, gravel and rock, is as a matter of law unreasonable within the meaning of the constitutional amendment. (See *Peabody*, 40 P.2d at 492.)

* * *

[P]laintiffs have not shown how their claimed use of the stream in the instant case, when measured by the constitutional mandate, is a reasonable one. In essence their position is that such use is a beneficial one encompassed within their riparian rights and that all beneficial uses are reasonable uses. Such a position ignores rather than observes the constitutional mandate. Article XIV, section 3, does not equate "beneficial use" with "reasonable use." Indeed the amendment in plain terms emphasizes that water must be conserved in California "with a view to the reasonable *and* beneficial use thereof in the interest of the people," that the right to use water "shall be *limited* to such water as shall be *reasonably* required for the beneficial use to be served," and that riparian rights "attach to, but to *no more than* so much of the flow" as may be required "in view of such reasonable *and* beneficial uses." (Emphasis added.) (Cal. Const., art. XIV, § 3.) Thus the mere fact that a use may be beneficial to a riparian's lands is not sufficient if the use is not also reasonable within the meaning of section 3 of article XIV and, as indicated, plaintiffs' use must be deemed unreasonable. Anything to the contrary in *Los Angeles Co. Flood Control Dist. v. Abbot*, 76 P.2d 188 (Cal. Dist. Ct. App. 1938), is disapproved.

Assuming *arguendo* the unreasonableness of their use of the stream, plaintiffs contend that in any event they are entitled to be compensated for the damage to their property interests. Article XIV, section 3, they say, was only a procedural as opposed to a substantive change in the law and had the effect of merely denying injunctive relief to protect certain riparian uses. Article I, section 14, on the other hand confers on them a cause of action for money damages for the injury to their real property resulting from the district's public improvement.

* * *

From the foregoing we arrive at the conclusion that since there was and is no property right in an unreasonable use, there has been no taking or damaging of property by the deprivation of such use and, accordingly, the deprivation is not compensable.

* * *

The judgment is affirmed.

NOTES

1. *Reasonable use: limits on private rights.* The vagueness of riparian rights, where they exist, has caused considerable problems. Uncertainty

among appropriators in several western states, like Oregon, was greatly diminished by freezing riparian rights when the state made the shift over to an appropriation system. Riparian landowners who were using water received authority to continue their uses at existing levels, but after a statutorily specified date, no new riparian water uses could begin. All new uses had to come under the prior appropriation scheme, which specified private water use rights with much greater clarity. Blocked by its state Supreme Court in its efforts to make this shift, Californiahas continued to struggle to achieve this same level of predictability in its water system.

In *Joslin*, the court made clear that all water rights in the state were legally protected as private property only when and so long as the water was used reasonably. And as the court also made clear, "reasonable" is a concept that varies over time and that depends upon changing circumstances. As the Joslins learned to their dismay, a water right that is protected property at one time can lose its property status over time. At any time, a court may rule (perhaps based on a jury finding) that a water use is not reasonable, and hence the water user has no property right in it. The idea is a troubling one to many observers of water law—indeed, terrifying to some. But the idea follows rather directly from the longstanding property law doctrine of *sic utere tuo*, which underlies the law of nuisance. Property owners have always been under a duty to use what they own so as to cause no harm to anyone else. That rule has been applied over the centuries in a way that kept it up to date: whether a property use creates "harm" is determined by the ideas of harm that prevail when the case is decided.

2. *Moving the land-water line.* The controversy in California that led to the 1928 constitutional amendment was entirely about the line between water attached to land and water that was available for acquisition as a discrete resource. According to the supreme court's early rulings, a riparian landowner could use as much water as she wanted, so long as she respected the rights of other riparians. Only water that riparians did not care to use was available for separate acquisition. The constitutional amendment, once interpreted and clarified by the court, moved this line in favor of making more water available as a discrete resource. After the amendment, a riparian was limited to the water that she could devote to a reasonable use. All water beyond reasonable uses was available for appropriators to take.

3. *Property rights and the law. Joslin* is also a useful case in that it gives us a glimpse of the necessary link between property rights and law, a link that was once well understood but has now become somewhat confused. Courts exist to enforce laws, not to apply abstract notions of natural law and justice—though the latter do creep in from time to time. On the general point, see William M. Wiecek, *Liberty Under Law: The Supreme Court in American Life* 44 (1988) (noting the Supreme Court's turning away from natural law as a basis for decision). In the case of property rights, they are protected only to the extent specified by law. E.g., *Board of Regents v. Roth*, 408 U.S. 564, 577 (1972) ("Property interests . . . are not created by the Constitution.") Indeed, as a jurisprudential matter, property is necessarily a product of law, and

exists when and to the extent lawmakers provide. We should again note that the Constitution does place minor limits on the ability of governments to redefine the meaning of property rights once in private hands—the "regulatory takings" jurisprudence—and the prohibition against the taking of property without due process of law.

But what body (or bodies) of law specifies the scope of property rights? One tendency is to look to the common law as the source of property rights, and to treat other types of laws as something else: regulations or restrictions on the use of property rights. Yet, how can this be, as a matter of jurisprudence, given that state legislatures have the power to alter the common law by passing statutes (which they frequently do), and given that federal law takes priority over state law? Is it more accurate to say that the content of property rights at any time is determined by looking to the full range of laws that apply in a given time and place? On this issue, *Joslin* provides a partial answer. According to the court, California altered the content of a riparian's property rights when it altered its constitution in the early twentieth century. Thus, a state constitutional amendment had the effect of altering the meaning of landownership, keeping it up to date.

4.   *Legal evolution, overt and covert.* For various reasons, courts are generally reluctant to make overt changes in the rules governing private property rights, for fear of disrupting settled expectations and being accused of interfering with the vested rights of individuals. We have seen this reluctance repeatedly in prior cases. In *Beacham* (p. 164), *Coffin* (p. 461), and *Pyle* (p. 450), courts nonetheless did change fundamental laws, yet claimed that they actually were not doing so.

In its prior rulings, particularly *Lux v. Haggin* (1886) and *Herminghaus* (1926), the California Supreme Court showed great hostility to any overt change in the reach and primacy of riparian rights. In *Joslin,* however, we see a far different attitude. The reasonable-use rule that the court accepts and applies is, in fact, a mechanism that can bring about substantial long-term change in water law, as society changes its ideas about the reasonableness of competing water uses. A water use that is reasonable one day can be unreasonable, and thus brought to an end, on the next. But there is a big difference in this kind of legal change. When courts apply the reasonable-use doctrine they *appear* to be applying a rule of law that is itself unchanging. In *form* the law stays the same, always banning unreasonable uses; in *application,* though, the content of the restriction can shift greatly as circumstances and prevailing attitudes change. Little wonder, then, that courts have found it appealing to define private rights in terms of "reasonableness" (or some synonym) so as to allow change to occur without having to change legal norms overtly.

Public appearances aside, is there a virtue to creating a system where legal change must occur covertly? What would the California court say if the California legislature got into the act, enacting a statute proclaiming, for instance, that it is unreasonable to use scarce water to irrigate pastures or to grow farm crops that are overabundant nationally (e.g., corn or cotton)? If a jury could make such a decision as a factual matter, interpreting reasonable use, why not let the legislature do so?

D. GROUNDWATER

A scientist would make no distinction between the molecular composition of water on the surface in rivers and lakes and water beneath the surface in aquifers (groundwater). But the law has long drawn a sharp distinction between surface water and groundwater. In the case of groundwater, there are at least four distinct allocation rules, which deviate from the parallel surface water rules. The decision below begins to explore them.

HIGDAY V. NICKOLAUS

Missouri Court of Appeals
469 S.W.2d 859 (1971)

[Higday and others owned some 6,000 acres of farmland overlying an alluvial water basin in Boone County known as the McBaine Bottom, bordering the Missouri River. The groundwater, trapped by an impervious layer of limestone, formed a huge aquifer. Higday and his colleagues devoted the overlying land to agricultural use, enjoying high yields due to the fertility of the soil. They used the groundwater for personal use and livestock watering, and intended to devote it also to agricultural irrigation. The city of Columbia, some twelve miles away, planned to withdraw groundwater of the McBaine Bottom for municipal supply to meet the demands of its burgeoning population, and acquired well sites (totaling 17.25 acres) for that purpose. Its plan called for pumping 11.5 million gallons per day. According to Higday, that pumping would have reduced the average level of the aquifer from ten feet below the surface to twenty feet below, damaging agricultural use of the overlying land. This planned withdrawal exceeded the rate at which groundwater migrated into the aquifer, estimated at 10.5 million gallons per day. Higday filed suit, seeking a declaration that the city had no right to transport the waters for use elsewhere to the deprivation of the overlying landowners' reasonable use of the groundwater. The trial court dismissed Higday's petition without hearing evidence.]

SHANGLER, J.

* * *

In legal contemplation, subterranean waters fall into two classifications, either underground streams or percolating waters. An underground stream is defined as water that passes through or under the surface in a definite channel or one that is reasonably ascertainable.

Percolating waters include all waters which pass through the ground beneath the surface of the earth without a definite channel and not shown to be supplied by a definite flowing stream. They are waters which ooze, seep, filter and otherwise circulate through the interstices of the subsurface strata without definable channel, or in a course that is not discoverable from surface indications without excavation for that purpose. The rule is that all underground waters are presumed to be percolating and therefore the burden of proof is on the party claiming that a subterranean stream exists.

The law with respect to rights in percolating waters was not developed until a comparatively recent period. Under the English common law rule, percolating waters constitute part and parcel of the land in which they are found and belong absolutely to the owner of such land who may without liability withdraw any quantity of water for any purpose, even though the result is to drain all water from beneath the adjoining lands. Under this rule, a municipality owing land may collect the underlying percolating waters and use them to supply its inhabitants regardless of the effect on adjoining landowners.

The English rule relating to percolating groundwater was generally followed by American courts through the mid-nineteenth century, although not always with the full rigor of the absolute ownership doctrine. At an early day, the courts expressed dissatisfaction with the English common law rule and began applying what has come to be known variously, as the rule of "reasonable use," or of "correlative rights." or the "American rule." By the turn of the century, a steady trend of decisions was discernible away from the English rule to a rule of reasonable use. The trend continues.

Generally, the rule of reasonable use is an expression of the maxim that one must so use his own property as not to injure another—that each landowner is restricted to a reasonable exercise of his own rights and a reasonable use of his own property, in view of the similar rights of others. As it applies to percolating groundwater, the rule of reasonable use recognizes that the overlying owner has a proprietary interest in the water under his lands, but his incidents of ownership are restricted. It recognizes that the nature of the property right is usufructuary rather than absolute as under the English rule. Under the rule of reasonable use, the overlying owner may use the subjacent groundwater freely, and without liability to an adjoining owner, but only if his use is for purposes incident to the beneficial enjoyment of the land from which the water was taken. This rule does not prevent the consumption of such groundwater for agriculture, manufacturing, irrigation, mining or any purpose by which a landowner might legitimately use and enjoy his land, even though in doing so he may divert or drain the groundwater of his neighbor.

The principal difficulty in the application of the reasonable use doctrine is in determining what constitutes a reasonable use. What is a reasonable use must depend to a great extent upon many factors, such as the persons involved, their relative positions, the nature of their uses, the comparative value of their uses, the climatic conditions, and all facts and circumstances pertinent to the issues. However, the modern decisions agree that under the rule of reasonable use *an overlying owner, including a municipality, may not withdraw percolating water and transport it for sale or other use away from the land from which it was taken if the result is to impair the supply of an adjoining landowner to his injury.* Such a use is unreasonable because non-beneficial and "is not for a 'lawful purpose within the general rule concerning percolating waters, but constitutes an actionable wrong for which damages are recoverable.' "

The "reasonable use" rule as developed in the law of ground waters must be distinguished from the "correlative rights" rule. In 1902, the California Supreme Court repudiated the English common law rule in favor of the distinctive correlative rights doctrine which is based on the theory of proportionate sharing of withdrawals among landowners overlying a common basin. Under the doctrine, overlying owners have no proprietary interest in the water under their soil. California remains the only important correlative rights state; Utah has abandoned it, and only Nebraska also applies it to some extent. The administration of such a system of rights has proved extremely difficult in times of water shortage and has tendered towards an "equalitarian rigidity" which does not take into account the relative value of the competing uses. However suitable this doctrine may be for California—the prime consumer of ground water in the country—or any other state which may follow it, the reasonable use rule offers a more flexible legal standard for the just determination of beneficial uses of ground water, particularly under the climatic conditions of Missouri.

Respondent City contends that the English common law rule of absolute ownership of percolating waters governs in Missouri by virtue of statute and judicial decision. The City seems to suggest that since the Territorial Laws of 1816 adopted the common law as the rule of action and decision in this state and present Sec. 1.010 V.A.M.S. continues that legislative policy, we have no power to change or abrogate it. As we have already noted, *Acton v. Blundell,* which is generally cited as having established the "English common law" rule of percolating waters, was decided in 1843 long after the Territorial Laws of 1816 were enacted. And not until 1860 was it decided that, without liability to an adjoining owner, an overlying owner might exhaust the groundwater to furnish a municipal water supply. Thus, there was no law of any kind on the subject at the time the common law was adopted by statute in this state. The subsequent English decisions declaring the common law on percolating waters are no more binding on us than the decisions of any court of another state. There is no impediment of inherited doctrine to our determination of the question presented according to the justice of the case.

* * *

Under the rule of reasonable use as we have stated it, the fundamental measure of the overlying owner's right to use the groundwater is whether it is for purposes incident to the beneficial enjoyment of the land from which it was taken. Thus, a private owner may not withdraw groundwater for purposes of sale if the adjoining landowner is thereby deprived of water necessary for the beneficial enjoyment of his land. Here, the municipality has acquired miniscule plots of earth and by the use of powerful pumps intends to draw into wells on its own land for merchandising groundwater stored in plaintiffs' land, thereby depriving plaintiffs of the beneficial use of the normal water table to their immediate injury and to the eventual impoverishment of their lands. "There is no apparent reason for saying that, because defendant is a municipal corporation, seeking water for the inhabitants of a city, it may therefore do what a private owner of land may not do. The city is a private owner of this land, and the furnishing of water to its inhabitants is its private business. It is imperative that the people of the city have water; it is not imperative that they secure it at the expense of those owning lands adjoining lands owned by the city." Under the rule we apply, however, plaintiffs could have no basis for complaint if the City of Columbia's withdrawals of groundwater for municipal purposes from the McBaine Bottom do not interfere with plaintiffs' beneficial use of such water. Under the facts pleaded, the water table could be maintained at its normal level and damage to plaintiffs avoided if the City were to limit its withdrawals to such quantity as would not exceed the daily recharge rate of 10.5 million gallons. If, on the other hand, the City perseveres in its declared intention to mine the water by at least one million gallons per day, it will become accountable to plaintiffs for whatever injury results from such diversion.

We have concluded that the pleaded averments of plaintiffs' petition raise in plaintiffs a property right to the reasonable use of the percolating waters underlying their lands, which right is shown to be threatened with wrongful and injurious invasion by the defendant City. . . . Plaintiffs' pleadings were sufficient to invoke the trial court's equitable jurisdiction to consider the request for injunctive relief thereby presented.

This is not to suggest that should proof follow upon the pleadings, perforce injunction will issue. Injunctive relief is a matter of grace, not of right. "The writ of injunction is an extraordinary remedy. It does not issue as a matter of course, but somewhat at the discretion of the chancellor. It is his duty to consider its effect upon all parties in interest, and to issue it only in case it is necessary to protect a substantial right, *and even then not against great public interest.*" (Emphasis added.) It requires the application of the principles of equity under all the circumstances. "The relative convenience and inconvenience and the comparative injuries to the parties and to the public should be considered in granting or refusing an injunction." This rule has been applied where "the allowance of an injunction would seriously interfere with or work detriment to public works or works of public benefit, where the issuance of the injunction asked would result in cutting off the water supply" to the public harm. "[A]nd, where the result of such public injury is so great on the one hand as compared to the injury complained of on the other, then it would be unconscionable to grant injunctive relief, and it will be denied." And this is so, even though the available remedy at law is not adequate.

The rule of comparative injury suggest that under the facts pleaded and concessions of counsel it may be more equitable to deny injunctive relief than to grant it. The evidence may prompt the trial chancellor to the same conclusion, but that must await the determination of existing circumstances. To be sure, the rights plaintiffs seek to preserve are substantial and may not be treated cavalierly, but they are to be weighed against "the immeasurable value of the health and welfare of the public." Few things are more vital or of such surpassing importance to the public well-being than the assurance of a wholesome water supply. At the time this appeal was submitted, the development of the City's water treatment and distribution system was nearing completion. Perhaps by now it has become operative. The evidence may also disclose, as the pleadings do not, whether the McBaine Bottom is intended to supplement the City's present source of water or to supplant it. Nor do we know the full extent of the City's financial commitment to the project. These and other factors will guide the trial chancellor in deciding whether to impose its restraint upon the City and in doing so, he will be mindful that "the public convenience and public mischief may mark the distinction between sound and unsound discretion in granting an injunction."

The City has resisted plaintiffs' requested declaratory and injunctive relief on the theory that the common law rule of absolute ownership of percolating waters has governed its relationship with plaintiffs and, therefore, any damage to them could not be a legal injury. It has not sought to exercise its power of eminent domain to acquire the right to withdraw water from beneath plaintiffs' lands doubtless on the premise that it was under no duty to do so. Should the trial court adjudge that plaintiffs are entitled to the declarations they seek, the rule of reasonable use will apply and defendant City will be answerable to plaintiffs for any damage from its unreasonable use of groundwater. Should the trial court adjudge injunctive relief for plaintiffs appropriate, it would be well within its discretion to condition the imposition of that restraint upon the exercise by the City within a reasonable time, of its power of eminent domain to acquire the water rights it has been violating. Failing that, plaintiffs would still have available to them a remedy in the nature of an inverse condemnation for any damage caused by the City's unreasonable use.

The judgment of the trial court is reversed and the cause is remanded for further proceedings consistent with the views we have expressed.

NOTES

1. *Place of use, revisited. Higday* introduces the common law of groundwater allocation. Just as the common law attached surface water to the land, so too did it attach groundwater to the land. Those who acquired land acquired, along with the land, a right to use groundwater. And for similar reasons, too, we see a place-of-use limit on this water right. How does the place-of-use rule in *Higday* compare with that of *Stratton* (p. 445)? With that of *Pyle* (p. 450)? At this point, how secure is the city's water right, even to the 10.5 million gallons per day that is the aquifer's apparent recharge rate?

2. *Alternative remedies.* The place-of-use rule applied in *Higday* essentially states that off-tract use is permissible unless the water use actually harms another water user who is using water on an overlying tract. Here, the city was pumping water for use miles away, and thus its water use was precarious. At any time an owner of land above the aquifer could show up and claim that the off-tract use was harming his or her own water use. The city, one might think, would be disinclined to rely on such a water source, given the catastrophic effects of having to shut down the city's water system in the event a court issued an injunction halting it. Yet, many cities in the United States do exactly what the City of Columbia did: buying up small tracts of land, miles away, installing wells, and pumping the water to the city. The same problem arises, in fact, even if a city's well is located within the city. The water is still being pumped off the tract where the well is located (owned, usually, by a water company) and onto properties throughout the city. Indeed, it would seem that cities everywhere which rely on groundwater are forced to distribute it for use off the overlying tract. How can this arrangement work? Why is there not more pressure to change state laws?

In fact, some state laws have been changed, but the key to the answer lies in the concluding paragraphs in *Higday*. In the court's view, municipal water use is a highly important activity. Even if a city is violating someone's landed property rights, an injunction halting the city's diversion will be issued only if it is equitable to do so. How likely is it that a court would order a city to shut down its water system, given the public health problems? More likely, the city would be given time to find an alternative. Perhaps even more likely, the court might refuse the injunction and instead award the plaintiff permanent damages for the invasion of private rights. In *Higday,* the court suggested that the city could exercise eminent domain to condemn the property rights needed to continue its water diversions. Sometimes cities will have this condemnation power, but often they will not because the land involved is outside of, or too far away from, the city's boundaries. Note, though, that a city essentially gains the power to condemn water rights when a court refuses to enjoin an unlawful water use and instead grants the plaintiff permanent damages.

3. *The correlative rights doctrine.* The dispute in *Prather v. Eisenmann,* 261 N.W.2d 766 (Neb. 1978), pitted three households, which gained their domestic water from groundwater wells, against another owner of land over the same aquifer who drilled a deeper well and extracted water for irrigation. The deeper irrigation well was sufficiently close to the household wells that it lowered the surrounding water table, creating an underground "cone of depression." The effect was to render the households unable to pump water unless they drilled their wells deeper while the defendant irrigator kept its well at the same depth. In resolving the dispute, the Nebraska court clarified how its groundwater law differed from that of other states, in terms of resolving disputes among landowners all using water on their overlying tracts. The standard American approach to reasonable use, the court (rightly) explained, evaluated the reasonableness of a water use in the abstract, without taking into account competing uses of the same water or the effects of a reasonable use on other water users:

> Under the reasonable use doctrine, two neighboring landowners, each of whom is using the water on his own property overlying the common supply, can withdraw all the supply he can put to beneficial and reasonable use. What is reasonable is judged solely in relationship to the purpose of such use on the overlying land. It is not judged in relation to the needs of others. (*Id.* at 770.)

Nebraska significantly modified this rule by grafting on to it two other rules. First and as a matter of common law, Nebraska landowners were entitled to a "reasonable proportion" of the water contained in a shared aquifer. This shared-use rule, the court explained, was similar to, but not as specific as, the correlative rights rule followed in California. Second, Nebraska law included a statute that provided a distinct preference, in case of conflict, for domestic water uses over all competing uses. All domestic users shared in this top priority. Among themselves they were each entitled to a proportionate (or fair) share of the whole. Because the irrigator was not a domestic user, the household users were entitled to a remedy for the invasion of their rights, without regard for whether the irrigator's use was also reasonable. By way of remedy, the court ordered the irrigator to pay the costs of deepening the plaintiffs' wells, and to refrain itself from deepening its own well.

4.   *Comparing Groundwater Regimes.*

The following chart highlights the differences among the various groundwater regimes.

Comparing Groundwater Right Systems

	"English"	"American"	Prior Appropriation	Correlative Rights
Place of use	No limit	overlying land only*	No limit	overlying land only
Temporal priority	first capture	Not important	first capture	Not important
Transferability?	Yes	only if no injury	Yes	Not clear–no injury?
Shortages shared?	No	Not overtly	imposed on juniors	Yes

The "English rule" is also known as "absolute ownership," although it provides no protection for overlying landowners until water is actually captured.

The "American rule" is also known as the "reasonable use" rule, although it differs from the surface-water reasonable use rule in that the reasonableness inquiry only looks at the details of a given water use (its purpose, efficiency, social value) and does not compare that use with other, competing ones. A variant of this rule appears in the Restatement (Second) of Torts, which employs a reasonable use definition that is essentially the same as the one used for surface water (riparian rights).

Correlative rights limits all water users to their fair shares. Nebraska has its own variant, which adds a correlative rights, fair-share element to the American rule, see discussion in *Spear T Ranch v. Knaub,* p. 568.

5.   *The so-called "absolute ownership" rule.* The English rule of absolute ownership of groundwater—essentially a free-wheeling rule of capture—has been largely rejected nationwide in favor of other alternatives, although in a thoughtful ruling the Supreme Court of Maine, in *Maddocks v. Giles*, 728 A.2d 150 (Maine 1999), retained the rule as well-suited for a state with ample water supplies. A more prominent example is Texas, as the following case indicates.

---

*   In many jurisdictions, may be used on non-overlying land so long as no injury to other uses, especially as applied to municipalities.

SIPRIANO V. GREAT SPRING WATERS

Supreme Court of Texas
1 S.W.3d 75 (1999)

[Plaintiffs Sipriano and Fain, landowners in Henderson County, sued Great Spring Waters of America (also known as Ozarka Natural Spring Water) for negligently draining the plaintiffs' wells by pumping from its own wells 90,000 gallons of groundwater per day, seven days a week. Ozarka defended on the ground that Texas has always recognized the English rule of absolute ownership. Both the trial and appellate courts agreed with Ozarka, and Sipriano appealed to the Texas Supreme Court.]

ENOCH, J.

For over ninety years, this Court has adhered to the common-law rule of capture in allocating the respective rights and liabilities of neighboring landowners for use of groundwater flowing beneath their property. The rule of capture essentially allows, with some limited exceptions, a landowner to pump as much groundwater as the landowner chooses, without liability to neighbors who claim that the pumping has depleted their wells. We are asked today whether Texas should abandon this rule for the rule of reasonable use, which would limit the common-law right of a surface owner to take water from a common reservoir by imposing liability on landowners who "unreasonably" use groundwater to their neighbors' detriment. Relying on the settled rule of capture, the trial court granted summary judgment against landowners who sued a bottled-water company for negligently draining their water wells. The court of appeals affirmed. Because we conclude that the sweeping change to Texas's groundwater law Sipriano urges this Court to make is not appropriate at this time, we affirm the court of appeals' judgment.

* * *

This Court adopted the common-law rule of capture in 1904 in *Houston & Texas Central Railway Co. v. East*, 81 S.W. 279 (Tex. 1904). The rule of capture answers the question of what remedies, if any, a neighbor has against a landowner based on the landowner's use of the water under the landowner's land. Essentially, the rule provides that, absent malice or willful waste, landowners have the right to take all the water they can capture under their land and do with it what they please, and they will not be liable to neighbors even if in so doing they deprive their neighbors of the water's use. Rooted in English common law, the rule of capture was perhaps first enunciated in 1843 in *Acton v. Blundell*:

> [T]hat person who owns the surface may dig therein, and apply all that is there found to his own purposes at his free will and pleasure; and that if, in the exercise of such right, he intercepts or drains off the water collected from underground springs in his

neighbor's well, this inconvenience to his neighbor falls within the description *damnum absque injuria* [an injury without a remedy] which cannot become the ground of an action.

In *East,* this Court faced a choice between the rule of capture and its counterpart, the rule of reasonable use. No constitutional or statutory considerations guided or constrained our selection at that time. Articulating two public-policy reasons, we chose the rule of capture. First, we noted that the movement of groundwater is "so secret, occult, and concealed that an attempt to administer any set of legal rules in respect to [it] would be involved in hopeless uncertainty, and would, therefore, be practically impossible." And second, we determined that "any . . . recognition of correlative rights would interfere, to the material detriment of the commonwealth, with drainage and agriculture, mining, the construction of highways and railroads, with sanitary regulations, building, and the general progress of improvement in works of embellishment and utility." Thus, we refused to recognize tort liability against a railroad company whose pumping of groundwater under its own property allegedly dried the neighboring plaintiff's well.

After droughts in 1910 and 1917, the citizens of Texas voted in August 1917 to enact section 59 of article 16 of the Texas Constitution, which placed the duty to preserve Texas's natural resources on the State:

> The conservation and development of all of the natural resources of this State . . . and the preservation and conservation of all such natural resources of the State are each and all hereby declared public rights and duties; and the Legislature shall pass all such laws as may be appropriate thereto.

This constitutional amendment, proposed and passed after our common-law decision in *East,* made clear that in Texas, responsibility for the regulation of natural resources, including groundwater, rests in the hands of the Legislature.

By 1955, this Court recognized that what was "secret [and] occult" to us in 1904—the movement of groundwater—was no longer so. But in *City of Corpus Christi v. City of Pleasanton,* 276 S.W.2d 798, 801 (Tex. 1955), we continued to adhere to the rule of capture. In so doing, however, we expressly recognized what was tacit in *East*—that the rule of capture is not absolute:

> Having adopted the . . . rule [of capture] it may be assumed that the Court adopted it with only such limitations as existed in the common law. What were those limitations? About the only limitations applied by those jurisdictions retaining the . . . rule [of capture] are that the owner may not maliciously take water for the sole purpose of injuring his neighbor, or wantonly and willfully waste it.

Thus, while we noted that the common law did not preclude a landowner from capturing and selling water for use off the land, we nonetheless made clear that the rule of capture has exceptions in Texas.

But our discussion of the rule of capture in *City of Corpus Christi* was incidental to the issue we decided. We were called on in that case to construe a statute that recognized the common-law right to use artesian water off the premises and to transport it in any of several enumerated ways, including by "river, creek or other natural water course or drain, superficial or underground channel, bayou, . . . sewer, street, road, [or] highway." But the statute also defined as "waste" any such transportation of water "unless it be used for the purposes and in the manner in which it may be lawfully used on the premises of the owner of such well." Specifically, we considered whether it was waste to transport water produced from artesian wells by flowing it down a natural stream bed and through lakes, given that loss of some of the water through evaporation, transpiration, and seepage was inevitable. While there was evidence that at times as much as 74% of the water was lost, we held that this use of underground water was not waste under the statute. Importantly, we expressly noted that the 1917 constitutional amendment imposed on the Legislature the duty to regulate groundwater:

> [T]he Amendment was not self-enacting. By the very terms of the Amendment the duty was enjoined upon the Legislature to implement the public policy found therein. It was said: ". . . and the Legislature shall pass all such laws as may be appropriate thereto." No such duty was or could have been delegated to the courts. It belongs exclusively to the legislative branch of the government.

Thus we recognized the Legislature's broad powers to regulate use of groundwater following the 1917 amendment, even within the common-law tort framework established by the rule of capture.

In 1978, in *Friendswood Development Co. v. Smith-Southwest Industries, Inc.,* 576 S.W.2d 21 (Tex. 1978), we were again invited to abandon the rule of capture and adopt the rule of reasonable use. Again, we declined. But again we recognized that the rule of capture is not without exception. Specifically, we "agree[d] that some aspects of the . . . common law rule as to underground waters are harsh and outmoded, and [that] the rule ha[d] been severely criticized since its reaffirmation by this Court in 1955." Thus, we used *Friendswood* to "discard an objectionable aspect of the court-made . . . rule [of capture] as it relates to subsidence." Specifically, we recognized an exception to the rule for a landowner's negligence that proximately causes the subsidence of another's land.

We most recently discussed the rule of capture in 1996 in *Barshop v. Medina County Underground Water Conservation District,* 925 S.W.2d

618 (Tex. 1996). In *Barshop,* we rejected facial constitutional challenges to the Edwards Aquifer Act. The Act imposed caps on groundwater withdrawals within the jurisdiction of the Edwards Aquifer Authority, and vested the Edwards Aquifer Authority with substantial authority to regulate groundwater withdrawals by well from the aquifer. The Legislature passed the Act because it was "necessary, appropriate, and a benefit to the welfare of this state to provide for the management of the [Edwards A]quifer." Our discussion of the rule of capture in that case was for the limited purpose of providing the historical common-law framework within which the Legislature acted and within which the plaintiffs made their claims against the Act. We found that the Act withstood various constitutional challenges. And in rejecting the plaintiffs' contentions that the Act had no rational basis and was overbroad, we reiterated the Legislature's constitutional charge to regulate groundwater:

> Water regulation is essentially a legislative function. The [1917 constitutional amendment] recognizes that preserving and conserving natural resources are public rights and duties. The Edwards Aquifer Act furthers the goals of the [1917 amendment] by regulating the Edwards Aquifer, a vital natural resource which is the primary source of water in south central Texas. The specific provisions of the Act, such as the grandfathering of existing users, the caps on water withdrawals, and the regional powers of the Authority, are all rationally related to legitimate state purposes in managing and regulating this vital resource.

Now, Sipriano asks us to fundamentally alter the common-law framework within which Texas has operated since the 1904 *East* decision. That common-law framework existed in 1917 when the citizens of Texas charged the Legislature with the constitutional duty to preserve groundwater through regulation. It persisted through our decisions in *City of Corpus Christi* in 1955 and *Friendswood* in 1978. And it was firmly in place when the Legislature passed the Edwards Aquifer Act and when we decided *Barshop.* Like the voters who passed the 1917 constitutional amendment, this Court has consistently recognized "the need for legislative regulation of water." Today, again, we reiterate that the people have constitutionally empowered the Legislature to act in the best interest of the State to preserve our natural resources, including water. We see no reason, particularly because of the 1917 constitutional amendment, for the Legislature to feel constrained from taking appropriate steps to protect groundwater. Indeed, we anticipated legislative involvement in groundwater regulation in *East:*

> *In the absence . . . of positive authorized legislation,* as between proprietors of adjoining lands, the law recognizes no correlative rights in respect to underground waters percolating, oozing, or filtrating through the earth.

With the allocation of responsibility for groundwater regulation contemplated by the 1917 amendment in mind, it is important that this case comes to us on the heels of Senate Bill 1, which has been described as a "comprehensive water management bill." Passed in June 1997, Senate Bill 1 revamped significant parts of the Water Code and other Texas statutes in an attempt to improve on this State's water management. Perhaps most relevant to our decision today is the Legislature's efforts to streamline the process for creating groundwater conservation districts and to make them more effective in the water management process. Indeed, the Legislature expressly stated that "[g]roundwater conservation districts . . . are the state's preferred method of groundwater management."

The Legislature first exercised its constitutional authority to create groundwater conservation districts in 1949. And since then the Legislature has repeatedly revisited and modified the operation of groundwater conservation districts. Now, with Senate Bill 1, the Legislature has given more authority to locally-controlled groundwater conservation districts for establishing requirements for groundwater withdrawal permits and for regulating water transferred outside the district. Senate Bill 1 also revised the "critical area" designation process to require the Texas Natural Resource Conservation Commission and the Texas Water Development Board to identify areas anticipated to experience critical groundwater problems, and streamlined the process by which the TNRCC or the Legislature can create a district in these areas. Senate Bill 1 also included various provisions calling for more comprehensive and coordinated water planning. While the efficacy of the groundwater management methods the Legislature chose and implemented through Senate Bill 1 has been a matter of considerable debate, as the *amicus* briefs filed in this case reflect, we cannot say at this time that the Legislature has ignored its constitutional charge to regulate this natural resource.

By constitutional amendment, Texas voters made groundwater regulation a duty of the Legislature. And by Senate Bill 1, the Legislature has chosen a process that permits the people most affected by groundwater regulation in particular areas to participate in democratic solutions to their groundwater issues. It would be improper for courts to intercede at this time by changing the common-law framework within which the Legislature has attempted to craft regulations to meet this state's groundwater-conservation needs. Given the Legislature's recent actions to improve Texas's groundwater management, we are reluctant to make so drastic a change as abandoning our rule of capture and moving into the arena of water-use regulation by judicial fiat. It is more prudent to wait and see if Senate Bill 1 will have its desired effect, and to save for another day the determination of whether further revising the common law is an appropriate prerequisite to preserve Texas's natural resources and protect property owners' interests.

We do not shy away from change when it is appropriate. We continue to believe that "the genius of the common law rests in its ability to change, to recognize when a timeworn rule no longer serves the needs of society, and to modify the rule accordingly." And Sipriano presents compelling reasons for groundwater use to be regulated. But unlike in *East,* any modification of the common law would have to be guided and constrained by constitutional and statutory considerations. Given the Legislature's recent efforts to regulate groundwater, we are not persuaded that it is appropriate today for this Court to insert itself into the regulatory mix by substituting the rule of reasonable use for the current rule of capture. Accordingly, we affirm the court of appeals' judgment.

NOTES

1.   *Reaffirming the capture rule.* In an era of widespread declines of aquifers, maintaining the capture rule for groundwater seems likely to encourage further declines, with attendant widespread social costs. Yet the court reaffirmed the capture rule. What reasons does it give? If the idea is deference to the legislature, how was the capture rule originally established in Texas? Notice that in *City of Corpus Christi v. City of Pleasanton,* 276 S.W.2d 798 (Tex. 1955), and *Friendswood Development Co. v. Smith-Southwest Industries, Inc.,* 576 S.W.2d 21 (Tex. 1978), the Texas Supreme Court approved changes in the rule of capture concerning waste and subsidence. Didn't the legislature signal a change in capture policy in enacting the Edwards Aquifer Act in 1993?

The capture rule of absolute ownership is subject to one exception: it bars the malicious wasting of water. Sipriano was unable to show waste in the case of Ozarka's pumping.

2.   *The nature of property rights under the capture rule.* What exactly is the nature of the property right in groundwater in Texas? In other words, what rights does the overlying landowner have to groundwater under the so-called absolute ownership doctrine? Could a landowner stop an adjacent neighbor from pumping on his land and mining groundwater under her land? If not, how absolute is her right? Is it not just as apt to say that the English rule of groundwater law is the "no ownership" rule? A landowner who cannot in any way limit the ability of neighbors to capture the water under her land has essentially no control over it, and thus nothing in the way of a substantial property right in it.

The name given to a legal doctrine may not seem as important as the substance, but names have important connotations. What if a state legislature bans all new groundwater withdrawals? If the governing law is no ownership, who can complain? After all, landowners have lost nothing that they own. If it is absolute ownership, on the other hand, the new law can seem like a significant disruption of existing property rights. As the Missouri court pointed out, the English rule dated from a time when the subsurface movement of groundwater and the contours of aquifers were largely mysterious. Knowing little about water movement beneath the ground, courts had trouble determining factually whether a withdrawal by one person was adversely affecting withdrawals by another. The absolute ownership (actually, no ownership) approach avoided any need to figure out who was harming whom. Only with advances in hydrogeology did it become possible to apply a reasonable use rule. Thus we have one of many instances in which the law has changed due to increased knowledge in other fields of inquiry.

What might be the reaction if we used, instead, one of two other ways of describing this legal arrangement: (1) the landowner has an exclusive *right to capture* the groundwater, but does not own it until capture; or (2) the landowner has a *right to exclude* others from entering his land to engage in capture (the verbal formulation that applies to wildlife resources located on private land)? Would these alternative verbal formulations resolve disputes the same way? Consider these various names in connection with the following principal case.

3. *The Edwards Aquifer.* The Edwards Aquifer is one of the most prolific artesian aquifers in the world, located in the Hill Country of south-central Texas. The aquifer serves over 2 million people, including the cities of San Antonio and San Marcos, and is also habitat for several cave species listed for protection under the federal Endangered Species Act. In 1993, to resolve some of the conflicts over use of the aquifer, the Texas legislature enacted the Edwards Aquifer Authority Act, which established an agency to administer a kind of correlative rights system in regulating groundwater pumping from the aquifer. The following case concerns implementation of the statute.

EDWARDS AQUIFER AUTHORITY V. DAY

Supreme Court of Texas
369 S.W.3d 814 (2012)

[Day bought some 380 acres of agricultural and cattle land overlying the Edwards Aquifer in 1994. Although the land had been irrigated in the past, Day's predecessor stopped irrigating in the 1970s. Under the artesian pressure, groundwater continued to flow down a ditch into a 50-acre lake on the property, fed also by an intermittent creek and used for recreation. To begin to irrigate again, Day needed a permit from the Edwards Aquifer Authority; the amount of water permitted was based on water used beneficially without waste between 1972 and 1993. An administrative law judge determined that the maximum amount of beneficial use by Day's predecessor for irrigation during the applicable period was 14 acre-feet per year. The Authority agreed. Day appealed to the district court, which found that Day was entitled to 150 acre-feet. But the court of appeals reversed, agreeing with the Authority that the groundwater became surface water in the lake, and therefore could not be considered in determining Day's permit amount. However, the appeals court also suggested that Day might have a takings claim. All parties appealed to the Texas Supreme Court, which handed down the following opinion.]

HECHT, J.

* * *

We begin by considering whether, under the EAAA [Edwards Aquifer Authority Act], the Authority erred in limiting Day's IRP [initial regular permit] to 14 acre-feet and conclude that it did not. Next, we turn to whether Day has a constitutionally protected interest in the groundwater beneath his property and conclude that he does. We then consider whether the Authority's denial of an IRP in the amount Day requested constitutes a taking and conclude that the issue must be remanded to the trial court for further proceedings. We end with Day's other constitutional arguments, concluding that they are without merit.

* * *

Groundwater provides 60% of the 16.1 million acre-feet of water used in Texas each year. In many areas of the state, and certainly in the Edwards Aquifer, demand exceeds supply. Regulation is essential to its conservation and use.

As with oil and gas, one purpose of groundwater regulation is to afford each owner of water in a common, subsurface reservoir a fair share. Because a reservoir's supply of oil or gas cannot generally be replenished, and because oil and gas production is most commonly used solely as a commodity for sale, land surface area is an important metric in determining an owner's fair share. Reasonable regulation aims at allowing an owner to withdraw the volume beneath his property and sell it. Groundwater is different. Aquifers are often recharged by rainfall, drainage, or other surface water. The amount of groundwater beneath the surface may increase as well as decrease; any volume associated with the surface is constantly changing. Groundwater's many beneficial uses—for drinking, agriculture, industry, and recreation—often do not involve a sale of water. It[s] value is realized not only in personal consumption but through crops, products, and diversion. Groundwater may be used entirely on the land from which it is pumped, or it may be transported for use or sale elsewhere. Consequently, regulation that affords an owner a fair share of subsurface water must take into account factors other than surface area.

* * *

As we have seen, chapter 36 [of the Water Code, which was previously the Groundwater Conservation District Act of 1949,] requires groundwater districts to consider several factors in permitting groundwater production, among them the proposed use of water, the effect on the supply and other permittees, a district's approved management plan. By contrast, the EAAA requires that permit amounts be determined based solely on the amount of beneficial use during the historical period and the available water supply. Under the EAAA, a landowner may be deprived of all use of groundwater other than a small amount for domestic or livestock use, merely because he did not use water during the historical period. The Authority argues that basing permits on historical use is sound policy because it recognizes the investment landowners have made in developing groundwater resources. But had the permit limitation been anticipated before the EAAA was passed, landowners would have been perversely incentivized to pump as much water as possible, even if not put to best use, to preserve the right to do so going forward. Preserving groundwater for future use has been an important strategy for groundwater rights owners. For example, amicus curiae Canadian River Municipal Water Authority argues that it has acquired groundwater rights to protect supplies for municipal use but has not produced them, waiting instead until they become necessary. The Authority's policy argument is flawed.

The Authority argues that this use-it-or-lose-it limitation is legally justified by *In re Adjudication of the Water Rights of the Upper Guadalupe Segment of the Guadalupe River Basin* [642 S.W.2d 438 (Tex. 1982)]. There we held that landowners who had not used water from the Upper Guadalupe River during a five-year historical period could be denied a permit for such water. We had previously upheld the cancellation of permits for use of river water after ten years' non-use. But riparian rights are usufructuary, giving an owner only a right of use, not complete ownership. Furthermore, non-use of groundwater conserves the resource, "whereas the non-use of appropriated waters is equivalent to waste." To forfeit a landowner's right to groundwater for non-use would encourage waste.

As already discussed, the Legislature last year amended section 36.002 of the Water Code to "recognize that a landowner owns the groundwater below the surface of the landowner's land as real property." Regarding groundwater regulation, section 36.002 continues:

(c) Nothing in this code shall be construed as granting the authority to deprive or divest a landowner, including a landowner's lessees, heirs, or assigns, of the groundwater ownership and rights described by this section.

(d) This section does not:

(1) prohibit a district from limiting or prohibiting the drilling of a well by a landowner for failure or inability to comply with minimum well spacing or tract size requirements adopted by the district;

(2) affect the ability of a district to regulate groundwater production as authorized under Section 36.113, 36.116, or 36.122 or otherwise under this chapter or a special law governing a district; or

(3) require that a rule adopted by a district allocate to each landowner a proportionate share of available groundwater for production from the aquifer based on the number of acres owned by the landowner.

(e) This section does not affect the ability to regulate groundwater in any manner authorized [for the Edwards Aquifer Authority, the Harris-Galveston Subsidence District, and the Fort Bend Subsidence District].

Subsections (c) and (e) appear to be in some tension. Under the EAAA, a landowner can be prohibited from producing groundwater except for domestic and livestock use. This regulation, according to subsection (e), is unaffected by the Legislature's recognition of groundwater ownership in subsection (a). But subsection (c) abjures all "authority to deprive or divest a landowner ... of ... groundwater ownership and rights". If prohibiting all groundwater use except for domestic and livestock purposes does not divest a landowner of groundwater ownership, then either the groundwater rights recognized by section 36.002 are extremely limited, or else by "deprive" and "divest" subsection (c) does not include a taking of property rights for which adequate compensation is constitutionally guaranteed. We think the latter is true. The EAAA itself states: "The legislature intends that just compensation be paid if implementation of this article causes a taking of private property or the impairment of a contract in contravention of the Texas or federal constitution." The requirement of compensation may make the regulatory scheme more expensive, but it does not affect the regulations themselves or their goals for groundwater production.

The Legislature has declared that "rules developed, adopted, and promulgated by a district in accordance with the provisions of [chapter 36]" comprise "the state's preferred method of groundwater management". Chapter 36 allows districts to consider historical use in permitting groundwater production, but it does not limit consideration to such use. Neither the Authority nor the State has suggested a reason why the EAAA must be more restrictive in permitting groundwater use than chapter 36, nor does the Act suggest any justification. But even if there were one, a landowner cannot be deprived of all beneficial use of the groundwater below his property merely because he did not use it during an historical period. . . .

In sum, the three *Penn Central* factors do not support summary judgment for the Authority and the State. A full development of the record may demonstrate that EAAA regulation is too restrictive of Day's groundwater rights and without justification in the overall regulatory scheme. We therefore agree with the court of appeals that summary judgment against Day's takings claim must be reversed.

The Authority warns that if its groundwater regulation can result in a compensable taking, the consequences will be nothing short of disastrous. A great majority of landowners in its area, it contends, cannot show the historical use necessary for a permit, and therefore the potential number of takings claims is enormous. The Authority worries that the financial burden of such claims could make regulation impossible, or at least call into question the validity of existing permits. Regulatory takings litigation is especially burdensome, the Authority notes, because of the uncertainties in applying the law that increase the expense and risk of liability. And the uncertainties are worse with groundwater regulation, the Authority contends, because there is no sure basis for determining permit amounts other than historical use. Moreover, the Authority is concerned that takings litigation will disrupt the robust market that has developed in its permits and that buyers will be wary of paying for permits that may later be reduced.

It must be pointed out that the Authority has identified only three takings claims that have been filed in the more than fifteen years that it has been in operation. While the expense of such litigation cannot be denied, groundwater regulation need not result in takings liability. The Legislature's general approach to such regulation has been to require that all relevant factors be taken into account. The Legislature can discharge its responsibility under the Conservation Amendment without triggering the Takings Clause. But the Takings Clause ensures that the problems of a limited public resource—the water supply—are shared by the public, not foisted onto a few. We cannot know, of course, the extent to which the Authority's fears will yet materialize, but the burden of the Takings Clause on government is no reason to excuse its applicability.

* * *

For these reasons, the judgment of the court of appeals is affirmed.

NOTES

1. *Dealing with a shortage of water.* As the court notes, the Edwards Aquifer does not supply enough water to meet the water demands of the people living above and near it. The demand is excessive, which means some

type of water-allocation system is needed. This allocation function is a key one in natural resources law, and arises in every resource setting when, as often occurs, demand exceeds supply. By now, you should be able to identify the chief allocation options available to law makers:

One option is to allow landowners to use water until the maximum use-level is reached and then to ban all new uses. This is the first-in-time allocation system.

A second option is to identify all possible users (all owners of land above the aquifer) and divide the available water among them on some sort of pro-rata basis. This is the correlative rights approach.

A third option is to evaluate possible water uses and to distinguish among them based on public interest criteria, perhaps of the type used in the *Shokal v. Dunn* ruling, considered earlier (p. 522). Public-interest allocation systems can consider a wide-variety of factors, including ones relating to the traits of the users themselves.

When a natural resource has gone unregulated and the time comes when regulation seems needed—when the resource is being overused—the near-universal practice of lawmakers and regulatory agencies is to do exactly what the EAAA did in this instance, to issue use rights to existing users of the resource based on their history of use. Typically this is done because the users have enough political influence to derail any regulatory approach that materially interferes with existing uses. Regulators then typically prohibit or severely curtail new uses of the resource so as to halt the increased overuse. The third step is then to find ways to prune existing uses, cutting them back to the point where overall use is in line with the supply. This is apparently what the EAAA intended to do.

The state supreme court's ruling in *Edwards Aquifer* threw a major wrench in this very familiar regulatory approach by severely criticizing the use of first-in-time as the initial allocation method for permits. In doing so, the ruling also increased the likelihood that existing groundwater users everywhere will fight even harder to forestall regulatory controls and permit requirements given that a new system could curtail their current uses. What is the EAAA to do at this point?

According to the court, each landowner has a right to a fair share of the underlying groundwater, and this is true whether or not the landowner has ever made use of the groundwater. The court endorses a fair-share, correlative rights approach to the extent that it says the law cannot deprive landowners of their fair shares. If this allocation principle were used strictly, the water in the aquifer would be divided among overlying landowners based (presumably) on the relative sizes of their surface landownership. But note that the court expressly rejects this idea, stating that landowners can use water off the tract and sell it for use by others. Yet, if surface area of land is not the basis for deciding a given landowners "fair" share, then what could be? The court proceeds to respond favorably to an allocation approach that considers various factors, many related to public interest considerations, as well as historic use. This language seems to push in the direction of the third allocation option considered above, allocation based on public interest. But historic use, the court notes, is also an appropriate factor to consider, as is the effect of a new water use on existing uses (a factor that similarly emphasizes priority in time). With surface-area rejected as the basis of fair-share allocation, the court seems to suggest that fair share might simply mean that each landowner should have the same right as any other to seek water under allocation principles that apply to everyone equally; no landowner should be denied water simply because the landowner has not used it in recent years. Of course, to the extent water is given to landowners who have not used it recently, the EAAA can protect the aquifer only by curtailing existing users by the same amount (actually, a greater amount given the need to prune overall existing uses). This brings us back to why existing water users might well be nervous.

The challenge that the EAAA faces—the challenge also of other groundwater water-management entities in Texas—is to develop an allocation scheme that qualifies as fair under the Supreme Court's ruling and that does not give too much weight to priority in time (still a relevant factor, but one that cannot be determinative). Under any allocation scheme, however, many landowners will be denied permits and thus have no right to capture the water beneath their lands. Can a scheme that denies all water to a landowner be consistent with the owner's vested property rights in a fair share of the water? Also, with historic use given less emphasis, many existing water users, when they apply for permits, will be told that they must halt their current uses. Can such a scheme be consistent with the constitution (see the following note), given its protection for existing, investment-backed expectations?

2.   *The* Penn Central *takings factors.* In *Penn Central Transportation Co. v. City of New York,* 438 U.S. 104 (1978), the U.S. Supreme Court established a three-part test for evaluating most takings claims in the course of rejecting a claim of the owner of the Grand Central Terminal that the City of New York's historic preservation ordinance worked a takings by limiting its development rights. The three factors are: 1) the economic impact of a regulation; 2) its effect on reasonable investment-backed expectations; and 3) the character of the governmental action. See, e.g., John D. Echeverria, *Making Sense of* Penn Central, 39 Envtl. L. Rep. 10471 (2009). Landowners usually fail to win takings claims under *Penn Central.* See F. Patrick Hubbard, et al., *Do Owners Have a Fair Chance of Prevailing under the Ad Hoc Regulatory Takings Test of* Penn Central Transportation Company?, 14 Duke Envtl. L. & Pol'y F. 121, 141 (2003) (providing statistics). Here, the Texas Supreme Court sent the dispute back to the trial court to undertake the detailed factual inquires required to apply the *Penn Central* factors.

3.   *The lack of groundwater takings litigation.* The court ended its opinion by stating that there had been few recent groundwater takings claims and expressing confidence that the legislature could act to protect

groundwater supplies without triggering takings liability. How likely is this lack of litigation to continue in the wake of this decision now that the court has explained, more clearly than ever, the constitutionally protected groundwater rights that landowners all enjoy?

4.   *The case on remand.* In the wake of the 2012 decision, the trial court concluded that both of the Braggs' takings claims had merit and awarded them over $700,000 in compensation. The court of appeals affirmed, applying the *Penn Central* factors, finding 1) a severe economic impact from the denial of the requested pumping permits, substantially diminishing the value of the Braggs' properties; and 2) an interference with the Braggs' reasonable investment-backed expectations, since it was reasonable to expect when the lands were purchased that unrestricted groundwater pumping would continue. The court of appeals also concluded that, although the character of the governmental action—protecting terrestrial and aquatic life and domestic and municipal water supplies, as well as the existing and future economic development of the state—weighed in favor of the Authority, this factor did not outweigh the first two factors or the fact that the Bragg's had no real alternative economically viable use of their pecan orchards. After announcing and applying this utilitarian calculus (and employing a highly subjective valuation), the court remanded the case to the district court with instructions to calculate just compensation based on the difference between the value of commercial-grade pecan orchards with unlimited use of groundwater for irrigation and the value of the orchards after application of the Authority's regulations. *Edwards Aquifer Authority v. Bragg,* 421 S.W.3d 118 (Tex. App. 2013).

The ruling on remand did not engage what would seem to be the central issue raised by the state supreme court. The landowners above the aquifer collectively have control of it, and each of them is entitled to a fair share. If we take the word "share" literally, it would seem that the water rights of all of the landowners collectively, once quantified in terms of acre-feet, should add up to the total amount of water that can be taken from the aquifer on an annual basis. The fair share for any landowner should then be his or her portion of this total allowable water use, however the shares are determined. The reasoning used by the court on remand, however, did not pay attention to the basic question of how much water overall was available to divide among all the landowners. It allowed landowners individually to claim shares, leaving the distinct possibility that the shares of all owners in combination could exceed (perhaps greatly) the total amount of water available for extraction. Under the court's reasoning, landowners in combination could have constitutionally protected rights to more than the total available water, an outcome inconsistent with the idea of fair shares.

5.   *Other groundwater takings litigation.* In a comprehensive survey of some 50 groundwater takings decisions over the past century, Professor Owen has suggested that "*Day* is probably the nation's most prominent groundwater takings case" and concluded that groundwater takings

claimants should enjoy no special constitutional protection against regulatory controls beyond that available to other property owners. Dave Owen, *Taking Groundwater*, 91 Wash. U. L. Rev. 253, 277, 307 (2013).

6. *Groundwater and the public trust doctrine.* In a provocative decision in 2014, a California Superior Court ruled that the public trust doctrine may constrain groundwater pumping where it harms navigable waterways. Environmentalists claimed that extensive pumping of hydrologically connected groundwater depleted the flow of the Scott River in northern California, often dewatering the river and damaging its fisheries and recreational uses. The court ruled that Siskiyou County, which issued groundwater-pumping permits, had an obligation as a subdivision of the state to consider public trust values before issuing permits. The court did note that it was incumbent upon the environmentalists to prove that the pumping was damaging the Scott River. *Envtl. Law Found. v. State Water Resources Control Bd.,* No. 34–2010–80000583 (Cal. Super. Ct. July 15, 2014).

––––––––––––

Some states have amended their water codes to adopt the prior appropriation system to allocate groundwater rights. One of those is Idaho, which also employs the prior appropriation system to allocate surface water rights. The effect is to unify surface and groundwater allocation under one doctrine, although that has hardly eliminated controversies, as reflected in the case below.

BAKER V. ORE-IDA FOODS, INC.

Supreme Court of Idaho
513 P.2d 627 (1973)

[This case concerned approximately 20 irrigation wells developed during the late 1950s and early 1960s in the Cottonwood Creek-Buckhorn Creek area of Cassia County in southern Idaho. The parties to this suit were engaged in farming operations in that area. Underlying this area is a limestone aquifer of unknown depth, recharged primarily by means of precipitation. The aquifer's annual recharge was inadequate to satisfy the needs of all the well owners during the summer irrigation season. Excess withdrawals during the period 1961 through 1968 caused a 20-foot per year drop in the aquifer's water level. In other words, the parties were apparently "mining" the aquifer, *i.e.* perennially withdrawing ground water at rates beyond the recharge rate. State law allocated groundwater pumping rights based on prior appropriation, and the trial court determined that the wells of the four senior-most appropriators extracted the full amount of the aquifer's recharge. The lower court enjoined pumping from all other wells and assigned administration of its decree to the Idaho Department of Water Administration (IDWA).]

SHEPARD, J.

This is an appeal from a judgment for plaintiffs enjoining defendants from operating their irrigation wells. Defendants' wells pumped from a ground water aquifer underlying both plaintiffs' and defendants' land. This Court must for the first time, interpret our Ground Water Act (I.C. §§ 42–226 *et seq.*) as it relates to withdrawals of water from an underground aquifer in excess of the annual recharge rate. We are also called upon to construe our Ground Water Act's policies of promoting "full economic development" of ground water resources and maintaining "reasonable pumping levels."

* * *

Appellants assert that Idaho's Ground Water Act, I.C. §§ 42–226 *et seq.*, has superseded Idaho's common law rules relating to ground water. Appellants argue that, although they are junior, they are nevertheless entitled, under the doctrine of correlative rights, to a mutual pro rata share of the water in the aquifer. Appellants further assert that pursuant to the Ground Water Act senior appropriators may only enjoin junior appropriators from pumping by showing that the juniors' pumping has exceeded reasonable pumping levels.

We must examine the evolution and development of water law to place these important ground water issues in their proper perspective. . . .

* * *

The early ground water decisions mirror the riparian doctrine by holding that ground water rights depend on land ownership. The oldest and most rigid theory of ground water allocation is the common law rule of absolute ownership under which a landowner has an unqualified right to remove unlimited amounts of the water underlying his land. *Greenleaf v. Francis*, 35 Mass. 117 (1836). American courts followed the absolute ownership doctrine until 1862 when the Supreme Court of New Hampshire modified the doctrine by adopting the rule of reasonable use as to percolating ground waters. *Bassett v. Salisbury Mfg. Co.*, 43 N.H. 569, 577–79 (1862). Under reasonable use a landowner could withdraw percolating waters under his land to the extent that such withdrawals were reasonably consistent with the similar rights of other neighboring landowners. However, the reasonable use doctrine prohibited the transportation of ground water for use in areas other than the overlying land.

California altered the reasonable use theory by creating its unique doctrine of correlative rights which requires that a common but insufficient water supply be divided among competing overlying landowners so that each receives an amount of the available water proportionate to his ownership of the overlying land. When there is more than enough water to meet the needs of the overlying owners surplus water may be used on non-overlying lands. However, such transportation is forbidden when there is not enough water to fill the pro rata shares of overlying owners.

In summary, American courts apply one of the following doctrines to ground water: 1). Absolute ownership; 2). Absolute ownership as modified by reasonable use; 3). Correlative rights; 4). Prior appropriation.

The courts and legislatures have drawn further distinctions in applying these doctrines depending on whether the ground water lies in a rechargeable or a non-rechargeable aquifer. In a non-rechargeable aquifer the water is simply a stock resource and it can reasonably be determined when it will be totally exhausted. Decisions must be made as to whether to use it, when to use it and how to use it. New Mexico pioneered this area by imposing strict controls on withdrawals from its numerous non-rechargeable aquifers.

A *rechargeable* aquifer, however, is a flow resource and the real problem is how best to utilize the annual supply without overdrafting the stock which maintains the aquifer's water level. In the years since World War II, most western states have enacted legislation establishing administrative controls over ground water withdrawals. Idaho was in the vanguard of this movement when we enacted our Ground Water Act in 1951; I.C. §§ 42–226 *et seq.*

The instant case requires construction of the Ground Water Act against the backdrop of the uneven development of our common law concerning ground water. Idaho has vacillated on the question of the appropriability of ground water. As early as 1899 our statutes listed "subterranean waters" as among those subject to appropriation. S.L. 1899, p. 380 § 2. In *Bower v. Moorman*, 147 P. 496 (Idaho 1915) the Court repudiated the absolute ownership doctrine and held that percolating waters may be appropriated. Seven years later the court apparently reversed itself in *Public Utilities Commission v. Natatorium Co.*, 211 P. 533 (Idaho 1922), and held that percolating waters underlying private land were not subject to appropriation. That case, however, suggested that waters in an underground stream might be appropriated.

In *Hinton v. Little*, 296 P. 582 (Idaho 1931), the court eradicated the questionable historical distinction between underground streams and percolating waters and stated that *all* underground waters are percolating waters. *Hinton* again rejected the absolute ownership doctrine and held that the litigants could appropriate a common body of artesian water under their land.

Silkey v. Tiegs, 5 P.2d 1049 (Idaho 1931) further expanded *Hinton* and ruled that percolating waters may be appropriated by diversion and application to a beneficial use. *Silkey* suggested that percolating waters may be appropriated by either the constitutional method or the statutory permit method.

In 1963 amendments to the Ground Water Act, I.C. § 42–229 (S.L.1963, ch. 216, § 1, p. 624), altered the traditional assumption that groundwater in Idaho could be appropriated by either the constitutional method or the permit method. We construed that amendment in *State ex rel. Tappan v. Smith*, 444 P.2d 412, 417 (Idaho 1968) and held:

> This section of the statute does not deny the right to appropriate ground water, but regulates the method and means by which one may perfect a right to the use of such water. The regulation is in accord with Article 15, Sections 1 and 3, of Idaho's Constitution, and with I.C. §§ 42–103 and 42–226. Thereby the legislature prescribed that from the effective date of the act which precedes the present action, the statutory method of appropriation would be the sole method of appropriating ground water. The trial court did not err in finding that our laws require an appropriator of ground water to follow the application, permit and license procedure of the Department of Reclamation.

Smith says the state may regulate appropriations of groundwater without violating our constitutionally mandated prior appropriation system.

We turn now to problems concerning the maintenance of water table levels. An early Idaho case dealing with assessments by an irrigation district set forth the following remarks concerning ground water:

> We conclude, however, that he had no right to insist the water table be kept at the existing level in order to permit him to use the underground waters. There is no proof that he secured water from a natural subterranean stream. The evidence tends to show that he secured it from water collected beneath the surface of the ground due to seepage and percolation. To hold that any land owner has a legal right to have such a water table remain at a given height would absolutely defeat drainage in any case, and is not required by either the letter or spirit of our constitutional and statutory provisions in regard to water rights. *Nampa & Meridian Irr. Dist. v. Petrie*, 223 P. 531, 532 (Idaho 1923).

In a subsequent water table case, *Noh v. Stoner*, 26 P.2d 1112, 1114 (Idaho 1933) the Court upheld an injunction forbidding a junior well owner from interfering with a senior's appropriation of ground water. The Court stated:

> If subsequent appropriators desire to engage in such a contest [a race for the bottom of the aquifer] the financial burden must rest on them and with no injury to the prior appropriators or loss of

their water. Otherwise, if the users [seniors] go below the appellants [juniors] and respondents were to go below them appellants would in turn, according to their theory, be deprived of their water with no redress.

Noh suggests that a senior appropriator of ground water is forever protected from any interference with his *method* of diversion. Under *Noh* the only way that a junior can draw on the same aquifer is to hold the senior harmless for any loss incurred as a result of the junior's pumping. If the costs of reimbursing the senior became excessive, junior appropriators could not afford to pump from the aquifer. See *Colorado Springs v. Bender*, 366 P.2d 552 (Colo. 1961). *Noh* was inconsistent with the full economic development of our ground water resources.

Apparently our Ground Water Act was intended to eliminate the harsh doctrine of *Noh:*

> It is hereby declared that the traditional policy of the state of Idaho, requiring the water resources of this state to be devoted to beneficial use in reasonable amounts through appropriation, is affirmed with respect to the ground water resources of this state as said term is hereinafter defined: *and, while the doctrine of "first in time is first in right" is recognized, a reasonable exercise of this right shall not block full economic development of underground water resources, but early appropriators of underground water shall be protected in the maintenance of reasonable ground water pumping levels as may be established by the state reclamation engineer* [director of the department of water administration] *as herein provided.* All ground waters in this state are declared to be the property of the state, whose duty it shall be to supervise their appropriation and allotment to those diverting the same for beneficial use. . . . (Emphasis in original.)

> *In the administration and enforcement of this act and in the effectuation of the policy of this state to conserve its ground water resources, the state reclamation* (director of the department of water administration) *is empowered*: (Emphasis in original) I.C. 42–237a.

> g.　To supervise and control the exercise and administration of all rights hereafter acquired to the use of ground waters and in the exercise of this power he may by summary order, prohibit or limit the withdrawal of water from any well during any period that he determines that water to fill any water right in said well is not there available. To assist the state reclamation engineer [director of the department of water administration] in the administration and enforcement of this act, and in making

determinations upon which said orders shall be based, he may establish a ground water pumping level or levels in an area or areas having a common ground water supply as determined by him as hereinafter provided. *Water in a well shall not be deemed available to fill a water right therein if withdrawal therefrom of the amount called for by such right would affect, contrary to the declared policy of this act, the present or future use of any prior surface or ground water right or result in the withdrawing the ground water supply at a rate beyond the reasonably anticipated average rate of future natural recharge.* (emphasis added) I.C. 42–237a(g).

* * *

Where the clear implication of a legislative act is to change the common law rule we recognize the modification because the legislature has the power to abrogate the common law. We hold *Noh* to be inconsistent with the constitutionally enunciated policy of optimum development of water resources in the public interest. *Noh* is further inconsistent with the Ground Water Act.

* * *

Appellant argues in essence that mutual pro rata rights in the aquifer should be established. This argument is based upon the doctrine of correlative rights. The correlative rights doctrine is based upon the riparian principle of land ownership. The doctrine of correlative rights is repugnant to our constitutionally mandated prior appropriation doctrine. . . .

* * *

We now hold that Idaho's Ground Water Act forbids "mining" of an aquifer. The evidence herein clearly shows that the pumping by all parties was steadily drawing down the water in the aquifer at the rate of 20 ft. per year. Since our statute explicitly forbids such pumping, the district court did not err in enjoining pumping beyond the "reasonably anticipated average rate of future natural recharge."

* * *

Appellants contend that our Act's use of the phrase "reasonable pumping levels" means that senior appropriators are not necessarily entitled to maintenance of historic pumping levels. We agree with appellants in this regard. However, our agreement avails appellants nothing because the trial court found the aquifer's water supply inadequate to meet the needs of all appropriators.

A senior appropriator is only entitled to be protected to the extent of the "reasonable ground water pumping levels" as established by the IDWA. 1.C. § 42–226. A senior appropriator is not absolutely protected in either his historic water level or his historic means of diversion. Our Ground Water Act contemplates that in some situations senior appropriators may have to accept some modification of their rights in order to achieve the goal of full economic development.

In the enactment of the Ground Water Act, the Idaho legislature decided, as a matter of public policy, that it may sometimes be necessary to modify private property rights in ground water in order to promote full economic development of the resource. The legislature has said that when private property rights clash with the public interest regarding our limited ground water supplies, in some instances at least, the private interests must recognize that the ultimate goal is the promotion of the welfare of all our citizens. See Clark, 5 *Water and Water Rights*, § 446 at 474 (1972). We conclude that our legislature attempted to protect historic water rights while at the same time promoting full development of ground water. Priority rights in ground water are and will be protected insofar as they comply with reasonable pumping levels. Put otherwise, although a senior may have a prior right to ground water, if his means of appropriation demands an unreasonable pumping level his historic means of appropriation will not be protected.

* * *

In the case at bar it is apparent under our Ground Water Act that the senior appropriators may enjoin pumping by the junior appropriators to the extent that the additional pumping of the juniors' wells will exceed the "reasonably anticipated average rate of future recharge." The seniors may also enjoin such pumping to the extent that pumping by the juniors may force seniors to go below the "reasonable pumping levels" set by the IDWA.

A necessary concomitant of this statutory matrix is that the senior appropriators are not entitled to relief if the junior appropriators, by pumping from their wells, force seniors to lower their pumps from historic levels to reasonable pumping levels. It should also be noted that those reasonable pumping levels are subject to later modification by the IDWA.

* * *

The judgment of the district court is affirmed.

NOTES

1. *The twists and turns of legal evolution. Baker* is a useful decision to consider carefully from various angles and its insights extend beyond water law. The court takes the time to review the history of water law over the

centuries. Why might it do this? Surely one reason is that it wants to emphasize how even the fundamental elements of private rights in water can change over time in response to physical circumstances, shifting human needs, and differing policy choices. The shift from riparianism and its groundwater equivalents (absolute ownership and reasonable use) was, of course, a very big redefinition of property rights. Idaho made the transition awkwardly in the case of groundwater, apparently shifting to prior appropriation, then pulling back, then shifting again. Appropriation at one time took place in accordance with the simple terms of the state constitution, then was done under both the constitution and a statutory permit system, then shifted so that the statutory method became exclusive. A fundamental element of prior appropriation is the protection senior users enjoy against withdrawals by junior users. On this issue, we also see a wandering course by Idaho lawmakers, shifting between absolute protection for senior users (adopted in the now-overruled decision in *Noh*), then protection for reasonable pumping levels, and then to a ban on groundwater mining. Perhaps the court assumed that present and future legal change appear more reasonable when seen as merely the latest installment of an on-going pattern of change.

2. *Reasonable pumping levels and the ban on mining.* The central challenge of the court in *Baker* was to make sense of two seemingly inconsistent statements in the new state groundwater statute. On the one hand, the statute repudiated any protection of historic pumping levels and stated that senior users were entitled to the maintenance only of reasonable levels. A pumping level can be reasonable even if the water table declines somewhat, and pumpers are forced to drill their wells deeper. A reasonable pumping level can be maintained even as an aquifer is slowly being mined. On the other hand, the statute bans groundwater mining, which is the withdrawal of water faster than the apparent recharge rate (which is often not well known). The ban on mining would seem to support maintenance of historic pumping levels, but as a matter of hydrology this is not always true. The *Baker* court chose to blend the two ideas. The stronger protection for the senior users is undoubtedly the ban on mining. Although this ban on mining does not fully ensure the maintenance of historic levels, it probably comes closest to doing so. On this issue, Idaho law differs from that of many states which allocate groundwater by prior appropriation. In those states, senior users are entitled to reasonable pumping levels but not to a total ban on junior withdrawals that exceed recharge.

3. *The conflict with priority in time and correlative rights.* The Idaho statute at issue in *Baker* aimed to promote the full "beneficial use in reasonable amounts" of the state's groundwater. Will it accomplish that goal, as interpreted in *Baker*? The end result in this litigation was that all of the water in the aquifer was turned over to the four senior-most appropriators. All others had to halt their uses entirely. The problem in this case was that the four senior-most users might be using water for purposes less socially worthy, or in ways less efficient, than the junior users. Another problem was

that rather minor changes in the water-use practices of the senior users could well save enough water to allow some of the junior users to continue pumping. Given the court's ruling, the four senior users had no legal obligation to change their practices at all. Perhaps junior users could approach them, offering to pay for conservation measures that would save enough water to allow more pumpers to use the aquifer. But if history is much guide, such transactions are unlikely to occur. Could the law, though, encourage them by creating opportunities for discussions to take place? If the aquifer had in place an aquifer-management team of some sort that could consider the practices and needs of all pumpers, might different outcomes be possible?

As we have seen, state lawmakers could have used a much-different method of resolving the dispute and thereby allocating water. The junior users pushed hard to get the court to require a sharing of the groundwater among all twenty pumpers on a fair-share, correlative rights basis. The court rejected that alternative as inconsistent with the state's commitment to prior appropriation. The other alternative was, of course, some form of public interest allocation in which water was divided among the twenty pumpers based on the relative public benefits generated by the various pumpers. But that approach would likely also have deviated substantially from the priority-in-time list, and seems to have been rejected just as quickly by the Idaho court. Yet another option would be to impose on all water users a duty of accommodation. When water is short, all users could be required to adopt reasonable available methods to conserve water; only after that took place and circumstances were reassessed would the court then curtail water uses by junior users. Such an "accommodation approach" could look a lot like the reasonable use approach employed in riparian rights law to allocate scarce water among riparian landowners. In any event, it is important to see clearly the rather stark conflict between the two basic ways of dealing with scarcity: 1) giving water to the senior-most users, or 2) reviewing all existing uses, and then giving the water to the uses that are the most socially beneficial and efficient. The Idaho statute embraces the former approach, even as the legislature announced that it wanted to promote the most beneficial use of state waters.

4. *Senior rights in a fossil aquifer.* What rights does a senior groundwater appropriator have in the case of an aquifer that has essentially no natural recharge? In such a case, any water withdrawal reduces the pool of water. Any water that a second or later appropriator pumps from the aquifer inevitably shortens the time period during which the first appropriator can pump. Is this a *per se* violation of the first appropriator's rights? Also, does it make sense to apply a ban on mining of such an aquifer, when the effect would be to leave the water completely untouched?

These issues arose in *Mathers v. Texaco, Inc.*, 421 P.2d 771 (N.M. 1966), in which an oil company, Texaco, applied to the state for a permit to withdraw water from a non-recharging aquifer and to use the water to recover additional oil from an underlying oil formation. Under state law, a new appropriator could gain a permit only by proving that the additional withdrawal would not impair existing water rights. The parties agreed that the additional withdrawal in this instance would force senior users to deepen their wells more rapidly and would lead to the quicker exhaustion of the aquifer. To promote full water use, the state engineer nonetheless decided to allow pumping from the aquifer up to the point where two-thirds of the aquifer's water would be gone in 40 years. Despite the legal requirement that new withdrawals respect existing rights, the state supreme court upheld the decision. To rule otherwise, the court announced, would be to allow only one user of the aquifer, since even a second user would lead to the more rapid depletion of it:

> The administration of a non-rechargeable basin, if the waters therein are to be applied to a beneficial use, requires giving to the stock or supply of water a time dimension, or, to state it otherwise, requires the fixing of a rate of withdrawal which will result in a determination of the economic life of the basin at a selected time.

> The very nature of the finite stock of water in a non-rechargeable basin compels a modification of the traditional concept of appropriable supply under the appropriation doctrine. Each appropriation from a limited supply of non-replaceable water of necessity reduces the supply in quantity and shortens the time of use to something less than perpetuity. Each appropriator, subsequent to the initial appropriation, reduces in amount, and in time of use, the supply of water available to all prior appropriators, with the consequent decline of the water table, higher pumping costs, and lower yields.

* * *

> In fact, if the position of protestants be correct, then each and all of the many permits to withdraw waters from this basin issued by the State Engineer, subsequent to the initial permit, have been issued wrongfully and unlawfully, because each withdrawal, to some degree, has caused a lowering of the water level, and thus an impairment of the rights of the initial appropriator.

* * *

> The only premise upon which the position of protestants can be logically supported is that "existing rights" embraces the element of perpetuity. As above stated, the beneficial use by the public of the waters in a closed or non-rechargeable basin requires giving to the use of such waters a time limitation. In the case of the Lea County Underground Water Basin, that time limitation was fixed by the State Engineer in 1952 at forty years, after having first made extensive studies and calculations. There is nothing before us to prompt a feeling that this method of administration and operation

does not secure to the public the maximum beneficial use of the waters in this basin.

The rights of the protestants to appropriate water from this basin are subject to this time limitation, just as are the rights of all other appropriators. A lowering of the water level in the wells of protestants, together with the resulting increase in pumping costs and the lowering of pumping yields, does not constitute an impairment of the rights of protestants as a matter of law. These are inevitable results of the beneficial use by the public of these waters.

Id. at 775–76.

5. *Conjunctive water management.* So far in our study we have looked at surface water allocation schemes and groundwater schemes in isolation from one another, just as the law has long done. In the *Cary v. Cochran* ruling (p. 504) we saw how courts handled disputes between two surface-water appropriators; in *Baker v. Ore-Ida Foods* (p. 557),we saw how the same kind of dispute was handled when the two appropriators had rights to groundwater. For decades, though, states have sought ways to integrate their surface- and groundwater allocation systems to take into account the hydrological connection of most water sources.

In the *Park County* decision, considered in chapter 1 (p. 29), we saw one seemingly successful way to achieve this result. Colorado assumes that all groundwater is tributary to surface water, so that groundwater withdrawals and surface withdrawals typically fit within a single priority list, thereby reducing conflict. By doing this, Colorado enables surface appropriators to store water in aquifers without risking that groundwater pumpers can thereby take it out. In that ruling, you will recall, the court authorized water owners to store water beneath the ground even when the water moved beneath the lands of neighboring owners who had not consented to it; this use of the subsurface, the court ruled, did not involve a subsurface trespass. This Colorado ruling was a ringing endorsement of the need to manage groundwater and surface water together; that is, to engage in what is often termed conjunctive management. Effective conjunctive management can allow for (among other benefits) the storage of large volumes of surface water underground during high water years and the pumping of large volumes of groundwater during drought years. Extensive rules on conjunctive management are in place in Idaho, a state like Colorado in which both ground and surface waters are governed by the prior appropriation doctrine. Idaho Water Resources Dept., Rules for Conjunctive Management of Surface and Ground Water Resources, IDAPA, § 37.03.11.

———————

In states without conjunctive management statutory authority and administrative rules, it is left to the courts to determine how to balance conflicting claims of ground and surface water users. The balancing can be quite challenging when different water law rules govern surface and subsurface waters, as they do in Nebraska.

SPEAR T RANCH, INC. V. KNAUB

Supreme Court of Nebraska
691 N.W.2d 116 (2005)

[Knaub and other appellees pumped groundwater for irrigation from their lands in the Pumpkin Creek Basin. Spear T Ranch diverted surface water from Pumpkin Creek for its own irrigation and stock-watering. According to Spear T, whose water use began earlier, the appellees' pumping of groundwater drained water from the creek and deprived Spear T of its surface water appropriations. The lower court rejected Spear T's claims.]

CONNOLLY, J.

This appeal presents the question whether a surface water appropriator has a claim against a groundwater user for interference with a surface water users' appropriation.

* * *

Analysis

The term "surface water" encompasses all waters found on the earth's surface. Here, the surface water is the stream on which Spear T has water appropriations. In contrast, ground water is defined as "that water which occurs or moves, seeps, filters, or percolates through the ground under the surface of the land."

Hydrologically, ground water and surface water are inextricably related. Ground water pumping can cause diminished streamflows. Streamflow can support the potential for subirrigation. Seepage from surface water supplies canals, and deep percolation of applied irrigation water from surface projects can recharge ground water aquifers. Water law commentators have colorfully described this phenomenon: "[A]ll water is interrelated and interdependent. If groundwater were red, most streams would be various shades of pink; if groundwater were poisoned, the streams would also be poisoned."

But Nebraska water law ignores the hydrological fact that ground water and surface water are inextricably linked. Instead of an integrated system, we have two separate systems, one allocating streamflows and the other allocating ground water. Under constitutional and statutory provisions, streamflows are allocated by priority in time. See Neb. Const. art. XV, § 6. Ground water, in contrast, is governed by a common-law rule of reasonableness and the GWMPA [Ground Water Management and Protection Act]. Moreover, the lack of an integrated system is reinforced by the fact that different agencies regulate ground water and surface water. The Department of Natural Resources regulates surface water appropriations. See Neb.Rev.Stat. §§ 61–201 *et seq.* In contrast, under the GWMPA, ground water is statutorily regulated by each Natural Resources District (NRD).

The tension between the two systems has long been recognized by commentators. See Richard S. Harnsberger et al., *Groundwater: From Windmills to Comprehensive Public Management,* 52 Neb. L. Rev. 179, 182 (1973) ("[g]round and stream diverters in Nebraska are on a collision course which may occur sooner than most people think"). That day has arrived.

1.   *Does Spear T Have a Common-Law Claim Against Appelles?*

We begin by determining whether Spear T has stated a claim. Spear T argues that it has stated a claim based either on the statutory rule of prior appropriation of surface water or on the tort of conversion; we reject these arguments. But as we explain below, we determine that the common law does recognize a tort claim by a surface water appropriator against a ground water user and that Spear T's complaint could be amended to state a claim.

(a)   *Prior Appropriation*

As noted, under constitutional and statutory provisions, streamflows are allocated by priority in time. In its first attempt to state a claim, Spear T relies on prior appropriation. Spear T argues that because the water is hydrologically connected and because it has a prior surface water appropriation, it has priority to the water. According to Spear T, the water is all one "stream" and, as such, Spear T's prior appropriation takes priority over other users of the water, including those who withdraw the water from under its lands. Thus, Spear T essentially asks this court to apply legislatively created surface water priorities to ground water use without considering existing common-law rules. We decline to adopt this approach for several reasons.

First, an application of surface water priorities to ground water requires this court to agree with a legal fiction that considers the ground water to be an "underground stream." We take as true that the water is hydrologically connected, but water rarely runs in a true underground stream. Adherence to such a view ignores reality.

Second, no statutory or case law authority supports applying surface water appropriations to ground water. We recognize that most legislatures in western states have developed comprehensive appropriation systems overseen by administrative agencies. See *Restatement (Second) of Torts*, ch. 41, topic 4 (1979). But in Nebraska, the Legislature has not developed an appropriation system that addresses direct conflicts between users of surface and ground water that is hydrologically connected.

Finally, the prior appropriation rule that Spear T advocates would give first-in-time surface water appropriators the right to use whatever water they want to the exclusion of later-in-time ground water users. This could have the effect of shutting down all wells in any area where surface water appropriations are hydrologically connected to ground water. Harnsberger et al., at 248 ("[i]f the doctrine of prior appropriation [was] carried to [its] logical conclusion, all Nebraska wells would be shut down"). This would unreasonably deprive many ground water users. Accordingly, we decline to apply the statutory surface water appropriation rules to conflicts between surface and ground water users.

(b) *Conversion*

Next, Spear T contends that it has stated a claim for conversion. Tortious conversion is any distinct act of dominion wrongfully asserted over another's property in denial of or inconsistent with that person's rights.

A right to appropriate surface water however, is not an ownership of property. Instead, the water is viewed as a public want and the appropriation is a right to use the water. As one article has stated in reference to ground water: "Trespass is unavailable in a typical well interference case because a physical invasion of the plaintiff's property is lacking. Similarly, an action in conversion is unavailable, since the plaintiff has no private property interest in groundwater, at least not prior to capture." Because Spear T does not have a property interest in its surface water appropriation and only has a right to use, it cannot state a claim for conversion or trespass.

(c) *Has Spear T Stated Claim Under Other Common-Law Doctrines or, Alternatively Should It Be Given Leave to Amend?*

Although Spear T cannot state a claim under the statutory surface water appropriation rules or for the tort of conversion, this does not end our analysis. The question remains whether it has stated a claim under other common-law principles or if it should be allowed leave to amend to state such a claim.

(i) *Review of Common-Law Rules*

We begin by reviewing common-law rules that courts have employed to adjudicate disputes between water users.

a.   *English Rule*

Under the English rule of water law—also referred to as the absolute ownership rule—a landowner had absolute ownership of the waters under his or her land. Therefore, the owner could withdraw any quantity of water for any purpose without liability, even though the result was to drain water from beneath surrounding lands.

* * *

Most American courts, however, have criticized the English rule, recognizing that the rule protected landowners from liability even when water was diverted for malicious purposes. The rule has also been criticized because, although a landowner theoretically had a property right in waters beneath his or her land, the overlying owner with the deepest well or largest pump could control water that would otherwise be available to all.

An extreme minority of jurisdictions still adhere to the English rule or a rule that has the same effect as the English rule. . . .

b.   American Rule

Because of disagreement with the English rule, American courts have modified it in different ways. Under what is termed the "American rule" of water law, the owner of the land is entitled to appropriate subterranean or other waters accumulating on the land, but cannot extract and appropriate them in excess of a reasonable and beneficial use of land, especially if the exercise of such use is injurious to others.

Under the American rule, the term "reasonable use" relates to the manner in which water is used upon the appropriator's land. The adjacent landowners' interests are in issue only when the appropriator uses water in excess of the reasonable and beneficial use of it upon his or her land and that excess use is injurious to the adjacent landowner. The American rule has at times also been referred to as a rule of "reasonable use," although it does not consider a balancing of the parties' interests. . . .

Under the American rule, a person who is deprived of surface water because of the use of ground water by a nearby landowner will recover only when the water was not used for a beneficial purpose on the ground water user's land. The adjacent landowners' interests are in issue only when the appropriator uses water in excess of the reasonable and beneficial use of it upon his or her land and that excess use is injurious to the adjacent landowner. *Prather v. Eisenmann,* 261 N.W.2d 766 (Neb. 1978). The American rule has at times also been referred to as a rule of "reasonable use," although it does not consider a balancing of the parties' interests. . . .

Under the American rule, a person who is deprived of surface water because of the use of ground water by a nearby landowner will recover only when the water was not used for a beneficial purpose on the ground water user's land.

c.   *Correlative Rights*

The correlative rights rule of water law originated in California and provides that the rights of all landowners over a common aquifer are coequal or correlative and that one cannot extract more than his or her share of the water even for use on his or her own land if other's rights are injured by the withdrawal. The rule first arose in Katz v. Walkinshaw, 70 P. 663 (Cal. 1902). Under the rule, the overlying landowners have no proprietary interest in the water under their ground and each owner over a common pool has a correlative right to make a beneficial use of the water on his or her land. Priority of use is irrelevant because in times of shortage, the common supply is apportioned among the landowners based on their reasonable needs.

* * *

d.   *Restatement*

The *Restatement (Second) of Torts* § 858 (1979) essentially adopts a correlative rights rule that allows for a balancing of many factors to determine reasonableness. Although the rule is initially stated in terms of "reasonable use" similar to the American rule, it adds exceptions that draw on principles of correlative rights. The Restatement rule finds its support in principles of nuisance law and has been suggested as the basic framework for well interference cases.

The Restatement, § 858 at 258, states in part as follows:

(1) A proprietor of land or his grantee who withdraws ground water from the land and uses it for a beneficial purpose is not subject to liability for interference with the use of water by another, unless

(a) the withdrawal of ground water unreasonably causes harm to a proprietor of neighboring land through lowering the water table or reducing artesian pressure,

(b) the withdrawal of ground water exceeds the proprietor's reasonable share of the annual supply or total store of ground water, or

(c) the withdrawal of the ground water has a direct and substantial effect upon a watercourse or lake and unreasonably causes harm to a person entitled to the use of its water.

Although § 858 is under chapter 41, topic 4, entitled "Interference With the Use of Water," *id.* at 253, a note on that topic's scope shows that it is intended to apply to water that is hydrologically connected to ground water. The note states in part: "This Topic covers the rights and liabilities of possessors of land and others withdrawing ground water. It also states the rules governing the rights and liabilities of persons using water where ground water is interconnected with the water of watercourses and lakes." *Id.* Several courts have adopted the Restatement approach. *Cline v. American Aggregates,* 474 N.E.2d 324 (Ohio 1984); *State v. Michels Pipeline Construction, Inc.,* 217 N.W.2d 339 (Wis. 1974); *Maerz v. U.S. Steel Corp.,* 323 N.W.2d 524 (Mich. Ct. App. 1982).

In addition, the Restatement keeps older definitions of ground water and surface water, but abandons any common-law distinctions between underground watercourses and percolating water. Ground water is defined as "water that naturally lies or flows under the surface of the earth." Comment *b.* of the Restatement recognizes that ground water may be connected to other forms of water. The comment states: "Most ground water is moving in the hydrologic cycle. It originates from infiltration of precipitation and inflow of streams; it discharges into springs, streams, lakes and oceans. Some ground water is sidetracked from the cycle in closed basins where geologic formations isolate it from recharge or discharge." *Id.* at 199.

Although the Restatement rule is derived from principles of reasonable use, the rule differs from the American rule because it balances the equities and hardships between competing users. The *Restatement (Second) of Torts* § 858, comment *b.* at 259 (1979), notes in part:

> The general rule is phrased in terms of non-liability in order to carry forward the policy of encouraging ground water use by permitting more or less unrestricted development of the resource by those who have access to it. The policy and the rule are justified by the fact that since most ground water basins are very large and contain vast quantities of water, it is usually impossible for a single water user to capture the entire supply and leave no water for others.

Comment *c.* at 259–60 provides:

> Exceptions to the general rule are stated in Clauses (a), (b), and (c) of Subsection (1). They incorporate all grounds of liability for use of ground water recognized by the common law but remove some of the restrictions contained in those rules of liability. The majority "American rule of reasonable use" ... was phrased in terms of the overlying landowner's right to capture ground water, limited by restrictions on the place of use of the water. In operation this protected small wells for domestic and agricultural uses from the harmful effects of large wells for municipal and industrial supply. The first exception to nonliability, contained in Clause (1)(a), continues this protection but follows a modern tendency to extend similar protection to

cases of harm done by unreasonably large withdrawals for operations conducted on overlying lands.

The second exception, Clause (1)(b), imposes liability upon a landowner who withdraws more than his reasonable share of the common supply. This has always been a possible outcome of a controversy concerning ground water if the source could be classified as an underground stream or if the rule of correlative rights were applied. The concept of underground streams was unscientific and its application could be quite arbitrary and the applicability of the rule of correlative rights was in doubt in many states. This exception merges the two rules and makes it possible to apportion shares of the water in the source to the owners of overlying land whenever total withdrawals reach such magnitude that it is necessary to protect the share of an individual landowner from appropriation by others.

The last exception, Clause (1)(c), restates the conditions for recognizing that ground water and surface water are often closely interrelated and should be treated as a single source. In the past this took many forms. Withdrawals of ground water have been called unreasonable when they reduced the flow of springs. A variant of the underground stream concept has enabled the courts to regulate some ground water as the underground segment of a surface stream. The part of an aquifer in contact with the bed and banks of a stream has been called the underflow of the stream and treated as part of it. This section substitutes a pragmatic test for determining the interconnection instead of employing these doubtful and unscientific categorizations.

Thus, under the Restatement, reasonableness of use is determined on a case-by-case basis and many factors can be considered; the test is flexible. The test for reasonableness is provided in the Restatement:

The determination of the reasonableness of a use of water depends upon a consideration of the interests of the riparian proprietor making the use, of any riparian proprietor harmed by it and of society as a whole. Factors that affect the determination include the following:

(a) The purpose of the use,

(b) the suitability of the use to the watercourse or lake,

(c) the economic value of the use,

(d) the social value of the use,

(e) the extent and amount of harm it causes,

(f)   the practicality of avoiding the harm by adjusting the use or method of use of one proprietor or the other,

(g)   the practicality of adjusting the quantity of water used by each proprietor,

(h)   the protection of existing values of water uses, land, investments and enterprises, and

(i)   the justice of requiring the user causing harm to bear the loss.

Restatement (Second) of Torts § 850A at 220 (1979).

e.   *Common-Law Claims in Disputes Between Ground Water Users in Nebraska*

We have never been confronted with whether a surface water appropriator may bring a common-law claim against the user of hydrologically connected ground water. We have, however, recognized that a ground water user may bring a common-law claim against another ground water user. We generally have stated the common law in a manner consistent with the American rule blended with a rule of correlative rights. For example, we have stated:

[T]he owner of land is entitled to appropriate subterranean waters found under his land, but he cannot extract and appropriate them in excess of a reasonable and beneficial use upon the land which he owns, especially if such use is injurious to others who have substantial rights to the waters, and if the natural underground supply is insufficient for all owners, each is entitled to a reasonable proportion of the whole, and while a lesser number of states have adopted this rule, it is in our opinion, supported by the better reasoning.

Olson v. City of Wahoo, 248 N.W. 304, 308 (Neb. 1933).

(ii) *Adoption of Restatement for Disputes Between Surface Water Users and Ground Water Users*

Having reviewed the common-law rules, we now consider whether we will recognize a common-law claim for interference with surface water by the user of hydrologically connected ground water.

Initially, we reject a rule that would bar a surface water appropriator from recovering in all situations. Such a rule would ignore the hydrological fact that a ground water user's actions may have significant, negative consequences for surface water appropriators.

Instead, the common law should acknowledge and attempt to balance the competing equities of ground water users and surface water appropriators; the Restatement approach best accomplishes this. The

Restatement recognizes that ground water and surface water are interconnected and that in determining the rights and liabilities of competing users, the fact finder needs broad discretion. Thus, when applying the Restatement, the fact finder has flexibility to consider many factors such as those listed in § 850A, along with other factors that could affect a determination of reasonable use.

Adoption of the Restatement is the modern trend. See *Cline v. American Aggregates,* 474 N.E.2d 324 (Ohio 1984); *State v. Michels Pipeline Construction, Inc.,* 217 N.W.2d 339 (Wis. 1974); *Maerz v. U.S. Steel Corp.,* 323 N.W.2d 524 (Mich. Ct. App. 1982). . . .

Accordingly, we adopt the Restatement to govern conflicts between users of hydrologically connected surface water and ground water. Specifically, we hold:

> A proprietor of land or his [or her] grantee who withdraws ground water from the land and uses it for a beneficial purpose is not subject to liability for interference with the use of water of another, unless . . . the withdrawal of the ground water has a direct and substantial effect upon a watercourse or lake and unreasonably causes harm to a person entitled to the use of its water.

Restatement (Second) of Torts § 858(1)(c) at 258 (1979). Whether a ground water user has unreasonably caused harm to a surface water user is decided on a case-by-case basis. In making the reasonableness determination, the Restatement, § 850A, provides a valuable guide, but we emphasize that the test is flexible and that a trial court should consider any factors it deems relevant.

We digress momentarily to offer a word of caution. Although the issue of available remedies is not yet before us, courts should be cautious when considering remedies for interference with surface water. For example, because the recharge of a stream that has dried up because of well pumping could take years, an injunction against pumping might only serve to deprive everyone in a water basin. Such a remedy would be unreasonable and inequitable. Likewise, a court can consider a surface water appropriator's ability to obtain an exception to stays on drilling new wells, or any additional programs that might provide relief.

(iii) *Has Spear T Stated a Claim Under the Restatement?*

Having adopted the Restatement approach, we next consider whether Spear T has stated a claim upon which relief can be granted. Our review of Spear T's complaint shows that it did allege—although not precisely— that the appellees' withdraw of ground water has directly and substantially affected Pumpkin Creek. However, although Spear T alleged that it has suffered harm, it did not allege that the appellees have unreasonably caused that harm. Thus, Spear T has failed to state a claim upon which relief can be granted.

We determine, however, that Spear T should be allowed to amend its complaint. Leave to amend should be granted liberally when justice so requires. Accordingly, we determine that the district court erred when it dismissed Spear T's complaint with prejudice for failure to state a claim.

* * *

V.　*Conclusion*

We adopt *Restatement (Second) of Torts* §§ 858 and 850A (1979) for resolving disputes between users of hydrologically connected ground water and surface water. Because we adopt the Restatement, we determine that the district court erred when it dismissed the complaint with prejudice for failure to state a claim. . . .

NOTES

1.　*The various options of groundwater rights. Spear T* is a good decision to read carefully concerning a number of natural resources issues, including the types of legal protections enjoyed by the owners of discrete rights to appropriate water. What level of protection does an appropriator have as against a groundwater pumper who is taking water from a hydrologically connected source? The decision is also valuable in clarifying further a rule of law that we have already seen: the reasonable use rule as it applies among groundwater users themselves. The court usefully distinguishes between the reasonable use rule as applied to groundwater by most American jurisdictions and the rather different reasonable use rule proposed in the *Restatement of Torts*. What exactly are the differences, and how important might they be in actual practice? One rule (the American) looks at the reasonableness of the landowner's activities largely in the abstract, paying little or no attention to competing uses of the water and larger social needs. The other (the Restatement approach, which Nebraska largely embraces) goes farther and looks to the particular needs and activities of other users and potential users of the same aquifer, much like the reasonable-use rule of riparian rights examines the relative merits of competing riparian water users.

The rules differ somewhat also on an issue considered at various places in this chapter: the question of where water can be used. Under the American rule (illustrated by *Higday*, p. 535), groundwater can be used off the overlying tract only if it causes no harm to a groundwater pumper who uses water on the tract. The Restatement approach, as we saw, considers place of use but only as one factor in assessing reasonableness. The correlative rights approach leans toward the American rule, allowing off-tract uses only when overall withdrawals are less than the recharge rate.

At first glance, it seems appropriate for a court to consider as many facts as possible to make the best judgment about how water should be used. But is there a downside to litigation that makes more facts and factual issues relevant? Who is supposed to gather this information, particularly if (as is true in many states) it is not publicly available in any way? Many water users are disinclined to tell other people what they are doing, even in terms of how much water they are pumping. Can we criticize the court in *Spear T* for not thinking more about the costs and difficulty of litigation?

2. *Priority in time versus reasonableness. Spear T* follows logically after *Cary v. Cochran* (p. 504) and *Baker v. Ore-Ida* (p. 557) in that it gives us another piece of the story about the protections that an appropriator of water enjoys as against competing users of the water. *Cary* told us about conflicts among surface appropriators; *Baker* about conflicts among groundwater appropriators. Here we see a conflict between a surface appropriator and a groundwater user. The surface appropriator, who was earlier in time, wanted its priority in time to be decisive. The court showed no interest in that argument, noting that priority in time was important only in disputes between and among surface appropriators.

Ultimately, the court in *Spear T* uses a reasonableness standard to limit the ability of a groundwater pumper to take water from a surface water user. The standard it embraces comes directly from the Restatement. But note that this reasonableness standard is quite different from the one that the state uses to resolve disputes between two groundwater pumpers. In the latter instance, the governing law includes an obligation to share the water; each pumper is allowed only a "reasonable proportion" of the available water. That language is what accounts for the court's statement that Nebraska embraces the American rule but grafts onto it the rule of correlative rights. Importantly, this sharing aspect is not present in the law governing disputes between surface water uses and groundwater pumpers, at least not directly. A groundwater pumper is liable to a surface water user only when the groundwater pumping directly and substantially affects the surface water source itself (that is, by lowering the water level in the river or lake) and "unreasonably harms" the surface water user. This legal standard makes no express reference to fair shares, and understandably so. Fair share makes sense in a dispute between two users of water from the same source. It is much harder to apply when the two water sources are merely connected and when each has its own governance system.

E. FEDERAL RESERVED WATER RIGHTS

As discussed above, the prior appropriation doctrine arose during the California Gold Rush out of water disputes among miners on federal lands. The federal government had no water law rule, so the states were free to develop their own rules. As we have seen, most states turned to prior appropriation. In *U.S. v. Rio Grande Dam & Irrigation Co.*, 174 U.S. 690, 703 (1899), the Supreme Court indicated that there were exceptions to this tradition of state primacy over water rights: 1) when water was necessary for the federal government to fulfill international treaty obligations; and 2) when water was required for the federal government to manage lands that it had set aside for particular purposes. As the ruling below recognized more expressly, water that the federal government implicitly reserved for these purposes was then unavailable for private parties to acquire under state law.

WINTERS V. UNITED STATES
Supreme Court of the United States
207 U.S. 564 (1908)

[In 1888, the federal government reserved the Fort Belknap Indian Reservation, which bordered on the Milk River in what is now Montana, for tribal homelands. The purpose of the reservation was to convert the tribes from nomadic hunters to "pastoral and civilized" agrarians. The following year, Montana was admitted as a state and adopted the prior appropriation system for allocating water rights. Sometime in the mid-1890s, a number of ditch companies (collectively referred to as Winters) began diverting substantial amounts of Milk River water under Montana law to serve their ranching and farming customers. In 1898, the federal government constructed an irrigation project to help fulfill the agrarian purpose of the Fort Belknap Reservation, but in 1905 a drought made satisfying both the Winters' diversions and the federal diversion impossible. The government filed suit, claiming that its diversion to benefit the Indian tribe had priority over the water rights of the private ditch companies, and a lower court agreed. The Supreme Court then issued the following opinion.]

MCKENNA, J.

* * *

The case, as we view it, turns on the agreement of May, 1888, resulting in the creation of Fort Belknap Reservation. In the construction of this agreement there are certain elements to be considered that are prominent and significant. The reservation was a part of a very much larger tract which the Indians had the right to occupy and use, and which was adequate for the habits and wants of a nomadic and uncivilized people. It was the policy of the government, it was the desire of the Indians, to change those habits and to become a pastoral and civilized people. If they should become such, the original tract was too extensive; but a smaller tract would be inadequate without a change of conditions. The lands were arid, and, without irrigation, were practically valueless. And yet, it is contended, the means of irrigation were deliberately given up by the Indians and deliberately accepted by the government. The lands ceded were, it is true, also arid; and some argument may be urged, and is urged, that with their cession there was the cession of the waters, without which they would be valueless, and "civilized communities could not be established thereon." And this, it is further contended, the Indians knew, and yet made no reservation of the waters.

We realize that there is a conflict of implications, but that which makes for the retention of the waters is of greater force than that which makes for their cession. The Indians had command of the lands and the waters,—command of all their beneficial use, whether kept for hunting, "and grazing roving herds of stock," or turned to agriculture and the arts of civilization. Did they give up all this? Did they reduce the area of their occupation and give up the waters which made it valuable or adequate? And, even regarding the allegation of the answer as true, that there are springs and streams on the reservation flowing about 2,900 inches of water, the inquiries are pertinent. If it were possible to believe affirmative answers, we might also believe that the Indians were awed by the power of the government or deceived by its negotiators. Neither view is possible. The government is asserting the rights of the Indians. But extremes need not be taken into account. By a rule of interpretation of agreements and treaties with the Indians, ambiguities occurring will be resolved from the standpoint of the Indians. And the rule should certainly be applied to determine between two inferences, one of which would support the purpose of the agreement and the other impair or defeat it. On account of their relations to the government, it cannot be supposed that the Indians were alert to exclude by formal words every inference which might militate against or defeat the declared purpose of themselves and the government, even if it could be supposed that they had the intelligence to foresee the "double sense" which might some time be urged against them.

Another contention of appellants is that if it be conceded that there was a reservation of the waters of Milk River by the agreement of 1888, yet the reservation was repealed by the admission of Montana into the Union, February 22, 1889, "upon an equal footing with the original states." The language of counsel is that "any reservation in the agreement with the Indians, expressed or implied, whereby the waters of Milk River were not to be subject of appropriation by the citizens and inhabitants of said state, was repealed by the act of admission." But to establish the repeal counsel rely substantially upon the same argument that they advance against the intention of the agreement to reserve the waters. The power of the government to reserve the waters and exempt them from appropriation under the state laws is not denied, and could not be. *United States v. Rio Grande Dam & Irrig. Co.*, 174 U.S. 690 (1899); *United States v. Winans*, 198 U.S. 371 (1905). That the government did reserve them we have decided, and for a use which would be necessarily continued through years. This was done May 1, 1888, and it would be extreme to believe that within a year Congress destroyed the reservation and took from the Indians the consideration of their grant, leaving them a barren waste,— took from them the means of continuing their old habits, yet did not leave them the power to change to new ones.

Appellants' argument upon the incidental repeal of the agreement by the admission of Montana into the Union, and the power over the waters of Milk river which the state thereby acquired to dispose of them under its laws, is elaborate and able, but our construction of the agreement and its effect make it unnecessary to answer the argument in detail. For the same reason we have not discussed the doctrine of riparian rights urged by the government.

Decree affirmed.

NOTES

1. *The canons of interpretation.* The *Winters* decision was importantly influenced by the canon of Indian treaty interpretation which instructs courts to interpret treaties (and treaty substitutes like statutes and executive orders) as the tribes would have understood them (similar to adhesion contracts, where the drafter of the contract has superior bargaining power) and liberally in their favor. For a recent analysis, see Richard B. Collins, *Never Construed to Their Prejudice*, 84 U. Colo. L. Rev. 1 (2013). In the Court's view, it made little sense for the tribe to retreat to a smaller tract of land to take up a farming-based mode of existence without adequate water to irrigate its crops. Interpreting the treaty in that manner allowed the tribe to retain adequate water for this purpose, meaning that water was then not available for any government of the United States—whether federal, state or local—to allocate to private parties, such as the ditch companies in this dispute.

2. *The* Winans *decision.* The Court cited *U.S. v. Winans,* 198 U.S. 371 (1905), a case involving treaty fishing rights on the Columbia River. Three years before *Winters*, the Court ruled that the tribes' treaty right "to take fish in common with the citizens of the territory" meant that tribal fisherman could not be excluded from privately-owned uplands, the crossing of which was necessary for them to access their historic salmon fishing grounds. The Court referred to the treaty fishing right as creating "a servitude" on private lands, providing the tribes what amounted to an easement. See Michael C. Blumm & James Brunberg, *"Not Much Less Necessary . . . Than the Atmosphere They Breathed": Salmon, Indian Treaties, and the Supreme Court—A Centennial Remembrance of* United States v. Winans *and Its Enduring Significance*, 46 Nat. Resources J. 489 (2006).

3. *Federal reserved water rights.* A federal reserved water right constitutes property, not just from the time the right is quantified, but from the time the reservation is created. The right arises on the date of the reservation and continues to exist even if it has not been asserted. The most

comprehensive analysis of federal reserved water rights is Brett Birdsong, *Federal Reserved Water Rights,* in 2 *Waters and Water Rights,* ch. 37 (Amy L. Kelley ed., 3d ed., 2014 ed.).

4.   *Equal footing.* The non-Indian irrigators in *Winters* raised the equal footing doctrine to assert (correctly, for the most part) that title to submerged lands vested in the state of Montana when it joined the union. With that ownership of submerged lands, they claimed, came state control of the water flowing in the rivers, which meant that the states had full power to allocate all the water. The equal footing doctrine—that is, the constitutional provision that new states enter the Union on an equal footing with the earlier states— was first explained by the Supreme Court in *Pollard v. Hagan,* 44 U.S. 212 (1845), where the Court concluded that new states at statehood gained ownership of the beds of navigable waters—just as the original thirteen states gained ownership from the King of England—and that during territorial status the federal government owned these lands in trust for future states until the territory became a state. However, equal footing is not absolute; there are exceptions. For example, in *Shively v. Bowlby,* 152 U.S. 1, 49–50 (1894), the Supreme Court stated that pre-statehood grants were valid where necessary to meet public exigencies or international obligations. In the case of Indian lands reserved by treaty, such lands were never owned by the federal government, and thus titles to them could not be passed from the federal government to the new states.

5.   *The* Klamath *controversy.* Reserved water rights have been at the center of a long-running controversy between non-Indian irrigators with federal water contracts and the Klamath Tribes in southern Oregon. See Holly D. Doremus & A. Dan Tarlock, *Water War in the Klamath Basin: Macho Law, Combat Biology, and Dirty Politics* (2008). The Ninth Circuit held that the tribes had "time immemorial" reserved water rights to hunt and fish, even though their reservation had been disestablished, in *United States v. Adair,* 723 F.2d 1394 (9th Cir. 1983); the same court ruled, in *United States v. Oregon,* 657 F.2d 1009 (9th Cir. 1981), that the state and its courts would determine the scope of those rights. The state finally did that in 2013, in *Klamath River Basin General Stream Adjudication,* Findings of Fact and Order of Determination (Oregon Water Resources Dept., March 7, 2013, available at http://www.oregon.gov/owrd/ADJ/docs/7_Findings_of_Fact _and_Order_of_Determination.pdf), in a result that was surprisingly favorable to the tribes. The tribes have since used their senior water rights (mostly instream flow rights to protect fisheries) to curtail upstream non-Indian junior irrigators. In 2014, the state and the tribes agreed to a settlement, but that agreement requires for implementation federal funding that is uncertain.

6.   *Non-Indian reserved water rights.* In *Arizona v. California,* 373 U.S. 546 (1963), the Supreme Court ruled that the reserved water rights doctrine applied not just to land reservations for Indian tribes, but to other lands which the federal government had set aside (reserved) for specific federal purposes such as national forests and wildlife refuges. At the time of each

such land reservation, water was also reserved by Congress, implicitly, on the date of the land reservation. The quantity of water thus reserved was the amount needed to meet the designated purposes of the federal land reservation.

As federal agencies began asserting their reserved water rights, they often created havoc in Western water law regimes. The priority dates of their water rights were sometimes quite early, which meant that the federal rights were interjected in the temporal priority lines of various rivers ahead of many other water rights holders. This disruption of longstanding assumptions about the stability of senior water rights was troubling enough. Even worse, the federal claims were not quantified in any specific way. Junior users did not know how many how many cubic feet per second, or acre feet per year, were needed to meet the water needs, for instance, of a particular national park or national forest. And given the sovereign immunity of the federal government, they could not file suit against a federal agency to force it to quantify its vague water rights claim. (The federal government can be forced to quantify its water rights in a general or whole-stream adjudication, but not in one-on-one litigation in state courts.)

For an assessment of the continuing significance of *Arizona v. California*, see Lawrence J. MacDonnell, Arizona v. California *Revisited*, 52 Nat. Res. J. 363 (2012). The Court applied the principle that reserved rights applied to non-Indian reservations in the following case.

CAPPAERT V. UNITED STATES

Supreme Court of the United States
426 U.S. 128 (1976)

[Devil's Hole, Nevada, is a deep limestone cavern on federal lands with an underground pool home to a unique species of desert fish. In 1952, President Truman declared the site a national monument under the American Antiquities Preservation Act, a statute that authorizes the President to proclaim national monuments to preserve "objects of historic or scientific interest" on federal lands. The Cappaerts owned a nearby ranch and were pumping groundwater to irrigate their ranch, reducing the water level of Devil's Hole and endangering its fish. The Cappaerts filed an application to change their use from several of their wells. The National Park Service protested the proposed change on the ground that the pumping interfered with the federal waters reserved for Devil's Hole. The state engineer denied the protest but the federal district court, reviewing the matter, agreed with the Park Service and enjoined new groundwater pumping. The Ninth Circuit affirmed, and the Supreme Court agreed to review the case to consider whether the reserved water rights doctrine included implied federal reservations of groundwater.]

BURGER, C.J.

The question presented in this litigation is whether the reservation of Devil's Hole as a national monument reserved federal water rights in unappropriated water.

* * *

The 1952 Proclamation notes that Death Valley was set aside as a national monument "for the preservation of the unusual features of scenic, scientific, and educational interest therein contained." The Proclamation also notes that Devil's Hole is near Death Valley and contains a "remarkable underground pool." Additional preambulary statements in the Proclamation explain why Devil's Hole was being added to the Death Valley National Monument [including that the "pool is of such outstanding scientific importance that it should be given special protection, and such protection can be best afforded by making the said forty-acre tract containing the pool a part of the said monument."

The Proclamation provides that Devil's Hole should be supervised, managed, and directed by the National Park Service, Department of the Interior. Devil's Hole is fenced off, and only limited access is allowed by the Park Service.

The Cappaert petitioners own a 12,000-acre ranch near Devil's Hole, 4,000 acres of which are used for growing Bermuda grass, alfalfa, wheat, and barley; 1,700 to 1,800 head of cattle are grazed. The ranch represents an investment of more than $7 million; it employs more than 80 people with an annual payroll of more than $340,000.

In 1968 the Cappaerts began pumping groundwater on their ranch on land 2 ½ miles from Devil's Hole; they were the first to appropriate groundwater. The groundwater comes from an underground basin or aquifer which is also the source of the water in Devil's Hole. After the Cappaerts began pumping from the wells near Devil's Hole, which they do from March to October, the summer water level of the pool in Devil's Hole began to decrease. Since 1962 the level of water in Devil's Hole has been measured with reference to a copper washer installed on one of the walls of the hole by the United States Geological Survey. Until 1968, the water level, with seasonable variations, had been stable at 1.2 feet below the copper marker. In 1969 the water level in Devil's Hole was 2.3 feet below the copper washer; in 1970, 3.17 feet; in 1971, 3.48 feet; and, in 1972, 3.93 feet.

When the water is at the lowest levels, a large portion of a rock shelf in Devil's Hole is above water. However, when the water level is at 3.0 feet below the marker or higher, most of the rock shelf is below water, enabling algae to grow on it. This in turn enables the desert fish (*cyprinodon diabolis*, commonly known as Devil's Hole pupfish), referred to in President Truman's Proclamation, to spawn in the spring. As the rock shelf becomes exposed, the spawning area is decreased, reducing the ability of the fish to spawn in sufficient quantities to prevent extinction.

* * *

Reserved-Water-Rights Doctrine

This Court has long held that when the Federal Government withdraws its land from the public domain and reserves it for a federal purpose, the Government, by implication, reserves appurtenant water then unappropriated to the extent needed to accomplish the purpose of the reservation. In so doing the United States acquires a reserved right in unappropriated water which vests on the date of the reservation and is superior to the rights of future appropriators. Reservation of water rights is empowered by the Commerce Clause, Art. I, § 8, which permits federal regulation of navigable streams, and the Property Clause, Art. IV, § 3, which permits federal regulation of federal lands. The doctrine applies to Indian reservations and other federal enclaves, encompassing water rights in navigable and nonnavigable streams.

Nevada argues that the cases establishing the doctrine of federally reserved water rights articulate an equitable doctrine calling for a balancing of competing interests. However, an examination of those cases shows they do not analyze the doctrine in terms of a balancing test. For example, in *Winters v. United States*, the Court did not mention the use made of the water by the upstream landowners in sustaining an injunction barring their diversions of the water. The "Statement of the Case" in *Winters* notes that the upstream users were homesteaders who had invested heavily in dams to divert the water to irrigate their land, not an unimportant interest. The Court held that when the Federal Government reserves land, by implication it reserves water rights sufficient to accomplish the purposes of the reservation.

In determining whether there is a federally reserved water right implicit in a federal reservation of public land, the issue is whether the Government intended to reserve unappropriated and thus available water. Intent is inferred if the previously unappropriated waters are necessary to accomplish the purposes for which the reservation was created. See, e.g., *Arizona v. California*, 373 U.S. at 599–601; *Winters v. United States*, 207 U.S. at 576. Both the District Court and the Court of Appeals held that the 1952 Proclamation expressed an intention to reserve unappropriated water, and we agree. The Proclamation discussed the pool in Devil's Hole in four of the five preambles and recited that the "pool . . . should be given special protection." Since a pool is a body of water, the protection contemplated is meaningful only if the water remains; the water right reserved by the 1952 Proclamation was thus explicit, not implied.

Also explicit in the 1952 Proclamation is the authority of the Director of the Park Service to manage the lands of Devil's Hole Monument "as provided in the act of Congress entitled 'An Act to establish a National Park Service, and for other purposes,' approved August 25, 1916 (39 Stat. 535; 16 U.S.C. §§ 1–3). . . ." The National Park Service Act provides that the "fundamental purpose of the said parks, monuments, and reservations" is "to conserve the scenery and the natural and historic objects and the wild life therein and to provide for the enjoyment of the same in such manner and by such means as will leave them unimpaired for the enjoyment of future generations." 39 Stat. 535, 16 U.S.C. § 1.

The implied-reservation-of-water-rights doctrine, however, reserves only that amount of water necessary to fulfill the purpose of the reservation, no more. *Arizona v. California*, 373 U.S. at 600–601. Here the purpose of reserving Devil's Hole Monument is preservation of the pool. Devil's Hole was reserved "for the preservation of the unusual features of scenic, scientific, and educational interest." The Proclamation notes that the pool contains "a peculiar race of desert fish . . . which is found nowhere else in the world" and that the "pool is of . . . outstanding scientific importance . . ." The pool need only be preserved, consistent with the intention expressed in the Proclamation, to the extent necessary to preserve its scientific interest. The fish are one of the features of scientific interest. The preamble noting the scientific interest of the pool follows the preamble describing the fish as unique; the Proclamation must be read in its entirety. Thus, as the District Court has correctly determined, the level of the pool may be permitted to drop to the extent that the drop does not impair the scientific value of the pool as the natural habitat of the species sought to be preserved. The District Court thus tailored its injunction, very appropriately, to minimal need, curtailing pumping only to the extent necessary to preserve an adequate water level at Devil's Hole, thus implementing the stated objectives of the Proclamation.

Petitioners in both cases argue that even if the intent of the 1952 Proclamation were to maintain the pool, the American Antiquities Preservation Act did not give the President authority to reserve a pool. Under that Act, according to the Cappaert petitioners, the President may reserve federal lands only to protect archeologic sites. However, the language of the Act which authorizes the President to proclaim as national monuments "historic landmarks, historic and prehistoric structures, and other objects of historic or scientific interest that are situated upon the lands owned or controlled by the Government" is not so limited. The pool in Devil's Hole and its rare inhabitants are "objects of historic or scientific interest." See generally *Cameron v. United States*, 252 U.S. 450, 455–56 (1920).

Groundwater

No cases of this Court have applied the doctrine of implied reservation of water rights to groundwater. Nevada argues that the implied-reservation doctrine is limited to surface water. Here, however, the water in the pool is surface water. The federal water rights were being depleted because, as the evidence showed, the "[g]roundwater and surface water are physically interrelated as integral parts of the hydrologic cycle." Here the Cappaerts are causing the water level in Devil's Hole to drop by their heavy pumping. It appears that Nevada itself may recognize the potential interrelationship between surface and groundwater since Nevada applies the law of prior appropriation to both. Nev. Rev. Stat. §§ 533.010 *et seq.*, 534.020, 534.080, 534.090 (1973). Thus, since the implied-reservation-of-water-rights doctrine is based on the necessity of water for the purpose of the federal reservation, we hold that the United States can protect its water from subsequent diversion, whether the diversion is of surface or groundwater.

* * *

We hold, therefore, that as of 1952 when the United States reserved Devil's Hole, it acquired by reservation water rights in unappropriated appurtenant water sufficient to maintain the level of the pool to preserve its scientific value and thereby implement Proclamation No. 2961. Accordingly, the judgment of the Court of Appeals is affirmed.

NOTES

1. *Water rights on federal government lands.* In *United States v. New Mexico*, 438 U.S. 696 (1978), the Supreme Court significantly curtailed the scope of federal reserved water rights by concluding that Congress implicitly reserved, in the instance of each land reservation, only sufficient water to meet the *primary* purposes of the land reservation, not to meet less important purposes. In the important case of land reserved for national forests, the primary purposes, the Court ruled, were only timber production and watershed protection. They did not include protection of fish and other aquatic life or recreation. This ruling limited the water rights of the largest category of the federal government's reserved lands.

An even greater limitation on federal reserved water rights came when a federal appellate court ruled that the vast landholdings of the Bureau of Land Management were not reserved lands for water purposes, *Sierra Club v. Watt*, 659 F.2d 203 (D.C. Cir. 1981) To acquire water for use on BLM lands federal managers must obtain the water in accordance with the water law of the state in which the lands are located. As *Cappaert* stated, lands in the National Park System are supported by extensive reserved water rights, as are the many landholdings of the Fish and Wildlife Service.

2. *The Black Canyon of the Gunnison case.* In *High Country Citizens' Alliance v. Norton,* 448 F.Supp.2d 1235 (D. Colo. 2006), the federal government entered into an agreement with the state of Colorado under which it relinquished a portion of the federal reserved rights to Black Canyon of the Gunnison National Park (part of which was a designated wilderness). The relinquished water rights had a priority date of 1933, leaving the government to seek new rights that would have a priority date of 2003— rights that would be subordinate to all appropriations acquired between 1933 and 2003. Recognizing that "the value of this property is its priority," the federal district court invalidated the agreement on the basis that the federal defendants had "unlawfully disposed of federal property without Congressional authorization." *Id.* at 1248. The court also concluded that the government had violated "nondiscretionary duties to protect the Black Canyon's resources," explaining that "the National Park Service has a legal obligation to protect the resources of national parks." *Id.* at 1248, 1250. Although the court relied on the National Park Service Organic Act of 1916 and the Wilderness Act of 1964 to impose an affirmative federal duty of protection—without mentioning the public trust doctrine—the results are comparable to what a federal public trust doctrine would accomplish: findings that: 1) the settlement unlawfully delegated federal decision-making authority to the state; 2) the government unlawfully disposed of federal property (reserved water rights) without congressional authorization; and 3) the government violated nondiscretionary duties. See Reed D. Benson, *A Bright Idea from Black Canyon: Federal Judicial Review of Reserved Water Rights Settlements,* 13 U.Denver Water L. Rev. 229 (2010).

CHAPTER 7

FOREST RESOURCES

■ ■ ■

Natural resources legal and policy professionals interested in forest management have tended to focus almost entirely on federally owned forests and to discount or ignore private forests. Yet federal forests make up only 35 percent of the nation's forestland. Of the remaining 65 percent of forests in "subnational" ownership, state governments own 5 percent and private landowners 60 percent. *See* U.N. Environment Programme, *Global Environment Outlook 3: Past, Present and Future Perspectives* 110 (2002), http://www.unep.org/geo/GEO3/english/pdf.htm. This chapter focuses on these often-overlooked private forests, shedding light on the chief property-related conflicts over them and introducing the overarching governance contexts within which these conflicts occur. Federally owned forests are best considered in the context of a broader study of federal lands management, taken up in chapter 8 of this book.

A. THE IMPORTANCE OF FOREST RESOURCES[1]

The U.S. alone contains nearly 8 percent of the world's total forest cover (of the world's approximately four billion hectares of forest, the United States maintains 302 million hectares. Jacek P. Siry et al., XIII World Forestry Congress, *Global Forest Ownership: Implications for Forest Production, Management, and Protection* 3 tbl.1 (2009)). Although forests have historically been thought of as a quintessentially local resource—anchored to the land of individual property owners—the national and global importance of local forests is becoming ever more apparent. Consider the variety of services that forests provide on local scales:

- a renewable source of building materials and associated jobs;
- a renewable source of paper products and associated jobs;
- a renewable source of energy in the form of biofuel;
- clean air services that filter and trap air pollutants;

---

[1] Portions of the following sections are excerpted from earlier drafts of Blake Hudson, *Dynamic Forest Federalism*, 71 Washington and Lee Law Review (forthcoming 2014).

- clean water services that prevent nutrient, chemical, and other non-point pollution run-off from entering waterways;

- protection of fisheries by mitigating run-off pollution that leads to "dead zones" in water bodies where fish cannot survive;

- flood control services;

- important habitat for diverse species;

- regulation of local ambient air temperatures in urban and rural areas;

- energy cost savings for households and businesses;

- aesthetic, spiritual, and cultural values; and

- recreational values.

See United States Department of Agriculture, Forest Service, *Ecosystem Services*, http://www.fs.fed.us/ecosystemservices/.

The role of forests as a global climate regulator and major carbon sink or source has assumed increasing prominence. Nearly 20 percent of yearly global carbon emissions in recent decades have resulted from forest loss and degradation, an amount greater than that emitted by the global transportation sector each year. *See* Erin C. Myers, *Policies to Reduce Emissions From Deforestation and Degradation (REDD)* in Tropical Forests, Resources For The Future 6 (2007), http://www.rff.org/documents/RFF–DP–07–50.pdf. As a result, mechanisms to protect forests globally are on the agenda of international climate negotiations.

Indeed, the issue of climate change has largely subsumed previous stand-alone negotiations related to establishing a global sustainable forest management regime. *See* United Nations Forum on Forests, http://www.un.org/esa/forests/. Not only is forest destruction a substantial *source* of atmospheric carbon, but a recent U.S. Forest Service report found that one-third of global carbon emissions are absorbed by forests each year, making forests the most significant terrestrial carbon sink on the planet., USDA Forest Service, *US Forest Service Finds Global Forests Absorb One-Third of Carbon Emissions Annually* (News Release, July 14, 2011), http://www.fs.fed.us/news/releases/us-forest-service-finds-global-forests-absorb-one-third-carbon-emissions-annually. As a result, forest preservation has a multiplier effect on greenhouse gas regulation and, correspondingly, forest destruction doubly amplifies concentrations of carbon in the atmosphere, since deforestation is both a source of carbon and the loss of a significant carbon sink.

B. THE FOREST REGULATORY AND MANAGEMENT FRAMEWORK

How exactly are U.S. privately-held forests managed, and what policy tools might be employed in their management? The 35 percent of forests in federal ownership are largely managed by the U.S. federal government (although states, as we have seen, play key roles in managing water and wildlife in them), and of course state governments manage the small percentage of forests in state ownership. American law has long considered private forest regulation a subject for state and local government regulatory action. *See* Jan G. Laitos et al., *Natural Resources Law* 849 (1st ed. 2006); Gerald A. Rose et al., *Forest Resources Decision-Making in the U.S.*, in The Politics of Decentralization: Forests, People and Power 238, 238–239 (Carol J. Pierce Colfer & Doris Capistrano eds., 2005) (stating that "[u]nder the US Constitution, the federal government has limited authority and responsibility; all other powers are reserved for the states. Forestland management and use was one such reserved power."). As a result, the management of private forests has been traditionally categorized within the body of zoning regulations and other local government regulatory spheres. While some may argue that the federal government cannot prescribe regulations within those spheres due to principles of constitutional federalism, at the very least, private forest management is an area where federal intrusion typically generates sharp political opposition. Notions of subnational control over forests stem from the concept of "dual federalism," which regards state and local governments as maintaining exclusive constitutional authority to regulate land use generally through their zoning and other police powers. Courts continue to declare that land use planning is the "quintessential state and local government activity." *See Rapanos v. United States*, 547 U.S. 715, 738 (2006) (excerpted in chapter 3, p. 224).

Recent legal controversies illustrate the resistance of subnational entities to federal involvement in private forest policy. For example, the Supreme Court case, *Decker* v. *Northwest Environmental Defense Center*, 133 S.Ct. 1326 (2013) involved a dispute over whether private foresters were required to receive a permit from the Environmental Protection Agency (EPA) under the Clean Water Act (CWA) for stormwater discharged from ditches along logging roads. In an amicus brief, the National Governors Association, National Association of Counties, National Conference of State Legislatures, International City/County Management Association, and Council of State Governments argued that such a requirement was unlawful because, among other things, the forest management activities in question were "traditionally regulated by state and local governments under their own laws." Brief for the National Governor's Association et al. as Amicus Curiae, *Decker* v. *Northwest Environmental Defense Center*, 133 S.Ct. 1326 (2013), at 15, http://www.

americanbar.org/content/dam/aba/publications/supreme_court_preview/
briefs/11–338_petitioneramcungaetal.authcheckdam.pdf. Moreover, this
coalition of subnational government organizations noted that "[the U.S.
Supreme] Court has held that the Constitution's Commerce Clause, U.S.
Const. art. I, § 8, cl. 3, limits Congress' power to enact laws that
'effectually obliterate the distinction between what is national and what
is local. . . .' " *Id.* at 17. The *Decker* case is a particularly lucid example of
how jealously subnational governments protect their forest management
authority, even if it means (in this instance) resisting federal regulation
(the CWA) aimed at managing an entirely different natural resource
(water).

It is true that the federal government maintains regulatory
mechanisms that may implicate private forest management activities,
such as the CWA and the Endangered Species Act. If a private forest
manager has an endangered species on her property or is discharging
sediment pollution from conveyances meeting the definition of a point
source under the CWA, these federal Acts may have a significant effect on
forest management activities. The federal government also maintains a
number of non-prescriptive, incentive-based programs that might be
employed to influence the management of private forests. *See* United
States Department of Agriculture, Forest Service, *Forest Legacy Program:
Protecting Private Forest Lands from Conversion to Non-Forest Uses*
http://www.fs.fed.us/spf/coop/programs/loa/aboutflp.shtml; Environmental
Easement Program, 16 U.S.C. § 3839 (2012); Conservation Stewardship
Program, United States Department of Agriculture, Natural Resources
Conservation Service, http://www.nrcs.usda.gov/wps/portal/nrcs/main/
national/programs/financial/csp; Healthy Forests Reserve Program,
United States Department of Agriculture, Natural Resources
Conservation Service, http://www.nrcs.usda.gov/wps/portal/nrcs/main/
national/programs/easements/forests. The federal government's role in
influencing private forest policy has remained extremely limited to date,
however.

So, what are states doing to facilitate management of private forests?
States are all over the board concerning their forest policies. As discussed
in the next section, a number of states maintain holistic prescriptive
regulations for private forests, protecting them not as a source of discrete
commodities but as complex biological communities. On the other end of
the spectrum are many states that maintain no prescriptive (or other)
regulation of private forest management, relying instead on voluntary
"best management practices" (BMPs). Before exploring these differences
in state policy, it is useful to review the two primary ways in which
forests can be managed and the types of forest management policy options
available to state and local governments.

1. METHODS OF MANAGING FORESTS: TIMBER EXTRACTION AND FOREST PRESERVATION

The first method of managing forests is to control how timber is cultivated and harvested so as to sustain timber flows and other economic and environmental goods and services. Management standards are important to regulate the effects of timbering on water, carbon, and other environmental resources and on the ability of forest lands to grow more trees. As described in the next subpart, this type of management involves crafting standards related to riparian buffer zones, stand density, afforestation/reforestation, clear-cutting, annual allowable cut, forest road building, controlled burning, fertilizer usage, among other standards. Many private forest operators, of course, implement these standards as best practices, but many may not in the absence of governmental regulatory standards.

The second primary method for managing forests entails policies that simply keep forests forested. These policies aim to prevent forested lands—whether used for timber production or for environmental services—from being replaced by industrial, residential, commercial, agricultural, or other developed uses. These policies may tip the scales toward primarily protecting the environmental goods and services provided by forests, rather than primarily emphasizing the extractive value of the resource—a more pure form of forest preservation. Even so, extractive timber operations may also occur on these lands, either intensively or selectively in order to balance timber extraction with other values such as carbon, biodiversity, or water quality protection. The primary means of achieving these management goals is through direct land use controls, such as the establishment of development density requirements, the use of urban growth boundaries or development "limit lines," or other outright restrictions or qualifications on the removal of forest acreage or even on the removal of individual trees.

2. FOREST MANAGEMENT POLICY OPTIONS

Forest policy, whether at the federal or state level, can be situated along a spectrum—depicted in Figure 1, below—based on the level of forest policy stringency and on the range of forest values protected. The scope of forest management standards can vary from virtually non-existent (in many states), to very basic (focusing primarily on timber extraction and fundamental silvicultural practices), to those fostering the full range of values provided by forests, including climate mitigation. Forest-management standard stringency might range from voluntary guidelines, to incentive-based programs, to prescriptive regulation. None of these, of course, are mutually exclusive and may overlap to a significant degree.

Thus, on one end of the spectrum is a policy of maintaining no policies at all for many or all categories of forest management, either through direct regulatory standard-setting or incentive provision. Next are voluntary procedural or substantive forest guidelines, whereby governments provide forest owners with information regarding suggested procedures (such as management plans or environmental impact assessment methods) or suggested substantive standards (which may range from basic timber extraction standards to standards related to the full scope of forest values). Farther along the spectrum are programs aimed at promoting, through monetary incentives or otherwise, voluntary forest management efforts that capture a range of values: from the very basic, timber extraction-centric forest standards to more robust standards related to carbon sequestration and forest ecosystem functions, including biodiversity.

Figure 1

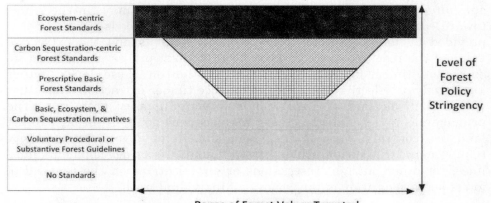

Still farther along the spectrum are prescriptive "basic" forest management regulatory standards that are fundamental for effective timber production. Such standards primarily focus on maximizing value from timber extraction, although they can also provide co-benefits, such as watershed protection and erosion control. These standards include (but are not limited to) five primary types of standards.

- First, *riparian streamside buffer zones* in forested watersheds prevent erosion that might interfere with timber production, prevent sedimentation of waterways, provide wildlife corridors, regulate water temperatures, and protect aquatic habitat.

- Second, *forest road standards* address the problems associated with road building, described as "one of the 'main causes [of] the environmental degradation of most forest regions'." Constance L. McDermott et al., *Global Environmental Forest Policies: An International Comparison* 16 (2010). Forest roads provide access for resource extraction and potential over-exploitation, cause erosion that damages watersheds, and lead to fragmentation of forest landscapes and habitat. As a result, decommissioning roads, limiting their location, reducing their extent, and placing limitations on culvert size at stream crossings are important forest management objectives.

- Third, *clearcut standards* aim to address "perhaps the most controversial forest harvesting practice[s]"—clearcutting— which, depending on how it is done, has been criticized by ecologists, civil society, and forest-market scholars alike. *Id.* at 18. Clearcutting effectively involves a complete removal and replacement of the forest, which cannot only impact long term forest productivity, but can also interfere with a variety of other ecological processes. Limiting clearcut size can avoid these negative effects.

- The final two forest management standards are *reforestation standards*, which specify time frames for replanting or achieving stocking levels, and *annual allowable cut standards*, which implement cut limits based on sustained yield. These standards are intended to keep harvesting to sustainable levels.

Moving along the spectrum beyond basic forest management standards are *carbon sequestration-centric standards* that are inclusive of protections provided by basic standards, but which are also aimed at maximizing carbon potential of forests (i.e., more robust clear-cutting prohibitions or stand density requirements than basic standards). Although these carbon-focused standards capture more values than basic standards, they may do so by prescribing practices that diminish other forest values, such as biodiversity and overall ecosystem functionality. Indeed, one concern in the climate change context is the replacement of ecologically functional and richly biodiverse forests with monoculture plantations of forests aimed at sequestering as much carbon as possible over short time scales. See Raquel Nunez Mutter & Winnie Overbeek, *The Great Lie: Monoculture Trees as Forests*, United Nations Research Institute for Social Development, Oct. 20, 2011, at http://www.unrisd.org; Kristin B. Hulvey, et al., *Benefits of Tree Mixes in Carbon Plantings*, 3 Nature Climate Change 869 (2013).

Last on the spectrum are *ecosystem-centric forest standards* that focus on ecosystem functionality by balancing a wide range of values, such as protection of biodiversity, species habitat, ecosystems, genetic resources, recreational and cultural values, and the provision of water purification, flood prevention, air quality regulation, and even timber commodity services. These standards basically amount to forest preservation standards, although they may allow selective cutting or controlled burns to, for example, prevent the buildup of fuel that may later result in a catastrophic fire.

Some degree of management may also be necessary because it is unclear whether a pure form of forest preservation maximizes forest carbon to the greatest degree possible if it occurs to such a degree that forest "succession" or natural fire events cease and the forest becomes carbon saturated and unable to sequester additional amounts of CO_2. Brian Finegan, *Forest Succession,* 321 Nature 109 (1984). It was long thought that saturation may exist in old-growth forests where human interference with natural processes (like fire) prevents regeneration of new, productive forest ecosystems that sequester even greater amounts of carbon from the atmosphere. Recently, however, scientific studies shed doubt on the idea that older, pristinely preserved forests are less productive at sequestering carbon. Bettina Boxall, *Big, Old Trees Keep Growing and Capturing Carbon, Study Finds*, Los Angeles Times, January 15, 2014; N. L. Stephenson et al., *Rate of Tree Carbon Accumulation Increases Continuously With Tree Size*, Nature, January 15, 2014. As a result, it may well be that simple forest preservation would maximize both carbon sequestration capabilities and capture the many other ecological values provided by forests; no tradeoff between them is needed. Regardless, even with pure, ecosystem-centric forest preservation standards it seems that some form of forest management may be needed to balance the full range of forest values, from carbon sequestration, to timber commodities, to biodiversity and other resource protections. In addition, not all forest ecosystems are the same, and so the broadest, ecosystem-centric forest preservation standards in one region of the country may look very different from those in another part of the country.

C. VARIABILITY AMONG U.S. STATE FOREST POLICIES

How do U.S. state forest policies differ from management of federal forests and from each other? To get a sense of the answer, let us first place U.S. state policies within a larger framework of assessment. Ben Cashore, Constance McDermott & Peter Kanowski have provided a framework for assessing and comparing the domestic forest policies of governments around the globe. *See* Constance L. McDermott et al., *Global Environmental Forest Policies: An International Comparison* 16 (2010).

Their study focuses primarily on the basic timber extraction policies highlighted above and does not expressly cover forest preservation. Even so, it supplies a useful tool for exploring the considerable variations among state policies. McDermott et al. identified four "styles" of forest policy regulation (*See id.* at 10):

1) Voluntary Procedural: *encourages* the voluntary development of forest management processes or plans, but does not require such plans to be developed;

2) Mandatory Procedural: *requires* the development of forest management plans or procedures;

3) Voluntary Substantive: *establishes* specific forest practice guidelines but without mandating their use; and

4) Mandatory Substantive: *imposes* forest-management requirements or restrictions, such as a rule that "no timber harvest may occur within x feet of a river of y width." These rules are, of course, legally enforceable and may be imposed when enforcement resources are available and the will to enforce exists.

In their important study, McDermott et al. used these four categories or styles of management to evaluate how stringently particular governments managed their forests. For each government analyzed, they looked at five types of forest-policy standards. For each standard, they evaluated a government relative to the management style it used (of the four outlined above) and based on particular indicators of how well the government achieved the standard's purpose or goal. The five policy standards that they studied, and the performance indicators associated with each, were as follows:

1) Protection of riparian zones in forested watersheds (*indicator*: riparian streamside buffer zone rules);

2) Protection from environmental damage caused by roads (*indicator*: rules for culvert size at stream crossings and road decommissioning);

3) Protection from clearcutting damage (*indicator*: clearcut size limits or other relevant cutting rules);

4) Reforestation (*indicator*: requirements for reforestation, including specified time frames and stocking levels); and

5) Limitations on annual allowable cut (*indicator*: cut limits based on sustained yield).

The authors then ranked particular governments based on an average of the "style" utilized for each of the five indicators. The consistent use of mandatory approaches placed governments nearer to "10" on the scale (with mandatory substantive the most stringent).

Governments that used voluntary measures or had no policy scored nearer to "0."

The state of California and the U.S. Forest Service (which manages federally owned forests) each scored a "9" on the scale, maintaining very high forest policy standards. The U.S. state of Washington scored a high "8" on the scale, while Oregon scored a "7," Idaho scored a "5," and Alaska scored a "4." Lowest on the scale were the states of Montana with a "2.5," Louisiana and Virginia with a "2," and the entire rest of the southeastern United States—Alabama, Arkansas, Georgia, Mississippi, North Carolina, South Carolina, and Texas—with a score of "1." To provide context for the southeastern U.S. states' level of forest policy stringency, consider that developing countries averaged a "6.7" on the scale while nine southeastern U.S. states averaged a "1.2," maintaining entirely voluntary "guidelines" or no standards at all. *See id.* 327. Of course, a forestry policy that looks sound on paper may not translate into good practices in actual forests: In nations with high scores, on-the-ground performance may be weak due to lax enforcement and widespread violations. In jurisdictions with low regulatory stringency (and thus low scores), large-scale operators may control vast acreages of forests and may manage their lands responsibly as a business matter.

Nonetheless, these rankings indicate that while some U.S. states maintain high forest management standards, others, particularly in the Southeast, maintain no enforceable standards at all. This is in no small part due to the fact that 86 percent of southeastern forests are privately owned. Yet this explanation alone is insufficient, since other states not analyzed by the McDermott survey, like Maine, have fairly stringent forest policies and high degrees of privately owned forests (in Maine, 94 percent of forests are privately owned). Maine Tree Foundation, *Forest Facts, Who Owns Maine's Forest* at www.mainetreefoundation.org. *See* Maine Forest Service Rules and Regulations, Timber Harvesting,; Maine Forest Practices Act,; Maine Forest Practices Act Rules Relating to Forest Regeneration and Clearcutting, all at www.maine.gov.

As noted, the governmental policies studied by the McDermott team were limited to those dealing with timber cultivation and harvesting—the policies categorized earlier as related to timber extraction. When we turn to the second broad category of forest management policies, those aimed directly at preservation (of forests and other associated natural components), we find pretty much the same wide variation in state policies. The use of *urban growth boundaries* is one mechanism that might be employed in this regard, but it is used sparsely across United States. Perhaps the most notable policy of the kind is Portland's urban growth boundary, or those of other Oregon municipalities, like Eugene. *See* Urban Growth Boundary, Oregon Metro, http://www.oregonmetro.gov/urban-growth-boundary.

Mirroring the geographical pattern uncovered by McDermott, states in the southeastern U.S.—where there are far more private landowners and a culture of resistance to government regulation—are less likely to use such policies. Tennessee is the only southern state that requires municipalities to enact growth boundaries. Although this mandate seems to contemplate the reduction of urban sprawl, the policy is primarily aimed at ensuring that growth occurs in the most economically efficient manner possible—which sometimes may continue a pattern of sprawl. *See* Tennessee Advisory Commission on Intergovernmental Relations, Tennessee Growth Policy, http://www.state.tn.us/tacir/growth.html. A handful of southern cities have growth boundaries as well, with Lexington, Kentucky's perhaps the most effective from an environmental perspective. *See* University of Delaware, *A Coastal Community Enhancement Initiative, Urban Growth Boundary (UGB)/Urban Services Boundary (USB)*, http://www.scc.udel.edu/sites/default/files/urbangrowth boundary.pdf. Other southern cities with purported growth boundaries, such as Miami, may be more concerned simply with controlling how land is inevitably developed than in halting land development that threatens forests and other resources. *See* Patricia Mazzei, *Miami-Dade commissioners expand Urban Development Boundary*, Miami Herald, Oct. 3, 2013. While it is important to control how land may be inevitably developed—to ensure that development is well-planned—the process of ever-expanding development itself needs to come to an end. More stringent growth boundary controls are required to make that happen.

Even without the use of urban growth boundaries, some state and local governments maintain policies to protect forestlands beyond focusing only on extractive values. For example, The Maryland Forest Conservation Act promotes *overall forest cover* by requiring that all counties in the State with less than 200,000 acres of forest cover adopt a forest-conservation ordinance. Md. Code Ann., Nat. Res. §§ 5–1601 to 1612. Washington County, Maryland maintains a Forest Conservation Ordinance pursuant to this state policy setting out a county-wide plan for forest preservation. *See* Forest Conservation Ordinance, Washington County, Maryland: Department of Planning and Zoning, http://www. washco-md.net/planning/forest.shtm. Some cities even maintain *tree preservation* ordinances, such as Tallahassee, Florida, as highlighted at the end of this chapter. *See* Leon County, Florida's Environmental Management Act, Chapter 10, Land Development Code (LDC), at http://cms.leoncountyfl.gov.

D. THREATS TO U.S. FORESTS— A SOUTHEASTERN CASE STUDY

The wide variability among both state timber-extraction and forest-preservation standards has stark implications for forest resources in the

United States. A recent U.S. Forest Service report highlighted that southeastern forests in particular face serious threats over the next 50 years. The Forest Service projects that southeastern U.S. states alone may lose up to 13 percent of their forests due to urbanization, population growth, invasive species, and climate change by 2060. *See* David N. Wear & John G. Greis, U.S. Forest Serv., *The Southern Forest Futures Project: Summary Report* 35 (2011), at www.srs.fs.usda.gov. For perspective, these 23 million acres of forestland would equal all of the forests in the state of Georgia. The report studied thirteen states, including Virginia, North Carolina, South Carolina, Georgia, Florida, Alabama, Tennessee, Kentucky, Mississippi, Arkansas, Louisiana, Oklahoma and Texas.

The Futures Report highlighted that urban development is "forecasted to result in forest losses, increased carbon emissions, and stress to other forest resources," including degradation of a variety of water ecosystem services such as flood control and water filtration—even to the point of threatening public health. *Id.* at 4. Population pressures in the Southeast would "result[ ] in declines in forest cover, increases in demand for ecosystem service[s], and restrictions that complicate the ability to manage forests for the full spectrum of uses." *Id.* at 26. Importantly, both population and economic growth have increased at higher rates in the Southeast than anywhere else in the United States, "with the resulting urbanization steadily consuming forests and other rural lands." *Id.* at 5.

Although reforestation of other lands or other intervening factors may mitigate these projections, a new phase of deforestation in the South would be a significant blow to both domestic forest resources and the services they provide as well as to the use of global forests to combat climate change. Further, the negative repercussions of these projections go beyond the environment, since the southeastern U.S. remains the most productive timber-producing region in the nation and has historically been among the most productive in the world. The timber production sector in the South contributed more than one million jobs and fifty-one billion dollars in employee compensation in 2009. *Id.* at 17. In fact, as the Forest Service report determined, "southern forests are the most intensively managed forests in the U.S." *Id.* at 29. A majority of the United States' lumber is harvested from southern forests, and "since 1986, if the South were compared with any other country, none would produce more timber than this one region of the United States." *Id.* at 17.

Forest losses due to rapid urbanization in the South would also affect the carbon storage capacity of southern forests. The amount of carbon sequestered in southern forests and their soils is projected to peak in 2020 and then decline by as much as 5 percent by 2060. Robert Hugget et al., *Forecasts of Forest Conditions*, *in* The Southern Forest Futures Project, Technical Report 17 (2011), http://www.srs.fs.usda.gov/futures/

reports/draft/Frame.htm. This decline in carbon storage capacity "would be a challenge for carbon mitigation policies, presenting a dynamic baseline where a first-order policy objective would be to *stabilize* rather than expand forest carbon stocks." David N. Wear & John G. Greis, U.S. Forest Serv., *The Southern Forest Futures Project: Summary Report* 34 (2011). The decline will increase the chances that southeastern forests may become an even greater *source* of carbon, much less sequester additional amounts of carbon in a way that would mitigate climate change impacts. Using southeastern forests as a more significant carbon sink would be especially difficult, if trends continue, since land use policies facilitating urbanization are also widespread, undermining conservation of southern forests. *See* Blake Hudson, *Federal Constitutions: The Keystone of Nested Commons Governance*, 63 Ala. L. Re. 1007, 1038–50 (2012).

NOTES

1. *A long row to hoe?* In *Decker*, discussed above at p. 591, if representatives of subnational forest interests were so willing to challenge federal regulations under the Clean Water Act—a statute aimed at protecting water quality—we can assume they would challenge any federal effort to manage state and private forests directly by, for instance, regulating clearcutting, stand density, afforestation and reforestation, road building, or forest preservation. How sound is this traditional allocation of regulatory power, given the wide variation in state approaches and the fact that so many states do almost nothing? Are there reasons, grounded in the benefits of decentralized governance, to allow states to vary so much in their forest policies? On the other hand, is more federal involvement needed given climate change, water-quality problems, and other interstate environmental issues? If you agree that states should remain variable in their approach to forest policy, is it acceptable that so many states maintain no forest management controls at all?

2. *Voluntary BMP's.* Alabama's position on voluntary "best management practices" is emblematic of the loose governance philosophy in the southeastern U.S. The Alabama Forestry Commission declared itself the "lead agency for forestry in Alabama" but announces also that it is "not an environmental regulatory or enforcement agency," and that it "[avoids] environmental problems through voluntary application of preventative techniques." McDermott et al., at 82. Yet, as evidenced by the *Futures Report's* projected loss of up to 13 percent of the region's forests over the next fifty years, a continued voluntary stewardship approach seems unlikely to protect the full range of a forest's ecological values. By and large, southeastern state administrative agencies operate pursuant to voluntary BMPs and "[t]he implementation of BMPs . . . generally involves agencies not directly responsible for environmental regulation." *Id.* at 82. The questions posed today are ones that have long been on the table: Will the voluntary

BMP approach lead to good results over time, particularly if greater efforts are made at educating forest owners and operators? Is there a role for economic incentive programs and, to the extent they involve taxpayer money, would these programs be fair to taxpayers? Finally, is it time for more states to follow the lead of California and the U.S. Forest Service and impose more stringent, mandatory controls to halt bad practices?

3. *Forest fragmentation.* One of the difficulties of crafting holistic forest policy in the southeastern U.S. is the degree to which forests are fragmented throughout the region. As noted, 86 percent of southern forests are privately owned, and forest industries and a vast array of non-industrial private forest owners manage privately owned forestlands. Governments in the region typically hesitate to place restrictions on private property rights. While 60 percent of privately owned forests are in tracts of 100 acres or more, 59 percent of private forest owners own fewer than nine acres of forestland, and family forest holdings in the region average only twenty-nine acres in size. *See* David N. Wear & John G. Greis, U.S. Forest Service, *The Southern Forest Futures Project: Summary Report* 62 (2011), http://www.srs.fs.fed.us/ pubs/gtr/gtr_srs168.pdf. How might this extensive fragmentation in forest ownership affect state and local government management efforts?

4. *Public forest policy "spillover effect."* The high number of private property owners in the Southeast correlates strongly with the low level of forest policy stringency adopted by the respective subnational governments. In the West, where the proportions of public forests are far greater (most of it federal), state private forest policy is far more stringent. So, for example, California, Washington, Oregon, Idaho, and Alaska maintain an average 67 percent of forests in public ownership. They embrace far more stringent forest policy standards for both state-owned and private forests (a "6.7" average) than do states in the southeastern United States (a "1.2" average), where 86 percent of forests are privately owned. McDermott et al., at 80 (hypothesizing that this constitutes a forest policy "spillover effect," where proximity to public forests, which tend to be managed more stringently, spills over into private forest management policy). It seems plausible that the U.S. Forest Service's "9" score on the forest policy ranking may have influenced western state forest policy in a way not seen in the Southeast. Southeastern states, according to one analysis:

> simply do[ ] not maintain the critical mass of publicly owned forests that would help facilitate a spillover effect . . . Though other factors, such as overall governance culture and the limited administrative capacity of southeastern governments, may also contribute to the region's lax standards, it seems that the lack of a spillover effect further exacerbates continuation of the status quo.

Blake Hudson, *Fail-safe Federalism and Climate Change: The Case of U.S. and Canadian Forest Policy*, 44 Conn. L. Rev. 925, 966 (2012).

The lack of publicly owned forests in southeastern states is an institutional issue that is difficult to change (even if it were desirable to do so, which it may not be). Given this reality, how might better forest related policy-making come about in the southeastern U.S.? As noted earlier, the state of Maine has been quite successful in effectively managing forests in the presence of a high degree of private ownership.

5.   *What to do in the absence of forest policies?: enter the common law.* One might ask what options a landowner has in the event that a neighboring forest owner engages in forest-management operations that damage the landowner's property. Say landowner B cuts timber to the edge of a stream that serves as the boundary shared with landowner A. In states with riparian buffer zone requirements, landowner A can report the violation to the appropriate agency. The agency might take action, curbing the damaging behavior. But what if a state only maintains voluntary BMPs, leaving landowners free to act as they see fit? Landowner A may look to the common law, and could perhaps bring a nuisance claim against landowner B if damages result (such as erosion leading to economic losses of timber). Is it sufficient to rely on common law doctrines like nuisance? What would landowner A need to prove to succeed on such a claim? What other limitations might landowner A face that would make the availability of such a claim ineffectual as a tool for managing forest resources? (See pp. 20–23, 66–72), on public and private nuisance, and *Washington v. Gillette* in chapter 4 (p. 280), on the power of states as trustee owners of wildlife to protect streams and aquatic life from streamside degradation.)

E. STATE TIMBER MANAGEMENT REGULATIONS

In the following cases, consider how states have used regulatory tools to shape the management of forests on private properties.

DEPARTMENT OF NATURAL RESOURCES V. MARR
Washington Court of Appeals
774 P.2d 1260 (Wash. App. 1989)

PEKELIS, J.

* * *

The relevant facts in this case are not in dispute. At issue is the scope of the Forest Practices Act (FPA) and the correct interpretation of certain provisions of the Act.

Bob Marr obtained a permit from the Department of Natural Resources (DNR) to log a 20 acre parcel of land, and at the same time obtained a permit to log a contiguous residential lot. With the permission of the landowners but without complying with the notification and application provisions of the FPA, Marr also commenced logging operations on nine nearby residential lots. These lots had been zoned residential for over 40 years and varied in size from 1/10th of an acre to 1 ¾ acres.

In response to a citizen complaint, Bernard Strachila, a DNR official responsible for enforcing the FPA, inspected the site of Marr's logging activities on January 9, 1987. During the inspection, Strachila discovered that Marr was logging areas for which he did not have a permit. Strachila issued and personally served a stop work order directing Marr to cease the unauthorized logging activities until he obtained an approved application or notification as required by the FPA. . . . However, in the order, Strachila made an error in the legal description of the property subject to the stop work order. The order read "SE ¼, NW ¼" instead of "SE ¼, NE ¼".

Strachila returned to the site on January 14, 1987 and saw that Marr had failed to comply with the stop work order. DNR then filed an action against Marr to enforce the order, obtaining a temporary restraining order on January 27, 1987, and a preliminary injunction on February 6, 1987. In its Order Granting Preliminary Injunction, the Superior Court found that Marr understood the stop work order to prohibit further logging on the residential lots.

Subsequently, both parties moved for summary judgment on the issue of whether the residential lots logged by Marr were "forest land" subject to the provisions of the FPA. The Superior Court concluded that the lots were forest land and permanently enjoined Marr from logging the lots until he complied with the FPA.

II.

Marr first contends that residential lots are not "forest land" subject to the provisions of the FPA. He argues that the Legislature intended the FPA to apply only to the commercial timber industry. DNR contends that the statutory definition of "forest land" is comprehensive and that the property logged by Marr falls within the definition.

In interpreting a statute, it is the court's duty to ascertain and give effect to the intent and purpose of the legislation as expressed in the act as a whole. Where an administrative agency charged with administering a special field of law is endowed with quasi-judicial functions because of its expertise, the agency's construction of the statute should be accorded substantial weight. However, the agency's interpretation is not conclusive. It is ultimately for the court to determine the purpose and meaning of the statute.

The paramount concern in interpreting a statute is to ensure that the interpretation is consistent with the underlying policy of the statute. The language of the statute is the court's primary guide in ascertaining its purpose.

The FPA regulates forest practices on public and private forest lands. The legislative findings which describe the purpose of the FPA show that the Legislature's intent in enacting the FPA was to foster the commercial timber industry while protecting the environment. RCW 76.09.010. Consistent with the underlying policy of protecting the environment, the Legislature gave the FPA broad application by broadly defining forest land:

> "Forest land" shall mean all land which is capable of supporting a merchantable stand of timber and is not being actively used for a use which is incompatible with timber growing.

RCW 76.09.020(6).

The parties agree that this definition of forest land incorporates a 2-part test. Marr first contends that the residential lots logged by him were not forest land because they did not contain "merchantable stands of timber."

The Forest Practices Board, acting pursuant to authority granted by the FPA, has defined "merchantable stand of timber" as follows:

> "Merchantable stand of timber" means a stand of trees that will yield logs and/or fiber:
>
> (a) Suitable in size and quality for the production of lumber, plywood, pulp or other forest products.
>
> (b) Of sufficient value at least to cover all the costs of harvest and transportation to available markets.

WAC 222–16–010(27). It is conceded by Marr that the sale of the logs removed from the lots realized more than it cost to remove and transport the logs to market. It may therefore be inferred that they were also suitable in size and quality for the production of forest products, and thus, constituted "merchantable stands of timber" satisfying the first part of the definition of "forest land".

Marr contends that the second part of the definition is not met because no active commercial timber growing was taking place on the lots. In making this contention, Marr reads an "active timber growing" requirement into the definition. However, there is no requirement that landowners be actively engaged in cultivating timber; the statute provides simply that land is forest land if it *"is not being actively used for a use which is incompatible with timber growing."* (Emphasis added.) RCW 76.09.020(6). As DNR points out, the fact that Marr realized a profit on the timber he logged would appear to conclusively show that the lots were not being put to a use incompatible with timber growing.

Marr does not directly address the logic of DNR's contention, but rather argues that designating residential lots as forest land would have the absurd result of requiring private landowners who want to cut down a few trees on their property to obtain a permit and to either reforest or state their intention to convert the property to another use. However, as DNR points out, that would not be the result under the FPA.

The FPA establishes four classes of forest practices. RCW 76.09.050; WAC 222–12–030; WAC 222–16–050. Class 2 forest practices may commence after written notification to DNR, and classes 3 and 4 require application and approval. RCW 76.09.050(1). Class 1 forest practices do not require either application or notification and include removal of less than 5,000 board feet of timber. RCW 76.09.050(1); WAC 222–16–050(3)(k). Thus, landowners who want to cut down a few trees on their property are not required to obtain a permit.

Similarly, cutting down a few trees would not necessarily require owners of forest land to reforest or to state their intention to convert their property to another use. Forest land is converted to a use other than commercial timber production only when it is converted to an active use which is incompatible with timber growing. RCW 76.09.020(4). Cutting down a few trees would not convert the land to another use and thus would not require landowners to submit an application stating their intention to convert to another use. See RCW 76.09.060(3). Moreover, reforestation is required in instances of partial cutting only

> where 50 percent or more of the timber volume is removed within any 5-year period, unless the department determines that the live trees remaining will reasonably utilize the timber growing capacity of the soils.

WAC 222–34–010(1)(a)(ii); see also RCW 76.09.070.

In addition, if we were to accept Marr's contention that the lots involved in this case are not forest land, it would effectively exclude all forest practices on residential lots from the coverage of the FPA. The fact that Marr removed over 326,000 board feet of timber from these lots illustrates the impact of such an exclusion. DNR would lose the ability to monitor the removal of a significant amount of timber, thereby losing the ability to effectively monitor the impact of logging on the environment.

The Legislature's broad definition of "forest land" in RCW 76.09.020(6) makes clear that it intended to bring logging activities such as Marr's within the purview of the FPA. The Superior Court correctly concluded that the residential lots logged by Marr are forest land subject to the requirements of the FPA.

III.

[Marr also contended "that DNR's action to enforce its stop work order must fail because the property was incorrectly described in the order." The court chose to "simply analyze whether the order provided adequate notice"].

In civil cases, the purpose of notice statutes is to fairly and sufficiently apprise those who may be affected of the nature and character of an action, and notice is deemed adequate in the absence of a showing that anyone was actually misled by the notice. *Nisqually Delta Ass'n v. DuPont*, 103 Wash.2d 720, 727, 696 P.2d 1222 (1985). Although Marr assigns error to the Superior Court's finding that he understood the stop work order to prohibit further logging on the residential lots, he cannot dispute that he knew what area was covered by the order. It is undisputed that when Strachila inspected Marr's logging operations, he clearly informed Marr that he must cease logging the lots until he obtained a permit. Thus, Marr received actual notice, if not the written notice required by RCW 76.09.080.

In light of the fact that Marr was not misled by the stop work order, and in light of the fact that the present action is not a criminal proceeding but simply an action to enjoin Marr from continuing his logging operations until he complies with the FPA, the stop work order is enforceable despite the error in the legal description. We thus affirm the Superior Court's order enjoining Marr from continuing his logging activities until he complies with the FPA.

NOTES

1. *Forest policy procedures.* Forestry laws are replete with notice, appeal, and other procedural protections like those highlighted in *Marr*. For example, in *Johnson Forestry Contracting, Inc. v. Washington State Department of Natural Resources*, 126 P.3d 45 (Wash. App. 2005), the state required a timber company to implement a 100-foot riparian buffer zone as a condition of approval for its planned logging operation. The company nonetheless proceeded to harvest timber within 25 feet of the riparian corridor. The state DNR assessed the company an $8,000 administrative penalty but gave it the chance to request "remission or mitigation" of the civil penalty under Washington statute RCW 76.09.170(3) by taking certain corrective steps. The company challenged the penalty by claiming that the state failed to comply with the enforcement processes required in the state statute by issuing the civil penalty *before* it issued its final order on pending "NTC's"—notices to comply. The court rejected the company's complaint. In doing so, it provided an overview of the administrative enforcement process, one that resembles processes followed in other states:

> Under RCW 76.09.090, "[i]f a violation, a deviation, material damage or potential for material damage to a public resource has occurred . . . then the department shall issue and serve upon the operator or land owner a notice." The Forest Practices Act provides specific processes for a violator to contest a NTC. Within 15 days of receiving a NTC, a violator may request a hearing in front of DNR. RCW 76.09.090(3). Within 10 days of such hearing, DNR is required to issue a final order "either withdrawing its notice to comply or

clearly setting forth the specific course of action to be followed by such operator." RCW 76.09.090(3). Once DNR issues a final order on the NTCs, a violator has 30 days to appeal the order to the Board. RCW 76.09.090(3).

Additionally, the legislature granted DNR authority to issue civil penalties under a separate section of the Forest Practices Act. Under RCW 76.09.170, "[e]very person who violates any provision of RCW 76.09.010 through 76.09.280 . . . shall be subject to a penalty in an amount of not more than ten thousand dollars for every such violation." RCW 76.09.170(1). The person incurring a penalty may apply in writing to DNR within 15 days for remission or mitigation of the penalty. RCW 76.09.170(3). The person incurring a penalty may also appeal the penalty to the Board within 30 days of receiving notice of the penalty. RCW 76.09.170(4). If a violator fails to apply for remission or mitigation to DNR and fails to appeal to the Board within the statutory timeframe, the penalty becomes "due and payable thirty days after receipt of notice." RCW 76.09.170(5).

The plain language of the Forest Practices Act grants DNR separate authority to issue both NTCs and civil penalties. . . . If the legislature intended the issuance of civil penalties to depend on the issuance of NTCs, the legislature would have maintained the reference to RCW 76.09.090 within the statutory language of RCW 76.09.170.

Here, under RCW 76.09.170, Johnson Forestry could have (a) filed for remission or mitigation of the civil penalty within 15 days of October 31, 2001; or (b) filed an appeal within 30 days of October 31, 2001. Johnson Forestry failed to do either within the statutory timeframe. Thus, the appeal filed on April 24, 2002, was not permissible under RCW 76.09.170.

Johnson Forestry. 126 P.3d at 50. This ruling illustrates that Washington state provides fairly broad procedural protections for timber operators, allowing for remission or mitigation of a civil penalty as well as opportunities to contest it. In other words, the state seems willing to give a forester every chance to remedy a violation. Might such procedural protections be employed as a political tool to calm the overregulation fears of the forest industry or individual property owners?

2.   *Is it forest land?* Do you think it is good policy to make residential lots subject to state timber extraction restrictions? Should homeowners wishing to cut trees on their lots be required to go through what they may view as an onerous state permitting process? On the other hand, should residential lots be subject only to local land use planning control? Or is the state level the appropriate locus of control over all forests, given that local governments may shortchange forest values in their efforts to promote short-term economic growth? *See* Blake Hudson, *Constitutions and the Commons* 55–73 (2014).

3.   *More forest procedure.* In some states, forest regulation works in conjunction with other environment-related statutes. Consider the state of California and its CEQA statute (the California Environmental Quality Act), California Public Resources Code § 21000 et seq. CEQA is a largely procedural statute, rather than imposing substantive limits on uses of the environment. The Act requires state and local agencies in California to comply with an environmental impact review (EIR) process under which they must notify the public of the environmental effects of certain proposed projects and mitigate adverse effects to the greatest degree possible. The statute operates similarly to the federal National Environmental Policy Act (NEPA), 42 U.S.C. § 4321 et seq., which also seeks to improve environmental outcomes by compelling federal actors to study carefully what they are doing and to consider alternatives. Consider the following explanation of the interplay between California's Forest Practice Act and CEQA.

> Timber harvesting operations in this state must be conducted in accordance with the provisions of the Forest Practice Act. The Act was intended to create and maintain a comprehensive system for regulating timber harvesting in order to achieve two goals: (1) to ensure that '[w]here feasible, the productivity of timberlands is restored, enhanced, and maintained'; and (2) to ensure that '[t]he goal of maximum sustained production of high-quality timber products is achieved while giving consideration to values relating to recreation, watershed, wildlife, range and forage, fisheries, . . . and aesthetic enjoyment.' ([Pub. Resources Code, 2] § 4513.) The Act vests in the [State Board of Forestry] the obligation to adopt forest practice rules and regulations specific to the various forest districts of the state in order 'to assure the continuous growing and harvesting of commercial forest tree species and to protect the soil, air, fish, and wildlife, and water resources, including, but not limited to, streams, lakes, and estuaries.' (§ 4551.)" (*Sierra Club v. State Bd. of Forestry*, 7 Cal. 4th 1215, 1236, 876 P.2d 505 (Cal. 1994) (*Sierra Club*).)

> The Forest Practice Act requires timber owners or operators on private land to submit a timber harvest plan specific to the site and planned logging activity to CDF for approval before harvesting. (§§ 4581–4582.5.) Timber harvest plans are available to the public and to public agencies for review and comment, and CDF's notice of approval must include a written response to significant environmental issues raised by commenters.

> CDF's approval of timber operations is generally subject to CEQA, but under section 21080.5, the Forest Practice Act's regulatory scheme has been certified for exemption from CEQA's requirements for preparation of an environmental impact report (EIR) before approval of a project. . . .

Serving as the functional equivalent of an EIR, a timber harvest plan must "provide public and governmental decisionmakers with detailed information on the project's likely effect on the environment, describe ways of minimizing any significant impacts, point out mitigation measures, and identify any alternatives that are less environmentally destructive." (*County of Santa Cruz v. State Bd. of Forestry*, 75 Cal.Rptr.2d 393 (Cal. App. 1998).) As in the preparation of an EIR, a timber harvest plan must consider cumulative impacts from the subject harvest together with other operations. The Forest Practice Act's implementing regulations, the Forest Practice Rules, adopt the CEQA regulations' definition of "cumulative impacts" from related projects: "the change in the environment which results from the incremental impact of the project when added to other closely related past, present, and reasonably foreseeable probable future projects. Cumulative impacts can result from individually minor but collectively significant projects taking place over a period of time." (Cal.Code Regs., tit. 14, § 895.1; see id., § 15355.)

The Forest Practice Rules further provide that "[c]umulative impacts shall be assessed based upon the methodology described in Board Technical Addendum Number 2. . . .

In turn, Technical Rule Addendum No. 2 provides in part: "The [preparer of a timber harvest plan] shall establish and briefly describe the geographic assessment area within or surrounding the plan for each resource subject to be assessed and shall briefly explain the rationale for establishing the resource area. This shall be a narrative description and shall be shown on a map where a map adds clarity to the assessment." The addendum's appendix further provides, "Biological assessment areas will vary with the species being evaluated and its habitat." (Technical Rule Addendum No. 2, appen. factor C.)

Ebbetts Pass Forest Watch et al. v. California Department of Forestry and Fire Protection, 43 Cal.4th 936, 942–944 (Cal.2008).

What seems to be the goal of requiring timber harvest plans? Does making them "available to the public and to public agencies for review and comment" provide a necessary and adequate check on forest operations? Does the requirement unduly interfere with forestry operations on private lands? On the other hand, is full disclosure enough when a forest manager after full disclosure might still proceed to operate in way that causes degradation? The California Department of Forestry, if it approves a plan, "must include a written response to significant environmental issues raised by commenters." Is this an appropriate check on agency discretion? As the court above explained, a properly prepared timber-harvest plan is the "functional equivalent of an EIR" under CEQA, which means the state agency can approve the plan without preparing a separate EIR. The next case explores this arrangement and how it works in practice.

KATZEFF V. CALIFORNIA DEPARTMENT OF FORESTRY AND FIRE PROTECTION

California Court of Appeal
181 Cal.App.4th 601 (2010)

RIVERA, J.

In this case, we are called upon to decide whether the California Department of Forestry and Fire Protection (CDF) properly granted an exemption allowing the harvesting of less than three acres of timber without environmental review, when one of the mitigation measures to two prior timber harvesting plans for the same property was that the trees in question remain in place to protect a neighboring property from excessive wind. The trial court decided CDF properly granted the exemption, and entered judgment on the pleadings in plaintiff Paul Katzeff's action for violations of the California Environmental Quality Act (CEQA) (Pub. Res.Code, 1 § 21000 et seq.), violations of the Z'Berg-Nejedly Forest Practice Act of 1973 (§ 4511 et seq.) (the FPA), and nuisance. We reverse.

I.   Background

This action was brought against CDF, Gregg Kuljian, and Ed Powers (collectively respondents) in April 2008, seeking to set aside CDF's approval of an exemption allowing the conversion of less than three acres of timber on Kuljian's property. According to the first amended complaint and petition for writ of mandate (the complaint), plaintiff and Kuljian own adjoining parcels of property. In 1988, CDF approved a Timber Harvest Plan (THP) on Kuljian's land (the property) (the 1988 THP). CDF concluded that the THP as proposed would allow wind to be funneled and accelerated, creating a threat of damage to Katzeff's property and home. Accordingly, as one of the conditions of approval, CDF required that " 'no trees . . . be removed from within 200 feet of [Katzeff's home] unless prior approval is obtained from [Katzeff].' "

CDF approved another THP for the same location 10 years later, in 1998 (the 1998 THP). Noting the apparent effectiveness of the wind buffer, CDF again required the landowner to refrain from cutting down trees within 200 feet of Katzeff's house.

Some years later, Powers sold the property to Kuljian. Kuljian could not afford to pay the purchase price, and so as a condition of the sale, he agreed to seek a "conversion exemption" pursuant to section 4584, subdivision (g), and to give Powers the right to log and sell the timber. In the application for the conversion exemption, Kuljian stated he intended to convert the timberland to an orchard. In April 2008, CDF "accepted and thereby approved" the conversion exemption.

In his first cause of action, Katzeff alleged that the conversion exemption violated the FPA and CEQA in that it would destroy a mitigation previously deemed necessary. In his second cause of action, he alleged that Kuljian did not have a bona fide intent to convert the land to an orchard. The third cause of action alleged a claim for private nuisance.

Powers moved for judgment on the pleadings on the ground that the complaint did not state a cause of action. The trial court granted the motion and dismissed the action in its entirety. Katzeff appealed.

II.   Discussion

* * *

B.   Requirements of FPA and CEQA

" 'Timber harvesting operations in this state must be conducted in accordance with the provisions of the Forest Practice Act. The [FPA] was intended to create and maintain a comprehensive system for regulating timber harvesting in order to achieve two goals: (1) to ensure that "[w]here feasible, the productivity of timberlands is restored, enhanced, and maintained"; and (2) to ensure that "[t]he goal of maximum sustained production of high-quality timber products is achieved while giving consideration to values relating to recreation, watershed, wildlife, range and forage, fisheries, . . . and aesthetic enjoyment." (. . . § 4513.) . . .' The [FPA] requires timber owners or operators on private land to submit a timber harvest plan specific to the site and planned logging activity to CDF for approval before harvesting. . . . CDF's approval of timber operations is generally subject to CEQA, but under section 21080.5, the [FPA's] regulatory scheme has been certified for exemption from CEQA's requirements for preparation of an environmental impact report (EIR) before approval of a project. 'Under the terms of section 21080.5, subdivision (c), that certification expressly exempts the timber harvesting plan process from the provisions of chapters 3 and 4 and section 21167 of CEQA. (§ 21080.5, subd. (c).) Chapters 3 and 4 deal, in large part, with the various requirements of an EIR at both the state level (chapter 3) and the local level (chapter 4). Section 21167 sets forth the time within which an action challenging a public agency's decision under the provisions of CEQA must be filed.' " (*Ebbetts Pass Forest Watch v. California Dept. of Forestry & Fire Protection,* 43 Cal. App. 4th 936, 912–13 (2008), 183 P.3d 1210 (Cal. 2008) (Ebbetts Pass).)

Division Five of the First Appellate District explained the relationship between the requirements of the FPA and CEQA in *Friends of the Old Trees v. Department of Forestry & Fire Protection,* 52 Cal.App.4th 1383, 1388 (1997), as follows: "Under the [FPA] and its implementing regulations, hereafter Forestry Rules ([rule] 895 et seq.), . . . logging. . . . [is] subject to [CDF's] approval of a site specific THP. The THP preparation and approval process is the functional equivalent of the preparation of an environmental impact report (EIR) contemplated by [CEQA]." "[W]ith the exception of certain specific provisions of CEQA relating to the 'procedural elements' of the EIR process, 'CEQA and its substantive criteria for the evaluation of a proposed project's environmental impact apply to the timber harvesting industry, and are deemed part of the [FPA] and the Forestry Rules.' The Supreme Court has . . . reiterated that timber harvesting is not exempt from adhering to the broad policy goals of CEQA. To the contrary, the court held 'that in approving timber harvesting plans, the [administrative body] must conform not only to the detailed and exhaustive provisions of the [FPA], but also to those provisions of CEQA from which it has not been specifically exempted by the Legislature.' Significantly, the [FPA] and the Forestry Rules establish a statutory and regulatory framework that, construed together with CEQA, confers on [CDF] the obligation to see that cumulative impacts and alternatives to the project, as well as other specified environmental information, be taken into consideration in evaluating THP's." (*Id.* at 1393) Moreover, "CDF has not only the authority but also the duty to approve, disapprove, and impose mitigation measures on timber harvest plans. . . ." (*Ebbetts Pass*, 43 Cal.4th at. 957.)

As explained in *Environmental Protection Information Center, Inc. v. Johnson*, 170 Cal.App.3d 604, 609–610 (1985), a THP "is an informational document designed to serve as an 'abbreviated' environmental impact report, setting forth proposed measures to mitigate the logging operation's potential adverse impact on the environment. CDF and public review of the THP prior to approval is intended to ensure that the adverse environmental effects are substantially lessened, particularly by the exploration of feasible less damaging alternatives to the proposed harvesting project. Section 21080.5 [part of CEQA], provides that the Secretary of the Resources Agency may certify a regulatory program of a state agency as exempt from the requirement of EIR preparation, if the program requires that a project be preceded by the preparation of a written project plan containing sufficient environmental impact information. To be certifiable, the agency's regulatory program must be governed by rules and regulations (1) which require that no project shall be approved if there are feasible alternatives or mitigation measures available which would substantially lessen any adverse impact on the environment (§ 21080.5, subd. (d)(2)(i). . . ."

C.   *Destruction of Mitigation Measure*

Katzeff's first cause of action alleges that CDF violated both the FPA and CEQA by approving a conversion exemption that would destroy a mitigation it had previously deemed necessary under those statutory schemes. Katzeff argues that CDF's actions constituted improper "piecemealing" of a project, and that an agency may not delete a mitigation required by CEQA without supplemental environmental review. Respondents take the position that the approval was a ministerial act not subject to CEQA and that it bore no relationship to the mitigation measures required by the 1988 and 1998 THP's. They also argue that the THP's have long since expired, and with them their mitigation requirements.

Several statutes and rules bear upon the parties' arguments. Section 4581 forbids anyone to conduct timber operations unless a THP has been submitted to CDF. Section 4590, subdivision (a) provides that a THP is effective for no more than three years, unless extended pursuant to specified procedures. Forest Practice Rules, rule 1039.1 provides that the "effective period of the plan" is "the 3-year period following the date the plan is determined to be in conformance or otherwise becomes effective pursuant to PRC 4582.7. Timber operations shall commence no earlier than the expected date of commencement stated in the plan," except under certain conditions. The THP's at issue here were approved in 1988 and 1998. There is no dispute that the right to conduct timber operations under these THP's has expired.

Conversion exemptions are governed by section 4584 and Forest Practice Rules, rule 1104.1. As we have explained, section 4584 allows the State Board of Forestry and Fire Protection, upon determining that the exemption is consistent with the purposes of the FPA, to exempt from the FPA's requirements anyone whose activities are limited to, among other things, "[t]he one-time conversion of less than three acres to a nontimber use." (§ 4584, subd. (g)(1); see § 4521.3.) Rule 1104.1 establishes the requirements for such exemptions. Under rule 1104.1(a), the conversion exemption "is applicable to a conversion of timberland to a non-timber use only, of less than three acres in one contiguous ownership, whether or not it is a portion of a larger land parcel and shall not be part of a THP." The notice of conversion exemption, which initiates the process, is required to contain certain material, including the names and addresses of the landowner, timber owner, and others; a legal description of the land at issue; certain maps; and a statement by the owner of the land to be converted certifying that the operation is a one-time conversion to non-timberland use, certifying that there is a bona fide intent to convert, specifying what the use will be after the conversion, and certifying that the landowner has not obtained a conversion exemption in the previous five years, unless a waiver had been granted. (FP Rules, rule 1104.1(a)(1).) As relevant here, timber operations conducted under rule 1104.1 are exempt from the conversion permit and THP requirements of the rules related to the conversion of timberland.

The presenting issue here is whether a conversion exemption that would destroy a mitigation required under now-expired THP's may be approved without additional environmental review. The parties have drawn our attention to no case precisely on point, and our own research has disclosed none.

Katzeff contends this case is analogous to *Orinda Assn. v. Board of Supervisors*, 182 Cal.App.3d 1145 (1986) (*Orinda*). There, a developer sought to build a project that included office, commercial, retail and theater space in downtown Orinda, on a site occupied by a historic theater and bank building that would have been demolished by the project as proposed. While environmental review of the project was proceeding under CEQA, the building inspection department issued an unconditional permit for demolition of the theater and bank building. Division Three of the First Appellate District concluded that this procedure violated CEQA because the "demolition was a phase of the overall Project; as such, it was subject to the same CEQA review as the rest of the Project, and the demolition permit could not be issued until the entire CEQA process was completed and the overall Project lawfully approved." (*Orinda*, at 1145, 1171.) The court reasoned: "A public agency is not permitted to subdivide a single project into smaller individual subprojects in order to avoid the responsibility of considering the environmental impact of the project as a whole. The requirements of CEQA, "cannot be avoided by chopping up proposed projects into bite-size pieces which, individually considered, might be found to have no significant effect on the environment or to be only ministerial." (*Id.*) The court noted that the demolition of the building had been considered part of the project from the outset, and that "[m]ost important, both the Board and the Planning Commission imposed conditions on the demolition of the Theatre and Bank Building as part of their approval of the Project. . . . If demolition could be segregated from other development activities and made nonreviewable, the requirements of CEQA would be avoided altogether. . . ." (*Id.* at 1172.)

Several points in *Orinda* are significant here. First, *Orinda* states the well-established principle that a project cannot be divided into smaller parts that individually will not have a significant effect on the environment. Second, this rule is applicable even if one of the smaller parts might require only ministerial, rather than discretionary, approval. Third, where conditions are imposed on a project, those conditions—and the policies behind CEQA—cannot be avoided by applying for another approval apart from the larger project. (*Orinda*, 182 Cal.App.3d at 1171–1172.).

Here, respondents contend, issuance of the conversion exemption was a ministerial action that required no environmental review. Under *Orinda*, however, even if we accept the argument that the exemption was ministerial, an applicant cannot avoid environmental review of a portion of a larger project simply by securing a separate ministerial permit, particularly where the permit would undo the protective effects of conditions imposed on a project's approval.

We recognize that *Orinda* is not precisely on point because the demolition permit there was issued while the overall project was under review, while here the conversion exemption took place years later. But if that distinction were dispositive, any mitigation required by CEQA or the FPA could be nullified simply by the passage of time. As Katzeff points out, under this line of reasoning, the wind buffer mitigation could permissibly be destroyed virtually as soon as it became necessary—that is, after the landowner had completed operations under the THP— because the landowner could simply seek a conversion exemption as soon as the right to conduct timber operations under the THP had expired. The conflict between this result and the intent of CEQA is self-evident. As noted in another context, "[e]xpiration of the [approval] was an abstract occurrence that had no effect on the project's environmental impacts." (*Moss v. County of Humboldt*, 162 Cal.App.4th 1041, 1056 (2008))

We see no principled distinction between a conversion exemption sought immediately after the right to harvest under a THP has expired, and one sought a decade later. Whether or not the legal right to harvest timber has expired, the environmental effects of the harvest are presumed to remain. The wind buffer was required in order to mitigate the effects of the timber harvest on Katzeff's property, and respondents offer no basis for a conclusion that the mitigation expires as a matter of law once the time to complete the timber harvesting—the very action that creates the need for the mitigation—has expired.

* * *

. . . *Napa Citizens for Honest Government v. Napa County Bd. of Supervisors*, 91 Cal.App.4th 342, 358–359 (2001), [ ] recognized that CEQA requires an agency to take steps to ensure that mitigation measures " 'will actually be implemented as a condition of development, and not merely adopted and then neglected or discarded.' " However, the court in *Napa Citizens* went on to conclude that nothing in the law required that "a mitigation measure, once adopted, is binding for all time." (*Id.* at 359.) Rather, "when an earlier adopted mitigation measure has been deleted, the deference provided to governing bodies with respect to land use planning decisions must be tempered by *the presumption that the governing body adopted the mitigation measure in the first place only after due investigation and consideration.* We therefore hold that a governing body must state a legitimate reason for deleting an earlier adopted mitigation measure, and must support that statement of reason with substantial evidence." (*Id.*, italics added; *see also Mani Brothers Real*

Estate Group v. City of Los Angeles, 153 Cal.App.4th 1385, 1388–1389, 1403 (2007), [no need for supplemental EIR rather than addendum to EIR where substantial evidence supported city's conclusion mitigation measures no longer necessary].). . . .

* * *

Consistent with the reasoning of the cases we have discussed, we conclude that where a public agency has adopted a mitigation measure for a project, it may not authorize destruction or cancellation of the mitigation—whether or not the approval is ministerial—without reviewing the continuing need for the mitigation, stating a reason for its actions, and supporting it with substantial evidence.

* * *

The judgment is reversed. . . .

NOTES

1. *Piecemealing projects*. Recall that a timber harvest plan made pursuant to California's Forest Practices Act is to be the "functional equivalent" of an Environmental Impact Report under CEQA (p. 609). One role of a procedural statute like CEQA is to forestall efforts to evade its requirements by disaggregating projects into component parts, each small enough in size to avoid triggering the requirement for a full-scale environmental review. Consider how this issue manifests under the federal National Environmental Policy Act, on which CEQA was modelled:

> Agencies may also try to avoid NEPA's reach by dividing up or "segmenting" projects. At the extreme, for example, consider how the Forest Service might try to avoid preparing an [Environmental Impact Statement (EIS)] for its decision to build a 20-mile road in a National Forest. This 20-mile road certainly would seem to be a major federal action significantly affecting the environment. But what if, instead, the Forest Service transformed the project into twenty separate decisions to build one-mile roads? By segmenting, the agency can transform major projects into innocuous minor ones. In isolation, none of these one-mile roads will likely trigger the requirements for an EIS. In scrutinizing examples like this, therefore, courts have asked whether the separate segments have independent utility. If the road segment along mile 16 makes no sense without miles 17 and 15, then they must be considered together. *See e.g.*, Taxpayers Watchdog, Inc. v. Stanley, 819 F.2d 294 (D.C. Cir. 1987) (upholding an agency EIS that addressed only a small segment of a much larger proposed subway system for Los Angeles because the segment was found to have sufficient independent utility to stand on its own, and did not irretrievably commit the agency to any particular future course of action).

A related problem concerns attempts to analyze individually separate but related actions. Imagine, for example, that the Forest Service decides to build a small road into a heavily-timbered section of forest and does not prepare an EIS because the road will not, by itself, have significant impacts. Soon thereafter, the Forest Service approves timber sales now accessible by the road into the area but does not prepare an EIS because the timber harvest will not have significant effects. Should the road and timber sales have been addressed together in a single EIS?

J.B. Ruhl, John Copeland Nagle, James Salzman, & Alexandra B. Klass, *The Practice and Policy of Environmental Law* 413 (3d. ed. 2014).

The segmentation issue posed under NEPA regularly arises in the context of forestry management. Land managers necessarily undertake their work on a project-by-project basis, cutting timber in one place, thinning it in another, and replanting in another still. Initial steps might well be part of a long-term overall management scheme. But the timing and details of later steps might well depend on future events, including the shifting prices of timber products. The kind of artificial segmentation for which the Forest Service has been criticized seems clearly wrong. But the issue remains: When are timber harvesting plans submitted years apart part of the same action? The *Katzeff* court cited the *Orinda* case for the proposition that "[a] public agency is not permitted to subdivide a single project into smaller individual subprojects in order to avoid the responsibility of considering the environmental impact of the project as a whole," and that the requirements of CEQA "cannot be avoided by chopping up proposed projects into bite-size pieces which, individually considered, might be found to have no significant effect on the environment. . . ." The rule is clear enough in general form, yet its application can be quite messy. For more information on CEQA, *see* California Environmental Quality Act 2014 Statute and Guidelines, at resources.ca.gov.

2. *Temporal considerations.* Regarding the expiration of the timber harvesting plan, the *Katzeff* court noted: "[w]hether or not the legal right to harvest timber has expired, the environmental effects of the harvest are presumed to remain." Often agencies look at projects in isolation, and while planning may take into account potential future adverse effects, policymakers may fail to make forward-looking decisions that limit future uses of land based upon past decisions regarding that parcel of land. Can you identify other ways CEQA and the California Forest Practices Act take into account sustainable management of California's forests over time?

PACIFIC LUMBER COMPANY V. STATE WATER RESOURCES CONTROL BOARD

California Supreme Court
37 Cal.4th 921 (2006)

MORENO, J.

* * *

I.   *Factual and Procedural Background*

This case involves proposed logging activity on approximately 700 wooded acres in Humboldt County's Elk River watershed. Until 1999, this land was owned by the Elk River Timber Company (Elk River). In 1997, Elk River submitted a timber harvesting plan (THP) as a precursor to logging this area. Under California law, an approved THP is a prerequisite to all nonexempt logging operations. (Pub.Res.Code, § 4581.) The Department of Forestry must review THP's to determine whether they comport with the Forest Practice Act and the rules and regulations of the State Board of Forestry and Fire Protection (Board of Forestry). (§ 4582.7.)

Elk River's THP underwent the multidisciplinary review spelled out in the Forest Practice Act and its associated regulations. (*See* § 4582.6, subds. (a), (b); Cal.Code Regs., tit. 14, § 1037.5.) The North Coast Regional Water Quality Control Board participated in this process, recommending that Elk River develop a sediment monitoring program along potentially affected waters. Elk River's forester agreed to the concept of a rigorous, cooperative monitoring program. But no mandatory monitoring program was ever written into the THP. The THP provided only that "[m]onitoring protocols, techniques and monitoring locations shall be chosen at the discretion of the landowner or representative." On August 24, 1998, Elk River's THP, known as THP 520, was approved by the Department of Forestry without any objection from the Regional Water Quality Control Board.

THP 520 and the land it encompassed were transferred to Pacific Lumber in 1999. [Immediately upon gaining control Pacific Lumber sought to make multiple amendments to the approved THP. This litigation had to do with its proposed amendment five, which would allow wintertime operations, "yarding" (removal of felled timber) by helicopter, and certain other changes. The amendments were substantial enough to require approval by the Department of Forestry under the Forest Practice Act.]

As part of the review process for amendment No. 5, a representative of the North Coast Regional Water Quality Control Board participated in on-site inspections of the THP 520 logging site on November 6, 2000 and November 29, 2000. In January 2001, the chairman of the review team for amendment No. 5 recommended that the Director of the Department of Forestry (Director) approve the amendment. (See Cal.Code Regs., tit. 14, § 1037.5, subd. (c).) Shortly thereafter, as allowed by the California Code of Regulations (id., subd. (e)), the Regional Water Quality Control Board submitted a "non-concurrence" disagreeing with the chairman's recommendation. The Regional Water Quality Control Board's non-concurrence letter voiced several concerns with the timber harvesting contemplated by the amended THP. Most relevant here, the letter stated that Pacific Lumber had not yet proposed a program that would adequately monitor the effects the harvesting would have on water quality. Without such monitoring, the Regional Water Quality Control Board argued, a chance existed that the timber harvesting authorized by THP 520 would violate state water quality law.

The Department of Forestry rejected the North Coast Regional Water Quality Control Board's concerns regarding inadequate monitoring, stating that the proposed amendment "is anticipated to reduce water quality issues below those in the existing unamended plan. That plan, as noted by [the Regional Water Quality Control Board], is in place and operable without the monitoring program being proposed in this non-concurrence." The Regional Water Quality Control Board's objections having been overruled, the Director approved amendment No. 5 on March 6, 2001.

On March 13, 2001, the North Coast Regional Water Quality Control Board asked the State Water Resources Control Board to invoke the Forest Practice Act's "head of agency appeal process," which would have allowed the Board of Forestry to review the amendment's approval. (§ 4582.9.) Two days later, the State Water Resources Control Board received a letter from the Director advising the agency that "the amendment and its proposed operations have been sufficiently restricted and mitigated to the point that there is minimal risk to water quality." The State Water Resources Control Board ultimately did not invoke the head of agency appeal process.

Undeterred, the North Coast Regional Water Quality Control Board issued Monitoring and Reporting Order No. R1–2001–19 on March 28, 2001. This order required Pacific Lumber to adopt a comprehensive water quality monitoring program that would include five new monitoring stations along the South Fork of the Elk River. The Regional Water Quality Control Board advised Pacific Lumber that the program was necessary "to assure that discharges from [logging contemplated by THP 520] comply with Basin Plan objectives and prohibitions, to assure that discharges do not impede recovery of the watershed, and to identify and address discharges of sediments to receiving waters in a timely manner."

Pacific Lumber filed a petition (see Wat.Code, § 13320, subd. (a)) with the State Water Resources Control Board, asking it to rescind the North Coast Regional Water Quality Control Board's order. In its petition, Pacific Lumber argued that the Forest Practice Act's provisions relating to THP approval precluded the Regional Water Quality Control Board from imposing monitoring requirements more stringent than those found within the applicable THP. The State Water Resources Control Board disagreed and upheld the Regional Water Quality Control Board's authority to require monitoring. However, the State Water Resources Control Board's final order required only two new monitoring stations, as opposed to the five demanded by the Regional Water Quality Control Board. The State Water Resources Control Board's order also imposed inspection, recordkeeping, reporting, and planning requirements associated with the monitoring.

[Pacific Lumber challenged the power of the state water board to impose these requirements, arguing that the Department of Forestry was the only agency that could regulate its timber management and that the regional and state water boards could only interject water-protection provisions if they were included in the final THP and approved by the Department of Forestry. The trial court agreed with Pacific Lumber. The Court of Appeal took the opposing view, concluding that the power of the water resources boards (regional and state) was in addition to the power of the Department of Forestry.].

* * *

II. Discussion

Pacific Lumber contends that the Water Boards' unilateral imposition of monitoring requirements subverted the procedures for THP approval incorporated within the Forest Practice Act, which Pacific Lumber characterizes as creating a "one stop" regulatory process for proposed logging activity that already incorporates detailed consideration of water quality impacts. This "one-stop" process, Pacific Lumber argues, cannot be reconciled with the after-the-fact imposition of additional water quality monitoring requirements by the Water Boards.

The Forest Practice Act promotes a state policy of "encourag[ing] prudent and responsible forest resource management calculated to serve the public's need for timber and other forest products, while giving consideration to the public's need for watershed protection, fisheries and wildlife, and recreational opportunities alike in this and future generations." (§ 4512, subd. (c).) The Forest Practice Act is designed to "create and maintain an effective and comprehensive system of regulation and use of all timberlands so as to assure that: (a) Where feasible, the productivity of timberlands is restored, enhanced, and maintained[, and] . . . (b) The goal of maximum sustained production of high-quality timber products is achieved while giving consideration to values relating to recreation, watershed, wildlife, range and forage, fisheries, regional economic vitality, employment, and aesthetic enjoyment." (§ 4513.)

Toward these goals, the Forest Practice Act requires the Board of Forestry to adopt rules pertaining to the effects of timber operations on water quality and watershed control, and rules controlling timber operations that will result or threaten to result in unreasonable effects on the beneficial uses of state waters. The Forest Practice Act also contains detailed procedures relating to the submission and approval of THP's. Subject to certain exemptions not implicated here, the Forest Practice Act requires parties who plan on harvesting timber to first submit a THP to the Department of Forestry for approval. The THP must contain information including "[a] description of the land on which the work is proposed to be done," "[a] description of the silvicultural methods to be applied, including the type of logging equipment to be used," "[a]n outline of the methods to be used to avoid excessive accelerated erosion from timber operations to be conducted within the proximity of a stream," "[s]pecial provisions, if any, to protect any unique area within the area of timber operations," "[t]he expected dates of commencement and completion of timber operations," "[a] certification by the registered professional forester preparing the plan that he or she or a designee has personally inspected the plan area," and "[a]ny other information the [Board of Forestry] provides by regulation to meet its rules and the standards of this chapter." (§ 4582, subds. (c)–(i); *see also* Cal.Code Regs., tit. 14, § 1034.)

Once submitted, the THP is made available for public inspection and comment. The Department of Forestry transmits copies of the THP to other agencies, including the Department of Fish and Game and the appropriate Regional Water Quality Control Board, for their review. A representative of the local Regional Water Quality Control Board participates in an interagency team that reviews the THP and assists the Director in evaluating the planned timber operations and their environmental impacts. (Cal.Code Regs., tit. 14, § 1037.5.) The review team may perform a preharvest inspection of the proposed logging site. The review team's chairperson makes a recommendation to the Director regarding whether the plan should be approved or rejected. Any member of the review team may submit a non-concurrence letter to the Director disagreeing with the chairperson's recommendation to approve a plan and offering advice on measures or actions that should be taken to address the asserted deficiency.

The Director then determines whether the THP conforms to the Forest Practice Act and the Board of Forestry's rules and regulations, taking into account the comments and recommendations that he or she has received. In this respect, the Director, or his or her designee, "shall have the final authority to determine whether a timber harvesting plan is in conformance with the rules and regulations of the [Board of Forestry] and with [the Forest Practice Act] for purposes of approval by the [D]epartment." (§ 4582.7, subd. (e).) Pertinent here, a THP may be rejected if "[i]mplementation of the plan as proposed would cause a violation of any requirement of an applicable water quality control plan adopted or approved by the State Water Resources Control Board." (Cal.Code Regs., tit. 14, § 898.2, subd. (h).)

An applicant whose THP has been disapproved by the Director may request a public hearing before the Board of Forestry, which then determines for itself whether the THP comports with the Forest Practice Act and related regulations. Conversely, at its option either the State Water Resources Control Board or the Director of Fish and Game may appeal to the Board of Forestry a decision to approve a THP. Any such appeal must be brought within 10 days of the THP's approval, and requires prior agency participation in the multidisciplinary THP review process. A hearing on an appeal shall be granted upon a Board of Forestry determination that the appeal raises substantial issues "with respect to the environment or to public safety." ((§ 4582.9, subd. (c).)

Pacific Lumber contends that the foregoing provisions signal an intent to make the THP approval process the exclusive forum for evaluating a proposed timber harvest's effects on water quality. This being the case, Pacific Lumber argues, the Water Boards cannot go outside of this process and unilaterally impose water quality requirements above and beyond those incorporated within an approved THP.

[The court next explained that the state's Porter-Cologne Water Quality Control Act (Wat.Code, § 13000 et seq.) (Porter-Cologne Act) clearly gave the Regional Water Quality Control Boards and the State Water Resources Control Board authority to require water quality monitoring of the type at issue here. The question was whether this power was curtailed in the context of forestry operations by the Forest Practice Act. Pacific Lumber argued that it was. It noted particularly that the water boards had full opportunities to participate in the review process of the THP and could challenge a plan if they did not like it. That prescribed process, Pacific Lumber argued, would be undercut if the water boards, having lost out in their challenges to the THP, could turn around and impose the monitoring requirements independently. If they could do that, why would they bother to participate in the THP review process? After summarizing this argument, the court then responded to it:]

This argument suffers from a fundamental flaw, in that it runs headlong into the Forest Practice Act's savings clause, which provides:

"No provision of this chapter or any ruling, requirement, or policy of the [Board of Forestry] is a limitation on any of the following: . . . (a) On the power of any city or county or city and county to declare, prohibit, and abate nuisances. . . . (b) On the power of the Attorney General, at the request of the [Board of Forestry], or upon his own motion, to bring an action in the name of the people of the State of California to enjoin any pollution or nuisance. . . . (c) *On the power of any state agency in the enforcement or administration of any provision of law which it is specifically authorized or required to enforce or administer.* . . . (d) On the right of any person to maintain at any time any appropriate action for relief against any private nuisance as defined in Part 3 (commencing with Section 3479) of Division 4 of the Civil Code or for any other private relief." (§ 4514, italics added.)

As the Court of Appeal ascertained, section 4514, subdivision (c)'s proviso that "[n]o provision of this chapter or any ruling, requirement, or policy of the [Board of Forestry] is a limitation on . . . the power of any state agency in the enforcement or administration of any provision of law which it is specifically authorized or required to enforce or administer" is fatal to Pacific Lumber's argument. Pacific Lumber's position boils down to the view that the Forest Practice Act implicitly precludes the Water Boards from exercising their authority under the Porter-Cologne Act to impose monitoring requirements, where those requirements relate to timber harvesting undertaken pursuant to an approved THP. Section 4514, subdivision (c) expressly provides that the contrary is true, that the Forest Practice Act in no way limits the Water Boards' authority in this respect. As a direct and pellucid expression of legislative intent regarding the precise issue before us, section 4514, subdivision (c) controls the present case.

* * *

. . . . The savings clause can be read as consistent with—and indeed, a vital part of—a regulatory scheme that encourages interagency teamwork in the THP approval process by providing forums for collaboration and the airing of any disagreements that may arise, but not at the cost of stripping state agencies of their respective authority to protect resources that may be affected by logging.

None of the terms of the Forest Practice Act that Pacific Lumber relies upon compels a contrary conclusion, for we perceive no irreconcilable conflict between any of these provisions and the Forest Practice Act's savings clause. . . . There is no inherent conflict between giving the Director final authority over the approval of THP's while at the same time preserving other state agencies' jurisdiction over the effects of timber harvesting on state resources under their purview. This approach simply creates a system of overlapping jurisdiction, an uncontroversial concept under our law even absent a savings clause like the one implicated here. . . . Being subject to regulation by both the Department of Forestry (to the extent Pacific Lumber proposed timber harvesting) and the Water Boards (to the extent this harvesting implicated the state's water resources and the Water Boards' authority under the Porter-Cologne Act), Pacific Lumber was bound to comply with the more stringent monitoring requirements imposed by the State Water Resources Control Board.

* * *

All in all, Pacific Lumber makes several reasonable arguments suggesting that a "one stop" process for THP approval might have some beneficial aspects, at least from the timber harvester's point of view. But there are also valid reasons to allow for concurrent jurisdiction among various regulatory agencies. The Forest Practice Act's savings clause, read in context, expresses a clear preference for the latter approach, and we are not free to substitute a contrary judgment for the Legislature's considered conclusions.

* * *

We affirm the judgment of the Court of Appeal.

NOTES

1.   *To coordinate or not to coordinate?* One criticism of environmental agencies is that they can be duplicative and inefficient, especially if multiple agencies maintain jurisdiction over the same resource and fail to coordinate. However, California's Forest Practices Act provides "multidisciplinary review" of potential timber harvesting plans in order to coordinate and avoid administrative inefficiencies. The North Coast Regional Water Quality Control Board participated in on-site inspections of the THP in this case, raising concerns that there was "a chance" the THP would violate state water quality laws. The Department of Forestry, Board of Forestry, and even the State Water Resources Control Board, refused to take action that would seek to increase water protection measures in the THP. The Department of Forestry even noted that the THP was "anticipated to reduce water quality issues below those in the existing unamended plan." Despite this substantial degree of oversight by numerous agencies, the regional water board required Pacific Lumber to go further and adopt a comprehensive water quality monitoring program—and the court upheld its action. Is this what the FPA intended? In seeking to reduce administrative inefficiencies and garner multidisciplinary agency involvement, has the statute increased those inefficiencies? Does the fact that the FPA included an explicit "multidisciplinary" agency review, with numerous opportunities for appeal, trump the savings's clause reservation of other state agencies' power to administer related laws?

As a policy matter, the issue is whether one state agency, with expertise in one field and with a given culture, is capable of looking after the full range of public interests at stake in a given project. Should the FPA be a "one-stop regulatory process," as Pacific Lumber argued? Or does the degree of regulatory oversight here, while adding to administrative costs, create valuable environmental protections, facilitating a precautionary approach that places a high burden on timber operators before they can engage in harvesting? The court seems to indicate as much when it states that "there are also valid reasons to allow for concurrent jurisdiction among various regulatory agencies." Observers who favor the outcome of the case might worry that the Department of Forestry could unduly favor timber production over other values. But there is the similar worry that an agency with only a protective mission (for instance, historic preservation) might unduly favor protection over competing public interests.

2.   *Timber management and water quality.* Forestry activities can have a number of effects on water sources critical for aquatic life, drinking water, and recreational use. Timber operations can affect sediment, nutrient, and chemical loads in streams and can alter stream flow and temperature. Pollutants that can enter waterways during forest operations include toxic chemicals and metals, organic matter, pathogens, herbicides, and pesticides. A number of forestry operations can lead to these adverse effects on water quality, including not only the cutting of trees themselves, but also construction of stream crossings, equipment use within stream corridors, and placement of slash or other debris generated by forestry activities within streams. Consider the following effects of forest operations on water quality:

> Forests play an important role in protecting the integrity of aquatic systems. Forest harvest can dramatically change the physical and biological characteristics of watersheds, removing vegetative buffers that protect surface waters from the elements and altering the movement of water. Other activities associated with timber operations, such as application of fertilizer and pesticides, and the waste disposal practices of pulp paper mills, also contribute to water pollution. The U.S. Environmental Protection Agency reports that the industry's use of best management practices has reduced water pollution in recent decades but that pollution remains a significant problem.

Sediment and Flow

> Forest vegetation helps to regulate water flow into surface waters. Water is absorbed from the soil by plant roots and released into the atmosphere from leaves—a process known as evapotranspiration. The roots of plants also bind soil and protect it from erosion. Rainwater and melted snow drain unhindered from harvested areas, causing higher baseline flow and increasing the chance of flooding. Unprotected soil is easily washed into water, and soil disturbance by other activities, such as road construction, can

exacerbate this problem. These results can have devastating effects on aquatic organisms that have adapted lifestyles to suit natural flow and sediment regimes. For instance, high flows during the spawning season may wash away fish eggs laid on the stream bottom. Many aquatic invertebrates require gravel or sand to live in and will not tolerate muddy stream bottoms. High flow and poor water clarity may also affect the ability of fish and invertebrates to capture prey. Problems caused by erosion are not restricted to fresh water habitats, as sediment travels downstream and collects in estuaries.

Chemical Pollution

Inorganic fertilizers and synthetic pesticides are often used by timber operations to enhance tree growth. These substances are typically spread by helicopter, a method that can lead to excess application and direct contamination of surface waters. Fertilizer nutrients promote surplus growth of aquatic algae and plants. Oxygen in the water is depleted when large amounts of plant matter are broken down by bacteria. Fish and aquatic invertebrates experience physiological stress in low-oxygen conditions, with some species—such as trout, salmon and mayflies—being more sensitive than others. A second source of chemical pollution is the effluent produced by pulp mills. Mills are required to treat their waste, but the effectiveness of treatment facilities in removing contaminants varies. Mill effluent contains large quantities of nutrients and organic matter. Mill waste and pesticides contain organic chemicals, such as dioxins and benzenes, which are toxic to aquatic life. Effects include tissue damage, reproductive and developmental problems, immune deficiency, reduced growth and female-biased sex-ratios.

Light Pollution

The amount of sunlight reaching surface waters increases dramatically when adjacent trees are harvested. Sunlight allows algae and plants to grow abundantly, leading to problems with oxygen depletion, and causes water temperature to rise. Warm water is less capable of holding oxygen than cold water, so this too can reduce levels of dissolved oxygen in the water. Cold-adapted fish species, like trout, are badly affected by high water temperature. Even a small increase in temperature accelerates fish metabolism, causing energy requirements to increase. Increased metabolic demand can reduce fish growth, as many forest streams and lakes do not contain enough prey to compensate for higher demand for food. Retaining forest buffers of 10 or more meters around surface waters helps to protect them from light and temperature effects.

Loss of Resources

Aquatic ecosystems in forested catchments are highly dependent on resources that fall from the surrounding forest. Many aquatic invertebrates feed on fallen leaves, organic particles and wood, and drift-feeding fish rely heavily on falling terrestrial invertebrates as a food source. Fallen logs create vital habitat for many aquatic creatures. Harvest of surrounding forest has mixed effects on aquatic organisms. For instance, forest clearance benefits invertebrates that feed on algae, while organisms that rely on leaves, wood and terrestrial prey can be negatively affected by short-term changes in food availability. Deciduous plant species re-establish within the first few years after harvest, but trees that provide other materials, such as conifer needles and large logs, take decades to re-establish.

Kirsten Campbell, *Timber Industry Effect on Water Pollution, Opposing Views*, Science, http://science.opposingviews.com/timber-industry-effect-water-pollution–23000.html. For more information *see* Environmental Protection Agency, *National Management Measures to Control Nonpoint Source Pollution from Forestry*, *available at* http://water.epa.gov.

F. STATE FOREST PRESERVATION

As noted at the beginning of this chapter, state and local governments in the U.S. may maintain not only policy tools aimed at timber extraction, but also tools aimed at the preservation of forests— that is, "keeping forests forested" regardless of whether timber extraction operations will be allowed on the land. Examples include the earlier referenced Maryland Forest Conservation Act, which requires, among other things, that all counties in the state with less than 200,000 acres of forest cover adopt an ordinance aimed at forest conservation. As you read through the Maryland forest preservation statute, consider the complexity and broad scope that forest preservation statutes may have.

MARYLAND FOREST CONSERVATION ACT
§ 5–1602

* * *

(a) Except as provided in subsection (b) of this section, this subtitle shall apply to any public or private subdivision plan or application for a grading or sediment control permit by any person, including a unit of State or local government on areas 40,000 square feet or greater.

Exceptions

(b) The provisions of this subtitle do not apply to:

(1) Any construction activity that is subject to § 5–103 of this title;

(2) Any cutting or clearing of forest in areas governed by the Chesapeake Bay Critical Area Protection Law (Title 8, Subtitle 18 of this article);

(3) Commercial logging and timber harvesting operations. . . .

(4) Any agricultural activity that does not result in a change in land use category, including agricultural support buildings and other related structures built using accepted best management practices;

(5) The cutting or clearing of public utility rights-of-way or land for electric generating stations . . . provided that . . . [t]he cutting or clearing of the forest is conducted so as to minimize the loss of forest;

(6) Any routine maintenance of public utility rights-of-way;

(7) Any activity conducted on a single lot of any size or a linear project provided that:

> (i) The activity does not result in the cutting, clearing, or grading of more than 20,000 square feet of forest; and

> (ii) The activity on the lot or linear project will not result in the cutting, clearing, or grading of any forest that is subject to the requirements of a previous forest conservation plan prepared under this subtitle;

(8) Any strip or deep mining of coal regulated under Title 15, Subtitle 5 or Subtitle 6 of the Environment Article and any noncoal surface mining regulated under Title 15, Subtitle 8 of the Environment Article;

(9) Any activity required for the purpose of constructing a dwelling house intended for the use of the owner, or a child of the owner, if the activity does not result in the cutting, clearing, or grading of more than 20,000 square feet of forest;

(10) A county that has and maintains 200,000 acres or more of its land area in forest cover;

(11) The cutting or clearing of trees to comply with the requirements of 14 C.F.R. § 77.25 relating to objects affecting navigable airspace, provided that the Federal Aviation Administration has determined that the trees are a hazard to aviation;

(12) Any stream restoration project for which the applicant for a grading or sediment control permit has executed a binding

maintenance agreement of at least 5 years with the affected property owner; and

(13) Maintenance or retrofitting of a stormwater management structure that may include clearing of vegetation or removal and trimming of trees, so long as the maintenance or retrofitting is within the original limits of disturbance for construction of the existing structure, or within any maintenance easement for access to the structure.

* * *

§ 5–1603.   Local forest conservation programs

* * *

(a)(1) A unit of local government having planning and zoning authority shall develop a local forest conservation program, consistent with the intent, requirements, and standards of this subtitle.

(2) By April 30, 1992 all units of government with planning and zoning authority shall submit a proposed forest conservation program, which meets or is more stringent than the requirements and standards of this subtitle, to the Department for its review and approval.

(3) A unit of local government which has an existing program of forest conservation, or subsequently adopts such a program prior to December 31, 1992, may continue to administer its program prior to approval by the Department of the local forest conservation program.

(4) A municipality which has planning and zoning authority may, with the concurrence of the county and the Department, assign its obligations under this subtitle to the county.

* * *

(c)(2) A local forest conservation program, which has been approved by the Department, shall include:

(i) A policy document and all applicable new and amended local ordinances relating to implementation of the regulated activities, exemptions, the review, approval and appeal processes, incentives, legal instruments for protection, enforcement program, and penalties; and

(ii) A technical manual which outlines submittal requirements for forest stand delineations, required information for the approval of a forest conservation plan, specific forest conservation criteria and protection techniques.

(3)(i) A local authority shall review and amend, as appropriate, all current local ordinances, policies and procedures that are inconsistent with the intent and requirements of this subtitle such as parking, road width, setback, curb and gutter, grading, and sidewalk requirements.

(ii) A local forest conservation program, when approved by the Department, may:

1. Allow clustering and other innovative land use techniques that protect and establish forests where open space is preserved, sensitive areas are protected, and development is physically concentrated; and

2. Waive the requirements of this subtitle for previously developed areas covered by impervious surface and located in priority funding areas at the time of the application for subdivision plan, grading, or sediment control permit approval.

* * *

§ 5–1605.   Proposed forest conservation plans

Submission of proposed forest conservation plan

(a) Upon receipt of notice that the forest stand delineation is complete and correct, the applicant shall submit to the State or local authority a proposed forest conservation plan for the site.

Development by qualified professionals

(b) The forest conservation plan shall be developed by a licensed forester, licensed landscape architect, or other qualified professionals that may be approved by the State or a local authority.

Contents of proposed forest conservation plan

(c) A proposed forest conservation plan shall contain:

(1) A map of the site drawn at the same scale as the grading or subdivision plan;

(2) A table listing the net tract area in square feet, the square foot area of forest conservation required for the site, and the square foot area of forest conservation provided by the applicant on-site and off-site, if applicable;

(3) A clear graphic indication of the forest conservation provided on the site showing areas where both retention of existing forest or afforestation, by any and all methods, is planned;

(4) An anticipated construction timetable, including the sequence for tree conservation procedures;

(5) An afforestation or reforestation plan with a timetable and description of needed site and soil preparation, species, size, and spacing to be utilized;

* * *

§ 5–1606.   Forestation level requirements

Afforestation standards

(a)(1) For the following land use categories, tracts having less than 20% of the net tract area in forest cover shall be afforested up to 20% of the net tract area:

> (i) Agriculture and resource areas; and

> (ii) Medium density residential areas.

(2) For the following land use categories, tracts having less than 15% of the net tract area in forest cover shall be afforested up to 15% of the net tract area:

> (i) Institutional development areas;

> (ii) High density residential areas;

> (iii) Mixed use and planned unit development areas; and

> (iv) Commercial and industrial use areas.

(3) Afforestation requirements must conform to the conditions in §§ 5–1607 and 5–1610 of this subtitle, including payment into the Forest Conservation Fund, if afforestation on-site or off-site cannot be reasonably accomplished.

(4)(i) The afforestation requirements under this subsection shall be accomplished within 1 year or 2 growing seasons after the completion of the development project.

> (ii) If afforestation cannot be reasonably accomplished on-site or off-site, the requirement to contribute money to a Forest Conservation Fund under § 5–1610 of this subtitle shall be met within 90 days after the completion of the development project.

(5) Linear projects that involve no change in land use may not be subject to afforestation requirements.

Forest conservation threshold

(b) There is a forest conservation threshold established for all land use categories as provided in subsection (c) of this section. The forest conservation threshold means the percentage of the net tract area at which the reforestation requirement changes from a ratio of ¼ acre planted for every 1 acre removed to a ratio of 2 acres planted for every 1 acre removed.

Exhaustion of efforts to minimize cutting or clearing of trees

(c) After every reasonable effort to minimize the cutting or clearing of trees and other woody plants is exhausted in the development of a subdivision plan and grading and sediment control activities and implementation of the forest conservation plan, the forest conservation plan shall provide for reforestation, or payment into the Forest Conservation Fund, according to the formula set forth in subsection (b) of this section and consistent with the following forest conservation thresholds for the applicable land use category:

> (1) Agricultural and resource areas: 50% of net tract area;
>
> (2) Medium density residential areas: 25% of net tract area;
>
> (3) Institutional development areas: 20% of net tract area;
>
> (4) High density residential areas: 20% of net tract area;
>
> (5) Mixed use and planned unit development areas: 15% of net tract area; and
>
> (6) Commercial and industrial use areas: 15% of net tract area.

* * *

§ 5–1607.   Afforestation and reforestation requirements, priorities

(a) The preferred sequence for afforestation and reforestation shall be established by the State or local authority in accordance with the following after all techniques for retaining existing forest cover on-site have been exhausted:

> (1) Those techniques that enhance existing forest and involve selective clearing or supplemental planting on-site;
>
> (2) On-site afforestation or reforestation may be utilized where the retention options have been exhausted. In those cases, the method shall be selected in accordance with subsection (b) of this section, and the location shall be selected in accordance with subsection (d) of this section;
>
> (3)(i) Off-site afforestation or reforestation in the same watershed or in accordance with an approved master plan may be utilized where the applicant has demonstrated that no reasonable on-site alternative exists, or where:
>
>> 1. Any on-site priority areas for afforestation or reforestation have been planted in accordance with subsection (d) of this section; and

2.   The applicant has justified to the satisfaction of the State or local jurisdiction that environmental benefits associated with off-site afforestation or reforestation would exceed those derived from on-site planting;

* * *

(iii) Off-site afforestation or reforestation may include the use of forest mitigation banks which have been so designated in advance by the State or local forest conservation program which is approved by the Department. . . .

* * *

Standards for afforestation or reforestation requirements

(b) Standards for meeting afforestation or reforestation requirements shall be established by the State or local program using one or more of the following methods:

(1) Forest creation in accordance with a forest conservation plan using one or more of the following:

(i) Transplanted or nursery stock;

(ii) Whip and seedling stock; or

(iii) Natural regeneration where it can be shown to adequately meet the objective of the forest conservation plan.

(2) The use of street trees in a municipal corporation with a tree management plan, in an existing population center designated in a county master plan that has been adopted to conform with the Economic Growth, Resource Protection, and Planning Act of 1992, or in any other designated area approved by the Department as part of a local program, under criteria established by the local program. . . .

* * *

(3) When all other options, both on-site and off-site, have been exhausted, landscaping as a mitigation technique, conducted under an approved landscaping plan that establishes a forest at least 35 feet wide and covering at least 2,500 square feet of area.

Priority for retention and protection

(c)(1) The following trees, shrubs, plants, and specific areas shall be considered priority for retention and protection, and they shall be left in an undisturbed condition unless the applicant has demonstrated, to the satisfaction of the State or local authority, that reasonable efforts have been made to protect them and the plan cannot reasonably be altered:

(i) Trees, shrubs, and plants located in sensitive areas including 100-year floodplains, intermittent and perennial streams and their buffers, coastal bays and their buffers, steep slopes, and critical habitats; and

(ii) Contiguous forest that connects the largest undeveloped or most vegetated tracts of land within and adjacent to the site.

(2) The following trees, shrubs, plants, and specific areas shall be considered priority for retention and protection, and they shall be left in an undisturbed condition unless the applicant has demonstrated, to the satisfaction of the State or local authority, that the applicant qualifies for a variance under § 5–1611 of this subtitle:

(i) Trees, shrubs, or plants identified on the list of rare, threatened, and endangered species of the U.S. Fish and Wildlife Service or the Department;

* * *

Priorities for afforestation or reforestation

(d) The following shall be considered priority for afforestation or reforestation:

(1) Establish or enhance forest buffers adjacent to intermittent and perennial streams and coastal bays to widths of at least 50 feet;

(2) Establish or increase existing forested corridors to connect existing forests within or adjacent to the site and, where practical, forested corridors should be a minimum of 300 feet in width to facilitate wildlife movement;

(3) Establish or enhance forest buffers adjacent to critical habitats where appropriate;

(4) Establish or enhance forested areas in 100-year floodplains;

(5) Establish plantings to stabilize slopes of 25% or greater and slopes of 15% or greater with a soil K value greater than 0.35 including the slopes of ravines or other natural depressions;

(6) Establish buffers adjacent to areas of differing land use where appropriate, or adjacent to highways or utility rights-of-way;

(7) Establish forest areas adjacent to existing forests so as to increase the overall area of contiguous forest cover, when appropriate; and

(8) Use native plant materials for afforestation or reforestation, when appropriate.

Md. Code Ann., Nat. Res. §§ 5–1601 to 1612. How would you assess the complexity and scope of this statute? Does it achieve a proper balance between protecting forest resources, facilitating development, and acknowledging private property rights? For an example of a local government that maintains a plan consistent with this statute, see Washington County, Maryland's Forest Conservation Ordinance. Forest Conservation Ordinance, Washington County, Maryland: Department of Planning and Zoning, *available at* http://www.washco-md.net/planning/forest.shtm. Consider the following case involving private property conflicts arising out of similar efforts by a state to preserve forest resources.

1000 FRIENDS OF OREGON V. LAND CONSERVATION AND DEVELOPMENT COMMISSION, LANE COUNTY

Oregon Supreme Court
752 P.2d 271 (1988)

JONES, J.

The principal issue in this land use case concerns Oregon's Statewide Planning Goal 4, which directs that forest lands be conserved for forest use. . . .

After several earlier attempts, Lane County presented its proposed comprehensive rural land use plan to the Land Conservation and Development Commission (LCDC). . . . In September 1984, LCDC acknowledged the Lane County plan as being in compliance with the statewide land use goals (goals). 1000 Friends of Oregon (1000 Friends) objected and sought judicial review by the Court of Appeals on seven assignments of error.

[NOTE: only the first assignment of error is reviewed here].

The Court of Appeals reversed LCDC on all but one of the assignments of error. *1000 Friends of Oregon v. LCDC*, 731 P.2d 457 (Or. App. 1987). Lane County, LCDC, and 1000 Friends petitioned this court for review. We reverse the decision of the Court of Appeals in part, affirm in part, and remand the case to LCDC for further action.

* * *

Dwellings on Forest Lands

The intent of Goal 4 is "to conserve forest lands for forest uses." The goal includes commercial forestry as well as wildlife habitat and watershed protection, forests as buffer zones, and several other uses of forest lands in Oregon. In its plan, Lane County zoned large portions of the county as forest land. Lane County established two types of forest zones, non-impacted forest lands and impacted forest lands. The latter lands Lane County defined as "impacted by non-forest uses." Lane County Development Code (LC) 16.211(1)(a). Residences were not permitted on non-impacted forest lands, but dwellings were permitted on impacted forest lands, if, among other reasons, they were "necessary and accessory" to forest management.

Specifically, LC 16.211(b)(3) provides that "[a] dwelling or mobile home, and any accessory structures, on a vacant legal lot containing at least 10 acres shall be deemed accessory and necessary to the forest management of the legal lot" if certain criteria are met. . . .

* * *

The "necessary and accessory" test incorporated in Lane County's LC 16.211(3)(b) originated in *Lamb v. Lane County*, 7 Or. LUBA 137 (1983). In that case [the Land Use Board of Appeals (LUBA)] stated:

> We understand petitioner to argue that Goal 4 prohibits uses not enumerated in Goal 4 unless the use is an essential part of one of the permitted, enumerated uses. In other words, unenumerated uses which are *necessary and accessory* to an enumerated forest use are permitted because they are, in effect, part of uses expressly authorized by Goal 4. For example, roads are not enumerated in Goal 4 as being an authorized use in lands zoned for forest uses. However, a logging road is a necessary accessory of commercial forestry production and would be permitted under petitioner's interpretation. We agree with that interpretation. Restrictions and conditions placed on unenumerated and accessory uses, such as buffering, are irrelevant because they fail to assure that forest lands are retained for the enumerated forest uses under this standard. Relevant conditions or restrictions would measure whether a use is, in fact, accessory. *Id.* [297 Or.] at 143 [681 P.2d 124] (emphasis added).

Lane County and LCDC rely on the use of the italicized phrase in prior acknowledged plans to support the validity of its use in LC 16.211(3)(b). The Court of Appeals observed on reconsideration of this case, 85 Or.App. 619, 622, 737 P.2d 975 (1987), that the county adopted the phrase as the sole criterion by which applications for building permits would be judged and that Lane County was the first to so use the phrase.

The real issue is not the meaning of the words "necessary and accessory," however. Rather, it is whether LCDC erred in allowing Lane County to provide that existence of a forest management plan *ipso facto* allows construction of a dwelling or mobile home as being "necessary and accessory" to whatever the forest management plan may contain. . . .

The relevant portion of LC 16.211(3)(b) provides:

A dwelling or mobile home, and any accessory structures, on a vacant legal lot containing at least 10 acres shall be deemed accessory and necessary to the forest management of the legal lot provided:

(i) A detailed forest management plan . . . is submitted for the legal lot which demonstrates forest production will be enhanced by on site forest management from the residence . . .

* * *

In its acknowledgment order, LCDC based its finding of compliance with Goal 4 on Lane County's requirement of a forest management plan. LCDC stated that the requirements for a forest management plan and the Lane County ordinance making it a violation to fail to implement the plan "assures that active forest management must occur on forest lands in order to establish a forest related dwelling; thus, satisfying the accessory and necessary test."

We do not believe that LCDC has adequately explained that conclusion. . . .

The present plan and acknowledgment order do not represent an articulation of a tenable basis for LCDC's application of Goal 4 to the facts of the plan. The order suggests that LCDC's legal conclusions are incorrect, but LCDC may be able to correct the record through a more extensive explanation of its reasoning so as to demonstrate the validity of the Lane County plan.

The key provisions in the Lane County plan concern the forest management plan. The language of the plan is such that if a landowner can file a proper forest management plan, the landowner can also construct a dwelling on forest land. This language raises questions unanswered in the acknowledgment order and leads to the conclusion that LCDC has not shown the plan to be in compliance with Goal 4.

The Court of Appeals held that . . . "Lane County's criteria would allow dwellings which can be done without, need not be had and are not absolutely required for a forest use; they therefore do not comply with the goal." 83 Or.App. at 282–83, 731 P.2d 457. . . .

. . . Lane County's ordinance provides that buildings may be erected whenever the details of a forest management are completed. Therefore, the question is actually whether the standards for compliance with the forest management plan are such that LCDC can properly conclude that what would otherwise be a non-forest use—a dwelling—is, because of the forest management plan, properly considered a forest use.

In their petitions, LCDC and Lane County argue that because a forest management plan requires certain minimum stocking of timber, a forest management plan will comply with Goal 4. Because there must be some range between minimum stocking and the maximum possible forest density for most forest lands, a minimum stocking requirement does not itself ensure that the land will not be put to other uses. Therefore, applying a forest management plan to the lot as a whole would not seem to ensure that all the uses on the lot were forest uses as defined by Goal 4. LCDC has not shown how a non-forest use on one part of a lot, even one which enhances forest uses on other parts of the lot, must thereby legally be considered itself to be a forest use.

In ordinary usage, when the term "enhance" is used in reference to a condition, the usage implies that the basic conditions already exist and that the addition will improve or, as LCDC says in its petition, that there will be "an increment of increase." Without LCDC's offering a more extensive explanation, it does not appear that enhancing existing forest uses on part of a lot necessarily makes a non-forest use into a forest use.

LCDC asserts that the standards set forth in the Lane County plan are an adequate substitute for a case-by-case application of the "necessary and accessory" test to construction permit requests. This assertion is the heart of LCDC's legal conclusions. LCDC must show the necessary legal connection between the policy of conserving forest land for forest uses and allowing dwellings on forest land. Goal 4 sets a high standard when it requires that "[e]xisting forest uses shall be protected unless proposed changes are in conformance with the comprehensive plan." This court is not prepared to suggest that no dwelling could be considered necessary and accessory to a forest use, but we cannot agree that allowing a dwelling on some part of a lot simply because it may enhance forest uses on the remainder of the lot protects existing forest uses to the extent required by Goal 4.

* * *

. . . The "necessary and accessory" test in the Lane County plan is neither precise nor strict enough to show that dwellings on forest lands will meet the stated intent of Goal 4 to conserve forest lands for forest uses.

* * *

Because there is not a sufficient showing in the record made by LCDC that the sole test in the Lane County plan used to evaluate dwellings on forest lands will protect Goal 4, the decision of the Court of Appeals on the first assignment of error is affirmed.

* * *

The decisions of the Court of Appeals and LCDC are reversed in part. . . .

NOTES

1. *The outcome.* To comply with Oregon's statewide planning goals, Lane County zoned portions of the county for forest uses. Within certain forested zones Lane County allowed dwellings if they were "necessary and accessory" to forest management. To determine if a dwelling was "necessary and accessory" to forest management, however, Lane County merely required the submission and approval of a forest management plan. In other words, if a party submitted a plan for the property on which it chose to build a dwelling, the county considered the dwelling to be *per se* necessary and accessory. The Land Conservation and Development Commission (LCDC) agreed, also noting that Lane County retained the power to compel compliance with forest management plans. This was not enough for the court, which sent the case back to the LCDC for a more "extensive explanation" as to how dwellings on land would meet the "forest use" requirement of Statewide Planning Goal 4, rather than just presuming such dwellings would be forest uses if a forest management plan were also in place on the property.

2. *Oregon's Statewide Planning Goal 4.* At the time of the case, Oregon's Statewide Planning Goal 4 sought "[t]o conserve forest lands for forest uses," and provided that: "[f]orest land shall be retained for the production of wood fibre and other forest uses. Lands suitable for forest uses shall be inventoried and designated as forest lands. Existing forest land uses shall be protected unless proposed changes are in conformance with the comprehensive plan." Goal 4 defined "forest lands" as:

> (1) lands composed of existing and potential forest lands which are suitable for commercial forest uses; (2) other forested lands needed for watershed protection, wildlife and fisheries habitat and recreation; (3) lands where extreme conditions of climate, soil and topography require the maintenance of vegetative cover irrespective of use; (4) other forested lands in urban and agricultural areas which provide urban buffers, wind breaks, wildlife and fisheries habitat, livestock habitat, scenic corridors, and recreational use.

Goal 4 defined "forest uses" as:

> (1) the production of trees and the processing of forest products; (2) open space, buffers from noise, and visual separation of conflicting uses; (3) watershed protection and wildlife and fisheries habitat; (4) soil protection from wind and water; (5) maintenance of clean air and water; (6) outdoor recreational activities and related support

services and wilderness values compatible with these uses; and (7) grazing land for livestock."

These and other descriptions of LCDC's goals are taken from "Oregon's Statewide Planning Goals 1985." *See 1000 Friends of Oregon v. LCDC (Curry Co.)*, 301 Or. 447, 452 n. 4, 724 P.2d 268 (1986). If you were LCDC on remand, what evidence would you require of Lane County to demonstrate that a dwelling on the property was a "forest use"? For an update on the status of these goals, *see* Oregon Department of Land Conservation and Development, Statewide Planning Goals, http://www.oregon.gov/LCD/Pages/goals.aspx.

3.   *1000 Friends of Oregon again.* In a different *1000 Friends of Oregon* case (*1000 Friends of Oregon v. Land Conservation and Development Comm'n (Tillamook County)*, 737 P.2d 607 (Ore. 1987)), 1000 Friends lodged a challenge against the LCDC's approval of county plans implementing Statewide Planning Goal 5 (Goal 5). Goal 5 stated:

To conserve open space and protect natural and scenic resources[,] [p]rograms shall be provided that will (1) insure open space, (2) protect scenic and historic areas and natural resources for future generations, and (3) promote healthy and visually attractive environments in harmony with the natural landscape character. The locations, quality and quantity of the following resources shall be inventoried:

a.   Land needed or desirable for open space;

* * *

d.   Fish and wildlife areas and habitats;

e.   Ecologically and scientifically significant natural areas, including desert areas;

* * *

g.   Water areas, wetlands, watersheds and groundwater resources;

h.   Wilderness areas;

* * *

Where no conflicting uses for such resources have been identified, such resources shall be managed so as to preserve their original character. Where conflicting uses have been identified the economic, social, environmental and energy consequences of the conflicting uses shall be determined and programs developed to achieve the goal.

* * *

Open Space—consists of lands used for agricultural or forest uses, and any land area that would, if preserved and continued in its present use:

(a) Conserve and enhance natural or scenic resources;

* * *

(e) Enhance the value to the public of abutting or neighboring parks, forests, wildlife preserves, nature reservations or sanctuaries or other open space;

(f) Enhance recreation opportunities;

* * *

(h) Promote orderly urban development.

Rather than develop their own plans to implement Goal 5, numerous Oregon counties sought to rely solely on Oregon's Forest Protection Act (FPA) to protect Goal 5 resources when conflicts arose regarding timber operations. The LCDC approved this approach, and 1000 Friends challenged it. The court of appeals held that the counties must do their own planning regarding Goal 5. But the Supreme Court of Oregon reversed, concluding that it was "legally permissible for the county to fulfill its planning responsibilities by deference to the administration of the FPA." The court noted that maintaining uniform regulations for forests was one of the primary goals of the FPA, and that counties could thwart this goal if allowed to maintain greater control over forest operations. Do you think that deference to the FPA will achieve Goal 5 directives as related to timber extraction? If not, should counties be able to go above the floor set by the FPA in order to better preserve the non-extractive values of timber, as Goal 5 seeks to do? Compare this outcome with the *Big Creek Lumber* case, below.

G. MUNICIPAL FOREST PRESERVATION

As long as local governments, including county and municipal governments, have regulatory authority delegated to them (through specific statutes or under broadly phrased home-rule laws), and so long as their efforts are not preempted by state legislative or constitutional provisions (a subject discussed in detail in this section), they may create their own forest-protection ordinances. These conditions, though, are not always met. Local governments may lack regulatory power over forests. Even when they possess this authority, their regulatory efforts may collide with state-level regulation.

1. PREEMPTION

BIG CREEK LUMBER CO. V. COUNTY OF SANTA CRUZ ET AL.

California Supreme Court
38 Cal.4th 1139 (2006)

WERDEGAR, J.

We must decide whether two county zoning ordinances relating to the permissible locations for timber operations are preempted by state forestry statutes. Concluding they are not, we reverse the judgment of the Court of Appeal.

Background

In 1999, the Board of Supervisors of the County of Santa Cruz (County) adopted several ordinances that would have affected timber harvesting operations in the County. As pertinent here, County's ordinances restricted timber harvesting to specified zone districts within the County (Santa Cruz County Res. No. 493–99 & Santa Cruz County Ord. No. 4577 (1999); hereafter the zone district ordinance), barred timber harvesting operations in certain areas adjacent to streams and residences (Santa Cruz County Ord. No. 4571 (1999); hereafter the stream ordinance), and limited the parcels on which helicopter operations associated with such harvesting could occur (Santa Cruz County Ord. No. 4572 (1999); hereafter the helicopter ordinance). County also requested and obtained from the California Coastal Commission a ruling certifying the zone district ordinance as an amendment to County's local coastal program.

Plaintiffs Big Creek Lumber Co. and Homer T. McCrary (jointly Big Creek) and the Central Coast Forest Association, a nonprofit association of landowners and forestry professionals in the County, filed a petition for writ of mandate against County and the California Coastal Commission, challenging County's timber-related ordinances and the Commission's certification of the zone district ordinance as a local coastal program amendment. Plaintiffs' petition alleged that County's and the California Coastal Commission's actions violated the California Environmental Quality Act (Pub. Resources Code, § 21000 et seq.), and County's ordinances violated the doctrine of preemption.

The preemption claim was bifurcated and heard separately. The trial court found in favor of plaintiffs except as to the zone district ordinance. On appeal, the Court of Appeal invalidated County's ordinances in their entirety. We granted County's petition for review of the Court of Appeal's invalidation of the helicopter and zone district ordinances.

Discussion

The zone district ordinance amends County's zoning laws to restrict timber harvesting operations to areas zoned for timber production, mineral extraction industrial, or parks, recreation and open space. The helicopter ordinance requires that helicopter staging, loading, and servicing facilities associated with timber operations be located either on a parcel of land zoned for timber harvesting or on a parcel adjacent to such, and within the boundaries of a timber harvesting plan that has been approved by the California Department of Forestry and Fire Protection.

Plaintiffs argue that the ordinances are preempted by the Z'berg-Nejedly Forest Practice Act of 1973 (FPA) (Pub. Resources Code, § 4511 et seq.) and the California Timberland Productivity Act of 1982 (TPA) (Gov.Code, § 51100 et seq.). For the following reasons, we conclude that County's ordinances are not preempted.

A.   Overview: State Forestry Law

1.   The Forest Practice Act

"Timber harvesting operations in this state must be conducted in accordance with the provisions of the Forest Practice Act. The Act was intended to create and maintain a comprehensive system for regulating timber harvesting in order to achieve two goals" (*Sierra Club v. State Bd. of Forestry*, 7 Cal.4th 1215, 1226 (1994): to restore, enhance, and maintain the productivity of timberlands where feasible; and to achieve the maximum sustained production of high-quality timber products, while giving consideration to values relating to recreation, watershed, wildlife, range and forage, fisheries, regional economic vitality, employment, and aesthetic enjoyment (*id.*; see § 4513).

As originally enacted in 1973, the FPA permitted individual counties to adopt stricter rules and regulations governing timber operations than those provided under the FPA. (Stats.1973, ch. 880, § 4, at 1615–1616 [adding former § 4516].) In 1982, the Legislature amended the FPA (Stats.1982, ch. 1561, § 3, at 6164–6166) to provide instead that counties may recommend to the California Board of Forestry and Fire Protection (Board) additional forest practice rules and regulations (§ 4516.5, subds.(a), (b)) but, except with respect to performance bonds or other surety for road protection, counties are forbidden to "regulate the conduct of timber operations" (§ 4516.5, subd. (d); hereafter section 4516.5(d)).

Pursuant to the FPA, "timber operations are controlled by means of a site-specific timber harvesting plan that must be submitted to the [state forestry] department before timber operations may commence (§§ 4581 and 4582.5.). The Legislature has specified that the plan include the name and address of the timber owner and the timber operator, a description of the land upon which the work is proposed to be done, a description of the silviculture methods to be applied, an outline of the methods to mitigate erosion caused by operations performed in the vicinity of a stream, the provisions, if any, to protect any 'unique area' within the area of operations, and the anticipated dates for commencement and completion of operations. (§ 4582, subds.(a)–(g).)" (*Sierra Club v. State Bd. of Forestry*, 7 Cal.4th at 1226.) The director of the state forestry department, and the Board on appeal, review timber harvesting plans for compliance with the FPA and applicable regulations. (§ 4582.7.)

2.   The Timberland Productivity Act

The TPA, as amended in 1982 (Stats.1982, ch. 1489, §§ 1–39, pp. 5748–5766), reflects state policy, inter alia, "That timber operations conducted in a manner consistent with forest practice rules adopted by the [Board] shall not be or become restricted or prohibited due to any land use in or around the locality of those operations" (Gov. Code, § 51102, subd. (b)). The TPA seeks to implement that policy "by including all qualifying timberland in timberland production zones." (*Id.*, § 51103.) "Timberland," the Legislature has stated, "means privately owned land, or land acquired for state forest purposes, which is devoted to and used for growing and harvesting timber, or for growing and harvesting timber and compatible uses, and which is capable of growing an average annual volume of wood fiber of at least 15 cubic feet per acre." (*Id.*, § 51104, subd. (f).)

In order to accomplish its purposes, the TPA relies on tax incentives and zoning mandates. The TPA restricts land in certain timberland production zones (TPZ's) to the growing and harvesting of timber and compatible uses. (See Gov. Code, §§ 51115, 51118.) In exchange, owners of land in a TPZ benefit by lower property tax valuations that reflect the enforceable statutory restrictions. (See Cal. Const., art. XIII, § 8 [Legislature may tax certain land consistently with use restrictions].)

* * *

B.   Preemption Principles

The party claiming that general state law preempts a local ordinance has the burden of demonstrating preemption. (*See, e.g., Kucera v. Lizza*, 59 Cal.App.4th 1141, 1153 (1997) We have been particularly "reluctant to infer legislative intent to preempt a field covered by municipal regulation when there is a significant local interest to be served that may differ from one locality to another." (*Fisher v. City of Berkeley*, 37 Cal.3d 644, 707 (1984); *see also Great Western Shows, Inc. v. County of Los Angeles*, 27 Cal.4th 853, 866–867 (2002).) "The common thread of the cases is that if there is a significant local interest to be served which may differ from one locality to another then the presumption favors the validity of the local ordinance against an attack of state preemption." (*Gluck v. County of Los Angeles*, 93 Cal.App.3d 121, 133 (1979), citing, inter alia, *Galvan v. Superior Court*, 70 Cal.2d 851, 862–864 (1969).)

Thus, when local government regulates in an area over which it traditionally has exercised control, such as the location of particular land uses, California courts will presume, absent a clear indication of preemptive intent from the Legislature, that such regulation is not preempted by state statute. . . . 'A county or city may make and enforce within its limits all local, police, sanitary, and other ordinances and regulations not in conflict with general laws.' (Cal. Const., art. XI, § 7, italics added.) ' "Local legislation in conflict with general law is void. Conflicts exist if the ordinance duplicates [citations], contradicts [citation], or enters an area fully occupied by general law, either expressly or by legislative implication. . . .' " (*Morehart v. County of Santa Barbara*, 7 Cal.4th 725, 747 (1994))

C.   *The Zone District Ordinance*

Plaintiffs contend the zone district ordinance is preempted by section 4516.5(d) of the FPA. With exceptions not relevant here, section 4516.5(d) provides that individual counties shall not "regulate the conduct of timber operations . . . or require the issuance of any permit or license for those operations." As neither ordinance at issue requires the issuance of any permit or license, this case concerns the import of the statutory phrase "conduct of timber operations."

In *Big Creek Lumber Co. v. County of San Mateo*, 31 Cal.App.4th 418, 428 (1995) (*Big Creek v. San Mateo*), the Court of Appeal held that section 4516.5(d) does not deprive California counties of authority to zone timberland outside TPZ's for uses other than timber production. The Court of Appeal acknowledged that section 4516.5(d) mandates that the "conduct" of timber harvesting operations be governed exclusively by state law, but held that San Mateo County's ordinance, which restricted the location of non-TPZ commercial timber harvesting, did not offend the statute because it spoke "not to how timber operations may be conducted, but rather [to] where they may take place." (*Big Creek v. San Mateo*, at 424–425.) The court also noted that numerous provisions of California forestry law reveal the Legislature's intention to preserve local zoning authority. (*See id.* at 425–426, citing statutes.) Harmonizing the FPA and the TPA, the court concluded that "the Legislature did not intend to preclude counties from using their zoning authority to prohibit timber cutting on lands outside TPZ's." (*Id.* at 426.) For the following reasons, we agree.

1.   Traditional local zoning power

Land use regulation in California historically has been a function of local government under the grant of police power contained in article XI, section 7 of the California Constitution. "We have recognized that a city's or county's power to control its own land use decisions derives from this inherent police power, not from the delegation of authority by the state." (*DeVita v. County of Napa*, 9 Cal.4th 763, 782 (1995).) And the Legislature, when enacting state zoning laws, has declared its " 'intention to provide only a minimum of limitation in order that counties and cities may exercise the maximum degree of control over local zoning matters.' " (*Id.*, quoting Gov.Code, § 65800.)

Thus, "[t]he power of cities and counties to zone land use in accordance with local conditions is well entrenched." (*IT Corp. v. Solano County Bd. of Supervisors*, 1 Cal.4th at 89.) "In enacting zoning ordinances, the municipality performs a legislative function, and every intendment is in favor of the validity of such ordinances." (*Lockard v. City of Los Angeles*, 33 Cal.2d 453, 460 (1949).)

2.   Express preemption

* * *

Section 4516.5(d) contains no express reference to "zoning," nor does it bar localities in terms from regulating the location of timber operations. Rather, counties are forbidden to "regulate the conduct" of timber operations. As the court in *Big Creek v. San Mateo* pointed out, in common parlance an ordinance that avoids speaking to how timber operations may be conducted and addresses only where they may take place falls short of being "a clear attempt to regulate the conduct" thereof. (*Big Creek v. San Mateo*, 31 Cal.App.4th at 424; cf. *Desert Turf Club v. Board of Supervisors*, 141 Cal.App.2d 446, 452 (1956). . . . Nevertheless, as the Court of Appeal below recognized, to the extent zoning by definition may have the consequence of excluding logging from some locations, it may in that sense be said to "regulate" that activity, at least in the excluded locations.

When as here a statute is susceptible to more than one reasonable interpretation, "we look to 'extrinsic aids, including the ostensible objects to be achieved, the evils to be remedied, the legislative history, public policy, contemporaneous administrative construction, and the statutory scheme of which the statute is a part.' " (*Hoechst Celanese Corp. v. Franchise Tax Bd.*, 25 Cal.4th 508, 519 (2001)). In this case, such indicia support the construction of section 4516.5(d) adopted by the Court of Appeal in *Big Creek v. San Mateo*, cited above.

First, in many places where it addresses timberland zoning, general state forestry law expressly preserves and plainly contemplates the exercise of local authority. The actual designation of TPZ's, for example, is left to local action. Owners of parcels desiring TPZ zoning must petition local authorities. If the parcel does not meet state timber stocking standards and forest practice rules, the owner must agree to do so within five years, and, if the owner fails to do so, local authorities are empowered to rezone the parcel and to "specify a new zone for the parcel, which is in conformance with the county general plan and whose primary use is other than timberland." Additionally, local bodies are authorized in certain circumstances to rezone TPZ parcels or convert them to another use.

"Thus, it is clear that the Legislature has deferred a number of important zoning decisions to local authority, even in the case of TPZ's." (*Big Creek v. San Mateo*, 31 Cal.App.4th at 425.) Certainly neither the TPA nor the FPA suggests localities are restricted in what uses they may prohibit outside TPZ zones. (*Big Creek v. San Mateo*, at 428.) "Nowhere in the statutory scheme," in fact, "has the Legislature expressly prohibited the use of zoning ordinances" (*id*. at 425).

. . . . That the Legislature intended the phrase "regulate the conduct" in section 4516.5(d) to preclude only local regulations that affect how timber operations are conducted is borne out by the kinds of issues the Board, under the rubric of "the conduct of timber operations," is in its rules and regulations statutorily required to address. (See § 4551.5.) Fire prevention and control, soil erosion control, site preparation, water quality and watershed control, flood control, disease prevention and control (*id*.)—these clearly are matters relating to the process of carrying out timber operations. (See *Big Creek v. San Mateo*, 31 Cal.App.4th at 426.)

* * *

When the Legislature wishes expressly to preempt all regulation of an activity, it knows how to do so. For example, the Legislature has provided in the TPA that "[p]arcels zoned as timberland production [i.e., located in TPZ's] shall be zoned so as to restrict their use to growing timber and to compatible uses. *The growing and harvesting of timber on those parcels shall be regulated solely pursuant to state statutes and regulations*." (Gov.Code, § 51115, italics added.) One implication of this provision, of course, is that the growing and harvesting of timber on non-TPZ parcels need not be regulated solely pursuant to state statutes and regulations.

* * *

The Legislature has had ample opportunity over the past decade to amend section 4516.5(d) to abrogate or modify the Court of Appeal's construction of the statutory phrase "regulate the conduct of timber operations" in *Big Creek v. San Mateo*. Yet, notwithstanding it has amended the FPA in numerous other particulars every year since that decision was filed, it has not done so. Several California judicial decisions, moreover, have relied on *Big Creek v. San Mateo* in the intervening years. " 'Where a statute has been construed by judicial decision, and that construction is not altered by subsequent legislation, it must be presumed that the Legislature is aware of the judicial construction and approves of it.' " (*Wilkoff v. Superior Court*, 38 Cal.3d 345, 353 (1985).) The Legislature's failure to amend section 4516.5(d), while not conclusive, "may be presumed to signify legislative acquiescence" in the *Big Creek v. San Mateo* decision. (*People v. Leahy*, 8 Cal.4th 587, 604 (1994), citing numerous authorities.)

For the foregoing reasons, we agree with the Court of Appeal in *Big Creek v. San Mateo* that "the 'conduct' of timber harvesting operations is exclusively governed by state law. 'Conduct' [however] is not given a specialized definition in the FPA. Its ordinary meaning is 'the act, manner, or process of carrying out (as a task) or carrying forward (as a business, government, or war).' " (*Big Creek v. San Mateo*, 31 Cal.App.4th at 426.) Accordingly, local zoning ordinances, like the County's zone district ordinance, that speak to the location of timber operations but not to the manner in which they are carried out, are not expressly preempted by section 4516.5(d).

[The court decided that there was no implied preemption of local regulation of forests since 1) the Forest Practices Act expressly preempted certain local regulations targeting the conduct of timber operations, thus impliedly permitting local regulation of other aspects of forests—that is, local regulation of not how timber operations occur, but rather where operations take place; and 2) the Timberland Productivity Act expressly recognized local zoning authority].

For the foregoing reasons, we reverse the judgment of the Court of Appeal and remand the cause for further proceedings consistent with our opinion.

<h2 style="text-align:center">JENSEN V. CITY OF EVERETT</h2>

Washington Court of Appeals
109 Wash.App. 1048 (2001)

BECKER, J.

Enforcing an Environmentally Sensitive Areas Ordinance, the City of Everett sanctioned appellant Jensen for clearing trees to create a view on his property. We affirm the trial court's order dismissing Jensen's challenge to the ordinance. The ordinance is not preempted by the Forest Practices Act.

[The court also addressed Jensen's claims that the ordinance was unconstitutionally vague and violated his right to due process and equal protection. This analysis has been omitted].

In 1990, Loren and Dianna Jensen bought three acres of undeveloped property in Everett, Washington. Jensen built a house at the top of a ravine designated as environmentally sensitive under Everett's Environmentally Sensitive Areas Ordinance. The ravine has steep slopes and potential wetlands linked to Narbeck Creek.

In August 1992, Jensen, through a consultant recommended by his lawyer, wrote a letter requesting the City's permission to clear the alder trees in the environmentally sensitive area in order to create a view of Puget Sound, plant gardens, and build a gazebo. The City responded that in a sensitive area, the ordinance forbids the removal of existing vegetation, including alder trees.

In January 1993, Jensen inquired whether a new city policy on views would allow Jensen to cut trees. The City Planning Department responded that the view policy would not permit Jensen to create a new view, but only allowed for the maintenance of existing views.

Jensen sought advice from his lawyer. The lawyer stated an opinion that the ordinance did not preclude cutting less than 5,000 board feet of timber for personal use because such cutting was permissible as a Class 1 forest practice under the Forest Practices Act. Jensen proceeded to clear approximately two acres of environmentally sensitive habitat one day in August, 1993. The City immediately posted a stop work notice on Jensen's property.

The City notified Jensen that the clearing of trees was a violation of the ordinance. The City gave him notice of a proposed short and long term mitigation plan, and suggested that Jensen post a $108,000 bond to cover the cost of mitigation. Jensen completed portions of the proposed short-term erosion control plan, including placing straw and a silt screen on the cleared bank, but did not engage in long-term environmental mitigation. The City requested a hearing on the notice of violation in order to enforce the mitigation requirements of the ordinance.

In May 1994, the City Hearing Examiner held a hearing. The City requested that Jensen be ordered to undertake anti-erosion measures, including grading contours, hydrological analysis, and replanting of the cleared wetland and buffer areas. The hearing examiner concluded that Jensen had violated the ordinance by conducting an unauthorized alteration on an environmentally sensitive area. The decision ordered him to prepare a habitat assessment and submit a schedule by which other required mitigation measures would be completed.

* * *

Preemption

Jensen contends the Forest Practices Act preempts the Everett ordinance. Initially, the City contends that Jensen's preemption argument is moot. In 1997, after the enforcement action from which this appeal arises, the Legislature amended the Forest Practices Act so that it now requires local authorities to regulate forest practices. The City contends the amendment is curative and remedial, and hence, retroactive.

. . . . The City has failed to demonstrate that the Legislature intended the amendment to be retroactive. . . . We conclude the preemption argument is not moot.

The version of the Act in effect before the 1997 amendment permitted municipalities to regulate forest practices in connection with land use planning and zoning, but only if such regulation was consistent with state forest practices regulations:

> No county, city, municipality, or other local or regional governmental entity shall adopt or enforce any law, ordinance, or regulation pertaining to forest practices, except that to the extent otherwise permitted by law, such entities may exercise any:
>
> (1) Land use planning or zoning authority: Provided, That exercise of such authority may regulate forest practices only: (a) Where the application submitted under RCW 76.09.060 as now or hereafter amended indicates that the lands will be converted to a use other than commercial timber production; or (b) on lands which have been platted after January 1, 1960: Provided, That no permit system solely for forest practices shall be allowed; that any additional or more stringent regulations shall not be inconsistent with the forest practices regulations enacted under this chapter; and such local regulations shall not unreasonably prevent timber harvesting[.]

Former RCW 76.09.240 (1993).

Parties asserting preemption bear the burden of overcoming the presumption that ordinances are constitutional. *Brown v. City of Yakima*, 116 Wn.2d 556, 559, 807 P.2d 353 (1991). Preemption occurs when the Legislature states its intention either expressly or by necessary implication to preempt the regulated field. *Kennedy v. City of Seattle*, 94 Wn.2d 376, 383–84, 617 P.2d 713 (1980).

The Forest Practices Act regulates forest practices. To show that the Act preempts the Everett ordinance from regulating his removal of the alder trees, Jensen must show that cutting the alder trees was a forest practice. A forest practice is "any activity conducted on or directly pertaining to forest land and relating to growing, harvesting, or processing timber". RCW 76.09.020(10).

Jensen contends that his residential lot is forest land, citing *Department of Natural Resources v. Marr*, 54 Wn.App. 589, 774 P.2d 1260 (1989). But *Marr* holds that a residential lot is forest land only if it meets the statutory definition: "land which is capable of supporting a merchantable stand of timber and is not being actively used for a use which is incompatible with timber growing." RCW 76.09.020(8). A merchantable stand of timber is:

a stand of trees that will yield logs and/or fiber:

Suitable in size and quality for the production of lumber, plywood, pulp or other forest products;

Of sufficient value at least to cover all the costs of harvest and transportation to available markets.

WAC 222–16–010.

Jensen introduced no evidence on summary judgment to establish that the harvested alder trees on his land were a merchantable stand or that the cost of harvesting was less than the commercial value of the timber. Because Jensen failed to establish that his property could be classified as forest land within the purview of the Forest Practices Act, the Forest Practices Act does not regulate the activities on his property and cannot preempt the ordinance as it applies to his property.

. . . Everett enacted [its] ordinance in 1991 under the mandate of the Growth Management Act, RCW 36.70A, et seq. The Growth Management Act's purpose and function, stated in its first section, is to bring about comprehensive land use planning:

The legislature finds that uncoordinated and unplanned growth, together with a lack of common goals expressing the public's interest in the conservation and the wise use of our lands, pose a threat to the environment, sustainable economic development, and the health, safety, and high quality of life enjoyed by residents of this state. It is in the public interest that citizens, communities, local governments, and the private sector cooperate and coordinate with one another in comprehensive land use planning. Further, the legislature finds that it is in the public interest that economic development programs be shared with communities experiencing insufficient economic growth.

RCW 36.70A.010 . . . . . It is plain that local governments acting under the Growth Management Act do not have the same function and purpose as the Department of Natural Resources enforcing its own regulations under the Forest Practices Act. Local governments have authority under the

Growth Management Act to designate critical areas, and regulate activities within the critical areas for the purpose of protecting the environment. RCW 36.70A.170, 36.70A.172, 36.70A.010. The Department of Natural Resources, on the other hand, enforces Forest Practices regulations for the purpose of protecting public, private and commercial forest lands. RCW 76.09.010. Because the Forest Practices Act and the ordinance have different functions and purposes, the Forest Practices Act does not preempt local government authority to regulate critical areas, even though the end result of regulation under both regimes may be restrictions on the cutting of trees.

We conclude the trial court properly dismissed Jensen's preemption claim.

* * *

NOTES

1. *To preempt or not to preempt?* Contrast the outcome of *Big Creek Lumber* with the second *1000 Friends of Oregon* case discussed in note 3, page 641, above. The Oregon court concluded that maintaining uniform regulations for forests was one of the primary goals of the Oregon Forest Practices Act, and that local governments could thwart this policy goal if allowed to maintain greater control over forest operations. Presumably, to achieve the goals of Statewide Planning Goal 5 local governments could have sought to exercise control over the siting of forest operations, rather than the direct management of those operations, as did the local government in *Big Creek Lumber*. Which is the better approach? To treat a Forest Practices Act as a floor above which local governments can regulate more stringently? Or is state preemption necessary to achieve uniform forest management? Does it matter if a local government is regulating the siting of forest operations rather than directly managing the forest operations themselves? Do you think the pre-1997 version of the Washington Forest Practices Act at issue in *Jenson* is a better approach, allowing local regulation but only if consistent with the FPA? The 1997 amendments to the Washington FPA, of course, give more control to local governments, much like the *Big Creek* court's interpretation of the California FPA.

2. *Timber operation siting versus control.* In *Big Creek Lumber v. San Mateo*, the court held that an ordinance that does not directly control timber operations—such as ordinances concerning fire prevention and control, soil erosion control, site preparation, water quality and watershed control, flood control, disease prevention and control—but that instead dictate where those operations may take place is not an attempt to regulate "timber operations." Is this true? The *Big Creek Lumber* court decided that controlling the siting of timber operations through zoning, potentially excluding timber operations from some locations, may be an appropriate form of regulating timber operations. Do you agree? Does the statute mean something very different

when it forbids counties from "regulat[ing] the conduct of timber operations"? Is "conduct" a key word here? Does "evidence by omission" lend evidence in this regard, in that the legislature never amended the FPA to reflect disagreement with the *Big Creek Lumber* ruling ("[w]here a statute has been construed by judicial decision, and that construction is not altered by subsequent legislation, it must be presumed that the Legislature is aware of the judicial construction and approves of it." *Wilkoff v. Superior Court*, 38 Cal.3d 345 (1985))? What weight do you give the fact that several California court decisions had relied on *Big Creek Lumber* decision?

3. *More state preemption.* In *Westhaven Community Development Council v. County of Humboldt*, 61 Cal.App.4th 365 (1998), a landowner sought to harvest timber on four acres of property zoned residential/single family. He submitted a proposed timber harvesting plan to the California Department of Forestry (CDF), which approved a modified version of the landowner's initial timber harvesting plan. The Westhaven Community Development Council (WCDC) sued to enjoin the timber harvest, arguing that the county's zoning ordinances did not allow single-family residential property to be principally used for commercial timber production. Instead, such production was only a conditionally permitted use of such property. WCDC therefore sought to require the landowner to apply for a conditional use permit. The property owners maintained that the FPA preempted the County's permit requirement, since the proposed harvest was larger than three acres. The trial court denied WCDC's request for a permanent injunction.

The lower court based its decision on the same FPA provision interpreted by the *Big Creek Lumber* court, which preempted individual counties from regulating "the conduct of timber operations" or—most relevant for this case—from requiring permits for timber operations. On appeal, the court distinguished *Big Creek Lumber v. San Mateo*, which differentiated between local ordinances that regulated the *location* of commercial timber harvesting rather than *timber operations* themselves. The court stated that the county ordinance at issue in *Big Creek Lumber* did not create a permit requirement, but instead prohibited commercial timber harvesting within a certain distance of dwellings. WCDC did not see the distinction as relevant,

> contend[ing] that each type of ordinance operates to determine whether timber activities may occur in a particular location. The ordinance in [*Big Creek Lumber v. San Mateo*] achieved this result by describing areas within which timber harvesting operations could not occur. According to WCDC, Humboldt County achieves this result by denying permits to individuals who seek to harvest timber in areas which Humboldt County concludes, subject to the limits of state law, should not be used for timber harvesting.

The court rejected WCDC's argument, determining that the ordinance at issue did not indicate *when* the county would deny a permit, whereas in *Big Creek v. San Mateo* forest owners had certainty regarding when their operations would be prohibited. The court also observed that a permit requirement "creates delays which an ordinance that expressly prohibits timber harvesting in a defined area does not create," and that the permit requirement raised more procedural due process concerns and burdens on landowners than did the ordinance at issue in *Big Creek Lumber v. San Mateo*. The court held that the FPA preempted the ordinance.

Can *Westhaven* and the two *Big Creek* cases be reconciled? Is the *Westhaven* court's analysis regarding the uncertainty of permit denial a valid assessment of the requirements of the FPA, or instead an assessment of procedural defects in the local zoning ordinance? Why does that matter? Are delays in obtaining permits, and the difficulty for timber operators to shape local decisions about where to allow timber harvests, administrative law critiques or valid critiques of the legal requirements of the FPA? In other words, is the court directly addressing the preemption question and the relationship between the FPA and the local ordinance, or is its ruling based on other grounds?

2. CONSTITUTIONAL CLAIMS

PALM BEACH POLO, INC. V. VILLAGE OF WELLINGTON
Florida Court of Appeal
918 So.2d 988 (2006)

WARNER, J.

* * *

Big Blue Reserve or Forest is an undeveloped tract of land, approximately ninety-two acres in size, in the Village of Wellington. It contains wetlands and many old-growth cypress trees, some more than 300 years old. Big Blue is the focus of this appeal.

In 1971 most of the Village of Wellington was owned by AlphaBeta, Inc. and Breakwater Housing Corp. Desiring to develop Wellington, they entered into a Planned Unit Development with Palm Beach County. The result became the Wellington PUD.

A Planned Unit Development is a zoning device used to permit flexibility in design and use of property. It is an agreement between the land owner and the zoning authority, and the terms of development are negotiated between the parties in accordance with the conditions set forth in the governing ordinances. A PUD plan, in compliance with zoning regulations, is submitted to the county for approval.

In 1972, the Zoning Resolution for Palm Beach County provided that, with respect to the Wellington PUD, "The intent and purpose of this section is to provide an alternative means of land development and to provide design latitude for the site planner." That year, the county approved the Wellington PUD submitted by AlphaBeta and Breakwater. It covered the development plan for 7400 acres. At the hearing approving the plan, several conditions were placed upon the approval. These included:

> Developer proposes an overall average of 2 dwelling units per acre with public open space of over 25%. Development expected to take at least until year 2000;

> Will enhance and preserve big blue areas and pine tree forests. Will develop a ring of water around it for protection. Will increase water level 1 foot (back to its original condition) and animal life can be restored to its original condition.

> Will preserve natural vegetation.

> A planned community of open spaces, bicycle paths, golf course and recreation areas, with restoration and preservation of big blue pristine forest areas.

The notes of the commission meeting reflect that as a reason for approval, the property, as zoned, could be developed with single-family dwellings with a density of four units per acre. However, the developer committed to an overall density of two units per acre, which was made one of the conditions of the plan. Big Blue was given an OS-R designation, meaning Open Space-Reserve, in an Agricultural/Residential zoning district.

A year later, in connection with an application for a binding letter of interpretation, the developer submitted an informational package to the State Department of Administration. In that package the developer stated the following regarding Big Blue:

> This 120-acre pristine forest containing some yet unnamed fern specimens, has been explored recently by a team of hardy souls who have ventured into this area to determine how best this untouched area can be preserved in its natural state.

> There have been claims of ferns 15 feet and higher as well as cypress trees reaching 85 to 100 feet in height flourishing in this wilderness area, along with abundant animal life. There is a definite contrast between the deafing [sic] quietness within the forest and the pure shrill sounds of literally dozens of species of birds.

> You can now walk into the Big Blue, very carefully, with proper guides; no vehicles will be allowed on the path. The Big Blue is a "must" evidencing an appreciation of the conservation, preservation and environmental attitude that is typical of the Wellington project.

In addition, the application by the Acme Improvement District for surface water management for the Wellington area noted that the environmental considerations upon most of the Wellington PUD property were not significant because it was abandoned agricultural land, except for Big Blue. In its application the District noted that Big Blue "will be preserved in its existing state. . . ."

In 1987 the surface water permit plan was modified with a particular emphasis on the Big Blue. This was done based upon application of the Landmark Land Company of Florida, Inc. The South Florida Water Management analysis refers to the proposed modification as completing the berm around Big Blue. The review stated, "The restoration of the Big Blue is dependent upon the perimeter berm being completed and constant inundation being maintained. . . . Constant inundation will kill most of the Brazillian Pepper [exotic vegetation present] and prevent further invasion."

The county adopted its Comprehensive Plan in 1988. The next year, the developer asked for another modification of the Wellington PUD. In the ordinance approving the modification, the county made it conditional upon the amending of the tabular data of the plan to reflect the "acreage of the OS-R natural reserve known as Big Blue reserve."

[In the following years, the developer of the PUD, Landmark, went bankrupt, and the project passed into the hands of Palm Beach Polo. Meanwhile, Wellington became an incorporated municipality and adopted its own plan, which essentially followed the county plan that it displaced. The Wellington plan, like its county predecessor, gave Big Blue a conservation designation and retained its OS-R zoning. Polo claimed that Wellington's actions violated its property rights in Big Blue. As the court explains, Wellington proceeded to file suit against Polo alleging that Polo was failing to maintain Big Blue as required by the approved PUD.]

Wellington then filed its own suit for declaratory judgment seeking to enforce the requirements of the 1972 PUD regarding Big Blue for flooding of the property and removal of exotic vegetation. Polo answered, contending that it had no legal obligation to preserve Big Blue. It asserted that the preservation boundaries were not legally described and that the restorative measures were too general in the original 1972 PUD to be enforced, nor were they properly implemented prior to Polo's acquisition in 1993. It counterclaimed for inverse condemnation, contending that the requirements for preserving Big Blue constituted an unlawful taking and a violation of the Bert J. Harris Act.

[The trial court ruled in favor of Wellington and upheld its power to enforce its land-use plan and the terms of the approved PUD. In so doing, it noted that these restrictions on the use of Big Blue had been in effect for years before Polo acquired the land. The trial court ordered Big Blue to comply with the applicable requirements, including those mandating affirmative conservation work. Polo appealed.]

We dispose first of Polo's claim that it is entitled to compensation under the Bert J. Harris Act, section 70.001, Florida Statutes. That statute creates a cause of action where a law, regulation, or ordinance, as applied inordinately burdens, restricts, or limits use of property without amounting to a taking. Section 70.001(2) provides:

> When a specific action of a governmental entity has inordinately burdened an existing use of real property or a vested right to a specific use of real property, the property owner of that real property is entitled to relief, which may include compensation for the actual loss to the fair market value. . . .

Section 70.001(3)(e) provides, in part:

> The terms "inordinate burden" or "inordinately burdened" mean that an action of one or more governmental entities has directly restricted or limited the use of real property such that the property owner is permanently unable to attain the reasonable, investment-backed expectation for the existing use of the real property or a vested right to a specific use of the real property with respect to the real property as a whole, or that the property owner is left with existing or vested uses that are unreasonable such that the property owner bears permanently a disproportionate share of a burden imposed for the good of the public, which in fairness should be borne by the public at large.

The statute defines "existing use" in section 70.001(3)(b) as follows:

> The term "existing use" means an actual, present use or activity on the real property, including periods of inactivity which are normally associated with, or are incidental to, the nature or type of use or activity or such reasonably foreseeable, nonspeculative land uses which are suitable for the subject real property and compatible with adjacent land uses and which have created an existing fair market value in the property greater than the fair market value of the actual, present use or activity on the real property.

We think it is fairly obvious from the abundant history of Big Blue that there was no "reasonable, investment-backed expectation" for an existing use of Big Blue at all. From 1972 forward it was designated as a natural reserve and extraordinary efforts were made to preserve this important pristine forest. As part of the PUD, any development density available to the acreage in Big Blue was transferred to other property in the Wellington PUD. At the time Polo purchased the Wellington property, Big Blue was designated as a nature reserve. Wellington's redesignation of it as a "conservation area" in its comprehensive plan changed nothing regarding the property. Polo failed to establish that at any time it was entitled to build on the property. In sum, Polo's claim that a violation of the Bert J. Harris Act occurred is frivolous.

Polo next argues that the 1972 Wellington PUD Master Plan is unconstitutional as applied to the Big Blue property because it is overly broad and vague, lacking definition of critical "technical" terms. It includes in those "technical" terms the words "big blue areas," "preserve," "restoration," "enhance," and the like. Even if we were to agree that these are "technical" terms, which we do not, both Polo's predecessors-in-title, as well as the regulating agencies, have given specific meanings to them.

"Generally, a reviewing court should defer to the interpretation given a statute or ordinance by the agency responsible for its administration. Of course, that deference is not absolute, and when the agency's construction of a statute amounts to an unreasonable interpretation, or is clearly erroneous, it cannot stand." . . . Here, the Director of the Department of Zoning testified at length to the interpretation of these terms. Some terms were defined in the zoning code, and some required the ordinary dictionary definition of the term. In its final judgment, the trial court also noted that Polo offered no alternative interpretations for the terms.

* * *

The trial court was correct in deferring to the agency's interpretation of its zoning code. The entire history of Big Blue and its regulation by the county and then the Village of Wellington shows that the meanings of the terms were well understood by all parties. Not only were they understood generally, but substantial evidence shows that specific requirements were also understood. The South Florida Water Management District Surface Water Management Permits are quite specific in the berming of Big Blue to inundate the property and also to remove exotic vegetation.

* * *

In this case, the original developers of the PUD property, AlphaBeta, Inc. and Breakwater Housing Co., included in their 1972 PUD application the specific conditions regarding Big Blue that were ultimately adopted and incorporated into the 1972 PUD plan. Stribling testified that in working up the PUD application he had several meetings with the Palm Beach County Planning and Zoning Board in which there was an exchange of information and ideas. Breakwater's and AlphaBeta's intentions were to preserve Big Blue and restore it to its original state. In return, the county permitted them to have great flexibility in their development plans, and the trial court found that the owner received compensating development rights for the preservation of Big Blue. It would be contrary to the original agreements to allow Polo to now avoid the obligations that its predecessors in title consented to, and which it had actual knowledge of through the extensive history in the public documents regarding the Wellington PUD.

Finally, we need not spend further time or effort in analyzing a takings claim. Although the Big Blue property will be flooded and thus unusable for development, that is precisely the condition of the property that Polo's predecessors agreed to in exchange for developing other property with higher densities. In *City of Riviera Beach v. Shillingburg*, 659 So.2d 1174 (Fla. 4th DCA 1995), a regulatory takings case, this court explained that the denial of use of some of a landowner's property does not itself constitute an unlawful taking, because the property must be considered in its entirety. In determining if a portion of the land should be considered as a whole or treated separately, the factors to be considered are whether the land is contiguous and whether there is unity of ownership. *Id.* at 1183. Whether there is a taking of Big Blue property requires a consideration of what occurred when the PUD was originally developed on the 7400 acres of Wellington in 1972. It was at that time that the owners bargained for development of vast sections at higher densities in return for preservation of Big Blue. This was an agreed restriction, compensated by the transfer of development rights to other property. No taking has occurred.

The trial court's judgment was thorough and correct. We affirm it in its entirety.

NOTES

1. *The saga continues.* Straub, the real estate developer in control of Palm Beach Polo and Country Club, again filed suit in 2014 "asking a Palm Beach County judge for an injunction declaring that Wellington—not Straub—must 'restore, enhance, maintain and preserve' the 92-acre wetland that lies in Palm Beach Polo and Country Club, which Straub owns." It appears that instead of just removing exotics, as stipulated in prior agreements, the club was removing native trees and clearing portions of the preserve. As a result, Wellington sent Palm Beach Polo stop-work orders to which it objected, arguing that the requirements went beyond its original obligations. *See* Kristen M. Clark, *Wellington, Straub in court again over Big Blue preserve*, Palm Beach Post, June 4, 2014.

Law is, of course, only as good as its enforcement. Are stiffer penalties warranted to enforce provisions like Wellington's PUD agreement? To what degree should forest preservation efforts be undertaken through flexible mechanisms like PUDs, the incorporation of which into case-by-case negotiated agreements runs the risk of being overlooked or challenged by subsequent purchasers of property? Would it be better to employ less flexible zoning ordinances that are more clearly part of the public record and provide more certainty regarding acceptable forest management options?

2.   *Pristine Big Blue.* The original developers of the area described Big Blue in rather glowing terms, noting that the "untouched area" should be preserved in its natural state, touting the abundant flora and fauna, and claiming that "Big Blue is a 'must' evidencing an appreciation of the conservation, preservation and environmental attitude that is typical of the Wellington project." While a great deal of effort may go into initial planning to protect resources like Big Blue, subsequent property owners may seek to undo preservation gains once the baseline of development shifts from an area that is predominantly pristine to one that is predominantly developed. The image below depicts Big Blue Preserve in the bottom left corner. As you can see, the Palm Beach Polo and Country Club is adjacent to the preserve, but the larger surrounding area has also been developed almost entirely. What should be the role of state and local law in protecting more areas of value like Big Blue? After all, flood protection services, water purification and retention services, air purification services, energy efficiency services, among a number of other ecosystem services, are most needed in areas where development exists. These services may be of less utility in rural areas removed from development.

3.   *Takings tests and statutes.* Florida's Bert J. Harris, Jr., Private Property Rights Protection Act and similar statutes aim to protect property owners from what is perceived as unnecessary regulatory intrusion into private property rights. These statutes typically require compensation for diminution in property value attributed to regulation in many circumstances

in which compensation is not required under the various constitutional takings tests—the *Penn Central* balancing test, the *Loretto* physical invasion test, and the *Lucas* complete elimination of economic value test. How do such statutes affect considerations of the public trust, discussed in chapter 3? If forests and the wildlife within them were considered public trust resources, could "property rights protection" statutes legally require compensation to be paid for forest preservation regulations? For more analysis on this question, see Blake Hudson, *The American Takings Revolution and Public Trust Preservation: A Tale of Two Blackstones*, 5 Sea Grant L. & Pol'y J. 57 (2013); Blake Hudson, *The Public and Wildlife Trust Doctrines and the Untold Story of the Lucas Remand*, 34 Colum. J. Envtl. L. 99 (2009); Michael C. Blumm & Lusas Ritchie, *Lucas's Unlikely Legacy: The Rise of Background Principles as Categorical Takings Defenses*, 29 Harv. Envtl. L. Rev. 321, 341-44 (2005) (discussing the public trust as a "background principle of state property law").

PEOPLE V. NOVIE

New York Supreme Court, Appellate Division
976 N.Y.S.2d 636 (2013)

* * *

By amended information dated November 18, 2011, defendant was charged with violating sections 176–6 (A) (1) and 176–7 (C) of the Tree Preservation and Landscape Maintenance Law of the Village of Montebello (Tree Law). Defendant moved to dismiss the accusatory instrument on the ground that the aforementioned sections of the Tree Law are unconstitutional for reasons set forth below. In support of his motion, defendant stated that when he and his wife had purchased the property in question, it consisted of almost an acre of land with trees on the front of the property facing the town road and a backyard area that had been "left unattended and as a result became overgrown with mainly Ash trees that grew in a crowded manner . . . resulting in scrawny, pole-like trees that became unhealthy due to reaching their life expectancy and other causes, such as illness, disease and damage from vines." At the time, defendant had three-year-old twins and wanted an attractive, safe backyard for his family. Therefore, in 2009, defendant hired a contractor to cut down some dead and dying trees, after which the Village of Montebello charged defendant with violating the aforementioned sections of the Tree Law, which required defendant to, among other things, obtain the Village's permission to remove any tree on his property.

In February 2010, defendant entered into a civil compromise with the Village by which, in lieu of prosecution, he agreed to pay the Village $250 and to "follow proper procedures with regard to any improvements/tree removal . . . concerning [his] property." In July 2010, defendant applied for a permit to remove from his property 15 dead ash and elm trees, two oak trees—to which defendant was allegedly allergic—and one birch tree, and agreed to pay professional consulting fees pursuant to chapter 65 of the Code of the Village of Montebello. In August 2010, defendant's application was approved to the extent of allowing 11 trees to be removed (eight dead or imminently dead trees, and three trees as of right). Defendant then hired a professional tree cutting company to remove the trees and alleges that, as the work was being performed, an officer of the Village stopped the work. By that time, 14 trees had, allegedly, been cut down. Thereafter, defendant was charged with violating sections 176–6 (A) (1) and 176–7 (C) of the Tree Law. . . . The Tree Law provides in pertinent part as follows:

§ 176–2 Legislative intent.

It is the intention of the Village of Montebello to retain the rural appearance of the community. Said rural appearance is a consequence of its existing wooded character and streetscape. Toward that end, the Village Board has implemented these regulations for the following purposes:

A. To preserve an important attribute of the Village, by encouraging owners of existing developed lands, and developers of lands, to save or replace as many native and mature tree species as possible when making improvements to real property.

B. To control and regulate indiscriminate and excessive removal, cutting, and destruction of trees in order to regulate and prevent conditions which cause increased surface runoff, soil erosion, and cause decreased soil fertility;

C. To maintain the stability and value of real estate by preserving existing woodlands and providing for the appropriate aesthetic of the streetscape; and

D. To ensure the continued maintenance of landscaping in accordance with site plan or subdivision plan approvals, or in accordance with the regulations contained herein. . . .

§ 176–6 Tree removal; permit; Planning Board review; licensing of contractors; fees.

A. Prohibited activities. Except as permitted herein, no person shall do or cause to be done by others, either purposely, carelessly, or negligently, any of the following acts upon privately owned property within the Village of Montebello:

(1) Cut, destroy, remove, or substantially injure any tree except as may be permitted in Subsection B, permitted activities, below. . . .

B.   Permitted activities. Notwithstanding the restrictions above, the following activities shall be permitted:

(1) The cutting, pruning, or trimming of trees in a manner that is not harmful to the health of the tree.

(2) The cutting, destruction or removal of trees which are dead or imminently dead or which endanger public safety and pose imminent peril, such condition confirmed by the Village Engineer, . . . [This provision went on to state that a person who without a permit removed a tree that was endangering public safety or that posed imminent peril could seek a permit within the following five days based on "independent proof" that the permit should be granted.] (3) Upon receipt of a permit after application to the Village Engineer or other designee of the Village Board and payment of a permit fee set by said Board by resolution, . . . the cutting or removal of not more than one tree per 10,000 square feet of lot area during any two-year period but, irrespective of lot area, in no event removal of more than eight trees per lot in any two-year period, or 12 trees in any six-year period, unless said removal is in accordance with a site or subdivision plan duly approved by the Planning Board. In the latter case, trees shall have been identified on said plans, and no additional trees shall be cut without approval of the Planning Board. For the purpose of this provision, 'year' shall be construed to be the calendar year. . . .

D.   Exceptions. [This provision authorized exceptions when enforcement was impractical or caused undue hardship due to peculiar conditions.]

E.   Planning Board review standards and fees. . . .

§ 176–7 Penalties for offenses.

A.   . . . [A]ny person violating any of the terms or provisions of this chapter or refusing to comply with the rules and regulations of this chapter shall, upon conviction, be subject to a fine not exceeding $250 for each offense. Each tree that is cut or damaged without appropriate approval from a Village agency shall constitute a single offense, up to a maximum penalty of $10,000 per lot. . . .

C.   [In addition, a violator was required to remediate the harm by planting new trees or, if that was not possible, paying money to the Tree Fund.]

In regard to tree preservation, General Municipal Law § 96–b, "Tree conservation," specifically allows for the adoption of tree preservation laws. The stated legislative intent behind the Village of Montebello's Tree

Law is to, among other things, preserve trees, provide appropriate aesthetic streetscapes, and regulate and prevent conditions which cause increased surface runoff, soil erosion, and decreased soil fertility (see Tree Law § 176–2). Such intent is supported by General Municipal Law § 96–b (1), which recognizes that trees

> abate noise, provide welcome shade to people, preserve the balance of oxygen in the air by removing carbon dioxide and fostering air quality, and add color and verdure to human construction. They also stabilize the soil and control water pollution by preventing soil erosion and flooding, yield advantageous microclimatic effects, and provide a natural habitat for wildlife. The destructive and indiscriminate removal of trees and related vegetation causes increased municipal costs for proper drainage control, impairs the benefits of occupancy of existing residential properties and impairs the stability and value of both improved and unimproved real property in the area of destruction, and adversely affects the health, safety, and general welfare of the inhabitants of the state.

In addition, an ordinance can have the purpose of promoting aesthetic considerations which bear substantially on the economic, social and cultural community. . . . Consequently, there is no merit to defendant's argument that the Tree Law is ultra vires because there is no enabling authority for it.

* * *

The Fifth Amendment of the United States Constitution—which applies to the states through the Fourteenth Amendment (see NY Const, art I, § 7 [a])—provides that "[n]o person shall be . . . deprived of life, liberty, or property, without due process of law; nor shall private property be taken for public use, without just compensation" [and] "Governmental regulation of private property effects a taking if it is 'so onerous that its effect is tantamount to a direct appropriation or ouster' " (*Consumers Union of U.S., Inc. v. State of New York*, 5 N.Y.3d 327, 357 (2005), quoting *Lingle v. Chevron U.S.A. Inc.*, 544 U.S. 528, 537 (2005)).

In the Justice Court, defendant argued that the Tree Law is unconstitutional in that (1) it takes his private property for public use without compensation since it "takes" all trees at least four inches in diameter and gives the Village the right to demand a tree cutting application and to intrude upon private property, to have the homeowner pay for consultant fees, and to demand restoration, (2) it takes his private property for public use by creating a de facto forest or nature preserve in his backyard and, therefore, he is entitled to just compensation under the Fifth and Fourteenth Amendments, and (3) the burdensome consultant fees, and other fees imposed by the Tree Law, amount to a taking in view of the "grossly burdensome, unreasonable and excessive governmental regulation."

[The court first found that "since defendant failed to show that he had sought compensation through state procedures providing for same, and had not received compensation, his claim is not ripe."]

. . . . Moreover, to the extent that defendant raises a substantive due process challenge to the consultant fees, such a challenge fails because defendant has not shown that chapter 65 is "so outrageously arbitrary as to constitute a gross abuse of governmental authority" (*Natale v. Town of Ridgefield*, 170 F.3d 258, 263 [2d Cir 1999]) and " 'so egregious, so outrageous, that it may fairly be said to shock the contemporary conscience' " (*Bullock v. Gerould*, 338 F. Supp. 2d 446).

Ordinances, like other legislative enactments, are presumed to be constitutional, and the party challenging the ordinance has the burden to prove its unconstitutionality beyond a reasonable doubt. . . . "In order for a[n] . . . ordinance to be a valid exercise of the police power it must survive a two-part test: (1) it must have been enacted in furtherance of a legitimate governmental purpose, and (2) there must be a 'reasonable relation between the end sought to be achieved by the regulation and the means used to achieve that end.' If the ordinance fails either part of this test, it is unreasonable and constitutes a deprivation of property without due process of law under our State Constitution" (*McMinn v. Town of Oyster Bay*, 66 N.Y.2d at 549 [citations omitted]).

Tree Law § 176–6 (A) (1) delineates what a person cannot do, with respect to trees, on privately owned property, and Tree Law § 176–6 (B) delineates the permitted activities on such property, and provides when a property owner must obtain a permit to remove a tree. As previously discussed, contrary to defendant's argument, the Tree Law was enacted for the legitimate governmental purpose of preserving trees, providing appropriate aesthetic streetscapes, and regulating and preventing conditions which cause increased surface runoff, soil erosion, and decreased soil fertility (see Tree Law § 176–2), and is supported by the home rule grant of authority. Moreover, we find that there is a reasonable relationship between the aforementioned ends sought to be achieved by the ordinance and the means used (i.e., the permit and fee process) to achieve that end. Consequently, defendant has not shown that the Tree Law is unreasonable and constitutes a deprivation of property without due process of law.

* * *

Pursuant to section 1 of the Fourteenth Amendment of the United States Constitution, a state is prohibited from "deny[ing] to any person within its jurisdiction the equal protection of the laws." The New York State Constitution provides that

> "[n]o person shall be denied the equal protection of the laws of this state or any subdivision thereof. No person shall, because of race, color, creed or religion, be subjected to any discrimination in his or her civil rights by any other person or by any firm, corporation, or institution, or by the state or any agency or subdivision of the state" (art I, § 11).

* * *

> .... There is a strong presumption that legislative enactments are constitutional, and a party contending otherwise bears the heavy burden of showing that a statute is 'so unrelated to the achievement of any combination of legitimate purposes' as to be irrational (*Affronti*, 95 N.Y.2d at 719).

To the extent that defendant argues that the Village's "preserve woodlands" mandate raises equal protection concerns because pre-Tree Law property owners are allowed to have lawns, whereas newer property owners face costly bureaucratic hurdles to create a lawn, defendant is incorrect. The Equal Protection Clause "permit[s] the exercise by the State of a wide scope of discretion in enacting laws which affect some groups differently than others, and a statutory determination will not be set aside if any state of facts reasonably may be conceived to justify it" (*Lighthouse Shores v. Town of Islip*, 41 N.Y.2d 7, 13 [1976]). Since the challenged portions of the Tree Law do not involve a suspect class or interfere with the exercise of a fundamental right, the scope of judicial review is limited to whether the legislation is rationally related to a legitimate governmental objective. The legislative intent behind the Tree Law, as previously discussed, advances a valid public policy basis for affecting some groups differently than others (i.e., those owning property in the Village of Montebello prior to the implementation of the Tree Law and those purchasing property in the Village of Montebello after the implementation of the Tree Law), and defendant has not shown that he has been intentionally treated differently from others similarly situated and that there is no rational basis for the difference in treatment. Consequently, defendant's equal protection challenge to Tree Law §§ 176–6 (A) (1) and 176–7 (C) fails.

* * *

Accordingly, the order is reversed and defendant's motion to dismiss the accusatory instrument is denied.

NOTES

1. *Constitutionally sound, politically burdensome?* Although the court's takings, due process, and equal protection analyses may seem sound from a legal perspective, do you think the statute is overly burdensome as a matter of policy? What degree of control over forest resources should state and local governments maintain? Is it better to employ zoning to designate areas as set-asides for forests and to require that certain acreages of forests be maintained free from timbering operations, or better instead to maintain specific ordinances related to the cutting of individual trees? Is requiring landowners to prove via "written application" that they cut a tree down due to public safety concerns, requiring that no more than eight trees be cut per lot in any two-year period or 12 trees cut per lot in any six-year period, and compulsory replanting of trees cut down in violation of the ordinance, an appropriate degree of control over local forests? After all, the many ecosystem services highlighted at the beginning of this chapter are more likely to remain intact with this stringent policy focus. But do statutes of this type properly balance private rights with the public interest in trees? Is there an argument that they may endanger the development of the good political will needed to have a broader forest protection focus? Or is this exactly the type of policy needed to place management of forest resources on private property owners' radars?

2. *Other tree-preservation ordinances.* Tallahassee, Florida maintains a tree preservation ordinance and is definitely a beautifully "treed" city. So these types of ordinances do seem to achieve the results they set out to achieve. Consider the provisions of Leon County (where Tallahassee is located), Florida's Environmental Management Act, Chapter 10, Land Development Code (LDC) related to tree cutting:

Key Definitions [LDC, Sec. 10–1.101]:

Critical protection zone (CPZ) shall mean that area surrounding a tree within a circle described by a radius of one foot for each inch of the tree's diameter at breast height (DBH) measured from the trunk.

DBH, diameter breast height, means the diameter of a tree measured at a height of 54 inches above the naturally occurring ground level. Trees with gross abnormalities or buttressing at breast height should be measured above and immediately adjacent to the irregularity. Trees that fork at breast height should be measured below the breast height and recorded as a single trunk. Trees that fork below breast height will be recorded as separate DBH for each stem.

Tree shall mean any self-supporting woody plant having at least one well-defined stem a minimum of two inches DBH, and which normally grows to a minimum height of 25 feet in the county area.

Tree removal shall include the following acts:

(1)   The actual removal of a live tree

(2)   Any unmitigated encroachment within a distance of three-fourths of the radius of the CPZ of a protected tree,

(3)   Any damage to 30% or more of the crown of a protected tree within the vertical projection of its critical protection zone; or

(4)   Any other action or activity likely to significantly damage or cause a premature death of a protected tree (ex: herbicide).

* * *

[Protected Trees Not to be Removed or Damaged Without Permit Approval Based on Each Type of Tree's DBH] ?

Any tree located within a canopy road protection zone, a special development zone, a required buffer or easement area, a preservation or conservation area as described in Sec. 10–4.202, including areas located within a wetland, waterbody, natural watercourse, undeveloped floodplain, severe or significant grades or native forest areas. Any tree planted to meet replanting, reforestation, or landscaping requirements?

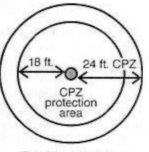

2"+ Trees two inches DBH or greater located on an undeveloped parcel?

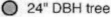

4"+ Dogwood (*Cornus florida*) trees of four inches DBH or greater. Trees with a DBH or four inches or greater which are located in the lot perimeter zone of any development site except for sites being developed for detached single-family residential use. The lot perimeter zone is the area of a development site which falls between a property line and the minimum building setback corresponding to that property line?

12"+Longleaf pine (*Pinus palustris*) or Live Oak (*Quercus virginiana*) trees of 12 inch DBH or greater?

18"+Trees having a diameter of 18 inches DBH or greater? Other Any exceptional specimen trees identified by the County Administrator or designee.

[Tree Removal Exemptions]

The Environmental Services Division shall be contacted prior to removing a tree via exemption in order to verify the exemption status.

1.   Single Family Residence: The removal of trees less than 36″ DBH on lots upon which there is an existing, lawfully occupied single family dwelling provided that such trees are not protected within the first tree protection category identified above.

2.   Emergency, Safety Hazard, Disease or Pest Infestation: Protected trees may be removed in cases of an emergency, acts of nature, disease or pest infestation where tree removal would protect the general public health, welfare or safety.

3.   Nursery Trees: The removal of any tree planted and grown in the ordinary course of business of a lawful plant or tree nursery.

4.   Bona Fide Silviculture: Activities associated with a bona fide silviculture operation on land that has received an agricultural exemption from the Leon County Property Appraiser are exempt from the tree removal requirements.

5.   Archaeological Project: Limited excavation within the CPZ of any protected tree when necessary for an archeological project.

6.   Invasive/Exotic Trees: The removal of invasive/exotic trees identified on Leon County's List of Invasive Plant Species.

As described by the county: "[a] tree removal permit is required for removing protected trees within Leon County. Tree removal permits can be issued as stand-alone permits for individual property owners, but are more frequently issued in conjunction with other environmental permits required for the development of a property." *See* Leon County Florida, Tree Removal Permit,   http://cms.leoncountyfl.gov/Home/Departments/Development–Support-and-Environmental–Management/Environmental–Services/STORMWATER–TREE–REMOVAL–PERMIT.

H. PRIVATE RIGHTS IN PUBLIC FORESTS— CONSTITUTIONAL AND LEGISLATIVE PROTECTIONS

Some forest preservation policies manifest not through state or local regulation of private forestlands, but rather through constitutional or legislative grants of authority to public entities to acquire forestlands and preserve them in perpetuity. Preservation of these public forests may conflict with potential private uses, as evidenced in the following cases.

ASSOCIATION FOR THE PROTECTION OF
THE ADIRONDACKS V. MacDONALD

New York Court of Appeals
253 N.Y. 234 (1930)

CRANE, J.

By chapter 417 of the Laws of 1929 the Conservation Commissioner is authorized to construct and maintain a bobsleigh run or slide on State lands in the Forest Preserve in the town of North Elba, Essex county, on the western slope of the Sentinel Range.

The act was passed for the purpose of providing facilities for the third Olympic winter games, which are to be held at or in the vicinity of Lake Placid, in the year 1932. The bobsleigh run will be approximately one and one-quarter miles in length and six and one-half feet wide, with a return route or go-back road. As additional land will have to be cleared on either side of the run, the width in actual use will be approximately sixteen feet, and twenty feet where the course curves. It is estimated that the construction will necessitate the removal of trees from about four and one-half acres of land, or a total number of trees, large and small, estimated at 2,500. The Forest Preserve within the Adirondacks consists of 1,941,403 acres. The taking of four acres out of this vast acreage for this international sports' meet seems a very slight inroad upon the preserve for a matter of such public interest and benefit to the people of the State of New York and elsewhere. The Legislature, recognizing the benefits of an international gathering of this kind, has sought in the public interest, by the enactment of the above law, to provide appropriately and in the spirit of hospitality, the necessary equipment and facilities for these games, and contests, incident to winter sport, of which tobogganing is a large feature. Winter sports of course must be held in a place where there will be an assurance of sufficient continual cold weather for snow and ice, and the vicinity of Lake Placid gives this assurance. The western slope of the Sentinel range, chosen for the toboggan slide, is the nearest and most appropriate place for its construction in connection with the center of attractions.

Considering the distinction of having one of the beauty spots of New York State selected as appropriate for the International Olympic winter games and the advantages afforded by Lake Placid and its vicinity, together with the good will promoted in the recognition by the State, through its Legislature, of the event, what possible objection can there be to the above law permitting this toboggan slide to be constructed on State land? One objection, and one only—the Constitution of the State, which prevents the cutting of the trees. This objection has been raised by the Association for the Protection of the Adirondacks, which has sought and obtained an injunction restraining the Conservation Commission of this

State and the Superintendent of Lands and Forests from constructing and maintaining the bobsleigh run on the ground that chapter 417 of the Laws of 1929 is unconstitutional and void.

The constitutional provision is section 7 of article VII, reading: "The lands of the state, now owned or hereafter acquired, constituting the forest preserve as now fixed by law, shall be forever kept as wild forest lands. They shall not be leased, sold or exchanged, or be taken by any corporation, public or private, nor shall the timber thereon be sold, removed or destroyed."

The lands and trees proposed to be taken for the toboggan slide are within the Forest Preserve and covered by this provision of the Constitution. Taking the words of section 7 in their ordinary meaning, we have the command that the timber, that is, the trees, shall not be sold, removed or destroyed. To cut down 2,500 trees for a toboggan slide, or perhaps for any other purpose, is prohibited. Some opinions, notably those of the Attorneys-General of the State, cited on the briefs and by the Appellate Division, have even gone so far as to state that a single tree, and even fallen timber and dead wood, cannot be removed; that to preserve the property as wild forest lands means to preserve it from the interference in any way by the hand of man.

. . . . The purpose of the constitutional provision, as indicated by the debates in the Convention of 1894, was to prevent the cutting or destruction of the timber or the sale thereof, as had theretofore been permitted by legislation, to the injury and ruin of the Forest Preserve. To accomplish the end in view, it was thought necessary to close all gaps and openings in the law, and to prohibit any cutting or any removal of the trees and timber to a substantial extent. The Adirondack Park was to be preserved, not destroyed. Therefore, all things necessary were permitted, such as measures to prevent forest fires, the repairs to roads and proper inspection, or the erection and maintenance of proper facilities for the use by the public which did not call for the removal of the timber to any material degree. The Forest Preserve is preserved for the public; its benefits are for the people of the State as a whole. Whatever the advantages may be of having wild forest lands preserved in their natural state, the advantages are for everyone within the State and for the use of the people of the State. Unless prohibited by the constitutional provision, this use and preservation are subject to the reasonable regulations of the Legislature.

The laws developing the Forest Preserve and the Adirondack Park, up to the Constitution of 1894, are reviewed in the opinion of this court in *People v. Adirondack Ry. Co.* (160 N. Y. 225). By chapter 707 of the Laws of 1892 the State Park, known as the Adirondack Park, was created within certain of the Forest Preserve counties. Such park is to be 'forever reserved, maintained and cared for as ground open for the free use of all the people for their health or pleasure, and as forest lands necessary to the preservation of the headwaters of the chief rivers of the State, and a future timber supply.'

Chapter 332 of the Laws of 1893, combining all previous acts, gave to the Forest Commissioners authority to sell certain timber on the Forest Preserve and also power to sell such of the lands as were not needed. They were also authorized to lease camp sites and lay out paths and roads in the park. Then came the Convention of 1894 with the debates indicating a change of policy regarding the sale and destruction of timber and the use of the lands.

At the time of the assembling of this Convention, the law of the State authorized the sale, lease, clearing and cultivation of lands in the Forest Preserve and the sale of standing or fallen timber thereon; also permitted the laying out of paths and roads through the property.

With these laws before them and the statements in the debates revealing the depredations which had been made on the forest lands, and the necessity for restricting the appropriation of trees and timber, section 7 of article VII was adopted and became part of the Constitution January 1, 1895, where it has remained ever since.

No longer was the land or timber to be sold or even condemned for public purposes. *(People v. Adirondack Ry. Co.,* cited above*)* The forests were to be preserved as wild forest lands, and the trees were not to be sold or removed or destroyed. Whereas the Legislature had authorized the building of roads through these lands, this power was thereafter conferred not through legislation, but by constitutional amendments adopted in 1918 and 1927. . . . If it were deemed necessary to obtain a constitutional amendment for the construction of a State highway, the use to which the Forest Preserve might be put with legislative sanction was greatly limited. Trees could not be cut or the timber destroyed, even for the building of a road. This seems to be a fair conclusion to be drawn from the adoption of these constitutional amendments after the Constitution of 1894.

What may be done in these forest lands to preserve them or to open them up for the use of the public, or what reasonable cutting or removal of timber may be necessitated in order to properly preserve the State Park, we are not at this time called upon to determine. What regulations may reasonably be made by the Commission for the use of the park by campers and those who seek recreation and health in the quiet and solitude of the north woods is not before us in this case. The Forest Preserve and the Adirondack Park within it are for the reasonable use and benefit of the public, as heretofore stated. A very considerable use may be made by campers and others without in any way interfering with this purpose of preserving them as wild forest lands.

But the question still remains whether the construction of a toboggan slide, which requires the cutting of 2,500 trees, is such a reasonable use, or is forbidden by the Constitution.

Counsel for the appellants has very ably argued that as the underlying purpose of all these restrictions upon the State lands is to preserve them for the free use of all the people for their health and pleasure, the erection of a toboggan slide for sport is within this purpose. He has pressed upon our attention the fact that outdoor sports do much to maintain the health, the happiness and the welfare of the people of this State; and that if a branch of these outdoor sports is to a minor extent permitted within the public lands, the very purpose which the framers of the Constitution of 1894 had in mind will be accomplished; that it is the benefit to the people which this constitutional provision sought to preserve in the preservation of the forest. What can be more beneficial, asks counsel, than the establishment of forest sports, among which is classed this toboggan slide? We must admit much, if not all, that counsel has so eloquently pleaded in behalf of outdoor games. Perhaps much may be due to international sports, such as the Olympic games, lawn tennis, golf, even aviation, for creating good will among the nations, and a desire to establish those friendly relationships so vigorously claimed and earnestly sought for through treaties and world conferences. However tempting it may be to yield to the seductive influences of outdoor sports and international contests, we must not overlook the fact that constitutional provisions cannot always adjust themselves to the nice relationships of life. The framers of the Constitution, as before stated, intended to stop the willful destruction of trees upon the forest lands, and to preserve these in the wild state now existing; they adopted a measure forbidding the cutting down of these trees to any substantial extent for any purpose.

Tobogganing is not the only outdoor sport. Summer sports in the Adirondacks attract a larger number of people than the winter sports, simply for the reason, if no other, that the summer time still remains the vacation period for most of us. The same plea made for the toboggan slide in winter might be made for the golf course in summer, or for other sports requiring the use or the removal of timber. In other words, this plea in behalf of sport is a plea for an open door through which abuses as well as benefits may pass. The Constitution intends to take no more chances with abuses, and, therefore, says the door must be kept shut. The timber on the lands of the Adirondack Park in the Forest Preserve, or that on the western slope of the Sentinel range cannot be cut and removed to construct a toboggan slide simply and solely for the reason that section 7, article VII, of the Constitution says that it cannot be done.

Consequently, chapter 417 of the Laws of 1929, permitting the erection of this bobsleigh slide and the destruction of the trees is unconstitutional, and the judgment should be affirmed, with costs.

SHAMBURGER V. DUNCAN

Kentucky Court of Appeals
244 S.W.2d 759 (1951)

STANLEY, COMMISSIONER.

The state, in the exercise of its police power to enact laws for the general welfare of the people, particularly for the conservation and development of its natural resources and adding to its wealth, enacted a statute authorizing the fiscal court of any county to acquire and maintain lands for 'a permanent public forest'. Acts of 1946, Chapter 93, KRS 149.200 et seq. Jefferson County acquired an area of about 2,000 acres as such a forest. It includes a tract of 168 acres on the edge of the forest which was formerly used as a clay pit or mine with facilities for the manufacture of sewer pipe. To 'a certain extent' it is denuded land. The conveyance was in fee simple without restriction as to its use. However, the recorded action of the fiscal court and the method of acquisition evidenced the purpose of its purchase, for which $3,365 of tax revenues were paid. The conditions and restrictions of the statute are in legal effect the same as if expressed in the deed.

It was recently discovered that this tract contains shale suitable for the making of light aggregate, which has many uses in the building industry, especially in the manufacture of concrete blocks. The fiscal court and the Jefferson County Forest Commission (an advisory body doubtless created under the terms of KRS 149.270) determined it would be to the public interest to execute a mineral lease of the tract for the term of fifty years for the mining of the shale. In response to advertising, the Ohio River Sand Co. submitted an offer to lease the property upon a royalty basis. It proposed to install mining and processing facilities costing between $200,000 and $500,000. It is agreed that Jefferson County now levies its constitutional limit of taxes and that there is very little, if any, tax revenue available for the maintenance of the forest. It is estimated that the mineral lease would yield a minimum annual revenue of $12,000, which would be used exclusively for the purpose.

The question of the authority of the fiscal court to execute the lease was submitted upon an agreed statement in accordance with the procedure provided in Sec. 637, Civil Code. The circuit court was of opinion that the statute restricts the use of the property as a forest exclusively with the sole exception of recreational purposes to the extent that they are consistent with the dominant purpose and that those uses only permit the granting of concessions or renting of small parts for refreshment stands and like conveniences. We concur in the opinion.

The statute outlines in definite language the objective of maintaining a permanent forest reservation. It authorizes cooperation with the State Division of Forestry in the Department of Conservation. It specifically directs the planting of trees upon denuded or bare land and authorizes the cutting of growing timber 'in accordance with approved forestry methods and in such manner as to perpetuate succeeding stands of trees.' The Legislature recognized that one of the reasons for preserving the forest is that it may be enjoyed by the people, so it was provided in KRS 149.260: "All lands acquired under the provisions of [the act] shall be protected at all times, as far as possible, from fire and grazing, and shall be kept and maintained as a permanent public forest, * * * All such forest lands shall be open to the use of the public for recreational purposes so far as such recreational purposes do not interfere with, or prevent the use of, such lands to the best advantage as a public forest."

We have analogous applicable law in the decisions denying authority of a city to divert to other or inconsistent purposes property acquired for a public park. Of particular application are the statutes governing a city of the third class, which is expressly authorized to acquire and maintain a park (KRS 97.530) and is given general authority by another statute to lease or convey property owned by the city, KRS 85.101. But such general authority does not embrace property dedicated to park purposes. Of special application is *Bedford-Nugent Co. v. Argue*, 281 Ky. 827, 137 S.W.2d 392, in which it was held that the City of Henderson was not authorized to lease part of land which had been dedicated for park purposes for the operation of a sand and gravel business, even though the part was a deep ravine, had never been improved and had long been used as a public dump for refuse.

Still more pertinent to the present case is *Association for the Protection of the Adirondacks v. MacDonald*, 170 N.E. 902, 903 (N.Y.1930). The State of New York had acquired about 2,000,000 acres for a Forest Preserve within the Adirondacks. A constitutional provision declared: "The lands of the State, now owned or hereafter acquired, constituting the forest preserve as now fixed by law, shall be forever kept as wild forest lands. They shall not be leased, sold or exchanged, or be taken by any corporation, public or private, nor shall the timber thereon be sold, removed or destroyed." Const. 1894 N.Y. art. 7, § 7. The Legislature enacted a statute authorizing the Conservation Commissioner to construct and maintain a bobsleigh run or slide within the Preserve to provide facilities for the forthcoming international Olympic winter games. The toboggan slide, about 1 1/4 miles in length, would have required the removal of 2,500 trees and the clearance of about 4 1/2 acres of land. The court fully recognized the desirability of having the facilities and appreciated the fact that the sports would be of great public interest and benefit to the people of the state. Nevertheless, it was constrained to hold the statute violated the constitutional provision against destroying timber and declared the act void. It expressly withheld deciding what could be done in the forest lands to preserve them or what reasonable cutting or removal of timber may be necessitated in order to properly preserve the state park.

In the present case the statute and order of the fiscal court are comparable to the constitution and statute in the New York case. Our statute requires that the county forest shall be permanently maintained as such and that denuded places shall be reforested. There is nothing to show that this area cannot be reforested in accordance with the objective of the statute. The permitted use for recreational purposes is consistent with the main purpose of the forest. But even that is permitted only so far as it does 'not interfere with, or prevent the use of, such lands to the best advantage as a public forest.' KRS 149.260, quoted above. The use of this property for industrial purposes does not conform. Quarrying shale or rock and operating machinery in the processing of it is inconsistent and unrelated.

The appellants rest the justification of their position in part on the word 'otherwise' in this provision of KRS 149.250: 'All revenue derived from such forest land by the sale of timber or otherwise shall accrue to the use of the county owning and holding such land.'

A definition of "otherwise" is, "In a different manner; in another way, or in other ways." Webster's International Dictionary. In the interpretation or application of the word consideration must be given the purpose and the object in view. We lift this from the above cited New York opinion: "Words are but symbols indicating ideas, and are subject to contraction and expansion to meet the idea sought to be expressed; they register frequently according to association, or like the thermometer, by the atmosphere surrounding them."

In this atmosphere we think the word "otherwise" refers to revenue derived from a source that is legally permissible within the purview of the statute. It is to be defined in a sense that is consonant with and which promotes the object and design of the statute. Unlimited, the word would open the door for unrestricted use of the property without respect to the purpose of its acquisition and maintenance.

We cannot accept the appellants' argument that the county forestry act is to be read in connection with Chapter 58 of the statutes (enacted at the same session) relating to the acquisition and development of public projects, although the term is defined therein as including lands and facilities suitable for or intended for public purposes or use in the promotion of the public welfare. KRS 58.010. The specific statute relating to public forests cannot be made subordinate to or in effect held to be repealed in part by this broad and general statute which looks to the acquisition and development of industries and public facilities through the issuance of revenue bonds. Each statute is to be construed in its own field of operation. The one is not enlarged or limited by the other.

The judgment is affirmed.

NOTES

1.   *No country for balancing public interests.* The *MacDonald* court acknowledged that the taking of four acres out of 2 million was a seemingly slight loss. Yet the court refused to engage in a balancing of public interests, as we typically see concerning natural resources on public lands. Consider the multiple use mandate for federal forestlands. *See* Multiple Use and Sustained Yield Act, 16 U.S.C. §§ 528–531. One arguably legitimate public use of the forest in *MacDonald* was to facilitate the publicly popular Olympics, as the court acknowledged in its eloquent oratory. But despite the very small adverse effect of the project on the state forest, no amount of countervailing public interest could intrude on the constitutional protection. Further, changes to the management of the forest can be made only through further—difficult to achieve—constitutional amendments. *MacDonald* demonstrates how much more strength constitutional provisions have relative to legislative and administrative protections, as also evident in the *Robinson Township* case in chapter 3. New York's Department of Environmental Conservation notes that "Article XIV's original wording . . . still survives today in spite of numerous efforts to modify it." *See* Article XIV of the New York State Constitution, http://www.dec.ny.gov/lands/55849.html.

2.   *To toboggan or not to toboggan?* Supporters of the Olympic development in *MacDonald* argued that the "underlying purpose of all these restrictions upon the State lands is to preserve them for the free use of all the people for their health and pleasure, the erection of a toboggan slide for sport is within this purpose." Do you agree that this four-acre development here was not sufficiently concerned with public health and pleasure? Or is the constitution clear in linking public health and pleasure to strictly forest uses? Consider that since its inception "[t]he Northway (I–87), Whiteface and Gore Mountain Ski Centers, the small airport at Piseco, an expanded cemetery in Keene, a new groundwater supply for Raquette Lake, and about 25 other amendments since 1895 have met with voter approval." Friends of the Forest Preserve, *Adirondack Wild*, http://www.adirondackwild.org/article14.html. Is an Olympic toboggan run that dissimilar from these developments? Or is it a matter of procedure, since the toboggan run development was not approved through the constitutional amendment process?

3.   *Shamburger and MacDonald.* Notice the *Shamburger* court relied on *MacDonald* to support its conclusion, even analogizing Kentucky's legislative enactment to New York's constitutional provision. Are there meaningful differences from forest preservation mandates arising out of

constitutional versus legislative enactments? Is it, again, a matter of procedure, since constitutional amendments are more difficult to change, whereas legislative instruments might be readily adjusted by subsequent legislatures?

4. *What are they now?* Today, the forest at issue in *Shamburger* has become the Jefferson Memorial Forest south of Louisville, KY, one of the largest municipal forests in the nation. Jefferson Memorial Forest, http:// louisvilleky.gov/government/jefferson-memorial-forest/. New York's Forest Preserve, as noted, is also still intact. Consider this description of the value of the preserve and the importance of the legal instruments that laid the foundation for its management:

> New York State is the only state, and the only government, which has a forest preservation mandate in its State Constitution. New York's three-million-acre publicly owned Forest Preserve in sixteen Adirondack and Catskill counties is protected by an ironclad, far-reaching covenant between a government and its people. We have an enduring wilderness for people and wild nature, a haven for the ultimate expression of our human partnership with nature.

> And that has been the case since 1894 when a constitutional convention in Albany and the voters approved the [constitutional protection provision].

* * *

> . . . The framers of Article XIV lived at a time of intense industrialization. The cutting and removal of trees on higher elevations with thin soils resulted in erosion, flooding, loss of soil moisture, and forest fires. Many European nations, as well as New England states, had already experienced severe loss of natural resources from exploiting their forests. New York's lawmakers were concerned with conserving watersheds, and assuring that rivers and streams which came from these mountains would continue to flow year-round to supply New York's canals, the highways of their day. Others knew that a constitutionally protected forest would serve as a refuge for wildlife and for the spirit of people seeking peace, respite, and recreation. Citizens were resolved that New York's "Forever Wild" clause would stand as a bulwark against unrestrained commercialism.

* * *

> Today, the Forest Preserve encompasses three-million-acres in the Adirondack and Catskill Parks. Article XIV acts not just as a restriction but as an opportunity for all that wild lands provide us at such little cost, and as an obligation for government to act comprehensively in ways that respect the health of our lands, our air, our atmosphere, and our watersheds. Rivers like the Upper

Hudson, Raquette, St. Lawrence, Black, Mohawk, and the Delaware all originate in these protected mountains. These great watersheds efficiently filter billions of gallons of water each day, and prevent flooding. The New York City metropolitan area is spared billions in water treatment costs by the Catskill "Forever Wild" watersheds. The smallest Adirondack stream flows year-round because of the stable base flow guaranteed by "Forever Wild" policies. The recreational, wildlife, and spiritual benefits of our wilderness are incalculable. The Forest Preserve acts as a buffer against a changing climate. The economic benefits are in the tens of billions of dollars annually and growing every year.

Judicial Decisions and Amendments

The most significant judicial interpretation of Article XIV came in 1930, after The Association for the Protection of the Adirondacks sued to block the construction of an Olympic bobsled run on the Forest Preserve. . . .

* * *

It is purposefully difficult to change our Constitution. "Forever Wild" amendments have to pass in two separately-elected legislatures. Ultimately, New York citizens decide whether an amendment constitutes a significant shift away from "Forever Wild." Voters have ratified defined amendments of limited geographic scope. The Northway (I–87), Whiteface and Gore Mountain Ski Centers, the small airport at Piseco, an expanded cemetery in Keene, a new groundwater supply for Raquette Lake, and about 25 other amendments since 1895 have met with voter approval. However, voters have rejected a dozen other proposals for massive dam projects, commercial cabins, roads, spreading ski resorts, and other development which would eviscerate the very wilderness which draws so many to these mountains. Paul Schaefer, founder of Friends of the Forest Preserve, personally led coalitions which defeated many of these proposals.

The Forest Preserve in the Adirondack and Catskill Parks is taxable. Taxes are paid by all New York residents to hundreds of affected towns, villages, and school districts, amounting to more than $80 million annually. Adirondack Wild helps lawmakers to recognize that the downstream benefits of protecting upstate watersheds in the Adirondacks and Catskills more than justify these costs spread among all taxpayers.

Challenges

There is a natural temptation by elected officials and state administrators to compromise and dilute "Forever Wild" for perceived short-term gain. There can be no Forest Preserve without a vigilant public that will not compromise on the long-term principles which undergird this law.

Strengthening Forever Wild

Adirondack Wild tells the story of how much wild nature benefits our society. We train students in wilderness stewardship, providing the background and tools they need. Young people know that the "Forever Wild" law should be strengthened, not compromised. With our help, students are showing how this can be done. Young people of all backgrounds, once introduced to the wilderness, learn teamwork, discipline, and may become influential leaders.

Friends of the Forest Preserve, *Adirondack Wild*, http://www.adirondackwild. org/article14.html.

CHAPTER 8

PUBLIC LANDS AND COMMODITY USES

■ ■ ■

A unique aspect of natural resources law in the United States is the amount of federal public lands, which in 2012 amounted to roughly 28 percent of the land mass of the country. These lands are the legacy of a national lands policy that changed directions in the early twentieth century. Originally, nearly all lands west of the original thirteen states (excepting Texas and many Indian reservations) were owned by the federal government, whose policy for roughly 150 years was to sell or otherwise dispose of the land to achieve various ends (funding the federal government high among them). That disposition policy over time became subject to exceptions as particular federal lands were set aside permanently as national parks (starting with Yellowstone and Yosemite), as national forests and defense installations, and for other purposes. The policy largely ended in the 1930s, with a decision to retain all remaining federal lands in federal ownership. By then, federal landholdings disproportionately comprised lands that were too dry or too mountainous for homesteaders, including remote lands in Alaska and in the inter-mountain West. Since then, the only major land dispositions have been the sizeable acreages turned over to the State of Alaska under its Statehood Act and in settlement of the claims of native inhabitants of Alaska. The upshot is a considerable federal public lands legacy owned by all members of the U.S. public, even though most Americans know little about their substantial inheritance.

The following report gives an overview of public lands in American history and law and of the federal government agencies principally responsible for managing them today.

FEDERAL LAND OWNERSHIP: OVERVIEW AND DATA
Ross Gorte, et al.
Congressional Research Service Report No. R42346, at 1–3, 8–10 (2012)

The formation of the U.S. federal government was particularly influenced by the struggle for control over what were then known as the "western" lands—the lands between the Appalachian Mountains and the Mississippi River that were claimed by the original colonies. The original states reluctantly ceded the lands to the developing new government; this cession, together with granting constitutional powers to the new federal government, including the authority to regulate federal property and to create new states, played a crucial role in transforming the weak central government under the Articles of Confederation into a stronger, centralized federal government under the U.S. Constitution.

Subsequent federal land laws reflected two visions: reserving some federal lands (such as for national forests and national parks) and selling or otherwise disposing of other lands to raise money or to encourage transportation, development, and settlement. From the earliest days, these policy views took on East/West overtones, with easterners more likely to view the lands as national public property, and westerners more likely to view the lands as necessary for local use and development. Most agreed, however, on measures that promoted settlement of the lands to pay soldiers, to reduce the national debt, and to strengthen the nation. This settlement trend accelerated with the federal acquisition of additional territory through the Louisiana Purchase in 1803, the Oregon Compromise with England in 1846, and cession of lands by treaty after the Mexican War in 1848.

In the mid to late 1800s, Congress enacted numerous laws to encourage and accelerate the settlement of the West by disposing of federal lands. Examples include the Homestead Act of 1862 and the Desert Lands Entry Act of 1877. Approximately 816 million acres of public domain lands were transferred to private ownership (individuals, railroads, etc.) between 1781 and 2010. Another 328 million acres were granted to the states generally (mostly through statehood acts), and an additional 142 million were granted in Alaska under state and Native selection laws. Most transfers to private ownership (97%) occurred before 1940; homestead entries, for example, peaked in 1910 at 18.3 million acres but dropped below 200,000 acres annually after 1935, until being fully eliminated in 1986.

Although some earlier laws had protected some lands and resources, such as salt deposits and certain timber for military use, new laws in the late 1800s reflected the growing concern that rapid development threatened some of the scenic treasures of the nation, as well as resources that would be needed for future use. A preservation and conservation movement evolved to ensure that certain lands and resources were left untouched or reserved for future use. For example, Yellowstone National Park was established in 1872 to preserve its resources in a natural condition and to dedicate recreation opportunities for the public. It was the world's first national park and, like the other early parks, Yellowstone was protected by the U.S. Army—primarily from poachers of wildlife [and] timber. In 1891, concern over the effects of timber harvests on water supplies and downstream flooding led to the creation of forest reserves (renamed national forests in 1907).

Emphasis shifted during the [twentieth] century from the disposal and conveyance of title to private citizens to the retention and management of the remaining federal lands. During debates on the 1934 Taylor Grazing Act, some western Members of Congress acknowledged the poor prospects for relinquishing federal lands to the states, but language included in the act left disposal as a possibility. It was not until the enactment of the [1976] Federal Land Policy and Management Act (FLPMA) that Congress expressly declared that the remaining public domain lands generally would remain in federal ownership. This declaration of permanent federal land ownership was a significant factor in what became known as the Sagebrush Rebellion, an effort that started in the late 1970s to pro[mote] state or local control over federal land and management decisions. To date, judicial challenges and legislative and executive efforts generally have not resulted in broad changes to the level of federal ownership. . . .

Today, the federal government owns and manages roughly 635–640 million acres of land in the United States. . . .

* * *

The four [major federal] land management agencies—the Forest Service, the National Park Service, the Fish and Wildlife Service, and the Bureau of Land Management—administer 609.4 million acres (about 95–96%) of the roughly 635–640 acres of federal land. . . .

Forest Service

The Forest Service (USFS) is the oldest of the four federal land management agencies. It was created in 1905 [and assigned to the Department of the Agriculture]. . . . The USFS administers 192.9 million acres of land, predominantly in the West, but the USFS manages more than half of all federal lands in the East.

Forest reserves were originally authorized to protect the lands, preserve water flows, and provide timber. These purposes were expanded in the Multiple Use-Sustained Yield Act of 1960. This act added recreation, livestock grazing, wildlife and fish habitat, and wilderness as purposes of the national forests, . . . direct[ing] that these multiple uses be managed in a "harmonious and coordinated" manner "in the combination that will best meet the needs of the American people." The act also directed sustained yield—a high level of resource outputs in perpetuity, without impairing the productivity of the lands.

National Park Service

The National Park Service (NPS) was created in 1916 to manage the growing number of park units established by Congress and monuments proclaimed by the President [under the authority of the Antiquities Act]. The National Park System has grown to 397 units with diverse titles—

national park[s], national monument[s], national preserve[s], national historic site[s], national recreation area[s], national battlefield[s], and many more. The Park Service administers 79.7 million acres of federal land in 49 states, with two-thirds of the lands (52.6 million acres, 66% of the NPS total) in Alaska.

The NPS has a dual mission—to preserve unique resources and to provide for their enjoyment by the public. Park units include spectacular natural areas (e.g., Yellowstone, Grand Canyon, and Arches National Parks), unique prehistoric sites (e.g., Mesa Verde National Park and Dinosaur National Monument), and special places in American history (e.g., Valley Forge National Historic Park, Gettysburg National Military Park, and the Statue of Liberty National Monument), as well as recreational opportunities (e.g., Cape Code National Seashore and Santa Monica Mountains National Recreation Area). The tension between providing recreation and preserving resources has caused many management challenges.

Fish and Wildlife Service

The first national wildlife refuge was established by executive order in 1903, although it was not until 1966 that the refuges were aggregated into the National Wildlife Refuge System administered by the Fish and Wildlife Service (FWS). Today, the FWS administers 88.9 million acres of federal land, of which 76.6 million acres (86%) are in Alaska. . . .

The FWS has a primary-use mission—to conserve plants and animals. Other uses (recreation, hunting, timber cutting, oil or gas drilling, etc.) are permitted, to the extent that they are compatible with the species' needs, but wildlife-related activities (hunting, bird-watching, hiking, education, etc.) are considered "priority uses" and are given preference over consumptive uses such as timber, grazing, and minerals. [Although management decisions can be challenged in terms of what secondary uses are compatible,] the relative clarity of the mission generally has minimized conflicts over refuge management and use.

Bureau of Land Management

The BLM was formed in 1946 by combining two existing agencies. One was the Grazing Service . . . , established in 1934 to administer grazing on public rangelands. The other was the General Land Office, which had been created in 1812 to oversee disposal of the federal lands. The BLM currently administers more federal lands than any other agency—247.9 million acres. BLM lands are heavily concentrated (99.8%) in the 11 western states.

As defined in FLPMA, BLM['s] management responsibilities are similar to those of the USFS—sustained yields of the multiple uses, including recreation, grazing, timber, watershed, wildlife and fish habitat, and conservation. Because of the similarity of their missions, merging the BLM and USFS occasionally has been proposed. However, each agency historically has emphasized different uses. For instance, most rangelands are managed by the BLM, while most federal forests are managed by the USFS. In addition, the BLM administers mineral development on all federal lands (about 700 million acres of federal subsurface minerals).

NOTES

1.   *The role of Indian title.* The federal government's hegemony in public land management (which is unusual among English-speaking countries such as Canada and Australia) can be traced to a decision of the U.S. Supreme Court in *Johnson v. M'Intosh*, 21 U.S. 543 (1823), in which the Court ruled that Native Americans lacked the ability to transfer land title to anyone but the U.S. government. This monopsony—along with the ceding to the federal government by the original states of their western land claims during the period of the 1780s to 1803—put the federal government in charge of western land settlement. As a result, virtually all contemporary land titles not subject to the claims of prior European sovereigns can be traced to the federal government.

2.   *The constitutional underpinnings of federal land ownership.* It is somewhat surprising that the legitimacy of federal public land ownership has been called into question in popular uprisings like that occasioned by the 2014 Cliven Bundy affair in Nevada. Such challenges to federal power have no colorable validity, at least legally. The Supreme Court has uniformly stated that the power of the federal government to manage its lands under the Property Clause of the Constitution (Art. IV, sec. 3, cl. 2, providing that "[t]he Congress shall have the Power to dispose of and make all needful Rules and Regulations respecting the Territory or other Property belonging to the United States") is "without limitation." *United States v. Gratiot*, 39 U.S. 526, 537 (1840); *Camfield v. U.S.*, 167 U.S. 518, 524–25 (1897); *United States v. City and County of San Francisco*, 310 U.S. 16, 29 (1940); *Federal Power Commission v. Idaho Power Co.*, 344 U.S. 17, 21 (1952); *Kleppe v. New Mexico*, 426 U.S. 529, 539 (1976). See also Matt Ford, *The Irony of Cliven Bundy's Unconstitutional Stand*, The Atlantic, Apr. 14, 2014. Bundy's claims largely repeated unsuccessful challenges to federal land ownership made by the so-called Sagebrush Rebellion in the 1970s (during the Carter Administration) and by the County Supremacy Movement in the 1990s (during the Clinton Administration), but unlike those predecessors, Bundy's lawless revolt may have some political resonance in an era of widespread antipathy toward the federal government.

3.   *Checkerboarded land ownership.* Most of the public does not realize that federal, state, and private land ownership is often discontinuous. Federal grants to railroads, commonplace in the nineteenth century, conveyed some 130 million acres as incentives to build rail lines (90 million

acres directly to railroads, nearly another 40 million acres to states for railroads, a total area roughly the size of Indiana, Illinois, Michigan, and Wisconsin combined), but they did so in a checkerboarded manner. The idea was that the new rail lines would attact settlers who would purchase lands at fair market value from the railroads and from the federal government. This federal plan was often undermined by local prevarications like "claims clubs," aimed at keeping land-sale prices low by rigging local auctions to favor squatters or, in some cases, timber companies. Checkerboarding also occurred as a consequence of federal land grants to states, usually at statehood, to support schools, roads, and other public needs. Some checkerboarding occurred when lands that had been homesteaded or sold into private hands later found themselves within national forests or other federal conservation units.

This federal land checkerboarding—discontinuous federal land ownership—has produced a jurisdictional nightmare. Federal lands are interspersed with state and private lands, making an ecosystem-management perspective difficult to implement and often causing access problems. An antidote to checkerboarding is land exchanges, which seek to consolidate federal land holdings through deals with states and private parties. The Federal Land Policy and Management Act (FLPMA) requires that land exchanges be in the public interest and that the lands that the federal government acquires in the exchanges be at least as valuable as those being conveyed. 43 U.S.C § 1716(a). Although this provision gives considerable discretion to federal land managers to exchange lands, courts have halted several exchanges because the discretion has been abused. See, e.g., *Center for Biological Diversity v. U.S. Dept. of Interior*, 623 F.3d 633 (9th Cir. 2010) (violation of FLPMA's "public interest" standard and the National Environmental Policy Act); *National Parks & Conservation Ass'n v. Bureau of Land Management*, 606 F.3d 1058 (9th Cir. 2010) (violation of FLPMA's "equal value" standard).

A paradigmatic example of the problems of checkerboarding is the so-called Oregon and California forest lands, whose fate is now a major congressional issue because tax revenues levied on the private lands are insufficient to fund local governmental services. See Michael C. Blumm & Tim Wigington, *The Oregon and California Railroad Grant Lands' Sordid Past, Contentious Present, and Uncertain Future: A Century of Conflict*, 40 B.C. Envtl. Aff. L. Rev. 1 (2013). The so-called "O & C" saga, undecided as we write, may be the quintessential federal-local conflict over public land in the twenty-first century, pitting concentrated local interests against diffuse national public concerns. The likely result is that the locals will prevail—as predicted by public choice political theory. See Michael C, Blumm, *Public Choice Theory and the Public Lands: Why "Multiple Use" Failed*, 18 Harv. Envtl. L. Rev. 405 (1994).

4.   *Modern public land litigation.* The typical modern public lands case involves a private party seeking review of federal agency action under the Administrative Procedure Act (APA), 5 U.S.C. § 551 *et seq.* The APA

establishes procedures for making agency policy, including informal rulemaking which governs most agency policy making, and requires that proposed rules be accompanied by a public statement of the "basis and purpose" of the rule. *Id.* § 553(c). The APA also allows the public to petition agencies to initiate rulemaking, *id.* § 555(e), and authorizes suits by "adversely affected" persons due to "agency action within the meaning of a relevant statute." *Id.* § 702. However, judicial review is limited by standing and ripeness doctrines to concrete cases brought by aggrieved people to resolve real disputes over agency actions fulfilling discrete congressional directives in a timely manner. See, e.g., *Lujan v. National Wildlife Federation*, 497 U.S. 871 (1990) (standing); *Ohio Forestry Ass'n, Inc. v. Sierra Club*, 523 U.S. 726 (1998) (ripeness); *Norton v. Southern Utah Wilderness Alliance*, 542 U.S. 55 (2004) (only implementation of discrete congressional directives are judicially reviewable). Agency decisions also generally receive considerable judicial deference. See 5 U.S.C. § 706(2)(A) (courts can set aside agency actions that are "arbitrary and capricious"); *Chevron, U.S.A. v. Natural Resources Defense Council*, 467 U.S. 837 (1984) (courts should defer to reasonable agency interpretations of statutes). See generally Sandra B. Zellmer & Jan G. Laitos, *Principles of Natural Resources Law* 33–56 (2014); George C. Coggins & Robert L. Glicksman, *Public Natural Resources Law,* § 8:47 (2d ed. 2014).

5. *Public lands and climate change.* Some federal public lands provide ecosystem services, including forested lands that serve as sinks for carbon and other greenhouse gas (GHG) emissions. Other federal lands offer open space that may be employed for renewable energy production like wind and solar energy production, for underground carbon sequestration or for new "smart" electric transmission lines. In all these ways, federal land managers can contribute to climate change mitigation.

Other federal lands contribute to GHG emissions through grazing permits and coal and oil and gas leasing. According to one report covering 2009, emissions linked to federal lands and resources accounted for roughly one-quarter of the nation's total GHG emissions. See Jessica Goad, *Stunner: One Quarter of Total U.S. Greenhouse Gas Emissions Come From Fossil Fuels Mined and Drilled on Public Lands* (Feb. 27, 2012), available at http://thinkprogress.org/cliimate/issue (discussing a report commissioned by the Wilderness Society).

Federal lands will also be adversely affected by climate change and rising temperatures. Consequently, adaptation measures will be necessary to respond to increased wildfires and their severity, insect infestations such as bark beetles that are devastating western forests, loss of biodiversity as species die off or migrate, and hydrological changes as water sources like wetlands dry up. According to a knowledgeable commentator, "managing the unavoidable" through adaptation measures is likely to be more challenging than mitigation measures like capping emissions, since it will require "considerable investment in information-gathering and science, which will almost certainly depend heavily on public funds." Moreover, adaptation measures will produce often uncertain and intangible benefits, compared to the jobs and profits produced, say, by green power projects. John D. Leshy, *Federal Lands in the Twenty-First Century*, 50 Nat. Res. J. 111, 131 (2010) (calling for green energy development to be linked with biodiversity reserves and other new conservation areas). See also Aimee Delach & Noah Matson, *Climate Change and Federal Land Management: A Comparison of the U.S. Fish & Wildlife Service, National Park Service, and U.S. Forest Service Climate Change Strategies* (Nov. 2010) (Defenders of Wildlife report calling for more specific adaption measures from the three federal agencies and a priority for wildlife conservation).

6. *Private rights in public lands.* That federal lands are owned by the public does not mean that there are not significant private rights in these lands. Even as the U.S. Supreme Court has declared that "All of the public lands of the nation are held in trust for the people of the whole country," *Light v. United States*, 220 U.S. 523, 537 (1911), citing *United States v. Trinidad Coal & Coking Co.,* 137 U.S. 160 (1890), private claims to use the lands remain strong and durable. See Bruce R. Huber, *The Durability of Private Claims to Public Property*, 102 Geo. L.J. 991 (2014). Thus, a considerable amount of public land law concerns private rights to mine, graze, and harvest timber—traditional commodity uses that are examined in this chapter.

A. MINING

1. PRIVATE MINING RIGHTS ON FEDERAL LANDS

Among the many private rights in public lands, mining claims are perhaps the most notable. Under the largely unamended 1872 General Mining Law, 30 U.S.C. §§ 22 *et seq.*, miners can claim property rights to "all valuable mineral deposits" if they discover them on federal lands that are open to mining. The most valuable minerals subject to this rule of capture are so-called "hard rock" minerals, particularly gold, silver, lead, tin, copper, diamonds, and gemstones (coal, oil, gas, and oil shale are leased; and stone, sand, and gravel are sold). Thus, the 1872 law is often referred to as the Hardrock Mining Act.

Once a valuable mineral deposit is discovered—the first step in the legal process—a miner must mark (locate) his claim properly and record it with the federal Bureau of Land Management (BLM). By doing that the miner acquires, under the statute, a constitutionally protected property right called an unpatented mining claim. Maintaining these property rights does require payment of an annual fee of $100 per claim or performance of "assessment work" but does not require actual mining— miners may in fact hold their mine claims indefinitely. When they do mine, they pay no royalties to the federal government.

Not all federal lands are subject to mining claims. Lands reserved for conservation purposes, such as national parks, national monuments, wildlife refuges, wild and scenic rivers, wilderness, and some national forests, are generally off-limits to mining entry, as are Indian reservations and defense lands. Other lands can be withdrawn from the Mining Law by executive action under the terms of the Federal Land Management and Policy Act, 43 U.S.C. § 1714(b)–(c).

A problematic issue with any capture rule, such as embodied in the 1872 Mining Law, is whether and how to protect those who are in the process of seeking to capture from competing capturers. Should there be some sort of pre-capture protection for those who invest labor in the search for capture but have yet to make an actual capture (or, in this setting, to discover a valuable mineral deposit)? In the case of mining on federal lands, the answer has been yes, in the form of *pedis possessio* (literally, a foothold) rights, which give prospectors who have yet to make an adequate discovery (and thus obtain a property right) some protection against competing prospectors. But as the following case indicates, *pedis possessio* rights are tenuous.

GEOMET EXPLORATION, LTD. V. LUCKY MC URANIUM CORP.

Supreme Court of Arizona
601 P.2d 1339 (1979)

[Lucky Mc posted some 200 mining claims covering roughly 4,000 acres of public land in western Arizona in 1976. It drilled a ten-foot hole on each claim and recorded notice of the claims as required by state statute. However, Lucky Mc made no discovery of valuable minerals and it was not present when Geomet, knowing of Lucky Mc's claims, peaceably entered some of them and began drilling. Lucky Mc sued, claiming trespass and seeking both possession and damages. The trial court awarded both, rejecting Geomet's argument that *pedis possessio* only protected miners who were actually present on a claim and diligently pursuing discovery. In the court's view, miners needed more protection than this; the requirement of actual possession, it concluded, was unrealistic in light of modern mining techniques and the expense involved in exploring large areas. The lower court also found that Geomet entered in bad faith, since it knew of Lucky Mc's claims. Geomet appealed.]

HAYS, J.

* * *

We must decide a single issue: Should the actual occupancy requirement of *pedis possessio* be discarded in favor of constructive possession to afford a potential locator protection of contiguous, unoccupied claims as against one who enters peaceably, openly, and remains in possession searching for minerals?

Pedis Possessio

Mineral deposits in the public domain of the United States are open to all citizens (or those who have expressed an intent to become citizens) who wish to occupy and explore them "under regulations prescribed by law, and according to the local customs or rules of miners in the several mining districts, so far as the same are applicable and not inconsistent with the laws of the United States." 30 U.S.C. § 22 (1970).

The doctrine of *pedis possessio* evolved from customs and usages of miners and has achieved statutory recognition in federal law as the "law of possession," 30 U.S.C. § 53 (1970):

> No possessory action between persons, in any court of the United States, for the recovery of any mining title, or for damages to any such title, shall be affected by the fact that the paramount title to the land in which such mines lie is in the United States; but each case shall be judged by the law of possession.

Regardless of compliance with statutory requisites such as monumenting and notice, one cannot perfect a location, under either federal or state law, without actual discovery of minerals in place. *Best v. Humboldt Placer Mining Co.*, 371 U.S. 334 (1963); 30 U.S.C. § 23 (1970). Until discovery, the law of possession determines who has the better right to possession.

The literal meaning of *pedis possessio* is a foothold, actual possession. Black's Law Dictionary 1289 (rev. 4th ed. 1968). This actual occupancy must be distinguished from constructive possession, which is based on color of title and has the effect of enlarging the area actually occupied to the extent of the description in the title. *Id.* at 1325. A succinct exposition of *pedis possessio* is found in *Union Oil Co. v. Smith*, 249 U.S. 337, 346–48 (1919):

> Those who, being qualified, proceed in good faith to make such explorations and enter peaceably upon vacant lands of the United States for that purpose are not treated as mere trespassers, but as licensees or tenants at will. For since, as a practical matter, exploration must precede the discovery of minerals, and some occupation of the land ordinarily is necessary for adequate and systematic exploration, legal recognition of the *pedis possessio* of a bona fide and qualified prospector is universally regarded as a necessity. It is held that upon the public domain a miner may hold the place in which he may be working against all others having no better right, and while he remains in possession, diligently working towards

discovery, is entitled—at least for a reasonable time—to be protected against forcible, fraudulent, and clandestine intrusions upon his possession. . . .

Whatever the nature and extent of a possessory right before discovery, all authorities agree that such possession may be maintained only by continued actual occupancy by a qualified locator or his representatives engaged in persistent and diligent prosecution of work looking to the discovery of mineral. (Emphasis added.)

If the first possessor should relax his occupancy or cease working toward discovery, and another enters peaceably, openly, and diligently searches for mineral, the first party forfeits the right to exclusive possession under the requirements of *pedis possessio. Cole v. Ralph*, 252 U.S. 286, 295 (1920); *Davis v. Nelson*, 329 F.2d 840 (9th Cir. 1964).

Arizona has recognized *pedis possessio* and the concomitant requirement of actual occupancy for a century. *Field v. Grey*, 25 P. 793 (Ariz. 1881). In *Bagg v. New Jersey Loan Co.*, 354 P.2d 40, 44 (Ariz. 1960), we said: "Location is the foundation of the possessory title, and possession thereunder, *as required by law and local rules and customs*, keeps the title alive, . . ." (Emphasis added.) It is perhaps more proper to speak of a possessory right than a title because, until discovery of mineral and issuance of a patent, absolute title in fee simple remains in the United States. *Bagg*, 354 P.2d 40; *Bowen v. Chemi-Cote Perlite Corp.*, 432 P.2d 435 (Ariz. 1967). Since this is a possessory action, the party with the better right is entitled to prevail. *Rundle v. Republic Cement Corp.*, 341 P.2d 226 (Ariz. 1959).

Conceding that actual occupancy is necessary under *pedis possessio*, Lucky urges that the requirement be relaxed in deference to the time and expense that would be involved in actually occupying and drilling on each claim until discovery. Moreover, Lucky points out that the total area claimed—4,000 acres—is reasonable in size, similar in geological formation, and that an overall work program for the entire area had been developed. Under these circumstances, Lucky contends, actual drilling on some of the claims should suffice to afford protection as to all contiguous claims. Great reliance is placed on *MacGuire v. Sturgis*, 347 F.Supp. 580 (D. Wyo. 1971), in which the federal court accepted arguments similar to those advanced here and extended protection on a group or area basis. Geomet counters that *MacGuire* is an aberration and contrary to three Wyoming Supreme Court cases upholding the requisite of actual occupancy. *Sparks v. Mount*, 207 P. 1099 (Wyo. 1922); *Whiting v. Straup*, 95 P. 849 (Wyo. 1908); *Phillips v. Brill*, 95 P. 856 (Wyo. 1908).

To adopt the premise urged by Lucky eviscerates the actual occupancy requirement of *pedis possessio* and substitutes for it the theory of constructive possession even though there is no color of title. We are persuaded that the sounder approach is to maintain the doctrine intact. In *Union Oil*, the Court considered the precise question of extending protection to contiguous claims and refused to do so:

> It was and is defendant's contention that by virtue of the act of 1903, one who has acquired the possessory rights of locators before discovery in five contiguous claims . . . may preserve and maintain an inchoate right to all of them by means of a continuous actual occupation of one, coupled with diligent prosecution in good faith of a sufficient amount of discovery work thereon, provided such work tends also to determine the oil-bearing character of the other claims. . . .

> In our opinion the act shows no purpose to dispense with discovery as an essential of a valid oil location or to break down in any wise the recognized distinction between the pedis possessio of a prospector doing work for the purpose of discovering oil and the more substantial right of possession of one who has made a discovery. . . . Union Oil v. U.S., 249 U.S. at 343, 353. (Emphasis added.)

We have canvassed the Western mining jurisdictions and found the requirement of actual occupancy to be the majority view. *Davis v. Nelson*; *United Western Minerals Co. v. Hannsen*, 363 P.2d 677 (Colo. 1961); *Adams v. Benedict*, 327 P.2d 308 (N.M. 1958); *McLemore v. Express Oil Co.*, 112 P. 59 (Cal. 1910).

There are always inherent risks in prospecting. The development of *pedis possessio* from the customs of miners argues forcefully against the proposition that exclusive right to possession should encompass claims neither actually occupied nor being explored. We note that the doctrine does not protect on the basis of occupancy alone; the additional requirement of diligent search for minerals must also be satisfied. The reason for these dual elements—and for the policy of the United States in making public domain available for exploration and mining—is to encourage those prepared to demonstrate their sincerity and tenacity in the pursuit of valuable minerals. If one may, by complying with preliminary formalities of posting and recording notices, secure for himself the exclusive possession of a large area upon only a small portion of which he is actually working, then he may, at his leisure, explore the entire area and exclude all others who stand ready to peaceably and openly enter unoccupied sections for the purpose of discovering minerals. Such a premise is laden with extreme difficulties of determining over how large an area and for how long one might be permitted to exclude others.

We hold that *pedis possessio* protects only those claims actually occupied (provided also that work toward discovery is in progress) and does not extend to contiguous, unoccupied claims on a group or area basis.

Lucky calls our attention to former A.R.S. [Arizona Revised Statutes] § 27–203(B), under which a potential locator was allowed 120 days to sink shafts to a specified depth. The contention is that during that period, Lucky should have been granted exclusive possession in order to discover mineral in place, and, since Geomet entered certain claims before the expiration of the 120 days, Lucky did not have the benefit of the full term in which to make discovery.

We point out, however, that the first statute concerning location of claims, A.R.S. § 27–201, reads as follows:

> *Upon discovery of mineral in place* on the public domain of the United States the mineral may be located as a lode mining claim by the discoverer for himself, or for himself and others, or for others. (Emphasis added.)

Discovery is the *sine qua non* that lends validity to other statutory procedures designed to complete a location. We have on two occasions held that acts of location confer no right in the absence of discovery. *State v. Tracy*, 257 P.2d 860, 862 (Ariz. 1953); *Ponton v. House*, 256 P.2d 246, 247 (Ariz. 1953). It is certainly true that, even after discovery, one may be held to have abandoned a location or forfeited his rights for failure to comply with additional statutory requirements. But *prior to discovery*, the only right one has to exclude others flows from *pedis possessio* and not from statutory law.

Finally, Lucky asserts that Geomet cannot invoke *pedis possessio* because Geomet, knowing that Lucky claimed the area, entered in bad faith. Lucky relies principally on *Bagg v. New Jersey Loan Co.* and *Woolsey v. Lassen*, 371 P.2d 587 (Ariz. 1962). It is true that a potential locator must enter in good faith. *Union Oil Co. v. Smith.*

There is language in our decisions that appears to indicate that mere knowledge of a prior claim constitutes bad faith. Although we are sure that our holdings were sound in the cases Lucky cites, certain statements may have been an inadvertent oversimplification of the issue of good faith and we take this opportunity to clarify the point.

In general terms, good faith may be defined as honesty of purpose and absence of intent to defraud. *People v. Bowman*, 320 P.2d 70 (Cal. Dist. Ct. App. 1958); *Thurmond v. Espalin*, 171 P.2d 325 (N.M. 1946). Both *Bagg* and *Woolsey* dealt with those who had discovered minerals in place and were in actual occupancy when others attempted to usurp their claims. These facts immediately distinguish them from the instant case, in which Lucky had neither made discovery nor was in actual occupancy of the areas Geomet entered.

* * *

In summary, both cases differ significantly from this case in their factual framework and did not depend for their resolution solely upon the element of knowledge. We stand by our conclusions in those cases but wish to emphasize that mere knowledge of a previous claim, in and of itself, does not constitute bad faith.

Since Geomet's entry concededly was open and peaceable, we hold that the entry was in good faith.

In conclusion, Lucky was not in actual occupancy of those areas Geomet entered and *pedis possessio* affords Lucky no protection as to those particular claims. Geomet is entitled to the exclusive possession of the disputed claims.

We reverse the trial court, order that the injunction be quashed, and remand for proceedings consistent with this opinion.

<h3 style="text-align:center">NOTES</h3>

1.   *The fair chase.* The issue in *Geomet* chiefly had to do with the rules of the hunt, mining style. How close can one prospector get to another, without acting unfairly? Prospectors today, of course, do not often go out with their mules, pick in hand. They more often go out with explosives and highly technical equipment, undertaking expensive seismic tests to look for underground ore formations. Once a likely formation has been found, they then need to go to the site and work on it. It is thus easy enough for other miners simply to watch what the big companies do and where they go, figuring that a company that sets up operation in a particular place must be doing so because its underground tests have turned up promising evidence of valuable deposits. The question here, then, is not simply about physically disturbing another miner. It is about taking advantage of information on underground ore formations that a miner has obtained at considerable expense. Should this contemporary reality have received more weight in the case than it did? On the other hand, note how much land Lucky was attempting to control, even though it had not actually discovered a valuable mineral deposit. As for the issue of Geomet's bad faith, how does the court now define "bad faith"? Under what circumstances might a person exhibit it? Is the issue of good or bad faith simply about whether Geomet is attempting itself to make a discovery, rather than attempting to disrupt Lucky's prospecting effort?

2.   *Discovery and the hidden evidence.* Note that whether a person has or has not discovered a valuable mineral deposit is based on evidence often known only to the miner. As the law operates, no one asks to see the evidence of discovery, nor is it judged unless one of two things happens: 1) someone

(the government, most likely) challenges a miner's claim to possess an unpatented mining claim, or 2) (see the *Coleman* case below) a miner goes to the government and asks for a patent, thus triggering a legal requirement to prove the deposit and satisfaction of the other legal requirements. In the meantime, a person can assert and enjoy exclusive use of mining claims without proving their validity (there is no limit to how many a person can have, so long as each claim is perfected). Note how Lucky Mc goes about conducting its business: once it finds a place where a valuable deposit might exist, it proceeds to locate its claims and file its papers, even though it has not yet discovered, and might never actually discover, a valuable mineral deposit. Lucky Mc is thus doing things a bit out of order, locating claims before the discovery is made. Yet, once Lucky Mc has asserted control over claims and located them, who is to know whether it has actually discovered valuable minerals, and thus who is to know whether Lucky Mc does or does not have unpatented mining claims?

Is this whole arrangement perhaps unfair, both to other miners and to the public? Is it sensible to allocate a resource based on first-in-time when only the actor knows whether he really has "captured" the resource? Isn't the purpose of the Mining Law to promote actual mining?

The 1872 law requires, in order to gain an unpatented mining claim, a (i) discovery of a (ii) valuable (iii) mineral (iv) deposit. The Supreme Court early on ruled that the statute required proof of a valuable discovery, not mere probabilities, speculation, and belief. *Sullivan v. Iron Silver Mining*, 143 U.S. 431 (1892). The Interior Secretary subsequently decided that a mineral deposit was valuable when "a person of ordinary prudence would be justified in the further expenditure of his labor and means, with a reasonable prospect of success, in developing a valuable mine. . . ." *Castle v. Womble*, 19 Pub. Lands Dec. 455, 457 (1894). Still, abuses of the General Mining Law were commonplace throughout its first ninety years, as so-called miners claimed federal land for non-mineral purposes like taverns and vacation cabins. One particularly notable claim failed in *U.S. v. Rizzinelli,* 182 F. 675 (D. Idaho 1910), when the court, upholding the power of the Forest Service to prohibit non-mining surface uses, disallowed a tavern owner from mining the pockets of local miners. This "prudent person" test, an objective one, remains the basic standard for judging whether a mineral deposit is valuable. In time the Interior Secretary refined the test in an effort to create greater certainty and to avoid frivolous claims of discovery, as the following case illustrates.

UNITED STATES V. COLEMAN

Supreme Court of the United States
390 U.S. 599 (1968)

[In 1956 respondent Coleman applied to the Department of the Interior for a patent to certain public lands based on his entry onto and exploration of these lands and his discovery there of a variety of stone called quartzite, one of the most common of all solid materials. Coleman contended that the quartzite deposits qualified as "valuable mineral deposits" under 30 U.S.C. § 22 and made the land "chiefly valuable for building stone" under 30 U.S.C. § 161. The Secretary of the Interior held that to qualify as "valuable mineral deposits" under 30 U.S.C. § 22, it must be shown that the mineral can be "extracted, removed and marketed at a profit"—the so-called "marketability test." The Secretary concluded that the quartzite deposits claimed by Coleman did not meet that criterion, since the deposits were a "common variety" of stone within the meaning of 30 U.S.C. § 611, and thus they could not serve as the basis for a valid mining claim under the mining laws. The Secretary denied the patent application, but Coleman remained on the land, forcing the government to bring an action in ejectment in the district court against Coleman. Coleman filed a counterclaim. The district court found for the government. On appeal, the Ninth Circuit reversed, holding that the test of profitable marketability was not a proper standard for determining whether a discovery of "valuable mineral deposits" under 30 U.S.C. § 22 had been made, and that building stone could not be deemed a "common variety" of stone under 30 U.S.C. § 611. The Supreme Court reversed the Ninth Circuit in the following opinion.]

BLACK, J.

* * *

We cannot agree with the Court of Appeals and believe that the rulings of the Secretary of the Interior were proper. The Secretary's determination that the quartzite deposits did not qualify as valuable mineral deposits because the stone could not be marketed at a profit does no violence to the statute. Indeed, the marketability test is an admirable effort to identify with greater precision and objectivity the factors relevant to a determination that a mineral deposit is "valuable." It is a logical complement to the "prudent-man test" which the Secretary has been using to interpret the mining laws since 1894. Under this "prudent-man test" in order to qualify as "valuable mineral deposits," the discovered deposits must be of such a character that "a person of ordinary prudence would be justified in the further expenditure of his labor and means, with a reasonable prospect of success, in developing a valuable mine * * *." *Castle v. Womble*, 19 L.D. 455, 457 (1894). This Court has approved the prudent-man formulation and interpretation on numerous occasions. See, for example, *Chrisman v. Miller*, 197 U.S. 313, 322; *Cameron v. United States*, 252 U.S. 450, 459; *Best v. Humboldt Placer Mining Co.*, 371 U.S. 334, 335–36. Under the mining laws Congress has made public lands available to people for the purpose of mining valuable mineral deposits and not for other purposes. The obvious intent was to reward and encourage the discovery of minerals that are valuable in an economic sense. Minerals which no prudent man will extract because there is no demand for them at a price higher than the costs of extraction and transportation are hardly economically valuable. Thus, profitability is an important consideration in applying the prudent-man test, and the marketability test which the Secretary has used here merely recognizes this fact.

The marketability test also has the advantage of throwing light on a claimant's intention, a matter which is inextricably bound together with valuableness. For evidence that a mineral deposit is not of economic value and cannot in all likelihood be operated at a profit may well suggest that a claimant seeks the land for other purposes. Indeed, as the Government points out, the facts of this case—the thousands of dollars and hours spent building a home on 720 acres in a highly scenic national forest located two hours from Los Angeles, the lack of an economically feasible market for the stone, and the immense quantities of identical stone found in the area outside the claims—might well be thought to raise a substantial question as to respondent Coleman's real intention.

Finally, we think that the Court of Appeals' objection to the marketability test on the ground that it involves the imposition of a different and more onerous standard on claims for minerals of widespread occurrence than for rarer minerals which have generally been dealt with under the prudent-man test is unwarranted. As we have pointed out above, the prudent-man test and the marketability test are not distinct standards, but are complementary in that the latter is a refinement of the former. While it is true that the marketability test is usually the critical factor in cases involving nonmetallic minerals of widespread occurrence, this is accounted for by the perfectly natural reason that precious metals which are in small supply and for which there is a great demand, sell at a price so high as to leave little room for doubt that they can be extracted and marketed at a profit.

We believe that the Secretary of the Interior was also correct in ruling that "[i]n view of the immense quantities of identical stone found in the area outside the claims, the stone must be considered a 'common variety'" and thus must fall within the exclusionary language of § 3 of the 1955 Act, 30 U.S.C. § 611, which declares that "[a] deposit of common varieties of . . . stone . . . shall [not] be deemed a valuable mineral deposit within the meaning of the mining laws . . ." Respondents rely on the earlier 1892 Act, 30 U.S.C. § 161, which makes the mining laws applicable to "lands that are chiefly valuable for building stone" and contend that the 1955 Act has no application to building stone, since, according to respondents, "[s]tone which is chiefly valuable as building stone is, by that very fact, not a common variety of stone." This was also the reasoning of the Court of Appeals. But this argument completely fails to take into account the reason why Congress felt compelled to pass the 1955 Act with its modification of the mining laws. The legislative history makes clear that this Act (30 U.S.C. § 611) was intended to remove common types of sand, gravel, and stone from the coverage of the mining laws, under which they served as a basis for claims to land patents, and to place the disposition of such materials under the Materials Act of 1947, 30 U.S.C. §§ 601 *et seq.*, which provides for the sale of such materials without disposing of the land on which they are found. . . . Thus we read 30 U.S.C. § 611, passed in 1955, as removing from the coverage of the mining laws "common varieties" of building stone, but leaving 30 U.S.C. § 161, the 1892 Act, entirely effective as to building stone that has "some property giving it distinct and special value" (expressly excluded under § 611).

For these reasons we hold that the United States is entitled to eject respondents from the land and that respondents' counterclaim for a patent must fail. The case is reversed and remanded to the Court of Appeals for the Ninth Circuit for further proceedings to carry out this decision.

NOTES

1.   *The marketability test.* On the facts of *Coleman*, it seems clear that the "miner" seeking a land patent had no interest at all in mining and every interest instead in owning a nice home "in a highly scenic national forest." His case may seem audacious except that it builds upon a long history of misuse of public land laws. Indeed, taking advantage of the government was (and for some, perhaps, still is) one of the prime forms of entertainment in the American West. Still, the marketability test as a means for judging the value of mineral deposits is not without its criticisms. A mineral deposit that cannot be exploited today, because the costs of exploitation or transport are too high, might well become usable in the future, when richer mines have been exhausted and more convenient mineral sources are gone. Note the final sentences of the Court's opinion: the marketability test is used chiefly for "nonmetallic minerals of widespread occurrence." The test is used far less in the case of precious metals such as gold and silver, even when ore concentrations are, for the time being, too low to mine at a profit.

2.   *Capturing minerals: the other elements.* To complete the capture of a mineral deposit, the claimant must do more than show that the deposit is "valuable" and "mineral." (As for the issue of "mineral," courts have ruled that it excludes both water and topsoil, even though both are valuable. Statutes enacted since 1872, including the Mineral Leasing Act of 1920, have

also excluded from the original act's coverage a variety of specific minerals, including oil, gas, and coal.) The miner must also stake out his claim, properly locating its boundaries. Once these steps are complete, the miner gains an "unpatented mining claim," which is a potentially perpetual property interest in the mineral deposit. The task of locating a claim can be complicated because the law divides mineral deposits into two types: lode claims and placer claims, depending upon whether the valuable mineral is or is not embedded in an ore formation (a lode claim is embedded). A miner who errs on this factual issue, treating a lode claim as a placer claim (or vice versa), has not properly completed the work of capture and thus does not gain an unpatented mining claim. Errors can also be made in establishing the exact dimensions of a claim. Note that the issues of "valuable" and "mineral" in this setting are essentially questions of statutory interpretation, as the Supreme Court recognized in *BedRoc Limited, LLC v. U.S.*, 541 U.S. 176 (2004), which ruled that a 1919 statute authorizing the sale of "nonmineral land," with the federal government reserving "valuable minerals," included ordinary sand and gravel. The term "mineral" can have widely different meanings in different legal settings (an issue explored in chapter 5).

    3.   *Excluding recreationalists from mine claims.* In *United States v. Curtis-Nevada Mines, Inc.*, 611 F.2d 1277 (9th Cir. 1980), Curtis asserted title to 203 unpatented mining claims on federal lands, covering some thirteen square miles. Although he claimed that the mining claims were worth "trillions," no mining was taking place, and only one employee was onsite, charged chiefly with keeping outsiders away. Curtis posted "no trespassing" signs around the area and excluded hunters, hikers, campers, and other recreational visitors. Under section 4(b) of the Surface Resources Act of 1955, 16 U.S.C. § 612(b), the rights of mining claimants are subject to "the right of the United States, its permittees, and licensees, to use so much of the surface thereof as may be necessary for such purposes," so long as such alternative uses do not "endanger or materially interfere with prospecting, mining, or processing operations or uses reasonably incident thereto." The Ninth Circuit ruled that the Surface Resources Act applied to recreational uses of the surface as well as to other consumptive land uses. The statutory language—"permittees and licensees"—thus included casual recreational visitors; it was not limited to individuals who held specific written permits or licenses to use the same land. Curtis therefore had to let them make free recreational use of the unpatented mining claims unless he could show material interference with his mining operations.

    4.   *Criminal sanctions.* In *U.S. v. Backlund*, 677 F.3d 930 (9th Cir. 2012), the court ruled that the Forest Service's regulation requiring prior approval of residential occupancy on national forest lands was not unenforceably vague in violation of the due process clause, and therefore upheld the conviction of one defendant under 36 C.F.R. § 261.10(b), for unlawfully occupying a residence not reasonably necessary to mining operations. However, the court ruled that the other defendant could challenge the denial of his mining plan, either under the Administrative Procedure Act

or in an ensuing criminal enforcement proceeding, and consequently denying him the right in the latter was impermissible.

———————

Prior to 1994, miners could obtain a land patent to the surface, which would effectively privatize the land, for a nominal filing fee. However, Congress passed an appropriations rider that year, Pub. L. No. 103–332, 108 Stat. 2499 (1994), that has for the last twenty years effectively foreclosed new surface land patents for mining claims, as Congress has continued the moratorium in annual appropriation statutes. The following case, which concerns a land patent application filed before the moratorium took effect, discusses the character of federal mining claims, the effect of conservation statutes like the Wilderness Act, and the concept of "valid existing rights" in public land law.

McMASTER v. UNITED STATES
Ninth Circuit Court of Appeals
731 F.3d 881 (2013)

[McMaster, the owner of the Oro Grande mining claim located in the Trinity Alps Wilderness area in northern California, filed an application for a land patent (the equivalent of a fee simple) in 1992. The Bureau of Land Management (BLM) granted McMaster a patent only to the mineral estate, after deciding that the surface estate was reserved to the federal government. McMaster filed suit under the Quiet Title Act (QTA), the Administrative Procedure Act, and the Declaratory Judgment Act (DJA), seeking to quiet title in fee simple. The district court dismissed all of McMaster's claims, and he appealed to the Ninth Circuit.]

BYBEE, J.

* * *

II.   *Legal Background*

A.   *Statutory History*

The General Mining Law of 1872 (Mining Law), 30 U.S.C. §§ 22 *et seq.*, was enacted to permit citizens to enter and explore unappropriated federal lands in search of "valuable mineral deposits," *id.* § 22. Citizens who discovered mineral deposits could then secure exclusive rights to the land by meeting certain statutory requirements. *Id.;* see *Independence Min. Co., Inc. v. Babbitt,* 105 F.3d 502, 506 (9th Cir. 1997). First, a claimant could validate his claim by meeting the legal requirements for "locating" and discovering the claim. See 30 U.S.C. § 28; see also *Cole v. Ralph,* 252 U.S. 286, 294–96 (1920). The holder of a valid, located claim is entitled to the "exclusive right of possession and enjoyment of all the surface included within the . . . location[ ]," as long as he continues to meet certain requirements. 30 U.S.C. § 26; see *id.* § 28; see also *Best v. Humboldt Placer Min. Co.,* 371 U.S. 334, 335–36 (1963). This possessory interest entitles the claim holder to "the right to extract all minerals from the claim without paying royalties to the United States," *Independence Min. Co.,* 105 F.3d at 506, but the United States retains title to the land, *United States v. Locke,* 471 U.S. 84, 104 (1985). Second, "an individual who possesses a valid mining claim may go through an additional process to obtain a patent," by applying to the BLM, in the Department of the Interior, and meeting additional statutory requirements. *Swanson v. Babbitt,* 3 F.3d 1348, 1350 (9th Cir. 1993); see 30 U.S.C. §§ 29, 35; *Independence Min. Co.,* 105 F.3d at 506. Under the General Mining Law, a patent generally conveyed fee-simple title to both the surface estate and the mineral deposits. See *Independence Min. Co.,* 105 F.3d at 506; see also *Andrus v. Shell Oil Co.,* 446 U.S. 657, 658 & n. 1 (1980).

In 1955, however, Congress enacted the Surface Resources and Multiple Use Act, 30 U.S.C. § 601–615, which established that any unpatented claim located after the effective date of the Act could not be used "for any purposes other than prospecting, mining or processing operations and uses reasonable incident thereto," *id.* § 612(a); see *United States v. Backlund,* 689 F.3d 986, 991 (9th Cir. 2012). Claimants would no longer receive the exclusive right of possession and enjoyment of the surface prior to patenting their claim; their claims would be subject to "the right of the United States to manage and dispose" of the surface of any such mining claim. 30 U.S.C. § 612(b); see *Backlund,* 689 F.3d at 991.

Then, in 1964, Congress enacted the Wilderness Act, 16 U.S.C. §§ 1131–36, which "established the National Wilderness Preservation System [(NWPS)] to be composed of federally owned areas designated by Congress as 'wilderness areas,'" *id.* § 1131(a). . . . Section 1133(d)(3) . . . limited the creation of future mining interests, while preserving some pre-existing mining interests and providing a grace period for discoveries. See 16 U.S.C. § 1133(d)(3). "[S]ubject to valid existing rights," patents that issued after the effective date of the Wilderness Act, would convey title only to the mineral deposits, with the surface estate being reserved to the United States. *Id.* New claims could also be located under the Act, but only until December 31, 1983. *Id.* After December 31, 1983, no patent would issue to claims located within a wilderness area, "except for valid claims existing on or before December 31, 1983." *Id.* And "[s]ubject to valid rights then existing," beginning on January 1, 1984, "all forms of appropriation under the mining laws" would no longer apply to any lands designated as wilderness areas. *Id.*

Twenty years later, the California Wilderness Act of 1984 made the Wilderness Act applicable to the Oro Grande mining claim as of September 28, 1984.

B.   *Regulatory History*

In 1966, the BLM promulgated a regulation to implement § 1133(d)(3) of the Wilderness Act. See 43 C.F.R. § 3638.5 (1996) (the regulation). The regulation states that any "patent issued under the U.S. mining laws for mineral locations established after [the effective date of the Wilderness Act], or validated by discovery of minerals occurring after [the effective date of the Wilderness Act]," would convey title only to the mineral deposits and would reserve title to the surface of the land to the United States. *Id.* Although § 3638.5 does not directly address whether such a reservation of surface rights to the United States applied to unpatented claims located prior to the effective date of the Wilderness Act [the Act allowed mineral entry in wilderness areas for twenty years— until the end of 1983–Eds.], in practice, the BLM regularly conveyed fee-[s]imple patents to such claims. See Solicitor's Opinion at 1, 19–20. In 1981, the BLM also published a policy stating that "[a] patent conveying both surface and mineral rights *may* be issued on a valid claim located prior to the date the area was included as part of the National Wilderness Preservation System." Bureau of Land Management, Wilderness Management Policy, 46 Fed. Reg. 47,180–01 (1981) (BLM policy). And in 1991, the BLM issued a manual stating that "[f]or claims located before enactment of the Wilderness Act . . . the claims must have a discovery as of the date of enactment to acquire the surface and mineral estates," BLM Manual H–3860–1, Mineral Patent Application Processing, VIII–7 (1991) (the Manual).

On May 22, 1998, the Solicitor of the Department of the Interior issued Opinion No. M–36994, *Patenting of Mine Claims and Mill Sites in Wilderness Areas*, available at http://www.doi.gov/solicitor/opinions/M–36994.pdf, disagreeing with BLM's practice of conveying fee-simple patents to all valid claims located before the wilderness designation. See Solicitor's Opinion, at 20. The Solicitor's Opinion recognized the BLM's policies and practices, see *id.* at 19–20, but ultimately instructed the BLM to follow a new policy:

> [M]ineral patents issued under the Mining Law for lands within the wilderness areas . . . should convey only the mineral deposits within the claim, unless the mining claim for which the patent is sought was located and validated by a discovery prior to designation of the wilderness area *and* the claimant complied with all the requirements for obtaining a patent under the Mining Law prior to the wilderness designation, as determined by the Secretary.

Id. at 21. This interpretation specified that the new policy should "be applied to . . . currently pending applications." *Id.*

III. *Discussion*

* * *

A.   *QTA [Quiet Title Act] Claims*

McMaster raised two independent QTA claims: (1) that the QTA required the government to convey fee-simple ownership of surface and mineral estates of the Oro Grande mining claim to McMaster; and (2) that McMaster properly holds title to all improvements and structures located on the Oro Grande mining claim. We consider each in turn.

1.   *Fee-simple title to Oro Grande mining claim*

In dismissing McMaster's first QTA claim, the district court held pursuant to the Wilderness Act that McMaster did not have a " 'valid existing right' to a patent conveying fee-simple ownership of the surface estate and structures associated with [its] mining claim." The relevant portion of the Wilderness Act states:

> [H]ereafter, *subject to valid existing rights,* all patents issued under the mining laws of the United States affecting national forest lands designated by this chapter as wilderness areas shall convey title to the mineral deposits within the claim . . . , but *each such patent shall reserve to the United States all title in or to the surface of the lands and products thereof,* and no use of the surface of the claim or the resources therefrom not reasonably required for carrying on mining or prospecting shall be allowed except as otherwise expressly provided in this chapter: Provided, That, unless hereafter specifically authorized, no patent within wilderness areas designated by this chapter shall issue after December 31, 1983, except for the valid claims existing on or before December 31, 1983. Mining claims located after September 3, 1964, within the boundaries of wilderness areas designated by this chapter shall create no rights in excess of those rights which may be patented under the provisions of this subsection.

16 U.S.C. § 1133(d)(3) (emphasis added).

McMaster argues that in passing the Wilderness Act, Congress intended for claimants to receive fee-simple title to their pre-existing valid claims. More specifically, McMaster contends that the "valid existing rights" language of the Wilderness Act protects claimants' legitimate expectations of fee-simple title, preserving the right to the surface estate for all those who had properly located a mining claim prior to the relevant wilderness designation.

* * *

a.   *BLM's regulation, Manual, and BLM policy*

McMaster argues that the regulation, Manual, and BLM policy are consistent with his interpretation and require that McMaster be issued a fee-simple patent. None of these, however, clearly requires issuing title to the surface estate for all valid claims.

First, the regulation contained in 43 C.F.R. § 3638.5 states that for "mineral locations established after [the effective date of the Wilderness Act], or validated by discovery of minerals occurring after [the effective date of the Wilderness Act]," title will issue to only the mineral deposits; the United States will retain title to the surface of the land. 43 C.F.R. § 3638.5. Section 3638.5 does not even address claims that were established prior to the effective date of the Wilderness Act. And stating that claims discovered after the effective date of the Act receive only limited patents does not necessarily mean that every valid claim located prior to the time announced in the Regulation is entitled to a fee-simple patent.

In contrast to the regulation, the Manual addresses claims that were established prior to the wilderness designation. The Manual states that "[f]or claims located before enactment of the Wilderness Act. . . . the claims must have a discovery as of the date of enactment to acquire the surface and mineral estates,". . . . Although the Manual indicates that a claim must be discovered prior to the wilderness designation to receive title to the surface estate, nowhere does the manual state that this is all that is required. Indeed, discovery is a necessary, but not a sufficient, condition for establishing a valid claim; the claim must also be located "by reference to some natural object or permanent monument as will identify the claim." 30 U.S.C. § 28. Moreover, even if the Manual could be read as stating that valid claims established before the wilderness designation are entitled to title to the surface state, BLM manuals are not legally binding. See *Schweiker v. Hansen,* 450 U.S. 785, 789–90 (1981). . . .

Finally, the BLM policy states that "[a] patent conveying both surface and mineral rights *may* be issued on a valid claim located prior to the date the area was included as part of the National Wilderness Preservation System." Bureau of Land Management, Wilderness Management Policy, 46 Fed. Reg. 47,180–01 (1981). Although the BLM policy indicates more clearly that valid claims may receive fee-simple title, the language of the policy is discretionary ("may be issued"). The policy thus leaves room for BLM to impose additional requirements for receiving fee-simple title. And, in any event, like the Manual, a BLM management policy is not legally binding. See *King's Meadow Ranches,* 126 IBLA 339, 341 n. 2 (IBLA 1993) (stating that policies "not established by regulation . . . lack[ ] the force and effect of law"); see also *Schweiker,* 450 U.S. at 789–90.

Thus, neither the regulation, nor the Manual, nor the BLM policy entitles McMaster to fee-simple title to the surface estate.

b.   *The Solicitor's Opinion*

In contrast to McMaster's interpretation of "valid existing rights," the Solicitor's Opinion concluded that the term refers to a claimant who had actually "filed a patent application, and established a right to a patent before the land in question was designated as wilderness" by "complying with all the requirements for obtaining a patent." Solicitor's Opinion, at 3, 21. Under this reading, the Wilderness Act does *not* preserve a right to a surface estate for those who "located a mining claim and made a discovery of a valuable mineral claim deposit before the land in question was designated as wilderness, but . . . had not established a right to a patent before the land was designated as wilderness." *Id.* at 3–4. Since the Solicitor's Opinion is contrary to McMaster's interpretation of the statute, we must determine whether it is owed deference.

* * *

[The court concluded that the Solicitor's Opinion was entitled to so-called *Skidmore* deference for its interpretation of "valid existing rights." Under *Skidmore v. Swift & Co.*, 323 U.S. 134 (1944), an agency's decision made through procedures less formal than notice-and-comment rulemaking is entitled to judicial deference if its reasoning is persuasive.]

iii.   *Application*

Applying the rule set forth in the Solicitor's Opinion to the facts of this case, it is undisputed that as of the effective date of the California Wilderness Act—September 28, 1984—McMaster had nothing more than a valid claim in the Oro Grande. McMaster did not fulfill the requirements for procuring a patent until at least August 14, 1992. Therefore, McMaster did not have a "valid existing right" to a fee-simple patent under the Wilderness Act at the time that he submitted its patent application, and was properly granted a patent with reservation of the surface estates. McMaster's only "valid existing right" was to a claim, not a patent. The district court did not err in dismissing McMaster's first QTA claim. . . .

* * *

To invoke the QTA, a complaint must "set forth with particularity the nature of the right, title, or interest which the plaintiff claims in the real property, the circumstances under which it was acquired, and the right, title, or interest claimed by the United States." 28 U.S.C. § 2409a(d). . . .

* * *

With regard to the origins of the title to the improvements, McMaster only generally alleges that the structures were constructed incident to mining operations, and specifically alleges that the cabin was built sometime in the early 1890s. Nowhere does McMaster allege whether or how Lynch obtained title, or whether he retained title until he sold the Oro Grande mining claim to McMaster. These particular facts are important because title to the structures may have passed to the Government at some time. When a claim is abandoned or deemed invalid, the title to surface structures passes to the United States. See *Brothers v. United States,* 594 F.2d 740, 741 (9th Cir. 1979). Thus, McMaster has failed to plead with particularly sufficient facts showing all of the circumstances under which his title to the structures was acquired, 28 U.S.C. § 2409a(d), and has failed to satisfy his burden under the QTA. See 28 U.S.C. § 2409a(d).

And, in any event, because McMaster no longer holds a valid claim to the Oro Grande lands, by virtue of the fact that he received only a mineral patent, he is required to obtain a special use permit prior to using the surface of the land. See 36 C.F.R. § 251.50. Thus, even if McMaster did "own" the structures, he would not have the right to use them, and could be required to remove them.

We conclude that McMaster's second QTA claim was properly dismissed under Federal Rule of Civil Procedure 12(b)(6).

* * *

NOTES

1.   *BLM patenting policies.* What was the 1981 BLM patenting policy in wilderness areas, and how did it compare to the 1998 Solicitor's Opinion? Is either binding on the courts? Note: the Interior Solicitor is basically the general counsel of the agency.

2.   *The patenting moratorium.* The 1994 moratorium on patenting is not necessarily permanent, since it is only the product of annual appropriation law riders. Should Congress fail to renew the moratorium (or amend the statute) it would expire and patenting would resume.

2. ENVIRONMENTAL REGULATION OF FEDERAL HARDROCK MINING

The 1872 law subjects mining claims to "regulations prescribed by law," 30 U.S.C. § 22. For most of its first century, few regulations affected mining claimants. In 1955 the Surface Resources Act, 30 U.S.C. § 612, made clear that miners could only use their unpatented mining claims fir mining purposes. It also asserted federal authority to manage the surface resources of claims and recognized rights of access for federal licensees across mine claims.

In the 1970s, environmentalists began pressuring the principal land management agencies, the Forest Service and the BLM, to adopt regulations to curb some of the adverse environmental effects of mining. The Forest Service clearly had sufficient authority to do so given its power under the Forest Service Organic Act of 1897, 16 U.S.C. § 551, to "regulate . . . occupancy and use" in national forests. In 1974, the Forest Service finally promulgated regulations. It required mining plans, designed to minimize environmental harms, for operations likely to entail "significant disturbance of surface resources." 36 C.F.R. § 228.4. These regulations were sustained by the Ninth Circuit in *United States v. Weiss*, 642 F.2d 296 (9th Cir. 1981). The agency thus had significant control over mining operations, although it remained unclear whether the agency could reject all mining on a valid unpatented mining claim, rendering it essentially worthless. See *Clouser v. Espy,* 42 F.3d 1522, 1536 (9th Cir. 1994) (enforcing a plan's banning of motorized access in a wilderness area but noting that a plan probably could not ban mining altogether on a valid claim).

On BLM lands, where most federal-lands mining takes place, environmental regulation arrived only with the Federal Land Policy and Management Act of 1976 (FLPMA), which authorized BLM to "take any action necessary to prevent unnecessary or undue degradation of the [public] lands." 43 U.S.C. § 1732(b). In 1980, BLM promulgated regulations requiring mine plans for operations of five acres or more. It required only notice of an intent to mine for smaller operations that produce more than negligible disturbances, so-called "causal use" mines. 43 C.F.R. § 3809.

In 2000, the outgoing Clinton Administration issued revised mine plan regulations. They interpreted the "unnecessary or undue degradation" standard in FLPMA to enable BLM to deny approval to mining when it would produce "substantial irreparable harm" to environmental or cultural resources that could not be effectively mitigated. 65 Fed. Reg. 69,998, 70,001 (Nov. 21, 2000). The incoming Bush Administration essentially rescinded that change in its 2001 regulations. Those regulations were challenged in the case below.

MINERAL POLICY CENTER V. NORTON

U.S. District Court for the District of Columbia
292 F.Supp.2d 30 (2003)

[Several environmental groups filed suit challenging federal mining regulations promulgated by the Bureau of Land Management (BLM) in 2001, claiming that the regulations weakened and sometimes eliminated BLM's authority to protect the public's lands, waters, cultural and religious sites, and other resources threatened by industrial mining operations in the West. The environmentalists maintained that the regulations were inconsistent with BLM's statutory duty under the Federal Land Policy and Management Act (FLPMA), 43 U.S.C. §§ 1701 *et seq.* (2000), to "take any action necessary to prevent unnecessary or undue degradation of the [public] lands." 43 U.S.C. § 1732(b). They asked the district court to vacate those parts of the 2001 regulations that violated the statute.]

KENNEDY, J.

* * *

I.   *Background Information*

A.   *Regulatory Background*

1.   *The Mining Law*

A correct resolution of the issues presented by this case requires an understanding and analysis of the pertinent legislative scheme and must begin with the General Mining Law, 30 U.S.C. §§ 21 *et seq.* (2000) (Mining Law), a law that was enacted in 1872. The Mining Law provides: "All valuable mineral deposits in lands belonging to the United States, both surveyed and unsurveyed, are hereby declared to be free and open to exploration and purchase . . . by citizens of the United States. . . ." 30 U.S.C. § 22. The Mining Law gives claimants the right to "a unique form of property." *Best v. Humboldt Placer Mining Co.,* 371 U.S. 334, 335 (1963). It gives any citizen the right to enter onto federal public lands, stake a claim on these lands, and obtain the exclusive right to extract the minerals thereon—all without payment to the United States and without acquiring title to the land itself. *Union Oil Co. v. Smith,* 249 U.S. 337, 348–49 (1919). Alternatively, the Mining Law gives a claimant the right to obtain title to the lands, by proving the location of a valuable mineral deposit on her mining claim, and paying a nominal fee ($5.00 per acre for certain claims, $2.50 per acre for others). 30 U.S.C. §§ 29–30, 37.

2.   *The Federal Land Policy and Management Act*

Much changed in this nation in the 100 years following the Mining Law's 1872 enactment. Accordingly, in 1976, Congress enacted FLPMA to amend the Mining Law and reflect the nation's changed view toward land and minerals. It is this law that is primarily at issue here.

FLPMA establishes standards for BLM to regulate hardrock mining activities on the public lands. Such regulation is vital. BLM administers roughly one-fifth of the land mass of the United States and, while the surface area of the land physically disturbed by active mining is comparatively small, the impact of such mining is not. . . . Mining activity emits vast quantities of toxic chemicals, including mercury, hydrogen, cyanide gas, arsenic, and heavy metals. The emission of such chemicals affects water quality, vegetation, wildlife, soil, air purity, and cultural resources. . . . The emissions are such that the hardrock/metal mining industry was recently ranked the nation's leading emitter of toxic pollution. . . .

FLPMA thus attempts to balance two vital—but often competing—interests. On one hand, FLPMA recognizes the "need for domestic sources of minerals, food, timber, and fiber from the public lands," 43 U.S.C. § 1701(a)(12), and, on the other hand, FLPMA attempts to mitigate the devastating environmental consequences of hardrock mining, to "protect the quality of scientific, scenic, historical, ecological, environmental, air, and atmospheric, water resource, and archeological values," *id.* § 1701(a)(8). . . .

The heart of FLPMA amends and supersedes the Mining Law to provide: "In managing the public lands the Secretary shall, by regulation or otherwise, take any action necessary to prevent *unnecessary or undue degradation* of the lands." 43 U.S.C. § 1732(b) (emphasis added); see *Rocky Mtn. Oil and Gas Ass'n v. Watt,* 696 F.2d 734, 738 n. 2 (10th Cir. 1982) . . . (recognizing that FLPMA amends the Mining Law). Also important for our purposes, FLPMA: (1) requires that the Secretary "manage the public lands under principles of multiple use and sustained yield," 43 U.S.C. § 1732(a); (2) encourages the "harmonious and coordinated management of the various resources without permanent impairment of the productivity of the land and the quality of the environment," *id.* § 1702(c); and (3) "declares that it is the policy of the United States that . . . the United States receive fair market value for the use of the public lands and their resources unless otherwise provided for by statute," *id.* § 1701(a)(9).

3. *The 1980, 2000, and 2001 Regulations*

After FLPMA was enacted in 1976, BLM commenced a rulemaking to implement it. BLM issued its proposed rules on December 6, 1976, and finalized them on November 26, 1980. See 41 Fed. Reg. 53,428 (Dec. 6, 1974); 45 Fed. Reg. 78,902 (Nov. 26, 1980). These rules, commonly known as the "1980 Regulations," established "procedures to prevent unnecessary or undue degradation of Federal lands which may result from operations authorized by the mining laws." 45 Fed. Reg. at 78,909–10 (Nov. 26, 1980). The 1980 Regulations defined "unnecessary or undue degradation," commonly referred to as "UUD," as being: (1) "surface disturbance greater than that which would normally result when an activity is being" conducted by "a prudent operator in usual, customary, and proficient operations"; (2) "failure to comply with applicable environmental protection statutes and regulations thereunder"; and (3) "[f]ailure to initiate and complete reasonable mitigation measures, including reclamation of disturbed areas or creation of a nuisance." *Id.* at

78,910. These rules, formerly codified at 43 C.F.R. § 3809.0–5(k) (1999), governed the mining industry for quite some time.

* * *

Interior finally amended the 1980 Regulations in 2000. . . . Most importantly, the 2000 Regulations replaced the 1980 Regulations' UUD "prudent operator" standard with a new and more restrictive UUD standard, commonly referred to as the "substantial irreparable harm" or "SIH" standard. 65 Fed. Reg. at 70,115 (formerly codified at 43 C.F.R. § 3809.5(f) (2001)).

The "substantial irreparable harm" standard is so named because in the 2000 Regulations, for the first time, BLM stated that it would deny a plan of operations, *i.e.,* a mining permit, if the plan failed to comply with performance standards or would result in "substantial irreparable harm" to a "significant" scientific, cultural, or environmental resource value of the public lands that could not be "effectively mitigated." *Id.* at 70,115. Thus, under the 2000 Regulations, BLM asserted its authority to deny a mining permit, simply because a potential site was unsuitable for mining because of, for instance, the area's environmental sensitivity or cultural importance. See *id.* at 70,016.

These 2000 Regulations were short lived, however. On March 23, 2001, after a change in the Administration, Interior published a Notice in the Federal Register stating its intention to amend the regulations once again. See Mining Claims Under the Gen. Mining Laws; Surface Mgmt., 66 Fed. Reg. 16,162 (Mar. 23, 2001).

In so doing, the Interior Solicitor issued a legal opinion examining FLPMA and concluding that the 2000 Regulation's SIH standard was *ultra vires,* a conclusion with which the Interior Secretary agreed. . . . The 2001 Regulations, promulgated on October 30, 2001, thus abolished the 2000 Regulations' SIH standard. 66 Fed. Reg. at 54,837–38. What was left after the revision was a standard more akin to the "prudent operator" standard utilized by the 1980 Regulations. *Compare* 65 Fed. Reg. at 70,115, *with* 66 Fed. Reg. at 54,860. The stated reason for the elimination of the SIH standard was that Interior determined that the standard's "implementation and enforcement . . . would be difficult and potentially subjective, as well as expensive for both BLM and the industry," and that "other means" would "protect the resources covered by the SIH standard." Id. at 54,846, 54,838. Interior further determined that the SIH standard would precipitate a "10%–30% decline overall in minerals production." 65 Fed. Reg. at 70,107.

The 2001 Regulations provide:

Unnecessary or undue degradation means conditions, activities, or practices that:

(1) Fail to comply with one or more of the following: the performance standards in § 3809.420, the terms and conditions of an approved plan of operations, operations described in a complete notice, and other Federal and state laws related to environmental protection and protection of cultural resources;

(2) Are not "reasonably incident" to prospecting, mining, or processing operations as defined in § 3715.0–5 of this chapter; or

(3) Fail to attain a stated level of protection or reclamation required by specific laws in areas such as the California Desert Conservation Area, Wild and Scenic Rivers, BLM-administered portions of the National Wilderness System, and BLM-administered National Monuments and National Conservation Areas.

43 C.F.R. § 3809.5.

* * *

III. *Analysis*

[P]laintiffs' essential argument is that the 2001 Regulations run contrary to key provisions of FLPMA. They contend that the 2001 Regulations suffer from three main deficiencies. First and foremost, plaintiffs argue that the 2001 Regulations fail to meet BLM's statutory mandate to "take any action necessary to prevent unnecessary or undue degradation of the [public] lands." 43 U.S.C. § 1732(b). Plaintiffs argue that in promulgating the 2001 Regulations, BLM essentially abdicated its duty to prevent "undue degradation" and instead, revised its definition of "unnecessary or undue degradation" to limit its authority to prevent only operations that are "unnecessary" for mining. Plaintiffs maintain that by reading "undue degradation" as superfluous to the statute, defendants contravene the plain language of FLPMA, in violation of the APA [Administrative Procedure Act].

* * *

In response to plaintiffs' claims, Interior offers three essential arguments. First, Interior asserts that the 2000 and 2001 Regulations are not as different from one another as plaintiffs contend. Interior maintains that "[t]he only change between the 2000 and 2001 rules in Interior's definition of UUD is the elimination of the provision defining UUD as 'substantial irreparable harm to significant scientific, cultural, or environmental resource values' because Interior determined the SIH proviso was contrary to statutory authority, subjective, potentially cumulative, and overbroad." . . . Second, Interior argues that no party in these rulemakings ever identified or defined the harm ostensibly prevented by the 2000 Regulations' SIH proviso. And third, Interior maintains that, in this case, plaintiffs espouse mere policy preferences for less or no mining on the public lands, untethered to the requirements of FLPMA or the Mining Law. Each claim will be explored in turn.

A. *Interior's Duty to Prevent Unnecessary or Undue Degradation of the Public Lands*

* * *

1. *Interior Must Prevent Both "Undue Degradation" and "Unnecessary Degradation" to the Public Lands*

The 2000 Regulations explicitly adopted the view that Congress had authorized the Secretary to prohibit mining activities found unduly degrading, although potentially lucrative. . . . This view was succinctly expressed in the preamble to the 2000 Regulations, which states:

> Congress did not define the term "unnecessary or undue degradation," but it is clear from the use of the conjunction "or" that the Secretary has the authority to prevent "degradation" that is necessary to mining, but undue or excessive. This includes the authority to disapprove plans of operations that would cause undue or excessive harm to the public lands.

65 Fed. Reg. 69,998 (Nov. 21, 2000).

Interior's interpretation of FLPMA's UUD standard potentially changed in 2001, however. Before the 2001 Regulations were promulgated, Interior's Solicitor, William G. Myers III, wrote an opinion in which he reviewed the meaning of the words "unnecessary" and "undue," as well as FLPMA's legislative history. Based on this analysis, Solicitor Meyers determined that the terms "unnecessary" and "undue" were not two distinct statutory mandates, as the 2000 Regulations presumed, but were instead "two closely related subsets or equivalents." . . .

Based on this interpretation of the UUD standard, Solicitor Meyers determined that as long as a proposed mining activity is "necessary to mining," the BLM has no authority to prevent it. [Solicitor's Opinion] at 14 ("FLPMA amends the Mining Law only as provided in four limited ways, and preventing necessary and due degradation is not one of them."). Solicitor Meyers found that:

> A definition that is more restrictive—that prevents degradation that would be caused by an operator who is using accepted and proper procedures in accordance with applicable federal and state laws and regulations when such degradation is required to develop a valuable mineral deposit—would inappropriately amend the Mining Law and impair the rights of the locator.

Id. at 12; see 66 Fed. Reg. 54,834, 54,837 (Oct. 30, 2001). Accordingly, Solicitor Meyers provided that the 2000 Regulations' SIH standard could not be sustained; BLM could *not* disapprove of an otherwise allowable mining operation merely because such an operation would cause "substantial irreparable harm" to the public lands. The Solicitor thus concluded that "relevant legal authorities require removal of the 'substantial irreparable harm' criterion from both the definition of 'unnecessary or undue degradation' in § 3809.5 and the list of reasons why BLM may disapprove a plan of operations in § 3809.411(d)(3)(iii) of the 2000 regulations, 65 Fed.Reg. 69,998, 70,115, 70,121, through the rulemaking process currently underway within the Department." *Id.* at 15.

Plaintiffs challenge the Solicitor's interpretation and argue that, based upon FLPMA's statutory language, it is clear that Congress intended to prevent "unnecessary degradation" *as well as* "undue degradation." Thus, according to plaintiffs, under FLPMA "BLM must prevent undue degradation, even though the cause of the degradation may be necessary for mining. . . ."

Upon careful consideration, the court agrees with plaintiffs' view. . . .

Three well-established canons of statutory construction compel the court's conclusion. First, it is well settled that the language of the statute should govern. As stated by the Supreme Court: "The starting point in interpreting a statute is its language, for 'if the intent of Congress is clear, that is the end of the matter.'" *Good Samaritan Hosp. v. Shalala,* 508 U.S. 402, 409 (1993) (quoting *Chevron, U.S.A., Inc. v. Natural Resources Def. Council,* 467 U.S. 837, 842 (1984)) . . .

The second rule is that when construing a statute, the court is "obliged to give effect, if possible, to every word Congress used." *Murphy Exploration & Prod. Co. v. U.S. Dep't of Interior,* 252 F.3d 473, 481 (D.C. Cir. 2001). . . . The court should "disfavor interpretations of statutes that render language superfluous." See *United States v. DBB, Inc.,* 180 F.3d 1277, 1285 (11th Cir. 1999). . . .

Third and finally, it is clearly established that "[i]n statutory construction the word 'or' is to be given its normal disjunctive meaning unless such a construction renders the provision in question repugnant to other provisions of the statute," *In re Rice,* 165 F.2d 617, 619 n. 3 (D.C. Cir. 1947) (citing *Gay Union Corp. v. Wallace,* 112 F.2d 192, 198 n. 15 (D.C. Cir. 1940)), or "the context dictates otherwise," *Reiter v. Sonotone Corp.,* 442 U.S. 330, 339 (1979). See *In re Espy,* 80 F.3d 501, 505 (D.C. Cir. 1996). . . .

Applying these well-established canons to the matter at hand, FLPMA provides that the Secretary "shall by regulation or otherwise, take any action necessary to prevent unnecessary *or* undue degradation of the lands." 43 U.S.C. § 1732(b) (emphasis added). Accordingly, in this case: (1) the disjunctive is used, (2) the disjunctive interpretation is neither "at odds" with the intention of the FLPMA's drafters, *Griffin v. Oceanic Contractors, Inc.,* 458 U.S. 564, 571 (1982), . . . nor contrary to the statute's legislative history; and (3) the "or" separates two terms that have different meanings. Consequently, the court finds that in enacting FLPMA, Congress's intent was clear: Interior is to prevent, not only unnecessary degradation, but also degradation that, while necessary to mining, is undue or excessive.

> 2.   *Plaintiffs Have Not Shown that the 2001 Regulations*
> *Fail to Prevent Unnecessary or Undue Degradation*

With that resolved, the question now before this court is whether the 2001 Regulations effectuate that statutory requirement. See *Chevron,* 467 U.S. at 843 n. 9 ("If a court, employing traditional tools of statutory construction, ascertains that Congress had an intention on the precise question at issue, that intention is the law and must be given effect."). Put another way, the court must determine whether the 2001 Regulations reasonably interpret and implement FLPMA, as properly understood. *Id.* at 843.

Plaintiffs contend that the 2001 Regulations ignore FLPMA's "undue" language and essentially limit BLM's authority to prevent only surface disturbance greater than necessary. Plaintiffs insist that "if an activity such as locating a waste dump on top of a Native American sacred site or dewatering an entire drinking water aquifer is 'necessary for mining,' and the mining company pledged to meet a few technical requirements, the BLM would be powerless to protect those resources." . . .

Interior, on the other hand, maintains that, despite the elimination of the 2000 Regulations' SIH standard, and the Solicitor's understanding that the terms "undue" and "unnecessary" "overlap in many ways," the 2001 Regulations nevertheless prevent UUD, as properly defined by this court. . . .

Specifically, Interior argues that it will protect the public lands from any UUD by exercising case-by-case discretion to protect the environment through the process of: (1) approving or rejecting individual mining plans of operations; (2) regulating in response to the requisite Notices that operators must submit before commencing exploration activities not requiring a plan of operations; (3) requiring financial guarantees for costs for mining activities; and (4) linking performance standards to those set forth in existing laws and regulations. These existing laws and regulations include: the Endangered Species Act, the Archeological Resources and Protection Act, the Clean Water Act, the Comprehensive Environmental Response, Control and Liability Act; Interior's authority under FLPMA to withdraw public land from mining entry, and Interior's authority under FLPMA to formally designate and withdraw from mining "areas of critical environmental concern[.]" 43 U.S.C. § 1712(c)(3). . . .

Plaintiffs, in response, have been unable to present evidence to contradict or undermine Interior's claim. Plaintiffs have not shown that, by the exercise of case-by-case discretion, Interior will fail to prevent unnecessary or undue degradation.

* * *

Because FLPMA is silent or ambiguous with respect to what specifically constitutes "unnecessary or undue degradation," and the means Interior should take to prevent it, the court shall review Interior's actions under the second prong of *Chevron.* . . . Consequently, the court must determine, not whether the 2001 Regulations represent the best interpretation of the FLPMA, but whether they represent a reasonable one. *Chevron,* 467 U.S. at 843. Here, upon careful consideration, the court finds that they do. Plaintiffs have neither demonstrated that the 2001 Regulations fail to prevent unnecessary or undue degradation of the public lands, in contravention of FLPMA, nor that Interior, in promulgating the 2001 Regulations, toiled under an erroneous view of its own authority. The 2001 Regulations are neither "procedurally defective" nor "arbitrary or capricious in substance," nor "manifestly contrary" to the FLPMA. *United States v. Mead Corp.,* 533 U.S. 218, 227 (2001). Thus, the regulations must be accorded due deference. . . .

[The court ruled that the Interior Solicitor misinterpreted FLPMA by conflating "unnecessary" or "undue" degradation but upheld Interior's regulations.]

* * *

NOTES

1.   *The outcome.* Who won this case? How does the court interpret FLPMA's "unnecessary or undue degradation" standard? Does the court give deference to the Interior Solicitor's interpretation of this term? Should a court defer to a legal opinion of the Solicitor?

2.   *"Undue degradation."* Since the 2001 regulations survived judicial review, can the Secretary now block a mining operation that produces environmental degradation that is "necessary" to the mining operation but in other ways "undue"?

3.   *The effect of the Endangered Species Act (ESA) on decisions not to require mine plans.* The ESA requires all federal agencies to ensure that their activities avoid jeopardizing the existence of listed species or damaging their critical habitat. 16 U.S.C. §§ 1531 *et seq.* In order to fulfill these responsibilities (as explained in chapter 4), the Act requires consultation with

federal wildlife agencies. The uneasy interaction of ESA procedures and federal mine plan requirements was exemplified by *Karuk Tribe of California v. U.S. Forest Service*, 681 F.3d 1006 (9th Cir. 2012) (en banc), which examined the Forest Service's practice of handling "notices of intent" covering smaller mining operations that could harm fish and wildlife. The agency maintained that such approvals did not invoke ESA consultation requirements, but the en banc Ninth Circuit disagreed, over four dissents. The court ruled that the Forest Service possessed control over such smaller mines, including the power to impose conditions to protect listed salmon habitat. This level of discretionary control was adequate to trigger the duty to consult with the Fish and Wildlife Service under the ESA. It was not relevant for this legal purpose, the court concluded, that the Forest Service's action was not sufficiently major to trigger also the duty to prepare an environmental impact statement under the National Environmental Policy Act .

4. *The Common Varieties Act.* Under this statute, which amended the 1947 Materials Disposal Act, Congress in 1955 withdrew so-called "common varieties" from the operation of the 1872 law, including sand, stone, gravel and other so-called "non-valuable minerals." 30 U.S.C. § 611. The statute authorizes the sale of these "common" minerals, usually to the highest bidder. Why would Congress withdraw these common minerals from the operation of the General Mining Law and leave gold, silver, copper, and other valuable minerals to individual initiative and the discovery doctrine?

NOTE ON RIGHTS-OF-WAY UNDER REVISED STATUTE 2477

The Mining Act of 1872 has been criticized as being a "lord of yesterday" by Charles Wilkinson in his engaging *Crossing the Next Meridian: Land, Water, and the Future of the West* (1993) because it retains nineteenth century "capture" and privatization values in twenty-first century public land management. An even more dramatic reflection of a nineteenth century lord of yesterday is from the 1866 Mining Act, the predecessor of the 1872 law, which was repealed nearly 40 years ago in the Federal Land Policy and Management Act (FLPMA), 43 U.S.C. § 4316(a). RS 2477 granted non-federal entities rights-of-way across public lands "for the construction of highways." When initiated these "roads" required no federal approval and were subject only to applicable state laws, if any. Since FLPMA kept alive all "valid existing rights," including RS 2477 rights-of-ways, RS 2477 roads remain an important issue in many places, including many national parks, monuments, forests, wildlife refuges, and wilderness areas. The state of Utah, for example, has filed claims to over 12,000 RS 2477 roads, spanning about 36,000 miles, in that state.

It is hardly clear, however, whether most of the claimed RS 2477 roads actually exist. Nor is it likely that there will be resolution of most claims any time soon because the Tenth Circuit, in *Southern Utah Wilderness Ass'n v. Bureau of Land Management*, 425 F.3d 735 (10th Cir. 2005), ruled that courts (not BLM) have primary jurisdiction over the validity of claims. Thus, contested claims will be judicially litigated. The Tenth Circuit also decided that, although federal law nominally governs the validity of the claims, state law governs when, as usual, no federal highway law applies (in which case the federal government "borrows" state law). Borrowing Utah highway law, the court determined that, despite the language of RS 2477 mentioning "construction", roads were legally valid even with no mechanical construction. The only requirement was for "continuous public use" prior to 1976 and no abandonment since then. These issues must be resolved in federal district courts, and the burden of proof is on the claimants, not the federal government.

Representative recent RS 2477 cases include *San Juan County, Utah v. United States*, 754 F.3d 787 (10th Cir. 2014) (county and state failed to meet their burden of proof concerning a jeep trail on a creek bed adjacent to Angel Arch in Canyonlands National Park; the creek bed did not have the intensity of use by the public to show the existence of a discernable road necessary to meet the state's standard for a highway in 1976, and thus is not an RS 2477 right-of-way); *Kane County, Utah v. United States,* No. 2:08–CV–00315, 2013 WL 1180764 (D. Utah Mar. 20, 2013) (quieting title to the county and/or state to 12 out of 15 roads, four of which run through Grand Staircase–Escalante National Monument); see also *Hale v. Norton*, 461 F.3d 1092 (9th Cir. 2006) (private claims of ditch rights, even when validly perfected under another provision of the 1866 law, nonetheless remain subject to federal regulation).

Utah has proved to be a hotbed of anti-federal land ownership. In 2012, the state passed H.B. 148, the "Transfer of Public Lands Act," which called upon the federal government to convey to the state most of the public lands within Utah's boundaries. See Nick Lawton, *Utah's Transfer of Public Lands Act: Demanding a Gift of Federal Lands*, 16 Vt. J. Envtl. L. (forthcoming 2014) (concluding that the state has no meritorious legal arguments but might prevail politically in Congress).

3.   THE MINERAL LEASING ACT

The Mineral Leasing Act (MLA) of 1920 was a landmark of natural resources law. The MLA reserved most fuel minerals from the operation of the 1872 Mining Law and made their development by private parties subject to a leasing system. The U.S. Supreme Court upheld the leasing of lead mines under a short-lived statute in an early case interpreting the Property Clause of the U.S. Constitution, *U.S. v. Gratiot*, 39 U.S. 526 (1840). During the Civil War, Congress authorized the sale of coal lands, but other minerals like oil and gas became subject to the location and patent system of the 1872 law, a stance reaffirmed in the Oil Placer Act of 1897. To avoid having the federal government paying oil companies for public lands' oil to power its ships in the run up to World War I, President Taft withdrew mineral lands in California and Wyoming from the operation of the 1872 law, effectively putting them off limits for private oil drilling. The Supreme Court upheld the withdrawal in *U.S. v. Midwest*

Oil Co., 236 U.S. 459 (1915) (on grounds of congressional acquiescence to longstanding Executive practice of public land withdrawals).

When finally passed in 1920, The Mineral Leasing Act supplied a capstone to the Progressive Conservation movement. The Act, 30 U.S.C. §§ 181–287, established a leasing system that empowered the government, not mineral developers, to control the exploitation of the various minerals covered by the Act (and by later expansions of it), including oil, oil shale, gas, coal, phosphate, sodium, and (under a 1947 statute) all minerals on lands acquired by the federal government (that is, lands other than those that the federal government had owned since territorial times). Unlike the 1872 law, the MLA reserved for the federal government a share of the revenues produced by mineral development: the government could obtain bonuses as a result of bidding for the leases, could charge rent for the leases, and could negotiate royalty payments. In effect, the MLA transformed what had been a first-in-time system of allocating rights to public land minerals into an administrative law system, with vast discretion on the part of the leasing agency. See *U.S. ex rel. McLennan v. Wilbur*, 283 U.S. 414 (1931) (upholding the Secretary's authority not to lease public lands).

The leasing system inaugurated by the MLA has been extended to offshore oil and gas leasing by the Outer Continental Shelf Lands Act, 43 U.S.C. §§ 1331–1356; and to geothermal resources in the Geothermal Steam Act, 30 U.S.C. §§ 1001–1028. Typically, these leasing statutes require the government to allocate leases by competitive bidding at fair market value. Much like private leases (considered in chapter 5), leases on federal lands require lessees to use reasonable diligence to exploit the minerals to avoid lease termination. None of these requirements apply to hardrock mining under the 1872 law.

Also, since implementation of the MLA is a function of administrative discretion, statutes like the National Environmental Policy Act (NEPA) and the Endangered Species Act (ESA) come into play. NEPA requires federal agencies to consider and publicly disclose the environmental effects of their proposals and to evaluate reasonable alternative courses of action. The ESA requires federal proposals to avoid jeopardy to listed species and their critical habitats and to not "take" listed species without a permit or its functional equivalent. The following case considers the effect of NEPA and the ESA on proposed mineral leases.

STATE OF NEW MEXICO EX REL. RICHARDSON V. BUREAU OF LAND MANAGEMENT

Tenth Circuit Court of Appeals
565 F.3d 683 (2009)

[The State of New Mexico and environmentalists challenged the Bureau of Land Management's (BLM's) decision to open to oil and gas development most of the Otero Mesa, a richly biodiverse area, home to the endangered Northern Aplomado Falcon, claiming violations of the National Environmental Policy Act (NEPA), the Federal Land Management Policy Act (FLPMA), the National Historic Preservation Act (NHPA), and the Endangered Species Act (ESA). The federal district court decided for BLM on most claims but concluded that BLM violated NEPA by beginning the leasing process on the Mesa before conducting additional analysis of the site-specific environmental effects of development on the leased lands. Both the plaintiffs and the opposing and intervening oil and gas producers appealed.]

LUCERO, J.

* * *

[In its draft Environmental Impact Statement (EIS), BLM's preferred alternative—Alternative A—opened 96.9% of the plan area to oil and gas leasing but placed significant limits on actual mining activities. In the case of 58.9% of the area, the lessee was subject to no-surface-occupancy (NSO) stipulations, which in effect banned all surface activities unless and until the lessee gained separate approval from the BLM of its plan of operations. The remaining lands in the plan were subject to lesser limits on the timing and nature of surface activities. In the case of 116,206 acres of the Otera Mesa and 16,256 acres of the adjoining Nutt Desert Grasslands, Alternative A included an NSO provision that allowed surface disturbance only within 492 feet of existing roads, in order to minimize habitat fragmentation. In the Final EIS and Proposed Resource Management Plan Amendment (RMPA), however, the agency adopted a modified version of preferred Alternative A, which the court explained].

This "modified version" of Alternative A (Alternative A-modified) differed in a crucial respect from Alternative A: Rather than limiting surface disturbances to areas within 492 feet of existing roadways, Alternative A-modified would instead limit disturbances to *any* 5% of the surface area of a leased parcel at a given time, regardless of location. In addition to the 5% disturbance cap, Alternative A-modified required "unitization," a management scheme under which different operators cooperate in exploration and well development with the goal of minimizing surface impacts. "Unitization" was a new creation, never previously used by BLM in managing surface resources. Although the sections of the Final EIS describing the management plan itself were modified to reflect these new requirements, the sections describing the plan's impacts on vegetation and wildlife were not substantially modified, because the EIS concluded that the changes "do not significantly alter . . . the analysis of the environmental consequences."

* * *

According to the State and NMWA [New Mexico Wilderness Association], NEPA requires BLM to complete a supplemental EIS [SEIS] specifically analyzing the likely environmental effects of Alternative A-modified before adopting that alternative as the new management plan for the area, and its failure to do so was arbitrary and capricious. An agency must prepare a supplemental assessment if "[t]he agency makes substantial changes in the proposed action that are relevant to environmental concerns." 40 C.F.R. § 1502.9(c)(1)(i). . . .

Rather than offer additional environmental analysis of Alternative A-modified, BLM concluded in the SEIS that no further analysis was necessary because the same or less surface area would ultimately be developed under Alternative A or A-modified. . . .

* * *

As described above, Alternative A and Alternative A-modified differ primarily in the restrictions they place on surface disturbances on the Otero Mesa. Alternative A proposed a qualitative restriction on development: Disturbances would only be allowed near existing roads. Thus, they would remain contiguous rather than scattering across the landscape. By contrast, A-modified imposes a quantitative restriction: Disturbances may occupy only five percent of the Mesa at any one time.

By arguing that a difference in the degree of habitat fragmentation did not require a fresh impacts analysis, BLM neglects the fundamental nature of the environmental problem at issue. As is well documented in the record before us, the location of development greatly influences the likelihood and extent of habitat preservation. Disturbances on the same total surface acreage may produce wildly different impacts on plants and wildlife depending on the amount of contiguous habitat between them. BLM's analysis of Alternative A assumed the protections of large contiguous pieces of habitat from development. Alternative A-modified muddied this picture, doing away with any requirement of continuity of undisturbed lands. Although A-modified also requires developers to work together to minimize impacts—potentially increasing the continuity of surface developments—BLM provided so little explanation of this "unitization" restriction that it is impossible to tell whether it would create the same clustering of impacts as would the proximity restriction in Alternative A.

* * *

BLM's unanalyzed, conclusory assertion that its modified plan would have the same type of effects as previously analyzed alternatives does not allow us to endorse Alternative A-modified as "qualitatively within the spectrum of alternatives" discussed in the Draft EIS. Because location, not merely total surface disturbance, affects habitat fragmentation, Alternative A-modified was qualitatively different and well outside the spectrum of anything BLM considered in the Draft EIS, and BLM was required to issue a supplement analyzing the impacts of that alternative under 40 C.F.R. § 1502.9(c)(1)(i).

BLM and IPANM [Independent Petroleum Association of New Mexico] also argue that even if the changes in fragmentation impacts between Alternative A and A-modified require further environmental analysis, such analysis was impracticable until the leasing stage because the overall level of development could not be sufficiently predicted at the RMPA stage. All environmental analyses required by NEPA must be conducted at "the earliest possible time." 40 C.F.R. § 1501.2. . . . Because the record reveals that BLM conducted an internal analysis of the fragmentation impacts of Alternative A-modified in 2004, we are convinced that such analysis was possible. Accordingly, we hold that NEPA requires BLM to release a supplemental EIS thoroughly analyzing its newly minted alternative at the planning stage.

* * *

Aside from the need to analyze the specific land use plan BLM eventually selected, NMWA also charges that BLM analyzed an unduly narrow range of alternatives during the EIS process. The Agency disagrees, arguing that Alternatives A and B and the No-Action Alternative were representative of the full range of reasonable planning alternatives for the area.

The "heart" of an EIS is its exploration of possible alternatives to the action an agency wishes to pursue. 40 C.F.R. § 1502.14. Every EIS must "[r]igorously explore and objectively evaluate all reasonable alternatives." 40 C.F.R. § 1502.14(a). . . . While NEPA "does not require agencies to analyze the environmental consequences of alternatives it has in good faith rejected as too remote, speculative, or impractical or ineffective," it does require the development of "information sufficient to permit a reasoned choice of alternatives as far as environmental aspects are concerned." *Colo. Envtl. Coalition v. Dombeck,* 185 F.3d 1162, 1174 (10th Cir. 1999). . . .

We apply the "rule of reason" to determine whether an EIS analyzed sufficient alternatives to allow BLM to take a hard look at the available options. [*Westlands Water Dist. v. U.S. Dep't of the Interior,* 376 F.3d 853, 868 (9th Cir. 2004).] The reasonableness of the alternatives considered is measured against two guideposts. First, when considering agency actions taken pursuant to a statute, an alternative is reasonable only if it falls within the agency's statutory mandate. *Westlands,* 376 F.3d at 866. Second, reasonableness is judged with reference to an agency's objectives for a particular project. See *Dombeck,* 185 F.3d at 1174–75. . . .

* * *

We begin with NMWA's argument that BLM was required to analyze an alternative prohibiting surface disturbances of the Otero Mesa. . . .

* * *

BLM argues that an alternative that closes the entirety of the Otero Mesa to development violates the concept of multiple use. But this argument misconstrues the nature of FLPMA's multiple use mandate. The Act does not mandate that every use be accommodated on every piece of land; rather, delicate balancing is required. See *Norton v. S. Utah Wilderness Alliance,* 542 U.S. 55, 58 (2004). "'Multiple use' requires management of the public lands and their numerous natural resources so that they can be used for economic, recreational, and scientific purposes without the infliction of permanent damage." *Pub. Lands Council v. Babbitt,* 167 F.3d 1287, 1290 (10th Cir. 1999) (citing 43 U.S.C. § 1702(c)); see also *Norton,* 542 U.S. at 58.

It is past doubt that the principle of multiple use does not require BLM to prioritize development over other uses. As we have reasoned in the past, " '[i]f all the competing demands reflected in FLPMA were focused on one particular piece of public land, in many instances only one set of demands could be satisfied. A parcel of land cannot both be preserved in its natural character and mined.' " *Rocky Mtn. Oil & Gas Ass'n v. Watt,* 696 F.2d 734, 738 n. 4 (10th Cir. 1982) (quoting *Utah v. Andrus,* 486 F.Supp. 995, 1003 (D. Utah 1979)). . . . Accordingly, BLM's obligation to manage for multiple use does not mean that development *must* be allowed on the Otero Mesa. Development is a *possible* use, which BLM must weigh against other possible uses—including conservation to protect environmental values, which are best assessed through the NEPA process. Thus, an alternative that closes the Mesa to development does not necessarily violate the principle of multiple use, and the multiple use provision of FLPMA is not a sufficient reason to exclude more protective alternatives from consideration.

BLM further argues that the purpose of the RMPA process was inconsistent with any management alternative more restrictive than Alternative B. See *Dombeck,* 185 F.3d at 1174–75. Specifically, BLM identifies the purpose of the RMPA as identifying lands suitable for fluid minerals development, and it concludes that any alternative that excludes or severely restricts such development would not be "reasonable." . . . To the contrary, the question of whether *any* of the lands in the plan area are "suitable" for fluid minerals development is left open, and is precisely the question the planning process was intended to address. . . . Accordingly, a management alternative closing the Otero Mesa would have been fully consistent with the objectives of the RMPA.

Applying the rule of reason, we agree with NMWA that analysis of an alternative closing the Mesa to development is compelled by 40 C.F.R. § 1502.14. Excluding such an alternative prevented BLM from taking a hard look at all reasonable options before it. . . .

* * *

The State contends that BLM's analysis of the environmental impacts of the various alternative management plans failed to sufficiently consider a crucial impact: possible contamination of the Salt Basin Aquifer (the "Aquifer"). BLM concluded in the Draft and Final EISs that any impacts of development on the Aquifer would be "minimal," and it defends that conclusion on appeal. The State argues that this determination is arbitrary and capricious because it is unsupported by evidence in the record.

* * *

Our first inquiry is whether BLM "examined the relevant data" regarding the likelihood of injection into, and resulting contamination of, the Aquifer. Strikingly, BLM points to no record evidence explaining (1) how much wastewater a natural gas well "typically" produces, (2) whether it is reasonable to believe that wells in the plan area will be "typical," or (3) how much wastewater can practicably be disposed of through evaporation. See *Citizens for Alternatives to Radioactive Dumping v. U.S. Dep't of Energy,* 485 F.3d 1091, 1096 (10th Cir. 2007). Upon our careful review, the evidence in the record instead tends to support New Mexico's view that nontrivial impacts are possible. The State points to studies concluding that geologically similar gas wells to those planned for the BRU [Bennett Ranch Unit] produced 38 barrels, or 1,596 gallons, of water per well per day. At this rate, under the level of development predicted by BLM, up to 603,000 acre-feet of water of the estimated 15 million acre-feet in the Aquifer could be contaminated. . . .

* * *

BLM also argues that state and federal injection well and water-quality regulations are designed to prevent the feared contamination. But the existence of these regulations does not preclude the possibility of contamination, even if the protections are intended to prevent such an outcome. Contravening the inference that existing protections are always 100% effective, the record contains evidence that, despite this regulatory scheme, groundwater contamination from gas wells has happened frequently throughout New Mexico in the past. . . .

We accordingly hold that BLM acted arbitrarily by concluding without apparent evidentiary support that impacts on the Aquifer would be minimal. . . .

* * *

We now reach the sole issue appealed by defendant-intervenor IPANM: Whether NEPA requires BLM to produce an EIS analyzing the specific environmental effects of the BRU lease before issuing that lease.

As discussed above, after issuing the Final EIS and adopting Alternative A-modified as the new management plan for the area, BLM opened bidding for a lease on the BRU Parcel. . . . HEYCO [Harvey E. Yates Company] purchased the lease. . . . IPANM contends on appeal that NEPA requires no more than (1) an EIS at the RMPA stage and (2) a later EIS when HEYCO submits an APD [application for permit to drill]. In other words, the parties dispute how the environmental analysis of drilling in the plan area should be "tiered" as planning progresses from the large scale to the small.

Oil and gas leasing follows a three-step process. "At the earliest and broadest level of decision-making, the [BLM] develops land use plans— often referred to as resource management plans. . . ." *Pennaco Energy, Inc. v. U.S. Dep't of Interior,* 377 F.3d 1147, 1151 (10th Cir. 2004); see also 43 U.S.C. § 1712(a). Next, BLM issues a lease for the use of particular land. The lessee may then apply for a permit to drill, and BLM will decide whether to grant it. § 1712(e); *Pennaco Energy,* 377 F.3d at 1151–52, 43 C.F.R. §§ 1610.5–3, 3162.3–1(c). The parties dispute whether our precedents create a hard rule that no site-specific EIS is ever required until the permitting stage, or a flexible test requiring a site-specific analysis as soon as practicable. If the latter, they dispute whether a site-specific EIS was practicable, and thus required, before issuance of the July 20 lease.

* * *

This court first addressed the tiering of impacts analysis in the oil and gas leasing context in *Park County Resource Council, Inc. v. U.S. Dep't of Agriculture,* 817 F.2d 609 (10th Cir. 1987). . . . We concluded that preparation of both plan-level and site-specific environmental impacts analysis was permissibly deferred until after leasing:

> As an overall regional pattern or plan evolves, the region-wide ramifications of development will need to be considered at some point. A singular, site-specific APD, one in a line that prior to that time did not prompt such a broad-based evaluation, will

trigger that necessary inquiry as plans solidify. We merely hold that, *in this case, developmental plans were not concrete enough at the leasing stage to require such an inquiry.*

Id. [at 623] (emphasis added). After leasing and prior to issuance of an APD, the agency had drafted an EIS, *id.* at 613, and NEPA was thus satisfied, *id.* at 624. IPANM argues that under *Park County,* BLM may routinely wait until the APD stage to conduct site-specific analysis, even without issuing a FONSI [finding of no significant impact].

We next had occasion to consider tiering in the oil and gas context in *Pennaco Energy.* . . . [W]e held that in the circumstances of that case, an EIS assessing the specific effects of coal bed methane was required before the leasing stage. As in *Park County,* the operative inquiry was simply whether all foreseeable impacts of leasing had been taken into account before leasing could proceed. Unlike in *Park County,* in *Pennaco Energy* the answer was "no."

Taken together, these cases establish that there is no bright line rule that site-specific analysis may wait until the APD stage. Instead, the inquiry is necessarily contextual. Looking to the standards set out by regulation and by statute, assessment of all "reasonably foreseeable" impacts must occur at the earliest practicable point, and must take place before an "irretrievable commitment of resources" is made. 42 U.S.C. § 4332(2)(C)(v); *Pennaco Energy,* 377 F.3d at 1160. . . . Each of these inquiries is tied to the existing environmental circumstances, not to the formalities of agency procedures. Thus, applying them necessarily requires a fact-specific inquiry. . . .

Applying these standards to the July 20 lease, we first ask whether the lease constitutes an irretrievable commitment of resources. [W]e conclude that issuing an oil and gas lease without an NSO stipulation constitutes such a commitment. The same regulation we cited in *Pennaco Energy* remains in effect and provides that HEYCO cannot be prohibited from surface use of the leased parcel once its lease is final. See 43 C.F.R. § 3101.1–2. . . . Because BLM could not prevent the impacts resulting from surface use after a lease issued, it was required to analyze any foreseeable impacts of such use before committing the resources.

Accordingly, the next question is whether any environmental impacts were reasonably foreseeable at the leasing stage. Considerable exploration has already occurred on parcels adjacent to the BRU Parcel, and a natural gas supply is known to exist beneath these parcels. Based on the production levels of existing nearby wells, the record reveals that HEYCO has concrete plans to build approximately 30 wells on the BRU Parcel and those it already leases, and it has obtained the necessary permits for a gas pipeline connecting these wells to a larger pipeline in Texas. We agree with the district court that the impacts of this planned gas field were reasonably foreseeable before the July 20 lease was issued. Thus, NEPA required an analysis of the site-specific impacts of the July 20 lease prior to its issuance, and BLM acted arbitrarily and capriciously by failing to conduct one.

* * *

NOTES

1.   *MLA leasing and NEPA.* The BLM's use of NSO stipuations became common after the ruling in *Conner v. Burford*, 848 F.2d 1441 (9th Cir. 1988). There, the court held that the BLM could not issue ordinary oil and gas leases without first undertaking detailed environmental studies in compliance with NEPA. NEPA compliance was necessary because the leases empowered the lessess to engage in mining—that is, to engage in actions that could significantly affect the environment. Issuance of the leases therefore circumscribed agency authority because it amounted to an "irretrieveable commitment of resources," of which NEPA requires prior analysis and disclosure. But when leases included NSO stipulations, they gave lessees no such power to alter the environment. Their issuance therefore did not require NEPA analysis. The BLM could therefore delay its environmental studies until later, when it would consider whether to approve a particular mining plan. The delay in the required environmental study made sense, in that the BLM was better able to assess likely environmental effects when it had a particular mining plan to consider. On the other hand, lessees were (and are) understandably less willing to pay up-front bonuses to acquire leases with NSO stipulations since they gain no power, from the leases alone, to engage in mining. Even with valid leases, their proposed mining can be curtailed or even halted by the BLM.

2.   *MLA leasing and fracking. Center for Biological Diversity v. Bureau of Land Management*, 937 F.Supp.2d 1140 (N.D. Cal. 2013), concerned a challenge to four BLM leases over 2,700 acres of federal land in central California for hydraulic fracturing (also known as fracking) of the Monterey Shale Formation. The court described the project in the following terms:

> Central California's Monterey Shale Formation is a massive sedimentary rock formation estimated to contain over 15 billion barrels of oil, equal to 64 percent of the nation's total shale oil reserve, most of which is not retrievable through conventional drilling techniques. Oil previously produced from the formation was dubbed "easy" oil, because it was released from the shale into other permeable formations and then pooled near the surface, where it could be extracted with conventional drilling techniques. What largely remains of the shale oil remains locked deep within the impermeable shale itself, which is currently only economically accessible through fracking.

Fracking is the artificial propagation of fractures in a rock layer by injecting large quantities of water and fracturing fluids at high volume and pressure. This fractures the geological formation, creating passages through which gas and liquids can flow and an overall increased permeability. Fracking typically uses "slick water," which is a mixture of water, sand, and a cocktail of chemical ingredients with a number of purposes, including increasing viscosity of the fluid and impeding bacterial growth or mineral deposition. Although fracking itself is not a new technology, it did not become a feasible means of deep shale gas production until the late 2000s. Whereas before fracking only increased permeability in a limited zone radiating from the well bore, more recently engineers have honed the fracking process by incorporating horizontal drilling, multi-stage fracturing, slick water, and improved equipment to allow the operator to fracture and extract resources from a larger volume from a single well. . . .

The effect of fracking on the oil and gas economies has been tremendous. An April 2011 Congressional report notes that "[a]s a result of hydraulic fracturing and advances in horizontal drilling technology, natural gas production in 2010 reached the highest level in decades." . . .

Whatever one view's of the virtue and vices of fracking, it is undisputed that fracking's potential—both good and bad—has not gone unnoticed. Advocates herald the technology as an economic method to meet our nation's energy needs by extracting vast amounts of formerly inaccessible hydrocarbon supplies. Opponents, however, warn of devastating environmental impacts, including contamination of ground water, deteriorating air quality, the flowbacks of gases and slick water, and surface pollution from spills. . . . In recent years, fracking has come under scrutiny in federal, state, and local governments alike, with some states contemplating enacting, or having already enacted, laws banning fracking altogether.

After stating that "[w]hat is not [at issue in the case] is the policy question of whether fracking in the Monterey Shale or anywhere else is a good thing or a bad thing," the court ruled that BLM violated NEPA by issuing two of the leases without an environmental impact statement, since those leases did not contain a "no surface occupancy" provision (prohibiting surface disturbance activities and essentially preserving for the lessee a right of first refusal) and were based on BLM's assumption that the leases would result in the drilling of only one exploratory well. However, the court did not interpret the MLA to require lessees to employ certain technologies to prevent natural gas emissions from fracking operations, as the MLA only requires lessees to use "reasonable precautions to prevent waste." 937 F.Supp. at 1151 (citing 30 U.S.C. § 225).

3.   *Split estates.* The material in this section so far has addressed mineral leases on lands to which the federal government holds fee simple title. The federal government sometimes owns the surface of land while subsurface minerals are owned by private parties. What power then does the federal government have to control surface activities? As we saw in chapter 5, the ownership of minerals includes the right to use the land surface as reasonably necessary to engage in mining, and the mineral estate is dominant over the interests of a private surface owner. In the case of a federal agency, however, the agency has broader powers. Not merely the surface landowner, the agency also has lawmaking power over the land surface. To what extent can a federal agency, wearing its law-making hat, protect its surface property rights against mining activities by a mineral estate holder which has vested property rights to use the land surface for this purpose? The issue is complex, and federal powers often turn on the precise nature of the mineral estate and the terms of the statutes that authorized the federal acquisition of the land surface. Illustrative cases include *Minard Run Oil Co. v. U.S. Forest Service*, 670 F.3d 236 (3d Cir. 2011); and *Duncan Energy v. U.S. Forest Service*, 50 F.3d 584 (8th Cir. 1995)

4.   *The Federal Onshore Oil and Gas Leasing Reform Act (FOOGLRA).* In 1987, Congress responded to the widespread perception that the federal government was not obtaining anywhere close to the statutorily mandated fair market value by passing FOOGLRA, 30 U.S.C. §§ 181 *et seq.* FOOGLRA substantially reworked MLA leasing to require competitive bidding for all leases. Only if tracts remain unsold after auction may they be offered for noncompetitive leasing, and only for two-year terms. (Before 1987, competitive bidding was required only for leases in places known to contain oil and gas.) The 1987 reforms also required minimum royalties and rents, gave the Forest Service a veto over BLM-proposed leases on national forest lands, and conditioned drilling on federal approval of plans of operations and reclamation bonds. See generally George C. Coggins & Robert L. Glicksman, 3 *Public Natural Resources Law* §§ 39:11 to 39:21 (2d ed. 2014).

5.   *The Surface Mining Control and Reclamation Act (SMCRA).* 30 U.S.C. §§ 1201 *et seq.*, regulates coal mining operations that remove over 250 tons per year on both public and private lands. The statute, largely implemented by approved states for non-federal lands, established environmental performance and reclamation standards for applicable surface mining operations. The standards include a requirement that strip-mined land be restored to its approximate original contour. 30 U.S.C § 1265(b)(3). New operations require SMCRA approval, including reclamation plans. The statute banned surface mining from several federal land reserves, like national parks, wilderness areas, wildlife refuges, and wild and scenic river corridors, and it also established a procedure to designate lands as unsuitable for surface mining operations. *Id.* § 1272. Opposition to the statute produced a suit unsuccessfully challenging its constitutionality. *Hodel v. Surface Mining & Reclamation Ass'n*, 452 U.S. 264 (1981) (upholding the statute on

commerce clause grounds and rejecting arguments based on state sovereignty protected by the Tenth Amendment).

B. GRAZING

Apart from recreation, grazing on federal lands is the most ubiquitous public land use nationwide. Around 250 million acres of federal lands are subject to grazing permits (roughly 155 million acres of Bureau of Land Management (BLM) lands and 95 million acres of U.S. Forest Service lands in 2014). Yet there are relatively few federal grazing permittees: only some 18,000 on BLM lands and just 8,000 on national forest lands in 2014. Nor is the meat produced from federal land grazing a significant part of production, amounting to just two percent nationwide. George C. Coggins & Robert L. Glicksman, 3 *Public Natural Resources Law* § 33:1 (2d ed. 2014).

Public land grazing is perhaps the quintessential subject for the "tragedy of the commons," where market forces encourage overconsumption of pasture land to the detriment of all. *See* Garrett Hardin, *The Tragedy of the Commons,* 162 Science 1243 (1968). Thus, shortly after the end of the Civil War era, westward migration brought immense numbers of cattle to arid western lands, resulting in widespread overgrazing of public lands. Congress forbade fencing of the public lands in the Unlawful Enclosures Act of 1885, 43 U.S.C. §§ 1061–1066, fostering an ideology of free use of the public domain. Cattle and sheep grazers, in particular, claimed the right to graze their livestock on the unenclosed public domain, and the federal government acquiesced to widespread overgrazing. As the Supreme Court noted, the federal government "suffered its lands" to be overused, thereby creating an implied license on the part of the grazers. *Buford v. Houtz*, 133 U.S. 320, 326 (1890).

Largely due to a lack of water, the federally-owned unenclosed grasslands were passed over by homesteaders. Consequently, they remained part of the public domain in the era before 1934, during which disposition of federal public lands into private ownership was the dominant federal policy.

The private rights that arose on federal lands were based more on custom (like the law of the mining camps) than on express state statutes. If we keep these points in mind—and remember, too, the long history of squatting in the American West—we can make better sense, legally and culturally, of the following decision which raises a question of considerable importance: What rights did private users of the public domain gain prior to the era of active federal government regulation? The decision also provides a helpful introduction to the law of grazing on federal lands, including a look at the federal government's longstanding insistence that grazing permits are not secure property rights.

1. THE NATURE OF GRAZING RIGHTS ON PUBLIC LANDS

DIAMOND BAR CATTLE COMPANY V. UNITED STATES

Tenth Circuit Court of Appeals
168 F.3d 1209 (1999)

[Diamond Bar and Laney Cattle Companies and their predecessors had grazed cattle on federal land since 1883, under federal permits since 1907. The companies' latest permits, issued by the U.S. Forest Service for ten years in 1985, authorized grazing on over 170,000 acres of land within the Apache and Gila National Forests. Neither company sought to renew their permits in the 1990s, although they offered to pay grazing fees. They claimed that they needed no permits because they possessed longstanding grazing rights under state law, rights that predated the national forests and that were protected under federal law as "valid existing rights." Their grazing rights, they asserted, arose when they acquired, under state law, rights to use water for grazing purposes. In short, they claimed that their state-law water rights included the ancillary right to graze their cattle on federal land near their water sources. The Forest Service denied the existence of such a grazing right and instituted a trespass case against the companies when their leases expired and they continued to refuse to seek renewal. The district court ruled in favor of the Forest Service, concluding that the existence of state water rights did not diminish the federal agency's control over the use and occupancy of national forest lands. Diamond Bar appealed.]

BRISCOE, J.

* * *

Federal Regulation of United States Lands

Article IV of the United States Constitution provides: "The Congress shall have Power to dispose of and make all needful Rules and Regulations respecting the Territory or other Property belonging to the United States." The Supreme Court has characterized Congress' power under the Property Clause to regulate the public lands as "without limitations." *United States v. City and County of San Francisco,* 310 U.S. 16, 29 (1940). Pursuant to this expansive grant of authority, Congress passed the Organic Administration Act of 1897, which authorized reservation of lands as national forests and directed the Secretary of Agriculture to issue rules and regulations concerning such forests. See 16 U.S.C. § 551. Since then, Congress has passed numerous additional statutes directing that grazing in national forests be by permit only. See, e.g., 16 U.S.C. § 580*l* ("The Secretary of Agriculture in regulating grazing on the national forests . . . is authorized, upon such terms and conditions as he may deem proper, to issue permits for the grazing of livestock for periods not exceeding ten years and renewals thereof."); 43 U.S.C. § 315b; 43 U.S.C. § 1752.

As early as 1906, the Secretary of Agriculture promulgated a regulation requiring that any person seeking to graze stock on national forest land first obtain a permit from the Forest Service. See *United States v. Grimaud,* 220 U.S. 506, 509 (1911). In upholding the Secretary's authority to issue this regulation, the Supreme Court iterated that an "implied license" to graze on public lands existed "so long as the government did not cancel its tacit consent." *Light v. United States,* 220 U.S. 523, 535 (1911). The fact that historically the government may not have objected to use of public lands for grazing was never intended to "confer any vested right on the complainant, nor did it deprive the United States of the power of recalling any implied license under which the land had been used for private purposes." *Id.*

The "implied license" theory discussed in *Light* was articulated by the Supreme Court as early as 1890, see *Buford v. Houtz,* 133 U.S. 320, 326 (1890), and has since been cited dominantly in cases reaffirming that use of public lands for grazing is not a right but a privilege. . . .

Current regulations provide that "all grazing and livestock use on National Forest System lands . . . must be authorized by a grazing or livestock use permit." 36 C.F.R. § 222.3. Permits are issued for terms of ten years or less and are issued only after submission and approval by the Forest Service of an appropriate application. See *id.* § 222.3(c)(1). A term permit holder has first priority for a new permit at the end of the term period, provided the holder has fully complied with the terms and conditions of the expiring permit. See *id.* Use of forest service lands for grazing purposes without a permit subjects the offender to unauthorized grazing use fees. See *id.* § 222.50(h). Grazing permits "convey no right, title, or interest held by the United States in any lands or resources." *Id.* § 222.3(b).

Plaintiffs concede the existence of the above law, but contend it does not apply to the specific situation presented here, namely the extent to which a permit is required when the rights were "appropriated" pursuant to state law before the federal government removed the land at issue from the public domain. However, plaintiffs misconstrue the law upon which they base their "vested private property rights."

New Mexico Law

In New Mexico, water rights are obtained and governed by the doctrine of prior appropriation. See N.M. Const. Art. XVI, § 2 ("Priority of appropriation shall give the better right."). Plaintiffs claim their predecessors in title obtained a valid, vested water right through appropriation. This vested water right allegedly entitled plaintiffs' predecessors, and now entitles them, to an inseparable but distinct right to use for grazing, without a permit, the rangeland known as the Diamond Bar and Laney allotments. See Plaintiffs' Br. at 17 ("Diamond Bar and Laney are the owners of the water right and the scope of that right includes possession of the range for the purpose of raising livestock.").

Plaintiffs premise their alleged rights upon N.M. Stat. Ann. § 19–3–13:

> Any person, company or corporation that may appropriate and stock a range upon the public domain of the United States, or otherwise, with cattle shall be deemed to be in possession thereof: provided, that such person, company or corporation shall lawfully possess or occupy, or be the lawful owner or possessor of sufficient living, permanent water upon such range for the proper maintenance of such cattle.

This section has been in effect since its passage in 1889 by the Territorial Legislature of New Mexico. Plaintiffs read this section as bestowing a private property right to graze cattle on the public domain upon all those with a valid water right. Plaintiffs' interpretation is negated by longstanding New Mexico law.

As early as 1915, the New Mexico Supreme Court rejected the proposition that what is now § 19–3–13 created, or was intended to create, a property right in land in the public domain superior or equal to the federal government's right in such land. In *Hill v. Winkler*, 151 P. 1014 (N.M. 1915), two private parties had conflicting claims to grazing land in the public domain. The court was asked to decide which party "had a first and prior right to graze the said tract of government land by reason of prior occupancy thereof, and by reason of the further fact that they had acquired and developed permanent waters in connection therewith for the proper maintenance of such cattle." *Id.* at 1015. The court conceded: "There is a serious question concerning the right of the Legislature to make provision such as is argued was here made." *Id.* The basis for the court's reservation was an 1885 federal statute prohibiting the "assertion of a right to the exclusive use and occupancy of any part of the public lands of the United States in any state or any of the territories of the United States, without claim, color of title." *Id.* In addressing the scope of the New Mexico law in light of the 1885 federal statute, the court stated "it seem[ed] clear . . . that the attempted granting of an exclusive right in the use of the public domain . . . would clearly violate the congressional act, and must therefore be held invalid, if that was the intention of the Legislature." *Id.* The court avoided this conflict by limiting the reach of the New Mexico statute:

> We are of the opinion, however, that the [New Mexico laws at issue] can be construed as not intending to grant any exclusive right in the use of the public domain, but, on the contrary, as attempting to provide that all those who seek to stock a range upon the public domain must, before doing so, lawfully possess, or be the lawful owner of, sufficient permanent water on such range for the proper maintenance of such cattle. This would be a sound and proper regulation of the use of the public lands which would be defended. It is clear, however, that any attempt on the part of the Legislature to grant exclusive right or occupancy upon a part of a public domain would be clearly . . . invalid.

Id. at 1015–16. Thus, contrary to plaintiffs' argument, § 19–3–13 has not been interpreted to bestow a private property right to graze upon the public domain if one has a concomitant right to the water upon the proposed grazing range. As *Hill* makes plain, § 19–3–13 purports only to limit access to the public domain for grazing purposes to those individuals who have first obtained a valid water right sufficient to maintain the cattle to be grazed.

* * *

Plaintiffs direct our attention to *First State Bank of Alamogordo v. McNew,* 269 P. 56 (N.M. 1928), where the New Mexico Supreme Court stated that McNew,

> having appropriated and stocked said range with cattle, and being the owner of permanent water for use upon said range for the maintenance of cattle thereon, had possessory rights in the said public lands, which he could protect as against one forcibly entering thereon without right. Equity would protect him in such possession by enjoining another stock-owner not owning or possessing water from willfully turning his cattle upon such range.

Id. at 59 (internal citations omitted). We do not read *McNew* as contravening *Hill* or *Yates,* but as restating that under § 19–3–13 McNew had a right to exclude from public lands anyone seeking to graze cattle upon those lands who did not have a vested water right. In any event, whatever McNew's rights may have been, they were superior only to those who were seeking to make use of public land "without right." As implicitly acknowledged in *Hill* and *Yates,* the government's right to possess, control, and exclude others from public lands is plenary and may not be negated by contrary state law. At best, McNew had a right to possession sufficient to allow him to exclude certain private parties. His own occupation of public lands for grazing was a privilege subject to withdrawal by the government.

* * *

Federal Law

The United States has long recognized the validity of private water rights obtained pursuant to state water law. See *Andrus v. Charlestone Stone Products Co., Inc.*, 436 U.S. 604, 614 (1978) (noting in 1866, 1870, and 1872, Congress affirmed the "view that private water rights on federal lands were to be governed by state and local law and custom"). This recognition was made explicit in the Mining Law of 1866, which provides in relevant part:

> Whenever, by priority of possession, rights to the use of water for mining, agricultural, manufacturing or other purposes, have vested and accrued, and the same are recognized and acknowledged by the local customs, laws, and the decisions of courts, the possessors and owners of such vested rights shall be maintained and protected in the same; and the right of way for the construction of ditches and canals for the purposes herein specified is acknowledged and confirmed.

43 U.S.C. § 661. Plaintiffs argue § 661 constitutes governmental recognition not just of their water right, but also of their "inseparable" range right, which they contend is within the scope of their water right and was likewise obtained by "priority of possession." In plaintiffs' words,

> The doctrine of prior appropriation is a doctrine which extends far beyond water. It can apply to any natural resource which can be reduced to the control of man by his own labor. . . .

> The doctrine applies to the water which the cattle consume and to the range upon which they forage.

Plaintiffs' Reply Br. at 9.

Plaintiffs' interpretation of the Mining Act is contrary not only to the language of the Act itself, which simply recognizes rights to the use of water, but also to the well-settled body of law holding no private property right exists to graze public rangelands. The Act cannot fairly be read to recognize private property rights in federal lands, regardless of whether proffered as a distinct right or as an inseparable component of a water right. . . .

* * *

Only one court has intimated that an interest in federal land, other than a ditch right-of-way or an easement for diversion of water from federal to private land, is obtainable under the Mining Act of 1866. In *Hage v. United States,* 35 Fed.Cl. 147 (1996), Nevada ranch owners brought suit alleging the government, by canceling plaintiffs' grazing permit and thereby denying them access to water to which plaintiffs had a vested right, had taken without just compensation plaintiffs' property interests in water rights, ditch rights-of-way, and rangeland forage. Plaintiffs claimed an interest in public land and water which their predecessors had used for cattle grazing since the 1800's. In 1907, Congress had designated the land as national forest. As relevant here, plaintiffs' complaint was twofold. First, plaintiffs claimed they had a "property interest in the permit because the federal government issued the permit in recognition of rights which existed prior to the creation" of the national forest. *Id.* at 168. This interest purportedly was recognized by the Mining Act of 1866: "Plaintiffs claim that the Act of 1866 merely enacted as federal law the custom and usage of the Western states and territories to recognize the rights of the first appropriator to acquire a priority right to the use and enjoyment of the public land over those who had not expended such labor." *Id.* at 170. Second, plaintiffs alleged that under Nevada law, their water right included the right ("inherently part of the vested stockwater right") to "bring cattle to the water, and for cattle to consume forage adjacent to a private water right." *Id.* at 175.

The court rejected plaintiffs' argument that the Mining Act recognized distinct property interests in public lands. See *id.* at 170 ("The Act does not address property rights in the public lands and the court declines to create such rights contrary to the clear legislative intention of Congress."). However, despite conceding grazing was a revocable privilege and plaintiffs had no property interest in the rangeland, the court denied the government's motion for summary judgment with respect to plaintiffs' claim that the water right included the right to adjacent forage.

> If Nevada law recognized the right to graze cattle near bordering water as part of a vested water right before 1907, when Congress created the Toiyabe National Forest, plaintiffs may have a right to the forage adjacent to the alleged water rights on the rangeland.

* * *

> When the federal government created the Toiyabe National Forest, it could not unilaterally ignore private property rights on the public domain. If Congress wanted to remove all private property interests in the public domain, which were created by the state under state law, the Constitution would have required the federal government to pay just compensation. Just as the federal government could not take private property rights in water or ditch rights-of-way when it created the Toiyabe National Forest, the government could not take any other form of private property right in the public domain. Plaintiffs will have the opportunity at trial to prove property rights in the

forage stemming from the property right to make beneficial use of water in the public domain within Nevada originating prior to 1907.

Id. at 175–76. In a subsequent order, the court explicitly recognized plaintiffs had a property interest in their ditch rights-of-way and forage rights appurtenant to their water right. See *Hage v. United States,* 42 Fed.Cl. 249, 251 (1998) ("[I]mplicit in a vested water right based on putting water to beneficial use for livestock purposes was the appurtenant right for those livestock to graze alongside the water."). The court held this forage right encompassed the "ground occupied by the water and fifty feet on each side of the marginal limits of the ditch." *Id.* See *Store Safe Redlands Assoc. v. United States,* 35 Fed.Cl. 726 (1996).

The circumstances here are appreciably different than in *Hage.* First, it is not the law in New Mexico that a water right includes the right to graze public lands. As noted, the New Mexico Supreme Court has specifically disavowed such an interpretation of N.M. Stat. Ann. § 19–3–13. See *Hill,* 151 P. at 1015. It is irrelevant to the present case that Nevada law may attach a forage right to a water right. Second, the property interest not explicitly recognized by the Mining Act but asserted by plaintiffs and recognized as potentially compensable in *Hage* was a narrow right to forage along the waterfront. Here, plaintiffs do not assert a right to forage only along the waterfront or a right to lead their cattle to water solely to drink, but a right to occupy and possess, without federal authorization, 174,396 acres of federal land for cattle grazing purposes.

* * *

At best, plaintiffs possess a valid water right that is protected by the Mining Act. However, the United States has not acted to take plaintiffs' water rights, has not denied access to the water, and has not sought to divert plaintiffs' use to a governmental purpose. In fact, the United States concedes if plaintiffs do hold a valid water right, the government may not usurp that right. Plaintiffs contend their water right is of little utility if their cattle have no place to graze. If true, the fault lies with plaintiffs, who were fully apprised of the consequences of failing to renew their permits. See *Hage,* 35 Fed.Cl. at 171 ("The court also understands that without a grazing permit, the ranch may become worthless. But the court emphasizes that plaintiffs' investment-backed expectations and reliance on the privilege to graze do not, in themselves, create a property interest in the rangeland or the permit.").

* * *

Affirmed.

NOTES

1.　*The durability of grazing rights.* Although it is clear that public land grazers have no right or title to public lands, their federal grazing rights have proved surprisingly durable. The first grazing permits went to grazers who had been using the lands at the time. Their permits thereafter were regularly renewed. Grazers formed a powerful special interest group, often formalized by their dominance of grazing advisory committees, and renewals were a matter of course absent sustained, gross misconduct by a grazer. See Bruce R. Huber, *The Durability of Private Claims to Public Property*, 102 Geo. L.J. 991, 1040 (2014)("[R]esource regimes tend to be mastered and manipulated by existing claimants and . . . vigilance is demanded of policymakers who would maintain even a weak form of equal access").

2.　*A grazing right attached to a water right?* At first glance, the grazers' arguments in *Diamond Bar* may seem frivolous—the idea that a person who gains a water right gains along with it a right to graze cattle. But is the idea so crazy in an arid land where land is worth virtually nothing without water? If water is the dominant resource (as commentators such as Wallace Stegner have long asserted), could not lesser resources be deemed incidental to it? For example, the holder of a water right in Colorado has incidental rights to cross private lands and to make use of natural water formations on them, all without the landowner's consent and without payment of compensation. See *Park County Bd. of County Comm'rs v. Park County Sportsmen's Ranch*, 45 P.3d 693 (Colo. 2002), excerpted on p. 29. The truth is, many natural resources have to be used in combination or not at all. What good is a water right with no way to use it? And what good is a grazing right if the animals have nothing to drink? Doesn't it make sense in arid lands to bundle the two resource rights?

In many resource settings, a person who acquires a natural resource gains the right to cross lands as needed to get to the resource and exploit it. This is commonly true when the person acquiring the resource buys it from the landowner, creating an implied easement. Yet a resource owner might be able to use the resource only if he can gain access by using land owned by someone who had no involvement in the resource acquisition. Note, though, that the plaintiffs in *Diamond Bar* went well beyond that idea. They asked not merely for the right to cross public lands to get to their water, but for the right to graze animals on the federal lands. Compare this request with the ruling by the Claims Court in *Hage v. United States,* 42 Fed. Cl. 249 (1998), discussed in *Diamond Bar*. The Federal Court of Claims recognized a land-use right, ancillary to the water right, but it was a land-use right of much more limited scope.

3.　*State water rights and public land management.* Courts have generally reached the same conclusion as the court in *Diamond Bar Cattle* when grazers have sought to gain secure grazing rights based on their ownership of state water rights. E.g., *Colvin Cattle Co. v. U.S.,* 468 F.3d 803 (Fed. Cir. 2006) (because water rights do not have an attendant right to graze, a governmental restriction on grazing on federal land was not a taking of the water rights); *Hunter v. U.S.*, 388 F.2d 148 (9th Cir. 1967) (rejecting a claim by a water rights holder that he could graze cattle on a national monument without a permit because his water right pre-dated the monument designation).

State water rights have also been important in federal land management when water withdrawals cause environmental harm and a federal agency has indirect power to modify the withdrawals. The issue has arisen when water users need to divert their water flows cross federal lands (in, for instance, irrigation ditches) and require a federal right-of-way to do so. Can a federal agency grant a right of way subject to the condition that the water right be exercised in a way that causes less harm? Several courts have said that they do, and ruled that, in some settings, a failure to consider imposing such conditions could be arbitrary and capricious. See *Nevada Land Action Ass'n v. U.S. Forest Serv.*, 8 F.3d 713 (9th Cir. 1993) (deciding that the Forest Service did not have to consider vested water rights in its planning process); *County of Okanogan v. Nat'l Marine Fisheries Serv.*, 347 F.3d 1081 (9th Cir. 2003) (upholding bypass flows to protect endangered species); *Trout Unlimited v. U.S. Dept. of Agriculture*, 320 F.Supp.2d 1090 (D. Colo. 2004) (decision not to require bypass flows in a right-of-way permit renewal was arbitrary and capricious by not minimizing damage as required by the Federal Land Policy and Management Act); *Sequoia Forestkeeper v. U.S. Forest Serv.*, No. CV F 09–392 LJO JLT, 2010 WL 5059621 (E.D. Cal. Dec. 3, 2010) (Forest Service has a duty to consider conditions to protect fish and wildlife and water quality in a water diversion permit in a national forest).

4. *Revoking the implied license to graze on public lands.* The implied license to graze on public lands was partially revoked when the Gifford Pinchot-led Forest Service began requiring grazing permits and charging fees shortly after its formation in 1905. Regulation did not come to the BLM lands, however, until the enactment of the Taylor Grazing Act in 1934, 43 U.S.C § 315, a response to the "dust bowl" of that era. The Taylor Act—along with a couple of ensuing executive orders—effectively ended the era of widespread disposition of federal lands and began tentative federal control of federal grazing. The statute called for establishing federal grazing districts, allocated grazing permits among established grazers, authorized charging fees for federal permits, and promised that the federal government would "adequately safeguard" grazing. One goal of the statute was to "stabilize the livestock industry on the public range." 43 U.S.C. § 315.

As noted above, the intial grazing permits on federal lands went largely to those who had grazed in the previous five years. These grazers, however, were often the ones who in prior years had been responsible for widespread overgrazing of the range. Despite the leasing system, overgrazing has remained a major problem. In 1988, the Government Accounting Office reported that over 50% of federally managed rangelands were in fair or poor ecological condition. U.S. Government Accountability Office, RCED–88–80, *Rangeland Management: More Emphasis Needed on Declining and*

Overstocked Grazing Allotments (1988). It is unlikely that conditions have materially improved in the quarter-century since that assessment.[1]

The Taylor Act made clear that a federal grazing permit, usually limited to five years, provided the permittee with "no right, title, or interest" in federal lands, apparently eliminating constitutional takings claims of just compensation for revocation of federal grazing permits. But in the following case the permittee nevertheless alleged a taking.

UNITED STATES V. FULLER

Supreme Court of the United States
409 U.S. 488 (1973)

[The federal government exercised its eminent domain power to acquire the "Fuller Ranch" for a government project. Fuller sought just compensation not only for the value of his privately-owned lands considered alone but also for the added value that those lands possessed by virtue of the federal permits to graze on adjacent lands that were, in a practical sense, attached to the private lands. The lower courts agreed with Fuller that the enhanced value of his fee land due to his federal grazing permits was compensable property in his takings claim. The federal government appealed.]

REHNQUIST, J.

* * *

The question presented by this case is whether there is an exception to that general rule where the parcels to be aggregated with the land taken are themselves owned by the condemner and used by the condemnee only under revocable permit from the condemnor.

To say that this element of value would be considered by a potential buyer on the open market, and is therefore a component of "fair market value," is not the end of the inquiry. In *United States v. Miller*, this Court held that the increment of fair market value represented by knowledge of the Government's plan to construct the project for which the land was taken was not included within the constitutional definition of "just compensation." The Court there said:

---

[1]   The 1988 GAO report concluded that range that is 26–50% similar to the natural plant community was in fair condition, while range that was 0–25% similar was in poor condtition (p. 22 n.2). The latest available assessment of rangeland health is BLM's Fiscal Year 2012 Rangeland Inventory, Monitoring, and Evaluation Report, available at http://www.blm.gov/pgdata/etc/medialib/blm/wo/Planning_and_Renewable_Resources/rangeland.Par.30896.File.dat/Rangeland2012.pdf, which inventoried 56% of BLM's acres (p. 5). Of those acres, 41% were in fair condition (so-called mid-seral), and 15% were in poor condition (early seral). Thus, 56% of BLM's surveyed acres remained in fair or poor condition in 2012.

But [respondents] insist that no element which goes to make up value . . . is to be discarded or eliminated. We think the proposition is too broadly stated. . . . 317 U.S. at 374.

* * *

A long line of cases decided by this Court dealing with the Government's navigational servitude with respect to navigable waters evidences a continuing refusal to include, as an element of value in compensating for fast lands which are taken, any benefits conferred by access to such benefits as a potential portsite or a potential hydroelectric site. *United States v. Rands*; *United States v. Twin City Power Co.*, 350 U.S. 222 (1956); *United States v. Commondore Park, Inc.*, 324 U.S. 386 (1945).

These cases go far toward establishing the general principle that the Government as condemnor may not be required to compensate a condemnee for elements of value that the Government has created, or that it might have destroyed under the exercise of governmental authority other than the power of eminent domain. If, as in *Rands*, the Government need not pay for value that it could have acquired by exercise of a servitude arising under the commerce power, it would seem *a fortiori* that it need not compensate for value which it could remove by revocation of a permit for the use of lands that it owned outright.

* * *

Seeking as best we may to extrapolate from these prior decisions such a "working rule," we believe that there is a significant difference between the value added to property by a completed public works project, for which the Government must pay, and the value added to fee lands by a revocable permit authorizing the use of neighboring lands that the Government owns.

* * *

[I]f the owner of the fast lands can demand port site value as part of his compensation, "he gets the value of a right that the Government in the exercise of its dominant servitude can grant or withhold as it chooses. . . . To require the United States to pay for this . . . value would be to create private claims in the public domain." 389 U.S. at 125, quoting *United States v. Twin City Power Co.*, 350 U.S. at 228.

We hold that the Fifth Amendment does not require the Government to pay for that element of value based on the use of respondents' fee lands in combination with the Government's permit lands.

* * *

Reversed.

NOTES

1.   *The dissent.* A four-member dissent, comprised of unlikely allies—
Justices Powell, Douglas, Brennan, and Marshall—would have sided with
Fuller in his claim. They noted that, under prior Court rulings, locational
value was compensable in a condemnation of a gasoline station adjacent to a
federal highway and a farm with access to irrigation water from a nearby
federal reservoir. The dissent thought these situations were indistinguishable
from the Fuller Ranch case.

2.   *Bank valuation.* Why is it not relevant that local banks typically
make loans to ranchers based not only on the value of their base property
owned in fee, but also based on the value of their federal grazing permits?

3.   *Due process claim.* In *Federal Lands Legal Consortium v. United
States*, 195 F. 3d 1190 (10th Cir. 1999), the court considered the applicability
of a due process claim to the reduction of grazing permits by the U.S. Forest
Service due to endangered species concerns. The 10th Circuit ruled that
grazing permits could be property for purposes of the due process clause, even
though they were not considered property for purposes of the takings clause.
It reached this conclusion based on the considerable discretion that the
federal government retained in altering the terms of a grazing permit on
renewal. In the course of its decision, the Tenth Circuit made the following
observations about the nature of the right to graze under federal permits:

> FLLC argues that the federal government has limited the Forest
> Service's discretion to change the terms or conditions from previous
> Gila Forest permits during the permit-renewal process. FLLC bases
> their argument, in part, on the fact that they have a priority for
> renewal. 43 U.S.C. § 1752(c) (providing for priority rights); 36 C.F.R.
> § 222.3(c)(1)(ii) (same). Although FLLC may have a priority during
> renewal, this court has repeatedly held that the decision whether to
> issue or deny a permit is a discretionary one: "[T]he very
> determinations of whether to renew grazing permits and whether
> public lands should even be designated for grazing purposes[, see 36
> C.F.R. § 219.20,] are matters completely within the Secretary of
> Interior's discretion." . . .
>
> More importantly, during the permit renewal process, an applicant
> has a priority for a permit only "[s]o long as . . . the permittee
> accepts the terms or conditions to be included by the Secretary . . ."
> 43 U.S.C. § 1752(c)(3); see also 16 U.S.C. § 580l ("The Secretary of
> Agriculture in regulating grazing on the national forest . . . is
> authorized, upon such terms and conditions as he may deem proper,
> to issue permits for the grazing of livestock. . . ."). The Forest
> Service, in turn, has discretion to require any change it deems
> necessary, see 16 U.S.C. § 580l; 43 U.S.C. § 1752(e); 36 C.F.R.
> § 222.3(c)(1)(vi), including discretion to set the "numbers of animals

to be grazed and the seasons of use," 43 U.S.C. § 1752(e); 36 C.F.R. § 222.3(c)(1)(i), which are, in essence, the permit changes at issue in this action. . . .

* * *

FLLC next argues that, historically, the Forest Service has renewed the permits without any changes in the permits' terms or conditions. [S]ee *Shufflebarger v. Commissioner,* 24 T.C. 980, 991–92, 997 (1955) (noting the historical practices of the Forest Service). According to FLLC, the Forest Service's practice thereby creates a legitimate entitlement to the terms and conditions of the previous permits. [S]ee also *Perry,* 408 U.S. at 602–03 (holding that a mutually implicit understanding may create a property right).

As an initial matter, it is not apparent that those historical practices survived the enactment of the Federal Land Policy and Management Act in 1976. Under that Act, "future adjudications of grazing use would be based on criteria vastly different than those provided" under the prior acts. *Public Lands Council v. Babbitt,* 167 F.3d 1287, 1295 (10th Cir. 1999). This court has therefore concluded that "[a]lthough it may well be the case that there were long periods in which the Secretary did not exercise his authority to change the permitted number . . . in new permits, this practice did not rise to the level of regulatory mandate." *Public Lands Council,* 167 F.3d at 1297–98.

Regardless, "in the absence of a statutory or contractual right to renewal, a person . . . can claim no property interest in the indefinite renewal of his or her contract." *Durant v. Independent Sch. Dist. No. 16,* 990 F.2d 560, 563 (10th Cir. 1993); . . . *Martin v. Unified Sch. Dist. No. 434,* 728 F.2d 453, 454–55 (10th Cir. 1984) (holding that a teacher whose one-year contract had been renewed every year for ten years did not have a protected property interest in renewal during the eleventh year). . . .

As noted above, the statutory scheme gives the Forest Service discretion to change the terms and conditions during the permit renewal process. That the Forest Service customarily did not exercise that discretion creates, at best, a unilateral expectation that the Forest Service would continue that practice. That expectation is insufficient to establish a property right. See *Roth,* 408 U.S. at 577 ("To have a property interest in a benefit, a person . . . must have more than a unilateral expectation of it.").

4.   *The effect of the National Environmental Policy Act (NEPA).* NEPA requires all federal agencies to analyze the environmental effects of their proposed major actions and to disclose those effects to the public and to other federal and state agencies. NEPA had a pronounced effect on BLM grazing regulation in the 1970s, largely through *Natural Resources Defense Council v.*

Morton, 388 F.Supp. 829 (D.D.C. 1974), *aff'd*, 527 F.2d 1386 (D.C. Cir. 1976), which ruled that BLM's livestock grazing program violated NEPA due to the lack of site-specific environmental analyses. (The court cited a BLM study that found that "[u]ncontrolled, unregulated or unplanned livestock use is occurring in approximately 85 percent of [Nevada's public lands]," causing extreme wildlife habitat and stream damage. *Id.* at 840.) In response, the BLM completed over 100 environmental impact statements (EISs), which revealed (as critics expected) West-wide damage to BLM lands and streams due to livestock grazing. The Reagan Administration's Secretary of the Interior James Watt criticized the EISs as "junk science" and forbade grazing reductions based on them.

In the early 1980s, guided by Secretary Watt, the BLM proposed a new generation of plans that did not call for grazing cutbacks. The approach received judicial sanction in *Natural Resources Defense Council v. Hodel*, 624 F.Supp. 1045 (D. Nev. 1985), *aff'd*, 819 F.2d 927 (9th Cir. 1987) (deferring to BLM's multiple-use mandate, declining to become a "rangemaster," and deciding that the lack of specificity in the statute governing BLM's land plans—the Federal Land Policy and Management Act—meant that the plans did not have to be effective in minimizing environmental damage). 624 F. Supp. at 1058–60, 1063.

5. *Rangeland reform.* With the inauguration of the Clinton Administration in 1993, Secretary of Interior Bruce Babbitt initiated a new effort to reform BLM rangeland regulation. Among other things, the initiative would have increased grazing fees, revised advisory committees, and established enforceable environmental standards. Secretary Babbitt quickly abandoned the effort to increase grazing fees after the Republican takeover of the House of Representatives in 1994, but he retained the other elements of the reform effort. These measures were challenged in the following case.

2.   REGULATION OF GRAZING RIGHTS

PUBLIC LANDS COUNCIL V. BABBITT

Supreme Court of the United States
529 U.S. 728 (2000)

[The Clinton-era grazing reform effort was promptly challenged by grazing interests. In the ensuing litigation, the district court struck down the elements of the reform plan that 1) changed the definition of "grazing preference" to tie grazing permits to land use plans instead of historic use; 2) permitted those not engaged in the grazing business to obtain permits; 3) granted the federal government title to all future permanent range improvements; and 4) authorized issuance of "conservation permits" that would allow no grazing at all. The district court upheld the new environmental standards and the changes to advisory committees. *Public Lands Council v. U.S. Dep't of Interior Sec'y*, 929 F.Supp. 1436 (D.

Wyo. 1996). The Tenth Circuit reversed the district court on the first three issues while upholding its ruling on the conservation permit issue. On review by the Supreme Court, the government chose not to appeal the conservation permit issue. A unanimous Court affirmed the Tenth Circuit in the decision below.]

BREYER, J.

This case requires us to interpret several provisions of the 1934 Taylor Grazing Act, 48 Stat. 1269, 43 U.S.C. § 315 *et seq.* The petitioners claim that each of three grazing regulations, 43 CFR §§ 4100.0–5, 4110.1(a), and 4120.3–2 (1998), exceeds the authority that this statute grants the Secretary of the Interior. We disagree and hold that the three regulations do not violate the Act.

I

We begin with a brief description of the Act's background, provisions, and related administrative practice.

A

The Taylor Grazing Act's enactment in 1934 marked a turning point in the history of the western rangelands, the vast, dry grasslands and desert that stretch from western Nebraska, Kansas, and Texas to the Sierra Nevada. Ranchers once freely grazed livestock on the publicly owned range as their herds moved from place to place, searching for grass and water. But the population growth that followed the Civil War eventually doomed that unregulated economic freedom.

A new era began in 1867 with the first successful long drive of cattle north from Texas. Cowboys began regularly driving large herds of grazing cattle each year through thousands of miles of federal lands to railheads like Abilene, Kansas. From there or other towns along the rail line, trains carried live cattle to newly opened eastern markets. The long drives initially brought high profits, which attracted more ranchers and more cattle to the land once home only to Indian tribes and buffalo. Indeed, an early-1880's boom in the cattle market saw the number of cattle grazing the Great Plains grow well beyond 7 million. See R. White, *"It's Your Misfortune and None of My Own": A History of the American West* 223 (1991); see generally E. Osgood, *The Day of the Cattleman* 83–113 (1929); W. Webb, *The Great Plains* 205–268 (1931).

* * *

B

The Taylor Act seeks to "promote the highest use of the public lands." 43 U.S.C. § 315. Its specific goals are to "stop injury" to the lands from "overgrazing and soil deterioration," to "provide for their use, improvement and development," and "to stabilize the livestock industry dependent on the public range." 48 Stat. 1269. The Act grants the Secretary of the Interior authority to divide the public range-lands into grazing districts, to specify the amount of grazing permitted in each district, to issue leases or permits "to graze livestock," and to charge "reasonable fees" for use of the land. 43 U.S.C. §§ 315, 315a, 315b. It specifies that preference in respect to grazing permits "shall be given . . . to those within or near" a grazing district "who are landowners engaged in the livestock business, bona fide occupants or settlers, or owners of water or water rights." § 315b. And, as particularly relevant here, it adds:

> So far as consistent with the purposes and provisions of this subchapter, grazing privileges recognized and acknowledged shall be adequately safeguarded, but the creation of a grazing district or the issuance of a permit . . . shall not create any right, title, interest, or estate in or to the lands. *Id.*

C

[The Court highlighted the "enormous administrative task" of implementing the Taylor Act and noted the lack of early implementation success.]

D

In the 1960's, as the range failed to recover, the Secretary of the Interior increased grazing fees by more than 50% (from 19 cents to 30 cents per AUM [Animal Unit Month]/year), thereby helping to capture a little more of the economic costs that grazing imposed upon the land. Department of Interior Ann. Rep. 66 (1963). And in 1976, Congress enacted a new law, the Federal Land Policy and Management Act of 1976 (FLPMA), 90 Stat. 2744, 43 U.S.C. § 1701 *et seq.,* which instructed the Interior Department to develop districtwide land use plans based upon concepts of "multiple use" (use for various purposes, such as recreation, range, timber, minerals, watershed, wildlife and fish, and natural and scenic, scientific, and historical usage), § 1702(c), and "sustained yield" (regular renewable resource output maintained in perpetuity), § 1702(h). The FLPMA strengthened the Department's existing authority to remove or add land from grazing use, allowing such modification pursuant to a land use plan, §§ 1712, 1714, while specifying that existing grazing permit holders would retain a "first priority" for renewal so long as the land use plan continued to make land "available for domestic livestock grazing," § 1752(c).

In 1978, the Department's grazing regulations were, in turn, substantially amended to comply with the new law. See 43 Fed. Reg. 29067. As relevant here, the 1978 regulations tied permit renewal and validity to the land use planning process, giving the Secretary the power to cancel, suspend, or modify grazing permits due to increases or decreases in grazing forage or acreage made available pursuant to land planning. . . .

* * *

E

[The Court explained that, in 1995, the BLM under the Clinton Administration amended the federal grazing regulations to "accelerate restoration" and encourage stewardship of rangelands. 60 Fed. Reg. 9894 (1995) (final rule). The Public Lands Council and other ranching interests challenged the regulations as exceeding BLM's authority under the Taylor Grazing Act.]

II

A

The ranchers attack the new "grazing preference" regulations first and foremost. Their attack relies upon the provision in the Taylor Act stating that "grazing privileges recognized and acknowledged shall be adequately safeguarded. . . ." 43 U.S.C. § 315b. Before 1995 the regulations defined the term "grazing preference" in terms of the *AUM-denominated amount* of grazing privileges that a permit granted. The regulations then defined "grazing preference" as

> the total number of animal unit months of livestock grazing on public lands apportioned and attached to base property owned or controlled by a permittee or lessee. 43 CFR § 4100.0–5 (1994).

The 1995 regulations changed this definition, however, so that it now no longer refers to grazing privileges "apportioned," nor does it speak in terms of AUMs. The new definition defines "grazing preference" as

> a superior or priority position against others for the purpose of receiving a grazing permit or lease. This priority is attached to base property owned or controlled by the permittee or lessee. 43 CFR § 4100.0–5 (1995).

The new definition "omits reference to a specified quantity of forage." 60 Fed. Reg. 9921 (1995). It refers only to a priority, not to a specific number of AUMs attached to a base property. But at the same time the new regulations add a new term, "permitted use," which the Secretary defines as

> the forage allocated by, or under the guidance of, an applicable land use plan for livestock grazing in an allotment under a permit or lease and is expressed in AUMs. 43 CFR § 4100.0–5 (1995).

This new "permitted use," like the old "grazing preference," is defined in terms of allocated rights, and it refers to AUMs. But this new term as defined refers, not to a rancher's forage priority, but to forage "allocated by, or under the guidance of *an applicable land use plan.*" *Ibid.* (emphasis added). And therein lies the ranchers' concern.

The ranchers refer us to the administrative history of Taylor Act regulations, much of which we set forth in Part I. In the ranchers' view, history has created expectations in respect to the security of "grazing privileges"; they have relied upon those expectations; and the statute requires the Secretary to "safeguar[d]" that reliance. Supported by various farm credit associations, they argue that defining their privileges in relation to land use plans will undermine that security. They say that the content of land use plans is difficult to predict and easily changed. Fearing that the resulting uncertainty will discourage lenders from taking mortgages on ranches as security for their loans, they conclude that the new regulations threaten the stability, and possibly the economic viability, of their ranches, and thus fail to "safeguard" the "grazing privileges" that Department regulations previously "recognized and acknowledged."

We are not persuaded by the ranchers' argument for three basic reasons. First, the statute qualifies the duty to "safeguard" by referring directly to the Act's various goals and the Secretary's efforts to implement them. The full subsection says:

> So far as consistent with the purposes and provisions of this subchapter, grazing privileges recognized and acknowledged shall be adequately safeguarded, *but* the creation of a grazing district or the issuance of a permit pursuant to the provisions of this subchapter shall *not* create any right, title, interest or estate in or to the lands. 43 U.S.C. § 315b (emphasis added).

The words "so far as consistent with the purposes . . . of this subchapter" and the warning that "issuance of a permit" creates no "right, title, interest or estate" make clear that the ranchers' interest in permit stability cannot be absolute; and that the Secretary is free reasonably to determine just how, and the extent to which, "grazing privileges" shall be safeguarded, in light of the Act's basic purposes. Of course, those purposes include "stabiliz[ing] the livestock industry," but they also include "stop[ping] injury to the public grazing lands by preventing overgrazing and soil deterioration," and "provid[ing] for th[e] orderly use, improvement, and development" of the public range. 48 Stat. 1269. . . .

Moreover, Congress itself has directed development of land use plans, and their use in the allocation process, in order to preserve, improve, and develop the public rangelands. See 43 U.S.C. §§ 1701(a)(2), 1712. That being so, it is difficult to see how a definitional change that simply refers to the use of such plans could violate the Taylor Act by itself, without more. Given the broad discretionary powers that the Taylor Act grants the Secretary, we must read that Act as here granting the Secretary at least ordinary administrative leeway to assess "safeguard[ing]" in terms of the Act's other purposes and provisions. . . .

Second, the pre-1995 AUM system that the ranchers seek to "safeguard" did not offer them anything like absolute security—not even in respect to the proportionate shares of grazing land privileges that the "active/suspended" system suggested. As discussed above, the Secretary has long had the power to reduce an individual permit's AUMs or cancel the permit if the permit holder did not use the grazing privileges, did not use the base property, or violated the Range Code. And the Secretary has always had the statutory authority under the Taylor Act and later FLPMA to reclassify and withdraw rangeland from grazing use, see 43 U.S.C. § 315f (authorizing Secretary, "in his discretion, to examine and classify any lands . . . which are more valuable or suitable for the production of agricultural crops . . . or any other use than [grazing]"); §§ 1712, 1752(c) (authorizing renewal of permits "so long as the lands . . . remain available for domestic livestock grazing *in accordance with land use plans*" (emphasis added)). The Secretary has consistently reserved the authority to cancel or modify grazing permits accordingly. Given these well-established pre-1995 Secretarial powers to cancel, modify, or decline to renew individual permits, *including the power to do so pursuant to the adoption of a land use plan,* the ranchers' diminishment-of-security point is at best a matter of degree.

* * *

B

The ranchers' second challenge focuses upon a provision of the Taylor Act that limits issuance of permits to "settlers, residents, and other *stock owners.* . . ." 43 U.S.C. § 315b (emphasis added). In 1936, the Secretary, following this requirement, issued a regulation that limited eligibility to those who "ow[n] livestock." But in 1942, the Secretary changed the regulation's wording to limit eligibility to those "engaged in the livestock business," 1942 Range Code § 3(a), and so it remained until 1994. The new regulation eliminates the words "engaged in the livestock business," thereby seeming to make eligible otherwise qualified applicants even if they do not engage in the livestock business. See 43 CFR § 4110.1(a) (1995).

The new change is not as radical as the text of the new regulation suggests. The new rule deletes the entire phrase "engaged in the livestock business" from § 4110.1, and seems to require only that an applicant "own or control land or water base property. . . ." *Id.* But the omission, standing alone, does not render the regulation facially invalid, for the regulation cannot change the statute, and a regulation promulgated to guide the Secretary's discretion in exercising his authority under the Act need not also restate all related statutory language. Ultimately it is *both* the Taylor Act and the regulations promulgated thereunder that constrain the Secretary's discretion in issuing permits. The statute continues to limit the Secretary's authorization to issue permits to "bona fide settlers, residents, and *other stock owners*." 43 U.S.C. § 315b (emphasis added).

Nor will the change necessarily lead to widespread issuance of grazing permits to "stock owners" who are not in the livestock business. Those in the business continue to enjoy a preference in the issuance of grazing permits. The same section of the Taylor Act mandates that the Secretary accord a preference to "landowners engaged in the livestock business, bona fide occupants or settlers." *Ibid.* And this statutory language has been extremely important in practice.

The ranchers nonetheless contend that the deletion of the term "engaged in the livestock business" violates the statutory limitation to "stock owners" in § 315b. The words "stock owner," they say, meant "commercial stock owner" in 1934, and a commercial stock owner is not simply one who owns livestock, but one who engages in the business. Hence, they argue, the Secretary lacks the authority to allow those who are not engaged in the business to apply for permits.

The words "stock owner" and "stock owner engaged in the livestock business," however, are not obvious synonyms. And we have found no convincing indication that Congress intended that we treat them as such. . . .

The ranchers' underlying concern is that the qualifications amendment is part of a scheme to end livestock grazing on the public lands. They say that "individuals or organizations owning small quantities of stock [will] acquire grazing permits, even though they intend not to graze at all or to graze only a nominal number of livestock— all the while excluding others from using the public range for grazing." The new regulations, they charge, will allow individuals to "acquire a few livestock, . . . obtain a permit for what amounts to a conservation purpose and then effectively mothball the permit."

But the regulations do not allow this. The regulations specify that regular grazing permits will be issued for livestock grazing or suspended use. See 43 CFR §§ 4130.2(a), 4130.2(g) (1998). New regulations allowing issuance of permits for conservation use were held unlawful by the Court of Appeals, see 167 F.3d at 1307–08, and the Secretary did not seek review of that decision.

Neither livestock grazing use nor suspended use encompasses the situation that the ranchers describe. With regard to the former, the regulations state that permitted livestock grazing *"shall be based* upon the amount of forage available for livestock grazing as established in the land use plan. . . ." 43 CFR § 4110.2–2(a) (1998) (emphasis added).

Permitted livestock use is not simply a symbolic upper limit. Under the regulations, a permit holder is expected to make substantial use of the permitted use set forth in the grazing permit. For example, the regulations prohibit a permit holder from "[f]ailing to make substantial grazing use as authorized for 2 consecutive fee years." § 4140.1(a)(2). If a permit holder does fail to make substantial use as authorized in his permit for two consecutive years, the Secretary is authorized to cancel from the grazing permit that portion of permitted use that the permit holder has failed to use. . . .

* * *

The judgment of the Court of Appeals is affirmed.

NOTES

1.   *The precarious nature of federal grazing rights. Public Lands Council* is a veritable catalog of the many ways that a grazing right on federal lands can come to an end, in whole or in part, either permanently or temporarily. The ruling is worth reading closely to make sure you understand the exact nature of these grazing rights. The governing federal statute provides that grazing rights will be "adequately safeguarded." But this statutory protection does not override any of the many limits concerning how long grazing rights last.

For starters, the Court tells us that a grazing right can be lost through non-use. That is, a holder of a permit must actually put livestock on the range that will eat the forage or else risk permit cancellation. The underlying policy, of course, is familiar to us already: Lawmakers want to see natural resources used, not left unused. In this setting, though, the forage would not go unused—it would be eaten by wild animals.

Note that this use-it-or-lose-it rule (common in natural resources law) effectively prohibits conservation groups from acquiring grazing permits and then allowing wild animals to graze. Could a conservation group fight back by litigating the definition of "livestock"? Given that many wild species (elk included) are captive-raised for meat, could a group claim that certain wild species qualify as livestock? What about wild species that are economically valuable because visitors come to view them? Can horse riding qualify as a livestock-based activity? Could a conservation group obtain a grazing permit and then decide to graze merely a few cows?

2.   *Nonrenewal, cancellation, suspension, and redefinition.* As you read *Public Lands Council* and try to get straight on the exact legal status of grazing rights, it may prove useful to consider four other ways that a grazing right might come to an end, partly or wholly.

Grazing permits are usually issued for 10-year terms; theoretically, they automatically end if they are not renewed. Permit holders have rights to renew, but they are qualified rights. What dangers are there that a permit will not be renewed? As you answer, consider *nonrenewal* that is caused by the permit holder's behavior (or misbehavior), and nonrenewal that is caused instead by decisions and preferences of BLM. As for the latter, note the ability of BLM to rewrite land use plans and to decide that particular lands might be better used if withdrawn from grazing and applied to other purposes. One of the key provisions in federal rangeland plans is the provision allocating forage between livestock and wild animals. For decades, BLM routinely allocated nearly all of the forage on ranges to domesticated livestock and was roundly criticized by conservation groups for doing so.

As for *cancellation,* this would take place during the term of a permit, mostly for misconduct by the permit holder. What actions could trigger cancellation, and how is cancellation related to physical conditions on the range itself—conditions that could be caused as much by drought or other weather patterns as by any grazing done by the permit holder?

There is also BLM's authority to *suspend* grazing rights to deal with drought, pest problems, and other ecological factors. Pay attention on this issue, not just to the grounds for which BLM might suspend rights, but to how the suspensions are implemented (as best we can tell). We saw, in the case of prior appropriation water rights, that shortages of water are dealt with by terminating the water rights of the most junior water users; only in particular settings (often within organized irrigation districts) is there an effort to force all users to cut back pro rata. In the case of grazing rights, suspensions take place within regions that are excessively grazed in relation to the land's carrying capacity. Within overgrazed regions, reductions are sometimes made among grazers pro rata, rather than using a system of temporal priority.

Finally, there is the danger that the terms of a permit will *change mid-stream* (during the 10-year term) due to changes in applicable land use plans. The specter of this risk underlaid *Public Lands Council,* even though the Court did not highlight it. Permits now typically contain express clauses that allow agencies to order grazers to reduce livestock on a range due to poor range conditions. Reductions ordered pursuant to reserved rights are not alterations of the terms of permits, given the reserved agency powers. From the grazer's point of view, however, they nonetheless entail reductions that can prove costly.

3. *Revising the grazing regulations.* The Bush Administration responded to the Supreme Court's affirmance of the Clinton Administration's grazing regulations by attempting to substantially revise them in 2006. The regulations aimed to make public participation in grazing permit renewal decisions more difficult, eliminated ecological criteria contained in the Clinton-era regulations as enforceable standards, and increased permittee ownership rights in range improvements and water rights, in what BLM described as an effort to improve working relationships with ranchers. BLM promulgated the regulatory changes despite criticism from three separate interdisciplinary teams of experts, all of which concluded that the regulations

would produce widespread adverse effects on wildlife, biological diversity, and riparian habitats.

Environmentalists filed suit, the District Court of Idaho granted their motion for summary judgment, and the Ninth Circuit affirmed in *Western Watersheds Project v. Kraayenbrink*, 632 F.3d 472 (9th Cir. 2011). Interestingly, between the district court decision and the Ninth Circuit decision, BLM switched positions (now siding with the environmentalists), but intervening grazing organizations continued the appeal. *Id.* at 477. The court affirmed that BLM violated both NEPA and the Endangered Species Act in promulgating the regulations by 1) not addressing the concerns raised by its own experts, other federal agencies, and state agencies, as well as claiming without foundation that the changes would not affect the environment, and 2) failing to satisfy the ESA by not consulting with U.S. Fish and Wildlife Service. *Id.* at 487–97. The decision induced BLM to end its efforts to amend the Clinton-era rangeland reforms.

4.   *Annual operation instructions.* Actual on-the-ground grazing is not simply a function of the AUMs (animal unit months) allowed in the permit because the environmental conditions of federal rangeland depend on annual precipitation, which cannot be anticipated in a long-term land plan. So, the AUMs in a land plan might be only a ceiling in what is referred to as "annual operating instructions" from BLM. In *Oregon Natural Desert Ass'n v. U.S. Forest Service*, 465 F.3d 977 (9th Cir. 2006), the court ruled that annual operating instructions to grazers were final federal actions for purposes of the Administrative Procedure Act, presumably also triggering NEPA and ESA responsibilities. The result could produce more scrutiny of annual grazing decisions on federal lands.

5.   *Grazing fees.* Cheap federal grazing fees have long characterized western ranching, from the time that Gifford Pinchot's Forest Service began charging fees in the early twentieth century. Fees have never returned the cost of administering federal rangeland management; for taxpayers, grazing makes no business sense. Secretary Babbitt's reform plan sought to increase grazing fees to approximate the higher fees typically charged in leases of private grasslands. The idea was dropped when Republicans gained control of the House of Representatives in 1994 and has not been revived. Environmentalists have long argued that below-market grazing encourages ranchers to graze on marginal lands, damaging their ecological functioning. Ranchers have steadfastly (and successfully) resisted all efforts to require fair-market returns. Below-market fees increase private profits, boost the sale prices of private ranches, and facilitate bank loans. See George C. Coggins & Robert L. Glicksman, 3 *Public Natural Resources Law* § 33:7 (2d ed. 2014).

6.   *Grazing buy-outs.* One potential solution to overgrazing is to encourage purchases of grazing rights by public-interest groups that do not use them. Grazing buy-outs seem to offer quick environmental improvements on overgrazed lands without the acrimony often attendant on regulatory

cutbacks, since they involve willing seller-willing buyer transactions. See John D. Leshy & Molly S. McUsic, *Where's the Beef? Facilitating Voluntary Retirement of Federal Lands from Livestock Grazing*, 17 N.Y.U. Envtl. L.J. 368 (2008).

There are, however, several problems with grazing buy-outs, chief among them the lack of assurance that the grazing reductions from buy-outs will be permanent. As we have just seen, the Tenth Circuit in the *Public Lands Council* litigation rejected the proposed conservation permits as inconsistent with the Taylor Act, 167 F.3d 1287, 1299 (10th Cir. 1999), a result the federal government did not challenge in the Supreme Court case. Consequently, lessees must graze livestock or forfeit their leases unless they can convince the BLM to suspend their grazing under one of the regulatory provisions that authorize suspensions. 43 C.F.R. § 4110.3–2 (2014). Alternatively, a public-interest group that acquired a grazing lease could encourage the BLM to amend its applicable land plan so as to retire the land from grazing. But such retirements are effective only for the life of the land plan, generally for 10 years, and the plan may be amended at any time. 43 C.F.R. § 4130.2(d) (2014). Funders of grazing permit buy-outs, such as environmentally-oriented foundations, generally want more lasting protection than this. One buy-out effort is explained in National Wildlife Federation, *Wildlife Conflict Resolution Program,* http://www.nwf-wcr.org/program.htm (describing the retirement of roughly 35 allotments on 618,197 acres in the Yellowstone Ecosystem and 5 allotments of 55,261 acres on the Charles M. Russell National Wildlife Refuge in Montana). See also http://www.nwf-wcr.org/SpecificAllotments.htm.

7. *State school trust lands.* As western states were admitted to the Union, Congress included in their separate enabling acts grants of federal land, including lands designated to support public schools. See Eric Biber, *The Price of Admission: Causes, Effects, and Patterns of Conditions Imposed on States Entering the Union*, 46 Am. J. Legal Hist. 119 (2004). School lands were transferred in trust, subject to federal-law duties to manage them to maximize income for the schools. Some states reiterated these trust duties in their state constitutions. For example, Article IX, section 8 of the Idaho constitution states:

> It shall be the duty of the state board of land commissioners to provide for the location, protection, sale or rental of all . . . lands . . . granted to or acquired by the state by or from the general government, under such regulations as may be prescribed by law, and in such manner as will secure the maximum long-term financial return to the institution to which granted. . . .

Often, states have leased these lands to grazers at low fees (commonly less than $1 per acre per year), ignoring complaints by school interests and notwithstanding the willingness of conservation groups, anxious to protect lands from overgrazing, to pay far more. Can such practices be legitimate when federal law requires that states maximize returns for the schools? The issue has engendered litigation in many Western states, including the following ruling.

3.   GRAZING RIGHTS ON STATE LANDS

IDAHO WATERSHEDS PROJECT V. STATE BOARD OF LAND COMMISSIONERS

Supreme Court of Idaho
982 P.2d 367 (1999)

[In 1996, the Idaho Watersheds Project (IWP), a conservation group, outbid ranchers to acquire several grazing leases on state school lands. The Idaho Land Board (Board), which oversaw the leasing, disqualified IWP on the basis of a state statute directing the Board, as it evaluated bids for leases, to consider the effects on the livestock industry and the state economy. I.C. § 58–310B. In effect, the Board ruled that the state lands were only subject to leasing by actual grazers, who would not need to outbid others to gain them.]

JOHNSON, J.

* * *

II.

I.C. § 58–310B Violates Article IX, § 8.

IWP asserts that I.C. § 58–310B violates Article IX, § 8 of the Idaho Constitution. We agree.

* * *

Article IX, § 8 directs that the Board provide "*rental* of all the lands heretofore, or which may hereafter be granted to or acquired by the state by or from the general government, *under such regulations as may be prescribed by law*...." (emphasis added). Therefore, we must determine whether I.C. § 58–310B is constitutional as a "regulation ... prescribed by law."

Article IX, § 8 provides that the objective of sales and leases of state endowment lands is to "secure the maximum long term financial return to the institution to which granted or to the state if not specifically granted." This is in keeping with the Idaho Admission Bill admitting Idaho into the union, which indicates that monies received from the sale or lease of school endowment lands "shall be reserved for school purposes only." Idaho Admission Bill, 26 Stat. L. 215, ch. 656, § 5(a).

Prior to the enactment of I.C. § 58–310B, hearings in the Senate Resources and Environment Committee (the committee) disclosed that the Idaho livestock industry contributes somewhere between $1.2 and

$3.8 billion to the economy of Idaho, as compared to only $78,000 earned from conflict bids for public grazing lands. Aside from the strict financial gain to the state, supporters of I.C. § 58–310B urged the committee to consider several other factors, all financially related, including the stability of the livestock industry, the effect on the overall economy of ranchers going out of business, jobs and additional tax funds generated by the livestock industry, and the effect on those who supply the livestock industry. As a result of those factors, the proponents argued that if the livestock industry were weakened, the monies to be obtained from bidding auctions would also be weakened since there would be fewer participants in the livestock industry to place bids in the first place.

During a December 1996 hearing before the Board, the Board indicated that it needed to consider sales, income, and property taxes from the businesses conducted on the leased lands in determining the "maximum long term financial return." The Board also stated that in the previous year, $22.4 million had been earned from rents on school endowment lands, which monies were funneled directly to the schools of Idaho, while an additional $800 million had been collected in various taxes that benefit the state as a whole. The factors considered by the Board in this case mirror the factors presented to the Senate and discussed prior to the enactment of I.C. § 58–310B.

Rather than seeking to provide income to the schools *and* the state in general, Article IX, § 8 requires that the State consider only the "maximum long term financial return" to the schools in the leasing of school endowment public grazing lands. Article IX, § 8 requires the Legislature to "provide by law that the general grants of land made by congress to the state shall be judiciously located and carefully preserved and held in trust, subject to disposal at public auction *for the use and benefit of the respective object for which said grants of land were made. . . .*" (emphasis added). By attempting to promote funding for the schools *and* the state through the leasing of school endowment lands, I.C. § 58–310B violates the requirements of Article IX, § 8. By the Board's application of the considerations contained in I.C. § 58–310B, IWP was denied the opportunity to participate in auctions for the leases for which it had applied.

We acknowledge that "[t]he Board is granted broad discretion in determining what constitutes the maximum long term financial return for the schools." *Idaho Watersheds Project v. Board of Land Comm'rs*, 918 P.2d 1206, 1210 (Idaho 1996) (*IWP I*). Section § 58–310B removes much of the Board's broad discretion, however, by impermissibly directing the Board to focus on the schools, the state, and the Idaho livestock industry in assessing lease applications, all to the detriment of other potential bidders like IWP, which might provide "maximum long term financial return" to the schools, but not to the state and the Idaho livestock industry.

Having declared I.C. § 58–310B to be unconstitutional, it necessarily follows that the 1996 leases the Board awarded for which IWP was an applicant but was not allowed to bid at an auction were improperly awarded and must be opened for applications again. . . .

III.

Conclusion

We reverse the judgment of the trial court upholding the decisions of the Board regarding IWP's grazing lease applications.

We remand to the Board for new auctions of the 1996 leases for which IWP was not allowed to bid.

NOTES

1.   *Fair market value permits in other states.* The duty to secure fair market value for state school trust land exists in many states, and the Idaho Supreme Court is not the only state court to allow conservationists to outbid grazing interests on the basis of that requirement. For example, Arizona and Montana courts also have upheld the proposition that revenue need not be generated by grazing but can be generated by other interests, such as conservation groups. *Forest Guardians v. Wells*, 34 P.3d 364 (Ariz. 2001) (the state land commissioner must at least consider whether the highest bidder for school trust land is best for the beneficiaries of the trust and cannot exclude a conservation group just because it does not intend to use the land for grazing); *Montanans for the Responsible Use of the School Trust v. State ex rel. Bd. of Land Comm'rs,* 989 P.2d 800 (Mont. 1999) (state land managers are required to obtain full market value for school trust lands). But see *WildEarth Guardians v. Hickman*, 308 P.3d 1201, 1205–07 (Ariz. App. 2013), which said the grazers' ability to monitor and protect the land and previous good stewardship of the property outweighed WildEarth's higher bid (which would have resulted in $79,344 additional rent over what the grazers were willing to pay over the 10-year lease period).

2.   *Enforcing Statehood Act promises.* The U.S. Supreme Court has ruled that statehood act promises of obtaining "full value" for state school lands are enforceable. *Lassen v. Arizona Highway Dept.*, 385 U.S. 458 (1967). Enforceability of Statehood Act promises is a largely overlooked area of natural resources law. See Erin Pounds, *State Trust Lands: Static Management and Shifting Value Perspectives*, 41 Envtl. L. 1333 (2011).

3.   *Managing state lands for conservation.* In *Branson School Dist. v. Romer*, 161 F.3d 619 (10th Cir. 1998), the court upheld an initiative that revised the provision in the state constitution governing school lands. The initiative placed some 300,000 acres under a "stewardship trust" to enhance "beauty, natural values, open space, and wildlife habitat." According to the

court the initiative was not facially inconsistent with the state's duties under its federal statehood act to manage lands solely to support schools.

C. TIMBER HARVESTING

Federal management of national forests began in 1891 when Congress authorized the President to reserve forested land from settlement and haphazard timber harvesting. Six years later, in the 1897 Organic Act, 16 U.S.C. §§ 473 *et seq.*, Congress required national forests to be managed for timber production and watershed preservation. *Id.* § 475. In 1905, Gifford Pinchot persuaded the conservationist President Theodore Roosevelt to transfer jurisdiction over the national forests from the Department of the Interior to a newly created Forest Service in the Department of Agriculture, where it has remained ever since—and also to appoint Pinchot as the first Chief of the Forest Service.

Under Pinchot and his successors, the agency gained a reputation for professionalism and practiced a utilitarian version of "multiple use, sustained yield," later codified by Congress in the Multiple-Use Sustained-Yield Act of 1960. 16 U.S.C. §§ 528–31. Pinchot's assertion of regulatory authority was ratified by the Supreme Court in *United States v. Grimaud*, 220 U.S. 506 (1911) (affirming the Forest Service's authority to regulate grazing); and *Light v. United States*, 220 U.S. 523 (1911) (ruling that Forest Service regulation preempted conflicting state laws).

Beginning in the 1920s, under the influence of foresters like Aldo Leopold and Arthur Carhart, the agency set aside some national forest land for preservation. Much of this land is today in the national wilderness system. In fact, timber harvesting on the national forests was not widespread in the years before World War II because of relatively low demand and competition from private timber lands; consequently, the Forest Service acted as more of a custodian than a promoter of timber harvests. However, the housing boom after the war caused timber harvests on national forests to accelerate dramatically throughout the 1950s and 1960s. This heavy logging drew the attention of the nascent environmental movement, which filed a suit alleging that the clearcut timber practices commonplace on national forests violated the provisions of the 1897 Organic Act. When the Fourth Circuit affirmed a trial court injunction on clearcutting in the Monongahela National Forest in *West Virginia Div. of Izaak Walton League of America v. Butz,* 522 F.2d 945 (4th Cir. 1975) (the Monongahela decision), and a federal court in Alaska followed suit in *Zieske v. Butz*, 406 F.Supp. 258 (D. Alaska 1975), the Forest Service and the timber industry turned to Congress to repeal pertinent provisions of the 1897 Act. Although they succeeded, the resulting legislation—the National Forest Management Act (NFMA) of 1976, 16 U.S.C. §§ 1600 *et seq.*—did much more than simply reinstate clearcutting.

NFMA promised a new era of forest management. The statute, among its other provisions, 1) required that harvested forest lands be physically and economically suitable for harvesting; 2) subjected clearcutting to several conditions, including that the Forest Service determine it to be the "optimum method" of harvest and be consistent with both land plans and number of environmental conditions, particularly watershed protection; and 3) required the protection of wildlife diversity. NFMA also required the Forest Service to prepare land plans for all national forests, to which all Forest Service actions—like conducting timber sales and constructing roads—must be consistent.

Litigation over timber harvests on national forest lands has involved both NFMA and NEPA (the National Environmental Policy Act). An important ruling was handed down in *Lands Council v. McNair,* 537 F.3d 981 (9th Cir. 2008), dealing with the requirement that national forest land-plans be adequate to sustain the "diversity" of species in the forst. A unanimous Ninth Circuit sitting en banc concluded that the Forest Service was not obligated by this requirement to undertake site-specific analyses of the timber harvests that it approved—analyses that would entail detailed studies before every harvest—so long as it had in hand reasonable scientific proxy evidence for concluding that a proposed timber harvest satisfied the requirement. Requiring more of the agency would, the court ruled, involve courts in stricter review of agency science than anticipated by the Administrative Procedure Act's arbitrary and capricious standard of review. *Id.* at 997–98.

Land Council's legacy is evident in several recent decisions upholding Forest Service decisionmaking. These cases include *Biodiversity Conservation Alliance v. Jiron,* 762 F.3d 1036, 1080–83, 2014 WL 3827171, at *25–29 (10th Cir. Aug. 5, 2014) (deferring to Forest Service's species and grazing suitability analyses in a plan amendment); *Conservation Congress v. U.S. Forest Service,* No. 2:12–CV–02800–TLN–CKD, 2014 WL 2092385, at *12–14 (E.D. Cal. May 19, 2014) (upholding a forest plan's use of habitat capability models to estimate species populations); *Lands Council v. U.S. Forest Service,* No. CV–12–619–FVS–1, 2014 WL 31869, at *8 (E.D. Wash. Jan. 6, 2014) (Forest Service need not demonstrate sufficient habitat to maintain species viability in the project area, only sufficient habitat throughout the entire Umatilla National Forest as a whole); *Alliance for the Wild Rockies v. Weber,* 979 F.Supp.2d 1118, 1137–38 (D. Mont. 2013) (approving different size buffers to protect fish in the Flathead National Forest Pre-commercial Thinning Project); *Earth Island Institute v. U.S. Forest Service,* 697 F.3d 1010, 1013–19 (9th Cir. 2012) (the Lake Tahoe Forest Plan did not have to demonstrate at the post-fire project level that harvesting both live and dead trees would maintain viable species population levels).

The deferential review the *Lands Council* decision called for under NFMA did not involve judicial review under NEPA, which requires agencies to evaluate the anticipated environmental effects of their proposals and reasonable alternatives and disclose those effects in writing to the public and other agencies. NEPA has been at the center of many disputes over timber harvesting. In fact, most challenges to federal timber involve both NFMA and NEPA claims, including the principal case below.

1. CLEARCUTTING

Clearcutting (euphemistically referred to as "even-aged management" by the Forest Service), which helped give birth to NFMA, has continued to be controversial under the statute. Clearcutting is favored largely on economic grounds, including reducing the costs of building and maintaining roads. It allows shade-intolerant trees, like the economically valuable Douglas firs of the Pacific Northwest, to regenerate in direct sunlight (helped by herbicides) without competition from other species. However, even-aged management typically involves the planting of a single tree species (a monoculture) and has adverse effects on most wildlife, soil, and watershed conditions. NFMA was pretty clearly aimed at authorizing some clearcuts that were enjoined as a result of the *Monongahela* decision and related litigation, but the statute also imposed limits on clearcutting. It was permissible only when the Forest Service found it be the "optimum" harvest method, consistent with the applicable forest plan, and protective of soils, watersheds, fish and wildlife, and recreational and esthetic resources. 16 U.S.C. § 1604(g)(3)(F). Just how restrictive of clearcutting NFMA's drafters intended these provisions to be has been the subject of considerable litigation.

Clearcutting has been especially controversial in eastern national forests, which acquired lands under the Weeks Act of 1911, 16 U.S.C. § 515, and often are composed of discontinuous tracts interspersed with non-federal lands Clearcutting was also the subject of the dispute in Montana that led to the decision below.

HAPNER V. TIDWELL
Ninth Circuit Court of Appeals
621 F.3d 1239 (2010)

[The Forest Service's Smith Creek Project in the Gallatin National Forest, adjacent to Yellowstone National Park, aimed to reduce the risk of wildfires and insect infestations and to promote wildlife habitat diversity (mostly for elk and cutthroat trout) by logging up to 810 acres and authorizing prescribed burning of another 300 acres. The project was roughly 35 miles north of Livingston, Montana, close to a residential area. One motivation for the project was to reduce fire intensity that could threaten nearby residences. The area had been previously logged, resulting in road construction, soil disturbance, and riparian damage. Historically, the area also experienced large-scale wildfires. The proposed logging would remove conifers to promote growth of aspen trees and would thin other areas, so that the conifer density would be reduced to approximately 300–500 trees per acre, down from up to 3,000 trees per acre. Environmentalists alleged violations of both the National Environmental Policy Act (NEPA) and the National Forest Management Act (NFMA). The federal District of Montana granted summary judgment for the Service on all of the plaintiffs' claims, and the environmentalists appealed.]

W. FLETCHER, J.

* * *

A.   *Plaintiffs' Claims Under NEPA*

NEPA is a purely procedural statute, intended to protect the environment by fostering informed agency decision-making. . . . "As a preliminary step, the agency may prepare an Environmental Assessment (EA) to determine whether the environmental impact of the proposed action is significant enough to warrant an EIS [environmental impact statement]." *High Sierra Hikers Ass'n v. Blackwell,* 390 F.3d 630, 639–40 (9th Cir. 2004) (citing 40 C.F.R. § 1508.9). An EA must include "brief discussions" of the need for the proposal, of reasonable alternatives, and of the anticipated environmental impacts. See 40 C.F.R. § 1508.9(b).

1.   *Effect on Wildfires*

Plaintiffs argue that the Service violated NEPA by failing to address scientific debate concerning whether forest thinning actually reduces wildfire intensity. A failure in an EA to "discuss and consider" evidence contrary to the Service's position suggests that the Service "did not take the requisite 'hard look' at the environmental consequences" of its proposed action. *Blue Mountains Biodiversity Project v. Blackwood,* 161 F.3d 1208, 1213 (9th Cir. 1998).

This case is different from those in which courts have identified significant controversies as to the efficacy of the Service's proposed methods. In *Sierra Club v. Eubanks,* 335 F.Supp.2d 1070, 1074, 1077–78 (E.D. Cal. 2004), the Service failed to respond to scientific studies showing that its activities would increase fire risk and, instead, relied on studies that did not actually support its position. In *Sierra Club v. Bosworth,* 199 F.Supp.2d 971, 979–80 (N.D. Cal. 2002), the literature review that accompanied the EIS included a report that called into question the Service's methodology, but that the EIS failed to disclose or analyze.

In this case, the EA acknowledges the limits of the benefits that would be provided by the Project. The EA does not claim that the Project would eliminate wildfires in the area altogether, but merely that it would reduce potential fire severity, in particular crown fires. The EA explains that limiting crown fires would enhance firefighter and public safety by reducing the average rate of fire spread from 1 to 3 miles per hour to 0.1 to 0.5 miles per hour. The Service's risk reduction calculations are supported by studies conducted in other regions, as well as by extensive modeling.

We therefore affirm the district court's grant of summary judgment to the Service on this claim.

2. *Global Warming*

Plaintiffs argue that the Service violated NEPA by failing to discuss global warming in the EA. The Service's decision to implement a project is arbitrary and capricious under NEPA if an EA or EIS "entirely failed to consider an important aspect of the problem." *Lands Council v. McNair,* 537 F.3d 981, 987 (9th Cir. 2008) (en banc). However, the Service is only required to focus on the issues "that are truly significant to the action in question." 40 C.F.R. § 1500.1(b). Also, "[i]mpacts shall be discussed in proportion to their significance." 40 C.F.R. § 1502.2(b).

Plaintiffs point out that global warming has been recognized by courts as an issue of national importance. See *Massachusetts v. EPA,* 549 U.S. 497, 521 (2007); *Ctr. for Biological Diversity v. Nat'l Highway Traffic Safety Admin.,* 538 F.3d 1172, 1221–24 (9th Cir. 2008). They also point out that the Deputy Chief for the National Forest System has issued a guidance document directing the Service to incorporate climate change analysis into its evaluations of projects. That guidance document suggests, for example, that a qualitative discussion of climate change would be necessary in an EA for a proposal to underburn 30,000 acres of ponderosa pine stands. It states, however, that proposals require no discussion if they are of a "minor scale [so] that the direct effects would be meaningless." The Project involves a relatively small amount of land and it will thin rather than clear cut trees. Further, we note that the Service addressed comments regarding climate change in its December 2007 notice of final decision.

We therefore conclude that the EA adequately considered the Project's impact on global warming in proportion to its significance.

* * *

B. *Plaintiffs' Claims under NFMA*

NFMA imposes procedural and substantive requirements on the Service's management of national forests. Procedurally, NFMA requires the Service to develop and maintain forest resource management plans.

See *Ecology Ctr. v. Castaneda,* 574 F.3d 652, 656 (9th Cir. 2009) (citing 16 U.S.C. § 1604(a)). After a forest plan is adopted, all subsequent agency actions must comply with that plan. *Id.* The Gallatin National Forest Plan is the relevant forest plan in this case. Substantively, NFMA requires that the forest plans adopted by the Service provide certain protections, such as protection of forest habitat and diversity of wildlife. See 16 U.S.C. § 1604(g)(3).

* * *

2.   *Old Growth Indicator Species*

The Gallatin Plan requires that designated management indicator species (MIS) "be monitored to determine population changes." The designated MIS for the habitat impacted by the Project are the northern goshawk and pine marten. Plaintiffs argue that the Service violated the Gallatin Plan, and therefore NFMA, by failing to monitor northern goshawk and pine marten. They also argue that the Service violated NFMA by not accurately determining the effect of the Project on those species. We reject both arguments.

The EA identifies a number of efforts to monitor the populations of both the northern goshawk and the pine marten in the region. Montana conducts annual studies of pine marten population trends that look at snow tracks of the birds. The studies have detected an average of 75 pine martens per 100 "transect miles" in southwest Montana over a ten-year period. A recent Service study on species viability in the Gallatin Forest concluded that habitat to support the pine marten is abundant in the Project area. The Service has also conducted habitat surveys and population monitoring for northern goshawks in the Gallatin Forest. The Service relied in its EA on several independent surveys concluding that goshawk viability is not a concern. One 2005 study involved a "systematic random survey" that "showed that the goshawk is relatively common and well-distributed in the Northern Region." Another study from 2005 concluded that "short-term viability of the goshawk in the Northern Region is not an issue."

In evaluating the effect of the Project on MIS populations, the Service appropriately relied on management of the species' habitat as a proxy for management of the species themselves. In *Lands Council,* 537 F.3d at 996, we approved "of the Forest Service's use of the amount of suitable habitat for a particular species as a proxy for the viability of that species." We concluded that such a method was appropriate even where the Service is taking actions that "will disturb some suitable habitat." *Id.* at 999.

We review the Service's application of the proxy approach under the arbitrary and capricious standard. *Id.* at 997–98. The Service "must both describe the quantity and quality of habitat that is necessary to sustain the viability of the species in question and explain its methodology for measuring this habitat." *Id.* at 998. We conclude that the Service's reliance on habitat as proxy in this case was not arbitrary and capricious. In the EA, the Service adequately demonstrated a "knowledge of what quality and quantity of habitat is necessary to support the species," and its "method for measuring the existing amount of habitat [was] reasonably reliable and accurate." *Lands Council,* 537 F.3d at 998–99. The EA describes in detail the habitat necessary for the viability of both the pine marten and the goshawk. It adequately describes existing habitat in the Gallatin Forest and the Project area, as well as the Project's limited effect on the habitat's ability to sustain MIS. Further, the EA provides for substantial mitigation measures to ensure that a nest is not disturbed in the unlikely event that one is located during implementation of the Project. The Service reasonably concluded that sufficient habitat currently exists for both species and that the Project would have "[n]o direct effects on the pine marten," and "little, if any, direct [e]ffect on goshawks."

Plaintiffs nonetheless argue that the Service's methodology for measuring existing habitat was flawed because the Service failed to adequately field-verify old growth stands. The Service conducted extensive examinations of stands in the field in the 1980s, as well as additional subsequent field verification. The Service is not required to use on-the-ground verification so long as alternative methodologies are reliable. "To always require a particular type of proof that a project would maintain a species' population in a specific area would inhibit the Forest Service from conducting projects in the National Forests." *Lands Council,* 537 F.3d at 997. The Service used multiple databases containing old growth stand information and multiple methods to verify its old growth information in the Project area. This analysis led the Service to predict a range of between 21.7% and 29.3% old growth in Gallatin Forest, with a 90% confidence interval, which places the old growth area well above the 10% minimum required by the Gallatin Plan.

We therefore conclude that the Service's conclusion that the Project would comply with the Gallatin Plan's monitoring requirements is not arbitrary and capricious.

* * *

5.   *Elk Cover*

Plaintiffs' single meritorious argument on appeal concerns the Gallatin Plan's elk-cover requirement. The Gallatin Forest Plan requires that the Service "[m]aintain at least two thirds of the hiding cover associated with key habitat components over time. Subsequent timber sale activity will be allowed after regeneration provides hiding cover." Elk are designated in the Plan as an indicator species of the Gallatin National

Forest, for which two-thirds hiding cover must be maintained. Plaintiffs argue that the Project violates the Plan because it would reduce elk cover to under two thirds. We agree.

In preparing the EA, the Service did not measure elk cover according to the definition provided in the Gallatin Plan. The Gallatin Plan defines elk cover as "[v]egetation, primarily trees, capable of hiding 90 percent of an elk seen from a distance of 200 feet or less." In the EA, the Service relied on two separate measurements of elk cover. One calculation of cover was based on the current prevalence of various tree classifications in the Project area. The Service measured 70–90% elk cover under this definition but does not explain what percent cover this translates to under the Plan definition. The other calculation suggested 62% elk cover under a canopy cover definition. According to a table in the Helena National Forest Plan, 60% elk cover as measured under the canopy cover definition translates to 42% elk cover as measured under the Gallatin Plan definition. The Project therefore violates the Gallatin Plan's two-thirds elk-cover requirement. The Service's failure to measure elk cover as defined by the Gallatin Plan renders us "unable to determine from the record that the agency is complying with the forest plan standard." *Native Ecosystems Council v. U.S. Forest Serv.,* 418 F.3d 953, 962 (9th Cir. 2005).

The Service argues that the Gallatin Forest Plan does not require that elk cover exceed 67% at all times, but only that any Service action retain two thirds of then-existing elk cover. The Service claims, in other words, that the Plan prohibits only timber sales that would reduce now-existing elk cover by more than 33%. The Service bases its argument on the wording of the Plan, which requires the Service to maintain "two thirds of the hiding cover" as opposed to merely "two thirds hiding cover." Because the Project would reduce now-existing elk cover by less than 33% under any measure, the Service claims that the Project complies with the Gallatin Plan.

"Agencies are entitled to deference to their interpretation of their own regulations, including Forest Plans." *Native Ecosystems Council,* 418 F.3d at 960. "[W]e have effectively treated forest plan directives as equivalent to federal regulations adopted under the APA [Administrative Procedure Act], deferring to the Forest Service's interpretation of plan directives that are susceptible to more than one meaning unless the interpretation is plainly erroneous or inconsistent with the directive." *Siskiyou Reg'l Educ. Project v. U.S. Forest Serv.,* 565 F.3d 545, 554–55 & n. 9 (9th Cir. 2009) (citing *Auer v. Robbins,* 519 U.S. 452, 461 (1997)). But the Service's interpretation of the elk-cover requirement in the Plan is plainly erroneous. The Plan requires that the two-thirds cover be maintained "over time." It further provides that "[s]ubsequent timber sale activity will be allowed after regeneration provides hiding cover." The Service's interpretation would allow iterative Service actions to whittle elk cover down to nearly nothing so long as each individual action removed only 33% of then-existing cover.

Alternatively, the Service argues that even if the Project violates the Gallatin Plan's elk-cover requirement, the error is harmless given the large elk populations in the Project area. But "[i]t is well-settled that the Forest Service's failure to comply with the provisions of a Forest Plan is a violation of NFMA." *Native Ecosystems Council,* 418 F.3d at 961. "If the Forest Service thinks any provision . . . of the Plan is no longer relevant, the agency should propose amendments to the . . . Plan altering its standards, in a process complying with NEPA and NFMA." *Id.* Although current elk populations may meet or exceed Montana objectives, those objectives cannot replace federal management objectives. . . .

We therefore conclude that the Service has violated the Gallatin Plan, and NFMA, by not ensuring that the Project complies with the current Gallatin Plan elk-cover requirement. . . .

NOTES

1. *Plan consistency.* Section 6(i) of NFMA, 16 U.S.C. § 1604(i), which proved to be determinative in this case, requires all Forest Service actions to be consistent with applicable forest plans.

2. *Ripeness and forest plans.* In *Hapner,* the Ninth Circuit cited *Ohio Forestry Ass'n v. Sierra Club,* 523 U.S. 726 (1998), in which the Supreme Court reviewed an environmentalist challenge to a new land plan for the Wayne National Forest in Ohio. The plan opened up areas to timber harvesting and clearcutting and expressed a preference for clear-cutting. In a unanimous opinion, the Supreme Court decided that the environmental challenge was not ripe for judicial review because the forest plan as such, without further agency action, did not expressly authorize any timber harvests; it merely opened up parts of the planning area to possible harvests in the future. The Court did suggest, however, that a land plan that opened up areas to, say, immediate off-road vehicle use would be justiciable. *Id.* at 738–39. Moreover, Justice Breyer's opinion for the Court indicated that a challenge to the environmental impact statement that accompanied the new land plan *was* ripe for challenge because the failure to comply with NEPA procedures would produce immediate injury. *Id.* at 737. So, it seems that bifurcated judicial review is the result: NEPA challenges are ripe upon land plan promulgation; NFMA challenges are ripe only when the agency takes an implementing action, like making a timber sale.

3. *Forest Service planning regulations.* The regulations governing Forest Service land plans have long been controversial, particularly with respect the NFMA's species diversity requirement. 16 U.S.C § 1604(g)(3)(B) (requiring forest plans to "provide for diversity of plant and animal communities based on the suitability and capability of the specific land area in order to meet overall multiple-use objectives. . . .") The 1982 regulations

interpreted the statutory provisions to require the agency to "maintain viable populations" of wildlife species. 36 C.F.R. § 219.12 (1982).

After the Clinton Administration interpreted the statute's species diversity provision to require forest plans to give primacy to ecological sustainability, 65 Fed. Reg. 67,514, 67,546 (Nov. 9, 2000), the Bush Administration reversed course in 2005, rejecting the emphasis on ecological sustainability, eliminating the minimum viable population requirement, and also eliminating the requirement that revised forest plans warrant preparation of an EIS. 70 Fed. Reg. 1023 (Jan. 5, 2005) (referring to the changes as a "paradigm shift in land management planning"). However, the 2005 regulations were enjoined for violating NEPA, the Administrative Procedure Act (APA), and the Endangered Species Act (ESA) in *Citizens for Better Forestry v. U.S. Dep't of Agriculture*, 481 F.Supp.2d 1059 (N.D. Cal. 2007). The Bush Administration's attempt to cure these statutory violations was also unsuccessful, *Citizens for Better Forestry v. U.S. Dep't of Agriculture*, 632 F.Supp.2d 968 (N.D. Cal. 2009).

The Obama Administration finally revised the forest planning regulations in 2012, 77 Fed. Reg. 21,162 (Apr. 9, 2012), which dispensed with the attempt to eliminate EIS review from forest plans but replaced the minimum viable populations provision with more discretionary provisions. The announced purpose of the regulations was to "promote the ecological integrity of the national forests," 36 C.F.R. § 219.1 (2012), although the regulations defined sustainability in social and economic terms as well as ecological. *Id.* § 219.8. Similar to the 2000 regulations, the 2012 regulations include both ecosystem and species-specific approaches to maintaining diversity, although the latter are required only as a backup if the ecosystem approach proves insufficient. As the leading commentators explain:

> [T]he Forest Service chose to emphasize protection of "species of conservation concern" . . . [and] chose not to require designation of management indicator species (MIS) [the approach of the 1982 regulations] or the monitoring of their population trends. . . . The 2012 planning rules therefore replaced the obligation to monitor MIS with the duty to monitor focal species ["[a] small subset of species whose status permits inference to the integrity of the larger ecological system to which it belongs and provides meaningful information regarding the effectiveness of the plan in maintaining or restoring the ecological conditions to maintain the diversity of plant and animal communities in the plan area."]

> Compliance with the regulation's ecosystem requirements is designed to provide the ecological conditions needed to maintain the diversity of plant and animal communities and support the persistence of most native species in the plan area. Compliance with the species-specific requirements is designed to provide additional ecological conditions not otherwise provided through compliance with ecosystem-related requirements.

George C. Coggins & Robert L. Glicksman, 3 *Public Natural Resources Law* § 16:59 (2d ed. 2014).

Although the 2012 regulations eliminated the requirements of maintaining minimum viable wildlife populations and monitoring numbers of indicator species—thereby weakening wildlife protections—motorized recreationalists and commodity users challenged them for still being inconsistent with multiple use, the Forest Service Organic Act, NFMA, and the APA. *Federal Forest Resource Coalition v. Vilsack,* No. 1:12–CV–01333 (D.D.C. Dec. 13, 2012) (claiming that the regulations' goal of ecological sustainability is not authorized by NFMA). See also discussion below at pp. 775–776.

4.   *NEPA, connected actions, and cumulative effects.* The Council on Environmental Quality's (CEQ's) NEPA regulations require federal agencies to consider in their EIS's "connected actions," defined as actions that "are closely related and therefore should be discussed in the same impact statement," 40 C.F.R. § 1508.25(a)(1). In *Thomas v. Peterson,* 753 F.2d 754 (9th Cir. 1985), the court enjoined construction of a timber road in a roadless area for violating NEPA. The court ruled that the Forest Service had to consider the effects of both the road and ensuing timber sales because they were "connected actions" within the meaning of CEQ's NEPA regulations (40 C.F.R. § 1508.25(a)(1)), since they were "inextricably intertwined." 753 F.2d at 759. Moreover, the cumulative effects of the road building and logging had to be considered together in a single EIS before the road was built, since they would produce cumulative adverse effects from sediment deposits in streams and destruction of wolf habitat. The combined effect on the streams and the wildlife habitat met the EIS trigger of raising "substantial questions" as to whether the road and the timber sales might have significant cumulative environmental effects. *Id.* Therefore, the court refused to allow the Forest Service to defer consideration of the effects of timber harvesting until after the road was built. On an unrelated issue the Ninth Circuit also decided that NFMA did not require that the proceeds of anticipated timber sales be sufficient to cover the costs of the timber road, thereby allowing the agency discretion to proceed with so-called "below-cost" timber sales. *Id.* at 762.

ALLEGHENY DEFENSE PROJECT, INC. V. U.S. FOREST SERVICE

Third Circuit Court of Appeals
423 F.3d 215 (2005)

[The Allegheny Defense Project (ADP) challenged the so-called East Side Project in the Allegheny National Forest (ANF). The project plan relied heavily on clearcutting, fertilizers, and herbicides to encourage the harvesting and regeneration of black cherry timber, the most economically remunerative tree species in the forest. ADP claimed the project violated the National Forest Management Act's (NFMA) provision proscribing the selection of a harvest method solely because of economics. The district court upheld the Forest Service's project, and ADP appealed.]

McKEE, J.

* * *

[I]n 1976, Congress enacted the NFMA, 16 U.S.C. §§ 1604, *et seq.* . . .

The NFMA . . . requires that the regulations issued by the Secretary of Agriculture include:

(3) . . . guidelines for land management plans developed to achieve the goals of the Program which—

* * *

(D) permit increases in harvest levels based on intensified management practices, such as reforestation, thinning, and tree improvement . . .

(E) insure that timber will be harvested from National Forest System lands only where—

(iv) the harvesting system to be used is not selected primarily because it will give the greatest dollar return or the greatest unit output of timber; and

(F) insure that clearcutting, seed tree cutting, shelterwood cutting, and other cuts designed to regenerate an even-aged stand of timber will be used as a cutting method on National Forest System lands only where—

(I) for clearcutting, it is determined to be the optimum method, and for other such cuts, it is determined to be appropriate, to meet the objectives and requirements of the relevant land management plan.

16 U.S.C. § 1604(g).

* * *

II. *Discussion*

* * *

C. *Alleged Deficiencies of the East Side Project*

ADP's main contention is that the Forest Service's decision to use even-aged harvesting combined with fertilizer and herbicide, and fencing, violates the APA [Administrative Procedure Act] and the NFMA "because it seeks primarily to achieve the highest dollar return by . . . emphasizing the logging and regeneration of black cherry timber, which is by far the most commercially valuable species in the Allegheny." ADP also contends that the Forest Service incorrectly determined that the even-aged logging authorized by the Project was "appropriate" and the clearcutting "optimal" when that logging was authorized primarily to give the greatest dollar return. The numerous factors ADP cites to support that position include:

- In its summary judgment brief, the Forest Service asserted that the ROD [record of decision] adopted the recommendations of the Northeastern Forest Experimental Station as set forth in the Marquis manuscript. [T]he manuscript states that it is designed primarily as a guidebook for practicing foresters whose goal is timber production. Also, the Magistrate Judge found that the object of the manuscript "was to produce the maximum profit from even-aged management."

* * *

- In its response to ADP's administrative appeal of the ROD, the Forest Service noted that more uneven-aged logging was not included because it would not regenerate black cherry. Additionally, the Forest Service explained that fertilizer would be applied to encourage more black cherry and not because the forest's soils were otherwise depleted.

ADP also maintains that the Forest Service's explanations for why it selected the particular silvicultural techniques are merely pretextual since "none of these justifications can even begin to explain the East Side Decision's overwhelming preference for even-aged logging and the accompanying techniques." For example, according to ADP:

- The Forest Service cannot justify its choice of silvicultural techniques by relying on the assertion that the success of uneven-aged management is uncertain since, according to the Magistrate Judge, uneven-aged management could work if it was supported by the same supplemental management—herbicides and fencing. . . .

- Health concerns also cannot justify the Forest Service's silvicultural practices since (1) thousands of acres that will be subjected to the Forest Service's management scheme are quite healthy and are not threatened by disease, and (2) even-aged management creates stands with their own health problems, including specific threats to the health of black cherry trees such as the Cherry Scallop Moth and Ground Level Ozone caused by pollution.

- The Forest Service's argument that it chose even-aged management to maintain diversity is not supported by the record. According to ADP, even-aged management would result in the least amount of old growth habitat, the highest amount of soil compaction, the lowest amount of standing dead and lying dead trees for wildlife habitat, the highest acreage of forest with more than 30% stocking of interfering ferns and grasses, and the lowest acreage of forest with an intact mid-story of all alternatives. Conversely, according to ADP, simply not logging or using more uneven-aged harvesting techniques would create the most diversity in the ANF.

* * *

D.   *Analysis*

The Forest Service maintains that the East Side Project is consistent with NFMA's prohibition against selecting a harvesting system primarily because it will give the greatest dollar return. We agree. Although it is beyond serious contention that the Forest Service considered the economic benefits of generating black cherry stands in structuring the Project, economic concerns may be considered under the Organic Act, MUSYA [Multiple-Use Sustained-Yield Act,] and NFMA. Indeed, Congress has mandated consideration of economic factors. See § 1604(g)(3)(A). . . . However, the record does not support ADP's claim that economic considerations were paramount or determinative in the Forest Service's selection of appropriate forest management techniques for the Project.

"When a party challenges agency action as arbitrary and capricious the reasonableness of the agency's action is judged in accordance with its stated reasons." *In re: Comptroller of the Currency,* 156 F.3d 1279 (D.C. Cir. 1998). . . . Here, the voluminous record illustrates that the Forest Service's decision to utilize even-aged management in MA [Management Area] 3 was not arbitrary and capricious. Rather, the record shows that decision was based on a thorough analysis of a variety of both economic and non-economic factors. As the ROD explains, the overall purpose of the Project is the implementation of the Forest Plan by "maintain[ing] and restor[ing] healthy and resilient watersheds and ecosystems." In order to do this, the Forest Service must initiate reforestation treatments, establish tree seedlings, improve the horizontal and vertical diversity in the ecosystem, regulate stocking and species composition, supply forest products to meet public demand and to contribute to the economic vitality of local communities, and restore wildlife habitat.

* * *

The ROD also documents why the Forest Service chose Alternative 1 (emphasizing even-aged management) over Alternative 4 (emphasizing uneven-aged management). The reasons include the following: (1) even-aged harvesting better achieves the desired future condition in MA 3 of Allegheny hardwoods because such shade-intolerant species regenerate better with larger forest opening; (2) several of the shade-tolerant tree species are experiencing decline or disease, and uneven-aged management could result in greater susceptibility to insect and disease outbreaks; (3) uneven-aged management is less cost effective; and (4) there are general uncertainties as to whether uneven-aged management could meet the needs of the Plan. Additional non-economic reasons for selecting Alternative 1 include the fact that: (1) clearcutting is the optimum method for maintaining aspen due to its intolerance for shade; (2) even-aged management provides abundant sunlight enabling seedlings to quickly grow out of the reach of deer; and (3) even-aged management improves age-class distribution, increases species diversity and moves the project toward the desired future forest condition for the various MAs.

ADP stresses the fact that even-aged management tends to increase the amount of black cherry, and we realize that black cherry is a very profitable species. Nevertheless, we cannot accept the inference that the Forest Service reached this result primarily because of the economic rewards endemic in even-aged management given the conditions in the ANF. . . .

The record demonstrates that the Forest Service's emphasis on black cherry is not based on the value of the tree alone. Black cherry also has numerous environmental benefits, including its superior resilience to drought, deer, and pests such as insects. The Forest Service is surely not required to ignore these benefits merely because black cherry has the additional benefit of its commercial value. Accordingly, we cannot conclude that the Forest Service's choice of silvicultural practices, which emphasized the regeneration of black cherry, was based primarily on financial concerns. Although ADP may disagree with the Forest Service's decision to manage MA 3 through even-aged harvesting, this disagreement is insufficient to establish that the Forest Service's choice of Alternative 1 was arbitrary, capricious, or an abuse of discretion. . . .

NOTES

1.   *Clearcutting in the southern pine forests.* The southern pine forests of east Texas have some of the remaining habitat of the red-cockaded woodpecker, listed under the Endangered Species Act largely because its habitat has been lost due to logging. The Sierra Club fought a decades-long battle over clearcutting on four national forests in east Texas, claiming that the clearcutting violated NFMA's provision limiting clearcutting to where it could be carried out "in a manner consistent with the protection of soil, watershed, fish, wildlife, recreation, and esthetic resources, and the

regeneration of the timber resource" (16 U.S.C. § 1604(g)(3)(F)(v)). A district court ruled that the provision limited clearcutting to exceptional circumstances, but the Fifth Circuit reversed in *Sierra Club v. Espy*, 38 F.3d 792, 799 (5th Cir. 1994) (deciding that clearcutting was not an exception to a general rule of selective harvesting, but instructing the Forest Service to "proceed cautiously in implementing [clearcutting] and only after a close examination of the effects that such management will have on other forest resources").

After the dispute returned to the district court, that court concluded that the clearcutting failed to satisfy a number of NFMA standards, including protection of "soil, slope, [and] watershed conditions [from] irreversibl[e] damage" (16 U.S.C. § 1604(g)(3)(E)(i)) and issued an injunction, but after the Fifth Circuit initially upheld the injunction, an en banc panel reversed on the ground that the Forest Service did not actually have forest-wide clearcutting programs in the east Texas forests. *Sierra Club v. Peterson*, 228 F.3d 559 (5th Cir. 2000). Presumably, however, individual timber sales involving clearcuts could still violate NFMA's provisions. See *Neighbors of Cuddy Mountain v. Alexander*, 303 F.3d 1059 (9th Cir. 2002) (allowing a challenge to an individual timber sale, even though the remedy was a programmatic change).

2.   *Challenging forest plans*. One of the hallmarks of NFMA is the requirement that all national forests have forest plans, which the Forest Service refers to as "land and resource management plans" (LRMPs). These plans govern all activities on national forest lands. 16 U.S.C. § 1604(d). LRMPs, which last up to fifteen years, are approved only after extensive public involvement, including NEPA compliance. *Id.* § 1604(f)(5), 36 C.F.R. § 219.7(c)(1). They identify areas suitable for, among other things, timber harvesting, recreational areas, and wilderness study and must protect soils, watersheds, and fish and wildlife. *Id.* §§ 1604(g), (k).

Public challenges to LRMPs became materially more difficult after the Supreme Court's decision in *Ohio Forestry Ass'n v. Sierra Club*, 523 U.S. 726 (1998), discussed above at pp. 689, 767, which ruled that challenges to approved plans were not ripe for judicial review unless there were immediate, concrete injuries that made the plan justiciable. Thus, a plan which opened up an area to timber harvesting would not be actionable until the Forest Service proposed specific timber sales. Curiously, however, the Court allowed public challenges to NEPA compliance to proceed at the time of LRMP approval, *id.* at 737 ("a person with standing who is injured by a failure to comply with the NEPA procedure may complain of that failure at the time the failure takes place, for the claim can never get riper"), creating a bifurcated system of judicial forest plan review.

One prominent recent legacy of *Ohio Forestry* was *U.S. Forest Service v. Pacific Rivers Council*, 689 F.3d 1012 (9th Cir. 2012), which ruled that a 2004 framework plan for eleven national forests in the Sierra Nevada Mountains, covering 11.5 million acres (more than 5% of Forest Service-managed land)— which significantly modified a 2001 framework plan by tripling the amount of acres available for timber harvesting, allowing the cutting of larger trees near streams, and substantially increasing road building and grazing—failed to satisfy NFMA by adequately considering the effects of the amendments on several species of fish. The 2001 Clinton Administration plan, prepared after over a decade of study, sought to ensure the ecological sustainability of the forests, but the 2004 Bush Administration plan significantly altered course, claiming that increased harvests were necessary to combat wildfire threats and to reduce economic effects on local communities. The environmentalists claimed that, because the 2004 plan opened up sensitive ecosystems, the plan was ripe for challenge and violated NEPA by failing to consider the effects of the plan on several fish and amphibian species.

The Ninth Circuit enjoined implementation of the 2004 plan, agreeing that the Forest Service violated NEPA by failing to consider the effects on fish. But after the Supreme Court granted *certiorari* to review the decision on NEPA standing and ripeness grounds as well as NFMA, the environmental plaintiffs sought and received from the Court an order dismissing the case and vacating the lower court decision, which they had won. 133 S.Ct. 2843 (2013). Thus, the 2004 framework plan and its call for increased timber harvesting in the Sierra Nevada remain in effect. See Hope M. Babcock, *Dismissal of the Certiorari Petition in Pacific Rivers Council: A Bullet Dodged in the Supreme Court's War Against Public Challenges to Flawed Federal Land Use Planning*, 32 Va. Envtl. L.J. 226 (2014) (explaining that environmentalists sought to avoid the Court's endorsing federal government arguments for imposing heightened standing and ripeness requirements as well as expanded agency deference to regulations). The dismissal also left intact, at least for a while, *Ohio Forestry*'s bifurcated judicial review in which NEPA challenges to forest plan EISs are ripe for challenge prior to NFMA challenges to the plans themselves.

2. DIVERSITY OF PLANT AND ANIMAL SPECIES

Section 6(g)(3)(B) of NFMA requires Forest Service plans to "provide for diversity of plant and animal communities . . . to meet overall multiple use objectives, and . . . provide, where appropriate, to the degree practicable, for steps to be taken to preserve the diversity of tree species. . . ." 16 U.S.C § 1604(g)(3)(B). Until 2012 (as noted above on pp. 768–769), Forest Service regulations required the identification of "indicator species" as proxies for the health of other species. The 2012 planning regulations eliminated its previous interpretation that the statute required maintenance of "viable populations" of plant and animal species. The new regulations emphasized instead what were termed "focal species"—a smaller subset of species that would become the focus of management if and when the statutory duty to protect species diversity was not satisfied through the Service's efforts to achieve broader ecosystem diversity goals. 77 Fed. Reg. 21,162 (Apr. 9, 2012). The Forest Service claimed that the new rule would impose procedures that are "adaptive and science-based, engage the public, and are designed to be efficient and effective" (as opposed to the previous rules which were "too complex, costly, lengthy, and cumbersome"). *Id.* at 21,164. But some critics claimed the new rule "significantly weakens longstanding protections for fish and wildlife resources on national forests." See Center for Biological Diversity, *Obama's Forest Service Weakens Protections for Wildlife on National Forests* (Mar. 23, 2012, press release), available at http://www.biologicaldiversity.org. The complex rule contained a regulatory preamble of 116 pages explaining its contents and the issues raised by commentators.

Implementation of the statute's diversity provision, no doubt a prominent source of the Forest Service's claim about "complex, costly, lengthy, and cumbersome" procedures, has been the subject of a considerable amount of litigation, including the following early ruling.

SIERRA CLUB V. MARITA
Seventh Circuit Court of Appeals
46 F.3d 606 (1995)

[The Sierra Club challenged two Forest Service land plans in northern Wisconsin, one that emphasized large diameter hardwood harvests, another that emphasized recreation, saw-timber, and aspen management. The Sierra Club maintained that the National Forest Management Act's (NFMA) diversity directive required the agency to manage the entire forest, as a single whole, in accordance with the newly embraced principles of the science of conservation biology. Those principles called for large forest tracts, unbroken by timber harvesting, connected by wooded corridors (also unbroken) that supplied protected routes for forest-dwelling wildlife to move among the major habitats. The district court rejected the claim that this science was sufficiently dominant that the Forest Service lacked discretion to manage its lands in any other way. The environmentalists appealed.]

FLAUM, J.

* * *

The Sierra Club argues that the diversity statute and regulations . . . required the Service to consider and apply certain principles of conservation biology in developing the forest plan[s]. These principles, the Sierra Club asserts, dictate that diversity is not comprehensible solely through analysis of the numbers of plants and animals and the variety of species in a given area. Rather, diversity also requires an understanding of the relationships between differing landscape patterns and among various habitats. That understanding, the Sierra Club says, has led to the prediction that the size of a habitat—the "patch size"—tends to affect directly the survival of the habitat and the diversity of plant and animal species within that habitat.

A basic generalization of conservation biology is that smaller patches of habitat will not support life as well as one larger patch of that habitat, even if the total area of the smaller patches equals the total area of the large patch. This generalization derives from a number of observations and predictions. First, whereas a large-scale disturbance will wipe out many populations in a smaller patch, those in a larger patch have a better chance of survival. Second, smaller patches are subject to destruction through "edge effects." Edge effects occur when one habitat's environment suffers because it is surrounded by different type of habitat. Given basic geometry, among other factors, the smaller the patch size of the surrounded habitat, the greater the chance that a surrounding habitat will invade and devastate the surrounded habitat. Third, the more isolated similar habitats are from one another, the less chance organisms can migrate from one habitat to another in the event of a local disturbance. Consequently, fewer organisms will survive such a disturbance and diversity will decline. This third factor is known as the theory of "island biogeography." Thus, the mere fact that a given area contains diverse habitats does not ensure diversity at all; a "fragmented forest" is a recipe for ecological trouble. On the basis of these submissions, the Sierra Club desires us to rule that

> [t]o perform a legally adequate hard look at the environmental consequences of landscape manipulation across the hundreds of thousands of hectares of a National Forest, a federal agency must apply in some reasonable fashion the ecological principles identified by well accepted conservation biology. Species-by-species techniques are simply no longer enough. Ecology must be applied in the analysis, and it will be used as a criterion for the substantive results.

As a way of putting conservation biology into practice, the Sierra Club suggested that large blocks of land (at least 30,000 to 50,000 acres per block), so-called "Diversity Maintenance Areas" (DMAs), be set aside in each of the forests. The Sierra Club proposed and mapped three DMAs for the Nicolet and two for the Chequamegon. In these areas, which would have included about 25% of each forest, habitats were to be undisturbed by new roads, timber sales, or wildlife openings. Neither forest plan, however, ultimately contained a DMA; the Chequamegon Forest Supervisor initially did include two DMAs, but the Regional Forester removed them from the final Chequamegon plan.

The Sierra Club contends that the Service ignored its submissions, noting that the FEISs [final environmental impact statements] and RODs [records of decision] for both the Nicolet and the Chequamegon are devoid of reference to population dynamics, species turnover, patch size, recolonization problems, fragmentation problems, edge effects, and island biogeography. According to the Sierra Club, the Service simply disregarded extensive documentary and expert testimony, including over 100 articles and 13 affidavits, supporting the Sierra Club's assertions and thereby shirked its legal duties.

The Service replies that it correctly considered the implications of conservation biology for both the Nicolet and Chequamegon and appropriately declined to apply the science. The Service asserts that it duly noted the "concern [of the Sierra Club and others] that fragmentation of the . . . forest canopy through timber harvesting and road building is detrimental to certain plant and animal species." The Service decided that the theory had "not been applied to forest management in the Lake States" and that the subject was worthy of further study. However, the Service found in both cases that while the theories of conservation biology in general and of island biogeography in particular were "of interest, . . . there is not sufficient justification at this time to make research of the theory a Forest Service priority." Given its otherwise extensive analysis of diversity, as well as the deference owed its interpretation of applicable statutory and regulatory requirements, the Service contends that it clearly met all the "diversity" obligations imposed on it.

* * *

The Sierra Club's arguments regarding the inadequacy of the Service's plans and FEISs can be distilled into five basic allegations, each of which we address in turn. First, the Sierra Club asserts that the law "treats ecosystems and ecological relationships as a separately cognizable issue from the species by species concepts driving game and timber issues." The Sierra Club relies on the NFMA's diversity language to argue that the NFMA treats diversity in two distinct respects: diversity of plant and animal communities and diversity of tree species. See 16 U.S.C. § 1604(g)(3)(B). . . . The Sierra Club concludes from these statutes and regulations that the Service was obligated to apply an ecological approach to forest management and failed to do so. In the Sierra Club's view, MISs and population viability analyses present only half the picture, a picture that the addition of conservation biology would make complete.

The Sierra Club errs in these assertions because it sees requirements in the NFMA . . . that simply do not exist. The drafters of the NFMA diversity regulations themselves recognized that diversity was a complex term and declined to adopt any particular means or methodology of providing for diversity. . . . We agree with the district court that "[i]n view of the committee's decision not to prescribe a particular methodology and its failure to mention the principles that plaintiffs claim were by then well established, the court cannot fairly read those principles into the NFMA. . . ." Thus, conservation biology is not a necessary element of diversity analysis insofar as the regulations do not dictate that the service analyze diversity in any specific way.

Furthermore, the Sierra Club has overstated its case by claiming that MIS and population viability analyses do not gauge the diversity of ecological communities as required by the regulations. Except for those species to be monitored because they themselves are in danger, species are chosen to be on an MIS list precisely because they will indicate the effects management practices are having on a broader ecological community. Indeed, even if all that the Sierra Club has asserted about forest fragmentation and patch size and edge effects is true, an MIS should to some degree indicate their impact on diversity. See Report of the Committee of Scientists, 44 Fed. Reg. at 26,627 (noting that MIS are chosen "because they indicate the consequences of management on other species whose populations fluctuate in some measurable manner with the indicator species."). . . . The Sierra Club may have wished the Service to analyze diversity in a different way, but we cannot conclude on the basis of the records before us that the Service's methodology arbitrarily or capriciously neglected the diversity of ecological communities in the two forests.

In a second and related argument, the Sierra Club submits that the substantive law of diversity necessitated the set-aside of large, unfragmented habitats to protect at least some old-growth forest communities. . . . Diversity, the Sierra Club asserts, requires the Service to maintain a range of different, ecologically viable communities. Because it is simply not possible to ensure the survival of any old-growth forest communities without these large, undisturbed patches of land, the Service has therefore reduced diversity. The Service was thus bound to protect and enhance the natural forest or explain why other forest uses prevented the Service from doing so. The Sierra Club believes the Service did neither.

The Sierra Club asserts that the diversity regulations require a certain procedure and that because the substantive result of the Service's choices will produce, in the Sierra Club's view, results adverse to "natural forest" diversity, the Service has violated its mandate. However, as the Service points out, the regulations do not actually require the promotion of "natural forest" diversity but rather the promotion of diversity at least as great as that found in a natural forest. The Service maintains that it did provide for such diversity in the ways discussed above. Additionally, the Service did consider the maintenance of some old-growth forest, even though the Sierra Club disputes that the Service's efforts will have any positive effects. And to the extent the Service's final choice did not promote "natural diversity" above all else, the Service acted well within its regulatory discretion. See *Sierra Club v. Espy,* 38 F.3d 792, 800 (5th Cir. 1994) ("That [NFMA diversity] protection means something less than the preservation of the status quo but something more than eradication of species suggests that this is just the type of policy-oriented decision Congress wisely left to the discretion of the experts—here, the Forest Service."). . . .

* * *

[T]he Sierra Club contends that the rejection of its "high quality" science argument on the basis of "uncertainty" in the application of conservation biology was unscrupulous. The Sierra Club asserts that conservation biology represented well-accepted and well-respected science even at the time the Service developed its management plans in the mid-1980s and that this evidence was before the Service when it drafted the forest plans. Thus, if the Service's only argument against applying the "high quality" science of conservation biology was its uncertainty, the Service has utterly failed to respond to the challenge of conservation biology.

A brief look at available evidence suggests that the district court's understanding of uncertainty was correct and the Service's explanation principled. The Service, in looking at island biogeography, noted that it had been developed as a result of research on actual islands or in the predominantly old-growth forests of the Pacific Northwest and therefore did not necessarily lend itself to application in the forests of Wisconsin. Literature submitted by the Sierra Club to the Service was not unequivocal in stipulating how to apply conservation biology principles in the Nicolet and Chequamegon. Likewise, a Sierra Club group member suggested during meetings regarding the Chequamegon that "the Forest Service should be a leader and incorporate this concept into the Plan. He indicated that it would set a precedent for other Forests and Regions." The Chequamegon Forest Supervisor also originally decided to include the DMAs in his forest plan not because science so compelled but as a way to research an as yet untested theory. Even recent literature has recognized that "new legislation may be necessary" in order to force the Service to adopt conservation biology. Robert B. Keiter, *Conservation Biology and the Law: Assessing the Challenges Ahead*, 69 Chi.Kent. L. Rev. 911, 916 (1994). Perhaps the Service "ha[s] the ability to reinterpret [its] own governing mandates to give species protection priority over visitor services and other concerns," *id.* at 921, but that is not and was not required.

The amici scientific societies suggest that the district court misunderstood the nature of scientific uncertainty. Their argument on this point boils down to the assertion that all scientific propositions are inherently unverifiable and at most falsifiable. . . .

Amici, like the Sierra Club, misapprehend the "uncertainty" of which the Service and the district court spoke. We agree that an agency decision to avoid a science should not escape review merely because a theory is not certain. But, however valid a general theory may be, it does not translate into a management tool unless one can apply it to a concrete situation. The Service acknowledged the developments in conservation biology but did not think that they had been shown definitively applicable to forests like the Nicolet or the Chequamegon. Thus, circumstances did not warrant setting aside a large portion of these forests to study island biogeography and related theories at the expense of other forest-plan objectives. Given that uncertainty, we appropriately defer to the agency's method of measuring and maintaining diversity. . . .

* * *

The creation of a forest plan requires the Forest Service to make trade-offs among competing interests. The NFMA's diversity provisions do substantively limit the Forest Service's ability to sacrifice diversity in those trades. . . . However, the Service neither ignored nor abused those limits in the present case. . . .

Affirmed.

NOTES

1. *Indicator species and their proxies.* Even if NFMA directed the Forest Service to adopt conservation biology principles (and the *Marita* court did not suggest that the agency lacked discretion to do so), that would not resolve how to measure the statutorily mandated species diversity.

One means of doing so is through inventorying species on the ground. But such inventories are expensive and resource consumptive. Agencies like the Forest Service prefer to measure diversity through proxies, such as a species whose presence or absence signals the presence or absence of other species, or whose abundance or loss indicates major changes in the ecosystem. Until 2012, Forest Service regulations relied on monitoring populations of so-called management indicator species. See 36 C.F.R § 219.12(a)(5)(iii).

Another, more controversial proxy is reliance on available habitat instead of species surveys. Courts have been generally unsympathetic to agency attempts to use surrogates for quantitative data on indicator species. See *Sierra Club v. Martin*, 168 F.3d 1 (11th Cir. 1999) (requiring the collection of population data before timber sales in the Chattahoochee and Oconee National Forests in northern Georgia); *Utah Environmental Congress v. Bosworth,* 439 F.3d 1184 (10th Cir. 2006) (determining that the Forest Service regulations required population data before selling timber in Utah's Fishlake National Forest); *Idaho Sporting Congress v. Rittenhouse*, 305 F.3d 957 (9th Cir. 2002) (using habitat as a proxy for population data for timber sales in the Boise National Forest was arbitrary when the Forest Service's own studies undermined that approach). The skepticism of courts toward using available habitat as a proxy for species viability is interesting considering that the "species-area relationship" ($S=cA^z$)—which establishes a direct correlation between the amount of habitat available and species' well-being—has "strong empirical support from many decades of field experiments." See James Rasband, James Salzman, & Mark Squillace, *Natural Resources Law and Policy* 330 (2d. ed. 2009). For more on the effects of habitat fragmentation on species survival see Richard Primack, *Essentials Of Conservation Biology* 181 (2002); Matthew H. Nitelki, *Extinctions* (1984).

2.   *"Best available science."* The 2012 planning regulations require the Forest Service to "use the best available scientific information." 36 C.F.R. § 219.3. Suppose in the future the best science endorses principles of conservation biology. Would a court overturn the *Marita* decision?

3.   *Ecological integrity.* The 2012 regulations require forest plans to "maintain or restore the ecological integrity of terrestrial and aquatic ecosystems and watersheds. . . ." 36 C.F.R. § 219.8(a)(1). Among the factors the Forest Service must consider as it seeks to maintain ecosystem integrity are "system drivers . . . such as natural succession, wildland fire, invasive species, and climate change. . . ." *Id.* at § 219.8(a)(1)(v).

4.   *Groundwater directive.* In May 2014, the Forest Service proposed a groundwater directive that would establish national policy for making groundwater management on national forests an integral component of watershed management. The proposed policy would require consideration of groundwater resources in agency activities, approvals, and authorizations; encourage source water protection and water conservation; establish procedures for reviewing new proposals for groundwater withdrawals on national forest lands; require the evaluation of potential effects of groundwater withdrawals on national forest resources; and require measurement and reporting for larger groundwater withdrawals. *Proposed Directive on Groundwater,* 79 Fed. Reg. 25815 (May 6, 2014).

The proposal drew fierce opposition from the Western Governors Association, which accused the Forest Service of misleadingly suggesting that the agency has equal authority with the states over groundwater management. In the governors' view, the Forest Service had no authority to limit groundwater withdrawals authorized by a state. The governors also objected to the proposed directive's suggestions that the agency would establish a rebuttable presumption that ground and surface water were connected and had authority to claim reserved rights in groundwater. See Western States Water Council, *Western States Water* (Oct. 3, 2014).

5.   *The Northwest Forest Plan.* The *Marita* case was essentially an effort by the Sierra Club to apply to a national forest in Wisconsin the conservation biology principles that had been used in the Northwest Forest Plan (NWFP). That 1994 plan, largely prompted by a desire to protect the Northern Spotted Owl), covers some 24 million acres of federal land, mostly

national forests and BLM lands within the range of the owl in northern California, Oregon, and Washington. The NWFP put conservation biology into practice by setting aside large, unfragmented habitats to maintain diverse, ecologically viable old-growth forest ecosystems capable of supporting sustainable populations of owls and salmon.

The plan created four primary categories of land: late successional reserves, riparian reserves, "matrix" lands, and adaptive management areas. The NWFP placed 7.4 million acres in the late successional reserves category, designed to protect and enhance old-growth forest conditions that are prime owl habitat. (Logging was already restricted on 8.8 million acres within the NWFP.) In these reserves, forests more than 80 years old cannot be clearcut unless doing so will create beneficial old-growth conditions. The NWFP also established 2.63 million acres of riparian reserves to protect aquatic systems and dependent species, restricting most timber harvesting, road building, grazing, mining, and off-road vehicle usage within 100–300 feet of most riparian areas, including the 100-year floodplain and landslide-prone areas.

The plan confined most logging to 4 million acres of so-called "matrix" lands. Finally, the plan placed 1.5 million acres in adaptive management areas, where land managers may explore alternative management techniques. Of the total plan area, approximately 77 percent of the land is in reserves, 16 percent in matrix lands, and 6 percent in adaptive management areas.

In addition to this zoning, the federal plan established the Aquatic Conservation Strategy (ACS), the first ecologically-based approach to managing watersheds and streamside forests on federal lands. The ACS, a science-based strategy of restoring and maintaining the ecological function and processes of watersheds and aquatic ecosystems, applies throughout the 24-million-acre NWFP. The ACS limits logging and road construction where the most harm results—for example, next to salmon streams and on steep slopes—while simultaneously allowing for active restoration through road decommissioning and other beneficial activities. The ACS calls for the restoration of "ecological health of watersheds and aquatic ecosystems contained within them on all public lands" and also establishes several restoration objectives, including specifying designated "key watersheds," in which no new roads may be built in "inventoried roadless areas," and no net increase of roads may occur within roaded areas.

The ACS requires a watershed analysis, which is a "systematic procedure . . . characteriz[ing] the aquatic, riparian, and terrestrial features within a watershed," that must precede management activities in designated areas. Information from this analysis forms the basis of an assessment of current watershed conditions and can lead to 1) revisions in riparian reserve boundaries, 2) plans for likely future conditions and restoration needs, and 3) monitoring programs for the watershed. A watershed analysis is not a decision document but instead is scientifically-based guidance meant to inform and, as such, usually included in NEPA documents.

A sleeper provision in the NWFP was its call for a "survey and manage" (S & M) program, requiring timber harvests to be preceded by studies of the presence of rare and sensitive species, including birds, mammals, and even snails and moss. If land managers find these animals, they must provide a buffer between their habitat and timber harvests.

The S&M provisions have been the subject of almost continuous litigation since approval in 1994. The implementing agencies have sought to reduce the number of species subject to the provision nearly from the beginning. However, the Bush Administration was unsuccessful in an attempt to downgrade the tree vole's status, *Klamath Siskiyou Wild Lands Center v. Boody,* 468 F.3d 549 (9th Cir. 2006) (violations of NEPA and the Federal Land Policy and Management Act) and to eliminate S&M entirely from the NWFP, *Conservation Northwest v. Rey,* 674 F.Supp.2d 1232 (W.D. Wash. 2009) (violations of NEPA). The latter decision led to a settlement agreement in which the Obama Administration largely agreed to reinstate the S&M requirements. That settlement, in turn, was successfully challenged because it did not go through the rulemaking process under which the S&M provisions were authorized. See *Conservation Northwest v. Sherman*, 715 F.3d 1181 (9th Cir. 2013) (ruling that a district judge's acceptance of a settlement agreement violated the Administrative Procedure Act).

6.   *The Oregon and California lands.* Not all federal forests are managed by the Forest Service. On the West Slope of the Cascades in Oregon, about ten percent of the lands now under the Northwest Forest Plan are managed by the Bureau of Land Management (BLM). These lands were the subject of violations of the terms of the Oregon and California Railroad (O & C) land grant, which led to a Supreme Court decision enjoining further land sales, *Oregon & California Railroad v. United States*, 238 U.S. 393 (1915), and eventually revestment of the lands in the federal government. In 1937, Congress assigned the management of these lands to the BLM, not the Forest Service, largely because the BLM promised localities a greater percentage of the revenues from timber sales. Oregon and California Sustained Yield Act, 43 U.S.C. §§ 1181a *et seq.* (O & C Act). Local pressure to keep timber harvest levels high to support local government services (and thereby keep property tax rates among the lowest in Oregon) has been a constant feature of the management of the federal O & C lands. See Michael C. Blumm & Tim Wigington, *The Oregon and California Railroad Grant Lands' Sordid Past, Contentious Present, and Uncertain Future: A Century of Conflict*, 40 B.C. Envtl. Aff. L. Rev. 1 (2013).

The 1937 O & C Act promised that the forest lands would be managed to produce sustained-use timber production, watershed protection, local economic benefits, and recreation. In practice, this meant that the forest was managed on an industrial timber harvest basis for a half-century. In *Headwaters v. Bureau of Land Management, Medford Dist.*, 914 F.2d 1174 (9th Cir. 1990), the Ninth Circuit endorsed a reading of the 1937 statute as calling for dominant-use timber production. But the same court later rejected government and timber industry arguments that the O & C Act exempted the lands from the effect of federal statutes like NEPA and the Endangered Species Act. *Portland Audubon Society v. Babbitt*, 998 F.2d 705 (9th Cir. 1993) (affirming a district court injunction). This decision effectively shut down the industrial timber harvesting on O & C lands and led to the Northwest Forest Plan, discussed above, which has curtailed timber production by roughly 90 percent.

The steep decline in timber receipts has produced a crisis in local services like police and fire protection, since the local governments have been unwilling to raise taxes, and voters have rejected several initiatives to do so. Congress intervened to provide temporary replacement funding in the form of the Secure Rural Schools and Community Self-Determination Act of 2000, 16 U.S.C §§ 7101–53, which was extended in 2008. But congressional willingness to continue to do so seems to be at an end, and funding dried up at the end of fiscal year 2013. This has led to initiatives on the part of members of the Oregon congressional delegation to restore some of the timber production to aid local governments. The House of Representatives passed the Restoring Healthy Forests for Healthy Communities Act (H.R. 1526, 113th Cong.) in September 2013, which would open up logging on about 1.5 million acres of O & C lands, while also designating wilderness lands and wild and scenic rivers. But as of this writing, the Senate had yet to take action.

Timber companies and trade associations also continue to challenge declining levels of federal timber sales in court. In *Swanson Group v. Salazar*, 951 F.Supp.2d 75 (D.D.C. 2013), they persuaded a district court that the O & C Act requires BLM to offer for sale the annual sustained yield capacity, once the agency declares that capacity (established by BLM land plans as 80 percent of the allowable sale quantity). The court also invalidated procedures for estimating the effects timber harvests have on the northern spotted owl because they were not authorized by rulemaking procedures.

3. THE ROADLESS RULE

In 1964, Congress enacted the world's first legal protection for wild lands in the Wilderness Act, 16 U.S.C. §§ 1131–36, also discussed below in chapter 9, pp. 809-18. The statute created some 9 million acres of "instant wilderness" by directly protected lands designated as wilderness by the Forest Service. It also established somewhat cumbersome procedures for additions to the wilderness system. These procedures called for the land management agencies—the U.S. Forest Service, the National Park Service, and the U.S. Fish and Wildlife Service (the statute overlooked BLM's lands)—to study lands of wilderness quality under their jurisdiction and make recommendations to the President, who in turn would make recommendations to Congress. Only Congress can designate wilderness areas, but the courts have interpreted the statute's study provisions broadly. For example, although the Wilderness Act only directed the Forest Service to study designated "primitive" areas, the

Tenth Circuit required study of adjacent roadless areas as well. *Parker v. United States,* 448 F.2d 793 (10th Cir. 1971) (affirming a district court's injunction of proposed timber sales).

In 1967, Forest Service Chief Edward Cliff ordered a study of roadless areas over 5,000 acres under the agency's jurisdiction as part of its effort to implement the study directives of the 1964 Wilderness Act. That study, the first Roadless Area Review Evaluation (RARE I), inventoried some 56 million acres but recommended only about 20 percent (12 million acres) for designation as wilderness. The RARE I recommendations foundered on requirements imposed by the newly enacted National Environmental Policy Act (NEPA), which requires (as we have seen) that federal actions producing significant environmental effects be accompanied by an environmental impact statement (EIS) that analyzes and publicly discloses those effects and that considers reasonable alternative courses of action. Two courts ruled that the Forest Service could not issue timber sales or mineral leases on lands that RARE I inventoried—on lands not recommended for wilderness protection—until they prepared an EIS that considered the environmental effects of nonprotection. The ruling effectively providing these *de facto* wild lands interim protection and, because of the high cost of such environmental studies, dealt a death blow to the RARE I process. *Sierra Club v. Butz,* 349 F.Supp. 934 (N.D. Cal. 1972); *Wyoming Outdoor Coordinating Council v. Butz,* 484 F.2d 1244 (10th Cir. 1973).

The Forest Service responded by undertaking a new nationwide study, called RARE II—this time encompassing some 62 million roadless acres—in an effort to release some inventoried lands to nonwilderness uses (some 36 million acres) while recommending others (some 15 million acres) for wilderness protection and still others for further planning (nearly 11 million acres). Unlike RARE I, the Forest Service accompanied RARE II with a 1979 EIS, but one the Ninth Circuit found deficient in *California v. Block,* 690 F.2d 753 (9th Cir. 1982), in part because it did not consider an adequate range of alternatives (including 100 percent protection). Thus, NEPA once again foiled Forest Service attempts to release wilderness-quality lands from the interim protection provided by the Wilderness Act's review provisions. See generally Michael C. Blumm & Lorena M. Wisehart, *The Underappreciated Role of the National Environmental Policy Act in Wilderness Designation and Management,* 44 Envtl. L. 323 (2014).

Before the Forest Service could undertake a RARE III study, Congress intervened and passed a series of statutes designating new wilderness areas. In 28 statutes enacted during the decade of 1984 to 1993 it added nearly 10 million acres of wilderness, mostly on a state-by-state basis. In the states affected by these statutes, lands not included in the wilderness system were not to be considered again for wilderness protection by the Forest Service until the agency revised applicable forest plans, in processes that would generally take ten or fifteen years. *Id.* at 344–45.

By the time of the Clinton Administration in the 1990s, there remained roughly 58 million roadless acres in national forests that had not been included in the wilderness system, about 30 percent of the lands in the national forest system. At the same time, the Forest Service had a large backlog of maintenance for its 380,000 miles of forest roads. Prompted by pressure from environmentalists and also from those wanting to save federal money, the agency promulgated a 2001 rule that prohibited road construction, reconstruction, and timber harvesting in all lands that had been studied for wilderness but not designated by Congress. 68 Fed. Reg. 3244 (Jan. 23, 2001), codified at 36 C.F.R. § 294. The rule was subject to limited timber harvesting exceptions where necessary to maintain and improve roadless area characteristics, to improve listed or sensitive species, or maintain or to restore ecosystems threatened by uncharacteristic wildfires. 36 C.F.R § 294.13(b) (2001). The rule drew a substantial amount of litigation, leading to decisions from both the Ninth and Tenth Circuits. A divided Ninth Circuit rejected claims of extractive industries, an Indian tribe, and the state of Idaho that the rule violated NEPA in *Kootenai Tribe v. Veneman*, 313 F.3d 1094, 1120 (9th Cir. 2002).

The roadless rule did not fare so well in the District Court of Wyoming, where Judge Clarence Brimmer enjoined it for violating not only NEPA but also the Wilderness Act (which reserves wilderness designations to Congress). *Wyoming v. U.S. Dept. of Agriculture*, 277 F.Supp.2d 1197 (D. Wyo. 2003). After a good deal of procedural wrangling, including the Bush Administration's failure to appeal the Brimmer decision, the Tenth Circuit eventually dismissed an environmentalist appeal as moot, since in the interim the Bush Administration had replaced the 2001 roadless rule with a so-called state petitions rule. *Wyoming v. U.S. Dept. of Agriculture,* 414 F.3d 1207 (10th Cir. 2005).

The 2005 state petitions rule allowed state governors to petition the Forest Service to establish particularized roadless rules for their states that would not necessarily protect all roadless areas, if they filed a petition within eighteen months. 70 Fed. Reg. 25,654 (May 13, 2005), revising 36 C.F.R. § 294. The Bush Administration approved a petition from Idaho in 2008 that established four categories of roadless protection, including one that allowed timber harvests, mining, and temporary roads. 73 Fed. Reg. 1135 (Jan. 7, 2008). The Idaho rule was eventually upheld in *Jayne v. Sherman*, 706 F.3d 994 (9th Cir. 2013). However, the Forest Service rejected petitions from other states.

California (joined by New Mexico, Oregon, and Washington) responded to the rejection of its petition by challenging the validity of the state petitions rule itself, and a district court agreed in *California ex rel. Lockyer v. U.S. Dept. of Agriculture*, 459 F.Supp.2d 874 (N.D. Cal. 2006) (finding violations of NEPA and the Endangered Species Act in the promulgation of the rule for failing to supply a "reasoned analysis" based on new evidence or new environmental analysis justifying the substantial change in government policy). The district court reinstated the 2001 roadless rule, a result affirmed by the Ninth Circuit. *California ex rel. Lockyer v. U.S. Dept. of Agriculture,* 575 F.3d 999 (9th Cir. 2009). This reinstatement caused the state of Wyoming to renew its challenge to the 2001 rule that the Tenth Circuit had vacated as moot, and Judge Brimmer once again concluded that the rule violated NEPA and the Wilderness Act, enjoining its implementation nationwide. *Wyoming v. U.S. Dept. of Agriculture,* 570 F.Supp.2d 1309 (D. Wyo. 2008). Both the Forest Service and intervening environmentalists appealed, and this time the Tenth Circuit reached the merits in the following decision.

WYOMING V. U.S. DEPARTMENT OF AGRICULTURE

Tenth Circuit Court of Appeals
661 F.3d 1209 (2011)

[Wyoming claimed that the roadless rule constituted a *de facto* designation of wilderness in violation of the Wilderness Act's reservation of wilderness designations exclusively to Congress. Wyoming also alleged that the rule violated NEPA by, among other things, failing to 1) examine a reasonable range of alternatives, 2) include site-specific analysis in the EIS, and 3) take an objective "hard look" at the environmental consequences of agency action. The Forest Service and the environmental intervenors disputed both claims. The court began its ruling by distinguishing the protections offered by the rule from those offered by the Wilderness Act.]

HOLMES, J.

* * *

As a general matter, the Roadless Rule restricts only two activities—road construction and commercial timber harvesting, unless an exception applies. On the other hand, although the Wilderness Act likewise prohibits permanent and temporary roads and commercial logging, it additionally prohibits all "commercial enterprise," "motor vehicles, motorized equipment or motorboats," all "form[s] of mechanical transport," and any "structure or installation," unless an exception applies. 16 U.S.C. § 1133(c). This rudimentary comparison of the general use prohibitions in IRAs [inventoried roadless areas] and wilderness areas demonstrates that they are not the same; the uses prohibited in wilderness areas under the Wilderness Act are greater in number and scope than those prohibited in IRAs under the Roadless Rule.

We acknowledge that the Wilderness Act and Roadless Rule do in fact overlap in coverage in many ways. However, the issue we are to consider is whether the IRAs governed by the Roadless Rule are de facto wilderness areas; that is, whether the Roadless Rule essentially mirrors the Wilderness Act by a different label. A closer examination of the precise differences between IRAs and wilderness areas further demonstrates that the Roadless Rule does not establish de facto wilderness. First, although the Wilderness Act prohibits permanent structures and installations, the Roadless Rule does not prohibit the construction of permanent or temporary structures or installations. Therefore, structures and installations that can be erected without the construction of a new road—for example, through the use of an existing road—are permitted in IRAs, but not in wilderness areas.

Second, the Wilderness Act imposes significantly more stringent prohibitions on recreational activities. Under the Wilderness Act, any "use of motor vehicles, motorized equipment or motorboats, . . . landing of aircraft, . . . [or] other form of mechanical transport" is prohibited. On the other hand, the Roadless Rule contains no prohibitions on the use of motorized vehicles or equipment, boats or aircraft, or other forms of mechanical transport. Therefore, many recreational uses allowed to continue under the Roadless Rule—such as off-road vehicle use, biking, snowmobiling, and other motorized and mechanical activities—would be prohibited under the Wilderness Act. See, e.g., 66 Fed. Reg. at 3245 (stating that "unlike Wilderness," the Roadless Rule permits the "use of mountain bikes, and other mechanized means of travel"); *id.* at 3249 ("The Roadless [Rule], unlike the establishment of wilderness areas, will allow a multitude of activities including motorized uses. . . ."); *id.* at 3267 ("[IRAs] provide a remote recreation experience without the activity restrictions of Wilderness (for example, off-highway vehicle use and mountain biking).").

Third, the Wilderness Act is more restrictive in terms of road maintenance, road construction, and use of existing roads. The Wilderness Act prohibits any "permanent road" or any "temporary road," and road maintenance activities, subject to limited exceptions, and prohibits any use of motor vehicles. On the other hand, the Roadless Rule allows all existing classified roads—defined as roads "wholly or partially within or adjacent to [NFS] lands that [are] determined to be needed for long-term motor vehicle access, including State roads, county roads, privately owned roads, National Forest System roads, and other roads authorized by the Forest Service," . . .—to be maintained. Therefore, unlike the Wilderness Act, the Roadless Rule permits unlimited maintenance of all existing roads and does not prohibit the use of motorized vehicles or other motorized transportation on such existing roads.

Furthermore, the Roadless Rule provides broader exceptions for when new road construction or reconstruction can occur. For example, unlike in wilderness areas, "a road may be constructed or reconstructed in an [IRA] . . . as provided for by statute or treaty," . . . when "needed to conduct a response action under the Comprehensive Environmental Response, Compensation, and Liability Act (CERCLA) or to conduct a natural resource restoration action". . . . The Wilderness Act includes no exceptions of this kind to its prohibition of temporary and permanent roads.

Fourth, the Roadless Rule is less restrictive in terms of "grazing." Under the Wilderness Act's mandate that "there shall be no commercial enterprise . . . within any wilderness area," . . . commercial livestock grazing is prohibited. The Act includes a grandfather clause that permits "the grazing of livestock . . . [that was] established prior to September 3, 1964," . . . but otherwise completely bars such activity. By contrast, the Roadless Rule does not explicitly prohibit *any* type of "commercial enterprise," with the exception of commercial logging, and therefore permits commercial grazing within IRAs. The district court found this distinction meaningless because "one could not meaningfully set cattle out to pasture in a roadless area with no way of rounding those cattle back up or trucking them in and out of the forest allotment," unless a new road was constructed. However, this conclusion does not take into account that all existing roads—as well as any roads constructed or reconstructed under exceptions to the Roadless Rule—could be used to facilitate commercial grazing. This would not be permitted in a wilderness area[ ] due to the general prohibition on commercial enterprises (unless such grazing was established more than four decades ago), as well as the Act's prohibition on the use of motorized vehicles or equipment. Accordingly, the court's dismissal of this distinction was unfounded.

Fifth, the Roadless Rule allows for mineral development to a greater extent than does the Wilderness Act. Although the Wilderness Act initially permitted mineral development under United States mining laws, wilderness areas governed by the Act are now closed to mineral-development activities. On the other hand, the Roadless Rule imposes no general prohibition on mining or mineral-development activities, other than the limitations imposed through the road-building prohibition. Therefore, "leasing activities not dependent on road construction, such as directional (slant) drilling and underground development," and mineral-leasing activities that could be carried out through utilization of existing roads, "would not be affected by the prohibition." 66 Fed. Reg. at 3265. . . .

The exceptions to the Roadless Rule's road-building prohibition would also permit new road construction or reconstruction for mineral development in certain situations. Under the exception for existing mineral leases, road construction is permitted "in conjunction with the continuation, extension, or renewal of a mineral lease on lands that are under lease by the Secretary of the Interior as of January 12, 2001[,] or for a new lease issued immediately upon expiration of an existing lease." 66 Fed. Reg. at 3272–73 (to be codified at 36 C.F.R. § 294.12(b)(7)). This exception "extends indefinitely the timeframe for which roads can be constructed on areas currently under lease." *Id.* at 3265–66. In addition, under the exception permitting road construction "as provided for by statute or treaty," *id.* at 3272 (to be codified at 36 C.F.R. § 294.12(b)(3)), "[r]easonable access to conduct exploration and development of valid claims for locatable minerals (metallic and nonmetallic minerals subject to appropriation under the General Mining Law of 1872)" would not be prohibited under the Roadless Rule. *Id.* at 3268. "Reasonable access" could "involve some level of road construction that, depending on the stage of exploration or development, could range from helicopters, temporary or unimproved roads, more permanent, improved roads, or nonmotorized transport." *Id.* In sum, the Roadless Rule is less restrictive than the Wilderness Act in regard to mineral development.

These distinctions clearly demonstrate that wilderness areas governed by the Wilderness Act and IRAs governed by the Roadless Rule are not only distinct, but that the Wilderness Act is more restrictive and prohibitive than the Roadless Rule. Accordingly, we conclude that the IRAs governed by the Roadless Rule are not de facto administrative wilderness areas; therefore, the district court erred by holding otherwise.

* * *

[The court also determined that the Forest Service acted within its authority under the Organic Act to regulate the "occupancy and use" of national forest lands and "to preserve the forests thereon from destruction" in promulgating the roadless rule. The court proceeded to conclude that the Forest Service had complied with NEPA, finding that the EIS on the rule considered a reasonable range of alternatives because the agency gathered information sufficient to permit a reasoned choice of alternatives as far as environmental aspects were concerned, and NEPA did not require more. The court made no mention of the Ninth Circuit's conclusion that actions protecting the environment required consideration of fewer alternatives than actions harming the environment.]

NOTES

1. *National roadless rule exceptions.* The Tenth Circuit decision in *Wyoming* reinstated the roadless rule nationwide. However, as mentioned

above, the Idaho roadless rule approved under the state petitions rule remains in effect. And in 2012 the Obama Administration implemented a roadless rule for Colorado that protected 4.2 million acres while increasing "flexibility" to accommodate wildfire protection, ski area expansion, and methane production by coal companies in North Fork Valley, 77 Fed. Reg. 39,576 (July 3, 2012).

Alaska's Tongass National Forest, the nation's largest national forest, apparently has no roadless rule. The Bush Administration exempted the Tongass from the 2001 rule in 2003, and its 2005 state petitions rule stipulated that the existing forest plan, not the roadless rule, would govern the forest. Environmentalists successfully challenged the exemption in district court, which concluded that the exemption was arbitrary and capricious in violation of the Administrative Procedure Act, but a divided Ninth Circuit reversed in *Organized Village of Kake v. U.S. Dept. of Agriculture,* 746 F.3d 970 (9th Cir. 2014) (deciding that the Forest Service gave a reasoned explanation for the exemption, which was "a strategy to attempt to end the constant and continuous litigation stemming from the 2001 Roadless Rule").

2. *Federal vs. state approaches to roadless protection.* What are the advantages and disadvantages of protecting roadless areas of national forests on a national versus a state basis? For more on the roadless area controversy as well as other federal "wild lands" protection, see Michael C. Blumm & Andrew B. Erickson, *Federal Wild Lands Policy in the Twenty-First Century: What a Long, Strange Trip It's Been*, 25 Colo. Nat. Resources, Energy & Envtl. L. Rev. 1 (2014).

D. TIMBER SALE CONTRACTS

The Forest Service issues timber sale contracts to private logging companies to harvest public timber. Agency regulations contain detailed provisions governing the advertising and awarding of contracts, their duration, and their termination. 36 C.F.R. § 223. Most sales are conducted by competitive bidding, although the Forest Service retains the right to reject all bids. *Id.* § 223.100; George C. Coggins & Robert L. Glicksman, 3 *Public Natural Resources Law* § 34:43 (2d ed. 2014). Normal rules of contract interpretation generally govern public timber sale contracts, *id.* at § 34:26. Nonetheless, the Forest Service's contracting flexibility is sometimes limited by statute. The following case involved an alleged limit on that flexibility—a claim that the Forest Service could not include in sale contracts a condition that allowed them to void the contract based on unexpected environmental dangers.

RESERVATION RANCH V. UNITED STATES

United States Court of Federal Claims
39 Fed. Cl. 696 (1997)

[In 1990, the Forest Service awarded a timber sale contract to Reservation Ranch to harvest some 1.16 million board-feet of timber from the Six Rivers National Forest in northern California. The contract included a contract provision permitting the Forest Service to cancel should the Forest Service determine that the logging would likely jeopardize the continued existence of a threatened or endangered species or cause an adverse impact to a sensitive species, and specifying there would be no recovery of lost profits, replacement cost of timber, or any other anticipatory losses. Due to a settlement in a suit brought by environmentalists who challenged the sale, the Forest Service cancelled the sale in 1992, and Reservation Ranch sought $5.5 million in damages. The Forest Service offered only $63,000, and the ranch filed suit in the Court of Federal Claims.]

MEROW, J.

* * *

I. *Validity of the Species Contract Provision*

Plaintiff claims that the Forest Service does not have the authority to adopt species contract provision C8.2(2)(d) permitting cancellation for species concerns, and limiting compensation for such cancellation. . . . In particular, plaintiff argues that this provision is invalid because it is purportedly inconsistent with Forest Service cancellation regulation 36 C.F.R. § 223.116(a)(5). Plaintiff maintains that this regulation, which permits cancellation for "serious environmental degradation or resource damage," but which does not limit compensation as provided by [the contract provision in this case] exclusively governs such cancellations. Plaintiff maintains that neither NFMA, nor the regulation, give the Forest Service the discretion to contract to different terms.

a. *Authority to Adopt the Species Contract Provision*

Forest management statutes do not speak directly to the question of adopting specific contract terms providing for the cancellation of timber contracts when species concerns prove paramount to harvesting. Where a statute is silent on the specific issue at hand, the agency interpretation of its statutory authority regarding that issue will be sustained if its interpretation is a permissible one. *Chevron U.S.A. Inc. v. Natural Resources Defense Council,* 467 U.S. 837, 842–44 (1984). . . .

NFMA directs the Forest Service to implement its timber sale program in a manner which promotes orderly harvesting consistent with the different values of the national forests, including fish and wildlife resources. 16 U.S.C. §§ 472a, 1604. While the Forest Service must balance timber production, recreation and fish and wildlife values in discharging this duty, 16 U.S.C. § 529, NFMA provides that the management of any given area may protect one resource value to the exclusion of another value. See 16 U.S.C. § 531(a) (recognizing that in managing national forests "some land will be used for less than all of the resources"). In view of this authority, the Forest Service's adoption of a contract term which provides that species considerations may preempt harvesting is a permissible implementation of its statutory charge to manage the timber program in a manner which insures the maintenance of wildlife diversity. See 16 U.S.C. §§ 529, 531(a), 472a(c), 1604(g)(3)(B).

* * *

b.   Contract Terms that Vary Regulatory Provisions

Plaintiff argues in the alternative that even if the Forest Service has the authority to adopt the species contract provision and compensation limitation, it restricted that authority by the promulgation of 36 C.F.R. § 223.116(a). According to plaintiff, this regulation prescribes the exclusive reasons for which the Forest Service may cancel timber contracts, and sets forth the sole measure of compensation for such cancellations. Contrary to this contention, while the Forest Service regulation may prescribe the exclusive circumstances under which the Forest Service may unilaterally cancel timber sale contracts, it does not limit the ability of the parties to contract otherwise. *Peters v. United States,* 694 F.2d 687, 692–96 (Fed. Cir. 1982). . . .

* * *

Plaintiff's reliance upon *Everett Plywood Corp. v. United States,* 651 F.2d 723 (Ct. Cl. 1981), for the proposition that the Forest Service regulation must be applied in this case is misplaced. In *Everett Plywood,* the Forest Service unilaterally canceled a timber sale contract for environmental reasons. Neither the contract, nor Forest Service regulations in effect at the time, however, provided for such cancellations. *Id.* at 728. On these facts, the Federal Circuit found that the Forest Service breached the contract, and applied the subsequently enacted Forest Service cancellation regulation to calculate compensation. *Id.* at 728–32; see also *Peters,* 694 F.2d at 692. Here, the contract did prescribe the relevant cancellation and compensation terms, rendering *Everett Plywood* inapposite.

Congress has not restricted the discretion of the Forest Service to adopt a contract term allowing for cancellation and limited compensation for species considerations. Nor has the Forest Service done so by the promulgation of 36 C.F.R. § 223.116. [The court therefore upheld the validity of the contract provision allowing cancellation for species concerns and limiting compensation. The court proceeded to consider whether the Forest Service could cancel the sale based on concerns over the northern spotted owl, even though the U.S. Fish and Wildlife Service had earlier concluded, in biological consultation under the Endangered Species Act (ESA), that the sale would not jeopardize the owl.]

* * *

II. *Forest Service Exercise of the Species Contract Provision*

Plaintiff alternatively claims that even if the species contract provision is valid, the Chief improperly relied upon that provision to cancel the POC sale. Plaintiff advances two main arguments in support of this claim. First, plaintiff argues that the Forest Service does not have the legal authority under the ESA to find jeopardy to the owl in the face of a contrary FWS opinion. Second, even if the Forest Service has the legal authority, plaintiff argues that this authority was arbitrarily exercised here. . . .

a. *Forest Service ESA Authority*

Plaintiff's first contention challenging the Forest Service's ESA authority fails under the plain language of the statute. The Forest Service, not the FWS [Fish and Wildlife Service], retained the ultimate authority under the ESA to decide whether to go forward with the POC sale. 16 U.S.C. § 1536(a)(2) ("[e]ach *Federal agency* shall . . . insure . . . [its actions are] not likely to jeopardize the continued existence of any endangered species or threatened species. . . .") (emphasis added); see also 50 C.F.R. § 402.15 ("Following the issuance of a biological opinion, the *federal agency* shall determine whether and in what manner to proceed with the action in light of its section 7 obligations and the Service's biological opinion.") (emphasis added).

* * *

Plaintiff alternatively argues that the FWS biological opinion is nonetheless effectively determinative of the issue of jeopardy because an agency which acts contrary to a FWS *jeopardy* determination "will almost certainly be found to have acted . . . contrary to law." *Lone Rock Timber v. U.S. Dept. of Interior,* 842 F.Supp. 433, 437 (D. Or. 1994). Plaintiff's reliance upon this proposition is misplaced because the rationale underlying it is not implicated where, as here, the agency acts contrary to a FWS *no jeopardy* determination.

* * *

This rationale does not apply . . . where the agency acts contrary to a FWS *no jeopardy* determination by finding jeopardy and canceling its proposed action. In such a case, the agency no longer runs the risk of violating the ESA. . . .

b. *Forest Service Jeopardy Determination*

Plaintiff claims in the alternative that even if the Forest Service has the legal authority under the ESA to find jeopardy, this authority was arbitrarily exercised by the Chief. . . . [P]laintiff alleges that there is no evidence to support the Chief's finding that harvesting a sale located in spotted owl habitat would jeopardize the continued existence of the owl. According to plaintiff, this evidentiary void, particularly when viewed in light of the contrary FWS determination, establishes that the Chief's determination was arbitrary. Second, plaintiff argues that the Chief's reliance upon the cancellation regulation to cancel other timber sales subject to the NEC [Northcoast Environmental Center] order supports the inference that the Chief's reliance upon the species contract provision here was arbitrary.

* * *

Plaintiff bears the burden of demonstrating that the Chief's jeopardy determination was arbitrary. . . . Here, the record reveals facts evidencing a rational relationship between the Chief's finding that the sale was to occur in spotted owl habitat, and his determination that harvesting the sale was likely to jeopardize the owl. Plaintiff has failed to present facts evidencing a reasonable dispute concerning this jeopardy determination premised upon habitat destruction.

* * *

[The court discussed Forest Service studies on the effect of the sale on the owl. These studies, taken in view of the ESA presumption that species conservation is accomplished through habitat protection, demonstrated a rational relationship between the Chief's finding that the sale was to occur in spotted owl habitat, and his determination that harvesting the sale was likely to jeopardize the continued existence of the owl.]

* * *

III. *Alternative Grounds for Cancellation*

* * *

a. *Forest Service NFMA Authority and Cancellation for Adverse Impact under C8.2(2)(d)*

[T]he Forest Service has not only the authority, but a legal duty independent from the ESA to protect the owl. See *Seattle Audubon Soc'y v. Evans,* 952 F.2d 297 (9th Cir. 1991). Pursuant to NFMA, the Forest

Service must maintain viable populations of the owl, a sensitive species under NFMA implementing regulations and policy. 16 U.S.C. § 1604(g)(3); 36 C.F.R. § 219(19). . . . Species contract provision C8.2(2)(d) reflected this independent duty by providing that the Chief could cancel if the sale would "cause unacceptable adverse impacts on sensitive species." . . .

Further, the terms of NFMA itself do not limit the consideration of wildlife diversity to the management planning process. See 16 U.S.C. § 1604(g)(3)(B). . . .

* * *

[The court denied the plaintiff's claim for $5.5 million and upheld the Forest Service's decision on compensation.]

NOTES

1. *Compensation for contract cancellation. Reservation Ranch* relied on *Everett Plywood Corp. v. United States,* 651 F.2d 723 (Ct. Cl. 1981), in which the court ruled in favor of the timber contractor when the Forest Service cancelled a sale upon determining that a timber road would cause unacceptable environmental damage. The *Everett Plywood* court emphasized the fact that the contract in that case had no provision for cancellation in the event of environmental damage and suggested that the agency could have either promulgated regulations or included a specific contract provision relieving it of liability in such an event. The government seems to have drafted the contract in the Reservation Ranch sale in light of the lesson learned from the *Everett Plywood* case.

2. *Cancellation regulations.* Forest Service regulations now provide for cancellation in the event of actions causing "serious environmental degradation or resource damage." The regulations also state that the contractor is entitled to "reasonable compensation . . . for unrecovered costs incurred under the contract and for the difference between the current contract value and the average value of comparable National Forest timber sold during the preceding 6-month period." 36 C.F.R. §§ 223.40, 223.116 (2004); see George C. Coggins & Robert L. Glicksman, 3 *Public Natural Resources Law* § 34:44 (2d ed. 2014). Do the regulations provide more compensation for contract cancellation due to environmental concerns than is reasonable?

CHAPTER 9

PUBLIC LANDS: PRESERVATION AND RECREATION

∎ ∎ ∎

The dominant public land policy during the nineteenth century was disposing of the public domain to states, railroads, and private parties. A crosscurrent of public land retention began in 1872 when Congress created the Yellowstone reserve, establishing the world's first national park as a "pleasuring ground." Two decades later, Congress authorized the President to set aside "any part of the public lands . . . covered with timber or undergrowth . . . as public reservations." This authorization would allow President Theodore Roosevelt to establish numerous forest reserves during 1905–09, which would be managed by his newly transformed Forest Service under the leadership of Chief Gifford Pinchot. In addition to establishing the lion's share of the national forest system, Roosevelt began to use non-statutory authority to reserve bird refuges in 1903, founding what is today the national wildlife refuge system. In 1916, Congress consolidated Yellowstone and a half-dozen other reserves into a national park system to conserve scenery and wildlife and to provide public enjoyment "without impairment" for future generations in the National Park Service Organic Act, 16 U.S.C § 1.

The retention impulse came to the remaining public lands through enactment of the Taylor Grazing Act in 1934, passed in response to the environmental catastrophe that was the Dust Bowl on the Great Plains. The Taylor Act brought regulation to grazing lands, aimed at "preserv[ing] the land and its resources from destruction or unnecessary injury" and "provid[ing] for the orderly use, improvement, and development" of federal rangelands. 43 U.S.C. §§ 315, 315a. Now managed by the Bureau of Land Management, rangelands—like national forests—are managed for multiple uses, balancing commodity use production with species and land preservation concerns; recreation is also a prominent multiple-use purpose. See 16 U.S.C. §§ 528–31 (Multiple Use-Sustained Yield Act); 43 U.S.C. § 1732(a) (Federal Land Policy and Management Act).

National parks and wildlife refuges are not multiple-use lands; they are instead managed primarily for preservation purposes, although public recreation is also a purpose of the parks (16 U.S.C. § 1), and so-called "compatible uses," including grazing, recreation, and even oil and gas development, are permissible on some refuges (*id.* § 668dd(d)(3)(A)). A more dominant preservationist management exists on wilderness areas, designed to be areas "untrammeled by man" by the 1964 Wilderness Act. *Id.* § 1131(c). Permanent roads and most commercial activities are proscribed, as are "structure[s] or installation[s]" unless necessary to meet "minimum requirements for the administration of the area." *Id.* §§ 1133(c), (d)(1). Primitive recreation, however, is permitted, including that provided by outfitters and guides, and can be allowed "to the extent necessary for activities which are proper for realizing the recreational or other wilderness purposes of the area." *Id.* § 1133(d)(5).

This chapter examines preservation and multiple-use lands through the lens of recreation, perhaps the most widespread and certainly the most economically remunerative use of federal public lands in the twenty-first century.

A. RECREATION AND NATIONAL PARKS

One of the crown jewels of the national park system is Grand Canyon National Park, through which, of course, runs the Colorado River, first navigated by the legendary John Wesley Powell in 1869. See Donald Worster, *A River Running West: The Life of John Wesley Powell* (2001). The first national park unit was Yellowstone, which was established in 1872, long before Congress established the national park system and the National Park Service to administer it in the 1916 Organic Act, 16 U.S.C. §§ 1 *et seq.* There are now over 400 units of the national park system— which includes not only parks but also monuments, battlefields, historic sites, landmarks, seashores, lakeshores, and recreation areas. Most of these areas have been congressionally designated, but national monuments may be established by the President under the Antiquities Act. *Id.* §§ 461 *et seq.*

The Organic Act directs the National Park Service to "promote and regulate" the national parks by "conserv[ing] the natural and historic objects and the wild life therein and to provide for the enjoyment of the same in such manner and by such means as will leave them unimpaired for the enjoyment of future generations." *Id.* § 1. The statute has sometimes been thought to require land managers to balance preservation against recreation, but a close reading suggests that the express requirement of preserving designated areas "unimpaired" for future generations is the dominant purpose of the law; recreation is a secondary purpose, to be pursued only where consistent with the non-impairment directive. After a long period of considering the dual purposes of the parks to be co-equal, the Park Service now finally agrees with the interpretation of the statute advanced above. National Park Service, Management Policies 2006, § 1.4.3 (2006). See discussion below at p. 808.

The recreation and preservation purposes of the Organic Act are at issue in the following case concerning river rafting in the Grand Canyon, an issue that had been subject to earlier litigation. See *Wilderness Public Rights Fund v. Kleppe*, 608 F.2d 1250 (9th Cir. 1979), in which the court upheld an allocation of river use that favored commercial users over non-commercial users. The case below concerns a challenge to motorized use, often used by commercial outfitters to reduce the length of time necessary to traverse the Colorado River through the Grand Canyon.

RIVER RUNNERS FOR WILDERNESS V. MARTIN

Ninth Circuit Court of Appeals
593 F.3d 1064 (2010)

[Environmental organizations challenged the National Park Service's decision to permit continued use of motorized watercraft in Grand Canyon National Park. The district court upheld the government's decision, and the environmentalists appealed. They contended that motorized activities impaired the wilderness character of the canyon, and maintained that the 2006 Management Plan was arbitrary and capricious under the Administrative Procedure Act (APA) because it violated Park Service policies. They also claimed that the plan violated the National Park Service Concessions Management and Improvement Act (Concessions Act) and the National Park Service Organic Act (Organic Act).]

PER CURIAM.

* * *

Enforceability of the Policies

Even though Congress has never acted on the Park Service's recommendation to designate a substantial portion of the Park as wilderness, Plaintiffs claim that the Park Service's own policies give rise to a legally binding obligation to maintain the wilderness character of the Park. Plaintiffs claim that the Park Service has breached this legal duty by authorizing the continued use of motorized activities in the 2006 Management Plan. Defendants and Intervenors argue that the Park Service policies do not have the force and effect of law and therefore may not be enforced against the Park Service in this action.

[The court determined that the Park Service's 2001 policies were not substantive rules, and are thus not enforceable under *United States v. Fifty-Three Eclectus Parrots*, 685 F.2d 1131 (9th Cir. 1982).]

* * *

The Policies Do Not Render the 2006 Management Plan
Arbitrary and Capricious

Citing *Ecology Center, Inc. v. Austin,* 430 F.3d 1057 (9th Cir. 2005), and related cases, Plaintiffs alternatively argue that the 2006 Management Plan is arbitrary and capricious even if the 2001 Policies do not have the force and effect of law. . . .

Plaintiffs base their argument on the fact that the Colorado River Corridor has been classified by the Park Service as potential wilderness. The 2001 Policies provide the following guidance with respect to the management of potential wilderness areas:

> The National Park Service will take no action that would diminish the wilderness suitability of an area possessing wilderness characteristics until the legislative process of wilderness designation has been completed. . . . This policy also applies to potential wilderness, requiring it to be managed as wilderness to the extent that existing non-conforming conditions allow. The National Park Service will seek to remove from potential wilderness the temporary, non-conforming conditions that preclude wilderness designation.

2001 Policies § 6.3.1. The FEIS [Final Environmental Impact Statement] makes this same commitment with respect to the Colorado River Corridor.

The language of § 6.3.1 makes clear that the Park Service is required to manage potential wilderness areas as actual wilderness only "to the extent that existing non-conforming conditions allow." This language does not require the Park Service immediately to remove existing non-conforming uses—in this case, motorized rafts. It requires the Park Service to manage the Colorado River Corridor as wilderness to the extent possible given the existing use of motors. In light of this clear provision, the court cannot conclude that the 2006 Management Plan is arbitrary and capricious for failing to remove motorized uses in the Colorado River Corridor immediately.

Section 6.3.1 further states that the Park Service "will seek to remove from potential wilderness the temporary, non-conforming conditions that preclude wilderness designation." 2001 Policies § 6.3.1. Seasonal uses of motors on the river do not preclude wilderness designation. Plaintiffs do not contend that such uses work any permanent change on the Corridor that would preclude later wilderness treatment. Seasonal float trips are not like the construction of a road or other physical improvements that might disqualify an area for wilderness designation in the future. Motorized float trips can readily be eliminated if Congress decides that the Corridor should be designated as wilderness. The FEIS concludes that the use of motors in the Corridor "is only a temporary or transient disturbance of wilderness values" and "does not permanently impact wilderness resources or permanently denigrate wilderness values.". . .

* * *

Finally, Plaintiffs argue that the 2006 Management Plan is arbitrary and capricious because it contradicts earlier Park Service decisions to phase out motorized boating in the Colorado River Corridor. As noted above, the 1979 Management Plan called for motorized watercraft between Lees Ferry and Separation Canyon to be phased out over a five-year period. The Court cannot conclude, however, that the 2006 Management Plan is arbitrary and capricious solely because it differs from earlier Park Service decisions. Part of the discretion granted to federal agencies is the freedom to change positions. . . . For reasons explained herein, the court finds the 2006 Management Plan sufficiently reasonable to pass APA muster.

* * *

The 2006 Management Plan and the Concessions Act

Plaintiffs first contend that the Park Service failed entirely to determine that the types and levels of commercial services authorized by the 2006 Management Plan are necessary and appropriate. We disagree. The Park Service made the following determinations:

> Since many visitors who wish to raft on the Colorado River through Grand Canyon possess neither the equipment nor the skill to successfully navigate the rapids and other hazards of the river, the [Park Service] has determined that it is necessary and appropriate for the public use and enjoyment of the park to provide for experienced and professional river guides who can provide such skills and equipment. . . . [S]ervices provided by commercial outfitters, which enable thousands of people to experience the river in a relatively primitive and unconfined manner and setting (when many of them otherwise would be unable to do so), are necessary to realize the recreational or other wilderness purposes of the park.

Plaintiffs argue that although the Park Service may have found commercial outfitters to be necessary and appropriate generally, it never made such a finding for *motorized* commercial services. Again we disagree. The ROD [Record of Decision] specifically states that "[d]etermination of the *types and levels* of commercial services that are necessary and appropriate for the Colorado River through Grand Canyon National Park were determined through [the FEIS]." Among the eight management alternatives considered by the Park Service in the [Draft Environmental Impact Statement] and FEIS were two that did not authorize any motorized uses in the Colorado River Corridor (Alternatives B and C). After evaluating these alternatives, the Park Service found that they "violated the basic premise of this planning effort; that of reducing congestion, crowding and impacts without reducing access of visitors to the Colorado River[.]" . . . [T]he Park Service quite clearly concluded that motorized commercial services were "necessary and appropriate for public use and enjoyment" of the Corridor. 16 U.S.C. § 5951(b).

Plaintiffs contend that even if the Park Service found that motorized services were necessary and appropriate, it made no determination as to the *amount* of such services that are necessary, and therefore failed to "limit" motorized uses to those that are necessary and appropriate as required by the Congressional policy statement of the Concessions Act. It is true that the FEIS and ROD do not contain a specific discussion of the amount of motorized traffic found necessary and appropriate for public use and enjoyment of the Corridor. But the absence of such a specific discussion does not necessarily require the agency's action to be overturned. . . . The Park Service's consideration of the amount of motorized traffic required in the Colorado River Corridor can reasonably be discerned from the FEIS.

Among the alternatives considered in the FEIS was a "no-action alternative"—an alternative that would have left the 1989 levels in place. . . . Alternative B would have eliminated all motorized traffic on the river and allocated 97,694 user days to commercial operators and 74,523 to non-commercial. Alternative C also would have eliminated all motorized trips, but would have increased commercial user days [calculated by multiplying the number of passengers by the number of days] to 166,814 and non-commercial to 115,783, presumably to accommodate sufficient numbers of visitors with the slower non-motorized trips. Alternatives D, E, F, and G would have permitted motorized uses, but varied the amounts for commercial and non-commercial traffic. . . .

User days were not the only variables evaluated by the Park Service. The FEIS also considered months without motors on the river, trip lengths, trip lengths during various parts of the year, group sizes, numbers of launches, numbers of passengers, and helicopter exchanges at the Whitmore helipad. . . .

The Park Service ultimately concluded that Alternatives B and C— the non-motor alternatives—would not meet the agency's objective of providing "a diverse range of quality recreational opportunities for visitors to experience and understand the environmental interrelationships, resources, and values of Grand Canyon National Park" because of the significantly reduced number of visitors who could experience the Colorado River Corridor. The Park Service evaluated a range of motorized use times in the other alternatives and, after considering all factors and variables, selected Modified Alternative H. . . .

* * *

In sum, the Park Service's decision concerning the amount of motorized trips on the river was made after considering competing alternatives and a significant number of variables. The Park Service chose an alternative that reduced motorized uses from current levels. The court is satisfied that the Park Service, as stated in the ROD, determined the "type and level" of traffic on the river that was "necessary and appropriate," including the type and level of motorized uses.

Plaintiffs argue that even if the Park Service made such a determination, the determination was arbitrary and capricious. As noted above, however, the decision occurred only after an extensive analysis of various alternatives. Defendants have identified a number of factors in the Administrative Record that support the Park Service's decision to allow motorized traffic to continue. First, because motorized trips take less time to complete (10 days as opposed to 16 days for non-motorized trips), substantially more people can see the Park each year from the river if motorized trips continue. Second, motorized trips are frequently chartered for special-needs groups, educational classes, family reunions, or to support kayak or other paddle trips. Third, because of their increased mobility, motorized trips help alleviate overcrowding at popular campsites and attractions in the Corridor. Fourth, some individuals feel safer when traveling in motorized rafts. In addition, studies performed as part of the [draft environmental impact statement] found that visitors are able to experience the river as wilderness in the presence of motorized uses and that those who took motorized trips were significantly more likely to stress safety and trip length as the most important factors in . . . choosing the type of trip they took.

Given the "judicial presumption favoring the validity of administrative actions" and the "administrative discretion" granted the Park Service under the Concessions Act, *Wilderness Pub. Rights Fund v. Kleppe,* 608 F.2d 1250, 1254 (9th Cir. 1979), the court cannot conclude that the agency acted arbitrarily and capriciously when it found that the Modified Alternative H levels of motorized uses were "necessary and appropriate for public use and enjoyment" of the Colorado River Corridor. . . .

* * *

The Organic Act

The Organic Act provides that the Park Service "shall promote and regulate the use of . . . national parks . . . in such manner and by such means as will leave them unimpaired for the enjoyment of future generations." 16 U.S.C. § 1. The Act also provides that "[n]o natural curiosities, wonders, or objects of interest shall be leased, rented, or granted to anyone on such terms as to interfere with free access to them by the public[.]" 16 U.S.C. § 3. Plaintiffs contend that the 2006 Management Plan is arbitrary and capricious because it permits commercial boaters to use the river at levels that interfere with free access by the public, and because it concludes that motorized uses do not impair the natural soundscape of the Park.

Free Access

Plaintiffs argue that the allocation of river access between commercial and non-commercial users is inequitable and thus limits the free access of members of the public. As noted above, however, the Park Service has significantly increased the access of non-commercial users. . . . [T]he allocation of river time between commercial and non-commercial user days changed from 66.5% commercial and 33.5% non-commercial under the 1989 Management Plan, to 50.4% commercial and 49.6% non-commercial under the 2006 Management Plan. . . .

Plaintiffs argue that non-commercial users are required to wait for permits to run the river—sometimes for 10 or more years—while clients of commercial rafting companies usually can book a trip within one year. They also assert that the current allocation favors the wealthy who can afford commercial trips, and they criticize the Park Service for not conducting a demand study that would have revealed the most equitable allocation. The court cannot conclude on this basis, however, that the Management Plan is arbitrary and capricious. The 2006 Management Plan significantly revised the system for private boaters to obtain permits by establishing a lottery system that is weighted to favor those who have not received a permit in previous years. Moreover, surveys show that 61% of private boaters have floated the Colorado River Corridor before, while only 20% of commercial boaters were on repeat trips. The existence of a waiting list therefore does not necessarily show that more private boaters than commercial customers are awaiting their first river trip. . . .

* * *

Impairment of the Natural Soundscape

* * *

Plaintiffs contend that [the Park Service's] cumulative [noise] analysis should have caused the Park Service to eliminate sounds from motorized river traffic. But if a cumulative analysis were to result in the elimination of all sounds that can be eliminated by the Park Service—in this case, all sounds other than aircraft over-flights, which are not within the jurisdiction of the Park Service—then all human activity in the Park would be eliminated. And still the aircraft overflights would create substantial and adverse sound effects in the Park. Plaintiffs have articulated no principled basis upon which the court can conclude that the Park Service should have eliminated motorized noises on the basis of such cumulative analysis, but not other human-caused noises such as hiking or non-motorized raft trips. The court cannot conclude that the Park Service acted arbitrarily and capriciously when it concluded from a cumulative-effects analysis that motorized river traffic noise was not the source of serious sound problems in the Park and that elimination of such noise would not significantly improve the overall soundscape.

Finally, Plaintiffs argue that the Park Service failed to consider earlier environmental impact statements and a number of studies conducted in the 1970s, some of which found that river use impacted the soundscape within the Park. The Park Service relied primarily on studies conducted by noise experts in 1993 and 2003. These studies included field acoustic measurements, including sounds from motorized and non-motorized raft trips. The studies determined the distance at which motorized rafts could be heard and the length of time they were audible while traveling down-river, when measured from fixed points in the Park. The studies also evaluated the effects of other sounds such as water flow, wind, wildlife, human voices, helicopters, and air-craft overflights. The studies provide a reasonable basis for evaluating sound effects within the Park.

* * *

[T]he court cannot conclude that the Park Service acted arbitrarily and capriciously when it concluded that motorized uses do not impair the soundscape of the Park within the meaning of the Organic Act. [The court also decided that the plaintiffs failed to establish that the Park Service acted arbitrarily and capriciously when it adopted the 2006 Management Plan.]

NOTES

1.   *The allocation.* In the predecessor case, *Wilderness Public Rights Fund v. Kleppe*, 608 F.2d 1250 (9th Cir. 1979), the court upheld a Park Service allocation of 92 percent to commercial uses, despite the Organic Act's promise of "free access" (16 U.S.C. § 3), largely on the grounds that commercial users served the larger proportion of the public without the necessary equipment, and the fact that during the litigation the Service initiated a study that yielded a proposed management plan that would increase non-commercial permits from 8 percent to 30 percent of the total allocation. In this case, the court approved the 2006 plan's increase in non-commercial use from roughly one-third of the allocation to roughly one-half. Why do you suppose that it took nearly 30 years for the agency to achieve a roughly 50–50 division of permits?

2.   *The Park Service Organic Act.* The 1916 statute which the court must interpret and which governs national park units calls for "promot[ing] and regulat[ing]" the parks to conserve their scenery, natural and historic objects, and wildlife "to provide for the enjoyment" of them "in such manner and by such means as will leave them unimpaired for the enjoyment of future generations." 16 U.S.C. § 1. Are there two possibly incompatible purposes here—public access and conservation? If so, on what grounds should Park Service officials make decisions? The district court in *Sierra Club v. Babbitt,* 69 F.Supp.2d 1202 (E.D. Cal. 1999), concerning reconstructing a road in Yosemite National Park, stated that the Organic Act established "two fundamentally competing values; the preservation of natural and cultural resources and the facilitation of public use and enjoyment. These competing values of conservation and public use have been actively in conflict since before the [enactment of the Organic Act, which] did not resolve the conflict in favor of one side or the other." *Id.* at 1246–47.

Even conceding the historic conflict between preservation and public access in the national parks, is the *Sierra Club* court's interpretation persuasive? Re-read the language of § 1. Doesn't it establish a kind of compatible use management instead of equality between so-called conflicting uses? In other words, Park Service managers may promote public access only so long as conservation values are not impaired. After a long period of inaction, the Park Service finally addressed the issue in 2001, determining that preservation predominates over public access where there are conflicts, and reaffirmed that position in 2006. Nat'l Park Serv., *Management Polices* § 1.4.3 (2006), available at http://www.nps.gov/policy/MP2006.pdf. The policies explicitly forbid impairment of park resources (*id.* § 1.4.7)—defined as an impact that "in the professional judgment of the responsible [park] manager, would harm the integrity of park resources or values, including the opportunities that otherwise would be present for the enjoyment of those resources or values"—but allow non-impairing "adverse impacts." *Id.* § 1.4.5. The Park Service must make impairment determinations in writing. *Id.* § 1.4.7. But it is not clear that these policies, which are not administrative rules, are publicly enforceable.

3.   *Park concessioners.* One reason that interpreting the purposes of the Organic Act is so significant concerns the historic influence of park concessioners over park management. Concessioners like Yosemite Park and Curry and their profit-making concerns (often quite lucrative) are commonly more evident to park visitors than Park Service personnel. However, the Organic Act imposes some limits on concessioners, stipulating that park resources should not be "leased, rented, or granted to anyone" on terms that interfere with the public's "free access." 16 U.S.C. § 3; see also 16 C.F.R. §§ 1– 2. Concessioners are governed by the 1998 Concessioners Management Act, which revoked a pre-existing preference for permit renewal and requires facilities to be consistent with the conservation of park values and resources. 16 U.S.C. §§ 5952(5), (7)(a).

4.   *The effect of NEPA.* Notice that when the Park Service revisited its management plan in *River Runners*, it triggered a National Environmental Policy Act (NEPA) obligation to study the allocation in an environmental impact statement, which allows the public to comment on the issue and requires the agency to consider alternative allocation methods. However, NEPA does not require the Service to select the most environmental or the most public-access favoring alternative (which might indeed not be the same). All that the Service must do is to fairly describe and publicly disclose the issues involved, consider a reasonable range of alternatives, and select one that is rational (not arbitrary and capricious) in light of the agency's study. On what grounds did the Park Service decide not to eliminate the adverse effects from motorized noise pollution *in River Runners*?

5.   *Land plans.* Like other federal land managers, the Park Service has a statutory directive to develop and implement land plans—called "general management plans"—for park units, required by the 1978 amendments to the Park Service Organic Act, see 16 U.S.C. § 1a–7(b). These plans trigger NEPA as well as Endangered Species Act requirements. What is the value of a generic land planning requirement on the public lands? Might this requirement help to make land managers think long-term, without the pressure of a particular proposed project, or a particularly influential concessioner, in mind? Might it require resource inventories and scientific studies?

6.   *The economics of it.* When desired resources become scarce, like access to rafting through the Grand Canyon, people are willing to pay for them. Consider what actually happens when the Park Service gives permits to commercial operators who then turn around and charge the public fees for access through their permits. People who obtain access through commercial outfitters effectively pay a premium for their access, which amounts to a governmental gift to the outfitters who re-sell their permits to the public for a profit. Wouldn't the government obtain something closer to fair market value if it auctioned the permits? On the other hand, when the government auctioned off public lands in the nineteenth century, there was a widespread practice of collusion on the part of bidders (through so-called "claims clubs") to keep bidding costs low.

7.   *Hunting in national parks.* Hunting is not permitted in national parks in the lower 48 states unless the individual park's legislation authorizes it, or the Park Service makes findings concerning consistency with public safety and sound resource management. 36 C.F.R. § 2.2(b)(2). However, hunting is a permissible use in national parks in Alaska.

8.   *Snowmobiles in Yellowstone National Park.* A long-running dispute over snowmobiles in Yellowstone might finally have been resolved by Obama Administration regulations in 2013, 78 Fed. Reg. 63,069 (Oct. 23, 2013). Snowmobiling in the park, which began in the 1960s, had dramatically expanded by the 1990s. The Clinton Administration in 2001, after settling an environmentalist lawsuit, promulgated a regulation that would have phased

out individual snowmobiles—due to their adverse effects on air quality, noise pollution, and disturbance to wildlife, especially bison—in favor of snowcoaches (bus-like vehicles), which would preserve access to the park in the winter while minimizing adverse effects but without the individual experience associated with snowmobiles. 66 Fed. Reg. 7260 (Jan. 22, 2001). These regulations were rejected by the new Bush Administration, which proposed to continue snowmobile use but capped it at 950 snowmobiles per day.

Environmentalists successfully challenged the Bush rule in the D.C. District Court, *Fund for Animals v. Norton*, 294 F.Supp.2d 92 (D.D.C. 2003) (finding violations of NEPA and the APA due to a dramatic and poorly reasoned change in policy, in light of the clear "conservation mandate" in the Organic Act, which "trumps all other considerations," *id.* at 108). But snowmobilers also successfully challenged the Clinton rule in Wyoming District Court. *International Snowmobile Manufacturers' Ass'n v. Norton*, 304 F.Supp.2d 1278 (D. Wyo. 2004) (due to a failure to take a "hard look" at the feasibility of snowcoaches and a "prejudged political decision" by the Clinton Administration, *id.* at 1291). The conflicting decisions left the pre-2001 regulation intact, which was essentially no regulation at all. The Park Service eventually allowed a total of 960 snowmobiles per day to enter Yellowstone and nearby Grand Teton National Park, basically the same amount as before the Clinton regulation.

The new Obama Administration's regulation changed course again, rejecting a fixed, maximum number of snowmobiles per day and establishing a system of regulating "transportation events," defined as a snowcoach or ten snowmobiles and allocating them among commercial outfitters and private individuals. The new rule requires snowmobilers to travel in guided caravans and also imposes a "new best available technology" requirement on both snowmobiles and snowcoaches in an effort to reduce air and noise pollution. 78 Fed. Reg. at 63,071.

9.   *Wild and scenic rivers.* The historical emphasis on damming rivers to tap their navigation, flood control, irrigation, and electric power potential was tempered by enactment of the Wild and Scenic Rivers Act of 1968, 16 U.S.C. §§ 1287 *et seq.* Unlike wilderness and national parks and forests, wild and scenic rivers can be designated by the executive (the Secretary of the Interior upon the initiative of a state), although of course Congress may also designate, usually upon the recommendation of the Secretary of Interior or Agriculture, *id.* §§ 1275(a), 1276(a). Rivers may be designated as wild, scenic, or recreational, depending on the amount of adjacent development (especially road access) they have.

The statute forbids construction of dams or other obstructions to the free-flowing nature of all designated rivers. *Id.* § 1278(a). Federal lands within one-quarter mile of a wild river are withdrawn from the operation of the 1872 Mining Law and the Mineral Leasing Act, but land uses in river corridors are affected mostly by management plans required of all designated rivers. These plans "may establish varying degrees of intensity for . . . protection and development, based on the special attributes of the area." *Id.* § 1281(a). Managing agencies must "protect and enhance the [outstandingly remarkable] values" that caused the river segment to be designated, without "limiting other uses that do not substantially interfere with . . . these values." *Id.*

Case law has established that the protection of the "outstandingly remarkable values" (ORVs) which gave rise to designation is the key management criterion. See *Friends of Yosemite Valley v. Norton*, 348 F.3d 789 (9th Cir. 2003) (management plan failed to protect and enhance ORVs by failing to set user limits and too narrowly drawing river corridor boundaries); *Wilderness Watch v. U.S. Forest Service*, 143 F.Supp.2d 1186 (D. Mont. 2000) (enjoining special use permits for hunting and fishing lodges on a wild river); *Oregon Natural Desert Ass'n v. Singleton*, 47 F.Supp.2d 1182 (D. Or. 1998) (finding a duty to eliminate grazing if adversely affecting ORVs).

10. *National trails.* The National Trails System Act of 1968 established a national system of trails for recreational, scenic, and historic purposes. 16 U.S.C. §§ 1241 *et seq.* Only Congress may designate scenic and historic trails, but land managers may designate recreational trails. *Id.* § 1244(b)(11). Condemnation of private rights is authorized, but only after negotiations with landowners and only those interests "reasonably necessary" to provide passage—and not more than 125 acres per mile of trail. *Id.* § 1246(g).

The Trails Act also authorizes federal agencies to facilitate conversion of unused railroad rights-of-way to trails, the so-called "rails-to-trails" program. *Id.* § 1247(d). The statute prohibits abandonment of a rail line if there is a qualified person able to manage it, assume legal responsibility, and pay taxes. *Id.* The language of the federal conveyance and the nature of state law, which govern the nature of the property interest in rails-to-trails conversions, determine whether a conversion has constitutionally taken a landowner's reversionary interest. The results of the cases vary. See *Preseault v. United States,* 100 F.3d 1525 (Fed. Cir. 1996) (concluding that there was a taking of a landowner's reversionary interest under Vermont law); *Toews v. United States*, 376 F.3d 1371 (Fed. Cir. 2004) (finding a taking due to a conversion, interpreting California law); *Mauler v. Bayfield County*, 309 F.3d 997 (7th Cir. 2002) (no taking, construing the language of the federal railroad grant). The Supreme Court construed an 1875 federal statute not to reserve a federal easement after the railroad abandoned the right-of-way in *Marvin M. Brandt Revocable Trust v. United States*, 134 S.Ct. 1257 (2014).

B. WILDERNESS AND RECREATION

Wilderness areas are managed with a more single-minded preservationist purpose than national parks. Under the Wilderness Act of 1964, 16 U.S.C. §§ 1131 *et seq.*, wilderness areas are defined in uncharacteristically poetic congressional language as areas "where the earth and its community of life are untrammeled by man, where man himself is a visitor who does not remain," lands retaining their "primeval character and influence, without permanent improvements or human habitation, . . ." *Id.* § 1131(c). The 1964 statute, the result of a long gestation period which can be traced as far back as the efforts of Aldo Leopold (concerning the Gila National Forest in New Mexico) and Arthur Carhart (concerning the White River National Forest in Wisconsin) to convince the Forest Service to begin to manage certain roadless areas of the national forests to perserve their natural state. These efforts began an administrative system of a dominant preservational use of select areas of national forests, eventually resulting in promulgation of so-called "U-Regulations" under the leadership of Bob Marshall in 1939.

The Forest Service retained discretion to alter the status of these protected areas, and that encouraged the nascent Wilderness Society led by Howard Zahniser to begin to lobby for more permanent, statutory protection. Eight years after the initial wilderness bill was introduced by Senator Hubert Humphrey, the effort finally bore fruit when President Lyndon Johnson signed the Wilderness Act into law in 1964, saying that he hoped that the statute would cause future generations to view his generation more favorably. The 1964 law designated some 54 wilderness areas, totaling over 9 million acres, that had been earlier set aside by the Forest Service and reserved the authority to designate future wilderness areas to Congress, although the statute prescribed a review process for federal land managers to study potential additions to the system and make recommendations to the President, who in turn would make recommendations to Congress.

This cumbersome process led to substantial additions to the wilderness system in the 1980s after a court rejected the Forest Service's attempt to release roadless lands it found ineligible for wilderness in *California v. Block*, 690 F.2d 753 (9th Cir. 1982) (violations of NEPA). Today, the wilderness system has expanded more than ten-fold, to 110 million acres, nearly five percent of the U.S. land mass. In addition, wilderness-like areas are subject to protection under the Forest Service's roadless rules, as described at pages 785–792 above, and the Bureau of Land Management protects wilderness study areas under the terms of section 603 of the Federal Land Policy and Management Act, 43 U.S.C. § 1782. See generally John D. Leshy, *Legal Wilderness: Its Past and Some Speculations on its Future,* 44 Envtl. L. 549, 593–95 (2014); Michael C. Blumm & Andrew B. Erickson, *Federal Wild Lands Policy in the 21st Century: What a Long, Strange Trip It's Been,* 25 Colo. Nat. Res. Energy & Envtl. L. Rev. 1 (2014).

Recently, the focus of attention concerning wilderness areas has turned to issues of wilderness management. The Act established no wilderness service to administer the areas; that chore falls on the existing land managers. 16 U.S.C. § 1131(b). The Wilderness Act forbids permanent roads, commercial activities, mechanized transport, and structures or installations unless necessary to meet the "minimum requirements for the administration of the area." *Id.* § 1133(c). These provisions are engendering substantial litigation. In the decision below, environmentalists challenged a management decision to eradicate non-native species in order to reinstitute native trout in a creek within a wilderness area in northern California.

CALIFORNIANS FOR ALTERNATIVES TO TOXICS V. U.S. FISH AND WILDLIFE SERVICE

U.S. District Court For The Eastern District Of California

814 F.Supp.2d 992 (2011)

[Environmental organizations challenged the Forest Service's (USFS) and Fish and Wildlife Service's (USFWS) decisions authorizing the Paiute Cutthroat Trout Restoration Project in Silver King Creek, located in the Carson-Iceberg Wilderness in Alpine County, California. The project called for applying pesticides to eradicate non-native trout, then restocking the creek with Paiute cutthroat trout (PCT). Environmentalists concerned about pesticide use argued violations of both NEPA and the Wilderness Act.]

DAMRELL, JR., J.

* * *

[I]n support of their claim that defendants failed to comply with the Wilderness Act, plaintiffs assert that the Project's use of a gasoline-powered auger does not qualify for an exception to the Act's prohibition against motorized equipment; that the Project elevates the goal of recreational angling over the goal of preserving wilderness character; and that the Agencies fail to prove that the Project is necessary to meet the Act's minimum requirements to administer wilderness. Specifically, plaintiffs assert that the Act prohibits the Project's use of the motorized equipment because the Project is not restoring a species fundamental to the overall natural health of the ecosystem, and the Combined Physical Removal Alternative would be feasible without potentially killing endemic or native invertebrate species in Silver King Creek.

Defendants respond, arguing that the Agencies met their burden of demonstrating that the use of motorized equipment was necessary to meet the goal of restoring PCT. Specifically, the Agencies determined that the use of a motorized auger at the neutralization site was the most effective method of applying potassium permanganate, compared to the drip system, and would minimize the human and ecological effects of the application. In addition, the Agencies assert that, while the Combined Physical Removal Alternative would avoid the effect of chemical treatment, that alternative would be unsuccessful in reaching the conservation goal of the project. Defendants point out that plaintiffs do not contest the proposition that recovery of the PCT is a conservation goal consistent with the purposes of the Act.

* * *

Conservation of PCT as Purpose Consistent with the Wilderness Act

An agency charged with administering a designated wilderness area is responsible for preserving its wilderness character. *High Sierra Hikers Ass'n v. Blackwell*, 390 F.3d 630, 645 (9th Cir. 2004) (citing 16 U.S.C. § 1133(b)). In addition, the agency must administer the area "for such other purposes for which it may have been established as also to preserve its wilderness character." *Id.* Specifically, the Act dedicates protected wilderness to "public purposes of recreational, scenic, scientific, educational, *conservation,* and historical uses." *Id.* (emphasis added).

In reference to this statutory language, the Ninth Circuit has noted that even though the Act is intended to enshrine the long-term preservation of wilderness areas as the ultimate goal, these sometimes conflicting responsibilities makes the purpose of the Act as to *conservation* ambiguous. *Wilderness Watch, Inc. v. U.S. Fish and Wildlife Serv.,* 629 F.3d 1024, 1033 (9th Cir. 2010). Therefore, in the absence of a plain meaning for conservation, this court must decide whether the conservation goal at issue here is consistent with the Act based on "the thoroughness evident in [the Agencies'] consideration, the validity of [their] reasoning, [and the] consistency with earlier and later pronouncements . . ." in accordance with the *Mead* standard of review. *U.S. v. Mead Corp.*, 533 U.S. 218, 228 (2001).

* * *

[T]he meaning of conservation is not plainly stated within the Act and is, therefore, ambiguous. 629 F.3d at 1033. Defendants argue that recovery of the PCT is plainly consistent with the Wilderness Act because it is supported by legislative intent, which plaintiffs do not dispute. See H.R. Rep. 98–40 (Mar. 18, 1983). However, the first step of *Chevron* analysis excludes any non-statutory material from the determination of plain meaning. *High Sierra Hikers Ass'n*, 436 F.Supp.2d at 1130.

Regardless, the USFS's decision here is persuasive in showing that restoration of the PCT to its native habitat is contained in the conservation goal of the Wilderness Act, in accordance with the *Mead* standard. The USFS's reasoning for complying with the Act reflects consistency with both the 1985 and 2004 Plans, as well as the limited legislative record for the designation of the Carson-Iceberg Wilderness.

More specifically, in the EIR/EIS [Environmental Impact Report/Environmental Impact Statement], the Agencies demonstrated a consistent history of federal agencies implementing projects to recover PCT in Silver King Creek. In fact, these efforts began before the designation of the Carson-Iceberg Wilderness by the California Wilderness Act of 1984, and have continued ever since. Second, although the PCT was not cited as a motivation for the Carson-Iceberg Wilderness designation, Congress did acknowledge in HR 98–40 that "certain wildlife management activities, designed to enhance or restore fish populations, are permissible and often desirable in wilderness areas to aid in achieving the goal of preserving the wilderness character of the area." . . .

Citing *High Sierra Hikers Ass'n,* plaintiffs contend that the Project's benefits to recreational fishing "elevate recreational activity over the long-term preservation of the wilderness character of the land," and render it entirely contrary to the Act. However, plaintiffs' reliance on *High Sierra Hikers Ass'n* is inapposite as their argument fails to distinguish the overall goal of this Project as opposed to the goal in *High Sierra Hikers.* 436 F.Supp.2d at 1123–24. The sole purpose of the project in *High Sierra Hikers Ass'n* was to maintain a local fishery that had been developed when cattlemen stocked the project area with trout at the beginning of the 20th century. *Id.* In contrast, the stated purpose of the Project here, as represented in the USFS ROD [Record of Decision] is: "to restore Paiute cutthroat trout to its historic range as stated in the 2004 Revised Paiute Cutthroat Trout Recovery Plan (USFWS 2004), and thereby satisfy[ ] one critical Recovery Plan component for delisting the species." Thus, unlike *High Sierra Hikers Ass'n,* reestablishing a native species in a wilderness area, independent of the means for reaching that goal, enhances the primitive character of an ecosystem and serves a conservation purpose (not a recreational purpose), permissible under the Act.

The Wilderness Act's Exception for Motorized Equipment that is "Necessary" to Meet the "Minimum Requirements" for Conserving PCT

The Act prohibits use of motorized vehicles and equipment, among other activities, subject only to one exception: "as necessary to meet minimum requirements for the purpose of this Chapter (including measures required in emergencies involving the health and safety of persons within the area)." 16 U.S.C. § 1133(c). . . .

* * *

In *High Sierra Hikers Ass'n* and *Wilderness Watch,* the Ninth Circuit articulated two ways that the Forest Service can violate the Wilderness Act in granting an exception to otherwise prohibited activities under § 1133(c): First, the Service may fail to make an adequately reasoned determination that the activity is necessary to achieve a purpose consistent with the Wilderness Act. "It is clear that the statutory scheme requires, among other things, that the Forest Service make a finding of 'necessity' before authorizing [otherwise prohibited activities] in wilderness areas." *High Sierra Hikers Ass'n,* 390 F.3d at 646.

* * *

Second, the Service may fail to explain why the extent of the activity is necessary. A finding of necessity is required, but not wholly sufficient, for allowing an otherwise prohibited activity. The Agency must explain why the extent of the otherwise prohibited activity is the necessary action as opposed to other strategies that could have met the goal of conserving the target species. *Wilderness Watch,* 629 F.3d at 1037. In explaining why the proposed extent of the activity is necessary, the agency must compare factors relevant to the decision in relation to each other. *High Sierra Hikers Ass'n,* 390 F.3d at 647. Therefore, the Ninth Circuit has held that if complying with the Act on one factor will impede progress towards another factor, "the administering agency must determine the most important value and [justify] its decision to protect that value." *High Sierra Hikers Ass'n,* 390 F.3d at 646.

* * *

Here, the USFS adequately reasoned that motorized equipment was necessary to achieve conservation of the PCT. Although the USFS misinterprets the standard in stating its overall conclusion that the Project is necessary, the Agency provides enough explanation for its decision throughout the Minimum Requirements Decision Guide (the "Guide"), to show a reasoned finding of necessity. Specifically, the USFS contends that § 1133(c) provides an exception to this Project because of the necessity of restoring PCT to its historic range. This assertion is misplaced because the standard requires that the necessity lies in the use of the otherwise prohibited activity, here the use of motorized equipment, and not the merits of the proposed project. The validity of the goal of restoring the PCT does not factor into this analysis.

* * *

However, while the Agencies justified the necessity of using motorized equipment as opposed to other methods, they nonetheless violated the Wilderness Act by failing to consider the potential extinction of native invertebrate species as a factor relevant to the decision of whether the *extent* of the project was necessary. . . .

[L]ike in *High Sierra Hikers Ass'n,* the USFS violated the Wilderness Act by failing to (1) balance competing values, (2) determine the most important value, and (3) justify the decision to protect that value. . . .

As a result of that failure, the Agencies charted Alternative Two as having a net positive impact on the wilderness character of the Carson-Iceberg Wilderness, based on the proposed benefit of restoring PCT. This characterization led to the final conclusion that the Project will create "improved long term natural conditions of wilderness character through restoration of a native species." But in fact, complying with the Act to conserve PCT by implementing this Project would *impede* progress towards preserving the overall wilderness character. Despite the benefits gained from restoring a PCT population, accounting for the potential loss of endemic species would create a net, *negative* impact; the loss of primitive species would depreciate the wilderness character of the Carson-Iceberg Wilderness.

* * *

As opposed to addressing process or practicalities, the Wilderness Act sets forth lofty goals about maintaining the naturalness of the wilderness. Indeed, Congress enacted the Wilderness Act "to assure that an increasing population, accompanied by expanding settlement and growing mechanization, does not occupy and modify all areas within the United States and its possessions, leaving no lands designated for preservation and protection in their natural condition. 16 U.S.C. § 1131(a). The Act established a National Wilderness Preservation System composed of "wilderness areas" which Congress directed "shall be administered for the use and enjoyment of the American people in such manner as will leave them unimpaired for future use and enjoyment as wilderness." *Id.* The Act defines wilderness "in contrast with those areas where man and his own works dominate the landscape, . . . as an area where the earth and its community of life are untrammeled by man, where man himself is a visitor who will not remain." *Id.* at § 1131(c).

It is against this backdrop that the court must evaluate the Agencies' decision in this case. The geographic context of this Project is highly significant. We are not considering the application of rotenone in a *reservoir,* but rather a *stream* in the Carson-Iceberg Wilderness, an unimpaired reference which would be impacted over a two to three year period. If the Project is successful, all living organisms within that eleven mile stretch of stream would be eradicated.

* * *

[T]his case is wholly distinguishable from *Wolf Recovery Foundation v. U.S. Forest Service*, 692 F.Supp.2d 1264 (D. Idaho 2010) heavily relied upon by defendants. There, the Idaho district court found that the use of helicopters to collect data on gray wolves in the Frank Church Wilderness was necessary to meet the minimum requirements for the administration of the area. In doing so, however, the court was careful to note that that "case . . . present[ed] the most rare of circumstances . . . [where] man [was] attempting to restore the wilderness character of the area by returning the wolf [an endangered species]." *Id.* at 1268. . . .

To the contrary, here, (1) the PCT is not an endangered species; (2) defendants have not established an imminent risk to the species should the Project not proceed; and (3) this Project is not a transient intrusion, like in *Wolf Recovery Foundation,* but rather a two to three year injection of rotenone to a wilderness stream which will eradicate all living organisms within the stream. Additionally, unlike *Wolf Recovery Foundation,* as well as *Wilderness Watch* and *High Sierra Hikers Ass'n,* the conservation efforts, in this case, on behalf of the PCT will be taken at the expense of other sensitive, and possibly rare or endemic, species. That fact is undisputed. Significantly, it also distinguishes this case from any others the court has reviewed. Indeed, the parties did not cite, nor is the court aware of, any other case where a project was found to be compliant with the Act's mandates despite the elevation of the interests of one species over another. . . .

In *High Sierra Hikers Ass'n* and *Wilderness Watch,* the Ninth Circuit emphasized that if complying with the Act on one factor will impede progress towards another factor, when deciding whether the extent of the project is necessary, the Forest Service must determine the most important value and justify a decision to protect that value. See, e.g., *High Sierra Hikers Ass'n.,* 390 F.3d at 646. That process involves a comparative and qualitative analysis where the variables are considered in relation to one another and the interests at stake are weighed.

It is precisely that type of analysis that was not performed in this case. The analysis is not contained within the Guide, and even were the court to independently consider the substantive findings of the Forest Supervisor's ROD, they too are insufficient. Approving the Project, the Supervisor concluded: "The short term negative effects to Wilderness are balanced by restoration of a native species to its historic habitat within the Carson-Iceberg Wilderness." However, like the Guide, the ROD does not perform the requisite comparative and qualitative analysis. While it does address more directly, and extensively, than the Guide the potential for long-term loss of aquatic invertebrates and the presence of rare and endemic species within the area, it does not balance the various interests at stake, comparing them to one another, nor does it explain a basis to elevate the PCT's interests over the other species at risk. The conclusory analyses set forth in both the ROD and the Guide are insufficient to me[e]t the Act's mandates.

At bottom, instead of choosing one competing value (conservation of the PCT) over the other (preservation of the wilderness character), the Agencies left native species, including invertebrate, out of the balance, and thus, improperly concluded that authorization of motorized equipment will comply with the Act by achieving the purpose of preserving wilderness character.

* * *

[The court held that the agencies violated the Wilderness Act and enjoined the Paiute Cutthroat Trout Restoration Project.]

NOTES

1. *The conservation project.* What was the U.S. Fish and Wildlife Service's purpose concerning this wilderness area? Was it a permissible purpose under the Wilderness Act? If so, what led to the judicial injunction? What sort of review does the court give to the Service's restoration project? Note the court's reliance on *United States v. Mead,* 533 U.S. 218 (2001) (ruling that where a statute has not delegated responsibility to an administrative agency to resolve an issue, the agency is still entitled to judicial deference to the extent that its decision is persuasive to the court).

2. *Recreational use conflicts in wilderness areas.* The court cited a number of other cases involving use conflicts in wilderness areas. In *High Sierra Hikers Ass'n v. U.S. Forest Service,* 436 F.Supp.2d 1117 (E.D. Cal. 2006), the court affirmed an injunction of artificial restocking of trout in a wilderness area to maintain a recreational fishery as inconsistent with the Wilderness Act's elevation of preservation of the natural environment over recreational fishing. In *Wilderness Watch v. U.S. Fish and Wildlife Service,* 629 F.3d 1024 (9th Cir. 2010), the court reversed a lower court decision and enjoined the installation of water tanks in the Kofa National Wildlife Refuge and Wilderness in southwest Arizona's desert to benefit big horn sheep suffering from low rainfall because it was inconsistent with the long-term preservation of the character of the area. The *Californians for Alternatives to Toxics* court distinguished *Wolf Recovery Foundation v. U.S. Forest Service,* 692 F.Supp.2d 1264 (D. Idaho 2010), which upheld a special use permit for the use of helicopters in the Frank Church Wilderness because they were necessary to monitor endangered gray wolf restoration to the area, despite the court's acknowledgment that helicopters were "antithetical to a wilderness experience." *Id.* at 1268.

In a case not cited in this excerpt, *Wilderness Watch & Public Employees for Environmental Responsibility v. Mainella,* 375 F.3d 1085 (11th Cir. 2004), the court ruled that the Park Service could not conduct motorized transport of tourists through the Cumberland Island Wilderness Area to access grave sites on slave plantations. Congress reversed the court (and upheld the Park Service's position) in an appropriations rider without affecting the wilderness designation of the area. See George C. Coggins, et al., *Federal Public Land and Resources Law* 943 (7th ed. 2014). Do these cases form a consistent body of law?

3.   *Other use conflicts in wilderness areas.* Use conflicts not involving recreation in wilderness areas include *Wilderness Society v. U.S. Fish and Wildlife Service*, 353 F.3d 1051 (9th Cir. 2003), where the court enjoined a permit introducing hatchery salmon into a wilderness lake to benefit commercial fishers downstream of the wilderness area as inconsistent with the statute's ban on commercial activities. In *Drakes Bay Oyster Co. v. Salazar,* 921 F.Supp.2d 972 (N.D. Cal. 2013), the court upheld a National Park Service denial of a permit renewal for an oyster farm on a potential wilderness within the Point Reyes National Seashore, concluding that the permit renewal was committed to the discretion of the Park Service.

C. RECREATION ON MULTIPLE USE AND COMPATIBLE-USE LANDS

Unlike national parks or wilderness areas, lands managed by the federal Bureau of Land Management (BLM)—like most lands managed by the U.S. Forest Service—are subject to multiple use management, first codified in the Multiple-Use and Sustained Yield Act of 1960, 16 U.S.C. §§ 528–31. According to some accounts, the almost unreviewable discretion afforded to the management agencies under this opaque standard has allowed concentrated local interests to maintain monopoly control of public resources. See, e.g., Michael C. Blumm, *Public Choice Theory and the Public Lands: Why "Multiple Use" Failed*, 18 Harv. Envtl. L. Rev. 405 (1994).

On BLM public lands, use conflicts are often intense. Frequently, those conflicts involve inter-recreational conflicts, such as between wilderness hikers and off-road vehicle enthusiasts. The case below epitomizes those conflicts.

UTAH SHARED ACCESS ALLIANCE V. CARPENTER
Tenth Circuit Court of Appeals
463 F.3d 1125 (2006)

[The members of Utah Shared Access Alliance (USA-ALL) used motorized vehicles to access lands throughout Utah lands managed by the Bureau of Land Management (BLM). After the BLM imposed several restrictions on off-road vehicle (ORV) use in certain parts of the state, USA-ALL filed suit under the Administrative Procedure Act (APA), alleging violations of the Federal Land Policy and Management Act (FLPMA) and the National Environmental Policy Act (NEPA). The federal district court upheld the BLM's restrictions. USA-ALL appealed.]

TACHA, C.J.

* * *

A. Federal Land Policy and Management Act

Nearly one-half of Utah is federal land managed by the BLM, which is an agency within the Department of Interior. *Norton v. S. Utah Wilderness Alliance,* 542 U.S. 55, 58 (2004) (*SUWA*). FLPMA, codified at 43 U.S.C. §§ 1701 *et seq.,* creates a "versatile framework" for governing the BLM's management of these lands. *Rocky Mountain Oil & Gas Ass'n v. Watt,* 696 F.2d 734, 737–38 (10th Cir. 1982). The statute directs the BLM to manage public lands "under principles of multiple use and sustained yield." 43 U.S.C. § 1732(a). . . . " 'Multiple use management' is a deceptively simple term that describes the enormously complicated task of striking a balance among the many competing uses to which land can be put. . . ." *SUWA,* 542 U.S. at 58 (citing 43 U.S.C. § 1702(c)). These uses include, but are not limited to, "recreation range, timber, minerals, watershed, wildlife and fish, and [uses serving] natural scenic, scientific and historical values." *Id.* The phrase "sustained yield" refers to the BLM's duty "to control depleting uses over time, so as to ensure a high level of valuable uses in the future." *Id.* (citing 43 U.S.C. § 1702(h)).

To assist in the management of public lands, FLPMA requires that the BLM "develop, maintain, and, when appropriate, revise land use plans." 43 U.S.C. § 1712(a). These land use plans, which the BLM regulations denote "resource management plans" (RMPs), see 43 C.F.R. § 1601.0–5(n) (2005), project both the present and future use of the land. 43 U.S.C. § 1701(a)(2). . . .

FLPMA prohibits the BLM from taking actions inconsistent with the provisions of RMPs. See *SUWA,* 542 U.S. at 69; 43 U.S.C. § 1732(a) ("The Secretary shall manage the public lands . . . in accordance with the land use plans developed by him. . . ."); 43 C.F.R. § 1610.5–3 ("All future resource management authorizations and actions . . . shall conform to the approved plan."). When needed, however, these plans may be amended. 43 C.F.R. § 1610.5–5. To do so, the BLM must prepare an environmental assessment or an environmental impact statement, see *id.,* and submit the proposed amendment to public notice and comment in the same way as when the plan was originally being prepared. 43 C.F.R. § 1610.2.

In any event, RMPs must further the purpose of FLPMA, which is to ensure that:

> the public lands be managed in a manner that will protect the quality of scientific, scenic, historical, ecological, environmental, air and atmospheric, water resource, and archeological values; that, where appropriate, will preserve and protect certain public lands in their natural condition; that will provide food and

habitat for fish and wildlife and domestic animals; and that will provide for outdoor recreation and human occupancy and use.

43 U.S.C. § 1701(a)(8). Further underscoring the BLM's duty to protect the environment is the statutory requirement that "[i]n managing the public lands the Secretary shall, by regulation or otherwise, take any action necessary to prevent unnecessary or undue degradation of the lands." 43 U.S.C. § 1732(b).

B.   Executive Orders and Federal Regulations Pertaining to ORV Use

* * *

Under 43 C.F.R. § 8342.1, all public lands must be designated as open, limited, or closed to off-road vehicles. See 43 C.F.R. § 8342.1. The designations must be made to minimize conflicts among the different users of the lands (i.e., hikers, ORV users, and birdwatchers). Id. In addition, care must be taken to avoid damage to natural resources and to prevent impairment of wilderness suitability. Id. The initial designation of areas as open, limited, or closed to ORVs is accomplished through the resource management planning process, and it must involve public participation and consideration of all viewpoints. 43 C.F.R. § 8342.2(a).

Short of promulgating or amending an RMP, the resource management planning process does not speak to the manner in which an ORV designation may be changed. As such, and in order to address Executive Order 11989, the BLM promulgated a regulation that requires the agency to close areas to ORV use, without resort to the route-designation process undertaken when promulgating or amending an RMP, when the BLM determines that ORVs "are causing or will cause considerable adverse effects" to "soil, vegetation, wildlife, wildlife habitat, cultural resources, historical resources, threatened or endangered species, wilderness suitability, other authorized uses, or other resources." 43 C.F.R. § 8341.2(a). Notably, such closures are nondiscretionary: the BLM "*shall immediately close* the areas affected to the type(s) of vehicle causing the adverse effect until the adverse effects are eliminated and measures implemented to prevent recurrence." Id. (emphasis added). "This provision creates a separate duty to close without regard to the designation process; it does not automatically become inoperative once the Secretary exercises his discretion to designate the land." Sierra Club v. Clark, 756 F.2d 686, 690 (9th Cir. 1985).

The BLM's authority to close or restrict the use of public lands notwithstanding the provisions of the governing RMP is not limited to 43 C.F.R. § 8341.2(a). It is also permitted to do so in order "to protect persons, property, and public lands and resources." 43 C.F.R. § 8364.1. An order closing or restricting the use of public lands under this authority must identify the lands that are closed to entry or restricted as to use; specify the uses that are restricted; specify the period of time during which the closure or restriction applies; identify any persons exempt from the closure or restriction; include a statement of the reasons for the closure; and be posted and published as provided in the regulation. 43 C.F.R. § 8364.1(b), (c).

* * *

C.   *The BLM Complied with Procedures Mandated by FLPMA and its Action is Supported by Substantial Evidence*

1.   *The Restrictions Are Not "De Facto Amendments."*

USA-ALL contends that the 2003 Box Elder Order and the two Grand County restrictions must be nullified because they are "de facto amendments" to the Box Elder and Grand County RMPs that were issued without public notice and participation and without the BLM having first conducted an EA [environmental assessment] as required by FLPMA. We disagree.

Although there is some support outside this jurisdiction for an argument relating to "de facto amendments," the cases of which this Court is aware have little—if any—bearing on the facts presented by this appeal. See, e.g., *House v. U.S. Forest Serv.,* 974 F.Supp. 1022 (E.D. Ky. 1997) (proposed timber sale approved on the basis of three policies that constituted "significant" changes to land use plan requires same public comment as land use plan itself); *Or. Natural Res. Council Fund v. Forsgren,* 252 F.Supp.2d 1088 (D. Or. 2003) (narrower definition of lynx habitat which led to reduction in such habitat is "significant" change to land use plan and requires public comment and preparation of EIS). This Court is not aware of any authority indicating that a closure order promulgated pursuant to 43 C.F.R. §§ 8341.2 and 8364.1 constitutes a "de facto" amendment to an RMP, thus triggering compliance with FLPMA's public participation and EA requirements. To the contrary, the Ninth Circuit has specifically held that "[n]othing in [§ 8364.1] or the authorizing statutory sections requires public hearings for temporary closures" to vehicular use—thereby foreclosing any argument that temporary ORV closures are essentially RMP amendments. *Humboldt County v. United States,* 684 F.2d 1276, 1283 (9th Cir. 1982).

Indeed, courts have consistently emphasized the distinction between the initial ORV-route-designation process reflected in an RMP—which is subject to public comment and requires the promulgation of an EA—and closures of those designated routes authorized under regulations promulgated pursuant to FLPMA, NEPA, and other statutes. For example, the Central District of California noted that:

The regulations took into account the amendments to E.O. 11,684 effected E.O. 11,989, 3 C.F.R. 120 (1978). See 43 C.F.R. s 8341.2. E.O. 11,989, among other things, amended E.O. 11,644 so as to require closure of ORV areas and trails whenever an agency finds that ORV use will cause or is causing "considerable adverse effects." *This closure standard is to be distinguished from the initial designation criteria set forth in E.O. 11,644 and mirrored in 43 C.F.R. § 8342.1.*

Am. Motorcyclist Ass'n v. Watt, 543 F.Supp. 789, 796 n. 14 (C.D. Cal. 1982) (emphasis added); see also *Sierra Club,* 756 F.2d at 690 (stating that 43 C.F.R. § 8341.2 "creates a separate duty to close without regard to the designation process; it does not automatically become inoperative once the Secretary exercises his discretion to designate the land."); *Am. Sand Ass'n v. U.S. Dept. of Interior,* 268 F.Supp.2d 1250, 1255 (S.D. Cal. 2003) (closure order under 43 C.F.R. §§ 8341.2 and 8364.1 done in accordance with FLPMA).

Moreover, this exemption of OHV [off-highway vehicle] travel restrictions from the resource management planning process reflects the realities of public land management and allows the BLM to timely comply with its statutory mandate to "take any action necessary to prevent unnecessary or undue degradation of the lands." 43 U.S.C. § 1732(b). Because the RMP revision process is much more time-consuming than enacting a temporary closure order, the BLM could not effectively respond to resource degradation only through the formal planning process. In this way, the BLM's exercise of its authority to address resource degradation—whether done pursuant to 43 C.F.R. § 8342.1(a) or 43 C.F.R. § 8364.1—is not "de facto" planning. Rather, it is a lawful discharge of the BLM's duty, independent of the planning process, to prevent undue degradation of resources.

2.   *An Emergency Is Not Required Before the BLM May Close Lands to ORV Use, and Its Decision is Supported by Substantial Evidence.*

USA-ALL also argues that there was no substantial evidence supporting a finding of an emergency, which it contends is necessary before the BLM may place ORV restrictions on the public lands. This contention is completely without merit. The regulation authorizing the challenged orders does not use the word "emergency," nor does it contain any language from which a requirement of an emergency could be inferred. See 43 C.F.R. § 8341.2; see also *Am. Sand Ass'n,* 268 F.Supp.2d at 1254 (holding that no emergency is necessary under FLPMA for the BLM to issue ORV closure orders). Rather, the BLM's authority under 43 C.F.R. § 8341.2 is tied to the existence of considerable adverse effects that are being caused by or will be caused by ORV use, and our review of the record convinces us that substantial evidence supports such a finding in this case. For this reason, we also disagree with USA-ALL's contention that the BLM's explanation as to why it issued the closure orders is implausible.

* * *

Conclusion

The BLM complied with required procedures under FLPMA and NEPA when it enacted the 2003 Box Elder Order and the Grand County ORV and Camping Restrictions, the BLM's decision [to] close various public lands to ORV use was supported by substantial evidence, and the BLM's reasoning in doing so was not implausible. . . . We therefore affirm.

NOTES

1.   *Off-road vehicle recreation.* Recreational use of public lands is now the dominant use of public lands. See Jan G. Laitos & Thomas A. Carr, *The Transformation on Public Lands*, 26 Ecology L.Q. 140 (1999). Off-road vehicle (ORV) recreation has burgeoned in recent years; sales of ORVs more than tripled between 1995 and 2003. Sandra B. Zellmer & Jan G. Laitos, *Principles of Natural Resources Law* 150 (2014). President Nixon began the regulation of ORVs on public land with Executive Order 11644 in 1972, which called for land managers to designate areas suitable for ORV use, an attempt to zone them to eliminate conflicts with other uses. President Carter banned ORV use where it was causing "considerable adverse [environmental] effects" in Executive Order 11989 in 1977. Under the executive orders, land managers assume public lands are closed to ORV use unless they are opened by land plans. BLM's regulations implementing the executive orders requiring, among other things, minimization of use conflicts, were at the center of the principal case above.

In the Federal Land Policy and Management Act of 1976, Congress included a separate title devoted to creating a plan for the California Desert Conservation Area, some 25 million acres in southeastern California described as a resource "extremely fragile, easily scarred, and slowly healed." 43 U.S.C. § 1781; Bureau of Land Management, *The California Desert Conservation Area Plan 1980 as Amended* 6 (1980). Nevertheless, a decision cited by the *Utah Shared Access* court, *Sierra Club v. Clark*, 756 F.2d 686 (9th Cir. 1985), upheld the BLM's approval of unrestricted ORV use in 3,000 acres of Dove Springs Canyon, despite the court's acknowledgement that the plan would amount to "the virtual sacrifice of a priceless natural area in order to accommodate a special recreational activity." *Id.* at 691. The court discounted these adverse effects by considering them in light of the entire planning area of 12 million acres, not just the affected canyon, leading to the conclusion that ORV damage would be limited to just 0.025 percent of the California desert. However, ORV use was subsequently curtailed by the BLM due to adverse effects on the desert tortoise, a threatened species under the Endangered Species Act. See George C. Coggins & Robert L. Glicksman, 3

Public Natural Resources Law § 31:10 (2d. ed. 2014), citing *American Motorcycle Ass'n*, 119 IBLA 196 (1991).

According to two respected commentators, increasing ORV use is leading to a "paradigm shift" in land management philosophy because the newer dominant motorized recreational uses are inherently incompatible with low-impact recreation like hiking, as ORV use produces a number of negative externalities like noise and air pollution, adverse effects on the land, public safety concerns, and harm to wildlife. They predict increasing conflicts between preservationists versus recreationists, historic allies in public land management. Zellmer & Laitos, cited above, at 151.

2.   *Deference to BLM.* In *Utah Shared Access*, the court deferred to the agency's multiple-use decision. Should a court defer to an agency decision that opened up public lands to consumptive use, as in *Sierra Club v. Clark*? BLM's organic statute, FLPMA, suggests that deference is appropriate, since it endorses multiple-use management, 43 U.S.C. §§ 1702(c), 1732(b), which the *Utah Shared Access* court described as "deceptively simple" but "enormously complicated." This is a notoriously opaque management standard. But the FLPMA's definition of multiple-use also includes the admonition that it does not include the "permanent impairment of the productivity of the land and the quality of the environment." *Id.* § 1702(c). Moreover, FLPMA also directs the BLM to "prevent unnecessary or undue degradation" of public lands. *Id.* § 1732(b). Perhaps FLPMA's multiple-use decision-making is cabined by these provisions, providing some limits on judicial deference to the BLM's discretion.

3.   *The importance of land plans.* FLPMA requires all BLM decisions to be consistent with applicable land plans (referred to as "resource management plans"). *Id.* § 1732(a). BLM amends land plans regularly, generally every 10–15 years. Amending a land plan triggers NEPA requirements, meaning that BLM must evaluate the resources in the planning area, publicly disclose these effects, consider alternatives, and respond to public comment. In short, amending a land plan is procedurally complex. Notice that the ORV users in *Utah Shared Access* suggested that BLM violated FLPMA's requirement of acting consistently with applicable land plans by restricting ORV use without amending the applicable land plan, in effect engaging in a "de facto" amendment that would require compliance with NEPA procedures. Why does the court reject this argument?

4.   *BLM conservation lands.* In recent years, BLM has acquired management responsibility for a number of nationally significant conservation units, including many national monuments, a variety of national recreation areas, national trails, and the Steens Mountain Cooperative Management and Protection Area in southeastern Oregon. These units were consolidated by Congress into the "National Landscape Conservation System" in the 2009 Omnibus Public Lands Act. Pub. L. No. 111–11, 16 U.S.C. § 7202. The system, now with 27 million acres, aims to "conserve, protect, and restore nationally significant landscapes that have

outstanding cultural, ecological, and scientific values for the benefit of current and future generations." Order No. 3308 of the Secretary of the Interior, § 1 (Nov. 15, 2010), available at http://www.blm.gov/or/news/files/ NLCS_Order.pdf. Uses on system lands must be managed to protect the values of the uses that warranted the designation, and BLM may prohibit uses conflicting with those values. *Id.* § 4.

5.   *National wildlife refuges.* Wildlife refuges—over a hundred years old, since Theodore Roosevelt began establishing them in 1903—now consist of some 95 million acres in 540 units located in every state. They are neither multiple-use lands nor preservation lands, but instead are "compatible use" lands. The National Wildlife Refuge System Administration Act of 1966, 16 U.S.C. §§ 668dd–668ee, consolidated a diverse array of wildlife reservations into a single system and required all uses authorized within a refuge to be "compatible" with the primary purposes for which the refuge was founded. *Id.* at § 668dd(d)(3)(A). This requirement was mostly ignored until *Defenders of Wildlife v. Andrus ("Ruby Lake" Decision)*, 455 F.Supp. 446 (D.D.C. 1978) (enforcing the compatibility requirement against a government regulation authorizing speed boating in the Ruby Lake National Wildlife Refuge). Decisions like the *Ruby Lake* case prompted Congress to enact a major reform statute in 1997.

The National Wildlife Refuge System Improvement Act of 1997, P.L. No. 105–57, established a unifying system conservation purpose, expressed in ecological terms. 16 U.S.C. § 668dd(a)(2). The statute directs the Fish and Wildlife Service to "sustain and, where appropriate, restore and enhance healthy populations of fish, wildlife, and plants [employing] . . . modern scientific [principles]." *Id.* § 668ee(4). Recognizing the interconnectedness of nature reserves, the 1997 law calls for a "national network" of refuges and requires all refuges to have a comprehensive conservation plan governing refuge uses. *Id.* § 668dd(a)(2), (e)(1)(A)(i). The act implements a dominant use paradigm on refuges, defining compatible uses as those "not materially interfer[ing] with or detract[ing] from the fulfillment of the mission of the System or the purposes of the refuge." *Id.* § 668ee(1). The Secretary may permit no new uses of refuges, or expand, renew, or extend existing uses, without a compatibility finding. *Id.* § 668dd(d)(3)(A)(i). Wildlife-dependent uses, including hunting and fishing, have priority over other uses like grazing, oil and gas development, timber harvesting, and non-wildlife dependent recreation. *Id.* § 668dd(a)(4)(H). The latter uses are prohibited if they conflict with the national wildlife refuge system's mission, conflict with the purposes of the individual refuge, or materially interfere with wildlife-dependent uses. 50 C.F.R. § 29.1. For a discussion of the wildlife refuge system and the 1997 statute's emphasis on biodiversity, see Robert L. Fischman & Bob Adamcik, *Beyond Trust Species: The Conservation Potential of the National Wildlife Refuge System in the Wake of Climate Change*, 51 Nat. Res. J. 1 (2011). The following case concerns the compatibility of farming genetically modified crops at the Prime Hook National Wildlife Refuge in Delaware.

DELAWARE AUDUBON SOCIETY V. SECRETARY OF THE INTERIOR

U.S. District Court for Delaware
612 F.Supp.2d 442 (2009)

[Environmentalists charged the Secretary with violating several statutes, including the National Wildlife Refuge System Administration Act (NWRSAA), by approving cooperative agreements which authorized commercial corn and soybean crops in the Prime Hook National Wildlife Refuge, whose 10,000 acres are managed primarily for migratory birds and their habitat. The Secretary made no compatibility finding concerning this agricultural use, which began in 1995 and was reauthorized in 2001. The same year the Fish and Wildlife Service (FWS) adopted a policy prohibiting the use of genetically modified crops or organisms (GMO policy) in national wildlife refuges, and the Prime Hook refuge adopted a goal of phasing out GMOs because they "do not contribute to achieving refuge objectives." However, the Service made repeated exceptions to the GMO policy, continued to allow GMO crops on Prime Hook, and in 2006 approved two additional one-season cooperative agreements permitting the use of GMO crops in Prime Hook, again without making compatibility findings, inducing the environmentalists to file suit. There has been no farming in the refuge since the end of 2006.]

SLEET, C.J.

[The court first ruled that the environmentalists' claims were not moot because the government did not voluntarily cease the farming practices and use of genetically modified crops at Prime Hook until after the suit was filed, and in the absence of any legally-binding assurances, the court was unconvinced that the practices might not resume in the future.]

* * *

Whether Summary Judgment Is Appropriate

* * *

According to the NWRSAA, the mission of the National Wildlife Refuge System "is to administer a national network of lands and waters for the conservation, management, and where appropriate, restoration of the fish wildlife, and plant resources and their habitats within the United States." 16 U.S.C. § 668dd(a)(2). In addition, the NWRSAA empowers the Secretary of the Interior to "permit the use of any area within the System for any purpose . . . whenever [he or she] determines that such uses are compatible with the major purposes for which such areas were established." *Id.* at § 668dd(d)(1)(A).

Under NWRSAA regulations, a national wildlife refuge may be opened "for any refuge use . . . only *after* the [FWS] determines that it is a *compatible use* and not inconsistent with any applicable law." 50 C.F.R. § 25.21(b) (emphasis added). [Eds. The term "refuge use" includes farming. See 50 C.F.R. § 25.12.] In particular, these regulations require that such compatibility determinations must: (1) be in writing; (2) identify the proposed or existing use that the compatibility determination applies to; and (3) state whether the proposed use is in fact a compatible use based on "sound professional judgment." See 50 C.F.R. § 25.12. In addition, the NWRSAA requires that a written compatibility determination be completed *before* farming is permitted on a national wildlife refuge. *Id.*

Here, there is no dispute that the defendants permitted farming on Prime Hook without first conducting or preparing a written compatibility determination. The defendants do not contest that from 1995 to 2007, they entered into no less than 37 cooperative farming agreements, and that under these agreements, farmers were permitted to harvest commodity corn or soybean crops at Prime Hook. The defendants also do not contest that prior to entering these cooperative farming agreements, they did not make any compatibility determinations, or conduct any studies to assess whether these uses were compatible with Prime Hook's purposes. The administrative record is simply devoid of anything that even purports to be a compatibility determination, much less a formal document that comports with the clear requirements set forth in the NWRSAA regulations.

Because there are no issues of material fact that the defendants failed to make a written compatibility determination—prior to permitting cooperative farming on Prime Hook—the court concludes that the defendants violated the NWRSAA as a matter of law.

* * *

[The court also concluded that the FWS violated NEPA and enjoined farming at Prime Hook until the FWS complied with both NEPA and the NWRSAA.]

NOTES

1.   *Eliminating farming in Prime Hook.* In 2013, the Fish and Wildlife Service completed a refuge plan and EIS that called for the elimination of farming in Prime Hook to stop attracting nuisance geese to the refuge and to reduce forest fragmentation.

2.   *Phasing out GMO and neonicotinoid pesticide use in national wildlife refuges.* In 2014, the Fish and Wildlife Service pledged to phase out the use of GMOs by January 2016 in all refuges, to use agriculture practices only where they specifically contribute to wildlife objectives, and banned the

use of neonicotinoid (neuro-active poisons, related to nicotine and linked to bee-kills) pesticides. The Service justified the decision on the basis of the agency's biodiversity policy, which calls for the maintenance and restoration of "the biological integrity, diversity, and environmental health of refuges and is based on the underlying principle of wildlife conservation that favors management that restores or mimics natural ecosystem processes or functions to achieve refuge purpose(s)." Memorandum from James W. Kurth, Chief of the National Wildlife Refuge System to Regional Refuge Chiefs (July 17, 2014) (also citing a precautionary approach to wildlife management).

3.   *Wildlife refuge funding.* There are now some 540 national wildlife refuges in all 50 states, providing habitat for hundreds of species of mammals, reptiles, and birds. Many of these were established by the President and later endorsed by Congress in statutes like the Migratory Bird Conservation Act of 1929. 16 U.S.C. §§ 715 *et seq.* Since many prime wildlife habitat areas were not on the (mostly arid) public domain but instead were lands the federal government conveyed to private owners, funding for wildlife refuge acquisition has always been important. The Migratory Bird Hunting Stamp Act of 1935, 16 U.S.C. §§ 718a *et seq.*, created a dedicated fund for habitat acquisition from sales of federal stamps that waterfowl hunters must purchase. Later, funds also came from the 1965 Land and Water Conservation Fund Act, 16 U.S.C. §§ 460*l*–4 to 460*l*–11, from funds generated by outer continental shelf oil and gas leases and a motorboat fuels tax. This statute, discussed in the following section, also provides funds for state and local acquisition of recreation lands. What are the advantages and disadvantages of relying on such dedicated funds for acquisition of wildlife habitat? Does the stamp act suggest why hunting has such a prominent place in wildlife refuge use priorities?

4.   *National wildlife refuge water rights.* As reserved lands, wildlife refuges would seem to benefit from the reserved water rights doctrine, established by the Supreme Court in *Winters v. United States* (p. 579) and applied to non-Indian reserved lands in *Arizona v. California* (p. 582). Unlike, say, national forest lands, which are often at the headwaters of streams, wildlife refuges are frequently located low in water basins. Thus, their water rights could disrupt the diversions of upstream water users. The 1997 National Wildlife Refuge System Improvement Act directed the Fish and Wildlife Service to acquire water needed for refuge purposes under state law, 16 U.S.C. § 668dd(a)(4)(G), and proclaimed that nothing in the 1997 Act "create[d] a reserved water right, express or implied," for any purpose. *Id.* § 668dd(n)(1). But the statute also disclaimed any intent to affect "any water right in existence" when the act passed or to affect any federal or state water quality or quantity law. *Id.* Did the 1997 law eliminate reserved water rights for national wildlife refuges? In *U.S. v. Idaho*, 23 P.3d 117 (Idaho 2001), without interpreting the 1997 statute, the Idaho Supreme Court ruled that the Deer Flat National Wildlife Refuge, established in 1937 and including nearly 100 islands in 110 miles of the Snake River "as a refuge and breeding ground for migratory birds and other wildlife," had no implied reserved water

rights primarily because the court interpreted the refuge's purpose to provide wildlife protection only from hunting by humans, not from other predators.

D. RECREATION ON STATE LANDS

The Land and Water Conservation Fund Act (L & WCFA), 16 U.S.C. §§ 460*l*–4 to 460*l*–11, discussed above at p. 830, has over the years generated sufficient revenues to purchase some 5 million acres of federal land and conservation easements. It has also provided funding to states and localities to purchase roughly 3 million acres of lands for public recreation purposes. However, this federal funding, often in the form of matching funds (so that state and local funding also contribute to the purchase), came with an important condition to ensure that the public recreational purpose of the acquired land is maintained, as the following case illustrates.

SIERRA CLUB V. DAVIES
Eighth Circuit Court of Appeals
955 F.2d 1188 (1992)

[The Crater of Diamonds State Park, located in Pike County, Arkansas, contains a 37-acre diamond-bearing "crater," at which the public is allowed to search for diamonds. The State of Arkansas received a federal grant under the L & WCFA to help acquire and develop the state park in 1976. In 1987, the Arkansas Legislature authorized the Department of Parks and Tourism to lease the park for exploration and diamond production, and the state sought to undertake investigatory drilling in the park. The National Park Service (NPS) decided that the drilling would not constitute an unlawful conversion from public use to commercial use under the L & WCFA and approved the activity. The Sierra Club and other conservation groups sued both the state parks department and the NPS. The district court enjoined the preliminary drilling, and the intervening mining companies appealed.]

MAGILL, J.

The [L & WCFA] requires all states that receive grants to maintain the benefited land as public outdoor recreational space forever. 16 U.S.C. § 460*l*–8(f)(3). Any conversion of park land to nonrecreational use must be approved by the Secretary of Interior and can come only after the Secretary: (1) finds the conversion in accord with the existing comprehensive statewide outdoor recreation plan, and (2) is assured that the state will substitute other recreational properties of at least equal fair market value and of reasonably equivalent usefulness and location.[1] *Id.*

---

[1] Since the public diamond mining at Crater of Diamonds State Park is unique, it would be nearly impossible to find equivalently useful land to substitute if the Secretary found a conversion. Nevertheless, the L & WCFA provides that wetlands within the state shall be

* * *

The heart of the L & WCFA is found in § 6(f)(3). The rather straightforward section provides:

> No property acquired or developed with assistance under this section shall, without the approval of the Secretary, be converted to other than public outdoor recreation uses. The Secretary shall approve such conversion only if he finds it to be in accord with the then existing comprehensive statewide outdoor recreation plan and only upon such conditions as he deems necessary to assure the substitution of other recreation properties of at least equal fair market value and of reasonably equivalent usefulness and location.

16 U.S.C. § 460l–8(f)(3). Appellees argue that Phase I testing constitutes just such a conversion under the Act. The acting regional director determined that Phase I testing would not constitute a conversion, but would be permitted as a "temporary non-conforming use." The agency's decision was emphatically limited to Phase I testing. Contrary to assertions by appellees and the determination of the district court, the agency's decision in no way ushers in a parade of horribles culminating in full-blown commercial mining. . . . [T]he director stated that any subsequent testing proposals would have impact inseparable from actual mining and would, therefore, have to comply with the procedural substitution requirements of § 6(f)(3), as well as the National Environmental Policy Act [NEPA]. 42 U.S.C. §§ 4321 to 4347.

Appellees contend, nonetheless, that the state's elaborate planning as well as the funding by the mining companies indicates that Phase I testing is just a precursor to the inevitable commercial mining of the park. Even if the link in planning between Phase I testing and mining is shown to be ironclad, and even if it is shown that commercial mining would constitute a conversion, our review is limited to the agency action. No matter what the evidence shows might happen in the future, it is beyond this court's power to render a speculative decision on postulated facts. It is possible that testing will reveal the potential for commercial mining at the park. If this occurs, it is possible that the elected representatives of the people of Arkansas will decide to mine the park commercially. If they do, they will need to comply with § 6(f)(3) and [NEPA]. The agency's approval, if granted, will be reviewable at that point.

Our task is to determine whether the Secretary's decision to permit limited Phase I testing without declaring it a conversion was arbitrary

---

considered of reasonably equivalent usefulness for all other property within the state. 16 U.S.C. § 460l–8(f)(3).

and capricious, an abuse of discretion, or otherwise not in accordance with law. 5 U.S.C. § 706(2)(A) (1988).

* * *

The L & WCFA does not define conversion. The question turns, then, on whether the agency's determination that Phase I testing would not constitute a conversion was a reasonable construction of the Act. See *Chevron, U.S.A., Inc. v. Natural Resources Def. Council, Inc.,* 467 U.S. 837, 842–43 (1984). The agency has determined that conversions generally occur in four situations:

(1) Property interests are conveyed for nonpublic outdoor recreation uses.

(2) Nonrecreation uses (public or private) are made of the project area, or a portion thereof.

(3) Noneligible indoor recreation facilities are developed within the project area without (National Park Service) approval.

(4) Public outdoor recreation use of property acquired or developed with L & WCFA assistance is terminated.

L & WCFA Grants Manual, Chapter 675.9.3(A).

The only one of these situations possibly pertinent here is the situation where a nonrecreational use is made of a project area. If Phase I testing constituted a nonrecreational "use," it plausibly could constitute a conversion. But under Phase I testing, there is "use" of the park land only in the strictest sense. The park's purpose is by no means turned nonrecreational. The exploratory drilling does not limit public use of the park, except for the ten-to-twelve-week period when a 5,000 square foot region will be cordoned off. No permanent damage will come to the land and the available supply of minerals available to public visitors will not be depleted. An interpretation of the regulations holding such activity a nonrecreational "use" would render virtually any temporary, de minimis, nondestructive activity a conversion.

The agency certainly does not read its own regulations so broadly. The record is replete with instances in which the agency has construed temporary, nondestructive activities as being other than conversions. The agency specifically exempts from the definition of conversion underground utility easements which do not have a significant impact on the recreational utility of the park. L & WCFA Grants Manual, Chapter 675.9.3(A)(5)(a). The administrative record also reveals an interpretation by the Director of the Bureau of Outdoor Recreation that the construction by a nonowner of a waterline, pipeline, underground utility or "similar construction" which does not impair the present or future recreational use of the property might not constitute a conversion if the surface area is restored to its "preconstruction condition" and there is no relinquishment of control over the property. The agency also has concluded that the sale of subsurface rights or the nondestructive extraction of oil and gas from Land and Water Conservation Fund-assisted land does not constitute a conversion under the Act. L & WCFA Grants Manual, Chapter 675.1(E).

The agency clearly has determined that the statute requires more than de minimis and temporary intrusions on small portions of fund-assisted land to constitute a conversion. Viewed in light of the reasonableness of the agency regulations and policies found in the administrative record, the acting regional director's determination that Phase I testing would not constitute a conversion clearly was a permissible construction of the statute, and therefore was not arbitrary and capricious.

* * *

[T]he agency's need for flexibility in determining whether nondestructive testing is a conversion is also dictated by the requirements of § 6(f)(3) itself. In order to convert a fund-assisted parcel to another purpose—such as commercial mining—the Secretary must first be assured the state will substitute land of equivalent values and usefulness. 16 U.S.C. § 460*l*–8(f)(3). But the Secretary must know the value of the converted parcel first. A requirement that the Secretary must first be assured of substituted lands, and then begin testing to determine the value of the converted land, is unworkable. It would require the Secretary to create a new park of reasonably equivalent usefulness and value even before he decides whether or not to convert the state park to a commercial diamond mine and even before he knows the value of the park he is charged to create. Further, it would virtually preclude states from considering whether to convert fund-assisted land to other recreational uses. Since the states would be forced to provide substituted land even before testing to determine which use of the subject land would be most beneficial, states would be discouraged from ever pursuing even beneficial changes. This outcome contravenes the Act. The L & WCFA does not forbid conversions, it merely dictates that the state must replace the converted land with a suitable substitute. Clearly, an agency construction of the statute that enables the state to make nondestructive tests on fund-assisted land to determine its commercial value or potential for other recreational purposes cannot be deemed unreasonable.

This interpretation is also well within the confines of the only circuit court case to address the definition of conversion. In *Friends of Shawangunks, Inc. v. Clark,* 754 F.2d 446, 449 (2d Cir. 1985), the Second Circuit ruled that the Park Service's interpretation of what constitutes a conversion must be given considerable deference. Nevertheless, the court overturned an agency determination that transforming a portion of land covered by a conservation easement funded by the L & WCFA into a limited-access, resort golf course did not constitute a conversion. *Id.* The court specifically found that the proposed development would directly contravene the agency's own regulations. By allowing the development, the agency would enable the holder of fee title to the land on which the easement rested to do precisely what the easement had precluded: change the character of the land from a conservation area for public enjoyment to a private golf course. *Id.* at 451. Unlike the virtual transfer of title in *Shawangunks,* no change in the character of the land at Crater of Diamonds State Park would take place. The only effect on park land would be a temporary disruption on approximately 5,000 square feet in the public access area.

* * *

For the foregoing reasons, we reverse the permanent injunction issued by the district court. . . .

NOTES

1.   *What is a "conversion"?* In *Friends of Shawangunks v. Clark,* 754 F.2d 446 (2d Cir. 1985), cited in the principal case, the Second Circuit (per Judge Oakes) ruled that an unlawful conversion took place when the state amended a conservation easement purchased with the help of federal matching funds from the L & WCFA, covering land adjacent to state park popular for hiking. The amendment would have allowed expansion of a preexisting private golf course, which would become part of a resort complex operated by the Marriott Corporation. The Department of the Interior determined that no conversion occurred because the golf course would become open for public use, thus increasing public access. The district court agreed, but the Second Circuit reversed, concluding that the golf-course expansion (eight new holes) in violation of the original easement terms amounted to a conversion despite the promised increased public access: "[i]t is plain that there is a conversion from public enjoyment of an unspoiled area to private golfing." *Id.* at 451.

2.   *Yankee Stadium conversion.* Plans for the new Yankee Stadium ran into L & WCFA problems. The new stadium was located on Macomb's Dam Park, which was purchased in part with L & WCFA money in 1978. However, a court rejected a challenge to federal approval of the conversion in *Save Our Parks v. Kempthorne,* No. 06 Civ.6859 NRB, 2006 WL 3378703 (S.D. N.Y. Nov. 15, 2006), deciding that replacement parcels that included a parking garage's rooftop ballfield and a pedestrian walkway were sufficient.

3.   *Other state parklands.* Of course, not all state and local parks are purchased with L & WCFA funding, and therefore involve no issues of what constitutes a conversion under that statute. But other questions may arise, such as the distinction under state law between state parks, state forests, and other preserves at issue in the following principal decision.

4.   *Recreation fees.* The L & W Conservation Fund Act also limited the ability of federal agencies to charge recreational fees, although agencies actually had little incentive to do so, since the revenue they generated went to the federal treasury, not to agency budgets. That situation changed due to an experimental program authorized in 1996 and made permanent in the Federal Lands Recreation Enhancement Act of 2004, 16 U.S.C. §§ 6801 *et seq.* The 2004 statute allows land management agencies to keep all of the revenues collected for recreational access fees, with 60–80 percent going to the site that collected them. Although all land managers may charge for use of "amenities," like campgrounds and motorized vehicle trails, only the National Park Service and the Fish and Wildlife Service may charge admission fees. *Id.* § 6802. Since taxpayers fund public land management, does charging the public for the use of lands it owns amount to a kind of double-taxation?

SIERRA CLUB V. KENNEY

Supreme Court of Illinois
429 N.E.2d 1214 (1981)

[In 1974, a 345-acre wildfire occurred in Camden Hollow, an area within Illinois's Pere Marquette State Park. In 1978, the Illinois Department of Conservation proposed a commercial timber harvest and sale in the burn area. The purposes of the sale were to salvage dead and injured trees for lumber or firewood, to remove damaged trees that would otherwise be susceptible to infestation and disease, to rehabilitate the area for growth and regeneration, and to improve wildlife habitat. 438 dead trees, and 1,625 live trees were marked for cutting. The Sierra Club challenged the sale. The circuit court denied an injunction, but the Illinois Court of Appeals reversed. The dispute then went to the state supreme court]

SIMON, J.

* * *

The Department's proposal to log the Camden Hollow section of Pere Marquette State Park was apparently a good-faith attempt to exercise its discretion in the management of the park consistent with advanced and scientific forestry practices. However, Pere Marquette is a State park, not a State forest, and the techniques developed to encourage productivity and growth in State forests or privately owned timberlands are inappropriate in State parks. The production of commercially valuable timber and forests is subordinated in parks to preservation and recreation. The decision is not left to the discretion of the Department; the policy has been mandated by statute. To the extent that the decision to log reflected a policy change in the Department, it was a change in policy the legislature had not authorized the Department to make.

* * *

In addition to State parks, the legislature has established State forests and State nature preserves. Each was similarly placed under the Department's control. Different interests are at stake in the management of each type of resource. The options are to develop the land for the commercial value of its timber, to use the land for recreation, or to preserve the land in its natural splendor for its aesthetic and cultural value. These uses are not necessarily conflicting, but are not perfectly reconcilable. The statutes governing the management of State forests, State parks and nature preserves reflect a legislative balancing of interests to allow a mix of different uses at each type of resource.

In State forests, the legislature has chosen to give priority to the production of continuous crops of timber for the use of the people and industries of the State. The Department is authorized to sell the timber, but is restricted to cutting and removing forest products in keeping with the best forestry practices. Commercial timber forests are also suitable for recreation and provide scenic beauty; thus, as a second priority the legislature has decreed that the Department must also make State forests accessible to the general public for recreation by providing improved highways through the forests. Residual uses are contemplated by the legislature as well—State forests protect watersheds and maintain the purity of streams and springs.

At the other end of the spectrum, nature preserves are established by the legislature to preserve and protect areas "against modification resulting from occupation or development which would destroy their natural condition." These lands have been set aside for research, teaching, natural and historic interest, and as "living illustrations of our original heritage wherein one may experience or envision primeval conditions in a wilderness type environment." In maintaining nature preserves, the legislature has commended the Department to conserve the "original character as distinguished from the artificial landscaping" of the land. In a nature preserve, then, the interest in the preservation of aesthetic and cultural values takes first priority, to the exclusion, if necessary, of conflicting commercial or recreational uses.

State parks strike a third balance; but while they are different from state forests they bear many similarities to nature preserves. They place the major emphasis on recreation but are also dedicated to preservation. State parks are established to preserve large forested areas and marginal lands near waters for recreation. But the types of recreation to be offered are limited. The legislature mandates that a State park offer recreation opportunities "different from that given by the typical city park." But recreation is not the sole priority; the parks are also preserved by legislative directive for their aesthetic and cultural value so that they "may remain unchanged by civilization, so far as possible, and be kept for future generations."

In addition, State parks are established to preserve the most important historical sites, to set aside areas of scenic and scientific interest, and to connect parks through a system of scenic parkways. Notably lacking from the purposes of a State park is any mention of improving or selling the timber grown in them.

To serve the prime recreational purpose of the State park the legislature allows some improvements, but these alterations of the park's original character are limited to those which aid recreation—roads, bridges, trails, camping sites, picnic areas, and the like. If natural plant areas in a park are devastated, the Department is authorized to replant, increase or supplement those areas. But the statutory authority for improving the parks is narrow—in maintaining a State park the Department is barred from artificial landscaping. As in a nature preserve, the mandate of the legislature is to conserve the original character of the park.

In summary, the scheme adopted by the legislature reserves State forests for commercial development and recreation, State parks for recreation and preservation, and nature preserves for preservation and recreation. In State forests there is little place for preservation of the forest in its natural state—improvement of the stand is the order of the legislature. In State parks and nature preserves there is little place for improvement of the forest for commercial development—preservation, for recreation or aesthetic or cultural values, and recreation are what the legislature has ordered.

When the question is the management of forested lands, the distinction between State parks and nature preserves, on the one hand, and State forests, on the other, crystallizes in the criminal penalty provisions of the statutes controlling each. It is a misdemeanor to remove individual *trees* or *timber* in a State park or nature preserve. By contrast, only removing *trees* is a misdemeanor in a State forest. The difference in wording can be readily explained by the differing legislative intent on the use to which parks, preserves and forest are to be put. State forests exist to grow trees for timber, and thus it is illegal to remove trees before their time but not illegal to harvest them as timber. State parks and preserves are not meant to provide commercial timber, and thus it is illegal to remove both trees and timber from them.

This interpretation of the statutes unifies both the general grants of power to the Department and the specific instructions given to the Department on how to manage the areas under its control. It does not defer to the interpretation adopted by the Department, the administrative agency delegated to carry out the statutes, because the

Department does not have a long experience with its interpretation or the policy it now proposes to pursue which has lent credence to it. This is, in fact, the first time the Department's interpretation has been put to the test.

The objectives stated by the Department's witnesses bear little relationship to the recreational, aesthetic or cultural uses of a State park. Salvaging timber before it rots is equivalent to the production of a crop of timber. Sanitation of a forest can protect it from disease or infestation that would threaten the proper uses of a State park, but no evidence here indicates any unusual threat of insect infestation or disease. Likewise, the safety of those in a park can be imperiled by dead or injured trees, especially near trails or campsites, but there is no evidence of such threats from the trees marked for logging. The evidence shows no need to rehabilitate the burn area; all that is required for the forest to regain its original vigor is time. By selective harvesting of trees in the burn area the productivity of the forest can be more than doubled, but stimulating forest growth in this manner is the work of civilization from which the legislature tells us the State parks are to be, so far as possible, immune.

* * *

The plan to log in Pere Marquette State Park is not authorized by statute. In addition, it runs afoul of several statutory provisions. Fires and their effects are part of the original character of Pere Marquette State Park. The source of a fire (natural or man-made) does not change its natural effect. However characterized, the Department's program constitutes artificial landscaping. The legislature has chosen not to permit this.

The effort to attenuate the effects of the fire by logging to speed regrowth does not leave the park unchanged by civilization, as the legislature intended. Even though the plan may be conservative forestry, there is no showing that *any* of the techniques of civilization are necessary to serve the recreational purpose of the park. It should be noted that by leaving the burn area alone, the Department would serve one park purpose—providing an area of scientific interest, a living laboratory in which the process of regeneration could be studied. In addition, the loss of two years of public access to the burn area of the park violates the legislative decree that State parks be kept open for the benefit of all the people.

* * *

Pere Marquette State Park in its present state is an irreplaceable natural resource. It is held in trust by the State, a holding designed by the legislature to serve the enjoyment and benefit of all the people of the State as a whole. Its future should not be charted by the Department's strained interpretation of guidelines the legislature has given to the agency entrusted with the management of this resource. Where the authority for the Department's irrevocable plan is at best ambiguous, and at worst nonexistent, it is prudent to adopt a "fail-safe" interpretation of the statutes governing the Department and the parks. If the legislature, when presented with the problem, should approve the logging proposal, the trees will still be there to cut. If this court allowed the logging despite our view that the legislature had not intended such a result, it would take decades for the area to regain its original character as a forest untouched by the improvements of man.

Accordingly, we find the logging proposal inconsistent with the legislative purpose for a State park. The Department should therefore be enjoined from proceeding with its logging proposal without more concise legislative directives. . . .

* * *

NOTES

1. *State land classifications.* Notice the similarity between the state's classifications of parks, forests, and nature preserves with federal parks, forests, and wilderness areas.

2. *Recreational use rights. Kenney* is useful in explaining the three basic management philosophies that apply on lands open to public recreational use. Nature preserves or wilderness areas are managed so as to ban or keep to an absolute minimum all human alterations. Parks are open for more active recreation. Developments (including roads, structures, and clearings) are permitted in them to the extent they promote recreation. Forests (and other multiple use lands) are managed actively for the production of particular natural resources with recreation allowed as an equal or (in Illinois) secondary land use.

The typical way to think about these land-use options is as philosophies of land management, considered from the point of view of the land management agency. But we can also consider them from the point of view of public visitors who possess and use recreational use rights in the lands. How might we define the public's use rights in these three categories of lands? What are the main elements of the rights, and how do they differ among the land types? Might it even help our thinking about public lands management to approach the issue from this unusual direction? A key issue, as we know, in the case of any natural resource use right is the right to halt interferences with the right. What legal enforcement powers do members of the public have, and are they adequate to protect the public's use rights?

It is worth noting that the original justification for protecting wilderness areas on federal lands, articulated by Aldo Leopold (then of the U.S. Forest Service) in the early 1920s, was as places set aside to promote particular forms of primitive recreation that were disappearing elsewhere, mostly due to the good roads movement. (That story is told in Paul S. Sutter, *Driven Wild: How The Fight Against Automobiles Launched The Modern Wilderness Movement* (2002), and in Julianne Lutz Newton, *Aldo Leopold's Odyssey* (2006).)

3. *"Natural incidents"?* The *Kenney* court tells us that the duty of the Department of Conservation (now the Department of Natural Resources) was to manage lands so as to leave them "unchanged by civilization," except as necessary to promote and enhance recreation. This standard, of course, is similar to the "natural incidents" line of thinking that we have seen in various cases involving private rights: landowners were entitled to the natural incidents of their lands, free of interference by other landowners. Once again, nature is providing a baseline for determining good from bad land use practices (as it does, as we have seen, in situations involving legal protections of wetlands, barrier islands, unstable slopes, and critical wildlife habitat). Recreational visitors to natural areas are entitled to enjoy the land's natural incidents. What difficulties, though, can we imagine in implementing this standard? Is it enough that an agency simply leave lands alone?

One problem with the hands-off approach is that it ignores how human activities in other places can alter the natural conditions within parks and nature reserves. Ecological "disturbance regimes" are a key component of nature's functioning. When humans develop surrounding lands they can easily alter such regimes—disrupting forest and prairie fires and routine flooding, for instance—in ways that significantly change the biological composition of the nature reserves. Land managers now know that active human intervention (for instance, burning prairies) is often required in order to keep lands in something close to the condition they were in before Europeans arrived on the scene. Has the court in *Kenney* shown adequate recognition of this ecological reality? Take note of the court's comment that the Department of Conservation can engage in timber harvesting and other actions in parks to the extent necessary for "preservation purposes" as well as recreation. After this ruling, could the Department return to court and assert that its logging plan is essentially an effort at preservation? In responding to this question, keep in mind that the fire in the park was apparently human-caused.

4. *Challenging agency inaction. Kenney* illustrates how a citizen group can successfully challenge the actions of a land management agency that impair recreational uses of lands in violation of statutes. But what about impairment that takes place while an agency sits and does nothing? Can that be challenged, and, if not, is the inability to bring suit a significant limit on public rights?

In *Norton v. Southern Utah Wilderness Alliance*, 542 U.S. 55 (2004), an environmental group sued the Bureau of Land Management (BLM) for failing to monitor and curtail increased off-road vehicle (ORV) use in an area set aside for study as a potential wilderness area under a process mandated by

Congress. The applicable federal statute, the Federal Land Management and Policy Act, obligated the agency to manage the lands so as "not to impair the suitability of such areas for preservation as wilderness." 43 U.S.C. § 1782(c). BLM stated that it would monitor ORV use and, if warranted, close an area to ORVs. The plaintiff environmental group sued to compel the agency to monitor the lands more carefully and otherwise to take steps to protect them against impairment of their wilderness characteristics. However, reversing the Tenth Circuit, the Supreme Court held that the BLM's alleged failure to protect the lands against impairment, even if true, did not amount to an "agency action" that the plaintiffs could challenge under the federal Administrative Procedure Act. The failure to act was an "inaction" that was not subject to judicial review. In addition, the agency's pledge in its land-use plan to use "supervision and monitoring" in designated areas did not create "a legally binding commitment" that the plaintiffs could enforce. It was instead a mere prediction of actions the agency would take in the future if resources were available and if the predicted action made sense relative to prevailing agency priorities. For criticism of the Court's *Norton v. SUWA* decision, see Michael C. Blumm & Sherry A. Bosse, Norton v. SUWA *and the Unraveling of Federal Public Land Planning*, 18 Duke Envtl. L. & Pol'y F. 105 (2007) (suggesting amendments to the Administrative Procedure Act to reverse the *Norton v. SUWA* result).

CHAPTER 10

RENEWABLE RESOURCES

■ ■ ■

For most of human history, society has perceived natural resources to be plentiful, and indeed limitless. It seemed as if human activity could hardly make a dent in the Earth's vast supplies of forests, fisheries, water, diverse species, clean air, and mineral energy resources. And indeed, in a world of fewer than one billion people up until the early nineteenth century, natural resources that we view as non-renewable today may very well have been renewable—the *rate* of human extraction and consumption was equal to or lower than the replenishment rate of the resources. In a world of 7 billion people, and projected to increase to 9 or 10 billion by 2050, even resources that we tend to think of as renewable are under severe strain.

Take groundwater aquifers as an example. The U.S. population relies on underground aquifers for nearly half of its drinking water by some estimates. See National Ground Water Association, *Groundwater Facts* (2010), *available at* http://www.ngwa.org/Fundamentals/use/Documents/gwfactsheet.pdf. Yet many important aquifer resources are being depleted at a rate much greater than they can naturally replenish. The Ogallala Aquifer, which supplies most of the water needed for agricultural operations in the "breadbasket of America," is a prime example. In some areas the aquifer is being drawn down six feet a year, while Mother Nature is putting back only an inch or two. See Jane Braxton Little, *The Ogallala Aquifer: Saving a Vital U.S. Water Source*, 19 Scientific American 32 (Mar. 1, 2009), *available at* http://www.scientificamerican.com/article/the-ogallala-aquifer/. Freshwater resources globally are under increasing strain, while rampant deforestation threatens global carbon sinks, pollution chokes waterways and regional atmospheres around the globe, more than three-quarters of all fisheries are being harvested before they can replenish, finite mineral resources are becoming more costly to extract (economically and environmentally), and society is entering a sixth, human-driven wave of extinction of earth's biodiversity.

Given this state of affairs, renewable resources are of increasing importance. Forests, fisheries, clean air, water, and even biodiversity may fall into the category of renewable or non-renewable resources, depending on relative extraction/replenishment rates. The finite mineral resources that are the subject of chapter 5, however—most frequently used as a source of energy—are non-renewable in the traditional sense. Once they are gone, they will not be coming back over human time scales. This chapter focuses on renewable resources related to energy production, with solar and wind power in particular acting as driving forces behind a shift in national energy portfolios the world over.

Even so, managing solar and wind as renewable natural resources is complicated by private property rights. What are the relative rights of neighbors to light and wind? If I have solar panels on my roof, can I bring a claim against you for letting your trees grow and blocking the light? What if you construct a building that blocks the light? Can you bring a claim against me if my solar panels are not aesthetically pleasing? Can a community ban solar panels on roofs of residences for the same reason? What about aesthetic or health and safety concerns over large-scale wind farms? These are just a few of the private right conflicts that arise in the context of renewable natural resource management.

A. RENEWABLES AND PRIVATE PROPERTY—SETTING THE STAGE

Renewable resources are often discussed in the context of "sustainable development," a phrase that has come to encapsulate a number of environmental themes. These renewables may be centralized or distributed. Centralized renewables might take the form, for example, of a solar array in the middle of a desert or a windfarm on the Texas plains, which operate by a transmission system carrying energy to some nearby city, industrial facility, or other development. Distributed renewables, on the other hand, include small-scale solar or wind units that fit on individual rooftops or properties where the energy is directly consumed. Both types of renewable energy can give rise to conflicts between private property owners and between property owners and the governments responsible for regulating land use and the siting of renewable technologies. Given the dispersion of distributed renewables across many different private properties and governmental jurisdictions, however, distributed renewables in particular have the potential to create greater conflict between private property owners, between property owners and governments, and even between governments due to federalism issues. Consider some of the conflicts that might arise in this context as described below by Professor Troy Rule, and what the appropriate governmental role is in balancing private rights with public interest in renewable energy use.

RENEWABLE ENERGY AND THE NEIGHBORS
Troy Rule
2010 Utah L. Rev. 1223, 1225–42 (2010)

Renewable energy devices are just one component of the global, decades-old sustainability movement. "Sustainable development" is development that "meets the needs of the present without compromising the ability of future generations to meet their own needs." Originating in a 1983 U.N. World Commission on Environment and Development report, the phrase has become a popular catchall for ecological, energy-efficient land use practices. Suburban growth boundaries, green building standards, renewable energy incentive programs, development density requirements, and programs for the preservation of trees and open space are all classifiable as sustainable land use policies.

Mounting fears of climate change and growing frustration with suburban sprawl have triggered a surge of popular interest in sustainable land use in recent years. Sustainable development practices reduce the country's dependency on fossil fuels and help curb carbon dioxide emissions. In an era of fierce global trade competition, sustainability policies are also increasingly viewed as a source of new domestic jobs and a means of safeguarding the nation's economic position.

Sustainability and the "Homevoter"

Although sustainable land use arguably offers valuable national and global benefits, not all sustainable development practices are equally appealing at the local level. Some sustainable land use policies can enrich a community's most influential landowners, while other policies threaten to have the opposite effect. Discussions about how to promote sustainable land use often fail to clearly distinguish those policies that are likely to garner neighborhood-level support from those that are not. State and federal strategies for promoting sustainable development will be most effective if they reflect the distinctly local interests and pressures that drive most land use decisions.

Sustainable development requires novel approaches to land use permits, building codes, and urban planning—all of which have historically fallen primarily under the control of municipalities and private community associations. Cities, counties, and homeowner associations are the primary regulators of land use in the United States. Municipal governments derive their land use authority primarily from the state delegation of police powers. Most states have empowered the local governments within their jurisdictions to regulate land use by enacting versions of the State Zoning Enabling Act. The vast majority of states have also implicitly granted land use regulatory authority to many of their cities and counties by affording them home rule status. In the past few decades, state-level regulation of land use has increased to address environmental concerns, which also falls within the scope of the state's police power. Nonetheless, local governments still retain the lion's share of land use regulatory authority. In recent years, homeowner associations have also become increasingly important regulators of land use.

Communities may derive their land use regulatory authority from the state, but they tend to formulate land use policies with distinctly local interests in mind. Professor William Fischel's *Homevoter Hypothesis* posits that "concern for home values is the central motivator of local government behavior." A home is often a voter's most valuable and highly leveraged asset, and land use regulations can greatly impact the market values of homes within a jurisdiction. Homeowners thus "tend to choose those policies that preserve or increase the value of their homes," recognizing that the package of taxes and public amenities that accompanies a home is capitalized into its value. Professor Fischel suggests that these "homevoters" are often a community's most influential voters and that they tend to favor policies that protect local home values even if alternative policies would better enhance the broader social welfare. Focused on the community-specific costs and benefits that predominate in their constituents' minds, local governments often pay less attention to the regional, national, or global effects of land use decisions.

The community-centric nature of local land use policy has important implications for state or federal policymaking aimed at promoting sustainable land use. Few municipal governments would voluntarily increase local taxes if they knew that 99% of the additional tax revenue raised would flow directly to the federal government. For similar reasons, most communities are reluctant to incur substantial new costs to support a sustainable development strategy whose benefits would flow primarily outside their jurisdictional boundaries.

Distributed renewable energy is less likely than many other sustainable land use practices to garner local political support. The following subsections attempt to categorize various sustainable land use policies based on their relative propensities for community acceptance, labeling the policies as "homevoter-favored," "homevoter-neutral," or "homevoter-feared." Such sorting is somewhat oversimplified, but it helps to illustrate why distributed renewable energy devices are more susceptible to local resistance than most other forms of sustainable development.

Homevoter-Favored Sustainability

Some sustainable land use policies substantially benefit a community's most influential voters. These homevoter-favored policies restrict or increase the cost of new real estate development, bolstering the market values of developed properties within a jurisdiction.

Several sustainable land use strategies directly or indirectly restrict real estate development. One aggressive growth-restricting policy is a growth boundary—a line drawn near the edge of an urban area beyond which new development within the jurisdiction is prohibited or highly restricted. Growth boundaries and other aggressive "smart growth" strategies are typically advocated as means of promoting infill development and reducing suburban sprawl, but they also reduce the supply of new development within the affected area. Particularly in "unique" communities where the demand for developed property is relatively inelastic, local citizens may support a smart growth policy at least partly for its capacity to buttress real estate values.

Growth boundaries and other direct development restrictions can be vulnerable to regulatory taking claims and political opposition, so community governments seeking to constrain growth often "fall back on more indirect controls" that are less susceptible to challenge. By increasing the cost of developing real estate within a jurisdiction, these indirect controls cause inward shifts in the supply curve for development that prop up market prices for existing homes and buildings.

Local ordinances that impose green building requirements on new developments are an indirect restriction on growth. Green building practices surely reduce the environmental impact of real estate development by incorporating stricter energy efficiency and sustainability standards into building construction and design. However, green building ordinances also diminish developers' flexibility in selecting materials and construction methods and are thus likely to raise the construction costs within a jurisdiction and thereby increase the value of developed real estate.

Not surprisingly, communities throughout the nation are increasingly embracing green building and other homevoter-favored sustainability practices. A growing number of local governments require that new, private development projects meet the U.S. Green Building Council's Leadership in Energy and Environmental Design (LEED) building standards or comparable green building requirements. Some cities also mandate that developers protect solar access in new subdivisions, conserve water, or preserve urban tree populations in connection with new development. Support for growth-restraining sustainability policies has seemingly been greatest in uniquely positioned cities with high real estate prices. Steep market values and a comparatively inelastic demand for real estate should theoretically mean greater property value increases from growth controls in these jurisdictions, which may partly explain why these cities have been swift to implement growth-restraining sustainability policies.

Green building and smart growth are laudable means of conserving scarce energy, water, and land without significantly compromising community aesthetics. However, given localities' increasing voluntary adoption of green development policies and the theoretical underpinnings for such local support, aggressive state or federal interventions aimed at accelerating their community-level adoption seem less justifiable than for the homevoter-neutral and homevoter-feared policies described below. Model green building ordinances, education programs aimed at local officials, and other more passive interventions are arguably more appropriate for promoting homevoter-favored policies.

Homevoter-Neutral Sustainability

A second category of sustainable development laws is not likely to substantially increase local property values but does not threaten home values either. Examples of these homevoter-neutral policies might include community garden programs, urban reforestation ordinances, pedestrian- or bicycle-friendly road construction for new developments, green building requirements for public projects, and mass transit-oriented planning strategies. Policies fitting within this category often involve discrete public expenditures, at least some of which may be offset by consequent improvements in the local tax base or by reductions in municipal energy consumption.

In regions where social norms strongly favor "going green," homevoter-neutral sustainability policies may have particular appeal as a means of cultivating a community's trendy, progressive image. Some city governments appear to adopt such policies at least partly as a means of distinguishing their locale from others in hopes of attracting employers or desirable economic development.

A prototypical homevoter would not strongly protest homevoter-neutral sustainable land use practices because any negative impacts that the measures might have on property values are usually minimal. Still, arguments that strong state or federal programs are needed to motivate communities to adopt homevoter-neutral sustainable land use policies are less convincing than for the homevoter-feared policies described below. Model ordinance provisions and intercommunity idea-sharing programs could simplify the adoption and implementation of these policies, making them better suited than state or federal programs to promote such policies at the local level.

Green LULUs: Homevoter-Feared Sustainability

A third set of sustainable land use policies are particularly susceptible to resistance [at the local level]. Rather than enhancing a community's property values or public image, these policies require neighborhoods to accommodate land uses that they have historically opposed.

Many landowners view distributed renewable energy devices as locally undesirable land uses (LULUs). State and federal programs aggressively promote distributed renewables, yet local land use restrictions across the nation have long inhibited their installation. Such opposition undermines federal and state efforts to promote sustainability, arguably imposing costs on the nation and the world.

Despite the numerous advantages of distributed renewables, these "green" LULUs commonly attract neighborhood opposition because of a perception that they could impose local costs in excess of the local benefits they would provide. Communities have restricted the installation of distributed renewables on countless occasions based on fears that the devices could diminish neighborhood aesthetics, disturb nearby landowners, or threaten property values.

An ordinance that invites distributed renewables into a municipality can arguably create greater uncertainty for local voters than an ordinance authorizing the siting of a single waste disposal site or power plant. Unlike large-scale, concentrated LULUs, distributed renewables are typically installed at unpredictable locations throughout host communities over time. Individual voters considering whether their town should host a large LULU often already know where it would be sited and thus may have greater certainty about how it could impact them. In contrast, distributed renewables-friendly ordinances create the risk that any resident could ultimately see a small wind turbine or unsightly solar panel array installed next door. Such broadly distributed risk can make it particularly difficult to build local support for land use controls favoring these devices. The following subsections discuss small wind turbines and solar panels—two common examples of green LULUs.

1. Small Wind Turbines

Small wind turbines are an increasingly popular renewable energy source in the United States. In contrast to their commercial-scale counterparts, small wind energy systems convert the kinetic energy in wind into electrical power that is typically consumed on-site.

Distributed wind energy development has distinctive characteristics that make it an attractive source of alternative energy. Unlike industrial-scale wind energy projects, small wind turbine installations do not require the construction of costly access roads and transmission lines across vast stretches of rural land and thus pose less of a threat to wildlife and conservation areas. Small wind turbines also diversify a region's renewable energy portfolio in ways that can ease pressure on utility grids because they often generate the most power during periods when solar panels are the least productive.

* * *

Unfortunately, despite aggressive government incentives for small wind turbines, local land use restrictions often discourage installation of the devices. Local height restrictions are perhaps the most common obstacle to small wind turbine installations. Height restrictions place limits on the permitted height of any building or structure erected within a zone or jurisdiction. Municipalities and homeowner associations have imposed height restrictions for decades to promote fire safety, and to preserve light, air, and a rural ambiance. Small wind turbines often must rise well above surrounding buildings and trees to be effective, necessitating heights that exceed local height restrictions, and can potentially damage a community's aesthetic appeal. Turbines have also been accused of creating safety hazards, noise, or flicker effects that can annoy neighbors and depress surrounding property values.

For these and other reasons, land use regulations in many communities directly or indirectly restrict or prohibit small wind turbine installations within their jurisdiction. Even when local zoning and subdivision covenants are silent as to small turbines, landowners' uncertainty over whether local authorities will challenge the turbines can still deter their installation.

2. Solar Energy Systems

Photovoltaic solar panels and other solar energy systems are also an important means of generating renewable energy. Rooftop and ground-mounted solar panels convert the radiant energy in sunlight into electric power. Given the myriad benefits of solar energy development, it is not surprising that new solar panel installations are eligible for many of the same federal tax credits and other incentive programs that apply to small wind turbines. Solar energy systems offer the unique benefit of being most productive on hot, sunny days when consumers are using air conditioning systems and utility grid demands are near their peak. The distributed nature of rooftop solar development also curbs energy sprawl, enabling renewable energy development without the need for new transmission lines through pristine rural areas.

However, some landowners also view solar energy systems as disruptive to neighborhood aesthetics or as threats to surrounding property values. Aware of popular objections to solar panels, numerous homeowner associations and local governments have adopted provisions that prohibit or severely restrict installation of the devices.

In spite of state and federal policies aimed at promoting distributed renewable energy, local land use regulations continue to deter many landowners from installing small wind turbines and solar panels. A handful of communities have voluntarily adopted provisions that accommodate these green LULUs, but most have proven reluctant to do so. . . .

Conflicts between neighbors and between landowners and local governments over distributed renewables become manifest either within court systems as common law claims like nuisance or through the decisions of local governments. We must remember, however, that private property owners and local governments are nested within a set of higher level governments that may influence their local policy preferences and decision-making. See Blake Hudson, *Constitutions and the Commons* 3–10 (2014). For example, federal or state governments could preempt local government efforts to allow distributed renewable generation. Or local regulations that prohibit the use of distributed wind or solar energy technologies might be preempted by state or federal regulations allowing distributed renewable energy development. Consider this issue as described by Professor Rule.

RENEWABLE ENERGY AND THE NEIGHBORS
Troy Rule
2010 Utah L. Rev. 1223, 1248–54 (2010)

Preemption of Local Regulations

The most aggressive means for states or the federal government to counter community resistance to distributed renewables is to invalidate local restrictions that stand in their way. Because most municipalities derive their land use authority from the state, state governments often have the power to preempt local regulations in order to advance statewide objectives. State governments can similarly invalidate private subdivision covenant provisions on public policy grounds.

Some researchers advocate the preemption of local land use regulations as the best strategy for overcoming neighborhood resistance to distributed renewables. State or federal government authorities have already used preemption to combat local opposition to the siting of cell towers, group homes, waste disposal sites, and myriad other LULUs. States have even defeated local resistance to *large*-scale wind energy projects based on their preemption power.

A growing number of states have enacted laws invalidating local land use ordinances that hinder renewable energy. A Florida law prohibits local governing bodies in that state from adopting any ordinance that "prohibits or has the effect of prohibiting the installation of solar collectors, clotheslines, or other energy devices based on renewable resources." Statutes enacted in California, Delaware, Indiana, Nevada, New Hampshire, Vermont, and Wisconsin similarly limit municipal land use restrictions on solar panels or small wind energy systems.

* * *

However, broadly preempting local ordinances to accommodate distributed renewables is an imprecise, one-size-fits-all approach that ignores local issues and concerns. No two neighborhoods are identical. Each has different geographic, topographic, cultural, and socioeconomic characteristics that create unique sets of values, social norms, and problems. Recognizing the vast diversity among local jurisdictions, scholars have long argued that municipal governments are ordinarily better situated to make local land use decisions than their state-level counterparts. Local officials typically reside within the jurisdictions they serve and tend to have a more specialized understanding than state officials of a community's unique characteristics and challenges. State statutes preempting local land use authority are thus prone to inefficiencies from inadequate consideration of localized factors in the policymaking process. State laws invalidating subdivision covenant restrictions on distributed renewables similarly overlook local concerns.

Consider the impact of a preemptive state law on the fictional city of Beachtown, a resort community known for its exceptional views and aesthetic appeal. Suppose that the existing ordinances in Beachtown protected the local ambiance by prohibiting structures (including wind turbines) from rising more than thirty-five feet above any parcel's surface, thereby protecting $200,000 in total property value premiums within the jurisdiction. If allowing turbines within the municipality would generate only $20,000 in aggregate social benefits but would diminish the aggregate value of Beachtown's viewshed by $100,000, then a state law preempting the local height restriction to allow wind turbines would generate an $80,000 deadweight loss.

Decentralized land use regulation mitigates such inefficiencies by empowering community officials with comparatively better information about a proposal's local costs and benefits to make policy decisions. A provision exempting communities from preemption upon a showing of undue hardship might inject some flexibility into a preemption statute but would likely cause additional problems. Such a provision would create incentives for communities to overstate their degree of potential hardship to qualify for exemption and could engender costly intergovernmental disputes over the issue.

An all-or-nothing preemption approach also hinders efficient Tieboutian sorting among the citizenry. The famous Tiebout hypothesis suggests that variations in local laws can increase social welfare by allowing citizens to "vote with their feet" in selecting communities to reside in that best suit their own respective preferences. Some citizens would undoubtedly be willing to pay a premium to live away from the sight of renewable energy systems that they deem aesthetically offensive. Others would gladly live in communities that accommodate distributed renewables, particularly if given financial incentives to do so. Localized policymaking on these issues can enhance the social welfare by enabling more citizens to reside in jurisdictions that regulate sustainable land use in ways that mirror their individual preferences.

Efficiency arguments aside, state laws that broadly preempt local land use restrictions on distributed renewables are probably politically infeasible in some states. Preemption statutes can provoke political hostility because they tend to marginalize the distinct interests and characteristics of a state's communities and fail to engage local governments in the policymaking process. Even where state legislatures succeed in passing preemption laws, the laws could prove costly and difficult to enforce amidst weak community support.

An ideal regulatory strategy would promote more efficient siting of distributed renewables by allowing for consideration of the costs and preferences unique to each community. Land use restrictions that exempt distributed renewables may be welfare-maximizing in many localities, particularly where aesthetics are of minimal concern. In communities such as Beachtown, however, the aggregate costs to landowners and neighbors from accommodating distributed renewables likely exceed the social benefits. The challenge lies in crafting equitable, low-cost rules that lead to distributed renewables installations only in "least-cost avoider" communities where accommodating the devices makes the most economic sense.

NOTES

1. *Scales of governance.* What is the appropriate role of local governments in resolving renewable energy-related property disputes? What is the role of state governments? How should local interests be balanced with state, national, and even global concerns? Consider the effect that decentralized decision-making over energy siting can have on efforts to create a holistic renewable energy policy:

> Since most states do not have land use laws requiring the inclusion of renewable energy, local governments have been left to their own devices in this area. The results have been haphazard.

> For example, New Jersey has 566 municipalities, each of which sets its own land use laws, including how to address renewable energy systems. By late 2007, there were approximately eight municipalities with ordinances expressly addressing the siting and management of wind turbines. Those ordinances run the gamut from expressly allowing wind energy to banning their installation.

The Township of Long Beach, New Jersey, which because of its location along the coast has good wind resources, also has sought to ban wind turbines completely within the town. Township of Long Beach, NJ Master Plan (2007). This decentralized regulatory approach is echoed in North Carolina. In Currituck County, small wind turbines are permitted in all zones. The county requires that the tower be one and a half times its height from the property line. Currituck also sets forth a process to waive the setback requirements. Currituck's ordinance provides for a maximum height of 120 feet. Currituck, NC, Unified Development Ordinance § 07–68 (2008). Camden County, North Carolina, is slightly different in that it requires a special permit for a small wind turbine in residential zones but has zoned for them in industrial areas. Camden, NC, Code § 151.334. The ordinances limit the height to 150 feet and provide for setbacks to be at least equal to the height of the tower and at least one and a half times the height from the nearest inhabited structure on the neighboring property. The owner of the tower also has to provide a surety bond or other guarantee in the amount of 120 percent of the anticipated cost of removing a wind energy system before its installation. *Id*. § 151.347(T).

In contrast, the state of Michigan has taken more of a "hands-on" approach and issued siting guidelines for both utility scale and on-site use (small-scale) turbines. Small-scale turbines can be no more than 40 meters while utility-scale systems can have towers up to 90 meters. The Michigan system permits small systems with towers less than 20 meters within all zoning districts while towers above 20 meters need to obtain a special land use approval. The Michigan siting guidelines require that the tower be set back from the property line at least 1.5 times the tower height, in order to "protect neighbors in the unlikely event of a tower failure." State of Michigan, Michigan Siting Guidelines for Wind Energy Systems (2007), www.michigan.gov/documents/Wind_and_Solar_Siting_Guidlines_Draft_5_96872_7.pdf. In contrast to the decentralized approach of New Jersey and some other states, Michigan and California have set up statewide policies that remove obstacles to the installation of renewable energy.

Zoning restrictions can create obstacles to those wishing to install renewable energy sources. Depending on the zoning requirements of the particular municipality, the installer and/or the homeowner may need to obtain permits from the construction officials or may even need to apply for special permissions or a variance from the agency in charge of the municipality's land use laws. In many instances, the municipalities will consider a wind turbine a nonpermitted use, therefore requiring a variance. In other instances, because of the lot size, exclusionary zoning, or height limitations, a person may be required to file an application for a variance for the wind turbine. The cost of obtaining a variance can be measured in both time and money. It can tack on thousands of extra dollars to an already-expensive undertaking and add weeks, if not months, to the permitting process. The installer also would have to hire lawyers, planners, and engineers for the variance hearing. At a hearing for a variance, the applicant would have to present testimony regarding the design, placement, and utility of their proposed renewable energy system. That testimony would not only have to come from the applicant, but likely from a professional planner and maybe an engineer. A land use hearing also would provide an opportunity for public participation. This public participation can add significant time and adversity to the process. Oftentimes the testimony of the public can be inflammatory. In many instances, such testimony only need cloud the issue enough to create doubt in the minds of the land use board members.

In Brigantine, New Jersey, an ordinance provides that the setback from the property line be equal to the diameter of the rotor of the wind turbine plus five feet. Brigantine, NJ, Code § 198–127. Brigantine's code promotes renewable energy and has zoned the systems for business and residential zones. In contrast, other towns in New Jersey require a minimum of five acres in order to put up a single wind turbine regardless of its height. Millville, NJ, Code § 30–220. In Kansas, the county of McPherson requires that the turbines be set back at least twice the height of the turbine but allows the turbines in all zoning districts. McPherson, KS, Zoning Regulations art. 6, § 100B(14). The setbacks for utility scale systems are 2000 feet from any residential structure.

These examples demonstrate that even if the wind turbine is a permitted use and the zoning does not preclude its installation, the setback or bulk requirements may discourage wind energy development. While the setback requirements may be argued as important from a safety perspective (even though most wind turbine systems are designed to withstand hurricane-force winds), they also can be perceived as out of step with other requirements in similar circumstances. Many other structures are comparable in height but not subject to similar requirements. Flagpoles, for example, also are subject to gravity and to extreme wind events, but there are no restrictions on where they may be located. Trees may be planted anywhere within a person's property, but, again, there is no requirement that the trees be situated so as to avoid falling onto a neighboring property.

Some municipalities have added a third set of hurdles by requiring installers to prepare and provide burdensome documents. For example, one town required avian studies for the installation of a single turbine. The town also required visualization studies showing how the turbine looks from various vantage points from the property. These requirements also add to the costs, delay the permitting/approval processes, and can discourage the implementation of renewable energy generation. In most cases these requirements do nothing to add real protection to the environment but do add to the costs and time for the project and increase the likelihood that the project will not happen.

Michael L. Pisauro Jr., *Renewables and Land Use Law*, 23 Nat. Res. & Env. 39, 40–41 (2008).

How do policymakers wade through this morass of segmented jurisdiction? Is greater coordination needed at the state level? At the federal level? Among local governments along the same horizontal plane of governance? What are the legal/institutional hurdles to such coordination? See Blake Hudson & Jonathan Rosenbloom, *Uncommon Approaches to Commons Problems: Nested Governance Commons and Climate Change*, 64 Hastings L.J. 1273 (2013). Many states have issued siting guidelines for wind energy systems in an effort to better coordinate wind energy development. See Michael Klepinger, *Michigan Land Use Guidelines for Siting Wind Energy Systems*, Extension Bulletin WO–1053 (Oct. 2007), *available at* http://www.michiganorganic.msu.edu/uploads/files/31/WO1053.pdf.

2.   *Renewables as a choice?* Given what we now know about the effects of fossil fuel consumption on the environment, and especially its role in exacerbating climate change, should citizens be allowed to "vote with their feet" by moving to communities that disallow renewable energy development? In other words, is it good policy to give citizens a Tieboutian choice (as described by Professor Rule) between living in communities that prohibit distributed and other forms of renewable energy and communities that allow it? Would the public interest be better served by making distributed and other renewable energy development an option in all jurisdictions through state or federal preemption? Or is legally decentralized (and thus locally controlled) governance in this area preferable? What are the pros and cons of higher level government preemption versus legal decentralization?

3.   *Preemption "one size fits all" or integral to holistic energy policy?* Do you agree or disagree with Professor Rule that preemption of local decision-making is likely an unworkable "one size fits all" approach? Or do the values of uniformity in national or state energy policy outweigh the downsides? The "negatives of a one size fits all approach" argument has purchase in the context of many natural resources like wetlands, which are very different from one region to the next. But does the interstate interconnectedness of the energy grid make coordination of energy rules and regulations more important? Consider that while many states leave a great deal of discretion to local governments to decide matters related to renewable energy facility or distributed unit siting, states are also increasingly seeking to integrate renewable energy into their energy portfolios. Indeed, as of March 2013, "renewable portfolio standards" existed in thirty-seven states, the District of Columbia, Guam, the Northern Mariana Islands, Puerto Rico and the U.S.

Virgin Islands. See U.S. Environmental Protection Agency, *Renewable Portfolio Standards*, http://www.epa.gov/agstar/tools/funding/renewable.html. If states will increasingly require renewable energy to be a part of production, should they take a more direct role in prohibiting local government efforts that would thwart renewable energy siting?

4. *Renewables versus fracking: to preempt or not to preempt?* As evidenced in chapter 3 in the *Robinson Township* case (p. 203), a number of state governments have attempted to preempt local efforts to prohibit natural gas fracturing ("fracking") within their jurisdictions. We can imagine a situation where a group of individuals would vehemently oppose state efforts to preempt local prohibitions on fracking while at the same time supporting state efforts to preempt local prohibitions on the use of solar or wind power. Can these positions be reconciled? Does the fact that the former regulates one's use of their property more generally, while the latter regulates one's use of their home draw a meaningful distinction? Does it matter that distributed renewables would generate electricity consumed directly by one's home, while fracked natural gas sold in an interstate market would not? If that distinction is meaningful enough to allow state preemption of local efforts to block renewables while disallowing preemption of state control over fracking, what about large-scale wind projects where electricity may not be consumed directly and primarily by the homeowner?

5. *The Beachtown hypo and social benefits.* Professor Rule provides a preemption hypothetical about a city named Beachtown, which enforces an ordinance prohibiting wind turbines taller than thirty-five feet to protect property values. Allowing taller turbines "would generate only $20,000 in aggregate social benefits" while "diminish[ing] the aggregate value of Beachtown's viewshed by $100,000." Professor Rule describes this as an $80,000 "deadweight loss." But how do you calculate aggregate social benefits, and over what time frame? $20,000 as compared to what? Could the aggregate value of transitioning to renewable energy today be far greater than $20,000 over longer time periods? What will the costs of energy be to future generations if we delay the transition? Will energy scarcity cause future generations to bear greater economic costs while we reap the short term economic benefits of relatively cheap fossil fuel consumption? Further, might aesthetic sensibilities shift over time in ways that diminish the costs of the taller turbines? Law and economics analysis is fraught with these types of valuation difficulties, primarily in the form of establishing appropriate discount rates into the future. On a finite planet it is difficult to know the exact and aggregated effects of today's consumption of resources on future generations. See Daniel A. Farber & Paul A. Hemmersbaugh, *The Shadow of the Future: Discount Rates, Later Generations, and the Environment*, 46 Vand. L. Rev. 267 (1993).

6. *Energy efficiency and the energy cycle.* Obviously, renewable energy is important, but extending the life of existing fossil fuels will be a key component of an effective transition to renewable fuels. In this way, land use planning can play a key role in facilitating that transition. Consider the

Homevoter-Favored Sustainability category discussed by Professor Rule. Growth boundaries that encourage infill and reign in urban sprawl could save the nation vast amounts of energy—transit times would be reduced since more people will live closer to work, shopping, and recreational opportunities; the need to create new infrastructure through energy intensive development would be reduced, and the energy grid would be more compact and less subject to leakage (which can result in transmission lines delivering only two-thirds of the power originally generated. See John Brian Shannon, *A Potential Solution For Long-Distance Power Transmission Leakage*, Clean Technica (Oct. 5, 2013), http://cleantechnica.com/2013/10/05/a-potential-solution-for-long-distance-power-transmission-leakage/). Yet only a handful of states have required growth boundaries, and only a handful of cities have implemented them elsewhere. See National League of Cities' Sustainable Cities Institute, *Urban Growth Boundaries*, http://www.sustainablecities institute.org/topics/land-use-and-planning/smart-growth/urban-growth-boundaries.

Why do you think that, in a nation of approximately 88,000 subnational governments, we only have a few hundred growth boundary policies? Steffen W. Schmidt et al., *American Government and Politics Today* 89 (14th ed. 2009); Paul Goldstein & Barton H. Thompson, Jr., *Property Law: Ownership, Use, and Conservation* 1048 (2006). One problem, of course, is that, while homevoters on the inside of the growth boundary may prefer them, those on the outside (and especially those just outside the boundary) are likely to disfavor them. It is simple economics that, once a limit is placed on development around a city, the supply of land decreases while demand is typically steady or increasing. As land becomes more valuable inside the line, the value of land outside the line plummets (since its development is limited). Imagine owning land inside the line worth $10,000 an acre, while your neighbor outside the line now owns land worth $2,000 an acre. We might characterize growth boundaries as Homevoter-Feared policies for those outside the boundary, just as distributed renewable promotion may constitute Homevoter-Feared policies under Professor Rule's analysis, while the same policies are Homevoter-Favored by those inside the boundary. Such a growth boundary would likely not be a Fifth Amendment taking, as economic value remains in the land, and because cases since *Euclid v. Ambler Realty*, 272 U.S. 365 (1926), have allowed public restrictions on property rights to greatly reduce the value of those properties without violating constitutional principles.

Is it the mere politics of land use regulation that inhibits the use of growth boundaries? Is it an institutional problem due to a lack of federal coordination of state and local land use planning—thus creating a race-to-the-bottom among state and local governments? See Blake Hudson, *Federal Constitutions: The Keystone of Nested Commons Governance*, 63 Ala. L. Rev. 1007, 1048–1052 (2012). What duties do private landowners owe the broader public in order to protect the public's interest in the availability of natural resources? Should urban sprawl, growth boundaries, and land use planning be reframed as a debate about energy usage and transitioning to renewable energy technologies? Would that shift the political discourse cause more states and municipalities to adopt these measures?

B. WIND, NUISANCE, AND ZONING

Global wind capacity increased sixty-four fold between 1992 and 2009—a growth rate of 28 percent a year. Jeremy Firestone & Jeffrey P. Kehne, *Wind*, in *The Law of Clean Energy* 363 (Michael Gerrard ed., 2011). Projections are that the U.S. could obtain 20 percent of its electricity from wind by 2030. *Id.* at 362. Wind energy is particularly likely to give rise to conflicts between private property owners, between property owners and the government, and between wind interests and those seeking to protect other natural resources. In the following cases, consider how both common law claims and regulatory tools have been used to shape the development of wind as a renewable energy technology utilized on private properties.

1. DISTRIBUTED WIND ENERGY

ROSE V. CHAIKIN
Superior Court of New Jersey
453 A.2d 1378 (1982)

GIBSON, J.S.C.

This action seeks to enjoin the operation of a privately owned windmill. Plaintiffs occupy neighboring properties and allege that the unit constitutes both a private nuisance and a violation of local zoning laws. Defendants deny the allegations and have counterclaimed. Based on the evidence presented at trial, the following factual findings may be made.

All of the parties are residents and/or owners of single-family homes located in a contiguous residential neighborhood in Brigantine, New Jersey. On or about June 18, 1981 defendants, in an effort to save on electric bills and conserve energy, obtained a building permit for the construction of a windmill. Pursuant to that permit they erected a 60'-high tower on top of which was housed a windmill and motor. The unit is located ten feet from the property line of one of plaintiffs. Shortly after the windmill became operational it began to produce offensive noise levels, as a result of which plaintiffs experienced various forms of stress-related symptoms, together with a general inability to enjoy the peace of their homes.

Relief was initially sought through city council. Although certain orders were issued reducing the times when the windmill could operate, the problem continued more or less until an action was instituted in this court. Following an initial hearing here, there was a preliminary finding of a nuisance and a temporary restraining order was issued restricting the use of the machine except for a period of no more than two hours a day, that being the time claimed to be needed for maintenance purposes. By consent, those restraints were continued up through the time of trial and still continue.

Although the evidence was in sharp dispute concerning the impact of the noise levels existing when the windmill is operational, this court is satisfied that those levels are of such a nature that they would be offensive to people of normal sensibilities and, in fact, have unreasonably interfered with plaintiffs' use and enjoyment of their properties. Measurements at the site reveal that the sound levels produced by the windmill vary, depending on the location, but generally show a range of 56 to 61 decibels (dBA). In all instances those levels exceed the 50 dBA permissible under the controlling city ordinance. Ordinance 11–1981, § 906.6.3, City of Brigantine. Although there are other sources of sounds in the area, for the most part they are natural to the site. These background (or ambient) sounds include the ocean, the sounds of sea gulls, the wind and the distant sounds of occasional boat traffic in the adjacent inlet. An exception to these "natural" sounds is the heat pump owned by plaintiffs Joel and Isadora Rose, of which more will be said later.

The sounds of the windmill have been variously described. Generally, however, they most resemble those produced by a large motor upon which there is superimposed the action of blades cutting through the air. The sounds are distinguishable not just by the level of the noise produced (noise being defined as unwanted sound) but because they are unnatural to the scene and are more or less constant. Although a reduction in the wind speed to below eight m.p.h. will automatically shut down the unit, the prevailing winds at this site are generally above that. Given the proximity of the homes involved, the net result is a noise which is both difficult to ignore and almost impossible to escape.

The impact on plaintiffs is significant. Both the lay and expert testimony support the conclusion that, in varying degrees, all of them experienced tension and stress-related symptoms when the windmill was operational. Those symptoms included nervousness, dizziness, loss of sleep and fatigue. The sounds disturbed many of the activities associated with the normal enjoyment of one's home, including reading, eating, watching television and general relaxation.

Defendants counterclaim and seek to enjoin the operation of the Rose heat pump. Although the unrebutted testimony indicated that it, too, produced sound levels in excess of 50 dBA, the impact on defendants was relatively small. Complaints were limited to some disturbance of certain activities, such as causing a distraction during reading and dinner. There is no evidence that it unreasonably interferes with defendants' health and comfort. What disturbance does occur is limited not only in duration but in frequency. The unit is rarely used by the Roses, and when used is on for relatively short periods of time.

I.   *Private Nuisance*

The basic standards for determining what constitutes a private nuisance were set forth by our Supreme Court in *Sans v. Ramsey Golf & Country Club*, 149 A.2d 599 (N.J. 1959). The court made clear that a case-by-case inquiry, balancing competing interests in property, is required.

> The essence of a private nuisance is an unreasonable interference with the use and enjoyment of land. The elements are myriad. . . . The utility of the defendant's conduct must be weighed against the *quantum* of harm to the plaintiff. The question is not simply whether a person is annoyed or disturbed, but whether the annoyance or disturbance arises from an unreasonable use of the neighbor's land. . . . [149 A.2d at 605]

Unreasonableness is judged

> ". . . 'not according to exceptionally refined, uncommon or luxurious habits of living, but according to the simple tastes and unaffected notions generally prevailing among plain people.' " [149 A.2d at 606]

Defendants resist plaintiffs' claim by advancing three basic arguments: first, that noise, standing alone, cannot constitute a private nuisance; second, that even if noise can amount to a nuisance, the noise from their windmill does not exceed the applicable threshold, and third, that in any event the circumstances of this case do not warrant the "extraordinary relief" of an injunction.

The first argument is without merit. New Jersey case law makes it clear that noise may, under the principles of unreasonable use, constitute an actionable private nuisance. Noise is an actionable private nuisance if two elements are present: (1) injury to the health and comfort of ordinary people in the vicinity, and (2) unreasonableness of that injury under all the circumstances. The "circumstances" may be multiple and must be proven by "clear and convincing" evidence.

> Broadly stated, the noises which a court of equity normally enjoins are those which affect injuriously the health and comfort of ordinary people in the vicinity to an unreasonable extent. . . . *Thus, the character, volume, frequency, duration, time, and locality are relevant factors in determining whether the annoyance materially interferes with the ordinary comfort of*

human existence. [Lieberman v. Saddle River Tp., 116 A.2d 809
(N.J. Super. Ct. App. Div. 1955); emphasis supplied]

To the factors listed in *Lieberman* may be added several others
gleaned from New Jersey cases and cases in other jurisdictions applying a
"reasonableness under the circumstances" test. For example, the
availability of alternative means of achieving the defendant's objective
has been found to be relevant. So, also, might the social utility of
defendant's conduct, judged in light of prevailing notions of progress and
the demands of modern life, be relevant. *See Protokowicz v. Lesofski*, 174
A.2d 385, 388 (N.J. Super Ct. Ch. Div. 1961) (in light of scientific
progress, noise from Diesel engine cannot be considered nuisance *per se*).
Whether a given use complies with controlling governmental regulations,
while not dispositive on the question of private nuisance, . . . does impact
on its reasonableness.

An application of these factors to the present case supports the
conclusion that defendants' windmill constitutes an actionable nuisance.
As indicated, the noise produced is offensive because of its character,
volume and duration. It is a sound which is not only distinctive, but one
which is louder than others and is more or less constant. Its intrusive
quality is heightened because of the locality. The neighborhood is quiet
and residential. It is well separated, not only from commercial sounds,
but from the heavier residential traffic as well. Plaintiffs specifically
chose the area because of these qualities and the proximity to the ocean.
Sounds which are natural to this area—the sea, the shore birds, the ocean
breeze—are soothing and welcome. The noise of the windmill, which
would be unwelcome in most neighborhoods, is particularly alien here.

The duration of the windmill noise is also significant. Since the
prevailing winds keep the unit operating more or less constantly, the
noise continues night and day. Interfering, as they do, with the normal
quiet required for sleep, nighttime noises are considered particularly
intrusive. Since ambient sounds are normally reduced at night, an alien
sound is even more offensive then. The sound levels are well documented
and clearly exceed permissible limits under the zoning ordinance.
Ordinance 11–1981. Independent of the ordinance, the evidence supports
the conclusion that the noise is disturbing to persons of ordinary
sensibilities. It can and does affect injuriously the health and comfort of
ordinary people in the vicinity to an unreasonable extent.

When consideration is given to the social utility of the windmill and
the availability of reasonable alternatives, the conclusion supporting an
injunction is the same. Defendants' purpose in installing the windmill
was to conserve energy and save on electric bills. Speaking to the latter
goal first, clearly the court can take judicial notice that alternative
devices are available which are significantly less intrusive. As to its social

utility, a more careful analysis is required. Defendants argue that the windmill furthers the national need to conserve energy by the use of an alternate renewable source of power. The social utility of alternate energy sources cannot be denied; nor should the court ignore the proposition that scientific and social progress sometimes reasonably require a reduction in personal comfort. On the other hand, the fact that a device represents a scientific advance and has social utility does not mean that it is permissible at any cost. Such factors must be weighed against the quantum of harm the device brings to others.

In this case the activity in question substantially interferes with the health and comfort of plaintiffs. In addition to the negative effect on their health, their ability to enjoy the sanctity of their homes has been significantly reduced. The ability to look to one's home as a refuge from the noise and stress associated with the outside world is a right to be jealously guarded. Before that right can be eroded in the name of social progress, the benefit to society must be clear and the intrusion must be warranted under all of the circumstances. Here, the benefits are relatively small and the irritation is substantial. On balance, therefore, the social utility of this windmill is outweighed by the quantum of harm that it creates.

That is not to say that all windmills constitute a nuisance or even that this windmill cannot be modified in a way to justify a different conclusion. Every case must be examined on an individual basis. Given the circumstances here, however, the evidence clearly and convincingly establishes a nuisance and the imposition of an injunction is warranted. . . .

* * *

Brigantine's Ordinance 11–1981 sets noise standards for windmills and is part of the city zoning ordinance. . . .

Defendants' violation of the zoning ordinance is uncontroverted. At all times the windmill operated in violation of the 50 dBA standard. . . .

* * *

Defendants nevertheless contend that the windmill ordinance is arbitrary and unreasonable. That position is unpersuasive. Defendants argue that the ordinance violates equal protection guarantees by arbitrarily singling out windmills for noise control, and due process because it unreasonably limits windmill noise to 50 dBA while other ambient sounds often rise above that level. The ordinance, however, is a zoning regulation and was promulgated under the police power. Since it is "social" legislation it need be justified only by a showing that, in any state of facts, it reasonably advances a legitimate state purpose. This same minimal standard satisfies the principle of substantive due process. Thus, a showing that the ordinance reasonably advances a legitimate state purpose would defeat both claims.

* * *

In conclusion, it is the view of this court that, for a variety of reasons, defendants' windmill constitutes an actionable nuisance. Under the same analysis plaintiffs' heat pump does not. An alternative basis for granting injunctive relief is defendants' violation of the municipal zoning ordinance. An order should be entered accordingly.

NOTES

1.   *Windmills and social utility.* In light of what we now know about climate change and ever-depleting fossil fuels, is the "social utility" of a windmill greater today than at the time of *Rose*? What of the aggregated social utility of both centralized and distributed wind power if it were to become in common use across "wind-rich" regions of the U.S.?

2.   *Availability of energy alternatives.* How "available" and "reasonable" are the energy alternatives highlighted by the majority in *Rose* likely to be in the future? Outside of the fossil fuel context, how much does alternative energy development depend upon regional variability, in that some areas have significant geothermal, hydroelectric, or wind resources while other areas do not? Consider the vast regional variability of wind resources in the United States, where wind energy tends to be concentrated more in the central United States than in the east and west (where it tends to be most prominent off the coast). See National Renewable Energy Laboratory, *Dynamic Maps, GIS Data, & Analysis Tools: Wind Maps*, http://www.nrel.gov/gis/wind.html.

3.   *Wind prohibitions through regulatory subterfuge?* The *Rose* court noted that the noise produced by the windmill exceeded the city's noise ordinance of 50 decibels (at 56–61 decibels). Other local governments in New Jersey prohibit noise levels below this range as well. See Township of Long Beach, N.J., Code § 123–6 (2007) (noise ordinance). How might localities use other valid regulatory tools, such as noise ordinances, to achieve prohibitions on renewable energy technologies like windmills? Are such actions grounded in legitimate concerns, or are they subterfuges for achieving other policy goals? Does it matter? The court decided that the Roses' heat pump, which also exceeded the 50 decibel noise limit, merely caused "a distraction during reading and dinner," and therefore was not a nuisance. Is the distinction between the windmill and the heat pump meaningful?

4.   *Scientific progress and renewable nuisances.* The *Rose* court observed that, in determining whether an activity constituted a nuisance, "the social utility of defendant's conduct, judged in light of prevailing notions of progress and the demands of modern life" might be a relevant factor. 453 A.2d at 217. The court cited the *Protokowicz* case for the proposition that, "in light of scientific progress, noise from Diesel engine cannot be considered

nuisance *per se*." *Id*. at 217–18. Given scientific progress in the area of renewable energy technologies, would the analysis in the *Protokowicz* case change the outcome of *Rose* in modern times?

2. CENTRALIZED WIND ENERGY

Rose concerned a single wind turbine on one landowner's property, but wind generation facilities may be much larger in size, like those at issue in the *Burch* and *Muscarello* cases below. Consider whether wind farms that are larger in size change the calculus regarding landowner claims of nuisance or local government zoning prohibitions on renewable development. Should the size and scope of the wind generation facility or unit be relevant in the allocation of rights to those seeking to implement renewable energy projects on their property?

BURCH V. NEDPOWER MOUNT STORM, LLC

Supreme Court of Appeals of West Virginia
647 S.E.2d 879 (2007)

MAYNARD, J.

* * *

I.   *Facts*

By final order dated April 2, 2003, the Public Service Commission ("the PSC") granted NedPower Mount Storm LLC, an appellee herein, a certificate of convenience and necessity to construct and operate a wind power electric generating facility along the Allegheny Front in Grant County. NedPower has entered into a contract with appellee Shell WindEnergy, Inc., to sell the entire facility to Shell upon its completion. It is contemplated that the wind power facility will be located on a site approximately 14 miles long with an average width of one-half mile. The facility is to include up to 200 wind turbines. Each turbine is to be mounted on a steel tower approximately 15 feet in diameter and 210 to 450 feet in height, and have three blades of approximately 115 feet.

The appellants are seven homeowners who live from about one-half mile to two miles from the projected wind turbines. On November 23, 2005, the appellants filed a complaint in the Circuit Court of Grant County seeking to permanently enjoin NedPower and Shell WindEnergy, Inc., from constructing and operating the wind power facility on the basis that it would create a private nuisance. Specifically, the appellants asserted that they will be negatively impacted by noise from the wind turbines; the turbines will create a "flicker" or "strobe" effect when the sun is near the horizon; the turbines will pose a significant danger from broken blades, ice throws, and collapsing towers; and the wind power facility will cause a reduction in the appellants' property values.

[The energy companies filed motions arguing that the lower court had no jurisdiction to enjoin, as a potential nuisance, projects authorized by the PSC. The circuit court agreed. The lower court also ruled that the landowners failed to set forth sufficient facts in their complaint alleging a private nuisance that would support the granting of a prospective injunction against the energy companies. The landowners appealed].

* * *

III. *Discussion*

The appellants raise two assignments of error in this appeal. The first assignment is that the circuit court erred in finding that the siting certificate granted by the PSC to the appellees for the construction of the wind power facility immunizes the appellees from liability under the common law doctrine of nuisance. Second, the appellants allege error in the circuit court's finding that the appellants failed to prove various allegations in their complaint, notwithstanding that on a motion for judgment on the pleadings the well-pled facts of the complaint must be taken as true.

As noted above, in its April 7, 2006, order, the circuit court dismissed the appellants' nuisance claim for an injunction on several independent grounds. This Court will now proceed to consider each of these separate grounds.

* * *

We begin our discussion with the recognition that our common law has always provided a remedy for a nuisance. This Court has explained that:

> "nuisance is a flexible area of the law that is adaptable to a wide variety of factual situations." *Sharon Steel Corp. v. City of Fairmont*, 334 S.E.2d 616, 621 (W. Va. 1985). In fact, "[i]t has been said that the term 'nuisance' is incapable of an exact and exhaustive definition which will fit all cases, because the controlling facts are seldom alike, and each case stands on its own footing." *Harless v. Workman*, 114 S.E.2d 548, 552 (W. Va. 1960). Nonetheless, "the term ['nuisance'] is generally 'applied to that class of wrongs which arises from the unreasonable, unwarrantable or unlawful use by a person of his own property and produces such material annoyance, inconvenience, discomfort, or hurt that the law will presume a consequent damage.'" *Harless*, 114 S.E.2d at 552. Stated another way, "nuisance is the unreasonable, unusual, or unnatural use of one's property so that it substantially impairs the right of another to peacefully enjoy his or her property." 58 Am.Jur.2d *Nuisances* § 2 (2002).

Booker v. Foose, 613 S.E.2d 94, 97 (W. Va. 2005). In the past, we described a nuisance as:

> anything which annoys or disturbs the free use of one's property, or which renders its ordinary use or physical occupation uncomfortable. A nuisance is anything which interferes with the rights of a citizen, either in person, property, the enjoyment of his property, or his comfort. A condition is a nuisance when it clearly appears that enjoyment of property is materially lessened, and physical comfort of persons in their homes is materially interfered with thereby.

Martin v. Williams, 93 S.E.2d 835, 844 (W. Va. 1956). More recently, we held that "[a] private nuisance is a substantial and unreasonable interference with the private use and enjoyment of another's land." *Hendricks v. Stalnaker*, 380 S.E.2d 198 (W. Va. 1989). The test to determine unreasonableness has been stated by this Court as follows: "An interference with the private use and enjoyment of another's land is unreasonable when the gravity of the harm outweighs the social value of the activity alleged to cause the harm." *Hendricks, supra*. With regard to remedying a nuisance, it has long been understood that "[j]urisdiction in equity to abate nuisances is undoubted and of universal recognition." *State v. Ehrlick*, 64 S.E. 935, 937 (W. Va. 1909).

* * *

[The court first analyzed whether the lower court maintained jurisdiction over electric generating facilities such that it could consider a common law nuisance claim against wind power facilities. The court found that legislation related to PSC authority did not strip the court of its jurisdiction.]

* * *

2.　*Private Nuisance Claim for a Prospective Injunction*

In addition to finding that it had no jurisdiction to hear the appellants' nuisance claim for an injunction, the circuit court ruled that the appellants failed to set forth sufficient facts in their complaint alleging a private nuisance that would support the granting of a prospective injunction against the appellees. Specifically, the circuit court found that even if the appellants alleged injuries for which remedies are available in nuisance, these alleged injuries do not support a prospective injunction because the injuries are speculative and contingent.

Our reading of the appellants' complaint indicates that the appellants allege, as private nuisances, that the wind turbines will cause constant noise when the wind is blowing and an increase in noise as the wind velocity increases; the turbines will create an eyesore as a result of the turbines' "flicker" or "strobe" effect when the sun is near the horizon; and proximity of the appellants' property to the turbines will result in a diminution in the appellants' property values. We will now determine the legal effect of each of these allegations under our settled law of nuisance.

First, the appellants allege that the noise from the turbines will constitute a nuisance. This Court has held that "[n]oise alone may create a nuisance, depending on time, locality and degree." *Ritz v. Woman's Club of Charleston*, 173 S.E. 564 (W. Va. 1934). We have further held that "[w]here an unusual and recurring noise is introduced in a residential district, and the noise prevents sleep or otherwise disturbs materially the rest and comfort of the residents, the noise may be inhibited by a court of equity." *Ritz, supra*. See also *Snyder v. Cabell*, 1 S.E. 241 (W. Va. 1886) (affirming injunction against skating rink's operation where it was found that noise from the rink materially interfered with the comfort and enjoyment of nearby residents.). These holdings are grounded on a principle that is essential to a civil society which is that "every person . . . has the right not to be disturbed in his house; he has the right to rest and quiet and not to be materially disturbed in his rest and enjoyment of home by loud noises." *Snyder*, 1 S.E. at 251. Thus, we find that the appellants' allegation of noise is cognizable under our law as an abatable nuisance.

Second, the appellants allege that a "flicker" or "strobe" effect from the turbines will create an eyesore. Traditionally "courts of equity have hesitated to exercise authority in the abatement of nuisances where the subject matter is objected to by the complainants merely because it is offensive to the sight." *Parkersburg Builders Material Co. v. Barrack*, 191 S.E. 368, 369 (W. Va. 1937). This Court has explained in further detail that

> [e]quity should act only where there is presented a situation which is offensive to the view of average persons of the community. And, even where there is a situation which the average person would deem offensive to the sight, such fact alone will not justify interference by a court of equity. The surroundings must be considered. Unsightly things are not to be banned solely on that account. Many of them are necessary in carrying on the proper activities of organized society. But such things should be properly placed, and not so located as to be unduly offensive to neighbors or to the public.

Barrack, 191 S.E. at 371. When an unsightly activity is not properly placed, when it is unduly offensive to its neighbors, and when it is accompanied by other interferences to the use and enjoyment of another's property, this Court has shown a willingness to abate the activity as a nuisance For example, in *Mahoney v. Walter*, 205 S.E.2d 692 (W. Va. 1974), it was held:

> The establishment of an automobile salvage yard with its incident noise, unsightliness, hazards from the presence of flammable materials, open vehicles, rodents and insects, and resultant depreciation of adjoining residential property values in an area which, though unrestricted and containing some commercial businesses, is primarily residential, together with the interference with the use, comfort and enjoyment of the surrounding properties caused by its operation, may be a nuisance and may be abated by a court of competent jurisdiction.

We hold, therefore, that while unsightliness alone rarely justifies interference by a circuit court applying equitable principles, an unsightly activity may be abated when it occurs in a residential area and is accompanied by other nuisances.

Third, the appellants allege that construction of the wind turbines will cause a reduction in their property values. With regard to the legal effect of mere diminution in the value of property, this Court has explained:

> Upon the question of reduction in value of the plaintiffs' properties, as the result of the establishment of the used car lot nearby, we find this statement in Wood on Nuisances, 3rd Edition, § 640: "Mere diminution of the value of the property, in consequence of the use to which adjoining premises are devoted, unaccompanied with other ill-results, is *damnum absque injuria*." Also in 66 C.J.S., Nuisances, § 19, P. 771, it is stated that: "However, a use of property which does not create a nuisance cannot be enjoined or a lawful structure abated merely because it renders neighboring property less valuable."

Martin, 93 S.E.2d at 843–44. However, the appellants in this case do not rely merely upon diminution of property values to support their nuisance claim, but also noise and unsightliness. According to *Martin*, *supra*,

> The establishment of what is commonly known as a "used car lot" with its incident noise, light, unsightliness and resultant depreciation of adjoining residential property values in an area which, though unrestricted and without the corporate limits of a town or city, was across a highway from zoned residential property lying within the corporate limits, and which area had previously been exclusively residential on both sides of the highway for a distance of approximately one-fourth of a mile, and which "used car lot" greatly interferes with the use, comfort and enjoyment of such surrounding residential properties,

constitutes a nuisance in fact, and may be abated by a court of equity.

See also *Mahoney*, cited above (holding that automobile salvage yard with noise, unsightliness, flammable materials hazards, rodents and insects, and resultant depreciation of adjoining residential property values may be a nuisance and may be abated). We hold, therefore, that an activity that diminishes the value of nearby property and also creates interferences to the use and enjoyment of the nearby property may be abated by a circuit court applying equitable principles. In addition, the landowners may seek compensation for any diminution in the value of their property caused by the nuisance.

Finally, the remedy sought by the appellants is an injunction against the construction and operation of the wind power facility.

It is a general rule that when the thing complained of is not a nuisance *per se*, but may or may not become so, according to circumstances, and the injury apprehended is eventual or contingent, equity will not interfere; the presumption being that a person entering into a legitimate business will conduct it in a proper way, so that it will not constitute a nuisance.

Chambers v. Cramer, 38 S.E. 691 (W. Va. 1901). We have recognized that a lawful business or a business authorized to be conducted by the government cannot constitute a nuisance *per se*. In the early case of *McGregor v. Camden*, 34 S.E. 936, 937 (W. Va. 1899), this Court succinctly stated that "[a] lawful business cannot be a nuisance *per se*, but from its surrounding places and circumstances, or the manner in which it is conducted it may become a nuisance." Further, according to *Watson v. Fairmont & S. Ry. Co.*, 39 S.E. 193 (W. Va. 1901),

When a person or corporation is authorized by the legislature by an express statute to do an act, or by the council of a city or town to which the power to authorize it has been delegated by a legislative act, such person or corporation cannot be regarded as committing a nuisance in the execution of such act nor proceeded against merely upon the theory that it is a nuisance, either at law or in equity.

Therefore, when we apply these holdings to the instant facts, we must conclude that, as a lawful business which has been granted a siting certificate by the PSC, the appellees' wind power facility cannot be considered a nuisance *per se*.

However, the fact that the appellees' electric generating facility does not constitute a nuisance *per se* does not mean that it cannot be abated as a nuisance. It is also true that a business that is not a nuisance *per se* may still constitute a nuisance in light of the surrounding circumstances. In *Mahoney,* cited above, this Court held:

> As a general rule, a fair test as to whether a business or a particular use of a property in connection with the operation of the business constitutes a nuisance, is the reasonableness or unreasonableness of the operation or use in relation to the particular locality and under all the existing circumstances.

Specifically, "[t]o sustain a[ ] [prospective] injunction inhibiting . . . [a] business, not *per se* constituting a nuisance, it must be shown that the danger of injury from it is impending and imminent, and the effect certain." *Pope v. Bridgewater Gas Co.,* 43 S.E. 87 (W. Va. 1903). With regard to whether an injury in nuisance is certain, this Court has explained that "[m]ere possible, eventual or contingent danger is not enough. That injury will result must be shown beyond question . . . not resting on hypothesis or conjecture, but established by conclusive evidence. If the injury be doubtful, eventual, or contingent . . . an injunction will not be granted." *Pope,* 43 S.E. at 89. . . .

Applying the above law to the allegations in the appellants' complaint, and taking these allegations as true, we conclude that the allegations are legally sufficient to state a claim to prospectively enjoin a nuisance. . . .

* * *

Reversed and remanded.

NOTES

1. *Wind farms, car lots, and salvage yards.* How does the utility of a wind farm compare with the used car lot from *Martin* or the rat-infested automobile salvage yard in *Mahoney,* the two cases cited by the court as exemplifying abatable nuisances? Further, how do you measure the "utility" of these uses of property? Utility for the local population? Utility for the state in setting and meeting renewable portfolio standards? Utility for the nation or the globe in capitalizing on a widespread source of renewable energy that in the aggregate produces a significant reduction in carbon emissions and helps combat climate change?

2. *Rejecting* Burch. Contrary to *Burch,* other courts that have considered whether noise and view associated with wind turbines support nuisance claims have rejected such claims. See *Rankin v. FPL Energy, LLC,* 266 S.W.3d 506 (Tex. App. 2008). For more information on nuisance claims against wind farms, see Stephen Harland Butler, *Headwinds to a Clean Energy Future: Nuisance Suits Against Wind Energy Projects in the United States,* 97 Calif. L. Rev. 1337 (2009).

3.   *Burch on remand.* Although the case was remanded to the lower court for consideration of whether the wind farm constituted a nuisance, the suit was ultimately settled. How would you structure such a settlement? Who would have the upper hand in the settlement talks? Do you think there is a high likelihood a court on remand would find a nuisance? If not, why would the wind farm settle? If a nuisance is likely, what concessions might the wind farm make in a settlement?

4.   *Contracting around renewable disputes.* Despite the potential for nuisance claims (as in *Rose* and *Burch* above) or local government prohibition of wind energy technologies, property agreements may be negotiated to facilitate wind energy development. These may take the form of options to purchase or lease, sale of a right of first refusal to wind developers, and creation of easements or covenants establishing wind rights, among a variety of other agreements. See Jessica Shoemaker, *Negotiating Wind Energy Property Agreements* (2007), *available at* http://www.flaginc.org/wp-content/uploads/2013/03/WindPropertyAgrmnts20071.pdf.

5.   *Federal wind incentives.* Notwithstanding local government control over wind energy siting, a number of federal incentive programs exist to encourage wind development, such as the Residential Renewable Energy Tax Credit, the Renewable Electricity Production Tax Credit, and the Business Energy Investment Tax Credit. See Energy.gov, Office of Energy Efficiency & Renewable Energy, *Frequently Asked Questions About Wind Energy*, http://energy.gov/eere/wind/frequently-asked-questions-about-wind-energy.

MUSCARELLO V. OGLE COUNTY BOARD OF COMMISSIONERS

Seventh Circuit Court of Appeals
610 F.3d 416 (2010)

WOOD, J.

Ogle County[, Illinois,] joined the alternative energy bandwagon in 2003 when it adopted an amendment to its zoning ordinances to allow special use permits for the construction of windmills used to generate power. In 2005, Baileyville Wind Farms, LLC ("Baileyville") took the county up on its offer by applying for and receiving a special use permit to construct 40 windmills.

Patricia Muscarello evidently did not share the county's enthusiasm for wind energy. Muscarello owns land adjacent to the proposed site of the Baileyville wind farm. She voiced her opposition through the political process and, when that failed, she repaired to federal court. At that point, this garden variety zoning dispute morphed into a federal case against 42 defendants, including Baileyville, its corporate parents, and the various Ogle County political actors involved in the decision to grant the permit. Muscarello's complaint invoked twelve theories of recovery, based on the U.S. Constitution, the Illinois Constitution, Illinois statutes, and the common law. In addition to objecting to the process that the county had followed, she attacked everything in the outcome (or anticipated outcome) from the loss of kinetic energy, to what she calls "shadow flicker," to the risk of a blade being hurled onto her property.

* * *

In late 2003, after a public hearing held by the Zoning Board of Appeals (the "ZBA"), the Ogle County Board of Commissioners (the "Board") adopted an amendment to the county zoning ordinances providing that special use permits would be available for systems that use wind energy and thereby reduce dependence on fossil fuels (the "Windmill Text Amendment").

In September 2005, Baileyville applied for a special use permit to build a wind-energy system on land in Ogle County adjacent to Patricia Muscarello's property. . . . Baileyville intended to construct 40 windmills, each of which was to be approximately 400 feet in height to the tip of the blade and 285 feet in diameter. The application specified the locations of the windmills on the property.

Sometime between November 7 and December 13, 2005, the ZBA held public hearings on Baileyville's application. On December 13, the ZBA issued its Findings of Fact in support of the application. On December 20, the Board issued the special use permit and adopted a Home Sellers Property Value Protection Plan (the "Protection Plan") to provide a mechanism for residential property owners to recover any diminution of value that resulted from the windmills if and when they decided to sell their homes. Nonresidential property owners were not eligible to take advantage of this procedure.

Muscarello objects to every stage of the process. On January 19, 2006, she filed her original complaint, in which she objected to the findings of fact for the Windmill Text Amendment, the Baileyville permit application, the notice for the public hearing, the public hearing itself, Baileyville's evidence at the hearing, the findings of fact for the special use permit, the decision to issue the permit, and the authorization of the Protection Plan. At the core of her substantive allegations is an assertion that the county has condoned an impermissible taking of her property. Muscarello presented a laundry list of charges in her first amended complaint; as she describes it, the issuance alone of the permit will harm her in numerous ways. . . .

[Muscarello claimed that she would be deprived of "the full extent of the kinetic energy of the wind and air as it enters her property;" that she would be subject to "shadow flicker" and reduction of light; that she would have to endure noise; that ice could be physically thrown onto her property by the rotating blades or that the blades themselves may come loose and be thrown onto her property; that she would suffer radar interference, interference with her cell phone network, GPS service, wireless communications, and television signals; that she would suffer an increased risk of sustaining damage from lightening and increased levels of electromagnetic radiation; and that she would be prevented from conducting crop-dusting operations on her fields, among other claims].

We glean from all this, taking it in the light most favorable to Muscarello, that she believes that the prescribed process was not followed and that the construction of windmills will have uncompensated adverse consequences for her and her fellow nonresidential property owners. Muscarello sued to stop the construction of the windmills and to require the Board to revoke the permit. To date, as far as the record before us reflects, no windmills have been constructed.

II

Muscarello's complaint includes 12 counts based on the U.S. Constitution, the Illinois Constitution, Illinois statutes, and Illinois common-law rights; as we noted earlier, it names 42 defendants. . . .

We divide our analysis of Muscarello's claims into three categories based on the type of jurisdiction pleaded: [only the first two of which are discussed here: (1) federal constitutional law, and (2) state common law]. . . .

1. . . . Muscarello alleges three violations of the Fourteenth Amendment of the U.S. Constitution: Count IV alleges a taking without just compensation; Count VI alleges a denial of due process; and Count VIII alleges a denial of equal protection. These counts stem from Ogle County's grant of the special use permit to Baileyville and the adoption of the Protection Plan that provides compensation only to residential property owners. Although the permit does not directly affect Muscarello's land, she asserts that it represents an unreasonable and illegal taking of her property, that the process by which it was awarded was defective, and that the Protection Plan unlawfully discriminates against nonresidential property owners. The district court dismissed her takings and equal protection claims as unripe, and it rejected her due process claim for failure to state a claim upon which relief could be granted.

2. . . . Two more of Muscarello's claims are based on state common law (trespass, in Count X, and nuisance, in Count XI). . . . [A]lthough Muscarello concedes that the windmills have yet to be constructed, she takes the position that she can recover under trespass and nuisance theories based solely on the county's decision to grant the permit for the future windmills. . . . [T]he district court rejected these speculative theories of trespass and nuisance as unripe.

* * *

III

We look first at the claims that allegedly arise under the federal Constitution's provisions relating to takings, due process, and equal protection. . . .

A

The core of Muscarello's claims is an allegation that Ogle County violated the Fourteenth Amendment of the U.S. Constitution through a violation of the Fifth Amendment's Takings Clause. The Takings Clause provides: "nor shall private property be taken for public use, without just compensation." U.S. CONST. amend. V. Muscarello asserts that Ogle County's decision to grant a permit to Baileyville constituted a taking without just compensation.

In order to invoke the protections of the Takings Clause, Muscarello must allege a taking of private property. Her complaint fails to meet that requirement. Muscarello does not allege any physical invasion of her property, a quintessential taking. See *Loretto v. Teleprompter Manhattan CATV Corp.*, 458 U.S. 419, 427 (1982) ("When faced with a constitutional challenge to a permanent physical occupation of real property, this Court has invariably found a taking."). Instead, she relies on the more elusive concept of the regulatory taking. See *Lucas v. S.C. Coastal Council*, 505 U.S. 1003 (1992) (finding a regulatory taking only where "all economically beneficial or productive use of land" is denied). But here, the alleged economic effects are a far cry from the denial of all economically beneficial or productive use of the land. The *Lucas* Court was careful not to create the impression that all zoning decisions that may diminish an owner's potential uses of her property, or compel a less valuable use, are takings. See *Covington Court v. Vill. of Oak Brook*, 77 F.3d 177, 179 (7th Cir. 1996) ("We frequently have reminded litigants that federal courts are not boards of zoning appeals."). In order to qualify as a regulatory taking, the measure must place such onerous restrictions on land as to render it useless. Muscarello would have us turn land-use law on its head by accepting the proposition that a regulatory taking occurs whenever a governmental entity lifts a restriction on someone's use of land. We see no warrant for such a step. See *Gagliardi v. Vill. of Pawling*, 18 F.3d 188, 191–93 (2d Cir. 1994) (holding that residential landowners had no property interest in the enforcement of zoning laws on adjacent property).

Even if we thought that Ogle County might have "taken" Muscarello's property when it issued the permit to Baileyville, Muscarello could not seek recovery in the way she has proceeded here. As we have observed in the past, in *Williamson County Regional Planning Commission v. Hamilton Bank*, 473 U.S. 172 (1985):

the Supreme Court articulated a special ripeness doctrine for constitutional property rights claims which precludes federal courts from adjudicating land use disputes until: (1) the regulatory agency has had an opportunity to make a considered definitive decision, and (2) the property owner exhausts available state remedies for compensation.

Forseth v. Vill. of Sussex, 199 F.3d 363, 368 (7th Cir. 2000). Muscarello concedes that she did not satisfy the exhaustion requirement. Therefore, her takings claim is unripe unless she is excused from that requirement. The district court found that Muscarello should not be excused, and we agree.

Muscarello attempts to save this part of her case through two exceptions to the exhaustion requirement: one for pre-enforcement facial challenges and one for situations in which relief is not available in state court. We conclude, however, that neither applies to this case. It is true that pre-enforcement facial challenges to the constitutionality of a law under the Takings Clause are not subject to the exhaustion requirement. But Muscarello's claim is not a pre-enforcement facial challenge. She has focused on the economic deprivation that she herself will suffer if and when the taking occurs—the characteristic "as applied" challenge. Although almost in passing she suggests that the alleged taking was not for a public purpose, this point is too undeveloped to require comment.

Second, plaintiffs are excused from the exhaustion requirement if state law does not provide relief. That rule does not fit Muscarello's case either, because Illinois provides ample process for a person seeking just compensation. See *Peters v. Clifton*, 498 F.3d 727, 733–34 (7th Cir. 2007). See also 735 ILCS 30/10–5–5 (providing a statutory basis for inverse condemnation actions under Illinois law); *Inn of Lamplighter, Inc. v. Kramer*, 470 N.E.2d 1205 (Ill. App. Ct. 1984) (noting that plaintiffs properly sought a writ of mandamus to compel an eminent domain action to compensate them for their alleged loss). Since Illinois law provides a remedy for Muscarello, her claims are not excused from the exhaustion requirement.

[The court next dispenses with Muscarello's Equal Protection and Due Process Clause claims, finding a lack of ripeness and a lack of a protectable property interest.]

IV

Muscarello also alleges two state common-law claims, which she apparently thinks fall outside the constitutional "case" she has presented under her federal theories. . . . Count X alleges trespass and Count XI alleges nuisance. The district court dismissed these claims as unripe, because the windmills, which ostensibly would cause the nuisance or trespass, have not been built and it is thus impossible to know how they might trespass upon her property. . . .

* * *

If Muscarello's trespass and nuisance claims were ripe, we would be able to consider them. But we conclude, as did the district court, that they are not. This provides an independent ground for dismissal.

The windmills have not been built yet, and so it is difficult to see how they might either be causing a trespass on Muscarello's land or creating a nuisance. Muscarello tries to argue that the permit itself creates an "interference with her property and her property rights," but this is too metaphysical for us. We cannot see how the permit, unexercised, causes a trespass or nuisance as Illinois law conceptualizes those causes of action. *In re Chicago Flood Litigation*, 680 N.E.2d 265, 277–78 (Ill. 1997), provides that nuisance and trespass both require an invasion. Nuisance requires only a perceptible invasion, but the permit did not even lead to this minor effect. Trespass is even tougher; it is usually defined by a "crass physical invasion." *Id.* at 278. Obviously the permit did not march onto Muscarello's land, nor, as far as this record shows, did any of the defendants in the effort to start building their wind facility. Limiting her claims to the permit, as she must, Muscarello cannot succeed at this time under either a nuisance or trespass theory.

* * *

NOTES

1. Muscarello II. The 2009 *Muscarello* case was not the only time Ms. Muscarello challenged wind energy projects near her lands. In *Muscarello v. Winnebago County Board*, 702 F.3d 909 (7th Cir. 2012) (*Muscarello II*), Ms. Muscarello alleged wind farm interference with her use of three land parcels in Winnebago County, Illinois. The court began its analysis by noting, rather tongue in cheek, that:

> A reduction in wind speed downwind is an especially common effect of a wind turbine. And that is the harm the plaintiff emphasizes— which is odd. For the only possible such harm that the wind farm could do to her would be to reduce the amount of wind energy otherwise available to her, and the only value of that energy would be to power a wind farm on her property—and she is opposed to wind farming.

Although the court did not reach the merits of the takings claim in *Muscarello I*, it did in *Muscarello II*. On the takings issue, the *Muscarello II* (702 F.3d. at 912–13) court stated:

> No one has yet applied for a zoning clearance or building permit for a wind farm in Winnebago County, and no wind farm has yet been

built anywhere in the county. As a result, a pall of prematurity hangs over the case. But injury need be neither certain nor great to confer standing under Article III of the Constitution. If the plaintiff's allegations regarding the prospective dangers from an adjacent wind farm are true or even if they are just widely believed, and if she must wait until a wind farm is built adjacent to one of her properties to proceed at law, she may find it difficult to sell the properties now (even before a wind farm is constructed) at the price they would command were the zoning amendment invalidated.

In fact the complaint alleges that her properties have lost $500,000 in value because of the 2009 ordinance. The number is suspiciously round, and unexplained. But the complaint was dismissed without a hearing on jurisdiction; and given the surprising number of potential adverse environmental consequences of wind farms (even though the energy they produce is clean and also reduces consumption of fossil fuels and so contributes to U.S. independence from foreign oil supplies), it is not beyond reason that the prospect of having a windmill adjacent to one's property might cause the value of the property to decline. The plaintiff has submitted a map on which, she argues, is marked a wind farm that a company wants to build near one of her properties, and she adds that a wind company once approached her about buying a wind easement from her. The injuries she alleges are speculative but not so speculative as to deny her standing to sue.

Yet it is germane to the merits if not to jurisdiction that no property of the plaintiff's has yet been taken, or will be until and unless a wind farm is built near her property—and probably not even then. A taking within the meaning of the takings clause of the U.S. Constitution has to be an actual transfer of ownership or possession of property, or the enforcement of a regulation that renders the property essentially worthless to its owner. *Lucas v. South Carolina Coastal Council*, 505 U.S. 1003, 1015–16 (1992); *Muscarello v. Ogle County Board of Commissioners, supra*, 610 F.3d 416, 421–22 (2010); *Gamble v. Eau Claire County*, 5 F.3d 285, 286 (7th Cir. 1993). The 2009 Winnebago ordinance does not transfer possession of any of the plaintiff's land or limit her use of it.

The Illinois takings clause, however, on which she also relies, is broader than the federal clause. Article I, section 15 of the state's constitution provides that "property shall not be taken or damaged for public use without just compensation." "Taken" is defined as under federal law . . . but "damaged" connotes merely "a direct physical disturbance" of the plaintiff's property that causes a loss of value. But as no wind farm has yet been built, there has been no direct, or for that matter indirect, physical disturbance of the plaintiff's property.

2. *Preemptive regulatory takings compensation?* The court in *Muscarello I* noted that the Board established a "Home Sellers Property Value Protection Plan" to "provide a mechanism for residential property owners to recover any diminution of value that resulted from the windmills if and when they decided to sell their homes." 610 F.3d at 419. Should provisions like this bear any relevance to whether a nuisance claim should succeed or whether a zoning regulation is upheld?

Interestingly, the Board was preemptively providing compensation to property owners similar to that mandated by some state legislatures in recent years. For example, Florida's Bert-Harris Property Rights Act requires compensation if new government regulation negatively impacts "an existing fair market value" of property. Fla. Stat. Ann. § 70.001(2), (3)(b) (West 2004). Another example is Oregon's "Measure 37." Or. Rev. Stat. § 197.352 (1), (2), (3)(E) (2005). Before Measure 37 was substantially replaced and its effects limited by Measure 49 in 2007, it either "require[d] state and local governments to compensate private property owners for the reduction in the fair market value of their real property that result[ed] from *any land use regulations* of those governmental entities that restrict[ed] the use of the subject properties," or "allow[ed] state and local governments to 'modify, remove or not apply the land use regulation' " at all. *MacPherson v. Dep't of Admin. Servs.*, 130 P.3d 308, 312 (Or. 2006) (emphasis added). See Michael C. Blumm & Erik Grafe, *Enacting Libertarian Property: Oregon's Measure 37 and Its Implications*, 85 Denv, U. L. Rev. 279 (2007).

Louisiana and Mississippi have also enacted similar legislation. See George Charles Homsy, *The Land Use Planning Impacts of Moving "Partial Takings" from Political Theory to Legal Reality*, 37 Urb. Law. 269, 278–79, 281 (2005). These statutes are primarily aimed at avoiding Fifth Amendment takings claim litigation. Why would the Board provide compensation to neighbors, given the low likelihood of those neighbors succeeding with a takings claim against the zoning authority or government that permitted the wind farm (as evidenced by the court's analysis in *Muscarello II*)? After all, under either the *Lucas* takings test or the *Penn Central* balancing test, a landowner would be hard pressed to prove that government siting of a wind farm adjacent to their property takes their property in some way. Is this a useful political tool to forge community support for wind projects?

3. *Anticipatory nuisance for wind farms?* Recall the case of *University of Montevallo v. Middle Tennessee Land Development Co., LLC* in chapter 7 (p. 431). That case involved anticipatory nuisance, a doctrine that allows the enjoining of activities that, *were they to occur in the future*, would with near certainty rise to the level of a nuisance. Since some courts have concluded that wind turbines located within a certain distance of households are nuisances, as in *Rose*, how likely is it that an anticipatory nuisance claim could succeed in a case where a wind farm or turbine has yet to be built?

4. *Wind turbine afflictions: real or imagined?* Some of the concerns raised by Ms. Muscarello, such as noise, ice throw, blade throw, shadow

flicker, and death of birds, are not out of the realm of possibility, although the probability and severity of their effects are debatable. See, e.g., Susan Combs, Texas Comptroller of Public Accounts, *The Energy Report: Wind Energy* (2008), www.window.state.tx.us/specialrpt/energy/renewable/wind.php; Carl Herbrandson & Rita B. Messing, Minnesota Department of Health, *Public Health Impacts of Wind Turbines*, May 22, 2009, www.health.state.mn.us/divs/eh/hazardous/topics/windturbines.pdf; American Wind Energy Association, *Wind Energy Siting Handbook* 5–33 to 5–48 (Feb. 2008), http://awea.files.cms-plus.com/Chapter_5_Impact_Analysis_and_Mitigation.pdf; Committee on Environmental Impacts of Wind Energy Projects, National Research Council, *Environmental Impacts of Wind-Energy Projects* 157–62 (2007), www.nap.edu/catalog/11935.html; Scott Larwood, California Wind Energy Collaborative, *Permitting Setbacks for Wind Turbines in California and the Blade Throw Hazard* 27 (June 16, 2005), http://newgenerationdri.capecodcommission.org/ng480.pdf; Kimberly E. Diamond & Ellen J. Crivella, *Wind Turbine Wakes, Wake Effect Impacts, and Wind Leases: Using Solar Access Laws as the Model for Capitalizing on Wind Rights During the Evolution of Wind Policy Standards*, 22 Duke Envtl. L. & Pol'y F. 195, 199–200 (2012).

One common complaint levied against wind farms, however, may have more purchase—the aesthetics of large fields of turbines. How do changing conditions affect notions of turbine aesthetics? Windmills, after all, are an iconic and historic symbol of nations like the Netherlands. Are oil derricks in Texas any more aesthetically pleasing? Given that aesthetics is sometimes a factor (never the sole one) that courts consider in the context of nuisance and zoning (*People v. Stover*, 191 N.E.2d 272 (N.Y. 1963)), how should aesthetics be weighed against developing renewable technologies to combat the worst effects of climate change?

5.   *NIMBYism and wind.* Often, opposition to wind project siting can seem to be a simple case of NIMBYism (Not in My Back Yard). This may be the case with the stalled siting of a wind project off of Nantucket Sound, which resulted in self-proclaimed environmentalists, like Edward Kennedy and Robert Kennedy, Jr., opposing this project due to its particular local effects while being generally supportive of windpower development. *See* Fred Bosselman et al., *Energy, Economics and the Environment* 856–60 (3d ed. 2010). The Alliance to Protect Nantucket Sound and its co-plaintiffs have actually lost no fewer than twenty-six legal challenges to the Cape Wind project in Massachusetts, and appear headed to even more litigation. See Todd Sperry, *Wind Farm Gets US Approval Despite Controversy*, CNN (Aug. 16, 2012) http://www.cnn.com/2012/08/16/us/wind-farm-faa/; Patrick Cassidy, *Cape Wind Foes Appeal Latest Legal Defeat*, Cape Cod Times (Aug. 28, 2014) http://www.capecodonline.com/apps/pbcs.dll/article?AID=/20140828/NEWS/408280310/–1/SPECIAL01; Cape Wind, *Cape Wind Project Status and Timeline*, http://www.capewind.org/when.

Bosselman et al. attribute the success of local resistance in part on the federal governance structure in which wind energy policies are embedded:

At times, opponents of renewable energy projects have been able to stymie progress by exploiting the federal, state, and local regulatory system that governs these projects to their advantage ... Opponents have recognized that there is no one single regulator or coherent regulatory strategy for these projects. With jurisdiction split among multiple local, state and federal regulators, it can be easy to find a way to halt or slow down a project.

Fred Bosselman et al., *Energy, Economics and the Environment* 854 (3d ed. 2010). What is the proper locus for control over these projects? The question is difficult to answer because of the considerable mismatch between the costs of such projects—which are imposed on local people—and the benefits, which are widespread. Local people, bearing a greater proportion of costs relative to the clean-energy benefits, are understandably inclined to give the costs considerable weight in decisionmaking. Outsiders, who enjoy the benefits without the costs, are more likely to highlight the benefits and discount or ignore the costs. See Ronald H. Rosenberg, *Diversifying America's Energy Future: The Future of Renewable Wind Power*, 26 Va. Envtl. L.J. 505 (2008); Richard J. Pierce, Jr., *Environmental Regulation, Energy, and Market Entry*, 15 Duke Envtl. L. & Pol'y F. 167 (2005); Carolyn S. Kaplan, *Congress, the Courts, and the Army Corps: Siting the First Offshore Wind Farm in the United States*, 31 B.C. Envtl. Aff. L. Rev. 177 (2004).

6. *Wind turbine vs. wind turbine.* Imagine a situation where two neighbors each want to develop wind energy resources. What if one neighbor's turbine creates a loss of wind energy productivity for a downwind neighbor? For more on how society might allocate property rights under such circumstances, *see* Troy Rule, *A Downwind View of the Cathedral: Using Rule Four to Allocate Wind Rights*, 46 San Diego L. Rev. 207 (2009).

C. WIND ENERGY AND OTHER NATURAL RESOURCES

Wind energy, whether distributed among individual households or contained within one project on a large acreage, has the potential to conflict with the protection and use of other natural resources, including biodiversity, water, and minerals. Each of these conflicts is explored through the cases presented below.

1. WIND AND BIODIVERSITY

ANIMAL WELFARE INSTITUTE V.
BEECH RIDGE ENERGY LLC

United States District Court, District of Maryland
675 F.Supp.2d 540 (2009)

TITUS, J.

This is a case about bats, wind turbines, and two federal polices, one favoring protection of endangered species and the other encouraging development of renewable energy resources. It began on June 10, 2009, when Plaintiffs Animal Welfare Institute ("AWI"), Mountain Communities for Responsible Energy ("MCRE"), and David G. Cowan (collectively, "Plaintiffs") brought an action seeking declaratory and injunctive relief against Defendants Beech Ridge Energy LLC ("Beech Ridge Energy") and Invenergy Wind LLC ("Invenergy") (collectively, "Defendants"). Plaintiffs allege that Defendants' construction and future operation of the Beech Ridge wind energy project ("Beech Ridge Project"), located in Greenbrier County, West Virginia, will "take" endangered Indiana bats, in violation of § 9 of the Endangered Species Act ("ESA"), 16 U.S.C. § 1538(a)(1)(B).

[The Court undertook a comprehensive review of the background of the federal Endangered Species Act].

Section 9 of the ESA, the cornerstone of the Act, makes it unlawful for any person to "take any [endangered] species within the United States." 16 U.S.C. § 1538(a)(1)(B). The ESA defines the term "take" as "to harass, harm, pursue, hunt, shoot, wound, kill, trap, capture, or collect, or to attempt to engage in any such conduct." 16 U.S.C. § 1532(19).

The U.S. Fish and Wildlife Service ("FWS" or the "Service") has passed regulations implementing the ESA that further refine what activities constitute an impermissible "take." The regulations define the term "harass" as:

> an intentional or negligent act or omission which creates the likelihood of injury to wildlife by annoying it to such an extent as to significantly disrupt normal behavioral patterns which include, but are not limited to, breeding, feeding, or sheltering.

50 C.F.R. § 17.3. The regulations also define the term "harm" as:

> an act which actually kills or injures wildlife. Such act may include significant habitat modification or degradation where it actually kills or injures wildlife by significantly impairing essential behavioral patterns, including breeding, feeding or sheltering.

Id. In 1981, the FWS added to its definition of the term "harm" the "word 'actually' before the words 'kills or injures' . . . to clarify that a standard of actual, adverse effects applies to section 9 takings." 46 Fed.Reg. 54,748, 54,750 (Nov. 4, 1981). See also *Babbitt v. Sweet Home Chapter of Communities for a Great Or.*, 515 U.S. 687, 703 (1995) (rejecting a facial challenge to invalidate the regulation and concluding that the Secretary's definition of harm to include habitat modification was consistent with "Congress' clear expression of the ESA's broad purpose to protect endangered and threatened wildlife").

Anyone who knowingly "takes" an endangered species in violation of § 9 is subject to significant civil and criminal penalties. 16 U.S.C. § 1540(a) (authorizing civil fines of up to $25,000 per violation); § 1540(b) (authorizing criminal fines of up to $50,000 and imprisonment for one year). In order to provide a safe harbor from these penalties, Congress amended the ESA in 1982 to establish an incidental take permit ("ITP") process that allows a person or other entity to obtain a permit to lawfully take an endangered species, without fear of incurring civil and criminal penalties, "if such taking is incidental to, and not the purpose of, the carrying out of an otherwise lawful activity." § 1539(a)(1)(B). Congress established this process to reduce conflicts between species threatened with extinction and economic development activities, and to encourage "creative partnerships" between public and private sectors. H.R.Rep. No. 97–835, at 30–31 (1982), reprinted in 1982 U.S.C.C.A.N. 2807, 2871–72. Some wind energy companies have obtained or are in the process of pursuing ITPs.

A person may seek an ITP from the FWS by filing an application that includes a Habitat Conservation Plan ("HCP"). See 16 U.S.C. 1539(a)(2)(A)(i)–(iv); see also generally 50 C.F.R. § 17.22. A[n] HCP is designed to minimize and mitigate harmful effects of the proposed activity on endangered species. Applicants must include in a[n] HCP a description of the impacts that will likely result from the taking, proposed steps to minimize and mitigate such impacts, and alternatives considered by the applicant including reasons why these alternatives are not being pursued. 16 U.S.C. § 1539(a)(2)(A)(i)–(iv); see also 50 C.F.R. § 17.22(b). If an ITP is issued, the FWS will monitor a project for compliance with the terms and conditions of a[n] HCP, as well as the effects of the permitted action and the effectiveness of the conservation program. 65 Fed.Reg. 35,242, 35,253–56 (June 1, 2000) (emphasizing the importance of periodic reports and field visits). The FWS may suspend or revoke all or part of an ITP if the permit holder fails to comply with the conditions of the permit or the laws and regulations governing the activity. 50 C.F.R. §§ 13.27, 13.28.

Congress also provided under Section 11 of the ESA that "any person" may bring a citizen suit in federal district court to enjoin anyone who is alleged to be in violation of the ESA or its implementing regulations. 16 U.S.C. § 1540(g). . . .

The ESA's plain language, citizen-suit provision, legislative history, and implementing regulations, as well as case law interpreting the Act, require that this Court carefully scrutinize any activity that allegedly may take endangered species where no ITP has been obtained.

II. *The Indiana Bat*

The FWS originally designated the Indiana bat (*Myotis sodalis*) as in danger of extinction in 1967 under the Endangered Species Preservation Act of 1966, the predecessor to the ESA. 32 Fed.Reg. 4,001 (Mar. 11, 1967). The species has been listed as endangered since that time. The Indiana bat is in the genus *Myotis* and shares some morphological similarities with other *Myotis* species. It closely resembles the little brown bat (*Myotis lucifugus*) and the northern long-eared bat (*Myotis septenrionalis*). An Indiana bat weighs approximately one quarter of an ounce (approximately seven grams), its forearm length is 1 3/8 inches to 1 5/8 inches (35–41 millimeters), and its head and body length is 1 5/8 inches to 1 7/8 inches (41–49 millimeters).

The current range of the Indiana bat includes approximately twenty states in the mid-western and eastern United States, including West Virginia. . . .

The Indiana bat population has declined since it was listed as an endangered species in 1967, and was estimated by the FWS in 2007 at approximately 468,184. However, research suggests that the West Virginia population of hibernating Indiana bats has increased since 1990, with an estimated current population of about 17,000. Approximately three percent of Indiana bats are located in West Virginia.

The Indiana bat is an insectivorous, migratory bat whose behavior varies depending on the season. In the fall, Indiana bats migrate to caves, called hibernacula. The bats engage in a "swarming" behavior in the vicinity of the hibernacula, which culminates in mating. Indiana bats ordinarily engage - in swarming within five miles of hibernacula, but may also engage in swarming beyond the five mile radius. During swarming, the bats forage for insects in order to replenish their fat supplies. In mid-November, Indiana bats typically enter hibernation and remain in hibernacula for the duration of winter.

In April and May, Indiana bats emerge from hibernation. After engaging in "staging," typically within five miles of the hibernacula, they fly to summer roosting and foraging habitat. In the summer, female Indiana bats form maternity colonies in roost trees, where they give birth to "pups," and raise their young. Studies suggest that reproductive female Indiana bats give birth to one pup each year. Male Indiana bats spend their summers alone or in small temporary groups in roost trees, changing roost trees and locations throughout the summer. Roost trees generally consist of snags, which are dead or dying trees with exfoliating bark, or living trees with peeling bark.

Like other bats, Indiana bats navigate by using echolocation. Specifically, bats emit ultrasonic calls and determine from the echo the objects that are within their environment. Call sequences are typically composed of multiple pulses.

The FWS published the original recovery plan for the Indiana bat in 1983 and a draft revised plan in 1999. In April 2007, the FWS published the current Draft Recovery Plan. See U.S. Fish and Wildlife Serv., Indiana Bat (*Myotis sodalis*) Draft Recovery Plan: First Revision (Apr. 2007). The current plan provides substantial background information regarding the behavior of the Indiana bat and the many threats that endanger the species. See *id.* at 7–8. The plan also sets forth a recovery program designed to protect the Indiana bat and ultimately remove it from the Federal List of Endangered and Threatened Wildlife. See *id.* at 8.

III. *Wind Turbines and Bat Mortality*

Research shows, and the parties agree, that wind energy facilities cause bat mortality and injuries through both turbine collisions and barotrauma. Barotrauma is damage caused to enclosed air-containing cavities (e.g., the lungs, eardrums, etc.) as a result of a rapid change in external pressure, usually from high to low. The majority of bat mortalities from wind energy facilities has occurred during fall dispersal and migration, but bat mortalities have also occurred in the spring and summer. At the Mountaineer wind energy facility in West Virginia, which is located approximately 75 miles from the Beech Ridge Project, a post-construction mortality study resulted in an estimated annual mortality rate of 47.53 bats per turbine.

The construction of wind energy projects may also kill, injure, or disrupt bat behavior. For example, the cutting of trees may kill or injure roosting bats and destroy potential roosting sites.

IV. *The Beech Ridge Project*

Defendant Invenergy is the fifth largest wind developer in the United States, with an aggregate wind-energy generating capacity of nearly 2,000 megawatts. Beech Ridge Energy, a wholly-owned subsidiary of Defendant Invenergy, intends to construct and operate 122 wind turbines along 23 miles of Appalachian mountain ridgelines, in Greenbrier County, West Virginia. The first phase of the project currently consists of 67 turbines and the second phase consists of 55 turbines.

The footprint for the transmission line will be approximately 100 acres and the footprint for the wind turbines will be approximately 300 acres. The lowest turbines are located at an elevation of approximately 3,650 feet above sea level and the highest are at approximately 4,350 feet. The towers are 263 feet tall and the rotors have a diameter of 253 feet. When the blade is pointing straight up at twelve o'clock, the turbine is 389 feet tall, and when the blade is pointing straight down at six o'clock, the bottom point of the blade is 137 feet off the ground.

The Beech Ridge Project will cost over $300 million to build and will produce 186 megawatts of electricity, equivalent to the amount of electricity consumed by approximately 50,000 West Virginia households in a typical year. The project is projected to operate for a minimum of twenty years. Invenergy has signed a twenty-year contract with Appalachian Power Company to sell all output from the first 105 megawatts of power. Sixty-seven turbines, the number of turbines in the first phase of the project, are required to produce this amount of electricity.

* * *

E.   *Indiana Bats are Present at the Beech Ridge Project Site*

Considering all of the evidence in the record, the Court concludes by a preponderance of the evidence that there is a virtual certainty that Indiana bats are present at the Beech Ridge Project site during the spring, summer, and fall. (Indiana bats are not likely to be present during winter, when the bats are hibernating.)

First, the Court finds that the close proximity of Indiana bat hibernacula to the project site, one cave located at 6.7 miles and another at 9.6 miles from the nearest turbines, supports a conclusion that Indiana bats are likely present at the Beech Ridge Project site. Indiana bats have been observed to travel far in excess of these distances in the spring, summer, and fall.

Second, the Court finds that the physical characteristics of the site also make the presence of Indiana bats more likely. The project site contains suitable roosting snags, and construction has further augmented the environment by creating habitat "sinks" that attract Indiana bats. Although the high elevation of the site makes it less likely, but not impossible, that maternity colonies are present during the summer, Indiana bats may still use the site during migration, fall swarming, and spring staging.

Third, the Court concludes that the acoustic data, collected by an entrepreneurial BHE subcontractor, confirms to a virtual certainty the presence of Indiana bats. [Plaintiffs' expert witnesses] Robbins and Gannon presented compelling testimony that their analysis of the AnaBat data identified Indiana bat calls. Because only four hours of acoustic data was collected over a mere two night period—during one summer survey session when Indiana bats are least likely to be present—more extensive acoustic surveys during different seasons and at different locations at the project site would almost certainly yield a greater number of Indiana bat calls.

Based on the evidence of nearby hibernacula, the physical characteristics of the project site, the acoustic data, and the behavioral traits of Indiana bats, the Court concludes by a preponderance of the evidence that Indiana bats are present at the Beech Ridge Project site during the spring, summer, and fall.

XII. *Likelihood of a Take of Indiana
Bats at the Beech Ridge Project Site*

It is uncontroverted that wind turbines kill bats, and do so in large numbers. Defendants contend, however, that Indiana bats somehow will escape the fate of thousands of their less endangered peers at the Beech Ridge Project site.

Defendants argue that Indiana bats do not fly at the height of the turbine blades. [Defendants' expert witnesses] Lacki and Tyrell stated that Indiana bats are "edge foragers," meaning they tend to forage for food directly below or at the tree canopy. Lacki opined that Indiana bats are not going to be in locations, such as the area above the tree canopy, where "their foraging approach is likely to render them vulnerable." Tyrell speculated that the tree canopy at the Beech Ridge Project site is 60 to 80 feet above the ground, which is below the lowest part of the rotor swept area.

However, Plaintiffs' expert Kunz, one of the leading bat biologists in the country, stated that with the development of acoustic technology and thermal cameras, there is growing research that bats can fly as high as a kilometer or more above the ground, and that Indiana bats may also fly at these altitudes. Kunz explained that bats fly above the tree canopy as warm air carries insects high above the surface of the earth. Kunz opined that "the fact that Indiana bats were detected at ground level . . . suggests that they would also . . . equally likel[y] be detected higher up in the rotor swept region." Moreover, the height at which Indiana bats forage has no relation to how high they fly during migration.

Defendants also point out that no Indiana bat has been confirmed dead at any wind power project in the country, which they contend supports a conclusion that Indiana bats, unlike other bat species, are somehow able to avoid harm caused by wind turbines.

However, other *Myotis* species have been reported killed at wind power projects. Plaintiffs' experts opined that biologically, Indiana bats are no less vulnerable than other *Myotis* species to turbine collisions and barotrauma.

In addition, post-construction mortality studies are generally inefficient (for example, due to scavenging), thus making the chances of finding the carcass of a rare species even smaller. At trial, Gannon criticized those mortality studies—like those proposed at the Beech Ridge Project site—that survey only a subset of the turbines: "[i]f you've got a haystack, and you're only looking at a very small portion of that haystack, what's the odds that you're going to find something rare in the haystack?"

* * *

The Court finds that there is no reason why Indiana bats would not fly at a height of 137 to 389 feet above the ground, within the rotor swept area of the turbines at the Beech Ridge Project site. Plaintiffs have presented compelling evidence that Indiana bats behave no differently than other *Myotis* species that have been killed by wind turbines and Defendants have failed to rebut this fact. Furthermore, the Court is not surprised that no dead Indiana bat has yet been found at any wind project because few post-mortality studies have been conducted, mortality searches are generally inefficient, and Indiana bats are rare.

Based on the evidence in the record, the Court therefore concludes, by a preponderance of the evidence, that, like death and taxes, there is a virtual certainty that Indiana bats will be harmed, wounded, or killed imminently by the Beech Ridge Project, in violation of § 9 of the ESA, during the spring, summer, and fall.

* * *

XIV.   *Injunctive Relief*

Because the Court has found that the Beech Ridge Project will take Indiana bats, injunctive relief is appropriate under § 11 of the ESA. The question, then, is what form that injunctive relief should take. The ITP process is available to Defendants to insulate themselves from liability under the ESA and, while this Court cannot require them to apply for or obtain such a permit, it is the only way in which the Court will allow the Beech Ridge Project to continue.

The Court sees little need to preclude the completion of construction of those forty turbines already under construction, but does believe that any construction of additional turbines should not be commenced unless and until an ITP has been obtained. The simple reason for this is that the ITP process may find that some locations for wind turbines are entirely inappropriate, while others may be appropriate.

There is, by the same token, no reason to completely prohibit Defendants from operating wind turbines now under construction once they are completed. However, in light of the record developed before this Court, that operation can only occur during the periods of time when Indiana bats are in hibernation, i.e., from November 16 to March 31. Outside this period, determining the timing and circumstances under which wind turbine operation can occur without danger of the take of an Indiana bat is beyond the competence of this Court, but is well within the competence of the FWS under the ITP process.

Accordingly, the Court will enjoin all operation of wind turbines presently under construction except during the winter period enumerated above. However, the Court invites the parties to confer with each other and return to the Court, if agreement can be reached, on the conditions under which the wind turbines now under construction would be allowed to operate, if at all, during any period of time outside of the hibernation period of Indiana bats.

* * *

NOTES

1. *Environmentalists versus environmentalists.* As *Animal Welfare* illustrates, natural resources law and policy disputes do not arise only between property owners and the government or between industry or developers and environmentalists. Natural resources management is multi-layered and complex, so advances in the management of one resource (energy in the form of renewables) can interfere with the management of another (biodiversity). Although wind energy is a clean, renewable source of energy that can alleviate society's dependence on fossil fuels and associated pollution, environmentalists are also concerned with the adverse impacts wind energy siting can have on wildlife, aesthetic values and scenic views, safety of citizens in the vicinity, economic value of residential properties, recreational use of land, and cultural resource values. Ronald H. Rosenberg, *Making Renewable Energy a Reality—Finding Ways to Site Wind Power Facilities*, 32 Wm. & Mary Envtl. L. & Pol'y Rev. 635, 640 (2008). How would you weigh the relative value of certain natural resources against others? Can a compromise always be struck, or must we sometimes sacrifice certain resources in order to protect others?

2. *The bird that could stop the wind.* Unlike *Animal Welfare*, which struck a balance between wind generation and species protection, some wind projects are completely forestalled by concerns over biodiversity. In 1999, for example, a Houston company sought to site a wind farm in California, but it was successfully opposed by the National Audubon Society on the basis that it might threaten the California condor. The condor is listed as endangered under the federal Endangered Species Act. Andrew Broman, *Environmentalists Pressure Houston-Based Firm to Drop Plans for Wind Farm*, Houston Chronicle, Nov. 4, 1999.

3. *Threats to biodiversity: wind farms versus climate change.* How might a court like that in *Animal Welfare* address a claim by defendants that the effects of climate change on biodiversity would be much more severe if energy projects like the one at issue are not allowed to go forward? In the long run, more biodiversity will be lost if society is unable to develop alternative energies where available—continued use of fossil fuels will contribute further to climate change impacts affecting many more species than just one bat. Is there a place for "conservation triage" when weighing the goals of different natural resources policies, whereby we focus on saving only those species most capable of being protected? See Blake Hudson, *Conservation Triage—"Should Conservationists Allow Some Species to Die Out?"*, Envtl. L. Prof Blog (May 16, 2011), http://lawprofessors.typepad.com/environmental_law/2011/05/conservation-triage-should-conservationists-allow-some-species-to-die-out.html.

4. *Did* Animal Welfare *get it right?* The *Animal Welfare* court allowed the turbines already under construction to be completed, and also allowed their operation to "only occur during the periods of time when Indiana bats are in hibernation, i.e., from November 16 to March 31," without requiring that the developer go through the ITP process. Given the danger to the bats, has the court adequately enforced the ban on taking by embracing this middle stance? Will forcing the company to go through the ITP process ultimately provide sufficient protections for the bats, notwithstanding the operation of the turbines already under construction? (For this question, you might revisit the materials on the ESA in chapter 4; a habitat conservation plan can gain approval even if it allows activities that clearly kill protected animals.) For more information on bats, birds, and wind turbines, *see* United States Geological Survey, *Bat Fatalities at Wind Turbines: Investigating the Causes and Consequences*, https://www.fort.usgs.gov/science-feature/96; National Wind Coordinating Collaborative, *Wind Turbine Interactions with Birds, Bats, and their Habitats: A Summary of Research Results and Priority Questions* (2010), *available at* http://www1.eere.energy.gov/wind/pdfs/birds_and_bats_fact_sheet.pdf.

2. WIND AND WATER

CONTRA COSTA WATER DISTRICT V. VAQUERO FARMS, INC.

California Court of Appeal
58 Cal.App.4th 883 (1997)

RUVOLO, J.

In this eminent domain proceeding, Contra Costa Water District (Water District) acquired approximately 3,500 acres of 6,000 acres owned by Vaquero Farms, Inc. (Vaquero) to be used by the Water District for the Los Vaqueros Reservoir Project (Reservoir Project). The issues on appeal involve the compensation awarded Vaquero for the taking of the property. Specifically, Vaquero contends: 1) the Water District must condemn its windpower rights, with a corresponding legal obligation to pay just compensation, even though the Water District chose to sever the property's windpower rights and reserve them to Vaquero; 2) the court erred in failing to award damages for the Water District's unreasonable precondemnation activities under *Klopping v. City of Whittier*, 500 P.2d 1345 (Cal. 1972); and 3) the jury's award of $1 million in severance damages for the diminution in value of the property remaining in Vaquero's ownership was unsupported by the evidence.

* * *

Background

The Vaquero property is located approximately six miles north of the City of Livermore, and approximately six miles south of the City of Brentwood. The property fronts over three miles of Vasco Road, which is a north-south traffic corridor. The 6,000 acres owned by Vaquero [were] and [are] primarily undeveloped. It varies tremendously in topographical features, ranging from relative flatlands adjacent to Vasco Road to steep ridge areas in the center and rugged ravines in the parcel's eastern portion. The property has been used as a working cattle ranch for nearly 50 years. In 1984, large portions of the ranch (over 2,100 acres) were leased for windpower electrical production and about 260 wind turbines have been installed on the property.

The Water District filed its complaint in eminent domain on June 14, 1993. By this action, the Water District sought to acquire four separate parcels of Vaquero's property, totaling approximately 3,500 acres, for the Reservoir Project. The Reservoir Project is a major public work including a reservoir, diversion facilities, pumping plants, and pipelines to convey water for storage and use. It is the largest public works project ever undertaken by the Water District. The project's primary purposes are to improve the quality of water supplied to the Water District's customers, to minimize seasonal changes in water quality, and to improve the reliability of the Water District's supply by providing for emergency storage. The project's secondary purposes include providing flood control benefits, maintaining and enhancing fish and wildlife resources, and offering recreational opportunities.

Each of Vaquero's four condemned parcels will be committed to a different use in connection with the Reservoir Project's implementation:

Parcel 1—a 2,743-acre parcel to be used for reservoir and watershed purposes;

Parcel 2—a 697-acre environmental mitigation parcel outside the reservoir/watershed area to be used to mitigate the environmental effects of the Reservoir Project on the habitat of the kit fox, an endangered species, and to mitigate the Reservoir Project's effect on the wetlands;

Parcel 3—a 4.8-acre parcel at the extreme southeast corner of the property to be used for road relocation. The proposed reservoir will inundate old Vasco Road, which provides the property's only public road access. Vasco Road will be relocated to the east of the reservoir and east of the property;

Parcel 4—a 52-acre area to be used as a combination cultural resource and environmental mitigation parcel outside the reservoir/watershed area.

Vaquero did not contest the right of the Water District to take its property. Instead, the focus of its answer to the complaint was the amount of "just compensation" to which appellant was entitled. Furthermore, in response to the complaint, Vaquero sought additional compensation for alleged damages sustained as a result of the Water District's precondemnation delays and other activities, and for severance damages.

By stipulation, the parties agreed to bifurcate the proceeding and to submit the pre-condemnation damages claim to a court trial in advance of the trial of other issues. The only issues which proceeded to trial by jury involved the fair market value of the property taken, generally measured by the highest and best use for which it is geographically and economically adaptable and an assessment of severance damages generally measured by the diminution in market value of the property remaining in the private property owner's possession. The presentation of evidence during the jury phase was protracted and extensive, consuming almost a month of court time. The ultimate issue of just compensation was a matter of widely conflicting expert opinion. The Water District presented witnesses who valued the property and severance damages between $6.1 million and $7.7 million. Vaquero's witnesses placed the total value of the take at over $30 million.

The jury returned a verdict in the total sum of $14,428,327. This verdict was comprised of $13,428,327 representing the fair market value of the property taken and $1 million representing severance damages to the land remaining in Vaquero's ownership by reason of the taking. After Vaquero's motion for new trial was denied, this appeal followed.

Severance of Windpower Rights

Vaquero advances the proposition that the Water District could not acquire the fee interest in its property while at the same time severing the windpower rights and windpower leasehold interests and reserving them to Vaquero. . . .

* * *

As noted, portions of the area being acquired and portions of Vaquero's remaining property are subject to leases with various companies engaged in the enterprise of generating and selling electricity derived from wind blowing across the property. At the time of trial, over 2,100 acres of the Vaquero property were subject to windpower leases, and approximately 260 wind turbines were built on that acreage between 1984 and 1986.

In anticipation of having to place a monetary value on these windpower rights, the Water District hired a windpower consulting firm charged with estimating the value of the existing machines to their operators, valuing the undeveloped windpower leases, and valuing Vaquero's present and future rental income streams. The consultants' findings are summarized by the Water District as follows: "Unfortunately, the range of values for the present worth of the future windpower income stream was highly speculative and varied wildly, depending on assumed long-term future energy prices, possible future royalty rates, and discount rates. It was not until 1991 that [the Water District] decided to attempt to avoid the problem entirely by reserving all windpower rights to the landowners."

The Water District's June 1993 resolution of necessity states that it is necessary to take Vaquero's fee interest but the Water District "does not, by the passage of this resolution of necessity, intend to acquire any of the windpower rights. . . ." Therefore, the Water District's complaint was limited to the acquisition of "[a]ll rights and incidents of the fee ownership interest vested in Vaquero Farms, . . . excepting and reserving to such defendants and their successors, and present and future assigns all rights for wind energy power conversion and the transmission of power generated by wind, including (1) the exclusive and perpetual right, . . . to develop, construct, install, maintain and operate windpower facilities, including but not limited to windmills, transmission lines and other facilities, necessary or advantageous for the purposes of generating or transmitting electric power from wind on the real property. . . ." The severance included reserving to Vaquero the exclusive right "to develop, construct, install, maintain and operate windpower facilities," the exclusive right to sell electric power generated by windmills, and the exclusive right to sell or lease the windpower rights. Vaquero was granted continued access to the property through non-exclusive easements for "roadway, ingress and egress, and utility purposes. . . ."

By subsequent amendment to the complaint, the Water District acquired all the windpower rights in certain areas where it was determined Vaquero's use of these rights would be inconsistent with the Reservoir Project's proposed uses. Specifically, the Water District decided to acquire Vaquero's rights in the following areas: 1) the 245-acre portion of Parcel 1 that the Reservoir Project will actually flood, 2) the area within Parcel 1 containing utility line relocation easements; and, 3) all of Parcel 3, the right-of-way for new Vasco Road. As a result, Vaquero's windpower rights were ultimately reserved in areas generally remaining undeveloped open space after the transfer from private to public ownership.

Vaquero filed a general demurrer to the Water District's complaint alleging it failed to state a cause of action because the Water District was prohibited, as a matter of law, from condemning the fee interest and severing the windpower rights. In opposition to the demurrer, the Water District contended that it was legally permissible to acquire the land needed for the Reservoir Project without appropriating the windpower rights because California law authorizes the condemner to sever rights it has determined are unnecessary for the public use. The court overruled Vaquero's demurrer, allowing the Water District to acquire the fee interest in the subject property while reserving and excepting the windpower rights to Vaquero.

The question before us may be stated as follows: When a public entity acquires property through eminent domain, are the windpower rights capable of segregation or are they so affixed to the underlying land that they must be acquired by the condemning authority? While the parties' dispute presents a question of first impression, its answer can be found by applying the reasoning of well-established California eminent domain law to this neoteric factual setting.

Under California's condemnation statutes, "... any person authorized to acquire property for a particular use by eminent domain may exercise the power of eminent domain to acquire any interest in property necessary for that use. ..." (§ 1240.110; see also §§ 1235.125, 1235.170.) The "interests" susceptible to condemnation under the statute, embrace "any right, title, or estate in property." (§ 1235.125.) Our Supreme Court has chronicled the interests considered to be property for condemnation purposes as including fee interest. ...

A review of the case law reveals California eminent domain law authorizes the condemner to select which right or combination of rights it needs to acquire from the full panoply of private ownership rights held within a fee simple estate. (See *Federal Oil Co. v. City of Culver City*, 179 Cal.App.2d 93, 96–97 (1960) [condemnation of lessee's surface rights without acquiring subsurface oil and gas rights]; *County Sanitation Dist. v. Watson Land Co.*, 17 Cal.App.4th 1268, 1273 (1993) [condemnation of permanent subterranean sewer easements and acquisition of temporary construction and occupational rights of way on the same properties]; [other citations omitted].) These cases remove any vestige of doubt that a condemner cannot be required to take more severable rights in property than what it needs for the public use.

When closely examined, the gravamen of Vaquero's argument rests on the premise that windpower rights must be rooted to the fee interest because no case, to date, has recognized windpower rights as capable of segregation or severance. In *Sacramento Mun. Util. Dist. v. Pac. G. & E. Co., supra*, 165 P.2d 741, the court was confronted with a problem similar to the one presented by this case. There, a public utility sought to acquire joint use of the condemnee's utility poles by condemnation. The condemnee argued the public utility could not condemn the "mere use in the poles in question instead of the fee therein or the poles themselves." (*Id.* at 751.) In support of its argument, the condemnee pointed out ". . . no right or interest known to the law is being acquired by such condemnation, . . ." (*Id.* at 750.) The court rejected this contention, declaring "[t]he precise legal designation which should be given to a joint use of a telegraph, telephone, or power-line pole, need not be determined herein. If the right to a joint or common use in a pole constitutes a substantial right—and we hold it does—then such a right is subject to condemnation." (*Id.* at 751.) In concluding the joint use of a utility pole constitutes a "substantial" right for purposes of condemnation, the court noted "[i]t is a compensable item in the acquisition of an electric distribution system . . ." which is capable of being assigned by contract. (*Id.*)

By parity of reasoning, windpower rights are "substantial rights" capable of being bought and sold in the marketplace, as evidenced by a 30-year lease which was entered into between Vaquero and a windpower developer, Altamont Energy Corporation, long before the Water District's condemnation action was initiated. The lease stands as irrefutable evidence that one may have a right to use windpower rights without owning any interest in the land. It memorializes Vaquero's agreement to convey the right to harness and develop windpower on its property until the year 2014 in exchange for monetary compensation, including a share of the gross annual revenue generated from the sale of electricity. Having itself derived economic benefit from the dissection of its property rights by separately leasing windpower rights to a third party, Vaquero's claim that these same rights are inextricably linked to the fee interest is unconvincing. Windpower rights clearly are "substantial" rights and thus may be condemned, or excluded from condemnation, despite their factual novelty under present law.

Vaquero complains that as a result of this partial take, its position has changed from fee owner with full and exclusive power over the use of the property to "an uncompensated lessor of land it does not own, with the theoretical right to develop wind production on someone else's property." According to Vaquero, this change of position prevents it from exercising even limited dominion as a lessor because "wind rights are dependent on control of the surface." Vaquero suggests to the court it can no longer give its windpower lessees authority to construct new windmills or relocate old windmills on land "it no longer owns."

These arguments are based on the erroneous premise that the Water District has acquired the sole right to occupy and use the entire surface of the land for public purposes to Vaquero's exclusion. As we have detailed earlier in this opinion, the record reflects otherwise. After the condemnation proceeding Vaquero will own all windpower rights in each of the affected parcels, together with an easement for ingress and egress and such other access rights as may be required for the maintenance and development of these windpower rights. Based on our request for supplemental briefing on the compatibility of the parties' joint use of the property, we are satisfied that private windpower generation is fully compatible with the Water District's public uses for the land being taken. The parcels involved are not physically encroached by the intended body of water and instead serendipitously must remain undeveloped to meet the environmental mitigation requirements of the Reservoir Project.

Vaquero's doubts that it could carry on windpower operations without ownership of the surface rights can be quelled by a simple comparison. It is well settled that subsurface minerals, gas and oil are distinct property rights which may be conveyed separately from the fee. We agree with the Water District's assertion that "[t]he right to generate electricity from windmills harnessing the wind, and the right to sell the power so generated, is no different, either in law or common sense, from the right to pump and sell subsurface oil, or subsurface natural gas by means of wells and pumps." The Water District persuasively points out, "[T]he argument that harvesting windpower somehow requires greater usage of the surface than harvesting oil and gas resources defies common sense to anyone who has seen a field of oil derricks."

Even without the assurances of the Water District, the law implies such surface rights of possession as are necessary and convenient to exercise the right to exploit the particular profit, estate or interest reserved. . . .

In conclusion, Vaquero's contention that the Water District cannot, as a matter of law, reserve windpower rights from a condemnation of property ignores the solidly established tenet of California law that a condemnation of property for public use need not be unqualified, total, and unconditional. For this reason, the authorities relied upon by Vaquero, which all involve fee simple takings without reservations, have little bearing on the issues at hand.

[The court then considered the question of whether the Water District's alleged improper pre-condemnation conduct entitled Vaquero to damages and concluded that the lower court committed no error in finding that it did not. The court also determined that Vaquero was not entitled to a greater amount of severance damages to compensate for the economic effect of the condemnation on the value of the remaining property in Vaquero's possession.]

The judgment is affirmed.

NOTES

1.   *Windpower rights, the elements.* This ruling addresses an issue that has arisen repeatedly in this book: the right to exploit a particular natural resource is often part of the bundle of rights that a person gains by acquiring ownership of land. Can an owner, however, sever that right from the land and sell it as a discrete asset? Rights in hardrock minerals can be severed, as we saw in chapter 5. Riparian water rights, however, typically cannot be severed as such, although a riparian landowner can allow outsiders to come on to the riparian tract and use the water (including transporting the water away after capture) (*Thompson v. Enz*, page 166 above; but compare *Pyle v. Gilbert*, page 450 above, allowing conveyance when reasonable). What position should the law take on this issue with respect to windpower rights? As noted below, several states have moved to ban severance. To get at the issue, we first need to think clearly about the elements of windpower rights and the inevitable need, at some point, to define them. That issue was immediately pertinent in this litigation, because the government needed to put a value on the rights. That cannot be done without first being clear on the bundle of legal entitlements that the holder of the rights would obtain.

At this point, we should have little trouble identifying many of the key issues to resolve in defining wind rights. In some way the definition needs to consider where turbines, roads, and other equipment might be installed, how many can be installed, and what surface use rights would be involved. As we have seen, conflicts will arise between the windpower owner and other holders of rights in the same land (the surface landowner and perhaps owners of other resource rights in the same land (e.g., mineral rights)). To what extent will the windpower rights be dominant? Will the holder of such rights be obligated to take steps to accommodate other users of the land? Will the windpower rights holder be obligated to pay for surface damages, and ultimately to clean up any messes? All of these need to be known—even if the answer is simply that the rights owner has full dominance and broad discretion.

2.   *Duration of the rights.* With the elements mentioned in the first note put in place, we still face a key issue about the duration of these windpower rights. How long will they last? This issue is wrapped up with the larger question of the nature of the property interest being conveyed (or in this instance reserved by the land seller). It also depends on whether the landowner is said to own the windpower in some sense—as a landowner owns hardrock minerals—or whether the landowner instead has an exclusive right to harvest or exploit a resource. Oil and gas rights in many states take this latter form (and do even in states that claim to embrace ownership in place).

In all states water rights also take this form; the water-rights holder enjoys a right to make use of a water source that, before the water is extracted, is owned by the people collectively and managed by the state. Wildlife law, as we saw in chapter 4, is the same: the landowner controls the land surface and can typically keep other hunters away but does not own the wildlife on her land.

Given that wind has no tangible form, and is even faster than migrating oil and moving animals in crossing over private land, it makes little sense to say that a landowner owns the windpower. It is more sensible to say that the owner has the exclusive right to harvest it. This articulation conveys the sense, rightly, that windpower rights involve the legal power to enter a tract of land and capture the wind energy on it; it is the right to make use of the landowner's exclusive right to harvest. That is, the landowner has no asset to sell; she instead has the power to let others come on the land and engage in a resource-related activity, much as a landowner gives a hunter the right to enter and hunt.

So what might this mean in terms of duration of the right? What kind of property interest is involved? The facts of this dispute suggest that the parties had in mind a type of perpetual affirmative easement: the owner of the windpower rights (Vaquero) would retain a permanent easement to enter the land, install wind turbines and other equipment, and export the energy developed. An easement, as we have seen, can be perpetual in nature but is subject to abandonment by the owner. It can also have an implicit duration limit based on the purpose of the easement; the easement could end when the purpose can no longer be fulfilled. On the issue of abandonment and purpose, we might compare such an easement with a railroad right-of-way; courts often conclude (too often, perhaps) that a railroad has abandoned its easement when it ceases rail service and removes its tracks. By similar reasoning, a windpower easement might end when turbines are removed, even though the easement itself might retain value. In contrast, hardrock mineral rights that are viewed as parts of the fee interest in the mineral estate are not lost through nonuse and are not subject to abandonment.

If we put the facts of this case to the side, we quickly realize that windpower rights can be crafted to have different durational limits. They could include a use-it-or-lose-it feature of the type often used in other resources settings (although usually when the landowner receives a royalty based on exploitation of the resource). They could be set up in the form of term permits, like grazing rights on federal lands, perhaps with conditional renewal rights. If this option were chosen, the arrangement would begin to look more like a lease than an easement. That terminology, though, is imprecise. A lease technically involves the transfer of a possessory interest to the lessee; the lease, that is, gives exclusive or near-exclusive rights to use some particularly defined place.

In the case of windpower rights, their duration could be viewed as leases of the specific spots where equipment is located, with ancillary rights of access. But the term lease is often used more generally, as in the oil and gas setting, to refer to a transaction that is not a true lease in this sense because it does not give any exclusive possessory rights to the lessee. An oil and gas lease, although structured as a lease, could just as readily be termed a bilateral easement agreement. In general, fee-type interests are presumed perpetual; easements are also presumed perpetual, although subject to abandonment and loss through fulfillment of purpose; and leases are presumed to have set time limits to them. But the categories are not clear, and ultimately private parties can structure a deal with whatever terms they like.

3. *Worries about severance.* Lawmakers in many states have expressed concerns about the severance of windpower rights, and some have moved to ban it. Wyoming prohibited severance of the wind and surface estates in the 2011 Wind Energy Rights Act. Wyo. Stat. Ann. § 34–27–103(a), (b). What worries underlie such legislation? A generic worry, it seems, is that owners of the severed rights will be able at any time to come on the land and use it as they like to promote wind power, with no concern for the consequences of their actions, particularly the effects on surface land uses. States that ban severance, however, do not bar landowners from entering into windpower leases.

What is the difference between the two approaches? The answer may be: perhaps not much, maybe even nothing. In both transactions, the parties need to define the surface-use rights of the windpower owner, and they could be more or less specific and may or may not require either accommodation or payment for surface damages. The problem of possible conflict arises in both settings. Leases, to be sure, tend to be shorter in duration, but the duration of a right is also subject to agreement by the parties and could be long or short under any legal arrangement. (A severance could last for 10 years, akin to a common law freehold term of years.) The underlying issue, then, is not well-highlighted by distinguishing severance from a lease. The issue is better addressed by focusing on the specific surface use rights of the windpower owner vis-à-vis the surface landowner and the duration of the arrangement, including powers of the surface landowner to terminate the arrangement for material breach. For more on the severance of wind rights from the surface estate, see Troy Rule, *Property Rights and Modern Energy*, 20 Geo. Mason L. Rev. 803, 811–12 (2013).

4. *The mitigation lands.* Note in the *Vaquero Farms* case that some of the wind turbines were going to be put on land being set aside as wildlife habitat to help address other concerns raised by the project. As we have seen, though, wind farms are by no means friendly for all wildlife. They are most visibly dangerous for flying animals. But their environmental consequences might well be harmful for many other species, in ways that we do not yet know. They could disrupt animal communications; they could disrupt a variety of necessary animal feeding and reproduction practices. The mere fact that animals such as foxes do not fly hardly means there is no possible conflict.

3. WIND AND MINERALS

OSAGE NATION V. WIND CAPITAL GROUP, LLC

U.S. District Court, Northern District of Oklahoma
2011 WL 6371384 (2011)

FRIZZELL, J.

* * *

Findings of Fact

Plaintiff, The Osage Nation, is a federally recognized Indian tribe (referred to herein as "Plaintiff" or "the Tribe"). In this case the Tribe is acting through its Minerals Council, an independent agency within the Osage Nation established by Article XV of the Osage Nation Constitution. The Osage Minerals Council manages the Osage Mineral Estate. In 1906, the U.S. Government severed the mineral estate from the surface of Osage County, retaining the Osage Mineral Estate in tribal trust ownership. . . . Defendants Wind Capital Group, L.L.C. and Osage Wind, L.L.C. (collectively "Defendants" or "Osage Wind") are the developers of a wind energy project in Osage County ("Wind Farm"). Construction of the Wind Farm had been planned to begin in November, 2011.

* * *

The Wind Farm has leased approximately 8,500 acres northeast of the town of Burbank, Oklahoma from a total of seven surface owners for the purpose of constructing a wind energy facility. The Wind Farm facilities will consist of 94 turbines, underground collection lines running between turbines and to a substation, one overhead transmission line, two permanent meteorological towers, and a network of access roads. After construction, the estimated surface footprint of the Wind Farm facilities, including the surface of the ground above where the collection lines will be installed, is less than 1.5% of the 8,500 or so acres the Wind Farm has under lease. . . .

Each turbine will be mounted on a tower at a height of 265 feet above the surface and will have three attached blades, with the tip of each blade extending approximately 165 feet from the center of the turbine. The turbine will rotate 360 degrees around the tower. The lowest clearance of the tip of the blade from the surface will be 100 feet and will occur when the blade is parallel with the supporting tower. The turbine foundations will be made from reinforced concrete, with each foundation initially being 16 feet in diameter down to four feet below the surface, then expanding in a conical shape with a maximum diameter of 50 feet, to a depth of 10 feet.

The turbines will be arranged by circuits, with an underground collection line buried four feet below ground running from turbine to turbine and then to a substation within the project boundary. From the substation, the electricity will then be transported to an interconnection facility via a 138kV overhead transmission line approximately 1.8 miles long. KAMO Electric Cooperative will construct and own the interconnection facility, which will connect to KAMO's already existing overhead transmission line. This line currently crosses the Wind Farm area and will continue to exist regardless of whether the Wind Farm is built.

The estimated time of construction for the Wind Farm is 9 to 12 months. The land in the Wind Farm area is largely unoccupied, [and] is currently used for grazing livestock, with some existing oil and gas production facilities. Two highways (U.S. Highway 60 and State Highway 18) and two existing overhead electric transmission lines run through parts of the planned Wind Farm.

The Tribe has leased its mineral interests within the Wind Farm area to Spyglass Energy Group, L.L.C., LINN Energy, L.L.C., Chaparral Energy, L.L.C., and Orion Exploration, L.L.C. The area lies just east of the town of Burbank, Oklahoma. The area was once the site of significant oil and gas activity following discovery of oil in 1920 from the Burbank sand. The area has recently seen increased drilling activity targeting the Mississippian formation. The Mississippian has recently become economical to explore because of relatively high oil prices combined with improvements in horizontal drilling technology and hydraulic fracturing ("fracking").

The Tribe's claims are generally predicated on the allegation the Wind Farm will unlawfully interfere with its rights to develop the Osage Mineral Estate. As more specifically set forth below, the Court finds that Plaintiff's evidence fails to establish either of the following propositions: first, under federal law, that the Wind Farm will interfere with the Tribe's right to use so much of the surface of the land within the Osage Mineral Estate as may be reasonable for oil and gas development; or second, under state law, that the Wind Farm will unlawfully interfere with the Tribe's right to make reasonable use of the surface estate, including the right of ingress and egress therefor, for the purpose of exploring, severing, capturing and producing the oil and gas.

* * *

Plaintiff's expert Michael Root did not establish that Wind Farm construction or operation would interfere with oil and gas mineral development. His opinion—that the Wind Farm will be detrimental to oil and gas exploration and development and will leave the oil and gas operator without reasonable use of the surface—is not supported by the evidence. The primary conflict predicted by the Tribe, through Mr. Root, is the potential for conflicts during Wind Farm construction. According to Mr. Root, a conflict would arise if a lessee attempts to drill a well at the same time and in the same area as turbine construction. Mr. Root's testimony with respect to alleged interference was speculative as to whether the lessee and the Defendants will be in the same place at the same time during construction. He admitted that, even then, they might be able to stagger and co-ordinate their work. He stated that, following construction and during operation and maintenance of the Wind Farm, there "would be an impact," but "it would not be as great as during construction." When asked whether maintenance and operation of the Wind Farm would unreasonably interfere with the development of the Mineral Estate, he stated "it might, possibly." The court finds Mr. Root's testimony speculative and insufficient to establish that the Wind Farm will interfere with development of the Osage Mineral Estate. This court is not persuaded that, following construction of the Wind Farm, continuing operations and maintenance will unreasonably interfere with the proposed oil and gas drilling program and/or oil and gas operations by Plaintiff's lessees.

* * *

The [C]ourt finds no evidence that the Wind Farm's surface use would prevent reasonable access to, and use of, the surface estate by oil and gas lessees. However, in the event an actual conflict occurs, the court finds that it can and should be resolved by the parties in accordance with their respective obligations under federal and state law. In the event a situation arises in which the defendants cannot accommodate an oil and gas lessee's request, the oil and gas industry has the ability, as defendant's expert John Campbell McBeath testified, to work around conflicts by modest adjustments in the form of directional drilling or moving the oil and gas wells slightly. Orion's Operations Manager, Mr. Brown, testified that he still doesn't know there's going to be a problem, and that he finds he "can usually work around most things." If a modest adjustment proves to be impossible, the lessee may seek redress of the specific dispute in a court of appropriate jurisdiction.

Each permanent turbine site will be 70 feet by 70 feet. During construction, there will also be a 40 foot by 80 foot temporary pad from which the turbine will be erected. Access to the turbine construction site can be staged from any direction—including the direction opposite the well site. A drilling rig would need roughly 100 feet from the edge of a drilling site to the wellhead, and from there drilling activities can typically be staged from any direction. In the event the location of a particular drill site is closer than these distances allow, a modest adjustment to the drilling schedule or location may solve the conflict.

The Court also finds that if a well location is selected within close proximity to a turbine center, or directly on a Wind Farm road or transmission line, Orion or other mineral lessees will likely be able to make modest adjustments to the well location. . . .

The Court further finds that the economics of the planned drilling program indicate that Orion will likely make necessary adjustments rather than forego development. Using information from Orion, the testimony of both expert witnesses support a finding that the wells are sufficiently promising that the additional expense associated with adjusting the location will not be prohibitive.

As to the oil and gas infrastructure such as flow lines, water lines, and tank batteries, the Court finds that any impact from the Wind Farm will be minimal. To the extent such infrastructure is buried, it will be at different depths than the underground collection lines. Orion can readily bore under Wind Farm roads if needed. And if a desired flow line or water line happens to intersect a turbine location, only a minor adjustment is necessary to circumnavigate the 16 foot diameter of the foundation at the four foot subsurface level. . . .

* * *

Facts Relevant to the Balance of Harms

The evidence at trial was insufficient to prove that the Tribe will be harmed by construction and/or operation of the Wind Farm. At this time, the alleged conflict between the Wind Farm and plaintiff's rights to develop the Osage Mineral Estate is speculative. An injunction prohibiting the construction of the Wind Farm will cause the following harms to Osage Wind: (a) it will lose approximately $40 million in expenses paid to date, including deposits for turbines and other equipment; (b) it will remain contractually obligated for more than $150 million of equipment purchases and construction contract penalties; and (c) it will lose the opportunity to make more than $30 million in estimated future profits.

Facts Relevant to the Public Interest

The Wind Farm project is expected to employ approximately 250 construction employees and 10–12 permanent employees. The State of Oklahoma would lose the economic benefit of those jobs if the Wind Farm is enjoined. The Wind Farm is projected to generate $20 million dollars in local tax revenues over 20 years, including $1.5 million for Shidler schools during the first few years of the project. Those benefits would be lost if the Wind Farm is enjoined. An injunction would harm the surface owners who have leased their property to Osage Wind. Under those leases, the surface owners would be entitled to receive lease payments over the 20-year life of the Wind Farm. The Wind Farm is projected to generate enough electricity to power 50,000 homes. This renewable, relatively stable energy source would be lost if the Wind Farm is enjoined.

[The court concluded by refusing to grant plaintiffs a permanent injunction. The court also found that the wind farm would not violate regulations promulgated under the federal Osage Allotment Act nor does it violate basic principles of Oklahoma state law related to servient surface estates and dominant subsurface mineral interests, as discussed earlier in chapter 5.]

NOTES

1. *Renewable energy and culture.* Not only does renewable energy development conflict at times with the management of other natural resources, such as biodiversity, water, and mineral resources, but also with cultural resources. In the tandem cases *Quechan Tribe v. U.S. Department of Interior I* and *II*, 755 F.Supp.2d 1104 (S.D. Cal. 2010); 927 F.Supp.2d 921 (S.D. Cal. 2013), the federal government sought to develop a solar array on federal lands. Importantly,

> The area where the project would be located has a history of extensive use by Native American groups. The parties agree 459 cultural resources have been identified within the project area. These include over 300 locations of prehistoric use or settlement, and ancient trails that traverse the site. The tribes in this area cremated their dead and buried the remains, so the area also appears to contain archaeological sites and human remains. The draft environmental impact statement ("EIS") prepared by the BLM indicated the project "may wholly or partially destroy all archaeological sites on the surface of the project area." The Tribe believes the project would destroy hundreds of their ancient cultural sites including burial sites, religious sites, ancient trails, and probably buried artifacts.

Quechan Tribe I, 755 F.Supp.2d at 1107. The tribe argued that the project threatened the habitat of the flat-tailed horned lizard, which was both under consideration for listing under the Endangered Species Act and also culturally important to the tribe. The tribe also claimed that the federal government failed to comply with the National Environmental Policy Act , the National Historical Preservation Act, and the Federal Land Policy and Management Act. In granting the tribe's motion for a preliminary injunction, the court did not bind the agency to any particular course of action, but did say that the Bureau of Land Management must consult with the tribe to comply with the requirements of the statutes in question before proceeding.

2. *Halting uncertain dangers.* The *Osage Nation* court stated that "testimony with respect to alleged interference was speculative as to whether the lessee and the Defendants will be in the same place at the same time during construction." How likely is it that such interference will occur? How

should those disputes be resolved? Is the mere specter of interference enough to give one form of resource development priority over the other? Will surface owners who wish to lease wind rights or otherwise engage in wind energy development be able to obtain investors if there is a chance that mineral estate owner activity might interfere with development? What about mineral estate owners who wish to develop the mineral estate? Will uncertainty over impacts at the surface chill investment in the mineral estate? Should this issue be resolved preemptively through contract? How would such agreements be structured? Contracting around such conflicts is one obvious approach, as described by DuVivier and Wetsel:

> Wind developers, particularly those from Europe, have been surprised to learn that under U.S. law their wind interest might be servient to dominant mineral estates. They have been rightfully concerned about investing hundreds of millions of dollars in a wind project that could be subject to interference by the owners of the mineral estate. Before providing financing, some investors require a title search and a mineral endorsement. These are available, however, only if the title company finds that there is little or no likelihood of mineral development.

> When mineral leases currently exist on the property, or if there is any future potential for mineral development, most wind investors require a more proactive approach. Instead of relying on a judge's resolution of potential conflicts, they seek instead to alter the common law regimes through express agreements.

* * *

[1] *If Wind Rights Are First In Time*

If the wind rights grantor owns the surface and mineral estates, and has not previously sold or leased any part of the estate, then wind developers have been able to negotiate clauses in their leases that greatly restrict oil, gas, and mining activities on the surface. Some clauses in early wind leases even attempted to reverse the dominant estate doctrine and make the mineral estate servient to the wind estate.

Additionally, wind companies have mandated that all future oil and gas leases entered into by the surface owner contain provisions referencing the wind lease and requiring the oil and gas lessee to enter into a surface use or accommodation agreement with the wind lessee. A surface accommodation agreement makes provision for any concurrent surface operations (including required distances from facilities), notice prior to the commencement of drilling or construction, use and maintenance of roads, indemnity for surface damages and personal injuries, and insurance. An accommodation agreement is now customary for an oil company which desires to drill on a wind farm.

As a further impediment, wind companies in their leases have sought to impose restrictions on surface use for oil and gas development. These clauses are very broadly written so as to prohibit the location of drilling rigs or other oil and gas facilities within a specified number of feet of any existing wind turbine, substation, or transmission line. Such clauses also provide that in any future oil and gas or mining lease, the surface owner must provide that the mineral company will not conduct any activities within the areas specified and will not otherwise unreasonably interfere with the wind company's rights under its lease. The term "minerals" is defined to include not only oil and gas but also other minerals such as coal, uranium, sand, gravel, and caliche.

Many wind leases also contain a broad "no-interference clause," which provides that the surface owner and its lessees shall not currently or prospectively disturb or interfere with the construction, installation, maintenance, or operation of the wind power facilities or the undertaking of any other activities permitted under the lease. As shown above, some wind companies have even gone so far as to provide in their leases that the surface estate of the property shall be dominant to the mineral estate. In this regard, there may be a serious issue as to whether the surface owner (who may or may not also own mineral rights) can affect the rights of non-executive mineral owners under the land with these provisions. If the surface owner also owns all of the mineral estate, it seems clear that he or she can reverse the doctrine. On the other hand, if there are non-executive mineral owners or non-participating royalty owners, it is unlikely that such a provision will be binding on those owners.

[2] *If Mineral Rights Are First In Time*

In conflict areas, it is more likely that the mineral estate has been severed and perhaps leased before a wind developer enters the scene. In these situations, wind developers first provide the mineral interest owner with notification.

Next, as a first line of defense when the mineral estate beneath a wind lease is severed from the surface, wind companies have sought to obtain a surface waiver or non-interference agreement from the mineral interest owners who did not also own the surface estate. Such non-disturbance agreements may be part of the county permitting requirements.

These efforts have often proved futile. With the assumption that they have the common law advantage of dominant estate ownership and have no obligation to accommodate the servient surface use of the wind lessee, some mineral owners have hindered development of wind projects by refusing to negotiate reasonable non-disturbance agreements or have requested exorbitant sums as compensation for them.

[3] *The Role of the Grantor*

Concurrent wind and mineral development is more likely when the grantor can act as referee between these separate interests. The grantor can try to negotiate clauses in the lease agreements that put pressure on lessees to work together. Also, even without express clauses, the intervention of the grantor may be enough to encourage open lines of communication.

However, the grantor can also be caught in the middle of battles between wind and mineral developers. For example, oil companies have fought back against wind development leases by requesting promises of their own from the grantors. Oil leases now frequently require that payment of the bonus consideration is contingent upon and subject to execution of an accommodation agreement by any wind lessee on the property. If the wind lessee does not agree to the accommodation agreement, the oil company may cancel the oil lease and has no obligation to pay the bonus consideration. Demands from wind lessees or mineral lessees that the grantor make their rights dominant can put the grantor in an untenable position, inviting litigation.

Furthermore, tensions between wind and mineral developers can be heightened if the grantor is not positioned to intervene. This occurs in at least two situations. First, the federal government's standard form lease reserves the right to lease different resources to different parties because the government believes that wind and mineral development are compatible. This leaves resolution of conflicts up to the various lessees.

Second, if a private grantor severed the mineral estate before executing the wind lease, a wind developer might be required to work with a mineral lessee who has interests that do not align with the wind grantor. The potential conflicts increase significantly with severance of the wind from the surface estate. When the wind rights are owned by one party and the mineral rights by another, there is little incentive for any of the parties to work together. The situation is further exacerbated if the surface owner, who is most impacted by both wind and mineral surface operations, receives no royalty or other benefit from the development of either resource.

K.K. DuVivier & Roderick E. Wetsel, *Jousting at Wind Mills: When Wind Power Development Collides with Oil, Gas, and Mineral Development*, 55 Rocky Mtn. Min. L. Inst. 9–1, 9–21 to 9–25 (2009). Should conflicts between a wind and mineral estate instead be resolved through legislative action clearly defining the rights and rules associated with overlapping wind and mineral development on the same surface estate?

D. SOLAR

Wind and solar, in their capacity as sources of renewable power, are inextricably linked—roughly 2 percent of solar energy entering the earth's atmosphere ends up being converted to kinetic energy in the form of wind. Joseph M. Moran et al., *Meteorology: The Atmosphere and the Science of Weather* 204 (5th ed. 1997). Solar capacity in the U.S. increased by 418 percent between 2010 and 2014 and continues to grow. Silvio Marcacci, *US Solar Energy Capacity Grew an Astounding 418% From 2010–2014*, Clean Technica (Apr. 24, 2014), http://cleantechnica.com/2014/04/24/us-solar-energy-capacity-grew-an-astounding–418–from–2010–2014/. Not surprisingly, private rights conflicts arise with solar similar to what we saw with wind. For example, structures may be built that restrict the flow of wind or block sunlight from one property to another. The siting of large solar arrays and wind farms may conflict with the management of other resources, like biodiversity, water, or minerals.

There are some important distinctions between wind and solar conflicts among private landowners, however. With distributed wind generation (installed on individual rooftops), the complaint is typically that a neighbor does not like the aesthetics of the device or is otherwise directly affected in some manner by the use of the device. Although the aesthetic concerns of neighbors may also be an issue with solar panels, typically the party claiming a grievance is the owner of the solar panel, claiming that a neighbor is interfering with light that would otherwise power the device. The following case was one of the first to address rights to light access, and lays a foundation for evolving law on the subject in the present day.

FONTAINEBLEAU HOTEL CORP. V.
FORTY-FIVE TWENTY-FIVE, INC.

District Court of Appeal of Florida
114 So.2d 357 (1959)

PER CURIAM.

This is an interlocutory appeal from an order temporarily enjoining the appellants from continuing with the construction of a fourteen-story addition to the Fontainebleau Hotel, owned and operated by the appellants. Appellee, plaintiff below, owns the Eden Roc Hotel, which was constructed in 1955, about a year after the Fontainebleau, and adjoins the Fontainebleau on the north. Both are luxury hotels, facing the Atlantic Ocean. The proposed addition to Fontainebleau is being constructed twenty feet from its north property line, 130 feet from the mean high water mark of the Atlantic Ocean, and 76 feet 8 inches from the ocean bulkhead line. The 14-story tower will extend 160 feet above grade in height and is 416 feet long from east to west. During the winter months, from around two o'clock in the afternoon for the remainder of the day, the shadow of the addition will extend over the cabana, swimming pool, and sunbathing areas of the Eden Roc, which are located in the southern portion of its property.

In this action, plaintiff-appellee sought to enjoin the defendants-appellants from proceeding with the construction of the addition to the Fontainebleau (it appears to have been roughly eight stories high at the time suit was filed), alleging that the construction would interfere with the light and air on the beach in front of the Eden Roc and cast a shadow of such size as to render the beach wholly unfitted for the use and enjoyment of its guests, to the irreparable injury of the plaintiff; further, that the construction of such addition on the north side of defendants' property, rather than the south side, was actuated by malice and ill will on the part of the defendants' president toward the plaintiff's president; and that the construction was in violation of a building ordinance requiring a 100-foot setback from the ocean. It was also alleged that the construction would interfere with the easements of light and air enjoyed by plaintiff and its predecessors in title for more than twenty years and "impliedly granted by virtue of the acts of the plaintiff's predecessors in title, as well as under the common law and the express recognition of such rights by virtue of Chapter 9837, Laws of Florida 1923 * * *." Some attempt was also made to allege an easement by implication in favor of the plaintiff's property, as the dominant, and against the defendants' property, as the servient, tenement.

The defendants' answer denied the material allegations of the complaint, pleaded laches and estoppel by judgment.

The chancellor heard considerable testimony on the issues made by the complaint and the answer and, as noted, entered a temporary injunction restraining the defendants from continuing with the construction of the addition. His reason for so doing was stated by him, in a memorandum opinion, as follows:

"In granting the temporary injunction in this case the Court wishes to make several things very clear. The ruling is not based on any alleged presumptive title nor prescriptive right of the plaintiff to light and air nor is it based on any deed restrictions nor recorded plats in the title of the plaintiff nor of the defendant nor of any plat of record. It is not based on any zoning ordinance nor on any provision of the building code of the City of Miami Beach nor on the decision of any court, nisi prius or appellate. It is based solely on the proposition that no one has a right to use his property to the injury of another. In this case it is clear from the evidence that the proposed use by the Fontainebleau will materially damage the Eden Roc. There is evidence indicating that the construction of the proposed annex by the Fontainebleau is malicious or deliberate for the purpose of injuring the Eden Roc, but it is scarcely sufficient, standing alone, to afford a basis for equitable relief."

This is indeed a novel application of the maxim *sic utere tuo ut alienum non laedas*. This maxim does not mean that one must never use his own property in such a way as to do any injury to his neighbor. It means only that one must use his property so as not to injure the lawful *rights* of another. In *Reaver v. Martin Theatres*, 52 So.2d 682, 683 (Fla. 1951), under this maxim, it was stated that "it is well settled that a property owner may put his own property to any reasonable and lawful use, so long as he does not thereby deprive the adjoining landowner of any right of enjoyment of his property *which is recognized and protected by law, and so long as his use is not such a one as the law will pronounce a nuisance*." [Emphasis supplied.]

No American decision has been cited, and independent research has revealed none, in which it has been held that—in the absence of some contractual or statutory obligation—a landowner has a legal right to the free flow of light and air across the adjoining land of his neighbor. Even at common law, the landowner had no legal right, in the absence of an easement or uninterrupted use and enjoyment for a period of 20 years, to unobstructed light and air from the adjoining land. . . .

There being, then, no legal right to the free flow of light and air from the adjoining land, it is universally held that where a structure serves a useful and beneficial purpose, it does not give rise to a cause of action, either for damages or for an injunction under the maxim *sic utere tuo ut alienum non laedas*, even though it causes injury to another by cutting off the light and air and interfering with the view that would otherwise be available over adjoining land in its natural state, regardless of the fact that the structure may have been erected partly for spite.

We see no reason for departing from this universal rule. If, as contended on behalf of plaintiff, public policy demands that a landowner in the Miami Beach area refrain from constructing buildings on his premises that will cast a shadow on the adjoining premises, an amendment of its comprehensive planning and zoning ordinance, applicable to the public as a whole, is the means by which such purpose should be achieved. (No opinion is expressed here as to the validity of such an ordinance, if one should be enacted pursuant to the requirements of law. Cf. *City of Miami Beach v. State ex rel. Fontainebleau Hotel Corp.*, 108 So.2d 614, 619 (Fla. Dist. Ct. App. 1959), *cert. denied*, 111 So.2d 437 (Fla. 1959).) But to change the universal rule—and the custom followed in this state since its inception—that adjoining landowners have an equal right under the law to build to the line of their respective tracts and to such a height as is desired by them (in the absence, of course, of building restrictions or regulations) amounts, in our opinion, to judicial legislation. As stated in *Musumeci v. Leonardo*, [75 A.2d 175, 177 (R.I. 1950)], "So use your own as not to injure another's property is, indeed, a sound and salutary principle for the promotion of justice, but it may not and should not be applied so as gratuitously to confer upon an adjacent property owner incorporeal rights incidental to his ownership of land which the law does not sanction."

* * *

The record affirmatively shows that no statutory basis for the right sought to be enforced by plaintiff exists. The so-called Shadow Ordinance enacted by the City of Miami Beach at plaintiff's behest was held invalid in *City of Miami Beach v. State ex rel. Fontainebleau Hotel Corp., supra.* It also affirmatively appears that there is no possible basis for holding that plaintiff has an easement for light and air, either express or implied, across defendants' property, nor any prescriptive right thereto—even if it be assumed, arguendo, that the common-law right of prescription as to "ancient lights" is in effect in this state. And from what we have said heretofore in this opinion, it is perhaps superfluous to add that we have no desire to dissent from the unanimous holding in this country repudiating the English doctrine of ancient lights.

[The court also considered and rejected the claim that the building should be halted because it violated the lot setback requirement that it be at least 100 feet from an established ocean bulkhead line; as approved, the project was set back only 76 feet 8 inches from the ocean bulkhead line, although it was 130 feet from the ocean measured from the mean high water mark. The court noted that the issue was raised late—when the structure was already eight stories high—and in any event the setback difference had no material effect on the solar blockage.]

Since it affirmatively appears that the plaintiff has not established a cause of action against the defendants by reason of the structure here in question, the order granting a temporary injunction should be and it is hereby reversed with directions to dismiss the complaint.

Reversed with directions.

NOTES

1. *Who decides?* Who is in the best position to adjudicate rights between property owners under the circumstances of *Fontainebleau*? Local zoning boards through regulations aimed at allocating these rights, or the courts through litigation? Do you agree with the court that ruling in favor of plaintiffs in *Fontainebleau* would amount to "judicial legislation"? Could it be argued that blocking access to light harms the plaintiffs in an appreciable way, either through their economic or environmental interests in renewable

energy growth? If so, do courts not regularly stop neighbors from harming each other through nuisance law? See *McCarty v. Natural Carbonic Gas Co.*, 81 N.E. 549 (N.Y. 1907) (finding that smoke from a neighboring carbonic acid plant constituted a nuisance).

2. *Keeping the common law up to date.* How do you think increased interest in solar and wind power should affect the outcome of cases like *Fontainebleau*, or should it? Common law property evolved over time to take into account changing circumstances and advances in scientific understanding. In other words, what once was a nuisance may be no longer so. In fact, governments are actively seeking through a number of initiatives to expand solar energy. Consider California's Million Solar Roofs campaign, which aims to get 1 million solar roofs in California by 2020. See http://www. environmentcalifornia.org/programs/million-solar-roofs. A recent report by Environment California details the key attributes of the solar policy in the ten U.S. states that lead in expansion of solar energy:

- Nine have strong *net metering policies*. In nearly all of the leading states, consumers are compensated at the full retail rate for the excess electricity they supply to the grid.

- Nine have strong statewide *interconnection policies*. Good interconnection policies reduce the time and hassle required for individuals and companies to connect solar energy systems to the grid.

- All have *renewable electricity standards* that set minimum requirements for the share of a utility's electricity that must come from renewable sources, and eight of them have *solar carve-outs* that set specific targets for solar or other forms of clean, distributed electricity.

- Nine allow for *creative financing options* such as third-party power purchase agreements, and eight allow Property Assessed Clean Energy (PACE) financing.

Jordan Schneider & Rob Sargent, *Lighting the Way: The Top Ten States that Helped Drive America's Solar Energy Boom in 2013*, Environment America (Aug. 2014), *available at* http://environmentamericacenter.org/sites/ environment/files/reports/EA_Lightingtheway_scrn.pdf. As states continue to promote solar installations, how should state common law adjust? Have states historically actively promoted nuisances? Can state nuisance law and zoning that is adverse to solar expansion be reconciled with state efforts to promote its use?

3. *A different take.* Another court, contrary to *Fontainebleau*, ruled that property owners have an interest in light and air access that can be protected through nuisance claims (although concluding that the parties did not meet their burden in that particular case). See *Tenn v. 889 Associates,*

Ltd., 500 A.2d 366 (N.H. 1985). Consider this perspective also in the following case:

PRAH V. MARETTI
Supreme Court of Wisconsin
321 N.W.2d 182 (1982)

ABRAHAMSON, J.

This appeal from a judgment of the circuit court for Waukesha [C]ounty . . . was certified to this court by the court of appeals as presenting an issue of first impression, namely, whether an owner of a solar-heated residence states a claim upon which relief can be granted when he asserts that his neighbor's proposed construction of a residence (which conforms to existing deed restrictions and local ordinances) interferes with his access to an unobstructed path for sunlight across the neighbor's property. This case thus involves a conflict between one landowner (Glenn Prah, the plaintiff) interested in unobstructed access to sunlight across adjoining property as a natural source of energy and an adjoining landowner (Richard D. Maretti, the defendant) interested in the development of his land.

The circuit court concluded that the plaintiff presented no claim upon which relief could be granted and granted summary judgment for the defendant. . . .

I.

According to the complaint, the plaintiff is the owner of a residence which was constructed during the years 1978–1979. The complaint alleges that the residence has a solar system which includes collectors on the roof to supply energy for heat and hot water and that after the plaintiff built his solar-heated house, the defendant purchased the lot adjacent to and immediately to the south of the plaintiff's lot and commenced planning construction of a home. The complaint further states that when the plaintiff learned of defendant's plans to build the house he advised the defendant that if the house were built at the proposed location, defendant's house would substantially and adversely affect the integrity of plaintiff's solar system and could cause plaintiff other damage. Nevertheless, the defendant began construction. The complaint further alleges that the plaintiff is entitled to "unrestricted use of the sun and its solar power" and demands judgment for injunctive relief and damages.

* * *

Plaintiff's home was the first residence built in the subdivision, and although plaintiff did not build his house in the center of the lot it was built in accordance with applicable restrictions. Plaintiff advised defendant that if the defendant's home were built at the proposed site it would cause a shadowing effect on the solar collectors which would reduce the efficiency of the system and possibly damage the system. To avoid these adverse effects, plaintiff requested defendant to locate his home an additional several feet away from the plaintiff's lot line, the exact number being disputed. Plaintiff and defendant failed to reach an agreement on the location of defendant's home before defendant started construction. . . .

* * *

We consider first whether the complaint states a claim for relief based on common law private nuisance. This state has long recognized that an owner of land does not have an absolute or unlimited right to use the land in a way which injures the rights of others. The rights of neighboring landowners are relative; the uses by one must not unreasonably impair the uses or enjoyment of the other. When one landowner's use of his or her property unreasonably interferes with another's enjoyment of his or her property, that use is said to be a private nuisance.

The private nuisance doctrine has traditionally been employed in this state to balance the conflicting rights of landowners, and this court has recently adopted the analysis of private nuisance set forth in the Restatement (Second) of Torts. The Restatement defines private nuisance as "a nontrespassory invasion of another's interest in the private use and enjoyment of land." Restatement (Second) of Torts sec. 821D (1977). The phrase "interest in the private use and enjoyment of land" as used in sec. 821D is broadly defined to include any disturbance of the enjoyment of property. The comment in the Restatement describes the landowner's interest protected by private nuisance law as follows:

> "The phrase 'interest in the use and enjoyment of land' is used in this Restatement in a broad sense. It comprehends not only the interests that a person may have in the actual present use of land for residential, agricultural, commercial, industrial and other purposes, but also his interests in having the present use value of the land unimpaired by changes in its physical condition. Thus the destruction of trees on vacant land is as much an invasion of the owner's interest in its use and enjoyment as is the destruction of crops or flowers that he is growing on the land for his present use. 'Interest in use and enjoyment' also comprehends the pleasure, comfort and enjoyment that a person normally derives from the occupancy of land. Freedom from discomfort and annoyance while using land is often as important to a person as freedom from physical

interruption with his use or freedom from detrimental change in the physical condition of the land itself."

Restatement (Second) of Torts, Sec. 821D, Comment *b*, p. 101 (1977).

Although the defendant's obstruction of the plaintiff's access to sunlight appears to fall within the Restatement's broad concept of a private nuisance as a nontrespassory invasion of another's interest in the private use and enjoyment of land, the defendant asserts that he has a right to develop his property in compliance with statutes, ordinances and private covenants without regard to the effect of such development upon the plaintiff's access to sunlight. In essence, the defendant is asking this court to hold that the private nuisance doctrine is not applicable in the instant case and that his right to develop his land is a right which is *per se* superior to his neighbor's interest in access to sunlight. This position is expressed in the maxim *"cujus est solum, ejus est usque ad coelum et ad infernos,"* that is, the owner of land owns up to the sky and down to the center of the earth. The rights of the surface owner are, however, not unlimited.

The defendant is not completely correct in asserting that the common law did not protect a landowner's access to sunlight across adjoining property. At English common law a landowner could acquire a right to receive sunlight across adjoining land by both express agreement and under the judge-made doctrine of "ancient lights." Under the doctrine of ancient lights if the landowner had received sunlight across adjoining property for a specified period of time, the landowner was entitled to continue to receive unobstructed access to sunlight across the adjoining property. Under the doctrine the landowner acquired a negative prescriptive easement and could prevent the adjoining landowner from obstructing access to light.

Although American courts have not been as receptive to protecting a landowner's access to sunlight as the English courts, American courts have afforded some protection to a landowner's interest in access to sunlight. American courts honor express easements to sunlight. American courts initially enforced the English common law doctrine of ancient lights, but later every state which considered the doctrine repudiated it as inconsistent with the needs of a developing country. Indeed, for just that reason this court concluded that an easement to light and air over adjacent property could not be created or acquired by prescription and has been unwilling to recognize such an easement by implication.

Many jurisdictions in this country have protected a landowner from malicious obstruction of access to light (the spite fence cases) under the common law private nuisance doctrine. If an activity is motivated by malice it lacks utility and the harm it causes others outweighs any social values. . . .

This court's reluctance in the nineteenth and early part of the twentieth century to provide broader protection for a landowner's access to sunlight was premised on three policy considerations. First, the right of landowners to use their property as they wished, as long as they did not cause physical damage to a neighbor, was jealously guarded.

Second, sunlight was valued only for aesthetic enjoyment or as illumination. Since artificial light could be used for illumination, loss of sunlight was at most a personal annoyance which was given little, if any, weight by society.

Third, society had a significant interest in not restricting or impeding land development. This court repeatedly emphasized that in the growth period of the nineteenth and early twentieth centuries change is to be expected and is essential to property and that recognition of a right to sunlight would hinder property development. The court expressed this concept as follows:

> "As the city grows, large grounds appurtenant to residences must be cut up to supply more residences. . . . The cistern, the outhouse, the cesspool, and the private drain must disappear in deference to the public waterworks and sewer; the terrace and the garden, to the need for more complete occupancy. . . . Strict limitation [on the recognition of easements of light and air over adjacent premises is] in accord with the popular conception upon which real estate has been and is daily being conveyed in Wisconsin and to be essential to easy and rapid development at least of our municipalities."

Miller v. Hoeschler, 105 N.W. 790 (Wis. 1905).

Considering these three policies, this court concluded that in the absence of an express agreement granting access to sunlight, a landowner's obstruction of another's access to sunlight was not actionable. These three policies are no longer fully accepted or applicable. They reflect factual circumstances and social priorities that are now obsolete.

First, society has increasingly regulated the use of land by the landowner for the general welfare. *Euclid v. Ambler Realty Co.*, 272 U.S. 365 (1926); *Just v. Marinette*, 201 N.W.2d 761 (Wis. 1972).

Second, access to sunlight has taken on a new significance in recent years. In this case the plaintiff seeks to protect access to sunlight, not for aesthetic reasons or as a source of illumination but as a source of energy. Access to sunlight as an energy source is of significance both to the landowner who invests in solar collectors and to a society which has an interest in developing alternative sources of energy.

Third, the policy of favoring unhindered private development in an expanding economy is no longer in harmony with the realities of our society. The need for easy and rapid development is not as great today as it once was, while our perception of the value of sunlight as a source of energy has increased significantly.

Courts should not implement obsolete policies that have lost their vigor over the course of the years. The law of private nuisance is better suited to resolve landowners' disputes about property development in the 1980's than is a rigid rule which does not recognize a landowner's interest in access to sunlight. As we said in *Ballstadt v. Pagel*, 232 N.W. 862 (Wis. 1930), "What is regarded in law as constituting a nuisance in modern times would no doubt have been tolerated without question in former times." We read *State v. Deetz*, 224 N.W.2d 407 (Wis. 1974), as an endorsement of the application of common law nuisance to situations involving the conflicting interests of landowners and as rejecting *per se* exclusions to the nuisance law reasonable use doctrine.

* * *

Yet the defendant would have us ignore the flexible private nuisance law as a means of resolving the dispute between the landowners in this case and would have us adopt an approach, already abandoned in *Deetz*, of favoring the unrestricted development of land and of applying a rigid and inflexible rule protecting his right to build on his land and disregarding any interest of the plaintiff in the use and enjoyment of his land. This we refuse to do.

Private nuisance law, the law traditionally used to adjudicate conflicts between private landowners, has the flexibility to protect both a landowner's right of access to sunlight and another landowner's right to develop land. Private nuisance law is better suited to regulate access to sunlight in modern society and is more in harmony with legislative policy and the prior decisions of this court than is an inflexible doctrine of non-recognition of any interest in access to sunlight across adjoining land.

We therefore hold that private nuisance law, that is, the reasonable use doctrine as set forth in the Restatement, is applicable to the instant case. Recognition of a nuisance claim for unreasonable obstruction of access to sunlight will not prevent land development or unduly hinder the use of adjoining land. It will promote the reasonable use and enjoyment of land in a manner suitable to the 1980's. That obstruction of access to light might be found to constitute a nuisance in certain circumstances does not mean that it will be or must be found to constitute a nuisance under all circumstances. The result in each case depends on whether the conduct complained of is unreasonable.

Accordingly we hold that the plaintiff in this case has stated a claim under which relief can be granted. Nonetheless we do not determine whether the plaintiff in this case is entitled to relief. In order to be entitled to relief the plaintiff must prove the elements required to establish actionable nuisance, and the conduct of the defendant herein must be judged by the reasonable use doctrine.

* * *

CALLOW, J. (dissenting).

* * *

The majority . . . concludes that this court's past reluctance to extend protection to a landowner's access to sunlight beyond the spite fence cases is based on obsolete policies which have lost their vigor over the course of the years. The three obsolete policies cited by the majority are: (1) Right of landowners to use their property as they desire as long as no physical damage is done to a neighbor; (2) In the past, sunlight was valued only for aesthetic value, not a source of energy; and (3) Society has a significant interest in not impeding land development. The majority has failed to convince me that these policies are obsolete.

* * *

The right of a property owner to lawful enjoyment of his property should be vigorously protected, particularly in those cases where the adjacent property owner could have insulated himself from the alleged problem by acquiring the land as a defense to the potential problem or by provident use of his own property.

The majority concludes that sunlight has not heretofore been accorded the status of a source of energy, and consequently it has taken on a new significance in recent years. Solar energy for home heating is at this time sparingly used and of questionable economic value because solar collectors are not mass produced, and consequently, they are very costly. Their limited efficiency may explain the lack of production.

* * *

I would submit that any policy decisions in this area are best left for the legislature. "What is 'desirable' or 'advisable' or 'ought to be' is a question of policy, not a question of fact. What is 'necessary' or what is 'in the best interest' is not a fact and its determination by the judiciary is an exercise of legislative power when each involves political considerations." *In re City of Beloit*, 155 N.W.2d 633, 636 (Wis. 1968). . . .

* * *

I conclude that plaintiff's solar heating system is an unusually sensitive use. In other words, the defendant's proposed construction of his home, under ordinary circumstances, would not interfere with the use and enjoyment of the usual person's property. See W. Prosser, *Law of Torts*, sec. 87, p. 578–79 (2d ed. 1971). "The plaintiff cannot, by devoting his own land to an unusually sensitive use, such as a drive-in motion picture theater easily affected by light, make a nuisance out of conduct of the adjoining defendant which would otherwise be harmless." *Id*. at 579.

* * *

Because I do not believe that the facts of the present case give rise to a cause of action for private nuisance, I dissent.

NOTES

1. *The shifting definition of land-use harm.* Do you agree with the majority or the dissent regarding the three policy considerations historically invoked for refusing to protect a landowner's access to sunlight? Should physical damage to a neighbor be the threshold? Does the expansion of solar energy capacity make loss of sunlight more than just a personal annoyance? Would facilitating the use of solar power impinge land development, or perhaps facilitate it?

2. *Threats to biodiversity: solar power versus climate change.* Recall that in the wind case of *Animal Welfare* defendants claimed that the adverse effects of climate change on biodiversity would be much more severe if energy projects like the one at issue were not allowed to go forward. The same issue arises in the context of solar power. Consider the Ivanpah Solar Energy Generating System, located in the Mohave Desert near the California-Nevada border. It is the largest solar thermal plant in the world, capable of producing 392 megawatts of power (enough electricity to power 140,000 homes). The project, completed in early 2014, has some 350,000 mirrors that generate heat to boil water and drive turbines with steam. Early reports have documented that the project has produced substantial bird mortalities—from collusions with the mirrors, the inability of waterfowl to launch themselves from the mirrors after they mistake them for a lake (stranded, the birds die of thirst, hunger, or prey), and some are even scorched in flight. One estimate had the project killing two birds per minute, or 100,000 per year; however, the project operator claimed that only 321 dead or injured birds were recovered.

Although fossil-fuel supporters and climate-change deniers cite such statistics to make it appear that renewable energy efforts seem counter-productive, traditional energy projects are in fact much more lethal to birds. For example, one study concluded that large nuclear power plants kill more than twice as many birds—and fossil-fuel plants more than 30 times as many—as wind farms per gigawatt hour. Moreover, the 2010 BP oil spill in the Gulf of Mexico killed over 600,000 birds and still is killing sea turtles and dolphins. And an Audubon Society study concluded that more than 50 percent of North American bird species will lose more than half of their current climatic range by 2080. See Rebecca Solnit, *Are We Missing the Big Picture on Climate Change?*, N.Y. Times Mag., Dec. 2, 2014, http://www. nytimes.com/2014/12/07/magazine/are-we-missing-the-big-picture-on-climate-change.html?_r=0.

3.   *Leaving it to the legislature.* Some courts considering the issue have refused to follow the rule in *Prah.* For example, in *Sher v. Leiderman*, 181 Cal.App.3d 867 (1986), a landowner claimed that a neighbor's trees grew so tall as to block light from reaching the landowner's solar panels. The California state legislature had already passed a Solar Shade Control Act to preemptively address these types of conflicts. As a result, the court decided to leave these judgments to the legislature. Harkening back to the question raised in note 1 after *Fontainebleau* (pp. 911–912), are courts or legislatures best situated to resolve these disputes? The dissent in *Prah* also reiterated this common refrain: "I would submit that any policy decisions in this area are best left for the legislature." Should a court's decision depend upon whether a regulation like a Solar Shade Control Act is already in place? Consider California's Solar Shade Control Act:

CALIFORNIA'S SOLAR SHADE CONTROL ACT
Cal. Pub. Res. Code §§ 25980–25986 (2008)

§ 25980 . . . It is the policy of the state to promote all feasible means of energy conservation and all feasible uses of alternative energy supply sources. In particular, the state encourages the planting and maintenance of trees and shrubs to create shading, moderate outdoor temperatures, and provide various economic and aesthetic benefits. However, there are certain situations in which the need for widespread use of alternative energy devices, such as solar collectors, requires specific and limited controls on trees and shrubs.

§ 25981. Solar collector

(a) As used in this chapter, "solar collector" means a fixed device, structure, or part of a device or structure, on the roof of a building, that is used primarily to transform solar energy into thermal, chemical, or electrical energy. The solar collector shall be used as part of a system that makes use of solar energy for any or all of the following purposes:

(1) Water heating.

(2) Space heating or cooling.

(3) Power generation.

(b) Notwithstanding subdivision (a), for the purpose of this chapter, "solar collector" includes a fixed device, structure, or part of a device or structure that is used primarily to transform solar energy into thermal, chemical, or electrical energy and that is installed on the ground because a solar collector cannot be installed on the roof of the building receiving the energy due to inappropriate roofing material, slope of the roof, structural shading, or orientation of the building.

(c) For the purposes of this chapter, "solar collector" does not include a solar collector that is designed and intended to offset more than the building's electricity demand.

(d) For purposes of this chapter, the location of a solar collector is required to comply with the local building and setback regulations, and to be set back not less than five feet from the property line, and not less than 10 feet above the ground. A solar collector may be less than 10 feet in height only if, in addition to the five-foot setback, the solar collector is set back three times the amount lowered.

§ 25982.

After the installation of a solar collector, a person owning or in control of another property shall not allow a tree or shrub to be placed or, if placed, to grow on that property so as to cast a shadow greater than 10 percent of the collector absorption area upon that solar collector surface at any one time between the hours of 10 a.m. and 2 p.m., local standard time.

§ 25982.1.

(a) An owner of a building where a solar collector is proposed to be installed may provide written notice by certified mail to a person owning property that may be affected by the requirements of this chapter prior to the installation of the solar collector. If a notice is mailed, the notice shall be mailed no more than 60 days prior to installation of the solar collector and shall read as follows:

SOLAR SHADE CONTROL NOTICE

Under the Solar Shade Control Act (California Public Resources Code § 25980 *et seq.*) a tree or shrub cannot cast a shadow greater than 10 percent of a solar collector absorption area upon that solar collector surface at any one time between the hours of 10 a.m. and 2 p.m. local standard time if the tree or shrub is placed after installation of a solar collector. The owner of the building where a solar collector is proposed to be installed is providing this written notice to persons owning property that may be affected by the requirements of the act no more than 60 days prior to the installation of a solar collector. The building owner is providing the following information:

Name and address of building owner:

Telephone number of building owner:

Address of building and specific location where a solar collector will be installed (including street number and name, city/county, ZIP Code, and assessor's book, page, and parcel number):

Installation date of solar collector:

_____

Building Owner, Date

(b) If the owner of the building where a solar collector is proposed to be installed provided the notice pursuant to subdivision (a), and the installation date is later than the date specified in that notice, the later date shall be specified in a subsequent notice to persons receiving the initial notice.

(c)(1) A transferor of the building where the solar collector is installed may provide a record of persons receiving the notice pursuant to subdivision (a) to a transferee of the building.

(2) A transferor receiving a notice pursuant to subdivision (a) may provide the notice to a transferee of the property.

§ 25983.

A tree or shrub that is maintained in violation of Section 25982 is a private nuisance, as defined in Section 3481 of the Civil Code, if the person who maintains or permits the tree or shrub to be maintained fails to remove or alter the tree or shrub after receiving a written notice from the owner or agent of the affected solar collector requesting compliance with the requirements of Section 25982.

§ 25984.

This chapter does not apply to any of the following:

(a) A tree or shrub planted prior to the installation of a solar collector.

(b) A tree planted, grown, or harvested on timberland as defined in Section 4526 or on land devoted to the production of commercial agricultural crops.

(c) The replacement of a tree or shrub that had been growing prior to the installation of a solar collector and that, subsequent to the installation of the solar collector, dies, or is removed for the protection of public health, safety, or the environment.

(d) A tree or shrub that is subject to a city or county ordinance.

§ 25985

(a) A city, or for unincorporated areas, a county, may adopt, by majority vote of the governing body, an ordinance exempting their jurisdiction from the provisions of this chapter. The adoption of the ordinance shall not be subject to the California Environmental Quality Act (commencing with Section 21000).

(b) Notwithstanding the requirements of this chapter, a city or a county ordinance specifying requirements for tree preservation or solar shade control shall govern within the jurisdiction of the city or county that adopted the ordinance.

§ 25986.

Any person who plans a passive or natural solar heating system or cooling system or heating and cooling system which would impact on an adjacent active solar system may seek equitable relief in a court of competent jurisdiction to exempt such system from the provisions of this chapter. The court may grant such an exemption based on a finding that the passive or natural system would provide a demonstrably greater net energy savings than the active system which would be impacted.

———————

Do you think this Act strikes the appropriate balance between the right of a property owner to have trees in their yard and the right of others to install solar panels? Section 25984(a) makes clear that the Act does not apply to "a tree or shrub planted prior to the installation of a solar collector." Does the timing of the tree/shrub planting or solar panel installation make a difference, particularly given that over time plants often grow taller? Does "first in time, first in right" bear any relationship with the broader policy of promoting solar development? Or is the Act merely meant to resolve the dispute as a property matter? In other words, does this provision make the statute less about natural resources management and more about allocating property rights? Other states have passed similar legislation, such as New Mexico (N.M. Stat. Ann. §§ 47–3–1 *et seq.*), Wyoming (Wyo. Stat. Ann. § 34–22–101 *et seq.*), and Iowa (Iowa Code § 564A.1 *et seq.*). For more information on renewable energy conflicts *see* Troy A. Rule, *Solar, Wind and Land: Conflicts in Renewable Energy Development* (2014).

INDEX

References are to Pages